AUFSTIEG UND NIEDERGANG
DER RÖMISCHEN WELT

II.21.1

AUFSTIEG UND NIEDERGANG DER RÖMISCHEN WELT

GESCHICHTE UND KULTUR ROMS
IM SPIEGEL DER NEUEREN FORSCHUNG

II

HERAUSGEGEBEN
VON

HILDEGARD TEMPORINI
UND
WOLFGANG HAASE

WALTER DE GRUYTER · BERLIN · NEW YORK
1984

PRINCIPAT

EINUNDZWANZIGSTER BAND
(1. HALBBAND)

RELIGION

(HELLENISTISCHES JUDENTUM IN RÖMISCHER ZEIT:
PHILON UND JOSEPHUS)

HERAUSGEGEBEN

VON

WOLFGANG HAASE

WALTER DE GRUYTER · BERLIN · NEW YORK
1984

Herausgegeben mit Unterstützung der Robert Bosch Stiftung, Stuttgart

CIP-Kurztitelaufnahme der Deutschen Bibliothek

Aufstieg und Niedergang der römischen Welt:
Geschichte u. Kultur Roms im Spiegel der neueren Forschung /
hrsg. von Hildegard Temporini u. Wolfgang Haase. — Berlin,
New York : de Gruyter.
NE: Temporini, Hildegard [Hrsg.]
2. Principat.
Bd. 21.
1. Halbbd. / Hrsg. von Wolfgang Haase. 1. Aufl. — 1984.
    ISBN 3-11-008845-2
NE: Haase, Wolfgang [Hrsg.]

© 1983 by Walter de Gruyter & Co., Berlin 30
Alle Rechte, insbesondere das der Übersetzung in fremde Sprachen, vorbehalten. Ohne ausdrückliche
Genehmigung des Verlages ist es auch nicht gestattet, dieses Buch oder Teile daraus auf photomechanischem Wege
(Photokopie, Mikrokopie) zu vervielfältigen.
Printed in Germany
Satz und Druck: Arthur Collignon GmbH, Berlin 30
Einbandgestaltung und Schutzumschlag: Rudolf Hübler
Buchbinder: Lüderitz & Bauer, Berlin

The United Library
Garrett-Evangelical/Seabury-Western Seminaries
Evanston, IL 60201

DG 209
.T28
v. 2
no. 21/1
GESW

Vorwort

Der vorliegende Band II 21 (1 und 2) des Gemeinschaftswerkes 'Aufstieg und Niedergang der römischen Welt' (ANRW) bildet in der Rubrik 'Religion' im II. Teil ('Principat') dieses Werkes zusammen mit den Bänden II 19 und II 20 eine Gruppe von Bänden, die der jüdischen Religion in römischer Zeit gewidmet sind. Während Bd. II 19, der bereits erschienen ist (2 Halbbände [Berlin – New York 1979]), Beiträge zu allgemeinen Themen und solche zum palästinischen Judentum (Bd. II 19,1), besonders zum Rabbinat (Bd. II 19,2), enthält und Bd. II 20, der sich in Vorbereitung befindet, Arbeiten zum helle-nistischen Judentum mit Ausnahme von Philon und Josephus vereinigen wird, ist Bd. II 21 in seiner ersten Hälfte Philon, in seiner zweiten Hälfte Josephus und einer kleinen Nachlese zum Programm des Bandes II 19 vorbehalten. Der zweite Halbband (II 21,2) wird dem ersten (II 21,1) mit kurzem Abstand im Frühjahr 1984 folgen. Was die Behandlung des Flavius Josephus in diesem Band (II 21,2) betrifft, so sei darauf hingewiesen, daß der ursprünglich vorgesehene umfassende kritische Forschungsbericht von Louis H. Feldman (New York, N.Y.), der zu einem eigenen starken Band herangewachsen ist, unter dem Titel 'Josephus and Modern Scholarship (1935–1980)' (ed. by W. Haase) gleichzeitig im selben Verlag (Walter de Gruyter, Berlin – New York) erscheint; an seine Stelle tritt hier eine synthetische Gesamtwürdigung des Josephus durch Prof. Feldman unter der Überschrift 'Flavius Josephus Revisited: the Man, his Writ-ings, and his Significance', die ihrerseits auf dem monographischen Forschungs-bericht fußt. Im übrigen ist zu Bd. II 21 und seiner Stellung im Gesamtwerk ANRW das Vorwort des Herausgebers zu Bd. II 19 (II 19,1, S. V–XI) zu ver-gleichen. Wie dort S. VII zur Orientierung des speziell interessierten Lesers der Inhalt der beiden anderen judaistischen Bände II 20 und II 21 angekündigt worden ist, sollen hier im Anschluß an das Vorwort die Inhaltsübersichten der Bände II 19 und II 20 in aktualisierter Form folgen.

Tübingen, im Oktober 1983   W. H.

Inhaltsübersichten:

ham (137–151); S. HOLM-NIELSEN (Kopenhagen), Religiöse Poesie des Spätjudentums (152–186). –
J. H. CHARLESWORTH (Durham, N. C.), The Concept of the Messiah in the Pseudepigrapha (188–
218); J. M. BAUMGARTEN (Baltimore, Md.), The Heavenly Tribunal and the Personification of Sedeq
in Jewish Apocalyptic (219–239); H. C. C. CAVALLIN (Uppsala), Leben nach dem Tode im Spätjudentum und im frühen Christentum. I. Spätjudentum (240–345); J. MAIER (Köln), Die Sonne
im religiösen Denken des antiken Judentums (346–412). – R. GOLDENBERG (Stony Brook, N.Y.),
The Jewish Sabbath in the Roman World up to the Time of Constantine the Great (414–447);
S. B. HOENIG (New York, N.Y.), The Ancient City-Square: The Forerunner of the Synagogue
(448–476); A. TH. KRAABEL (Minneapolis, Minn.), The Diaspora Synagogue: Archaeological and
Epigraphic Evidence since Sukenik (477–510). – A. HULTGÅRD (Uppsala), Das Judentum in der
hellenistisch-römischen Zeit und die iranische Religion – ein religionsgeschichtliches Problem
(512–590). – B. WARDY (Montreal, Quebec), Jewish Religion in Pagan Literature during the Late
Republic and Early Empire (592–644). – J. F. STRANGE (Tampa, Florida), Archaeology and the
Religion of Judaism in Palestine (646–685); E. M. MEYERS (Durham, N. C.), The Cultural Setting
of Galilee: The Case of Regionalism and Early Judaism (686–702). – H. BIETENHARD (Bern), Die
Handschriftenfunde vom Toten Meer (Ḥirbet Qumran) und die Essener-Frage. Die Funde in der
Wüste Juda (704–778); H. GABRION (Paris), L'interprétation de l'Ecriture dans la littérature de
Qumrān (779–848). – P. HOLLENBACH (Ames, Iowa), Social Aspects of John the Baptizer's
Preaching Mission in the Context of Palestinian Judaism (850–875).

2. Halbband: J. NEUSNER (Providence, R. I.), The Formation of Rabbinic Judaism: Yavneh
(Jamnia) from A. D. 70 to 100 (3–42); P. SCHÄFER (Köln), Die Flucht Joḥanan b. Zakkais aus Jeru-
salem und die Gründung des 'Lehrhauses' in Jabne (43–101). – G. PORTON (Urbana, Ill.), Midrash:
Palestinian Jews and the Hebrew Bible in the Greco-Roman Period (103–138); B. M. BOKSER
(Berkeley, Cal.), An Annotated Bibliographical Guide to the Study of the Palestinian Talmud
(139–256); D. GOODBLATT (Haifa), The Babylonian Talmud (257–336). – G. STEMBERGER (Wien),
Die Beurteilung Roms in der rabbinischen Literatur (338–396); M. HADAS-LEBEL (Paris), Le paga-
nisme à travers les sources rabbiniques des IIe et IIIe siècles. Contribution à l'étude du synchrétisme
dans l'empire romain (397–485). – E. STIEGMAN (Halifax, Canada), Rabbinic Anthropology (487–
579); H. BIETENHARD (Bern), Logos-Theologie im Rabbinat. Ein Beitrag zur Lehre vom Worte
Gottes im rabbinischen Schrifttum (580–618); W. S. GREEN (Rochester, N.Y.), Palestinian Holy
Men: Charismatic Leadership and Rabbinic Tradition (619–647). – L. I. LEVINE (Jerusalem), The
Jewish Patriarch (Nasi) in Third Century Palestine (649–688).

Band II. 20 (in Vorbereitung): RELIGION (HELLENISTISCHES JUDENTUM IN
RÖMISCHER ZEIT: ALLGEMEINES): G. DELLING (Halle), Die Begegnung zwischen Hellenis-
mus und Judentum. – C. AZIZA (Paris), Moise et le récit de l'Exode chez les écrivains paiens de
langue grecque (Manéthon, Chaerémon, Lysimaque, Apion). – N. WALTER (Naumburg), Jüdisch-
hellenistische Literatur vor Philon von Alexandrien (unter Ausschluß der Historiker); R. DORAN
(Cincinnati, Ohio), The Jewish-Hellenistic Historians before Josephus; A. BARZANÒ (Bergamo),
Giusto di Tiberiade; A. PAUL (Paris), Le IIIe Livre des Macchabées comme texte antiphilonien. –
L. GREENSPOON (Clemson, S. C.), (Zum griechischen A. T. im hellenistischen Judentum); A. PAUL
(Paris), Le mouvement d'anti-Septante clôturé par Aquila; O. MUNNICH (Paris), Contribution à
une interprétation de la première révision de la Septante; M. HADAS-LEBEL (Paris), L'évolution de
l'image de Rome auprès des Juifs en deux siècles de relations judéo-romaines 164 avant – 66 après
J. C.; G. LEASE (Santa Cruz, Calif.), Jewish Mystery Cults since Goodenough; D. M. HAY (Cedar
Rapids, Iowa), The Psychology of Faith in Hellenistic Judaism. – J. H. CHARLESWORTH (Durham,
N. C.), Jewish Interest in Astrology during the Hellenistic and Roman Period; A. STROBEL (Neuen-
dettelsau), Weltenjahr, Große Konjunktion und Messiasstern in späthellenistischer und römischer
Zeit. – M. DE JONGE (Leiden), The Testaments of the Twelve Patriarchs: Central Problems and
Essential Viewpoints; J. J. COLLINS (Chicago, Ill.), The Development of the Sibylline Tradition;
V. NIKIPROWETZKY (Paris), La Sibylle Juive et le IIIe livre des pseudo-oracles sibyllins depuis
Ch. Alexandre; J. H. CHARLESWORTH (Durham, N. C), The Treatise of Shem: Introduction, Text
and Translation; CHR. BURCHARD (Heidelberg), Der jüdische Asenethroman und seine Nach-
wirkung. Von Egeria zu Anna Katharina Emmerick oder zu Moses aus Aggel zu Karl Kerényi. –
J. RIAUD (Paris), Les Thérapeutes d'Alexandrie dans la tradition et dans la recherche critique jusqu'aux découvertes de Qumran.

Inhalt

RELIGION
(HELLENISTISCHES JUDENTUM IN RÖMISCHER ZEIT:
PHILON UND JOSEPHUS)

Band II.21.1:

NACHTRAG ZU BAND II.19

RELIGION

(HELLENISTISCHES JUDENTUM IN RÖMISCHER ZEIT: PHILON UND JOSEPHUS)

Philo Judaeus:
An Introduction to the Man, his Writings, and his Significance

by Samuel Sandmel†, Cincinnati, Ohio

Contents

I. Introduction

This essay presupposes a reader with little or no previous knowledge of Philo. Another essay, by Peder Borgen, is dedicated to a bibliography of the Alexandrian.[1]

Writing about 42 A.D., Philo Judaeus of Alexandria described himself as an old man. On the premise that he was at that time at least sixty, it is often concluded that he was born between 25 and 20 B.C. The unknown date of his death is

---

[1] There one will find data on the editions and translations of Philo (below, pp. 98–154).

presumed to have occurred between 42 and 45 A.D. His lifetime coincided, partly or fully, with the Rabbinic sage Hillel, with Jesus, and with Paul. His abundant writings illuminate the age of the incipient transition from the biblical religion, centered in the Temple in Jerusalem, to the Synagogue Judaism which survived the destruction of the Temple and the termination of the Temple cult in 70 A.D. Since earliest Christianity was a Judaism, his writings have significance for an understanding of Christianity too. Because he was in a sense a Platonist,[2] as well as a Stoic too, he is of some consequence in the understanding of the unfolding in his age of significant currents of hellenistic philosophy. Indeed, one might say wryly that often Philo has been of interest to scholars not for himself but for the light he sheds on presumably more significant matters.

Alexandria, his native city, was in his day a leading metropolis of the world. About its size, especially the population statistics, various conjectures exist, but however these differ in detail, they united in ascribing a hugeness to the city, and a cultural hegemony in the realms of sculpture, painting, poetry, theater, and philosophy.[3]

There is also universal testimony respecting the size, and significance of the Jewish community. The community appears to have been formed at the time of the founding of the city by Alexander the Great in 332. Some seventy-five years later that community had largely forgotten the ancestral Hebrew in which Scripture was written, and the spoken Aramaic of Judaea. Fidelity to Judaism, and some noticeable abundance of Jews, impelled a translation of the Five Books of Moses into Greek. It is reported in 'The Letter of Aristeas' that that translation was made in 250 B.C., by seventy-two priests invited from Jerusalem for that purpose; from the Greek word for seventy [two] comes the title 'Septuagint', the customary way of alluding to the Greek translation of Scripture.

The Septuagint was used in a variety of related ways. It was the textbook in Judaism of Greek-speaking Jews. It was utilized in the divine worship in the synagogues, or, more precisely, the proto-synagogues. It spurred the production of other writings, such as histories, apologies, dramas, and epic poems. Between the origin of the Septuagint and Philo's time, there arose, accordingly, a body of material derived from Scripture which, preliminarily, we might allude to as interpretive literature. Philo is the culmination, in significance and probably in time of that body of interpretive literature.

Direct information about Philo the man is scanty. The greatest abundance of direct information comes from his account of a calamitous experience of the Alexandrian Jewish community. In 38 or 39 A.D., the ship bearing Herod Agrippa, newly designated as the 'client-king', from Rome to Judaea, stopped at Alexandria, and touched off severe anti-Jewish riots. At that time Rome ruled Egypt. The Jewish community believed that the Roman governor, Avillius Flaccus, had been insufficiently interested in or energetic about protecting Jewish

---

[2] The statement, "Either Philo platonizes or Plato philonizes," is ascribed to Numenius.

[3] See: E. SCHÜRER, The Jewish Encyclopedia, I (1901), pp. 361–366, s.v. Alexandria, Egypt-Ancient.

lives and property. Hence, a delegation of leading Jews went to Rome to present their complaints to the Emperor Gaius Caligula; Philo was one of the members of the deputation. Hence, he was certainly a man of some eminence. This is confirmed in that his brother, Lysimachus,[4] was an official ('alabarch') of the community, and indeed possibly its head. Many passages in Philo's writings reflect a knowledge of how the wealthy live; the high quality of his education in Greek would have been readily possible only for someone from a wealthy family. We know almost nothing about Philo's daily activities, or about the character of his relationship to the Jewish community; he may have been an active leader, but it is more likely that he was the solitary scholar, greatly admired by his fellow Jews, relatively few of whom may be presumed to have read him. The current word 'elitist' seems appropriate to describe him; though he had a concern for all his fellow Jews, he also had a scorn for the common man that all too often marks the intellectual. That Philo was preeminently an ivory tower figure, rather than a man engaged in committee work in the community, is to be inferred from the tremendous quantity that he wrote. Such a volume of writing could come only from a full preoccupation to it. His literary manner is 'Atticistic', that is, he uses that form of *koine* ("common") hellenistic Greek which consciously imitated the style of hellenic Athens. Such a style is hostile to simplicity, and it is not surprising that Philo wrote sentences that are endless and utilized compound words with two or more gratuitous prepositional prefixes. He was prolix; he was repetitious; he found tangents irresistible. Much of what he wrote suffers from an indisposition to emphasize or subordinate. He could not readily restrain an irrelevant intrusion of his truly wide learning and erudition into what he was writing. If, then, he has been the victim of some lamentable manner of writing, and if to read him, in Greek or in translation, is often a tedious chore or even an ordeal, there is nevertheless a content in him that makes him a person of genuine consequence. It has been his fate that Jewish scholars have ordinarily neglected him because he wrote in Greek, not in Hebrew-Aramaic, and Christian scholars because he was Jewish.

That he was a Jew who wrote in Greek has raised a series of issues and scholarly controversies respecting the interpretation of his writings. Was he at all hellenized? Was he only superficially hellenized? Was he hellenized to the maximum that a Jew, still loyal to Judaism, could be? Was he kindred in his religiosity to the Judean sage Hillel, or does his religiosity differ substantially? Did he know no Hebrew, or a little Hebrew, or a lot? Was he presumably in touch with the contemporary academies of Judaea, such as the Schools of Hillel and of Shammai, or completely independent of them? Was he primarily a preacher who knew philosophy? Or was he a philosopher who wrote hortatory essays? Or was he a psychologist? Was he an original mind of consequence, or is it right to follow those who dismiss him as merely an electic, and a poor one at that? Why were his writings preserved by Christians and why did he influence Clement of Alexandria and Origin as much as he did? In a sense, the issues and controversies about Philo are like those about Paul. There is a significant difference in the case of Paul, for

---

[4] See note 30.

some of the acuteness of the controversies results from the existence of Acts of the Apostles in which there is a portrait of Paul which may or may not be congruent with the inferences about him to be derived from the Epistles alone. But had we only Paul's Epistles, and lacked Acts, and were we free of the issue of whether or not Paul wrote Ephesians, Colossians, and the Pastoral Epistles, the similar controversies would still arise. Both Philo and Paul were Jews. Both of them wrote fluently in their native Greek. Were they more Jewish than Greek, or more Greek than Jewish?

II. The Writings

It has become customary to divide the writings of Philo into four categories:[5]

For the first of these, the term 'historical' is occasionally used; perhaps a better term would be 'non-biblical', that is, those writings that are not inter-pretations of Scripture. The following principal writings in this category can be cited. The first one of these has survived in two extracts quoted in Eusebius.[6] Its name, 'Hypothetica', is unclear and disputed, one view being that it means "sup-positions", that is, diverse premises among which the readers can choose; the other that it connotes "exhortations".[7] The work is also alluded to as 'Apology for the Jews'. The first extract treats of the Exodus, explaining that the Jews had left Egypt as a result of the inability of the land to sustain their large population, coupled with their yearning for their fatherland. Philo also defends the character of Moses against allegations of deception and knavery. He turns rather quickly to the settlement in Canaan, and the building of the Temple. The respect for law and obedience which Jews exhibit reflects their veneration of their lawgiver, Moses. In the lapse of more than two thousand years since the time of Moses, Jews have not altered a single word of what Moses wrote. The laws are most rigorous, being replete with the death penalty for a wide range of trespasses. Besides the laws, there are unwritten customs and institutions. Philo lauds the Sabbath as exemplifying self-control, and describes the Sabbath gatherings in synagogues where people heard the Law expounded. Philo lauds equally the Sabbatical seventh year of Scripture.

The second extract is a description of the Essenes, similar to a description of them given in another essay called 'Peri tou Panta Spoudaion Eleutheron Einai' ('That Every Good Man is Free'; it is alluded to as 'Probus').

---

[5] The scholarly classification ordinarily follows, though not without disagreement, M. L. MASSEBIEAU, Le classement des œuvres de Philon, Bibliothèque de l'Ecole des Hautes Etudes . . . Sciences religieuses, I, Paris, 1889, pp. 1–91.

[6] In: Preparation for the Gospel, VIII, 6,1–9; 7,1–20 and VIII, 11,1–8.

[7] See the discussion by F. H. COLSON, Loeb Classical Library (LCL), Philo, IX, 1941, revised and reprinted 1954, pp.410–411.

The opening words of this essay allude to a previous one, which is lost, but seemingly had some such title as 'That Every Fool is a Slave'. 'Probus' has been described as filled with Stoic paradoxes and dialectic. It has been correctly assessed as an essentially secular treatise, with no more than five allusions to or quotations from the Law. The passage on the Essenes in 'Probus' (75—91) is quoted in Eusebius, Preparation for the Gospel, VIII,12, as is the similar passage noted above from the 'Hypothetica'.

A third book in this category is 'Peri Biou Theoretikou E Hiketon' ('On the Contemplative Life or Suppliants', alluded to a 'Vita'). The quiet life of 'vision' of this book is contrasted in the opening lines with a preceding treatise Philo had written on the Essenes as exemplars of the active (praktikon) life of the Essenes. Some scholars take "the preceding treatise" to be 'That Every Good Man is Free'; others take it to be that essay part of which is reproduced in Eusebius, as mentioned above. Another view holds that there may well have been a third, now lost, treatise, one entirely on the Essenes.[8] The substance of 'On the Contemplative Life' is the description of an ascetic community of Egyptian Jews who had a center of some kind on Lake Mareotis. Controversies have raged over this essay. It has been denied that there ever were monastic Jewish communities, and, accordingly, Philo's authorship has been denied, with the deniers deeming the essay as Christian in origin. Disputes have existed, also, about the credibility of the substance of the treatise, as if to suppose that Philo, or whoever was the author, so idealizes the community that his description bears little relationship to what the community may actually have been.[9]

Another of the non-biblical treatises is 'Eis Phlakkon' ('Against Flaccus'). There is a broadly held opinion that this treatise is the second part of a longer work, with the first half not having survived. This opinion rests on the observation that in the first words of the treatise there seems to be a summary of something preceding relative to the misdeeds of Seianus[10], and possibly there is another comparable allusion to him at the very end; it also rests on a passage cited as if from 'Against Flaccus' by St. John of Damascus;[11] since the passage cited is not found in the surviving text, it is conjectured that it comes from the lost part one.

Avillius Flaccus had been named governor (prefect) of Alexandria and Egypt about 32 A.D., and was recalled in disgrace by the Emperor Gaius Caligula about 39, though exactly why is not clear. Disgraced and exiled, Flaccus wandered about in despair, exposed to public shame; finally he was cruelly and painfully

---

[8] This latter is the hypothesis of F. H. Colson, op. cit., p. 106.

[9] The significant denial of Philo's authorship came in 1880 from P. E. Lucius, but might be said to go back to Eusebius, Ecclesiastical History, II,17, where the Therapeutae are viewed as the first Christian converts, though the treatise is there ascribed to Philo. The refutation of Lucius came from F. C. Conybeare, Philo about the Contemplative Life . . . Critically Edited with a Defense of its Genuineness, Oxford, 1895. S. Sandmel, Philo's Place in Judaism, Augm. edit., New York, 1971, pp. 194—196, notes the abundant use in this treatise of Philo's allegorical treatment of Abraham, this in support of Philonic authorship.

[10] Lucius Aelius Seianus was the minister to the emperor Tiberius who had Seianus executed in 31 A.D. as a murderer; see, e.g., Tacitus, Annals, IV, 1—38, 39—59, 74; V, 6—9.

[11] A theologian of the Eastern Church, probably 8th century.

put to death by Caligula's executioners. That Flaccus had not protected Jews in the pogrom of 38, and, indeed, had contributed to their suffering and had come to be deposed, humiliated, and executed could appear to reflect cause and effect, and the example of Flaccus could be used as an object lesson respecting the fate that awaited anyone foolhardy enough to harm Jews.[12] This is the theme that dominates the treatise; the events described in the treatise are very much sub-ordinated to the theme. In the framework of the description of the events, Philo provides information, regrettably not always clear, about the political rights and the demography of the Alexandrian Jewish community to which we revert below.

The fifth treatise in this category is 'Tes Presbeias Pros Gaion' ('On the Embassy to Gaius', often alluded to in the Latin, 'Legatio'). The ending of the treatise appears to be lost, for we are led to expect a 'palinode', or 'reversal', an account of a reversal of imperial policy towards Jews. But if the palinode was written it has not survived.[13] 'Legatio' was written after the death of Gaius and the accession to the throne of Claudius; it would have been foolhardy to have written such a treatise while Gaius Caligula was still alive. The treatise tells that a few months after being crowned emperor, Caligula became demented. To the difficulties the Alexandrians suffered from Flaccus there were now added troubles that ensued when Gaius, imaging himself a god, indeed the Supreme God, decreed that his image be set up in places of worship. Synagogues in Alexandria were defiled, and when Alexandrian mobs encountered Jewish resistance, syn-agogues were destroyed. The Alexandrian community sent a deputation to Gaius to protest against the violation of their consciences and their rights.[14] Philo was the leader of the deputation.[15]

'Legatio' in part covers the difficulties suffered by the Alexandrian com-munity described also in 'Against Flaccus', though there are some differences that border on contradiction. Only in the latter third of the treatise does it deal, caustically and bitterly, with the arrogance of Caligula. Apparently the point of the treatise, that whoever damages the Jews will be punished by God, is diluted by the absence of the palinode which is presumed to have described the details of the punishment Caligula underwent.

This treatise has a subtitle that associates it with a set of writings 'On the Virtues'. This subtitle has raised unimportant problems about the classification[16]

---

[12] See, for example, Flac. 116.

[13] Eusebius (Ecclesiastical History, II, 5) speaks of "five books" which Philo wrote about events in the time of Gaius. Considerable confusion exists about exactly what Philo wrote. This is especially the case because 'Legatio' is part of a series of essays called 'On the Virtues'; a traditional subtitle of 'Legatio' is 'The First Part of the Treatise on Virtues'. There are several historical confusions (see F. H. COLSON, Loeb Classical Library, Philo, X, 1962, pp. XVI—XXXI).

[14] On 'Flacc.' and 'Legatio' see ERWIN R. GOODENOUGH, The Politics of Philo Judaeus, Practice and Theory, New Haven, 1938 and literature cited there, pp. 1—20.

[15] He speaks of five members of the deputation (370), Josephus of three (Ant. XVIII, 8,1).

[16] Apparently the subtitle was the original title, since it might have been dangerous in Philo's own lifetime to write so explicitly; the content here, and that in 'Flacc.', may have suggested the names of these treatises we now inherit.

of Philo's work. The view adopted here involves ignoring the subtitle and setting into a later category the works 'On the Virtues' and some similar other writings.

The second category consists of 'Questions and Answers to Genesis' and 'Questions and Answers to Exodus'. A few fragments of this lengthy work survive in Greek; the largest amounts we possess have survived in a translation into Armenian.[17] In form the work consists of the asking of a brief question about the meaning of a biblical passage or verse, immediately followed by an answer to the question.[18] It is usual for the answer to suggest that the literal meaning of Scripture is clear, and to turn promptly to the allegorical meaning (about allegory, see below, p. 13ff.). Scholars have wondered whether Philo wrote similarly about Leviticus, Numbers, and Deuteronomy, and some conjecture that he did, but these writings were lost. It is more likely that he never got around to writing about these books, simply for lack of time and out of the conviction that Genesis and Exodus were of primary importance. Biblical materials from Leviticus, Numbers, and Deuteronomy appear in abundance within the essays that he wrote. It has been suggested[19] that the verse by verse exposition in 'Questions and Answers' were preliminary notes on the basis of which Philo in part later composed some treatises and in part did not.

The third category is called the 'Allegory of the Laws'. The treatises in this category all bear names, as will presently be seen. In form each of the treatises begins with the citation of a biblical passage.[20] The treatise proceeds to give the allegorical meaning of sentences, phrases, and words. There is usually a clear relationship in the content of a particular treatise to its title; the main thrust of the content, though, derives from the sequence of the biblical phrases or words, rather than from the chosen title. It is particularly in the treatises in this category that Philo's prolexity and his tangential digressions are to be found. The published treatises are arranged in the sequence of the biblical passages (except that the essay 'On Creation', not a part of this category, is normally given the first position in Philo's writings).

---

[17] The Armenian was translated into Latin by J. B. AUCHER (Philonis Iudaei Paralipomena Armena, Venice, 1826). A translation from the Armenian into English by RALPH MARCUS is found in the two supplementary volumes (XI—XII) to the Loeb Classical Library Philo, 1953.

[18] That the form was derived from comparable commentaries on Homer is suggested by E. E. HA-LEVI, Tarbit, XXXI (1961), pp. 157—159. An English summary of this Hebrew article ('Biblical Midrash and Homeric Exegesis') is given there on pp. III—IV.

[19] S. SANDMEL, Philo's Environment and Philo's Exegesis, Journal of Bible and Religion, XXII (1954), p. 249.

[20] These lemmata, as well as quotations within the treatises, are regarded as throwing light on questions related to the Septuagint. While in general Philo's quotations conform to the so-called Septuagint, there are disagreements too. See PETER KATZ, Philo's Bible: The Aberrant Text of Bible Quotations in Some Philonic Writings . . ., Cambridge, 1950. KATZ seems to regard the aberrant verses as the result of the interpolation of a late recension of the Septuagint, one influenced by Aquila into the text of Philo.

The following are the surviving[21] treatises in the category, the 'Allegory of the Laws', and the biblical passages on which the treatises are based. In parentheses are given the Latin abbreviations by which it is customary to cite the treatises. About the first title given, there is this comment to be made, that its name, applicable to three related treatises, was at one time applied to cover all the treatises in this category; however, those treatises subsequent to the first three came to bear their own titles. Curiously, then, the three parts of 'The Allegory of the Laws' are part of the total category known also as the 'Allegory of the Laws'.

Commentary On		Latin Abbrev.
Genesis 2.1–17	Legum Allegoriae I	Leg. I
Genesis 2.18–3.1	Legum Allegoriae II	Leg. II
Genesis 3.8b–19	Legum Allegoriae III	Leg. III
Genesis 3.24–4.1	De Cherubim	Cher.
Genesis 4.2–4	De sacrificiis Abelis et Caini	Sacrif.
Genesis 4.8–15	Quod deterius potiori insidiari soleat	Deter.
Genesis 4.16–25 (in parts)	De posteritate Caini	Poster.
Genesis 6.1–4a	De gigantibus	Gig.
Genesis 6.4b–12 (in parts)	Quod Deus sit immutabilis	Deus
Genesis 9.20–21	De agricultura	Agric.
Genesis 9.20–21	De plantatione	Plant.
Genesis 9.20–21	De ebrietate	Ebr.
Genesis 9.24–27	De sobrietate	Sobr.
Genesis 11.1–9	De confusione linguarum	Confus.
Genesis 12.1–6 (in parts)	De migratione Abrahami	Migr.
Genesis 15.2–18	Quis rerum divinarum heres sit	Her.
Genesis 16.1–6	De congressu eruditionis gratia	Congr.
Genesis 16.6b–14	De fuga et inventione	Fug.
Genesis 17.1–5, 16–22	De mutatione nominum	Mutat.
Genesis 28.10–22	De somniis, I	Somn. I
Genesis 31.10–13	De somniis, I	Somn. I
Genesis 37.8–11	De somniis, II	Somn. II
Genesis 40.9–11, 16–17	De somniis, II	Somn. II
Genesis 41.17–24	De somniis, II	Somn. II

The fourth category of writings is known as the 'Exposition of the Law'. The treatises in it are no less allegorical than those in the 'Allegory of the Law'. In the treatises in the 'Exposition', there is no beginning biblical quotation. The

---

[21] There is evidence that some treatises in this category have been lost. See Somn. I,1 and Heres, 1 for allusions to treatises not extant.

contents of these treatises are intimately bound to the title. In the 'Allegory' the individual treatise expounds a biblical passage; in the 'Exposition' the individual treatise expounds a topic. The surviving treatises ordinarily ascribed to the 'Exposition' are the following:

De opificio Mundi	Opif.
De Abrahamo[22]	Abr.
De Iosepho	Ios.
De vita Mosis	Mos.
De Decalogo	Decal.
De specialibus legibus	Spec.
De virtutibus	Virt.
De praemiis et poenis, de exsecrationibus	Praem.

There is an overlap in the content of the 'Allegory' and the 'Exposition'; for example, most of what is contained in 'De Abrahamo' (a treatise in the 'Exposition') is found scattered throughout the 'Allegory'.

It has seemed to scholars that aspects of Philo's manner suggest that the 'Allegory' and the 'Exposition' were written for different audiences. The 'Allegory' seems to assume that the reader knows the content of Scripture, and Philo serves him, as it were, by deepening his knowledge; the 'Exposition' seems to assume that the reader knows little or nothing of Scripture, and needs to be inducted into that knowledge, and to the deeper meaning of Scripture. It came to be a usual view that the 'Allegory' was written for Jews, the 'Exposition' for Gentiles; this view is found in much of the older literature.[23] An inquiry by VIKTOR TCHERIKOVER[24] concluded that there is little evidence that Gentiles in any number read Jewish writers, and hence he denied that the 'Exposition' was written for Gentiles. S. SANDMEL suggested that the 'Exposition' was for a Jewish audience, those who seemed ignorant of their Jewish heritage and inclined to or on the verge of apostasy; the 'Exposition' was an effort to retain these Jews for Judaism. Philo's own nephew, Tiberius Alexander,[25] became an apostate and quite anti-Jewish. The tone of the entire 'Exposition' is defensive and apologetic,

---

[22] This treatise ought not be confused with 'Migratio Abrahami' of the 'Allegory'.

[23] It reappears with great frequency in the writings of ERWIN R. GOODENOUGH. See next note.

[24] In 'General Observations' in the Hebrew memorial volume (Sefer Zikkaron) to Hans (Johanan) Lewy, pp. 139—160. That the treatises on Joseph, Abraham, and Moses are hellenistic aretologies (see A. PRIESSNIG, Die literarische Form der Patriarchenbiographien des Philon von Alexandrien, Monatsschrift für die Geschichte und Wissenschaft des Judentums, LXXIII [1929], pp. 143—155) does not prove they were written for Gentiles. That Philo adopted hellenistic literary forms is noted by a number of authors. The view of ERWIN R. GOODENOUGH (Harvard Theological Review, XXVI [1933], pp. 109—125) that 'De Vita Mosis' was an introduction to Judaism for Gentiles ought not be followed.

[25] A brief sketch is found in: S. KRAUSS, The Jewish Encyclopedia, I (1901), pp. 357—358, s.v. Alexander, Tiberius Julius. I have not seen A. LEPAPE, Tiberius Julius Alexander, Préfet d'Alexandrie et d'Egypte, Bulletin de la Société royale d'Archéologie d'Alexandrie, N.S., VIII (1934), pp. 331—341.

and, in passages, indignant.[26] The defensive-apologetic tone is not that of a
Josephus in 'Contra Apionem II' in replying to Egyptian slanders; it is rather a
contention that the noble heritage of Jews is at least as good, and indeed even
better, than the heritage of the Greeks. The 'Exposition' is not a reply to outside
slanders.

Apparently Philo wrote treatises about Isaac and Jacob, but these have not
survived.

To summarize the treatises in the 'Allegory' and the 'Exposition' would con-
sume space beyond what is allotted. Much of their content will be cited in the
ensuing double presentation of Philo's thought. Here it may be said that the
essays, especially those in the 'Exposition', conform in form, and greatly in content, to hellenistic biographical essays.[27] The external form of both 'Abr.' and
'Decal.' is the same; a balance on the one hand between piety to God, and the four
Stoic cardinal virtues on the other. This same pattern is found in IV Maccabees.
The treatises 'Abr.', 'Ios.' and 'Mos.' conform to the biographical aretologies of
the hellenistic world.

It remains to mention some other treatises, some authentically by Philo and
some not, which might have appeared in category one, rather than here. The
treatise 'On the Indestructability of the World'[28], which has not survived in
totality, is ordinarily ascribed to Philo. The conviction that the world exists
because God created it leads to the contention that through the will and power of
God the world is eternal. Most of the surviving portion, however, provides the
arguments in favor of the world's destructability, as a prelude to a refutation to
ensue but which has been lost. Concerning 'Providence'[29], preserved as an entity
in Armenian translation, though some portions are preserved in Greek in Eusebius, is a dialogue between Philo, in support of the doctrine of providence, and
an Alexander who expresses doubts. Perhaps this is Tiberius Alexander, the
nephew who later abandoned Judaism. The matter of providence, or, better, fate,
was a usual topic in Greek philosophy and was a divisive issue between Stoics
(whom Philo admires) and Epicureans whom he does not. Philo's view, derived
from Scripture, affirms providence.

The treatise 'Alexander', with the subtitle 'On Whether Dumb Animals have
the Power of Reason', is again a dialogue, but not with Alexander; rather,
Philo and his eminent brother Lysimachos[30] discuss an essay written by Philo's

---

[26] After Philo explains the great deed of Abraham, as related in Gen. ch. 22, of course lauding
the uniqueness of the patriarch, he says that the captious critics of Abraham, who had
alleged that there was nothing unique, ought now set "bolt and bar to their mouths" (Abr.
179–184).

[27] See above, note 24.

[28] The Latin is 'De Aeternitate Mundi'.

[29] The Latin is 'De Providentia' (Prov.). The treatise has two parts; in the first part, some
later scribal activity obliterated the dialogue form and also provided a number of inter-
polations.

[30] On Philo's family, see J. SCHWARTZ, Note sur la famille de Philon d'Alexandrie, Annuaire
de l'Institut de philologie et d'histoire orientales et slaves, XIII (1953), pp. 591–602 and his
'L'Egypte de Philon', in: Philon d'Alexandrie, 11–16 Septembre 1966, a colloquium pub-

nephew Tiberius Alexander. Philo, of course, argues that animals do not possess the capacity to reason. Treatises on Sampson and Jonah are usually regarded as not by Philo.

III. Allegory

The import of the term 'allegory' is consistent with the meaning of the Greek word, namely, "to say something other." Allegory is a device used relative to a text which, being old, can become contemporary by some freedom in interpretation. Moreover, allegory is useful when an ancient text is both sacred and also troubling. In its very nature, allegory tends to make into merely a symbol something which in the work being allegorized is presented as if a reality. Strictly speaking, in the Olympian pantheon, in which Aphrodite represents female beauty, or Pallas Athene wisdom, such representations are not to be classified as allegories, though a comparable impulse is at work. As to unmistakable allegory, it is common to ascribe its broad use to the Stoics in their interpretation of Homer. The Stoics raised allegory from a previous occasional or inchoate use into a rather fullfledged, common interpretive device. That the 'Iliad' is about the wrath of Achilles, whose wench Briseis was taken from him by Agamemnon; that the Achaeans were at Troy to regain the faithless Helen who had fled from her husband Menelaus; that in due course Agamemnon was murdered by his wife Clytemnestra and her lover Aegisthus — all this to a Stoic could represent unseemly lust, the abominable loss of self control, and a capitulation to base passion. Moreover, the narratives about Zeus the philanderer, with his array of conquests despite the jealousy of his watchful Hera, ascribe to the Olympian gods an even more unseemly departure from Stoic standards of virtue. To convert either the divine pantheon, or the Homeric personalities, into symbols representing aspects of human characteristics or dispositions could enable one to continue a sense of personal connection with the ancient past, this by making it contemporary and universal in the sense that these human characteristics still abided among men. The particular item which seems most clearly to illustrate Stoic allegory insofar as this relates to Philo is derived from the 'Odyssey', the account of faithful Penelope. In Odysseus' absence, she was the object of the lust of many suitors, but at no time succumbed to them. Her maid, though, did succumb. Plutarch, in his treatise 'De Liberis Educandis', presents the allegory that the suitors wished to master philosophy, Penelope, but were not able to go beyond the maids, the 'preliminary studies', the so-called encyclical studies.[31] In Philo's allegory, Sarah

---

lished in 1967, pp. 35—44. On Alexander Lysimachus, see WILCKEN, RE, I, 1 (1893), 1441, s.v. Alexandros no. 26. The effort to align Philo's treatises with his career appears in LEOPOLD COHN, Einleitung und Chronologie der Schriften Philos, Philologus, Supplement 7,3, Berlin, 1899, pp. 387—435.

[31] There are extant other Stoic versions of this rather well-known allegory; see F. H. COLSON, Philo on Education, Journal of Theological Studies, XVIII (1917), pp. 153—154; HARRY A.

is philosophy and her Egyptian maid Hagar is the preliminary studies (as we shall see in greater detail). It is not wrong to state that Philo[32] has borrowed from the Stoics both the manner of allegory and also some of the content, and has utilized these with respect to Scripture. The biblical personalities through allegory become universal and contemporary types of men, or else aspects of human personality: Adam is the ordinary mind, Eve sense perception, Abraham the capacity to learn, Lot the disposition to pleasure, and the Pharaoh of Gen. 12 the hypocrite.

The allegory in Philo, however, has a significance far beyond that of manner. It is in addition the device by means of which Philo can interpret Scripture as a huge repository of Platonism and Stoicism. The immensity of the quantity of Platonism and Stoicism in Philo is astounding.[33]

Moreover, the crotchet is found in him, as well as in other Jews, that whatever there was of value in the Greek heritage was a latter-day borrowing from the original source, Scripture. The crotchet was a concession that Greek philosophy in its main substance (that is, except for Epicureanism) was valid, edifying, and noble; its legitimacy was established on the basis that it was all derived from Moses. Plato was right because Moses in effect taught him[34]. That the content of Greek philosophy was in Scripture attested to the greater antiquity of Judaism compared with Greek civilization, this latter a repeated theme in hellenistic Jewish apologetics.[35]

This conversion of Scriptural narratives and Scriptural laws into the universal, contemporary understanding of man entailed both the need to find a Scriptural forerunner for a Platonic doctrine, and, in an understandable reversal of the process, to explain a bizarre or embarrassing Scriptural item by fitting it into the complex of Pythagoreanism, Platonism and Stoicism. Yet, as we shall see, the motive in this capricious allegorizing was more than merely explanatory; it extended into the conviction that Scripture, properly understood, was the personal, contemporary experience of every man: we all have minds (there is the Adam in us); we all have sense perception (there is the Eve in us); we all incline to material things (there is the Lot in us) — und so on, both endlessly, yet arranged in the light of a particular controlled focus and purpose. That is, Philo does not

---

WOLFSON, Philo, 2 vols., Cambridge, Mass., 1947, I, pp. 145—146; and H. VON ARNIM, Stoicorum Veterum Fragmenta, Stuttgart, 1964, I, p. 78.

[32] Of the abundant literature, see LOUIS GINZBERG, The Jewish Encyclopedia, I (1901), pp. 403—411, s.v. Allegorical Interpretation; JACOB Z. LAUTERBACH, The Ancient Jewish Allegorists in Talmud and Midrash, Jewish Quarterly Review, N.S., I (1910—1911), pp. 291—333, 503—531; LEOPOLD TREITEL, Ursprung, Begriff und Umfang der allegorischen Schrifterklärung, Monatsschrift für Geschichte und Wissenschaft des Judentums, LV (1911), pp. 543—551.

[33] The literature on the Greek philosophy in Philo is enormous; see E. R. GOODENOUGH and HOWARD L. GOODHART, A General Bibliography of Philo (published in: GOODENOUGH, The Politics of Philo Judaeus), New Haven, 1938, section XIII, listing some 61 direct items. The treatment by HARRY A. WOLFSON, Philo, 2 vols., Cambridge, Mass., 1947, is a magnum opus in this area, even to the neglect of 'Religionsgeschichte'.

[34] This frequent view is perpetuated among Christian writers too.

[35] The great antiquity of Judaism is set forth at length in Josephus, Against Apion, I.

explain for the mere purpose of explaining, but rather for his goal of guiding us — this is his focus and purpose — to what he conceives of as the higher life.

This conception that there is a higher life is to Philo the essence and the goal of his inherited Judaism. What one might call the premises, or possibly the intuitions of Philo, are Jewish; his explanations of the content of Judaism are Greek. The role of Platonism and Stoicism is to tell us how it is that the Jewish intuitions and goals work. For example, we, like Abraham, should control our passions and have our higher minds correct the errors that inhere in sense perception; and recourse to Stoicism replains the nature and the role of passions and senses, and how the higher mind can control them.

The abundance of philosophy in Philo has led to a variety of assessments[36] of him as a philospher, whether disparaging as in the case of RICHARD REITZENSTEIN or unreserved adulation by HARRY A. WOLFSON. In either case, the philosophy, whether REITZENSTEIN or WOLFSON is right, is subordinate to the religious guidance and exhortation which is the true clue to Philo.

The social and religious problems which confronted an Alexandrian Jew such as Philo cannot really be separated from each other. Analytically we may perhaps view them separately, but they are intertwined. Socially, the Alexandrian community, as said above, had forgotten the ancestral Hebrew, even of Scripture, but had retained its high Jewish loyalty. It had its synagogues. It had certain political rights[37], usually honored, but sometimes ruptured, as in the pogroms of 38.[38] It lived side by side partly with transplanted Greeks and partly with hellenized Egyptians, and all were ruled over by Romans. Clearly not all Jews had the remarkable education[39] in Greek literature that Philo had; clearly there were carpenters and cobblers as well as the intelligentsia. Yet plain people — whom Philo scorns as the *ochlos*, the mob — and Philo and his coterie were all affected by the environment. The frictions in an age which had not made a principle out of toleration inevitably existed even when there were no demagogues to stir up hatreds. The difference in religion, entailing the dietary prohibitions of Judaism, or the refusal to worship emperors, contributed to the frictions, as is historically recorded. The denigration of Jewish laws, and, indeed, of Scripture could and did take place on the lowest of popular levels.

In this context, there was a special focus on Scripture and its legal content as a divisive matter. This is to be approached initially from the curious title which

---

[36] See WOLFSON, op. cit., I, pp. 97—99 for some of the assessments, and, for a much wider assembly, V. NIKIPROWETZKY, Le Commentaire de l'Ecriture chez Philon d'Alexandrie, Arbeiten zur Literatur und Geschichte des Hellenistischen Judentums, 11, Leiden, 1977, pp. 1—3.

[37] See ERWIN R. GOODENOUGH, Politics, pp. 1—20, and, especially, V. TCHERIKOVER, Hellenistic Civilization and the Jews (transl.), Philadelphia, 1959, pp. 309—322, 409—415.

[38] Disputes about whether Jews were citizens, or, better, full citizens center around a rescript of the Emperor Claudius; it is likely that there were limits on their rights, but protection within the ethnic rights granted. See V. TCHERIKOVER, The Jews in Egypt (Hebrew), pp. 154ff. The rescript of Claudius is found in V. TCHERIKOVER and Corpus Papyrorum Judaicarum, ed. V. TCHERIKOVER and A. FUKS, vol. I, Cambridge, Mass. 1960, 153. See V. TCHERIKOVER, Hellenistic Civilization and the Jews, pp. 313—314.

[39] See preceding note. Apparently the rescript of Claudius barred Jews from the *gymnasia*.

Greek Jews gave to the Five Books of Moses, namely, the *Nomos*, "the Law."
Jews in Alexandria lived in the center of three concentric circles of law, the
Jewish, around it the local hellenistic, and around that the over-arching Roman.
Challenges to the Jewish claims of the unique and divine character of the Mosaic
legislation, coming from rude outsiders on matters such as the dietary laws, could
be met by responsive rudeness.

Challenges from sophisticated, skeptical insiders who knew of hellenistic or
Roman statutes almost or actually identical with Mosaic statutes could be met
only by a sophistication or level of knowledge that could be, or seem to be, considerably superior to that of the skeptic.

It may be useful here to set forth preliminarily some motifs common to Plato
and the Stoics: Reality does not inhere in anything material or corporeal, but
only in the incorporeal. The 'real' world is the *cosmos noetos*, the world of concept; the *cosmos aesthetikos*, the world of perception, is unreal. The mechanism
by which one rises from the *cosmos aesthetikos* to the *cosmos noetos* is by freeing
the soul or the higher mind (its synonym), from the body, its prison, so that the
soul or higher mind can enter into the *cosmos noetos* where are found ideas and/or
archetypal forms. Moreover, and most significantly, Scripture is both the record
of eminent men of antiquity, but also — here I repeat — the universal experience
of contemporaneous man.

Lastly, the question could be asked, and seemingly was, in what way is it
appropriate that Genesis, a book almost exclusively narration, be included in
what is called the *Nomos*, "the Law?" The procedure now to follow, viewing
Philo's use of Scripture, will give the clue to the philosophy thereafter to be
presented. To set forth the quasi-existential approach to Scripture is required if
we are to grasp the essence of Philo; thereafter a summary of his philosophy finds
its contest. Partial repetition is involved; it seems unavoidable if we are to do
justice to Philo.

There are two narratives in Scripture of the origin of man. In Gen. 1.1–2.4
it is told that God 'created' man; in Gen. 2.7, that God 'made man', out of dust of
the earth, breathing into him the breath of life. The 'created' man is the ideal of
man; the 'made' man is men such as we. The 'created' man has never come to
earth there has been only the 'made' man. The dust of which the latter was made
alludes to the corporeal[40] aspect of man, and by assumption what is corporeal
is bad, while by assumption the immaterial spirit is good.

In the corporeal part of man (in the body) lie both the senses which are prone
to error and also the passions which distort conduct and impede correct understanding. Hence, man is caught in tension in that he is tugged in opposite directions by his evil body and his good spirit. But Adam, allegorically, is the mind,

---

[40] Issues as to the distinctions between body and flesh, or between soul, spirit, and higher
   mind ought not be raised here. The presentation here deliberately uses words in the most
   neutral sense, for scholars have based acute distinctions on such words, supplying their own
   emphasis, and often arriving both at partisanships and at subtleties which I am persuaded
   Philo would neither have accepted nor understood.

neither a good nor a bad mind, but rather any mind. Any mind functions basically through its senses; Eve is sense perception. The senses convey perceptions to the mind, which can assemble them and sort them out; a dog sees a bone under a tree and goes to it. Adam and Eve are joined together; the mind can function only when joined to the senses, and the senses are meaningless except when joined to the mind. An ordinary lower mind, such as that of a dog, is incapable of what a more gifted mind can do, namely, to infer concepts from perceptions. A dog sees bones or trees, yet cannot have a concept of boneness, or treeness, but a man can have such concepts; the more gifted the human mind, the more readily it can fashion concepts out of antecedent perceptions.

Historically, Adam, mind, and Eve, sense perception, inclined to the serpent, pleasure. When the mind and the senses become bent on pleasure, they lose Eden, ideal virtue — virtue as a concept;[41] the four rivers which flowed from Eden are the perceptible virtues of justice, bravery, prudence, and moderation (Leg. I, 63 and Quaest. in Genes. I, 12f.). They are perceptible in that we all know just or brave or prudent men. But virtue as a concept is with in the *cosmos noetos*. You and I, like the first man, can lose what perceptible virtues we may have by following pleasure, and thereafter fall into despair.

But man is distinguished from all other creatures[42] in the possession of hope, the allegory of Enos, which means "man" in Hebrew; Gen. 4.26 tells that Enos h o p e d to call on the name of God. Our possession of hope can move us to a next stage, that of Enoch, allegorically repentance. Next we can move on to Noah, allegorically tranquility. The stage of Noah is the third of the preliminary stages, preliminary in that Noah represents a relative righteousness rather than a pure one. Tranquility is not the goal of living; it is the third stage in preparing to move on further to the goal.

If through hope and repentance we have come to a relative tranquility, we can then move even further, provided we have the gifts that will enable us to do so. These gifts are the innate, natural endowments with which men can be born. These gifts number three: the capacity to be taught, the gift of intuition, and the ability to practice. The patriarchs allegorically are these three innate gifts: the patriarchs were not so much men as they were qualities of the soul. Abraham is the capacity to be taught, Isaac intuition, and Jacob the ability to practice. Historically the three patriarchs reached perfection; each possessed all three innate gifts, but in Abraham the capacity to be taught was dominant, in Isaac it was intuition, and in Jacob it was the ability to practice. We too can move on towards perfection in the measure that we possess the gifts with which the patriarchs were endowed. The divine gift of the capacity to learn is the Abraham in us, the divine gift of intuition is the Isaac in us, the ability to practice is the Jacob in us. If we have the appropriate endowments, we can recapitulate the experiences of the

---

[41] Ideal virtue is synonymous with true philosophy, Sarah, as we shall see.

[42] The readiest Philonic exposition here summarized is found in his 'De Abrahamo'. On the additional materials, see S. SANDMEL, Philo's Place in Judaism, an assembly from the total Philonic corpus of what Philo sets forth briefly in 'De Abrahamo'.

historical patriarchs. Abraham left Ur; we can do so too.[43] He made an allegorical journey to Charran; we can make the same journey. What was Abraham's departure from Ur? It was a departure from the astrology into which he was born and under which he was raised. Astrology arises from letting the eyes roam the heaven; it stems, then, from sense perception; it is a procedure within the perceptible world. Astrology, in relying on the sense of sight, is a wrong process; it reaches an erroneous conclusion, namely, that the stars control the future. To believe this is to ascribe to the stars, created things, the capacity of the Creator. Such was the error that Abraham abandoned; we too can abandon such errors of method and conclusion and journey on to the truth.

Charran means "holes, orifices," and reminds one of the body; allegorically it means introspection. In journeying to Charran, Abraham abandoned all reliance on the senses. He turned to introspection. Discovering that there existed a *logos* ("mind")[44] within him, he reasoned (that is, he did not any more rely on the senses) that there must be a Logos in the universe. This attainment by his reason was Abraham's momentous achievement, his discovery of the existence of God. (At this point let us define Logos in this context as the best possible conception of God man can attain to and experience; Logos is by no means God Himself.) In epitome, then, the Abraham of history learned to abandon astrology and by dialectic learned the existence of God.

But his learning encompassed other matters. He learned also to control his senses and passions (as you and I can do), rather than to be controlled by them. Gen. ch. 14 is the account of this experience.[45] The four kings of the east are the four passions; the five kings of the Dead Sea region are the five senses. It was not a battle between the four and the five that took place (though so Scripture relates!), but rather a battle between the nine and the higher mind which was learning and progressing. Abraham's nephew Lot is 'inclination',[46] the universal inclination of all men towards material pleasures, before they attain to maturity (Gen. ch. 13). By contrast, Abraham moved beyond such inclination to material pleasures. Rather, his higher mind controlled and regimented his senses and passions. To have killed these would have distorted his existence (as, for example, to 'kill' sexual desire could result in race suicide). Rather, Abraham established democracy in his soul. By definition, democracy is the state of affairs under which a true king — a philosopher king — has all the components of his kingdom in their proper array. Democracy in the soul similarly arrays the components of a man in proper manner.

Further in his progress, Abraham's mating with Hagar was his mastery of the encyclical studies. These are within the perceptible world, though on the

---

[43] Abraham is the example we can follow of moving from error to truth. W. L. Knox, Abraham and the Quest for God, Harvard Theological Review, XXVIII (1935), pp. 55–60, portrays Abraham as the prototype of the convert, a view affirmed by S. Sandmel in: Abraham's Knowledge of the Existence of God, Harvard Theological Review, XLIV (1951), pp. 137–139.

[44] On Logos, see below, p. 24.

[45] See S. Sandmel, Philo's Place, p. 147, note 221.

[46] Ibid.

border of the world of concept. When we are mated with Hagar, we can beget only Ishmael ("hearing God"); Ishmael was an archer whose arrows hit the target but seldom the bull's eye. Allegorically, Ishmael is the sophist, a status much lower than that of the philosopher. Only after one has mated with Hagar can one mate with true[47] philosophy, Sarah, this in the world of concept.

The consequence of the progress Abraham made is described in Gen. ch. 18, the account of three visitors who come to Abraham.[48] The three, though a triple vision, are in reality a single vision, entailing a unity transcending all other unities. One of the three visitors is the divine *dynamis* ("power") of creation; a second is the divine *dynamis* of ruling the world; the third of the three is the divine Logos. The progressing person who arrays his inner being, as carefully and effectively as in Gen. ch. 18 Abraham had arranged his household, has the experience that the three — the Logos and the two powers — enter into his spiritual household. God in Philo is *To On*, or *To Ontos On*, and is not attainable to man. The creative *dynamis* is the biblical *theos*, usually to be rendered "God," but not at all to be regarded as identical with *To On*; the ruling power is the biblical *kyrios*, "Lord." The powers are aspects of God, not the totality of Him; *To On* is the totality, and, of course, much more than just the sum of merely the facets. A man even of low mentality can discern in the perceptible world that creation has taken place; he can with his senses discern *theos*. A better mind, though still in the perceptible world, can discern *kyrios*, that is, that the universe is governed, as in the parade of the seasons and in their annual repetition. The best minds, through entering into the world of concept, can there encounter the divine Logos. From the standpoint of man in his ascent towards the divine, Logos is the ultimate to which man can rise. From the standpoint of God, in His descent towards man, Logos is the lowest to which He descends. Hence, to be united with the Logos, or for the Logos to enter into a man's spiritual household, is the maximum human attainment of the union of God and man. Union with the Logos is a "second best journey," for the first best is beyond man.

Abraham, accordingly, became united with the Logos. To him was accorded the privilege of mating with Sarah, this in the world of concept. She is true philosophy, ideal virtue. As ideal virtue (and within the world of concept) Sarah is virgin,[49] free of any contact with anything material. She is the mother of Isaac, "laughter," namely, the spiritual joy which comes to a sage as a result of his virtue; that is, 'Sarah' is the mother of 'Isaac', but 'Abraham' cannot be the father, for no man begets his spiritual joy. The father and begetter is God, who mates with the virgin Sarah, who, bearing Isaac, presents him to Abraham.[50]

But, returning to the topic, in what way is Genesis appropriate within a writing called the *Nomos*, a passage depicts Abraham being addressed as "king."[51]

---

[47] The various Greek systems are philosophy; it is Judaism which is true philosophy.

[48] S. SANDMEL, Philo's Place, pp. 180—183.

[49] Based on Gen. 18.11, which Philo interprets as restoration to virginity. See next note.

[50] This allegory, occurring three times in Philo, is deemed a mystery, not suitable for all ears, and not to be passed on as gossip by those inducted into it. See S. SANDMEL, Philo's Place, pp. 174—175, and the many references there in note 340.

[51] LXX Gen. 23.6.

A true king, being a philosopher, can free his mind from the prison of the body, and have his mind rise to the world of concept and there encounter the ideal law, the unwritten law of nature. He absorbs this ideal law, and, reverting to the perceptible world, proceeds to decree particular laws. These particular laws, coming from a philosopher-king, are consistent with nature and reliable substitutions of it. Such a philosopher-king is a *nomos empsychos kai logikos*, a law made incarnate and vocal.[52] Abraham was such a figure, an embodiment of the law of nature. Genesis is the Book of the Law of Nature. Abraham, Isaac, and Jacob were each a *nomos empsychos*. Moreover, Abraham was a prophet, a member of God's own family, to whom God spoke as one does to members of his family.

If you and I wish to live like Abraham, and attain what he did, there are two different ways open to us. One is for us to do exactly what Abraham did: abandon Ur, regiment our senses and passions, mate with Hagar, and so array our inner spiritual life that we too experience the Logos. But to travel this route we must possess the innate endowments of Abraham (or of Isaac, or of Jacob), and in particular we must possess *orthos logos*, impeccably accurate, error-free dialectic.

But suppose we lack these innate endowments? Are we denied the goal of religion? No. There is another way which God has graciously provided, namely, the laws of Moses. These laws are a record of what Abraham did. Anyone who obeys the laws of Moses is living like Abraham. If he is unschooled and deficient in innate gifts, he lives like Abraham[53] coincidentally, that is, without awareness that he is doing so. But if he has better gifts, he can rise above mere coincidence. The laws like the narratives are subject to allegory. The literal law — Philo associates it with Aaron — is the bare requirement. The allegory of the law — the level of Moses — is the law's spiritual significance. Passover means the soul's passing out of rule by the body; circumcision prunes away passion; abstention from a delicacy such as pork is commendable self-control.[54] One can, then, observe the laws of Moses and live like Abraham consciously, with fullest awareness. Moreover, recalling that thought is unuttered speech and is pure, while speech is uttered thought and is impure, we can understand that Aaron represents uttered thought (*logos prophorikos*) and Moses unuttered speech (*logos endiathetos*). Indeed, Moses allegorically is the divine and holy Logos.

Moses is by far the most important of the biblical characters to Philo. Paradoxically, he devotes in the 'Allegory' much less space to him than he does to the characters of Genesis. The two[55] treatises, called 'Vita Mosis', in the 'Exposition'[56], are more than twice as long as 'De Abrahamo'. The first (Mos. I) is primari-

---

[52] See Abr. 5; Mos. II, 4. The translation is that of ERWIN R. GOODENOUGH. On the origin of the phrase, see his 'The Political Philosophy of Hellenistic Kingship', Yale Classical Studies, I (1928), pp. 55–102. See, for a brief survey of the sources, LCL, Philo, VI, p. 605.

[53] S. Abr. 5.

[54] Mos. I, 155–159. Cf. Deter. 38–40, 126–135.

[55] Manuscripts and early printings treat the work as if three treatises.

[56] Differences of judgment have existed as to whether 'De Vita Mosis' is to be classified with the 'Exposition' or not. On the question, see ERWIN R. GOODENOUGH, Philo's Exposition of the Law and his De Vita Mosis, Harvard Theological Review, XXVI (1933), pp. 109–125, and LCL, Philo, VI, 1935, pp. XV–XVI.

ly biographical; Philo himself states this in the preamble to the second treatise. He proposes, so he says, to write the life of Moses whom some describe as the legislator of the Jews, others as the interpreter of the holy laws. The exact intent in 'interpreter' is elusive, but clearly something beyond legislation itself is intended. In his biographical treatment, Philo follows Scripture,[57] but he adds many items not found there, for example, an imaginative description of Moses' broad and deep education, kindred to Philo's own, and the quality of his mind (Mos. I, 18–24).

The second treatise (Mos. II) deals with Moses as lawgiver, as high priest, and prophet; king here is the philosopher-king and lawgiver. Devoted as the treatise is to topics, it is presented without reference to narrative or chronology. As to Moses as a lawgiver, he was the best of all in all countries, since his laws came truly from God. Only the laws of Moses have remained unchanged and unaltered. Because Gentiles admired them, Ptolemy Philadelphus determined to have them translated into Greek.[58] Philo then justifies the arrangement in which the historical materials (Genesis and Exodus chs. 1–19) precede the legislative in the structure of Scripture. In the legislative Moses suggests and admonishes, rather than commanding.[59] The legislation is in conformity with eternal nature (Mos. I, 12–65).

Moses as a high priest established the cult, having arranged for the construction of the cult-objects, and thereafter selected Aaron to become the high priest in his stead (abstaining from designating his own sons, Mos. II, 142).

As to prophecy and Moses, there are three types of material in the sacred writings. One type are those divine utterances spoken by God with the prophet being His interpreter; the second are the results of questions to God and His answers; the third are those spoken by Moses when he was possessed by God and in *ekstasis*. God had given Moses His own power of foreknowledge and the ability to reveal future events (such as the splitting of the Red Sea and the fall of manna). When it became time for Moses to journey from earth to heaven, God transformed his mortal two-fold nature, body and soul, into a single entity, mind, pure as the sun. Moses then prophesied about the tribes (Deut. ch. 32) and then about his own death. He was buried not by mortal hands but by immortal powers.

Moses, allegorically the divine Logos, accordingly set forth in Genesis and Exodus chs. 1–19 the law of nature, and in the rest of the Pentateuch the special laws which are substitutes for the law of nature.

Hence, granted that the Mosaic laws, being written, are in the perceptible world and are to be classified as special, or particular, laws,[60] they are the best possible imitations of nature and thoroughly consistent with it. In Athens, a new king abolishes or alters laws, or introduces new ones; the laws of Moses are immutable. If one moves from Athens to Sparta or to Ephesus, the laws change;

---

[57] Curiously, Philo omits the Sinai episode. It appears, however, in Dec. 32–49.
[58] Philo repeats the substance of the 'Letter of Aristeas' (II, 31–44).
[59] Mos. II, 50.
[60] Abr. 3–5.

the laws of Moses, however, are everywhere the same. For these two reasons, they surpass the laws of all other peoples.

Accordingly, one can reach perfection as Abraham did through living like him and exercizing *orthos logos*; or else one can reach it by observing the laws of Moses. In the first instance one is, as it were, on his own, and few men have this capacity. Scripture was graciously given to mankind so that all men may be able to do what otherwise only few could do.

IV. Philo's Philosophy

Philo is a preacher in the sense that he encourages, indeed he urges, his readers to travel the route to communion with God. Judaism, true religion, is the journey to communion with God. Philo is a philosopher at least in the sense that he utilizes Plato and Stoicism in his explanation of how an Abraham or a Jacob progressed, or how an Isaac was born perfect.

Philo does not present a systematic exposition of his philosophy. Modern scholars, such as JAMES DRUMMOND,[61] HARRY A. WOLFSON,[62] and EMILE BRÉHIER[63] have done so.[64] The absence of his own system occasions a number of problems. The main problem is that of incompleteness, the nature of which needs to be clear. The philosophic materials present in Philo are there because there are biblical passages which he interprets as philosophic items. All too often, where there is nothing in the Bible which could occasion a philosophical explanation, Philo has no reason to present one. Again, Scripture is repetitious, and so is Philo, and he does not always repeat himself in the same way. Consistent as he is, he is also guilty of that imprecision which inheres in non-systematic expositions. Thus, he can confuse us by the variety of terms for mind, higher mind, soul, reason, and the like, and we can err if we try to commit him by words alone to precise meanings of his philosophic explanations, and if we try unduly to distinguish, for example, among terms such as *nous, logismos, logos, sophia, episteme* and the like. At times there are distinctions legitimately to be drawn from Philo's present-ations, and at times acute distinctions need to be sturdily resisted. To present his philosophy independent of the biblical basis is to run the risk of ascribing either too much or too little to some particular item.

The following is a brief outline of main aspects of his philosophy.

---

[61] Philo Judaeus; or the Jewish-Alexandrian Philosophy in its Development and Completion, 2 vols., London, 1888.

[62] Previously cited, note 33.

[63] Les idées philosophiques et religieuses de Philon d'Alexandrie, Paris, 2nd ed., 1925.

[64] Such works have been criticized by W. VÖLKER, Fortschritt und Vollendung bei Philo von Alexandrien, Texte und Untersuchungen zur Geschichte der altchristlichen Literatur, 49, 1, Leipzig, 1938, as being wrong in supposing that Philo can be systematized. VÖLKER also denies that mysticism can be ascribed to Philo.

1. God

Philo's God (*To On*) is thoroughly transcendant. In no way is He directly within the perceptible world. He is shapeless and formless. He was, is, and will be eternal. He is beyond man's cognitive attainment. His attributes can never be expressed in positive ways, for so to do is in effect to define God; to define is to limit, and by assumption God is unlimited. His totality (*pleroma*, "fullness") is too vast for man's comprehension. He is nameless. (Philo shows little concern with the Tetragrammaton; *YHWH*, the name of the Deity which, ineffable in the Judean tradition, was to be pronounced only by the high priest and only on the Day of Atonement when the high priest entered the holy of holies; see Mos. II, 208 for the single allusion known to me.)

God is the 'good' or the 'true'. He is pure being, in that He is unmixed with anything corporeal. He lacks and needs nothing, being all selfsufficient.

God is not identical with, but is superior to the world of ideas, and is, indeed, their creator. (Here Philo seems to depart from Plato, who viewed ideas as pre-existent and hence uncreated.) As superior to the ideas, and as their Creator, there is a series of appellative synonyms for God: Craftsman, Maker, Planter, Steersman, Parent, Father, and Cause (some of which are also Scriptural appel-latives). By analogy to a well of water and to the sun in the sense that each is a source, one for water, the other for light, well and sun are used also metaphoric-ally in speaking of the Deity.[65]

2. Proof of God's Existence

Though God in His essence is unknowable,[66] even philosophically, proof of His existence can be formulated. The formulation and oral articulation of such proof is more difficult than is the silent mental conception of that proof. There are what appear to be four different proofs. One is the argument from effect to cause, that is, since it is obvious that the world exists, its existence is the effect of an antecedent cause. A second argument, derived from the Aristotelianism which Philo partly rejects (namely, the Aristotelian view of the eternity of matter), the world is a passive object on which the active cause works; God is proved through the eternity of motion in that God is the immovable prime mover. The third proof is derived from applying the principle of causality to the orderly processes of nature. The fourth proof, arrived at by analogy, contends that just as a mind exists in man, so much there be a God existent in the universe. Just as the mind is separable from the body, so is God separable from the world. (In part this argument is directed against what might be called pantheism.)

---

[65] WOLFSON, II, pp. 94—149.
[66] WOLFSON, II, p. 73.

3. Logos

The Logos, we have said, is the immanent facet of the transcendant *To On*. In any situation in which contact between Deity and this world, or between Deity and man, is to be expressed, it is the Logos which is in contact. As a facet of God, Logos is, of course, less than the *pleroma*. Moreover, the *pleroma* is made up of more than the Logos itself; the activities of God (as distinct from the analyzable essence of God) are at times to be described as having been accomplished each by a *dynamis*, a power of God; that is, a *dynamis* is a clue to what God has done or does, and is not a clue to God's essence. Indeed, a *dynamis* can be a single activity of the Logos, rather than of *To On*. That Philo uses Theos, the creative *dynamis*, does not obstruct his ascribing the creation of the world to the Logos. Kyrios, the ruling *dynamis*, likewise can be treated either as separate from the Logos, or else as contained within it. The point is that Logos is attainable to man (or, at least to some men), if such can rise into the world of concept. The *dynamis* are attainable to less gifted men in that they enter into the perceptible world as the Logos does not.

The events at creation entailed God's creation of the perfect Logos[67], an act that is by analogy comparable with the work of an architect who requires an idea or plan; Logos is the center, or focus, of the divine plan of creation. The Logos is the ideal macrocosm; an aspect of the Logos, breathed into man, makes the spiritual side of man a corresponding microcosm. The created world, imperfect because it is material, is in its way a microcosm, reflecting the Logos, the perfect macrocosm which is immaterial.

What thoughtless men might in ordinary speech ascribe to God, thoughtful men, in their guarded, philosophical speech ascribe to Logos. In a sense (in anticipation of later Christian gnostics) God created the Logos in order that the Logos might in turn create the world. While passages suggest that in Philo the Logos is involved in and responsible for creation, there is no clear-cut expression in Philo of the Logos as the creator such as appear elsewhere, for example in the prologue to the Gospel According to John. Indeed, the question has properly been raised whether the Logos in Philo is any more than merely a convenient philosophical construct and, if the ensuing words are clear, it can be contended that the Logos is not a real reality, but is only a manner of speaking. In other aspects of Philo's doctrines it is essential to note that there is a disparity between what he seems to accept religiously and what he defines philosophically.

4. Scripture

Thus, religiously Scripture for him is a vessel containing God's revelation. Indeed that revelation occurred at historic moments, and was graciously conveyed to the spiritual giants, such as Abraham and especially Moses. Yet the basic meaning of revelation implies an action on the part of God, an action that

---

[67] Opif. 24—25.

impinges on men. For Philo this is reversed: revelation is the action of men, such
as these giants among them who ascended to God. The content of revelation —
the audible words of Scripture — become metamorphosed in Philo into the ascent
of the soul, freed from the impediment of the body, into the world of archetypal
Platonic forms, all this in the most rational of ways. Scripture — which rabbinic
Jews called *Torah*, divine teaching — becomes altered from narratives into
accounts of universal personality traits, and divine commandments into norms of
virtue that are rational, rather than being divine demands and prohibitions. When
Philo tells us that Moses never commands, but only encourages and exhorts, he is
in effect removing from Scripture what ordinary people might consider its prime
characteristic, its divine prohibitions and demands.

The Scriptural commandments — both the affirmative demands and the
prohibitions[68] — emerge in Philo's treatment in that the cardinal virtues, which
characterize many humans in their dealings with men, derive from the prohibitions in Scripture. Generic or ideal virtue, on the other hand, derives from the
affirmative demands, and is to be equated with man in relationship to God, that
is, in terms of piety. Scripture provides in the written Mosaic laws the cardinal
virtues, which are applications of the unwritten law of nature, with the consequence that Scripture and natural law are in effect identical.

Philo portrays faith[69] — which can arise initially from doubt — as belief in
God, in His unity and providence; belief in the Scriptural revelation, and unreserved trust in Him. Faith is in effect a synonym for piety.

In Philo, prayer[70] is presented as within the ambit of the virtue. Sacrifices,[71]
as offered in the Temple in Jerusalem, are a worthy form of worship, provided
that these include the intent of the heart and are not simply mechanical. Similarly,
prayer devoid of the intent of the heart is of no value. Indeed, earnest prayer is
superior to sacrifices. Silent prayer is superior to spoken prayer. Spoken prayer
is at its best when it is soft-spoken.[72]

Repentance[73] is likewise within the ambit of the virtues. It is, of course,
derived from Scripture. Absolute sinlessness characterizes only God. While
perfection is superior to repentance, repentance is the younger brother to guilt-
lessness. Yet it is unmistakable that Philo, paradoxically, regards Scriptural law
as commandments. The solution of this problem would seem to lie in a distinction
to be drawn between religion and philosophy. Religion can be, in addition to
supernatural, both capricious and also illogical; philosophy, however, must be
rational. Accordingly, when the philosopher applies rationalism to the supernatural, or the capricious, or the illogical, the end result is to turn everything into
the pleasingly rational. Philosophy can remove the deterrent to a skeptic's willingness to believe in a religion, with the consequence that the skeptic can thereby in

[68] WOLFSON, II, p. 200.
[69] Ibid. II, p. 218.
[70] Ibid. II, p. 238.
[71] Ibid. II, p. 244.
[72] Ibid. II, pp. 245—250.
[73] Ibid. II, pp. 256—258.

effect accept both the irrational religion and the rational philosophical explana-tion. This is the case even when, or especially when, the philosophy in reality is in direct contradiction with the religion. A Philo, then, believes in literal revelation, and explains it as if it is not revelation at all. To define revelation in Philo, as has been done above, correctly reflects revelation as he explains it, but one must add that he also believes in biblical revelation.

The content of revelation religiously is Scripture. Philosophically it is the ideas, ideas in the Platonic sense, of archetypal forms which the mature and disciplined mind can rise to, on its ascent from the perceptible world into the world of concept. At times Philo seems to conceive of the ideas as contained within the Logos; at times they appear to be outside and apart from the Logos. One might say that Philo inclines to view the Logos as the sum total of the separate archetypal forms.

The powers of God appear to derive from Philo's view of ideas. Since God created the ideas, they in a sense are reflective of Him. One might say that an idea is a passive power, while a divine power is an idea that is active. An idea which can come into the mind of a man and stir him to some deed is a power of God; from man's standpoint, a power is that which a man can recognize as some single limited action in the context of abundant divine activity. The two principal powers, as we have seen, are the creative and the ruling powers; from the stand-point of man, they represent two different grades in the human capacity of acquiring knowledge about God; lowest minds can recognize the creative power, and better minds the ruling.

5. Israel and Man

The recipient of revelation is the collective Israel,[74] which means "seeing[75] God." Philo makes a few direct allusions in his allegory to the collective people.[76] In general, however, he means by Israel anyone, Jew or not, who rises to the 'vision' of God. Ordinarily Jews rise readily to the vision, and non-Jews only rise sporadically.

It is the series of Jewish individuals, that is, the Patriarchs and Moses, and the prophets who exemplify revelation. Because they are men, Philo must give fullest attention to the nature of man, a mixture of the material and the im-material. He speaks of the widest range of men, for example, the fool, the hypocrite, and the sage, because his philosophy compels him to, and because innumerable passages in Scripture lend themselves readily to alignment with this sense or that passion, or with topics such as memory or learning, or physiology, or the virtue of prudence. The gifted individuals of the Jewish past are those who were endowed with innate high qualities.

---

[74] See below, p. 29, on *politeia*.
[75] On the variety and gradation of the senses, see LCL, Philo, X, p. 334.
[76] They are the "beloved of God" (Migr. 113) and the "best of races" (Congr. 51).

Philo's explanation of prophecy is borrowed from Plato. He proceeds to assert, however, that in the case of the prophet, it is the Deity speaking through the mechanism of a body prepared for the purpose through the ascension of the soul to the highest level of the world of concept.

His view of man is appropriately to be called dualistic. Compared with the monism — the absence of tension between body and soul, which characterizes Palestinian Judaism — his dualism is advanced; compared with the extreme dualism of second century Christian gnostics, his dualism is relatively restrained.

6. Miracles; Angels

In a general way, Philo accepts the historicity of biblical accounts of miracles but he usually supplies a naturalistic explanation that in effect denies what is usually meant by a miracle, namely, an event in which the divine has intervened to alter the course of nature or of cause and effect. At times his naturalistic explanation accompanies an assertion of the supernatural character of the intervention.[77]

Philo appears to ascribe souls to the stars.[78] Souls are, of course, incorporeal. There are different ranks of souls[79] (as in Plato). Souls which abstain from entering into bodies can be called angels (though philosophers call them demons[80]). Angels appear to inhabit either the supper air, or even[81] heaven. They seem also to be identified with powers of the Deity, that is, the abundance of divine functions of which creation and ruler are the two principal ones. Philo does not reject the literal accounts of angels[82] (though he usually allegorizes the passages); the angels of popular folklore, as in Daniel or Revelation, are thoroughly absent.

7. Soul — Mind — Spirit

Since in a sense soul, mind, and spirit are synonymous, just as there is in man, and even in animals, a lower mind which assembles and sorts out the perceptions of the senses, and a higher mind in man which draws concepts out of perceptions, one can speak of a lower and a higher soul. The lower mind and lower soul, being incapable of concept, and operating strictly within the world of perception, must necessarily be destructible and mortal[83] (as is the body); the higher mind-soul is indestructible and immortal. As to the fate of the soul after the death

---

[77] WOLFSON, I, p. 351.
[78] Ibid. I, p. 365.
[79] Ibid. I, p. 366.
[80] Ibid. I, p. 367.
[81] Ibid. I, pp. 372—373.
[82] Ibid. I, p. 379.
[83] Ibid. I, p. 395.

of the body, Philo lists a series of views,[84] apparently accepting finally the view that the immortal soul joins the angels (souls which have never entered a body) in heaven; but some souls rise to become ideas in the world of concept. Special souls,[85] Moses for example, rose to the presence of God.

Souls can undergo rebirth; this is a spiritual rebirth, not a physical rebirth as would be implied by resurrection, a doctrine alien to Philo.

8. Free Will − Providence

Philo ascribes to the higher mind (found in gifted men) the capacity of free will.[86] The best rational mind avoids domination by the passions and the senses; poor minds lack free will.[87] Knowledge of good and evil is a precondition for the best minds freely to choose. Poor minds lack accurate knowledge, and hence they lack the freedom of choice.

9. Sin

Philo distinguishes (as does Scripture) between involuntary evil[88] and sin (namely, an accidental evil event, like the head of an axe falling from its handle and striking someone) and deliberate, intended sin. Often involuntary sin is an indirect way by means of which God can punish those who deserve punishment. Deliberate sin, though, is purely human, and is free from direct or indirect divine causation.

Both grace (the gift to man of something he has not earned) and providence (God's concern for man, and His direction of the flow of events so that man can avoid the untoward) are warmly affirmed. Providence in no way compromises free will. Grace[89] can most readily come to the man whose virtue puts him into the position of receiving it (Abraham prepared himself, but it was God's grace which determined whether or not he received the 'vision of God').

Earthly rewards[90] are to be given to the righteous, but a higher spiritual reward also awaits these.

10. Political Theory

Philo's theories about government presuppose kingship[91], this on the basis of Scripture. The accounts of the divine selection of a Saul or a David − though

---

[84] Ibid. I, pp. 398−401.
[85] Ibid. I, p. 403.
[86] Ibid. I, p. 431.
[87] Ibid. I, p. 437.
[88] Ibid. I, p. 441.
[89] Ibid. I, p. 451.
[90] Ibid. II, pp. 301−302.
[91] Ibid. II, p. 329.

Philo does not mention prophetic anointment — turn him away from kingship determined by lot or by the vote of those whose ballots can be bought. True
kingship[92], as exemplified in Moses, results not from the possession of military
power, but from nobility of conduct. From biblical accounts, such as the confirmation of David as king by all the people, Philo seems opposed to limiting the
assent to the election of a king to only a portion of the population, such as
property owners or those who are of good family. In his view, Moses was
designated king by God, but with the free consent of the governed. A king rules
for life. Though Philo says nothing directly about hereditary kingship, he
endorses it indirectly[93] (since this too is biblical).

He sets forth requirements about the king:[94] One, the king is to judge the
people in full accord with the laws. Two, he is to delegate minor matters to
subordinates. Three, he is to rule people for their benefit. Four, he must have
recourse in ambiguous cases to men learned in the laws.

Moses, in the Scriptural account, was in effect the high priest until he invested
Aaron[95] in that office and then designated who should be the ordinary priests.
The same person can scarcely serve both as king, guarding the obligations to men,
and as high priest, guarding the obligations to God, though the great Moses
uniquely could do this.

The Jewish people constitute a *politeia*,[96] an entity governed by laws derived
from the constitution devised by Moses. A citizen of that polity is someone
willing to be ruled by the Law. An alien who wishes to live under the Law cannot
be barred from citizenship. Scripture has defined the rights both of temporary and
of permanent 'residents'.[97] Those who are born Jews are all fully equal under the
constitution. Proselytes (Philo also uses the term 'epelytes'),[98] are to be admitted
on equal terms (though Philo pays lip service to restrictions found in Deut.
23.4—9). The born Jew receives God's favor not because of his Jewish birth, but
because he has been faithful to his inherited nobility. Proselytes receive God's
favor because they have abandoned their past and have moved to piety. Only
analytically is there a distinction between the born Jew and the proselyte; in rights
they are equal and in effect are the same.

Philo makes provision for the person who, though abstaining from actually
becoming a Jew (as by undergoing circumcision) is spiritually the equivalent of
a proselyte.[99]

The constitution of Moses is not imperfect, as are the constitutions of the
Greek city-states or kingdoms. The Platonic state, whether that presented in the
'Republic' or that presented as a second best in the 'Laws', could not be the ideal
state. Indeed, the Mosaic constitution is the true ideal state. The laws of Moses

---

[92] Ibid. II, pp. 330—331.
[93] Ibid. II, p. 332.
[94] Ibid. II, p. 334.
[95] Ibid. II, p. 338.
[96] Ibid. II, p. 354.
[97] Ibid. II, p. 364.
[98] Ibid. II, p. 356.
[99] Ibid. II, pp. 369—373.

were promulgated in the wilderness, and were a revelation from God, not inventions of men out of their experience.[100] They were designed for a society that was to come into existence in the future, not one already existing. The people of this society (the Hebrews) had become purged in the wilderness of the wrong opinions and the passions acquired from their residence in Egypt. The true ruler of the ideal state is not its human king but rather God.[101] The Mosaic state is free from possible oligarchy, tyranny, and lawlessness; rather, it is true democracy[102] through its inner harmony, order, and stability.

Philo makes no mention of the Messiah.[103] However, he recognized the disparity between the ideal state expressed in his philosophy and the reality of his time. Palestine was in Roman hands; the dynasty of Herod was disreputable (except for Herod Agrippa I); Jews were scattered throughout the world, and lacked an overall Jewish sovereignty. Accordingly, Philo looks to the future, to what we might call the Messianic age for the renewal of the ideal, the Jewish constitution. At that future time the scattered of Israel would be gathered back to the land of the fathers. In that land cities would be rebuilt,[104] and the barren land would become fruitful. Great prosperity would prevail. Peace, both among men, and between men and beasts, would arise. The wicked — the enemies, by implication the Romans,[105] and also those who rioted against the Jews in 38 — would be punished in that they would undergo God's curses.

The pre-condition for the great change was to be man's repentance,[106] followed by divine forgiveness and redemption, this for the sake of the Patriarchs. Thereafter, the entire world would abandon ancestral customs and turn to the Jewish laws alone.[107]

If the foregoing brief sketch is tolerably clear, it may perhaps now become clear why the assessments of Philo as a philosopher have been so diverse. No one denies the presence in Philo of an immense quantity of philosophy; it is the quality, or lack of it, that has stirred extreme statements, ranging from the denigration of his philosophy to the unreserved praise of it. The disputes are as to whether he is to be viewed as a learned man devoid of all creativity and originality, or as a learned man of perception, insight, and penetrating understanding. In general, those scholars interested in Philo for himself seem to value him; those who read him for the light he is presumed to shed on other, presumably weightier matters, are the ones who denigrate him.

---

[100] Ibid. II, p. 380.

[101] Ibid. II, p. 381.

[102] The treatise 'De Josepho', in the 'Exposition', is both a biography and a treatment of high statesmanship. In the 'Allegory', however, Joseph is treated pejoratively, namely, as a politician.

[103] But see GOODENOUGH, Politics, pp. 115—116, for the view that the idea is present in synonyms, though the word itself is absent.

[104] WOLFSON, ibid. II, p. 408.

[105] Ibid. II, p. 411.

[106] Ibid. II, p. 412.

[107] Ibid. II, pp. 415—420.

V. Jew or Greek

The presence in Philo's writings of so vast a quantity of Greek philosophy is the clue to one of many scholarly disputes, namely, was Philo more Greek than Jewish, or more Jewish than Greek? At the extreme there are views which regard him as Greek, not Jewish, and others as Jewish, not Greek. Perhaps antecedent conclusions are involved in viewing him as Jewish, not Greek, for, as we shall see, there exists a premise that since Philo was loyal to the Jewish community, he therefore must have been essentially Jewish, and whatever reflection there is in him of hellenism is of no real consequence. On the other hand, there is on the surface a marked difference in manner from that of the Rabbis in the Talmud and the Midrash, or from Jesus in the Synoptic Gospels. Specifically, Philo abstains almost completely − perhaps my word 'almost' is excessive caution − from the use of parable; I can recall not a single one of the Rabbinic type. Nor does one find the kind of brief aphorism found in both the Rabbinic literature and in the Synoptic Gospels. The lack of such 'typical' Jewish modes of instruction are regarded by some as evidence of Philo's being essentially Greek.

Since there can be no doubt of the quantity of Greek content in Philo, is it possible for a balanced judgment about his hellenization to arise? If it is assumed that for Philo to merit the epithet Jew, that epithet must connote a Hillel, or a Rabbi Johanan ben Zakkai, or a Rabbi Aqiba, or the author of 'Tobit' or of 'Judith', then perhaps it is such an assumption that beclouds many interpreters. Philo is little like any of these. But how similar are ultra-orthodox residents of Meah Shearim in Jerusalem and the late Professor BELKIN of Yeshivah University? How similar as Christians are Thomas Aquinas, JACOB BÖHME, MARY BAKER EDDY, and RUDOLF BULTMANN?

The statement seems irrefutable that Philo as a type is quite different from the Rabbis of his age and of the immediate subsequent decades. What makes them all Jews is their Jewish loyalty, their devotion to Scripture, and their obedience to Jewish laws. What makes them different from each other is, first and foremost, that they were individuals, and second that they lived in different environments and therefore confronted different situations. Certainly they possessed many elements in common, as we shall see. But the differences are also of consequence.

Three main factors contribute to the conclusion that Philo was essentially Greek,[108] despite his undoubted Jewish loyalty. His bible was the Greek Bible, not the Hebrew or the Aramaic Targum. Indeed, almost the only Hebrew knowledge he displays might not have been his personal possession.[109] This Hebrew is for the most part limited to the etymologies of biblical names. But such lists of

---

[108] The best work on this topic is ISAAC HEINEMANN, Philons griechische und jüdische Bildung, Breslau, 1932. HEINEMANN concludes that Philo knew virtually nothing of the Judean *halacha*; he was a loyal Jew, but thoroughly Grecianized.

[109] One should read, but with caution, A. T. HANSON, Philo's Etymologies, Journal of Theological Studies, XVIII (1967), pp. 128−139.

names were in circulation, certainly after Philo's time. The conclusion of
SANDMEL has been approved by other scholars, that Philo had at best a useless
knowledge of Hebrew.[110]

The second factor is the nature of Philo's use of Greek philosophy, namely,
that at no point does he treat Greek philosophy as something peripheral or
extrinsic. His recourse to it is artificial only in the mechanism of his allegory,
never in substance. It is otherwise so natural to him as to be to the experienced
reader of Philo who knows some Greek philosophy no less than predictable as to
how he will treat a scriptural passage. The exposition Philo gives of his inherited
Judaism — it is, of course, his Judaism that he explains — is quintessentially
Grecian; it is consistently and universally so. This is the case because he has not
only studied Greek philosophy, but also because he has absorbed it that it is as
much a part of him as was his breathing.

The third factor is the matter of what can be called his religiosity. If it is
conceded that a Quaker represents a religiosity different from that of a Roman
Catholic, both of course being Christian, some comments can be made about
Philo's religiosity (comments which can be misunderstood by any one who
desires to do so). Philo conceivably could have observed the same religious
calendar, the same aggregate of biblical laws, acknowledged the same religious
authority as did Judean sages, but nevertheless could view what he did as a Jew
from a stance quite different from that of the Judeans. Specifically, he could
conceivably have viewed his Judaism in a way similar to the Greek pagan intellectuals and their view of the Greek religions. If a view commonly accepted is
right that Greek religion, especially the mysteries, was regarded as the means of
salvation of man out of this miserable world, then a Philo could have viewed
Judaism similarly without noticeable deviation from the cult practices of Judaism.[111] It is conceded on all sides that Philo does use the language of the
mysteries; it is conceded on all sides that he expresses scorn for the pagan religions;
it is conceded that at least on the surface he treats Judaism as if it is the one true
Mystery, whereas the pagan mysteries are error and delusion. Does Philo truly
regard Judaism as a mystery religion? If so, then his religiosity is kindred to that

---

[110] S. SANDMEL, Philo's Place, pp. 11–13. That Philo knew Hebrew seemed likely to CARL
SIEGFRIED, Philo von Alexandria als Ausleger des Alten Testamentes, Jena, 1875, reprinted
Aalen–Amsterdam, 1970 and even then the issue had long been disputed, pp. 142–144.

[111] This view is expressed in several places by ERWIN R. GOODENOUGH, e.g., in: An Introduction to Philo Judaeus, New Haven, 1940, pp. 184–187. This citation of GOODENOUGH is
not meant as an unreserved endorsement of GOODENOUGH's views; too often these seem to
go much too far. 'By Light, Light: the Mystic Gospel of Hellenistic Judaism', New Haven,
1935, has a needlessly flamboyant title. It is a brilliant, overstated, and erratic work.
GOODENOUGH's thesis that Philo represents a peripheral Judaism, different from Judea,
led him into a theory of a sub-rosa Judaism which was extra-Talmudic and anti-Pharisaic.
His multi-volume 'Jewish Symbols in the Greco-Roman Period', I–XIII, New York,
1953–68, is a study of pagan symbols found widely in Jewish art. GOODENOUGH saw in
these symbols what one might call 'pictorial allegorization'; he tries to give literary expression to non-literary pictorial representation, by way of JUNGian psychology. See further
S. SANDMEL, The First Christian Century in Judaism and Christianity, New York, 1969,
pp. 86–88.

of pagan intellectuals, and remote from the varieties of Palestinian Judaism where the motif of salvation from this world is noticeably missing. If Philo indeed represents a Grecian religiosity, then this accommodation or syncretism is considerably more significant than an item such as his utilization of the Bible in Greek; rather, Philo would thereby represent a hellenization so basic as to render this or that detail of conformity or lack of conformity with Palestinian Judaism of little account. Precisely such a view of Philo as essentially a Greek, though loyally Jewish, has been warmly advocated by ERWIN R. GOODENOUGH.[112] If it be granted that GOODENOUGH has overstated the case (as I hold he has), nevertheless a more restrained advocacy of the basic view might well be tenable. That is, Philo seems to shift the center of gravity of Judaism. Palestinians viewed Judaism as centered in divinely revealed laws, the observance of which was the goal of an 'objective' type of religion, whereas in Philo the laws are a means to salvation in a 'subjective' type of religion.

The case can be made, then, that the Jew Philo is a Greek in his basic religious assumptions and inferences.[113]

Then what is there Jewish in Philo? The prompt answer, if we will not insist that Jewish means Pharisaic-Rabbinic, needs to be, quite as much as, or even more than, what is Greek.[114] For example, his Logos doctrine, however strongly it reflects Stoic notions of his environment, is genealogically to be traced to Jewish 'wisdom' (I Kings 3.5—12) according to which wisdom is a gift bestowed by God, as being neither acquired by schooling nor by experience. That 'wisdom' was available to the Creator at the time of creation (Prov. 8.22—31). Moreover, wisdom and Torah had become identified with each other long before Philo, as in Ecclesiasticus 4.24; 9.1, and Wisdom of Solomon 4.11—19. The precise steps in the development from Hebrew ḥokmah ("wisdom") to Philo's logos are not fully traceable.[115] Antecedent to Philo, there had taken place, when Jews and Greeks had encountered each other, the identification of ḥokmah — Torah with sophia, and thereafter the identification of ḥokmah — Torah — sophia — logos. However Grecian Philo's explanation of logos might be, the basic supposition in the term is Jewish. The divine Logos is both divine wisdom and also divine revelation, and this union of the two is Jewish.

---

[112] A key passage, Spec. I, 319—323, is as clear and specific a rejection of the Greek mysteries as one could find. GOODENOUGH interprets this passage as only denouncing pagan mysteries. Against this, see NIKIPROWETZKY (op. cit.), pp. 16—18; 30—32, in support of the criticism of GOODENOUGH leveled by VÖLKER.

[113] NIKIPROWETZKY (op. cit.) interestingly provides two chapters, one which he calls 'Philo Alexandrinus' (his first chapter) and the other 'Philo Judaeus' (his second) as a means of discussing the respective Greek and Jewish elements.

[114] See NIKIPROWETZKY (op. cit.), p. 241, and his citation of A. JAUBERT, pp. 260—261.

[115] On the backgrounds of Logos, see, for a brief statement, WOLFSON, I, pp. 20—26, and the references there to Ecclesiasticus, Wisdom of Solomon, and the like. The topic of Wisdom has become a central concern in current New Testament scholarship. One fears that too often it has become exaggerated to the point of distortion.

Moreover, it is Scripture, the Jewish sacred writings, which Philo expounds. However much he may echo Plato's 'Timaeus' in 'Opif.', it is Genesis that he expounds by means of the 'Timaeus', not the 'Timaeus' by means of Genesis. It is Abraham, Joseph, and Moses about whom he wrote surviving essays, not Pythagoras, Heraclitus, or Zeno. It is the Decalogue and biblical laws that he expounds, not the codes of the Greek city-states.

The delineation of Philo as if he were a Pharisaic-Rabbinic Jew, found in some scholars,[116] tends to cloud the issues. The emergence of Synagogue Judaism properly raises for its historians questions about the origin and the manner of the unfolding of *halaka*, the post- and non-biblical Jewish law, which climaxes in the later collections known as the Midrash and the Mishna. In Philo's treatrise 'On the Special Laws', there are instances in which the materials presented are non-biblical. Does Philo owe to Palestinian sages some debt in the realm of *halaka*? Possibly he does; it is equally possible that he provides inferences which should be ascribed to Scripture rather than to his knowledge of the discussions and debates in the Judean academies. A work published in 1879, 'Philo und die Halacha', by BERNHARD RITTER, assembled an array of parallels between halakic passages in Philo and those in the Midrash, with the assumption there being that such parallels settled the issue of source (Judean academies) and derivation (Philo). The works of SAMUEL BELKIN, The Alexandrian Halakah in Apologetic Literature of the First Century C.E., Philadelphia, 1936, and: Philo and the Oral Law, Cambridge, Mass., 1940, were dedicated to demonstrate a greater number of parallels than RITTER had uncovered. BELKIN then proceeds to contend, gratuitously, that such halakic similarity proves that Philo's Judaism was not essentially different from the Pharisaic-Rabbinic Judaism of Judea. It can be legitimately doubted that Philo needed Judean precedents in order to arrive at his halakic conclusions, and, moreover, even if one conceded that he did derive the halakic items from Judea, such a concession scarcely touches the issue of Philo's similarity to or dissimilarity from the Rabbis, for it is not in *halaka* that the distinction lies.

The entire question is fraught with complex problems. Thus, the Midrash and the Mishnah were recorded at least a century after Philo. The Midrash and the Mishnah, though, quote sages contemporary with Philo and sages earlier. But there intrudes chronologically between the age of Philo and the age when the Midrash and the Mishnah were set down in writing the catastrophic event of 70 A.D. The non-historic character of the Midrash and the Mishnah presents the problem of control, namely, how reliable are the attributions made in the post-70 period to the pre-70 period? The precise dating of Rabbinic materials is most precarious.[117]

The case is even more precarious respecting *haggada*, the term used for Pharisaic-Rabbinic materials which are not strictly halakic. In part, haggadic

---

[116] This presumption is omnipresent in WOLFSON. For a review of the literature, see NIKIPRO-WETZKY, op. cit., pp. 40—49.

[117] See, for example, BERNARD BAMBERGER, The Dating of Aggadic Materials, Journal of Biblical Literature, LXVIII (1949), pp. 115—123 and S. SANDMEL, Philo's Place, pp. 13—26.

materials entailed narratives. For example, it is told that Terah, the father of Abraham, owned a shop where idols were sold. Terah left Abraham in charge; he returned to find the shop in shambles, with all the idols broken except the largest, in whose hands there rested an axe. Abraham, who had chopped the idols to pieces, explained to his father that the biggest idol had won the chopping. In part, however, haggadic materials can be a non-legal deduction that falls short of being a narrative. For example, did Father Abraham have no daughters? Perhaps the verse, "The Lord blessed Abraham *ba-kol* ("in everything")" is the clue to Abraham's having had an unnamed daughter; or perhaps the daughter was not nameless, but, indeed, bore the name Bakol. This matter of *ba-kol* falls short of being a narrative in the sense of a story with a beginning, a middle, and an end. Again, some haggadic materials are less than rounded narratives, but more than simply the ingenious manipulation of a verse.

Pseudepigraphic works such as 'Jubilees' prove the case that *haggada* arose earlier than Philo. Haggadic materials of 'Jubilees' reappear in Josephus,[118] in whose writings an abundance of still other haggadic (and halakic) materials are provided. Some of the haggadic materials in Josephus are assembled in his citations from Alexander Polyhistor and consist in what one might call legends, these in the works of hellenistic Jewish writers who wished to show the antiquity of the Jews. The materials are quite distinct from the haggadic embellishments of the Pharisaic-rabbinic tradition. This legendary material is often alluded to as 'hellenistic midrash'.[119]

But Philo reproduces none of this hellenistic *midrash*. Did he know it? Did he know it and disdain it as alien to his purposes? He does reproduce in Mos. II, 25—44 the substance of the origin of the Septuagint as set forth in the 'Letter of Aristeas', and there one sees a direct relationship between Philo's usual predilections and the origin of the Greek Bible. But the other legends of hellenistic *midrash* are absent. The best hypothesis would seem to be that Philo knew this hellenistic *midrash*, but scorned using it.

Reverting to the Judean Pharisaic-Rabbinic *midrash*, it needs to be said first of all that Philo nowhere engages in narratives such as that of Abraham smashing idols. The fanciful embellishments such as Abraham's having had a daughter are completely missing from Philo. The most that Philo presents is an occasional item such as that Abraham left Harran "with only a few, or even alone,"[120] or that he did not grieve out of measure at the death of Sarah.[121] At least on the surface there is no relationship between the bits of *haggada* in Philo and the *haggada* of the Rabbis of Judea.

But perhaps there are similarities that are latent. Philo and the Rabbis unite in ascribing to Abraham the momentous discovery of the existence of God. The

[118] See S. RAPPAPORT, Agada und Exegese bei Flavius Josephus, Vienna, 1930.
[119] See S. SANDMEL, Philo's Place, pp. 16—17. The term appears to go back to J. FREUDENTHAL, Hellenistische Studien, I, Breslau—Berlin, 1875, pp. 76—77.
[120] Abr. 66.
[121] Abr. 257.

manner of describing this discovery is different.[122] So is the treatment of Gen.
4.26B, a verse which by implication attributes to Enos an anticipation of the great
discovery by Abraham, so that that verse undergoes manipulation to remove the
offending complication. Nevertheless, the manipulations are different in Philo
from what they are in the Rabbis.[123]

The contention is made that Philo does know the Judean *midrash* but that he
dresses it into a superficial philosophical garb. WOLFSON, denying that Philo is
substantially different from the Rabbis, repeats ad infinitum that some item in
Philo was already taught by the Rabbinic sages. SANDMEL's 'Philo's Place in
Judaism' was intended as a direct refutation of this procedure of WOLFSON; that
is, for the most part what WOLFSON adduces as parallels are not parallels at all,
and WOLFSON abstains from noting what is idiosyncratic in Philo.

But borrowing,[124] either by Philo from Judean, or Judean sages, is neither
to be denied, nor is it relevant, for the distinctiveness of Philo within Judaism is
not substantially affected, whether he borrowed or not. Philo is quite external to
the Rabbinic tradition in his basic religiosity.

Rather, Philo, Fourth Maccabees, the fragments from Aristobulus, and the
Wisdom of Solomon can be described as a blend of Judaism and hellenism, and
this blend is neither identical with any Palestinian Judaism, nor with pagan hel-
lenism. It is a unique blend, a cultural anomaly.[125] It is the offspring of the
Septuagint, furthered by hellenistic *midrash*, heightened by philosophy, especially
Stoicism, and it culminates in Philo.

VI. Philo and Christianity

What is the relationship between Philo and New Testament writings?[126]
The scholarly views are diverse and mutually contradictory.

---

[122] See S. SANDMEL, Philo's Place, p. 60, note 228.

[123] See S. SANDMEL, Genesis 4.26B, in: Hebrew Union College Annual, XXXII (1961),
pp. 19—29.

[124] Naturally enough, there have been those who suggest a reversal, namely, that Judean sages
were the borrowers and Alexandria the source. See, for example, DAVID DAUBE, Rabbinic
Methods of Interpretation and Hellenistic Rhetoric, Hebrew Union College Annual, XXII
(1951), pp. 239—264, and SANDMEL's comments, in: Philo's Place, pp. 14—15.

[125] See S. SANDMEL, The First Christian Century in Judaism and Christianity, p. 137: ". . .
When any two civilizations encounter each other, as in the encounter by the Jewish civilization of the Greek civilization, they . . . fashion an intermediary civilization . . . always
fraught with some sense of being alien to those in the respective civilizations who have not
been part of the encounter. It is in such terms that a Paul and a Philo seem so un-Jewish to
so many Jewish commentators, and so un-Greek to so many classical commentators."

[126] There is no modern book that I know of on this topic, but it appears, in passing, in an
abundance of essays. See GOODENOUGH and GOODHART, Bibliography, pp. 290—297, and
LOUIS H. FELDMAN, Scholarship on Philo and Josephus (1937—1962), New York, no date,
pp. 19—22.

But a prior issue of consequence needs exposition. Obviously there is a Judean basis to Christianity; obviously Christianity spread into the Greek world, and among Gentiles. If one accepts the year 29 or 30 as the date of the death of Jesus, and that Paul's activity begins within a decade, that is, before 40, and notes that Paul writes in Greek, then would it not appear that Christianity underwent a most rapid hellenization, whether superficially or deeply? No Christian documents in Aramaic have survived; the entire New Testament is in Greek. It is often suggested that the Revelation of John derives from an Aramaic or Hebrew original; it is occasionally also suggests that the Gospels, in whole or in part, are translated documents. But, to repeat, no Christian, Aramaic or Hebrew documents have survived, if indeed any were written.

The earliest Jewish Christian convictions or views obviously were translated into Greek, or else Christianity could not have been preached in the Greek world. Did the translation take place in the oral period, before any Aramaic documents were written? If so, then was not such translation of ideas a most speedy hellenization?

The issue of the supposed rapid hellenization of Christianity has been one of the most divisive in the New Testament scholarship. This is especially the case with the Apostle Paul, and for good reasons. On the one hand Epistles which bear Paul's name, such as I and II Timothy and Titus have been denied to Paul. Less often Ephesians is denied to him, and Colossians veers from denial to acceptance and back. That is, modern scholars do not accept as genuinely Pauline as many as five or more New Testament writings which bear his name. The bases for the denials can be stated in this way, that the rejected Epistles reflect a church at a stage of development (respecting an officialdom in the case of the Pastorals or the Christology in Colossians) which seems necessarily later than the early time of Paul, according to what is found in Galatians, Corinthians, or Romans.

But the problem of hellenization about Paul is complicated by the way Acts of the Apostles presents him, namely, a student of Gamaliel, a resident of Judea before his 'conversion', a man able to speak Hebrew, and who goes to the Temple to pay a vow. The Paul of Acts is surely not an acutely hellenized figure; he is, rather, virtually a Judean, bilingual, and devoid of any special suitability for depiction as a hellnized Jew. If we did not possess Acts, but the Epistles alone, we should not be reluctant to view Paul as fully hellenized in his own unique way as Philo was in his.

The issue of the rapidity of the hellenization of Christianity has agitated more than one generation of scholars. The 'Tübinger Schule' of F. C. BAUR in the 1830's treated the issue of rapidity by denying that the hellenization was rapid, this by assigning to many New Testament documents the label pseudepigraphs and a second century provenience. In our own time, ERWIN R. GOODENOUGH, vigorously advocating the rapid hellenization, has contended that the existence of a hellenized Judaism, exemplified in Philo, helped to bring about the very rapid hellenization of Christianity. Opposed to him has been W. D. DAVIES[127] who,

---

[127] St. Paul and Rabbinic Judaism, Cambridge, 1955.

brushing Philo aside, and affirming the materials in Acts, has contended that Paul can be explained from the content of Rabbinic literature.[128]

The views, then, ignoring the question of rapidity, are diametrically opposed to each other: Paul was a hellenized Jew, Paul was not a hellenized Jew. In Britain and in the United States, especially since the discovery of the Dead Sea Scrolls, there has been a general tendency to treat the hellenistic world as of no great consequence in the unfolding of Christianity, and, indeed, there are those who deny that there ever was a distinction between Judean Judaism or Christianity and hellenistic Judaism or Christianity. The almost century and a half of skepticism in New Testament scholarship about the historical reliability in Acts has latterly given way to an acceptance of its reliability, either by ignoring its inherent problems or else by exegetical legerdemain. The view adopted here is that Paul does represent a hellenistic Jewish figure.

That there are echoes of Paulinism in Philo and Philonism in Paul is beyond dispute, even on the part of those who are free of skepticism about Acts of the Apostles. WILFRED L. KNOX[129] and HENRY CHADWICK[130] have presented the evidence for this. A far-fetched view was expressed by GERALD FRIEDLANDER[131] that Paul had read Philo. A more likely possibility is that both are representatives of hellenized Judaism, and inevitably they reflect a community of interest. Let it at this point, though, be noted that Paul and Philo are also different from each other! Distinctiveness within a setting is quite other than two distinctive settings. However much British and American democracy have in common, and however much American law utilizes precedents from British law, the impeachment inquiry into President Nixon could not have occurred in Britain, nor the abdication of Edward VIII in the United States. Gerald Ford and Ronald Reagan, or Ford and Hubert H. Humphrey, despite differences, and opposition to each other, come from the same American cultural milieu, and not from Britain. So too Paul and Philo.

What Paul and Philo have in common is a view of the transcendance of God, and the need to find a way to bridge the gap. They share in common a reserved dualism, in which the material side of man is evil, the immaterial good. For both 'reality' is Platonic-Stoic, a function of the world of concept.

Their differences are striking. Philo was, shall we say, a pedantic master of the Greek legacy; Paul was relatively unlearned. Philo was a rationalist; Paul was emphatically not so. In Philo, allegory is architectonic; in Paul, allegory is sporadic and arbitrary. Paul lived in a world inhabited by a devil, and governed by principalities, the 'elements' of this world; Philo, a rationalist, reflects none of this.

---

[128] A comparable general presupposition underlies H. L. STRACK and PAUL BILLERBECK, Kommentar zum Neuen Testament aus Talmud und Midrasch, 5 vols., Munich, 1922–1956. It is presented also in some surprising extensions in DAVID DAUBE, The New Testament and Rabbinic Judaism, Cambridge, 1955.

[129] St. Paul and the Church of the Gentiles, Cambridge, 1939 (1955, 1961).

[130] St. Paul and Philo, Bulletin of the John Rylands Library, XLVIII (1965–66), pp. 286 ff.

[131] Hellenism and Christianity, London, 1912, pp. 84 ff.

Each in his own way has 'difficulties' with the Laws of Moses. Philo is put to defend it, and does so laboriously and with grandeloquence. Paul turns his back on the Laws of Moses. Philo argues that he who moves from hope through repentance to tranquility can elect to proceed further on the road to salvation; Paul knows no tranquility, and denies that man can elect to proceed to salvation, or can, unaided, get there. Philo is certain that man can observe the Law, Paul that man cannot. In Philo a man can, under providence, merit reward or punishment; in Paul man cannot work his own salvation, but must have it done for him divinely, and the saved are those whom God has predestined for salvation.

Yet the solution of the problem of God's transcendence is essentially the same, in that the Logos in Philo and the Christ in Paul are synonymous, for both are the immanent aspect of the transcendant God. The difference, though, is also acute. Philo has little sense of history, and even less of his own fitting into history. The Logos in Philo is timeless and unconnected with space. Paul, on the other hand, deals with an event, that the Christ became the man Jesus in Judea, and that historically the Christ had appeared to Paul. That Philo reports that at times the Logos has permeated his being is never raised to a crucial event. There is no echo in Philo of Paul's doctrine of justification by faith alone.

The salvation they seek is similar, release from what one might call bondage to the flesh, to death, and to 'this world'. The impulse to rise above corporeality is similar. The utilization of the terminology of the mystery religions is often similar.

Yet the two men arose, not in Mithraism, nor from the cult of Cybele, but from hellenistic Judaism. Philo by no means explains Paul himself, nor by any means all that is in Paul. But Philo is a major resource in the understanding of significant presuppositions in Paul and is much more significant than the apocalyptic writings of the Pseudepigrapha and the Rabbinic Literature in grasping the great apostle.

There are on record affirmations and denials respecting the relationship between Philo and the Gospel According to John.[132] This is the case both respecting the Logos-prologue to John, and about the Gospel as a totality. Were there some unanimity among scholars on the Gospel According to John, it would be easier to compare it with Philo. There are views which regard the Logos-prologue as permeating the entire Gospel, and views which seem to consider the prologue as if engrafted onto the Gospel and as forgotten thereafter.

That the prologue or the Gospel owes a debt directly to Philo in the sense of being derived from him and only from him seems unlikely. The Logos-prologue is better illumined by an understanding of the Logos in Philo than by any other non-New Testament material; Philo is the largest available source on the Logos. But, as in the case of Paul, it is the Christ-event which is crucial to John, and John in this respect owes no direct debt to Philo.

---

[132] See, on the one hand, A. W. ARGYLE, Philo and the Fourth Gospel, Expository Times, LXIII (1951), pp. 385—386, which affirms direct Philonic influence on John, and, on the other hand, ROBERT McLACHLEN WILSON, Philo and the Fourth Gospel, ibid., LXV (1953), pp. 47—49, which contends that both were drawing on a relatively common environment.

Philo writes explicitly that the three visitors to Abraham (Gen. ch. 18) were incarnate as men.[133] Indirectly his views of Abraham, Isaac, and Jacob as *nomoi empsychoi,* "Laws incarnate in men", can be cited; so too that Moses allegorically is the Logos can also be mentioned. But it is scarcely possible to go beyond the statement that there are motifs in Philo that bear on the understanding of John's *Logos*-doctrine and the incarnation but they fall short of explaining John.

In neither the case of John nor Philo is it prudent to equate the Logos with the Memra[134] of the Targum. *Memra* does mean 'word'. Its use in the Targum is not so much a device to bridge the gap between man and a transcendent deity, but rather the opposite, namely, to introduce a gap, by eliminating many instances of anthropomorphisms and anthropopathisms in the Hebrew text. The *memra* is to be classified with euphemism, not with philosophic constructs.

It is widely known that RUDOLF BULTMANN in his 'Commentary on John' treated the Logos-prologue by ascribing it to a gnostic source; that is, the prologue was borrowed by John from a gnostic hymn. The objection has been repeatedly expressed that BULTMANN is quite unable to cite some gnostic precursor to the hymn since no such precursor exists beyond BULTMANN's speculation. Indeed, among those who reject BULTMANN's speculation (and often with indignation), there are those who deny that John is a hellenistic Gospel. John, so the argument runs, reflects a dualism. But the Dead Sea Scrolls also reflect a dualism. The Scrolls are Judean, and, hence, the dualism in John is not necessarily hellenistic. Indeed, WILLIAM F. ALBRIGHT[135] contended that John was the earliest Gospel — not the latest as most scholars hold — and was written in Palestine. Such views ought to be regarded as desperate efforts to shield Christianity from any influence from the Greek world. The erudite volumes by MARTIN HENGEL[136] contribute besides an extraordinary quantity of learning, an open invitation to the unlearned and the half-learned. It is HENGEL's contention that all of Judaism, including the Rabbinic Literature, is influenced, or shaped, or permeated by hellenism. The usual prudence of HENGEL himself has been followed by an imprudence on the part of others. To search in Palestinian Judaism for the dualism in the Gospel According to John rather than in hellenistic writings such as Philo is to prefer the sporadic and marginal rather than the omnipresent and the explicit.

John's manner is surely not identical with that of Philo in the matter of the material and the immaterial worlds. But a comparable contrast is present and, indeed, constitutes the nub of John. The device in the soliloquies ascribed to Jesus is for a topic to be misunderstood: rebirth, bread, water, to the end that the con-

---

[133] Abr. 118.

[134] See WOLFSON, I, p. 287 and literature there cited.

[135] Recent Discoveries in Palestine and the Gospel of St. John, in: W. D. DAVIES and D. DAUBE, The Background of the New Testament and its Eschatology, Cambridge, 1956, pp. 153—171.

[136] Judentum und Hellenismus, Wissenschaftliche Untersuchungen zum Neuen Testament, 10, Tübingen, 2nd ed., 1973.

trast can be drawn between the material (by implication, what is in the perceptible world) and the spiritual (what is in the world of concept). The manner is different, but not the essence.

This Johannine sense of two worlds available in the present, appears to be a development from an antecedent contrast, found in Judaism as well as in the Gospel, between this age and the future age to come. Linear time here becomes obliterated. The Jewish eschatological views respecting 'the end of time', as in Isa. 2.14 and Micah 4.1, were altered in the messianic movements to the conviction that the future, once deemed eschatological and remote, had suddenly become near at hand. Then the frustration of vivid messianic expectations led to the abandonment of a sole reliance on time, and to an alteration of the linear, horizontal view of the world to come into one in which the world to come was, as it were, disengaged from time. Rather it was universally and immediately available, to be entered into on an individual's death. The world to come was now deemed already at hand, already existing in heaven, in a paradisaic setting. It was to this world to come already at hand that the departed patriarchs had gone, enabling Luke to portray an Abraham to welcome Lazarus to his bosom, or the rabbinic sages to attend an 'academy on high' to continue their pious study of Torah. In short, the future world to come became transformed by non-philosophic Judean minds into a rough equivalent of the philosophic *cosmos noetos*. John, however, has gone far beyond this transformation, for in his Gospel, futurity is not clearly present nor is eschatology present except by overtone. "My kingship is not of this world" is but one of several passages in which 'this world' and a 'spiritual world' are set into sharp contrast. The profundity in John triumphs over the naiveté of its device of recurrent misunderstanding; the naiveté clearly indicates that John emerges not from the elite setting of a Philo but rather from popular folk echoes of philosophic motifs (much as today the use of "inferiority complex" echoes not FREUD himself, or a mastery of psychoanalysis, but a vulgarization of the latter). It is scarcely Philo himself who is reflected in John but rather the broad Jewish hellenism.

In Colossians[137] there occurs a uniquely Christian development, namely, the progressive deepening of the Christology. The progressive tendency to exalt the Christ prompted the inevitable query: in what way is the Christ like God? Partly? Completely? In what way was he human? Partly? Fully? That Godness could be subject to analysis, whether by poetic assertion or analytical philosophy, and a distinction drawn between the *pleroma* ("the fullness") and between such aspects of God as Philo ascribes to the powers and the Logos were more crucial to Christianity with its greater bondage to event than such matters were to Philo.

---

[137] The most relevant passage in Colossians is 1.15–20; compare 2.9. I have not seen S. LYONNET, L'Hymne christologique de l'Epître aux Colossiens et la fête juive du Nouvel An, Recherches de Sciences Religieuses, LVIII (1960), pp. 93–100. FELDMAN, op. cit., p. 20, cites the work as contending that Colossians 1.20 echoes Spec. Leg., II, 192; quoting FELDMAN's paraphrase, "Paul was thinking of [Philo's] use of the term . . ." I find this particular connection a bit extravagant.

The Logos-doctrine in Philo is in a sense central in his thought, but it is there scarcely crucial. In unfolding Christianity, the Christ was no less than crucial. Hence, Christianity inevitably demanded acute definitions, as if the fate of the church depended on them, and then in due course differences led to the delineation of Arianism as a heresy. Out of Philonism we can see the kinds of issues that arose in Christianity as between God and the Logos, or the Christ and the man Jesus which Christianity heightened from diversity into controversy. Nothing in Philo leads us to expect from him a doctrine of the trinity, but the raw materials of the trinity are present, requiring only the event, namely, that Jesus was viewed as the human interval in the pre-existent and eternal Christ. *To On*, Logos, and holy spirit are present in Philo; without the Christ-event the three did not need to be welded into a formula. When the author of Colossians declares that the Christ is the *pleroma* of God, he has gone far beyond where Philo could have gone. But the assertions in Colossians have a character that might elude our ready understanding, were it not for Philonic doctrines.

In Hebrews,[138] insofar as essential philosophic aspects are concerned, we encounter still another metamorphosis of the two worlds, the perceptible and the conceptual. In Hebrews ideal and imitation become shifted into still another pattern of time, namely, that imitation precedes the ideal: Judaism is the substitution, the imitation which preceded; Christianity is the progression in time to the ideal (not, as is usual, that the ideal precedes the substitution). There is no great harm in the word frequently used, typology, to describe Hebrews, that is, that the Jewish practices which, though imperfect, were the type that foreshadowed the perfection which time and development were to effect in Christianity. The harm can lie in the assumption that typology is essentially different in substance from the patterns of ideal and substitute as taught in Plato and the Stoics. What is different in Hebrews is the manner of the presentation of imitation and ideal, not the substance of it. Where in Philo there are a literal tabernacle and an allegorical one, in Hebrews there is a worthy but imperfect tabernacle, followed by a perfect Temple, the 'body' of the Christ.

As explicitly stated in Philo, so too Hebrews asserts that the sage is a stranger on earth, for his commonwealth is from heaven. It is within Christianity that a

---

[138] It is especially Hebrews for which Philonic influence is frequently asserted. GOODENOUGH and GOODHART (p. 294) cite JOHANNES BENEDICTUS CARPZOVIUS, Sacrae exercitationes in S. Pauli epistolam ad Hebraeos ex Philone Alexandrino . . ., Helmstedt, 1750. C. SPICQ, Le philonisme de l'Epître aux Hébreux, Revue Biblique, LVI (1949), pp. 542—572 and LVII (1950), pp. 212—242, not only ascribed Philonic influence on Hebrews in ways such as vocabulary, rhetorical devices, themes, and structure, but even supposes that the author of Hebrews was personally acquainted with Philo. For the most part, however, even those who discern connections ascribe these to the general environment rather than to direct Philonic influence. R. WILLIAMSON, Philo and the Epistle to the Hebrews, Arbeiten zur Literatur und Geschichte des hellenistischen Judentums, 4, Leiden, 1970, provides an extreme rejection of SPICQ's views, in effect denying all influence of Philo on Hebrews. A most recent study is LALA KALYAN KUMAR DEY, The Intermediary World and Patterns of Perfection in Philo and Hebrews, Missoula, Mont., 1975.

man is enabled, through the loving self-sacrifice of the Christ, to rise above corporeality. Revelation in the previous ages, as through the prophets through whom God spoke, had prepared the way for the climax in which God has recently spoken through a Son.

The Pastoral[139] and the Johannine Epistles reflect doctrinal dissensions in the church. These are not always precisely identifiable. Two principal 'heresies' are known in the second century, encratism and docetism. Encratism[140] is excessive self-mortification, and is perhaps what Philo opposes when he advocates regimenting the senses and passions, rather than the destroying them; such destruction would be kindred to encratism. Docetism[141] is the heresy ascribed to gnostics who denied that Jesus had come in the flesh; according to them, Jesus only 'seemed' (docetism means 'seemingness') to be real. Both heresies arise from dualism, and from a contempt for the body and its functions. If Jesus was real, he was subject to the ingestion, digestion, and egestion of foods; from such supposedly unseemly frailties, the gnostics wished to protect Jesus. At least one passage in Philo reflects docetism: The three angels of Gen. ch. 18, for whom Abraham provides a sumptuous meal, only seem to eat.[142]

In no sense are Philo and his doctrines directly related to these Christian heresies. Yet an understanding of his dualism discloses those overtones of the currents of thought that rose to issues in developing Christianity. The basic concern that arises between literalism on the one hand and the allegorical on the other focuses on the sense of actuality ascribed to this world. The allegorical in Philo by implication ascribes to this world, and to the events that have taken or take place, a lack of actuality that can appear to deny that the events have truly occurred, while encratism can seem to contradict the essential character of a man. If it is denied that a Jesus came eating and drinking (Mt. 11.19), then in what sense can it be contended that he is the top rung in the historical ladder of revelation that began with Abraham? Was it actual that he appeared on earth in a part of the world called Judea, and was it actual that he was executed under Pontius Pilate? Was it actual that he died, was dead, and on the third day was raised from the dead? Just as Philo dehistoricized patriarchal narratives (asserting as he does at the end of 'Congr.' that Hagar and Sarah were never real women), so too the gnostics appear to have dissolved the Jesus of history and to have viewed him only as a symbol. In modern times there have been those who have questioned the divinity of Jesus; in early Christianity it was, instead, his true humanity that was ques-

---

[139] FELDMAN cites also H. G. MEECHAM, The Epistle of St. James, Expository Times, XLIX (1937—1938), pp. 181—183, which suggests that this epistle was edited by a disciple of Philo. I have not seen F. R. M. HITCHCOCK, Philo and the Pastorals, Hermathena, LVI (1940), pp. 113—135, which FELDMAN cites (op. cit., pp. 19—20). It notes the similarity in the vocabularies of the Pastorals and Philo.

[140] This is mentioned in the writings of Irenaeus, Adv. Haer. I, 28; Clement of Alexandria, Stromata VII, 17 and elsewhere.

[141] Some see docetism in Col. 2.8, but this is disputed. Clearer reflections are in I Jn. 4.1—3 and II Jn. 7.

[142] Abr. 107—118.

tioned. Philo furnishes us with ample basis to understand the tendency in aspects of Christianity to question the true humanity of Jesus.

It had been the usual view until the rise of the school of scholars known as the 'Religionsgeschichtliche Schule' to view gnosticism as a development within second century Christianity. The phrase of HARNACK was often cited that gnosticism was the hellenization of the Gospel. But the 'Religionsgeschichtliche Schule' inaugurated an inquiry which supposed that Christian gnosticism had a much longer and more complex background, as suggested above in connection with the view of RUDOLF BULTMANN respecting the gnostic origin of the Logos-prologue to John. The theory of a pre-Christian, non-Christian gnosticism gained increasing acceptance in some circles. There arose the usual scholarly differences of judgment. These seem to have been increased by some semantic confusions, for there are on record scholarly disputations, a key to which is a lack of agreement on some basic terms.[143] At a conference on gnostic origins at Messina[144] the proposal was made in a document that was published in French, German, English, and Italian that the term 'Gnosis' be reserved for the earlier pre-Christian, non-Christian phenomenon, and 'Gnosticism' for the second century Christian phenomenon.

The semantic problems may some day be solved, in future research. How to solve such problems in the past research is difficult to envisage. Thus, the phenomena which my teacher ERWIN R. GOODENOUGH ascribes to the Mysteries seem to me to be largely right, but I should prefer to ascribe these instead to Gnosis.[145] Let it be noted that it is the ascription, whether to the Mysteries or to Gnosis, that is at stake, not the presence of the phenomena.

Philo may be considered as a witness to Gnosis, a phenomenon contemporary with him, and not to Gnosticism which was a later, Christian development from Gnosis. Under Gnosis the suppositions would include elements such as the following: The goal of religion is union with God (and hence Gnosis and Mysticism are in some senses synonymous). A person who achieves such union does so through divine illumination. At least in part such illumination is the result of 'wisdom' entering into the person. The man so illuminated escapes bondage to the world of perception and rises into the world of concept. The 'knowledge' in Gnosis is a combination of human acquisitions and of divine inspiration.

The question was raised by MARCEL SIMON[146] as to whether Philo should be termed a 'gnosticizer' or a 'pre-gnostic'. At stake, he says correctly, are the

---

[143] See my 'Philo's Place in Judaism', Augmented Edition, New York, 1971, pp. X–XVI, and 'The First Christian Century', pp. 198–199, written prior to my having seen the volume mentioned in the following note.

[144] The proceedings were published in: Le Origini dello Gnosticismo, ed. UGO BIANCHI, Studies in the History of Religions, 12, Leiden, 1967. 'The Proposal for a Terminological and Conceptual Agreement with regard to the Theme of the Colloquium' is found, in the four languages, on pp. XX–XXXII.

[145] See S. SANDMEL, Philo's Place in Judaism, Augmented Edition, pp. XVI–XVIII.

[146] Eléments gnostiques chez Philon, in: Le Origini dello Gnosticismo, pp. 360–374.

definitions and the views on the origins of Gnosis and Gnosticism. It would appear to contribute little to the ambiguities to use the word 'gnostic' for Philo; more would misunderstand than would understand. But no violence is done by an assertion that Philo stands very near to Gnosis.

It is essential, however, to avoid what HANS JONAS termed a "semantic disservice to clarity" on the part of GERSHOM SCHOLEM who introduced the phrase "Jewish Gnosticism" relative to certain Rabbinic writings, about sages who ascended to heaven, called *Hekalot* literature. Gnosis and this Jewish gnosticism have precious little in common.[147]

Perhaps to emphasize the distinctions in the matter of relations of Philo to Gnosis and Gnosticism, one might quote HANS JONAS on the ingredients of Gnosticism: "A Gnosticism without a fallen god, without benighted creator and sinister creation, without alien soul, cosmic captivity and acosmic salvation, without the self-redeeming of the Deity – in short: A Gnosis without divine tragedy will not meet specifications."[148] As a sequel, SANDMEL wrote, respecting Philo, "I see no trace of a fallen god; I see, however, fallen man, in Eden. I see no benighted creator; I, however, see the logos as the creator. As to a sinister creation, I see in Philo the view that this world of appearance is rather sinister, and that the sage is indeed an alien soul in this world. I do not see cosmic captivity or acosmic salvation; I do see salvation of the soul from the prison of the body. I do not wonder at the absence of a fallen god for Philo was a staunch Jew; in the light of Genesis I and the repeated refrain of 'God saw and it was good', Philo could scarcely admit of a benighted creator . . . Philo contains no myths . . . he reflects no magic such as is known to have characterized other marginal Jews of his age; he believes in prophecy, but in so exalted a form that apocalyptic, so frequent in his age, is totally missing from his writings. He is a God-intoxicated rationalist, and an austere and sometimes modest, sometimes arrogant man."[149]

In 1882 MICHEL NICOLAS described him as an ecstatic.[149a] SANDMEL calls him a "philosophic mystic,"[150] but expressed a preference for the characterization by Professor MARGUERITE HARL,[151] who describes Philo as reflecting an "interiorization of the Jewish religion . . . He is the first representative of a new type of religious man."

Some significant portion of current New Testament scholarship involves acute debates on the issues reflected among Christian partisans as alluded to in Paul, especially in the Corinthian correspondence. The writings of WALTER SCHMITHALS (Die Gnosis in Korinth, Forschungen zur Religion und Literatur

---

[147] See the discussion and bibliographical references in: S. SANDMEL, Philo's Place in Judaism, Augmented Edition, pp. XIV–XV.

[148] In: Gnosticism and the New Testament, in: PHILIP HYATT, The Bible in Modern Scholarship, London, 1966, pp. 279–293.

[149] Philo's Place in Judaism, Augmented edition, p. XXIV.

[149a] MICHEL NICOLAS, Etudes sur Philon d'Alexandrie, Revue de l'Histoire des Religions, V (1882), p. 328.

[150] Ibid.

[151] In her introductory essay 'Quis rerum divinarum heres sit', Paris, 1966 in the French edition, Les Œuvres de Philon d'Alexandrie, vol. XV, p. 153.

des Alten und Neuen Testaments, N.F. 48, Göttingen, 1956, and: Das kirchliche
Apostelamt, Göttingen, 1961, Engt. tr., Nashville, 1969) have stirred vehement
denunciation, indeed completely out of proportion. Philo himself does not come
directly into focus in such academic quarrels. The exposition by HANS JONAS,
'Gnosis und spätantiker Geist',[152] is an illuminating array of quasi-gnostic
elements, patent or latent in Philo. One can scarcely enter the fray, on whatever
side one is a partisan, without some consideration of Philo.

Subjectivity alone determines whether a scholar admires or denigrates Philo.
Only a determination to remain uninformed can explain the curiosity that many,
many New Testament scholars ignore him entirely, or substitute reading about
him for reading him. The unwary pick up phrases or passages in excerpt, and rush
into independent judgments without adequate knowledge of the context. There
have been those who have used him on the Essenes without having read any more
of him than the passage in 'Probus'.

There is no purpose to be achieved here in either praising or scorning the
quality of Philo's philosophy. If one finds it admirable and is enriched by it, or
tedious and is bored by it, that is all secondary to the circumstance that Philo is
crucial in understanding the unfolding of Synagogue Judaism and of Christian
doctrine. If unimportant in himself, he is nevertheless the hinge on which so
much turns. The legend that he became a Christian has no substance, but it does
suggest why a Clement of Alexandria, an Origen, or a Eusebius saw in his
doctrines an affinity with Christian doctrines. Hellenistic Christianity emerged
from a world about which Philo tells us more than does any writer. Completeness
in scholarship should compel a rounded study of Philo as an accompaniment to
New Testament scholarship. Prudence and caution should never be abandoned;
clearly there is a difference between the influence of a milieu and the specific influence of a single man. Partial overlap ought not mean total identity, nor should
striking similarity obstruct real and distinctive differences. Parallelomania or
arbitrary theories of source and derivation ought to undergo at least a bit of
restraint. But not to know Philo is a serious disqualification for a would-be New
Testament scholar.

---

[152] Forschungen zur Religion und Literatur des Alten und Neuen Testaments, N.F., 45, vol. II,
Göttingen, 1954, pp. 70—121.

Bibliographia Philoniana 1935–1981

by Earle Hilgert, Chicago, Ill.

Contents

Preliminary Note

The bibliography of scholarship on Philo of Alexandria presented here is intended to continue that compiled by H. L. Goodhart and E. R. Good-

ENOUGH, A General Bibliography of Philo, published in GOODENOUGH's 'The Politics of Philo Judaeus', in 1938.

During the four decades since that notable bibliography appeared, several other listings and surveys of literature on Philo, covering parts of this period, have been published, including those by GERHARD DELLING, LOUIS H. FELDMAN, RALPH MARCUS, ANTONIO V. NAZZARO, HARTWIG THYEN, WILHELM TOTOK, and the present writer's bibliographies in Studia Philonica (listed below in Sections II and XX). Several other continuing bibliographical services include significant, systematic listings of Philonic scholarship: L'année philologique (Paris), Elenchus Bibliographicus Biblicus (Rome), Gnomon (München), Internationale Zeitschriftenschau für Bibelwissenschaft und Grenzgebiete (Düsseldorf), and New Testament Abstracts (Cambridge MA). For articles in Hebrew, reference should be made to Kiryath Sefer (Jerusalem). All of these bibliographies have been important in identifying the literature on Philo listed here.

In compiling this bibliography, the question has repeatedly arisen as to what should be included and what omitted. In a number of instances I have included works which concern themselves with Philo only briefly, but in which the discussion involves a significant point or insight in regard to Philo's writing. On the other hand, I have included only a general reference (in Section XIX) to GERHARD KITTEL and GERHARD FRIEDRICH, Theologisches Wörterbuch zum Neuen Testament / Theological Dictionary of the New Testament, which systematically presents many discussions of Philo's theological and philosophical use of words that also appear in the New Testament.

In as far as possible I have sought to derive the data offered from an examination of the book or article itself. When this has been impossible, the source of the information given is indicated by a symbol following the entry. These symbols are included in the list of abbreviations.

In the case of titles of books and articles in less familiar languages, a translation has been given in brackets. When a second title in English it not so enclosed, it is to be understood as a subtitle or translation which appears in the work itself.

A number of colleagues have shown the kindness of directing my attention to materials I otherwise would have missed. For such information I am especially grateful to SAMUEL AKSLER, formerly of Spertus College of Judaica, HANS DIETER BETZ of the University of Chicago, GERHARD DELLING of the University of Halle, LOUIS H. FELDMAN of Yeshiva University, ZDISŁAW KAPERA of Cracow, JEAN LAPORTE of Notre Dame University, BURTON L. MACK of the Claremont Graduate School, VALENTIN NIKIPROWETZKY of the University of Paris-Vincennes, HERBERT OPALEK of Philadelphia, DAVID C. REEVES of McCormick Theological Seminary, WOLFGANG REISTER of the Institutum Judaicum, Tübingen, and JAMES R. ROYSE of San Francisco State University. Particular thanks are deserved by CALVIN H. SCHMITT, formerly General Director of the Jesuit-Krauss-McCormick Library in Chicago, for his support in a multitude of ways.

Abbreviations for sources from which data have been drawn:

ADD   American Doctoral Dissertations
B   Brinkman's Catalogus van Boeken

BM	British Museum, General Catalogue of Printed Books
BN	Catalogue de la Bibliothèque Nationale, Paris
BS	Bulletin signalétique
D	Personal Letter from GERHARD DELLING
DA	Dissertation Abstracts
DB	Deutsche Bibliographie
DHS	Jahresverzeichnis der deutschen Hochschulschriften
E	Elenchus Bibliographicus Biblicus
EB	Catalogue de l'Ecole Biblique, Jérusalem
F	Personal Letter from LOUIS H. FELDMAN
G	H. L. GOODHART, E. R. GOODENOUGH, A General Bibliography of Philo
IAJS	Index to Articles in Jewish Studies
IZBG	Internationale Zeitschriftenschau für Bibelwissenschaft und Grenzgebiete
M	Personal Letter from BURTON L. MACK
N	ANTONIO V. NAZZARO, Recenti studi filoniani (1963–70)
Ni	Personal Letter from VALENTIN NIKIPROWETZKY
NUC	National Union Catalog
PAL	Philon d'Alexandrie, éd. par R. ARNALDEZ et C. MONDÉSERT, Lyon 11–15 septembre 1966, Paris 1967 (Colloques nationaux du Centre national de la Recherche scientifique)
R	Personal Letter from WOLFGANG REISTER
T	WILHELM TOTOK, Handbuch der Geschichte der Philosophie

I. Texts, Translations and Selections

BARON, SALO W., and BLAU, J. L., eds. Judaism: Postbiblical and Talmudic Period. New York, 1954. [Philo: 31–53.]

BARRETT, CHARLES K. The New Testament Background: Selected Documents. London, 1961. (Harper Torchbooks/The Cloister Library) New York, 1961. [Philo: 173–89.]

CORSINI, EUGENIO. Filone d'Alessandria. In: La filosofia antica. Antologia di testi, 451–62. Ed. NICOLA ABBAGNANO. Bari, 1963. [Introduction, excerpts.]

FRÜCHTEL, LUDWIG. Griechische Fragmente zu Philons Quaestiones in Genesin et in Exodum. ZAW N.F. 14 (55) (1937) 108–15.

GLATZER, NAHUM. The Rest is Commentary. A Source Book of Judaic Antiquity. Boston, 1961. [Philo: 83–97, 113–33.]

HEGERMANN, HARALD. Philon von Alexandrien. In: Umwelt des Urchristentums, 2. 281–314. Ed. JOHANNES LEIPOLDT, WALTER GRUNDMANN. Berlin, 1967, ⁴1975.

PETIT, FRANÇOISE. L'ancienne version latine des Questions sur la Genèse de Philon d'Alexandrie. I: Édition critique. II: Commentaire (TU 113–114). Berlin, 1973.

PETIT, FRANÇOISE. Les fragments grecs du livre VI des Questions sur la Genèse de Philon d'Alexandrie. Édition critique. Muséon 84 (1971) 93–150.

Philo Judaeus. De la charité et Amour pour son prochain [par] Philon d'Alexandrie dans la traduction de PIERRE BELLIER. In: De la charité et Amour de son prochain, 89–121 (Éditions du Cercle intellectuel pour le rayonnement de la pensée et de la culture juive, Marseille). Marseille, 1954. [NUC]

Philo Judaeus. La creazione del mondo. Ed. GIANMARIA CALVETTI. Le allegorie delle legge.
    Ed. RENATA BIGATTI. Intro. GIOVANNI REALE (Centro di Ricerche di metafisica dell'Uni-
    versità Cattolica del Sacro Cuore di Milano). Milano, 1978. [Ni]
Philo Judaeus. The Essential Philo. Ed. NAHUM M. GLATZER. New York, 1971.
Philo Judaeus. Filone Alessandrino. De opificio mundi. De Abrahamo. De Josepho. Ed.
    CLARA KRAUS REGGIANI (Bibliotheca Athena 23). Roma, 1979. [NUC]
Philo Judaeus. La migration d'Abraham. Ed., trans. R. CADIOU (SC 47). Paris, 1957.
Philo Judaeus. Obras completas de Filón de Alejandría. Ed., trans. JOSÉ MARÍA TRIVIÑO.
    5 vols. Buenos Aires, 1975—76.
Philo Judaeus. Les œuvres de Philon d'Alexandrie. Ed. CLAUDE MONDÉSERT et al. Paris,
    1961—.
    Vol. 1. Introduction générale. De opificio mundi. Ed., trans. ROGER ARNALDEZ. 1961.
    Vol. 2. Legum allegoriae I—III. Ed., trans. CLAUDE MONDÉSERT. 1962.
    Vol. 3. De Cherubim. Ed., trans. JEAN GOREZ. 1963.
    Vol. 4. De sacrificiis Abelis et Caini. Ed., trans. ANITA MÉASSON. 1966.
    Vol. 5. Quod deterius potiori insidiari soleat. Ed., trans. IRÈNE FEUER. 1965.
    Vol. 6. De posteritate Caini. Ed., trans. ROGER ARNALDEZ. 1972.
    Vols. 7, 8. De gigantibus. Quod Deus sit immutabilis. Ed., trans. ANDRÉ MOSÈS. 1963.
    Vol. 9. De agricultura. Ed., trans. JEAN POUILLOUX. 1961.
    Vol. 10. De plantatione. Ed., trans. JEAN POUILLOUX. 1963.
    Vols. 11, 12. De ebrietate. De sobrietate. Trans. JEAN GOREZ. 1962.
    Vol. 13. De confusione linguarum. Ed., trans. JEAN-GEORGES KAHN. 1963.
    Vol. 14. De migratione Abrahami. Ed., trans. JACQUES CAZEAUX, S.J. 1965.
    Vol. 15. Quis rerum divinarum heres sit. Ed., trans. MARGUERITE HARL. 1966.
    Vol. 16. De congressu eruditionis gratia. Ed., trans. MONIQUE ALEXANDRE. 1967.
    Vol. 17. De fuga et inventione. Ed., trans. ESTHER STAROBINSKI-SAFRAN. 1970.
    Vol. 18. De mutatione nominum. Ed., trans. ROGER ARNALDEZ, CLAUDE MONDÉSERT,
        JEAN POUILLOUX. 1964.
    Vol. 19. De somniis I—II. Ed., trans. PIERRE SAVINEL. 1962.
    Vol. 20. De Abrahamo. Ed., trans. JEAN GOREZ. 1966.
    Vol. 21. De Josepho. Trans. JEAN LAPORTE. 1964.
    Vol. 22. De vita Mosis I—II. Ed., trans. ROGER ARNALDEZ, CLAUDE MONDÉSERT, JEAN
        POUILLOUX, PIERRE SAVINEL. 1967.
    Vol. 23. De decalogo. Ed., trans. VALENTIN NIKIPROWETZKY. 1965.
    Vol. 24. De specialibus legibus I et II. Ed., trans. SUZANNE DANIEL. 1975.
    Vol. 25. De specialibus legibus III et IV. Ed., trans. ANDRÉ MOSÈS. 1970.
    Vol. 26. De virtutibus. Ed. ROGER ARNALDEZ, trans. PAULETTE DELOBRE, MARIE-ROSE
        SERVEL, ANNE-MARIE VERILHAC. 1962.
    Vol. 27. De praemiis et poenis. De exsecrationibus. Ed., trans. ANDRÉ BECKAERT, A.A.
        1961.
    Vol. 28. Quod omnis probus liber sit. Ed., trans. MADELEINE PETIT. 1974.
    Vol. 29. De vita contemplativa. Ed. FRANÇOIS DAUMAS, trans. PIERRE-JEAN-LOUIS
        MIQUEL, O.S.B. 1963.
    Vol. 30. De aeternitate mundi. Ed. ROGER ARNALDEZ, trans. JEAN POUILLOUX. 1969.
    Vol. 31. In Flaccum. Ed., trans. ANDRÉ PELLETIER, S.J. 1967.
    Vol. 32. Legatio ad Caium. Ed., trans. ANDRÉ PELLETIER, S.J. 1972.
    Vol. 33. Quaestiones in Genesim et in Exodum: fragmenta Graeca. Ed., trans. FRAN-
        ÇOISE PETIT. 1978.
    Vol. 34 A. Quaestiones et solutiones in Genesim: e versione armeniaca, 1. Ed., trans.
        CHARLES MERCIER. 1979.
    Vol. 35. De providentia I et II. Ed., trans. MIREILLE HADAS-LEBEL. 1973.
Philo Judaeus. Philonis Alexandrini opera quae supersunt. Ed. LEOPOLD COHN, PAUL WEND-
    LAND. 7 vols. in 8. Berlin, 1896—1930; reprinted Berlin, 1962.

Philo Judaeus. Philo; in Ten Volumes (and Two Supplementary Volumes), with an English Translation. Ed. F. H. Colson, G. H. Whittaker, Ralph Marcus (The Loeb Classical Library). Cambridge MA, London, 1929–53.
Vol. 6. Ed., trans. F. H. Colson [Abr; Jos; Vita Mos I–II]. 1935.
Vol. 7. Ed., trans. F. H. Colson [Dec; Spec Leg I–III]. 1937.
Vol. 8. Ed., trans. F. H. Colson [Spec Leg IV; Virt; Praem]. 1939.
Vol. 9. Ed., trans. F. H. Colson [Quod Omn; Vita Cont; Aet; Flacc; Hyp; Provid]. 1941.
Vol. 10. Ed., trans. F. H. Colson [Gaium; Indices to Vols. 1–10, J. W. Earp]. 1962.
Supplement Vol. 1. Ed., trans. Ralph Marcus [Quaes Gen I–IV]. 1953.
Supplement Vol. 2. Ed., trans. Ralph Marcus [Quaes Ex I–II]. 1953.
Philo Judaeus. Philo of Alexandria: About the Life of Moses. Trans. David L. Dungan. In: Sourcebook of Texts for the Comparative Study of the Gospels, 297–345. Ed. David L. Dungan, David R. Cartlidge (Sources for Biblical Study 1). Missoula, 1971, ⁴1974. [Excerpts from Vita Mos].
Philo Judaeus. Philo: Philosophical Writings. Selections. Ed. Hans Lewy. Oxford, 1946.
Philo Judaeus. Philo von Alexandrien von den Machterweisen Gottes: eine zeitgenössische Darstellung der Judenverfolgungen unter dem Kaiser Caligula. Ed., trans. Hans Lewy. Berlin, 1935.
Philo Judaeus. Philon. de ebr. § 223 – de poster. Cain. § 34. In: Papiri greci e latini 11 (1935) 90–91 (Pubblicazioni della Società Italiana). [G]
Philo Judaeus. Philonis Alexandrini In Flaccum. Ed., trans. Herbert Box. London, 1939; reprinted New York, 1979.
Philo Judaeus. Philonis Alexandrini Legatio ad Gaium. Ed., trans. E. Mary Smallwood. Leiden, 1961, ²1970.
Philo Judaeus. Philonis Alexandrini libellus de opificio mundi. Ed. Leopold Cohn. Breslau, 1889; reprinted Hildesheim, 1967.
Philo Judaeus. Le traité de la Vie Contemplative de Philon d'Alexandrie. Ed., trans. Pierre Geoltrain (Sem 10). Paris, 1960.
Philo Judaeus. Die Werke Philos von Alexandria in deutscher Übersetzung. 7 vols. Breslau, Berlin, 1909–64.
Vol. 6. Ed. Isaak Heinemann, Maximilian Adler [Congr; Fuga; Mut; Somn I–II]. Breslau, 1938.
Vol. 7. Ed. Leopold Cohn et al. [Quod omn; Vita cont; Aet; Flacc; Gaium; Provid]. Berlin, 1964.
Philo Judaeus. חיי איש המדינה, הוא על יוסף. The Life of the Statesman; that is, On Joseph. Trans. Naomi Goldstein Cohen. Jerusalem, 1965.
Philo Judaeus. כתבי הסטוריה; נגד פלאקום, המלאכות אל קיום. בנספחות: על אסיים, קטעים ושרידים [Historical Writings; Contra Flaccum; Legatio ad Gaium; Appendices: On the Essenes; Fragments and Remains]. Ed., trans. Menahem (Edmund) Stein. Tel Aviv, 1936–37.
Philo Judaeus. כתבים הפילוסופיים של פילון [The Philosophical Writings of Philo]. Ed. Yohanan (Hans) Lewy; trans. Yehoshua Amir. Jerusalem, 1964.
Philo Judaeus. על בריאת העולם [De opificio mundi]. Ed. Moshe Schwabe; trans. Yitshak (Isaac) Mann (כתבי פילון האלכסנדרוני מתורגמים מיוונית לעברית 1) [The Writings of Philo Alexandrinus Translated from Greek into Hebrew 1]). Jerusalem, 1931; reprinted 1970/71.

Siegert, Folker. Drei hellenistisch-jüdische Predigten (WUNT 20). Tübingen, 1980. [De Jona, De Sampsone, De Deo.]

II. Bibliographies, Concordances and Abstracts

Abstracts of Recent Articles on Philo. SP 2 (1973) 55–73.
Abstracts of Selected Articles on Philo, 1966–1970. SP 1 (1972) 72–91.
Abstracts of Recent Articles on Philo. SP 4 (1976–77) 87–108.
Abstracts of Recent Articles on Philo. SP 5 (1978) 121–36.
Abstracts of Recent Articles on Philo. SP 6 (1979–80) 201–22.
BORGEN, PEDER, and SKARSTEN, ROALD. Complete KWIC-Concordance of Philo's Writings.
    Trondheim, Bergen, 1973. [Magnetic tape.]

DELLING, GERHARD. Bibliographie zur jüdisch-hellenistischen und intertestamentarischen
    Literatur, 1900–1965 (TU 106). Berlin, 1969; 2., überarbeitete und bis 1970 fortgeführte
    Auflage, 1975.

FÜRST, JULIUS. Bibliotheca Judaica. Bibliographisches Handbuch umfassend die Druckwerke
    der jüdischen Literatur. 3 vols. Leipzig, 1863; reprinted Hildesheim, 1960. [Philo: 3.
    87–94.]

GÄRTNER, H., and HEYKE, W., Bibliographie zur antiken Bildersprache (Bibliothek der klas-
    sischen Altertumswissenschaft, N.F. 1). Heidelberg, 1964. [Philo: 289–94.]

GOODHART, H. L., and GOODENOUGH, ERWIN R. A General Bibliography of Philo. In:
    GOODENOUGH, ERWIN R. The Politics of Philo Judaeus, 125–348. New Haven, 1938;
    reprinted Hildesheim, 1967.

HAELST, JOSEPH VAN. Catalogue des papyrus littéraires juifs et chrétiens. Paris, 1976.
HILGERT, EARLE. A Bibliography of Philo Studies in 1971, with Additions for 1965–1970.
    SP 2 (1973) 51–54.
HILGERT, EARLE. A Bibliography of Philo Studies, 1963–1970. SP 1 (1972) 57–71.
HILGERT, EARLE. A Bibliography of Philo Studies, 1972–1973. SP 3 (1974–75) 117–25.
HILGERT, EARLE. A Bibliography of Philo Studies, 1974–1975. SP 4 (1976–77) 79–85.
HILGERT, EARLE. A Bibliography of Philo Studies, 1976–1977. SP 5 (1978) 113–20.
HILGERT, EARLE. A Bibliography of Philo Studies, 1977–1978. SP 6 (1979–80) 197–200.

MARCUS, RALPH. Selected Bibliography (1920–1945) of the Jews in the Hellenistic-Roman
    Period. Proceedings of the American Academy for Jewish Research 16 (1946–47) 97–181.
MAYER, GÜNTER. Index Philoneus. Berlin, 1974.

PAUL, ANDRÉ. Bulletin de littérature intertestamentaire. Du Judaïsme ancien au Judéo-
    Christianisme. RechSR 66 (1978) 343–87.

RAPPAPORT, URIEL. ביבליוגרפיה לתולדות ישראל בתקופה ההלניסטית והרומית. Bibliography of
    Works on Jewish History in the Hellenistic and Roman Periods, 1946–70. In: מחקרים
    בתולדות עמיישראל וארץ־ישראל [Studies in the History of the Jewish People and the Land
    of Israel], 2.247–321. Ed. B. ODED et al. Haifa, 1972.

RAPPAPORT, URIEL. ביבליוגרפיה נבחרת לתולדות ישראל בתקופת הבית השני. A selected Bibliog-
    raphy of Jewish History in the Period of the Second Temple. Haifa, 1969.

SHUNAMI, SHLOMO. Bibliography of Jewish Bibliographies. Jerusalem, 1936, ²1965; reprinted
    with corrections, 1969. [Esp. 2089, 4109–12.]

TOTOK, WILHELM. Handbuch der Geschichte der Philosophie, unter Mitarbeit von HELMUT
    SCHRÖER. Frankfurt/Main, 1964. [Philo: 1.328–31.]

III. General Studies

ADORNO, FRANCESCO. La filosofia antica. 2 vols. Milano, 1965. [Philo: 2.171–228.] [N]

AGOURIDIS, SAVAS. Φίλων ὁ Ἰουδαῖος [Philo Judaeus]. Γρηγόριος Παλαμᾶς [Gregorios Palamas] 50 (1967) 441–50.

AMIR, YEHOSHUA. Philo Judaeus. EJ 13 (1971) 409–15.

ARGYLE, A. W. Philo, the Man and his Work. ExT 85 (1973–74) 115–17.

ARNALDEZ, ROGER. Introduction. PAL 13–16.

ARNALDEZ, ROGER. Philo Judaeus. NCE 11 (1967) 287–91.

BARNARD, L. W. The Background of Early Egyptian Christianity. Church Quarterly Review 164 (1963) 300–10, 428–41.

BENTWICH, N. DeM. Philo Judaeus of Alexandria. Philadelphia, 1910; reprinted, 1940.

BONAFEDE, GIULIO. Storia della filosofia greco-romana. Firenze, 1949. [Philo: 343–50.]

BRÉHIER, ÉMILE. Philo Judaeus. In: ID. Études de philosophie antique, 207–14 (Publications de la Faculté des lettres de Paris). Paris, 1955.

CHADWICK, HENRY. Philo. In: The Cambridge History of Later Greek and Early Medieval Philosophy, 137–57. Ed. A. H. ARMSTRONG. Cambridge, 1967.

COLPE, CARSTEN. Philo. RGG 5 (³1961) 341–46.

COMAY, JOAN. Philo Judaeus. Who's Who in Jewish History after the Period of the Old Testament, 320. London, 1974. [Portrait.]

DANIÉLOU, JEAN. Philon d'Alexandrie. Paris, 1958.

DRUMMOND, JAMES. Philo Judaeus, or The Jewish-Alexandrian Philosophy in its Development and Completion. With Introductory Chapters on Greek Philosophy and the Blending of Hellenism and Judaism till the Time of Philo. With Critical Notes and Indexes of Subjects and Names and of References to Passages in Philo. London, 1888; reprinted Amsterdam, 1969.

FELDMAN, LOUIS. Philo of Alexandria. The New Encyclopaedia Britannica. Macropaedia 14. 245–47. Chicago, 1974.

Filonas. Lietuvių Enciklopedija 6.262. South Boston, 1955.

GALLI, DARIO. Il pensiero greco (Il pensiero antico 1, 1). Padova, 1954. [Philo: 306–09.]

GOODENOUGH, ERWIN R. An Introduction to Philo Judaeus. New Haven, 1940; 2d ed., Oxford, 1962.

GOODENOUGH, ERWIN R. By Light, Light: the Mystic Gospel of Hellenistic Judaism. New Haven, 1935.

GOODENOUGH, ERWIN R. Jewish Symbols in the Greco-Roman Period. 13 vols. (Bollingen Series 37). New York, 1953–68. [Esp. 13.13–15.]

GOODENOUGH, ERWIN R. Philo Judaeus. IDB 3 (1962) 769–99.

GOODENOUGH, ERWIN R. Philo of Alexandria. Jewish Heritage 1, 4 (Winter 1959) 19–22; reprinted: Jewish Heritage Reader, 173–77. Ed. MORRIS ADLER. New York, 1965.

GOODENOUGH, ERWIN R. Philo of Alexandria. In: Greek Jewish Personalities in Ancient and Medieval Times, 98–119. Ed. SIMON NOVECK (B'nai Brith Great Books Series). New York, 1959. German: Philo von Alexandria. In: Große Gestalten des Judentums, 1.9–32. Ed. SIMON NOVECK. Zürich, 1972. [E]

GUASTALLA, R. M. Judaïsme et hellénisme. La leçon de Philon d'Alexandrie. REJ 7 (107) (1946–47) 3–38.

HEGERMANN, HARALD. Griechisch-jüdisches Schrifttum. In: Literatur und Religion des Frühjudentums: eine Einführung, 163–80. Ed. JOHANN MAIER, JOSEF SCHREINER. Würzburg, 1973. [Esp. 175–78.]

HEGERMANN, HARALD. Das griechischsprechende Judentum. In: Literatur und Religion des Frühjudentums: eine Einführung, 328–52. Ed. JOHANN MAIER, JOSEF SCHREINER. Würzburg, 1973.

HEGERMANN, HARALD. Philo von Alexandria. In: Umwelt des Urchristentums, 1.326–42. Ed. JOHANNES LEIPOLDT, WALTER GRUNDMANN. Berlin, 1966, ⁴1975.

HEGERMANN, HARALD. Philon von Alexandria. In: Literatur und Religion des Frühjudentums: eine Einführung, 353–69. Ed. JOHANN MEIER, JOSEF SCHREINER. Würzburg, 1973.

HEINEMANN, ISAAK. Philo. UJE 8 (1948) 495–96.

JAUBERT, ANNIE. Philon d'Alexandrie. Encyclopaedia Universalis, 12 (1975) 969–70.

JAY, B. Le monde du Nouveau Testament (Collection théologique). Yaoundé, 1978.

KARAVIDOPOULOS, IOANNES D. Φίλων. Ὁ Ἀλεξανδρεύς [Philo Alexandrinus]. Θρησκευτικὴ καὶ Ἠθικὴ Ἐγκυκλοπαιδεία [Religious and Ethical Encyclopedia] 11.1157–62. Athens, 1967.

KIESEWETTER, K. Philon d'Alexandrie. Rencontre orient-occident 10 (1973) 10–15. [IAJS]

LAUER, SIMON. Philon von Alexandrien. Sein Leben und seine Welt, sein Werk und seine Wirkung. Israelitisches Wochenblatt 69, 37 (1969) 88–90. [IZBG]

LEISEGANG, HANS. Philon. PW (Neue Bearbeitung) 20,1.1–50.

LEWY, YOHANAN (HANS). עולמות נפגשים, מחקרים על מעמדה של היהדות בעולם היווני־הרומאי. Studies in Jewish Hellenism. Jerusalem, 1960; reprinted 1969.

LOEWE, R. Philo and Judaism in Alexandria. In: Jewish Philosophy and Philosophers, 20–40. Ed. RAYMOND GOLDWATER. London, 1962.

LOHSE, EDUARD. Umwelt des Neuen Testaments (Grundrisse zum N.T. Das Neue Testament Deutsch. Ergänzungsreihe, 1). Göttingen, 1971. [Esp. 62, 97–101.]

MARCUS, RALPH. The Hellenistic Age. In: Great Ages and Ideas of the Jewish People, 95–139. Ed. LEO W. SCHWARZ. New York, 1956. [Esp. 132–35.]

MARCUS, RALPH. Hellenistic Jewish Literature. In: The Jews, their History, Culture and Religion, 2.1077–1148. Ed. LOUIS FINKELSTEIN. London, Philadelphia, 1949; New York, ³1960. [Esp. 1107–15.]

MARLOWE, JOHN. The Golden Age of Alexandria from its Foundation by Alexander the Great in 331 B.C. to its Capture by the Arabs in 642 A.D. London, 1971. [Esp. 241–244.]

MARSHALL, I. H. The Jewish Dispersion in New Testament Times. Faith and Thought 100 (1972–73) 237–58.

MONDÉSERT, CLAUDE. Philon von Alexandrien. Lexikon für Theologie und Kirche 8 (1963) 470–71.

MONDÉSERT, CLAUDE et al. Philon d'Alexandrie ou Philon le Juif. DBS 7 (1966) 1288–1351.
    I. MONDÉSERT, CLAUDE. Bibliographie, 1288–90.
    II. CADIOU, R. La Bible de Philon, 1290–99.
    III. MÉNARD, JACQUES-É. Les rapports de Philon avec le Judaïsme palestinien et Josèphe, 1299–1304.
    IV. ARNALDEZ, ROGER. Philon et les 'disciples de Moïse', 1305–06.
    V. ARNALDEZ, ROGER. Moïse et la loi, 1306–12.
    VI. ARNALDEZ, ROGER. Figures et historicité, 1312–20.
    VII. ARNALDEZ, ROGER. La méthode allégorique, 1320–29.
    VIII. ARNALDEZ, ROGER. Philosophie, théologie et mystique, 1329–48.
    IX. FEUILLET, ANDRÉ. Les rapports de Philon avec S. Jean, S. Paul et l'Epître aux Hébreux, 1348–51.

PARUZEL, HENRIKO. Filono el Aleksandrio. Biblia Revuo 11 (1975) 81–114.

PAUL, A. Littérature intertestamentaire. RechSR 62 (1973) 401–34. [Esp. 401–21.]

PETERS, F. E. The Harvest of Hellenism. A History of the Near East from Alexander the Great to the Triumph of Christianity. New York, 1970. [Esp. 300–06.]

PFEIFFER, ROBERT H. History of New Testament Times. New York, 1949. [Esp. 221–24.]

Philon d'Alexandrie. Lyon 11–15 septembre 1966 (Colloques nationaux du Centre national de la recherche scientifique). Paris, 1967.

PROOST, KAREL FREDERIK. Tussen twee werelden. Philo Judaeus (Gastmaal der eeuwen. Taferelen uit de cultuur geschiedenis van Europa 17). Arnhem, 1952. [B]

RABINOWITZ, H. R. פילון; הדרשן היהודי הראשון בגולה [Philo, the First Jewish Preacher of the Dispersion]. ניב המדרשה [Nib Hamidrashah], 1971, 192–99. [E]

REALE, GIOVANNI. Storia della filosofia antica (Cultura e storia 12–15; Pubblicazoni della Università Cattolica di Milano). 5 vols. Milano, 1976–80. [Esp.: 4.247–306.] [Ni]

REITZENSTEIN, RICHARD. Hellenistic Mystery Religions. Their Basic Ideas and Significance. Trans. JOHN E. STEELY (Pittsburgh Theological Monograph Series 15). Pittsburgh, 1978. [Originally published: Die hellenistischen Mysterienreligionen. Leipzig, 1910.]

RICHARDSON, W. Philo and his Significance for Christian Theology. Modern Churchman 30 (1940) 15–25.

SANDMEL, SAMUEL. The First Christian Century in Judaism and Christianity: Certainties and Uncertainties. New York, 1969. [Esp. 107–42.]

SANDMEL, SAMUEL. Philo of Alexandria. An Introduction. New York, 1979.

SCHALLER, B. Philon, 10. Der kleine Pauly, 4.772–76. Ed. K. ZIEGLER, W. SONTHEIMER. München, 1972.

SCHNEIDER, CARL. Kulturgeschichte des Hellenismus. 2 vols. München, 1967, 1969. [Esp. 1.876–81, 891–900, 2.558–59, 620, 840.]

SCHÜRER, EMIL. The History of the Jewish People in the Age of Jesus Christ (175 B.C.–A.D. 135); a New English Version. Rev., Ed. GÉZA VERMÈS, FERGUS MILLAR, PAMELA VERMÈS, MATTHEW BLACK. Edinburgh, Vol. 1, 1973. [NUC]

SCHÜRER, EMIL. The Literature of the Jewish People in the Time of Jesus. Ed. NAHUM N. GLATZER. New York, 1972. (= The Jewish People in the Time of Jesus Christ, Vol. 3) [Esp. 243–44; 321–81.]

SELTZER, ROBERT M. Jewish People, Jewish Thought. The Jewish Experience in History. New York, London, 1980. [Esp. 205–13.]

SIMON, MARCEL. La civilisation de l'antiquité et le christianisme (Collection Les grandes civilisations). Paris, 1972. [Esp. 54–56.]

SIMON, MARCEL, and BENOÎT, ANDRÉ. Le judaïsme et le christianisme antique d'Antiochus Epiphane à Constantin (Nouvelle Clio 10). Paris, 1968. [Esp. 204–06.]

STEIN, MENAHEM (EDMUND). פילון האלכסנדרוני. הסופר וספריו ומשנתו הפלוסופיה [Philo Alexandrinus. The Writer, his Writings and his Philosophical Teachings]. Warsaw, 1935.

STEMBERGER, GÜNTER. Geschichte der jüdischen Literatur. Eine Einführung (Beck'sche Elementarbücher). München, 1977. [Esp. 60–64.]

SURBURG, RAYMOND F. Introduction to the Intertestamental Period. St. Louis, 1975. [Esp. 153–61.]

THOMA, CLEMENS. Judentum und Hellenismus im Zeitalter Jesu. Bibel und Leben 11 (1970) 151–59. [Esp. 157.]

THYEN, HARTWIG. Philon von Alexandria. Lexikon der Alten Welt, 2301–02. Zürich, 1965.

TREVES, PIERO. Philon. Oxford Classical Dictionary, 684. Oxford, 1949; 2d ed., 822, Oxford, 1970.

WENDLAND, PAUL. Die hellenistisch-römische Kultur in ihren Beziehungen zum Judentum und Christentum. 4. Aufl. erweitert um eine Bibliographie von HEINRICH DÖRRIE. Tübingen, 1972. [Esp. 203–11.]

WOLFSON, HARRY A. Philo: Foundations of Religious Philosophy in Judaism, Christianity, and Islam. 2 vols. (ID. Structure and Growth of Philosophic Systems from Plato to Spinoza 2). Cambridge MA, 1947.

WOLFSON, HARRY A. Philo Judaeus. The Encyclopedia of Philosophy, 6.151—55. Ed. PAUL EDWARDS. New York, 1967; reprinted, WOLFSON, H. A. Studies in the History of Philosophy and Religion, 60—70. Ed. ISADORE TWERSKY, GEORGE H. WILLIAMS. Cambridge MA, 1973.

WOLFSON, ZVI (HARRY) A. פילוסופיה הדתית היהודית יסודות; פילון [Philo; Foundations of Jewish Religious Philosophy], Trans. MOSHE MEISELS, 2 vols. ספרית יעקב מיכאל, 30—29 תרגומים ואסופות מחכמת ישראל [Yaakob Michael Library, Translations and Collections from the Wisdom of Israel 29—30]). Jerusalem, 1970.

אוצר ישראל; אנציקלופידיא לכל מקצועות תורת ישראל, ספרותו ודברי ימיו פילון [Philo]. Ozar Yisrael; an Encyclopedia of All Matters Concerning Jews and Judaism in Hebrew, 7.230—34. Ed. JUDAH DAVID EISENSTEIN. 10 vols. Jerusalem, 1951; reprinted 1970/71.

IV. Studies of Individual Treatises and Passages

ADLER, MAXIMILIAN. Das philonische Fragment De deo. MGWJ 80 (1936) 163—70.

BOLOGNESI, G. Postille sulla traduzione armena delle 'Quaestiones et solutiones in Genesim' di Filone. Archivio Glottologico Italiano 55 (1970) 52—77. [E]

BOTTE, BERNARD. La vie de Moïse par Philon. Cahiers Sioniens 8,2—4 (1954) 56 (174)—62 (180) reprinted in: Moïse, l'homme de l'alliance, 55—62. Paris, 1955. German: Das Leben des Moses bei Philo. In: Moses in Schrift und Überlieferung, 173—81. Trans. FRIDOLIN STIER, ELEONORE BECK. Düsseldorf, 1963.

BOYANCÉ, PIERRE. Études philoniennes. REG 76 (1963) 64—110. [On Opif.]

HECHT, RICHARD D. Preliminary Issues in the Analysis of Philo's De Specialibus Legibus. SP 5 (1978) 1—55.

KÜCHLER, MAX. Frühjüdische Weisheitstraditionen: zum Fortgang weisheitlichen Denkens im Bereich des frühjüdischen Jahweglaubens (Orbis Biblicus et Orientalis 26). Freiburg, Schweiz; Göttingen, 1979. [Esp. pp. 222—35: Die Gesetzesepitome bei Philo, Hyp. 7, 1—9.]

LAMEERE, W. Sur un passage de Philon d'Alexandrie (De Plantatione 1—6). Mn 4th series, 4 (1951) 73—80. [F]

LEBRAM, JÜRGEN C. H. Eine stoische Auslegung von Ex. 3, 2 bei Philo. In: Das Institutum Judaicum der Universität Tübingen in den Jahren 1971—1972, 30—34. Tübingen, 1972.

LEISEGANG, HANS. Philons Schrift über die Ewigkeit der Welt. Philologus N.F. 46 (92) (1937) 156—76.

LEISEGANG, HANS. Philons Schrift über die Gesandtschaft der alexandrinischen Juden an den Kaiser Gaius Caligula. JBL 57 (1938) 377—405.

LUCCHESI, ENZO. La division en six livres des 'Quaestiones in Genesim' de Philon d'Alexandrie. Muséon 89 (1976) 383—95.

MARCUS, RALPH. A Note on Philo's Quaestiones in Gen. ii.31. Classical Philology 39 (1944) 257—58.

MARCUS, RALPH. Notes on the Armenian Text of Philo's Quaestiones in Genesin, Book I—III. Journal of Near Eastern Studies 7 (1948) 111—15.

MÉASSON, ANITA. Le De sacrificiis Abelis et Caini de Philon d'Alexandrie. Bulletin de l'Association Guillaume Budé 25 (1966) 309—16.

NIKIPROWETZKY, VALENTIN. Κυρίου πρόσθεσις. Note critique sur Philon d'Alexandrie, De Josepho 28. REJ 127 (1969) 387—92.

NIKIPROWETZKY, VALENTIN. Schadenfreude chez Philon d'Alexandrie? Note sur *In Flaccum* 121 sq. REJ 127 (1968) 7–19.

NIKIPROWETZKY, VALENTIN. Sur une lecture démonologique de Philon d'Alexandrie, *De Gigantibus*, 6–18. In: Hommage à Georges Vajda. Études d'histoire et de pensée juives. Ed. GÉRARD NAHON, CHARLES TOUATI, 43–71. Louvain, 1980.

NORDEN, E. Das Genesiszitat in der Schrift vom Erhabenen. In: Abhandlungen der deutschen Akademie der Wissenschaften zu Berlin, Klasse für Sprachen, Literatur und Kunst 1954, 1, 1–23. Berlin, 1955. [Esp. 11–23.] Reprinted in: ID. Kleine Schriften zum klassischen Altertum, 286–313. Berlin, 1966. [Esp. 294–313.]

PETIT, MADELEINE. A propos d'une réminiscence probable d'Isaïe dans le Quod omnis probus liber sit. In: Hommages à André Dupont-Sommer, 491–95. Paris, 1971.

POUILLOUX, JEAN. Le calendrier et un passage de Philon d'Alexandrie REA 66 (1964) 211–13.

ROYSE, JAMES R. The Original Structure of Philo's *Quaestiones*. SP 4 (1976–77) 41–78.

RUNIA, DAVID T. Philo's De Aeternitate Mundi: the Problem of its Interpretation. VC 35 (1981) 105–51.

SANDMEL, SAMUEL. The Confrontation of Greek and Jewish Ethics: Philo, *De Decalogo*. CCAR Journal 15 (1968) 54-63, 96; reprinted in: ID. Two Living Traditions: Essays on Religion and the Bible, 279–90. Detroit, 1972.

SCHWARZ, W. A Study in pre-Christian Symbolism: Philo, *De somniis* I.216–218, and Plutarch *De Iside et Osiride* 4 and 77. Institute of Classical Studies Bulletin 20 (1973) 104–17.

SCROGGS, ROBIN J. The Last Adam. A Study in Pauline Anthropology. Oxford, Philadelphia, 1966. [Appendix on Philo, Quaes Gen I–III.]

SIJPESTEIJN, P. J. The Legationes ad Gaium. JJS 15 (1964) 87–96.

SOLOMON, DAVID. Philo's Use of γενάρχης in *In Flaccum*. JQR 61 (1970) 119–31.

TROIANI, L. Osservazioni sopra l'apologia di Filone: Gli *Hypothetica*. Athenaeum 66 (1978) 304–14.

VERNHES, J. V. Philon d'Alexandrie, De sacrificiis Abelis et Caini. Revue de philologie 94 (3d series, 42) (1968) 298–305.

V. Problems of Manuscripts, Text and Language

ALAND, KURT. Eine neue Schrift Philos? TLZ 68 (1943) 169–70.

ALEXANDER, PAUL J. A Neglected Palimpsest of Philo Judaeus: Preliminary Remarks editorum in usum. In: Studia Codicologica. Ed. KURT TREU (TU 124) 1–14. Berlin, 1977.

BARTELINK, G. J. M. Μισόκαλος, épithète du diable. VC 12 (1958) 37–44.

BARTHÉLEMY, D. Est-ce Hoshaya Rabba qui censura le ʿCom(mentaire) All(égorique)? À partir des retouches faites aux citations bibliques, étude sur la tradition textuelle du ʿCom. All.ʾ PAL 45–79.

BOLOGNESI, G. Note al testo del ʿDe providentiaʾ di Filone. In: Armeniaca, 190–200. Venise, 1969. [E]

CADIOU, R. Sur un florilège philonien. REG 70 (1957) 93–101.

CADIOU, R. Sur un florilège philonien. Notes complémentaires. REG 71 (1958) 55–60.

COHEN-YASHAR, YOHANAN (KAHN, JEAN-GEORGES). הבעיות המיוחדות הכרוכות בתרגום כתבי פילון האלכסנדרוני לעיברית [Special Problems in Translating the Writings of Philo of Alexandria into Hebrew]. Proceedings of the Fifth World Congress of Jewish Studies 3.203–07. Jerusalem, 1972.

Früchtel, Ludwig. Griechische Fragmente zu Philons Quaestiones in Genesin et in Exodum. ZAW 55 (N.F. 14) (1937) 108–15.

Früchtel, Ludwig. Zum Oxyrhynchos-Papyrus des Philon (Ox.-Pap. XI 1356). Philologische Wochenschrift 58 (1938) 1437–39.

Giusta, M. ἀνευπροφάσιστος: un probabile ΑΠΑΞ ΕΙΡΗΜΕΝΟΝ in Filone De aeternitate mundi § 75. Rivista di filologia e d'istruzione classica 100 (1972) 131–36.

Grønbech, Vilhelm P. Philon. Et fragment (Studier fra Sprog- og Oltidsforskning 58, 209). København, 1949.

Lake, Kirsopp. Introduction. In: Eusebius. The Ecclesiastical History, 1.xl–xliv (Loeb Classics). Cambridge MA, 1953. [Regarding fragments of Philo in Eusebius.]

Lewy, Hans. The Pseudo-Philonic de Jona. I: The Armenian Text with a Critical Introduction (Studies and Documents 7). London, 1936. [Discussion of Armenian mss. of Philo.]

Mercier, C. La version arménienne du Legum Allegoriae. In: Armeniaca, 9–15. Venise, 1969. [E]

Merell, Jean. Nouveaux fragments du Papyrus 4. RB 47 (1938) 5–22.

Roberts, Colin H. Buried Books in Antiquity: Habent sua fata libelli. A Public Lecture Delivered at the Library Association, Chaucer House, London on 25 October 1962 (Arundell Esdaile Memorial Lecture, 1962). London, 1963. [Esp. 11–13.] [NUC]

Royse, James R. The Oxyrhynchus Papyrus of Philo. Bulletin of the American Society of Papyrologists 17 (1980) 155–65.

Royse, James R. The Text of Philo's Quis Rerum Divinarum Heres 167–173 in Vaticanus 379. Theokratia. Jahrbuch des Institutum Judaicum Delizschianum 3 (1973–75) 217–23.

Smith, J. P. Γένος in Philo on the Essenes (Hypoth. = Eus. Pr. Ev. 8. 11) = νόμος? Bib 40 (1959) 1021–24.

Stahlschmidt, Klara. Eine unbekannte Schrift Philons von Alexandrien (oder eines ihm nahestehenden Verfassers). Aegyptus 22 (1942) 161–76.

Winden, J. C. M. van. The first fragment of Philo's Quaestiones in Genesim. VC 33 (1979) 313–18.

VI. Literary Style, Source and Form Criticism

Barnes, E. J. Petronius, Philo and Stoic Rhetoric. Latomus 32 (1973) 787–98.

Belkin, Samuel. לשאלת המקורות של פרשנות פילון האלכסנדרוני [On the Question of the Sources of the Commentaries of Philo of Alexandria]. Horeb 9 (1946) 1–20.

Cazeaux, Jacques. Aspects de l'exégèse philonienne. RSR 47 (1973) 262–69; reprinted in: Exégèse biblique et Judaïsme, 108–15. Ed. Jacques-É. Ménard. Strasbourg, Leiden, 1973.

Cazeaux, Jacques. Littérature ancienne et recherche des 'structures'. Revue des études Augustiniennes 18 (1972) 287–92.

Dillon, John M. The Transcendence of God in Philo: Some Possible Sources. Center for Hermeneutical Studies in Hellenistic and Modern Culture. Protocol of the Sixteenth Colloquy: 20 April 1975. Ed. Wilhelm Wuellner (Protocol Series of the Colloquies of the CHSHMC 16). Berkeley, 1975. [With responses by Gerard E. Caspary and David Winston and discussion by a group of participants.]

Grumach, Ernst Israel. Zur Quellenfrage von Philos De opificio mundi § 1–3. MGWJ 83 (N.F. 47) (1939) 126–31.

HAMERTON-KELLY, ROBERT G. Sources and Traditions in Philo Judaeus. Prolegomena to an Analysis of his Writing. SP 1 (1972) 3–26.

HAY, DAVID M. Philo's Treatise on the Logos-Cutter. SP 2 (1973) 9–22.

MICHAELSON, S., and MORTON, A. Q. The new stylometry: a One-Word Test of Authorship for Greek Writers. Classical Quarterly 22 (1972) 89–102. [Esp. 95–96.]

MICHEL, A. Quelques aspects de la rhétorique chez Philon. PAL 81–103.

THYEN, HARTWIG. Der Stil der jüdisch-hellenistischen Homilie (FRLANT 65) 1955.

TRISOGLIO, F. Apostrofi, parenesi e preghiere in Filone d'Alessandria. Rivista Lasalliana 31 (1964) 357–410; 32 (1965) 39–79, 192; reprinted Torino, 1964. [E]

VII. Life of Philo; Philo as a Person

COHEN-YASHAR, YOHANAN (KAHN, JEAN GEORGES). (על פי ?האם ידע פילון האלכסנדרוני עברית (פירושיו האטימולוגיים) [Did Philo of Alexandria Know Hebrew? (Based on the Testimony of the Etymologies)]. Ta 34 (1964–65) 337–45. [English summary, p. IV–V.]

FOSTER, S. STEPHEN. A Note on the 'Note' of J. Schwartz. SP 4 (1976–77) 25–32.

FUCHS (FUKS), ALEXANDER. (לתולדות משפחת פילון האלכסנדרוני) מרקום יוליוס אלכסנדר [Marcus Julius Alexander (Relating to the History of Philo's Family)]. Zi 13–14 (1948–49) 10–17. [English summary, p. I.]

GUTMAN, YEHOSHUA. פילון האפיקון [Philo the Epicist]. Esh 1 (1954) 49–72.

MANTEL, HAIM DOV. ?האם ידע פילון עברית [Did Philo Know Hebrew?] Ta 32 (1962–63) 98–99, 395.

NAZZARO, ANTONIO V. Il problema cronologico della nascita di Filone Alessandrino. Rendiconti della Accademia di archeologia, lettere e belle arti, Napoli N.S. 38 (1963) 129–38.

SCHWARTZ, JACQUES. L'Égypte de Philon. PAL 34–44.

SCHWARTZ, JACQUES. Note sur la famille de Philon d'Alexandrie. In: Mélanges Isidore Lévy, 591–602 (Université libre de Bruxelles. Annuaire de l'Institut de philologie et d'histoire orientales et slaves 13 [1953]). Bruxelles, 1955.

TERIAN, ABRAHAM. The Implications of Philo's Dialogues on his Exegetical Works. In: Society of Biblical Literature 1978 Seminar Papers. Ed. PAUL J. ACHTEMEIER (SBL Seminar Papers Series 13), 1.181–90. Missoula, 1978.

VIII. Jewish and Roman History

ABEL, ERNEST L. Were the Jews Banished from Rome in 19 A.D.? REJ 127 (1968) 383–86.

ADRIANI, MAURILIO. Note sull'antisemitismo antico. Studi e materiali di storia delle religioni 36 (1965) 63–98. [Esp. 95–98.]

APPLEBAUM, S. The Legal Status of the Jewish Communities in the Diaspora. In: The Jewish People in the First Century, 420–63. Ed. S. SAFRAI et al. (Compendium rerum Iudaicarum ad Novum Testamentum 1, 1). Assen, 1974. [Esp. 434–40.]

ARGYLE, A. W. The Ancient University of Alexandria. Classical Journal 69 (1973–74) 348–350.

BARNETT, P. W. "Under Tiberius all was Quiet." NTS 21 (1975) 564–71.

BELKIN, SAMUEL. The Jewish Community in a Non-Jewish World: Problems of Integration and Separation. In: ID. Essays in Traditional Jewish Thought, 121–143. New York, 1956. [Esp. 125–30]

BELL, HAROLD IDRIS. The Constitutio Antoniniana and the Egyptian poll-tax. JRS 37 (1947) 17–23.

BELL, HAROLD IDRIS. P. Giss. 40 and the Constitutio Antoniniana. Journal of Egyptian Archaeology 28 (1942) 39–49; 30 (1944) 72–73.

BERTRAM, GEORG. Philo als politisch-theologischer Propagandist des spätantiken Judentums. Theologisches Literaturblatt 64 (1939) 193–99. [T]

BERTRAM, GEORG. Philo und die jüdische Propaganda in der antiken Welt. In: Christentum und Judentum, 79–105. Ed. W. GRUNDMANN. Leipzig, 1940.

BILDE, PER. The Roman Emperor Gaius (Caligula)'s Attempt to Erect his Statue in the Temple of Jerusalem. ST 32 (1978) 67–93.

BOKSER, BARUCH. Philo's Description of Jewish Practices. Protocol of the Thirtieth Colloquy: 5 June 1977. The Center for Hermeneutical Studies in Hellenistic and Modern Culture. Ed. WILHELM WUELLNER. Berkeley, 1977.

BRANDON, SAMUEL G. F. Religion in Ancient History. London, 1969. [Esp. 256–58.]

BURKE, J. B. Philo and Alexandrian Judaism. Dissertation, Syracuse University, 1963. [DA]

COLIN, J. Philon d'Alexandrie et la 'lâcheté' du préfet d'Égypte. Rheinisches Museum für Philologie 110 (1967) 284–85.

DELLING, GERHARD. Philons Enkomion auf Augustus. Klio 54 (1972) 171–92.

DOYLE, A. D. Pilate's Career and the Date of the Crucifixion. JTS 42 (1941) 190–93.

FELDMAN, LOUIS H. The Orthodoxy of the Jews of Hellenistic Egypt. Jewish Social Studies 22 (1960) 215–37.

FOSTER, SAMUEL STEPHEN. The Alexandrian Situation and Philo's Use of Dike. Dissertation, Northwestern University, 1975.

FRY, VIRGIL ROY LEE. The Warning Inscriptions from the Herodian Temple. Dissertation, Southern Baptist Theological Seminary, 1974. [Esp. Ch. 3.] [DA]

GOODENOUGH, ERWIN R. Archeology and Jewish History. JBL 55 (1936) 211–20. [Review of: J.-B. FREY, Corpus inscriptionum Iudaicarum, IIIᵉ siècle avant J.-C. au VIIᵉ siècle de notre ère 1 (Rome, Paris, 1936).]

GOODENOUGH, ERWIN R. The Jurisprudence of the Jewish Courts in Egypt. Legal Administration by the Jews under the Early Roman Empire as Described by Philo Judaeus. New Haven, 1929; reprinted Amsterdam, 1968.

GRANT, MICHAEL. The Jews in the Roman World. New York, 1973. [Esp. 126–29.]

HENNIG, DIETER. Zu der alexandrinischen Märtyrerakte P. Oxy. 1089. Chiron 4 (1974) 425–440.

KASHER, ARIÉ. הנסיבות לפירסום האדיקט של קלאודיוס קיסר ומכיתבו אל אלכסנדרונים [The Circumstances of the Edict of Claudius Caesar and of his Letter to the Alexandrians]. Zi 39 (1974) 1–7.

KASHER, ARIÉ. Les circonstances de la promulgation de l'édit de l'Empereur Claude et de sa lettre aux Alexandrins (41 ap.J.-C.). Sem 26 (1976) 99–108.

KASHER, ARIÉ. ירושלים כ'מטרופולים' בתודעתו הלאומית של פילון [Jerusalem as a 'Metropolis' in Philo's National Consciousness]. Cathedra 11 (Apr 1979) 45–56.

KASHER, ARIÉ. יהודי מצרים ההלניסטית והרומית במאבקם על זכויותיהם. The Jews in Hellenistic and Roman Egypt ש"ע היהדות למדעי הספר בית פרסומי; 23, התפוצות לחקר המכון פרסומי) רוזנברג חיים). Tel-Aviv, 1978. [Esp.: 212–38; Eng. summary, VII–XXII.]. [Ni; NUC]

KASHER, ARIÉ. עדות פילון על זכויותיהם של יהודי אלכסנדרייה [The Testimony of Philo on the Rights of the Jews of Alexandria]. In: דברי הקונגרס העולמי הששי למדעי היהדות. Proceedings of the Sixth World Congress of Jewish Studies, 2.35–45. 4 vols. Jerusalem, 1975. [Eng. summary, "Philo on the Rights of Alexandrian Jews," 2.411–12.]

KATZ, ROBERT S. The Illness of Caligula. Classical World 65 (1972) 223–25.

KRAUS, CLARA. Filone Alessandrino e un'ora tragica della storia ebraica. Napoli, 1967.

LE MOYNE, JEAN. Les Sadducéens (Études bibliques). Paris, 1972. [Esp. 60–62.]

MAIER, PAUL L. The Episode of the Golden Roman Shields at Jerusalem. HTR 62 (1969) 109–21.

MENDELSON, ALAN. Encyclical Education in Philo of Alexandria. Dissertation, University of Chicago, 1971.

REYERO, S. Los textos de Flavio Josefo y de Filón sobre las residencias de los procuradores romanos en Jerusalén. Studium 1 (1962) 527–56. [E]

RICHNOW, WOLFGANG. Untersuchung zu Sprache und Stil des zweiten Makkabäerbuches. Ein Beitrag zur hellenistischen Historiographie. Dissertation, Göttingen, 1966. [D]

SAFRAI, S. Relations between the Diaspora and the Land of Israel. In: The Jewish People in the First Century, 184–215. Ed. S. SAFRAI et al. (Compendium rerum Iudaicarum ad Novum Testamentum 1, 1). Assen, 1974.

SEVENSTER, JAN N. The Roots of Pagan Anti-Semitism in the Ancient World (NTSup 41). Leiden, 1975.

SHERWIN-WHITE, A. N. Philo and Avilius Flaccus: a Conundrum. Latomus 31 (1972) 820–828.

SIMON, MARCEL. Situation du judaïsme alexandrin dans la diaspora. PAL 17–33.

SMALLWOOD, E. MARY. The Chronology of Gaius' Attempt to Desecrate the Temple. Latomus 16 (1957) 3–17.

SMALLWOOD, E. MARY. The Jews under Roman Rule. Leiden, 1976 [Esp. 222–46.]

STERN, M. The Jewish Diaspora. In: The Jewish People in the First Century, 117–83. Ed. S. SAFRAI et al. (Compendium rerum Iudaicarum ad Novum Testamentum 1, 1). Assen, 1974. [Esp. 122–33.]

TAMM, B. Ist der Castortempel das Vestibulum zu dem Palast Caligulas gewesen? Eranos 62 (1964) 146–69. [E]

TCHERIKOVER, VICTOR A. The Decline of the Jewish Diapora in Egypt in the Roman Period. JJS 14 (1963) 1–32.

TCHERIKOVER, AVIGDOR (VICTOR A.). היהודים במצרים בתקופה ההלניסטית־הרומית לאור הפאפירולוגיה. The Jews in Egypt in the Hellenistic-Roman Age, in the Light of the Papyri. Jerusalem, 1945, 1963.

TCHERIKOVER, AVIGDOR (VICTOR A.). היהודים בעולם היווני והרומי. The Jews in the Greco-Roman World. Tel-Aviv, 1961.

TCHERIKOVER, VICTOR A., FUKS, ALEXANDER, eds. Corpus Papyrorum Judaicarum. 3 vols. Cambridge MA, 1957–1964.

TREU, KURT. Die Bedeutung des Griechischen für die Juden im römischen Reich. Kairos N.F. 15 (1973) 123–44. [Esp. 126.]

TROIANI, LUCIO. L'opera storiografica di Ellanico di Lesbo, di Delfino Ambaglio. Gli ebrei e lo stato pagano in Filone e in Guiseppe, di Lucio Troiani (Bibliotheca di studi antichi 24; Ricerche di storiografia antica 2). Pisa, 1980.

VISSCHER, F. DE. La politique dynastique de Tibère. In: Synteleia Vincenzo Arangio-Ruiz, 54–65. Napoli, 1964. [E]

WOLFSON, HARRY A. Philo on Jewish Citizenship in Alexandria. JBL 63 (1944) 165–68.

YOYOTTE, JEAN. L'Égypte ancienne et les origines de l'anti-judaïsme. RHR 163 (1963) 133–43.

ZEITLIN, SOLOMON. Did Agrippa Write a Letter to Gaius Caligula? JQR 56 (1965) 22–31.

IX. The Therapeutae, the Essenes and Qumrân

ADAM, ALFRED. Antike Berichte über die Essener (Kleine Texte für Vorlesungen und Übungen 182). Berlin, New York, 1961, ²1972. [Esp. (2d ed.) 1–22: Quod Omn 72–91; Judaeis defensio (Eus., PE 8.2); Vita Cont 1–90.]

AGOURIDIS, SAVAS. Οἱ Θεραπεῦται [The Therapeutae]. Θεολογία [Theologia] 38 (1967) 246–69.

AMUSIN, IOSIF DAVIDOVICH. Тексты Кумрана. Выпуск I: Перевод с древнееврейского и арамейского. Введение и комментарии (Памятники письменности Востока 33,1) [The Texts of Qumran. Part I: Translation from Ancient Hebrew and Aramaic. Introduction and Commentary (Literary Monuments of the East 33, 1)]. Moskva, 1971. [Russian translations of: Quod Omn 75–87 (341–44), Judaeis defensio (Eus., PE 8.2) (345–47), Vita Cont (376–91).]

BAUMGARTEN, JOSEPH M. Studies in Qumran Law (SJLA 24). Leiden, 1977. [Esp. 134–38.]

BRAYER, MENACHIM M. Psychosomatics, Hermetic Medicine, and Dream Interpretation in the Qumran Literature. JQR 60 (1969) 112–27, 213–30. [Esp. 119–24.]

BROOKE, GEORGE JOHN. 4Q Florilegium in the Context of Early Jewish Exegetical Method. Dissertation, Claremont Graduate School, 1978.

CARMIGNAC, J. Étude sur les procédés poétiques des Hymnes. RQ 2 (1959–60) 515–32. [Esp. 30–32: Appendice. – Témoignage de Philon.]

DANIEL, CONSTANTIN. Filon din Alexandria membru de seamă al mişcării eseniene din Egipt [Philo of Alexandria, an Important Member of the Essene Movement of Egypt.] Studii teologice 27 (1975) 602–25.

DANIEL, CONSTANTIN. Vederea lui Dumnezeu în Noul Testament şi teofaniile esenienilor [The View of God in the New Testament and the Theophany of the Essenes]. Studii teologice 25 (1973) 188–206. [Esp. 197–200.]

DANIEL, CONSTANTIN. 'Le voyant', nom cryptique des Esséniens dans l'œuvre de Philon d'Alexandrie. Studia et Acta Orientalia (Bucureşti) 9 (1977) 25–47.

DAUMAS, FRANÇOIS. Philon d'Alexandrie et le problème des Thérapeutes. Compte rendu et commentaire de la conférence donnée le 12 décembre 1963 au siège de la Y.M.C.A. sous les auspices de la Société archéologique d'Alexandrie (Conférences 1). Alexandrie, 1964. [BN]

DAUMAS, FRANÇOIS. La 'solitude' des Thérapeutes et les antécédents égyptiens du monachisme chrétien. PAL 347–59.

DELCOR, MATHIAS. Repas cultuels esséniens et thérapeutes, thiases et ḥaburoth. RQ 6 (1968) 401–25; reprinted in: ID. Religion d'Israël et Proche Orient ancien. Des Phéniciens aux Esséniens, 320–44. Leiden, 1976. [Esp. 327–29.]

ELIZAROVA, MARGARITA MIKHAĬLOVNA. Сведения о Ессеях и Терапевтах в «Хронике» Георгия Амартола [Some Information Concerning the Essenes and the Therapeutae in the 'Chronicle' of Georgios Hamartolos]. Палестинский Сборник [Palestinskiĭ Sbornik] 25 (88) (1974) 73–76.

ELIZAROVA, MARGARITA MIKHAĬLOVNA. Община терапевтов. (Из истории ессейского общественно религиозного движения I в. н. э.) [The Community of the Therapeutae.

(From the History of the Essene Socio-Religious Movement of the First Century.)]. Moskva, 1972.

FARMER, WILLIAM R. Essenes. IDB 2 (1962) 143–49. [Esp. 143–44, 147.]

HENDRIX, P. J. G. A. Een Paasvigilie in Philo's 'De vita contemplativa'. Nederlands Theologisch Tijdschrift 25 (1971) 393–97.

LOHSE, BERNHARD. Askese und Mönchtum in der Antike und in der alten Kirche (Religion und Kultur der alten Mittelmeerwelt in Parallelforschungen 1. Ed. C. COLPE, H. DÖRRIE). München, 1969. [Esp. 102–10.]

MARCUS, RALPH. Philo, Josephus and the Dead Sea Yaḥad. JBL 71 (1952) 207–09.

MORARD, FRANÇOISE-E. Monachos, moine: histoire du terme grec jusqu'au 4ᵉ siècle. Freiburger Zeitschrift 20 (1973) 332–411. [Esp. 357–62.]

NIKIPROWETZKY, VALENTIN. Le 'De Vita Contemplativa' revisité. In: Sagesse et Religion. Colloque de Strasbourg (octobre 1976) (Bibliothèque des Centres d'Études Supérieures spécialisés. Travaux du Centre d'Études Supérieures spécialisé d'Histoire des Religions de Strasbourg), 105–25. Paris, 1979.

RIAUD, J. Les Thérapeutes d'Alexandrie dans la tradition et dans la recherche critique jusqu'aux découvertes de Qumrân. Mémoire de maîtrise, Université de Paris-Vincennes, 1977.

ROWLEY, HAROLD H. L'histoire de la secte qumranienne. In: Donum natalicium Iosepho Coppens septuagesimum annum complenti, 1.270–301. Ed. H. CAZELLES et al. Gembloux, Paris, 1969. [Esp. 284–85.]

SCHIFMAN, LAWRENCE HARVEY. The Halakhah at Qumran. 2 vols. Dissertation, Brandeis University, 1974. [DA]

SCHÖNFELD, HANS-GOTTFRIED. Zum Begriff 'Therapeutai' bei Philo von Alexandrien. RQ 3 (1961) 219–40.

STRICKER, B. H. De praehelleense ascese (vervolg.) Oudheidkundige mededelingen uit het Rijksmuseum van oudheiden te Leiden 49 (1968) 18–39.

SCHUHL, PIERRE-MAXIME. Philon, les banquets et le Séder pascal. In: Miscellanea di studi alessandrini in memoria di Augusto Rostagni, 54–55. Torino, 1963.

VERMÈS, GÉZA. Essenes and Therapeutae. In: ID. Post-Biblical Jewish Studies, 30–36 (SJLA 8) 1975.

VERMÈS, GÉZA. Essenes–Therapeutai–Qumran. Durham University Journal 52 (1960) 97–115.

VERMÈS, GÉZA. The Etymology of 'Essenes'. RQ 2 (1959–60) 427–43; reprinted in: ID. Post-Biblical Jewish Studies, 8–29 (SJLA 8) 1975. [Esp. 9–10, 19–23.]

WAGNER, SIEGFRIED. Die Essener in der wissenschaftlichen Diskussion vom Ausgang des 18. bis zum Beginn des 20. Jahrhunderts (BZAW 79). Berlin; Giessen 1960. [Esp. 146–56, 194–202.]

X. Apocrypha, Pseudepigrapha and Other Jewish-Hellenistic Literature

BELKIN, SAMUEL. The Alexandrian Halakah in Apologetic Literature of the First Century C.E. Philadelphia, 1946. [NUC]

CERESA-GASTALDO, ALDO. ΑΓΑΠΗ nei documenti anteriori al Nuovo Testamento. Aegyptus 31 (1951) 269–306.

DALBERT, PETER. Die Theologie der hellenistisch-jüdischen Missionsliteratur unter Ausschluß von Philo und Josephus (Theologische Forschung: Wissenschaftliche Beiträge zur kirchlich-evangelischen Lehre 4). Hamburg-Volksdorf, 1954. [Includes some consideration of Philo.]

DELCOR, MATHIAS. Le testament d'Abraham. Introduction, traduction du texte grec et commentaire de la recension grecque longue suivi de la traduction des Testaments d'Abraham, d'Isaac et de Jacob d'après les versions orientales (Studia in Veteris Testamenti pseudepigrapha 2). Leiden, 1973. [Esp. 279: parallels with Philo.]

DELLING, GERHARD. Die Bezeichnung 'Söhne Gottes' in der jüdischen Literatur der hellenistisch-römischen Zeit. In: God's Christ and his People: Studies in Honour of Nils Alstrup Dahl. Ed. JACOB JERVELL, WAYNE A. MEEKS, 18ff. Oslo, 1977.

DENIS, A. M. Les pseudépigraphes grecs d'Ancien Testament. NT 6 (1963) 310–19.

DENIS, A. M., and DE JONGE, M. The Greek Pseudepigrapha of the Old Testament. NT 7 (1965) 319–28.

FABER VAN DER MEULEN, HARRY E. Das Salomo-Bild im hellenistisch-jüdischen Schrifttum. Dissertation, Kampen, 1978.

GILBERT, MAURICE. La critique de dieux dans le Livre de la Sagesse (Sg 13–15) (Analecta Biblica 53). Rome, 1973.

HENGEL, MARTIN. Judentum und Hellenismus. Studien zu ihrer Begegnung unter besonderer Berücksichtigung Palästinas bis zur Mitte des 2. Jh. v. Chr. (WUNT 10). Tübingen 1969, ²1973.

HERRMANN, LÉON. La lettre d'Aristée à Philocrate et l'empereur Titus. Latomus 25 (1966) 58–77. [Esp. 58–64.]

LARCHER, C. Études sur le Livre de la Sagesse (Études Bibliques). Paris, 1969. [Esp. Ch. 2.]

MEEKS, WAYNE A. Moses as God and King. In: Religions in Antiquity. Essays in Memory of Erwin Ramsdell Goodenough, 354–71. Ed. JACOB NEUSNER (SHR 14). Leiden, 1968. [Esp. 354–61.]

NIKIPROWETZKY, VALENTIN. La troisième Sibylle. Recherches sur la signification, l'origine et la date du troisième poème pseudo-sibyllin, suivies du texte d'Oracula sibyllina III, établi, traduit et annoté (Collection Études juives 9). Paris, 1963, ²1970.

REIDER, JOSEPH, ed. The Book of Wisdom (Jewish Apocryphal Literature 6). New York, 1957.

RICKEN, FRIEDO. Gab es eine hellenistische Vorlage für Weisheit 13–15? Bib 49 (1968) 54–86.

ROBBINS, WILLIAM J. A Study in Jewish and Hellenistic Legend with Special Reference to Philo's Life of Moses. Dissertation, Brown University, 1948. [ADD]

SCHMIDT, FRANCIS. (Without title.) Annuaire, École Pratique des Hautes Études, Vᵉ section – sciences religieuses 80–81, 3 (1972–73; 1973–74) 321–25; 82, 3 (1973–74) 191–94. [Report of lectures on traditions regarding Abraham in Jewish Hellenistic literature. Esp. 82, 3, 191–94.]

SMITH, JONATHAN Z. The Prayer of Joseph. In: Religions in Antiquity. Essays in Memory of Erwin Ramsdell Goodenough, 253–94, Ed. JACOB NEUSNER (SHR 14). Leiden, 1968. [Esp. 265–67.]

STEIN, EDMUND. Zur apokryphen Schrift 'Gebet Josephs'. MGWJ 81 (1937) 280–86. [Esp. 282–83.]

TALBERT, CHARLES H. The Concept of Immortals in Mediterranean Antiquity. JBL 94 (1975) 419–36. [Esp. 424, 430.]

TEEPLE, HOWARD M. The Mosaic Eschatological Prophet (JBL Monograph Series 10). Philadelphia, 1957. [Esp. 34–38.]

WACHOLDER, BEN ZION. Pseudo-Eupolemos' Two Greek Fragments on the Life of Abraham. HUCA 34 (1963) 83–113.

XI. Rabbinic and Later Jewish Literature

ALON, GEDALYAHU (GEDALIAH). לחקר ההלכה של פילון [Research on the Halakah of Philo]. Ta 5 (1933–34) 28–36, 241–46; 6 (1934–35) 30–37, 452–59; reprinted in: ID. מחקרים בתולדות ישראל בימי בית שני ובתקופת המשנה והתלמוד. Studies in Jewish History in the Times of the Second Temple, the Mishna and the Talmud, 1.83–114. 2 vols. Tel-Aviv, 1957.

ALON, GEDALYAHU. On Philo's Halakha. In ID., Jews, Judaism and the Classical World. Studies in Jewish History in the Times of the Second Temple and Talmud. Trans. Israel Abrahams, 89–137. Jerusalem, 1977.

AMIR, YEHOSHUA. דרשותיו של פילון על היראה והאהבה ויחסן למדרשי ארץ-ישראל [The Homilies of Philo on Fear and Love and their Relation to Palestinian Midrashim]. Zi 30 (1965) 47–60. [English summary, p. II–III.]

BAER, YITSHAK F. החסידים הראשונים בכתבי פילון ובמסורת העברית [Ancient Hasidim in the Writings of Philo and in Hebrew Tradition]. Zi 18 (1953) 91–108.

BAMBERGER, BERNARD J. The Dating of Aggadic Materials. JBL 68 (1949) 115–23.

BAMBERGER, B. Philo and the Aggadah. HUCA 48 (1977) 153–85.

BELKIN, SAMUEL. Levirate and Agnate Marriage in Rabbinic and Cognate Literature. JQR 60 (1969–70) 275–329. [Esp. 294–303.]

BELKIN, SAMUEL. Philo and the Oral Law: the Philonic Interpretation of Biblical Law in Relation to the Palestinian Halakah (Harvard Semitic Series 11). Cambridge MA, 1940; reprinted New York, 1970.

BELKIN, SAMUEL. The Relation of Philo to the Pharisaic Halakah. Dissertation, Brown University, 1935. [ADD]

BELKIN, SAMUEL. Some Obscure Traditions Mutually Clarified in Philo and Rabbinic Literature. In: The Seventy-Fifth Anniversary Volume of The Jewish Quarterly Review, 80–103. Ed. ABRAHAM A. NEUMAN, SOLOMON ZEITLIN. Philadelphia, 1967.

BELKIN, SAMUEL. מדרש הנעלם ומקורותיו במדרשים האלכסנדרוניים הקדומים [The Midrash ha-Ne'elam, its Origins in the Ancient Alexandrian Midrashim]. Su 3 (1958) 25–92.

BELKIN, SAMUEL. המדרש הסמלי אצל פילון בהשוואה למדרשי חז"ל [The Symbolic Midrash in Philo Compared with Rabbinic Midrash]. In: ספר היובל לכבוד צבי וולפסון. Harry Austryn Wolfson Jubilee Volume, Hebrew Section, 33–68. Jerusalem, 1965.

BELKIN, SAMUEL. המדרש הגדול ומדרשי פילון [The Midrash ha-Gadol and the Midrashim of Philo.] In: ספר היובל לכבוד י. פינקל [J. Finkel Jubilee Volume], 7–58. New York, 1974. [IAJS]

BELKIN, SAMUEL. מדרש שאלות ותשובות על בראשית ושמות לפילון האלכסנדרוני ויחסו למדרש הארץ-ישראל [The Midrash Quaestiones et solutiones in Genesin et in Exodum of Philo Alexandrinus and its Relation to the Palestinian Midrash]. Horeb 14 (1960) 1–74.

BELKIN, SAMUEL. מדרשי פילון האלכסנדרוני לאור מדרשי א"י [The Midrashim of Philo Alexandrinus in Light of the Palestinian Midrashim]. Su 5 (1960) 1–68. [E]

BELKIN, SAMUEL. מדרשים בכתבי פילון ומקבילותיהם למאמרים במדרש הגדול ש"מקורם נעלם" [Midrashim in the Writings of Philo and their Parallels to Sayings in the Midrash ha-Gadol which are of "Unknown Origin"]. In: הגות עיברית באמריקה [Hebrew Thought in America] 1. Ed. M. ZOHARI. Tel-Aviv, 1972. [E]

BELKIN, SAMUEL. מקור קדום למדרשי חז"ל מדרש שו"ת על בראשית ושמות לפילון האלכסנדרוני [The Earliest Source of the Rabbinic Midrash – Quaestiones et solutiones in Genesin et in Exodum of Philo Alexandrinus]. In: ספר יובל לכבוד הרב ד"ר אברהם וייס. The Abraham Weiss Jubilee Volume, Hebrew Section, 579–633. Ed. SAMUEL BELKIN. New York, 1964.

BELKIN, SAMUEL. פילון ומסורה מדרשית ארץ ישראלית [Philo and the Midrashic Tradition of Palestine]. Horeb 13 (1958) 1–60.

BLACK, MATTHEW. The Origin of the Name Metatron. VT 1 (1951) 217–19.

COPPENS, J. Philon et l'exégèse targumique. ETL 24 (1948) 430–31. [EB]

DAHL, NIELS ALSTRUP, and SEGAL, ALAN F. Philo and the Rabbis on the Names of God. JSJ 9 (1978) 1–28.

DAUBE, DAVID. Rabbinic Methods of Interpretation and Hellenistic Rhetoric. HUCA 22 (1949) 239–64.

DEXINGER, F. Ein 'messianisches Szenarium' als Gemeingut des Judentums in nachherodianischer Zeit? Kairos 17 (1975) 249–78. [Esp. 250–55.]

FINKEL, JOSHUA. The Alexandrian Tradition and the Midrash Ha-Neʿelam. In: The Leo Jung Jubilee Volume. Essays in his Honor on the Occasion of his Seventieth Birthday, 77–103. Ed. MENAHEM M. KASHER et al. New York, 1962.

GINZBERG, LOUIS. Legends of the Jews. 7 vols. Philadelphia, 1909–38. [Esp. Indexes, Vol. 7.]

HALEVI, E. E. (EPSTEIN-HALEVI, ELIMELECH). עולמה של האגדה; האגדה לאור מקורות יווניים [The World of the Aggadah; the Aggadah in Light of Greek Sources]. Tel-Aviv, 1972. [NUC]

HALEVI, E. E. (EPSTEIN-HALEVI, ELIMELECH). פרשיות באגדה לאור מקורות יווניים [Passages in the Aggadah in Light of Greek Sources]. Haifa, Tel-Aviv, 1973.

HENGEL, MARTIN. Proseuche und Synagoge. Jüdische Gemeinde, Gotteshaus und Gottesdienst in der Diaspora und in Palästina. In: Tradition und Glaube. Das frühe Christentum in seiner Umwelt. Festgabe für Karl Georg Kuhn zum 65. Geburtstag, 157–84. Ed. GERT JEREMIAS et al. Göttingen, 1971.

JACKSON, BERNARD S. Essays in Jewish and Comparative Legal History (SJLA 10). Leiden, 1975. [Esp. 213–23, 235–40).

KAMINKA, A. Die mystischen Ideen des R. Simon ben Johai. HUCA 10 (1935) 149–68. [Esp. 157–58, 160–64.]

KNOX, WILFRED L. Abraham and the Quest for God. HTR 28 (1935) 55–60.

LEVINE, ISRAEL. Philo and Maimonides. In: ID. Faithful Rebels: a Study in Jewish Speculative Thought, 43–56. London, 1936; reprinted Port Washington NY, 1971.

LIEBERMAN, SAUL. Response to the Introduction by Professor Alexander Marx. Rabbinical Assembly Proceedings 12 (1948); reprinted in: The Jewish Expression, 117–133. Ed. JUDAH GOLDIN. New York, 1970.

MEYER, RUDOLF. Hellenistisches in der rabbinischen Anthropologie; rabbinische Vorstellungen vom Werden des Menschen (BWANT, 4. Folge 22). Leipzig, 1937.

NEUSNER, JACOB. The Idea of Purity in Ancient Judaism. JAAR 43 (1975) 15–26.

NISSEN, ANDREAS. Gott und der Nächste im antiken Judentum. Untersuchungen zum Doppelgebot der Liebe (WUNT 15). Tübingen, 1974. [Esp. 417–502.]

PELLETIER, ANDRÉ. La nomenclature du calendrier juif à l'époque hellénistique. RB 82 (1975) 218–33.

REVEL, BERNARD. The Karaite Halakah and its Relation to Sadducean, Samaritan and Philonian Halakah. Philadelphia, 1913; reprinted in: Karaite Studies, 1–88. Ed. PHILIP BIRNBAUM. New York, 1971. [Esp. 51–88.]

SANDMEL, SAMUEL. Abraham's Knowledge of the Existence of God. HTR 44 (1951) 137—39.
    [Reply to W. L. KNOX, Abraham and the Quest for God.]
SCHOLEM, GERSHOM. Kabbalah. EJ 10 (1971) 489—653. [Esp. 495—96.]
SEGAL, ALAN FRANKLIN. Two Powers in Heaven: the Significance of the Rabbinic Reports
    about Binitarianism, Ditheism and Dualism for the History of Early Christianity and
    Judaism. Dissertation, Yale University, 1975. [DA]
SEGAL, ALAN F. Two Powers in Heaven. Early Rabbinic Reports about Christianity and
    Gnosticism (SJLA 25). Leiden, 1977. [Esp. 159—81.]

TOWNER, WAYNE SIBLEY. The Rabbinic 'Enumeration of Scriptural Examples'. A Study of a
    Rabbinic Pattern of Discourse with Special Reference to Mekhilta d'R. Ishmael (SPB
    22) 1973. [Esp. 109—16.]

VERMÈS, GÉZA. He is the Bread. In: ID. Post-Biblical Jewish Studies, 139—46 (SJLA 8) 1975.
    [Esp. 143—44.]
VIVIANO, B. TH. Study as Worship. Aboth and the New Testament (SJLA 26). Leiden, 1978.

WÄCHTER, LUDWIG. Der Einfluß platonischen Denkens auf rabbinische Schöpfungsspekula-
    tionen. ZRGG 14 (1962) 36—56. [Esp. 41—48.]
WATERHOUSE, P. The Figure of Melchizedek in Rabbinic and Philonic Literature. Thesis,
    University of Leeds, 1977(?).
WERBLOWSKY, R. J. ZWI. Philo and the Zohar: a Note on the Methods of the scienza nuova
    in Jewish Studies. JJS 10 (1959) 25—44, 113—35.
WOLFSON, HARRY A. The Terms 'Holy Spirit,' 'Divine Light' and their Equivalents in Hallevi.
    In: ID. Studies in the History of Philosophy and Religion, 2.86—119. Ed. ISADORE
    TWERSKY and GEORGE H. WILLIAMS. Cambridge MA, 1973. [Esp. 104—06.]

XII. Classical Literature

ALEXANDRE, MONIQUE. La culture profane chez Philon. PAL 105—30.
ALFONSI, LUIGI. Il Περὶ βίου θεωρητικοῦ di Filone e la tradizione protrettica. Wiener
    Studien 70 (1957) 5—10.
AMIR, YEHOSHUA. האליגוריה של פילון ביחסה לאליגוריה ההומרית [The Allegory of Philo
    Compared with Homeric Allegory]. Esh 6 (1970) 35—45.

BARBEL, JOSEPH. Christos Angelos. Die Anschauung von Christus als Bote und Engel (Theo-
    phaneia 3). Bonn, 1941, ²1964. [Esp. 19—33.]
BAUMGARTEN, HANS. Vitam brevem esse, longam artem. Gymnasium 77 (1970) 299—323.
    [Esp. 315—16.]
BETZ, HANS-DIETER. The Delphic Maxim ΓΝΩΘΙ ΣΑΥΤΟΝ in Hermetic Interpretation.
    HTR 63 (1970) 465—84.
BLOOMFIELD, MORTON W. A Source of Prudentius' Psychomachia. Speculum 18 (1943) 87—
    90.
BOYANCÉ, PIERRE. Le culte des muses chez les philosophes grecs: études d'histoire et de
    psychologie religieuses (Bibliothèque des Écoles françaises d'Athènes et de Rome 141).
    Paris, 1937. [NUC]
BOYANCÉ, PIERRE. Écho des exégèses de la mythologie grecque chez Philon. PAL 169—88.
BOYANCÉ, PIERRE. Études philoniennes. REG 76 (1963) 64—110.
BOYANCÉ, PIERRE. Note sur la φρουρά platonicienne. Revue de philologie 89 3ᵉ série 37 (89)
    (1963) 7—11.
BOYANCÉ, PIERRE. Sur l'exégèse hellénistique du Phèdre (Phèdre, p. 246c). In: Miscellanea di
    studi alessandrini in memoria di Augusto Rostagni, 45—53. Torino, 1963.

CHROUST, ANTON H. A Fragment of Aristotle's *On Philosophy* in Philo of Alexandria, *De opificio mundi* I, 7. Divus Thomas 77 (1974) 224–35.

CHROUST, ANTON H. A Fragment of Aristotle's On Philosophy. Some Remarks about Philo of Alexandria, De Aeternitate Mundi 8, 41. Wiener Studien, N.F. 8 (87) (1974) 15–19.

CHROUST, ANTON H. 'Mystical Revelation' and 'Rational Theology' in Aristotle's *On Philosophy*. Tijdschrift voor Filosophie 34 (1972) 500–12. [BS]

CHROUST, ANTON H. Some Comments on Philo of Alexandria, *De aeternitate mundi*. Laval théologique et philosophique 31 (1975) 135–45.

CONLEY, THOMAS. 'General Education' in Philo of Alexandria. Center for Hermeneutical Studies in Hellenistic and Modern Culture. Protocol of the Fifteenth Colloquy: 9 March 1975. Ed. WILHELM WUELLNER (Protocol Series of the CHSHMC 15). Berkeley, 1975. [With responses by JOHN DILLON, ALAN MENDELSON, DAVID WINSTON and discussion by a group of participants.]

COURCELLE, PIERRE. Connais-toi toi-même, de Socrate à saint Bernard. 2 vols. Paris, 1974. [NUC]

COURCELLE, PIERRE. Le corps-tombeau (Platon, *Gorgias*, 439*a*, *Cratyle*, 400*c*, *Phèdre*, 250*c*). REA 68 (1966) 101–22. [Esp. 102–05.]

DE RIJK, L. M. Ἐγκύκλιος παιδεία. A Study of its Original Meaning. Vivarium 3 (1956) 24–93. [Esp. 73–85.]

DILLON, JOHN. Ganymede as the Logos: Traces of a Forgotten Allegorization in Philo. SP 6 (1979–80) 37–40.

DÖRRIE, HEINRICH. Praepositionen und Metaphysik. Wechselwirkung zweier Prinzipienreihen. Museum Helveticum 26 (1969) 217–28; reprinted in ID. Platonica minora, 124–36 (Studia et Testimonia antiqua 8). München, 1976. [Esp. 130–32.]

DÖRRIE, HEINRICH. Ὑπόστασις. Wort und Bedeutungsgeschichte. Nachrichten der Akademie der Wissenschaften zu Göttingen, phil.-hist. Kl. 1955, Nr. 3, 35–92; reprinted in: ID. Platonica minora, 12–61 (Studia et Testimonia antiqua 8). München, 1976. [Esp. 39.]

EFFE, BERND. Studien zur Kosmologie und Theologie der Aristotelischen Schrift 'Über die Philosophie' (Zetemata 50). München, 1970. [Esp. 7–23.]

FALLON, FRANCIS T. The Law in Philo and Ptolemy: a Note on The Letter to Flora. VC 30 (1976) 45–51.

GAGER, JOHN G. Moses in Greco-Roman Paganism. Nashville, 1972.

GOODENOUGH, ERWIN R. Literal Mystery in Hellenistic Judaism. In: Quantulacumque: Studies Presented to Kirsopp Lake, 227–241. Ed. R. P. CASEY et al. London, 1937.

GUNDEL, WILHELM, and GUNDEL, HANS GEORG. Astrologumena. Die astrologische Literatur in der Antike und ihre Geschichte (Sudhoffs Archiv. Vierteljahrschrift für Geschichte der Medizin und der Naturwissenschaften, der Pharmazie und der Mathematik. Beiheft 6). Wiesbaden, 1966. [Esp. 180–83.]

HALEVI, E. E. (EPSTEIN-HALEVI, ELIMELECH). מוטיבים יווניים באגדה [Greek Motifs in the Aggadah]. Ta 40 (1970–71) 293–300.

HARL, MARGUERITE. Cosmologie grecque et représentations juives dans l'œuvre de Philon d'Alexandrie. PAL 189–205.

HEINEMANN, ISAAK. Philons griechische und jüdische Bildung. Kulturvergleichende Untersuchungen zu Philons Darstellung der jüdischen Gesetze. Breslau, 1932; reprinted Hildesheim, 1962.

HÉRING, J. Eschatologie biblique et idéalisme platonicien. In: The Background of the New Testament and its Eschatology . . . in Honour of Charles Harold Dodd, 444–63. Cambridge, 1954. [Esp. 446–50.]

KAHN, JEAN-GEORGES. 'Connais-toi toi-même' à la manière de Philon. RHPR 53 (1973) 293–307.

KNOX, WILFRED L. Pharisaism and Hellenism. In: Judaism and Christianity 2: The Contact of Pharisaism with other Cultures, 59–111. Ed. H. M. J. LOEWE. London, 1937.

KOESTER, HELMUT. ΝΟΜΟΣ ΦΥΣΕΩΣ. In: Religions in Antiquity. Essays in Memory of Erwin Ramsdell Goodenough, 521–41. Ed. JACOB NEUSNER (SJLA 14) 1968. [Esp. 530–41.]

KRÄMER, HANS JOACHIM. Der Ursprung der Geistmetaphysik. Untersuchungen zur Geschichte des Platonismus zwischen Platon und Plotin. Amsterdam, 1964. [Esp. 266–84.]

KROKIEWICZ, A. Sceptycyzm grecki. Od Filona do Sekstusa. Warszawa, 1966. [E]

LÉVY, ISIDORE. Recherches esséniennes et pythagoriciennes (Centre de recherches d'histoire et de philologie de la IVᵉ section de l'École Pratique des Hautes Études III; Hautes études du monde gréco-romain 1). Genève, Paris, 1965. [Esp. Chs. 4, 5.]

LUSCHNAT, OTTO. Thukydides. PW Supplement 12 (1970) 1085–1354 [Esp. 1296–97.]

MÉNARD, JACQUES-É. Le mythe de Dionysos Zagreus chez Philon. RSR 42 (1968) 339–45.

MONDIN, BATTISTA. Il problema dei rapporti tra fede e ragione in Platone e in Filone Alessandrino. Le parole e le idee 9 (1967) 9–15.

MORAUX, PAUL. Une nouvelle trace de l'Aristote perdu. Les études classiques 16 (1948) 89–91.

MÜHL, MAX. Zu Poseidonios und Philon. Wiener Studien 60 (1942) 28–36.

NEUMARK, HERMANN. Die Verwendung griechischer und jüdischer Motive in den Gedanken Philons über die Stellung Gottes zu seinen Freunden. Dissertation, University of Würzburg, 1937. [DHS]

NOCK, ARTHUR DARBY. The Exegesis of Timaeus 28 C. VC 16 (1962) 79–86. [Esp. 82.]

NORTH, HELEN. Sophrosyne: Self-Knowledge and Self-Restraint in Greek literature (Cornell Studies in Classical Philology). Ithaca, 1966. [Esp. 323–28.]

PEASE, ARTHUR S. Caeli enarrant. HTR 34 (1941) 163–200. [Esp. 189–90.]

POHLENZ, MAX. Philon von Alexandreia. Nachrichten der Akademie der Wissenschaften zu Göttingen, phil.-hist. Kl. 1942, Nr. 5, 409–87; reprinted in ID. Kleine Schriften 1.305–83. Ed. HEINRICH DÖRRIE. Hildesheim, 1965.

POHLENZ, MAX. Die Stoa. Geschichte einer geistigen Bewegung. 2 vols. Göttingen, ³1964. [Esp. 1.369–78, 2.180–84.]

RAVAISSON–MOLLIEN, FÉLIX. Essai sur la métaphysique d'Aristote. Fragments du Tome III (Hellénisme–Judaïsme–Christianisme). Ed. CHARLES DEVIVAISSE (Bibliothèque des textes philosophiques). Paris, 1953. [Esp. 33–35, 62–70.]

SCARPAT, G. Cultura ebreo-ellenistica e Seneca. Rivista Biblica 13 (1965) 3–30. [E]

STEIN, MENAHEM (EDMUND). היהדות והיוונות [Judaism and Hellenism]. זרמים [Zeramim] 12 (1931) 62–69; reprinted in: ID. בין תרבות ישראל ותרבות יוון ורומא. The Relationship between Jewish, Greek, and Roman Cultures, 112–16. Ed. JUDAH ROSENTHAL. Tel-Aviv, 1970.

SUDER, W. On Age Classification in Roman Imperial Literature. Classical Bulletin 55 (1978) 5–9.

THEILER, WILLY. Gott und Seele im kaiserzeitlichen Denken. In: Recherches sur la tradition platonicienne, 65–91 (Entretiens sur l'antiquité classique 3). Vandoeuvres-Genève, 1955. [Esp. 68–72.] Reprinted in: ID. Forschungen zum Neuplatonismus, 104–23. Berlin, 1966. [Esp. 106–10.]

THEILER, WILLY. Philo von Alexandria und der Beginn des kaiserzeitlichen Platonismus. In: Parusia . . . Festgabe für Johannes Hirschberger, 199–218. Ed. KURT FLASCH. Frankfurt/Main, 1965; reprinted in: ID. Untersuchungen zur antiken Literatur, 484–501. Berlin, 1970. [E]

THEILER, WILLY. Philo von Alexandria und der hellenisierte Timaeus. In: Philomathes: Studies and Essays in the Humanities in Memory of Philip Merlan, 25–35. Ed. ROBERT B. PALMER and ROBERT G. HAMERTON-KELLY. The Hague, 1971.

UNTERSTEINER, MARIO. Aristotele. Della filosofia. Introduzione, testi, traduzione e commento esegetico (Temi e testi 10). Roma, 1963. [Esp. 24–27, 34–41, 46–49, 240–45.]

VANDERLINDEN, E. La foi de Virgile. Bulletin de l'Association Guillaume Budé 4 (1964) 448–58.

VERBEKE, GÉRARD. Ethische paideia in het latere stoïcisme en het vroege christendom. Tijdschrift voor Filosofie 27 (1965) 3–53. [E]

WASZINK, J. H. Der Platonismus und die altchristliche Gedankenwelt. In: Recherches sur la tradition platonicienne, 137–79 (Entretiens sur l'antiquité classique 3). Vandoeuvres-Genève, 1955. [Esp. 166–67.]

WILLMS, H. Εἰκών. Eine begriffsgeschichtliche Untersuchung zum Platonismus. 1. Teil: Philon von Alexandreia. Mit einer Einleitung über Platon und die Zwischenzeit. Münster, 1935. [DHS]

WOLFSON, HARRY A. Extradeical and Intradeical Interpretations of Platonic Ideas. Journal of the History of Ideas 22 (1961) 3–32; reprinted in: ID. Religious Philosophy. A Group of Essays, 27–68. Cambridge MA, 1961.

WOLFSON, HARRY A. The Philosophy that Faith Inspired. Greek Philosophy in Philo and the Church Fathers. In: The Crucible of Christianity, 309–16, 354. Ed. ARNOLD TOYNBEE. New York, 1969; reprinted as: Greek Philosophy in Philo and the Church Fathers. In: ID. Studies in the History of Philosophy and Religion, 71–97. Ed. ISADORE TWERSKY and GEORGE H. WILLIAMS. Cambridge MA, 1973.

WOLFSON, HARRY A. Plato's Pre-Existent Matter in Patristic Philosophy. In: The Classical Tradition; Literary and Historical Studies in Honor of Harry Caplan, 409–20. Ed. LUITPOLD WALLACH. Ithaca, 1966. [Esp. 410–12, 415–17.] Reprinted in: ID. Studies in the History of Philosophy and Religion, 170–81. Ed. ISADORE TWERSKY and GEORGE H. WILLIAMS. Cambridge MA, 1973. [Esp. 176–80.]

ZICÀRI, MARCELLO. Nothus in Lucr. V 575 e in Cat. 34, 15. In: Studia Florentina Alexandro Ronconi sexagenario oblata, 525–29. Roma, 1970. [Esp. 527–28.]

XIII. The Old Testament

AMIR, YEHOSHUA. Philo and the Bible. SP 2 (1973) 1–8.

AMIR, YEHOSHUA. פירושי שמות עבריים אצל פילון. Explanation of Hebrew Names in Philo. Ta 31 (1961) 297.

AMIR, YEHOSHUA. דיוקנו של משה אצל פילון [Philo's Portrait of Moses]. מחניים [Mahanayim] 115 (1967), 42–49.

BEAUCHAMP, P. La cosmologie religieuse de Philon et la lecture de l'Exode par le livre de la Sagesse: le thème de la manne. PAL 207–219.

BERTRAM, GEORG. ΊΚΑΝΟΣ in den griechischen Übersetzungen des ATs als Wiedergabe von schaddaj. ZAW N.F. 29 (70) (1958) 20–31. [Esp. 28–31.]

BROCK, S. P., FRITSCH, C. T. and JELLICOE, S. A Classified Bibliography of the Septuagint (ALGHJ 6) 1973.

BYRNE, BRENDAN. 'Sons of God' – 'Seed of Abraham' (Analecta Biblica 83). Rome, 1979. [Esp. 57–59.]

COHEN-YASHAR, YOHANAN (KAHN, JEAN-GEORGES). על ריאה יש מאין בכתבי פילון [On the Proof of 'Something from Nothingness' in Philo's Writings]. Bar-Ilan 4–5 (1967) 60–66.

COLSON, F. H. Philo's Quotations from the Old Testament. JTS 41 (1940) 237–51.

DELLING, GERHARD. Biblisch-jüdische Namen im hellenistisch-römischen Ägypten. Bulletin de la Société d'Archéologie copte 22 (1974–75) 1–42.

ERVIN, HOWARD MATTHEW. Theological aspects of the Septuagint of the Book of Psalms. Dissertation, Princeton Theological Seminary, 1962. [DA]

FASCHER, ERICH. Abraham, Φυσιολόγος und Φίλος θεοῦ. Eine Studie zur außerbiblischen Abrahamtradition im Anschluß an Deuteronomium 4, 19. In: Mullus. Festschrift Theodor Klauser, 111–24. Ed. A. STUIBER, A. HERMANN (JAC, Ergänzungsband I). Münster, Westfalen, 1964.

GEOLTRAIN, P. Quelques lectures juives et chrétiennes des premiers versets de la Genèse, de Qoumrân au Nouveau Testament. In: In Principio. Interprétations des premiers versets de la Genèse, 47–60 (Études Augustiniennes). Paris, 1973. [BS]
GRANT, ROBERT M. Miracle and Natural Law in Greco-Roman and Early Christian Thought. Amsterdam, 1952. [Esp. 89–91, 185–87.]

HANSON, ANTHONY. Philo's Etymologies. JTS N.S. 18 (1967) 128–39.
HOWARD, GEORGE E. The 'Aberrant' Text of Philo's Quotations Reconsidered. HUCA 44 (1973) 197–209.

JELLICOE, SIDNEY. Aristeas, Philo, and the Septuagint *Vorlage*. JTS N.S. 12 (1961) 261–71.
JOBLING, DAVID. "And Have Dominion . . ." The Interpretation of Genesis 1, 28 in Philo Judaeus. JSJ 8 (1977) 50–82.

KAHLE, PAUL. The Cairo Geniza. London, 1947; reprinted New York, 1960.
KARNI, P. (פילון ואחרים ,'הז"ל) עיון בדרכי־פרשנות שונות; עיון לשון האדם מוצא על סיפור [Story of the Origins of Human Language; a Study in Different Ways of Exegesis (the Rabbis, Philo et al.)] Hagut Ba-Miqra' 2 (1976) 223–32.
KATZ, PETER. Notes on the Septuagint. JTS 47 (1946) 30–33. [Esp. 31–33.]
KATZ, PETER. Οὐ μή σε ἀνῶ, οὐδ᾽ οὐ μή σε ἐγκαταλίπω, Hebr. xiii. 5: the Biblical Source of the Quotation. Bib 33 (1952) 523–25.
KATZ, PETER. Philo's Bible: the Aberrant Text of Bible Quotations in Some Philonic Writings and its Place in the Textual History of the Greek Bible. Cambridge, 1950.
KATZ, PETER. Das Problem des Urtextes der Septuaginta. TZ 5 (1949) 1–24. [Esp. 15–16.]
KATZ, PETER. Septuagintal Studies. Their Links with the Past and their Present Tendencies. In: The Background of the New Testament and its Eschatology . . . in Honour of Charles Harold Dodd, 176–208. Ed. W. D. DAVIES, DAVID DAUBE. Cambridge, 1956. [Esp. 205–07.]
KLIJN, ALBERTUS F. J. Seth in Jewish, Christian and Gnostic Literature (NTSup 46). Leiden, 1977.
KNOX, WILFRED L. A Note on Philo's Use of the Old Testament. JTS 41 (1940) 30–34.
KRAFT, ROBERT A. Philo (Josephus, Sirach and Wisdom of Solomon) on Enoch. In: Society of Biblical Literature 1978 Seminar Papers. Ed. PAUL J. ACHTEMEIER (SBL Seminar Papers Series 13) 1.253–57. Missoula, 1978.

LAPORTE, JEAN. Philo in the Tradition of Biblical Wisdom Literature. In: Aspects of Wisdom in Judaism and Early Christianity, 103–41. Ed. ROBERT L. WILKEN (University of Notre Dame Center for the Study of Judaism and Christianity in Antiquity 1). Notre Dame IN, 1975.

MARCUS, RALPH. A Textual-Exegetical Note on Philo's Bible. JBL 69 (1950) 363–65.
MERODE, MARIE DE. «Une aide qui lui corresponde.» L'exégèse de Gen. 2, 18–24 dans les écrits de l'Ancien Testament, du judaïsme et du Nouveau Testament. Revue théologique de Louvain 8 (1977) 329–52. [Esp. 341–43.]

MILGROM, JACOB. Cult and Conscience. The *Asham* and the Priestly Doctrine of Repentence (SJLA 18). Leiden, 1976. [Esp. 111–14.]

MYRE, ANDRÉ. Les caractéristiques de la loi mosaïque selon Philon d'Alexandrie. Science et esprit 27 (1975) 35–69.

MYRE, ANDRÉ. La loi de la nature et la loi mosaïque selon Philon d'Alexandrie. Science et esprit 28 (1976) 163–81.

NIKIPROWETZKY, VALENTIN. Note sur l'interprétation littérale de la loi et sur l'angélologie chez Philon d'Alexandrie. In: Mélanges André Neher, 181–90. Paris, 1975.

NIKIPROWETZKY, VALENTIN. Rébecca, vertu de constance et constance de vertu chez Philon d'Alexandrie. Sem 26 (1976) 109–36.

NIKIPROWETZKY, VALENTIN. ΣΤΕΙΡΑ, ΣΤΕΡΡΑ, ΠΟΛΛΗ et l'exégèse de I Sam. 2, 5, chez Philon d'Alexandrie. Sileno, rivista di studi classici e cristiani 3 (1977) 149–85.

OLMO LETE, G. DEL. Teología bíblica de la lluvia y la sequía. Cultura bíblica 27 (1972) 38–43. [E]

PETIT, MADELEINE. A propos d'une traversée exemplaire du désert du Sinaï selon Philon (*Hypothetica* VI, 2–3.8): texte biblique et apologétique concernant Moïse chez quelques écrivains juifs. Sem 26 (1976) 137–42.

POUILLOUX, JEAN. Philon d'Alexandrie: recherches et points de vue nouveaux. RHR 161 (1962) 135–37.

REICKE, BO. Die zehn Worte in Geschichte und Gegenwart (Beiträge zur Geschichte der biblischen Exegese 13). Tübingen, 1973. [Esp. 21–22, 24–25.]

ROKEAH, D. A New Onomasticon Fragment from Oxyrhynchus and Philo's Etymologies. JTS 19 (1968) 70–82.

SCHMITT, ARNIM. Interpretation der Genesis aus hellenistischem Geist. ZAW 86 (1974) 137–163.

STAROBINSKI-SAFRAN, ESTHER. Exode 3, 14 dans l'œuvre de Philon d'Alexandrie. In: Dieu et l'être. Exégèse d'Exode 3, 14 et de Coran 20, 11–24 (Recherches du Centre d'Études des Religions du Livre. École Pratique des Hautes Études – 5e Section), 47–55. Paris, 1978.

STAROBINSKI-SAFRAN, ESTHER. La prophétie de Moïse et sa portée d'après Philon. In: La figure de Moïse. Écriture et relectures. Ed. R. MARTIN-ACHARD et al. (Publications de la faculté de théologie de l'Université de Genève 1) 67–80. Genève, 1978.

STEIN, EDMUND. Alttestamentliche Bibelkritik in der späthellenistischen Literatur. 'Collectanea Theologica' Societatis Theologorum Polonorum 16 (1935); reprinted, Lwów, 1935. [G]

STEWART, R. A. The Sinless High-Priest. NTS 14 (1967) 126–35. [Esp. 131–34.]

SUNDBERG, ALBERT C. The Old Testament of the Early Church (Harvard Theological Studies 20). Cambridge MA, 1964. [Esp. 67–74, 99.]

TEEPLE, HOWARD M. The Mosaic Eschatological Prophet (JBL Monograph Series 10). Philadelphia, 1957. [Esp. 34–38.]

TRUDINGER, LEONHARD PAUL. The Text of the Old Testament in the Book of Revelation. Dissertation, Boston University, 1963. [DA]

WALTERS (KATZ), PETER. The Text of the Septuagint; its Corruptions and their Emendation. Ed. D. W. GOODING. London, 1973.

ZAMPAGLIONE, GERARDO. L'idea della pace nel mondo antico. Torino, 1967. English: The Idea of Peace in Antiquity. Trans. RICHARD DUNN. Notre Dame IN, 1973. [Esp. 172–174.]

XIV. The New Testament

ARGYLE, A. W. Philo and the Fourth Gospel. ExT 63 (1951—52) 385—86.

BAJSIĆ, A. Pilatus, Jesus and Barrabas. Bib 48 (1967) 7—28.

BASKIN, JOE ROBINSON. Words for Joy and Rejoicing in the Writings of the Apostle Paul and Philo Judaeus. Dissertation, Princeton Theological Seminary, 1966.

BATEY, RICHARD. The μία σάρξ Union of Christ and the Church (Eph 5, 21—33). NTS 13 (1966) 270—81. [Esp. 273.]

BAUER, BRUNO. Philo, Strauss und Renan und das Urchristentum. Berlin, 1874; reprinted Aalen, 1972.

BERGER, KLAUS. Zu den sogenannten Sätzen Heiligen Rechts. NTS 17 (1970) 10—40. [Esp. 37—38.]

BERNARD, JACQUES. La guérison de Béthesda: harmoniques judéo-hellénistiques d'un récit de miracle un jour du sabbat. Mélanges de science religieuse 33 (1976) 3—34.

BETZ, HANS-DIETER. Der Apostel Paulus und die sokratische Tradition. Eine exegetische Untersuchung zu seiner 'Apologie' 2 Korinther 10—13 (BHTh 45). Tübingen, 1972. [Esp. 30—31, 67—68, 128—130.]

BETZ, HANS-DIETER. 2 Cor 6:14—7:1: an Anti-Pauline Fragment? JBL 92 (1973) 88—108. [Esp. 93—94.]

BETZ, HANS-DIETER. Zum Problem des religionsgeschichtlichen Verständnisses der Apokalyptik. ZTK 63 (1966) 391—409. English: On the Problem of the Religio-Historical Understanding of Apocalypticism. Journal for Theology and Church 6 (1969) 134—56. [Esp. 140—42, 150, 155.]

BONNARD, PIERRE. Contemplation johannique et mystique hellénistique. In: La Notion biblique de Dieu (Bibliotheca ETL 41) 351—60. Gembloux, Leuven, 1976. [Esp. 358—59.]

BORGEN, PEDER. Eine allgemein-ethische Maxime. Temenos 5 (1969) 37—53. [Esp. 40—41.]

BORGEN, PEDER. Bread from Heaven; an Exegetical Study of the Concept of Manna in the Gospel of John and the Writings of Philo. Leiden, 1965.

BORGEN, PEDER. Brød fra himmel og fra jord. Om haggada i palestinsk midrasj, hos Philo og i Johannesevangeliet. Norsk Teologisk Tidsskrift 61 (1960) 218—40.

BORGEN, PEDER. God's Agent in the Fourth Gospel. In: Religions in Antiquity; Essays in Memory of Erwin Ramsdell Goodenough, 137—48. Ed. JACOB NEUSNER (SHR 14). Leiden, 1968. [Esp. 144—48.]

BORGEN, PEDER. Logos var det sanne lys. Momenter til tolkning av Johannesprologen. Svensk exegetisk årsbok 35 (1971) 79—95. [Esp. 84—85.] English: Logos was the True Light. Contributions to the Interpretation of the Prologue of John. NT 14 (1972) 115—30. [Esp. 120.]

BORGEN, PEDER. Der Logos war das wahre Licht. Beiträge zur Deutung des johanneischen Prologs. Studien zum Neuen Testament und seiner Umwelt 2 (1977) 99—117. [D]

BORGEN, PEDER. Observations on the Theme 'Paul and Philo.' Paul's Preaching of Circumcision in Galatia (Gal. 5:11) and Debates on Circumcision in Philo. In: Die Paulinische Literatur und Theologie. The Pauline Literature and Theology. Ed. SIGFRED PEDERSEN (Skandinavische Beiträge, Teologiske Studier 7) 85—102. Århus, Göttingen, 1980.

BORGEN, PEDER. Response concerning the Jewish Sources. NTS 23 (1976) 67—75. [Response to B. LINDARS, The Place of the Old Testament in the Formation of New Testament Theology. NTS 23 (1976) 59—66.]

BORGEN, PEDER. Some Jewish Exegetical Traditions as Background for Son of Man Sayings in John's Gospel (Jn 3, 13—14 and Context). In: L'Évangile de Jean. Sources, rédaction, théologie. Ed. M. DE JONGE (Bibliotheca ETL 44) 243—58. Gembloux, Leuven, 1977.

BORIG, RAINER. Der wahre Weinstock. Untersuchungen zu Jo 15, 1–10 (Studien zum Alten und Neuen Testament 16). München, 1967.

BRANDENBURGER, E. Fleisch und Geist. Paulus und die dualistische Weisheit (WMANT 29). Neukirchen, 1968.

BRAUN, HERBERT. Das himmlische Vaterland bei Philo und im Hebräerbrief. Verborum veritas. Festschrift für Gustav Stählin zum 70. Geburtstag, 319–27. Ed. OTTO BÖCHER, KLAUS HAACKER. Wuppertal, 1970.

BÜHNER, JAN-A. Der Gesandte und sein Weg im 4. Evangelium (WUNT 2. Reihe, 2). Tübingen, 1977. [Esp. 359–60.]

BURCH, VACHER. The Epistle to the Hebrews: Its Sources and Message. London, 1936. [Esp. 17–19, 85–89.]

BURTNESS, JAMES H. Plato, Philo, and the Author of Hebrews. Lutheran Quarterly 10 (1958) 54–64.

CANTALAMESSA, RANIERO. Il papiro Chester Beaty III (P⁴⁶) e la tradizione indiretta di Hebr. 10, 1. Aegyptus 45 (1965) 194–215. [Esp. 209–10.]

CARLSTON, CHARLES. The Vocabulary of Perfection in Philo and Hebrews. In: Unity and Diversity in New Testament Theology: Essays in Honor of George E. Ladd. Ed. ROBERT A. GUELICH, 133–60. Grand Rapids, 1978.

CAVALLIN, HANS CLEMENS CAESARIUS. Life after Death: Paul's Argument for the Resurrection of the Dead in 1 Cor 15. I. An Inquiry into the Jewish Background (Coniectanea biblica, N.T. Series 7, 1). Lund, 1974. [Esp. 135–40.]

CHADWICK, HENRY. St. Paul and Philo of Alexandria. BJRL 48 (1966) 286–307.

CHEEK, JAMES EDWARD. Eschatology and Redemption in the Theology of Origen: Israelite-Jewish and Greek-Hellenistic Ideas in Origen's Interpretation of Redemption. Dissertation, Drew University, 1962. [DA]

COCKERILL, GARETH LEE. The Melchizedek Christology in Heb. 7:1–28. Dissertation, Union Theological Seminary in Virginia, 1976.

COLPE, CARSTEN. Der Begriff Menschensohn und die Methode der Erforschung messianischer Prototypen. Kairos 11 (1969) 241–63. [Esp. 253–54.]

CONGDON, LOIS MARGARET. The False Teachers at Colossae: Affinities with Essene and Philonic Thought. Dissertation, Drew University, 1968.

COULON, G. L. The Logos High Priest: an Historical Study of the Theme of the Divine Word as Heavenly High Priest in Philo of Alexandria, the Epistle of Hebrews, Gnostic Writings and Clement of Alexandria. Dissertation, Institut Catholique, Paris, 1966. [M]

CRABB, R. WELDON. The κεφαλή Concept in the Pauline Tradition with Special Emphasis on Colossians. Dissertation, San Francisco Theological Seminary, 1966. [DA]

CROSSAN, JOHN DOMINIC. Imago Dei. A Study in Philo and St. Paul. Rome, 1961.

CROUCH, JAMES E. The Origin and Intention of the Colossian Haustafel (FRLANT 109). Göttingen, 1972. [Esp. 77–88.]

CULPEPPER, R. ALAN. The Pivot of John's Prologue. NTS 27 (1980) 1–31. [Esp. 20–21.]

DAHL, NILS ALSTRUP. Das Volk Gottes. Eine Untersuchung zum Kirchenbewußtsein des Urchristentums (Skrifter utgitt av Det Norske Videnskaps-Akademi i Oslo. II. Historisk-Filosofisk Klasse, 1941, 2). Oslo, 1941; reprinted Darmstadt, 1963. [Esp. 92–118.]

DELLING, GERHARD. Die Bezeichnung 'Söhne Gottes' in der jüdischen Literatur der hellenistisch-römischen Zeit. In: God's Christ and His People. Studies in Honour of Nils Alstrup Dahl, 18–28. Oslo, 1977. [Esp. 23–24.]

DEY, LALA KALYAN KUMAR. The Intermediary World and Patterns of Perfection in Philo and Hebrews (SBL Dissertation Series 25). Missoula MT, 1975.

DODD, CHARLES H. Hellenism and Christianity. In: Independence, Convergence, and Borrowing in Institutions, Thought, and Art (Harvard Tercentenary Publications). Cambridge MA, 1937; reprinted Harvard Divinity School Bulletin, April 24, 1937, 24–44. [G]

ECCLES, ROBERT S. The purpose of the Hellenistic Patterns in the Epistle to the Hebrews. In: Religions in Antiquity. Essays in Memory of Erwin Ramsdell Goodenough, 207–26. Ed. JACOB NEUSNER (SHR 14), 1968.

FABER VAN DER MEULEN, HARRY E. Zum jüdischen und hellenistischen Hintergrund von Lukas 1, 31. In: Wort in der Zeit. Neutestamentliche Studien. Festgabe für Karl Rengstorf zum 75. Geburtstag. Ed. WILFRID HAUBECK, MICHAEL BACHMANN, 108–55. Leiden, 1980. [Esp. 114–15.]

FRIESENHAHN, PETER. Hellenistische Wortzahlenmystik im Neuen Testament. Leipzig, 1935; reprinted Amsterdam, 1970. [Esp. 89–98.]

GÄRTNER, BERTIL. The Pauline and Johannine Idea of "To Know God" against the Hellenistic Background. The Greek Philosophical Principle "Like by Like" in Paul and John. NTS 14 (1968) 209–31. [Esp. 213–15.]

GEORGI, DIETER. Die Gegner des Paulus im 2. Korintherbrief. Studien zur religiösen Propaganda in der Spätantike (WMANT 11). Neukirchen, 1963.

GOODENOUGH, ERWIN R. New Light on Hellenistic Judaism. Journal of Bible and Religion 5 (1937) 18–28.

GOODENOUGH, ERWIN R. Religious Tradition and Myth. New Haven, 1937. [Esp. 68–72.]

GOODENOUGH, ERWIN R. and KRAABEL, A. T. Paul and the Hellenization of Christianity. In: Religions in Antiquity. Essays in Memory of Erwin Ramsdell Goodenough, 23–68. Ed. JACOB NEUSNER (SHR 14). Leiden, 1968. [Esp. 40–43, 62–68.]

GOULDER, M. D. The Evangelists' Calendar. A Lectionary Explanation of the Development of Scripture (The Speaker's Lectures in Bible Studies 1972). London, 1978. [Esp. 47–48.]

GRANT, ROBERT M. The Early Christian Doctrine of God. Charlottesville VA, 1968.

HAGNER, DONALD A. The Vision of God in Philo and John: a Comparative Study. Journal of the Evangelical Theological Society 14 (1971) 81–93.

HENGEL, MARTIN. Der Sohn Gottes. Die Entstehung der Christologie und die jüdisch-hellenistische Religionsgeschichte. Tübingen, 1975. [Esp. 82–89.] English: The Son of God: the Origin of Christology and the History of Jewish-Hellenistic Religion. Philadelphia, 1976. [Esp. 51–56.]

HILL, DAVID. New Testament Prophecy. Atlanta, 1979. [Esp. 31–33.]

HOFIUS, OTFRIED. Katapausis. Die Vorstellung vom endzeitlichen Ruheort im Hebräerbrief (WUNT 11). Tübingen, 1970.

HOFIUS, OTFRIED. Die Unabänderlichkeit des göttlichen Heilsratschlusses; Erwägungen zur Herkunft eines neutestamentlichen Theologumenon. ZNW 64 (1973) 134–45.

HOLLADAY, CARL R. Theios Aner in Hellenistic Judaism: a Critique of the Use of this Category in New Testament Christology (SBLDS 40). Missoula, 1977. [Esp. 133–98.]

HOMMES, N. J. Philo en Paulus. Philosophia Reformata 2 (1937) 156–87; 193–223. [T]

HORSLEY, RICHARD A. Pneumatikos vs. Psychikos: Distinction of Spiritual Status among the Corinthians. HTR 69 (1976) 269–88.

HORSLEY, RICHARD A. Wisdom of Word and Words of Wisdom in Corinth. CBQ 39 (1977) 224–39.

HORTON, FRED L. The Melchizedek Tradition. A Critical Examination of the Sources to the Fifth Century and in the Epistle to the Hebrews (SNTSMS 30). Cambridge, 1976. [Esp. 54–60.]

HUGEDÉ, NORBERT. Saint Paul et la culture grecque. Genève, 1966. [Esp. 40–48.]

ISAACS, MARIE E. The Concept of Spirit: a Study of Pneuma in Hellenistic Judaism and its Bearing on the New Testament (Heythrop Monographs 1). London, 1976.

JACOBS, IRVING. Midrashic Background for James 2:21–3. NTS 22 (1976) 457–64. [Esp. 459–461.]

JAUBERT, ANNIE. Approches de l'Évangile de Jean. Paris, 1976. [Esp. Eclairages philoniens, 168–74.]

JOHNSSON, WILLIAM G. Apocalyptic or Philonic – the Religionsgeschichtliche Conundrum of Hebrews. In: Society of Biblical Literature, One Hundred Fourteenth Annual Meeting, Abstracts. Ed. PAUL J. ACHTEMEIER, 14. Missoula, 1978.

KAMLAH, ERHARD. Die Form der katalogischen Paränese im Neuen Testament (WUNT 7). Tübingen, 1964. [Esp. 50–53, 104–15.]

KAMLAH, ERHARD. Philos Beitrag zur Aufhellung der Geschichte der Haustafeln. In: Wort und Wirklichkeit. Studien zur Afrikanistik und Orientalistik. Eugen Ludwig Rapp zum 70. Geburtstag. Ed. BRIGITTA BENZING et al., 1.90–95. Meisenheim am Glan, 1976.

KNOX, WILFRED. Parallels to the New Testament Use of σῶμα. JTS 39 (1938) 243–46.

KNOX, WILFRED. Some Hellenistic Elements in Primitive Christianity (The Schweich Lectures, 1942). London, 1944. [Esp. 34–54, 78–94.]

KÖSTER, HELMUT. Einführung in das Neue Testament im Rahmen der Religionsgeschichte und Kulturgeschichte der hellenistischen und römischen Zeit. Berlin, 1980. [Esp. 284–93.]

KRAFT, ROBERT A. The Multiform Jewish Heritage of Early Christianity. In: Christianity, Judaism and Other Greco-Roman Cults. Studies for Morton Smith at Sixty, 174–99. Ed. JACOB NEUSNER (SJLA 12). Leiden, 1975. [Esp. 190–96.]

KRIJBOLDER, PIERRE. Jezus de Nazoreër. En studie over de historiciteit van Jezus en de oorsprong van het christendom. Amsterdam, 1976. [Esp. 92–98.]

LAGRANGE, M.-J. Les origines du dogme paulinien de la divinité du Christ. RB 45 (1936) 5–33. [Esp. 15–20.]

LEISEGANG, HANS. Der Gottmensch als Archetypus. Eranos Jahrbuch 18 (1950) 9–45.

LUCCHESI, ENZO. Nouveau parallèle entre Saint Paul (Gal. iii 16) et Philon d'Alexandrie (*Quaestiones in Genesim*)? NT 21 (1979) 150f.

LUCCHESI, ENZO. Précédents non-bibliques à l'expression néo-testamentaire: « les temps et les moments.» JTS 28 (1977) 537–40.

LUCCHESI, ENZO. Réminiscence philonienne dans le discours de Paul devant l'Aréopage. Revue des études arméniennes, N.S. 11 (1975–76) 179–81.

MAAR, O. Philo und der Hebräerbrief. Dissertation, University of Vienna, 1964 [E]

MACKENZIE, R. Hellenistic Background of Early Christianity. Dissertation, University of Edinburgh, 1977(?).

MACRAE, GEORGE W. Heavenly Temple and Eschatology in the Letter to the Hebrews. Semeia 12 (1978) 179–99.

MARE, W. H. The Greek Altar in the New Testament and Intertestamental Periods. Grace Journal 10 (1969) 26–35. [E]

MATUSZEWSKI, S. Filozofia Filona z Aleksandrii i jej wpływ na wczesne chrześcijaństwo [The Philosophy of Philo of Alexandria and its Influence on Early Christianity] (Rozprawy i materjały 5). Warszawa, 1962. [E]

McCASLAND, S. VERNON. 'The Image of God' according to Paul. JBL 69 (1950) 85–100. [Esp. 92–93, 97–100.]

McGAUGHEY, DON HUGH. The Hermeneutic Method of the Epistle to the Hebrews. Dissertation, Boston University, 1963. [DA]

McNICOL, ALLAN JAMES. The Relationship of the Image of the Highest Angel to the High Priest Concept in Hebrews. Dissertation, Vanderbilt University, 1974. [DA]

MEEKS, WAYNE A. The Divine Agent and his Counterfeit in Philo and the Fourth Gospel. In: Aspects of Religious Propaganda in Judaism and Early Christianity. Ed. ELISABETH SCHÜSSLER FIORENZA (Center for the Study of Judaism and Christianity in Antiquity 2), 43–67. Notre Dame, 1976.

MERCADO, LUÍS FIDEL. The Language of Sojourning in the Abraham Midrash in Hebrews 11: 8–19: its Old Testament Basis, Exegetical Traditions and Function in the Epistle to the Hebrews. Dissertation, Harvard University, 1967. [Abstract, HTR 60 (1967) 494–95.]

MESSEL, N. 'Guds folk' som uttrykk for urkristendommens kirkebevissthet. Innlegg ved cand. theol. Nils Alstrup Dahls disputas for doktorgraden i teologi 12. sept. 1941. Norsk Teologisk Tidsskrift 42 (1941) 219—37. [Esp. 229—37.]

MIDDLETON, R. D. Logos and Shekinah in the Fourth Gospel. JQR 29 (1938—39) 101—33. [Esp. 101—04.]

MÜLLER, PAUL-GERHARD. ΧΡΙΣΤΟΣ ΑΡΧΗΓΟΣ: der religionsgeschichtliche und theologische Hintergrund einer neutestamentlichen Christusprädikation (Europäische Hochschulschriften 23, 28). Bern, 1973. [Esp. 90, 193—212.]

NAKAGAWA, HIDEYASU. Christology in the Epistle to the Hebrews. Dissertation, Yale University, 1955. [DA]

NASH, RONALD H. The Notion of Mediator in Alexandrian Judaism and the Epistle to the Hebrews. Westminster Theological Journal 40 (1977) 89—115.

NOCK, ARTHUR D. Christianisme et hellénisme (Lectio Divina 77). Paris, 1973.

ORBÁN, Á. P. Les dénominations du monde chez les premiers auteurs chrétiens (Graecitas christianorum primaeva 4). Nijmegen, 1970.

OWEN, H. P. The 'Stages of Ascent' in Hebrews v. 11—vi. 3. NTS 3 (1956—57) 243—53.

PEARSON, BIRGER A. Hellenistic-Jewish Wisdom Speculation and Paul. In: Aspects of Wisdom in Judaism and Early Christianity, 43—66. Ed. ROBERT L. WILKEN (University of Notre Dame Center for the Study of Judaism and Christianity in Antiquity 1). Notre Dame IN, 1975.

PEARSON, BIRGER A. The Pneumatikos-Psychikos Terminology in 1 Corinthians: a Study in the Theology of the Corinthian Opponents of Paul and its Relation to Gnosticism (SBLDS 12). Missoula, 1973.

PELLETIER, ANDRÉ. Deux expressions de la notion de conscience dans le judaïsme hellénistique et le christianisme naissant. REG 80 (1967) 363—71.

POKORNÝ, PETR. Der Gottessohn. Literarische Übersicht und Fragestellung (Theologische Studien 109). Zürich, 1971. [Esp. 18—21.]

RANDALL, JOHN HERMAN. Hellenistic Ways of Deliverance and the Making of the Christian Synthesis. New York, 1970. [Esp. 113—16.]

RONCAGLIA, M. Histoire de l'Église copte (Histoire de l'église en Orient). Beyrouth, 1966. [Esp. 1.14—21.]

SANDELIN, KARL-GUSTAV. Die Auseinandersetzung mit der Weisheit in 1. Korinther 15 (Meddelanden från stiftelsens för Åbo Akademi Forskningsinstitut 12). Åbo 1976. [Esp. 26—44.]

SANDERS, EDWIN P. Paul and Palestinian Judaism. A Comparison of Patterns of Religion. Philadelphia, 1977. [Esp. 553—55.]

SANDMEL, SAMUEL. Judaism and Christian Beginnings. New York, 1978. [Esp. 279—301.]

SANDMEL, SAMUEL. Palestinian and Hellenistic Judaism and Christianity: The Question of the Comfortable Theory. HUCA 50 (1979) 137—48.

SCHOEPS, HANS-JOACHIM. Paulus. Die Theologie des Apostels im Lichte der jüdischen Religionsgeschichte. Tübingen, 1959; reprinted Darmstadt, 1972. [Esp. 21—22.]

SCHRAGE, W. Zur Ethik der neutestamentlichen Haustafeln. NTS 21 (1974) 1—22. [Esp. 7—8.]

SCHRÖGER, F. Der Verfasser des Hebräerbriefes als Schriftausleger (Biblische Untersuchungen 4). Regensburg, 1968.

SCHULZ, ANSELM. Nachfolgen und Nachahmen. Studien über das Verhältnis der neutestamentlichen Jüngerschaft zur urchristlichen Vorbildethik (Studien zum Alten und Neuen Testament 6). München, 1962. [Esp. 215—21.]

SCHWEIZER, EDUARD. Christianity of the Circumcised and Judaism of the Uncircumcised. The Background of Matthew and Colossians. In: Jews, Greeks and Christians. Religious Cultures in Late Antiquity. Essays in Honor of William David Davies. Ed. ROBERT HAMERTON-KELLY, ROBIN SCROGGS, 245—60. Leiden, 1976. [Esp. 249—60.]

SCHWEIZER, EDUARD. Gottesgerechtigkeit und Lasterkataloge bei Paulus (inkl. Kol und Eph).
    In: Rechtfertigung. Festschrift für Ernst Käsemann zum 70. Geburtstag. Ed. JOHANNES
    FRIEDRICH et al., 461–77. Tübingen, Göttingen, 1976.

SCHWEIZER, EDUARD. Die hellenistische Komponente im neutestamentlichen σάρξ-Begriff.
    ZNW 48 (1957) 237–53. [Esp. 246–50.]

SCHWEIZER, EDUARD. Zum religionsgeschichtlichen Hintergrund der 'Sendungsformel' Gal 4,
    4f. Rm 8, 3f. ZNW 57 (1966) 199–210. [Esp. 204–06.]

SEIBEL, JAMES WILLIAM. Shepherd and Sheep Symbolism in Hellenistic Judaism and the New
    Testament. Dissertation, Yale University, 1964. [ADD]

SEVENSTER, JAN N. Het verlossingsbegrip bij Philo vergeleken met de verlossingsgedachten
    van de synoptische evangeliën (Van Gorcum's Theologische Bibliotheek 4). Assen, 1936.

SIMPSON, R. T. Creation and Matter in the Epistle to the Hebrews. NTS 12 (1966) 284–93.

ŠKRINJAR, A. Theologia epistolae 1 J(oh.) comparatur cum philonismo et hermetismo. VD 46
    (1968) 224–34.

SOWERS, SIDNEY G. The Hermeneutics of Philo and Hebrews. A Comparison of the Inter-
    pretation of the Old Testament in Philo Judaeus and the Epistle to the Hebrews (Basel
    Studies of Theology 1). Zürich, Richmond, 1965.

SPICQ, CESLAUS. Alexandrinismes dans l'Épître aux Hébreux. RB 58 (1951) 481–502.

SPICQ, CESLAUS. Le philonisme de l'Épître aux Hébreux. RB 56 (1949) 542–72.

STAPLES, AUSTIN. The Book of Hebrews in its Relationship to Philo Judaeus. Dissertation,
    Southern Baptist Theological Seminary, 1951. [ADD]

STELMA, JUURD HARI. Christus' offer bij Paulus vergeleken met de offeropvattingen van Philo.
    Wageningen, 1938. [BM]

STEWART, ROY A. Creation and Matter in the Epistle to the Hebrews. NTS 12 (1966) 284–93.

TERNUS, JOSEPH. Paulinische, Philonische, Augustinische Anthropologie. Scholastik 11 (1936)
    82–98.

THERON, DANIËL J. Paul's Concept of ἀλήθεια (Truth), a Comparative Study with Special
    Reference to the Septuagint, Philo, the Hermetic Literature, and Pistis Sophia. Disserta-
    tion, Princeton Theological Seminary, 1950. [ADD]

THISELTON, A.C. The 'Interpretation' of Tongues: a New Suggestion in the Light of Greek
    Usage in Philo and Josephus. JTS 30 (1979) 15–36.

THOMPSON, JAMES W. Hebrews 9 and Hellenistic Concepts of Sacrifice. JBL 98 (1979) 567–
    578.

THOMPSON, JAMES WELDON. 'That Which Abides': Some Metaphysical Assumptions in the
    Epistle to the Hebrews. Dissertation, Vanderbilt University, 1974. [DA]

THOMPSON, JAMES WELDON. 'That which cannot be Shaken.' Some Metaphysical Assump-
    tions in Heb 12:27. JBL 94 (1975) 580–87.

THURÉN, JUKKA. Das Lobopfer der Hebräer. Studien zum Aufbau und Anliegen von Hebräer-
    brief 13 (Acta Academiae Aboensis, Ser. A: Humaniora 47, 1). Åbo, 1973.

THYEN, HARTWIG. Studien zur Sündenvergebung im Neuen Testament und seinen alttesta-
    mentlichen und jüdischen Voraussetzungen (FRLANT 96). Göttingen, 1970.

URBAN, LINWOOD, and HENRY, PATRICK. "Before Abraham was I am": Does Philo Explain
    John 8:56–58? SP 6 (1979–80) 157–95.

VAN CANGH, J. M. La multiplication des pains et l'eucharistie (Lectio Divina 86). Paris, 1975.
    [Esp. 50–53.]

WILCKENS, ULRICH. Weisheit und Torheit. Eine exegetisch-religionsgeschichtliche Unter-
    suchung zu 1. Kor. 1 und 2 (BHTh 26). Tübingen, 1959. [Esp. 139–59.]

WILLIAMSON, RONALD. Philo and the Epistle to the Hebrews (ALGHJ 4). Leiden, 1970.

WILLIAMSON, R. Philo and New Testament Christology. ET 90 (1979) 361–65.

WILSON, R. McL. Philo and the Fourth Gospel. ExT 65 (1953) 47–49.

WINTER, MARTIN. Pneumatiker und Psychiker in Korinth: zum religionsgeschichtlichen Hintergrund von 1. Kor. 2,6–3,4 (Marburger Theologische Studien 12). Marburg, 1975.

ZIMMERMANN, HEINRICH. Das Bekenntnis der Hoffnung. Tradition und Redaktion im Hebräerbrief (Bonner Biblische Beiträge 47). Köln, 1977. [Esp. 91–92.]

XV. The Christian Fathers

ALEXANDRE, MONIQUE. L'exégèse de *Gen*. 1, 1–2a dans l'*In Hexaemeron* de Grégoire de Nysse: deux approches du problème de la matière. In: Gregor von Nyssa und die Philosophie. Zweites internationales Kolloquium über Gregor von Nyssa, Freckenhorst bei Münster 18.–23. September 1972. Ed. HEINRICH DÖRRIE et al., 159–92. Leiden, 1976. [Esp. 166–67, 181–82.]

ALTANER, BERTHOLD. Augustinus und Philo von Alexandrien. Eine quellenkritische Untersuchung. ZKT 65 (1941) 81–90; reprinted in: ID. Kleine patristische Schriften 181–93. Ed. GÜNTER GLOCKMANN (TU 83). Berlin, 1967.

BEYSCHLAG, KARLMANN. Zur εἰρήνη βαθεῖα (I Clem. 2, 2). VC 26 (1972) 18–23.

BIENERT, WOLFGANG A. 'Allegoria' und 'Anagoge' bei Didymos dem Blinden von Alexandria (Patristische Texte und Studien 13). Berlin, 1972. [Esp. 36–40, 52–53.]

BIETZ, WOLFGANG KARL. Paradiesesvorstellungen bei Ambrosius und seinen Vorgängern. Dissertation, Giessen, 1973. [R]

BIGG, CHARLES. The Christian Platonists of Alexandria (The Bampton Lectures, 1886). Second ed., with additions and corrections, Oxford, 1913; reprinted Amsterdam, 1969. [Esp. 32–53.]

BRUNS, J. EDGAR. The *Altercatio Jasonis et Papisci*, Philo, and Anastasius the Sinaite. TS 34 (1973) 287–94.

CANTALAMESSA, RANIERO. Origene e Filone: a proposito di *C. Celsum* IV, 19. Aevum 48 (1974) 132–33.

CHESNUT, GLENN F. The First Christian Histories. Eusebius, Socrates, Sozomen, Theodoret, and Evagrius (Théologie historique 46). Paris, 1978. [Esp. 147–55.]

CLASSEN, C. J. Der platonisch-stoische Kanon der Kardinaltugenden bei Philon, Clemens Alexandrinus und Origenes. In: Kerygma und Logos. Beiträge zu den geistesgeschichtlichen Beziehungen zwischen Antike und Christentum. Festschrift für Carl Andresen. Ed. ADOLF MARTIN RITTER, 66–88. Göttingen, 1979.

COLPE, CARSTEN. Von der Logoslehre des Philon zu der des Clemens von Alexandrien. In: Kerygma und Logos. Beiträge zu den geistesgeschichtlichen Beziehungen zwischen Antike und Christentum. Festschrift für Carl Andresen. Ed. ADOLF MARTIN RITTER, 89–107. Göttingen, 1979.

CORNÉLIS, H. Les fondements cosmologiques de l'eschatologie d'Origène. RSPT 43 (1959) 32–80.

COURCELLE, PIERRE. Saint Augustin a-t-il lu Philon d'Alexandrie? REA 63 (1961) 78–85.

DANIÉLOU, JEAN. L'être et le temps chez Grégoire de Nysse. Leiden, 1970. [Esp. 116–32.]

DANIÉLOU, JEAN. Message évangélique et culture hellénistique aux IIe et IIIe siècles (Bibliothèque de théologie. Histoire des doctrines chrétiennes avant Nicée 2). Tournai, 1961. English: Gospel Message and Hellenistic Culture. Translated, Edited and with a Postscript by JOHN AUSTIN BAKER (A History of Early Christian Doctrine Before the Council of Nicaea 2). London, Philadelphia, 1973.

DANIÉLOU, JEAN. Philon et Grégoire de Nysse. PAL 333–46.

DANIÉLOU, JEAN. Sacramentum futuri. Études sur les origines de la typologie biblique (Études de théologie historique). Paris, 1950. [Esp. 177–90.] English: From Shadows to Reality. Studies in the Biblical Typology of the Fathers. Trans. DOM WULSTAN HIBBERD. Westminster MD, 1960. [Esp. 202–16.]

DANIÉLOU, JEAN. Les tuniques de peau chez Grégoire de Nysse. In: Glaube, Geist, Geschichte. Festschrift für Ernst Benz zum 60. Geburtstage, 355–67. Ed. GERHARD MÜLLER, WINFRIED ZELLER. Leiden, 1967. [Esp. 357–8, 362.]

DASSMANN, E. Die Frömmigkeit des Kirchenvaters Ambrosius von Mailand. Münster, 1965.

DRIJVERS, H. J. W. Edessa und das jüdische Christentum. VC 24 (1970) 4–33. [Esp. 25.]

ESCRIBANO-ALBERCA, IGNACIO. Glaube und Gotteserkenntnis in der Schrift und Patristik (Handbuch der Dogmengeschichte 1, 2. Ed. M. SCHMAUS, A. GRILLMEIER, L. SCHEFFCZYK). Freiburg i. B., 1974. [Esp. 7–11.]

ESCRIBANO-ALBERCA, IGNACIO. Die spätantike Entdeckung des inneren Menschen und deren Integration durch Gregor. In: Gregor von Nyssa und die Philosophie. Zweites internationales Kolloquium über Gregor von Nyssa, Freckenhorst bei Münster 18.–23. September 1972. Ed. HEINRICH DÖRRIE et al., 43–60. Leiden, 1976.

Gregory of Nyssa. The Life of Moses (Classics of Spirituality). New York, 1978.

GUILLAUMONT, A. Philon et les origines du monachisme. PAL 361–74.

HEINEMANN, ISAAK. Philo als Vater der mittelalterlichen Philosophie? TZ 6 (1950) 99–116.

HENAO ZAPATA, L. San Justino y las anteriores dialécticas Platónicas. Franciscanum 13 (1971) 91–124. [BS]

HOCHSTAFFL, JOSEF. Negative Theologie. Ein Versuch zur Vermittlung des patristischen Begriffs. München, 1976. [Esp. 33–35.]

HORN, H. J. Antakoluthie der Tugenden und Einheit Gottes. JAC 13 (1970) 5–28. [Esp. 22–24.]

KANNENGIESSER, CHARLES. Philon et les Pères sur la double création de l'homme (Gen 1, 26s; 2, 7). PAL 277–97.

KATZ, PETER. The Johannine Epistles in the Muratorian Canon. JTS N.S. 8 (1957) 273–74.

KRETSCHMAR, GEORG. Studien zur frühchristlichen Trinitätstheologie (BHTh 21). Tübingen, 1956. [Esp. 82–94, 112–13.]

LANNE, E. La *xeniteia* d'Abraham dans l'œuvre d'Irénée. Irenikon 47 (1974) 163–87. [BS]

LAPORTE, JEAN. La chute chez Philon et Origène. In: Kyriakon. Festschrift Johannes Quasten 1.320–35, Ed. PATRICK GRANFIELD, JOSEF A. JUNGMANN. 2 vols. Münster, 1970.

LILLA, SALVATORE R. C. Clement of Alexandria. A Study in Christian Platonism and Gnosticism (Oxford Theological Monographs). Oxford, 1971. [Esp. 191–92, 199–220.]

LILLA, SALVATORE R. C. Middle Platonism, Neoplatonism and Jewish-Alexandrine Philosophy in the Terminology of Clement of Alexandria's Ethics. Archivo italiano per la storia della pietà 3 (1962) 1–36.

LUCCHESI, ENZO. L'usage de Philon dans l'œuvre exégétique de Saint Ambroise: une 'Quellenforschung' relative aux commentaires d'Ambroise sur la Genèse (ALGHJ 9). Leiden, 1977.

MONDÉSERT, CLAUDE. Clément d'Alexandrie: introduction à l'étude de sa pensée religieuse à partir de l'écriture. Paris, 1944. [Esp. 163–83.]

MONDIN, BATTISTA. Filone e Clemente. Saggio sulle origini della filosofia religiosa (Studi superiori). Torino, 1968.

PAULSEN, H. Erwägungen zu Acta Apollonii 14–22. ZNW 66 (1975) 117–26.

PERI, C. *La Vita di Mosè* di Gregorio di Nissa: un viaggio verso l'aretè cristiana. Vetera christianorum 11 (1974) 313–32.

PETIT, PIERRE. Emerveillement, prière et esprit chez saint Basile le Grand (suite). Collectanea cisterciensia 35 (1973) 218–38. [Esp. 220–22.]

PIZZOLATO, LUIGI FRANCO. La dottrina esegetica di sant'Ambrogio (Studia patristica Mediolanensia 9). Milano, 1978.

POPMA, K. J. Patristic Evaluation of Culture. Philosophia reformata 38 (1973) 97–113. [BS]

RAASCH, J. The Monastic Concept of Purity of Heart, III: Philo, Clement of Alexandria and Origen, Studia monastica 10 (1968) 7–55. [Esp. 7–13.]

SAVON, HERVÉ. Saint Ambroise critique de Philon dans le De Cain et Abel. In: Studia patristica 13 (1971) 273–79. Berlin, 1957.

SAVON, HERVÉ. Saint Ambroise devant l'exégèse de Philon le Juif. 2 vols. Paris, 1977.

SCHMIDT, KARL LUDWIG. Jerusalem als Urbild und Abbild. Eranos-Jahrbuch 18 (1950) 207–48.

SCHWARTZ, JACQUES. Philon et l'apologétique chrétienne du second siècle. In: Hommages à André Dupont-Sommer, 497–507. Paris, 1971.

SHOTWELL, W. A. The Biblical Exegesis of Justin Martyr. London, 1965. [Esp. 41–45, 93–103, 109–115.]

SMULDERS, P. A Quotation of Philo in Irenaeus. VC 12 (1958) 15–56.

STRITZKY, MARIA-BARBARA VON. Zum Problem der Erkenntnis bei Gregor von Nyssa (Münsterische Beiträge zur Theologie 37). Münster, 1973. [Esp. 7–8, 14–15.]

SZABÓ, FRANÇOIS. Le Christ et le monde selon S. Ambroise. Augustinianum 8 (1968) 225–260.

THUNBERG, LARS. Microcosm and Mediator. The Theological Anthropology of Maximus the Confessor (Acta Seminarii neotestamentici Upsaliensis 25). Lund, 1965. [Esp. 142, 155–156, 195–97, 248, 253–54.]

UNNIK, WILLEM C. VAN. Tiefer Friede (1 Klemens 2, 2). VC 24 (1970) 261–79.

VERHOEVEN, TH. Monarchia dans Tertullien, *Adversus Praxean*. VC 5 (1951) 43–48.

VÖLKER, WALTHER. Die Vollkommenheitslehre des Clemens Alexandrinus in ihren geschichtlichen Zusammenhängen. TZ 3 (1947) 15–40.

WAGNER, WALTER HERMANN. The Paideia Motif in the Theology of Clement of Alexandria. Dissertation, Drew University, 1968. [DA]

WASZINK, JAN HENDRIK. Bemerkungen zu Justins Lehre vom Logos Spermatikos. In: Mullus. Festschrift für Theodor Klauser, 380–90. Ed. A. STUIBER, A. HERMANN (JAC, Ergänzungsband 1). Münster, 1964. [Esp. 389.]

WOLFSON, HARRY A. Negative Attributes in the Church Fathers and the Gnostic Basilides. HTR 50 (1957) 145–56.

WOLFSON, HARRY A. Philosophical Implications of Arianism and Apollinarianism. Dumbarton Oaks Papers 12 (1958) 3–28; reprinted in: ID. Religious Philosophy. A Group of Essays, 126–57. Cambridge MA, 1961. [Esp. 137–46.]

WOLFSON, HARRY A. The Philosophy of the Church Fathers 1: Faith, Trinity, Incarnation. Cambridge MA, 1956. [See Index, 624–25.]

WOLFSON, HARRY A. St. Augustine and the Pelagian Controversy. Proceedings of the American Philosophical Society 103 (1959) 554–62; reprinted in: ID. Religious Philosophy. A Group of Essays, 158–76. Cambridge MA, 1961. [Esp. 159–63.]

XVI. Gnosticism

BETZ, OTTO. Was am Anfang geschah. Das jüdische Erbe in den neugefundenen koptisch-gnostischen Schriften. In: Abraham unser Vater. Festschrift für Otto Michel zum 60. Geburtstag, 24–43. Ed. O. BETZ, M. HENGEL, P. SCHMIDT (Arbeiten zur Geschichte des Spätjudentums und Urchristentums 5). Leiden, Köln, 1963. [Esp. 39–40.]

BIANCHI, UGO. Le gnosticisme: concept, terminologie, origines, délimitation. In: Gnosis. Festschrift für Hans Jonas. Ed. BARBARA ALAND et al., 33–64. Göttingen, 1978. [Esp. 53–55.]

COLPE, CARSTEN. New Testament and Gnostic Christology. In: Religions in Antiquity; Essays in Memory of Erwin Ramsdell Goodenough, 227–43. Ed. JACOB NEUSNER (SHR 14). Leiden, 1968.

FESTUGIÈRE, A. M. J. Philon. In: ID. La révélation d'Hermès Trismégiste 2.519–85 (Études bibliques). Paris, 1949.

FRIEDLÄNDER, MORIZ. Der vorchristliche jüdische Gnosticismus. Göttingen, 1898; reprinted Farnborough, 1972.

GRANT, ROBERT M. Les êtres intermédiaires dans le judaïsme tardif. In: Le origini dello gnosticismo, 141–57. Ed. UGO BIANCHI (SHR 12). Leiden, 1967. [Esp. 142, 148.]

GRANT, ROBERT M. Gnosticism and Early Christianity. New York, 1959.

HELDERMAN, JAN. Anachorese zum Heil. Das Bedeutungsfeld der Anachorese bei Philo und in einigen gnostischen Traktaten von Nag Hammadi. In: Essays on the Nag Hammadi Texts in Honour of Pahor Lahib, 42–55. Ed. MARTIN KRAUSE. Leiden, 1975.

JONAS, HANS. Gnosis und spätantiker Geist (FRLANT N.F. 33/45). Göttingen, 1934/54. [Esp. Part. 2, 1: Von der Mythologie zur mystischen Philosophie.]

JOSSA, GIORGIO. Considerazioni sulle origini dello gnosticismo in relazione al giudaismo. In: Le origini dello gnosticismo, 413–26. Ed. UGO BIANCHI (SHR 12). Leiden, 1967. [Esp. 416–19.]

KLEIN, FRANZ-NORBERT. Die Lichtterminologie bei Philon von Alexandrien und in den hermetischen Schriften. Leiden, 1962.

McNEIL, BRIAN. The Narration of Zosimus. JSJ 9 (1978) 68–82. [Esp. 77–81.]

MÉNARD, JACQUES-É. L'Évangile de vérité et le dieu caché des littératures antiques. RSR 45 (1971) 146–61. [Esp. 154–55.]

PEARSON, BIRGER A. Friedländer Revisited. Alexandrian Judaism and Gnostic Origins. SP 2 (1973) 23–39.

PEARSON, BIRGER A. Philo and the Gnostics on Man and Salvation. Protocol of the Twenty-ninth Colloquy: 17 April 1977. The Center for Hermeneutical Studies in Hellenistic and Modern Culture. Ed. WILHELM WUELLNER. Berkeley, 1977.

POKORNÝ, PETR. Počátky gnose: Vznik gnostického mýtu o božstvu Člověk [Gnostic Origins: the Beginning of the Gnostic Myth of the Heavenly Man]. Praha, 1969. [Esp. 5–7.] [English summary.]

POKORNÝ, PETR. Der Ursprung der Gnosis. Kairos 9 (1967) 94–105. [Esp. 101–02.]

QUISPEL, GILLES. Ezekiel 1:26 in Jewish Mysticism and Gnosis. VC (1980) 1–13.

QUISPEL, GILLES. Der gnostische Anthropos und die jüdische Tradition. Eranos-Jahrbücher 22 (1953) 195–234.

QUISPEL, GILLES. Jewish Gnosis and Mandaean Gnosticism. In: Les textes de Nag Hammadi. Colloque du Centre d'histoire des religions (Strasbourg, 23–25 octobre 1974), 82–122. Ed. JACQUES-É. MÉNARD. Leiden, 1975. [Esp. 93–94.]

QUISPEL, GILLES. Philo und die altchristliche Häresie. TZ 5 (1949) 429–36.

SCHENKE, HANS MARTIN. Der Gott 'Mensch' in der Gnosis; ein religionsgeschichtlicher Beitrag zur Diskussion über die paulinische Anschauung von der Kirche als Leib Christi. Göttingen, 1962.

SIMON, MARCEL. Éléments gnostiques chez Philon. In: Le origini dello gnosticismo, 359–76. Ed. UGO BIANCHI (SHR 12). Leiden, 1967.

STEAD, G. C. Valentinian Myth of Sophia. JTS N.S. 20 (1969) 75–104.

STEUR, K. Poimandres en Philo. Een vergelijking van Poimandres § 12 – § 32 met Philo's uitleg van Genesis I, 26–27 en II, 7. Purmerend, 1935.

WILSON, R. McL. Philo of Alexandria and Gnosticism. Kairos 14 (1972) 213–19.

WLOSOK, ANTONIE. Laktanz und die philosophische Gnosis. Untersuchungen zu Geschichte und Terminologie der gnostischen Erlösungsvorstellung (Abhandlungen der Heidelberger Akademie der Wissenschaften. Phil.-hist. Klasse, 1960, 2). Heidelberg, 1960. [Esp. 48–114.]

ZANDEE, JAN. 'Les enseignements de Silvanos' et Philon d'Alexandrie. In: Mélanges d'histoire des religions offerts à Henri-Charles Puech, 337–45. Paris, 1974.

ZANDEE, JAN. Die Person der Sophia in der vierten Schrift des Codex Jung. In: Le origini dello gnosticismo, 203–14. Ed. UGO BIANCHI (SHR 12). Leiden, 1967. [Esp. 208–12.]

ZANDEE, JAN. 'The Teachings of Silvanus' and Clement of Alexandria. A New Document of Alexandrian Theology (Mededelingen en Verhandelingen van het Voorziatisch-Egyptisch Genootschap 'Ex Oriente Lux' 19). Leiden, 1977.

XVII. Neoplatonism

ARNOU, RENÉ. Le désir de Dieu dans la philosophie de Plotin. Deuxième édition revue et corrigée. Ed. PAUL HENRY. Rome, 1967. [Esp. 260–65.]

THEILER, WILLY. Die Vorbereitung des Neuplatonismus (Problemata 1). Berlin, 1930; reprinted ²1964).

WOLFSON, HARRY A. Albinus and Plotinus on Divine Attributes. HTR 45 (1952) 115–30; reprinted in: ID. Studies in the History of Philosophy and Religion, 115–30. Ed. ISADORE TWERSKY, GEORGE H. WILLIAMS. Cambridge MA, 1973. [Esp. 115–17, 126–29.]

XVIII. Philo's Exegesis

AMIR, YEHOSHUA. פירושי שמות עבריים אצל פילון. Explanation of Hebrew Names in Philo. Ta 31 (1961–62) 297.

ARNDT, OTFRIED. Zahlenmystik bei Philo – Spielerei oder Schriftauslegung? ZRGG 19 (1967) 167–71.

BASKIN, JUDITH REESA. Reflections of Attitudes towards Gentiles in Jewish and Christian Exegesis of Jethro, Balaam and Job. Dissertation, Yale University, 1976.

BELKIN, SAMUEL. מדרש השמות בפילון [The Interpretation of Names in Philo]. Horeb 12 (1956) 3–61.

BORGEN, PEDER, and SKARSTEN, ROALD. Quaestiones et Solutiones: Some Observations on the Form of Philo's Exegesis. SP 4 (1976–77) 1–12.

CAZEAUX, JACQUES. Interpréter Philon d'Alexandrie (sur un commentaire du De Abrahamo, nos 61–84). REG 84 (1972) 345–52.

CAZEAUX, JACQUES. Système implicite dans l'exégèse de Philon. Un exemple: le De Praemiis. SP 6 (1979–80) 3–36.

CHRISTIANSEN, IRMGARD. Die Technik der allegorischen Aulegungswissenschaft bei Philon von Alexandrien (Beitr. z. Gesch. d. bibl. Hermeneutik 7). Tübingen, 1969.

DANIÉLOU, JEAN. Die Entmythologisierung in der alexandrinischen Schule. In: Kerygma und Mythos 6, 1, 38–43 (Theologische Forschung 30). Hamburg, 1963.

DANIÉLOU, JEAN. La symbolique du Temple de Jérusalem chez Philon et Josèphe. In: Le symbolisme cosmique des monuments religieux, 83–90 (Série orientale 14). Roma, 1957. [EB]

DELLING, GERHARD. Wunder – Allegorie – Mythus bei Philon von Alexandreia. In: Gottes ist der Orient. Festschrift für Prof. D. Dr. Otto Eissfeldt D.D., 42–68. Berlin, 1959.

DÖRRIE, HEINRICH. Zur Methodik antiker Exegese. ZNW 65 (1974) 121–38.

GAZZONI, LAURA. L'"erede' nel *Quis rerum divinarum heres sit* di Filone Alessandrino. Rivista di filologia e di istruzione classica 102 (1974) 387–97.

GNILKA, CHRISTIAN. Aetas spiritalis; die Überwindung der natürlichen Altersstufen als Ideal frühchristlichen Lebens (Theophaneia 24). Bonn, 1972. [Esp. 73–96. 114.]

HAMERTON-KELLY, ROBERT G. Some Techniques of Composition in Philo's Allegorical Commentary with Special Reference to *De Agricultura* – a Study in the Hellenistic Midrash. In: Jews, Greeks and Christians. Religious Cultures in Late Antiquity. Essays in Honor of William David Davies. Ed. ROBERT HAMERTON-KELLY and ROBIN SCROGGS, 45–56. Leiden, 1976.

HAY, DAVID M. Philo's References to Other Allegorists. SP 6 (1979–80) 41–75.

HECHT, RICHARD D. Patterns of Exegesis in Philo's Interpretation of Leviticus. SP 6 (1979–1980) 77–155.

HEINEMANN, ISAAK. Altjüdische Allegoristik. Breslau, 1936. [NUC]

KOHNKE, F. W. Das Bild der echten Münze bei Philon von Alexandria. He 96 (1968) 583–90.

KUHR, FRIEDRICH. Die Gottesprädikationen bei Philo von Alexandrien. Dissertation, Marburg, 1944. [DHS]

LERCH, DAVID. Isaaks Opferung christlich gedeutet (BHTh 12). Tübingen 1950. [Esp. 20–25.]

LEVIN, ARNOLD GUNNAR. The Tree of Life: Genesis 2:9 and 3:22–24 in Jewish, Gnostic and Early Christian Texts. Dissertation, Harvard University, 1966. [Abstract: HTR 59 (1966) 449–50.]

LEWIS, JACK P. A Study of the Interpretation of Noah and the Flood in Jewish and Christian Literature. Leiden, 1968. [Esp. 42–74.]

LOEWE, RAPHAEL. The 'Plain' Meaning of Scripture in Early Jewish Exegesis. In: Papers of the Institute of Jewish Studies London, 1.140–85. Ed. J. G. WEISS. Jerusalem, 1964. [Esp. 146–52.]

LOHSE, EDUARD. The New Testament Environment. Nashville, 1976. [Originally published: Umwelt des Neuen Testaments. Göttingen, 1971.]

LONGENECKER, RICHARD. Biblical Exegesis in the Apostolic Period. Grand Rapids, 1975. [Esp. 45–50.]

LORD, JAMES RAYMOND. Abraham: a Study in Ancient Jewish and Christian Interpretation. Dissertation, Duke University, 1968. [DA]

LOWY, SIMEON. The Principles of Samaritan Bible Exegesis (SPB 28). Leiden, 1977.

MACK, BURTON L. Exegetical Traditions in Alexandrian Judaism: a Program for the Analysis of the Philonic Corpus. SP 3 (1974–75), 71–112.

MACK, BURTON L. Weisheit und Allegorie bei Philo von Alexandrien. SP 5 (1978) 57–105; Theokratia 3 (1979) 23 ff.

MARTÍN, JOSÉ PABLO. Filón de Alejandría y el actual problema semiótico. Revista de filosofía latinoamericana 3:5–6 (1977) 181–99.

MARTIN-ACHARD, ROBERT. Actualité d'Abraham (Bibliothèque théologique). Neuchâtel, 1969. [Esp. 132–37.]

MAYER, GÜNTER. Aspekte des Abrahambildes in der hellenistisch-jüdischen Literatur. ET N.F. 27 (32) (1972) 118–27.

MAYER, GÜNTER. Exegese II (Judentum). RAC 6 (1966) 1194–1211. [Esp. 1205–07.]

MAYER, REINHOLD. Geschichtserfahrung und Schriftauslegung. Zur Hermeneutik des frühen Judentums. In: Die hermeneutische Frage in der Theologie, 290–355. Ed. O. LORETZ, W. STROLZ (Schriften zum Weltgespräch 3). Freiburg i. B., 1968.

MEEKS, WAYNE A. Moses as God and King. In: Religions in Antiquity. Essays in Memory of Erwin Ramsdell Goodenough, 354–71. Ed. JACOB NEUSNER (SHR 14), 1968.

MEEKS, WAYNE A. The Prophet-King: Moses Traditions and the Johannine Christology. Leiden, 1967. [Esp. 100–31.]

MOEHRING, HORST R. Arithmology as an Exegetical Tool in the Writings of Philo of Alexandria. In: Society of Biblical Literature 1978 Seminar Papers. Ed. PAUL J. ACHTEMEIER (SBL Seminar Papers Series 13) 1.191–227. Missoula, 1978.

MOEHRING, HORST R. Moses and Pythagoras: Arithmology as an Exegetical Tool in Philo. In: 6th International Congress on Biblical Studies, Oxford, 3–7 April 1978. Ed. ELIZABETH A. LIVINGSTONE (Journal for the Study of the Old Testament Supplement Series 2: Studia Biblica 1978) 205–08. Sheffield, 1979.

MÖLLER, CHRISTA. Die biblische Tradition als Weg zur Gottesschau. Eine Hermeneutik des Judentums bei Philon von Alexandria. Dissertation, Universität Tübingen, 1976.

NAZZARO, ANTONIO V. Filone Alessandrino e l'ebraico. Rendiconti della R. Accademia di archeologia, lettere e belle arti di Napoli 42 (1968) 61–79.

NIKIPROWETZKY, VALENTIN. Le commentaire de l'Écriture chez Philon d'Alexandrie. Lille, 1974. [BS]

NIKIPROWETZKY, VALENTIN. Le commentaire de l'écriture chez Philon d'Alexandrie: son caractère et sa portée. Observations philologiques (ALGHJ 11). Leiden, 1977.

NIKIPROWETZKY, VALENTIN. L'exégèse de Philon d'Alexandrie. RHPR 53 (1973) 309–29.

NIKIPROWETZKY, VALENTIN. Problèmes du 'Récit de la Création' chez Philon d'Alexandrie. REJ 124 (1965) 271–306.

NIKIPROWETZKY, VALENTIN. La spiritualisation des sacrifices et le culte sacrificiel [sic] au temple de Jérusalem chez Philon d'Alexandrie. Sem 17 (1967) 97–116.

OPELT, I. Etymologie. RAC 6 (1966) 797–844. [Esp. 822–26.]

OTTE, K. Das Sprachverständnis bei Philo von Alexandrien. Sprache als Mittel der Hermeneutik (Beiträge zur Geschichte der biblischen Exegese 7). Tübingen, 1968.

PARENTE, FAUSTO. La Lettera di Aristea come fonte per la storia del giudaismo alessandrino durante la prima metà del I secolo a. C. Annali della Scuola normale superiore di Pisa 2 (1972) 177–237, 517–67. [Esp. 517–49.]

PEISKER, MARTIN. Der Glaubensbegriff bei Philon, hauptsächlich dargestellt an Moses und Abraham. Aue i. Sa., 1936. [NUC]

PÉPIN, JEAN. Mythe et allégorie. Les origines grecques et les contestations judéo-chrétiennes (Philosophie de l'esprit). Aubier, 1958. [Esp. 231–42.]

PÉPIN, JEAN. Mythe et allégorie. Les origines grecques et les contestations judéo-chrétiennes. Nouvelle édition, revue et augmentée. Paris, 1977.

PÉPIN, JEAN. Remarques sur la théorie de l'exégèse allégorique chez Philon. PAL 131–68.

PETER, MICHAŁ. Melchizedek w egzegezie judaistycznej [Melchizedek in Jewish Exegesis]. Analecta cracoviensia 3 (1971) 171–81. [Summary in German.] [Esp. 174–75.]

RICHARDSON, W. The Philonic Patriarchs as Νόμος Ἔμψυχος. Studia Patristica 1.515–25 (TU 63). Berlin, 1957.

SANDMEL, SAMUEL. Philo's Environment and Philo's Exegesis. JBR 22 (1954) 248–53.

SANDMEL, SAMUEL. Philo's Place in Judaism: a Study of Conceptions of Abraham in Jewish Literature. HUCA 25 (1954) 209–37; 26 (1955) 151–332; reprinted Cincinnati, 1956; with new introduction by the author, New York, 1972.

SHROYER, MONTGOMERY J. Alexandrian Jewish Literalists. Dissertation, Yale University, 1935. Condensed in JBL 55 (1936) 261–84.

Siegfried, Carl Gustav Adolf. Philo von Alexandria als Ausleger des Alten Testaments; die griechischen und jüdischen Bildungsgrundlagen und die allegorische Schriftauslegung Philo's; das sprachliche Material und die Literatur an sich selbst und nach seinem geschichtlichen Einfluß betrachtet. Nebst Untersuchungen über Philo's Gräcität, mit einer Einleitung über die innere Entwicklung des Judentums und einem Register. Jena, 1875; reprinted Aalen, Amsterdam, 1970.

Stein, Menhem (Edmund). המדרש ההלניסטי [The Hellenistic Midrash]. In: Id. בין תרבות ישראל ותרבות יוון ורומא. The Relationship between Jewish, Greek and Roman Cultures, 93–105. Ed. Judah Rosenthal. Tel-Aviv, 1970.

Stein, Menahem (Edmund). "המקום" במובן אדנות אלוהית הביטוי [The Term "The Place" in the Sense of Divine Lordship]. בדרך [Baderech (Warsaw)] 1934, 7–10; reprinted in: Id. בין תרבות ישראל ותרבות יוון ורומא. The Relationship between Jewish, Greek and Roman Cultures, 109–111. Ed. Judah Rosenthal. Tel-Aviv, 1970.

Starobinski-Safran, Esther. Signification des noms divins – d'après Exode 3 – dans la tradition rabbinique et chez Philon d'Alexandrie. RTP 3e serie 23 (1973) 426–35.

Tiede, David Lenz. The Charismatic Figure as Miracle Worker (SBL Dissertation Series 1). Missoula, 1972. [Esp. 101–37.]

Tobin, Thomas H., S.J. The Creation of Man: Philo and the History of Interpretation. Dissertation, Harvard University, 1980.

Vermès, Géza. He is the Bread; Targum Neofiti Exodus 16:15. In: Neotestamentica et Semitica: Studies in Honour of Matthew Black, 256–63. Ed. E. Earle Ellis, Max Wilcox. Edinburgh, 1969. [Esp. 261–63.]

Vidal, J. Le thème d'Adam chez Philon d'Alexandrie. Mémoire de maîtrise, University of Paris IV, 1971. [BS]

Walter, Nikolaus. Anfänge alexandrinisch-jüdischer Bibelauslegung bei Aristobulos. Helikon 3 (1963) 353–72; revised and expanded in: Id. Der Thoraausleger Aristobulos, 124–29 (TU 86). Berlin, 1964.

Wedderburn, A. J. M. Philo's 'Heavenly Man'. NT 15 (1973) 301–26.

Wilson, R. McL. The Early History of the Exegesis of Gen. I, 26. In: Studia Patristica 1.423–37 (TU 63). Berlin, 1957.

XIX. Philosophy, Theology and Ethics

Altman, A. Homo Imago Dei in Jewish and Christian Theology. JR 48 (1968) 235–59.

Amir, Yehoshua. Die Begegnung des biblischen und des philosophischen Monotheismus als Grundthema des jüdischen Hellenismus. ET 38 (1978) 2–19. [Esp. 13–14.]

Amir, Yehoshua. פירוש דתי למושג פילוסופי אצל פילון [A Religious Commentary on a Philosophical Point in Philo]. In: ספר זכרון לפרופ' בנציון כ"ץ ז"ל ... מחקרים בתרבות הקלאסית. Commentationes ad antiquitatem classicam pertinentes in memoriam viri doctissimi Benzionis Katz, 112–18. Ed. Marc Rozelaar, B. Shimron. Tel-Aviv, 1970.

Amir, Yehoshua. הרעיון המשיחי ביהודות ההלניסטית [The Messianic Idea in Hellenistic Judaism]. מחנים [Mahanayim] 124 (1970) 54–67; English summary: The Messianic Idea in Hellenistic Judaism. Trans. Chanah Arnon. Immanuel 2 (1973) 58–60.

Amir, Yehoshua. הסוואה ראציונאלית להגות אירראציונאלית אצל פילון מאלכסנדריה [Rational Disguise for Irrational Thought in Philo of Alexandria]. Ešel Beer Šebaʿ 1 (1975–76) 68–77.

Amstutz, Joseph. ΑΠΛΟΤΗΣ. Eine begriffsgeschichtliche Studie zum jüdisch-christlichen Griechisch (Theophaneia 19). Bonn, 1968. [Esp. 52–59.]

ANDRESEN, C. Erlösung. RAC 6 (1966) 54–219. [Esp. 72–76.]

ARGYLE, A. W. The Logos of Philo: Personal or Impersonal? ExT 66 (1954–55) 13–14.

ARNALDEZ, ROGER. La dialectique des sentiments chez Philon. PAL 299–331.

ARNALDEZ, ROGER. Les images du sceau et de la lumière dans la pensée de Philon d'Alexandrie. L'Information historique 15 (1963) 62–72. [E]

ARNALDEZ, ROGER. L'œuvre de l'École d'Alexandrie. In: Les Mardis de Dar el-Salam, 1952, 25–121. Le Caire, 1952. [Esp. 45–64: Moïse et Platon dans la philosophie de Philon d'Alexandrie.] Arabic: موسى وافلاطون في فلسفة فيلون الإسكندري [Moses and Plato in the Philosophy of Philo of Alexandrial]. In: احاديث الثلاثاء بدار السلام [The Tuesdays of Dar el-Salam], 29–39. Cairo, 1952. [Cited from RONCAGLIA, M., Section XIV above.]

BAËR, DIDIER. Incompréhensibilité de Dieu et théologie négative chez Philon d'Alexandrie (I). Présence orthodoxe 8 (1969) 38–46.

BAER, RICHARD A. Philo's Use of the Categories Male and Female (ALGHJ 3). Leiden, 1970.

BELKIN, SAMUEL. יסוד ושורש במוסר היהדות [A Fundamental Principle in Jewish Ethics]. In: ספר יובל . . . שמואל קלמן מירסקי. Samuel K. Mirsky Jubilee Volume 5–25. Ed. SIMON BERNSTEIN, GERSHON A. CHURGIN. New York, 1958.

BENGIO, A. La dialectique de Dieu et de l'homme chez Platon et chez Philon d'Alexandrie: une approche du concept d'ἀρετή chez Philon. Mémoire de maîtrise, University of Paris IV, 1971. [BS]

BERGMEIER, ROLAND. Entweltlichung. Verzicht auf religions-geschichtliche Forschung? NT 16 (1974) 58–80.

BIGATTI, R. Sui significati del termine 'Logos' nel trattato 'Le Allegorie delle Leggi' di Filone di Alessandria. Rivista di filosofia neo-scolastica 72 (1980) 431–51.

BILLINGS, THOMAS HENRY. The Platonism of Philo Judaeus. New York, 1979. [Reprint of: Chicago, 1919.]

BORMANN, KARL. Die Ideen- und Logoslehre Philons von Alexandrien. Eine Auseinandersetzung mit H. A. Wolfson. Dissertation, Köln, 1955. [DHS]

BOYANCÉ, PIERRE. Le dieu très haut chez Philon. In: Mélanges d'histoire des religions offerts à Henri-Charles Puech, 139–49. Paris, 1974.

BRAUN, HERBERT. Wie man über Gott nicht denken soll, dargelegt an Gedankengängen Philos von Alexandria. Tübingen, 1971.

BRAVO GARCIA, A. La concepción filoniana de εἰρήνη y πόλεμος: ideas sobre el pensamiento antropológico del filósofo de Alejandría. Ciudad de Dios 192 (1979) 193–238.

BRÉHIER, ÉMILE. Les idées philosophiques et religieuses de Philon d'Alexandrie. Paris, 1908, ²1925; reprinted 1950.

CHADWICK, HENRY. Betrachtungen über das Gewissen in der griechischen, jüdischen und christlichen Tradition (Rheinisch-Westfälische Akademie der Wissenschaften, Vortrag G 197, 183. Sitzung vom 28. 2. 1973 in Düsseldorf). Opladen, 1974. [R]

COHEN-YASHAR, YOHANAN (KAHN, JEAN-GEORGES). ישראל–רואה אל [Israel–Beholding God]. Ta 40 (1970–71) 285–92.

COHON, SAMUEL S. The Unity of God: a Study in Hellenistic and Rabbinic Theology. HUCA 26 (1955) 425–79. [Esp. 433–36.]

COURCELLE, PIERRE. Philon d'Alexandrie et le précepte delphique. In: Philomathes: Studies and Essays in the Humanities in Memory of Philip Merlan, 245–50. Ed. ROBERT B. PALMER and ROBERT HAMERTON-KELLY. The Hague, 1971.

DALBERT, PETER. Die Theologie der hellenistisch-jüdischen Missionsliteratur unter Ausschluß von Philo und Josephus (Theologische Forschung: Wissenschaftliche Beiträge zur kirchlich-evangelischen Lehre 4). Hamburg–Volksdorf, 1954.

DANIEL, SUZANNE. La Halacha de Philon selon le premier livre des "Lois Spéciales". PAL 221–41.

DELASSUS, D. Le thème de la Pâque chez Philon d'Alexandrie. Mémoire de maîtrise, University of Lille III, 1972. [BS]

DELCOR, M. Pentecôte. SDB 7 (1966) 858–79.

DIHLE, A. Ethik. RAC 6 (1966) 646–796. [Esp. 698–701.]

DILLON, JOHN. The Middle Platonists. A Study of Platonism 80 B.C. to A.D. 220. London, 1977. [Esp. 139–83.]

DILLON, JOHN and TERIAN, ABRAHAM. Philo and the Stoic Doctrine of Εὐπάθειαι. SP 4 (1976–77) 17–24.

DÖRRIE, HEINRICH. Präpositionen und Metaphysik. Wechselwirkung zweier Prinzipienreihen. In: ID. Platonica Minora (Studia et Testimonia Antiqua 8) 124–36. München, 1976. [Originally published: Museum Helveticum 26 (1969) 217–28.] [Esp. 130–32.]

DÖRRIE, HEINRICH. Ὑπόστασις. Wort und Bedeutungsgeschichte. In: ID. Platonica Minora (Studia et Testimonia Antiqua 8) 12–61. München, 1976. [Originally published: Nachrichten der Akademie der Wissenschaften zu Göttingen, phil.-hist. Kl. 1955, 3.35–92.] [Esp. 39.]

DREYER, OSKAR. Untersuchung zum Begriff des Gottgeziemenden in der Antike. Mit besonderer Berücksichtigung Philos von Alexandrien (Spudasmata 24). Hildesheim, New York, 1970.

DUPONT, JACQUES. Gnosis; la connaissance religieuse dans les épîtres de saint Paul (Universitas Catholica Lovaniensis. Dissertationes ad gradum magistri in Facultate theologica consequendum conscriptae. Series 2, 40). Louvain, 1949.

EHRHARDT, ARNOLD. The Beginning. A Study in the Greek Philosophical Approach to the Concept of Creation from Anaximander to St. John. Manchester, 1968. [Esp. 188–89, 196–98, 202–05.]

ELMGREN, HENR. Philon av Alexandria, med särskild hänsyn till hans eskatologiska föreställningar [Philo of Alexandria, with Particular Regard for his Eschatological Concepts]. Stockholm, 1939.

ELSAS, CHRISTOPH. Das Judentum als philosophische Religion bei Philo von Alexandrien. In: Altes Testament – Frühjudentum – Gnosis. Neue Studien zu 'Gnosis und Bibel'. Ed. KARL-WOLFGANG TRÖGER, 195–220. Gütersloh, 1980.

FARANDOS, GEORGIOS D. Kosmos und Logos nach Philon von Alexandria (Elementa 4). Amsterdam, 1976.

FEIBLEMAN, JAMES K. Religious Platonism: the Influence of Religion on Plato and the Influence of Plato on Religion. London, 1959. [Esp. 96–127, 131–34.]

FIEDLER, MARTIN JOHANNES. Δικαιοσύνη in der diaspora-jüdischen und intertestamentarischen Literatur. JSJ 1 (1970) 120–43. [Esp. 123–29.]

FISCHER, ULRICH. Eschatologie und Jenseitserwartung im hellenistischen Diasporajudentum (BZNW 44). Berlin, 1978.

FOÀ, VIRGINIA GUAZZONI. Ricerche sull'etica delle scuole ellenistiche (Pubblicazioni dell'Istituto di filologia classica e medievale 44). Genova, 1976. [Esp. 67–83.]

FOAKES JACKSON, F. J. Philo and Alexandrian Judaism. In: A History of Church History: Studies of Some Historians of the Christian Church, 39–55. Cambridge, 1939.

FRÜCHTEL, URSULA. Die kosmologischen Vorstellungen bei Philo von Alexandrien. Ein Beitrag zur Geschichte der Genesisexegese (ALGHJ 2). Leiden, 1968.

GERHOLD, GERHARD. Mystik und Mysterienreligion bei Philo von Alexandrien. Dissertation, Erlangen, 1939/1966. [R]

GERSHENSON, DANIEL E. Logos. EJ 11.460–62. [Esp. 461–62.]

GIBLET, J. L'homme image de Dieu dans les commentaires littéraires de Philon d'Alexandrie. Studia hellenistica 5 (1948) 93–118.

GIVERSEN, SØREN. L'expérience mystique chez Philon. In: Mysticism. Based on Papers Read at the Symposium on Mysticism Held at Åbo on the 7th–9th September, 1968, 91–98

(Scripta Instituti Donneriani Åboensis 5). Ed. SVEN S. HARTMAN, CARL-MARTIN EDS-MAN. Stockholm, 1970.

GOODENOUGH, ERWIN R. Philo on Immortality. HTR 39 (1946) 85–108.

GOODENOUGH, ERWIN R. The Politics of Philo Judaeus. New Haven, 1938.

GRANT, ROBERT M. The Letter and the Spirit. New York, 1957.

GRÉGOIRE, F. Le Messie chez Philon d'Alexandrie. ETL 12 (1935) 28–50.

GUTTMANN, JOSHUA. God (in Hellenistic Literature, Philo). EJ 7.651–54.

HAMERTON-KELLY, ROBERT G. Pre-Existence, Wisdom and the Son of Man. A Study of the Idea of Pre-Existence in the New Testament (SNTSMS 21). Cambridge, 1973. [Esp. 20–21, 120–121, 145–47.]

HARL, MARGUERITE. Adam et les deux arbres du Paradis (*Gen.* II–III) ou l'homme *milieu entre deux termes*, μέσος–μεθόριος chez Philon d'Alexandrie. Pour une histoire de la doctrine du libre-arbitre. RechSR 50 (1962) 321–88.

HAUSSLEITER, J. Erhebung des Herzens. RAC 6 (1966) 1–22. [Esp. 10–11.]

HEGERMANN, HARALD. Die Vorstellung vom Schöpfungsmittler im hellenistischen Judentum und Urchristentum (TU 82). Berlin, 1961. [Esp. 6–87.]

HEINEMANN, YITSHAK (ISAAK). היחס שבין עם לארצו בספרות היהודית־היליניסטית. The Relationship between the Jewish People and their Land in Hellenistic-Jewish Literature. Zi 13–14 (1948–49) 1–9. [English abstract, p. I.]

HENRICHS, A. Philosophy, the Handmaiden of Theology. Greek, Roman and Byzantine Studies 9 (1968) 437–50.

HORSLEY, RICHARD A. Spiritual Marriage with Sophia. VC 33 (1979) 30–54.

JAUBERT, ANNIE. La notion d'alliance dans le judaïsme aux abords de l'ère chrétienne (Patristica sorbonensia 6). Paris, 1963. [Esp. 375–442, 477–94.]

JAUBERT, ANNIE. Le thème du 'Reste Sauveur' chez Philon. PAL 243–54.

JAVIERRE, ANTONIO MARÍA. El tema literario de la sucesión en el judaísmo, helenismo y cristianismo primitivo; prolegómenos para el estudio de la sucesión apostólica (Bibliotheca theologica salesiana. Series 1, Fontes 1). Zürich, 1963. [Esp. 267–79.]

JERVELL, JACOB. Imago Dei. Gen. I, 26f. im Spätjudentum, in der Gnosis und in den paulinischen Briefen (FRLANT N.F. 58 [76]). Göttingen, 1960. [Esp. 52–70.]

JONAS, HANS. Heidegger und die Theologie. ET 24 (1964) 621–42. [Esp. 622–24.] English: Heidegger and Theology. Review of Metaphysics 18 (1964) 207–33. [Esp. 207–11.]

KÄSEMANN, ERNST. Das wandernde Gottesvolk; eine Untersuchung zum Hebräerbrief (FRLANT N.F. 37 [55]). Göttingen, 1939, ²1957. [Esp. 45–52.]

KARAVIDOPOULOS, IOANNES D. Ἡ περὶ Θεοῦ καὶ ἀνθρώπου διδασκαλία Φίλωνος τοῦ Ἀλεξανδρέως [The Teaching of Philo Alexandrinus Regarding God and Man]. Θεολογία [Theologia] 37 (1966) 72–86, 244–61, 372–89.

KAUFMANN, PIERRE. Don, distance et passivité chez Philon d'Alexandrie. Revue de métaphysique et de morale 62 (1957) 37–56.

KAUFMANN-BÜHLER, D. Eusebeia. RAC 6 (1966) 985–1052. [Esp. 1020–23.]

KELBER, WILHELM. Die Logoslehre. Von Heraklit bis Origenes. Stuttgart, 1976. [Originally published, 1958.] [Esp. 95–130.]

KOVEL'MAN, A. B. Филон Александрийский о труде рабов и свободных в римском Эгипте. [Eng. summary, p. 157: Philo Judaeus on the Labor of Slaves and Freemen in Roman Egypt.]Vestnik Drevneĭ Istorii 1978, No. 3, 150–57.

KRONER, RICHARD. Speculation in Pre-Christian Philosophy (Speculation and Revelation in the History of Philosophy, Vol. 1). Philadelphia, 1956. [Esp. 237–40.]

LADNER, G. B. Eikon. RAC 4 (1959) 771–86. [Esp. 773–74.]

LANGSTADT, E. Zu Philos Begriff der Demokratie. In: Gaster Anniversary Volume, 349–64. London, 1936. [EB]

LAPORTE, JEAN. La doctrine eucharistique chez Philon d'Alexandrie (Théologie historique 16). Paris, 1972.

LARSON, CURTIS W. Prayer of Petition in Philo. JBL 65 (1946) 185–203.

LAUER, S. Philo's Concept of Time. JJS 9 (1958) 39–46.

LAURENTIN, ANDRÉ. Le pneuma dans la doctrine de Philon. ETL 27 (1951) 390–437; reprinted Bruges, 1951.

LENTNER, LEOPOLD. Glaube und Mythos im jüdisch-hellenistischen Schrifttum. Wien, 1976–1977.

LEVI, ADOLFO. Il problema dell'errore in Filone d'Alessandria. Rivista critica di storia della filosofia 5 (1950) 281–94.

LUCCHESI, ENZO. Un trait platonicien commun à Virgile et Philon d'Alexandrie. RÉG 89 (1976) 426–27, 615–18.

LÜHRMANN, DIETER. Pistis im Judentum. ZNW 64 (1973) 19–38.

LUNEAU, A. Les âges du monde. État de la question à l'aurore de l'ère patristique. In: Studia patristica 5.509–18. Ed. F. L. CROSS (TU 80). Berlin, 1962. [Esp. 515–17.]

MACDONALD, DUNCAN BLACK. The Hebrew Philosophical Genius: a Vindication. Princeton, 1936.

MACK, BURTON L. Imitatio Mosis: Patterns of Cosmology and Soteriology in the Hellenistic Synagogue. SP 1 (1972) 27–55.

MACK, BURTON L. Logos und Sophia. Untersuchungen zur Weisheitstheologie im hellenistischen Judentum (SUNT 10). Göttingen, 1973.

McLELLAND, JOSEPH C. God the Anonymous. A Study in Alexandrian Philosophical Theory (Patristic Monograph Series 4). Cambridge MA, 1976.[Esp. 23–44.]

MADDALENA, ANTONIO. L'ἔννοια e l'ἐπιστήμη Θεοῦ in Filone ebreo. Rivista di filologia e d'istruzione classica 96 (1968) 5–27.

MADDALENA, ANTONIO. Filone Alessandrino (Biblioteca de filosofia saggi 2). Milano, 1970.

MALINGREY, ANNE-MARIE. 'Philosophia'. Étude d'un groupe de mots dans la littérature grecque, des Présocratiques au IVᵉ siècle après J.-C. (Études et commentaires 40). Paris, 1961. [Esp. 77–91.]

MEALAND, D. L. Philo of Alexandria's Attitude to Riches. ZNW 69 (1978) 258–64.

MELNICK, R. On the Philonic Conception of the Whole Man. JSJ 11 (1980) 1–32.

MEYER, ALBRECHT. Vorsehungsglaube und Schicksalsidee in ihrem Verhältnis bei Philo von Alexandria. Würzburg, 1939. [DB]

MILGROM, JACOB. On the Origins of Philo's Doctrine of Conscience. SP 3 (1974–75) 41–45. [Originally published in: WALLIS, RICHARD T. The Idea of Conscience in Philo of Alexandria (Protocol Series of the Center for Hermeneutical Studies in Hellenistic and Modern Culture 13). Berkeley, 1975.]

MONDIN, BATTISTA. Esistenza, natura, inconoscibilità e ineffabilità di Dio nel pensiero di Filone Alessandrino. SCa 95 (1967) 423–47.

MONDIN, BATTISTA. L'universo filosofico di Filone Alessandrino. SCa 96 (1968) 371–94.

MÜHLENBERG, EKKEHARD. Das Problem der Offenbarung in Philo von Alexandrien. ZNW 64 (1973) 1–18.

MUFFS, YOCHANAN. Joy and Love as Metaphorical Expressions of Willingness and Spontaneity in Cuneiform, Ancient Hebrew, and Related Literatures. In: Christianity, Judaism and Other Greco-Roman Cults. Studies for Morton Smith at Sixty, 3.1–36. Ed. JACOB NEUSNER (SJLA 12), 1975. [Esp. 30–31.]

MUSSNER, FRANZ. ZΩH. Die Anschauung vom 'Leben' im vierten Evangelium unter Berücksichtigung der Johannesbriefe. Ein Beitrag zur Biblischen Theologie (Münchener Theologische Studien, I. Historische Abteilung, 5). München, 1952. [I.3: Die griechische Metamorphose des jüdischen Lebensbegriffs bei Philo von Alexandria, 32–35.]

MUTIUS, H. G. VON. Die Trennung von Licht und Finsternis in Philo von Alexandriens 'De Opificio Mundi.' Biblische Notizen 1980, Nr. 11, 32 ff.

MYRE, ANDRÉ. La loi dans l'ordre cosmique et politique selon Philon d'Alexandrie. Science et esprit 24 (1972) 217–47.

MYRE, ANDRÉ. La loi dans l'ordre moral selon Philon d'Alexandrie. Science et esprit 24 (1972) 93–113.

MYRE, ANDRÉ. La loi et le Pentateuque selon Philon d'Alexandrie. Science et esprit 25 (1973) 209–25.

NAZZARO, ANTONIO V. Il γνῶθι σαυτόν nell'epistemologia filoniana. Annali della Facoltà di lettere e filosofia dell'Università di Napoli 12 (1969–70) 49–86; republished Napoli, n.d. [E]

NAZZARO, ANTONIO V. Nota a Filone De migratione Abrahami 8. Rivista di filologia e di istruzione classica 98 (1970) 188–93.

NEUMARK, HERMANN. Die Verwendung griechischer und jüdischer Motive in den Gedanken Philos über die Stellung Gottes zu seinen Freunden. Dissertation, Universität Würzburg, 1937.

NEUSNER, JACOB. The Idea of Purity in Ancient Judaism. The Haskell Lectures, 1972–1973. With a Critique and a Commentary by MARY DOUGLAS (SJLA 1), 1973. [Esp. 44–50.]

NIKIPROWETZKY, VALENTIN. La doctrine de l'elenchos chez Philon, ses résonances philosophiques et sa portée religieuse. PAL 255–74.

PASCHER, JOSEPH. Η ΒΑΣΙΛΙΚΗ ΟΔΟΣ. Der Königsweg zu Wiedergeburt und Vergottung bei Philon von Alexandreia (Studien zur Geschichte und Kultur des Altertums 17, 3–4). Paderborn, 1931; reprinted New York, n.d. [1968].

PELLETIER, ANDRÉ. Les passions à l'assaut de l'âme d'après Philon. REG 78 (1965) 52–60.

PELLETIER, A. La philanthropia de tous les jours chez les écrivains juifs hellénisés. In: Paganisme, judaïsme, christianisme: . . . mélanges offerts à Marcel Simon, 35–44. Paris, 1978.

PETIT, MADELEINE. Les songes dans l'œuvre de Philon d'Alexandrie. In: Mélanges d'histoire des religions offerts à Henri-Charles Puech, 151–59. Paris, 1974.

PFEIFER, GERHARD. Ursprung und Wesen der Hypostasenvorstellungen im Judentum (Arbeiten zur Theologie 1. Reihe 31). Stuttgart, 1967. [Esp. 47–59.]

PULVER, MAX. Das Erlebnis des Pneuma bei Philon. In: Der Geist, 111–32 (Eranos-Jahrbuch 13). Zürich, 1945. English: The Experience of the Pneuma in Philo. In: Spirit and Nature. Papers from the Eranos Yearbooks, 107–21 (Bollingen Series 30, 1). New York, 1954.

REALE, GIOVANNI. Filone de Alessandria e la prima elaborazione filosofica della dottrina della creazione. In: Paradoxos politeia. Studi patristici in onore di Giuseppe Lazzati. Ed. RANIERO CANTALAMESSA and L. F. PIZZOLATO (Studia patristica Mediolanensia 10) 247ff. Milano, 1979.

REISTER, WOLFGANG. Die Sophia im Denken Philons. In: LANG, BERNHARD. Frau Weisheit. Deutung einer biblischen Gestalt, 161–64. Düsseldorf, 1975. [R]

RINGGREN, HELMER. Word and Wisdom. Studies in the Hypostatization of Divine Qualities and Functions in the Ancient Near East. Lund, 1947. [Esp. 124–25.]

RIST, JOHN M. The Use of Stoic Terminology in Philo's Quod Deus immutabilis sit 33–50 (Protocol Series of the Colloquies of the Center for Hermeneutical Studies in Hellenistic and Modern Culture 23). Berkeley, 1976.

RONDET, HENRI. Le péché originel dans la tradition. Bulletin de littérature ecclésiastique 67 (1966) 115–48. [Esp. 126–30.]

ROYSE, JAMES R. Philo and the Immortality of the Race. JSJ 11 (1980) 33–37.

SANDMEL, SAMUEL. Apocalypse and Philo. In: Essays on the Occasion of the Seventieth Anniversary of the Dropsie University (1909–1979). Ed. ABRAHAM I. KATSH and LEON NEMOY, 383–87. Philadelphia, 1979.

SANDMEL, SAMUEL. The Rationalist Denial of Jewish Tradition in Philo. In: A Rational Faith. Essays in Honor of Levi A. Olan. Ed. JACK BEMPORAD, 137–43. New York, 1977.

SANDMEL, SAMUEL. Virtue and Reward in Philo. In: Essays in Old Testament Ethics. In Memoriam J. Philip Hyatt, 215–23. Ed. JAMES L. CRENSHAW, JOHN T. WILLIS. New York, 1974.

SAVIGNAC, JEAN DE. Le messianisme de Philon le juif. NT 4 (1960); also published in: Труды двадцать пятого международного конгресса востоковедов, Москва, 1960 [Proceedings of the International Congress of Orientalists, Moscow, 1960] 25, 1, 385–86. Moskva, 1962.

SCHNIEWIND, JULIUS. Euangelion: Ursprung und erste Gestalt des Begriffs Evangelium (Beiträge zur Förderung christlicher Theologie, 2. Reihe 13). Gütersloh, 1927; reprinted Darmstadt, 1970. [Esp. 79–94.]

SCHOEPS, HANS-JOACHIM. Religionsphänomenologische Untersuchungen zur Glaubensgestalt des Judentums. ZRGG 2 (1949–50) 293–310; reprinted in: ID. Studien zur unbekannten Religions- und Geistesgeschichte, 123–39 (Veröffentlichungen der Gesellschaft für Geistesgeschichte 3). Göttingen, 1963.

SEGALLA, G. Il problema della volontà libera in Filone Alessandrino. Studia Patavina 12 (1965) 3–31. [E]

SÉROUYA, HENRI. Les étapes de la philosophie juive 1: Antiquité hébraïque. Paris, 1969. [Esp. 189–341.]

SICILIANO, FRANCESCO. Alla luce del Logos: Filone d'Alessandria. Cosenza, 1975. [NUC]

SOWERS, SIDNEY G. On the Reinterpretation of Biblical History in Hellenistic Judaism. In: Oikonomia, Heilsgeschichte als Thema der Theologie. Oscar Cullmann zum 65. Geburtstag gewidmet, 18–25. Ed. FELIX CHRIST. Hamburg-Bergstedt, 1967.

SPICQ, CESLAUS. Agapè: prolégomènes à une étude de théologie néo-testamentaire (Studia hellenistica 10). Louvain, Leiden, 1955. [Esp. 171–83.]

STACHOWIAK, LECH. Die sittlichen Mahnungen in der intertestamentlichen Literatur. Collectanea Theologica 18 (1978) 41–60. [Esp. 58–59.]

VANDERLINDEN, E. Les divers modes de connaissance de Dieu selon Philon d'Alexandrie. Mélanges de science religieuse 4 (1947) 285–304.

VERBEKE, GERARD. L'évolution de la doctrine du pneuma du stoïcisme à S. Augustin (Bibliothèque de l'Institut supérieur de philosophie. Université de Louvain). Paris, Louvain, 1945. [Esp. 236–60.]

VILLENEUVE, F. Philon d'Alexandrie et le judaïsme antique. Histoire 23 (1980) 45–54.

VOELKER, W. Fortschritt und Vollendung bei Philo von Alexandrien: eine Studie zur Geschichte der Frömmigkeit (TU 49, 1). Berlin, 1938.

WAGNER, WALTER HERMANN. Philo and Paideia. Cithara 10 (1971) 53–64.

WALLIS, RICHARD T. The Idea of Conscience in Philo of Alexandria. Center for Hermeneutical Studies in Hellenistic and Modern Culture. Protocol of the Thirteenth Colloquy; 12 January 1975. Ed. WILHELM WUELLNER (Protocol Series of the CHSHMC 13). Berkeley, 1975. [With responses by JOHN M. DILLON, WILLIAM S. ANDERSON, JACOB MILGROM, SAMUEL SANDMEL, DAVID WINSTON, WILHELM WUELLNER and discussion by a group of participants, and a reply by the author.]

WALLIS, RICHARD T. The Idea of Conscience in Philo of Alexandria. SP 3 (1974–75) 27–40. [Originally published: Protocol Series of the Center for Hermeneutical Studies in Hellenistic and Modern Culture 13. Berkeley, 1975.]

WARNACH, W. Selbstliebe und Gottesliebe im Denken Philons von Alexandrien. In: Wort Gottes in der Zeit. Festschrift Karl Hermann Schelkle, 198–214. Ed. HELMUT FELD, JOSEF NOLTE. Düsseldorf, 1973.

WEAVER, M. J. Πνεῦμα in Philo of Alexandria. Dissertation, Notre Dame University, 1973. [DA]

WEISS, HANS-FRIEDRICH. Untersuchungen zur Kosmologie des hellenistischen und palästinischen Judentums (TU 97). Berlin, 1966. [Esp. 18–74.]

WHITTAKER, JOHN. God and Time in Philo of Alexandria. In: ID. God Time Being. Two Studies in the Transcendental Tradition in Greek Philosophy, 33–57 (Symbolae Osloenses, fasc. supplet. 23). Oslo, 1971.

WINSTON, DAVID S. Freedom and Determinism in Greek Philosophy and Jewish Hellenistic Wisdom. SP 2 (1973) 40–50.

WINSTON, DAVID S. Freedom and Determinism in Philo of Alexandria (Protocol Series of the Center for Hermeneutical Studies in Hellenistic and Modern Culture 20). Berkeley, 1976. [Also published: SP 3 (1974–75) 47–70.]

WINSTON, DAVID S. Philo's Theory of Cosmogony. In: Religious Syncretism in Antiquity. Essays in Conversation with Geo Widengren, 157–71. Ed. BIRGER A. PEARSON (Series on Formative Contemporary Thinkers 1). Missoula, 1975.

WINSTON, DAVID S. Philo's Theory of Eternal Creation: De Prov. 1.6–9. In: American Academy for Jewish Research Jubilee Volume (AAJR Proceedings 46–47). Ed. SALO W. BARON and ISAAC E. BARZILAY, 593–606. Jerusalem, 1980.

WINSTON, DAVID S. Was Philo a Mystic? In: Society of Biblical Literature 1978 Seminar Papers. Ed. PAUL J. ACHTEMEIER (SBL Seminar Papers Series 13), 161–80. Missoula, 1978.

WINTER, MARTIN. Pneumatiker und Psychiker in Korinth. Zum religionsgeschichtlichen Hintergrund von 1. Kor. 2,6–3,4 (Marburger theologische Studien 12). Marburg, 1975. [Esp. 96–157.]

WOLFSON, HARRY A. Answers to Criticisms of my Discussions of the Ineffability of God. HTR 67 (1974) 186–90.

WOLFSON, HARRY A. Causality and Freedom in Descartes, Leibniz, and Hume. In: Freedom and Experience: Essays Presented to Horace M. Kallen, 97–114. Ed. SIDNEY HOOK, MILTON R. KONVITZ. Ithaca, 1947; reprinted in: ID. Religious Philosophy. A Group of Essays, 196–216. Cambridge MA, 1961.

WOLFSON, HARRY A. Philo on Free Will. HTR 35 (1942) 131–69.

WOLFSON, HARRY A. The Philonic God of Revelation and his Latter-Day Deniers. HTR 53 (1960) 101–24; reprinted in: ID. Religious Philosophy. A Group of Essays, 1–26. Cambridge MA, 1961; reprinted in: The Jewish Expression, 87–108. Ed. JUDAH GOLDIN. New York, 1970.

WOLFSON, HARRY A. Spinoza and the Religion of the Past. The Menorah Journal 1950, 146–167; reprinted in: ID. Religious Philosophy. A Group of Essays, 246–69. Cambridge MA, 1961.

WOLFSON, HARRY A. Two Comments Regarding the Plurality of Worlds in Jewish Sources. JQR 56 (1965–66) 245–47.

WOLFSON, HARRY A. The Veracity of Scripture in Philo, Halevi, Maimonides, and Spinoza. In: Alexander Marks Jubilee Volume, English Section 603–30. Ed. SAUL LIEBERMAN. New York, 1950; reprinted as: The Veracity of Scripture from Philo to Spinoza. In: ID. Religious Philosophy. A Group of Essays, 217–45. Cambridge MA, 1961.

WOLFSON, HARRY A. What is New in Philo? In ID. From Philo to Spinoza: Two Studies in Religious Philosophy. New York, 1977.

XX. History and Criticism of Philo Sholarship; Selected Book Reviews

BELKIN, SAMUEL. Review of: GOODENOUGH, ERWIN R. An Introduction to Philo Judaeus. JBL 60 (1941) 61–69.

BELKIN, SAMUEL. Goodenough's By Light, Light. JQR 28 (1937–38) 279–82.

BEVAN, E. Review of: BELKIN, SAMUEL. Philo and the Oral Law. JTS 44 (1943) 201–03.

BOLOGNESI, GIANCARLO. Giacomo Leopardi recensore e critico di testi armeni. In: Leopardi e l'ottocento. Atti del II Convegno internazionale di studi leopardiani. (Recanati, 1–4 ottobre 1967) 65–79. Firenze, 1970. [Ni]

BORGEN, PEDER, and SKARSTEN, ROALD. Bibelvitenskap, gresk og EDB [Biblical Studies, Greek and Electronic Data Processing]. Forskningsnytt fra Norges almenvitenskapelige forskningsråd 16, 3 (1971) 37–39, 50.

BOYANCÉ, PIERRE. Philon d'Alexandrie selon le P. Daniélou. REG 72 (1959) 377–84.

CAZEAUX, JACQUES. Review of: MADDALENA, A. Filone Alessandrino. Gn 44 (1972) 651–58.

CHURGIN, GERSHON A. שלשה פילוסופים יהודים [Three Jewish Philosophers]. In: ספר יובל אלפנביין ישראל ד"ר הרב לכבוד מוגש [Israel Elfenbein Jubilee Volume], 102–10. Jerusalem, 1962–63. [Discusses H. A. WOLFSON's contributions.]

COURCELLE, PIERRE. Review of: PM 4, 14, 15, 20. REA 69 (1967) 175–80.

DANIÉLOU, JEAN. The Philosophy of Philo. The Significance of Professor Harry A. Wolfson's New Study. TS 9 (1948) 578–89.

DAUBE, DAVID. Review of: BELKIN, SAMUEL. Philo and the Oral Law. Bibliotheca orientalis 5 (1948) 64–65.

DAVIDSON, HERBERT. Harry Austryn Wolfson: an Appreciation. SP 3 (1974–75) 1–9.

DELLING, GERHARD. Die Fortschritte der französischen Bearbeitung der Werke Philons. OLZ 64 (1969) 229–33. [EB]

DELLING, GERHARD. Die französische Bearbeitung der Werke Philons vor dem Abschluß. OLZ 72 (1977) 5–11.

DELLING, GERHARD. Perspektiven der Erforschung des hellenistischen Judentums. HUCA 45 (1974) 133–76.

DELLING, GERHARD. Studia Philonica. Deutsche Literaturzeitung 96 (1975) 40–42.

DELLING, GERHARD. Zum Corpus Hellenisticum Novi Testamenti. ZNW 54 (1963) 1–14.

DILLON, JOHN. Some Thoughts on the Commentary. In: The Commentary Hermeneutically Considered. Protocol of the Thirty-first Colloquy: 11 December 1977. Ed. EDWARD C. HOBBS, 14–16. Berkeley, 1978.

FELDMAN, LOUIS H. Scholarship on Philo and Josephus (1937–1962). Classical World 54 (1960–61) 281–91; 55 (1961–62) 36–49, 236–44, 252–55, 278–92, 299–301; reprinted as: Studies in Judaica 1. New York, n.d.

FELDMAN, LOUIS H. Corrigenda to Scholarship on Philo and Josephus (1937–1962). SP 1 (1972) 56.

FRANCOTTE, A. A propos d'un livre récent. Revue philosophique de Louvain 70 (1972) 212–219. [Review of: MADDALENA, ANTONIO. Filone d'Alessandria.]

GOODENOUGH, ERWIN R. A Collection of Philo Judaeus. Yale University Library Gazette 25 (1951) 155–56.

GOODENOUGH, ERWIN R. Problems of Method in Studying Philo Judaeus. JBL 58 (1939) 51–58. [Review of: VÖLKER, W. Fortschritt und Vollendung.]

GOODENOUGH, ERWIN R. Review of: BELKIN, SAMUEL. Philo and the Oral Law. JBL 59 (1940) 413–19.

GOODENOUGH, ERWIN R. Symbolism in Hellenistic Jewish Art: the Problem of Method. JBL 56 (1937) 103–14.

GOODENOUGH, ERWIN R. Wolfson's Philo. JBL 67 (1948) 87–109.

GRAESER, ANDREAS. Review of: EFFE, BERND. Studien zur Kosmologie und Theologie der Aristotelischen Schrift 'Über die Philosophie'. Gn 44 (1972) 335–39.

GRIGORIAN, G. Փիլոն Աղեքսանդրացու աշխատությունների հայ մեկնությունները [The Armenian Commentaries on the Works of Philo of Alexandria]. Բանբեր Մատենադարանի [Herald of Matenadaran] 5 (1960) 95–116 [includes résumé in Russian]. Abstract in French: Revue des études arméniennes 3 (1966) 426; abstract in English: SP 2 (1973) 57.

GROSSI, V. Filone e Clemente. Saggio sulle origini della filosofia religiosa. SCa 49 (1971) 239—42. [Review of: MONDIN, BATTISTA. Filone e Clemente.]

HAUSLEITER, JOHANNES. Nacharistotelische Philosophen . . . Bericht über das Schrifttum der Jahre 1931—36. In: Jahresbericht über die Fortschritte der klassischen Altertumswissenschaft 281 (1943) 1—177. [Esp. 107—16.]

HEINEMANN, ISAAK. Um Philons geschichtliche Stellung. MGWJ N.F. 45 (81) (1937) 355—68. [Reviews of: GOODENOUGH, E. R. By Light, Light; STEIN, M. (E.). פילון האלכסנדרוני (Philo Alexandrinus).]

HILGERT, EARLE. Central Issues in Contemporary Philo Studies. Biblical Research 23 (1978) 15—25.

KRAFT, ROBERT A. Jewish Greek Scriptures and Related Topics. NTS 16 (1970) 384—96. [Esp. 389—90.]

LLAMAS, J. Reseña del estado de las cuestiones: Fílon de Alejandría. Sefarad 2 (1942) 437—47.

MARCUS, RALPH. Recent Literature on Philo (1924—1934). In: Jewish Studies in Memory of George A. Kohut, 463—91. New York, 1935.

MARCUS, RALPH. A 16th Century Hebrew Critique of Philo (Azariah dei Rossi's *Meor Eynayim*, Pt. I, cc. 3—6). HUCA 21 (1948) 29—71.

MARCUS, RALPH. Wolfson's Reevaluation of Philo: a Review Article. Review of Religion 13 (1949) 368—81.

MENDELSON, ALAN. A Reappraisal of Wolfson's Method. SP 3 (1974—75) 11—26.

News and Notes. SP 4 (1976—77) 109—12.

News and Notes. SP 5 (1978) 137—39.

News and Notes. SP 6 (1979—80) 223—24.

NAZZARO, ANTONIO V. A proposito di un recente libro su Filone Alessandrino. Vichiana 6 (1969) 200—03. [Review of: MONDIN, BATTISTA. Filone e Clemente.] [F]

NAZZARO, ANTONIO V. Realtà e linguaggio in Filone d'Alessandria. Le Parole e le Idee 11 (1969) 339—46. [Review of: OTTE, K. Das Sprachverständnis bei Philo.]

NAZZARO, ANTONIO V. Recenti studi filoniani (1963—70). Vichiana, N.S. 1 (1972) 280—329; republished Napoli, 1973.

NEUSNER, JACOB. The Rabbinic Traditions About the Pharisees Before 70. 3 vols. Leiden, 1971. [Esp. 175—79, regarding methodology for parallels.]

NIKIPROWETZKY, VALENTIN. Review of: MADDALENA, ANTONIO. Filone Alessandrino. RHR 187 (1975) 204—15.

NIKIPROWETZKY, VALENTIN. 'Recherches esséniennes et pythagoriciennes'. À propos d'un livre récent. REJ 125 (1966) 313—52. [Review of: LÉVY, ISIDORE. Recherches esséniennes et pythagoriciennes.]

NOCK, ARTHUR D. Philo and Hellenistic Philosophy. Classical Review 57 (1943) 77—81; reprinted in: ID. Essays on Religion in the Ancient World, 2.559—65. Ed. ZEPH STEWART. Cambridge MA, 1972. [Review of: PLCL 9.]

NOCK, ARTHUR D. The Question of Jewish Mysteries. Gn 13 (1937) 156—65; reprinted in: ID. Essays on Religion in the Ancient World, 1.459—68. Ed. ZEPH STEWART. Cambridge MA, 1972. [Review of: GOODENOUGH, E. R. By Light, Light.]

NOCK, ARTHUR D. Religious Symbols and Symbolism II. Gn 29 (1957) 524—33; reprinted in: ID. Essays on Religion in the Ancient World, 2.895—907. Ed. ZEPH STEWART. Cambridge MA, 1972. [Esp. 897—99.] [Review of: GOODENOUGH, E. R. Jewish Symbols 5—6.]

PFEIFER, G. Zur Beurteilung Philons in der neueren Literatur. ZAW 77 (1965) 212—14.

POUILLOUX, JEAN. Philon d'Alexandrie: recherches et points de vue nouveaux. RHR 161 (1962) 135—37.

REISTER, WOLFGANG. Zur Problematik eines Philo-Index. ZRGG 27 (1975) 166—68.

SANDMEL, SAMUEL. Parallelomania. JBL 81 (1962) 1–13; reprinted in: ID. Two Living Traditions: Essays on Religion and the Bible, 291–304. Detroit, 1972.

SANDMEL, SAMUEL. Philo's Knowledge of Hebrew: the Present State of the Problem. SP 5
(1978) 107–12.

Samuel Sandmel, 1911–1979. SP 6 (1979–80) 1–2.

SAVON, HERVÉ. Review of V. NIKIPROWETZKY, Le commentaire de l'Écriture (ALGHJ 11).
Leiden, 1977. In: RÉG 92 (1979) 574–77.

SCHOEPS, HANS-JOACHIM. Review of: WOLFSON, HARRY A. Philo. TLZ 76 (1951) 680–82.

SCHOEPS, HANS-JOACHIM, and HEINEMANN, ISAAK. Rund um Philo. MGWJ 82 (1938) 269–
280.

SHIEN, J. The Philo Institute. Journal of Ecumenical Studies 9 (1972) 208–09.

SMITH, MORTON. The Image of God: Notes on the Hellenization of Judaism, with Especial
Reference to Goodenough's Work on Jewish Symbols. BJRL 40 (1957–58) 473–512.

SMITH, MORTON. Goodenough's *Jewish Symbols* in Retrospect. JBL 86 (1967) 53–68.

S.N.T.S. Committee on Computer Aids. NTS 18 (1972) 459–61. [Esp. 460.]

THYEN, HARTWIG. Die Probleme der neueren Philo-Forschung. TR N.F. 23 (1955) 230–46.

UNNIK, WILLEM C. VAN. Corpus Hellenisticum Novi Testamenti. ETR 49 (1974) 55–56.

WALTER, NIKOLAUS. Jüdisch-hellenistische Literatur im Rahmen der 'Griechischen christlichen Schriftsteller' und der 'Texte und Untersuchungen.' (TU 120. Berlin, 1977)
173–77.

WATKIN, E. I. New Light on Philo. Downside Review 86 (1968) 287–97. [Review of: PAL.]

ZEITLIN, SOLOMON. A Survey of Jewish Historiography: from the Biblical Books to the *Sefer
ha-Kabbalah* with Special Emphasis on Josephus. JQR 59 (1969) 171–214. [Esp. 176–
177.]

XXI. Miscellaneous

AREVŠATYAN, SEN. The Date of the Armenian Version of the Works of Plato [in Armenian].
Banber Matenadarani 10 (1971) 7–18. [Abstract by H. BARBÉRIAN, Revue d'études
arméniennes, N.S. 9 (1972) 482–83.]

BRUNS, J. EDGAR. Philo Christianus: the Debris of a Legend. HTR 66 (1973) 141–45.

CLAYTON, ALAN J. Remarques sur deux personnages camusiens: Hélicon et Scipion. Revue des
sciences humaines, N.S. 129 (Jan–Mar 1968) 79–90. [Esp. 84.]

CROSS, J. E., and TUCKER, S. J. Appendix on Exodus 11.289–90. Neophilologus 44 (1960)
38–39.

EYDOUX, EMMANUEL. À Philon d'Alexandrie [poem]. In: De la charité et Amour de son prochain, 7–86 (Éditions du Cercle intellectuel pour le rayonnement de la pensée et de la
culture juive, Marseille). Marseille, 1954. [NUC]

GOLDKORN, GEORGES. Hommage à Philon d'Alexandrie. 15 eaux-fortes originales et 20 bois
gravés. Extraits d'œuvres de Philon. Avant-propos et étude du peintre graveur. Paris,
1962. [BN]

HAMBROER, JOHANNES. Theogonische und kosmogonische Mythen aus Rumänien. ZRGG 17
(1965) 289–306. [Esp. 299–304.]

HEMMERDINGER, BERTRAND. Karabas ou l'origine alexandrine du Chat Botté. Chronique
d'Égypte 38 (1963) 147–48.

MALINA, MARILYN. Sailing to Alexandria: Philo's Imagery. SP 4 (1976–77) 33–39.

MILLS, LAWRENCE HEYWORTH. Zaraθuštra, Philo, the Achaemenids, and Israel: Being a Treatise upon the Antiquity and Influence of the Avesta. New York, 1977. [Originally published: Leipzig, 1905–06.]

MONDOLFO, RODOLFO. Un precorrimento di Vico in Filone Alessandrino. In: Miscellanea di studi alessandrini in memoria di Augusto Rostagni, 56–60. Torino, 1963; reprinted in: ID. Momenti del pensiero greco e cristiano, 53–58. Napoli, 1964. [E]

PAGLIALUNGA DE TUMA, M. Filón de Alejandría en la temática calderoniana. Cuadernos del sur, 1969, 90–105. [F]

SANDMEL, SAMUEL. Philo and his Pupils: an Imaginary Dialogue. Judaism 4 (1955) 47–57; reprinted in: ID. Two Living Traditions: Essays on Religion and the Bible, 265–78. Detroit, 1972.

SCHADE, HERBERT. Die Tiere in der mittelalterlichen Kunst. Untersuchungen zur Symbolik von zwei Elfenbeinreliefs. Studium generale 20 (1967) 220–35.

TREU, URSULA. Ein merkwürdiges Stück byzantinischer Gelehrsamkeit. Byzantinische Zeitschrift 58 (1965) 306–12. [Esp. 310–11.]

WEISBART, GLADYS. Terah, Terah, Terah! Reconstructionist 37 (1972) 7–13.

WILPERT, PAUL. Philon bei Nikolaus von Kues. In: Antike und Orient im Mittelalter. Vorträge der Kölner Mediaevistentagungen 1956–1959, 69–79. Ed. PAUL WILPERT (Miscellanea mediaevalia, Veröffentlichungen des Thomas Instituts an der Universität Köln 1). Berlin, 1962.

ZIEGLER, J. Judentum in Alexandria und Philo: Koptische Kunst. In: Christentum am Nil, 37–41. Exhibition catalogue, Essen, 1936. [D]

Philo of Alexandria.
A critical and synthetical survey of research since World War II

by PEDER BORGEN, Trondheim

Contents

I. Bibliography

1. Abbreviations

AIPHOS   Annuaire de l'Institut de Philologie et d'Histoire Orientales et Slaves.
ALGHJ   Arbeiten zur Literatur und Geschichte des hellenistischen Judentums. Leiden.

BGBE   Beiträge zur Geschichte der Biblischen Exegese.
BJRL   The Bulletin of the John Rylands Library.
BZAW   Beihefte zur ZAW. Giessen, now: Berlin.

CPJ   Corpus papyrorum Judaicarum. Ed. VICTOR A. TCHERIKOVER and A. FUKS. 3 v. Cambridge, Mass. 1957—64.
CRJNT   Compendia Rerum Judaicarum ad Novum Testamentum. Assen.
CW   Classical World.

EJ   Encyclopaedia Judaica.
ETL   Ephemerides Theologicae Lovanienses.

FRLANT   Forschungen zur Religion und Literatur des Alten und Neuen Testaments. Göttingen.

HTR   Harvard Theological Review.
HUCA   Hebrew Union College Annual.

IDB   The Interpreter's Dictionary of the Bible. Ed. G. A. BUTTRICK. 4 v. Nashville, N.Y. 1962.

JBL   Journal of Biblical Literature.
JBR   Journal of Bible and Religion.
JEA   Journal of Egyptian Archaeology.
JJS   Journal of Jewish Studies.
JJurP   Journal of Juristic Papyrology.
JRS   Journal of Roman Studies.
JTS   Journal of Theological Studies. ·

MGWJ   Monatsschrift für Geschichte und Wissenschaft des Judentums.

NCE   New Catholic Encyclopedia. 15 v. New York 1967.
NT   Novum Testamentum.
NTSuppl. Novum Testamentum Supplements. Leiden.
NTT   Norsk teologisk tidsskrift.
Nu   Numen.

PAL   Philon d'Alexandrie, Lyon 11—15 Septembre 1966: colloque. Ed. R. ARNALDEZ, C. MONDÉSERT, J. POUILLOUX. Editions du Centre National de la Recherche Scientifique. Paris 1967.
PCH   Die Werke Philos von Alexandria in deutscher Übersetzung. Ed. L. COHN, I. HEINEMANN, et al. 6 v. Berlin 1962.
PCW   Philonis Alexandrini opera quae supersunt. Ed. L. COHN, P. WENDLAND. 8 v. Berlin 1896—1930.
PLCL   Philo, with an English Translation. Ed. F. H. COLSON et al. (Loeb Classical Library.) 12 v. Cambridge, Mass. 1929—62.
PM   Les Oeuvres de Philon d'Alexandrie. Ed. C. MONDÉSERT, et al. Paris 1961—.
PW   Realencyclopaedie der classischen Altertumswissenschaft. Ed. A. F. VON PAULY, GEORG WISSOWA, et al. Stuttgart 1894—.

RAC	Reallexikon für Antike und Christentum. Ed. TH. KLAUSER. Stuttgart 1950–.
RGG	Religion in Geschichte und Gegenwart. 3rd ed. Ed. K. GALLING. 7 v. Tübingen 1957–65.
SHR	Studies in the History of Religions (Supplement to Nu). Leiden.
SJLA	Studies in Judaism in Late Antiquity. Leiden.
SNTSMS	Studiorum Novi Testamenti Societas Monograph Series. Cambridge.
SO	Symbolae Osloenses.
SP	Studia Philonica.
SUNT	Studien zur Umwelt des Neuen Testaments.
Ta	תרביץ (Tarbitz).
TR	Theologische Rundschau.
TU	Texte und Untersuchungen zur Geschichte der altchristlichen Literatur. Leipzig, now: Berlin.
TZ	Theologische Zeitschrift.
ZAW	Zeitschrift für die alttestamentliche Wissenschaft.
ZNW	Zeitschrift für die neutestamentliche Wissenschaft.
ZRGG	Zeitschrift für die Religions- und Geistesgeschichte.

2. Selected Philo studies since World War II

M. ALEXANDRE, De congressu eruditionis gratia, PM, 16, Paris 1967.

G. ALON, Jews, Judaism and the Classical World, Jerusalem 1977.

Y. AMIR, Philo and the Bible, SP, 2, 1973, 1–8.

Y. AMIR, Philo Judaeus, EJ, 13, cols 409–15.

S. APPLEBAUM, The Legal Status of the Jewish Communities in the Diaspora, CRJNT, I:1, Assen 1974, 434–40.

R. ARNALDEZ, Philo Judaeus, NCE, 11, New York 1967, 287–91.

R. BAER, JR., Philo's Use of the Categories Male and Female, ALGHJ, 3, Leiden 1970.

H. I. BELL, The Constitutio Antoniniana and the Egyptian poll-tax, JRS, 37, 1947, 17–23.

H. I. BELL, Egypt from Alexander the Great to the Arab Conquest, Oxford 1948.

H. I. BELL, P. Giss. 40 and the Constitutio Antoniniana, JEA, 28, 1942, 39–49; 30, 1944, 72–3.

P. BORGEN, God's Agent in the Fourth Gospel, in: Religions in Antiquity, E. R. Goodenough Memorial Volume, ed. J. NEUSNER, Leiden 1968, 137–48.

P. BORGEN, Eine allgemein-ethische Maxime, Temenos, 5, 1969, 37–53.

P. BORGEN, Logos was the true Light, NT, 14, 1972, 115–30.

P. BORGEN and R. SKARSTEN, Complete KWIC-Concordance of Philo's Writings, Magnetic tape, Trondheim and Bergen, 1973.

P. BORGEN, Some Jewish exegetical traditions as background for Son of Man sayings in John's Gospel (John 3:13–14 and context), in: ETL, Leuven 1976, 243–58.

P. BORGEN and R. SKARSTEN, Quaestiones et solutiones. Some observations on the form of Philo's exegesis, SP, 4, 1976/77, 1–15.

P. BORGEN, Observations on the theme 'Paul and Philo', in: Die Paulinische Literatur und Theologie, ed. S. PEDERSEN, Aarhus and Göttingen 1980, 85–102.

P. BORGEN, Bread from Heaven, NT Suppl., 10, Leiden 1965, 2nd ed. Leiden 1981.

P. BORGEN, Philo of Alexandria, CRJNT, II:2, Assen forthcoming.

H. CHADWICK, St. Paul and Philo of Alexandria, BJRL, 48, 1966, 286–307.

I. CHRISTIANSEN, Die Technik der allegorischen Auslegungswissenschaft bei Philon von Alexandrien, Beiträge zur Geschichte der bibl. Hermeneutik, 7, Tübingen 1969.

C. COLPE, Philo, RGG, 3rd ed., 5, 1961, cols 341–6.

F. H. COLSON, Every good man is free, PLCL, 9, London 1941, reprinted 1960, 1–101.

F. H. COLSON and G. H. WHITAKER, PLCL, 1–10, London 1929–62.

F. H. COLSON, The Embassy to Gaius, PLCL, 10, London 1962.

F. H. COLSON, Philo's quotations from the Old Testament, JTS, 41, 1940, 237–51.

N. A. DAHL, Das Volk Gottes, Oslo 1941.

J. DANIÉLOU, Philon d'Alexandrie, Paris1958.

D. DAUBE, Jewish Law in the Hellenistic World, in: Jewish Law in Legal History and the Modern World, ed. B. S. JACKSON, Leiden 1980, 45–60.

G. DELLING, Perspektiven der Erforschung des hellenistischen Judentums, HUCA, 45, 1974, 133–76.

G. DELLING, Wunder – Allegorie – Mythus bei Philon von Alexandreia, in: ID., Studien zum Neuen Testament und zum hellenistischen Judentum. Gesammelte Aufsätze, Göttingen 1970, 72–129.

F. DEXINGER, Ein „messianisches Scenarium" als Gemeingut des Judentums in nach-herodianischer Zeit?, Kairos, 3–4, 1975, 250–78.

J. DILLON, The Middle Platonists, London 1977.

W. FARMER, Essenes, IDB, 2, New York 1962, 143–9.

L. H. FELDMAN, Scholarship on Philo and Josephus (1937–59), CW, 54, 1960/61, 281–91, and 55, 1961/62, 36–39; also published in: ID., Studies in Judaica. Scholarship on Philo and Josephus (1937–62), New York 1963.

U. FRÜCHTEL, Die kosmologischen Vorstellungen bei Philo von Alexandrien, Arbeiten zur Literatur und Geschichte des hellenistischen Judentums, 2, Leiden 1968.

K.-H. GERSCHMANN, Gegen Flaccus, PCH, 7, Berlin 1964, 122–65.

E. R. GOODENOUGH, An introduction to Philo Judaeus, New Haven 1940; 2nd rev. ed. Oxford 1962.

E. R. GOODENOUGH, Philo Judaeus, IDB, 3, New York 1962, 796–99.

E. R. GOODENOUGH, Jewish Symbols in the Greco-Roman Period, 1–13, New York 1953–68.

R. M. GRANT, The Letter and the Spirit, London 1957.

K. HAACKER and P. SCHÄFER, Nachbiblische Traditionen vom Tod des Mose, in: Josephus-Studien. Festschrift für Otto Michel, ed. O. BETZ, et al, Göttingen 1974, 147–174.

R. HAMERTON-KELLY, Some techniques of composition in Philo's Allegorical Commentary with special reference to De Agricultura – A study in the Hellenistic Midrash, in: Jews, Greeks and Christians. Essays in honour of W. D. Davies, ed. R. HAMERTON-KELLY and R. SCROGGS, SJLA, 21, Leiden 1976.

R. G. HAMERTON-KELLY, Sources and Traditions in Philo Judaeus, SP, 1, 1972, 3–26.

M. HARL, Cosmologie grecque et représentations juives dans l'œuvre de Philon d'Alexandrie, PAL, Paris 1967.

D. M. HAY, Philo's References to Other Allegorists, SP, 6, 1979–1980, 41–75.

R. D. HECHT, Preliminary Issues in the Analysis of Philo's De Specialibus Legibus, SP, 5, 1978, 1–55.

HARALD HEGERMANN, Griechisch-Jüdisches Schrifttum, in: Literatur und Religion des Frühjudentums, eds. J. MAIER and J. SCHREINER, Würzburg 1973, 163–180.

HARALD HEGERMANN, Philon von Alexandria, in: Literatur und Religion des Frühjudentums, ed. J. MAIER and J. SCHREINER, Würzburg 1973, 353–69.

E. HILGERT, A bibliography of Philo studies, 1963–70, SP, 1, 1972, 57–71; 1972–1973, Sp, 3, 1974–1975, 117–125; 1974–1975, SP, 4, 1976–1977, 79–85; 1976–1977, Sp, 5, 1978, 113–120; 1977–1978, SP, 6, 1979–1980, 197–200.

E. HILGERT et al, Abstracts of selected articles on Philo, 1966–70, SP, 1, 1972, 72–91.

E. HILGERT, Abstracts of recent articles on Philo through 1971, SP, 2, 1973, 55–73.

E. Hilgert, A bibliography of Philo studies in 1971 with additions for 1965–70, SP, 2, 1973, 55–73.

E. Hilgert, et al, Abstracts of Recent Articles on Philo, SP, 4, 1976–1977, 87–108; SP, 5, 1978, 121–136; SP, 6, 1979–1980, 201–222.

G. E. Howard, The 'aberrant' text of Philo's quotations reconsidered, HUCA, 44, 1973, 197–209.

H. Jonas, Gnosis und spätantiker Geist, II:1 (Von der Mythologie zur mystischen Philosophie), FRLANT, 63 (N.S. 45), Göttingen 1954.

H. Jonas, Discussion of M. Simon, Eléments gnostiques chez Philon, in: U. Bianchi (ed.), Le origini dello gnosticismo, SHR, 12, Leiden 1967, 374f.

E. Käsemann, Das wandernde Gottesvolk, FRLANT, 55 (N.S. 37), Göttingen 1939.

P. Katz, Das Problem des Urtextes der Septuaginta, TZ, 5, 1949, 15ff.

P. Katz, Philo's Bible. The aberrant text of Bible quotations in some Philonic writings and its place in the textual history of the Greek Bible, Cambridge 1950.

P. Katz, Septuagintal Studies in the mid-century, in: The Background of the New Testament and its Eschatology, in honour of C. H. Dodd, Cambridge 1956, 205ff.

F.-N. Klein, Die Lichtterminologie bei Philon von Alexandrien und in den Hermetischen Schriften, Leiden 1962.

W. L. Knox, A note on Philo's use of the Old Testament, JTS, 41, 1940, 30–4.

F. W. Kohnke, Gesandtschaft an Caligula, PCH, 7, Berlin 1964, 166–266.

Robert A. Kraft, The multiform Jewish heritage of early Christianity, in: Christianity, Judaism and other Greco-Roman Cults, Studies for Morton Smith at Sixty, ed. J. Neusner, SJLA, 12, Part three, Leiden 1975, 174–199.

H. Leisegang, Philon, PW, 20,1, Stuttgart 1941, cols 1–50.

B. L. Mack, Imitatio Mosis. Patterns of cosmology and soteriology in the Hellenistic Synagogue, SP, 1, 1972, 27–55.

B. L. Mack, Logos und Sophia: Untersuchungen zur Weisheitstheologie im hellenistischen Judentum, SUNT, 10, Göttingen 1973.

B. L. Mack, Exegetical Traditions in Alexandrian Judaism: A Program for the Analysis of the Philonic Corpus, SP, 3, 1974/5, 71–112.

B. L. Mack, Weisheit und Allegorie bei Philo von Alexandrien, SP, 5, 1978, 57–105.

R. Marcus, Philo: Questions and answers on Exodus, PLCL, Suppl. 2, 1953.

R. Marcus, Philo: Questions and answers on Genesis, PLCL, Suppl. 1, 1953.

G. Mayer, Index Philoneus, Berlin 1974.

R. Mayer, Geschichtserfahrung und Schriftauslegung. Zur Hermeneutik des frühen Judentums, in: Die hermeneutische Frage in der Theologie, ed. O. Loretz and W. Stolz, Freiburg 1968, 290–353.

W. Meeks, The Prophet-King, NT Suppl., 14, Leiden 1967.

A. Mendelson, Secular Education in Philo of Alexandria, Cincinnati 1982.

N. Messel, 'Guds folk' som uttrykk for urkristendommens kirkebevissthet. Innlegg ved cand. theol. Nils Alstrup Dahls disputas for doktorgraden i teologi, 12. sept. 1941, NTT, 42, 1941, 229–37.

C. Mondésert, R. Arnaldez, J. Pouilloux, et al, PM, 1, Paris 1961.

E. Mühlenberg, Das Problem der Offenbarung in Philo von Alexandrien, ZNW, 64, 1973, 1–18.

Y. Muffs, Joy and love as metaphorical expressions of willingness and spontaneity in cuneiform, ancient Hebrew, and related literatures, in: Christianity, Judaism and other Greco-Roman cults, SJLA, 12, Part three, Leiden 1975, 1–36.

A. V. Nazzaro, Recenti Studi Filoniani (1963–70), Napoli 1973.

V. Nikiprowetzky, Le Commentaire de L'Ecriture chez Philon d'Alexandrie, ALGHJ, 11, Leiden 1977.

K. Otte, Das Sprachverständnis bei Philo von Alexandrien, BGBE, 7, Tübingen 1968.

B. Pearson, Friedländer revisited. Alexandrian Judaism and Gnostic Origins, SP, 2, 1973, 23–35.
B. A. Pearson, Philo and the Gnostics on Man and Salvation. Protocol of the Twenty-ninth Colloquy, ed. W. Wuellner, Berkeley 1977.
A. Pelletier, In Flaccum; Introduction, Traduction et Notes, PM, 31, Paris 1967.
F. Petit, Philo Judaeus. Quaestiones in Genesim et Exodum, Introduction, texte critique et notes, PM, 33, Paris 1978.

Wolfgang Reister, Zur Problematik eines Philo-Index, ZRGG, 27, 1975, 166–168.

S. Safrai, Relations between the Diaspora and the Land of Israel, CRJNT, I:1, Assen 1974, 122–33.
S. Sandmel, Philo's Environment and Philo's Exegesis, JBR, 22, 1954, 248–53.
S. Sandmel, Philo's Place in Judaism, New York 1956; Augmented Edition, New York 1971.
S. Sandmel, Philo's Knowledge of Hebrew, SP, 5, 1978, 107–111.
S. Sandmel, Philo of Alexandria. An Introduction, New York 1979.
J. Schwartz, L'Egypte de Philon, RAL, Paris 1967, 35–44.
J. Schwartz, Note sur la famille de Philon d'Alexandrie, AIPHOS, 13, 1953, 591–602.
M. Simon, Eléments gnostiques chez Philon, in: U. Bianchi (ed.), Le origini dello gnosticismo, SHR 12, 1967, 359–74 (Discussion, 374–76).
E. M. Smallwood, The Jews under Roman Rule, SJLA, 20, Leiden 1976.
E. M. Smallwood, Philonis Alexandrini Legatio ad Gaium, edited with an Introduction, Translation and Commentary, Leiden 1961.
M. Smith, Goodenough's 'Jewish Symbols' in retrospect, JBL, 86, 1967, 53–68.
Sidney G. Sowers, The Hermeneutics of Philo and Hebrews, Richmond, Va. 1965.
M. Stern, The Jewish Diaspora, CRJNT, I:1, Assen 1974, 122–33.

V. A. Tcherikover, Syntaxis and Laographia, JJurP, 4, 1950, 179–207.
V. A. Tcherikover and A. Fuks, Corpus Papyrorum Judaicarum, 1–3, Cambridge, Mass. 1957–64.
V. A. Tcherikover, Hellenistic Civilization and the Jews, Philadelphia 1959; 3rd impr. 1966.
V. A. Tcherikover, The Decline of the Jewish Diaspora in the Roman Period, JJS, 14, 1963, 1–32.
A. Terian (ed., trans.), Philonis Alexandrini de Animalibus: The Armenian Text with an Introduction, Translation and Commentary, Chico, Cal. 1981.
W. Theiler, Philo von Alexandria und der hellenisierte Timaeus, in: Philomathes. Studies and Essays in the Humanities in Memory of Philip Merlan, The Hague 1971, 25–35.
W. Theiler, Philo von Alexandria und der Beginn des kaiserzeitlichen Platonismus, in: Parusia. Festgabe für Johannes Hirschberger, Frankfurt a. M. 1965, 199–217.
W. Theiler, Forschungen zum Neuplatonismus, Quellen und Studien zur Geschichte der Philosophie, 10, Berlin 1965.
H. Thyen, Der Stil der Jüdisch-Hellenistischen Homilie, FRLANT, 65 (N. F. 47), Göttingen 1955.
H. Thyen, Die Probleme der neueren Philo-Forschung, TR, N. S. 23, 1955, 230–46.

A. J. M. Wedderburn, Philo's 'Heavenly Man', NT, 15, 1973, 301–26.
R. McL. Wilson, Philo of Alexandria and Gnosticism, Kairos, 14, 1972, 213–19.
J. Whittaker, God, time, being, SO, Fasc. Suppl. 23, Oslo 1971.
H. A. Wolfson, Philo, 1–2, Cambridge, Mass. 1947, 4th printing revised 1968.

3. Other works discussed

M. ADLER, Studien zu Philon von Alexandreia, Breslau 1929.

C. ANDRESEN, Logos und Nomos. Die Polemik des Kelsos wider das Christentum, Arbeiten zur Kirchengeschichte, 30, Berlin 1955.

L. BAECK, Aus drei Jahrtausenden, Tübingen 1958.

H. I. BELL, Jews and Christians in Egypt, London 1924.

H. I. BELL, Juden und Griechen im römischen Alexandreia, Leipzig 1926.

H. BOX (ed.), Philonis Alexandrini In Flaccum, Oxford 1939.

A. BLUDAU, Juden und Judenverfolgungen im alten Alexandria, Münster 1906.

A. BÖHLIG, Der jüdische Hintergrund in gnostischen Texten von Nag Hammadi, in: Le origini dello gnosticismo, ed. U. BIANCHI, SHR 12, Leiden 1967.

W. BOUSSET, Die Religion des Judentums, 3rd ed. by H. GRESSMANN, Tübingen 1926.

E. BRÉHIER, Les idées philosophiques et religieuses de Philon d'Alexandrie, Paris 1908, 2nd ed. 1925.

R. BULTMANN, Weissagung und Erfüllung, Glauben und Verstehen, 2, Tübingen 1965.

L. COHN, Einteilung und Chronologie der Schriften Philos, Philologus, Suppl. 7, Berlin 1899, 385−435.

L. COHN and P. WENDLAND, PCW, 1−7, Berlin 1896−1930, repr. Berlin 1962.

N. A. DAHL, The Johannine Church and history, in: Current issues in New Testament, Essays in honour of O. A. Piper (eds. W. KLASSEN and G. F. SNYDER), New York 1962.

D. DAUBE, The New Testament and Rabbinic Judaism, London 1956.

G. DELLING, Die biblische Prophetie bei Josephus, in: Josephus-Studien. Festschrift für Otto Michel (ed. O. BETZ, et al), Göttingen 1974, 109−21.

H. DÖRRIES, Erotapokriseis, RAC, 6, 1966, cols 347−70.

H. EWALD, Geschichte des Volkes Israel, 6, Göttingen 1852.

Z. FRANKEL, Über den Einfluß der palästinischen Exegese auf alexandrinische Hermeneutik, Leipzig 1851.

Z. FRANKEL, Über palästinische und alexandrinische Schriftforschung, Programm zur Eröffnung des jüdisch-theologischen Seminars zu Breslau 1854.

L. GINZBERG, The Legends of the Jews, 6, 5th impr., Philadelphia 1968.

E. R. GOODENOUGH, By Light, Light, New Haven, Conn. 1935.

E. R. GOODENOUGH, Philo's Exposition of the Law and his De Vita Mosis, HTR, 26, 1933, 109−25.

E. R. GOODENOUGH, The Politics of Philo Judaeus, New Haven, Conn. 1938, repr. Hildesheim 1967.

E. E. HALLEWY, Biblical Midrash and Homeric Exegesis, Ta, 31, Dec 1961, 157−69, with English summary on pp. III−IV.

I. HEINEMANN, Altjüdische Allegoristik, Leipzig 1936.

I. HEINEMANN (transl.), Über das Zusammenleben um der Allgemeinbildung willen, PCH, 6, Breslau 1938, 2nd ed. Berlin 1962.

M. HEINZE, Die Lehre vom Logos in der griechischen Philosophie, Oldenburg 1872.

R. P. C. HANSON, Allegory and Event, London 1959.

M. HENGEL, Judaism and Hellenism, 1−2, 2nd rev. and enl. ed., London 1974.

M. HENGEL, The Son of God, Philadelphia 1976.

H. LEISEGANG, Der Heilige Geist, I:1, Berlin 1919.

L. I. LEVINE, Caesarea under Roman Rule, SJLA, 7, Leiden 1975.

L. I. LEVINE, The Jewish-Greek conflict in first Century Caesarea, JJS, 26, 1975.

S. LIEBERMANN, Hellenism in Jewish Palestine, New York 1950.

R. MEYER, Hellenistisches in der rabbinischen Anthropologie, Stuttgart 1937.

J. PASCHER, Ἡ Βασιλικὴ Ὁδός, der Königsweg zu Wiedergeburt und Vergottung bei Philon von Alexandrien, Paderborn 1931.

M. POHLENZ, Philon von Alexandria, Nachrichten von der Akademie der Wissenschaften in Göttingen, philos.-hist. Klasse, N.F. 1, 5, Göttingen 1942.

R. REITZENSTEIN, Die hellenistischen Mysterienreligionen, 3rd ed., Leipzig and Berlin 1927.

S. SANDMEL, The first Christian Century in Judaism and Christianity, New York 1969.

CHR. SCHÄUBLIN, Untersuchungen zu Methode und Herkunft der Antiochenischen Exegese, Köln and Bonn 1974.

G. SCHOLEM, Gnosticism, Merkabah Mysticism and Talmudic Tradition, New York 1960.

G. SCHOLEM, Major Trends in Jewish Mysticism, 1941, 3rd rev. ed., New York 1961.

H. SCHRADER, Porphyrii Quaestionum Homericarum ad Iliadem Pertinentium reliquias, Fasc. I, Leipzig 1880.

E. SCHÜRER, Geschichte des jüdischen Volkes im Zeitalter Jesu Christi, 3rd and 4th ed., 1, Leipzig 1901; 2nd ed., 2, Leipzig 1886; 4th ed., 3, Leipzig 1909.

E. M. SIDEBOTTOM, The Christ of the Fourth Gospel in the Light of First-Century Thought, London 1961.

C. SIEGFRIED, Philo von Alexandria als Ausleger des Alten Testaments, Jena 1875.

E. STEIN, Die allegorische Exegese des Philo aus Alexandria, BZAW, 51, Giessen 1929.

M. STONE, Judaism at the Time of Christ, American Schools of Oriental Research, Newsletter No 1, 1973/4, 1—6.

M. STONE, Scriptures, Sects and Visions, London and New York 1980.

A. TERIAN, The Implications of Philo's Dialogues on his Exegetical Works, SBL Seminar Papers Series, 13, ed. P. J. ACHTEMEIER, Missoula, Mt. 1978, 181—190.

L. TREITEL, Ursprung, Begriff und Umfang der allegorischen Schrifterklärung, MGWJ, 55, N.S. 19, 1911, 543ff.

E. E. URBACH, The Sages — their Concepts and Beliefs, 1, Jerusalem 1979.

W. VÖLKER, Fortschritt und Vollendung bei Philo von Alexandrien, TU, 49, Leipzig 1938.

U. WILCKEN, Griechische Ostraka aus Ägypten und Nubien, 1, Leipzig and Berlin 1899.

U. WILCKEN, Zum alexandrinischen Antisemitismus, Abhandlungen der Königl. Sächsischen Gesellschaft der Wissenschaften, phil. hist. Klasse, 27, Leipzig 1909, 783—839.

H. WINDISCH, Die Frömmigkeit Philos, Leipzig 1909.

E. ZELLER, Die Philosophie der Griechen in ihrer geschichtlichen Entwicklung, III:2 (Die nacharistotelische Philosophie), 4th ed., Leipzig 1903.

4. Additional note on bibliographies

The basic bibliography of Philo studies is that of H. L. GOODHART and E. R. GOODENOUGH, A bibliography of Philo, in: E. R. GOODENOUGH, The Politics of Philo Judaeus, New Haven, Conn. 1938, repr. Hildesheim 1967, 130—321. This bibliography covers works through 1936.

For the period discussed in the present article, the following bibliographies are the most important ones:

a) L. H. FELDMAN, Scholarship on Philo and Josephus (1937—59), CW 54, 1960/61, 281—91 and 55, 1961/62, 36—9. This bibliography is included in: L. FELDMAN, Studies in Judaica, Scholarship on Philo and Josephus (1937—62), New York 1963.

b) *E. Hilgert, A bibliography of Philo studies, 1963–70, in: SP, 1, 1972, 57–71, Id., A
   bibliography of Philo studies in 1971 with additions for 1965–70, SP, 2, 1973, 55–73; Id.,
   A bibliography of Philo studies, 1972–1973, SP, 3, 1974–1975, 117–125; 1974–1975, SP,
   4, 1976–1977, 79–85; 1976–1977, SP, 5, 1978, 113–120; 1977–1978, SP, 6, 1979–1980,
   197–200.
c) A. V. Nazzaro, Recenti Studi Filoniani (1963–70), Napoli 1973.

L. H. Feldman's bibliography is annotated. His comments often conclude with points of
evaluation. A. V. Nazzaro summarizes the works listed, often rendering comments made by
others in reviews, etc.

II. Introduction

Philo's writings provide significant background material both for New
Testament research and for studies in patristics. In New Testament research
Philonic exegesis has especially been utilized to throw light upon the concept of
Logos in John's gospel and upon the platonizing exegesis and thoughts in the
Epistle to the Hebrews. Philo's writings can illuminate other New Testament
ideas as well, and his use of exegetical techniques and forms produces comparative
material of interest. Moreover, when Philo — or the other exegetes to whom he
refers — can be shown to draw on common Jewish exegetical traditions, also
preserved for example in the later rabbinic writings, then he can give support for
the understanding that these traditions existed in New Testament times. It has
also been realized that Philo's writings reflect a variety of movements within
Judaism, and this observation has proved fruitful to throw light upon some of the
conflicts and debates in the early Christian Church. For example, the question
raised concerning observance of feasts and circumcision in the Alexandrian community (Migr 86–93) illuminates the corresponding discussion in the Galatian
churches, according to St. Paul's Letter to the Galatians. (See B. Lindars and
P. Borgen, The place of the Old Testament in the Formation of New Testament
Theology: Prolegomena and Response, NTS, 23, 1976, 67–8; A. V. Nazzaro,
Recenti Studi Filoniani [1963–70], Napoli 1971, 80–9; P. Borgen, Observations on the theme 'Paul and Philo'.)

Similarly, it is a long tradition in patristic studies to draw extensively on
Philo in research on Justin Martyr, Clement, Origenes, etc. and on particular
subjects as the monastic movement. (For studies since 1963, see A. V. Nazarro,
op. cit., 89–94.)

In recent years, however, more attention has been given to Philo as a major
representative of Diaspora Judaism, and, as such, as an extensive source for
Judaism during the first half of the first century A.D. The present critical and

---

* E. Hilgert has kindly made available to me additional titles which he has collected for the
  bibliography which is published above, pp. 47–97. He also made available to me the
  bibliography by Nazzaro.

synthetical survey will concentrate on these aspects of research (during and) since World War II.

World War II brought a setback to Philonic research, and the discoveries of the Dead Sea scrolls and the Nag Hammadi Library caught much of the attention of the scholarly world in the period following after the end of the war. Philonic studies were pushed more into the background but important contributions were not withstanding made both during the War and afterwards. Among these works H. A. WOLFSON, Philo 1–2, 1947, marks itself out.

Renewed interest in Philo and Diaspora Judaism was seen towards the end of the fifties and the beginning of the sixties. Important signs of the new impetus were the publication of V. A. TCHERIKOVER and A. FUKS, Corpus papyrorum Judaicarum, 1957–64, the Greek-French edition of Philo's works, Les oeuvres de Philon d'Alexandrie, ed. C. MONDÉSERT et al, 1961 –; and the annotated and critical bibliography of Philo studies by L. H. FELDMAN, Studies in Judaica, Scholarship on Philo and Josephus (1937–1962), 1963.

Various works on Philo throughout the sixties led to increased and more organized efforts in the seventies: The Philo Institute was organized in Chicago in 1971. Its yearbook began in 1972, containing articles, bibliographies and abstracts of articles. In 1972/73 P. BORGEN and R. SKARSTEN, Norway, completed the production of a machine-readable text of Philo's works preserved in Greek, the fragments included. On this basis, a complete KWIC-Concordance was produced by computer in 1973. In the following year G. MAYER published his 'Index Philoneus', Berlin 1974, based on the treatises and the text in: L. COHN and P. WENDLAND (ed.), Philonis Alexandrini opera quae supersunt, Editio Minor. In his review W. REISTER (Zur Problematik eines Philo-Index, ZRGG, 27, 1975, 166–8), regrets that the Greek fragments are not covered by this index, except Apologia pro Iudaeis.

Since 1974/75, the Center for Hermeneutical Studies at the Graduate Theological Union and University of California has organized an international team on Philonic research. More recently, in 1977, the initiative was taken by the Institute of Antiquity and Christianity at Claremont, California, U.S.A., to form a research team on Philonic studies, under the direction of Professor BURTON MACK.

As for research on manuscripts, textual criticism and new editions of the text of Philo's writings, no major new contributions have been made in the period surveyed. The basis is still the text published by L. COHN and P. WENDLAND, Philonis Alexandrini opera quae supersunt, I–VI, Berlin 1896–1915, reprinted 1962. Some textual revisions are made, however, in the editions by F. H. COLSON and G. H. WHITAKER, Philo, with an English translation (Loeb), London 1929–62, and the yet incomplete edition by C. MONDÉSERT et al, mentioned above, as well as in other editions of individual treatises. As for fragments in Greek and treatises and fragments preserved in Armenian, the basic editions were also made before World War II. See F. H. COLSON and G. H. WHITAKER, PLCL, 9, 1960, 407–507, and R. MARCUS, Suppl. 1 and 2, London 1953. Research in these areas is in progress, however. Thus, the Greek fragments of the Quaestiones, edited by F. PETIT, were published in 1978, as volume 33 in the French series PM. In 1981 A. TERIAN published the Armenian text with

an introduction, translation and commentary of Philonis Alexandrini de Animalibus ('On whether animals possess reason').

The areas in which Philonic research has proved to be most active and
fruitful since World War II are in the present survey indicated by the headings
'Philo's Situation', 'Philo as interpreter of the Pentateuch' and 'Conqueror or
conquered'. The last heading refers to the debate about Philo's place in
relationship to Judaism and the wider Hellenistic world. In these areas the
surveyor attempts to give a brief description of the background before World War
II and then discuss works published in the period that followed. Since the task is
to analyse and evaluate the scholarly debate and emerging trends, the selection of
works in these areas has been made with that aim in mind.

III. Philo's Situation

1. The social and political situation

The situation of the strong Jewish community in Alexandria from the
Roman take-over in 30 B.C. to the settlement of the increasing unrest by the
Emperor Claudius in 41 A.D. has already been subject to thorough examination
earlier in this century by such scholars as U. WILCKEN, A. BLUDAU and H. I.
BELL.[1]

V. TCHERIKOVER (Hellenistic, 320–28, 409–15; CPJ, 1, 1–111), M. STERN
(CRJNT, I:1, 122–33), S. SAFRAI (CRJNT, I:1, 184–215) and S. APPLEBAUM
(CRJNT, I:1, 434–40) build on these earlier studies and have added new points
to the discussion. The general conclusions can be summed up in this way: The
Romans made a distinction between, on the one hand, the citizens of the Greek
cities and the Hellenes of the provincial towns and villages, and on the other,
the native Egyptian population. The first group was either exempted from the poll
tax, as in the case of the Greek citizens, or paid a lower rate, as did the Hellenes,
while the native Egyptians paid the tax in full. For the Jews in Alexandria, therefore, the question of their legal status was a burning issue, and they pressed for
equal status with the Greek citizens of the city. The Greek citizens, on the other
hand, tried to deprive the Jews of the privileges granted them by the Emperor
Augustus, and wished the Jews to be classified together with the native Egyptians.

After Gaius Caligula became Emperor in 37 A.D., this state of cultural,
judicial and religious strife led to anti-Jewish riots which grew into a pogrom. A
military uprising by the Jews against the Greeks followed in 41 C.E. on the death
of Gaius Caligula and the accession of Claudius to the throne. It is worth noting

---

[1] U. WILCKEN, Zum alexandrinischen Antisemitismus. Abhandlungen der Königl. Sächsischen Gesellschaft der Wissenschaften, phil. hist. Klasse, 27, 1909, 783–839; A. BLUDAU,
Juden und Judenverfolgungen; H. I. BELL, Juden und Griechen.

that many Jews from Palestine and Egypt took part in the armed revolt, as can be seen from the fact that Claudius forbade the Alexandrian Jews to permit Jews from Syria and Egypt to enter the city. The Emperor, furthermore, would not permit Jews to infiltrate into the environment and the various activities connected with the *gymnasion*.

These points are largely accepted by scholars who since 1940—45 have examined the situation of the Jews in Alexandria in the early Roman period.

Some specific issues have been subject to further debate, however:

a) The poll-tax. H. I. BELL (JRS, 37, 1947, 17ff.; ID., JEA, 28, 1942, 39ff.; 30, 1944, 72f.; ID., Egypt, 68ff.) suggested that the poll-tax, *laographia*, was a normal feature of the financial system of Roman Egypt, taken over by Augustus from the Ptolemies but remodelled by him, with a grant of exemption to certain classes which he wished to distinguish from the general mass. V. A. TCHERIKOVER (JJurP, 4, 1950, 179—207, V. A. TCHERIKOVER and A. FUKS, Corpus, 1, 60) convincingly objects that Roman *laographia* was not a continuation of the Ptolemaic *syntaxis*, since the meaning of *syntaxis* as poll-tax is nowhere attested and since the introduction of a poll-tax by the Ptolemies seems very unlikely. It was an innovation of Augustus, admirably suited to the general principle of Roman rule in the provinces: A conquered people had to pay a *vectigal*, or a *tributum*. Thus TCHERIKOVER revives the view of earlier scholars, such as U. WILCKEN (Griechische Ostraka, 1, 230ff.). Against this background it becomes evident that the situation of the Jews in Alexandria had grown more complicated and critical under Roman rule up to the time of Philo.

b) Concerning citizenship and Philo, S. APPLEBAUM (CRJNT, I:1, 439—40) sums up some of the points found in Philo's writings: For Philo, the collective rights enjoyed by the Jewish community constitute a *politeia*, which appears to possess both an abstract and a concrete significance. Thus, Flaccus' attempt to abolish it (Flac 53) means the abolition both of Jewish rights and of the organization which exists to apply them. Philo also refers to the established rights of the Alexandrian Jews as "our rights" (Gaium 366 ἡμετέρων . . . . . δικαίων), "political right" (ibid. 371 πολιτικὸν . . δίκαιον) and "communal rights" (ibid. τὰ κοινὰ . . . δίκαια); the political rights are referred to again in Flac 53. These references hardly imply that the Jews enjoyed the status of full citizenship in Alexandria. On the other hand Philo constantly refers to the Jews of the city as Ἀλεξανδρεῖς (Alexandrians). In Gaium 183 the Jewish Alexandrians are distinguished from the party of other Alexandrians. In Gaium 350 the term refers to the Alexandrian Jews. It is very difficult to know whether Philo is using the term 'Alexandrians' in anything more than a broad geographical sense; none of his other expressions are such as to suggest a more specific status within the framework of the Alexandrian *polis*, and his use of *politeia* in relation to the Jews of the city seems rather to refer to the Jewish communal organization (*politeuma*) only. In Flac 47, when he refers to the Jews as *politai*, he may therefore equally mean Jews as members of their own Jewish *politeuma*. TCHERIKOVER (Hellenistic, 315) has pointed out that elsewhere Philo (Flac 172) calls the Jews κάτοικοι, a status not reconcilable with that of *politai* in the sense of members of the Greek *polis* of Alexandria. Philo does state that the Alexandrian Jews 'enjoyed' the privilege of being corporally punished with rods instead of with whips (Flac 79); this information would also be consistent with the assumption that they possessed, corporately, not Alexandrian citizenship, but an intermediate status somewhat above that of the native Egyptians.

Thus, the Jews were not full citizens, but they fought for their civil rights. The Emperor Claudius accordingly rebukes the Jews in his letter in 41 A.D., where he bids them remain content with their existing position and not strive to win extra privileges. In the view of H. I. BELL (Jews and Christians, 16 and ID., Juden und Griechen, 17) and of H. BOX (In Flaccum, Oxford 1939, XLIX) all the Jews in Alexandria wanted Greek citizenship. E. M. SMALLWOOD (Legatio, 12—14 and EAD., The Jews, 234—5) does not accept this view. She rather maintains that the strict and orthodox Jews were content with the *status quo*, and only individuals who belonged to the liberal, 'modernist' party wanted to obtain Greek citizenship.

Observations in Philo's writings offer some evidence in support of SMALL-WOOD's view that there were Jews who were anxious to gain the social and political advantages which Greek citizenship would give them, even at the price of some slackening of their religious principles. For example, in Leg all III 167 Philo criticizes those who pursue their education out of desire for office under the rulers, and in Migr 89—93 he condemns some who abandon the Jewish way of life, although maintaining some ideas tied to the Pentateuch.

Nevertheless, SMALLWOOD's alternatives are too simple and schematic. The Jews understood themselves to be the chosen people, and their laws were the God-given laws to be accepted by all. TCHERIKOVER and FUKS (Corpus, 1, 78) were therefore right in their interpretation of Philo's attitude: "The chosen people, who could play the role of priests for the whole universe and had received from God the divine Law, equally suitable for Jews and Greeks, were at least worthy of civic rights, in order that they might not be forced to pay the poll-tax or be scourged publicly like an Egyptian fellah."

Philo even expects that the laws of Moses, which had been announced to the Greek world since the Septuagint translation, would be accepted by the other nations: "But if a fresh start should be made to brighter prospects, how great a change for the better might we expect to see: I believe that each nation would abandon its peculiar ways, and, throwing overboard their ancestral customs, turn to honouring our laws alone" (Vita Mos II 44; see P. BORGEN, Philo of Alexandria, CRJNT, II:2.)

In this connection it is also relevant to mention E. R. GOODENOUGH's (The Politics, 62) characterization of the treatise De Iosepho: "De Iosepho seems to me, then, to have been written from first to last with a single purpose, namely to . . . suggest that the real source for the highest political ideal of the East, the ideal of a divinely appointed and guided ruler, had had its truest presentation in Jewish literature, and highest exemplification at a time when a Jew was, in contemporary language, prefect of Egypt. In a sense the treatise presents at the same time another aspect of the familiar and fantastic claim of hellenistic Jews, that the Greeks had some great ideas in philosophy because they had had the sense to borrow them from their source, the Jewish scriptures."

From these observations the following hypothesis can be formulated: It is probable that some Jews in Alexandria were content with the *status quo* under which they were permitted to live according to their own laws and customs as a separate *politeuma* of its own. Furthermore, it is certain that others coveted Greek citizenship for the sake of higher social and political prestige and of economic advantages.

Strong forces among the Alexandrian Jews, however, seem to have entertained the eschatological expectations that the other nations would acknowledge the Law of Moses, and the people of God, the Jews, as the center of the world. Among these Jews there seem to have been two different views as to methods which should be used: Some would be in favour of using force, even arms, if necessary.[2] The armed revolt by the Jews in Alexandria in 41 seemed to have been inspired by such convictions, since they were even able to motivate Jews from Syria and Egypt to come and join them. (See the Emperor Claudius' letter, Col. V, 95ff.; TCHERIKOVER and FUKS, Corpus 1, 69 and 2, 54; KRAFT, Christianity, Judaism, Part three, 195.)

Others among the Alexandrian Jews would advocate that the Jews were to conquer their surroundings by peaceful means, i. e. by their religion, based on the laws given by the Creator, and by their growing prosperity. Philo belonged to this group: in Vita Mos II 44 he expresses the conviction that increased prosperity and progress among the Jews will lead other nations to accept the laws of Moses; and Philo's writings serve the general aim of interpreting these laws to the surrounding world, and preparing the Jews for their universal task.

Accordingly, in Somn II 83 Philo advises his fellow Jews to be cautious and not to use revolutionary provocations in their dealings with the non-Jewish political authorities: ". . . . . Surely then they are all lunatics and madmen who take pains to display untimely frankness, and sometimes dare to oppose kings and tyrants in words and deeds. They do not perceive that not only are their necks under the yoke like cattle, but that the harness also extends to their whole bodies and souls, their wives and children and parents, and the wide circle of friends and kinsfolk . . . . ." (Cf. E. R. GOODENOUGH, The Politics, 5—7.) Similar views were current among the Pharisees, G. ALON, Jews, 18—47. Against the background of Philo's active ideological 'warfare', it is quite inadequate to describe him as primarily a solitary and non-eschatological mystic, as is done by KRAFT (Christianity, Judaism, Part three, 192). The view of TCHERIKOVER and FUKS (Corpus 1, 67) is also inadequate when they regard Philo as a representative of the policy of reconciliation and adaptation championed by the higher circles of the Jewish population in Alexandria. Philo wanted rather to further the universal claim and cause of the Jewish nation, but by peaceful means.

c) With regard to Philo and social life, it is commonly accepted by scholars that Philo and his family possessed full citizenship in Alexandria (SCHWARTZ, Annuaire, 597; ID., PAL, 35—44; TCHERIKOVER and FUKS, Corpus 2, 197;

---

[2] Cf. the combination of ideological and military measures in the Jewish-Greek conflict in Caesarea; see L. I. LEVINE, Caesarea under Roman Rule, 29—30 and ID., JJS, 26, 1975.

APPLEBAUM, CRJNT, I:1, 473). Varying views are put forth, however, with regard to the participation of Philo and other Jews in the social life in Alexandria.

WOLFSON (Philo, 1, 80—1) suggested that there were Jewish organizations for sport and theatrical performances in Alexandria: "When Philo, therefore, speaks of his own presence at a contest of Pancratiasts, or at chariot races, or at the performance of a tragedy by Euripides, it may refer to events which took place within such strictly Jewish organizations, or it may perhaps only indicate that he had the curiosity to see these things performed by non-Jews and had the money to pay the admission fee; it does not indicate any participation, even on the part of men of the type of Philo, in the general sporting and intellectual life of the city." (ibid., 81).

WOLFSON (ibid., 81—2) admits, however, that the letter of the Emperor Claudius to the Alexandrians refers to Jews who infiltrate into the gymnastic or cosmetic games.

These Jews, however, belong only to a group of uprooted Jewish intellectuals, and do not represent a trend or attitude among the faithful Jews.

In contrast to WOLFSON's view TCHERIKOVER and FUKS (Corpus 1, 39, n. 99) maintain that "Philo speaks of the gymnastic contests, gymnasium education, etc. as of every day interests. There is no suggestion that these Greek habits in any way affected his religious scruples as a faithful Jew . . ." Similar evidence of Jewish participation in the Greek milieu centered around the gymnasium is also found in other cities. For example, in Miletos a special place in the theatre was reserved for the Jewish members of the audience.

The view of TCHERIKOVER and FUKS is correct, and consequently Philo belonged to the strong movement among the Alexandrian Jews who entered — and infiltrated — the Greek social and cultural center in and around the gymnasium. It only should be added that Philo stressed that the Jews should follow their Jewish principles and pursue Jewish aims in their social life, as examples from Ebr 20ff. 95; Agr 110—21; Jos 42ff. 56—7, 202—6 demonstrate.

Among the burning issues are mentioned the paying of fees and participation in the life of the clubs. Reluctantly, Philo says: ". . . when the object is to share in the best of possessions, prudence, such payments are praiseworthy and profitable; but when they are paid to obtain that supreme evil, folly, the practice is unprofitable" (Ebr 20ff.), and it can lead to Egyptian animal worship (95). Another issue is participation in the triennial festivals of wrestling, boxing, etc. which are organized by the cities. To Philo, these festivals are examples of contests in rivalry, lust, anger and licentiousness. A Jew should try to avoid participation in these, but if compelled to take part, he should not hesitate to be defeated (Agr 110—21). In Babylonian Talmud, Gittin 47a we find an example of this attitude. According to Gittin 47a Simeon S. Lakish at one period of his life was a professional gladiator. He justified this on the ground of grim necessity.

The treatise De Iosepho reflects problems related to sexual ethics and to table fellowship. In Jos 42ff. and in 56—7 the difference is pointed out between the Hebrew nation and other nations in sexual ethics and marriage laws. The Hebrews have strict customs and strict laws on marital matters, while licentiousness has destroyed the youth of the Greek race and the barbarians also. And in Egypt it is easy for Jewish youth to leave the ancestral way of life and change to alien ways, because the Egyptians deify things created and mortal, and are blind to the true God (254).

Another area of tension was that of table fellowship. Joseph gave a feast both for his own family and for Egyptians together with them. Joseph feasted each party according to its ancestral practice, but Philo adds that the Egyptians followed the same seating order as the Hebrew. The Egyptians indicated that in other times the style of life in their country was less civilized, until Joseph introduced good order (Jos 202–6)!

Philo himself participated actively in public social life: he took part in banquets (Leg all III 155f.); he frequented the theatre, saw plays and heard concerts (Ebr 177, Quod Omn 141), watched contests of pancratiasts (Quod Omn 26), and horse-racing (Apol Jud in Eusebius, Praep Ev VII 14.58).

The conclusion drawn from this evidence is that Philo supported the policy that Jews should participate actively in the social life of Alexandria. He therefore belonged himself to those who infiltrated the Greek milieu centered around the gymnasium. At the same time, however, he attacked and passionately criticized pagan worship and pagan life standards (see BORGEN, Philo of Alexandria, CRJNT, II:2).

2. Philo and the Jewish community

Many scholars realize that Philo lived as a faithful Jew within the context of Judaism (GOODENOUGH, Symbols, 1, 54; WOLFSON, Philo, 1, 55–86; SANDMEL, Philo's Place, 2; H. HEGERMANN, Literatur, 353, etc.). One of the basic questions in Philonic research, however, is to determine the relationship in Philo's thinking and attitude between the concrete Jewish nation and his universal and abstract (mystical) notions about it. The research on Philo's use of the term Israel, "he who sees God", can illustrate this problem. SMALLWOOD (Legatio, 153f., referring to previous research by other scholars) states that the etymology was presumably based on the reading of 'Israel' as אִישׁ רָאָה אֵל or יְשֻׁר אֵל. The etymology was well known, occurring in a Jewish apocryphon, in Syriac sources and in the Church Fathers. P. BORGEN (Bread, 115, n. 5) also points out that the etymology occurs in a rabbinic writing, i.e. in a text preserved in Hebrew: Seder Eliahu zuta, ed. M. FRIEDMANN, Wien 1902, 27 (138–9).

E. M. SMALLWOOD recognizes that Philo frequently used this etymology to support his theological doctrine of the place of Israel in the world. In his mystical interpretation of Jewish history, Jacob became "the man who sees God" through his wrestling with the angel. In this way Jacob gained the vision of reality or of the existence of God. SMALLWOOD refers at this point to GOODENOUGH, but without posing sharply the problem as to whether this etymology is a spiritual and universal concept, or whether it refers to the concrete nation of the Jews.

These two alternative interpretations were formulated by scholars before World War II. Among those who believed that Philo used the etymology as a

spiritual concept, GOODENOUGH may serve as representative[3]. GOODENOUGH
(By Light, Light, 136) writes: "This race has got the name of Israel, that is 'Seeing
God', and is distinguished by the fact that it has the vision of God at the end of
the mystic Road, the highest possible achievement, to which vision God draws
the soul up by the Road by the action of the divine Powers. This is not a reference
to the race of Israel, but first to the Patriarchs, and then to those who got the
vision, whether Jew or Gentile, and only those."

Strangely enough, GOODENOUGH also represents the alternative viewpoint,
i.e. that this etymology refers to the concrete nation of the Jews. Thus
GOODENOUGH (The Politics, 12) writes the following comment on Gaium 1–7:
"This race is, of course, the Jews, and Philo begins, strangely, to plunge the
reader into the Mystery. The Jews are Israel, which means, he says, 'seeing God'.
The mystic vision given to Jews, vision of that Deity which is beyond all
categories, even the categories of virtue, is hidden from other men . . .". It is,
indeed, surprising that GOODENOUGH has not discovered that his two
contradictory presentations of Philo's etymological interpretation of Israel
undermines his own understanding of Philo's mysticism. He should at least have
connected them and discussed them together.

During the Second World War, N. A. DAHL (Das Volk, 108ff.; 113) made
an attempt to mediate between these two conflicting views of 'the nation of vision',
and to place both within a pattern of ascent from earth to heaven. The concept of
Israel in Philo thus moves from the empirical Jewish nation, through other stages
such as the invisible 'church' of universal character, to the abstract vision of God
and, finally, to Logos as the one who has the vision. According to DAHL, Philo
has, therefore, the perspectives of both nationalism and universalism, but on
different levels.

N. MESSEL (NTT, 42, 1941, 229–37) criticizes DAHL's understanding at this
point, maintaining that Philo takes his philosophical and mystical ideas from the
surrounding world outside Judaism, transforms them, and employs them to show
the unique and superior position of the Jewish nation. On the basis of MESSEL's
position, GOODENOUGH's comments upon the concept of Israel in Gaium 1–7
should be extended to characterize Philo's viewpoint in general: The mystical
understanding of Israel, – he who sees God –, serves to define the concrete (and
faithful) Jewish nation, including the proselytes.

In various ways scholars as H. A. WOLFSON (Philo, 2, 51f.), BORGEN (Bread,
115–8) and H. HEGERMANN (Literatur, 354 and 369) follow the same interpretation of Israel, "he that sees God." Even GOODENOUGH (Symbols, 1, 57)
seems later to have reached the one conclusion that Israel, "the man who sees
God," is a description of Judaism.

Against this background it should be emphasized that Philo had the Jewish
community and its institutions as the base and context for his life and his
knowledge of Jewish traditions. His writings give some specific information
about this context: the large number of synagogues in Alexandria and all around
the world, the central significance of the celebration of the Sabbath, the

---

[3] Concerning similar views expressed by other scholars, see BORGEN, Bread, 116.

recognition of Jerusalem as mother city of the Jews, and Philo's very sharp condemnation of those who betray Judaism (see BORGEN, Philo of Alexandria, CRJNT, II:2). Philo therefore clearly belonged to the main body of Judaism, which recognized the religious jurisdiction of the Jerusalem Temple. Moreover, the Jewish nation was the life-setting even for his philosophical and mystical ideas.

Thus, S. SAFRAI's general conclusion also applies to Philo: "Various documents discovered in Egypt during the present century show us how closely the Jews were attached to institutions of Hellenistic law and to concepts tributary to this sphere. But the Jews of Egypt and the Hellenistic world, like the Jews of the other Diaspora centres, generally remained loyal to the Torah both in public and in private life" (CRJNT, I:1, 184—5).

These observations make difficult any understanding of Philo, which divorces Philo's spiritual interpretation of the Jerusalem Temple from the fact that he regarded the defence of its pure worship as a life-and-death issue (Gaium, 225—35, etc.). It is therefore a very superficial and mistaken approach to Philo's thinking, when FRÜCHTEL (Vorstellungen, 81, n. 2), without examining Philo's many references to Jerusalem, nevertheless concludes: „Indirekt läßt sich aus der Art und Weise, wie Philo die beiden großen Traditionen über den Tempel weiterüberliefert, erschließen, was er vom Jerusalemer Heiligtum hält: Es ist ganz uninteressant.“

Correspondingly, Philo's ties to the milieu of the synagogue were not of pragmatic nature so that he just made the necessary adaptations to his community. Philo's various descriptions of the gatherings in the synagogue rather suggest that his writings to a large extent should be regarded as a product of exegetical traditions and methods from the activities in the synagogue. G. DELLING, HUCA, 45, 1974, 139—45, rightly stresses that all of Philo's writings ought to be examined from this point of view.

3. Philo and the encyclia

The connection between Philo's philosophy of religion and his Jewish community on the one hand and the non-Jewish surroundings on the other is reflected in Philo's understanding of the encyclical education.

Before World War II such scholars as SIEGFRIED, ZELLER, BRÉHIER and VÖLKER interpreted the encyclia as a preliminary stage in the moral and religious progress of individuals, although their interpretations give very different emphases to details. GOODENOUGH considered the encyclia as a preliminary stage in ascent towards the vision of the Mystery. (C. SIEGFRIED, Philo von Alexandria, 260—2; E. ZELLER, Die Philosophie der Griechen, III:2, 4th ed., 457f.; 460f.; E. BRÉHIER, Les idées philosophiques et religieuses, 279—95; W. VÖLKER, Fortschritt und Vollendung, 158—98; R. R. GOODENOUGH, By Light, Light.)

In the time after World War II the same general approach to Philo's philosophy of education is pursued by scholars such as WOLFSON, FRÜCHTEL and A. MENDELSON. WOLFSON (Philo, 1, 145—51) discusses the relationship among the *encyclia*, philosophy and Scripture from the view-point of the philosophical question of cognition, and concludes that Philo regards Scripture as being superior to the others. FRÜCHTEL also (Vorstellungen, 153f.) discusses the *encyclia* from the view-point of cognition. She regards it as a preparatory stage of the perfect goal of the philosopher, even wisdom itself. A. MENDELSON (Secular Education, 25−33; 81−82, also points to Philo's philosophical and theological interpretation of the *encyclia*, but stresses that he places them within a Jewish framework.

Even before and during World War II, I. HEINEMANN and M. POHLENZ saw that the issue of Judaism and paganism was involved in Philo's evaluation of the *encyclia*. (I. HEINEMANN, PCH, 6, 4; M. POHLENZ, Nachrichten von der Akademie der Wissenschaften in Göttingen, phil.-hist. Klasse, 428ff.)

After World War II, it has become more and more clear that Greek education and the gymnasium were burning issues to the Jews in Alexandria, since they served as the condition for full civil rights. The *encyclia* therefore played an important part both in matters of taxes and in the question of gaining access to political offices. The works of TCHERIKOVER and FUKS (Corpus 1, 37−41; 64f.) and TCHERIKOVER (Hellenistic, 311ff.; ID., JJS, 14, 1963, 4−8) have brought this aspect to the foreground.

Although Philo has a concentrated discussion of these questions in Congr, he deals with it again in his writings. BORGEN (Bread, 122−7, cf. G. DELLING, HUCA, 45, 1974, 141) has examined the way in which the situation of the Alexandrian Jews is reflected in Leg all III 162−8. In 167 Philo describes the wrong objectives for education: "Many, then, have acquired the lights in the soul for night and darkness, not for day and light; all elementary lessons, for example, and what is called school-learning (τὰ προπαιδεύματα) and philosophy itself when pursued with no motive higher than parading their superiority, or from desire of an office under the rulers." Here Philo is concerned with the motives which stimulated Jews to acquire the necessary education and try to make a political and social career in their pagan surroundings.

The central Pentateuchal text for Philo's discussion of education is Gen 16:1−6 on Abraham's relationship to Sarah and Hagar. When Philo interprets Abraham's relationships in terms of educational ideas, he is dependent upon the allegorical interpretation of the figure of Penelope in Homer (see BORGEN, Bread, 108). For example Plutarch tells that those who, being unable to win philosophy, wear themselves out in the encyclical disciplines, are like the suitors of Penelope, who when they could not win the mistress, contented themselves with her maids. Correspondingly, when Abraham did not, at first conceive a child with Sarah, he took the maid, Hagar, in her place (see BORGEN, Bread, 108).

In his understanding of Philo FRÜCHTEL (Vorstellungen, 153−4) stresses that the figures of Abraham, Sarah and Hagar have been transformed in such a way that they in Greek fashion illustrate the progress of a philosopher from preliminary education to philosophy.

BORGEN (Bread, 108; cf. M. ALEXANDRE, PM, 16, 79, etc.) draws rather on the insights from the situation of the Jewish community in Alexandria: The transformation of Penelope and her maids into Sarah and Hagar means that Philo claims this allegory for Judaism, so as to interpret its point of view regarding encyclical education. Abraham's double relationship both to Hagar and Sarah, reflects the dual aspects of Judaism in Alexandria, i.e. its outward and inward relations. This is the reason why Philo often emphasizes the notion that Hagar was an Egyptian woman (Quaes in Gen III 19. 21; Abr 251 and especially Congr 20ff.). Hence the offspring of Abraham and Hagar, Ishmael, is logically enough characterized as a bastard, Sobr 8. Sarah, on the other hand, represents the inward aspect of Judaism, and is therefore called the mother of the Jews, 'the most populous of nations', Congr 2—3.

Accordingly, Abraham, representing the Jewish nation, receives education from two schools: the encyclical education is the bastard school which the Jews have in common with their pagan surroundings; the other school is the genuine school of Jewish philosophy. Philo expresses this situation clearly in his interpretation of Abraham, Sarah and Hagar in Congr 35: ". . . . . the virtue that comes through teaching, which Abraham pursues, needs the fruits of several studies, both those born in wedlock, which deal with wisdom, and the baseborn, those of the preliminary lore of the schools." Philo thus places encyclical education on the borderline between Judaism and paganism, as an *adiaphoron* which in itself is neither good nor bad. It is in harmony with this view of the *encyclia* that Philo describes it as the "well 'between Kadesh and Bered'", that is, "on the borderland (μεθόριος) between the holy and the profane", Fug 212—213; The term ἡ μέση παιδεία, which Philo used in Mut 255, etc., expresses the same evaluation of the *encyclia* and means therefore "education on the borderland" or "neutral education". Philo does not only deal with these questions of profane education at the level of principle, but also gives glimpses of educational activities in lecture halls and theatres filled with students (Congr 64).

IV. Interpreter of the Pentateuch

1. Philo's writings

There has long been general agreement among scholars on the classification of Philo's expository writings. See especially L. COHN, Philologus, Suppl. 7, 385—435. These fall into two main groups: 1. The exposition of the Law of Moses (Op; Abr; Jos; Dec; Spec; Leg; Virt; Praem). These writings are but parts of one comprehensive re-writing of the Law of Moses. 2. The exegetical commentaries, which fall into two subordinate series: a) Quaestiones et solutiones in Genesim et Exodum, which is a brief commentary in the form of questions and answers on parts of the first two books of the Pentateuch. b) Legum allegoriae, which consists of Leg all; Cher; Sacr; Quod Det; Post; Gig; Quod Deus; Agr; Plant; Ebr; Sobr; Conf; Migr; Heres; Congr; Fuga; Mut; Somn. This series covers the main parts of Gen 2—41.

There has been more uncertainty on the classification of the remaining writings. In general they have been divided into purely philosophical writings (Act; Prov; Alexander; Quod Omn) and historical and apologetic treatises (Flac;

Gaium; Vita Cont; Apol Jud; Vita Mos). E. R. GOODENOUGH (HTR, 26, 1933, 109–25) has rightly challenged the placement of De Vita Mosis among the historical and apologetic writings. He has shown that this treatise and The exposition of the Law of Moses were companion pieces. GOODENOUGH moreover argues that they were all written for non-Jewish readers.

DANIÉLOU (Philon, 87–8) and AMIR (EJ, 13, col 410) and DELLING (Studien, 73–4) are in general agreement with GOODENOUGH's understanding of Vita Mos. ARNALDEZ (NCE, 11, 287) and HEGERMANN (Literatur, 177) on the other hand follow the former classification which places Vita Mos among the so-called historical and apologetical writings.

Although GOODENOUGH's view is on the whole convincing, his emphasis on gentiles as the addressee needs further be examined more closely. He is right in stating that Vita Mos is written for gentile readers to tell them about the supreme law-giver whose laws they are to accept and honour. GOODENOUGH overlooks, however, that at the same time, this book is also written for Jews to strengthen them for their universal role. The same dual purpose also runs through The Exposition of the Law of Moses. GOODENOUGH rightly makes the observation that, in this series, Philo in some places tells about the assemblies in the synagogues in a way which shows that he has non-Jews in mind. At the same time Philo's use of the first person plural, ἡμᾶς, in Op 170 seems to refer to man in general, including the Jews. In the situation in Alexandria, when Jews infiltrated into the environment of the Gymnasium, Philo's work thus offered an ideological basis for the activities of the Jews and their attempt to overcome the non-Jews through their religion and philosophy. (See BORGEN, Philo of Alexandria, CRJNT, II:2.)

Apart from the questions related to Vita Mos, the classification of other writings as historical and apologetic is also rather unsatisfactory. The main weakness of this heading is that it fails to integrate these treatises with the other works of Philo. It therefore also seems pertinent here to start from the fact that Philo was an exegete. Against this background the classification of these writings should be given the heading: Pentateuchal principles applied to contemporary issues and events.

These writings fall into three groups: 1. Writings in which Pentateuchal material, in the form of literal narrative or/and of deeper principles, is applied to socio-religious factors in the Jewish community. Apol Jud and Vit Cont fall into this category. 2. Writings in which Pentateuchal principles are applied to, or are developed in dialogue with contemporary philosophical issues and religious phenomena: Quod Omn, Aet, Provid and Alexander, sive de eo quod rationem habeant bruta animalia. 3. Writings in which Pentateuchal principles are applied to specific historical events and persons: Flac and Gaium.

Some points on each of these groups should be added. First, some remarks on the writings on socio-religious issues: The preserved fragments of Apol Jud deal with events and laws which cover parts of the Pentateuch from Jacob (Gen 25) to the conquest of Palestine in the Books of Joshua and Judges. The emphasis in Apol Jud is placed on a characterization of Judaism in Philo's own time, and it can therefore be listed among Philo's writings on contemporary issues.

In Vita Cont Philo tells about the religious community of the Therapeutae to illustrate the aspect of heavenly ascent (Vita Cont 11): they are citizens of Heaven even in this life in the world (Vita Cont 90). They are in this way model Jews, since to be a true Jew is to be a citizen of Heaven; cf. that a proselyte receives a place in Heaven when he becomes a Jew (see for instance Praem 152).

The second group of treatises deals with philosophical issues. In these writings Philo uses his interpretation of the laws of Moses in evaluating and developing philosophical notions (see especially Quod Omn 42 ff.; 53—57; 75—91; Aet 13—19; Prov I 22; 35; 84).

Even the view expressed by Philo in the treatise Alexander seems to be selected on the basis of his Jewish attitude, and can be combined with ideas which he puts forward in other writings: the animals know nothing of God, cosmos, law, ancestral customs, state and political life. These attributes are exclusive to man. Some of these Stoic ideas are part of Philo's exposition of the laws of Moses. Thus, in saying that the animals know nothing about man's conscious and purposeful art, τέχνη, Philo in Congr 141 gives the full Stoic definition of art as part of the exposition of Gen 16:5. And the philosophical ideas of God, cosmos, ancestral customs, state and political life are points which in several places are central to Philo's interpretation of the Pentateuch. The conclusion is that Philo's views stated in Alexander etc. are influenced by his attitudes and views as a Jew in the sense in which he himself defines the Jewish ideas in his other writings. LEISEGANG (PW, 20, col 8) is therefore wrong when he states that nothing in this dialogue reveals that the persons taking part are Jews.

When Philo draws on Pentateuchal passages and principles in his philosophical writings, he presupposes the kind of exegesis which he has developed in his various expository works. They therefore presuppose Philo's work as an exegete, and do not, as L. COHN suggests, belong to a period of his life before he had settled down to interpret the Laws of Moses. Thus, COHN's view (Philologus, Suppl. 7, 389) which has been accepted by scholars such as COLSON (PLCL, 9, 2) needs to be revised.

This hypothesis championed by COHN, COLSON and others is built on the doubtful assumption that Philo had less interest in philosophy after he began to interpret the Pentateuch. But his expositions betray that all the time he was drawing on Greek philosophy and philosophical works. Some of the philosophical writings point rather to a later period than that of youth: Alexander, sive de eo quod rationem habeant bruta animalia, for example, must have been written some time after the year 12 C.E., and in it Philo even refers to a journey of his own to the Temple at Jerusalem to offer sacrifice. And if, as it seems, his own nephew Alexander was old enough to be his dialogue partner, Philo was most probably of mature age.

It is, therefore, doubtful whether Philo's life should be divided into the philosophical period of young man and his exegetical period as a mature and old man. He lived all his life in the double context of the Jewish community and the Alexandrian Greek community. See A. TERIAN, The Implication of Philo's Dialogues on his Exegetical Works, who presents evidence to indicate that Philo's dialogues were written when he was of old age. Philosophy was Philo's life interest. The dialogues seem to be apologetic writings and thus seem to fall in line with the rest of his works. See further A. TERIAN, De Animalibus, 33−34.

The third group, the writings on contemporary matters, deals with the historical events connected with the pogrom in Alexandria 38 A.D. − Since World War II the two treatises concerned, Flac and Gaium have been published, with introductions and notes, by K.-H. GERSCHMANN (Gegen Flaccus, PCH, 7, 1964, 122−65), A. PELLETIER (In Flaccum, PM, 31, 1967), F. H. COLSON (The Embassy to Gaius, PLCL, 9, 1962, IC−XXXI; 1−187); F. W. KOHNKE (Gesandtschaft an Caligula, PCH, 8, 1964, 166−266) and E. M. SMALLWOOD (Legatio, 1961). All these render Philo's treatises in translation. PELLETIER, COLSON and SMALLWOOD also edit and publish the Greek text. They follow the text version of COHN, WENDLAND and REITER, although some alternative readings are preferred.

These publications illustrate that scholars have difficulties in integrating these books closely into Philo's general authorship. The introductions, notes and commentaries deal mainly with historical and chronological questions. For example, SMALLWOOD (Legatio, and ID., The Jews, 243) argues convincingly for the conclusions drawn by E. SCHÜRER (Geschichte des jüdischen Volkes, 1, 3rd and 4th ed., 1901, 501, n. 174) that the Jewish envoys went to Rome in 39−40 and not as early as in 38−9, as maintained by scholars as COLSON (PLCL, 9, XXX).

GERSCHMANN and KOHNKE, however, attempt to a larger extent to understand Flacc and Gaium on theological grounds also. They conclude that Philo interprets the events in Alexandria and Rome in 38 A. D. and after from the perspective of a conflict between the Jewish belief that they were the elected people of the one God, the Creator, and the usurpatory claim of power and of divine prerogatives of the Greek *polis* and the Roman emperor. KOHNKE (PCH, 7, 170) also links Philo's understanding of the events in 38 A. D. and after to his previous convictions, as stated by Philo in Praem 172: In persecution, "if in the soul a tiny seed be left of the qualities which promote virtue, . . . still from that little seed spring forth the fairest and most precious things in human life, by which states are constituted, manned with good citizens, and notions grow into a great population."

The connection between the historical writings Flac and Gaium and Philo's expository writings can be even more closely drawn. In his exegetical works also Philo at times applies Pentateuchal principles to historical events and persons. Thus as an example of persons who (as seen in Gen 37:9−11) exalt themselves above men and the world of nature, he lists Xerxes, who was punished by insanity. Another example was a governor over Egypt who attempted to disturb the ancestral customs of the Jews (Somn II 123 ff.).

In Flacc and Gaium the same approach is followed, in such a way that the Pentateuchal principles, − as understood by Philo, − are used as an interpretative key, and the actual Biblical passages are presupposed as background.

Of particular interest is Gaium 3−7, where Philo gives a summary of the main points of his interpretations of the Laws of Moses and thus of the Jewish religion. He places emphasis here, as elsewhere, on God's creative, kingly, providential powers and such of the other powers which serve both beneficial and punitive purposes. (Cf. Quod Deus 77–8; Plant 50. Cf. also SMALLWOOD, Legatio, 156–7.)

This nation, whose God is the Creator, is according to Philo the race of suppliants (§ 3) in the sense that they serve as link between God and man. God's care for all men is in a sense the outcome of His care for the Jews. (Cf. Praem 44 and GOODENOUGH, Politics, 13 and SMALLWOOD, Legatio 152.)

Philo then tells how Flaccus and Gaius Caligula proved to be enemies of the Jews (Flacc 24 etc. Gaium 373), but were in reality enemies of God himself: Flaccus was puffed up with arrogance (Flac 124; 152), and Gaius even overstepped the bounds of human nature and claimed to be god (Gaium 75; 367f., etc.).

Philo here narrates theologically interpreted history, as indicated by KOHNKE (PCH, 7, 168). In this respect these treatises show a similarity to history writing in the Old Testament, in Judaism and in the New Testament. In the New Testament especially, the Passion narrative in the Gospels and the persecutions of the early church according to the Acts of the Apostles describe similar historical events and interpret them on the basis of the Old Testament. As for Philo's specific point about rulers being punished for their blasphemous arrogance, the brief story in Acts 12:20–23 applies this principle to the same king Herod who aided the Alexandrian Jews: "And the people shouted, 'The voice of a god, and not of a man!' Immediately an angel of the Lord smote him, because he did not give God the glory; and he was eaten by worms and died."

2. Philo's Bible

Philo's works are based on the interpretation of the Pentateuch, although also other Septuagint books are used. This predominance of the Pentateuch has produced various hypotheses. At the time of World War II, scholars such as W. L. KNOX and F. H. COLSON discussed this phenomenon. KNOX (A note on Philo's use of the Old Testament, JTS, 41, 1940, 30–4) supposed that Philo knew only the Pentateuch apart from 'testimonies' of a few passages from other Septuagint books. COLSON (Philo's quotations from the Old Testament, JTS, 41, 1940, 237–51), on the other hand, suggested that Philo concentrated on the exegesis of the Pentateuch because of its higher authority and because of his personal predilections.

The new recognition of the synagogue as Philo's primary milieu points in another direction. The predominance of his use of the Pentateuch probably reflects the reading practice in the Alexandrian synagogues (THYEN, Der Stil, 74; BORGEN, Bread, 55, and n. 3). In this case, Pentateuchal pericopes would have been used in the regular reading, while other Biblical books would have been drawn upon only in expositions or in other parts of the services. It should also be added here that the Pentateuchal books would be of special interest to the Jewish community in Egypt, since Egypt and the Exodus are central geographical and theological elements in these books.

Since Philo builds his exegesis on the Greek text of the Septuagint, he develops a theological understanding of this translation: The Septuagint is an exact and inspired translation of the Hebrew original. Moreover, it has a central role, since it serves as a revelation of the Sacred Writings to the Greek-speaking part of mankind.

In spite of this fact, many details as to Philo's Septuagint text are uncertain and at the very least, complicated to unravel, particularly as he sometimes departs from the Septuagint readings. In his discussion of this problem DANIÉLOU (Philon, 95 ff.) starts out from KAHLE's understanding of the Septuagint. Accordingly, to DANIÉLOU therefore Philo's variant readings are due to the fact that the Septuagint was a Greek form of 'targum'. The Septuagint was thus used as the interpretative translation of the Hebrew text in the Greek-speaking synagogues. This function meant that a rich variation of readings existed. DANIÉLOU is right in searching for an explanation in synagogal practices. It is doubtful, however, whether Philo's exegesis presupposes the reading of the Hebrew text supplemented by a 'targumic' use of the Septuagint.

P. KATZ (TZ, 5, 1949, 15 f; ID., Philo's Bible, 3—4; 103; cf. ID., The Background, 205 f.) maintains that the quotations in the lemmata of the majority of manuscripts represent the original Septuagint-text of Philo, while the differently phrased quotations found in the lemmata of the manuscripts UF (L) represent an aberrant text adapted to a modernized revision of the LXX and Aquila. KATZ attempts to reconstruct Philo's original text from the exegetical paraphrase of his expositions.

G. E. HOWARD, HUCA, 44, 1973, 197—209 offers several points of criticism against KATZ' analysis: HOWARD reaches the following conclusions:

1. ". . . . the aberrant text of manuscripts UF (L) does represent at times the type of text used by Philo. However, it must be emphasized that the Septuagint text as represented by the early Christian Codices is the text which is reflected most often by the exposition. But the percentage of verifiably authentic LXX lemmata is not as great as one might think.

In the first place there is a large number of instances where the exposition reads in a way that does not disclose which text Philo had before him. There are other instances where the exposition does not verbally support any lemma at all. In these cases it is difficult to decide whether Philo is merely paraphrasing or whether he is commenting on a form of the Greek Bible which is no longer extant. Then there are the instances where the readings of UF are reflected in the exposition. This considerably reduces the number of clearly authentic LXX readings.

2. The fact that Philo at times used a text type different from the Christian codices of the Septuagint has implications for our understanding of the nature of the Greek Bible at the beginning of the first century C.E. Though it is possible that Philo used two versions of the Greek Bible, sometimes LXX and sometimes the aberrant text, it is also possible that he used only one version of the Greek Bible which contained a mixed text, some parts coming from LXX and some from the aberrant text. One could also argue (though it does not seem likely) that Philo used an unmixed version which from its very beginning included

at least those elements of the aberrant text which his exposition supports. If so, it would imply that the original Greek was not characteristically uniform in its methods of translation.

3. The present study again raises the issue of the nature of the aberrant text. One of its most striking characteristics is its often close relationship to Aquila. It was for this reason that KATZ wanted to date it somewhere in the early Middle Ages at a time when an interpolator, who, being interested in Philo from the point of view of his scripture quotations only, could bring together such conflicting elements as Philo and Aquila.

The publication of the first century C.E. Greek Twelve Prophets Scroll by BARTHÉLEMY and his identification of it with the early pre-Aquila καίγε text places this issue in an entirely different light. It is possible that Philo made use of the καίγε text and by this means occasionally overlapped with Aquila. If this is the case, the aberrant text preserves for us some of the earliest extant remnants of the καίγε text in the Pentateuch.

At the same time, however, we must not make the mistake of equating the aberrant text in toto with καίγε."

These observations and conclusions made by HOWARD are on the whole convincing. The weakness of his and the other scholars' analyses are, however, that they to some extent ignore the fact that in the paraphrasing expositions Philo deals with the text as an active exegete, and he works, moreover, exegetical traditions into his paraphrase. Thus, it is impossible to reconstruct an original Septuagint text on the basis of his exegesis. The understanding that Philo basically is to be understood as an exegete, has received strong emphasis by the work of V. NIKIPROWETZKY, Le commentaire.

The question whether Philo knew Hebrew or not, has been much discussed, but no general consensus has been reached. C. SIEGFRIED (Philo, 142—145), and H. A. WOLFSON (Philo, 1, 88), think that Philo knew Hebrew. S. SANDMEL (Philo's Place, repr. 1971, 11—13, and ID., SP, 5, 1978, 107—111) and A. HANSON (JTS, 18, 1967, 128—139) think that Philo knew a little Hebrew, but drew most of his Hebrew etymologies from a source, probably an etymological list or dictionary.

On the other hand, I. HEINEMANN (Bildung, 524f.), and V. NIKIPROWETZKY (Le Commentaire, 50—81) reach the conclusion that Philo had no knowledge of Hebrew. In a recent study D. DAUBE (Jewish Law in the Hellenistic World, 45—50) has made such a negative assessment less confident.

The question whether Philo knew Hebrew is not of decisive importance, however. The basic fact is that he renders etymological interpretations based on Hebrew, and that he employs some traditions which were common to Greek-speaking and Hebrew-speaking Jews. He may here rely on written documents or on oral traditions in the synagogues. Philo's broad knowledge and his role and place in the Jewish community suggest that he used both kinds of sources.

3. Philo and the haggada and halaka

In many places in his writings Philo indicates that he draws on sources beyond the Bible itself. Of special interest is Vita Mos I 4 where he has learned the life and teachings of Moses "both from the sacred books (κἀκ βίβλων τῶν ἱερῶν), the wonderful monuments of his wisdom which he has left behind him, and from some of the elders (παρὰ . . . πρεσβυτέρων) of the nation; for I always interwove (ἀεὶ συνύφαινον) the narrated things (τὰ . . . . . λεγόμενα) with the things read (aloud) (τοῖς ἀναγινωσκομένοις), and thus believed myself to have a closer knowledge (ἀκριβῶσαι) than others of his life's history."

Philo weaves together the points read from the Sacred books and the traditions heard from the elders of the nation. This means that he has reworked the material to some extent, and that he has probably made some creative impact on it. Philo says that he always follows this approach in his writings.

Since Philo draws on tradition, the question to be asked is whether he depends on Palestinean haggada and halaka. This problem has remained on the agenda for more than one century, without any consensus being reached. SANDMEL (Philo's Place, 9—10) has summed up the alternatives in this way: A) Palestinian Jewry, especially rabbinic Judaism, was the acknowledged leader and authority in religious matters for Alexandria, as early as 20 B.C.—40 A.D. Philo was dependent on authoritative rabbinic statements. B) Alexandrian Jewry was not a cultural suburb of Palestine, but self-contained and almost self-sufficient. Philo was thus independent of Palestinian traditions. C) Alexandrian Judaism and Palestinian Judaism each developed along its own lines of creativity but without complete loss of communication. SANDMEL himself represents this view.

During the last decades the basis of this discussion has been challenged, namely, the thought that a sharp distinction existed between 'normative' Palestinian Judaism and Hellenistic Judaism. Among those who argue against this former consensus are D. DAUBE, E. M. SIDEBOTTOM, S. LIEBERMANN, R. MEYER, V. A. TCHERIKOVER and M. HENGEL.[4] The author of the present article has reviewed the works of some of these scholars (BORGEN, Bread, 3, 58—60) and he is in agreement with their main point of view. He has also attempted to add some observations on the similarities between Philonic and midrashic exegesis.

Since no sharp distinction can be drawn between Palestinian Judaism and Hellenistic Judaism, it is a subordinate question to ask whether Philo was dependent on Palestinian traditions or the Palestinian Jews drew on Alexandrian traditions, as exemplified in Philo's writings. The main question is then to uncover traditions current in Judaism at that time and examine the various usages, emphases and applications within this common context.

---

[4] D. DAUBE, The New Testament and Rabbinic Judaism, IX; E. M. SIDEBOTTOM, The Christ of the Fourth Gospel, 15—16; S. LIEBERMANN, Hellenism in Jewish Palestine; R. MEYER, Hellenistisches in der rabbinischen Anthropologie; M. HENGEL, Judaism and Hellenism, see especially 1, p. 1ff.; V. A. TCHERIKOVER, Hellenistic.

With regard to Philo, he — and the Alexandrian Judaism which he represents, — belonged to the main body of Judaism, that is, the Judaism which recognized Jerusalem and its temple. Moreover, there is evidence which proves that there were frequent and close contacts between Alexandrian and Palestinian Jews. Philo himself reflects this contact, since he visited Jerusalem at least once to offer sacrifice in the temple. These considerations suggest that in some areas there was a common Jewish halaka to a greater extent in Philo's time than was possible after the destruction of Jerusalem and its temple in 70 A.D.

As for more specific agreements between Philo's works and the rabbinic material, scholars have indicated detailed and specific agreements. BORGEN (Bread) has discussed the close agreements in form and content in traditions about the manna and the well, seen together as a reversal of the regular processes of rain from heaven and bread being produced from earth (Philo, Vita Mos I 202—2; II 267, ExR 25:2, 25:6; Mek Ex 16:4). Specific agreements in form and content also exist in the discussion as to why Adam was created last (Op 77—8 and Tosephta, Sanhedrin 8:7—9; see BORGEN, Philo of Alexandria, CRJNT, II:2). At these points Philo and the rabbis seem to reflect the same common exegetical traditions.

W. MEEKS (The Prophet-King, 110f, 192—4) has examined the interpretation of Ex 7:1 in Vita Mos I 155—8 and Tanchuma, ed. BUBER, IV, 51f. In both places the words "see, I have made you a god to Pharaoh" (Ex 7:1) is understood to mean that Moses was appointed God and King. The reason is that the same exegetical tradition behind the passages implied that the role of 'king' was one aspect of the scriptural term 'God'. MEEKS (Prophet-King, 194) concludes: "The central element of the midrash, therefore, turns out to be older than Philo: that is, it was current prior to 40 A.D."

Y. MUFFS (Christianity, Judaism, Part three, 30ff.) examines another exegetical tradition common to Philo and the rabbis, based on Ex 4:27: "The Lord said to Aaron, 'Go to meet Moses in the wilderness'". Both in Vita Mos I 85—6 and in Tanhuma Yashan to Exodus 4:27 the verse is interpreted to mean that God had made Aaron predisposed to obedience and to accepting his own secondary role. MUFFS' view is formulated in this way: "A much later midrash (Tanhuma Yashan to Exodus 4:27; cf. KASHER, Torah Shelemah, ad loc.), reflects the same ancient tradition already found in Philo's free-flowing pashtanic narrative." (31)

Another example is produced by the widespread Jewish belief that Moses did not die, but was taken up to heaven. This view is found in B Sot 13b, and its existence in 1st century A.D. and earlier is evidenced by Philo, Quaes Gen I 86; Josephus, Ant 4, 326; and the New Testament, Mk 9:2—8 par; Mt 17:1—17; Rev 11:3—6; see K. HAACKER and P. SCHÄFER, Josephus-Studien, 170—1.

Of special interest is the study of G. ALON, Jews. He has shown that at several places where Philo's juridical views are in disagreement with Rabbinic halaka, Philo represents earlier views, which also were held in Palestine. This applies to Philo's views on gifts to be brought to the Temple, on capital cases, on lynching punishment, and on the blowing of the shofar (G. ALON, Jews, 89—137).

At times Philo, rabbinic Judaism and the New Testament have traditions in common which they also share with the Hellenistic world in general. This is the case with regard to the socalled Golden rule, Apol Jud 7:6, Targum Pseudo Jonathan Lev 19:18; Luke 6:31; Isocrates, Nicocles 24 and 61, Mt 7:12, etc. See BORGEN, Temenos, 5, 1969, 37—53.

Among the recent scholars who stress the difference between Philo and the rabbis, Y. AMIR (SP 2, 1973, 1—8) can be mentioned. AMIR maintains that Philo's understanding of the Law of Moses was in complete contradiction to the rabbinic view. AMIR writes on the basis of B Sanhedrin 99a (see L. GINZBERG, The Legends, 5th impr., 6, 47, note 248), that the rabbis had a clear antithesis: "The Bible is either from God or from man . . . the rabbis would have classified Philo among the mockers of the Torah", since he thought that Moses gave the laws.

A similar conclusion is reached by E. E. URBACH, The Sages, 1, 364—5: no parallel can be drawn between Philo's discussion of the Decalogue and rabbinic discussion of the Ten commandments. R. D. HECHT, SP, 5, 1978, points out that URBACH does not consider the evidence of Targum Pseudo-Jonathan, Ex 24, 12. — Philo develops systematically the notion present also in Palestinian traditions that the Decalogue contained all the commandments of the Mosaic corpus. The Decalogue was given by God himself directly, and the other laws by Moses (Vita Mos II 188ff., etc. and Mekhilta de-R. Ishmael on Ex 20:19, etc.). Thus the view stated by H. A. WOLFSON, Philo, 2, 201, has been strengthened: the rabbis and Philo understood the Decalogue in a similar manner.

Although S. SANDMEL is more open for mutual influences between Philo and Palestinian (rabbinic) Judaism, he also often stresses the difference between them. For example, SANDMEL (Philo's Place, 49) describes the different views on Abraham in this way: "The rabbis say that Abraham observed the Law; Philo says that the Law sets forth as legislation those things which Abraham did." It should be added, however, that Philo himself knew the view of those who, like the rabbis, would claim that Abraham obeyed the law: "Such was the life of the first, the founder of the nation, one who obeyed the law, some will say, but rather, as our discourse has shown, himself a law and an unwritten statute." (Abr 276). Philo was, therefore, aware of this rabbinic picture of Abraham, and referred to it explicitly as background for his interpretation. See further S. SAND-MEL, Philo, 127—134.

4. Various groups of interpreters

The traditional distinction made between Hellenistic and Palestinian Judaism needs to be replaced by a closer examination of various groups among the Diaspora and the Palestinian Jews. In Egypt three separate groups existed: 1. Jews who recognized the religious jurisdiction of the temple of Onias in Leontopolis (TCHERIKOVER and FUKS, Corpus, 1, 44—6. 52. 80), 2. Samaritans (Josephus, Ant XIII, 74—79) and 3. Jews who recognized the jurisdiction only of the Temple in Jerusalem.

Among the Jews who had the Jerusalem Temple as their center, various groupings can also be traced. The letter of the Emperor Claudius to the Alexandrians seems to reflect a division between the Jews who, like Philo, wanted to fight by non-military means, and the Jews who instigated armed revolt in Alexandria. As a result, the Alexandrian Jews sent two delegations to the Emperor (see TCHERIKOVER and FUKS, Corpus, 2, 50—3).

Philo's writings also testify to the existence of various groups and tendencies within Alexandrian Jewry, based on different interpretations of the Laws of Moses. J. DANIÉLOU (Philon, 104f.) offers a good starting point when he distinguishes between the primitive literalists and the syncretistic literalists. This distinction might be made sharper so that the primitive literalists should be called literalists who were faithful to Judaism, while the syncretistic literalists rather were unfaithful scoffers who attacked the Pentateuch and Judaism.

Several examples of the exegesis of the faithful literalists could be listed (see BORGEN, Philo of Alexandria, CRJNT, II:2). For example, the term 'beginning' in Gen 1:1 meant chronological beginning (Op 26; Leg all I 2); in Gen 2:8 Paradise is a real garden (Quaes Gen I 8), etc. It is probable that the Alexandrian Jews who took up arms and revolted in 41 A.D. were primarily to be found among such faithful literalists, who would then also take the Scriptural war-theology literally. It is also probable that they championed eschatological expectations, as indicated by KRAFT, Christianity, Judaism, Part three, 195—6.

Philo also renders examples of the exegesis developed by the scoffing and unfaithful literalists. They ridicule the change of one letter in Abram/Abraham and Sarah/Sarai (Mut 60—62 and Quaes Gen III 43 and 53). The treatise Mut served as a defence against such a scoffing literalist, whom Philo himself had heard, and who committed suicide as punishment from God (Mut 60—2). (See further examples in DANIÉLOU, Philon, 104ff. and BORGEN, Philo of Alexandria, CRJNT, II:2.)

Correspondingly, the difference between Jews and gentiles also created two groups of allegorists. One group, although Jews, used allegorical exegesis to spiritualize the meaning of customs and observances so that they lived as gentiles (Migr 89—93). See P. BORGEN, Observations, 86—8; HAY, SP, 6, 1979—1980, 47—9.

Although scholars in general agree in their understanding of these extreme allegorists, they vary in their evaluation of Philo and his fellow exegetes who attempted to combine both the symbolic and the literal meanings. Scholars such as GOODENOUGH (An Introduction, 2nd rev. ed., Oxford 1962, 139ff.), KRAFT (Christianity, Judaism, Part three, 192) and FRÜCHTEL (Vorstellungen, 120) think that the deeper allegorical meaning represents Philo's real understanding of the Scriptures, and the literal exegesis and observance are adaptations to the life of the Jewish community and the Scriptural texts, or the external points of comparison for spiritual truth.

Others, like WOLFSON (Philo, 1, 125f.), DELLING (Studien, 102), SOWERS (The Hermeneutics, 22), AMIR (EJ, 13, 411ff.), P. BORGEN (Observations, 86—8) maintain in various ways that the historical events and persons and the external observance and institutions are integral parts of Philo's religious life and thinking.

It should be emphasized that Philo and his fellow exegetes do not just offer a compromise between literal and allegorical methods. They are rather allegorists who used the Jewish people, its history, institutions, its religious convictions and values, and its relationship to the pagan surroundings as a hermeneutical key, not only to the literal wording but also to the spiritual principles found in Scriptures. Thus, Philo's allegorical system of ideas does not have as its primary 'locus' the spiritual life of each individual, but rather a collective, − the elected nation. Praem 65−66 makes this point in an explicit way in the treatment of the rewards given to Jacob's children: "This is the household, which kept safe from harm, perfected and united both in the literal history and in the allegorical interpretation, received for its reward, as I have said, the chieftaincy of the tribes of the nation. From this household, increased in the course of time to a great multitude, were founded flourishing and orderly cities, schools of wisdom, justice and religion, where also the rest of virtue and how to acquire it is the sublime subject of their research."

Philo applies this general attitude in such a way that at times he can discard the literal meaning altogether in specific passages (Quod Det 95. 167, etc.), or he can allow it to play only a limited role. (See HAY, SP, 6, 1979, 51.) Accordingly, he sometimes characterizes the faithful Jewish literalists as men of narrow citizenship (Somn I 39) and selfsatisfied pedantic professors of literalism (Somn I 102). He can also criticize the spiritualists correspondingly as those who "in a petty spirit find fault with the literal sense of the word, urging that it is irreligious and dangerous to speak of God as the portion of man" (Plant 70f.). Philo may then in several places stress the literal meaning, for example in Sobr 65.

In his replies to the scoffers who attack the Pentateuch and Judaism, Philo may stress the use of the allegorical method. At the same time he remarks that other Jews attempt to answer the attacks by means of literal exegesis (Conf 14; Mut 65ff.). It should also be added that Philo occasionally discusses the views of others which do not readily fall into the classifications of literal and symbolic exegesis, although they may be combined with such an approach. As an example, Agr 128−9 can be listed: "There are some whose definition of reverence is that it consists in saying that all things were made by God, both beautiful things and their opposites. We would say to these, one part of your opinion is praiseworthy, the other part on the contrary is faulty . . . ." (Cf. Leg all I 35; 59; III 204f.)

5. Allegorical interpretation

Much discussion has evolved around Philo's allegorical method and form of interpretation. The discussion mainly has centered on the question whether Philo here has as a background Greek allegorical methods (especially those employed by the Stoics in their interpretation of Homer), or Palestinian ones.

I. HEINEMANN (Altjüdische Allegoristik) found several parallel features of a general nature between Greek exegesis of Homer and Jewish exegesis of the Torah: 1. Both Homer and the Torah were classical and authoritative writings which were thought to contain all wisdom. 2. Greek and Jewish exegetes elaborated upon and developed the epic style and metaphoric style found in the texts. Nevertheless, two entirely different kinds of exegesis developed, due to different systems of thought: Greek exegesis, on the one hand, used both 'scientific' philological exegesis and philosophical and mystical allegories. The Jewish rabbis, on the other hand, interpreted the Biblical books into a concrete world picture, in which the analogy between earth and heaven was essential, and even philological knowledge served a practical interpretative purpose and was not 'scientific'. Jewish allegory was also used within this same context. According to HEINEMANN, the allegorical interpretations of the Bible in Hellenistic Judaism followed the Greek exegesis of Homer and adapted the Jewish writings to a way of thinking completely foreign to them.

A similar distinction to that made by HEINEMANN between Palestinian exegesis and Philo's allegory is made by L. TREITEL, MGWJ, 55 (N.F. 19), 1911, 551 (a concrete world view as opposed to an esoteric and mystical one) and R. P. C. HANSON, Allegory and Event, 63f. (typology versus non-historical speculations).

E. STEIN (Die allegorische Exegese, BZAW, 51) found that Philo follows the Stoic allegorical method with its natural and ethical allegorical interpretations, pushing natural allegory into the background and placing strong emphasis on ethical allegory. His ethical ideas are based on the concept of God. Moreover, this allegory finds a point of contact in the idealized picture of the Biblical persons in the haggada. His allegory is thus largely developed as an interpretation of the patriarchs and other Biblical persons, often by means of etymologies. Cf. B. MACK, SP, 5, 1978, 59–60, etc., who emphasizes the close connection between allegory and the praise (the Encomium) of the patriarchs.

FRANKEL thought that Philo drew on rabbinic principles and rules of exegesis and made them into rules for developing an allegorical interpretation: the text itself points in the direction of allegory when particular features occur, such as reduplicated expressions, seemingly superfluous words, tautologies, contradictory expressions placed closely together, etc. SIEGFRIED stresses that Philo has combined such 'rabbinic' points with the Stoic notions that allegory is to be used when a text does not make sense otherwise, or when something unworthy or immoral seems to be stated. At the same time, SIEGFRIED and FRANKEL realize that Philo usually keeps the literal meaning of the text. (Z. FRANKEL, Über den Einfluß der palästinischen Exegese auf alexandrinische Hermeneutik, 1 and 90ff., also 33, n.g. and 191, n.b.; ID., Programm zur Eröffnung des jüdisch-theologischen Seminars zu Breslau, 1ff. and 33ff., and C. SIEGFRIED, Philo von Alexandria als Ausleger des Alten Testaments, 160–97; cf. R. M. GRANT, The Letter and the Spirit, 35ff.)

The main contributions to the discussion of Philo's allegorical interpretation are made by H. A. WOLFSON, U. FRÜCHTEL, I. CHRISTIANSEN and G. DELLING in the period since World War II.

WOLFSON (Philo, 1, 117–38) stresses Philo's Jewish heritage: "The principle that Scripture is not always to be taken literally and that it has to be interpreted allegorically came to him as a heritage of Judaism; his acquaintance with Greek philosophic literature led him to give a philosophical turn to the native Jewish allegorical method of interpretation. The example of the Greek allegorical method, of course, helped and encouraged him and served him as a model" (138).

According to WOLFSON, no allegorical interpretation of a scriptural story meant the rejection of the story itself as a fact (126).

WOLFSON draws on HEINEMANN's study, Altjüdische Allegoristik. HEINEMANN concluded, however, that Philo's allegories adapted the Biblical writings to a way of thinking completely foreign to them, while WOLFSON regards Philo's allegories rather as having a philosophical bent developing out of the Jewish heritage.

FRÜCHTEL (Vorstellungen, esp. 119—26) and CHRISTIANSEN (Die Technik) understand Philo's allegorical interpretation within the context of Greek hermeneutical tradition. FRÜCHTEL writes that Philo took over the approach used in the exegeses of Homer: On the basis of a *tertium comparationis*, often in the form of a superficial similarity, physical, cosmological and general philosophical insights were found in the texts. Philo's interest in etymological interpretations, in play on words, etc. is also evidence for his dependence on Homer-exegesis. More specifically, Philo has as background Middle Platonism, where the philosophers no longer wanted to develop new and independent systems, but interpreted the old authorities and found their philosophical ideas present in their authoritative writings.

CHRISTIANSEN (Die Technik) agrees with FRÜCHTEL's approach: Philo followed the Greek philosophers of Middle Platonism in their recognition of the ancient authorities, and in their method of etymology and analogy (11f.). Like FRÜCHTEL she stresses the importance of the *tertium comparationis*, but does not find the point of comparison to be external and arbitrary. Such an understanding would divorce Philo's interpretation completely from the Biblical text. CHRISTIANSEN finds rather that the *tertium comparationis* has logical force. There is therefore a logical relationship between the Biblical text and the allegorical exposition (26—7).

On the basis of C. ANDRESEN, Logos und Nomos, CHRISTIANSEN moves on to a comprehensive study of the technique of allegorical interpretation. CHRISTIANSEN (Die Technik, 13—4) brings out four main points from AN-DRESEN's work: 1. Allegory is applied Platonic philosophy. 2. Allegory is not meant to be arbitrary exposition. 3. Allegorical exegesis reveals ideas. 4. The allegorical exegesis is a method of cognition which leads to the vision of God.

ANDRESEN does not deal in a specific way with the technique of allegory, which is played by CHRISTIANSEN in the center of the examination: Philo follows the dialectical method of *diairesis* in his exegesis. In this way he builds up a pyramid of concepts from the specific to the general and universal ideas: „*Das 'Allgemeine' zu erkennen, das sich im 'Besonderen' der heiligen Schrift offenbart, ist das systematische Ziel Philons von Alexandrien bei seinen Erklärungen des Alten Testaments*" (42 and 44).

Furthermore, the technique of symbolic interpretation is important for Philo's exegetical undertakings. In a symbol two concepts participate in one idea. The Scriptural word formulates one of the concepts. The other concept is defined by similarity or analogy. For example in Somn I 102—4 the Biblical term 'garment' (Ex 22:26) is a symbol of Logos, because of the following similarities: the garment 1. keeps off the mischiefs that are wont to befall the body from frost and heat; 2. it conceals nature's secret parts; 3. the raiment is a fitting adornment to the person. Similarly, Logos 1. is a weapon of defence against those who threaten him with violence; 2. Logos is a most necessary covering for men's sin; 3. Logos serves as an adornment of the whole life.

In his expository techniques Philo employs the ten Aristotelian categories, which he himself lists in Dec 30: substance, quality, quantity, relation, activity, passivity, state, position, time and place. For example, in Cher 26 it says that the flaming sword is the sun, that packed mass of flame, which is the swiftest of all existing things and whirls round the whole universe in a single day. Here, both the flaming revolving sword and the sun have the same substance, which makes them two concepts within the context of one idea (CHRISTIANSEN, Die Technik, 91).

To sum up, CHRISTIANSEN's definition of allegory is as follows: „*Die Allegorese ist eine Interpretationsform, mit der eine Ideeneinheit entfaltet wird, die das Schriftwort unentfaltet enthält, indem neben das Schriftwort ein gleichartiger Begriff gestellt wird, der allgemeiner ist als das entfaltete Schriftwort.*" (CHRISTIANSEN, 134).

CHRISTIANSEN shows that allegorical exegesis is not just arbitrary expositions of the Biblical text, but it has its method and inner logical structure. She also rightly stresses that, according to Philo, Moses — and his laws, — give a faultless revelation of the reality and the nature of all things. Her use of the ten Aristotelian categories needs to be modified, however, since they do not function as so important thought-categories throughout Philo's works (cf. B. MACK, SP, 3, 1974/75, 83, and SP, 5, 1978, 97. CHRISTIANSEN to a large extent overlooks, however, how allegorical methods and concepts are used by Philo to express and serve the cause of Judaism: In Philo's works the general and cosmic ideas and principles form a superstructure of the Laws of Moses as they governed and govern the self-understanding and the life of the Jewish nation. In this connection it must be added that CHRISTIANSEN unfortunately ignores the midrashim, Qumran, the New Testament and Josephus in her examination of background material and comparative material for the understanding of Philo's exegesis.

Further investigation should also consider this material and analyse further how Philo attempts to make the allegorical method serve his Jewish aims. Some of the points are: 1. Philo's allegorical interpretation is akin to the concept of prophecy and fulfillment: It spells out the abstract principles hidden in the Biblical text, so that these may be applied to the experience of the individual (cf. S. SANDMEL, JBR, 22, 1954, 249ff.; ID., Philo, 24—28; M. STONE, Judaism at the Time of Christ, 4—5) and the whole Jewish community, and can serve as key to the interpretation of specific events. In this way Philo uses allegorical interpretations for example in Somn I and II, and shows how Biblical dreams give foreknowledge of things to come (Somn I 2). In his allegories Philo thus develops principles which can in turn be applied to specific events such as the pogrom in Alexandria in 38. Flac and Gaium give examples of this kind of application as well as Somn II 110—38, etc. — R. BULTMANN, Glauben und Verstehen, 2, 1965, 162—3, has seen that there is a close relationship between the

Jewish concept of prophecy and fulfillment and Stoic allegory. Cf. also G.
DELLING, Josephus-Studien, 109–21, esp. 110 in his discussion of Josephus' view
on Biblical prophecy: „. . . *nicht zuerst die Vorstellung des Vorhersagens,
sondern die des Hervorsagens, des Heraussagens von Unbekanntem, des
öffentlichen Verkündens."* Moreover, Philo states that the Essenes make wide use
of the allegorical method. In this way he characterizes the kind of exposition
found in the Dead Sea Scrolls, in which the Biblical texts are applied to the life and
history of the Qumran community. See W. FARMER, IDB, 2, 149. 2. Philo makes
his allegory serve the Jewish conviction of election. This enables him to claim
elements from Greek philosophy of religion, of education and ethics, and
elements from mystery religions, etc. for the Jews and their sacred writings. Cf.
M. STONE, Scriptures, Sects and Visions, 88–89. 3. The allegorical interpretation is one way in which the wisdom of the Laws of Moses and the religious
practices of the Jewish nation can be declared to the Hellenistic world. In
this way it contributes to the task of making these laws known, a task in
Philo's view specially begun by the Septuagint translation of the Hebrew Torah
into the Greek language. 4. In his expositions, – both literal and allegorical, –
Philo weaves into the paraphrase elements and fragments from common Jewish
exegetical traditions. By doing this he fuses them with the extra-Jewish elements which he also uses. 5. The Jewish concept of unity between the people
and the patriarchs has encouraged Philo's allegorical interpretations. Consequently, Philo's ideas of the various aspects of the life of the Jewish nation
is attributed to the patriarchs and this interpretation of the patriarchs and of
Biblical events, makes his views into authoritative criteria for Jewish values.
Moreover, the Laws of Moses deal both with creation, – and thereby with the
cosmos and cosmic principles, – and also with the founding period of the chosen
people of the Jews. This fact gives Philo a Pentateuchal basis for his interpretation
of the Jewish nation and the rest of mankind within the context of cosmic
concepts of God, and of man's experience and ethical life.

6. Expository use of sources

A survey of the research on sources and traditions in Philo is given by R. G.
HAMERTON-KELLY, SP, 1, 1972, 3–26. HAMERTON-KELLY is too optimistic when
he maintains that the methods of source analysis as traditionally employed still
can be used. The history of research has shown that attempts to uncover sources
on a larger scale have not proved successful. Only limited and individual sources
have been identified with some degree of certainty.

This limited result of source analysis is due to the nature of Philo's writings:
they take the form of expositions. These expositions consist of exegetical
paraphrases of words and phrases from the Pentateuchal texts together with other
words and phrases. Philo (together with other exegetes in Alexandria) thus
weaves together parts of the Pentateuchal text and fragments from Jewish and
non-Jewish (Greek) traditions.

M. HARL has analysed along these lines cosmological ideas in the fragment De Deo, preserved only in Armenian. In this fragment there are both Greek and Jewish elements woven together. The chief Greek element is the idea that God is pilot of the world chariot; the chief Jewish element is the concept of God riding upon the chariot of the Cherubim. As Philo combined such varied traditions, his organizing force was the Jewish convictions and attitudes. The Greek terms are made to serve the Jewish point of view that God as creator governs the world. See M. HARL, PAL, 189—203; cf. the mixture of Jewish and Greek elements in Philo's exposition of Gen 1:3, where "God said" is interpreted as meaning Logos; BORGEN, NT, 14, 1972, 115—30.

The author of the present article has attempted to analyse in detail some parts of Philo's works along these lines. As an illustration, elements of Philo's exegesis of Gen 16:4 in Leg all III 162—8 can be mentioned. (See BORGEN, Bread, 1—20; 122—46.)

Leg all III 162: "That the food of the soul is not earthly but heavenly, we shall find abundant evidence in the sacred Word:

'Behold I rain upon you bread out of heaven,
and the people shall go out and they shall gather
the day's portion for a day,
that I may prove them whether they will walk by my
Law or not' (Ex 16:4.)

You see that the soul is fed not with things of earth that decay, but with such words as God shall have poured like rain out of that lofty and pure region of life to which the prophet has given the title of heaven."

167b: "And this is why he goes on with the words: that I may prove them whether they will walk in My law or not; for this is the divine law, to value excellence for its own sake . . . . . ."

Here the words from the Pentateuchal quotation are spaced. These words are in 167b paraphrased together with the stoic phrase 'to value excellence for its own sake', which also has close parallels in Palestinian Jewish traditions. See VON ARNIM, SVF, 3, 11; for Palestinian parallel, see Siphre on Deut 32:2 referred to in H. A. WOLFSON, Philo, 2, 279—303 and BORGEN, Bread, 122 and 126—7.

In the exposition in § 162, the words from Ex 16:4 are paraphrased together with terms from natural science, such as 'lofty' (μετάρσιος) and 'pure' (καθαρός) heaven. And the combination of the heavenly bread of manna and bread from the earth seems to be a fragment from haggadic stories about bread from heaven and bread from the earth, such as found in ExR 25:2; Mek Ex 16:4, Vita Mos I 201—2 and II 267.

The use of this distinction, in the form of a contrast between the heavenly food of the soul and the earthly food of the body, also reflects Platonic thought patterns and ideas. See Plato, Phaedrus 247 CD; 248 BC; 246 DE; Protagoras 313 C; Phaedo 84 AB.

The other expositions of Philo are also to be analysed from the view point that elements of Jewish tradition are woven into the exegetical paraphrase. For example, in Leg all I 48 Philo bases his argumentation on the common Jewish maxim that man is to imitate God (Ex R 26:2; Mek Ex 15:2, etc.; cf. BIL-LERBECK, I, 372). — In Leg all III 65 and in Gen R 20:2 and Num R 19:11 and B. Talmud Sanhedrin 29a the same question is taken up, why the serpent was not allowed to defend himself. — In Leg all III 251 Philo seems to draw on elements from exegetical traditions when he, as is also done in Jer. Targum, Gen 3:17f. (cf. Vita Adae and Evae chs 1—9), characterizes the grass that man had to eat, according to Gen 3:18, as the food of animals.

Even in details interesting features can be traced, for example about the ways in which philological observations serve an exegetical purpose. Thus a different reading can be rendered to confirm and define the meaning of a given text. (BORGEN, Bread, 64):

Migr 1 and 43:
"'into the land which I shall shew thee' (Gen 12:1) . . .
. . . He says not 'which I am shewing thee' but 'which I will shew thee'."

This form of philological exegesis occurs frequently in the midrashim, as for example in Mek Ex 15:11, where a corresponding formula occurs: אין כתיב כאן־אלא.

Examples of philological exegesis of just the opposite kind can also be given. Here the reading of a given text is changed or corrected in the same way as in the rabbinic אל תקרי־אלא (ibid., 63 and C. SIEGFRIED, Philo von Alexandria, 176):

Quod Det 47—48:
"'Cain rose up against Abel his brother and slew him' (αὐτόν) (Gen 4:8) . . .
It must be read in this way 'Cain rose up and slew himself' (ἑαυτόν), not someone else . . ."

Both problem-solving exegesis in the form of questions and answers and direct exegesis ('this is', 'this means', etc.) are employed. As the name indicates, Philo's Quaestiones et solutiones in Genesim et Exodum is a commentary in the form of questions and answers.

The Quaestiones has been compared with Philo's other commentary series, Legum allegoriae, since both have the form of running commentary based on verse(s) which are quoted from Pentateuchal books. E. SCHÜRER (Geschichte des jüdischen Volkes, 2, 1886, 836 and 838 and 4th ed., 3, 1909, 644 and 648, and C. COLPE, RGG, 3rd ed., 5, 342) have suggested that Quaestiones is a catechetical work of questions and answers, while Legum allegoriae is Philo's scholarly work.

SANDMEL (JBR, 22, 1954, 249; ID., Philo, 79—80) and BORGEN and SKARSTEN (SP, 4, 1976/77, 1—15) have, however, attempted to show that this hypothesis cannot be upheld since several passages in Legum allegoriae display the same form, method and problems as those found in Quaestiones. Such passages of question and answer are even built into the Exposition of the Laws of Moses, although in general it does not have the formal structure of an exegetical commentary. A similar conclusion is reached by V. NIKIPROWETZKY, Le Commentaire, 231—4.

Among the passages which have the same form of *quaestiones et solutiones* in the Exposition of the Laws of Moses, BORGEN and SKARSTEN examine Op 72–75 (what reason there could be for ascribing the creation of man, not to one Creator, but, as the words would suggest, to several), Op 77–88 (why man comes last in the world's creation) and Dec 36–43 (why, when all these many thousands were collected in one spot, He thought good in proclaiming His ten oracles to address each as to one). See also other examples of the form in Dec 2–17; 176–8, etc. In Op 77 as for example also in Quaes Gen I 43 the problem is that of an unexpected order and rank in the Pentateuchal story. In Op 72 and Dec 36, as in Quaes Gen I 15, the problems discussed are those of unexpected plural or singular forms of the verb.

The same form of *quaestiones et solutiones* are also found in the allegorical commentary. In Leg all I 101–4 (God first addresses the command to a single person, then He speaks to more than one) the very question is raised as in Quaes Gen I 15, with reference to Gen 2:16–17. Similarly, in Leg all I 85–87 and in Quaes Gen I 13 almost the same question is asked on the basis of surprising omissions in the text of Gen 2:10–14.

As indicated by these examples, there is no difference of content or substance where Quaestiones overlaps with parts of Legum allegoriae, a fact which shows that the same method and form of questions and answers are used in Philo's various writings.

Scholars as L. COHN (Einteilung und Chronologie, Philologus, Suppl. 7, 1899, 402f.) and R. MARCUS (PLCL, Suppl. 1, IX) have observed that Philo's *quaestiones et solutiones* in their form resemble Greek commentaries on the Homeric poems. E. E. HALLEWY (TA, 31, Dec 1961, 157–69, with English summary on pp. III–IV) has pointed out that the rabbinic expositions also show similarities with Homeric exegesis. See examples of Homeric commentary in H. SCHRADER, Porphyrii Quaestionum. For its use in Christian Exegesis, see CHR. SCHÄUBLIN, Untersuchungen, 49–51, and H. DÖRRIES, RAC, 6, 1966, cols 347–70.

As the investigation moves beyond the observations made by these scholars, it is seen that the form of *quaestiones et solutiones* seems to have been common to (Greek commentaries on Homer and both) Philo's and rabbinic expositions of the Laws of Moses. For example, a close parallel both in form and content exists between Philo's Op 77–78 and rabbinic exposition in Tosephta, Sanhedrin 8:7–9. In both places the problem raised is the biblical statement that Adam was created last. In both passages the problem is formulated as a question. Moreover, in both the answers are partly the same: the comparison is drawn between God and a human host, who invites the guest when the meal is made ready. Likewise God made man after the world had been created. Although the agreements do not prove that Tosephta's version is the source, Philo and the rabbinic Tosephta here are clearly rendering two versions of the same tradition. This conclusion is supported by Op 77 where Philo explicitly states that he has received the tradition from others, "those, then, who have studied more deeply than others the laws of Moses and who examine their contents with all possible minuteness . . . ."

BORGEN (Bread, 82–3) has analysed the argumentation and the phraseology used in one such kind of *quaestiones et solutiones*. The example is found in Mut 141a, 142b–144.

In this passage the following five points can be found: Point (1) has a quotation from the Old Testament, Gen 17:16. Point (2) gives the interpretation of the quotation. (No words from the Old Testament quotation are paraphrased here in Mut 142b, but the central term 'mother' clearly refers to the phrase 'from her' in the quotation cited in § 141a.)

Point (3) then raises the objection to the interpretation. Point (4) refers to and repeats the interpretation in point (2), which has been questioned.

Finally Point (5) refutes the objection and gives the solution of the problem. The end of this point refers back to point (2), the interpretation, by paraphrasing parts of it.

These five points and the exegetical and stylistic terminology in this passage show similarity to the expository passages in John 6:31b, 41–48 and Mek Ex 12:2, although there is no overlapping in the subject matter discussed.

The passage	Mut 141a. 142b–144	John 6,31b. 41–48	Mek Ex 12,2
1	Old Testament quotation	Old Testament quotation	Old Testament quotation
2	τρίτοι δέ εἰσιν οἱ – λέγοντες	εἶπεν	רבי שמעון בן יוחאי אומר
3	πρὸς δὲ τοὺς ζητοῦντας, εἰ	καὶ ἔλεγον οὐχ οὗτός ἐστιν	והלא
4	οἱ χρησμοὶ νῦν ὅτι – ὁμολογοῦσι	πῶς νῦν λέγει ὅτι	כיצד
5	λεκτέον ἐκεῖνο, ὅτι	ἀπεκρίθη ᾽Ιησοῦς καὶ εἶπεν αὐτοῖς	רבי אליעזר אומר

In the other, and often simpler, forms of *quaestiones et solutiones* Philo also uses exegetical formulas, even though he may do it in a flexible way. Some examples are collected by BORGEN and SKARSTEN (SP, 4, 1976/77, 1–15):

In Op 77–88 and Leg all I 91–92 the questions are introduced by phrases which have (ἐπι)ζητεῖν as the verb, followed by words for 'why': ἐπιζητήσειε δ᾽ ἄν τις τὴν αἰτίαν, δι᾽ ἣν . . . (Op 77); and ζητητέον δέ, διὰ τί . . . (Leg all I 91). In Op 72–75, Leg all I 85–87; 101–104 and Dec 36–43 the questions are introduced by phrases which have (δι)απορεῖν as verb: ᾽Απορήσειε δ᾽ ἄν τις οὐκ ἀπὸ σκοποῦ, τί δήποτε . . . (Op 72); ῎Αξιον δὲ διαπορῆσαι, διὰ τί . . . (Leg all I 85); διαπορητέον. ὅτε . . . (Leg all I 101); and δεόντως δ᾽ ἄν τις ἀπορῆσαι, τοῦ χάριν . . . (Dec 36).

The answers in Leg all I 85–87; 91–92; 101–104 and Dec 36–43 are introduced with phrases which contain the word λεκτέον: λεκτέον οὖν ὅτι . . . (Leg all

I 85—87); τί οὖν λεκτέον (Leg all I 19—92); λεκτέον οὖν τάδε, ὅτι . . . (Leg all I 101—104) and λεκτέον οὖν ἓν μὲν, ὅτι . . . (Dec 36).

The introductory phrases ἐπιζητήσειε δ'ἄν τις τὴν αἰτίαν, δι' ἥν . . . . . (Op 77) and Ἀπορήσειε δ'ἄν τις οὐκ ἀπὸ σκοποῦ, τι δήποτε . . . . . (Op 72), as well as the other phrases listed, are long forms for the corresponding use of διὰ τί which occurs frequently in the Quaestiones. This can be seen from the Greek fragments to Quaes Gen I 1; II 13, 62; IV 144, 145; Quaes Ex II 64, 65. This conclusion is also confirmed by passages such as Quaes Gen I 13, 15 and 43 where the Armenian equivalent to διὰ τί is used exactly like these longer phrases in the corresponding passages in Op, Leg all and Dec.

Finally, the phrases with λεκτέον which introduce the answers in Leg all and Dec are employed in cases for which in the Quaestiones there is often no introductory formula, or where διότι or ὅτι is used (Quaes Gen I 94; IV 145), or where another term (such as 'first', 'second', etc.) may be used.

As for Philo's direct exegesis, there is still much work to be done. M. ADLER (Studien zu Philon von Alexandreia) made a start in analysing the simple and complex structures of Philo's allegorical commentaries, but he did not pay sufficient attention to the exegetical activity which produced the commentaries and the exegetical paraphrase employed.

One example given by M. ADLER (Studien, 9—15) on the simple and brief structure of direct exegesis is found in Leg all I 16: "'He rested therefore on the seventh day from all His works which He had made' (Gen 2:2). This is as much as to say (τοῦτο δ' 'εστὶ τοιοῦτο) that God ceases moulding the masses that are mortal whenever He begins to make those that are divine and in keeping with the nature of seven. But the interpretation of the statement in accordance with its bearing on human life and character is this, that, whenever there comes upon the soul the holy Reason of which Seven is the keynote, six together with all mortal things that the soul seems to make therewith comes to a stop."

From the point of view of form, this example of brief and direct exegesis gives support to the view of R. MAYER (Die hermeneutische Frage in der Theologie, ed. O. LORETZ and W. STOLZ, 320—1) that Philo's exegesis shows formal agreements with the Pesher method of exegesis used among the Essenes of the Qumran: a brief scriptural quotation is followed by an exposition, and a transitional phrase, such as 'this means', etc., ties the quotation and the commentary together.

MAYER's classification of Philo's expositions as being similar to those in the Dead Sea scrolls is, however, inadequate. One reason is that the Dead Sea scrolls do not contain the kind of problem solving exegesis examined above. Here Philo and the rabbis show close agreement. What is more, even Philo's direct exegesis often demonstrates a much more complex structure and is far broader than the Essene expositions found in the Dead Sea scrolls.

Such a longer form of direct exegesis has been investigated by BORGEN (Bread, 28—58). The structure shows the following characteristics: A quotation from the Pentateuch is followed by an exegetical paraphrase which determines its exposition; this exposition can also be identified as a united whole by the similarity between the opening and concluding statements. Besides the main

10*

quotation from the Pentateuch (the text), there are subordinate quotations. Direct exegesis of this nature is found in Leg all III 162–8; 169–73; Sacr 76–87; and Mut 253–63, etc. Similar expository structures are found in the midrashim, for example Ex R. 15–52.

It is relevant to present afresh ADLER's (Studien, 22–3) list of formular phrases which are found in Philo's direct exegesis. Examples from Leg all I–III are:

ὃ δὲ λέγει, τοιοῦτόν ἐστιν (I 22).

τὸ δὲ τοιοῦτόν ἐστιν (I 27; III 78) τὸ δὲ τοῦτ᾽ ἐστιν (III 57) τοῦτ᾽ οὖν φησιν (III 60).

τουτέστι (a word explained by another word): I 29.54.74.92; II 45.62.77. 87.103; III 11.14.15.20.25.28.32.34.35.45.46.95.123.142.143.145.172. 230.231.232.242.244.

τουτέστι (a word or a phrase explained by a sentence) I 98; I 65; II 92.93; III 16.126.157.176.

τοῦτο δέ ἐστι (I 26.52.66; II 31.60).

ἴσον ἐστὶ τῷ (I 65; III 219.246).

(τὸ) ἴσον τῷ (III 51.189; III 119).

ὅπερ ἐστὶν ἴσον τῷ (III 247.253).

ὅπερ ἐστὶν (III 128), ὅπερ ἦν (I 74; III 37).

ὃ ἐστιν (III 45), ὃ ἦν (III 37).

ἀντὶ τοῦ (II 44).

On the basis of analyses of Philo's expository techniques also whole treatises should be examined to see how he weaves various elements of traditions together. A beginning along this line is made by HAMERTON-KELLY, in: Jews, Greeks, SJLA, 21, Leiden 1976 and aspects of such an approach are built into the program for the analysis of the Philonic Corpus, proposed by B. MACK, SP, 3, 1974/75, 71–112.

V. Conqueror or Conquered

1. Background

In this critical survey of research on Philo's writings and related matters it has so far been stressed that he worked as an exegete and wove together traditions and elements from various writings in his exposition. He was an interpreter of the Pentateuch among several in the Jewish community in Alexandria. Some differences and agreements among them are reflected in his writings. Philo's Pentateuchal interpretations have been produced within the context of his own and his compatriots' historical situation. They lived within the synagogal community, and at the same time they infiltrated the community of the Greek full citizens and pressed for full civil rights for the Jews. Correspondingly, Philo's writings reflect how the Jews in Alexandria sought for points of contact with the surrounding culture. They also evidence the hatred and enmity between Jews and gentiles, which reached its climax in the pogrom in 38 C.E. Philo, therefore, makes the Pentateuch interpret Jewish community life, and the fateful historical events which took place.

Was Philo then basically a Jew, or an intellectual pagan wearing Jewish robes? H. Ewald (Geschichte des Volkes Israel, 6, 243) thought that Philo was a Jew at heart and only put on Greek language and culture as an overcoat. Several scholars, however, have placed Philo fundamentally within the context of non-Jewish (pagan) Hellenism. M. Heinze (Die Lehre vom Logos, 259) saw in Philo a Hellenistic philosopher who adapted himself to Old Testament ideas. W. Bousset (Die Religion des Judentums, 3rd ed., 449—52) regarded Philo as a representative of ecstatic mystery piety. H. Windisch (Die Frömmigkeit Philos) laid emphasis on the Platonic form of dualism in Philo's theology and piety.

H. Leisegang (Philon, PW, 20,1, 1941, cols 1—50, and Id., Der Heilige Geist, I:1) interpreted Philo on the basis of Greek mysticism and the mystery cults. With variations in approach and emphasis R. Reitzenstein (Die hellenistischen Mysterienreligionen, 3rd ed., 223ff.), E. Bréhier (Les idées, 1908, 2nd ed., 1925) and J. Pascher ('Η Βασιλικὴ 'Οδός) set the Egyptian mystery cult in the center of their interpretations. E. R. Goodenough (By Light) also stressed the importance of the mystery cults, but he does not think that Philo himself originated this interpretation of Judaism. He was rather a witness to a wider tendency within Hellenistic Judaism to regard itself as a mystery. Goodenough (By Light, 6—10) formulates this hypothesis in this way:

The shreds of literature we have from Greek Judaism before Philo, and the full achievement recorded by Philo's time, indicate that the Jews were captivated by their neighbours' religion and thought. Yet since a Jew could not now simply become an initiate of Isis or Orpheus and remain a Jew as well, the . . . clever trick was devised . . . of representing the biblical personalities as Orpheus and Hermes-Tat, and explaining that the Jewish 'Wisdom' figure, by translation *Sophia*, was identical with that 'Female Principle in nature' which Plutarch identified as Isis. By Philo's time, and long before, Judaism in the Greek-speaking world, especially in Egypt, had been transformed into a Mystery.

The objective of this Judaism was salvation in the mystical sense. God was no longer only the God presented in the Old Testament: He was the Absolute, connected with phenomena by His Light-Stream, the Logos or Sophia. The hope and aim of man was to leave created things and to rise to immortality by climbing the mystic ladder, traversing the Royal Road, of the Light-Stream. The commandments of the Law were still carefully followed by most Jews, but they were secondary to the true Law in a platonizing sense, the streaming Logos-Nomos of God. Philo is the chief source for knowledge of details of this Mystery . . . He is, however, far beyond a crude stage of syncretism. He is looking not directly at Gentile mythology but at the Hellenistic mystic philosophy which made any mythology only a typology for its doctrines. The allegories of Philo are then not attempts at making Abraham, Moses, Sophia, and the Logos types of Orpheus, Isis or the Persian *pleroma,* but rather types of the ideas which Greek thinkers were forcing upon all mythology.

2. E. R. Goodenough, S. Sandmel and H. A. Wolfson

During and after World War II, Goodenough continued his research on his interpretation of Hellenistic Judaism as a mystery, especially in: An Introduction to Philo Judaeus, 1940, 2nd ed., 1962), in the monumental 'Jewish Symbols', 1–13, and in: IDB, 3, 796–99. In his 'An Introduction', 1940, 178–211, Goodenough discusses the transformation of the Biblical story and that of the Jewish rite. The transformation of story was done through the technique of the Greek Mystic philosophers. In this way Philo interpreted the Patriarchs as the royal priesthood which had the priestly power to bring others up into their own experience.

Is then Philo's Mystery a real mystery, or, as an ideological rather than a ritualistic mystery, only a figurative one? Goodenough finds this dilemma to be false, since real mystery in ancient usage is to be understood as teaching, with or without rites, which would lead the ' initiate' or ' disciple' out of matter into the eternal. And if mystic Judaism made use of rites, it would have used Jewish rites, transformed with pagan ideology, but externally unchanged. According to Goodenough, this latter alternative proves to be Philo's approach to the Jewish festivals. There is no trace of an initiatory rite for Jews into the Mystery. But for proselytes Philo changed circumcision into a sacrament, just as he made every Festival into a sacrament in the sense that it was a visible sign of an invisible, a mystic, grace.

In his 'Jewish Symbols' Goodenough tries to trace evidence for this widespread Judaism by means of archeological data on the use of mystical symbols. In order to recover the theology of this Jewish mystery religion, one has to rely on Philo. But most of the Jews were not theologians. They only felt and experienced by means of symbols and rites what Philo tried to explain.

Goodenough's research has many merits: He interpreted Philo as a representative of a movement in Judaism, and not as an isolated individual. Although Goodenough thought that pagan philosophy and mysteries had conquered this kind of Judaism, he nevertheless managed at the same time to observe that Philo was a patriotic Jew. It is also important that Goodenough drew on archeological material to throw light on Judaism in that period. In this way he follows the important trend championed by Tcherikover and Fuks in their use of papyrus. Finally, Goodenough is right in his emphasis on Philo's practical aim, namely, to lead men to the vision of God.

Many points of criticism can also be given: Goodenough's notion of a widespread pagan sacramental mystery was an exaggeration. His attempts to show that there existed an empire-wide, antirabbinic Judaism based on the idea and rites of a mystery, have failed. Although Goodenough was aware of (Jewish Symbols, 1, 8, 19f.) G. Scholem's research on early Jewish mysticism (Major Trends, 1941, 3rd rev. ed., 1961), his schematic and uniform understanding of rabbinic and normative Judaism made it impossible for him to see the variety of Palestinean Judaism before 70 A.D. and also after that time (see M. Smith, JBL, 86, 1967, 53–68). Moreover, Goodenough did not offer much help on Philo's exegetical activity and method.

S. SANDMEL follows GOODENOUGH's basic contention that Philo's view of Judaism differed from that of the rabbis as philosophical mysticism based on the Bible differed from halakic legalism. Philonic Judaism was the result of a hellenization which was as complete as was possible for a group which retained throughout its loyalty to the Torah, and the separateness of the group. SANDMEL does not, however, accept GOODENOUGH's view that Philo represented a large movement within Judaism. He thinks that Philo and his associates reflected a marginal, aberrative version of Judaism (SANDMEL, Philo's Place, Augm. ed., 1971, 211; ID., Philo, 140–7).

SANDMEL has, rightly, moved away from GOODENOUGH's emphasis on the transformation of Judaism to the model of mystery religions. SANDMEL rather defines Philo's practical aim as an existential actualization of the Biblical material: Philo's exegesis of Scripture includes his reading Scripture in full accord with his own view of Jewish religiosity; see SANDMEL, JBR, 22, 1954, 249–53. The philosophical matters were only secondary to Philo. They illustrated his principal purpose, to exhort his readers to travel on the 'royal road' to perfection (SANDMEL, Philo's Place, Augm. ed., 1971, XX–XXIV; ID., Philo, 24–5).

A different approach to Philo to that of GOODENOUGH and SANDMEL is attempted by H. A. WOLFSON. WOLFSON's study on Philo is part of a comprehensive project under the general title 'Structure and Growth of Philosophic Systems from Plato to Spinoza' (Philo, 1, VI), and he finds in Philo's writings the "foundations of religious philosophy in Judaism, Christianity, and Islam" as it is said in the sub-title of his two volume work.

While GOODENOUGH thought that Hellenization had transformed Judaism into a mystery, WOLFSON says that Philo represents "a Hellenization in language only; not in religious belief or cult . . . it did not cause them (the Jews) to change their conception of their own religion" (Philo, 1, 13). Philo uses terms borrowed from the mysteries in the same way as he uses terms borrowed from popular religion and from mythology, all of them because they were part of common speech (Philo, 1, 45–6), not because Philo meant Judaism to be a mystery.

According to WOLFSON, Philo was a great and unique philosopher: Philo ushered in the period of 'Mediaeval Philosophy' which was based on Scripture and revelation. In this way mediaeval philosophy was the history of the philosophy of Philo (Philo, 2, 439–60). Philo was the first religious thinker to make philosophy a handmaid to religion, and he first formulated the problem of the reconciliation of faith and reason: Just as the truths of revelation are embodied in Scripture, so the truth discovered by reason are embodied in a philosophic literature written primarily in Greek. Since God is the author both of the truths made known by revelation and of the truths discovered by reason, there can be no real conflict between them (Philo, 2, 446ff.).

In WOLFSON's interpretation Philonic thoughts are a philosophical derivation and development of Pharisaic Judaism. In his use of Greek philosophy Philo is rather critical of Stoicism, although he draws heavily on Stoic expressions. His philosophy of religion comes closer to Platonic ideas, but every Platonic teaching is examined critically.

With his belief derived from Scripture that from eternity God was alone and hence that God alone is uncreated Philo gave his own version of the philosophy of Plato, partly as an interpretation of Plato and partly as a departure from him. According to Philo God is superior to virtue and knowledge, and He created the intelligible world as well as the visible world (Philo, 1, 200—17). One of the most important features of Philo's revision of the Platonic theory of ideas is his application of the term Logos to the totality of ideas and his description for it as the place of the intelligible world, which in its turn consists of the ideas (Philo, 1, 293). With regard to the doctrine of God as such, Philo was the first philosopher known to have stated that God, in His essence, is unknowable and indescribable. Scripture teaches that God is not to be named, and under the influence of philosophic reasoning, this notion came to mean that God cannot be described or known. Those terms which in Scripture are predicated of God are according to Philo either used only for the purpose of instruction, or they are what philosophers call properties (Philo, 2, 149ff.).

In this way WOLFSON step by step discovers in Philo's writings a comprehensive and consistent system of philosophy of religion, a system of religious ethics included.

WOLFSON's work is a rich collection of important material on Philo, Judaism, Greek philosophy, etc. In spite of his main interest in philosophy of religion, he also pays attention to the actual situation of Hellenistic Judaism, with special reference to Alexandrian Judaism and Philo. Moreover, the large amount of parallels to Philonic ideas from rabbinic traditions give support for the hypothesis that Philo and at least parts of Palestinian Judaism had traditions in common and also that they at points show kinship where the ideas are formulated in different and independent ways.

WOLFSON's critics are right, however, when they maintain that he is much more systematic than Philo ever was. Thus, a Philonic system rather than Philo has been reconstructed. (See L. H. FELDMAN, CW, 54, 1960/61, 288.) As for WOLFSON's picture of Alexandrian Judaism, some critical remarks have been given previously (see above on page 112). Another point of criticism has to be emphasized: although WOLFSON realizes that Scripture and Scriptural exposition play a central role in Philo, he does not take seriously that Philo was an exegete, and not a systematic theologian. Philo's inconsistencies, varied emphases and forms of presentation point in the direction that he, as an exegete, found all true wisdom in Scripture, that he drew on various exegetical traditions, and reflected different applications in different situations (Cf. L. H. FELDMAN, op. cit., 288 and BORGEN, Bread, 99f.; V. NIKIPROWETZKY, Le Commentaire.) Consequently, Philo was not a unique individual philosopher as WOLFSON thinks, but an exegete among fellow-exegetes, and a representative of a trend in Alexandrian Jewry.

3. Gnostic and other interpretations

Although Philo clearly draws on various philosophical schools and religious traditions and cults, many scholars have felt that it was inadequate to refer his different ideas to these various schools and religious traditions. One reason was the fact that what he owed to each school of philosophy, etc., could not be clearly distinguished. As a result, scholars attempted to interpret Philo on the background of the religious syncretism of the period, as in gnosticism, or the mixture of philosophical schools in Middle Platonism or Middle Stoicism. The interpretation of Philo on the background of the gnostic movement is to be treated first. The main contributions are here made by E. KÄSEMANN, Das wandernde Gottesvolk, and H. JONAS, Gnosis, II:1. These scholars understand Philo as a person who lived in the tensions and contradictions mainly between Judaism and hellenistic-oriental gnosis.

KÄSEMANN (Gottesvolk, 45ff.) draws on PASCHER's study, ῾Η Βασιλικὴ ῾Οδός, der Königsweg zu Wiedergeburt und Vergottung bei Philon von Alexandrien, 1931, where the royal road means the journey of the soul from the visible world to the spiritual world and then to God. KÄSEMANN goes beyond PASCHER's study, however, when he discusses Philo's concept of Logos in its relationship to the concept of the high priest and the idea of an 'Urmensch'. He concludes that Philo's concept of Logos has received features from the gnostic 'Urmensch'. And, since Philo also gives Logos the role of being high priest, he has the idea of an 'Urmensch — Erlöser' as well (Gottesvolk, 132—4).

FRÜCHTEL (Vorstellungen, 35, n. 1) criticizes KÄSEMANN (Gottesvolk) that he was overlooked the fact that there is not in Philo identity between the Prototype (= Logos) and Adam. There is in Philo no evidence for the hypothesis of an 'Urmensch — Erlöser'. She maintains, however, that Philo has contributed to the kind of exegesis of Gen 1:26f., which in gnosis developed into the idea of the god Anthropos (FRÜCHTEL, Vorstellungen, 4 and 34, n. 6). A similar conclusion is reached by A. J. M. WEDDERBURN, NT, 15, 1973, 301—26. According to FRÜCHTEL (Vorstellungen, 17f. and 40) rather the world view of Middle Platonism was known to Philo and was used by him. It consisted of the following points: 1. the trans-heavenly God, 2. the divine reason or the place of the ideas, as a second god, 3. soul as part of cosmos. This world view is then in gnosis developed into a soteriological system, but there is no relation of dependency between Philo and gnosis.

In a corresponding way M. SIMON, in: Le origini, SHR, 12, 1967, 359—76, stresses that Philo only has a modified dualism, which does not agree with any of the gnostic systems. The reason is that Philo is committed to the Bible as source of revelation. S. SANDMEL, Philo's Place, Augm. ed., 1971, XVI, rightly finds that Philo can produce elements which are akin to gnostic thoughts and attitudes, but on the whole central gnostic ideas are lacking: "I see no trace of a fallen god; I see, however, fallen man in Eden. I see no benighted creator; I see, however, the logos as the creator. As to a sinister creation, I see in Philo the view that this world of appearance is rather sinister, and that the sage is indeed an alien soul in this world. I do not see cosmic captivity or acosmic salvation; I do see salvation of the prison of the body. I do not wonder at the absence of a fallen god, for Philo was a staunch Jew; in light of Genesis 1, and the repeated refrain of 'God saw and it was good', Philo could scarely admit of a benighted creator." A similar conclusion is reached by B. A. PEARSON, Philo and the Gnostics and by R. McL. WILSON, Kairos, 14, 1970, 213–19.

JONAS (Gnosis II:1, 38; ID., in: Le origini, SHR, 12, 1967, 374–5) attempts to trace gnostic elements in Philo's use of the term "virtue", ἀρετή. He thinks that in Philo the Stoic-Platonic concept of virtue is hollowed out by Jewish and crypto-gnostic motives on the basis of a dualism between heaven and earth, soul and body. This transformation is seen by the non-Greek idea that virtue comes from above, like the manna, without co-operation by men (Mut 258, etc.), leaving the soul to have no καλόν of her own. THYEN (TR, N. S. 23, 1955, 243) accepts JONAS' interpretation.

BORGEN (Bread, 99–121) analyses one of the texts referred to by JONAS, namely Mut 258. He shows that in Philo's exposition of Gen 17:19ff. and Ex 16:4 in Mut 253–63 there is no such dualism between heaven and earth, soul and body, being developed. JONAS is right when he thinks that the Greek concept of virtue is transformed, but this transformation is caused by a collision between Greek educational ideas on the one hand, Ex 16:4 and fragments from haggadah about the manna on the other.

This collision reflects moreover the actual position of Judaism in Alexandria, where the relationship between the Jewish philosophy of the Synagogue, and the non-Jewish encyclical education was a burning question. Hence the teaching of the *encyclia* is compared to farming by help of teachers as laborers, while the 'virtue' and 'wisdom' of the synagogal philosophy are the bread from heaven which comes without co-operation by men, i. e. comes as God-given revelation. JONAS is positively wrong when he cites Mut 258 to show that Philo does not leave any καλόν to man. In Mut 253–63 Philo clearly says that the earthly and human aspect also has its virtue, although of a different kind from the heavenly one: "Thus each virtue (ἑκατέρας ἀρετῆς), one where the teacher is another, one where the teacher and learner are the same, will be open to human kind" (Mut 263).

Under the influence of H. JONAS and his teacher C. MENSCHNIG, F. N. KLEIN (Lichtterminologie) also employs a gnostic interpretation of Philo. KLEIN's concern is not to use philological and historical method as such to understand Philo, but to analyse the structure of religious language (IXf., etc.).

He wants to find out the way in which God is called light, whether light is part of the divine reality itself or it is a way in which the divine reality is expressed. The alternatives are therefore a concrete and 'physical' use of light as a religious term or a metaphorical use for the religious reality as *das ganz Andere* (74, 204f.).

KLEIN's analysis shows that there is a similarity in outlook between Philo and the Hermetica: they represent a spiritual form of religious piety over against a materialistic and external form. Although this conclusion has some truth in it, KLEIN has difficulties in fitting Philo into his alternatives of either concrete or metaphorical use of the term light. Philo mixes both together (68–78, 207f.).

This difficulty indicates that KLEIN imposes modern categories ('*das ganz Andere*', etc.) on Philo to make his analysis inadequate.

Moreover, KLEIN ignores almost completely the question of possible agreements between Philo and Palestinian Judaism, and the question of common Jewish traditions being interpreted differently in various parts of Judaism. Thus KLEIN mentions only in passing, in a footnote (41, n. 3), Philo's use of the common Jewish idea that the religion and piety of the Jews are characterized as light (Leg Spec I 54).

Another modernizing approach to Philo's thoughts is made by KLAUS OTTE, Das Sprachverständnis. In this book HEIDEGGER's existentialism determines the argument. Consequently, the book revolves about the problem of the relation between speech and Being (p. 3f.) and the concluding chapter relates Philo's understanding of language to the contemporary discussion concerning speech, mainly the discussion among HEIDEGGER and his disciples. Philo's theory of language belong to the same type as that of HEIDEGGER: language is created by man's encounter with the subject matter, it is a result of this encounter (148).

There is, however, a basic difference between HEIDEGGER and Philo: the Being which evolves itself in language is according to HEIDEGGER a historical Being, whereas it is an eternal Being according to Philo. In other words, according to HEIDEGGER, speech is the house of Being, whereas, according to Philo, it is only the door, only a means through which Being expresses and reveals itself (149f.). Thus, Philo's theory of language is imbedded in an idealism. He understands, however, the relationship between the pattern and the copy, between the divine Logos and wordly events, as a dynamic relation between the Creator and the world, a *creatio continua*. In this way Philo avoids the static and passive schematism which often belongs to idealism (101).

This modern presentation of Philo's thoughts has its merits: it removes to some extent the feeling of distance and estrangement which modern men, scholars included, sometimes experience when they try to understand Philo, especially his use of etymologies, allegory, etc. Furthermore, OTTE points to the fact that Philo's understanding of reality gives a new context and new meaning to the many various elements to which he takes over from Greek philosophy, etc. For example, when Philo draws on the ten Aristotelian categories in his allegories (see I. CHRISTIANSEN, Die Technik), his selection and use of these categories have to be understood within the context of Philo's specific understanding of Being (OTTE, Das Sprachverständnis, 58–9, and 59, n. 44). Although OTTE's understanding of Philo's allegory is inadequate, he touches one significant aspect of it when he defines Philo's allegorical method as a way in which Being is brought to expression (19ff.).

OTTE's study shows severe weakness, however. The main weakness is the anachronistic treatment of Philo. In this way the term 'Being' is introduced at almost every point of the argument and it gives to Philo's thoughts a colour that is more Heideggerian than Philonic. There is rather a need for an energetic study of Philo's understanding of language against the background of his own contemporary time, i. e. against the background of the understanding of language elsewhere in Judaism and in the Hellenistic world.

R. A. BEAR (Male and Female) is much more cautious in his method, almost too cautious. Thus he only examines the correlations of ideas and motifs between Philo and some gnostic texts without defining the relationship further.

For Philo the male-female polarity symbolizes the dichotomy between the rational and eternal, on the one hand, and the irrational and perishable, on the other, according to BEAR. In other words, the term 'female' generally refers to the material, sense-perceptible realm, which includes the sexual male-female relation, whereas 'male' refers to the realm which is intrinsically asexual, the sphere of Logos and ultimately of God himself.

BEAR makes a comparison between Philonic ideas and ideas in some gnostic texts. Philo is distinct from most of the gnostics insofar as he never uses sexual-mythical metaphors in describing the creation of the world and the rational soul of man. For Philo, the categories male and female function within the realm of creation and are not used, as they are, for example, in Valentinianism, to describe the fallible, erring part of the Godhead. For Philo, God is asexual, i.e. completely beyond or outside of the male-female polarity (Male and Female, 66). Nevertheless, both in Philo's writings and in the Pseudo-Clementines, for example, man is understood to make progress in the moral and spiritual life by fleeing from that which is female (Male and Female, 68).

BEAR has taken up a topic that to some extent has been neglected in Philonic research. His work serves well as an initial examination of the subject. Some aspects should be dealt with more fully, such as ideas of conception, birth and rebirth. The background of the ideas in Pythagorean traditions, Greek religion, Jewish traditions, etc. is only touched in passing.

Moreover, the relationship between the various ideas about male-female and Philo's view of the Jewish nation needs to be discussed. For example, BEAR stresses that the forsaking of the sphere of sense-perception — the realm of the female — means the change from duality to unity, the quality of the monad. Philo sees the number seven (the virgin, the motherless, begotten by the father of the universe alone, well-gifted by nature for sovereignty and leadership, etc.) as being most closely related to the monad, the beginning of all things. BEAR's main reference is Dec 102. This passage however, is part of Philo's interpretation of the main institution of the Jews, the Sabbath (Dec 96–105). Thus, the number seven and the monad are fundaments of the people of the Sabbath, the Jews, and the change from the sphere of sense-perception therefore means the change from heathen qualities to Jewish.

More independently of the gnostic interpretation of Philo, B. L. MACK, Logos und Sophia, interprets Philo largely on the basis of the Isis-Osiris mythology (cf. BRÉHIER, PASCHER, GOODENOUGH). According to MACK the Wisdom theology between Proverbs and Philo developed after certain thought-models. Three models were typical: 'the hidden', 'the near', and 'the disappeared' Wisdom. In the creation of 'the hidden' and 'the disappeared' types of Wisdom the Jews took Egyptian Isis-mythology as category of thinking.

In Philo the traditional dualism between 'the hidden' and 'the near' aspects of Wisdom was replaced by 'the heavenly' and 'the earthly' Wisdom. Moreover, the Logos concept was in the process of replacing the term Sophia. The Logos term was employed as the (Stoic) 'right reason', the *nomos* (Torah), etc. Although the Isis-Osiris mythology served as the most important analogy to these thoughts of Philo, the influence from Greek philosophy is quite obvious.

Mack realizes rightly the creative thinking of the Jews in the development of the Wisdom theology, and so also in Philo. Thus the thought of Philo expresses and serves Jewish concerns and aims. He seems, however, to overestimate the role played by the Isis-Osiris mythology. Therefore it would have proved fruitful to his study if he had paid more attention to cosmological trends within Palestinian Judaism (with its emphasis on the categories of heaven and earth) on the one hand, and on the Hellenistic developments of Greek philosophy (Middle Platonism, etc.) on the other hand. Moreover, more emphasis should also be placed on Philo's thoughts as a result of his activity as an exegete in discussion with other Jewish exegetes as well as with persons and groups in the Hellenistic world around him.

4. Middle Platonism and Philo

In the study of Greek philosophy an understanding has developed that the time before Neo-Platonism, i.e. before 200 A.D., should be characterized as a period of its own, Middle Platonism. This period began in the first half of the 1st century B.C., and the leading philosophers were Poseidonios, Antiochos from Askalon, Albinos, and Gaius and his school.

Some recent studies place Philo within this context. The main works are Theiler (in: Parusia. Festschrift für Johannes Hirschberger, 1965, 199—218, Id., in: Philomathes. In Memory of Philip Merlan, 1971, 26—35), Früchtel (Vorstellungen), Christiansen (Die Technik) and Whittaker (God, time, being), J. Dillon (The Middle Platonists, 139—83); cf. M. Hengel, The Son of God, 51 ff., esp. n. 103.

The most comprehensive work among these studies is Früchtel's monograph, 'Die kosmologischen Vorstellungen bei Philo von Alexandrien'. Her thesis is as follows: Philo was challenged by the contemporary philosophy, and he has accordingly interpreted Scripture on the basis of specific philosophical presuppositions. Through Philo ideas and attitudes from Middle Platonism have made history.

Früchtel analyses on this background Philo's cosmological concepts, centered around the ideas of cosmos as God's *polis*, as God's plant, and as God's temple. Philo's idea of creation by means of division is also discussed (Vorstellungen, 7—115). These cosmological traditions present many differences and express contradicting tendencies. As a result, scholars have characterized Philo's ideas very differently. They have called him a Neo-Pythagorean, a Neo-Platonic, a thinker to be compared with Middle-Stoicism, and in ethics his thoughts show similarities with Cynic-Stoic *diatribe*.

According to Früchtel, it is insufficient to refer Philo's different ideas to various philosophical schools, or characterize him as an eclectic. „Was Antiochos,

*der Vertreter des mittleren Platonismus, und Philo, der am Alten Testament
orientierte Theologe, machen, ist eigentlich keine Auswahl, sondern ein Sammeln mit Methode unter einem bestimmten Telos. Dieser Sammelvorgang ist
nur verständlich, wenn Philo wie alle mittleren Platoniker davon überzeugt ist,
daß diese Lehren ein- und dieselben Aussagen enthalten und sich nur
terminologisch unterscheiden. Philosophie treiben heißt, wie schon gesagt, der*
ratio *und der* auctoritas *der veteres folgen . . . . . Dieses Sammeln von Lehren bei
der gleichzeitigen Überzeugung von der einen Wahrheit hat eine Parallele im
gleichzeitigen Mysterienverständnis. Es gibt viele Mysterien, sie meinen aber alle
ein und dasselbe . . . Dieselbe Tendenz finden wir bei Philo. Er würde es
natürlich weit von sich weisen, sich in verschiedene heidnische Mysterien einweihen zu lassen, aber er kennt neben den 'Mysterien des Mose' noch andere
Mysterien innerhalb des Alten Testaments und fordert seine Leser auf, sich in sie
alle einweihen zu lassen."* (Vorstellungen, 129–30). Corresponding to the philosophical interpretations of the mysteries in Middle Platonism, Philo's mystery
is developed at the desk in the study and not in mystery cult (ibid. 112, 130f).

In her analysis FRÜCHTEL offers interesting criticism of WOLFSON and
GOODENOUGH. WOLFSON is criticized for regarding Philo a synthesizing philosopher who draws in an eclectic way on ideas from various schools. In this
way WOLFSON ignores the approach by Middle Platonic philosophers, their
respect for the old authorities, their concept of truth behind their seemingly
eclectic method (Vorstellungen, 2 and n. 2, 107, n. 1).

FRÜCHTEL agrees with GOODENOUGH that Philo has no independent and
purely cosmological ideas. They rather serve the aim of cognition, more precisely,
the aim of knowing and seeing God (Vorstellungen, 144–63). She criticizes,
however, GOODENOUGH in particular at two points: 1. Philo does not organize
the powers in a hierarchical 'stream of Light-Power', as GOODENOUGH thinks
(By Light, 243, etc.) Neither is it adequate to talk about emanations to describe
Philo's understanding at this point. FRÜCHTEL (Vorstellungen, 21–7) rightly
stresses that the main passages on this question, Quaes Ex II 66ff. and Fug 94f.,
each give different pictures about the structures of the powers. And Logos is not
to Philo an emanation from God nor is Logos product of divine intercourse. To
Philo, Logos is rather God's created *eikon* (FRÜCHTEL, Vorstellungen, 15, 26f.).
2. GOODENOUGH defended the theory of a Jewish mystery cult, while FRÜCHTEL
regards Philo's mystery as a philosophical product only (see above).

FRÜCHTEL's study needs to be modified and supplemented at two points:
1. Philo's writings should not onesidedly be regarded as works developed at the
desk in the study, since they reflect their background in the synagogues. 2. Philo
fuses together Jewish exegetical traditions and philosophical ideas. Philo's interpretation of the parable of the architect illustrates how he weaves together Jewish
exegetical traditions and philosophical ideas:

In Op 15–25 Philo interprets the phrase 'one day' in Gen 1, 5. The main
body of the exposition consists of a parable about the architect who built a city,
to illustrate how God created the world.

The picture of the Creator as an architect also occurs in the rabbinic writings.
Without discussing the dating of this material, we shall use it for comparison

with Philo, Op 15—25, to examine features which are common to both, and in this way also to define Philo's distinctive philosophical exegesis.

Philo tells about an architect who made a model of the various parts of the city he was to build. Similarily, Pirqe de-R. Eliezer III, portrays a king who wanted to build a palace, and first modelled on the ground its foundations, entrances and exists. According to Philo, the architect thought out in his mind how he should build. Similarly, in an anonymous midrash, it is stressed that the man first sat and calculated how he wanted the building, E. E. URBACH, The Sages, 200—1. An important point to Philo is the idea of the Word of God, when he was engaged in the act of creation. Similarly, the parable of the architect in the anonymous midrash is supported by Psalm 33:6: "By the word of the Lord the heavens were made".

In his use of the parable of the architect Philo thus to a large degree stays within the context of Jewish exegesis of the creation story. Nevertheless, Philo develops a philosophical exegesis on this basis. He focuses the attention on the intellectual activity of the architect, and in this way the model is not an empirical sketch or model, but the image of the city in the mind of the architect. Thus, the parable expresses the idea that the model of the world is the intelligible world (of ideas) conceived by God before he created the world perceived by the senses.

Here Jewish exegetical tradition about God as architect and Platonic terminology and thought categories are brought together in a synthesis. Philo transforms the Platonic elements, however. First he understands these Platonic ideas to be teachings present in the Torah revealed to the Jewish people through Moses. Second, the Platonic ideas are modified due to Philo's Jewish emphasis on God's exclusive character. While the model (*paradeigma*) of Plato's 'Timaeus' was something independent of the Demiurge, the model in Philo's exegesis becomes God's creation. As shown by J. DILLON, The Middle Platonists, 93—5; 158—9 Philo's interpretation probably has been furthered by similar trends in Middle Platonism, as for example in Antiochus of Ascalon (born 130 B.C.). Antiochus identified the Demiurge with the Stoic Pneuma-Logos, and thus the paradigm of 'Timaeus' is but the content of the intellect of the Logos, on the pattern of which the physical world was constructed. Philo is the first, however, known to explicitly state that the model, the intelligible world, is God's creation.

A corresponding philosophical exegesis is found in Philo's understanding of God's Word, Logos. Philo's phrase "the Logos of God who brings creation about (Op 24 ..... θεοῦ λόγον ... κοσμοποιοῦντος), may echo Psalm 33:6 "By the Word of the Lord the heavens were made", and can in itself be understood as God's creative and spoken word, as in the Old Testament. Philo blends this concept of God's Logos, however, with Platonic and Stoic terminology, in a way resembling the views of Middle Platonists. (See J. DILLON, Middle Platonists, 5 and 159—60.) He thus identifies Logos, a technical term of Stoicism, with the Platonic intelligible world. Logos is then not here defined as God's spoken word, but as his reasoning activity when He is engaged in the act of creation. As a Jew, Philo stresses, however, that Logos is G o d's, the Creator's, Logos. In this way Philo saw in Gen 1—2 the description of a double creation, first that of the intelligible world — which is Philo's interpretation of Gen 1:5 "one day" —, and then that of the sensible world.

5. A conqueror, on the verge of being conquered

It remains to give a summary of some main points and to add some concluding remarks on the approach to follow in the interpretation of Philo's ideas and concerns.

1. Philo was an exegete who interpreted the Pentateuch and Jewish exegetical traditions into his contemporary situation, without cutting off their historical basis in the Biblical events. The contemporary situation of Philo's Jewish community contained such factors as the Jews' relationship to Greek education, to political and economic career, and to mixed social life. It also comprised political and sociological factors and events, as the tension and interaction among Jews, Egyptian and Greek communities in Alexandria as well as Rome. Moreover, Philo's situation was influenced by Greek philosophy of religion and education, and by pagan religions.

Philo was not a system-building philosopher, but he was one exegete among the other exegetes in the synagogues, and he represented one trend among the Jews to meet the challenge of their time.

2. Philo shared the common Jewish view that the Jewish nation was the center of the world, and that this nation was called by God to have world dominion. This point has been demonstrated by TCHERIKOVER and FUKS (Corpus, 1, 78): Philo regarded the Jews as the chosen people who played the role of priests for the whole universe and had received from God the divine Law, equally suitable for Jews and Greeks.

Against this background further research is needed on Philo's (eschatological) expectations and goals for the chosen people as world conquerors. For example, according to Philo, the offices of Moses are fundamental to the Jewish people and their divine call in the world. As for kingship, Moses was the king of a nation destined to be consecrated above all others to offer prayers forever on behalf of the human race that it might be delivered from evil and participate in what is good (Vita Mos I 149).

As for his office as law-giver, Moses was the best of all law-givers in all countries, and his laws are most excellent: they are firm and secure and will endure as long as the universe exists, and almost every other people to some extent shows respect to the laws of the Jews, such as the Sabbath and the Day of Atonement. And the supreme proof of the universal acceptance of the laws of Moses is the Septuagint translation of them into Greek, ordered by king Ptolemy Philadelphus himself, an occasion celebrated annually on the island of Pharos, where both Jews and others participate (Vita Mos II 12—186).

As for his office as high priest, Moses established the priesthood in Israel, and the priestly tribe was the nucleus of all mankind as regards the blessed eschatological life to come (Vita Mos II 186). Finally, his office of prophet was particularly applied to the defence of the Jewish religion, and to prophecies about the things which were to come to pass for Israel (Vita Mos II 187—291).

Philo's purpose is in this way to show the divine calling of Moses and the Jewish people to worship God, keep the Sabbath and serve the whole world. Philo expects that the new (eschatological) era might come when all nations will throw overboard their ancestral customs and honour the laws of Moses alone (Vita Mos II 43—44).

Especially in Praem Philo draws on common Jewish eschatological expectations (see F. DEXINGER, Kairos, 3—4, 250—5 and G. DELLING, HUCA, 45, 1974, 158—9). When the cosmic Law (made concrete in the Laws of Moses) is kept, the era of peace among animals and nations will materialize. Also here the Jews are to serve as head nation (Praem 93 ff., 114, 125, cf. Vita Mos II 44 and Somn I 175—6, 215). In Gaium 3 this central role of the Jews is stated explicitly: The Jewish nation, whose God is the Creator, is the race of suppliants in the sense that they serve as link between God and man. God's care for all men is in a sense the outcome of this care for the Jews.

SANDMEL (Philo's Place, Augm. ed., 1971, XXf.) is right when he states that Philo is concerned with the religious experience of every man. It should be added, however, that Philo does not therefore ignore the notion of the Jewish nation and its Biblical history. To Philo, true man is a Jew, and therefore his doctrine of man and his doctrine of the chosen nation are one. Accordingly, the others are to become Jews and obey God's revealed Laws in order to be true men. It is therefore correct when B. L. MACK, SP, 1, 1972, 27—55, states that Philo's cosmology is not merely the result of speculation, but is intended to interpret anew the nature and destiny of Israel in cosmic-universal terms.

3. When Philo draws on Greek philosophy and various notions from pagan religions, etc., his intention is not to compromise Jewish convictions and aims. He is not interested in making a synthesis between Judaism and Hellenism as such, nor does he intend to transform Judaism on the basis of Hellenistic philosophy and religion. Philo's intention is to conquer the surrounding culture ideologically by claiming that whatever good there is has its source in Scripture and thus belonged to the Jewish nation and its heritage. In this way Philo represents the dynamic and offensive movement of the Jews who infiltrated the environment of the Alexandrian citizens around the *gymnasium*, as reflected in Claudius' letter to the Alexandrians (see above p. 112f.).

Some examples of Philo's attitude and view should be given. When Philo in his philosophy of education transforms allegorical ideas about Penelope and her maids into Sarah and Hagar, he claims this allegory for Judaism so as to interpret its point of view as to encyclical education on the borderline between Jews and gentiles. Philo thinks that ideas which he found in Hellenistic philosophy of Platonic/Pythagorean/Stoic nature were already present in the writings of Moses. In that way he makes claim on them for his Jewish religion and for the high self-understanding of the Jews as the chief nation of the world. The Jews who observe the Laws of Moses are the ones who are cosmopolitan, since these laws are universal and cosmic (Op 3). The treatise Jos is written with the purpose to suggest that the real source for the highest political ideal, the ideal of a divinely appointed and guided ruler, has had its truest presentation in Jewish literature, and highest exemplification at a time when a Jew, Joseph, was prefect of Egypt (cf. GOOD-ENOUGH, The Politics, 62).

Greek ideas of the virtues are according to Philo Scriptural, as he shows by examples from the Pentateuch (Leg Spec IV 136—238, etc.). In his references to examples and persons outside Judaism, Philo can use various lines of argumentation. In his discussion of the free men (in: Quod Omn) he says that the various levels of freedom of the worthy man receives their full dimension and true expression in Moses and in those who follow him in worshipping the Self-existent only. At several places Philo maintains that the Greek philosophers drew their thought from Moses and his Laws, Heres 214, Leg all I 108, Leg spec IV 61, Post 133, Quaes Gen IV 152, Quod Omn 53—7, Congr. 176. In agreement with this Philo pictures Moses as the embodiment of all knowledge and wisdom. Although Moses had Egyptian and Greek teachers, he was independent in his apprehension so that he seemed a case rather of recollection than of learning (Vita Mos 21 ff.).

4. A basic problem and concern reflected in Philo's expositions is the question: what do the Jews share in common with all other men and what is their own distinctive character? This question is dealt with in a variety of ways. For example, in his philosophy of education Philo at times draws a sharp distinction between the *encyclia* (i. e. Hagar and Ishmael), which is based on cultivation and training by teachers, and the Jewish wisdom (i. e. Sarah) which is selftaught and intuitive, based on vision. In twentieth century terminology this viewpoint would be expressed by drawing a distinction between the human knowledge communicated by teachers and the knowledge which comes by revelation. (See BORGEN, Bread, 108—11). According to Philo, therefore, the Jews have school-knowledge in common with other men, but the wisdom and vision of God revealed in Scripture and coming especially on the Sabbath (Mut 253—63) are distinctive to the Jews.

Against this background also aspects of Philo's doctrine of God are better understood. Several scholars have pointed to his contradicting statements between the knowability and unknowability of God. FRÜCHTEL as one deals with this problem in various ways. She distinguishes in Philo's thought between the lesser mystery in which God is known through creation and the greater mystery in which man experiences the vision of God himself. The distinction can also be made between gaining knowledge of God through reason, and knowledge through revelation. Philo's basic notion is the view that no man can by his own power know God, because God is unknowable and invisible to men. Revelation thus is God's sovereign act: to know God means that man is being known by God, to see God means that God sees man (Post 11, Abr 79f., Somn I 68). See FRÜCHTEL, Vorstellungen, 107—10, 144—71; cf. E. MÜHLENBERG's discussion of the problem of revelation in Philo, ZNW, 64, 1973, 1—18. — FRÜCHTEL's and MÜHLENBERG's discussions of these questions need to be placed more sharply within the distinction presupposed and made by Philo between Jews and other men: The chosen people, the Jews, have received the revelation of God and they are therefore the visionary nation. They share with other men, however, a certain knowledge of God through creation and reason, but only the revelation received by the Jews through Moses gives vision of God. In his ascent to God Moses was transformed from the realm of human reason to the realm of revelation and he thereby had the vision of God, and thus the Jews who imitate him are the visionary people of God.

Also Philo's dualism must be connected with the distinction made between the chosen people, the Jews, and other men. Philo combines an ethical dualism between heaven and earth and between soul and body with the dualism between Judaism and the pagan world. For example, the Jews who make education, wealth and office serve the heavenly values, as manifested in the Laws of Moses, bring heaven to rule over earth. If, on the other hand, the Jews have luxurious living, political careers and licentiousness as their objectives, they join with the earthly, pagan disorder. (See BORGEN, Bread, 118—21 and 143.) Accordingly, when Philo often interprets Egypt and Egyptians to mean the body, passions, mortal values, etc. (see PLCL, 10, 303—06), he combines these two aspects of his dualism: Egypt and Egyptians represent the pagans in difference to the Jewish nation, and at the same time they represent evil body over against the Jewish nation which has the heavenly quality of the soul (Leg all III 162f.: Ebr 36—7, see BORGEN, Bread, 133—6). When Jews yield to the somatic passions and other evils, they then join with the Egyptians in their vices.

5. No basic and sharp distinction should be made between Hellenistic Judaism and Palestinian Judaism. The main reason is the observation that Hellenistic methods and motives have also penetrated Palestinian Judaism, although to a lesser degree. What trend within Judaism forms then basis for Philo's interpretation of the Jewish religion? This trend needs to show kinship with Philo's combination of motives of Platonic and Stoic nature and of the nature of mystery religions, like combinations made in Middle Platonism and Middle Stoicism. This trend of Judaism must then combine ideas of man's heavenly ascent and his function as ruler and law-abiding person.

The most probable answer seems to be that Philo draws on traditions from early Jewish mysticism. Concerning the early stages of mystical Judaism, see G. SCHOLEM, Major Trends, 3rd rev. ed., 1961, 40—79; ID., Gnosticism, Merkabah Mysticism and Talmudic tradition, New York 1960; L. BAECK, Aus drei Jahrtausenden, 244—255; S. SANDMEL, The First Christian Century, New York 1969, 98f., P. BORGEN, in: Religions in Antiquity, 1968, 137—148; cf. ID. Bread, 147. See also N. A. DAHL, Current Issues in New Testament, 1962, 286—287.

GOODENOUGH (Jewish Symbols, 1, 8, 19f.) raised the question of Jewish mysticism on the basis of G. SCHOLEM's studies on the subject, but he did not succeed to relate it to Philo nor to Palestinian/rabbinic Judaism. CHADWICK (BJRL, 48, 1966, 286—307) shows the far-reaching, but independent agreements of Paul and Philo, which may have come from a common background in mystical Judaism. BORGEN (Bread, 177, ID., Religions in Antiquity, 137—48) finds that Philo and mystical Judaism share the idea of a heavenly being/angel, Israel, 'the one who sees God'. Importantly, both Philo and mystical Judaism combine ideas of heavenly beings, concepts and vision with moral/legal ideas and precepts. Furthermore, such ideas from mystical Judaism, as the heavenly Israel, who sees God, etc., have contributed to gnosticism, as can be seen from Jewish traditions

found in texts from Nag Hammadi in Egypt. (Cf. A. Böhlig, Le origini, SHR,
12, 1967, 109—40.)

In the article 'Some Jewish exegetical traditions as background for Son of
Man sayings in John's Gospel (John 3:13—14 and context)', in: ETL, 1977,
243—58, Borgen has made the observation that Philo, Quaes Ex II:46, interprets Moses' ascent at Mt. Sinai as rebirth, as also in the same way the experience of the burning bush and the revelation at Sinai are interpreted as birth
in rabbinic traditions (Cant R 8:2, Ex R 3:15, Tanchuma, ed. Buber, Shemoth
18, Ex R 30:5, cf. John 3:13). Such features of Jewish mysticism, therefore,
have given Philo (and his exegetical milieu) religious thought-categories which
could be developed along the lines of the Platonizing notion of the ascent of
the soul and the Stoic notion of life in accordance with divine law (cf. Middle
Platonism).

Philo's Jewish base makes him maintain that Moses, although understood as
'mind' by him, nevertheless has a basic significance also as a historical and bodily
man when he ascended: "As for eating and drinking, he had no thought for them
for forty successive days, doubtless because he had the better food of
contemplation, through whose inspiration sent from heaven above, he grew in
grace first of mind, then of body also through the soul, and in both so advanced in
strength and wellbeing that those who saw him afterwards could not believe their
eyes" (Vita Mos II 69—70).

Similarily, W. A. Meeks (The Prophet-King, 192—5) has shown that when
Philo in Vita Mos I 155—8 says that Moses shared God's Kingship, he relied on
traditional Jewish exegesis. Such Jewish exegetical traditions and elements of
mysticism about heavenly ascents and kingship are then by Philo (and his exegetical milieu) interpreted along the lines of the Platonic notion of ascent, and the
Stoic notion of the wise man as king.

Was Philo then fundamentally a Jew? Yes, even such an extreme Jew in his
loyalties and his claims that he seemed to refer all ideas and phenomena of value,
also including those outside Judaism, to Moses as their origin and authentic
formulation. Consequently, being so extreme in his claims, he was on the verge of
ending at the other extreme, that of being overcome by the ideas he wished to
conquer. In this way, Philo's extreme form of particularism was on the point of
ending up in a universalism where Jewish distinctiveness was in danger of being
lost.

Philon d'Alexandrie, exégète

par Jacques Cazeaux, Lyon*

Table des matières

* CNRS.

Limites et plan de l'étude

Nous traiterons ici de l'exégèse de Philon dans ses caractères spécifiques. Nous dirons ce que sont devenues dans ses traités allégoriques[1] les applications du symbolisme et de l'*interpretatio*. C'est dire que nous supposons connus les principes de l'allégorie hellénistique, leur usage alexandrin. Bien plus, nous considérons que le lecteur possède déjà une idée suffisante des habitudes propres de Philon. Qu'il connaît les notions courantes: Adam s'opposant à Ève, comme le principe intellectuel, mâle, au principe femelle de la sensibilité. Nous supposons connues les définitions allégoriques des personnages bibliques: Abraham est l'ami de la science; Isaac, la nature qui sait de soi-même; Jacob, l'athlète; Noé, repos et justice; Joseph, d'une manière plus subtile, est le symbole ordinaire du 'politique', puisqu'il vit en Égypte, dont le nom signifie le corps, tout en appartenant à la vertu et à Dieu[2]; et toutes les autres 'traductions'. Nous supposons encore que le lecteur distingue les types courants d'exégèse: cosmologique (*naturalis*), ou psychologique (*moralis*), dont nous redirons en conclusion qu'elles peuvent être associées, comme le montrera ici un passage des

---

[1] Pour la commodité du lecteur, nous utiliserons surtout les traités du cycle d'Abraham, du 'De migratione Abrahami' au 'De mutatione nominum'.
[2] Par exemple, dans le 'De migratione Abrahami', § 158 à 163.

'Quaestiones in Genesin', III, 3, milieu et fin. Trois animaux destinés au sacrifice d'Abraham dans la scène d'alliance (Genèse, ch. 15) se voient successivement interprétés par un symbolisme cosmologique et psychologique. Ils sont tout d'abord symboles de la terre (la génisse), de l'eau (c'est la chèvre, agitée et capricieuse), de l'air (voici le bélier, impétueux et nécessaire à la vie, pour la laine qu'il donne); ils sont ensuite des symboles moraux, du corps (le bovidé, pour son obéissance à l'homme, qui est l'esprit), de la sensibilité (c'est la chèvre, pour ses impulsions désordonnées), et du *logos* (le bélier, un principe mâle).

Nous nous servirons de ces réalités. Mais nous montrerons essentiellement à travers elles la construction savante, subtile parfois, du texte ordinaire de Philon. Nous montrerons la cohérence des citations, des images, des idées, entre elles et avec l'intention globale du traité considéré. Nous montrerons qu'il y a derrière le symbolisme de l'allégorie simple, un autre symbolisme, celui d'une s t r u c t u r e[3]. Dans une première partie, nous établirons une liste de procédés d'exégèse plus simples, plus extérieurs et donc plus apparents, ceux que le lecteur de Philon remarque immédiatement, c'est à dire les procédés de la g r a m m a i r e allégorique et de la r h é t o r i q u e. Dans une deuxième partie, nous donnerons un exemple d'interprétation complet, afin que le lecteur se souvienne que les moyens les plus ordinaires sont toujours dans Philon au service d'un ensemble, d'une exégèse vaste et compréhensive. Une troisième partie, ainsi préparée, expliquera les procédés plus cachés, de la d i a l e c t i q u e et de la p h i l o s o p h i e. Par là, nous rejoindrons l'esprit profond de l'exégète alexandrin. Une quatrième partie précisera quelques-uns des procédés les plus généraux et les plus féconds. Au terme, nous aurons montré l'unité et la l o g i q u e spécifique du commentaire philonien.

Deux présupposés

Pour comprendre l'exégèse de Philon, il servira de supposer deux principes. Le premier n'est autre que sa c o n t i n u i t é: Philon n'est pas d'abord un philosophe, si l'on entend par là l'auteur d'ouvrages spéculatifs; il part de la Bible et il y revient. C'est toujours[4] dans la citation biblique de départ qu'il convient de chercher l'explication de tous les éléments apparus dans le développement[5]. Les concepts philosophiques entrent dans le discours, mais comme une matière entre autres. Ce principe reçoit des applications variées; le problème de l'interprète de Philon est justement de retrouver la logique spécifique et l'unité. Le second principe s'énonce encore plus brutalement: il n'existe pas de digression. Non seulement le thème, l'idée directrice continuent leur chemin dans des pages

---

[3] Le mot 'structure' désigne ici une construction rigoureuse, souvent représentable par une figure symétrique, et qui combine à plusieurs niveaux un certain nombre de valeurs.

[4] Nous parlons ici des traités allégoriques.

[5] Plus loin, nous nuancerons cette affirmation: le commentaire de Philon s'appuie également sur la citation future.

apparemment improvisées, mais il y a un grand nombre de liens, voire de silences, qui rattachent la prétendue digression au traité, et cela avec précision.

Le commentaire de Philon veut agir sur la mémoire: il ne craint pas de poser à distance les uns des autres une série d'éléments, mots, citations, images, qui ont entre eux des rapports étroits, composent une sorte de schéma symétrique et déterminent un sens global. Pour saisir ce sens, il convient de garder en mémoire la succession et le contenu des différentes étapes parcourues. Par exemple, lorsque Philon énumère plusieurs hypothèses exégétiques, plusieurs interprétations d'un mot rencontré dans le texte biblique dont il traite, le lecteur doit se demander comment la série est disposée. Souvent, Philon donne dans cette série l'image d'une 'odyssée' de l'âme, un itinéraire spirituel. Ainsi, la liste des cinq sens à donner éventuellement au mot 'source', dans les § 177 à 201 du 'De fuga et inventione', n'est pas simplement une énumération fortuite. Les exemples donnés par Philon sont les suivants:

a) la source qui arrose le jardin d'Éden (Genèse, ch. 2, v. 6);
b) les sources d'Élim, étape des Hébreux dans le Désert (d'après l'Exode, ch. 15, v. 27);
c) la 'source' de la femme dans ses règles (Lévitique, ch. 20, v. 18);
d) la source où Rébecca puise l'eau pour le serviteur d'Abraham (Genèse, ch. 24, v. 16);
e) enfin, selon Jérémie, ch. 2, v. 13, la Source qui est Dieu même et que les impies abandonnent pour se creuser des citernes lézardées.

Si l'on regarde avec attention, le commentaire du premier exemple, celui de l'Éden, rejoint le commentaire du cinquième et dernier exemple, car, si l'on se souvient que l'esprit de Dieu et l'esprit de l'homme se répondent comme la Nature à la nature (ce qui est rappelé juste avant dans le texte du 'De fuga'), on voit l'homme et Dieu occuper les extrêmes dans cette série. Or, les exemples d'Élim et de Rébecca (c'est à dire le deuxième et le quatrième) ont en commun de désigner dans la 'source' les valeurs de la science propédeutique, à savoir l'éducation moyenne avec Élim, la patience avec Rébecca. Déjà a) et e), puis b) et d) déterminent une certaine symétrie[6]; au centre l'exemple c), celui des règles de la femme, représente un aspect négatif, misérable, opposé à l'aspect positif des quatre autres exemples qui l'entourent: l'abîme du Mal ouvre ses horizons maléfiques. La succession des cinq étapes décrit le chemin qui conduit l'âme de la nature initiale à la Nature parfaite qui l'achève et qui l'appelle, Dieu même. La présence du Mal, au milieu du voyage, est pour ainsi dire enveloppée et conjurée par la sagesse moyenne, celle, plus négative, des portails d'Élim, qui est située avant l'hypothèse funeste des règles féminines, et celle, plus positive, de la patience (Rébecca), qui est située après. On peut représenter ainsi la suite des cinq interprétations:

---

[6] Nous nous contentons ici de jeter ces indications: on pourrait, bien entendu, préciser ces rapports et en montrer tout le détail.

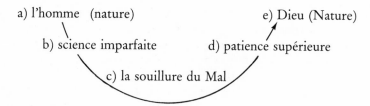

a) l'homme (nature)   e) Dieu (Nature)

b) science imparfaite   d) patience supérieure

c) la souillure du Mal

La science, imparfaite (hypothèse b), n'empêche pas la tentation (hypothèse c); seule, la patience de l'athlète, sa persévérance dans la lutte (hypothèse d), le conduiront auprès de Dieu, qui le délivrera définitivement (hypothèse e). Cet exemple est loin d'être unique, et nous le plaçons ici pour que le lecteur aperçoive du premier coup dans quelle direction l'exégèse de Philon et notre propre inter-prétation se situent. Nous fournirons plus loin d'autres occasions d'apprécier le travail subtil du commentaire philonien. Retenons de cet exemple que Philon compose avec soin de longs développements, sans révéler nettement les articu-lations, parce qu'il confie à la mémoire de son lecteur le soin de noter les rapports et d'en tirer un sens[7]. Tous les autres procédés exégétiques de Philon sont employés en vue de pareilles formules, synthétiques et, telles des symboles, destinées à enseigner tout en voilant.

I. Les procédés de 'grammaire' et de 'rhétorique'.
Le fond et la forme

La première réalité que le lecteur de Philon doit posséder, c'est le chapitre des équivalences entre les personnages bibliques et les valeurs morales. Le réper-toire existe[8] et nous le supposons connu. Il contient donc la substance même de l'allégorie philonienne: chaque fois que tel personnage entre en scène, il est accompagné de sa définition. Cette définition est complexe: on peut la comparer à un blason, orné de pièces diverses. Elle est fondée en général à la fois sur une

---

[7] Souvent, une figure comme la parabole ci-dessus est reprise à l'intérieur même des éléments qui la composent. Ainsi, les § 183 à 187 du même 'De fuga et inventione', c'est à dire l'hypothèse b), où 'source' évoque les eaux et les palmiers d'Élim, présentent une composition subtile: la notion d'imperfection enveloppe celle de perfection, de la manière suivante:

a) Élim = portails, et   a') les Hébreux, auprès
non pas l'intérieur   et non pas dans
b) nombre 12, parfait   b') nombre 70, parfait

Ce qui veut dire: la Sagesse est un fruit caché dans une enveloppe. On note que ce schéma est l'inverse du schéma général, où le Mal restait au milieu du progrès moral.

[8] L'édition anglaise de Philon, dans la collection Loeb, contient, avec le volume X, l'index établi par J. W. Earp, p. 269 à 433, base indispensable à toute lecture de Philon.

étymologie de type populaire[9], plus ou moins traditionnelle, et sur des références concrètes : Isaac désigne la n a t u r e   q u i   s a i t   d e   s o i - m ê m e, pour deux séries de raisons. Tout d'abord, son nom signifie « Rire », d'après le livre de la Genèse, lui-même, ch. 17, v. 17 ; ch. 18, v. 12 à 15, qui appuient lourdement ; or le rire est un effet de la 'joie', et la joie, à son tour, marque l'accomplissement de la perfection spirituelle. Mais, d'autre part, Isaac bénéficie d'un rapport spécial avec le temps : la Genèse, ch. 21, v. 2, ne dit-elle pas que « Sara conçut e t enfanta à Abraham un fils » ? La conjonction 'et', placée entre 'conçut' et 'enfanta', signifie pour l'allégoriste que 'concevoir' et 'enfanter' sont une seule et même chose, placée dans un seul et même temps. De là vient la notion d'un Isaac retiré aux vicissitudes de la temporalité, n a t u r e   d o n n é e   d ' u n   c o u p, sans devenir ; et comme tout est transposé, dans l'allégorie philonienne, en projet intellectualiste, empruntant l'image de l'itinéraire intellectuel de l'âme, l'absence de devenir est traduite par l'absence d'apprentissage : Isaac est bien la n a t u r e   q u i   s a i t   s p o n t a n é m e n t. De la même manière, si L o t est l'âme qui 'dévie' ou quitte le droit chemin, c'est à la fois par raison d'étymologie et parce qu'Abraham lui dit un jour : « Si tu vas à droite, j'irai à gauche ; si tu vas à gauche, je prendrai à droite ! » (dans la Genèse, ch. 13, v. 9), ce que l'allégorie interprète immédiatement : Lot est incapable de faire autre chose que d'aller 'à droite ou à gauche', en perdant de vue le droit chemin . . .

Philon combine donc deux systèmes, l'un d'apparence formelle, l'étymo-logie fantaisiste ou réelle ; l'autre, plus lié aux réalités de l'Écriture. En parcourant la liste des procédés de 'grammaire' et de 'rhétorique', nous en resterons tout d'abord à des phénomènes plus visibles, sachant bien que Philon ne distingue pas comme nous l'accessoire du sérieux, et qu'il n'établit pas une progression dans les arguments. Il ne commence pas nécessairement par une observation formelle qui le conduirait petit à petit jusqu'à des recoupements de fond. Dans chaque rencontre, la décision peut être enlevée grâce à un argument très extérieur aussi bien que par un raisonnement fondé. Pour la simplicité, mais aussi pour suivre les étapes de l'antique *paideia*, nous distinguerons entre les procédés 'apparents', ceux qui vont faire la matière de cette première partie, et les procédés plus subtils, par lesquels Philon organise son texte en laissant au lecteur la tâche de reconstituer la forme et le sens.

1. Procédés de 'grammaire'

D'un point de vue pratique, les procédés simples de l'interprétation gram-maticale servent dans l'allégorie à susciter l'attention du lecteur : en soulignant un détail de forme verbale ou de syntaxe, Philon oblige le lecteur à lire véritablement, à secouer la monotonie. D'un point de vue théorique, l'attention portée à ce détail signifie que l'Écriture formule un discours tout à fait suivi et significatif lui-même ; rien n'y est laissé au hasard : c'est une manière inattendue d'appliquer l'adage : « Pas un apex, pas un iod écrits dans la Loi ne passeront. »

---

[9] On ne saurait trancher par là la question de savoir si Philon connaissait ou non l'hébreu.

a) L'article

La présence ou l'absence de l'article défini suffit déjà pour entraîner une interprétation. Le double récit de la création de l'homme (Genèse, ch. 1, v. 26 et 27) permet d'opposer 'l'Homme', idée pure et générique de l'humanité, à 'un homme'[10], grâce à la précision du texte inspiré, qui met dans un cas l'article défini, et l'omet dans le second. Lorsque la nécessité s'en fait sentir, 'l'Homme', ainsi exalté par cet article hyperbolique, devient un modèle: il est, absolument, le sage: ὁ ἄνθρωπος – σπουδαῖος[11]. Une exégèse très subtile est provoquée dans le 'De fuga et inventione', § 212 à 213, par la succession dans la même phrase biblique des deux formes τὸ φρέαρ, φρέαρ οὗ ἐνώπιον εἶδον[12]: la forme accompagnée de l'article désigne l'Absolu, Dieu, quand la seconde, sans article, renvoie à son reflet, l'Ange.

b) Le temps des verbes

Le caractère absolu de la divinité ou de la splendeur originelle est aussi bien représenté par le jeu des temps verbaux. Le présent ne marque-t-il pas l'immobilité de l'éternel? Le temps présent qui est celui de la formule célèbre « Je Suis » exprime naïvement, s'il le faut, la stabilité divine[13]. Moïse atteint un sommet de perfection quand il recontre Dieu et s'entretient avec lui: Philon souligne que ce dialogue est noté par un imparfait, temps de la durée éternelle[14]. Un oracle annonçant «Je serai avec toi!» est analysé deux fois: une première exégèse en tire la notion de futur et commente l''espérance' rattachée à l'avenir; une seconde insiste sur la valeur du verbe[15] 'être', pour enseigner que la présence divine est déjà donnée. Un impératif tel que cet ordre: «Sors au-dehors!» permet à Philon de proposer une exhortation, à l'impératif elle-même[16]. Plus subtilement, Philon déduira un présent de la rencontre dans la même phrase biblique des deux autres parties du temps, le futur et le passé: il s'agit de la promesse que Moïse reçoit de sa propre mort, «Tu n'entreras pas dans la terre que Je t'ai fait voir!»[17] Philon déduit une présence actuelle des deux autres pôles du temps, «Tu n'entreras pas» s'opposant à «Je t'ai fait voir». Une forme verbale sans sujet exprimé, διεῖλεν, «il divisa», oblige à croire, d'après l'allégorie, que l'Absolu en est le sujet: c'est donc Dieu qui 'divisa', et cette remarque de Philon ouvre l'immense chapitre 'De la division en parts égales' qui occupe le tiers du 'Quis heres'[18].

[10] Dans le 'De fuga et inventione', § 68 à 72.
[11] Quis heres, § 258.
[12] Nous expliquons ce passage dans: La trame et la chaîne, Leiden, 1983, p. 468–469.
[13] De mutatione nominum, § 27.
[14] Quis heres, § 17.
[15] De migratione Abrahami, § 28 et 43.
[16] Quis heres, § 74.
[17] De migratione Abrahami, § 45.
[18] Quis heres, § 130 à 236; l'exégèse de διεῖλεν est au § 130.

c) Les conjonctions et les prépositions

Les petits mots de la syntaxe produisent de grandes conséquences philosophiques. Nous avons rappelé ci-dessus l'exploitation de l'expression complète «Sara conçut et enfanta un fils», où le ʿetʾ reçoit le sens forcé de ʿéquivalemmentʾ, ʿou bienʾ, de sorte que l'enfantement et la conception ne soient pas distingués. Ailleurs, c'est un neutre, ʿcelaʾ, qui en vient à signifier: ʿune essence particulièreʾ, et comme Pharaon est dit par la Bible «ne même plus penser à cela», Philon comprend: Pharaon s'applique, lui symbole de l'esprit-roi, à ne pas penser à une essence quelconque; Pharaon ne pense à rien; en définitive, Pharaon pense le rien: paradoxalement, le roi de l'Égypte occupe son esprit au ʿrienʾ, vide pour ainsi dire devenu substance pleine, ʿnéantʾ fait objet de pensée. Tout ce jeu signifie la perversion totale de l'esprit dominé par le corps (l'Égypte est traduite régulièrement par le ʿcorpsʾ)[19]. Ailleurs, Philon tire un grand parti de l'alternance de deux prépositions passées en préfixes dans les synonymes ʿextaseʾ / ʿenthousiasmeʾ, où ἐκ- / ἐν- échangent donc leurs significations locales: c'est lorsqu'il est ʿhorsʾ de soi que l'esprit est ʿenʾ Dieu[20]. Parce que le texte dit κατὰ τὸν νόμον, il est possible de comprendre cette précision, ʿselonʾ, d'une manière concrète et absolue: le sage marche ʿselon la Loiʾ, c'est à dire en la suivant point par point, adhérant à elle sans omission[21]. L'héritage du juste s'étend «de l'Égypte vers l'Euphrate»: prenons ces deux prépositions, ʿdeʾ et ʿversʾ, de manière disjonctive, brutale: elles désignent alors la distance entre deux points, et non pas les frontières extrêmes d'un territoire; un vide et non pas un plein — ce que le texte biblique imposait[22]. Elle est déjà plus simple, l'allégorie voulant que les Hébreux qui posent leur camp «entre Béred et Qadès» s'établissent ainsi ʿentreʾ deux valeurs supérieures, et donc reconnaissent leur situation ʿmoyenneʾ[23]. Un développement immense reçoit son impulsion de la différence dénoncée par Philon entre deux perfections du sage: s'il est simplement ʿagréable à Dieuʾ, c'est qu'il est perdu dans la mystique séparée; c'est un ascète exténué, inutile. Mais s'il est, comme c'est le cas d'Abraham, à la différence d'Énoch, ʿagréable devant Dieuʾ, il est plus parfait: il fait de surcroît retomber sur les autres hommes la bénédiction qui l'exalte lui-même[24]. Une subtilité permet de retourner la ʿfuiteʾ, thème du développement, en ʿfuite devant le bienʾ: en effet, si Jacob ʿfuit vers Laban, symbole du sensible[25]ʾ, on peut aussi bien dire qu'il ʿfuit le suprasensibleʾ, ʿvers le sensibleʾ équivalant à ʿloin du suprasensibleʾ[26].

---

[19] De fuga et inventione, § 123.
[20] Quis heres, § 252 à 256.
[21] De migratione Abrahami, § 127.
[22] Quis heres, § 314 à 315.
[23] De fuga et inventione, § 213 et dernier.
[24] De mutatione nominum, § 34 à 39.
[25] On sait que Laban est traduit par «blancheur»; la couleur devient par généralisation le signe de toute la sensibilité.
[26] De fuga et inventione, § 24 à 38.

d) Les pronoms et la métaphysique

Nous avons vu un Pharaon occupé 'pas même à cela', c'est dire pas même à 'une essence particulière'[27]. L'interrogatif «Que me donneras-tu, toi qui m'as déjà tout donné?» signifie dans le contexte: 'Quelle essence particulière, limitée, pourras-tu ajouter aux dons illimités, infinis, que j'ai déjà reçus de toi'?, et l'on peut dire que tout le 'chapitre' formé des § 1 à 30 du 'Quis heres' utilise comme base du commentaire les pronoms, interrogatifs, personnels, tels cet ἐγώ prononcé enfin par Abraham et qui manifeste, au bout du développement, qu'Abraham a trouvé une consistance personnelle, lui qui était au début menacé de disparaître, d'avoir à se taire. Un adverbe démonstratif, οὕτως, est analysé successivement comme signifiant simplement 'ainsi', et, de manière absolue, ontologique, 'en soi, tel qu'en soi-même'[28]. L'interrogation d'Isaac aveugle, s'étonnant que son fils revienne si vite de la chasse: «Qui est celui qui a ainsi chassé?», signifie qu'il admire la n a t u r e supérieure de Jacob: celui-ci n'a-t-il pas surpassé Ésaü, le chasseur entraîné[29]? Ailleurs, Philon observe que le texte sacré distingue soigneusement entre le personnage qui reçoit la ville de refuge et celui qui bénéficie de son asile: «Je te donnerai un Lieu où il (le meurtrier) se réfugiera»; cette distinction sert admirablement l'exégèse de Philon, qui, dans le contexte, s'efforce de faire évoluer très lentement la notion de 'fugitif' vers celle de 'suppliant'[30]. Le nom hébreu de la Manne n'est autre que l'interrogatif «Qu'est-ce que c'est?»: la valeur métaphysique apparaît tout de suite[31]. Un commentaire plus subtil s'attache à expliquer l'interrogation de Moïse, figé de surprise devant le buisson ardent: Τί ὅτι;, que, dans le contexte, il faut comprendre de façon analytique: 'Qu'est ce par quoi? — Qu'est ce qui est la Cause?', valeur métaphysique à nouveau, puisque Moïse apprend qu'il ne saura de Dieu qu'une chose, sa raison de causalité à l'endroit de l'univers, et non point son Être[32]. Encore plus subtile, voici, pour terminer, une exégèse fondée sur l'absence du pronom démonstratif: opposée à toute essence particulière, m o n t r a b l e[33], la 'voix' dont parle le texte biblique ne peut être que La Voix par excellence, celle de Dieu.

e) Le singulier ou le pluriel

Souvent, dans une même exégèse, Philon oppose un s i n g u l i e r, porteur de vérité, de solidité, d'unité, à un p l u r i e l, symbole de la dispersion, de la mul- tiplicité vite associée à la prostitution, c'est-à-dire à l'idolâtrie, le pire des crimes. Lorsque les Puissances, au pluriel, se mettent à fabriquer l'homme, il s'agit de

---

[27] De fuga et inventione, § 123.
[28] Quis heres, § 86 à 87.
[29] Quis heres, § 251 à 256.
[30] De fuga et inventione, § 76 à 77.
[31] De fuga et inventione, § 137 à 138.
[32] De fuga et inventione, § 161 à 163.
[33] Quis heres, § 67 à 68, où justement δεῖξις signifie «valeur du pronom démonstratif».

l'homme empirique, déjà compromis dans la sensibilité et donc le mal[34]. Lorsque le mot 'source' appelle plusieurs traductions, de subtils échanges font que la Manne, au singulier, s'oppose par son excellence[35] à la valeur inférieure des 'eaux', forme plurielle de la sagesse, auprès desquelles les Hébreux campèrent. Philon prend beaucoup de temps et de peine quand il doit expliquer la formule: «Tu t'en retourneras vers tes pères» — qui, dans la Bible, annonce à Abraham la mort qui suivra une longue vieillesse. La paternité désigne toujours pour le sage un monde qui est plus ou moins explicitement rapproché de Dieu, Cause du tout; mais le pluriel gêne Philon[36], et il tourne autour du mot 'pères' jusqu'à ce qu'il puisse le traduire, brusquement et de manière détournée à la fois, par l'''éther', c'est-à-dire par une nature supra-céleste déjà, mais encore éloignée de Dieu: on le voit, l'''éther' est un singulier, traduisant subrepticement un pluriel. Tout le détour[37] est provoqué par cette question de mystique grammaticale.

f) L'étymologie, ou l'optimisme de la langue

Laissons de côté les étymologies classées, tout le lot des 'blasons'. Il est des endroits de Philon où le commentaire s'appuie sur une traduction du grec au grec, à la manière du 'Cratyle'. Δεσπότης est interprété en fonction de δεσμός; ou κύριος, en fonction de κῦρος[38]. La 'justice', δίκη, rime avec δίχα, «en deux parts», ce qui permet de glisser de l'égalité à la justice[39]. Quand Philon spécule sur l'âme en progrès, il évoque l'''agneau' pascal, le πρόβατον étant interprété d'après προβαίνειν, «aller de l'avant»[40]. Dans le même contexte, la Pâque, Πάσχα évoque les souffrances dues aux 'passions' — πάσχειν sert ainsi un jeu de mots double[41]. Tout cela est banal et attendu. Plus curieux sera l'effort de l'Alexandrin pour dissocier φίλημα de φιλεῖν comme, dit-il, il faut évidemment distinguer ἵππος, «le cheval», de μάρσιππος, «le sac»[42]. On peut encore rattacher à l'étymologie le procédé qui consiste à détacher dans un verbe ou dans un mot un élément qui entre dans sa composition: en soulignant le préverbe dans ἀνά-βλεψον — «lève les yeux», Philon se prépare à traduire ce regard levé vers le ciel par la notion capitale de sacrifice, ἀνα-τίθημι[43]. La traduction appuyée du verbe ἀποκάθημαι, «être assise à l'écart (à cause des règles)», par ce commentaire ἀπωτάτω καθέζομαι, «se tenir à bonne distance», permet à l'exégèse de souligner la séparation de la sensibilité féminine et du principe masculin

---

[34] De fuga et inventione, § 68 à 70.

[35] De fuga et inventione, § 188 à 193.

[36] A la vérité, Philon n'est pas 'gêné': il tire toujours parti de l'occasion, et fait servir les détours à des fins précises.

[37] Quis heres, § 281 à 283.

[38] Quis heres, § 23.

[39] Quis heres, § 161 à 162.

[40] Quis heres, § 192. Cf. le 'De sacrificiis Abelis et Caini', § 112 ou le 'De congressu eruditionis gratia', § 106.

[41] Ibid.

[42] Quis heres, § 40 à 41.

[43] Quis heres, § 74.

d'unité: Rachel est éloignée dangereusement de Jacob[44]. Une décomposition plus intérieure fait que la forme λαλήσω contient deux valeurs: le sujet en indique la transcendance, Dieu qui parlera; le sens nous enseigne que Dieu s'exprime en 'parole', c'est à dire par le Logos; la même forme nous livre l'Être et sa première Puissance, le Logos[45]. Une variante du même procédé étymologique entraine tout un développement sur l'apparence et la réalité: Pharaon, parlant du Peuple des Hébreux, n'a-t-il pas dit que c'était là μέγα πλῆθος, alors qu'il aurait dû, suivant l'association naturelle des mots, prononcer plutôt l'expression: πολὺ πλῆθος? De cette sorte de 'lapsus' l'Écriture tire un enseignement profond sur la grandeur et le nombre, l'apparence et la vérité[46].

g) Les synonymes et les disjonctions, inversés

Philon n'hésite pas à renverser l'évidence, et il fait servir à rebours de leur sens obvie des associations ou des séparations du texte sacré. Pour lui, les r e d o n d a n c e s indiquent plutôt une différence. Si nous lisons «Il le fit sortir au-dehors»[47], ce pléonasme n'en est pas un; le texte inspiré a voulu attirer notre attention sur la complexité du concept moral d''entrée / sortie', étant donné qu'on peut très bien 'sortir' au-dedans, etc. Il existe d'ailleurs des pléonasmes cachés, au second degré, mais que l'allégorie dépiste: si nous lisons 'homme de Dieu', et si nous sommes informés que déjà le nom[48] d''homme' désigne un être qui est 'la possession de Dieu', force nous est de sentir tout d'abord une répétition étrange, 'homme de Dieu' devant être compris ainsi: 'possession-de-Dieu, de Dieu' Mais ce pléonasme n'en est plus un si nous l'acceptons comme le signe d'une différence entre les deux formules, et si nous comprenons que le premier 'de Dieu' renvoie à la condition de dépendance pure et simple où l'homme se trouve par rapport à Dieu, quand le second 'de Dieu' ajoute l'idée d'une providence par laquelle le sage imite la générosité divine et reverse sur l'humanité la pluie des bienfaits qu'il a reçus. Lorsque la Bible semble donner aux 'sources' d'Élim le s y n o n y m e des 'eaux'[49], nous devons apprendre à distinguer: la 'source' renvoie à la Sagesse inaccessible; les 'eaux' en apportent le flot, mais divisé, pluriel, abaissé au niveau des sciences propédeutiques.

h) Le jeu de mots

Le jeu de mots forme la pointe extrême de ce procédé: au lieu d'être répété, un sens est dédoublé dans un seul vocable. Ainsi, τέλος désignera simultanément le 'terme', c'est à dire la Fin suprême, et le 'terme de l'impôt', la dîme du sacrifice, la reconnaissance[50]. Une dialectique, très subtile et très simple en même temps,

[44] De fuga et inventione, § 189.
[45] Quis heres, § 166.
[46] De migratione Abrahami, § 53.
[47] Quis heres, § 81.
[48] De mutatione nominum, § 25 à 26.
[49] De fuga et inventione, § 183 à 187.
[50] De migratione Abrahami, § 134 à 142.

naît ailleurs d'une cascade de jeux de mots fondés sur ce premier: βάτος veut dire «buisson», mais aussi «accessible»; et cependant Moïse, devant ce βάτος, reçoit la défense d'avancer, d'ʽaccéder à l'accessible'. C'est là-dessus que se greffe l'interprétation du Τί ὅτι;[51]. Le plus surprenant de tous les exemples se trouve sans doute dans le début du ʽDe mutatione nominum'[52]. Philon introduit une ample dialectique sur le nom de la Puissance divine désignée par le mot Κύριος, en commençant par dire: le nom de la seconde Puissance majeure, Θεός, ne saurait être prononcé de manière «propre» — κυρίως. Inutile d'avertir le lecteur que ce début annonce de subtiles analyses et une savante composition.

Nous avons vu comment, au contraire, la distinction réelle indiquée par ʽet', dans «Sara conçut et enfanta un fils» devient une équivalence symbolique: Sara n'a pas mis neuf mois pour former Isaac; en elle il a été conçu et produit tout ensemble, et il peut être le symbole de l'Instant sans durée, mais non sans profondeur, qui est celui de la Nature parfaite. Plus subtile parce qu'occasionnelle, la synthèse suivante forgée par Philon: Abraham interroge Dieu pour apprendre de lui qui héritera; en grec, la formule est la suivante: πυνθάνεται φάσκων· τί μοι δώσεις; — nous n'expliquons pas ici les subtilités des analyses. Or, plus loin, au terme de l'apparition d'Abraham suffisamment stable et assuré en lui-même, Philon conclut sans en avoir l'air: ἐπιζητῶ μαθεῖν τε καὶ κτήσασθαι. C'est là un hendiadys improvisé par l'exégète, mais qui calque l'interrogation originelle du texte, et surtout qui prétend réunir comme une seule réalité la possession (κτήσασθαι reprend τί μοι δώσεις;) et le savoir (μαθεῖν reprend πυνθάνεται). La coordination forte τε καί est là pour relier et confondre ce qui, à l'origine, restait différent. Pourquoi? Parce que l'Abraham né avec l'interrogation, se définit — c'est même son ʽblason' — comme interrogateur de Dieu. Pour lui, ʽposséder les biens divins' c'est ʽexister'; mais ʽexister', c'est être comme interrogeant Dieu: d'où l'innocente association, ἐπιζητῶ μαθεῖν τε καὶ κτήσασθαι[53]. Un exemple pris ailleurs, mais exactement semblable en ce qu'il constitue un passage subreptice, presque caché, d'une distinction à une réunion de concepts, se trouve dans le même traité[54]. Philon a disserté de la moitié du ʽdidrachme' offert pour le rachat en impôt de capitation; il a montré que l'Écriture n'a pas dit, comme il serait naturel, ʽune drachme', mais la ʽmoitié du didrachme': nous partons donc dans le sens de la division. Or le commentaire, soudain, tourne dans une autre direction et Philon d'enchaîner: «. . . la drachme et monade» — δραχμῇ τε καὶ μονάδι — avec toujours cet innocent τε καί, comme si la chose allait de soi, alors que Philon passe de la division à l'unité. D'autres distinctions de concepts sont ramenées ainsi à la confusion: «Qui fuit là-bas, vivra», est-il dit à Jacob; Philon, voyant déjà dans l'adverbe[55] ʽlà-bas' quelque chose comme notre ʽAu-delà', c'est à dire Dieu, et sachant que ʽla vie'

---

[51] De fuga et inventione, § 161 à 163.

[52] De mutatione nominum, § 11 à 17. Nous reprenons souvent les mêmes contextes pour que notre lecteur se familiarise avec le cumul des procédés dans une même exégèse.

[53] Quis heres, § 33.

[54] Quis heres, § 187.

[55] De fuga et inventione, § 77 à 78.

s'identifie, d'autre part, avec le même Dieu, conclut sans effort que 'fuir', à ses yeux simplement redoublé par 'là-bas', c'est donc la même chose que 'vivre', leçon inattendue et tirée d'une suite de glissements tendant à rassembler ce que les mots originaux laissaient à distance. Mais, au contraire, une liaison évidente, fournie par le texte de l'Exode à propos du buisson qui à la fois brûle et ne brûle pas pour les yeux émerveillés de Moïse, devient sous la plume de Philon[56] une disjonction: il nous explique tout uniment que Moïse voit d'un c ô t é des éléments qui se consument, et d'un a u t r e c ô t é, des éléments qui ne passent point, du corruptible et de l'incorruptible, p r i s s é p a r é m e n t. Terminons par la plus étonnante proposition, qui veut que 'descendre' soit synonyme de 'monter'[57], pourvu, il est vrai qu'entre les deux opérations, contraires d'apparence, l'âme ait 'rempli sa cruche', à l'instar de Rébecca puisant pour le serviteur d'Abraham.

i) La syntaxe, source de symbolisme

Lot est condamné[58] d'avance par les mots, comme nous l'avons dit, mais aussi par la syntaxe même des propos d'Abraham. Celui-ci dit à son adresse: «Si tu vas à droite, j'irai à gauche; si tu vas à gauche, j'irai à droite.» Or, le simple balancement régulier des deux hypothèses disjonctives revient à signifier l'i n d i f-f é r e n c e coupable de Lot. Au fond, peu lui importe la direction, le sens, le but. La répétition, avec l'article, puis sans article, mais accolés l'un à l'autre, des deux 'puits' où Agar rencontra l'Ange — τὸ φρέαρ, φρέαρ οὗ ἐνώπιον εἶδον[59] suffit pour entraîner la pensée vers l'image du 'miroir': «Ne devais-tu pas, âme qui progresses et qui approfondis par la science propédeutique, voir comme à travers un miroir, celui de la culture, la Cause de la science?» C'est la juxtaposition qui a produit la notion d'image. Ailleurs, un g é n i t i f a b s o l u suggère le caractère quasi mécanique dont le vice et la vertu se succèdent dans l'âme: «Rachel, la trop aimée, étant stérile, Lia enfante nécessairement aussitôt»[60]. Plus important, Joseph est placé dans le cortège «au milieu, entre ses frères et le Pharaon», c'est-à-dire entre le bien et la mort; il suffit pour le savoir de lire le texte sacré: le nom de Joseph vient précisément entre le nom de Pharaon et les noms de ses frères, les fils bénis d'Israël[61]. Un effet de la syntaxe atteint même en un cas précis des dimensions étonnantes: tout le premier chapitre du 'De mutatione nominum'[62] s'explique par un seul trait. Philon a devant lui la phrase suivante: «Le Seigneur fut vu d'Abraham, et lui dit: Je serai ton Dieu». L'observation, tacite mais évidente à l'habitué de Philon, qui sous-tend le commentaire n'est autre que celle-ci: l'Écriture a prononcé les deux noms des Puissances majeures de l'Être, 'Seigneur' et 'Dieu', dans une seule émission de voix, pour ainsi dire — et donc ces deux

---

[56] De fuga et inventione, § 161.
[57] De fuga et inventione, § 194 à 195.
[58] De migratione Abrahami, § 148 à 150.
[59] De fuga et inventione, § 212 à 213.
[60] Quis heres, § 50 à 51.
[61] De migratione Abrahami, § 159.
[62] Les § 1 à 33.

noms sont en relation étroite; mais chacun occupe une extrémité de la phrase, 'Seigneur' étant au début, et 'Dieu', à la fin de l'oracle. Il n'en faut pas plus pour déterminer une dialectique complexe et subtile, mais simple en réalité, pour peu qu'on ait saisi ce fil d'Ariane de la syntaxe.

j) Les silences

Rattachons à la 'syntaxe' les silences de l'Écriture exploités par Philon. La seconde 'moitié du' fameux 'didrachme' ne fait dans la législation de Moïse l'objet d'aucun commentaire: Philon interprète ce silence en disant qu'elle est du 'rien', du néant positif, si l'on ose dire[63]. Si Caïn n'est pas déclaré mort dans la Bible, c'est qu'il est toujours en vie[64].

On l'a vu, ces procédés réveillent le lecteur de la Bible. Mais il est difficile d'en parler comme s'ils restaient à l'extérieur de l'interprétation. Chaque fois, nous avons engagé le lecteur dans un commencement d'analyse, plus profond qu'on ne pouvait s'y attendre, plus ramifié, plus enfoncé lui-même dans la pensée de l'auteur. Et pourtant, les procédés grammaticaux possèdent en eux-mêmes une vertu symbolique: sans doute Philon y voit-il le moyen, très humble, de rester fidèle à la lettre. Il pense que rien n'a pris place au hasard, et l'attention accordée à ces détails rejoint certainement, à ses yeux, la Nature qui affecte de se cacher — non pas de disparaître dans l'énigme, mais de se laisser rejoindre à partir des traces qu'elle imprime dans la lettre même de la Bible, à partir des minces anomalies que les initiés de l'allégorie viennent relever, deviner, interpréter comme des signes de vérité.

2. Procédés de 'rhétorique'

Mais la Bible est un livre, le livre même. Et le discours sur ce livre ne serait pas conforme à sa nature, il le trahirait, s'il ne formait pas lui-même une sorte d'image du livre premier. C'est pourquoi, plus que d'autres, Philon a composé: la rhétorique s'en mêle. Ne dit-il pas lui-même que la contemplation a besoin de l'expression composée; que Moïse, dans toute sa science de Dieu, doit communiquer par l'intermédiaire de son frère, Aaron? Abel n'a-t-il pas péri sous les artifices de la fausse rhétorique, et que lui a-t-il servi d'être juste et sage, tant qu'il ne disposait point des armes de la véritable éloquence? Pour rendre hommage à l'harmonie naturelle de l'Écriture, Philon savait bien qu'il fallait sans doute brider le *logos*, toujours trop prompt à se répandre, mais qu'il fallait aussi le 'diviser', l'ordonner et l'orner, en faire une 'tapisserie' subtilement ourdie[65]. Nous allons parcourir les procédés qui sont l'effet de ce travail où l'auteur se manifeste comme

---

[63] Quis heres, § 186 à 187.
[64] Quod deterius, § 177; De confusione linguarum, § 122; De virtutibus, § 200; De praemiis, § 68 à 73; De fuga et inventione, § 60 à 62.
[65] Voir, à ce sujet, le 'De sacrificiis Abelis et Caini', § 81 à 85; ou le 'De migratione Abrahami', § 74 à 85.

tel bien plus que dans l'interprétation des particularités de grammaire. L'ordre le plus simple sera encore celui d'une exposition naturelle: nous parlerons d'abord des procédés de commencement, c'est-à-dire ceux qui ouvrent le développement exégétique; puis des procédés fondamentaux du discours lui-même, du milieu, en ce sens; et enfin des procédés qui achèvent l'exégèse, ceux de la fin.

a) Les procédés du 'commencement', le paradoxe

Philon use volontiers pour commencer soit l'ouvrage, soit un développement particulier, du paradoxe. C'est ainsi que tout le début du 'De migratione Abrahami' procède. Abraham reçoit l'ordre de quitter; mais très vite, sur le point de partir, le voici comme arrivé: la terre, la parenté, le langage, qu'il doit fuir, se transforment très vite en valeurs positives. Plus loin, nous voyons que la nation d'Israël, désignée par Pharaon comme 'grand nombre', est rapidement gratifiée de l'unité et donc bénie[66]. Plus loin encore, la Fin, terme du voyage, est présentée au milieu de l'itinéraire, à propos d'un texte qui déclare: « Il marchait selon Dieu »[67], texte qui tendrait plutôt à décrire les étapes. Le comble de l'intelligence revient à l'ignorance[68], et la perfection du sacrifice rejoint l'accueil que l'âme peut faire de la providence divine[69]. La fin du livre n'est pas moins paradoxale: l'émigration dont on attendait la description a déjà disparu plus ou moins derrière la Fin; la dernière partie de l'ouvrage nous raconte les autres émigrations d'Abraham, en remontant ainsi le cours du temps. Nous assistons au départ d'Abraham, quittant Ur en Chaldée. Le 'Quis heres' prend son essor de la même manière, par un paradoxe: Abraham, que les bienfaits de Dieu invitent au silence, parle. Et Philon de spéculer longuement[70] sur cette dialectique du silence et de la parole. Un autre paradoxe ouvre un autre développement du même traité: lorsque Philon nous explique pourquoi Abraham a raison d'appeler Masek d'un nom équilibré, 'servante', mais 'servante née à la maison', il veut que la gamme des sentiments familiaux et domestiques soit parcourue lentement et dans un ordre donné: aussi distingue-t-il paradoxalement dès le début φιλεῖν et φίλημα, soit 'aimer' de 'donner un baiser'; ce premier paradoxe en prépare un second: 'la femme haïe' passe aux yeux de Dieu avant 'la femme chérie', Lia avant Rachel. Et ces paradoxes, à leur tour, trouvent justification dans l'erreur manifeste du premier homme, Adam, qui appela Ève, « vie », une compagne source de mort[71]. Il est des paradoxes que Philon construit. Il en est d'autres qu'il recueille dans le texte sacré. Pourquoi l'Écriture dit-elle cet oracle surprenant: « Reçois pour Moi! »[72]? Pourquoi parle-t-elle audacieusement d'« oiseaux qui descendent », alors que l'aile est faite pour monter[73]? Pourquoi Isaac est-il meilleur chasseur

---

[66] De migratione Abrahami, § 53 à 69.
[67] De migratione Abrahami, § 127.
[68] De migratione Abrahami, § 127 à 142.
[69] De migratione Abrahami, § 139 à 142.
[70] Quis heres, § 1 à 30.
[71] Quis heres, § 40 à 57.
[72] Quis heres, § 102 à 111.
[73] Quis heres, § 237 à 243.

qu'Ésaü, dont la chasse est le métier[74]? Pourquoi Abraham prophétise-t-il au moment de son sommeil[75]? Et comment lui parle-t-on de 'paix' quand son existence vit tant de 'guerres'[76]? Tous ces paradoxes, décelés à même le Texte, appellent une réflexion et lancent l'exégèse. Ils sont relevés par Philon, pour que le disciple averti apprenne à son tour comment briser l'apparence de l'Écriture.

b) Les procédés du 'milieu', l'anticipation

Voici la curiosité lancée: il faut maintenant expliquer le paradoxe. Le procédé majeur de l'exposition philonienne est celui de l'anticipation. La plupart des exégèses d'une certaine étendue sont 'téléologiques': Philon commente la phrase du texte de base qu'il a citée au départ, mais il le fait les yeux fixés sur la citation qui terminera l'exégèse. Le plus souvent, il faut, dans son texte, savoir où il va, c'est à dire toujours quelle nouvelle citation il invoquera au terme du raisonnement, pour comprendre en cours de route les éléments de son commentaire et ne pas croire qu'il s'égare ou procède par association d'idées. Dans une courte section du 'De migratione Abrahami'[77], la citation finale, «J'envoie mon Ange», survient quand tous les termes en ont été pour ainsi dire annoncés. Les mots «Lève les yeux!» apparaissent seulement au § 76 du 'Quis heres', mais ils ont influencé au moins les § 74 et 75, ne fût-ce qu'en leur imposant la forme de l'impératif d'exhortation. Le passage du même traité qui ouvre le chapitre de la 'Division'[78], introduit le Logos de manière soudaine: il suffit d'achever la lecture de ce petit ensemble pour voir qu'il est une traduction anticipée du grand-prêtre qui coupe en cheveux les plaques d'or destinées au tabernacle. Plus largement encore, tout le développement des § 65 à 85 du traité 'De fuga et inventione' exploite les notions de 'séparation' et de 'communauté' dans des termes et au moyen d'images qui présupposent les § 86 à 118, où Philon met en scène le personnage du Lévite: son influence s'est fait sentir bien auparavant, et sa définition a été comme subrepticement introduite avant son nom et son titre. Plus subtil: Philon est en possession d'une division logique qui permettra d'expliquer le verbe 'trouver'. La double division suivante occupe un long chapitre: «on ne cherche pas et l'on ne trouve pas; on cherche et on trouve; on cherche sans trouver; on trouve sans avoir cherché». Or, traitant la troisième hypothèse, où l'on cherche sans réussir à trouver, Philon glisse un commentaire sur l'histoire de Thamar, qu'on cherche parmi les prostituées sans, bien sûr, l'y trouver, de telle sorte que ce soit la transcendance de la vérité qui la fasse manquer: mais cette transcendance fait en réalité l'objet de la quatrième hypothèse, et le commentaire de la troisième a donc anticipé sur elle[79]. L'effet de l'anticipation est de rendre

---

[74] Quis heres, § 252 à 256.

[75] Quis heres, § 258 à 265.

[76] Quis heres, § 284 à 289.

[77] Les § 170b à 175.

[78] Les § 130 à 132.

[79] Nous avons évoqué certains exemples plus difficiles: le discours de Philon est souvent rusé; il convient de lui faire confiance. La solution des difficultés de lecture est souvent en avant, et non pas en arrière.

facile la transition d'un texte à un autre, et de faire paraître naturelle et brillante une phrase de l'Écriture appelée par une première phrase, de même famille.

Une très belle anticipation se trouve dans le passage du traité 'De mutatione nominum' que nous avons déjà cité[79a]. Si Philon parle d'Énoch, 'agréable à Dieu' au moment d'achever l'explication des mots «Je serai ton Dieu», c'est qu'il vise la phrase suivante de son texte de base: «Sois agréable devant moi!». L'opposition des deux formules, 'devant' et 'à', a été trouvée à partir de la seconde citation, et elle a, de proche en proche, orienté l'exégèse précédente. Comme par miracle, il n'y a en tout cela rien de forcé: Philon n'introduit pas brutalement les concepts à venir, mais il combine les informations données par la citation initiale et par la citation vers laquelle il se dirige, qu'elle soit présente dans le texte à commenter, qu'elle soit simplement invoquée pour son parallélisme avec la première.

c) Le chiasme

L'anticipation est une sorte de ruse du discours. Il faut maintenant observer des procédés plus sûrs et plus simples. Nous allons successivement répertorier quelques phénomènes ordinaires dans Philon, le chiasme, entendu d'une façon un peu large, comme une figure symétrique courant sur un ensemble de texte réduit, et non seulement sur une phrase; la technique qu'on pourrait appeler 'du filet', consistant à tenir au début et à la fin d'un développement deux points fixes, deux citations sœurs par exemple, et à faire perdre de vue dans l'intervalle le thème initial: des citations, des exemples, apparemment différents ou étrangers, prennent le relais. On s'aperçoit seulement à la fin du rapport qui réunissait en fait l'ensemble du commentaire. Lorsque deux barques supportent chacune une extrémité du filet, on ne voit leur collaboration qu'au moment où le filet est relevé, fermé et rapproché du rivage. Un troisième procédé philonien consiste à fournir deux points de vue à l'exégèse: d'abord par une observation de la forme, et ensuite du contenu.

Le chiasme est, en petit, l'analogue de ce que nous observerons à la fin en parlant des symétries, chères à Philon. Il y a tout d'abord les simples chiasmes stylistiques, tel celui-ci, pris dans le 'De migratione Abrahami', § 18: Philon annonce que Joseph a conservé des «formes incorruptibles et mémorables», et les deux développements qui suivent traitent, le premier des formes mémorables, le second, des formes incorruptibles[79b]. Plus loin dans le même traité, deux mentions de l''injuste' encadrent la mention du 'nombre', et là nous avons un sens symbolique: le multiple, le pluriel, est perdu dans les formes de l'injustice[79c]. Et autour de ce chiasme, Philon a disposé une figure symétrique enveloppante[80], qui donne la disposition inverse: c'est au tour de l''injustice' d'être placée à l'intérieur du 'nombre'. En voici le détail, que nous représentons pour plus de commodité:

[79a] Les § 34 à 38.
[79b] Soit le § 18, puis les § 19 à 23.
[79c] De migratione Abrahami, § 61.
[80] De migratione Abrahami, § 59 à 63.

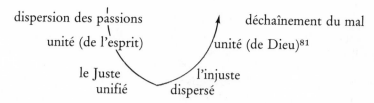

dispersion des passions   déchaînement du mal

unité (de l'esprit)   unité (de Dieu)[81]

le Juste   l'injuste
unifié   dispersé

Avec une plus ou moins grande subtilité d'intention, des croisements supplé-mentaires[82], par exemple, ce système se rencontre souvent. Toujours dans le 'De migratione Abrahami', les § 164 à 170 nous proposent une réflexion sur la 'vision' de Jacob devenu Israël, coupée d'une référence au personnage d'Isaac, comme si le patriarche avait besoin de la lumière supérieure apportée par la Nature illuminée directement. Ailleurs, voici un chiasme doublé d'un parallélisme secondaire[83]:

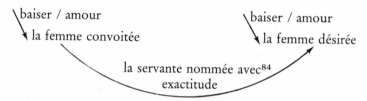

baiser / amour   baiser / amour

la femme convoitée   la femme désirée

la servante nommée avec[84]
exactitude

C'est encore une suite harmonieuse que nous lisons dans la discussion des § 86 à 88 du 'Quis heres': une sorte de conque symbolique permet à Philon de montrer que le sage est une image du ciel, grâce aux thèmes suivants ainsi disposés:

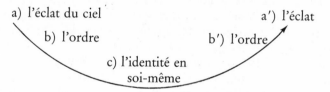

a) l'éclat du ciel   a') l'éclat

b) l'ordre   b') l'ordre

c) l'identité en
soi-même

La force mystique de cette structure n'a pas besoin d'être soulignée. Plus loin[84], au cœur d'une dialectique[85] destinée à changer un reproche fait par l'impie à l'Écriture naïve en une exhortation du Logos, un nouveau chiasme permet à Philon de dérouler une sorte d'échelle morale que le lecteur doit d'abord descendre puis remonter: de Dieu, nous descendons vers le monde sensible qui provoque

---

[81] Le lecteur reconnaît dans cette symétrie secondaire de l''unité de l'esprit humain' et de l''unité divine' la figure que nous trouvons dans les cinq hypothèses du mot 'source' (De fuga et inventione, § 177 à 201), ci-dessus, p. 159.

[82] Dans les § 97 à 100 du 'De migratione Abrahami', le 3ᵉ exemple d'une série de cinq est fait de deux parties: la première annonce le contexte qui suivra; la seconde fait écho à ce qui précède.

[83] Quis heres, § 42.

[84] Les § 92 à 94 du même 'Quis heres'.

[85] Ce mot est à comprendre dans le sens que nous montrerons ci-dessous, p. 195. Philon marque en général le centre des grandes symétries, dialectiques ou non, au moyen de procédés complexes.

une souillure et appelle une purification (c'est alors le point le plus bas de la courbe); nous remontons les degrés naguère descendus pour retrouver un Dieu pleinement reconnu pour ce qu'il est.

Bien entendu, un grand nombre de chiasmes purement stylistiques ornent le discours de Philon: nous ne les prenons pas en considération, et personne n'est obligé de trouver une portée considérable au fait que le § 126 du 'De fuga et inventione', par exemple, résume la double histoire de la femme de Lot, ἄψυχος, et de Pharaon, ἄλογος, en inversant les deux qualificatifs, les déclarant: ἄλογον καὶ ἄψυχον. Mais il faut trouver un sens à la disposition qui nous fait passer de la 'guerre' à la 'guerre éternelle' par l'intermédiaire de l'orgueil': la précision apportée par le troisième élément, guerre 'éternelle', vient de la faute essentielle aux yeux de Philon, la suffisance et l'autonomie de l''orgueil': il est ici un moyen terme logique tout autant que le pivot d'une élégante construction[86]. La diversité et la complication des chiasmes recontrés dans l'œuvre de Philon interdisent qu'on songe ici à les classer. On l'a noté, nous appelons chiasme une symétrie à mi-chemin entre le chiasme de phrase et la symétrie, beaucoup plus importante, dont nous traiterons plus loin[87]. C'est, de même, par un mot de notre invention, le 'filet', que nous poursuivons l'étude des procédés d'exposition.

d) La technique du 'filet'

C'est un procédé qui consiste à donner, à retirer, à rendre. Ainsi, dans les § 53 à 69 du 'De migratione Abrahami', Philon pose une citation des Nombres, ch. 14, substitut d'une citation de l'Exode, ch. 32, puis s'éloigne apparemment dans des citations et des commentaires divergents, pour boucler au terme en reprenant la citation de Nombres, ch. 14: «Je ferai un Peuple encore plus grand et plus nombreux que celui-ci» (§ 68). La fin du même traité[88] spécule sur le nombre 75: il est posé au § 198, on l'oublie pour le retrouver au § 215. Ce procédé est différent du chiasme, dont tous les éléments intermédiaires se laissent apercevoir clairement et en position symétrique; il ne ressemble pas non plus, pour la même raison, aux symétries plus vastes que le chiasme, mais tout aussi apparentes; il ne répond pas davantage à la dialectique, passage réglé par un centre médiateur d'un point à son contraire. Il sert à manifester les correspondances d'un texte avec d'autres textes: il est un effet de la conversation qui, aux yeux de Philon, règle les échanges des mots de l'Écriture entre eux et avec la totalité de la révélation. Il arrive que Philon, apparemment désinvolte, avertisse son lecteur qu'il arrête son exploration: «En voilà suffisamment sur cette question . . .»; la barque rentre au port. Mais il faut rester méfiant, et de telles formules cachent souvent des liaisons et des transitions plus subtiles. On se souviendra que la technique de la 'digression' dans les auteurs classiques répond à ce principe, et l'on

---

[86] De fuga et inventione, § 209b à 211.
[87] Ci-dessous, p. 211s.
[88] Déjà prévu au § 176, le nombre 75, premier terme des trois mots commentés: «A soixante-quinze ans, il sortit de Haran », sera traité le dernier; Haran, le dernier, est traité le premier.

peut, plus près de Philon, en donner un exemple remarquable. Les Épîtres de
Paul la pratiquent volontiers, et, par exemple, les fameux chapitres 8 à 10 de la
Première aux Corinthiens, sur les idolothytes. Paul y rédige une contre-rhétorique
à l'usage des orgueilleux de Corinthe qui se considèrent comme libres à l'endroit
des usages, des viandes, des idoles. Or, au milieu de l'explication, voici surgir un
immense développement sur le mystère de l'Écriture, l'exemple des Pères, lui-
même précédé de l'exemple de l'apôtre[89], étiré de telle sorte qu'on oublie le thème
fondamental, la question des idolothytes, qui se retrouve à la fin[90], presque
brutalement. En réalité, Paul, dans cette 'digression', dans ce 'filet' apparemment
distendu, a conduit la notion initiale de liberté — la pseudo-liberté où prétendent les Corinthiens — à celle de la lutte pour Dieu; puis de la lutte d''un
seul contre tous' (avec l'image du stade) à la lutte plus subtile qui exténue le
Peuple dans le Désert et les anéantit tous jusqu'à n'être plus que très peu à
entrer dans la Terre promise; puis la lutte de Dieu, lutte que, Lui, il n'a pas
achevée, condamne la suffisance de ces pseudo-libérés, s'imaginant avoir, eux,
vaincu les dieux. En cours de route, Paul a déployé les grandes figures du salut: la
digression a modifié insensiblement les concepts de départ; elle a opéré une
variation lente, mais puissante et efficace. De même, dans Philon, telle suite de
citations.

e) La double exégèse: par le fond et par la forme

Il n'est pas rare de surprendre dans Philon une double exposition. Parti de
l'observation grammaticale, qui a donné un premier sens et une première suite de
raisons, il redouble l'exégèse en prenant l'aspect, plus intérieur à nos yeux, du
contenu, du fond. Le premier chapitre du 'Quis heres'[91] va sans cesse d'un type
d'exégèse à l'autre: il s'interroge sur la possibilité d'interroger Dieu quand on a
tout reçu de lui, ce qui est une exégèse de forme, car Philon s'étonne que le
'serviteur' (Abraham dit bien: «Maître!») ait la hardiesse de demander. Peu
importe, en ce premier sens, le contenu de la demande. Vient ensuite la considération des mots et de leur valeur interne. A vrai dire, les deux aspects alter-
nent, à la fois dans l'ensemble du chapitre et dans chaque section, ce dont nous ne
pouvons ici rendre un compte détaillé. Le même traité du 'Quis heres' rencontre
plus loin le nom d'Éliézer[92]. Il est deux fois interprété: pour sa forme, Philon y
discernant un appel, «Mon Dieu, (viens) à mon secours!»; pour sa signification:
«Dieu (est) mon secours», formule qui contredit à l'autonomie coupable des
athées. Nous avons déjà noté l'effet produit par un impératif sur le commentaire
des mots: 'Échappe-toi!'; il entraîne un développement à l'impératif, une exhortation. Mais Philon, bien entendu, explique le thème de la 'sortie de soi', conforme au contenu de l'expression[93]. Le chapitre sur la division en parts égales

---

[89] L'ensemble couvre le ch. 9 et les 22 premiers versets du ch. 10.
[90] Première aux Corinthiens, ch. 10, v. 23 à 33.
[91] C'est-à-dire l'ensemble des § 3 à 39.
[92] Quis heres, § 58 à 62.
[93] Quis heres, § 74.

et contraires est ouvert par une double analyse du verbe διεῖλεν: l'absence de sujet renvoie à Dieu; la signification introduit la thème de la 'division'. Philon en général s'ingénie à fondre les différences que ces deux aspects pourraient introduire: une idée continue s'accommode très bien des deux, et le passage est d'ordinaire souple d'une exégèse à l'autre. Il est quelquefois dissimulé: les § 252 à 256 du 'Quis heres' montrent l'étonnement d'Isaac devant le prompt retour de son fils – qu'il ne sait pas être Jacob; c'est un exemple de l'extase d'admiration, et Philon le traite ici à partir du contenu: c'est l'idée du miracle, de l'action merveilleuse de Dieu qui domine. Mais plus loin, dans les § 258 à 262, apparemment éloignés du cas précédent, c'est la forme qui domine le commentaire. Ailleurs, parlant des «plantes qui poussent toutes seules», puis des «semailles et des moissons», Philon s'occupe du contenu dans les développements extrêmes; mais au milieu, il introduit[94] une réflexion fondée sur l'aspect formel, le style déclaratif du texte biblique: «(Le Texte) n'exhorte pas; il produit une sentence déclarative – γνώμην ἀποφαίνεται. Pour exhorter, il aurait dit: Ne semez pas; ne moissonnez pas; mais pour déclarer: Vous ne sèmerez pas; vous ne moissonnerez pas». Plus loin dans le même traité 'De fuga et inventione', une série de versets reçoivent un commentaire accéléré, tantôt pris du point de vue de la forme, tantôt du fond, sans que, peut-être, on puisse y discerner autre chose qu'une élégance d'exposition[95]. Il reste que chaque section du commentaire, dans Philon, a des chances de recourir aux deux exégèses, de forme et de fond: les nécessités particulières du contexte, l'importance relative des enseignements pourront faire varier la place de chacune, et surtout leur caractère d'évidence: on peut aller de la juxtaposition claire à l'intrication la plus subtile des deux aspects.

Tels sont, avec l'anticipation[96], le chiasme, entendu comme nous l'avons dit un peu largement, la technique du 'filet', la double exégèse, de fond et de forme, les procédés fondamentaux de l'exposition. Ils participent de ce que nous appelons la 'rhétorique' en ce sens qu'ils ordonnent la matière de l'ouvrage par des moyens d'expression artificiels, conscients[97], tout le temps employés et ordonnateurs du discours, lui conférant la tenue, l'efficacité, la forme originale qui contraint le lecteur à parcourir un certain cheminement intellectuel et affectif. Beaucoup restent relativement cachés, ou du moins effacés.

f) Les procédés de la 'fin', l'inclusion

Il existe au contraire des artifices très évidents. Bien des développements, sans comporter ni chiasme ni symétrie quelconque, se voient délimités clairement par une inclusion, qui marque de façon limpide le commencement et donc la fin de l'exégèse. Le thème du nombre ouvre et ferme le chapitre que constituent les

---

[94] De fuga et inventione, § 170 à 174.

[95] Ce qui ne veut pas dire gratuité pure, car Philon mêle toujours les points de vue les plus extérieurs à l'étude.

[96] Répétons que ce procédé forme l'âme de tous les autres.

[97] Par 'conscients' nous entendons moins l'attention claire et explicite de l'auteur que la volonté ordonnatrice, vigilante, quel que soit le degré d'aperception où elle atteigne.

§ 68 à 89 du traité 'Quis heres'. La section des § 103 à 124 du même ouvrage nous conduit d'une formule où l'homme 'reçoit' pour Dieu à une autre formule, où, cette fois, Dieu feint de 'recevoir' des mains de l'homme — λαβέ μοι et λαμβάνει. Ce sont les 'oiseaux' du sacrifice qui permettent de commencer et de terminer le chapitre de la division dans le même 'Quis heres'[98]. Dans le cas d'unités plus modestes, Philon se contente d'un mot: le verbe spécialisé, 'aiguiser', marque les frontières d'une courte section, celle des § 130 à 140 du même traité. L''art' divin, la τέχνη, délimite pareillement les § 156 à 160. Dans des sections plus vastes, Philon insiste. Peut-être le lecteur inattentif laissera-t-il échapper une inclusion comme celle qui clôt les § 174 à 200 du 'Quis heres': les 'douze pains de proposition' et les 'douze tribus d'Israël', formules renforcées d'ailleurs par d'autres indices. Mais il ne lui échappera pas que Philon a intentionnellement réuni les § 250 à 265 grâce à une expression imagée, qu'on ne risque pas de négliger: au début, l''extase' suppose que l'homme ne soit pas immobilisé dans le 'midi' de sa raison, et qu'il accueille au contraire la clarté divine au plus noir de son renoncement; à la fin, cette clarté divine est appelée lumière de 'midi'. On peut aisément embrasser d'un coup d'œil l'ensemble des § 299 à 306, toujours dans le 'Quis heres', fermés sur eux-mêmes par le mot caractéristique 'se détourner'. Il faut déjà plus d'attention ailleurs[99] pour se souvenir que le même verbe 'se détourner', utilisé de façon péjorative pour stigmatiser la femme de Lot et Pharaon, revient quelques pages plus loin pour donner occasion de féliciter Moïse. Terminons sur deux beaux exemples. Les § 180 à 199 du traité 'De fuga et inventione' sont délimités par le retour d'une expression également typique: 'les réalités olympiennes'. Enfin, la pseudo-digression qui occupe les § 89 à 120 du traité 'De congressu eruditionis gratia', si l'on prend soin d'y inclure les § 86 à 88, apparaît prise dans une immense inclusion: au début, la Loi protège Israël des vices de Canaan; à la fin le chiffre 10 de la même Loi met à mal l'impiété de l'Égypte; les deux pays, de l'arrivée et du départ, les deux pays ennemis d'Israël sont vaincus moralement par un même héros, la Loi.

g) Le procédé caché du silence

C'est aussi une façon d'arrêter le commentaire, en tout cas d'éviter un long détour, que de taire certains mots du texte de base. Philon connaît trois formes de ce s i l e n c e. Il y a tout d'abord les silences de l'Écriture, comme ceux dont nous avons déjà parlé: Caïn ne meurt pas dans la Bible, et c'est donc qu'il continue de vivre effectivement, dans les forces du mal toujours à l'œuvre dans le monde. Mais Philon omet lui-même un renseignement fourni par son texte: il ne dit rien du départ de Lot, dans le traité 'De migratione Abrahami', § 175; il ne dit rien du Désert, à la fin du traité 'De fuga et inventione', au moment où il rassemble pour les commenter rapidement tous les termes de son texte de base; il ne dit rien

---

[98] Les § 126b à 128 et les § 230 à 236.
[99] De fuga et inventione, les § 121 à 124 et le § 141.

surtout de cet enfant 'mâle' que la servante Agar doit enfanter, parce que cette précision emporterait le commentaire dans des directions trop compliquées[100]. Une troisième catégorie de silence entraîne le lecteur dans l'obligation de surveiller davantage le texte de Philon. Il s'agit d'un procédé subtil. Philon n'omet pas, en réalité, un commentaire donné; il le déplace et pratique une sorte d'exégèse 'indirecte', dissimulée. Par exemple, il ne dit rien au début du traité 'De migratione Abrahami' sur la formule employée par le texte de la Genèse, ch. 12, v. 1: «Dieu dit à Abraham». Mais une autre phrase du Texte, «Je te ferai voir» lui permet, à partir du § 47, donc assez loin dans le livre, de mettre en valeur des données équivalentes: le commentaire de la 'diction' divine est différé, dissimulé derrière un autre texte, mais effectif. Ailleurs et plus subtilement, Philon donne au silence une valeur symbolique: les § 121 à 124 du 'De fuga et inventione' prennent pour thème de discussion l'hypothèse où l'on ne cherche ni ne trouve, mais les mots exprès, 'chercher' — 'trouver', ne paraissent pas dans le commentaire. C'est que Philon ne veut pas les avancer dans une hypothèse négative: il leur trouve des substituts, tels que le verbe 'délibérer'; les mots propres seraient sans doute profanés dans cette hypothèse. De même, le premier chapitre du 'Quis heres' ne commente pas les mots du texte de base: «Il s'informe en disant . . .». En réalité, le commentaire est tout entier commandé par ces mots, invisibles mais actifs, et la fin du chapitre, comme nous l'avons signalé, traduit, exalte, honore ces mots cachés: Philon conduit toute l'exégèse de telle sorte que les expressions apparues à la fin définissent Abraham comme 'celui qui interroge Dieu'. Les mots du texte de base, «Il s'informe en disant . . .» reçoivent alors seulement leur véritable commentaire, bien que Philon ne les cite pas explicitement[101]. Lorsque Joseph entreprend de vaines recherches dans la plaine, Philon néglige d'utiliser les mots qui définissent le thème sacré de la 'recherche'[102], par un souci analogue à celui que nous avons noté ci-dessus. Lorsque le Peuple hébreu frôle la vérité, établi qu'il est «auprès des douze sources d'Élim», Philon, dans le commentaire, évite précisément de nommer les 'douze sources', parce que les âmes en progrès ne sont pas encore dignes des 'sources', non plus que du nombre parfait 'douze'[103].

Ce procédé connaît des formules plus subtiles encore. Il arrive qu'un développement annoncé ne soit pas réalisé, sinon dans un chapitre ultérieur. Ainsi, les § 18 à 28 du 'De mutatione nominum', théoriquement chargés d'expliquer les mots 'ton Dieu', en appuyant sur le possessif 'ton', commentent plutôt le substantif 'Dieu'; mais les § 29 à 38, théoriquement chargés du substantif, 'Dieu', s'attachent en fait au possessif 'ton'. Cette substitution des commentaires n'est pas une exception dans l'exégèse de Philon, et son lecteur doit toujours rester en éveil.

---

[100] En fait, l'exégèse utilise bien ce verset, mais uniquement de façon formelle: l'Ange, capable d'annoncer un garçon, lit donc dans l'avenir. Philon se tait complètement sur la signification positive du caractère masculin. Cf. § 203 à 205, et 207 à 208 du 'De fuga et inventione'.
[101] Les § 3 à 39.
[102] De fuga et inventione, § 127.
[103] De fuga et inventione, § 183 à 187.

h) L'accélération' ou l'évidence de l'Écriture

Dans plusieurs endroits, le texte de Philon marque une sorte de précipitation. Les citations ou les concepts sont rassemblés en peu d'espace, au terme d'une explication linéaire. Ainsi, les § 125 à 126 du traité 'De migratione Abrahami' rassemblent les trois personnages de la Triade mystique, Abraham, Jacob, Isaac, en imitation des trois moments du temps, le passé, l'avenir, le présent immobile, et cela dans une sorte d''accélération' du style. Au § 157 du même traité, les témoignages conjoints d'Homère et des Psaumes, les poètes des deux civilisations, entourent l'apparition décisive d'Isaac. L'accélération peut marquer de son style la fin d'un ouvrage: le traité 'De migratione Abrahami' et le traité 'De fuga et inventione' se trouvent dans ce cas. Ce procédé porte en soi une signification très claire: au terme d'une certaine étendue de commentaire, la raison humaine fait place à l'évidence de la Bible. Il suffit de citer rapidement, d'évoquer brièvement des figures bibliques ou des citations correspondantes, et l'initié comprend, interprète rapidement. Il écoute purement la voix de la vérité. L'exemple du traité 'De fuga et inventione' est tout à fait révélateur: Philon accumule en conclusion tout ce qu'il a laissé du texte de base, jusque là paresseusement commenté à partir de trois thèmes venus de trois mots, la 'fuite', la 'découverte', la 'source'. Les quelques pages qui terminent l'ouvrage, les § 202 à 213, se partagent plus de mots que le reste du traité; l'accélération subie par le commentaire n'est pas le signe d'un oubli, d'une hâte réparatrice: de façon délibérée, Philon entend que son disciple franchisse désormais tout seul le désert de l'analyse, qu'il comprenne pour ainsi dire à même le Texte ce que jusque là sa patiente analyse a meurtri, découvert, expliqué. La fin du traité 'Quis heres', moins rapide cependant, a déjà quelque chose de cette éducation de l'oreille: en un nombre relativement réduit de pages, Philon achève le commentaire du plus long chapitre qu'il ait jamais abordé, le chapitre 15 de la Genèse, intégralement analysé[104]. L'Écriture sans explication pesante, l'Écriture en soi-même brillant et expliquée, telle est l'ambition de l'exégèse.

i) L'élégance

On n'aurait encore rien dit de la 'rhétorique' sans avoir noté le bonheur de dire qui anime le discours de Philon. Lorsqu'Aaron retrouve son frère Moïse, c'est la 'joie' qui éclate. Ce symbole vaut du texte philonien. Très vite, comme il est dit dans une page du 'De migratione Abrahami'[105], où Moïse trouve Aaron comme la pensée trouve son expression heureuse, «le langage connaît la joie et l'exultation, lorsqu'une conception de l'esprit apparaît, dégagée de toute obscuri-

---

[104] Les § 275 à 315 vont en rapidité croissante, ce qui n'empêche nullement Philon de surveiller lucidement la suite des notions et de ménager une splendide conclusion, parfaitement ordonnée, mesurée, calculée: le symbolisme du 'four' et toute la dialectique du 'feu', de la braise à l'embrasement, dont nous reparlerons, donnent au traité du 'Quis heres' une conclusion symbolique d'une rare puissance. Seulement, la discrétion émousse les effets. L'Alexandrin sert l'Écriture, sans jamais l'offusquer par trop d'éclat.

[105] Au § 79.

té: pour sa clarté, il peut utiliser dans une traduction infaillible et heureuse son trésor de vocables propres et qui ont un sens et de l'expressivité. » Le traité 'De migratione Abrahami' abonde en recherches agréables, en effets plus ou moins savants: lorsque Philon réunit, par exemple[106], les conclusions de deux développements étranges en une seule phrase qui stigmatise ensemble et les animaux 'dépourvus de pattes' et les animaux 'qui ont trop de pattes', il joint l'agrément à l'utilité. Quand il compose le portrait de trois types d'hommes, le 'ramassis' d'une foule misérable et perdue, dévoyée, le 'mixte' représenté par un Joseph hésitant entre Pharaon et Israël, les sages enfin, et qu'il décompose ensuite la troisième catégorie à nouveau en trois modèles, il faut voir là une recherche de rhétoricien[107]. S'il veut combiner les variations des 'larmes' et de la 'joie' de sorte que l'agencement allie chiasme et paralléllisme suivant le schéma

larmes de deuil   larmes de joie

joie du deuil   joie de la délivrance

nous devons reconnaître là une élégance apprise[108]. S'il veut montrer les mérites de Joseph[109] en trois tableaux, dont le premier parle de son action, le second, de son action conjointe à sa parole, et le troisième, de sa parole, le sens ne justifie pas seul l'agencement harmonieux: la joie de bien s'exprimer participe de près à cette élégance. Quelquefois, le souci de plaider agréablement touche les limites du paradoxe: après avoir prouvé la transcendance de Dieu par la coordination des deux domaines, '. . . là-haut dans le ciel et sur terre, ici-bas', il apporte une seconde preuve d'un texte qui est, lui, en asyndète: «Je (suis) ici, en avant de toi »[110]. Élégance encore, la manière dont le second thème, annoncé dès le § 133, des parts égales mais contraires, est inséré à l'intérieur du chapitre de la Division: la liste d'une cinquantaine de 'contraires' vient se loger au milieu de la dissertation qui a pour titre le Logos médiateur[111]. Cette place, symbolique à tous égards, répond également au souci esthétique de Philon. Il n'est pas rare qu'une annonce soit à la fois respectée et bousculée: le programme est rempli, mais dans un ordre différent de celui qui était prévu; dans une proportion et une dialectique accommodées aux véritables relations du thème à la vérité exégétique.

j) La conscience d'écrire

Enfin, il est impossible de traiter de la rhétorique philonienne sans évoquer un dernier artifice, évidemment plus subjectif encore. Souvent tout se passe

---

[106] Au § 69.
[107] De migratione Abrahami, § 148 à 175.
[108] De migratione Abrahami, § 155 à 156.
[109] De migratione Abrahami, § 159 à 162.
[110] De migratione Abrahami, § 183.
[111] 'Quis heres': les 'contraires' se trouvent énumérés dans les § 207 à 214, dans un ensemble formé des § 201 à 206, avant, et les § 215 à 225, après l'enclave.

comme si Philon imitait dans la composition l'effet intellectuel produit par les notions qu'il élabore. Un exemple tout simple indiquera la direction: les § 137 à 139 du traité 'De fuga et inventione' dissertent sur la Manne, c'est à dire sur l'interrogation «Qu'est-ce là?» (traduction de ce mot). Or, dans ce contexte, le commentaire procède par interrogations. Nous avons plusieurs fois cité le cas de l'exhortation à l'impératif qui entoure, ou plutôt annonce, une citation à l'impératif: «Échappe-toi!»[112]. Une sorte de coquetterie affecte certains commentaires, qu'on pourrait appeler 'croisés': ainsi les § 40 à 51 du 'Quis heres', théoriquement consacrés au thème de la 'mère', traitent en réalité du 'fils', tandis que les § 52 à 62, théoriquement consacrés au 'fils' de la servante d'Abraham, parlent en fait de la 'mère'. Dans ces cas, la recherche de l'effet n'est pas seulement esthétique, mais il serait hors de propos ici d'en montrer la signification. De cette sorte de conscience réflexe de l'écriture nous avons des témoignages plus simples encore, lorsque Philon évite des mots qui occasionneraient dans le commentaire un détour qu'il juge excessif: nous avons vu qu'il n'appuyait pas sur le fait que l'enfant attendu par la servante Agar soit un enfant 'mâle'[113]. Ailleurs, il semble corrompre le texte de base: une législation destinée à protéger un aîné contre la jalousie de son père devient une loi symétrique, protégeant toujours le cadet, en raison d'un système proprement philonien qui donne comme πρεσβύτερος le plus jeune[114]. Par tous ces traits, Philon montre qu'il domine son écriture. Mais il ne saurait être entièrement libre: l'Écriture lui impose sa loi. Il écrit moins qu'il ne lit.

k) La conscience de lire

A peine peut-on parler de procédé dans ce qui va suivre. Nous voulons indiquer une sorte de consentement qui pourrait définir la mystique de Philon devant l'Écriture. En certains endroits de son exégèse, Philon 'déçoit' le lecteur et trompe une attente qu'il a cependant créée: et cela imite l'autorité de l'Écriture, l'enlèvement que la Parole de Dieu impose aux forces de l'intelligence humaine, à ses yeux. Par exemple, les § 60 à 63 du 'De migratione Abrahami' commencent bien par suggérer l'idée d'un combat où le nombre impie doit être vaincu; mais cette première description reste à l'état statique. Or, la fin de la section montre soudain que le combat est mené et gagné par l'Unique, Dieu, avant même d'avoir eu lieu, en tout cas sans que l'âme ait eu à combattre. Cette brusquerie logique traduit symboliquement l'invasion du Dieu transcendant. De même dans un autre contexte[115], le lecteur s'attend à voir discuter le problème de l'apparence et de la réalité à l'intérieur de catégories morales, humaines. Or, soudain, c'est l'apparence de la Loi qui entre en discussion, par un passage du point de vue subjectif, moral, au point de vue métaphysique, objectif. Un troisième exemple

---

[112] Quis heres, § 74.
[113] Les § 203 à 204 utilisent cette donnée comme signe de la science angélique, et non pour elle-même. Il s'agit du 'De fuga'.
[114] Quis heres, § 48.
[115] De migratione Abrahami, § 88 à 93.

instruira le lecteur sur la variété et le génie de Philon: l'image de la Tente arrive brusquement dans un contexte paisible, pour tout bouleverser, introduire le souvenir des fautes quand on parlait de justice[116]. Cette surprise imite l'arrivée du salut au milieu de notre monde — tel est en effet le thème fondamental du chapitre. La conclusion du traité 'De fuga et inventione' est en réalité introduite par un verset inattendu: la mention du puits fait bien suite au thème des 'sources', mais Philon ne l'avait pas évoqué dans le texte de base. Il apparaît comme une sorte d'exaltation donnée au raisonnement par l'Écriture elle-même, et cela d'autant mieux que le 'puits' fait partie du verset qui suit le texte de base[117].

Tous ces procédés de 'rhétorique' ont pour destination le discours, composé, suivi, orné même, en tout cas rendu cohérent à force de soin. Au discours inspiré dont les procédés de 'grammaire' ont rendu justice en respectant ses plus humbles nuances, le discours de l'interprète répond ainsi, par une composition, elle-même volontaire et achevée. Avant d'en venir à une autre catégorie de remarques touchant l'exégèse philonienne, il nous paraît indispensable de rendre plus concrètes les indications passées et à venir. Pour cela, nous proposons au lecteur l'analyse complète d'une unité littéraire prise en dehors des traités qui nous ont jusqu'ici servi de référence. L'analyse sera, disons-nous, complète: c'est à dire qu'elle parcourra les étapes théoriques d'une interprétation de Philon, sans prétendre épuiser l'enseignement ni même la totalité des procédés mis en œuvre. Dans ce genre d'application, la véritable preuve réside dans la possibilité de généraliser une méthode: aussi bien est-ce l'ensemble de l'analyse qui donnera le sens plénier à des détails qui paraîtront gratuits au premier abord.

II. Un exemple de l'exégèse de Philon, pris dans le 'Quod deterius', § 119 à 140

1. Présentation

Nous avons pu voir jusqu'ici avec quelle vigilance le lecteur de Philon doit surveiller son texte, même quand il s'agit de noter des procédés ou des signes encore bien apparents. A plus forte raison lorsque l'on est surpris ou déçu, faut-il y regarder de plus près. Tel développement d'apparence étrangère au contexte permet, une fois qu'il a été expliqué et remis par la mémoire en bonne place, d'apercevoir des rapports plus vastes dans le traité où il se situe, et de dominer plus sûrement le panorama moral dessiné par la succession des exégèses. C'est ce que nous montrerons en choisissant dans le 'Quod deterius potiori insidiari soleat' le passage étrange où Philon introduit soudain la rencontre d'Aaron et de Moïse,

---

[116] Quis heres, § 112 et 113, dans l'ensemble des § 102 à 124. Il s'agit, on le voit, du centre de ce chapitre.
[117] De fuga et inventione, § 211 à 213.

et célèbre la joie qui marque le rapprochement harmonieux de la parole et de la pensée inspirée. L'ensemble où l'épisode s'inscrit va du § 119, semble-t-il, au § 140.

Nous voyons donc que l'harmonie du verbe et de la pensée est 'joie'. Or, Caïn, sujet du traité, n'est-il pas atteint de la malédiction et montré 'en proie à la tristesse et à la peur'? Ce premier couple de contraires moraux, tristesse et joie, pourrait aider le lecteur à situer d'autres éléments et ouvrir ainsi une interprétation. Nous verrons par quels détours. Où sommes-nous au début du chapitre? Dans la description des châtiments de Caïn. Il est à la fois abandonné de Dieu (§ 141 et la fin du livre) et d'abord « maudit du côté de la terre » (§ 96 à 140, justement). Or, par le jeu des contrastes, Philon évoque d'autres personnages saints: Noé, puis Sara, Isaac, Moïse précisément, accompagné d'Aaron, Énos enfin, opposent tous au sinistre meurtrier d'Abel le rayonnement d'une vertu contraire. Plus précisément, si Caïn connaît la 'tristesse' et la 'peur', les héros de Dieu incarnent une 'joie' ou une 'espérance' paradisiaques auprès de l'enfer qui mure Caïn. C'est ce développement qui occupe les § 119 à 140 du 'Quod deterius' et que nous avons décidé de mettre en valeur, sobrement puisqu'il suffira d'en manifester le caractère savamment concerté, le 'schème' imaginatif.

Une inclusion évidente délimite ce qu'on peut appeler un 'chapitre'. Les mots-clefs de la citation biblique, 'tristesse' et 'peur', apparaissent dans le § 119, pour revenir au § 140: ils encadrent ainsi le raisonnement. Partis de Caïn, nous le perdons de vue durant un long espace, pour le retrouver au terme. A vrai dire, les mots de l'Écriture étaient exactement ceux-ci: «gémissant et tremblant», mais le système classique des quatre 'passions' de l'âme s'offrait de lui-même pour engendrer l'allégorie: 'gémissant' devient aisément 'triste', et 'tremblant' aboutit sans effort à 'peureux'. Par ce biais, les deux passions négatives livrent accès à leur contraire: l''espérance' et la 'joie'. Mais Philon ne s'en tient pas à cette opposition rhétorique et morale. Le lien formel ne lui permet pas seulement d'ouvrir le dossier des personnages que Dieu bénit, mais d'en exploiter une suite ordonnée selon la logique de l'Écriture et de ses expressions. Logique dit relation intérieure: il existe un rapport entre Caïn et le premier modèle des favorisés, Noé. Car ce dernier porte un nom qui se traduit par « Repos », ou mieux par une formule: « il nous fait reproser loin de la terre que le Seigneur a maudite ». La malédiction du sol, enfin levée par l'intermédiaire de Noé, n'est-elle pas précisément le premier signe de la punition qui frappe Caïn, « maudit du côté de la terre »? On pourrait imaginer que Philon se contente de cette opposition: Noé se trouve placé au terme d'une dialectique dont Caïn marque le début, par sa malédiction. Mais en fait, Noé, nous allons le constater, Noé qui voit se défaire la malédiction contractée par la terre avec Caïn, n'est pourtant pas présenté comme le contraire de Caïn en tous points. Philon, au § 120 a soigneusement précisé que 'joie' et 'espérance' regardaient respectivement le présent et l'avenir. Il se glisse du même coup une distance entre les deux sentiments, entre les deux états, et Philon respecte cette distance, lui fait droit, en prépare l e n t e m e n t la reconnaissance, en prévoyant un itinéraire où les étapes seront marquées avec soin. Le rapprochement 'intellectualiste', spéculatif, entre Caïn et Noé ne l'intéresse pas tant que l'étoffe patiemment historiée d'une tapisserie . . . Dans le panneau tissu à cette occasion, nous commencerons par le centre, pour éviter nous-même toute précipitation. Il s'agit de la rencontre de Moïse et d'Aaron, de leur 'joie', du confort né d'une pensée en harmonie avec son expression.

2. La joie du présent éternel: § 123b à 137

Ce passage impose sa loi à l'ensemble de la liste, ne fût-ce que par sa longueur. On devine rapidement que Philon ne songeait pas simplement à jeter des 'exemples' dont le nombre ou l'autorité démontreraient une thèse. Il veut composer une pièce importante dans l'économie du traité. N'est-ce pas à partir d'Isaac, la nature parfaite, que nous sommes conduits jusqu'à Moïse maintenant, et qu'avec Moïse nous suivons à l'intérieur du 'langage' une sorte de philosophie développée? Le lecteur, pressé ou surpris par le tour que prennent alors les choses croira sans peine à l'égarement, c'est-à-dire à la digression. Plus méfiants, nous allons d'abord observer la suite exacte des notions.

Pour commencer, nous dirons que le personnage mis en cause dans les § 123b à 125 est Sara, relayée, expliquée par Abraham; l'Isaac dont il est également question ne figure là qu'au titre d'objet: Abraham est le père d'Isaac, et Sara à cause d'eux se réjouit — ce qui est la traduction biblique du nom même d'Isaac. Bien mieux, le § 124b et le § 125 restent dans le même horizon. Ils commentent le texte de la Genèse, ch. 21, v. 6: «Le Seigneur a fait pour moi le Rire; et tous ceux qui l'entendront se réjouiront avec moi». Ceux qui 'entendent' ainsi le Rire sont bien les âmes aptes à entendre la poésie de Dieu. L'activité 'poétique' de Dieu renvoie à la formule également évoquée de la Création: «Le Seigneur a fait . . . ». Augustin se réjouirait à dire là aussi un peu de grec pour démêler devant son bon peuple l'art divin et la joie bondissante du salut. Pour nous, pour Philon, il n'y a pas de solution de continuité entre le début et la fin du § 124.

Et l'insistance soudaine mise par l'exégèse sur cette poétique — Κύριος ἐποίησεν — et sur l'heureuse audition de la 'joie' qui lui est associée, contribue à faire du couple de Sara et d'Abraham en présence d'Isaac, le Rire, une réplique anticipée du couple heureux par excellence, celui que formeront bientôt Moïse et Aaron, son frère. Moïse est sur le même plan théorique que le fils de la promesse, Isaac; Aaron, sur le même plan que les parents, Sara ou Abraham. Après l'image, voici le modèle. Voici la grande analyse de la rencontre que Dieu ménage, ordonne et réussit entre Moïse et son 'prophète', Aaron; entre la pensée divinement inspirée, l'Idée, et le langage exprimé.

Les § 126 à 137 analysent donc terme après terme le texte de l'Exode, ch. 4, v. 14: «N'est-ce pas là Aaron, ton frère, le Lévite? Je sais qu'il parlera pour toi; et voici que lui, il sortira à ta rencontre: à te voir, il se réjouira en lui-même»[118].

---

[118] Nous citons non pas la Bible, mais ce que Philon en comprend. Selon une règle presque toujours appliquée, Philon déploie les différents aspects du thème adopté au fil d'une analyse qui suit tous les éléments du texte invoqué. Les mots «Je sais qu'il parlera pour toi» supposent une distinction entre pensée et expression de la pensée (§ 127 à 128); les

Dans le commentaire, on peut reconnaître trois chefs principaux, qui correspondraient, pour faire bref, à trois études successives: une première analyse (les § 127 et 128), d'ordre 'psychologique', fait mention des nécessités qui rattachent la pensée à l'expression: celle-ci aide la première, sans se contenter de la suivre servilement. Une deuxième analyse (celle des § 129 à 131) montre que la parole doit tout de même rester dans son rôle subalterne: simple interprète, elle ne peut évoluer seule; toujours agitée par nature, prompte à se manifester, elle risque toujours de voir déborder ses flots[119] et de compromettre gravement l'harmonie. Cette section peut être dite 'morale': on peut y lire une critique des sophistes ou plus simplement de tout abus de la parole. La troisième section (qui recouvre les § 132 à 135) atteint le domaine 'religieux': une frontière sépare la Parole de Dieu et le langage impie, et cela permet au langage saint de 'rencontrer' en vérité la perfection.

La première période interprète ces mots du texte de base: « Il parlera pour toi », en voyant dans le datif λαλήσει αὐτός σοι un datif d'intérêt; la deuxième explicite les mots « à ta rencontre » à l'aide d'un verbe de mouvement, très significatif dans Philon[120], « il sortira », de telle sorte que la rencontre donne toute l'importance à Moïse: Aaron 'sort' de lui-même, se renonce en quelque sorte, pour venir au-devant de Moïse; la troisième section, enfin, s'arrête sur la précision capitale apportée par la Bible: « Aaron, ton frère, le Lévite ». Du fait que le Lévite est, par définition, 'à Dieu', Philon voit dans ce qualificatif une confirmation du renoncement à soi-même, déjà indiqué par le verbe 'il sortira'. Et Caïn, le monstre dont nous scrutons le châtiment dans tout le chapitre, n'est-il pas tout entier consacré à soi-même, par la pire des perversions? Aussi la conclusion de l'exégèse revient-elle au thème de départ, la 'joie' d'Aaron, mais en évitant de trop l'exalter: Philon voit bien que l'expression du texte à cet endroit, « il se réjouira en lui-même » risquerait de rappeler l'autonomie coupable de Caïn, si elle n'était pas comprise comme son opposé. Il suffit d'admettre pour ces mots dangereux, « en lui-même », un sens psychologique et moral: l'âme se réjouit des biens premiers.

Loin d'être produit par un jeu d'associations de fantaisie, ce chapitre prend place dans le traité. Qu'il suffise d'indiquer ici que le 'Quod deterius' démontre l'utilité de la rhétorique, et l'on verra tout de suite la portée que prend la mise en place et en ordre des règles du langage juste que les trois sections, psychologique, morale et religieuse, assurent. En ce sens, le personnage essentiel n'est autre qu'Aaron, dans son rapport étroit avec Moïse: Moïse combat les sophistes égyptiens; Aaron lui sert d'interprète, puiqu'il parle, alors que son frère reste

---

mots « Il sortira à ta rencontre » manifestent l'exigence qui impose au verbe de s'adapter à une pensée et non à soi-même (§ 128 à 131); mais Aaron nous est présenté comme 'le Lévite': l'idéal de la pensée vertueuse est d'être dite par une parole vertueuse, consacrée à Dieu (§ 132 à 134); enfin, après le rappel de la citation entière (§ 135), Philon en vient aux mots qu'il visait depuis le début: « il se réjouira en lui-même » (§ 136 à 137). Nous allons voir que le déroulement littéral accompagne une division plus savante.

[119] Sur la dangereuse précipitation du langage, voir par exemple le traité 'De sacrificiis Abelis et Caini', § 81.

[120] Développé, entre autres passages, dans le 'Quis heres', § 40 à 89.

embarrassé de langue, au point même de s'excuser auprès de Dieu: «Je ne sais pas parler: envoie quelqu'un d'autre!»[121]. Dans la première partie de ce traité, Abel s'est laissé détruire, lui qui incarne la vertu, par la sophistique d'un Caïn[122]. Au contraire, Moïse refuse de rencontrer les sophistes tant qu'il ne voit pas son frère à ses côtés (§ 38 à 44, déjà). Dans le débat sur l'utilité de la rhétorique ou de l'éloquence juste, notre chapitre entre donc tout à fait bien. Cette première réponse est nécessaire, juste, solide en dépit de sa généralité. Mais elle n'explique pas tout. Elle ne dit pas exactement pourquoi Philon a choisi cet endroit du livre pour amener l'anti-Caïn et pour développer ce thème, secondaire en apparence, de la 'joie' qui célèbre le juste emploi de la dialectique. L'analyse du chapitre en son entier nous permettra d'apporter une précision.

L'idée que les § 119 à 140 obéissent à une structure précise et efficace peut déjà venir à l'esprit quand on observe que les trois étapes décrites possèdent entre elles des liens et une progression. L'analyse 'psychologique' a montré la profonde unité du langage et de la pensée; l'analyse 'morale' donne une règle à cette harmonie, en soumettant la parole à la pensée: la réalisation de la parole, plus passive qu'active, lui procure la 'joie' (§ 129 b); à partir de là, l'interprétation 'religieuse' vient naturellement, et elle accorde au langage des titres de noblesse en faisant de lui l'interprète de la Parole. Une sorte de naissance à soi-même est suivie d'un renoncement, qui prépare une exaltation[123]. Et, couronnement notable, nous apprenons à la fin que la rhétorique sainte et puissante tire sa valeur d'un discours qui existe déjà et qui est la Loi: elle apparaît soudain, comme la révélation suprême dans Platon. Ce sont tout d'un coup les 'décrets divins' (début du § 133) qui occupent l'attention. La Loi accomplit la montée subjective des personnages; elle lui donne une portée objective. Tout cela demande maintenant à être situé dans l'ensemble des personnages appelés en renfort par l'allégorie. De ce point central, nous allons redescendre pour discerner tout autour les degrés d'une logique plus large, tout aussi simple à la vérité, mais peut-être moins visible tout d'abord.

3. De part et d'autre: Noé, le passé; Énos, l'avenir. La lenteur de la 'dialectique'

Il ne sera pas inutile de mettre sous les yeux du lecteur une synopse du développement qui groupe les deux attributs du sage, cette 'joie' et cette 'espérance' qui s'opposent au malheur de Caïn, à sa 'peur', à sa 'tristesse'.

---

[121] Voir l'Exode, ch. 4, v. 13; cf. ch. 6, v. 30.

[122] Dans le traité 'Quod deterius', voir les § 32 à 37, où Philon commente l'imprudence d'Abel s'avançant dans la plaine.

[123] En un sens très général, on peut signaler que le traité 'Quis heres' développe dans ses trois parties la même dialectique: Abraham commence par acquérir droit de cité en présence de l'infini; son sacrifice et son sommeil mystique le font 'mourir', au terme de quoi il entre en possession de l'héritage.

Caïn: tristesse et peur	§ 119
le sage: joie et espérance	§ 120
a) la joie 1) repos, apporté par Noé	§ 121−123
2) joie de Sara (Isaac = Rire)	§ 124a
3) joie des auditeurs de Dieu-poète	§ 124b−125
4) joie du langage, Aaron	
− psychologie	§ 127−128
− morale	§ 129−131
− métaphysique	§ 132−134
joie en soi-même	§ 135−137
b) l'espérance, Énos	§ 138−139
Caïn: tristesse et peur	§ 140

Caïn, présent au début, revient inchangé à la fin. Entre-temps, nous avons suivi une ligne simple, rhétorique, prenant argument des deux vertus qui ornent le sage, la joie, puis l'espérance. Mais ce tableau ordonné n'est que provisoire. Son apparente régularité néglige le détail; et le détail importe ici, surtout quand il concerne les transitions. Nous devrons en particulier retoucher le passage entre les figures de Noé et de Sara; comme entre Sara et les auditeurs du Dieu-poète, qui nous conduisent enfin à la rencontre de Moïse et d'Aaron. Nous devrons nous interroger sur l'équilibre des masses, observer que le partage entre les deux vertus, symbolisées par Noé puis Énos, est loin d'être équitable: l'espérance de la fin n'a pas droit à autant de considération, semble-t-il, que la joie (les § 138−139 font l'affaire, contre les § 120 à 137).

Prenons cette dernière remarque: si l'espérance ne reçoit pas un développement comparable à celui de la joie, la raison en est peut-être dans le fait que l'exégète nous a quelque peu égarés en formulant une division rhétorique satisfaisante: «Nous avons montré», reprend-il même au § 138, «que la joie appartient en propre au sage; montrons maintenant qu'il en est de même pour l'espérance»[124]. Si, au lieu des thèmes prévus, joie et espérance, le lecteur de Philon prend comme points fixes les personnages bibliques, l'équilibre devient bien plus satisfaisant. Énos répond alors à Noé, dont le sort littéraire apparaît même identique, puisque chacun reçoit 18 lignes de commentaire. Sans préjuger du résultat où conduisent de pareilles observations, il convient de les poser. Le schéma se corrige donc de la manière suivante, en ce qui touche aux extrémités, du moins:

Caïn tristesse et peur	§ 119
Noé . . . / . . .	§ 121−123
. . . / . . .	
Énos (espérance)	§ 138−139
Caïn tristesse et peur	§ 140

---

[124] L'annonce s'en trouve au § 120.

Peu importe pour l'instant que l'espérance d'Énos soit mise en relation, non plus avec la joie, mais simplement avec le repos symbolisé par le personnage de Noé. Nous verrons que leur symétrie réelle n'est autre que celle de l'avenir et du passé. Déjà nous pouvons recueillir un enseignement symbolique: le personnage négatif, Caïn, n'a pas d'histoire, pour ainsi dire. Son destin est stéréotypé, immobile; tel il est au début, tel on le retrouve à la fin. Au contraire, le juste possède et engendre toute une histoire, des figures multiples qui l'enrichissent et le révèlent. Ce n'est donc pas un hasard qu'Énos, signe de l'espérance, bien que placé à la fin, ouvre «le livre des origines de l'humanité» (§ 139). Il existe, on le sait, deux triades mystiques, celle de Énos, Énoch et Noé; celle d'Abraham, Isaac et Jacob. Noé, dans la première, ferme et accomplit une première idée de la vertu; et la seconde Triade mène cette idée à son achèvement en Isaac, par la science d'Abraham et l'entraînement de Jacob. Philon a disposé aux deux extrémités Noé et Énos, appartenant à la première série, pour encadrer le modèle idéal dont ils ne sont que l'image anticipée. Nous verrons même plus loin pourquoi Énos, le premier des trois premiers, apparaît au terme du raisonnement, laissant à Noé le soin d'ouvrir la série des nobles figures.

En introduisant Noé tout d'abord, Philon a évité d'exploiter immédiatement le thème de la ʿjoieʾ, cependant annoncé dès le § 120. Il nous retient un instant sur le palier intermédiaire, celui du ʿreposʾ: les dispositions ennemies de la joie, à savoir les ʿchagrinsʾ mérités par Adam, perdent leur virulence devant Noé. Du coup, le dessein de Philon se révèle plus clairement: il veut privilégier le thème de la ʿjoieʾ en lui faisant occuper le cœur du chapitre, mais non point brusquement. Avec lenteur, il en prépare la signification profonde: une sorte d'itinéraire nous permettra d'en explorer le sens exact, sans erreur ni précipitation. Aussi la fait-il précéder par le repos, et la fait-il suivre par l'espérance, comme pour lui ménager des degrés et lui donner une place de reine. On voit alors que Philon assouplit de deux manières l'annonce du § 120: il ne traitera pas à égalité les deux vertus qui font à égalité la tranquillité du sage, ʿjoie et espéranceʾ; d'autre part, un thème nouveau, même s'il est connexe, s'interpose, celui du ʿreposʾ. Deux personnages bibliques, Noé, Énos, vont rendre acceptables et même esthétiques ces dérogations. De surcroît, ils confirmeront ce que nous avons présumé naguère: à l'immobile destinée du méchant, Caïn, s'oppose l'histoire du juste, puisque sa joie connaît des époques, une sorte de vie, dont la première étape se lit dans le modèle de Noé.

La transition de Noé jusqu'à Sara, sur laquelle nous nous interrogions aussi, se trouve éclairée. Il suffit de ne pas oublier que les § 123b à 125 ne mettent pas tellement en scène le personnage idéal d'Isaac, mais plutôt celui de Sara. De fil en aiguille, nous tenons la solution d'un autre problème laissé en souffrance, le passage de Sara au langage d'Aaron. L'exégète s'est emparé du texte de la Genèse, ch. 21, v. 6: après avoir très sommairement expliqué ces mots: «Le Seigneur a créé pour moi le Rire» par la référence à la paternité divine, il poursuit: «Si quelqu'un est capable d'entendre la création de Dieu, il est lui-même dans la joie, et il partage la joie de ceux qui l'ont d'abord entendue» (§ 124b). Sara proclamait Dieu ποιητής, créateur de son fils, du Rire, Isaac; Philon insiste sur la fonction ποιητική de celui qui rassemble art et nature, Dieu, et il l'entend désormais dans le sens d'une création lyrique et 'poétique'. Mais c'est que le passage est rendu possible par la lettre de la Bible: «Tous ceux qui l'entendront se réjouiront avec moi» (ibid. v. 6 b). Les § 124 b à 125 ne font que poursuivre l'exégèse du verset proposé dans la fin du § 123. Par choc en retour, Sara, qui proclama pour des auditeurs avertis la 'poétique' divine, invite ces auditeurs à se transformer en prophètes, pour célébrer comme elle les mystères de cette création. Le texte de la Bible ne dit-il pas lui-même ensuite: «Qui dira à Abraham que Sara allaite un fils?». Du trop-plein de la connaissance rejaillit la volonté ou la nécessité de la communiquer par la parole. De la sorte, le passage des auditeurs de Sara à la rencontre de Moïse et d'Aaron procède, lui aussi, d'une exégèse suivie. On devra même aller un peu plus loin et comprendre encore que la définition de la 'poésie' divine comme Loi — ces «règles de la vérité gravées sur la pierre» — et comme œuvres de la Nature, définies comme «parfaites, avec l'héritage d'une harmonie propre», cette définition annonce depuis le § 125 le personnage de Moïse, législateur et scrutateur véridique de la Nature des choses.

On voit donc la précision et l'ordre régner partout, et précisément à cette jonction décisive entre le passage de Sara et celui d'Aaron, qu'un tableau présentera mieux:

Noé = éloignement des passions, r e p o s
des { peines
     { joie de Sara

«Dieu a fait . . .   Isaac { fabrication
                                              { 'poésie'   de Dieu

Qui entendra!   e n t e n d u e   } Loi
                                                           } Nature
(et qui dira? . . .)»   d i t e   }
                            pour Moïse   (= Loi, Nature)
                                 par Aaron

A gauche, la séquence scripturaire lue dans sa suite régulière. Si la troisième proposition, «et qui dira?», figure en parenthèse, c'est que Philon ne la cite pas: il se devait de la garder implicite, puisque le thème de la 'joie' exige désormais qu'on enchaîne des citations contenant le substantif de la 'joie', ou le verbe 'se réjouir'. Mais le verset «et qui dira?» reste en filigrane, comme souvent dans Philon, et il anime un autre texte: la rencontre d'Aaron et de Moïse calque, exagère et donc explicite celle des 'prophètes' suscités par Sara avec Sara elle-même . . . De là, cette osmose des deux systèmes: le texte sous-entendu, «et qui dira?», permet l'apparition du texte de l'Exode, et l'un des personnages de l'Exode, celui qui est, comme Sara, situé du côté de l'oreille, de l'intelligence directe des réalités divines, c'est à dire Moïse, est précédé dans le discours progressif de l'Alexandrin par son ombre comme le voyageur qui se présente à la porte contre le soleil couchant. Moïse explique seul la traduction de la 'poétique' divine en Loi et en Nature. La phrase de Sara, «Qui dira?», définit par avance et dit seule ce qui, en Moïse, obligera son frère Aaron à se montrer, car Moïse

demandera lui aussi: ʿQui parlera pour moi? Qui dira pour moi?ʾ Le contenu de
l'Exode, Moïse, est anticipé au § 125 a; l'expression de la Genèse, ch. 21, v. 7,
absent et actif, subsiste discrètement dans le § 125 b:

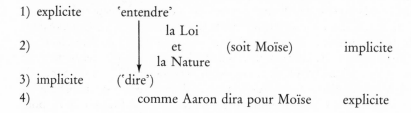

1) explicite   ʿentendreʾ

                       la Loi

2)   et   (soit Moïse)   implicite

                       la Nature

3) implicite   (ʿdireʾ)

4)   comme Aaron dira pour Moïse   explicite

A travers ce contrepoint subtil de l'exégèse apparente et cachée, le thème de la
ʿjoieʾ suit son chemin, d'un rythme constant: joie de Sara; joie des âmes capables
d'ʿentendreʾ la poétique de Dieu; joie des ʿprophètesʾ, qui déjà expriment; joie
d'Aaron, expression par excellence du secret de Moïse . . . On ne serait pas loin
du vrai en pensant même qu'ici la forme littéraire de l'exégèse imite le contenu et
cette correspondance discrète des personnages saints. La ʿraisonʾ du jeu précédent
doit être lue plus simplement comme suit:

    explicite   ʿentendreʾ ⎫
        implicite   ⎰ Moïse ⎰
        implicite   ⎱ ʿdireʾ ⎱
    explicite   Aaron. ⎭

Une alternance des conditions de l'exégèse assure secrètement la cohérence et
l'harmonie du discours.

4. Le temps

   L'économie générale du chapitre peut maintenant montrer toute son efficacité, sa subtile simplicité, ses lenteurs. Placés sous le signe d'Isaac, ses père et
mère, qui sont Abraham et Sara, participent à la présence de Dieu. Ils sont, à en
croire le § 120, en possession de la ʿjoieʾ. Or nous apprenons aussi que «la vie
vertueuse qui a fait l'acquisition du bien, détient la joie», par contraste avec celle
qui n'en est qu'à l'espérance. Mais l'insertion de Noé complète le tableau et le
nuance. Car, s'il est par définition le ʿreposʾ, il l'est en quelque sorte négative-
ment: il fait cesser la lutte et relâche les tourments du vice; en ce sens, il est tourné
vers le passé, et son existence forme une sorte de barrage moral entre le Mal qui a
nom Caïn et un Isaac, décidément parfait. Le § 123 b ne dit-il pas au moment de
présenter Sara: «Quand le juste a repoussé les vices . . .» — ce qui suppose que
l'étape de purification est accomplie, en Noé précisément.
   A l'autre bout du texte, voici Énos, qui «espéra pour la première fois
invoquer le nom du Seigneur». Cette définition du patriarche, toute due à la

Bible, possède aux yeux de Philon plusieurs mérites (nous sommes aux § 138 à 139). Tout d'abord, elle rattache Énos à la fin du commentaire donné au personnage d'Aaron, car la sublimation du langage en Loi nous a fait parvenir jusqu'à Dieu, dont il faut exprimer la Parole; or, maintenant, l'espérance de celui qui est aussi traduit par l'Homme a pour objet 'l'invocation du Nom du Seigneur'. Cette finalité théocentrique définit non seulement l'espérance, mais l'essence de l'homme. Ainsi défini, par l''extase', la 'sortie de soi' exigées pour avoir l'espérance, Énos est orienté vers l'avenir. Il s'oppose du fait de sa reconnaissance du Nom divin à la fausse humanité que Caïn représente, faite de tromperie, de fausse éloquence et surtout de ce vice qui lui donne son nom, Caïn voulant dire 'possession' autonome et orgueilleuse. Dans ces conditions, Philon peut faire revenir Caïn tout à fait naturellement (§ 140), grâce à cette oposition claire: celui qui croyait 'posséder' n'a rien en réalité, sinon les marques du néant que lui donnent la peur et la tristesse, tandis que l'Homme, Énos, accompli justement grâce à sa démission devant Dieu, «obtient en partage et possède» tous les biens (début du § 140). Mais Philon s'intéresse également au problème du temps: la division annoncée au § 120, de la 'joie' et de l''espérance', plaçait la joie dans le temps du présent, τὸ μὲν οὖν ἔχειν ἀποτελεῖ χαράν, ce qui veut dire que la vérité essentielle des personnages saints est aperçue dans une actualité, un temps présent: Sara et Abraham bénéficient de l'immobilité d'Isaac; Aaron, d'autre part, est éclairé par Moïse et placé dans la même éternité de la Loi. La seconde vertu, l'espérance, ouvre l'homme à l'avenir: c'est la part du représentant de l'Homme, Énos; il est rattaché à l'espérance et donc à l'avenir, tandis que Noé, nous délivrant du mal passé, est rattaché au passé. Énos et Noé, l'un au début du chapitre, l'autre à la fin, occupent des positions symétriques et rendent ainsi objective cette relation au temps. Un indice supplémentaire attire l'attention du lecteur de Philon: tous deux, Énos et Noé, sont aussi rattachés au thème du Logos-langage. Au milieu, Aaron exprime en mots et en sons les Idées perçues par Moïse; au début, Noé assume le rôle du «raisonnement juste» — ὁ δίκαιος λογισμός — tandis qu'à la fin, Énos est défini comme «participant de la nature rationnelle» — λογικῆς φύσεως. Tous deux, ils entourent donc, mais sans y habiter la demeure immobile de l'éternité: Isaac et Moïse font entrer Abraham et Sara, puis Aaron, dans l'instant privilégié de la 'joie'. Nous savons par Philon lui-même qu'il a voulu représenter ici les étapes de l'itinéraire moral: en présentant Noé, il dit: «Le premier effet de la justice[125] est de remplacer un travail pénible par le repos» (§ 122). Ce premier effet doit bien être suivi d'autres considérations.

Le temps présent des personnages centraux participe de l'éternité divine qui les éclaire constamment par la Loi, parole de Dieu. Les deux figures latérales et symétriques de Noé et d'Énos, sont placées dans l'histoire: Noé rachète le passé;

---

[125] Cette définition réunit les deux traductions du nom de Noé: il est 'juste' (cf. Legum Allegoriae, III, § 77; De posteritate Caini, § 173; De gigantibus, § 5; De migratione Abrahami, § 125, etc). Il est 'le repos', comme ici.

Énos hérite de l'avenir. Mais à cette logique du temps Philon a surajouté une logique de la logique, pour ainsi dire: au centre, Aaron représente le λόγος προφορικός; au début, Noé dit le raisonnement juste, λογισμός; au terme, Énos a la lumière de ce qui rend le langage correct, la λογικὴ φύσις. Nous pouvons représenter ces systèmes autour des personnages qui en sont le symbole. On voit maintenant que la succession des idées, de linéaire qu'elle semblait au départ, et disproportionnée, est apparue circulaire, complexe, mais parfaitement régulière. C'est que Philon a construit lentement un édifice que seule la mémoire du lecteur, lente et patiente, reconstruit à partir des ensembles. Voici une image de cette exégèse.

Décrets divins (Loi)
Moïse
Aaron
λόγος προφορικός

Sara	(Isaac)	Abraham
thème: ʿentendreʾ	Joie	thème: ʿdireʾ
Noé λογισμός		λογικός Énos

Passé	Présent	Avenir

Or, si l'on continue dans cette direction, il apparaît qu'entre Noé placé au début de l'itinéraire, et Énos, qui en ferme l'évolution, il s'est passé quelque chose; un progrès a été réalisé. Et du même coup, nous pouvons interpréter plus fermement le fait que le commencement et la fin du chapitre soient en rapport avec Caïn. La répétition pure et simple des passions qui le définissent désormais, ʿpeur et tristesseʾ — ʿtristesse et peurʾ veut dire que, pour Caïn, il n'arrive rien, ni progrès ni conversion. Il est, lui aussi, dans un présent, mais un présent immobile et mortel. C'est une caricature de l'immobile richesse intérieure de Moïse communiquée à Aaron, d'Isaac communiquée à Sara ou Abraham, ou ces ʿauditeurs du Dieu-poèteʾ, qui forment le Peuple de la Loi. Noé se rattache de façon précise à Caïn: il met un terme à sa malédiction; il pose une barrière infranchissable au mal. Énos, de l'autre côté, empêche le vice de Caïn de revenir à l'intérieur du territoire de la sainteté: par son espérance et son action de grâces, il oppose une barrière à l'autonomie qui définit Caïn, à la «possession» pervertie. Noé abolit la ʿmalédiction de la terreʾ; Énos ʿpossèdeʾ en vérité. Énos et Noé dominent Caïn, pour le contredire: mais ils le font en association avec une foule d'autres personnages, donnant la main, l'un à Sara, l'autre au Lévite Aaron, et, par eux, à tout un peuple. Caïn, pour sa part, ne rejoint que lui-même, et son autonomie est vaine, ʿtristeʾ. Avec Noé, le ʿpasséʾ touche au ʿprésentʾ; avec Énos, l'ʿavenirʾ envahit déjà le ʿprésentʾ. Au contraire, la durée qui prolonge éternellement les misères de Caïn forme un présent inutile et faux: la ʿtristesseʾ le fixe dans son expérience mauvaise du crime passé; la ʿpeurʾ rend présent un avenir redoutable. Nous pouvons compléter le schéma précédent:

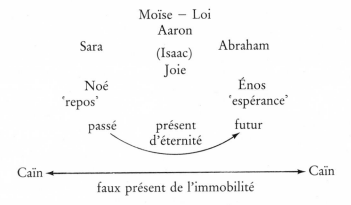

Nous avons par ce détour répondu à la question de savoir pourquoi Noé pré-cédait Énos dans la série des patriarches, malgré la chronologie biblique. Noé délivre l'homme du mal, du Déluge ou de Caïn; Énos empêche le mal de revenir: comme «il invoque le Nom de Dieu», il est d'une valeur plus positive que Noé; il est plus proche d'Aaron, le Lévite, tout «consacré à Dieu».

Il faut encore justifier la place de ce chapitre dans le traité. Il possède une structure en lui-même, une masse, et donc pour Philon une solidité; nous devons aller plus loin, et déterminer sa relation exacte avec le corps du livre. A titre de conclusion, nous allons indiquer brièvement l'économie du 'Quod deterius potiori insidiari soleat' qui répond à cette seconde question.

Le traité comprend deux parties, l'une consacrée au meurtre d'Abel par Caïn, l'autre, au châtiment de Caïn (soit, les § 1 à 95; puis les § 96 à 178). Or, on peut montrer qu'elles sont ainsi menées que l'une répond à l'autre comme la v é r i t é répond à l ' a p p a r e n c e. La première se contente de l'apparence: elle a même un centre, les § 47 à 56, où Philon spécule explicitement sur ce thème; la seconde décrit la réalité: elle a même un centre où Philon explique comment Caïn, meurtrier de son frère, est destiné au 'rien' (c'est là la vérité mortelle de son apparente survie, comme la fin du traité le confirme en 'immortalisant' le mal dans Caïn)[126]; ce centre est formé des § 141 à 149, juste après le chapitre que nous venons d'analyser. Aussi l'on peut comprendre que la 'réalité' de la rhétorique saine n'apparaisse que dans la seconde partie, pays de la vérité. Un simple phéno-mène, immédiatement vérifiable, permettra de l'entrevoir. Le 'Quod deterius' évoque deux fois la rencontre d'Aaron et de Moïse. Or, ces deux développements (les § 38 à 44; les § 126 à 137, pris dans le contexte maintenant éclairci), en principe semblables, sont également dissemblables. Pour résumer, disons que le premier (§ 38 à 44) est 'philosophique': il donne en clair les règles pour le bon usage de la parole et de l'éloquence, nécessaires à la lutte que le sage doit mener contre les sophistes. Le second (notre chapitre, si l'on est fidèle à l'extension donnée par notre analyse), le second prend à témoins un grand nombre de

---

[126] La belle conclusion, des § 167 à 178, reprend le jeu de la mort dans la vie, de l'apparence et de la réalité.

personnages bibliques; et il suit une dialectique raffinée, qui n'est pas dénuée de philosophie, nous l'avons vu, mais bien plus cachée. La supériorité naturelle de l'Écriture et de ses figures symboliques fait que la réponse est donnée seulement dans ce second exposé. Le langage est ici seulement pleinement justifié, placé qu'il se trouve désormais entre l'indépendance et l'autonomie perverse d'un Caïn, d'une part, et, d'autre part, le silence impuissant d'un Moïse privé d'Aaron ou d'un Abel.

Ce n'est pas tout: une ressemblance formelle semble nous permettre de tenir ces considérations pour objectives par rapport à l'intention de Philon[127]. Les deux sections du livre qui ont pour objet la rencontre d'Aaron et de Moïse se trouvent l'une et l'autre juste avant le centre de chacune des deux parties du traité. On le voit bien, Philon confie à la m é m o i r e du lecteur, et non pas seulement à son intelligence, une sorte de tableau, large, composite, régulier. Le s e n s a besoin, pour être dégagé, de l'i m a g i n a t i o n du lecteur.

Notons, à propos de ces deux spéculations de Philon sur Aaron et Moïse, l'une 'philosophique', et donc provisoire, l'autre conduite par l'Écriture, et donc décisive et assurée, que l'on retrouve souvent dans l'œuvre allégorique de Philon cette alternance d'une exégèse qui prend appui sur la 'philosophie', disons sur la considération 'morale', et d'une autre exégèse, qui, elle, déroule un cortège plus ou moins étiré de figures bibliques, de citations et d'images venues de la révélation mosaïque. En général, comme nous le verrons, la seconde exégèse est complexe, ornée de procédés variés. Il faut dire que la distance entre les deux exposés est ici plus grande peut-être que partout ailleurs dans les autres ouvrages de l'Alexandrin. Mais c'est un exemple parfait, à ce titre, pour faire comprendre au lecteur ce que nous voulons dire en parlant de la nécessaire l e n t e u r de l'exégèse philonienne, et du rôle que joue la m é m o i r e.

III. Les procédés de 'dialectique' et de 'philosophie'

Philon a, semble-t-il, fabriqué ou du moins utilisé d'autres moyens techniques d'exposition. Plus cachés que les procédés de grammaire et de rhétorique, ils sont trop souvent employés pour n'être qu'un fruit du hasard littéraire. Nous avons voulu décrire dans ce chapitre les procédés de la 'dialectique'. Nous désignons par ce mot, 'dialectique', un système complexe dans lequel Philon part d'un mot, d'un texte, d'une notion, pour atteindre son c o n t r a i r e logique, et cela par l'intermédiaire d'un mot, d'un texte, d'une notion, qui assure une

---

[127] L'intention n'est pas nécessairement la 'conscience'. Encore une fois, l'objectivité du texte a son domaine propre, que nous ne pouvons confondre avec la subjectivité d'un auteur. Le nom de 'Philon' désigne, si l'on veut, dans ce cas, non point l'ambassadeur de la communauté juive d'Alexandrie, mais l'auteur des exégèses écrites.

médiation effective[128]. Dans un chapitre ultérieur, nous parlerons d'autres procédés, appelés de 'philosophie': tout se passe comme si l'exégète cachait sous un discours moral, biblique, la position de réalités qu'il est plus simple de décrire comme des alliances de concepts philosophiques, telle l'alternance de l'Un et du multiple, d'un aspect statique et d'un aspect dynamique, et ainsi d'autres concepts, le plus souvent antithétiques. Dans ces questions, la terminologie importe moins que l'analyse correcte des faits littéraires. Et c'est d'eux que nous allons nous efforcer de rendre compte.

1. Procédés de 'dialectique'

a) Définitions

La complexité des développements de Philon pour qui cherche à la mettre en évidence, et surtout la variété qu'il met dans l'utilisation de procédés identiques en leur nature rendent impossible l'énumération de tous les cas, ni même d'un grand nombre. Il vaut mieux se limiter à quelques exemples, pour en analyser la genèse. Nous appelons donc 'dialectique' le passage d'un concept dans son opposé, quand ce passage est réglé au moyen d'un troisième terme, à égale distance logique des deux autres. Cette définition sommaire et pratique suppose trois données. En parlant de 'concepts', nous pensons à des couples d'une certaine importance, dont le traitement exégétique témoigne qu'ils sont fondamentaux. C'est le cas des oppositions fécondes, de 'parole / silence', de 'Seigneur / Dieu', les deux grandes Puissances de l'Être; d''être / paraître', dont l'étude du chapitre précédent a fait usage . . . En disant qu'il se produit un 'passage', nous voulons simplement rappeler cet effet de la mémoire dont nous avons également traité précédemment: Philon sépare d'abord avec soin les concepts opposés, et il élabore ensuite leur rapprochement par une transition qui prend entre les deux un certain temps littéraire. Le passage est dit 'réglé', parce qu'un élément médiateur adapté aux deux partis vient les rendre à la coopération, sinon à l'unité: par exemple, le nombre 12, qui est un nombre, donc un pluriel imparfait, mais un nombre symbole d'une certaine perfection, autorise le passage de l'Unité à une multiplicité dominée, saine; ou l'inverse, de la pluralité douteuse à l'unité dominatrice. C'est dire qu'au centre du développement il y a toujours une sorte de concentration, de nœud, de densité particulière.

b) L'exemple du 'miroir', médiation du paraître à l'être, dans le 'De migratione Abrahami', § 94 à 104

Pour faire l'exégèse du quatrième 'don' fait à Abraham, à savoir le 'grand nom', qui fait rejoindre la réalité et l'apparence, Philon invoque le témoignage de

---

[128] Une 'dialectique' prend toujours la forme d'une symétrie, puisque la fin du développement est le contraire du début; mais la réciproque n'est pas exacte: il existe des 'symétries' de simple juxtaposition des éléments, et dénuées de dialectique, c'est à dire de ce passage 'réglé' dont nous allons donner des exemples.

cinq citations bibliques: Lia veut être félicitée à la fois par les femmes (apparence sensible) et par les hommes (vérité mâle); Abraham, déjà, voulait donner un double héritage, de réalités fondamentales et de biens apparents; ce sont des femmes et des hommes qui confectionnent les ornements de l'arche d'alliance, et leur association avec des hommes évite à ces femmes de sombrer dans l'anarchie et de compromettre l'âme, comme le firent les femmes qui incendièrent Moab; quatrième exemple, celui d'Isaac, appelant sur Jacob les dons du ciel et de la terre, nouvelles expressions de l'être et de l'apparence; enfin, le grand-prêtre associe dans le culte l'esprit et la sensation.

Déjà, le lecteur de Philon doit être mis en éveil par le nombre des citations; cinq elles sont, et c'est là un nombre impair qui appelle la disposition symétrique: 2 / 1 / 2. Le troisième cas, celui des femmes associées à des hommes pour la fabrication des ornements cultuels, possède effectivement une particularité qui le détache des autres: il est dédoublé et formé de deux tableaux opposés entre eux, car les femmes de Moab sont uniquement tournées vers le sensible et le malheur, tandis que les femmes mises à l'ouvrage par Moïse produisent du travail de qualité et de vérité[129]. Cette complexité confirme le lecteur dans l'idée qu'il est en présence d'un foyer plus dense. Qu'il regarde plus attentivement.

Portons-nous aux deux extrémités. D'un côté, le § 94 montre qu'Abraham donne en héritage les 'lois de nature' et les 'lois positives'; mais il faut tout de suite observer que les deux séries sont simplement juxtaposées: les bâtards se contenteront des petites donations, mais l'héritier, le fils légitime, possédera les substances. Comme donations et substances représentent les valeurs en question dans le chapitre, à savoir l'être et l'apparaître, disons qu'au début de cette série d'exemples l'être et l'apparaître restent juxtaposés, bien que réunis. Or, ce concept de 'juxtaposition' passe, au terme de la série, dans son contraire, la conjugaison harmonieuse: les § 102 à 104 montrent le grand-prêtre portant sur son vêtement le dessin des réalités sensibles et des puissances intelligibles; cette fois, un seul et même personnage réunit ce que les destinataires des parts d'héritage séparaient au nom de la légitimité ou de la bâtardise.

Continuons cette lecture en considérant maintenant les exemples intermédiaires, l'exemple deuxième, de Lia réclamant la louange des femmes et des hommes; le quatrième, celui d'Isaac, bénissant son fils Jacob d'une double bénédiction, pour la rosée du ciel et pour la graisse de la terre. Avertis par les résultats précédents, nous observons ceci: l'exemple de Lia reste encore dans une certaine juxtaposition des deux valeurs, de l'être (louange masculine) et de l'apparence (louange féminine). C'est un procédé subtil, en effet, qui permet à Philon d'interpréter la citation: «Je suis bienheureuse, parce que (ou: de ce que) les femmes me diront bienheureuse» (d'après la Genèse, ch. 30, v. 13). La première proposition: «Je suis bienheureuse» est absolue, et donc, suppose Philon, elle vient de la vérité directe: c'est une vérité mâle, par opposition à la seconde

---

[129] Dans les § 97 à 98, opposés aux § 99 à 100. Le lecteur retrouve ici une structure déjà rencontrée au début de cet article, dans l'examen d'un passage du 'De fuga et inventione', § 177 à 201; cf. ci-dessus, p. 159–160.

proposition, qui répète la bénédiction[130], mais au compte des femmes, ce qui lui confère une moindre certitude, un caractère sensible et apparent. Les deux phrases sont bien réunies et prononcées de la même bouche, mais leur redoublement est de simple juxtaposition: il n'existe pas de lien, en tout cas pas de lien manifesté, entre l'affirmation absolue, «Je suis bienheureuse», et la redondance: «les femmes me diront bienheureuse». Au contraire, dans le texte invoqué dans l'épisode symétrique (§ 101), la double réalité, «rosée du ciel» et «graisse de la terre» manifeste déjà beaucoup plus de connivence entre les deux termes: pour la simple raison que la graisse du sol dépend de l'irrigation accordée par le ciel. Philon parle avec précision ici: la pluie douce et bienfaisante, capable de féconder la terre, s'oppose à des flots dévastateurs, et il s'agit bien de marquer le rapport, implicite mais réel, qui rapproche les deux bienfaits, du ciel et de la terre. On ajoutera même un détail qui paraîtra gratuit à celui dont la familiarité avec Philon n'est pas encore suffisante: l'exégèse du § 101 est énoncée de façon continue, d'une seule émission de voix, si l'on peut dire, d'une seule phrase; de plus, le texte cité de la Genèse, ch. 27, v. 28 est non seulement commenté, mais prolongé: la fin du paragraphe suppose en effet qu'on lise encore le v. 29 de ce ch. 27 de la Genèse, sur la victoire[131] promise à Jacob. Dè toute manière, tout se déroule entre des personnages singuliers: Isaac possède en soi l'autonomie magnifique de la Nature; Jacob reçoit les deux bienfaits, et il est en lui-même, unifié par la Sagesse qu'il désire. Or, les exemples d'Abraham distribuant son héritage ou de Lia recherchant la félicitation de deux catégories morales, restaient, à prendre les acteurs de l'épisode, dans la division, la dualité. Ici, tout se rapproche au point d'honorer un seul et même citoyen de la vertu.

Au résultat, nous pouvons opposer les deux premiers cas aux deux derniers, comme ceux de la juxtaposition de l'être et de l'apparaître à ceux de la communauté harmonieuse, en précisant que cette formule vaut précisément du premier opposé au cinquième, et qu'elle se reporte de manière plus discrète dans les exemples voisins. On peut représenter ce processus cohérent:

§ 94 héritier / bâtards   § 102−104 vêtement unique
juxtaposition   communauté
§ 95−96 deux chœurs   § 101 la continuité de
pour une même bénédiction   la pluie à la richesse
juxtaposition plus   communauté encore
resserrée   implicite

Mais cela n'est jamais qu'une symétrie. Nous avons besoin de l'exemple des femmes travaillant pour Moïse: il est le troisième; il est le pivot. Et non seulement les deux rapports de l'être et de l'apparence se disposent autour de lui dans une

---

[130] Il faudrait dire, plus techniquement, 'béatitude'.

[131] Cette possibilité d'enchaîner un verset avec le verset suivant signifie, dans l'habitude de Philon, qu'il sont en partie synonymes; et donc, ici, si nous revenons au v. 28, il comprend également comme pratiquement synonymes les deux parties de l'oracle prononcé par Isaac, au sujet du ciel, au sujet du sol.

figure symétrique, mais, nous allons le montrer, c'est lui qui fait passer la juxtaposition en communauté et dans cette harmonie du 'chœur' unique dont parle le § 104, encore élargi par le trait final du § 105, prenant son symbolisme dans l'union conjugale[132].

Nous voici donc en possession d'une structure claire et significative d'une transformation d'un concept: la juxtaposition deviendra la communauté harmonique. Que faut-il logiquement pour ce passage? Un élément intermédiaire, où l'on retrouve explicités les éléments caractéristiques des deux volets. Il faut encore un élément dynamique[133], capable de donner le mouvement nécessaire à la transition: car les deux parties ci-dessus analysées restent immobiles, donnant, d'un côté, les personnages séparés, de l'autre, les personnages réunis. Or ces deux conditions de la 'médiation' sont magnifiquement remplies dans les § 97 à 100, l'épisode dédoublé des femmes d'Israël et des femmes de Moab. Voici comment, et la réalisation est très simple: Philon a trouvé dans le symbole du 'miroir' l'élément dynamique et médiateur. L'héritier ou les bâtards d'Abraham reçoivent leur part; Lia sollicite la bénédiction des hommes comme des femmes; Isaac veut pour Jacob la chaîne de la prospérité; le grand-prêtre porte sa tunique historiée[134]: tout ce monde est là, immobile, arrêté dans une attitude chaque fois exemplaire[135]. Mais les femmes de Moïse agissent. Leur action est une transformation d'un même objet, le 'miroir'. Il a servi à flatter la sensibilité par la coquetterie; désormais, il servira la pureté: le prêtre s'y regardera pour déceler la plus petite souillure. Il n'est guère besoin d'insister: l'image parle d'elle-même. Et non seulement l'episode fournit un mouvement, mais il participe des deux séries qui l'entourent. Bien mieux, les relations des § 97 à 100 avec les deux volets antithétiques sont croisées, en chiasme, si l'on veut. En effet, l'épisode des femmes confectionnant les broderies a trait au culte, comme le dernier exemple, du grand-prêtre entrant dans le sanctuaire avec son vêtement[136] composite; dans les deux, précisément, il est question des parures corporelles[137]. L'épisode des femmes pieuses évoque également le 'jeûne' (§ 98), quand le quatrième exemple, celui d'Isaac appelant la bénédiction sur Jacob, évoque la 'richesse' et la 'graisse de la terre' (§ 101), comme si la purification introduisait de l'ascèse à la prospérité. De façon homologue, le second épisode de la section centrale, celui des femmes de Moab (§ 99b à 100), est

---

[132] Il aurait d'abord fallu démontrer, sans doute, que le § 105 donne la conclusion de tout le chapitre, en relation étroite avec notre section des § 94 à 104, mais sans faire partie de la série.

[133] On le voit, notre étude de la 'dialectique' fait appel à des valeurs que nous avons annoncées comme procédés 'philosophiques', tellement l'exégèse de Philon use de complexité.

[134] Le vêtement du grand-prêtre portrait une représentation de l'univers astral. Cf. Mos., II, § 12 et 117.

[135] Nous ferons une distinction tout à l'heure à propos du dernier: synthèse de l'ensemble des figures, lui aussi, il se meut, s'avançant dans le sanctuaire (début du § 104 – εἰσιόντος εἰς τὰ ἅγια).

[136] Philon a pris soin, nous dirons pourquoi tout à l'heure, de dire la chose – οἱ μέλλοντες ἱερουργεῖν – sans dire le mot, qui ne paraîtra qu'au § 102 – ἀρχιερεύς.

[137] Le vêtement lui aussi est un 'lieu' de l'échange mystique: d'objet de coquetterie, il devient décor pour le sanctuaire.

en direction inverse: il souligne le mal dans lequel l'abandon à la sensibilité entraînerait l'âme[138]; or, cet aspect proprement dangereux, féminin, rappelle la double présence, dans la première série, des 'femmes', dont il est dit et souligné qu'elles sont compromettantes, «toujours soumises à l'apparence» (fin du § 95), d'une part, et, d'autre part, des 'bâtards' d'Abraham, qui sont, au début du texte (§ 94), le signe d'une existence mixte, comme ils sont les «fils des concubines», d'autres 'femmes'. Il faut ajouter que dans l'épisode central, que nous comparons en ce moment avec les quatre autres, deux à deux, les 'femmes' pieuses cessent de l'être en réalité: Philon leur fait enlever les attributs féminins de la sensibilité, parures et miroir; à la vérité il ne dit pas qu'elles cessent d'être des femmes, mais il emploie une image équivalente dans son code: «elles ont des raffinements de citadines, par opposition à ces autres femmes . . . qui n'ont pas de cité» (§ 99). Il sera utile de tracer un schéma qui résume toutes ces observations:

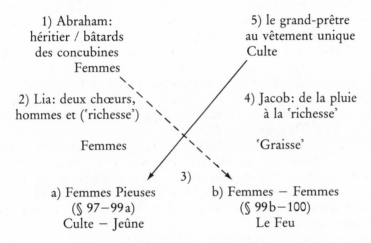

1) Abraham:
héritier / bâtards
des concubines
Femmes

5) le grand-prêtre
au vêtement unique
Culte

2) Lia: deux chœurs,
hommes et ('richesse')

4) Jacob: de la pluie
à la 'richesse'

Femmes

'Graisse'

3)

a) Femmes Pieuses
(§ 97–99 a)
Culte – Jeûne

b) Femmes – Femmes
(§ 99 b–100)
Le Feu

Un indice, peut-être, de la transformation des femmes pieuses elles-mêmes sera trouvé dans l'absence du nom des officiants, au § 98. La périphrase, οἱ μέλλοντες ἱερουργεῖν a pour effet d'atténuer la différence entre les femmes, qui tissent les voiles ou qui fondent leur bronze, et ces personnages en train de se purifier. Elles-mêmes, par le dépouillement, se purifient, et ces officiants ne sont là que pour redoubler le schème de la transformation. Comme en un 'miroir' — s'il faut prendre à Philon l'exégèse de Philon — au milieu de cette dialectique, les deux réalités, mâle et féminine, se regardent, se révèlent mutuellement, échangent leur pureté. Les unes se purifient en perdant leur 'sensibilité'; les autres — et ce sont les mêmes, dans le symbole[139] — les autres se purifient en profitant du sacrifice, mais en gardant la «mémoire des miroirs» que c'était là — κατὰ μνήμην ἐσόπτρων. Ce

---

[138] Même cet épisode contient une transformation: le feu détruira ce qui était valeur mâle et noétique.

[139] Il s'agit bien d'un σύμβολον, où les deux fragments rapprochés rendent la figure initiale et entière.

dernier détail du texte, étrange au premier abord, est fondamental: il signifie que, par une sorte de croisement des idées, quand les femmes visent la pureté en abandonnant leur miroir, les officiants cherchent ce miroir sensible pour achever leur propre pureté . . . Un pareil détail révèle la structure souterraine du discours, sa logique réelle. Et s'il fallait une preuve décisive que notre analyse correspond à la réalité, qu'il suffise de signaler maintenant que Philon a bien conscience d'achever ici la séquence des femmes, en ouvrant celle des vertus viriles, puisque nous retrouvons au milieu même de toute la section, au début du § 99, la mention des «femmes dont Lia désire le témoignage»[139a]. Le nom de Lia clôt en effet le premier volet.

La transformation intéresse le problème fondamental de l'être et de l'apparence: Philon a conduit la 'preuve' scripturaire de telle sorte qu'elle ait la forme d'un itinéraire moral, où, une fois de plus, le mal se laisse entrevoir en plein milieu, mais racheté par les figures avoisinantes. Faut-il de plus faire observer que l'entrée et la sortie de ce chemin sont gardés, l'une par la Loi (les biens distribués comme héritage par Abraham reproduisent les deux catégories de lois, § 94), l'autre par l'harmonie des intelligibles (§ 104) que seul, le culte permet d'entendre? Au milieu, avec l'épisode des femmes et de la transformation, la conversion, venue de la Loi et cherchant l'adoration, prend toute sa valeur de moyen. Entre ces éléments, deux bénédictions, celle de Lia, celle de Jacob, font descendre, à mi-chemin, la splendeur de la Fin dans les étapes de l'émigration — qui forme le sujet de l'ouvrage 'De migratione Abrahami'.

C'est ainsi qu'une suite d'exemples empruntés de-ci de-là à l'histoire biblique, loin d'être une preuve par accumulation, apparaît comme une dialectique précise, parfaitement mesurée, riche d'enseignements qu'on peut arrêter à plusieurs niveaux de profondeur et de subtilité, sans jamais prendre en défaut la cohérence du texte, ni sa sobriété, ni les détails dont il se sert pour préciser le mouvement essentiel.

Pour en finir avec cette analyse, nous dirons à titre d'hypothèse ceci: il n'est pas impossible que l'organisation générale de ces § 94 à 104 du 'De migratione Abrahami' ait pris une certaine forme paradoxale. Le troisième exemple, en principe destiné à opérer la médiation, le passage souple d'une juxtaposition à une communauté de l'être avec l'apparence, est, parmi les cinq, celui qui se présente en deux parties brusquement tranchées: le tableau des femmes de Moab ne semblait pas prévu, et, en dehors de la structure que nous avons esquissée, il paraîtra aberrant ou comme l'effet d'une association d'idées. La souplesse et la fermeté sont associées dans le travail de Philon, et toutes les exégèses répondent simultanément à plusieurs canevas. C'est ainsi que ce troisième exemple, dont nous avons jusqu'ici affirmé légitimement qu'il était dédoublé entre deux types de

---

[139a] Rien n'est moins sûr que la restitution souvent admise, d' αἰσθήσεις à la suite de γυναῖκες (début du § 99). Pour mieux comprendre l'idée qui permet d'opposer les femmes vertueuses aux dévastatrices de Moab, comme des ἀσταί τε καὶ ἀστεῖαι à des ἀπόλιδες, on se souviendra que la Bible (Nombres, ch. 21, v. 30) ne donne pas l'ethnique des secondes. Pour l'idée, cf. Legum allegoriae, III, 1—2: le méchant est ἄπολις.

femmes, peut en même temps obéir à une autre forme littéraire simple: Philon[140], dans les § 97 à 100, n'a pas montré réellement la conjonction des hommes et des femmes. Contrairement aux autres exégèses, de l'héritage, de la double béné-diction de Lia ou de Jacob, et du vêtement sacerdotal, l'exégèse des femmes pieuses avec son complément (§ 97 à 100) ne dit qu'au début et à la fin, rapidement et hors commentaire littéral, «Moïse a confié l'exécution des ornements sacrés à des femmes aussi bien qu'à des hommes» (début du § 97), et «les faveurs des sensations en même temps que celles des hommes, les raisonne-ments . . .» (fin du § 100). Le commentaire proprement dit est ainsi composé:

§ 97—98a femmes pieuses   § 99b—100 femmes déchaînées
        seules   seules
              § 98b officiants (hommes)
                         seuls

Chaque groupe est indépendant. Mais la différence entre les premières femmes et le bataillon des secondes réside en ceci: les premières, parce qu'elles sont ἀσταί τε καὶ ἀστεῖαι[140a], restent, même à distance, dans la communauté des hommes, tandis que les secondes, ἀπόλιδες, perdent toute direction du bien. Une sorte de république est ainsi fondée, libre. La communauté n'est pas une force de type mécanique: la distance relative ne la diminue pas. Aussi, le dernier mot de toute cette exégèse est-il en faveur de de la liberté: l'image du chœur (§ 104), où la symphonie naît de la contribution de chacun, s'achève bien sur cette expression: κατὰ μέρος χορευταῖς ἀπεικάζεται. Ce qui apparaît en notion à la fin vient de la troisième hypothèse, située au milieu. C'est là le s i g n e d'une 'dialectique' bien conduite. L'exégèse du vêtement porté par le grand-prêtre ne réunit-elle pas, de surcroît, des traits propres à chacune des quatre hypothèses précédentes? Elle traite des objets intelligibles, dans la même perspective intellectualiste que les exemples de Lia et de Jacob; elle part du vêtement cultuel, comme l'exemple des femmes pieuses, et elle en adopte même l'aspect dynamique: le prêtre «entre dans le sanctuaire» (§ 104), et tout vient s'ordonner en un chœur de musique; enfin, elle rejoint la première exégèse des lois distribuées par l'héritage d'Abraham (§ 94), mais d'une manière plus subtile: le culte complète la loi. Le § 105, conclusion de tout le chapitre consacré au quatrième présent fait par Dieu à Abraham, nomme la Loi: Συνόλως γὰρ, ἥ φησιν ὁ νόμος . . . et ce que dit alors la Loi n'est autre chose que la réunion des trois thèmes illustrés par les cinq exemples bibliques: τὰ δέοντα reprend les ὑπάρχοντα – ὑπαρκτά d'Abraham (§ 94); τὸν ἱματισμόν reprend les parures et la tunique sacerdotale (§ 97 et 102); enfin, l'ὁμιλία d é s i g n e l'aptitude à tenir ensemble l'intelligible et le sensible (§ 105, fin): or, Lia a enfanté Asher, «symbole de la richesse sensible et bâtarde» (deuxième exemple, § 95), comme Jacob doit hériter de «la richesse sensible et

---

[140] Il convient, on le voit, de renoncer à suivre mentalement l'idée intellectuelle, pour surveiller la présentation littéraire.

[140a] Ce jeu de mots est à la fois une élégance et un symbole d'origine stoïcienne, celui de la citoyenneté de la vertu.

terrestre» (quatrième exemple, § 101), mais dans la conjonction étroite[141] avec la raison masculine ou le ciel[142].

c) La nécessité de ces analyses et le sens de la 'dialectique'

La difficulté d'une telle structure et de sa mise au jour vient en partie des habitudes mentales qui nous font projeter sur la technique de Philon des catégories vérifiées dans d'autres exégèses, celles des Pères de l'Église, par exemple. La compréhension de l'exégèse spécifique de Philon exige ces reconstructions. Les citations bibliques ne sont pas pour lui de simples 'témoins', successivement appelés pour 'prouver' une affirmation initiale; et nous avons dû passer de l'idée simpliste d'une énumération à celle, simple mais ordonnée et approfondie, d'une dialectique. Mais quel est l'intention de pareilles élaborations? La réponse à cette question fondamentale n'est pas facile. Tout d'abord, affirmons qu'il suffit qu'on puisse les constater: en faire l'analyse, montrer les relations de tous les termes, voilà déjà un premier travail, légitimé par son succès même. Il est ensuite possible d'aller un peu plus loin. Philon use de ce procédé non seulement dans le cas d'une liste d'exemples (la liste des sens du mot 'source', dont nous avons parlé au début; ou la liste des personnages heureux telle que nous l'avons développée dans notre deuxième partie[143]; ou celle des couples réunissant l'intelligible et le sensible, comme nous venons de la voir), mais encore dans des exégèses libres. On ne peut pas prévoir où Philon décide de s'en tenir à un commentaire linéaire, sans symétrie ni donc dialectique; où il veut une simple composition régulière et symétrique[144]; où, enfin, l'idée exige une élaboration plus forte, celle de la dialectique. Mais, là où elle existe, cette forme d'exposition correspond à une notion intellectuelle et mystique très simple, mais assez féconde pour produire des exégèses nombreuses et diverses, tantôt brèves, tantôt prolongées. Cette idée pourrait être ainsi exprimée: la Bible est une en son fond; elle est multiple en son discours, et, par là, semblable apparemment au *logos* dont Philon dit plusieurs fois qu'il court trop vite en un flot désordonné. Mais, de même que le *logos* humain doit, pour être juste, se laisser diviser[145], de même le Discours de la Bible est-il parsemé d'indications, ténues mais fermes, qui permettent de l'ordonner, ou plutôt d'en apercevoir l'ordre pré-existant. C'est ainsi que toutes les formules de la 'joie'[146] risquent de ne rien nous expliquer, même réunies en faisceau ou en liste exhaustive, jusqu'à ce que l'une d'entre elles, plus complexe, permette non seulement de rassembler, mais de hiérarchiser les autres: bref, l'une d'entre elles

---

[141] Il faut même préciser, d'après l'analyse ci-dessus: une conjonction qui reste juxtaposition dans le cas de Lia, mais qui atteint à la communication dans le cas de la pluie produisant la 'graisse de la terre'.

[142] Le § 105 entre finalement dans la dialectique: Philon possède une habileté consommée pour conclure, lier sans confusion.

[143] Ci-dessus, p. 182—194.

[144] La 'symétrie' fera comme telle l'objet d'un développement ultérieur, ci-dessous, p. 211—216. Il n'y a pas de dialectique sans symétrie, mais le contraire n'est pas vrai.

[145] Cf. le traité 'De sacrificiis Abelis et Caini', § 81 à 85.

[146] Dans le texte du 'Quod deterius potiori insidiari soleat', analysé ci-dessus, § 119 à 140.

est médiatrice. Elle rend seule intelligible la somme des autres, et de même leur éventuelle contrariété (la même 'joie' peut faire 'rire' et provoquer les 'larmes'[147]), qu'il convient de sauver[148]. L'Écriture est habitée d'un seul Logos, dont les échos multiples ne sont pas indifférents: tel et tel, dans telle catégorie morale, dans telle constellation d'Idées, possède un caractère spécial qui aux avertis donne le signe attendu. Ainsi, le troisième exemple d'une âme capable de réunir le sensible et l'intelligible, dans la dialectique précédente. Ainsi, en dehors de toute série, la médiation de Moïse dans le premier 'chapitre' du 'Quis heres', qui va nous offrir un modèle plus large du même principe.

d) La 'médiation' de l'excès dans le 'Quis heres', § 3 à 39

Plus rapidement, le beau départ du 'Quis heres' nous permettra de surprendre plusieurs ressorts cachés de l'exégèse philonienne. De quoi s'agit-il en ce début de traité? De comprendre pourquoi Abraham, comblé de biens, peut encore demander quelque chose à Dieu; et comment il peut sortir du silence, que la joie[149] ou du moins le respect inspirent. Sans entrer dans le détail, bien trop complexe, nous disons que le début affirme la nécessité du silence, et que la fin (§ 30) consacre en Abraham le fait qu'il ait pris la parole: Moïse lui-même «a gravé sur la stèle ce que j'ai éprouvé: Abraham s'approcha, dit-il, pour déclarer: J'ai maintenant commencé de parler au Seigneur, mais je suis terre et poussière». Philon pour réussir ce passage entre deux contraires, parole et silence, a essayé deux voies, si l'on peut s'exprimer ainsi. Il expose d'abord (§ 3 à 9)[150] une sorte de philosophie du bon sens et de la convenance (ἐν τῷ δέοντι du § 5, et ἄξιον du § 7), qui autorise le bon serviteur à prendre la parole devant son maître. Mais, au § 10, l'exégèse repart comme si rien n'était vraiment prouvé ou acquis. Et Philon d'entreprendre une vaste exploration du couple 'silence' / 'parole'. La péripétie décisive a lieu dans les § 14 à 19, que le lecteur voudra bien relire ici. Philon nous fait alors monter et descendre, une fois de plus, l'échelle des sons: les ignorants doivent se taire (§ 14, début); mais, symétriquement, Moïse est montré en train de 'crier' (§ 14b): le texte suit les degrés de la voix, λέγειν – λέγειν σὺν ἠρεμίᾳ – μετὰ κραυγῆς μείζονος ἐκβοᾶν (§ 14b à 15), pour revenir ensuite au 'parler', à l'entretien de Dieu et de Moïse (§ 17), installés dans un imparfait d'éternité, puis au 'parler' prophétique du médiateur (§ 19), et enfin au 'silence' des ignorants (ibidem).

Les citations de l'Exode et de son contexte ont pris le relais des citations de la Genèse. Moïse semble avoir pris la place d'Abraham. Sans qu'on puisse déterminer, semble-t-il, une symétrie analogue à la précédente, les § 14b et 15 se

---

[147] Ainsi dans le traité 'De migratione Abrahami', § 151 à 158.

[148] 'Sauver', au sens de la science antique, σῴζειν τὰ φαινόμενα.

[149] Quis heres, § 3 et 22.

[150] Il faudrait toute l'analyse de détail pour justifier cette césure et la différence des deux sections. Disons simplement à titre d'indication: le § 9, comme le § 30 renferment une épitaphe d'Abraham, une sorte d'éloge funèbre, qui sert de conclusion aux deux parties du commentaire.

présentent comme le milieu logique de l'épisode. Or, que s'y passe-t-il? Ceci, de
tout à fait remarquable: quelque chose en Dieu permet le passage, en Moïse, du
silence à la parole. Une exégèse subtile de l'interrogation de Moïse, «Que cries-tu
vers Moi?», fait observer que Dieu interroge tout en connaissant la réponse. Or,
de son côté, Moïse n'a rien dit . . . du moins extérieurement. Philon met
ensemble ces deux excès, ces deux abus du langage: quelqu'un parle sans voix;
quelqu'un parle au-delà du sens. Telle est la médiation cherchée. Le passage de
Moïse qui le conduit du silence − n'oublions pas que Moïse était tout d'abord
muet, incapable de parler (le § 4 nous le rappelle expressément − βραδύγλωσ-
σος) − à la parole et au cri, est réglé par un moyen terme, l'interrogation inutile
et abusive de Dieu: celui-ci devrait logiquement se taire, puisqu'Il sait tout. Il
rejoint, en parlant, un Moïse qui ne devrait logiquement pas être entendu,
puisqu'il se tait: οὐ στόματι καὶ γλώττῃ[151]. Désormais, Abraham revenant
pourra user du langage: il ne le fera plus en 'serviteur' louable, comme la première
justification le disait (§ 3 à 9), mais en 'ami', comme la seconde preuve le souligne
(§ 21: πρὸς ἑαυτοῦ φίλον). Abraham, au début noyé dans le flot de l'infinité
divine, existe à la fin, dans la définition même que Philon lui accorde régulièrement, à savoir comme interrogateur de Dieu. Cela est devenu possible grâce au
'cri' absurde de Moïse et à la question abusive de Dieu (§ 15). Alors, capable de
parler sans violer le silence, Abraham connaît la jouissance de soi-même ('jouissance': ἀπλήστως οὖν εὐωχοῦμαι τοῦ κράματος, au § 29, premiers mots; 'de
soi': l' ἐγώ de l'épitaphe du § 30 sera développé dans les § 31 à 39). Du néant
marqué par le silence et l'infinité divine, Abraham est venu à l'existence mesurée.
Seule l'analyse complète montrerait que nous ne faisons ici que lire.

e) Autres exemples de la 'médiation'

Le traité 'Quis heres' contient lui-même plusieurs exégèses semblables. Mais
l'une des plus subtiles manifestations du procédé se rencontre dans le premier
chapitre du 'De mutatione nominum'. Philon y traite de la distinction et de la
communauté des trois appellations divines, l'Être, Seigneur, Dieu; l'analyse concrète est menée de telle sorte que, autour de l'Être immobile, les deux titres
adverses et complémentaires, de Κύριος / Θεός, échangent leurs propriétés en
une série de traitements impossibles à résumer. Pour passer du titre divin de Θεός
à celui de Κύριος, tous deux impropres et tous deux échangeant leurs valeurs,
Philon place au milieu du développement un élément médiateur: un témoin de cet
échange et en même temps de l'impropriété des noms divins surmontée par une
sorte de ruse. Cet élément de médiation est donné par la scène fameuse où Jacob
lutte avec l'Ange de Yahvé. L'Ange refuse son nom à Jacob. Mais l'Ange lui
accorde sa bénédiction. Or, bien analysée (§ 14 à 17 du 'De mutatione nominum'), la bénédiction conduit à la notion de Cause; et la notion de Cause
conduit à son tour jusqu'à la reconnaissance du Seigneur − Κύριος, ce titre même

---

[151] C'est au § 18 que Philon précise bien: Dieu ayant 'répondu', il faut poser que Moïse a
interrogé, car la Bible commence *ex abrupto*: «Dieu répondit à Moïse . . .».

qui, au début, ne pouvait être prononcé qu'improprement − οὐ κυρίως[152] (d'après le § 11 et le § 13). La même citation biblique contient et donc surmonte les deux réalités contraires, de l'ineffable et du communiqué.

Il y aurait toute une étude à faire des héros ou des citations de passage dans Philon. La double transgression, de Dieu et de Moïse dans le 'Quis heres', § 15, la transmutation du miroir en bassin de purification, dans le 'De migratione Abrahami', § 98, la ruse de l'Ange pour dire à Jacob sans lui dire, sont des éléments symboliques évidents. Terminons en évoquant deux héros de passage, d'ailleurs associés, Nadab et Abiud, que nous trouvons à la fin du 'Quis heres', § 309, au milieu d'une exégèse qui combine avec une extraordinaire virtuosité tous les aspects du feu. Le commentaire porte sur le «four fumant» qui passe entre les parts égales qu'Abraham a disposées pour son sacrifice (Genèse, ch. 15, v. 17). Il s'agit toujours de passer d'une image à son contraire, et d'une façon réglée. Ici, Abraham doit aller de la 'fumée', la manifestation la plus obscure et la moins chaude, à la flamme brillante des 'torches' (qui suivent, au v. 17b). Philon a su réunir tous les degrés: nous avons la fumée passant dans l'eau des larmes, le four cuisant les nourritures et faisant passer du cru au cuit, l'étincelle prête à bondir en flamme, la cendre prête à redevenir feu éteint, la lumière réalisée du feu ou des torches brillantes et immobiles. Or, au milieu de cette liste, le § 309 exprime très clairement le passage. Philon y montre les deux transformations possibles et contraires, du four en cendre refroidie ou en feu sacré. Nadab et Abiud dont considérés au moment de leur embrasement, en ce point de sublimation où le four cesse de fumer pauvrement pour flamber. Or, en même temps, Nadab et Abiud font la synthèse du divin et de l'humain: ils se sont sacrifiés, et c'est là un effort humain; mais ils «reçoivent leur transformation» (fin du § 309), et le lecteur de Philon doit tout observer: le mot 'transformation' dit éloquemment ce que nous cherchons à montrer en parlant de 'dialectique', et le passif δέξασθαι annonce la passivité des héros. Cette observation resterait intéressante sans plus, si elle ne permettait de comprendre l'ensemble du texte considéré: c'est qu'au début (§ 307), la flamme était celle de la 'vertu', c'est à dire de l'effort humain, et qu'à la fin (§ 312), il s'agit de la flamme des 'Puissances divines'. Le symbolisme du feu a servi l'idée théologique. Tous deux ont trouvé une médiation dans l'exemple privilégié de Nadab et Abiud. Dans toute la série des occasions où la Bible parle des éléments du feu, elle contient aux yeux de Philon un caractère spécifique, actif et révélateur, qui permet de l'utiliser comme outil de médiation.

Mais, en parlant de la 'dialectique', nous avons souvent touché à d'autres problèmes, et, en particulier, nous avons désigné des couples de notions 'philosophiques': le début du traité 'Quis heres' ne fait-il pas venir Abraham d'une sorte d'anéantissement à une 'existence' personnelle, rendue concrète par le mélange (κρᾶμα, au § 29, et, déjà, dans la fin du § 28) de deux sentiments contraires, la crainte et le respect? Et ce 'mélange' n'annonce-t-il pas la 'division', qui forme tout un immense chapitre dans le même traité?

---

[152] Ce jeu de mots, entre Κύριος − «Seigneur», et κύριον ὄνομα − «nom propre», «nom proprement attribué», revient plusieurs fois dans ce chapitre. C'est lui qui introduit même le titre divin dans la discussion, au § 11.

2. Procédés de 'philosophie'

a) Définitions

Nous ne désignons pas ici la philosophie propre à Philon. Ce sont des 'procédés' intérieurs à la composition littéraire que nous voulons mettre en évidence, et non pas le système métaphysique, physique ou moral de l'Alexandrin. Les chapitres précédents de cet article ont déjà montré au lecteur l'emploi que nous faisions de ces couples de concepts antithétiques, 'néant / existence'; ou 'statique / dynamique', etc. Nous rangeons cette étude dans celle de l'exégèse, et même des procédés d'exégèse, parce qu'ils servent, dans Philon, à équilibrer le commentaire: Philon bâtit pour ainsi dire une interprétation de tel texte biblique en distribuant la matière, vocables, images, citations annexes, style — et jusqu'à des omissions[153] — entre deux volets d'un diptyque 'philosophique', en ce sens que les couples de concepts ci-dessous permettent de comprendre de la façon la plus simple l'économie du développement[154]. Bien entendu, les 'concepts' ainsi révélés ne sont pas exprimés par Philon: ils restent implicites, ou plus exactement c'est l'interprète de Philon qui les nomme. Les noms que nous emploierons restent donc provisoires; mais les faits littéraires qu'ils permettent d'expliquer appartiennent, eux, à l'écriture de Philon, à son exégèse.

b) Les cadres de l'imagination

Il arrive fréquemment dans la littérature biblique de toutes les époques[155] que telle composition emprunte la forme d'un diptyque, dont les volets sont dominés, l'un par le schème du temps, et l'autre, par celui de l'espace. Le traité 'Quis heres' s'emploie à confirmer Abraham dans une existence mesurée, comme nous l'avons dit: or, le début repose sur une démonstration du temps où Abraham peut exister, l'avenir qui donnera au patriarche la nouveauté, l'héritier ou l'héritage, le sauvant de l'infinité des dons passés (cf. § 30 à 39, au terme de la

---

[153] Nous avons touché un mot des 'silences', ci-dessus, p. 177–178.

[154] Le problème d'une interprétation est, dans un premier temps, celui que nous tenons dans cet article, de ramener dans la mesure du possible les faits littéraires multiples à des foyers d'unité les plus simples possible, et sans privilégier un thème, aussi riche qu'il puisse être dans l'ouvrage étudié. Les faits littéraires du texte de Philon obéissent de la manière la plus générale à la symétrie, dialectique ou non. Il contraint son lecteur à projeter dans un espace imaginaire deux séries de valeurs que la mémoire fait ensuite interpréter l'une par l'autre. Il n'est pas 'philosophe' pur, et ses 'idées' ne suivent pas la logique conceptuelle. Ses traités allégoriques illustrent le 'schème transcendantal' kantien ou son héritière, l'Imageation de FICHTE.

[155] Le livre de Jonas est partagé en deux époques: le premier épisode le montre parcourant des lieux éloignés de sa mission; le second est sous le signe de l'impatience. Les symboles de l'espace, dans le premier, du temps, dans le second, vont jusqu'au détail. Les deux grandes aventures d'Élie (I Rois, ch. 18 et 19) se déroulent, l'une sous le signe du temps (le sacrifice du Carmel), l'autre sous le signe de l'espace (la fuite au mont Horeb). Le prologue de Matthieu associe une généalogie (temps) et le récit de plusieurs voyages (espace), avec les Mages et Joseph.

dialectique des § 3 à 29). A la fin du traité, Philon donne un contenu réel à ce 'temps' nouveau: il s'agit du temps exact de la 'prophétie', le midi du sacrifice et de l'illumination. Mais, dans l'intervalle, le commentaire du ch. 15 de la Genèse et le symbolisme de la Division composent un espace symbolique: le monde entier, astres et éléments, les images matérielles du culte dessinent un lieu ordonné, une représentation étalée de l'univers, un parcours que l'âme, capable de diviser le *logos,* suit en compagnie du Logos. Dans le traité 'De migratione Abrahami', théoriquement destiné à montrer le départ d'Abraham, l'exégèse est menée de telle façon que la notion de la Fin — τέλος — occupe le centre du commentaire; bien mieux, la troisième partie de l'ouvrage nous reporte dans le lointain passé d'Abraham, c'est à dire la première émigration qui le conduisit d'Ur des Chaldéens jusqu'à la ville de Haran. Une savante combinaison des schèmes spatiaux et temporels donne une sorte de sentiment de la totalité: la Fin, dans la seconde partie, n'est-elle pas décrite sous la forme d'un itinéraire, d'après les mots du texte biblique commenté, «Abraham allait selon la parole de Dieu», où le verbe 'aller' prend et garde l'accent tout au long de l'exégèse?

Un certain nombre d'antithèses jouent dans le discours de Philon le rôle d'organisatrices. Les § 118 à 122 du traité 'De migratione Abrahami' expliquent comment le sage attire la bénédiction sur les autres hommes. Or, le développement part d'un juste placé en position de force: il est 'surveillant'; il jouit d'une certaine autonomie, d'un mérite personnel, en quelque sorte; mais, au terme, ce juste n'est plus présenté que comme 'suppliant'. Le commentaire est divisé en deux parties: les § 118 à 119 montrent l'activité du sage, qui donne à tous la santé et la sauvegarde; les § 121 à 122 montrent sa passivité: de créateur de vie, il devient d'abord suppliant, puis petit reste, chétif devant la Cause unique. Philon a fait usage de deux axes 'philosophiques' dissimulés: l'axe 'statique / dynamique' et l'axe 'multiple / Un'. Ajoutons que le § 120, entre les deux parties, propose un schème dialectique de transformation: l'image du feu[156].

Un très beau chapitre du 'Quis heres' est construit sur une variation du schème 'activité/passivité'[157]. Autour d'un centre également dialectique, à savoir les § 112 à 113, consacrés à l'image de la Tente plantée au milieu du Camp des Hébreux, le problème du dépôt confié à l'homme par la divinité reçoit deux explications opposées. Les § 104 à 111 soulignent la valeur d'un intendant fidèle: c'est le mérite qui lui donne droit à la reconnaissance de Dieu. Au contraire, les § 114 à 124, sous le signe de la fragilité, du mal que Dieu doit sans cesse racheter, l'idée d'un dépôt confié à l'homme évolue complètement et devient l'idée d'une miséricorde de Dieu, qui fait semblant même de recevoir à son tour . . . Comme signe de cette évolution, nous pouvons relever l'opposition, aux deux extrémités du texte, du mot χάριν χάριτι δικαίως καὶ προσηκόντως ἀμειψάμενος (§ 104), et de cet

---

[156] Nous avons parlé des couples de concepts 'philosophiques' en traitant de la 'dialectique'; nous ne pouvons davantage éviter de mentionner les ressorts dialectiques qui agissent entre les termes des couples 'philosophiques'.

[157] Pour reprendre le même exemple, disons que le livre de Jonas utilise cette même opposition: Jonas est passif dans le premier épisode; il est actif, têtu, obstiné et volontaire, dans l'affaire de Ninive. Entre les deux états, il célèbre Yahvé, à la fois passif et actif.

autre (§ 124), λύτρα: d'un côté, le côté de l'activité, voici la ʿjustice d'un échangeʾ entre l'homme et Dieu; du côté de la passivité, voici l'acceptation d'une ʿrançonʾ.

Nous avons répété que le premier chapitre du ʿQuis heresʾ faisait passer Abraham du ʿnéantʾ à l'ʿexistenceʾ[158]. Or, le traité ʿDe fuga et inventioneʾ conduit le sage jusqu'à la philosophie de l'oracle delphique et socratique: ʿConnais-toi toi-mêmeʾ. Mais, si l'on regarde bien, avant d'en arriver là, Philon nous a fait passer d'une catégorie de l'extérieur à la catégorie de l'intérieur. Les § 23 à 38 définissent la vertu en termes de politique et d'action extérieure, telle celle du commerce (§ 35); les § 39 à 47 montrent que Jacob doit fuir aussi bien la fiction, symbolisée par le nom d'Ésaü, que l'offrande, symbolisée par la maison de ses parents (§ 42 à 43): quand il se réfugie chez Laban, Jacob s'éloigne en effet de ses parents, qui l'aiment, en même temps que de son frère, Ésaü, qui le hait. Mais que signifie cette double fuite? Que Jacob doit d'abord se trouver lui-même (§ 46, avec l'oracle delphique), c'est-à-dire quitter, si l'on peut dire, les deux pays qui lui sont extérieurs: et le mal, Ésaü, et les réalités intelligibles, dont il n'est pas capable. Or, sous une autre forme et pour une autre exégèse, telle était bien la dialectique du premier chapitre du ʿQuis heresʾ: Abraham ne pouvait subsister en lui-même, tant que l'infinité des biens divins le débordait; il fallait qu'il trouve, pour être soi-même, un bien fini: l'interrogatif neutre, τί μοι δώσεις, devant être compris dans le sens que nous avons indiqué, ʿQuelle essence particulière, finie, me donneras-tu?ʾ On croirait écrite pour ce début du ʿQuis heresʾ la formule du ʿDe fuga et inventioneʾ, § 43: «Il est périlleux de vivre en compagnie du bien parfait». Dans le ʿDe fugaʾ, le schéma est simplement inversé: au lieu de chercher, comme le fait Abraham, un bien fini, pour rester lui-même en lui-même, Jacob doit se trouver lui-même en lui-même (l'oracle delphique du § 46) pour éviter les deux domaines qui lui sont extérieurs, le bien parfait et le mal. Dans les deux cas, à cette nuance près, nous progressons de l'extérieur vers l'intimité de l'ἐγώ, vivant d'une existence mesurée et moyenne[159].

Un autre ressort à l'œuvre dans l'exégèse de Philon: l'opposition de l'ʿapparenceʾ à la ʿréalitéʾ. Rappelons pour mémoire l'immense diptyque ainsi réalisé par les deux parties du ʿQuod deteriusʾ[160]: le meurtre d'Abel par Caïn correspond à une étude de l'apparence; le commentaire du châtiment de Caïn établit la vérité dans sa paradoxale solidité. Du même schème on peut donner au contraire un exemple très bref: Philon démontre avec virtuosité, dans les § 43 à 44 du ʿQuis heresʾ, que les paroles hypocrites de Laban poursuivant Jacob et ses filles appartiennent au double registre, de la vérité et de l'apparence mensongère. Laban, explique-t-il en substance, Laban trouve le moyen de prononcer faussement des paroles ʿvraiesʾ; mais ensuite Moïse et Aaron viennent au secours des filles de Laban contre lui, et prononcent ʿvraimentʾ la fausseté de Laban.

---

[158] Exactement, du néant devant l'infinité divine, à l'existence mesurée, donc finie.

[159] Bien que difficiles, ces analyses permettraient de montrer que l'exégèse de Philon use de schémas qui ne sont pas en nombre excessif: cette ʿarchéologieʾ du commentaire philonien reste à faire.

[160] Ci-dessus, p. 193–194.

c) Les couples de concepts visibles

Avant de signaler d'autres applications du procédé ʿphilosophiqueʾ, précisons que Philon utilise parfois explicitement les concepts antithétiques dont nous trouvons l'emploi caché dans d'autres passages. Ainsi, il existe tout un développement clair sur le jeu des deux prépositions ἐκ et ἐν, dans le traité ʿQuis heresʾ, § 81 à 85, à propos du pléonasme lu dans le texte biblique: «Il le fit sortir au-dehors». Le développement spécule sur la dialectique ʿintérieur–extérieurʾ.

Lorsque le chapitre prolongé sur la Division, dans le même ʿQuis heresʾ, se partage en deux sections, la première (§ 141 à 200) entend le verbe διεῖλεν d'une manière transitive, objective; la seconde (§ 201 à 229) le considère comme donnant la position du Logos, placé ʿau milieuʾ pour diviser les réalités en parts égales, et non plus la division des parts égales: c'est un point de vue subjectif. Mais ce même schème va être pour ainsi dire enfoui dans une autre exégèse, dont nous allons parler.

d) Autres exemples

Les § 40 à 51 du ʿQuis heresʾ peuvent être éclairés par l'interprétation à partir d'un schéma emprunté à ces catégories de ʿsubjectif / objectifʾ. Voici comment. Deux exemples bibliques servent à illustrer l'idée que le sage doit employer avec discernement le vocabulaire de l'amitié, sans se laisser tromper par des liens extérieurs: ainsi, Abraham est-il capable de nommer exactement sa servante, sans excès ni mépris, alors que Laban renie ses propres filles, tout en affirmant qu'il les aime; ainsi, Jacob se trompe en aimant trop Rachel et en détestant Lia, que Dieu bénit. Or, pour des raisons d'ensemble que nous ne pouvons expliquer ici, Philon a disposé habilement ces deux tableaux. L'histoire comparée d'Abraham et de Laban met en scène deux personnages séparés: entre eux il y a une distance objective. L'histoire de Jacob se déroule dans le seul Jacob, qui nourrit en lui-même deux sentiments contraires, et tous deux contraires à la vérité: ce drame est subjectif. Mais, chose curieuse, la solution trouvée par Philon est inversée par rapport aux deux problèmes. Pour conclure la double histoire de Laban et d'Abraham, il recourt à la justice subjective d'Abraham, qui sait nommer sa servante sans hésitation (§ 42, milieu de la section); pour conclure l'ambiguïté double des sentiments de Jacob, Philon recourt à une sorte d'intervention mira-culeuse, extérieure, objective, d'un Dieu qui «ouvre le sein de Lia», et qui sauve du dehors un héros en danger de s'égarer dans le sensible (§ 50 à 51). De tels procédés ont quelque chose de subtil; mais si l'on veut justifier le texte de Philon pas à pas sans l'accuser d'étrangeté ou d'illogisme, il est nécessaire de recourir à une patiente analyse de moyens littéraires sans doute originaux[161]. Nous avons

---

[161] L'idée théologique qui explique l'exemple précédent est celle ci: le sage est toujours ʿsauvéʾ par Dieu; comme l'intendant dont nous parlions naguère, il est peut-être fidèle, mais d'abord appelé par la miséricorde de l'Un. Or, les chapitres 3 et 4 d'un ouvrage sans doute alexandrin, la Sagesse, usent de la même dialectique: nous partons d'un juste «digne de Dieu» (ch. 3, v. 5) et nous aboutissons à un juste «enlevé» de peur qu'il trébuche (ch. 4, v. 11).

indiqué ci-dessus[162] que Nadab et Abiud, en brûlant à Dieu, faisaient une synthèse du divin et de l'humain, du fait qu'ils ʻreçoivent' leur transformation. Disons maintenant que ce tableau final du ʻQuis heres' répond au développement initial de la manière suivante: ils donnent une synthèse objective, réalisée dans le sacrifice, d'une synthèse subjective, où Abraham existait bien devant Dieu, mais au nom d'un ʻmélange' de deux sentiments personnels, le respect et l'audace (Quis heres, § 307 à 312; et § 28 à 30). Il existe encore d'autres couples de catégories, par exemple celles de ʻcontiguïté / communauté' qui permettent d'expliquer en particulier toute la première partie du traité ʻDe fuga et inventione'. Mais il faut en venir à l'alternance la plus importante, plus manifeste aussi: celle qui fait se succéder deux exégèses pour un même commentaire, l'exégèse naturelle ou ʻphilosophique' et l'exégèse par l'Écriture elle-même.

e) De la philosophie à l'Écriture

Philon use souvent de ce procédé. Il permet de faire passer deux fois les yeux du lecteur sur le même texte. Il correspond, en théorie, à l'opposition de l'apparence et de la réalité. Car la première interprétation, morale, psychologique ou philosophique, ne conclut pas: elle reste dans la δόξα. C'est le cas dans le premier chapitre du ʻQuis heres': la dialectique des § 10 à 30 est rendue justement nécessaire par l'incapacité des premières preuves à expliquer l'audace d'Abraham. Disons exactement: c'était une apparence d'explication, fondée sur la convenance et le bon sens; elle paraissait suffire. Or, la reprise du commentaire relègue cette suffisance dans la simple conjecture: de fait, Abraham trouve bien plus à la fin, lorsque les citations de l'Exode ont prouvé par Moïse la teneur exacte du silence et du cri. Il n'est guère besoin d'insister. Pour exposer, dans le ʻDe migratione Abrahami', § 194 à 197, la nécessité de rentrer en soi-même pour philosopher, l'exégète commence par citer Homère et exposer en clair la signification morale de ce thème; Moïse prend ensuite le relais, et c'est le livre de Samuel qui apporte la lumière décisive. Ce sont les figures de la grammaire, étymologies, distinctions sémantiques, qui commencent à expliquer le vocabulaire affectif des § 40 à 42 du ʻQuis heres'; mais bientôt la vérité de l'Écriture s'empare du thème et le conduit à bonne fin (§ 43 à 44). Dans le cas de l'intendant du ʻQuis heres', § 104 à 124, de même, la première section (§ 104 à 111) disserte honnêtement de réalités morales; la seconde exploite les mystères de l'Écriture (§ 114 à 124). La seconde fait appel à des notions de risque, tandis que la première restait dans la prudence. Parlant ensuite de la ʻpaix' promise à Abraham (Quis heres, § 284 à 286a), Philon commence par en décrire les effets; c'est seulement quand il cite ensuite l'Écriture (§ 285 à 286a) que le commentaire est complet; un signe de sa vérité peut être discerné dans le fait suivant: le nom de la ʻpaix' ne figure pas dans le premier raisonnement, comme si son essence ne pouvait être montrée que grâce à l'Écriture. Nous citerons, pour terminer, le cas du ʻDe fuga et inventione' pris dans son entier. La première partie répond à une division psychologique: il existe trois motifs pour ʻfuir'; la deuxième partie répond à une division logique: soit le

---

[162] Ci-dessus, p. 205.

couple 'chercher / trouver', il existe quatre hypothèses pour les combiner, suivant qu'on ne cherche ni ne trouve, qu'on cherche sans trouver, qu'on cherche et qu'on trouve, ou enfin qu'on trouve sans chercher — cas idéal et divin. Mais la troisième partie commente le mot 'source' par cinq interprétations prises dans la Bible: l'Écriture a succédé à la 'philosophie', à partir de là.

Ainsi, bien des pages de Philon obéissent implicitement à une autre loi que celle des procédés de rhétorique. Des lignes de force plus secrètes organisent le donné littéraire: nous les avons évoquées en parlant de 'dialectique' et de 'philosophie'. Le dernier système, celui de l'alternance de la philosophie et de la Bible, est fondamental: son évidence seule nous a dispensé d'insister davantage: on ne mesurera pas son importance à la place relative qu'il tient dans cet exposé.

Par tous ces procédés, de grammaire, de rhétorique simple, de dialectique subtile et de philosophie cachée, l'exégèse de Philon constitue un livre, composé comme doit l'être le Livre. Mais, s'il tient souvent dans la discrétion les moyens dont il se sert, il y a sans doute une raison profonde à cela. Cette raison est dans le désir de servir la lecture du Livre. Il en imite suffisamment l'unité et l'harmonie pour ne pas en donner une idée trop triste; il cache en partie la composition, savante et même recherchée, pour ne pas se substituer à l'Écriture, et pour que le disciple apprenne dans le commentaire à chercher une vérité qui «aime à se cacher», suivant l'adage héraclitéen, tant dans la Bible que dans la 'nature'.

IV. L'exégèse de Philon

Nous avons vu à travers plusieurs exemples que les procédés qui permettent à Philon de construire son livre participent de plus ou moins près à une forme imaginaire, quasi spatiale, celle de la symétrie, dialectique ou non. Nous avons, dans notre introduction annoncé notre projet: montrer la cohérence du discours de Philon; et les analyses précédentes en ont largement témoigné. Avant de donner un aperçu du procédé de la substitution ou de la suppléance d'un texte par un autre texte, tous deux tirés de la Bible, nous fournirons un dernier exemple d'exégèse qui décrira une symétrie sans dialectique, et qui nous permettra de faire voir, de plus, qu'il ne faut pas parler trop vite de 'digression' dans les traités allégoriques de Philon.

1. Une forme essentielle d'exposition: la symétrie

La symétrie règne à peu près partout dans Philon. Les unités littéraires couvertes sont de grandeur très diverse, allant de quelques paragraphes à un traité (la place de la Fin au milieu du 'De migratione Abrahami' équilibre tout le traité). Les § 25 à 42 du même traité disposent symétriquement les deux modèles de Jacob, resté le Jacob de l'exercice, à Jacob devenu Israël, c'est à dire capable de voir Dieu, suivant son blason. A la suite, les § 53 à 69 contiennent deux développements sur l'Un et le multiple, et chacun s'arrête sur le thème de la victoire. Une section plus courte, au centre de ces §§, les § 60 à 63, est construite sur une belle symétrie que nous avons schématisée ci-dessus[163]. Les § 72 à 75, toujours à la suite, offrent en petit une même symétrie: d'un côté (§ 72), Philon présente un tableau abstrait de la séparation de la pensée et de l'expression; puis les § 74 à 75 montrent Dieu rendant l'unité à ces deux principes, tandis qu'au milieu (§ 73) l'histoire d'Abel, perdu devant Caïn par manque d'expression, sert de pivot à la symétrie. Plus loin, dans les § 94 à 104 (une page plus abondante), cinq exemples, réunissant apparence sensible et réalité intelligible, obéissent à la dialectique et donc à la symétrie que nous avons expliquée[164]. Plus loin, deux séries de cinq exemples scripturaires démontrent successivement le discernement intellectuel d'Abraham (soit les § 127 à 132, d'une part, et, d'autre part, les § 139 à 142). Dans les § 159 à 162, deux citations prouvent, l'une que Joseph est supérieur à Pharaon, l'autre, qu'il est inférieur à Israël. La spéculation sur le nombre 75, l'âge d'Abraham quittant Haran, commence par 75, continue sur 70 puis 5, et revient à 75: au milieu, le passage du développement sur 70 au développement sur 5 est assuré par le symbole de l'Égypte, qui termine l'exégèse de 70 (par le deuil de 70 jours) et inaugure l'exégèse de 5 (par les cinq sens, liés au 'corps' dont l'Égypte est le symbole ordinaire). Ainsi, de proche en proche, tout le 'De migratione Abrahami' pourrait être représenté comme une suite de figures symétriques, quelquefois prises elles-mêmes dans d'autres systèmes plus enveloppants.

a) La 'digression' du 'De congressu', § 81 à 121

Il arrive qu'on prenne les § 86 à 121 du 'De congressu eruditionis gratia' pour une sorte de traité dans le traité: le développement sur le nombre 10 serait une unité autonome, voire étrangère. On peut donner à cette vue des choses un démenti qui tient au fond, et montrer qu'il existe des liens réels entre les idées de la 'digression' et le corps du traité. Mais une autre démonstration, plus instructive, peut venir de la forme. C'est elle que nous allons proposer ici. Elle nous permettra de reprendre d'une manière synthétique plusieurs procédés de Philon.

Nous avons parlé de l'anticipation, ou encore exégèse téléologique. Or, si l'on se demande dans le cas présent, où commence le commentaire du nombre 10, la réponse n'est pas forcément: au § 89, «Ce qui fait la raison du nombre 'dix' a été l'objet d'une étude attentive de la part des enfants de la Musique». Et il est possible qu'il faille se reporter avant l'exégèse explicite. D'autre part, un lecteur de Philon peut soupçonner dans un développement de cette importance (§ 89 à 121) que le début rejoint la fin, par exemple. Voici le résultat de cette enquête. La dernière section du chapitre, à savoir les § 111 à 118, correspondent par symétrie à la section qui précède le § 89, à savoir les § 83 à 88. L'inclusion la plus remarquable est évidemment, dans ces deux sections éloignées, celle qui fait que la Loi figure de part et d'autre. Le § 86 dit en effet: «Vous ferez les ordonnances et vous pratiquerez mes commandements; vous marcherez en eux!» — toutes expressions techniques de la législation d'Israël; et nous lisons au § 120 l'exemple des 'dix' commandements qui composent la Loi. A partir de là, d'autres symétries s'établissent entre les extrêmes: la Loi, des deux côtés, vient mettre un terme à un voyage: l'âme (§ 83 à 88) a quitté l'Égypte; Éliézer (§ 111 à 119) s'avance dans un royaume de perfection, en quête d'une femme pour Isaac, le fils de son maître Abraham. De plus, au début, la Loi vient s'opposer aux vices de Canaan; à la fin, la Loi sanctionne les dix plaies d'Égypte (ici, prend place une symétrie intermédiaire, qu'il serait trop long de manifester). Enfin si l'on récapitule les deux sections, on obtient, de part et d'autre, une même suite des éléments exégétiques: voyage, Loi, rappel du délai indiqué par le nombre 10:

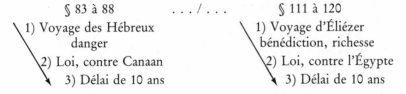

On peut observer encore plusieurs détails, que nous indiquons sommairement. Philon a combiné une symétrie directe (les trois éléments se suivent dans le même ordre de part et d'autre, avec un effet indirect: les Hébreux arrivent en Canaan après avoir quitté l'Égypte: or, cette indication du début est équilibrée à la fin seulement, car, à la fin, c'est l'Égypte qui ressent le contrecoup de la manifestation de la Loi (elle reçoit dix plaies, pour dix commandements . . .). La section initiale de ce qui nous apparaît maintenant comme l'unité naturelle du texte (du § 83 au § 121) évolue selon la catégorie du discontinu (la Loi s'interpose brutalement entre le Peuple et Canaan), alors que la section finale (§ 111 à 118) est sous le signe de la continuité (l'exégèse explicite du nombre 10 permet d'enchaîner de manière progressive).

Déjà, ce résultat en produit un autre. S'il est vrai que les § 83 à 88 entrent de façon si étroite, formellement, dans le chapitre de l'exégèse consacré au nombre 10, la conclusion est qu'il fallait prendre en considération la toute première annonce de ce thème, du nombre 10, celle qui commence le § 81: «(Sara) donne (Agar à Abraham) dix ans seulement après son arrivée en la terre de Canaan . . .». C'est là que commence en réalité le chapitre. Et les premiers paragraphes sont attirés, par exégèse téléologique, vers la totalité du chapitre. Il n'y a pas de digression.

De proche en proche, une lecture, attentive aux faits littéraires plutôt qu'aux notions, aura tôt fait de construire tout ce chapitre selon une figure parfaitement régulière et symétrique. Le tableau suivant donnera les détails à qui voudrait reconstituer le système avec précision. Disons ceci: il s'agit d'une réflexion de type arithmologique, où Philon utilise des données pourtant simples sur la 'raison' mathématique du 9. Or, les § 89 à 93 prennent le nombre 10 comme le produit de 9 + 1; et c'est ce que font, à l'autre extrémité, les § 103 à 110. Dans l'intervalle, les § 94 à 102 célèbrent, au contraire, un nombre 10 plein, si l'on peut dire, sans composition ni décomposition. Il est le symbole de l'offrande pure et totale, alors que, de part et d'autre, les § 89 à 92 et les § 103 à 110 parlent de victoire, puis de libération, c'est à dire de deux approches de la perfection, seulement. De cette différence capitale, entre la formule 9 + 1 et cette autre, 10 absolument pris, nous avons une preuve remarquable: le lecteur attentif aura noté que la 'dîme' offerte par Abraham (§ 93) est à nouveau mentionnée à un endroit surprenant. Au § 93, la 'dîme' fait partie du 9 + 1 et du thème de la victoire; au § 99, nous sommes d'après la théorie précédente, dans le domaine de la perfection: n'y a-t-il pas là une dissymétrie fâcheuse pour la théorie? Or, justement, ce retour de la 'dîme' montre bien le travail caché de Philon. Au § 93, la 'dîme' est en liaison manifeste avec les thèmes de l'imperfection, victoire, etc.; mais au § 99, Philon ne fait plus paraître ni Dieu, avec qui Abraham l'échangeait, ni la victoire, qui en fut l'occasion: le mot du texte biblique qui intéresse ici Philon est le mot 'tout', dans la phrase: «Il lui donna la dîme de tout». Abraham n'est pas nommé, lui-même; et c'est Melchisédech, le prêtre, le parfait, qui prend pour ainsi dire son rôle: sa présence fait que la dîme, au § 99, entre dans le mystère de la totalité, c'est à dire de l'offrande pure et totale qui est le contexte dont nous avons dit qu'il définissait les § 93 à 102. Ce qu'il fallait démontrer. Une symétrie nouvelle orne les § 93 à 102: la première section, formée des § 94 à 97, montre la réunion des sens; les § 98 à 102 s'attachent à montrer l'harmonie des trois parties de l'âme: sens, parole, esprit[165].

Tout est parfaitement agencé dans ce modèle exemplaire. Jusqu'aux transitions d'une section à l'autre. Nous indiquons sur le tableau que les § 94 et 102, aux frontières de la section médiane, mais lui appartenant encore ou déjà, contiennent chacun une expression qui rappelle ou annonce la situation inférieure des sections qui précèdent ou suivent: le § 94 dit que le «nombre 9 est apparenté à notre espèce, mortelle»; le § 102 reprend: «le nombre 9 restera chez nous», munis que nous sommes «de mesures mensongères et injustes». On ne peut mieux composer.

b) L'impérialisme de la 'symétrie'

Ce mode d'exposition domine le travail ordinaire de Philon. On verra même à quel point par ce dernier exemple, d'une exégèse fort curieuse. Dans le chapitre de la Division, qui occupe une partie notable du 'Quis heres', et qui prête d'autant mieux à la 'symétrie' que son sujet est la 'division en parts égales et contraires', nous rencontrons à nouveau le thème des dix commandements. Philon veut cette fois indiquer leur division exacte en deux groupes, le premier dictant nos devoirs envers Dieu, et le second, envers les hommes. La difficulté apparente réside en ceci: le cinquième commandement ordonne de respecter père et mère. La belle symétrie est compromise, et nous avons un déséquilibre: 4 commandements, contre 6. Philon ne dit rien de cette difficulté. Il affirme (§ 168) que les deux tables gravées devant Moïse contiennent chacune cinq préceptes, distingués par leur objet, Dieu ou nos semblables. Et d'entamer le commentaire de la première série.

---

[165] Il n'y a pas de désordre, non plus, dans l'énumération des § 103 à 110; mais la démonstration serait ici déplacée, trop onéreuse.

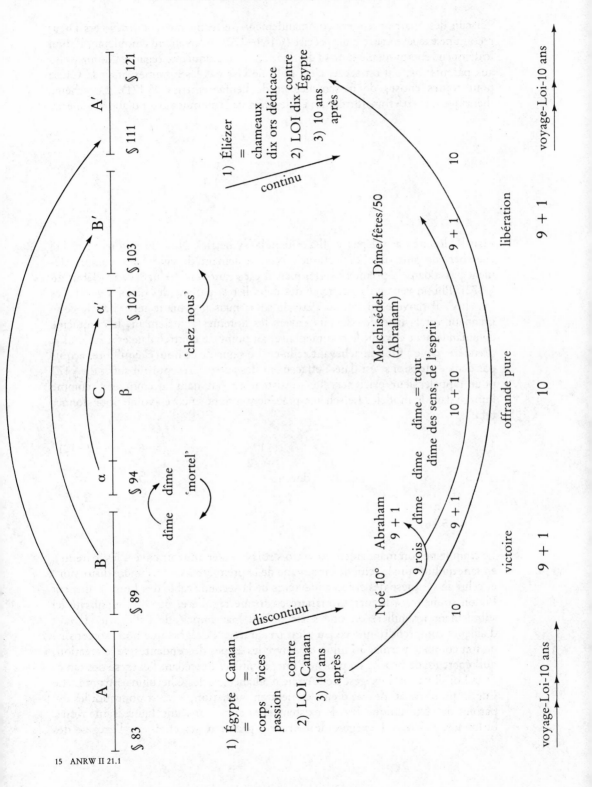

Chacun des quatre premiers commandements, effectivement tournés vers Dieu, reçoit une exégèse sobre mais précise (§ 169–170). Arrivant au cinquième, Philon le détourne énergiquement de sa destination: «Le cinquième regarde l'honneur dû aux parents: or, s'il est sacré, c'est qu'il ne vise pas les hommes, mais la Cause pour toutes choses de la semence et de l'enfantement» (§ 171). Le schéma théorique de cette transformation est le suivant: le cinquième est d'abord annexé.

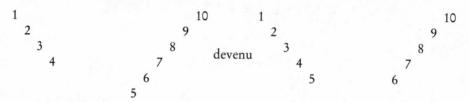

Mais Philon ne s'arrête pas là. Il a obtenu la 'symétrie'. Nous le voyons en réalité chercher, de plus, une 'dialectique'. Non seulement, le cinquième commandement passe dans la première série, mais il est «mitoyen» – μεθόριος (début du § 172). Philon veut qu'il participe des deux listes: parlant des devoirs envers les 'parents', il renvoie en fait au Père de tout; mais il projette un reflet de cette grandeur sur la liste des devoirs envers les hommes. Finalement, le cinquième commandement envahit le commentaire, au point de contrebalancer à lui seul la première 'table', tout en achevant celle-ci. Le signe de ce nouvel équilibre, acquis par deux distorsions, est dans l'effacement des autres préceptes: il suffit du § 173 pour rappeler leur existence. Ils subsistent en fait dans le cinquième comme l'image dans le modèle. Le schéma précédent a donc encore évolué pour donner ceci:

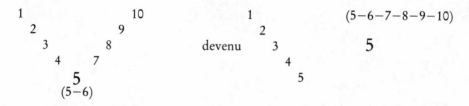

Le cinquième commandement joue trois rôles: le sien (devoir envers les 'parents', en tant qu'humains), celui de cinquième de la première liste (première distorsion) et celui de synthèse des commandements de la seconde table des Lois. Tellement Philon souhaite ordonner sa matière en forme régulière, de cette régularité ici subtilement irrégulière en une sorte de jeu 'par impar' de l'allégorie. Il faut d'ailleurs comprendre que ce jeu n'est pas gratuit: l'exégèse que nous sortons ici de son contexte permet à Philon de suivre les étapes descendantes de la création, qui répercute de proche en proche l'Image initiale. Précédant l'exégèse des tables de la Loi, il y avait l'exégèse de l'Arche d'alliance, et des Chérubins affrontés. Le Logos qui plane au-dessus d'eux les tient en médiation, et c'est pourquoi les dix paroles de cette unique Parole existent elles aussi dans une figure symétrique, ordonnée, médiate. L'exégèse de l'Arche a prolongé ses effets sur l'exégèse des

Lois. Tel est en effet le dernier principe de l'allégorie philonienne. C'est lui que nous allons maintenant considérer: une exégèse ne vit jamais isolée; une sorte de redondance fait, aux yeux de Philon qu'un verset de la Bible reçoit un redoublement d'expression dans le verset suivant.

2. De l'Écriture à l'Écriture: la 'suppléance'

Le procédé de la 'symétrie' ne serait qu'une fantaisie d'auteur, si l'Écriture n'était pas, aux yeux de Philon, une sorte de république, où les personnages, les textes, participent à une vie commune suivant un usage réglé. Et Philon use d'un procédé qui s'appuie sur ce principe: il explique souvent, sinon toujours, un personnage par un autre, Abraham par Moïse, pour donner un exemple fréquent; en second lieu, il arrange de telle sorte son commentaire que la fin d'une exégèse particulière rejoigne exactement le verset de la Bible qui vient juste à la suite. Examinons les deux effets de ce principe unique.

a) La suppléance des personnages

Philon commence à parler d'un héros biblique. Soudain, il donne l'impression de l'oublier. Il arrive que cet oubli se prolonge très longtemps: on ne se souvient plus d'Agar, dans le 'De fuga et inventione', dès qu'on a franchi le § 6, et il faut attendre le § 202 pour la retrouver! Les absences sont en général plus courtes. Mais il ne faudrait pas croire que Philon a perdu de vue le personnage abandonné, ou qu'il suit plutôt une 'idée' qu'une figure biblique. En réalité, le personnage survit dans ceux qui prennent sa place. Mieux, il profite d'eux, de leur blason. Combien de fois Jacob prend-il le rôle d'Abraham[166]? Moïse supplée Abraham, également, parce que tous deux peuvent être dits μετέωροι, «montés dans la contemplation du ciel»[167]. Noé peut montrer par son caractère de sauveur qu'un Abraham sauve le monde[168]. Et notre Agar, si longtemps absente du 'De fuga', y est tout de même présente, derrière Jacob, par exemple: Philon insiste sur le «séjour à l'étranger» que Jacob doit faire: or c'est la traduction même du nom d''Agar'[169]. Un moment important d'une dialectique réunit souvent les trois personnages de la triade, Abraham, Isaac, Jacob; mais l'un ou l'autre n'est pas explicitement désigné, si le contexte général ne s'y prête pas.

Les exemples sont aussi nombreux que les pages de Philon. Insistons plutôt sur ce qui arrive dans cette suppléance. Si, par exemple, Moïse remplace pour un temps le personnage d'Abraham, lorsqu'Abraham revient en scène, Moïse continue de lui apporter son commentaire vivant: une sorte de lumière continue,

---

[166] Par exemple dans le 'De migratione Abrahami', du § 25 au § 42; du § 207 au § 215; dans le 'Quis heres', du § 48 au § 51. Plus subtilement, dans le 'Quis heres', § 48 à 51, Isaac à son tour permet à Jacob de suppléer Abraham . . .

[167] De migratione Abrahami, § 168 à 170a.

[168] De migratione Abrahami, § 125 à 126.

[169] De fuga et inventione, § 48 à 52.

après son départ, à briller du personnage suppléant sur le personnage suppléé. Dans le premier chapitre du 'Quis heres'[170], Philon commence par exposer le problème d'Abraham: doit-il vraiment parler? Nous avons dit que la réponse vient de Moïse: Moïse, lui aussi, mais pour d'autres raisons, ne pouvait pas s'exprimer; seulement, il a franchi lentement une étape, puis une autre, qui l'ont mené jusqu'au «hurlement» — ἐκβοᾶν (§ 14 à 15). Donc Abraham a la possibilité de parler, pourvu que le lecteur de la Bible comprenne que la dialectique de Moïse existe dans Abraham. Il semblerait qu'on doive s'en tenir là. En fait, le passage de Moïse a révélé dans Abraham cette capacité de parler; mais il a révélé bien d'autres valeurs, grâce à des valeurs identiques de Moïse. Par exemple, celle-ci: Moïse, dans ses 'cris', reproche à Dieu d'avoir fait sortir d'Égypte un Peuple qu'il va faire mourir; au nom du passé, des promesses jadis faites aux Patriarches, Moïse demande à Dieu de poursuivre le salut des Hébreux. Cette dimension du passé va venir enrichir le personnage d'Abraham[171]. Abraham, lui, reproche à Dieu ne pas songer à son avenir: il s'inquiète de ne pas voir venir d'enfant pour hériter de lui. Or, Philon, à partir du § 22, fait exprimer ce désir de l'avenir grâce à une série de réflexions en même temps dominées par le thème de la création, c'est-à-dire de l'origine, du passé. Moïse a servi de catalyseur[172]. De même dans le début du 'De mutatione nominum', il se passe quelque chose d'inattendu. Philon annonce qu'il existe trois degrés de vie religieuse; or, le second, en principe représenté par Abraham, ne correspond pas exactement à la définition: c'est que le personnage de Moïse, entrevu au cours de l'exégèse, a communiqué à Abraham une valeur supérieure. Là encore, Philon n'improvise pas: s'il a d'abord énoncé trois degrés de conscience, et s'il arrange le commentaire de telle sorte qu'Abraham, théoriquement placé sur le deuxième degré, soit plutôt entre le deuxième et le troisième, c'est pour la raison que le texte biblique de base dit: «Abraham était âgé de 99 ans . . .» (§ 1). Qui dit 99, dit un nombre tout proche de 100, c'est à dire presque parfait, au seuil de l'accomplissement. Mais c'est la proximité de Moïse, sa suppléance, qui ont donné à Abraham le supplément nécessaire.

La suppléance des personnages est indéfiniment à l'œuvre. Mais il existe un rythme constant, que nous devons signaler ici: Philon fait souvent alterner les citations de la Genèse et celle de l'Exode. La raison en est objective: il est vrai que le livre de l'Exode est beaucoup plus dramatique, et l'existence du Peuple bien plus mouvementée, révélatrice du cœur humain et des repentirs de Yahvé, que la Genèse. Le premier livre de la Torah présente, à partir du chapitre 12, la vie exemplaire de trois héros de la Promesse. Leurs aventures sont inscrites dans le cadre de la fidélité, tant la fidélité de Yahvé que celle d'Abraham, d'Isaac, de Jacob. On pourrait dire sans se tromper, du moins sur le plan pratique et littéraire, que Philon se sert de la différence de ton. Il sait que la Genèse dit bien toute la vérité spirituelle; mais elle le fait de manière concise, ou, pour ainsi dire,

---

[170] Nous revenons souvent sur les mêmes textes, pour que le lecteur, plus familier, en voie la richesse et la complexité.

[171] Non pas tant le personnage que l'intelligence que le lecteur de l'Écriture doit en acquérir.

[172] Les § 22 à 23 parlent du 'Créateur'; les § 24 à 28a, de la création, les § 28b à 30, de la créature, consistante en soi-même.

plate; alors que l'Exode introduit le drame, le volume. Comme l'Écriture ne dit, au fond, qu'une seule Parole, il est donc légitime de montrer la profondeur inaperçue de la Genèse en utilisant l'image qu'en offre l'Exode. L'histoire agitée du Peuple rebelle explique les révoltes de Caïn, les paresses de Lot, les efforts de Jacob, et surtout la vision d'Israël, auquel les débats ouverts par Moïse auprès du Dieu qu'il cherche à v o i r apportent toutes les précisions désirables, lui dont le nom signifie: « Qui voit Dieu »[173].

De plus, l'alternance de la Genèse et de l'Exode permet l'alternance des notions complémentaires de création et de salut. Or Philon se sert également de ces deux pôles pour organiser son discours, par exemple dans le grand chapitre de la Division (Quis heres, § 130 à 230). Ce procédé paraîtrait peut-être fortuit s'il ne correspondait à une division qui existe dans les livres bibliques. Le livre de Jonas, que nous avons déjà évoqué, bâtit son premier chapitre autour d'une définition catéchétique tirée de la Genèse: le Dieu du prophète est celui « qui a fait la mer et la terre » (ch. 1, v. 9); mais le second épisode, à Ninive, prend son sens de l'objection que Jonas fait à Dieu en partant de la définition traditionnelle de l'Exode: « Dieu de tendresse et de pitié, lent à la colère . . . » (ch. 4, v. 2 de Jonas, citant l'Exode, ch. 34, v. 6−7, dans l'épisode du veau d'or). Les aventures majeures du prophète Élie, d'ailleurs caricaturé avec d'autres par le livre de Jonas, font appel à une semblable alternance: le 'jugement de Dieu' qui restaure sur le Carmel la foi d'Israël est centré sur le rappel des Patriarches et des douze pierres de la fondation en Jacob des douze tribus d'Israël (I Rois, ch. 18, v. 36), tandis que la fuite d'Élie vers le mont Horeb dit suffisamment son inspiration, venue de Moïse séjournant dans la montagne de Dieu (ibid., ch. 19). Le prologue de Matthieu évoque la généalogie, ce qui nous fait descendre de la Genèse, alors qu'ensuite il utilise les souvenirs de l'Exode pour raconter la persécution de Jésus, son exil: « J'ai appelé mon fils d'Égypte » (ch. 2, v. 15).

b) La redondance de l'Écriture

La conversation des figures bibliques entre elles a pour principe l'unité de l'Écriture: elle se répète dans la variation des épisodes de l'histoire sacrée. Mais, à suivre uniquement cette direction, l'exégète n'aurait aucune raison de borner son discours: il trouverait toujours un biais pour que tous les passages de la Loi viennent appuyer le moindre verset. Or, il n'en rien. Philon revient périodiquement au texte de base. La raison en est dans le même principe, appliqué différemment. L'unité de l'Écriture est l'unité d'un discours suivi. Et Philon ordonne son commentaire d'un verset de façon à ce qu'il vienne juste à la frontière du verset suivant. Le procédé de l'exégèse téléologique facilite évidemment les choses: donnons-en un exemple. Pourquoi la dialectique mettant en cause la

---

[173] Des exemples de cette alternance entre la Genèse et l'Exode se trouvent partout; on peut évoquer: De migratione Abrahami, § 53 à 69; Quis heres, § 3 à 30, bien entendu, dont nous avons analysé le contenu: l'Exode connaît un 'drame' de la parole que les formules trop simples de la Genèse − πυνθάνεται φάσκων − ne laissaient pas deviner; § 112; § 166 à 173; § 179 à 181; § 196 à 200; § 201 à 206; De mutatione nominum, § 19 à 28, etc.

possibilité pour l'homme de nommer les Puissances de l'Être, le Κύϱιος et le Θεός, aboutit-elle au personnage d'Hénoch, sinon parce que Hénoch fut 'agréable à Dieu', et qu'Abraham, sujet du traité, fut, pour sa part, 'agréable devant Dieu'? Si l'on prend l'exégèse de Philon en commençant par la fin, c'est à dire, chaque fois, par ce qui est juste après la fin de tel commentaire, la 'raison' de bien des passages surprenants apparaîtra naturellement. Un tel phénomène s'observera, par exemple, dans les § 1 à 42 du traité 'De migratione Abrahami': Philon illumine le départ d'Abraham et les ruptures auxquelles il consent, par une sorte de vision anticipée de la Fin, comme nous l'avons dit. Dans l'exégèse, cela veut dire que le verset ultérieur: «Abraham allait selon Dieu», agit par avance et apporte le présent de la présence divine, quand la notion de départ n'impliquait pas autre chose qu'un avenir. Plus exactement, Philon a sans cesse gardé devant les yeux la notion impliquée dans le verset suivant, tout en commentant le verset: «Quitte ton pays, ta famille et la maison de ton père». Aussi Philon parle-t-il de la 'vision' (§ 35 à 42)[174]; mais la vision attire le personnage de Jacob-Israël (§ 38 à 39), et celui-ci paraîtra auparavant sous la forme élémentaire de Jacob (§ 26 à 36). Ce passage, encore approfondi, donnera un exemple précis du travail de tapisserie auquel Philon s'est livré. Qu'on suive bien: nous voyons que le thème de la Fin (qui paraît formellement au § 127, donc loin dans la suite) a influencé le début de l'ouvrage, en ce sens que «aller selon la Parole de Dieu» semble à Philon répéter partiellement ce qu'il lit dans le verset précédent, «Quitte . . .», accompagné des promesses de bénédiction. Mais, de plus, tout se passe comme si Philon avait également orienté le commentaire du départ d'Abraham en fonction d'un mot du texte qu'il ne cite pas, «Va vers le pays que je te ferai voir», où le verbe 'voir' sert de soutien implicite à l'exégèse de Jacob-Israël et de la 'vision'. En ce sens, très précis du point de vue de la fabrication littéraire, le verset «Quitte . . . Je ferai de toi une grande nation» équivaut en partie à cet autre: «Va vers la terre que Je te ferai voir»[175]. Il y a si bien redondance d'un mot à l'autre du texte de base que commenter l'un permet de passer l'autre sous silence.

Mais en général, le procédé suit son cours ordinaire: la fin d'un commentaire rejoint très exactement le début du commentaire suivant. La plus grande part du 'Quis heres' le manifeste. Et la dernière partie, qui concentre en si peu d'espace l'exégèse de presque tout le chapitre 15 de la Genèse, est ordonnée par ce procédé. Déjà, par exemple, les § 74 à 76 supposent que le verset «Il le fit sortir au-dehors» équivaut pratiquement au verset suivant: «Lève les yeux . . .». Ce sont des redondances qui expliquent ensuite que l'extase d'Abraham ait lieu au coucher du soleil, car l'extase prophétique dont jouit Abraham disait déjà ce refus du soleil de midi (Quis heres, § 258 à 266); le verset annonçant l'exil de quatre-

---

[174] Un triple développement souligne le thème de la 'vision': les § 34 à 36 l'ayant préparé, nous avons ensuite: l'objet de la vision, l'Être (§ 37), le voyant, Israël (§ 38 à 39), et enfin Celui qui fait voir, la Source de toute illumination (§ 40b à 42).

[175] Le silence de Philon, relatif comme on le voit, s'explique également ici par le fait que les mots «vers la terre» auraient dû recevoir leur explication dans le verset: «Va vers la terre que Je te ferai voir», mais que ce commentaire aurait entraîné Philon loin du thème de l'exil: «Quitte ta terre!» Tout concorde dans le commentaire Philon, depuis l''idée' jusqu'aux ruses de l'allégorie et du silence.

cents ans confirme le verset précédent, qui parlait de terre étrangère, parce que les 'passions', au nombre de quatre, sont pour l'âme une terre d'exil (§ 269 à 271). Plus ou moins visible, le procédé existe partout. Il porte en soi une signification: le commentateur est soumis au Texte. Il reçoit du Texte son début et sa fin. L'activité de Philon est immense: le souci qu'il a de composer son livre apparaît dans la richesse incroyable, la souplesse et la fermeté des procédés de la 'rhétorique' ou de la 'dialectique'[176]. Mais cette activité, que peu de ses propres exégètes ont reconnue dans toute sa rigueur, est justement c a c h é e: or c'est précisément la raison de l'allégorie, de déceler dans un texte son discours implicite, et Philon, au lieu de décrire en petit grammairien les traces de l'Idée divine cachée dans l'Écriture, a composé un ouvrage qui cache à son tour, en même temps qu'il éclaire.

Philon lui-même a comparé le discours bien ordonné à une tapisserie: «Le *logos*, qui est le meilleur des vêtements, est tissé dans l'harmonie . . . Plus précieux que l'or, il forme une broderie de mille formes; il est achevé en ouvrage admirable lorsqu'il est divisé jusque dans ses chapitres les plus ténus, et comme la chaîne, reçoit en guise de trame les démonstrations adaptées» (De sacrificiis Abelis et Caini, § 83). Il n'y a rien d'étonnant à ce que la description de son exégèse soit obligée de défaire patiemment et avec peine un travail serré.

Conclusion:
La 'tapisserie'. Les procédés apparents et les procédés cachés

L'étude de l'exégèse philonienne peut être faite à des niveaux de profondeur très divers. Elle peut déterminer des plans de cohérence variés, mais dont la synthèse est toujours possible, car Philon mène à la fois plusieurs recherches. La 'broderie' ou la 'tapisserie' est une image qu'il a lui-même appliquée au *logos*, et elle correspond à son extraordinaire habileté. En forme de conclusion, nous donnons un dernier exemple, qui montrera justement rassemblés un grand nombre des procédés analysés ci-dessus.

Les § 120 à 176 du traité 'De fuga et inventione' exploitent les quatre hypothèses engendrées par les deux termes 'chercher / trouver'. La première est celle des âmes qui ne cherchent pas et ne trouvent pas. L'exégèse de ce type maudit occupe les § 121 à 125:

«Ceux qui ne s'attachent ni à la découverte ni à la recherche émoussent gravement leur raisonnement par le manque d'éducation et d'exercice: ils pouvaient y voir très clair, mais ils sont devenus aveugles. Le (texte) dit bien: La femme de Lot s'est retournée en arrière; elle est devenue une stèle. Ce n'est pas une invention fantastique, mais l'expression caractéristique d'une réalité. 122 Car celui qui fait peu de cas de son précepteur à cause de sa paresse, innée ou invétérée, abandonne ce qui est devant lui et qui lui per-

---

[176] Résumées, en un sens, par la symétrie.

mettrait d'user des moyens de voir, d'entendre ainsi que des autres facultés, pour juger des réalités de la nature; il se tord le cou, au contraire, et le tend vers ce qui est en arrière, plus ardent pour l'aveuglement des choses de la vie que des parties du corps: à la manière d'une pierre inanimée et sourde, elle est devenue stèle.

123 Ces manières d'être n'ont pas, dit Moïse, un cœur pour comprendre, des yeux pour voir, des oreilles pour entendre (Deutéronome, ch. 29, v. 3); elles se sont fabriqué à elles-mêmes une vie sans vie, aveugle, sourde, inintelligente, de toute manière privée d'usage de leurs membres, pour ne s'être attachées à rien de ce qu'il fallait.

124 Le chef de ce chœur est le roi de la région corporelle: Pharaon se retourna, dit le (texte) et entra dans sa maison: il n'appliqua pas même son esprit à 'cela' (Exode, ch. 7, v. 23), c'est-à-dire qu'il l'appliqua au 'rien', absolument parlant; il le laissa se dessécher comme une plante qu'on ne cultive pas, devenir stérile et sans graines. Ceux qui délibèrent, examinent, observent partout soigneusement aiguisent et affûtent leur (esprit). Celui-ci, par l'exercice, porte des fruits convenables à sa nature, la sagacité et l'intelligence, qui lui font vaincre les tromperies, mais l'autre, à force d'irréflexion, émousse et brise les pointes de la pensée. »

Sans entrer dans tout le détail[177], nous montrerons rapidement ce qui se dissimule sous des phrases parfois étranges. On se souviendra[178], par exemple, que la 'traduction' donnée par Philon aux mots du texte « il n'appliqua même pas son esprit à cela » suppose que le pronom 'cela' signifie « une essence particulière »; Pharaon néglige donc toute 'essence', et il en vient à ne penser 'à rien', sinon à penser − lui, symbole de l'esprit, en tant que 'roi' − le 'rien'.

Ainsi, le commentaire de la formule 'ne pas chercher / ne pas trouver' est obtenu à partir de deux personnages bibliques, la femme de Lot, venue de la Genèse; Pharaon, venu de l'Exode. Or, on notera, dans les deux exégèses, l'absence des mots-clés 'trouver / chercher'. Philon les a remplacés par des synonymes d'ordre noétique: 's'attacher à' − 's'appliquer' − 'examiner' − 'observer' − 'vaincre les tromperies', ou, avec la citation de Moïse, 'comprendre'. Sans doute Philon refuse-t-il l'emploi de ces mots sacrés, 'chercher / trouver'[179], quand il s'agit d'une hypothèse entièrement négative et impie.

Deuxième remarque: si les vocables se rapportant au thème fondamental, 'trouver-chercher', ne paraissent pas, il en est un au contraire, qui revient dans les deux récits: un même geste caractérise l'attitude de la femme de Lot et de Pharaon (§ 121 et 124): tous deux 'se retournèrent'. Or, c'est là le thème qui définit Lot. Ce mot, de la 'perversion', renvoie donc implicitement au héros de Sodome.

---

[177] Ainsi, les mots du début (§ 121), « il pouvaient y voir très clair, mais ils sont devenus aveugles » renvoient à deux éléments de la suite: la faculté de voir et d'user des autres sens; mais aussi la royauté de Pharaon: symbole de l'esprit, il en a le pouvoir.

[178] Ci-dessus, p. 163.

[179] Ces mots ont chez les Prophètes, en particulier, une résonance.

Troisième observation: précisément, Sodome se traduit, d'après le code philonien, par deux noms, que nous trouvons ici, l'un et l'autre: 'stérilité' ou 'aveuglement'[180]. Sodome est le lieu que Lot et sa famille doivent fuir; plus loin, Pharaon doit entrer dans sa maison — geste à la fois semblable, puisque le roi d'Égypte fuit Moïse qui lui annonce la vengeance divine, mais dissemblable, car il mène du dehors au dedans. Tout se passe comme si Philon, toujours implicitement, avait ordonné ces deux exemples, de Pharaon et de la femme de Lot, en les faisant rejoindre de manière invisible dans les deux thèmes de Sodome et de la fuite, thèmes eux-mêmes rapprochés par la fuite de Lot.

Encore: la femme de Lot représente les sens; Pharaon, roi de l'Égypte[181], représente l'esprit. Mieux: les sens deviennent aveugles; l'esprit devient stérile. Philon compare l'esprit à une plante (§ 124, fin); la Bible fait déchoir la femme de Lot jusqu'à la stèle de pierre. Le végétal, représentant l'esprit, est, en Pharaon, stérilisé; la pierre tient d'une vie sans vie. Et c'est de la sorte que Philon a combiné deux exégèses, cosmologique et psychologique. Réunis, la femme de Lot et Pharaon, sens et esprit, composent l'homme tout entier, corps et âme; c'est la psychologie. Combinés, les quatre termes issus des deux sujets et des deux perversions: sens — pierre; esprit — plante, donnent une échelle des êtres, toute schématique mais réelle (c'est la cosmologie):

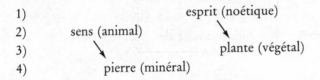

1)   esprit (noétique)
2)   sens (animal)
3)   plante (végétal)
4)   pierre (minéral)

Dans le texte, la comparaison avec la plante vient en fin de commentaire, parce qu'elle permet de montrer l'opposition d'une plante qu'on ne cultive pas et du fruit produit par l'application: par là, Philon rejoint les hypothèses suivantes, plus glorieuses.

Ce n'est pas tout: entre les deux exégèses, Philon a placé une citation du Deutéronome. Elle ne s'applique pas seulement au cas de la femme de Lot, car la première perversion dénoncée par Moïse est celle du «cœur, qui ne comprend pas». Or, la perversion de l'intelligence est celle de Pharaon[182]. En chiasme, donc, la citation médiane résume et soutient les deux types de perversion. Bien mieux, si on fait maintenant attention à l'exégèse elle-même dans chacun des deux tableaux, on observera ceci: le premier tableau est expliqué par la Bible elle-même; la femme de Lot devient dans le texte une statue pétrifiée; au contraire, dans le second récit, il faut que l'exégète Philon tire une image d'un texte sans image, à

---

[180] Στείρωσις καὶ τύφλωσις, par exemple De ebrietate, § 222; De confusione linguarum, § 28; De somniis, II, § 192; De congressu eruditionis gratia, § 109; 'Quaestiones in Genesin', IV, § 31.

[181] Philon dit bien au début du § 124 βασιλεύς. Il est 'roi', non pas directement de l'Égypte, corps mauvais, mais de 'la région corporelle', encore indécise. C'est l'irréflexion du roi, l'esprit, qui pervertira à son tour le corps.

[182] On sait qu'en hébreu, le cœur, lev, désigne souvent l'intelligence.

partir de sa ʿgrammaireʾ (le pronom ʿcelaʾ). Si bien qu'on peut encore ajouter cette symétrie à toutes les autres: d'un côté l'exégèse immédiate; de l'autre, l'exégèse allégorisée. Telles sont en effet les deux voies qui ouvrent l'accès de l'Écriture.

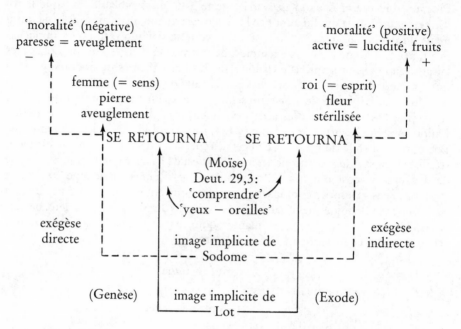

Apparemment, seul le mot commun ʿse détournaʾ associe Pharaon à la femme de Lot; en réalité, tout un réseau, complexe et naturel à la fois, rend les deux images inséparables, comme si elles étaient prédestinées à symboliser non seulement une vérité locale, mais tout l'univers que le schéma précédent déploie dans les symétries. Les données sont devenues inextricables, comme la trame et la chaîne d'un ouvrage de tissage.

Pour conclure, rappelons que l'exégèse de Philon n'est pas didactique, mais pédagogique: les allégories, comme celle de Pharaon, doivent reconduire le lecteur de la Bible à la simplicité des récits, comme celui de Sodome. Philon, au terme d'un commentaire plus ou moins long, accumule soudain plusieurs citations qu'il n'explique pas, ou très vite: la dernière partie du ʿQuis heresʾ accorde moins de place à plusieurs versets que la seconde partie n'en a concédé au seul mot «il les partagea en deux» — διεῖλεν. De même, la fin du ʿDe fuga et inventioneʾ. De même, à l'intérieur d'un traité, arrive-t-il que le texte parle pour ainsi dire de lui-même. Philon se conduit alors envers son lecteur comme Dieu à l'endroit du progressant: «Il veut manifester l'indépendance du disciple, et montrer que ses leçons, bien que le maître ne soit plus là, apparaissent spontanément; qu'il y est libre, avec son consentement et son élan; qu'il agit par soi. Le maître accorde à son élève l'espace d'un usage indépendant, qui ne répond pas à une admonition de sa part; il lui imprime la forme la plus assurée d'une mémoire sans faute» (telles sont les dernières lignes du traité De mutatione nominum, § 270). L'appel à la 'mémoire', en effet, caractérise le procédé de la symétrie; et la symétrie ordonne toute l'exégèse de Philon.

Bibliographie

P. WENDLAND, Philo und die kynisch-stoische Diatribe. Beiträge zur griechischen Philosophie und Religion, Berlin, 1895, 1–75.

W. BOUSSET, Jüdisch-christlicher Schulbetrieb in Alexandria und Rom. Literarische Untersuchungen zu Philo und Clemens von Alexandria, Justin und Irenäus, Göttingen, 1915.

E. STEIN, article 'Allegorische Auslegung', in: Encyclopaedia Judaica, 2, 1928, 338–351.

J. HELLER, article 'Aristobul', in: Encyclopaedia Judaica, 3, 1929, 321–324.

E. STEIN, Die allegorische Exegese des Philo aus Alexandreia, Giessen, 1920, et: Beihefte zur Zeitschrift für alttestamentliche Wissenschaft (BZAW), 51, Giessen, 1929.

KARL STAEHLE, Die Zahlenmystik bei Philon von Alexandreia, Leipzig–Berlin, 1931.

E. STEIN, Philo und der Midrasch, BZAW, 57, Giessen, 1931.

F. BUECHSEL, article 'ἀλληγορία,' in: Theologisches Wörterbuch zum NT, 1, 1933, 260–264.

W. L. KNOX, Parallels to the NT use of sôma, Journal of Theological Studies, 39, 1938, 243–246.

D. DAUBE, Rabbinic method of Interpretation and Hellenistic Rhetoric, Hebrew Union Coll. Ann. 22, 1949, 239–264.

P. KATZ, Philo's Bible, Cambridge, 1950.

H. THYEN, Der Stil der Jüdisch-hellenistischen Homilie, Forschungen zur Religion und Literatur des Alten und Neuen Testaments (FRLANT), 47, Göttingen, 1955.

S. BELKIN (en hébreu), The Interpretation of Names in Philo, Horeb 12, 1956, p. 3–61.

S. SANDMEL, Philo's Place in Judaism. A Study of Conceptions of Abraham in Jewish Literature, Cincinnati, 1956.

F. BUFFIÈRE, Les mythes d'Homère et la pensée grecque, Collection d'études anciennes, Paris, 1956.

JEAN PÉPIN, Mythe et allégorie, Paris, 1976.

S. BELKIN (en hébreu), Philo and the Midrashic Tradition of Palestine, Horeb, 13, 1958–59, 1–60.

S. BELKIN (en hébreu), The Philonic Exposition of the Torah in the Light of the Ancient Rabbinic Midrashim, Sura, 4, 1960, 1–68.

J. POUILLOUX, Philon d'Alexandrie. Recherches et points de vue nouveaux, Revue d'histoire des Religions, 161, 1962, 136–137.

P. BOYANCÉ, Études philoniennes, Revue des Études Grecques, 76, 1963, 64–110.

RAPHAËL LOEWE, The 'plain' meaning of Scripture in early Jewish exegesis, Jerusalem, 1964.

SIDNEY G. SOWERS, The Hermeneutics of Philo and Hebrews, Basel Studies of Theology, 1, Richmond, 1965.

S. BELKIN (en hébreu), Symbolic theories in Philo compared with rabbinical theories, in: Harry Austryn Wolfson Jubilee, American Academy for Jewish Research, Jerusalem, 1965.

V. NIKIPROWETZKY, Problèmes du récit de la Création (Genèse 1–3) chez Philon d'Alexandrie, Revue des Études Juives, 124, 1965, 271–306.

J. CAZEAUX, De migratione Abrahami, introduction et traduction, Les œuvres de Philon d'Alexandrie, 14, Paris, 1965.

ANTHONY HANSON, Philo's etymologies, Journal of Theological Studies, 18, 1967, 128–139.

CH. KANNENGIESSER, Philon et les Pères sur la double création de l'homme, in: Philon d'Alexandrie. Colloques nationaux du Centre national de la Recherche scientifique, Lyon, 11–15 sept. 1966, éditions du CNRS, Paris, 1967, 277–296.

A. Michel, Quelques aspects de la rhétorique chez Philon, ibid., 81–103.

J. Pépin, Remarques sur la théorie de l'exégèse allégorique chez Philon, ibid., 131–168.

U. Fruechtel, Die kosmologischen Vorstellungen bei Philo von Alexandrien. Ein Beitrag zur Geschichte der Genesis-Exegese, Arbeiten zur Literatur und Geschichte des hellenistischen Judentums (ALGHJ), 2, Leiden, 1968.

Reinhold Mayer, Geschichtserfahrung in Schriftauslegung. Zur Hermeneutik des frühen Judentums, Freiburg, 1968.

S. G. Sowers, On the Reinterpretation of Biblical History in Hellenistic Judaism, in: Oikonomia. Heilsgeschichte als Thema der Theologie, O. Cullmann gewidmet, Hamburg, 1967, 18–25.

K. Otte, Das Sprachverständnis bei Philo von Alexandrien. Sprache als Mittel der Hermeneutik, Beiträge zur Geschichte der biblischen Exegese, 7, Tübingen, 1968.

Irmgard Christiansen, Die Technik der allegorischen Auslegungswissenschaft, Beiträge zur Geschichte der biblischen Hermeneutik, 7, Tübingen, 1969.

V. Nikiprowetzky, Κυρίου πρόσθεσις, Note critique sur Philon d'Alexandrie, De Josepho, 28, Revue des Études Juives, 127, 1969, 387–392.

Richard Baer, Philo's use of the categories male and female, ALGHJ, 3, Leiden, 1970.

P. Courcelle, Philon d'Alexandrie et le précepte delphique, in: Philomathes. Studies and essays in the humanities in memory of Ph. Merlan, La Haye, 1971, 245–250.

J. Cazeaux, Littérature ancienne et recherche des 'structures', Revue des Études augustiniennes, 18, 1972, 287–292.

J. Cazeaux, Interpréter Philon d'Alexandrie, Revue des Études Grecques, 85, 1972, 345–352.

J. Cazeaux, Aspects de l'exégèse philonienne, Revue des Sciences religieuses, 47, 1973, 262–269.

V. Nikiprowetzky, Le commentaire de l'Écriture chez Philon d'Alexandrie, ALGHJ, 11, Leiden, 1977.

J. Cazeaux, La trame et la chaîne: Structures littéraires et exégèse dans cinq traités de Philon d'Alexandrie, ALGHJ, Leiden, 1983.

J. Cazeaux, L'épée du Logos et le Soleil de Midi, Maison de l'Orient méditerranéen, 1 Rue Raulin, Lyon, 1983.

J. Cazeaux, Philon d'Alexandrie: De la grammaire à la mystique, Supplément au Cahier-Évangile 44, Le Cerf, Paris, 1983.

Philo Judaeus and Exegetical Traditions in Alexandria

by Burton L. Mack, Claremont, Cal.

Contents[1]

---

[1] A selected biliography on Philo and the interpretation of the scriptures in Hellenistic Judaism is given at the end of the article. Items listed there will be cited in the notes by author and abbreviated title only. Other references to works not included in the bibliography will be cited in full at first appearance. Thereafter an abbreviated title will be used. The standard bibliographies for the history of Philo studies are: H. L. Goodhart and E. R. Goodenough, A General Bibliography of Philo Judaeus. In: The Politics of Philo Judaeus, by E. R. Goodenough (New Haven: Yale, 1938; reprinted Hildesheim: Olms, 1967); E. Hilgert, Bibliographia Philoniana 1935–1981. ANRW II, 21, 1 (1983), p. 47–97 (above in this same volume).

Introduction

The history of Philo scholarship has turned again and again to the question of his place in the complex syncretism of Hellenistic religions and philosophies. His place has not yet been determined. This is so in spite of the many excellent studies devoted to investigations on the one hand of his relationship to various aspects of the philosophical and religious milieu, and on the other to attempts to delineate or reconstruct his own system of thought. Recent studies have been suggesting that a large part of the problem has been a lack of clarity about the form and intention of his work as commentary upon or interpretation of the Pentateuch.[2] If the intention was exegetical, and the authority was a religious

---

[2] Cf. CHRISTIANSEN, Technik; NIKIPROWETZKY, Le commentaire; MACK, Exegetical Traditions. — These studies have called for a thorough investigation of the Philonic material as interpretation of the Pentateuch. This call is to be distinguished from repeated refer-

corpus, it may indicate a system of meaning which cannot be reconstructed adequately by using only the models of the Hellenic and Hellenistic schools. Instead it becomes necessary to discover the hermeneutic which determined how the Hellenistic school languages used were meant to be taken precisely as interpretations of the scriptures. Thus an analysis of the Philonic corpus seems to be called for which investigates the hermeneutical principles of the various types of exegesis to be found there and seeks to determine the contribution which Alexandrian Judaism may have made in the poetics of interpretation, and which Philo himself may have made to the history of Alexandrian-Jewish thought.

This narrowing of the focus of investigation with respect to the place of Philo in the history of Alexandrian Judaism may indeed be the precision required of the next period in Philo research as a necessary preparation for the eventual placement both of Philo and of Alexandrian Judaism within the larger Hellenistic world. It is the purpose of this essay to review the scholarship on Philo in such a way as to clarify the question with regard to his relationship to exegetical traditions in Alexandria and thus contribute to the current investigations of Philo as an interpreter of the scriptures and repository of Alexandrian exegetical traditions. In order to do this it will be helpful to begin by assessing the scholarship on the question of sources and traditions in Philo in general.

I. The Sources of Philo's Religious Thought

A. The Greek Sources

1. The School Traditions

Characteristic of the long and rich history of Philo studies has been the attempt to delineate his system of religious thought and to derive its conceptuality from the Greek school traditions of philosophy. The great works of the last century reflect the early recognition that in Philo both a religious tradition (Jewish) and a philosophical tradition (Greek) combined to form a new 'religious

ence, especially in the German scholarship, to the role which the scripture may have played in determining its interpretation. There the acknowledgment of the role of scripture, frequently described as 'Zwang' (cf. THYEN, Probleme, 235) has been introduced mainly as an explanation for curious developments and inconsistencies of thought which cannot be understood strictly as expressions of Greek thought and logic. Here, in the recent studies, it is the essential and continuous function of the scriptures as that which is being interpreted which has been noted. In the article reference will be made to the Pentateuch as the scriptural authority for Philo; but the designation 'Pentateuch' does not intend a foreclosure on the question of the exact nature and delimitation of scriptural authority for Alexandrian Judaism. It refers only to the phenomenon of Philo's special concern with the Five Books of Moses.

philosophy.'³ It was understood that the religious heritage had modified significantly the philosophical traditions reflected in the new conceptuality, but it was
assumed, nevertheless, that the new philosophy could be reconstructed as a
system of thought comparable to those of the Greek philosophers and schools.
Many attempts were made to discover its structure and determine its position
with regard to the classical issues of the history of Greek philosophy. Especially
important appeared to be Philo's concept of Logos which was traced repeatedly to
its supposed source in the Greek philosophical tradition and was understood to be
a major idea of the new philosophy making possible a unified conception of the
ideas of God, world, and human being.⁴

This approach to the Philonic corpus was challenged by the rise of the
history of religions school and the discovery that much of the Philonic language
could be traced rather to the Hellenistic religions of mystery and their mythologies. But the challenge did not bring to an end the effort to account for Philo as a
philosopher. Instead the search for the Hellenic and Hellenistic origins of certain
remarkable Philonic conceptualities was intensified and resulted in a number of
major monographs tracing the development of certain specific terms from their
background in the philosophical traditions into their usage in the Philonic corpus.⁵
In the work of H. A. WOLFSON, then, it was even the case that a marvelous
attempt was made to reconstruct the Philonic system as a whole, showing in every
instance the precise point at which Philo as a Jewish thinker parted ways with the
Greek philosophical traditions upon which he was dependent for his new philosophical theology.⁶

The problem with this approach to Philo has been the need in every case to
assume Philonic interests in systematic philosophy which are simply not in evidence in the commentaries. Lacking express developments of philosophical position-taking in the corpus as a whole it has been necessary for scholars to determine Philo's views on a matter by collecting the passages which appear to be
relevant and making the attempt to equalize seeming contradictions in the interest
of some consistent logic assumed by the scholar. At this point the scholar has
usually been aided by a general impression of Philo's system as a whole, frequently
unacknowledged, which could be used to make judgments about the intention of
specific statements which might not appear otherwise to have a clear philosophical
intention in keeping with the supposed logical system. Invariably the process of

---

³ One needs only to notice the titles given to the following works: A. GFRÖRER, Philo und
die alexandrinische Theosophie. Stuttgart, 1831; A. F. DÄHNE, Geschichtliche Darstellung
der jüdisch-alexandrinischen Religions-Philosophie. Halle, 1834; J. DRUMMOND, Philo
Judaeus, or the Jewish-Alexandrian Philosophy in its Development and Completion.
London, 1888; reprinted: Amsterdam, 1969.

⁴ As an example, see M. HEINZE, Die Lehre vom Logos in der griechischen Philosophie.
Oldenburg, 1872.

⁵ The following works may serve as examples: H. LEISEGANG, Pneuma Hagion. Leipzig,
1922; H. WILLMS, EIKΩN, Eine begriffsgeschichtliche Untersuchung zum Platonismus.
1. Teil: Philon von Alexandreia. Münster, 1935. One might also review the bibliographical
article by HILGERT, section 12 (Classical Literature). There it is clear that the main
methodology has been to trace concepts, themes and motifs.

⁶ H. A. WOLFSON, Philo 1–2. Cambridge, Mass.: Harvard, 1945–48.

selection of material to be investigated has taken it out of its commentary context for discussion.[7]

In the history of scholarship the judgment has been made frequently that Philo's system can be understood as a modification of Stoic views by means of middle Platonic conceptuality in the interest of a theology of transcendence.[8] As a general impression this judgment may indeed continue to give some guidance to those investigating Philo's own persuasions. But it can not account for the presence of large quantities of material which can not be classified in this way, including material from other Greek school traditions, nor has it been able to establish an objective criterion by which the Philonic preference for Platonic categories can be ascertained. This failure to demonstrate the Philonic system by those convinced of his systematic intentions is an impasse well known to Philonic scholars. Thus one frequently reads the opposite opinion, namely, that the corpus contains a confusing version of Hellenistic eclecticism which reflects no system at all.

In view of this impasse one can hardly avoid the conclusion that the assumption which has guided this scholarship, that namely Philo is to be viewed primarily in terms of the Greek philosophical tradition, is inadequate. It is the thesis of this article that this conclusion is true. The inadequacy has been due to a failure to recognize the form and intention of the Philonic corpus as scriptural interpretation, as well as a failure to explore the possibility that the corpus may contain a great deal of material from the traditions of Jewish interpretation which can not be attributed directly to Philo at all. The presence of vital interest in Greek language and conceptuality in the Philonic corpus and the Jewish interpretive enterprise is not therefore to be denied. But the intention of its usage as commentary seems to indicate a logic governed by some system of meaning whose essential components extend beyond the interests of the philosophical schools. This has been acknowledged implicitly in the history of Philo studies by other scholarly traditions which have sought Philo's place rather among the mystagogues, or religious apologists, and so on. It is thus the inability of the philosophical school model to account for the range of material in Philo, and its form of commentary, which requires a revision in research methodology.

2. The Literary Sources

In addition to the immense investment in philosophical and philological investigation just mentioned, scholarship in Philo has produced some significant

---

[7] Two recent examples of this approach are: R. A. BAER, Philo's Use of the Categories Male and Female. ALGHJ 3. Leiden: Brill, 1970 and F.-N. KLEIN, Die Lichtterminologie bei Philon von Alexandrien und in den hermetischen Schriften. Leiden: Brill, 1962.

[8] Examples are to be found in the following studies: M. POHLENZ, Philon von Alexandria. Nachrichten der Akademie der Wissenschaften zu Göttingen, phil.-hist. Klasse (1942) 409–487; H. A. WOLFSON, Philo 1, 111–113; A. WLOSOK, Laktanz und die philosophische Gnosis. Untersuchungen zu Geschichte und Terminologie der gnostischen Erlösungsvorstellung. AHAW Heidelberg (1960) 59–60.

source-critical studies which have sought to determine the dependence of certain specific passages in Philo upon the Greek literature of the Hellenistic period. The only study which was able to point to specific extra-Philonic comparative material which could be viewed as a literary source in the documentary sense, however, has been that portion of H. VON ARNIM's work in which he could show that in Ebr 164-205 Philo was dependent upon the 'Ten Tropes' of Aenesidemus.[9] Most of the other attempts to determine literary sources have found it necessary to argue for the probability of a Hellenistic source on the basis of some similarity in matters of form and/or content between the Philonic passages under investigation and other generally comparable examples of Hellenistic literature.[10] Many studies have been content simply to establish the correlation of certain aspects of Philonic style, or certain patterns of literary organization with known Hellenistic genre. Areas in which important correlations have been established include the *diatribe*,[11] the biography,[12] and the doxography.[13] It is a significant curiosity indicative of the history of Philonic scholarship that the literary comparison most obviously called for, that of the form of the commentary, has received little investigation.[14]

3. The Enduring Problem

As important as this scholarship in the Greek sources of Philo's thought and works has been, its meager and inconclusive results indicate that its assumptions about Philo's philosophical and literary intentions have been misleading. It has become necessary therefore to consider whether Philo was interested in constructing a philosophical system at all. If it is granted that some form of systematic

---

[9] H. VON ARNIM, Quellenstudien.

[10] Examples of this kind of investigation are: A. H. CHROUST, A Fragment of Aristotle's 'On Philosophy.' Some Remarks about Philo of Alexandria, De aeternitate mundi 8, 41. Wiener Studien N.F. 8 (1977) 15—19; A. J. FESTUGIÈRE, La revélation d'Hermès Trismégiste 2: Le Dieu cosmique. Paris (1949) 492—496 (Philo's use of περὶ κόσμου); E. R. GOODENOUGH, A Neo-Pythagorean Source in Philo Judaeus. Yale Classical Studies 3 (1932) 115—164; P. WENDLAND, Eine doxographische Quelle Philos. Sitzungsbericht der königlich-preussischen Akademie der Wissenschaften zu Berlin (1897) 2, 1074—1079; W. LAMEERE, Sur un passage de Philon d'Alexandrie. Mnemosyne IV/4 (1951) 73—80. LAMEERE relates Plant 1—6 to Aristotle's lost treatise περὶ φιλοσοφίας. For an overview see R. HAMERTON-KELLY, Sources and Traditions in Philo Judaeus. SP 1 (1972) 3—26.

[11] P. WENDLAND, Philo und die kynisch-stoische Diatribe. Beiträge zur Geschichte der griechischen Philosophie und Religion. Ed. P. WENDLAND and O. KERN. Berlin: Reimer, 1895, 1—75; H. THYEN, Stil.

[12] A. PRIESSNIG, Die literarische Form der Patriarchenbiographien des Philo von Alexandrien. MGWJ N.F. 37 (1929) 143—155.

[13] P. WENDLAND, Eine doxographische Quelle.

[14] It should be mentioned that M. ADLER, Studien, saw the allegorical treatises as commentaries and made some helpful observations about the types of exegetical procedure encountered in them. See R. HAMERTON-KELLY, Sources and Traditions, 14—15. Cf. also A. D. NOCK, The Exegesis of Timaeus 28 C. VC 16 (1962) 79—86, esp. 82.

conceptuality must be, or appears to be, in evidence in his writings, it should also be acknowledged that it does not appear to be the intention of those writings to present such a system systematically. That Philo was at home in the language and literature of the Greek philosophical traditions is clear; but what he intended by his usage of them is not. The language of the schools has been found often to work another way at his hand;[15] and the organizing principles both of his thought and of his literary formations appear to be determined by logics other than those which control the Hellenic philosopher. Until the peculiar logic of the Philonic corpus is discovered in relationship to its specific intention as commentary on the Pentateuch it must be that Philo's place in the history of Greek philosophy, if indeed he is to be given one, cannot be established.

B. Sources in Hellenistic Religions

1. The Mystery Religions

As early as 1894 PAUL ZIEGERT wrote an article indicating that Philo may have been influenced by the Hellenistic mystery religions.[16] Thus an aspect of Philonic language was noticed which pointed to religious concerns not immediately recognizable as Jewish and, in so far as this was true, at variance with the older view of Philo as one who sought to understand Jewish religious tradition solely in terms of Greek thought. This new perspective was explored and confirmed in the monumental study on Philo by ÉMILE BRÉHIER in 1907.[17] He was able to show that much of the conceptuality in Philo frequently borders on mythological imagery and that it was used in the interest of a theological and religious concern. This concern was fully syncretistic, intending to support a particularly Jewish understanding of social order, but seeking to explicate its Jewish traditions in terms understandable to its Hellenistic setting. This setting was found to be characterized by a kind of religious thought which had interpreted or used Stoic terminology to conceptualize oriental ideas about the knowledge of God and the immortality of the soul as the two highest soteriological values. This *culte spirituel* BRÉHIER was able to identify as a Hellenistic Egyptian mystery religion.[18]

---

[15] An example would be the use of Pneuma in Philo. H. LEISEGANG, Pneuma Hagion, sought to derive its meaning from the Greek philosophical traditions. But H. LEWY, Sobria Ebrietas. Beiheft ZNW 9. Giessen, 1929, 63 ff., brought a telling critique against such a derivation. Similar findings could be documented for a sizable number of important terms.

[16] P. ZIEGERT, Über die Ansätze zu einer Mysterienlehre bei Philo. Theologische Studien und Kritiken 67 (1894) 706—732.

[17] É. BRÉHIER, Les idées philosophiques et religieuses de Philon d'Alexandrie. Études de philosophie médiévale 8. Paris: Vrin, 1907; second edition, 1925; reprinted, 1950.

[18] BRÉHIER, Les idées, 237—249. It should be noted that R. REITZENSTEIN already had explored the possibility of an Hellenistic-Egyptian religious syncretism in: Zwei religions-

BRÉHIER's work inaugurated a series of studies which sought more information both about the Hellenistic mystery upon which Philo was dependent, and about the significance of the mystery terminology as it was used by Philo.[19] Now it was possible to understand the intention of the Philonic language another way and to see how it could be that apparently philosophical terminology might be working in the interest of a religious view of reality. The watch words now were 'mystery,' 'mystic,' and the 'piety' of Philo. It was a very important discovery, the significance of which for the question of Philo's sources and traditions has not yet been assessed fully.

2. The Pattern of the Mystery

The quest for the mystery religion reflected in the works of Philo has not succeeded in identifying a particular non-Jewish Hellenistic mystery as the source of influence, although it has become clear that the religion and mythology of Isis in their Hellenistic forms do provide the closest parallels to much of the imagery and mythological metaphor in Philo. Nevertheless, working with commonplace conceptions about the Hellenistic mysteries in general, this scholarship has succeeded in organizing the Philonic material itself in such a way as to show an amazingly consistent pattern of thought which appears to be at work throughout the corpus and which commends itself as a systematic principle able to account in part for the form and intention of the corpus. This, it will be remembered, the thesis of Philo as philosopher could not achieve. The pattern has to do with the conception of the 'path' to God with its two stages consisting first of preliminary practice, and then of ultimate perfection. Already in 1909 H. WINDISCH had discovered that the image of the soteriological path was a major organizing principle in the corpus and had used it to interpret Philo's work as a whole, and explicate it as an expression of a religious piety seeking the knowledge of God and immortality.[20] He did this, however, without engaging the issue of the source or background for such a pattern.

In 1931 J. PASCHER developed the thesis that the terminology of 'the path' had its source in Hellenistic mystery mythology.[21] He collected a great deal of comparative material to show that various Philonic metaphors and allegories could be correlated and understood as expressions of a single unified system of soteriology according to which the first stage eventuated in a rebirth of the initiate

---

geschichtliche Fragen. Strassburg, 1901 and Hellenistische Theologie in Ägypten. Neue Jahrbücher für das klassische Altertum 13 (1904), 177—194.

[19] In addition to the studies by WINDISCH, PASCHER and GOODENOUGH see the following: L. CERFAUX, Influence des mystères sur le Judaisme alexandrin avant Philon. Le Muséon 37 (1924) 28—88; G. GERHOLD, Mystik und Mysterienreligion bei Philo von Alexandrien. Dissertation, Erlangen, 1966.

[20] H. WINDISCH, Die Frömmigkeit Philos und ihre Bedeutung für das Christentum. Leipzig: Hinrichs, 1909.

[21] J. PASCHER, Η ΒΑΣΙΛΙΚΗ ΟΔΟΣ. Der Königsweg zu Wiedergeburt und Vergottung bei Philon von Alexandreia. Paderborn: Schöningh, 1931.

as the Logos, the second in a rebirth as God himself. The major allegory depicting the first stage was found to be that of the High Priest as the Logos; the major imagery of the second stage was that of the ascent-vision. Both were combined, according to PASCHER, as two sequential stages of the 'King's Highway' – an allegory of the exodus story.

PASCHER's work has not been found to provide a solid basis upon which to initiate further explorations. This is because the system which he discovered has appeared to others more as a construct of his own than as an exegetical or historical finding. The schema itself, moreover, appears to have governed the collection of the comparative materials both from without and from within the corpus, and its intention either as an allegory or as a mystery *logos* is far from clear. But he did succeed in quickening the imagination of subsequent scholarship which would want to explore the possibility that some such pattern of soteriological achievement might provide the key to understand the allegorical interpretation of the Pentateuch intended by the corpus, and thus explain the form of the corpus as commentary. It is at least in this sense that one can understand the indebtedness to PASCHER which E. R. GOODENOUGH acknowledged.[22] It is GOODENOUGH's work which continues to stand as the classic attempt to understand Philo as mystagogue of the mystery.

GOODENOUGH developed the thesis that one could speak in general about the Hellenistic age as a time of mystic religion – a quest for religious experience and certainty which interpreted the oriental mythologies as symbols of metaphysical truth and submerged the classical traditions of rationalistic philosophy beneath the recurring waves of the new mystic systems. The Jews of Alexandria participated in this quest, according to GOODENOUGH, and so transformed by means of allegory not only their scriptural traditions but their rites and practices as well into symbols of the mystery. The mystery was about a path of ascent which fled the oppression of a determinist world and ended in the vision of the transcendent God. It could be rediscovered in the scripture by means of allegory if only the patriarchs, Aaron and Moses were transformed into symbols which represented the stages on the way.

The mystery then was the key by which the allegorical interpretation of the Pentateuch could be understood, and GOODENOUGH organized his book according to this grand scheme of correspondence which he found rationalized in Philo's commentary series on the Exposition of the Law. This discovery of a correspondence between a system of religious thought and an allegory of the Pentateuch as a whole, as well as the profundity implicated by the correlation of an interpretive method (transformation of literal text into religious symbol) with its religious intention (enabling the experience of transformation itself) will be one of GOODENOUGH's lasting contributions to scholarship on Philo. Unfortunately GOODENOUGH himself did not pursue the significance of these correlations, perhaps because he was interested mainly in delineating what he termed the mystery itself, rather than in exploring the allegorical method and its possible role

---

[22] E. R. GOODENOUGH, By Light, Light: The Mystic Gospel of Hellenistic Judaism. 5. New Haven: Yale University Press, 1935.

in the creation of the mystery. His view was that the mystery essentially was the Jewish form of a common Hellenistic religio-cultural phenomenon, and that the Jews had learned or copied it from their neighbors. The allegorical method merely enabled the mystery to be reflected in the Pentateuch for initiates to see. Thus the source of the commentary was understood to be the mystery which GOOD-ENOUGH understood to be literally experienced and practiced.[23] The question of the function of the scriptures and the allegory to the experience of the mystery was not engaged.

3. The Enduring Problem

GOODENOUGH's thesis about a literal Jewish religion of mystery has not found wide support. The problem has to do with the understandable unwillingness of scholars to take the language of the mystery itself literally, suspecting rather that the graphic, abstract and often mythological depictions of the mystery were intended to be taken some other way. GOODENOUGH himself seemed to understand the 'spiritualizing' and figurative function of the allegorical language in relation to the literal text being interpreted. It is curious that he argued for its intention then as referring to a literal mystery of any kind. The usual suggestion at this point is that the mythological language was intended metaphorically or figuratively to enhance certain aspects of the process of allegorizing itself as an initiation into 'mystery.' But if this is true, as it appears indeed in some sense to be, the question remains as to the nature of that mystery. It is the nature of the interpretative enterprise itself, then, and not the reconstructed systems of philosophical and religious thought, which needs to be understood if Philo is to be understood.

C. The Jewish Sources

1. Palestinian Judaism

That Philo was a Jew, and that his commitment to Judaism is clearly expressed in his writings, has always been acknowledged in modern scholarship. But opinions about the form of his Judaism have varied greatly. On the one hand there is a tradition of scholarship which has preferred to emphasize the existence of a common 'normative' Judaism of the time and to regard Philo as a participant in and representative of such a configuration. On the other there are those who have wanted to distinguish clearly between a 'Palestinian' and a 'Hellenistic' Judaism, and to regard Philo as a representative only of the latter. It is a curiosity of Philonic scholarship that those who have held to the monolithic view of Judaism have argued for Palestinian influence on Philo; those who have

---

[23] See E. R. GOODENOUGH, Literal Mystery in Hellenistic Judaism. In: Quantulacumque: Studies Presented to Kirsopp Lake, 227—241. Ed. R. P. CASEY et al. London, 1937.

distinguished sharply between Palestinian and Hellenistic varieties of Judaism have tended to argue that there was little or no Palestinian influence at all. The research which has addressed this issue directly has concentrated on comparative studies between Philo and the Palestinian midrashim.

2. Comparative Midrash

a) Haggada

In 1875 C. Siegfried[24] brought together a few references from the Palestinian midrashim in order to show that Philo was acquainted with the haggadic traditions there. In 1890 L. Treitel[25] expanded the basis for comparison a bit, and in 1910 N. Bentwich[26] used the evidence to argue for the essential 'catholicity of Judaism,' accounting for the divergencies between Palestinian and Alexandrian Judaism by hypothesizing a 'fluidity' of ancient traditions for the period under consideration and speaking of a 'break between the two schools' only after the time of Philo.

It was not until the work of M. Stein[27] in 1931 that the relationship between the haggada in Philo and in the Palestinian midrashim was investigated seriously. He distinguished between two types of haggada — one which embellished by 'historicizing,' another which interpreted by allegorizing — and argued that the allegorical haggada characteristic of Hellenistic Judaism was a development of, and dependent upon, the earlier historicizing haggadic traditions of Palestine. Stein's purpose in the study was to find a way to argue for the direction of influence in the development of haggadic tradition, but his thesis may also have significance still for the search for the origins of Jewish allegory itself in earlier haggada, irrespective of the question of the provenance of that haggada.[28] This aspect of his work has not yet found the thorough scholarly critique it deserves.

In 1954 S. Sandmel[29] produced a major study which called into question the thesis that Philo was dependent upon Palestinian (rabbinic) haggadic traditions for his allegories. Sandmel concentrated upon the story of Abraham and produced extensive data for a thorough investigation. His conclusion was that most

---

[24] C. Siegfried, Philo als Ausleger.

[25] L. Treitel, Agadah bei Philo.

[26] N. Bentwich, Philo-Judaeus of Alexandria. Philadelphia: Jewish Publication Society, 1910.

[27] M. Stein, Philo und der Midrasch.

[28] The question is the more pressing in light of the fact that the Philonic corpus itself contains both the 'historicizing' and the 'allegorizing' modes of interpretation. An excellent example of their employment side by side is to be found in the treatise 'De Abrahamo.' Stein's thesis would indicate that the allegories here are in some way dependent upon earlier haggadic embellishments of a non-allegorizing mode, examples of which may also be extant in the treatise. If that could be substantiated a sequential development of exegetical activity could be seen which might put one in touch with the origins of a particular allegory or allegorical mode.

[29] S. Sandmel, Philo's Place.

of the apparent parallels are superficial or to be explained as natural developments given the general similarity of purpose — the interpretation of the scriptural traditions. The differences, however, were found to be striking, reflecting what he called distinct "religiosities."[30] The Abraham of Philo, he contended, was interpreted as being a sage unique in his achievement of philosophical and mystical knowledge, because Philo himself was a Hellenized Jew who regarded such achievement highly. "Philo," he said, "creates his Abraham independent of the rabbis."[31]

It is clear that the studies by STEIN and SANDMEL are in some respects contradictory in conclusion, and point to the need for a refinement of method in future investigations which can relate the categories of tradition and creativity.

In the work by P. BORGEN[32] in 1965, which is the only other major study in Philo and the midrash haggada to be mentioned here, the argument is made that there was an oral haggadic tradition about the manna common both to Palestinian and Hellenistic Judaism. BORGEN's concern was rather with the way in which the haggada may have contributed to the form of the homily, than with an investigation of the origin and method of haggadic development itself. But his study is very important, providing as it does a 'literary' context and a setting in life in which haggada can be observed. The question is whether the homily may be more than that, i.e. the matrix in which certain haggadic developments actually originated. We know far too little about the hermeneutical principles of haggadic development to make full use of comparative studies between Philonic and Palestinian traditions.[33]

b) Halaka

In 1879 B. RITTER[34] produced a work intending to strengthen the thesis of Philo's dependence on Palestinian traditions. Whereas SIEGFRIED had made the point of dependence in respect to the haggada, RITTER collected the halakic par-

---

[30] SANDMEL, Philo's Place, 199.

[31] SANDMEL, Philo's Place, 199.

[32] P. BORGEN, Bread from Heaven.

[33] Promising explorations for the hermeneutical principles of Jewish exegesis are beginning to appear: R. BLOCH, Ecriture et tradition dans le Judaisme: Aperçus sur l'origine du Midrash. Cahiers Sioniens 8 (1954) 9—34; R. BLOCH, Article 'Midrash,' Supplément au Dictionnaire de la Bible 5 (1951) 1263—1280; J. BOWER, The Targums and Rabbinic Literature. London: Cambridge University Press, 1969; R. LE DÉAUT, Apropos a Definition of Midrash. Interpretation 25 (1971) 259—282; R. MAYER, Geschichtserfahrung und Schriftauslegung. Zur Hermeneutik des frühen Judentums. In: Die hermeneutische Frage in der Theologie. Ed. O. LORETZ, W. STROLZ. Schriften zum Weltgespräch 2. Freiburg: Herder, 1968; M. MILLER, Article Midrash. IDB Supplementary Volume, 1976; M. MILLER, Targum, Midrash and the Use of the Old Testament in the New Testament. JSJ 2 (1971) 29—82; D. PATTE, Early Jewish Hermeneutic in Palestine. SBL Dissertation 22. Missoula, Montana: Scholars, 1975; G. VERMÈS, Scripture and Tradition in Judaism. Studia Post-Biblica 4. Leiden: Brill, 1961; A. WRIGHT, The Literary Genre Midrash. Staten Island: Alba, 1967.

[34] B. RITTER, Philo und die Halaka.

allels. The argument was based upon the apparent similarity of many points of interpretation and, though not accepted by the historians of religion who emphasized rather Philo's Hellenistic character,[35] stood as the authoritative study on the subject until HEINEMANN's investigation in 1932.[36]

H. HEINEMANN's study was concerned primarily with the larger question of the extent to which Philo stood under the cultural influence of Jewish or Greek ways of thought. He chose the Philonic material having to do with the interpretation of the laws as the basis for his study, and came to the conclusion that Philo was indebted not to pre-rabbinic oral traditions, but to Alexandrian Jewish traditions which had interpreted the laws in terms of Greek philosophy. He was able even to identify a rather consistent use of Cynic categories in Philo's discussion of the Jewish festivals, and posited a written source which must have originated within the Hellenized Jewish community in Alexandria.[37] HEINEMANN did not want to deny the loyalty of Alexandrian Jews to Judaism — a conception which he did not define precisely; but he was convinced that the influence of the Greek philosophical traditions had transformed its meaning for them in a development which was quite distinct from, and independent of, Palestinian directions. In 1938 E. R. GOODENOUGH[38] provided support for this view by emphasizing the indigeneity of Jewish jurisprudence in Alexandria.

In the last major work in this area, S. BELKIN[39] argued just the reverse. He did agree with GOODENOUGH and HEINEMANN to the extent that Philo reflects the jurisprudence of local Jewish courts in Egypt,[40] and that he represents a group of Jews who allegorized the laws in terms of Greek philosophy. But he differed from both of them in his insistence that the Alexandrian development itself followed what he called the "principles of the Tannaitic Halaka."[41] His thesis was that Philo and his group "combined a Pharasaic Halakism, practical allegorism, and mysticism."[42] He collected halakic parallels to show the ultimate agreement of the two traditions at the point of literal or Pharasaic interpretation.

3. The Enduring Problem

It will be clear to scholars of the Hellenistic period that the studies in Philo which have concerned themselves with the question of his Jewish sources have reflected certain generalized views about the forms of Judaism of the time, and have been hindered by the imprecision of those views. It is now commonplace to understand the inadequacy of the old contrasts between 'Jewish-Greek' and

---

[35] For example, see M. FRIEDLÄNDER, Geschichte, 205.
[36] HEINEMANN, Bildung.
[37] HEINEMANN, Bildung, 142—146. See below Section D, 2, c, pp. 246f.
[38] E. R. GOODENOUGH, The Jurisprudence of the Jewish Courts of Egypt. New Haven: Yale University Press, 1929.
[39] BELKIN, Philo and the Oral Law.
[40] BELKIN, Philo and the Oral Law, 5.
[41] BELKIN, Philo and the Oral Law, 6.
[42] BELKIN, Philo and the Oral Law, 28.

'Palestinian-Hellenistic' as very helpful descriptions; but it is just these which have dominated the discussion in this area of research and it is they which account for its many disappointments. It is true that BELKIN attempted to delineate a spectrum of 'sects' which were to be distinguished in terms of their method of interpretation of the law — an observation which if critically investigated could lead to very important findings.[43] But his characterizations of the groups were quite subjective, untested, and constructed in such a way as to support a thesis which others have found improbable on other grounds.[44] More significant was the actual identification of a type of interpretation of the festivals by HEINEMANN which now needs to find some actual social setting in Alexandrian Judaism in order to explain its existence and make its full contribution to our knowledge of that community as a whole.

The overriding concern of this scholarship has been to trace the Palestinian 'influences' operative in Philo, or to deny them. This is not an insignificant question, of course, but the impasse at the end of both discussions — STEIN and SANDMEL on the question of haggadic influence; BELKIN and HEINEMANN on the question of halakic influence — does indicate that some refinement in methodology would be in order before engaging further merely comparative studies.

It is the thesis of this paper that the refinement should be sought in terms of an exploration of the formal characteristics of both the haggadic and the halakic materials as midrash, i.e. as interpretation of the scriptures. One is struck by the lack of consideration for this obvious intention of the Jewish material which has been investigated. The attempt has been mainly to compare and characterize the content. And where discussion of 'methods' or 'principles' of midrash have occurred it has been assumed that the Tannaitic and Rabbinic models are clear and sufficient to explain the phenomenon of interpretive concern itself.[45] There has

---

[43] BELKIN distinguished between the 'extreme allegorists,' who advocated the abrogation of the law; the 'literalists,' who kept but refused to interpret the law; and a party taking the middle position which both kept the law and interpreted it allegorically. He later combined these with a tri-partite description of Palestinian positions which included 'Sadducean literalists,' 'Pharisaic halakists,' and 'Palestinian practical allegorists' (27—28). It is clear that BELKIN theorized on the basis of certain schematic understandings of Jewish 'sects' at the time, and that his main concern was to associate Philo with the Pharisaic tradition. This aspect of his work has not been found acceptable. But the attempt to distinguish sects in Alexandria was helpful. WOLFSON expanded upon this by distinguishing: 1) the 'traditionalists' who upheld the literal meaning of the texts both in legal and narrative parts, and rejected allegory; 2) the 'extreme allegorists,' who rejected the literal meaning altogether; and 3) 'apostates' (Philo 1, 57—86). It was Philo, according to WOLFSON, who combined the traditional method with the allegorical (57). The inadequacy of these schematizations is clear. But the phenomenon of conflicting attitudes toward, and diverse methods of, the interpretation of the law in Alexandrian Judaism is also clear. Precision about these positions will be essential in any reconstruction of the history of exegesis in Alexandria.

[44] Cf. GOODENOUGH, Light, 78; An Introduction to Philo Judaeus 12. New Haven: Yale, 1940; second edition revised, Oxford: Blackwell, 1962; D. DAUBE, Review of Belkin, BO 5 (1948) 64—65.

[45] It should be noted that SANDMEL's position is an exception to this generalization. He has emphasized instead the particularity of cultural setting and individual creativity to account

been little discussion of types and methods of interpretation other than to note repeatedly the distinction between haggada and halaka itself. There has been little discussion of the strange practice of what has been called 'theoretical halaka' in distinction from 'practical' jurisprudence. There has been little investigation of the various views of authority which diverse interpretive methods imply for a text. There has been very little sensitivity to the problem of whether the cultic ethos or the written scripture is actually providing the 'text' or tradition being interpreted.[46] And, with the exception of M. STEIN, few have addressed the question of how traditions developed as a clue to tracing historical trajectories of hermeneutical activity.[47] Only by means of careful attention to matters such as these can advancement in the area of comparative midrash be made.

D. The Alexandrian Traditions

1. Exegetical Schools

In distinction from the quests for the sources of Philo in the Greek philosophical traditions, the Hellenistic religions, and the Jewish midrashim, each quest of which can be characterized as a self-conscious tradition of scholarly endeavor, the discoveries of pre-Philonic Alexandrian exegetical traditions must be characterized as a series of isolated findings. No one has noticed these findings as a class, collected the pertinent material about them, or investigated what the contours of the historical community must have been to which they all belonged. Here a first attempt is made to note what the scholarship has held, theorized, or discovered, often inadvertently, about the phenomenon of Philo's relationship to intellectual and exegetical activity in the Alexandrian Jewish community both prior to and during his own time.

Characteristic of the scholarship of the last century was the frequent mention of the 'school of Alexandria' by which generally the similarity of exegetical method (allegory) and theological system (the Logos as continuum for creation and redemption) of Philo, Clement of Alexandria and Origen was acknowledged. In 1915 W. BOUSSET[48] sought to clarify the Alexandrian institution which could account for such interdependence by arguing for the existence of Jewish and Christian schools which produced written exegetical and theological works and so

---

for the separate developments of exegetical tradition. This is extremely helpful as a corrective to mechanistic views of transmission; but it does not provide a basis for further definition of the several exegetical methods which may be at work. These must be understood before either similarities or differences between comparable material can be evaluated.

[46] A significant example of this problem is the question of the role of the second temple institutions in the development of the symbolism which was used to interpret the Pentateuchal descriptions allegorically.

[47] But cf. above, note 33.

[48] BOUSSET, Schulbetrieb. Note that BOUSSET did not include Origen; but that he included Justin Martyr and Irenaeus in his study of Philo and Clement of Alexandria.

made possible the conservation and transmission of the compendium-like works which these authors produced. He did this by identifying a major source for Philo's series of allegorical commentaries and arguing that such a source and its use by Philo could only be understood as activities within a school organized for that kind of education, exploration and production.

Bousset's thesis has not found wide acceptance among Philonists, mainly due to the lack of reference to, or other evidence for, such an institution.[49] It has not been denied that Philo stood within some tradition of exegetical endeavor and worked with ideas which came to him from that tradition. But the emphasis has been upon the oral character of the tradition, its homiletical form, and its probable setting within the synagogue as primarily a religious instead of a scholastic institution.[50] Thus the debate has clarified the difficulty of accepting Bousset's conclusion with regard to the existence of a social institution of a certain kind, and it has revealed in that clarification the embarrassment of Philonic scholarship with regard to the question of the social setting in general for the literature it has studied. But while finding reasons not to accept Bousset's thesis with regard to the school the scholarship all but forgot the major contribution which he made, a contribution which still needs to be acknowledged, accounted for, analyzed, and related to other similar discoveries in Philo's works, that, namely, an exegetical source could be identified at all.

The peculiar nature of that source will be indicated below along with mention of other pre-Philonic 'exegetical traditions' which have been discovered. First, however, it will be helpful to indicate what it is the scholarship as a whole has said about pre-Philonic exegetical activity in Alexandria in general.

From an early time it has been customary to acknowledge that Philo did, after all, make mention of others who were engaged in the interpretation of the scriptures. With the exception of his description of the Therapeutae as exegetes, which is descriptive of their method,[51] however, the references are all made in passing in the context of introducing the interpretation to be discussed. Among others Philo mentions predecessors,[52] contemporary persons (groups?) with interpretations he might consider helpful;[53] contemporary persons (groups?) with divergent methods of interpretation,[54] persons (groups?) with whose interpretations as a system he was in strong disagreement,[55] and persons who had come to

---

[49] Cf. H. Thyen, Philoforschung, 234—235; Stil, 79; A. Culpepper, The Johannine School. SBL Dissertation 26. Missoula, Montana: Scholars, 1975. 205. The issue has to do with Bousset's understanding of 'school' in an institutional sense. Cf. Sandmel, Philo's Place, 17.

[50] An excellent summary of this debate is given by Culpepper, Johannine School, 197—214, and expecially 204—206.

[51] Vita Cont 28—29.

[52] Vita Mos I 4; Spec Leg I 8. Cf. Siegfried, Philo als Ausleger, 26—27.

[53] Cher 21—28; Heres 280—281; Mut 141—143; Somn I 188; Abr 99; Jos 151.

[54] Literalists (?): conf 14; Somn I 102; II 301; Quod Deus 21; 133; Quaes Gen I 8; 10; II 28; 58. Extreme allegorists (?): Migr 89—90.

[55] Cf. the Chaldaean polemic in B. L. Mack, Logos und Sophia. Untersuchungen zur Weisheitstheologie im hellenistischen Judentum, 124—130. SUNT 10. Göttingen: Vandenhoeck und Ruprecht, 1973.

ridicule the scripture as the basis for any significant interpretation at all.[56] Taken together the evidence is overwhelming that Philo was consciously in an interpretative enterprise in which large numbers of Jewish exegetes were, and had been at work, and which appears to have been the occasion for lively debate and serious position-taking.[57]

Only small beginnings have been made to reconstruct the views and methods of other persons mentioned by Philo. It has been customary to associate those whom Philo called 'physicians' with BOUSSET's source, for instance, but without a thorough investigation of the probabilities. There has been a brief indication of the possible system of those whom Philo called the 'Chaldaeans,' but without an investigation of their exegetical method.[58] There have been suggestions that the descriptions of the interpretive methods of the Therapeutae give us a picture of the origins and practice of Jewish allegory as a whole.[59] And, especially in the context of the research on Philo and the halaka, it has been customary to relate his statements about 'literalists' and 'extreme allegories' to a supposed spectrum of Jewish attitudes toward the Law.[60] But major studies investigating the material which expressly mentions others engaged in the interpretive enterprise in Alexandria have not yet been forthcoming.

The only other not-so-commonplace acknowledgment of Alexandrian predecessors for Philo to be found in the scholarship, with the exception of the implicit assumption of pre-Philonic traditions involved in the various quests to determine the influence of this or that tradition, and especially of the Palestinian midrash, upon him, would be the occasional reference to Aristobulos as predecessor, or to evidences here and there in the Hellenistic-Jewish literature, especially Ps Arist and Wisd, of pre-Philonic interpretive activity of an allegorical type.[61] Thus it must be concluded that the question of pre-Philonic exegetical traditions in Alexandria has not succeeded in becoming a focus for any stream of Philonic scholarship.

But to this kind of judgment should be added now a number of significant reconstructions of pre-Philonic sources which, while not intended by the scholars as a contribution to this question at all, do, when taken together, present a body of knowledge about the complexion of Philo's Jewish milieu which appears to be very instructive indeed.

---

[56] Conf 2; Migr 45; Agr 157; Quaes Gen I 53; III 43; IV 168.

[57] It should be noted also that Philo could give more than one interpretation of a given text without apparent need to decide in favor of one above the other(s). This phenomenon of multiple interpretation reminds one of a similar capacity in Rabbinic literature; but it also occurs in Hellenistic collections as, for instance, in the multiple etymologies in Cornutus. The logic at work here needs to be understood.

[58] MACK, Logos und Sophia, 124–130.

[59] R. P. C. HANSON, Allegory and Event. A Study of the Sources and Significance of Origen's Interpretation of Scripture, 46. Richmond: Knox, 1959.

[60] See above note 43. Cf. SHROYER, Literalists.

[61] See below Section II, A, 1, pp. 250ff. The best study of this Jewish development from Aristobulos to Philo will be found in WALTER, Thoraausleger, 124–149.

2. Exegetical Traditions

a) Bousset's Q[62]

The importance of Bousset's work for the question of the existence of Jewish schools in Alexandria has been mentioned above. Now the significance of his thesis concerning the use of an exegetical source by Philo deserves some explication. The arguments for the existence of school activity were based upon a series of investigations which focused upon disparate cosmological ideas in Philo which Bousset arranged by theme and studied in relation to the question of pre- and/or extra-Philonic provenance.[63] Once the probability of Philonic dependence on 'school traditions' in general had been established, however, Bousset turned to an analysis of the allegorical commentary as a unit in order to show that much of the material occurring there bore the marks of tradition which Philo must have taken over and reworked in various ways. In the course of this analysis it happened that the contours of a rather coherent allegory of the anthropological figures of the Pentateuch came into view with which Philo appeared to be in some disagreement. The source (Q) began with an allegory of Adam and Eve as symbols for *nous* and *aisthesis*, described in terms of Stoic psychology but understood in a soteriological way, and continued, apparently, through the patriarchal narratives. Philo used the source for some reason, probably because he was interested in the epistemological dimensions of the allegory, but disagreed with what he understood to be a glorification of both *nous* and *aisthesis*. His own preference, Bousset found, was an emphasis upon the need for revelation of which the *nous* was not capable, and for which Platonic rather than Stoic categories seemed to be more appropriate.

It may be admitted that Bousset did not succeed either in a precise delineation of the source as a whole, or in a convincing separation of it from its reinterpretation by Philo in every instance. But scholars have generally not rejected Bousset's conclusion that a pre-Philonic exegetical tradition was at work there. Stein,[64] in fact, accepted Bousset's thesis and devoted a special study to it with the purpose of finding additional support for it. The brief discussion about it by

---

[62] Bousset, Schulbetrieb.

[63] Bousset, Schulbetrieb, 14—43. Bousset found conflicting philosophical and theological views in the corpus and was able to make judgments about points at which Philo's own position could be ascertained in contrast to those of his source. He could detect Philo's hand where Platonic categories were introduced to qualify an essentially Stoic discussion, for instance, and where ethical-religious concerns were introduced to qualify an otherwise apparently secular discussion of Stoic epistemology. Most scholars would tend to agree with Bousset's judgments to be sure, but they are based on impressions of Philo's concerns as a whole and have not yet been tested in terms of controlled literary-critical argumentation. Bousset's achievement was to use these insights in an analysis of the entire allegorical commentary and succeeded in the delineation of a rather coherent pre-Philonic 'source.' It is this extent to which Bousset tested his impression which gives his thesis such weight.

[64] Stein, Allegorische Exegese.

HEINEMANN[65] was concerned mainly with the problem of understanding its pre-occupation with Stoic-epistemological categories which BOUSSET and STEIN had characterized as 'theoretical' and 'profane.'[66] HEINEMANN's critique is probably to be sustained, that, namely, the interest in epistemology in the source was not 'profane' at all. But it does remain one of the most curious and curiously most neglected hypotheses of Philonic research either way. That there is some evidence for a sustained allegorization of the Pentateuch in the interest of a Stoic view of the psychology of perception by Alexandrian Jews is a remarkable phenomenon indeed. Sustained, the thesis could point to extremely diverse theological positions implicit in a complex spectrum of exegetical endeavors not yet disclosed much less understood.[67]

b) STEIN's Etymological Source[68]

It was mentioned above that M. STEIN accepted BOUSSET's thesis in regard to an exegetical source for Philo's allegorical commentary. His critique had to do only with BOUSSET's methods which, he thought, were 'subjective' — based mainly on BOUSSET's own views of Philo's own position against which the Stoic source appeared in contrast. STEIN intended to contribute some 'objective' evidence by a close and thorough analysis of one means by which the allegory appeared to be derived from the Pentateuch, namely, the etymology.

STEIN was impressed with the fact that BOUSSET's source did not use the etymologies for its allegorization and sought to prove that it did not do so because the etymologies reflected theological concerns which it did not share. In order to develop this thesis, it was necessary for STEIN to do a major investigation of the etymologies themselves, and it is here that his real contribution was made. He distinguished between etymologies proper which presupposed knowledge of the Hebrew, and symbolic interpretations which presupposed a Greek form. He theorized that the etymologies of the Hebrew names were earlier than interpretations based on the Greek, studied them as a class, and discovered in them the reflection of an ethical-soteriological system which distinguished the virtues from

---

[65] HEINEMANN, Bildung, 139—140.

[66] BOUSSET, Schulbetrieb, 74ff.; STEIN, Allegorische Exegese, 49.

[67] The possibility that a Stoic conceptuality was determinative for a Jewish philosophical theology is in itself worthy of thorough investigation. When one considers that such a position may have arisen by means of an identification of wisdom and *physis* the cultural dynamics of the phenomenon become even more interesting. This is especially so in light of the fact that the other clearly pre-Philonic philosophical Hellenization of wisdom categories in the Wisdom of Solomon does not make use of the *physis* concept, even though the presence of wisdom as structuring element in the world is being understood in Hellenistic terms. This means that the evidence in Philo for a Jewish tradition of Wisdom-*physis* theology must be regarded as a surprising development in need of clarification. This is also the place to mention the strong probability that the figure of Adam, which appears to have been the point of departure for BOUSSET's source, itself may have given rise to a history of interpretation partially recoverable by analysis from the Philonic corpus.

[68] STEIN, Allegorische Exegese.

the vices and exemplified the process by which the virtues could be achieved. Because Philo himself knew no Hebrew STEIN theorized that both the etymologies as a class and the allegory of the virtues and vices as a system were pre-Philonic exegetical traditions. Thus both the profane Q and the ethical allegory were found to be pre-Philonic traditions.

STEIN's thesis is yet to be reviewed and substantiated. But the convergence of exegetical method, theological system, and pre-Philonic tradition in an identifiable set of textual materials strongly points to the probability of vigorous and self-conscious exegetical enterprise of a very specific kind. When one considers the possible theological contrast between the etymological source and BOUSSET's source, which STEIN discovered, the complexity and seriousness of the pre-Philonic exegetical endeavor in Alexandria begins to come into view. In any reconstruction of the Jewish exegetical history in Alexandria a place will have to be found for the etymologies, and STEIN's thesis about an etymological source and its development as a basis for one type of allegorical system will certainly have to be taken into consideration.

c) HEINEMANN's Cynic Source[69]

HEINEMANN's work has already been mentioned in regard to the question of Philo's relation to Palestinian Jewish halaka. In order to control that investigation HEINEMANN focused upon the interpretation of the Jewish festivals in the treatises on the special laws, and distinguished three general views about them.[70] There was an allegorical interpretation which intended to supercede the practice of the cult entirely. There was a literal interpretation which proposed that only the fulfillment of the rites as prescribed mattered. And there was a mediating view which advocated both a participation in the actual cult and an understanding of its significance in symbolic terms. It was in support of this third view that HEINEMANN argued for a pre-Philonic source in Spec Leg II 41–207.

HEINEMANN called this source 'Cynic' because it interpreted the festivals and the Jewish religious ethos in general in terms of Cynic-Stoic views and values. This ability to see facets of cosmic order reflected in the rites appeared to HEINEMANN to be a phenomenon quite different from the Platonizing allegorization found in the allegorical commentaries and warranted the hypothesis of an entirely distinct tradition of interpretation available to Philo as a written source.

HEINEMANN's thesis has yet to be tested in scholarly debate. But its occurrence as another instance of hypothesization on the part of a major Philonist with regard to pre-Philonic Jewish sources is important in its own right and adds to the picture of vigorous and diverse intellectual enterprise in Alexandrian Judaism. An important issue in the case of HEINEMANN's source has to do with the form of the authority being interpreted. Here one must question whether the symbolism might not be rooted in the actual cult itself, and investigate the extent to which the system of symbolic interpretation was intended primarily as an interpretation of

---

[69] HEINEMANN, Bildung, 142–146.
[70] HEINEMANN, Bildung, 137ff.

the Pentateuch or of the empirical cult. But, either way, HEINEMANN's thesis of a pre-Philonic interpretive tradition won from the Philonic corpus by means of literary-critical analysis needs to be taken seriously and accounted for in any holistic reconstruction of the Alexandrian situation.

d) The Chaldaeans

In 1960 A. WLOSOK[71] published an important study tracing the development of the ascent-vision conceptuality from Plato through Philo, the Hermetica and Clement of Alexandria to Lactantius. In her investigation of Philo she worked out the precise point at which the Platonic intellectual ascent had been reinterpreted by what she called a mystic understanding of the ultimate vision − not now merely of the noetic ideas, but of the transcendent God. In the course of her work she set this development in the context of what she perceived to be a very complex intellectual quest among the Jews of Alexandria, the evidence for which frequently pointed to the existence of diverse allegorical traditions.[72] In 1973 it was possible for the present author[73] to point to one of these traditions more specifically − the interpretation of Abraham's migration which those whom Philo called Chaldaeans understood as an allegory of the ascent of the *nous*. It could be shown, moreover, that Philo was in strong disagreement with the Chaldaean view of the ascent vision, and that he may have stood in a polemical relationship to them on the issue of the correct understanding of the Abraham allegory as well. This possibility was not thoroughly investigated, however, so that the position of the Chaldaeans as exegetes remains to be investigated. But as another indication of the possibility of a pre-Philonic exegetical tradition Philo's debate with the Chaldaeans certainly deserves to be mentioned.

e) The Symbolism of the Temple and the High Priest

In 1961 H. HEGERMANN[74] was able to show that a great deal of the material in Philo which deals with the High Priest's robes, the temple, and the Sinai story reflects a coherent symbolical interpretation of Jewish cult as cosmic mystery. His thesis was that these interpretations belonged to a pre-Philonic Jewish tradition of exegesis and Hellenistic mission which Philo used metaphorically in the interest of yet another conception of Jewish piety. If HEGERMANN was right another instance of pre-Philonic exegetical tradition can be observed here.

HEGERMANN's work may be important for other reasons too. The obvious interest in cultic symbolism vies with exegetical activity in the source, and thus points to the possibility of provenance in circles directly related to the institution of the temple in Jerusalem. HEGERMANN was also able to show that the Logos

---

[71] WLOSOK, Laktanz.

[72] WLOSOK, Laktanz, 43, note 24.

[73] See above note 55.

[74] H. HEGERMANN, Die Vorstellung vom Schöpfungsmittler im hellenistischen Judentum und Urchristentum. TU 82. Berlin: Akademie, 1961.

figure, though certainly firmly rooted in the tradition before Philo took it up, did
not belong to its earliest formulations. HEGERMANN reconstructed a development
or trajectory of the interpretations from an original cosmic symbolism, through a
Logos allegorization, to use as a metaphor by Philo in the interest of ethical instruction. It is clear that the possibility of the existence of such a trajectory needs
to be investigated in relationship to other evidence for pre-Philonic exegetical
activity and integrated in some picture of the origin and development of Alexandrian exegesis as a whole. HEGERMANN's thesis indicates that the origins of
allegorization may have to be sought in several disparate settings, one of which
may have very close relations with the temple institutions in Jerusalem.

f) The Wisdom Tradition

It is something of a surprise to discover that so little has been done in the
history of Philonic scholarship on the possibility of the Wisdom tradition as a
source for Philo's theology. Even those who have emphasized the language of
mystery in Philo and have noted the possibilities of relationships on the one hand
between Philonic mystery and Isis mystery, and on the other between Isis mythology and Wisdom mythology, have not pursued the clue.[75] The Wisdom discussions has been limited pretty much first to the debate about the relationship of
Wisdom to Logos in the works of Philo, and then to the question of the relationship of the figure of Wisdom in Philo to the figure of Wisdom in Jewish Wisdom
literature. The usual statement is that Wisdom and Logos are functionally identical in Philo, even though the Wisdom language may have developed earlier.[76]
GOODENOUGH[77] spoke vaguely about both a Logos tradition and a Wisdom
tradition which came together in Philo.

Nevertheless, three recent works have established the thesis that Philo was
strongly influenced by Jewish Wisdom traditions.[78] In 1966 H. F. WEISS[79]
showed that Philo's conception of the Logos as a mediator of creation was a
development of earlier Jewish views of Wisdom. In 1968 EGON BRANDENBUR-
GER[80] argued for a Hellenistic Jewish background for Paul's conception of 'flesh'
and 'spirit' in antithesis by reconstructing what he called a tradition of dualistic
wisdom. He traced its roots to the Jewish Wisdom tradition and found Philo as its
major extant Hellenistic representative. In 1973 the present author[81] published a
1967 Göttingen dissertation which worked out a typology of Wisdom mythology,

---

[75] See a brief discussion and review in MACK, Logos und Sophia, 108—110.

[76] MACK, Logos und Sophia, 110, note 10.

[77] GOODENOUGH, Light, 165.

[78] Cf. also J. LAPORTE, Philo in the Tradition of Biblical Wisdom Literature. In: Aspects of
Wisdom in Judaism and Early Christianity, 103—141. Ed. R. L. WILKEN. Notre Dame:
University Press, 1975.

[79] H.-F. WEISS, Untersuchungen zur Kosmologie des hellenistischen und palästinischen
Judentums. TU 97. Berlin: Akademie, 1966.

[80] E. BRANDENBURGER, Fleisch und Geist. Paulus und die dualistische Weisheit. WMANT
29. Neukirchen, 1968.

[81] MACK, Logos und Sophia.

argued for its theological intention, and traced its influence into the works of Philo.

None of these studies has explored the possibility that Wisdom theology might be involved in the development of allegorical or other exegetical endeavors. But they have established the probability that certain aspects of Philo's thought, including the importance of mythological patterns for his systems of correlation between Pentateuchal narrative and the structure of the pattern of soteriological transformation, have their origin here. This means that the 'sources' of Philo's religious thought should be sought in a form of Jewish Wisdom tradition which made possible the assimilation of Hellenistic philosophical and religious thought by organizing it to serve Jewish theological concerns. The Wisdom tradition could do this by taking such language metaphorically – i.e. as conceptual image for explication of the structures of Jewish Wisdom mythology itself.[82] If it could be shown that such a mode of thinking had turned to the task of interpreting the ancient scriptural traditions – a not impossible thought – the question of the 'source' of Philonic thought and exegetical activity would be clarified and focused in a most helpful way.

3. The Enduring Problem

The cumulative force of the disparate observations on, and discoveries of, pre-Philonic Alexandrian traditions is quite impressive. The problem is that each has remained an isolated finding and that no one has made the attempt to integrate the evidence in any larger reconstruction of the Alexandrian Jewish community which could have produced such phenomena. One needs at least one or two clear trajectories of the development of relatively coherent systems of exegetical and theological activity in the pre-Philonic period in order to begin. To do this, however, requires knowledge about the compatability of various methods of interpretation within a single system, tradition, or circle of interpreters engaged in theological exegesis. This knowledge is not yet available.

II. Exegetical Methods in Philo's Commentaries

It has been indicated that the history of Philo studies has failed generally to take account of the exegetical form and intention of the major portion of the Philonic corpus as a factor which could contribute to the explication of Philo's system of thought. This does not mean that the exegetical function has been overlooked completely, however. Several very significant studies have been devoted to its investigation and they must be reported below. But even here it has been the

---

[82] On Wisdom mythology as theology see B. L. MACK, Wisdom Myth and Mythology. Interpretation 24 (1970) 46–60.

rule that a stereotype conception of the interpretive process has prevailed. The many exegetical procedures to be found in Philo have been reduced in this history of scholarship to 'allegory.' And allegory has been understood primarily in terms of its Greek development. Since it appears there as a method by which philosophical systems could be found reflected in the ancient poetry, its employment in Philo has been viewed as the super-imposition of a Greek method (allegory) and a Greek conceptuality (philosophy) upon a scripture completely foreign to it. This has been taken implicitly to mean that the scripture could not be the real source of Philo's system of thought and thus the quest for that system was allowed without consideration for its possible scriptural correlate.

It is true, of course, that the Philonic methods may be compared with those of the Greek allegorists, and the points of similarity have frequently been noted. Both intend an interpretation of a scripture in some sense archaic and sacred. Both acknowledge the offensiveness of 'mythological' and 'anthropomorphic' statements about (the) God(s). Philo used the technical terminology of the Greeks for allegorical interpretation, and distinguished as they did between a 'physical' and an 'ethical' interpretation. And the categories of abstraction into which the texts were transformed were expressed in terms of the Greek systems of cosmology and anthropology. While a thorough comparison of the form of the commentaries on the Pentateuch and on Homer has not yet appeared, it is to be expected that here, too, comparables will be observed.

But in spite of the numerous evidences for Greek influence upon the allegorical enterprise in Alexandrian Judaism, the Greek analogue has not proven sufficient to clarify the Jewish intention. Not only has the scholarship in general not been able to determine the system of religious thought to be assumed for the enterprise; those who have studied the method itself have not been able to determine the principles of correlation which allowed the scripture to be interpreted just such a way and no other. H. THYEN was right when he said that the unsolved problem in Philo studies has to do with the relationship between the text and the system of thought which was intended as its interpretation.[83]

A. The Allegorical Method

1. The Limits of the Greek Analogue

The major milestones of the investigation of Philo as exegete are the works by S. SIEGFRIED (Philo als Ausleger, 1875), M. STEIN (Allegorische Exegese, 1929), I. CHRISTIANSEN (Technik, 1969), JACQUES CAZEAUX[84] and V. NIKIPRO-

---

[83] THYEN, Philoforschung, 237.

[84] J. CAZEAUX, Aspects; Interpréter; and: Philon d'Alexandrie, Exégète, ANRW II, 21,1 (1983) pp. 156—226 (below in this same volume). CAZEAUX has argued rather consistently for the priority of literary analysis before taking up either comparative or trajectory studies. He has insisted on beginning with the literary units as given, namely the treatises, in order to inquire about their structure. His exemplary analyses in this area

WETZKY (Le commentaire, 1974). SIEGFRIED's contribution, in addition to its achievement as the first great work which summarized the evidence for the origins and development of both Greek and Jewish allegorization, was the attempt to list the 'rules' which governed the use of allegory in the interpretation of the scriptures. He distinguished between scriptural statements which could not be accepted without allegorization (anthropomorphic statements about God; logical contradictions; statements already figuratively intended), and those for which allegorization could offer a supplemental significance. He then listed 24 'rules' or textual circumstances which invited allegorization, including such things as grammatical, syntactical, philological and stylistic peculiarities of the text, and noting that the occurrence of single words such as names and numbers could become the occasion for allegorization too. It is now obvious that SIEGFRIED's 'rules' were nothing more than a collection of observations about the range of triggering devices which occurred in the process of allegorization.[85] They did not address the question of why precisely a certain interpretation occurred and not some other. SIEGFRIED could not be aware of this problem, however, because for him the Alexandrian allegory was merely a superimposition of Greek philosophy upon the Pentateuch and could have had no deeper rationale in any case. Given this understanding the process of deriving another significance from the text was arbitrary in essence.

In 1929 M. STEIN devoted a study (Allegorische Exegese) to the origin and development of Jewish allegory. He wanted to support BOUSSET's thesis about a pre-Philonic tradition of allegorical exegesis and worked out a sequential development from early beginnings in haggadic symbolism, through Aristobulos and the Hellenistic Wisdom literature, into a spectrum of pre-Philonic allegorical endeavors in Alexandria which were reflected in the Philonic corpus. STEIN's study is full of valuable observations and reflections, not the least important of which is his attempt to determine the precise point at which one can speak technically about an haggadic interpretation as allegorical. Allegory was defined for him, of course, in terms of its Greek manifestation, and thus his understanding of the phenomenon in Judaism agreed with the traditional view. But to his credit are

---

have produced remarkable insights into what he has begun calling an 'implicit system' which controls both Philo's theology and his exegetical mode. His work is extremely valuable and his discoveries may indeed provide a way to begin to visualize the subtle relationship between systematic thought and exegetical method in Philo's works themselves. The question we are raising with regard to Philo's predecessors and his indebtedness to allegories already won, as well as to his polemics, and to the question of the origins and development of conceptualities which could eventuate in such a profound endeavor — all are understood as quests which can be related to CAZEAUX's concerns in much the same manner as form-critical and trajectory investigations in New Testament studies relate to and enhance redaction-critical and compositional investigations.

[85] It should be noted, however, that SIEGFRIED's 'rules' were accepted as sufficient clarification of the phenomenon until quite recently. In 1955 THYEN, Stil, 81, could still refer to them as an adequate way in which to understand both the reasons for and the methods of the allegorical mode of exegesis. For a recent discussion of this problem in the history of scholarship on allegory in general see I. CHRISTIANSEN, Technik, 1–29.

some observations about some distinctions between Jewish allegory and the Greek.[86] In the first place, he found, the 'ethical' interpretation was emphasized above the 'physical' in the Jewish allegory. Secondly, a theological principle seemed to govern the ethical interpretation. Thirdly, the object or person to be interpreted first had to be turned into a symbol before it could be related to the 'physical' or 'ethical' orders. And fourthly, the accumulative effect of the allegory was that the biblical history was turned thereby into a story of the soul. STEIN could not know that these sensitive perceptions amounted to a description of a phenomenon which could not be clarified adequately in terms of Greek practices, and so the remainder of his study was organized with the Greek analogue in mind. But his discovery of the possibly unique characteristics of Jewish allegory is nonetheless significant. We will return to it below.

The most recent critical study of Philonic allegory is that of I. CHRISTIANSEN (Technik). She addressed the question of the principles which governed the correlation of text and interpretation in Philo, and set forth a novel and striking thesis. According to CHRISTIANSEN Philo was a Platonist whose mind had been trained in the dieretic technique by which all of reality could be ordered in pyramid-like structures from the most universal categories on down to the most specific and disparate phenomena. But whereas Plato began his dialectic with the world of the ideas, Philo began with the sacred scriptures. The first step was to win from the scriptures a symbol, which meant that a scriptural term would be found to stand in a dieretic relationship to another extra-biblical term. The dieretic relationship meant that each term, the biblical and the extra-biblical, could be placed in a dieretic scheme, usually as subdivisions of a more general category which assumed and expressed some aspect of similarity between them. An inquiry into the possibility of classifying the categories of similarity led CHRISTIANSEN to the conclusion that Philo was working primarily with the ten Aristotelian categories for the attributes of existing things. Thus the allegorical technique may be described as the scholastic means by which the words of the Pentateuch could be taken as symbols for a world of existent phenomena ordered dieretically.

CHRISTIANSEN has engaged an essential problem in the quest for an understanding of Philonic allegory, and she has shown that dieretic structuring is indeed in evidence in many of the Philonic pericopes. But she is less convincing in her claim that dieretic logic is the essential technique by which symbolical equivalence was derived, and her argument as to the significance of the Aristotelian categories is really very weak. Her contribution is that she has raised finally the question as to the logic of the Philonic allegory and suggested an intriguing solution. The solution itself, however, still stands in the tradition of those who have seen Philo primarily in terms of philosophical enterprise, and it will fail to satisfy those who want to understand his religious concerns as well.

In 1974 V. NIKIPROWETZKY published a study (Le commentaire) in which he reviewed the history of the scholarship on Philo precisely from this point of view. He could show that many of the enduring problems in Philonic research could be resolved in principle if it were acknowledged that Philo's essential concern was

---

[86] STEIN, Allegorische Exegese, 3—6.

with a religious interpretation of the Pentateuch, and that his employment of conceptual systems was determined by that concern. He did not engage the question of the logic or method of allegorization directly, but he did lay the foundation for such an investigation by showing clearly the presuppositions for the allegorical enterprise. These are found to be the series of identifications of Wisdom, the Law of Moses, and the Law of nature, as well as the series of distinctions between Greek philosophy, Wisdom, and the practical wisdom of life according to the Law of Moses. NIKIPROWETZKY called for a study of Philo which takes seriously the form of the writings as commentary and their intention as a guide for the life lived according to wisdom. He has seen clearly the limits of the Greek analogue.

2. The Contrast of the Jewish Method

Returning now to STEIN's observations on points at which Jewish allegory must be distinguished from the Greek, it will be helpful to relate them to certain findings of the scholarship on Philo as a whole, and use them as a point of departure for some considerations of the directions in which subsequent studies may be well advised to move.

STEIN's first point had to do with the predominance of the 'ethical' allegory over the 'physical.' STEIN himself thought that the essential religious concern of the commentaries resided precisely in the 'ethical' allegory, which was in turn based upon the etymological source, in distinction from the 'physical' or cosmological allegory. Since he did not investigate the theological function of the cosmological mythology in Philo, one may beg to differ with him about its lack of religious concern. But he was probably right about the extent to which Jewish allegory was carried out primarily in the interest of a religious concern and that that concern gave the Jewish enterprise a different character from that of the Greek parctice with its orientation to philosophical equivalences. This agrees with the judgment of many Philonists that a religious concern can be perceived as the basis for Philo's work including his usage of philosophical conceptuality.

STEIN's second point was that it was a theological principle which governed the ethical allegory. By this he was referring to such things as the schematization between the ethically good and bad, the 'stages' into which the types of virtue were arranged, the casting up of paradigms or examples for moments of transition from stage to stage, and the exhortations to imitate the examples. This 'theological principle' according to which STEIN saw the ethical allegory organized is none other than the structure of Philo's religious system as reconstructed by a number of scholars and discussed above. Here then the possibility of a pattern of thought at work in the allegory as a whole has been seen — a pattern which may not correspond to a system of Greek philosophy at all.

STEIN's third point had to do with the transformation of the biblical terms into what he called symbols by means of an interpretive process not characteristic of the Greek allegoristic. His attempt to clarify the distinction as that between seeing the Greek heroes as 'patterns' (*Muster*) for virtue, and taking the Jewish patriarchs as 'symbols' of virtue, may not have proven too helpful. But his insight into a distinction between the Greek and Jewish allegories at the point of characterization is very perceptive indeed. We shall return to this consideration below.

STEIN's fourth point was that the Jewish allegory functioned to transform the biblical story into a story of the soul. Since he could find no Greek analogue for the idea of a progressive formation of the soul he concluded that the conception must have been a Jewish development. STEIN's perception here is extremely important, for it suggests the integral relationship which may exist between the structure of the Pentateuchal narrative and the allegory of the soul. If such a relationship can be imagined — and it reminds one of the correlation which PASCHER discovered between the 'mystery' (Philo's system of religious thought) and the King's Highway (the scriptural pattern of the path) — one might want to ask how the allegory worked to make it happen.

Taken together the uniquely Jewish characteristics of the Hellenistic Jewish allegory which STEIN noticed suggest a phenomenon of integrity controlled by its own logic and determined by serious theological and religious concerns. If he was right about the overall intention and effect — the transformation of biblical history into a model for personal salvation — the hermeneutical aspects of the process may actually be quite profound.

STEIN's third point, mentioned above, may provide a way to begin reflection upon the peculiar nature of Jewish allegory by contrasting it with its Greek and Egyptian analogues. The contrast is to be seen in that the Jewish allegory performed not one but two interpretive intentions in order to arrive at the allegorical equivalent of an agent. This double interpretation mechanism marks the procedure as complex in contrast to that which appears to have happened in Greek and Egyptian allegoristic.[87] In the case of Stoic allegorization of Homer, for instance, the given text which contained the stories of the gods and heroes was interpreted so as to reflect the system of philosophy and ethics which was given in the school. Since the Stoic system of thought was given prior to and independently of the process of allegorization, the process itself may be called 'simple.' This does not mean that the various *tertia comparationis* (principles of analogy) were simply obvious, nor that the stories themselves may not have contributed in a variety of complex ways to the process of their interpretation. It means that the correlation took place between two expressions of truth equally at home in a common cultural tradition. In the case of Egyptian allegoristic this feature of common cultural tradition for both the text and the interpretive system is even more obvious. But in the Jewish Alexandrian process the systems of thought do not appear to have been so clearly defined nor so obviously 'given' prior to the interpretive enterprise. Not only are several (!) 'philosophic' systems of thought reflected in the Philonic corpus; the 'systems' themselves are, by and large, not taken from the cultural

---

[87] Much of what follows in the remainder of this paragraph and in the next four paragraphs has been argued by the author in a written response to a paper by B. PEARSON for a colloquy at the Center for Hermeneutical Studies, Berkeley. It is published by the Center as Colloquy 29, 1977. The title of PEARSON's paper is: Philo and the Gnostics on Man and Salvation.

tradition to which the text belonged, but from the new cultural situation in which the exegetes found themselves. This fact distinguishes the Alexandrian allegoristic from the classical forms and leads to the designation 'complex.' A closer analogy might be found in the Hellenistic allegorization of Egyptian myths, for here too syncretistic concerns are determinant.[88]

In relation to the text this complexity of Alexandrian Jewish allegoristic frequently demanded not one but two moments of interpretation. It is the second moment with which we are the more familiar — the translation of the text into 'physical' and 'ethical' categories. This is the easier to perceive because it is articulated as the express intention of the interpretations in the commentaries themselves, and because it corresponds to the form and intention of Stoic allegoristic. But in order to achieve this second and intended interpretation a prior interpretive moment must be assumed. That moment is the recognition of the text (the Five Books of Moses) as containing the stories of the god(s) and heroes! It is this moment which STEIN recognized as unique and which may account for the phenomenon often noted by scholars of Hellenistic Judaism and sometimes called 'remythologization' of the scriptural traditions. It is not easy to detect in the Philonic commentaries because the form of the mythology which is used in the process of recognition is already abstract and related as an abstraction to both the physical (cosmological) and ethical (anthropological) orders which the eventual interpretation intends. But it is certainly there in the figures of Sophia and Logos, as well as in the preponderance of mythological metaphor. Thus, for example, Sarah is identified with mythological Wisdom 'before' being interpreted as virtue. The High Priest is identified with the mythological Logos 'before' being interpreted as the conscience within. God is identified with the Demiourg 'before' being interpreted as the cosmic principle of rationality. And in the case of Adam and the patriarchs there is the prior identification with certain high mimetic anthropological types (King, Sophos, First Man) before being interpreted in terms of Hellenistic psychologies and ethics. This complicating factor would not be a serious hinderance to our explorations, however, if the mythologies thus employed were found to be coming from a single cultural tradition in which a prior allegoristic had worked out a correlation compatible with a single system of thought (for example, the Stoic). Unfortunately, not only are all of the disparate and competing Hellenistic systems of thought reflected in the Philonic commentaries; there is evidence of the use of oriental mythologies from diverse backgrounds and of deep dependence upon the Jewish wisdom mythology as well to do the work of allegorization.

This means that the 'system' or 'structure' or 'pattern' of what really should be called a mythology is not to be found simply derivable from any of the contemporary extra-Jewish philosophical or religious systems. This is true even though it is clear that aspects of the syntax and conceptuality of certain Hellenistic systems of thought are certainly reflected in the Jewish ordering of things. But the ordering itself may actually have been governed by some pattern of perception

---

[88] See J. G. GRIFFITHS, Allegory in Greece and Egypt. Journal of Egyptian Archaeology 53 (1967) 79–102.

peculiar to the Jewish vision. Whence then the 'pattern' which appears to be in control?

One hypothesis with which the present author has been intrigued is that a very early allegoristic occurred when Wisdom mythology was used to re-read first the stories of the creation and the giving of the Torah,[89] then the exodus story,[90] and finally the stories of the patriarchs as the story of Wisdom herself — her part in the ordering of creation, her quest for a people, her call to and deliverance of her sons in trouble, and her exaltation of them to positions of vindication and authority.[91] This hypothesis has the advantage of visualizing an early stage of Jewish allegoristic in which both the text and the system of conceptuality were indigenous to the religious-cultural tradition. It could also account for many of the later Hellenistic systems of conceptuality being taken up to do the work of allegorization. Both the Stoic and the Platonic systems, as well as neo-Pythagorean and certain esoteric and occultic traditions could well have found entrance into the allegorical enterprise by means of the recognition of their implicit correlation with Wisdom mythologumena and conceptuality. The question is whether systematic conceptuality continued to be a concern for the resulting allegories and, if so, what one is to make of Philo's curious employment of traditions of diverse and possibly competing conceptions.

The possibility that Jewish allegorization was a product of Jewish Wisdom theologians would mean that Jewish allegory, in spite of its eventual complexity as a Hellenistic phenomenon, was originally and essentially as 'simple' as either the indigenous Greek or Egyptian allegoristics were. This in turn would mean that it could be understood as legitimate interpretation of authentic cultural traditions instead of as a superficial superimposition of extraneous ideas from a strange cultural syncretism. Recent studies in the allegorical mode as such could then be used to understand its potentially profound social function for Jews during this time.[92] These studies have pointed to the serious function of allegory as

---

[89] Cf. Prov 1—9; Job 28; Sirach.

[90] Cf. Wisdom of Solomon and the significance of the redaction which combines chapters 1—10 with the midrashic interpretation of the exodus in chapters 11—19.

[91] Cf. especially Wisd 10.

[92] Recent studies on allegory as a literary and interpretive mode include: E. HONIG, Dark Conceit. The Making of Allegory. Evanston: Northwestern, 1959 and A. J. S. FLETCHER, Allegory: The Theory of a Symbolic Mode. Ithaca, New York: Cornell, 1964; 1970. Historical-literary studies in the origin and development of Greek allegory include: F. BUFFIÈRE, Les mythes d'Homère et la pensée grecque. Paris: Les belles lettres, 1956; F. BUFFIÈRE, Héraclite. Allégories d'Homère. Paris: Les belles lettres, 1962; PÉPIN, Mythe et allégorie; J. A. COULTER, The Literary Microcosm: Theories of Interpretation of the Later Neoplatonists. Leiden: Brill, 1977. Discussions of Jewish allegory include: PLANCK, Commentatio de principiis, 1806; FRANKEL, Schriftforschung, 1854; LAUTERBACH, Ancient Jewish Allegorists, 1910/11; TREITEL, Ursprung, Begriff und Umfang der allegorischen Schrifterklärung, 1911; STEIN, Allegorische Exegese, 1929; STEIN, Alttestamentliche Bibelkritik, 1935; HEINEMANN, Altjüdische Allegoristik, 1936; HEINEMANN, Die Allegoristik der hellenistischen Juden, 1952. Discussions of Philonic allegory (other than those already mentioned above and in the article) include: BRÉHIER, La méthode allégorique, 1907; DELLING, Wunder — Allegorie — Mythus, 1957; DANIÉLOU, L'Exégèse de Philon,

legitimate and powerful re-visualization of older cultural tradition and value in a time of cultural transition. But first there needs to be careful analysis of the range of methods and modes of exegesis employed in the Philonic corpus in the interest of a quest for the earliest pre-Philonic interpretive systems. Without clear evidence it will be difficult to sustain the thesis that any interpretive system was at work, much less one as profound as the Wisdom allegoristic suggested above.

B. A Typology of Exegetical Methods

It is the allegorical method which has been associated with the Alexandrian interpretation of the scriptures and upon which the major focus of scholarly investigation has fallen. But if the point about the complexity of Jewish allegory be taken seriously it may well be that there are more than one type of allegory to be observed in the corpus, and that there may have been several allegories or allegorical systems interpreting various aspects of the biblical material which can be distinguished. Added to this is the consideration that allegory was not the only method of interpretation mentioned or used in the corpus. This means that precision in the search for any coherent interpretive system, whether Philonic or pre-Philonic, demands a typology of exegetical methods found to be employed. A beginning has been made in a paper which the author presented to the Philo Institute at its annual meeting in 1975.[93] The typology suggested there is reproduced here essentially as it appeared in its subsequent published form.

1. The Anti-anthropomorphic Apology

This kind of interpretation does not appear to have produced a systematic corpus of interpretation of the Pentateuch as a whole, but does occur regularly where anthropomorphic statements about God are encountered in the Pentateuch. It is characterized by some apologetic reference to the anthropomorphism and a suggestion as to how one might re-interpret the statement acceptably. Frequently the anthropomorphism is interpreted as a reference to the 'powers' of God which are active in the world, or to the order of the creation itself, a solution which is already in evidence in the work of Aristobulus. The intention is to overcome what is termed a 'mythic' reading of the Pentateuch and this determines the concern to develop a theology in keeping with acceptable Hellenistic views of the nature of God and the world. Philo often used these traditional *topoi* to argue for the necessity of allegorical interpretation of the Pentateuch, but this appears to be a later rationale. Whether the earlier apologetic was controlled by a single theology or conceptual system needs to be investigated. In its form the inter-

---

1958; FRÜCHTEL, Die kosmologischen Vorstellungen, 1968; BOYANCÉ, Echo des exégèses de la mythologie grecque, 1967; PÉPIN, Remarques sur la théorie de l'exégèse allégorique, 1967; AMIR, האליגוריה של פילון, 1970.

[93] MACK, Exegetical Traditions, 81—88.

pretation is quite simple: Pentateuch reference; apology; interpretation. The interpretation can be supported and explained by an analogy to show the correspondence of the interpretation to the biblical image, and may be a very early kind of allegorical interpretation. Later methods of allegorical procedure, to be discussed below, are not yet in evidence.[94]

2. The Encomium

Basic to the Exposition appears to be a kind of description of the patriarchs which retells the biblical story in such a way as to minimize or overlook offensive traits or deeds and idealize those which can illustrate certain virtues. Because the old stories are changed in this way one may certainly speak of a kind of interpretation which is achieved. But this interpretation is accomplished without setting up a contrast between the biblical text and the interpretation. The biblical text receives its 'interpretation' in the retelling itself, which is set forth as an independant and sufficient account. Judging from similar material to be found in other Jewish literature of the time (such that in the 'Book of Jubilees,' or Josephus' 'Antiquities') this kind of paraphrase and embellishment of the scriptures was also an early form of interpretation with its own intention as well as formal and material characteristics.[95]

---

[94] An example of the anti-anthropomorphic apology is found in Leg All I 43—44. The text Gen 2:8 has been cited in the normal course of the commentary: "And God planted a pleasaunce in Eden toward the sun-rising, and placed there the man whom He had formed." After indicating that the Garden of Eden is to be understood as a reference to Wisdom (following the form of the identification allegory to be discussed below) the apology is given as follows: "Far be it from man's reasoning to be the victim of so great impiety as to suppose that God tills the soil and plants pleasaunces. We should at once be at a loss to tell from what motive He could do so. Not to provide Himself with pleasant refreshment and comfort. Let not such fables even enter our mind. For not even the whole world would be a place fit for God to make His abode, since God is His own place, and He is filled by Himself, and sufficient for Himself, filling and containing all other things in their destitution and barrenness and emptiness, but Himself contained by nothing else, seeing that He is Himself One and the Whole." (PLCL I 175) Here one sees that the apology is occasioned by what is taken to be a mythic statement. This statement is found to be offensive if taken at face value and is re-interpreted by means of a conceptuality which safeguards both the text and a certain understanding of the transcendence of God. In this case the important term is τόπος; other terms which occur frequently in the anti-anthropomorphic apology are δύναμις and φύσις. As is usually the case, the apology appears here in the context of the commentary as an aside which has little or no relation to the other interpretations being given to the verse or pericope.

[95] An example of the encomium is found in De Abrahamo 91—98. Here the story of Abraham and Sarai in Egypt (Gen 12:10—20) is (re)told in such a way as to heighten the danger of Sarai's being violated by the Pharaoh in order to set the stage for the intervention of God, to keep that from happening, and the declamation of the virtues of Abraham and Sarai which are vindicated in this way. The encomium is introduced by appropriate remarks about the greatness of the deeds to be recounted.

That encomia are to be found in the Philonic corpus is highly significant, providing as they most probably do traditional material which has been taken up into more highly developed systems of Pentateuch interpretation. They are the basis, in fact, for the Exposition series itself which is governed by a very sophisticated schema of correspondences between *physis*, Torah (as *nomos*) and the lives of the patriarchs. Careful analysis will show that this schema presupposes a series of conceptual developments through which the history of the encomium form must have gone. To determine the stages of this development would require careful consideration of the relationship of this history to the developmental histories of the other forms of interpretation to be discussed. But its significance as a traditional form of interpretation may already be seen in the tenacity with which the characterization of the patriarchs, though becoming highly idealized as types of virtue and pictures of the life (*bios*) lived according to nature (*physis*), remains nevertheless on the level of historical personification. If Philo wanted to allegorize the patriarchal stories in the context of the Exposition, as he did, he expressly had to distinguish between the encomium which had been given and the allegorical interpretation to follow. To do this he used the technical terminology of τὸ ῥητόν – τὸ πρὸς διάνοιαν, and it may very well be that this distinction (which is also basic to the formal structure of the 'Quaestiones') is a direct result of the desire to combine two traditional modes of interpretation. Thus there are at least three major stages in the development of a treatise like that of 'De Abrahamo': the development of the schema of the Exposition; the development of the Allegory; the combination of the two which presumambly has its own intention as well as formal characteristics.

3. The Reasoned Allegory

The study by I. CHRISTIANSEN has shown that some of the Philonic allegorization proceeds according to definite patterns of symbol association and dieretic clarification. Her generalizations and conclusions appear a bit hasty, and she is not convincing at the point of suggesting that the symbolic equivalents of the allegory are determined by associations with the Aristotelian categories of the attributes which Philo discovered in the words of the biblical text. But the structural patterns of the allegorical interpretations she discusses are quite helpful. If one takes a somewhat larger sampling, irrespective of the incidence of dieretic structure, the following outline of the Philonic allegorical procedure emerges:

a. The biblical text is cited.

b. Attention is called to certain words or aspects of the text, often in the form of a question as to what is meant.

c. The answer is given in a brief statement, often in the form of a simple identification of 'equivalence' between the word or phrase to be interpreted and the allegorical meaning.

d. The 'reasons' for the equivalence are then given which frequently consist of various syllogisms of analogy and association, or some analogical correspondence to some schema with which he may be working. The 'logic' intended by the correspondence is indicated also in the very frequent usage of αἰτία, γάρ and ἐπειδή to develop the correspondence or to introduce further analogies.

e. The establishment of the equivalence may then be supplemented by giving further examples or illustrations of the meaning which has been derived, sometimes from everyday experience, sometimes from philosophical *topoi*, frequently from another statement in the Pentateuch introduced as a 'witness' to the phenomenon under discussion.

f. After the establishment of the allegorical meaning and its clarification or illustration an appropriate exhortation or application to the 'reader' may be given. It is significant, however, that this component is frequently missing and does not appear to be essential. Neither is a concluding summary or statement essential, even though Philo is quite adept at formulating such.[96]

4. The Identification Allegory

A formal distinction must be made between the reasoned allegory just discussed and those allegorical interpretations which are given without that kind of support. These may be called 'identification' allegories, because the procedure is simply to identify a biblical figure with some other figure and proceed to a discussion in keeping with the new characterization or ethos which is achieved. This kind of identification appears to be normative for a series of semi-mythological figures such as those of Wisdom, Logos, *dynamis*, *arete* and *physis*. It probably indicates an earlier kind of allegorization which was achieved by some system of association and analogy which did not require the kind of explanation characteristic of the reasoned allegory. Here it would be important to establish the primary biblical points of departure for a given figure (say for Wisdom or *dynamis*) in order to discover the scope and ask about the tertium comparationis for the allegorical system. It is probable that the discovery of such a system would put one very close to the beginning of the history of Alexandrian exegesis.[97]

---

[96] An example of the reasoned allegory is found in Migr 216—225. The Text is cited: "Abraham) travelled through (διοδεῦσαι) the country as far as the place of Shechem, to the lofty oak tree (Gen 12:6)." The Question is raised: "Let us consider what 'to travel through' means." The Answer is immediately given: It is characteristic of the Love of learning (τὸ φιλομαθές). The Reasons for the correspondence are given: Love of learning pries into everything, explores all material and immaterial things, and follows its quest through its own country to foreign parts. Examples follow: Merchants, traders and seekers after wisdom are all questers. The Application is addressed to the Psyche: "Travel then through man . . . Travel again through the universe . . ." The difficulty of attaining the learning sought for leads then to a focus upon the symbolism for Shechem ("shouldering" equals 'toil') and the oak (which symbolizes *paideia*). But now the Text has been reintroduced and the form of the reasoned allegory has another point of departure, i.e., it begins over again.

[97] An example of the identification allegory is found in Conf 62—63. The Text is introduced: "Behold a man whose name is the rising (Zech 6:12)." The strangeness of the designation taken literally is noted (a device not always employed which, therefore, may not belong to

5. The Development of a Theme

Another kind of interpretation may be called the 'development of a theme,' although as a formal indicator this only serves to distinguish a wide variety of thematic material from the preceding forms of interpretation. Thus there is a thematic development underlying many of the treatises themselves. There are blocks of material large and small which handle themes suggested by the allegories but which are only indirectly related to the biblical text. There are also collections of biblical texts according to them and combinations of such lists with a development of the theme using extra-biblical material. In general one has the impression that the thematic organization of interpretive materials is a very late form of commentary. But this could be deceiving in some cases (as for instance in the case of some of the short descriptions of the *encyclia* in Congr), and the material offers in any case an important basis for inquiry into the final form and intention of the series of commentary themselves. The function of this material and form to the interpretation of the Pentateuch is certainly unclear and needs to be investigated.[98]

6. The Clarification of the Literal Meaning

Under the 'literal' meaning of the biblical text Philo could discuss a variety of grammatical and historical matters in addition to encomium motifs. This is especially true in the Quaestiones, but can occur elsewhere as well. Here he shows that he was fully capable of reading the Pentateuch as a literary and historical document. Since he polemicized on occasion against those who read it 'literally,' it would be helpful to study those polemics in connection with his own discussions of the literal meaning. It may be that this would not put one in touch with a tradition or system of interpretation at all, but it might reveal a great deal about the primary understanding of the Pentateuch from which Philo himself moved into allegorization. It would appear, for instance, that miracle-accounts presented no problem for him and would therefore not have been a cause for apologetic interpretation. It would appear, too, that he was quite able to understand the history in the Pentateuch as empirically significant, and the laws and

---

the primary form of the identification allegory) and the identification is made: The "man" is the *eikon*. This identification is made on the basis of the name 'rising' which can be associated with a Logos-mythological motif, but once introduced interest in the description of the *eikon* takes over without need to give further reason for, or evidence of, the appropriateness of the description as interpretation of the verse at hand. One might compare Migr 5–6: The 'house of God' is taken to refer to the 'Logos' which, however, is then described as an entity in its own right without further consideration of its correspondence with the verse being interpreted.

[98] For an exemple, one might look at Leg All II 65–70 where the mention of 'shamelessness' gives rise to a short development of 'three kinds of shamelessness.' The treatise 'De agricultura' presents a case in which an entire work has been developed thematically on the basis of a single word in the story of Noah — that he was a 'husbandman'!

regulations as making good sense without appeal to allegory. This ability to deal with the biblical text according to its 'literal' meaning should caution against the hasty assumption that it was the offensiveness or vagueness of the old stories and laws which demanded allegorization. Only in the case of the anthropomorphisms and isolated verses where Philo made a point of noting some unclarity or logical contradiction does that appear to be a major consideration. A study of the 'literal' meaning may provide, then, a significant control for the investigation of the impulses which led to the various systems of interpretation including the allegorical systems.

C. Exegetical Systems and Trajectories

A typology of exegetical methods is not sufficient for a reconstruction of the exegetical history in Alexandria. Ways must be found to determine systems of interpretation and their historical and theological interrelationships.

1. Exegetical Systems

The determination of an exegetical system requires evidence for the integral relationship of identifiable method, delimited textual basis, and a coherent intention in interpretation. 'Textual basis' refers to the form of the authority to be interpreted and the way in which its authority is understood. Thus the uncertainty about the cultic-scriptural range of authority for the allegory of the priest and temple becomes an important consideration for the determination of a cultic-cosmic system of allegory. And in the case of certain types of interpretation it would be important to determine their Pentateuchal scope — i. e. the range or selection of material which is focused upon for interpretation. The question of Pentateuch itself, especially in the form Pentateuch vs. other Jewish scriptures as basic authority belongs here as well.

To discover a 'coherent intention' requires consideration of the system as a whole, especially in terms of its conceptuality and rhetorical functionality. Examples of possible systems of interpretation in the Philonic corpus may be given for purposes of illustration.

Beginning with the encomia as a set, i. e. taking one's point of departure from an identifiable type of interpretive activity (method), one might reasonably inquire as to a possible intention prior to and independently of their function in the grand scheme of Philo's Exposition of the Law. Considerations of scope indicate that the encomia may have been limited originally to the patriarchal narratives, especially the stories of Abraham. Content considerations show that the encomia share a pre-allegorical understanding of the 'virtues' of the patriarchs and may be compared with the non-allegorical embellishments of these stories to be found in 'Jubilees' and Josephus. One might well conclude that a coherent system of interpretation was in evidence and be justified in the quest for some historical and social setting distinct from and/or prior to its usage by Philo.

For a second example, one might begin with the observation that a method (identification allegory) and a material identifier (Wisdom) sometimes converge. The search for a system would need not only to substantiate this convergence, but establish its textual scope as well. A preliminary textual-scope study indicates that the Wisdom-identification allegory may have focused upon the creation and exodus stories by means of locating terms there which could be taken as symbols for the mythological equivalents of 'source,' 'path,' and 'place.' Since these abstractions are derivable from the mythology of the figure of Wisdom, and since they can easily be correlated with an abstract reduction of the structure of the Pentateuchal account read as cosmogony, the possibility that a system of interpretation is in evidence can be entertained. One might want to investigate whether such a finding can be substantiated and, if it can, whether it reflects any theological concern which can be assigned to a believable historical-social setting.

Here would be the place, too, to re-investigate the exegetical traditions discussed above in Section D, 2 in the attempt to determine whether exegetical systems may be in evidence there.

2. Trajectories

The determination of an exegetical system in the sense described above is not sufficient for historical reconstruction. That is because it does not guarantee the engagement of the questions of historical and social setting. Without engaging these questions one cannot know the limits of a particular system's compatibility with other systems which may have been employed by the same person or group. To determine historical place one must begin with questions of sequence as exegetical systems are compared.

In the history of the scholarship there have been some attempts to work out sequences and trajectories in the development of interpretations. M. STEIN argued for a development from early non-allegorical haggada, via symbolic interpretations to eventually allegorization. If one could find a way to relate the hypothetical system of the encomia, mentioned above, to other haggadic traditions and to the eventual development of an allegorical interpretation of the patriarchal narratives, one might well be on the way to the reconstruction of such a line of development as a trajectory. HEGERMANN's thesis for a development from early cosmic symbolism, through Logos allegorization, to ethical and psychological reduction of the significance of the image of the High Priest, etc., provides another example of a possible trajectory. And in a recent study the present author[99] analyzed the treatise 'De congressu eruditionis' and discovered at least four layers in the history of the interpretation of the Hagar story in Gen 16:1—6 which might be arranged in chronological order.

---

[99] B. L. MACK, Weisheit und Allegorie bei Philo von Alexandrien: Untersuchungen zum Traktat 'De congressu eruditionis'. A paper read at the Neutestamentliches Seminar, München, 1975; the Institutum Judaicum, Tübingen, 1975; and the Philo Institute, Chicago, 1975.

Other criteria for the reconstruction of trajectories will be given as the
various systems of interpretation are compared with extra-Philonic Jewish
literature. Thus a comparison of the anti-anthropomorphic apology with the
fragments of Aristobulos might contribute to the reconstruction of a trajectory.
Determination of the development from Wisdom theology to Wisdom allegory
would provide another development. Taken together the possibilities for
reconstruction of what must have been an exceptionally rich history of interpretation in Alexandrian Judaism seem to be quite good.

D. Philo's Place on the Trajectories

We return now to the question of Philo's place in cultural history, having
narrowed the field of inquiry to concentrate upon Alexandrian Judaism and its
exegetical traditions as the specific and immediate cultural manifestation within
which his place should be sought. We have been led to this inquiry by means of a
review of the scholarship which has indicated firstly, that derivations of his
thought from more broadly defined configurations of his cultural milieu have not
succeeded; secondly, that Philo's explicit references to those with whom he knew
himself to be in conversation are references to other Jewish exegetes or exegetical
traditions; and thirdly, that, although a comprehensive picture of the history of
Alexandrian exegesis has not yet been achieved, evidence for a number of
exegetical traditions and their developments has been indicated with some
frequency in the scholarship. Some observations appear then to be in order concerning that nature of the evidence which may help to disclose Philo's own
position with regard to these traditions.

1. Philo's Critique of the Traditions

a) Traditions Rejected

There are several groups or types of persons representing theological,
exegetical, and philosophical positions which Philo rejected. He disagreed
radically with the view which the 'Chaldaeans' had of God.[100] He disagreed
radically with some 'extreme allegorists' on the importance of the practice of the
actual cult.[101] He was troubled, too, by some whom he dubbed 'sophists,' whom
he accused of failing in principle to practice what they preached. And he disagreed with some literalists about the validity of allegorical interpretation.[102]
With the possible exception of the 'sophists' each of these groups of persons
appears to represent a position vis à vis the Jewish cult related to specific views or
interpretations of the scriptures.

---

[100] See above note 55.
[101] Migr 89—90. Cf. WOLFSON, Philo 1, 66—71.
[102] See above note 54.

b) Traditions Qualified

There is also evidence that other exegetical traditions were used by Philo, but seriously qualified at certain points. This is true of the source which BOUSSET discovered. Philo could use it apparently as long as its (Stoic) conception of the power of the *nous* could be corrected in the direction of a concept of revelation, and as long as its positive evaluation of *aisthesis* could be negated or discounted in some way. It is probably also true of certain traditions which had interpreted certain stories of the patriarchs in terms of ascent-visions and heavenly enthronements. Philo could use the mythology of ascent, but only by qualifying it in one of two ways. One qualification was his insistence upon the necessity for a guide on the path. The other was his well-known reservation about the possibility of the ultimate vision of God.

c) Traditions Collected

It is frequently the case, as every Philonist knows, that multiple interpretations of a particular term or verse will be given in a series without argument for one above another. Preference may indeed be indicated, and infrequently a personal opinion appended and noted to be such. Here it is clear that the exegetes were in conversation with one another and that Philo was as interested in hearing and reporting the views of others as in making his own contribution. The apparent lack of debate in these cases must be contrasted with the evidence noted above for Philo's capacity for violent disagreement. The range of attitude toward other interpretations revealed here indicates a broad and complex context in which his work was done.

2. His Capacity for System and Logic

The older quests for Philo's system of thought failed for two reasons. One was that systems were assumed which were philosophical or discursive instead of exegetical. The other was that Philo was held to be the author of every statement and opinion in the commentaries, as strange as that may sound given the many logical contradictions which invariably ensued. We have now seen that Philo's contributions to the traditions of exegesis in Alexandria must be won by redaction-critical methods and that the systems to be assumed may have mythological structure. The interpretations intended may reveal logics of analogy which differ from the conceptual ordering of a philosophical theology. Allegory may have its own logic after all.

This being the case a renewed search for Philo's own position is called for.

a) The Commentaries as Systems

One way to begin is with the observation that the three series of commentaries offer examples of systematic thought and intention. Each differs from

18*

the other two in principles of organization, and comparative studies therefore would be possible. Here the series on the Exposition of the Law will be used as an example of what may be learned.

In Abr 1—6 and in Praem 1—3 Philo expressly mentions the plan for the series as a whole. The underlying conception is that a correlation exists between the Pentateuch (as law) and the world-order (as *physis, nomos*). This correlation provides the hermeneutical principle by which the contents of the Pentateuch can be classified and treated as a unit. There are three components: the cosmogony, the history and the legislation of the laws. The cosmogony includes the account of the creation of man and is treated in 'De opificio mundi.' History refers to the stories of the patriarchs, including Moses, and is handled in the treatises ascribed to them. The laws are treated in the tractates on the decalogue and the special laws. The series ends with treatises on the virtues and on rewards and punishments. Since the correlation of the cosmogony with the legislation is readily enabled by the hermeneutical principle (cosmos — *nomos*), it is with the historical narratives that additional imagination is called for. These appear to be aligned with the overall plan by means of the Stoic conception of the *sophos* who lives in accordance with nature. Because the patriarchs lived before the legislation of the laws they become examples of life in accordance with the unwritten law of nature (in distinction from the written laws) and are called 'laws' themselves. This plan of exposition is clear evidence of a holistic and systematic approach to the hermeneutical task. It reveals sustained reflection about the nature of the material contained in the Five Books of Moses, and works with a theological conception most profound. But it will be discovered in the analysis of the treatises that the plan is at best unevenly developed, and at worst merely a framework rationale used to organize great amounts of diverse material, much of which does not compliment the theme at all. It is such incongruity which makes the comparison of exegetical types possible, however, and which may lead to the identification of exegetical traditions appearing in the Exposition, but not compatible with it.

b) The Dualistic Frame

In spite of the fact that there has been no consensus among the scholars about Philo's philosophical or theological system as a whole, there appears to be some agreement about his preference for middle Platonic conceptuality. This observation should not be forfeited, but tested, for it provides a solid scholarly judgment as a point of departure for the investigation of the function of a preferred philosophical conceptuality to the allegorical enterprise. The reasons for such a preference would need thorough researching, of course, but it is already possible to begin to develop some theories.

There is a significant amount of evidence to suggest that there were major systems of interpretation which had used essentially Stoic conceptualities to work out the implications of what must have been a Wisdom understanding of the cosmic dimensions of Jewish Torah. And it is clear that, for some theological purposes, such interpretive systems could have proved helpful. But the dangers implicit in such conceptuality for certain Jewish theologumena are obvious too.

And it is just such dangers which appear to have been the reasons for Philo's many critiques of the several exegetical traditions which, in his opinion, did not overcome the immanentist tendencies. It is quite within the realm of possibility that Philo found the middle-Platonic conceptuality preferable to the Stoic at just those points of theological concern – the transcendence of God, the dependency of humankind on God, the world as sphere of potentiality, and some sort of teleological reservation in subtle tension with the affirmation of the goodness and significance of life lived in the present in accordance with the divine intentions. The theological point of departure could also have been given in the Wisdom tradition which knew of the divine and transcendent as well as the immanent forms of wisdom. And it appears to be that a convergence of Wisdom mythology and Platonic conceptuality has indeed taken place in Philo. The exegetical task would have been to ascertain the truth of the dualist frame in the Torah itself – a task which most Philonists would acknowledge had been achieved. Philo's insistence on the absolute transcendence of God, his reservation about the possibility of the ultimate vision, his distinction between the Spirit (of revelation) from God and the human mind, and all the ambiguities about the ontological status of the archetypes and patterns into which creation account and patriarchal narrative were transformed – all indicate a coherent and logical mind at work in the interest of a specific theological concern. That concern was for a conceptual grasp of some older persuasions expressed then in terms of wisdom. For this the concepts of the Greeks were at hand. But in the grasping it was the older persuasions which remained in control, transforming the Greek conceptuality into metaphors of a new Jewish Wisdom.

And the purpose could then be found in the psychological reduction which the allegory of the soul would make possible. The Torah as paradigm for creation and redemption, pattern for the way in which the soul was called to go! If some such correlation could be shown which brings together a philosophical conceptuality, a wisdom-theological concern, a unified grasp of the Torah, and an appropriate method of interpretation – that would suggest a very profound program indeed and indicate a kind of systematic mind heretofore not imagined for Philo.

Conclusion

It has been suggested that the writings of Philo may yield a picture of an exciting and significant era of Jewish intellectual creation. The scholarship has been reviewed to show both the necessity and the possibility for studies which would explore it. The thesis has been that the intellectual activity was essentially hermeneutical debate which was carried by means of exegetical traditions which had roots in theological systems. Philo's works can be seen to be both a repository for such traditional exegetical accomplishment, and the result of systematic efforts of his own. The logic of the theological systems has been difficult to establish because the systems themselves merely intended explication of the older poetries of wisdom, creation and law. To discover them and reconstruct their developmental histories in Alexandrian Judaism will require new methods of research which begin with the observation that the commentaries are intended as interpretation of the Pentateuch after all.

A Selected Bibliography on Philo and the Interpretation of the Scriptures in Hellenistic Judaism

Abbreviations will be used in keeping with the article by EARLE HILGERT, Bibliographia Philoniana 1935–1981. ANRW II, 21,1 (above, pp. 47–97).

ADLER, M., Studien zu Philon von Alexandreia. Breslau: Marcus, 1929.

AMIR, Y., האליגוריה של פילון ביחסה לאלגוריה ההומרית [The Allegory of Philo Compared with Homeric Allegory]. Esh 6 (1970) 35–45.

AMIR, Y., דרשותיו של פילון על היראה והאהבה ויחסן למדרשי ארץ־ישראל [The Homilies of Philo on Fear and Love and their Relation to Palestinian Midrashim]. Zi 30 (1965) 47–60.

ARNIM, H. VON, Quellenstudien zu Philo von Alexandria. Philologische Untersuchungen 11. Berlin: Weidmann, 1888.

BELKIN, S., The Alexandrian Halakah in Apologetic Literature of the First Century C.E. Philadelphia: Jewish Publication Society, 1936.

BELKIN, S., מדרש הנעלם ומקורותיו במדרשים האלכסנדרוניים הקדומים [The Midrash ha-Ne'elam and its Origins in the Ancient Alexandrian Midrashim]. Su 3 (1958) 25–92.

BELKIN, S., המדרש הסמלי אצל פילון בהשוואה למדרשי חז"ל [The Symbolic Midrash in Philo Compared with Rabbinic Midrashim]. In: ספר היובל לכבוד צבי וולפסון [Harry Austryn Wolfson Jubilee Volume]. Hebrew Section, 33–68. Jerusalem, 1965.

BELKIN, S., המדרש הגדול ומדרשי פילון [The Midrash ha-Gadol and the Midrashim of Philo.] In: ספר היובל לכבוד י. פינקל [J. Finkel Jubilee Volume], 7–58. New York, 1974. [IAJS].

BELKIN, S., מדרש שאלות ותשובות על בראשית ואמות לפילון האלכסנדרוני ויחסו למדרש הארץ־ישראל [The Midrash 'Quaestiones et solutiones in Genesin et in Exodum' of Philo Alexandrinus and its Relation to the Palestinian Midrash]. Horeb 14 (1960) 1–74.

BELKIN, S., מדרשי פילון האלסנדרוני לאור מדרשי א"י [The Midrashim of Philo Alexandrinus in Light of the Palestinian Midrashim]. Su 4 (1964) 1–68.

BELKIN, S., מדרשים בכתבי פילון ומקבילותיהם למאמרים במדרש הגדול ש'מקום נעלם' [Midrashim in the Writings of Philo and their Parallels to Sayings in the Midrash ha-Gadol which are of 'Unknown Origin']. In: הגות עיברית באמריקה [Hebrew Thought in America] 1. Ed. M. ZOHARI. Tel-Aviv, 1972.

BELKIN, S., מקור קדום למדרשי חז"ל מדרש שו"ת על בראשית ושמות לפילון האלכסנדרונו [The Earliest Source of the Rabbinic Midrashim – the Midrash 'Quaestiones et solutiones in Genesin et in Exodum' of Philo Alexandrinus]. In: ספר יובל לכבוד הרב ד"ר אברהם וויים [The Abraham Weiss Jubilee Volume]. Hebrew Section, 579–633. Ed. S. BELKIN. New York, 1964.

BELKIN, S., פילון ומסורה מדרשית ארץ ישראלית [Philo and the Midrashic Tradition of Palestine]. Horeb 13 (1958) 1–60.

BELKIN, S., מדרש השמות בפילון [The Interpretation of Names in Philo]. Horeb 12 (1956) 3–61.

BELKIN, S., Philo and the Oral Law. Harvard Semitic Series 11. Cambridge, Massachusetts: Harvard University Press, 1940; Reprinted, New York: KTAV, 1970.

BORGEN, P., Bread from Heaven. An Exegetical Study of the Concept of Manna in the Gospel of John and the Writings of Philo. NT Suppl 10. Leiden: Brill, 1965.

BOUSSET, W., Jüdisch-christlicher Schulbetrieb in Alexandria und Rom. Literarische Unter-
    suchungen zu Philo, Clemens von Alexandria, Justin und Irenäus. FRLANT N.F. 6.
    Göttingen: Vandenhoeck und Ruprecht, 1915.
BOYANCÉ, P., Echo des exégèses de la mythologie grecque chez Philon. PAL, 169—186.
BRÉHIER, É., La méthode allégorique chez les Juifs avant Philon. In: Les idées philosophiques
    et religieuses de Philon d'Alexandrie, 45—61. Paris: Vrin, 1907. Second edition, 1925;
    reprinted, 1950.

CAZEAUX, J., Aspects de l'exégèse philonienne. RSR 47 (1973) 262—269. Reprinted in: Exégèse
    biblique et Judaïsme, 108—115. Ed. JACQUES-É. MÉNARD. Strasbourg, Leiden, 1973.
CAZEAUX, J., Interpréter Philon d'Alexandrie (sur un commentaire du De Abrahamo, nos 61—
    84). REG 84 (1972) 345—352.
CHRISTIANSEN, I., Die Technik der allegorischen Auslegungswissenschaft bei Philon von Alex-
    andrien. BBH 7. Tübingen: Mohr, 1969.
COPPENS, J., Philon et l'exégèse targumique. ETL 24 (1948) 430—431.
CULPEPPER, P. A., Philo's School. In his: The Johannine School, 197—214. SBL Dissertations
    26. Missoula, Montana: Scholars, 1975.

DANIEL, S., La Halacha de Philon selon le premier livre des 'Lois Spéciales.' PAL 221—242.
DANIÉLOU, J., L'Exégèse de Philon. In his: Philon d'Alexandrie, 119—142. Paris: Fayard, 1958.
DANIÉLOU, J., Die Entmythologisierung in der alexandrinischen Schule. In: Kerygma und
    Mythos 6.1, 38—43. Theologische Forschung 30. Hamburg, 1963.
DANIÉLOU, J., La symbolique du Temple de Jérusalem chez Philon et Josèphe. In: Le sym-
    bolisme cosmique des monuments religieux, 83—90. Serie orientale 14. Roma, 1957.
DAUBE, D., Alexandrian Methods of Interpretation and the Rabbis. In: Festschrift Hans Lewald,
    27—44. Basel: Helbing und Lichtenhahn, 1953.
DELLING, G., Wunder—Allegorie—Mythus bei Philon von Alexandreia. Wissenschaftliche
    Zeitschrift der Martin-Luther-Universität Halle-Wittenberg 6 (1957) 713—740. Reprinted
    in: Gottes ist der Orient. Festschrift für Prof. D. Dr. Otto Eissfeldt D. D., 42—68.
    Berlin, 1959.

FINKEL, J., The Alexandrian Tradition and the Midrash Ha-Ne'elam. In: The Leo Jung Jubilee
    Volume, 77—103. Ed. MENAHEM M. KASHER, et al. New York: KTAV, 1962.
FRANKEL, Z., Über den Einfluss der palästinischen Exegese auf die alexandrinische Hermeneu-
    tik. Leipzig: Barth, 1851.
FRANKEL, Z., Über palästinische und alexandrinische Schriftforschung. Breslau: Breslauer
    Seminar, 1854.
FRIEDLÄNDER, M., Geschichte der jüdischen Apologetik als Vorgeschichte des Christentums.
    Zürich, 1903; Leipzig, 1906; reprinted: Amsterdam: Philo Press, 1973.
FRÜCHTEL, U., Die kosmologischen Vorstellungen bei Philo von Alexandrien. Ein Beitrag zur
    Geschichte der Genesis-Exegese. ALGHJ 2. Leiden: Brill, 1968.

HAMERTON-KELLY, R., Some Techniques of Composition in Philo's Allegorical Commentary
    with Special Reference to De Agricultura — A Study in the Hellenistic Midrash. In: Jews,
    Greeks and Christians: Religious Cultures in Late Antiquity, 45—56. Ed. R. HAMERTON-
    KELLY and R. SCROGGS. Leiden: Brill, 1976.
HANSON, A., Philo's Etymologies. JTS N.S. 18 (1967) 128—139.
HEINEMANN, I., Die Allegoristik der hellenistischen Juden ausser Philo. Mnemosyne IV/5
    (1952) 130—138.
HEINEMANN, I., Altjüdische Allegoristik. Breslau: Marcus, 1936.
HEINEMANN, I., Philons griechische und jüdische Bildung. Breslau: Marcus, 1932. Reprinted:
    Hildesheim: Olms, 1962.
HEINISCH, P., Der Einfluss Philos auf die älteste christliche Exegese. Alttestamentliche Ab-
    handlungen 1.1/2. Münster: Aschendorff, 1908.

JERVELL, J., Imago Dei. Gen 1.26f. im Spätjudentum, in der Gnosis und in den paulinischen Briefen. FRLANT N.F. 58. Göttingen: Vandenhoeck und Ruprecht, 1960.

LAUTERBACH, J. Z., Ancient Jewish Allegorists in Talmud and Midrash. JQR 1 (1910/11) 291–333; 503–531.

LEVIN, A. G., The Tree of Life: Genesis 2:9 and 3:22–24 in Jewish, Gnostic and Early Christian Texts. Dissertation, Harvard University, 1966.

LEWIS, J. P., A Study of the Interpretation of Noah and the Flood in Jewish and Christian Literature. Leiden: Brill, 1968.

LOEWE, R., The 'Plain' Meaning of Scripture in Early Jewish Exegesis. In: Papers of the Institute of Jewish Studies London 1,140–185. Ed. J. G. WEISS. Jerusalem, 1964.

LORD, J. R., Abraham: a Study in Ancient Jewish and Christian Interpretation. Dissertation, Duke University, 1968.

MACK, B. L., Exegetical Traditions in Alexandrian Judaism: A Program for the Analysis of the Philonic Corpus. SP 3 (1974/75) 71–112.

MAYER, G., Exegese II (Judentum). RAC 6 (1966) 1194–1211.

MYRE, A., La loi et le Pentateuque selon Philon d'Alexandrie. Science et Esprit 25 (1973) 209–225.

NIKIPROWETZKY, V., Le commentaire de l'Écriture chez Philon d'Alexandrie. Lille: Université de Lille, 1974.

NIKIPROWETZKY, V., L'exégèse de Philon d'Alexandrie. RHPR 53 (1973) 309–329.

NIKIPROWETZKY, V., Note sur l'interprétation littérale de la loi et sur l'angélologie chez Philon d'Alexandrie. In: Mélanges André Neher, 181–190. Paris, 1975.

NIKIPROWETZKY, V., La spiritualisation des sacrifices et le culte sacrificiel au temple de Jérusalem chez Philon d'Alexandrie. Sem 17 (1967) 97–116.

OTTE, K., Das Sprachverständnis bei Philo von Alexandrien. Sprache als Mittel der Hermeneutik. Beiträge zur Geschichte der biblischen Exegese 7. Tübingen: Mohr, 1968.

PÉPIN, J., Mythe et allégorie. Les origines grecques et les contestations judéo-chrétiennes. Philosophie de l'esprit. Paris: Aubier, 1958.

PÉPIN, J., Remarques sur la théorie de l'exégèse allégorique chez Philon. PAL, 131–167.

PLANCK, H., Commentatio de principiis et causis interpretationis Philonianae allegoricae. Dissertation, Göttingen, 1806.

RITTER, B., Philo und die Halacha. Eine vergleichende Studie unter steter Berücksichtigung des Josephus. Leipzig: Hinrichs, 1879.

RYLE, H. E., Philo and the Holy Scriptures. London: Macmillan, 1895.

SANDMEL, S., Philo's Environment and Philo's Exegesis. JBR 22 (1954) 248–253.

SANDMEL, S., Philo's Place in Judaism: a Study of Conceptions of Abraham in Jewish Literature. HUCA 25 (1954) 209–237; 26 (1955) 151–332; reprinted Cincinnati: Hebrew Union College, 1956; with new introduction by the author, New York: KTAV, 1972.

SCHMITT, A., Interpretation der Genesis aus hellenistischem Geist. ZAW 86 (1974) 137–163.

SHROYER, M. J., Alexandrian Jewish Literalists. Dissertation, Yale University, 1935. Condensed in: JBL 55 (1936) 261–284.

SIEGFRIED, C., Philo von Alexandria als Ausleger des Alten Testaments. Jena: Dufft, 1875; reprinted Amsterdam, Aalen, 1970.

SOWERS, S. G., The Hermeneutics of Philo and Hebrews. Basel Studies in Theology. Zürich, Richmond, 1965.

SOWERS, S. G., On the Reinterpretation of Biblical History in Hellenistic Judaism. In: Oikonomia. Heilsgeschichte als Thema der Theologie. Festschrift für Oscar Cullman, 18–25. Ed. FELIX CHRIST. Hamburg-Bergstedt, 1967.

STEIN, M. (EDMUND), Die allegorische Exegese des Philo aus Alexandria. Beihefte zur ZAW 51. Giessen: Töpelmann, 1929.

STEIN, M. (EDMUND), Alttestamentliche Bibelkritik in der spät-hellenistischen Literatur. In: Collectanea Theologica 16, 38—83. Societas Theologorum Polonorum, 1935; reprinted: Lwow, 1935.

STEIN, M. (EDMUND), המדרש ההלניסטי [The Hellenistic Midrash]. In his: בין תרבות ישראל ותרבות יוון ורומא [The relationship between Jewish, Greek and Roman Cultures], 93—105. Ed. JUDAH ROSENTHAL. Tel-Aviv, 1970.

STEIN, M. (EDMUND), Philo und der Midrasch. Beihefte zur ZAW 57. Giessen: Töpelmann, 1931.

THYEN, H., Die Probleme der neueren Philo-Forschung. Theologische Rundschau N.F. 23 (1955) 230—246.

THYEN, H., Der Stil der jüdisch-hellenistischen Homilie. FRLANT N.F. 47. Göttingen: Vandenhoeck und Ruprecht, 1955.

TREITEL, L., Agadah bei Philo. Monatsschrift für Geschichte und Wissenschaft des Judentums 53 (1909) 28—45; 159—173; 286—291. Reprinted in: Philonische Studien, 85—113. Ed. M. BRANN. Breslau, 1915.

TREITEL, L., Ursprung, Begriff und Umfang der allegorischen Schrifterklärung. Monatsschrift für Geschichte und Wissenschaft des Judentums 55 (1911) 543—554.

WALTER, N., Der Thoraausleger Aristobulos. TU 86. Berlin: Akademie, 1964.

WILSON, R. McL., The Early History of the Exegesis of Gen 1,26. In: Studia Patristica 1, 423—437. TU 63. Berlin, 1957.

WOLFSON, H. A., The Allegorical Method. In his: Philo I, 115—138. Cambridge, Massachusetts: Harvard University Press, 1962.

A Critical Introduction to Philo's Dialogues

by ABRAHAM TERIAN, Berrien Springs, Mich.

Contents

Introductory Remarks

    Philo of Alexandria, our best representative of Hellenistic Judaism, continues to attract readers and researchers from a broad spectrum of disciplines. The

Abbreviations:

    Authors and titles of Greek classical works are abbreviated in the forms given in H. G. LIDDELL and R. SCOTT, A Greek-English Lexicon (9th ed. by H. S. JONES, rev. with a supplement by E. A. BARBER; Oxford, 1968), pp. xvi—xxxviii; and those of Latin classical works, with the exception of Pliny (the 'Elder'), in the forms given in the Oxford Latin Dictionary, ed. P. G. W. GLARE (Oxford, 1982), pp. ix—xx. Titles of Philonic treatises are abbreviated in the forms listed in: Studia Philonica, 1 (1972), 92; with some additions, they are as follows:

Abr	De Abrahamo
Aet	De aeternitate mundi
Agr	De agricultura
Anim	De animalibus
Apol Jud	Apologia pro Iudaeis
Cher	De Cherubim
Conf	De confusione linguarum
Congr	De congressu eruditionis gratia
Dec	De Decalogo
Deo	De Deo
Ebr	De ebrietate

cumulative scholarship[1] accurately reflects the diversity of interests and opinions among those attracted to this literary giant of the 1st century. We have extant over

Flacc	In Flaccum
Fuga	De fuga et inventione
Gaium	Legatio ad Gaium
Gig	De gigantibus
Heres	Quis rerum divinarum heres sit
Jos	De Iosepho
Leg All I–III	Legum allegoriae I–III
Migr	De migratione Abrahami
Mut	De mutatione nominum
Num	De numeris
Op	De opificio mundi
Plant	De plantatione
Post	De posteritate Caini
Praem	De praemiis et poenis
Provid I–II	De Providentia I–II
Quaes Ex I–II	Quaestiones et solutiones in Exodum I–II
Quaes Gen I–IV	Quaestiones et solutiones in Genesin I–IV
Quod Det	Quod deterius potiori insidiari soleat
Quod Deus	Quod Deus immutabilis sit
Quod Omn	Quod omnis probus liber sit
Sacr	De sacrificiis Abelis et Caini
Sobr	De sobrietate
Somn I–II	De somniis I–II
Spec Leg I–IV	De specialibus legibus I–IV
Virt	De virtutibus
Vita Cont	De vita contemplativa
Vita Mos I–II	De vita Mosis I–II

[1] See the critical surveys by W. Völker, Fortschritt und Vollendung bei Philo von Alexandrien. Eine Studie zur Geschichte der Frömmigkeit, Texte und Untersuchungen zur Geschichte der altchristlichen Literatur, 49 (Leipzig, 1938); H. Thyen, Die Probleme der neueren Philo-Forschung, Theologische Rundschau, 23 (1955), 230–246; and V. Nikiprowetzky, L'exégèse de Philon d'Alexandrie, Revue d'histoire et de philosophie religieuses, 53 (1973), 309–329. For the vast literature on Philo, see the following bibliographies: H. L. Goodhart and E. R. Goodenough, The Politics of Philo Judaeus, Practice and Theory [with] General Bibliography of Philo (New Haven, 1938); J. Haussleiter, Nacharistotelische Philosophen, 1931–1936, Jahresbericht über die Fortschritte der klassischen Altertumswissenschaft, 281–282 (1943), 107–116; L. H. Feldman, Scholarship on Philo and Josephus (1937–1962), Studies in Judaica, 1 (New York, n. d.), 1–25; G. Delling and R. M. Maser, Bibliographie zur jüdisch-hellenistischen und intertestamentarischen Literatur, 1900–1970, Texte und Untersuchungen zur Geschichte der altchristlichen Literatur, 106 (Berlin, 1975); E. Hilgert, A Bibliography of Philo Studies, 1963–1970, Studia Philonica, 1 (1972), 57–71; A Bibliography of Philo Studies in 1971 with Additions for 1965–70, Studia Philonica, 2 (1973), 51–54; A Bibliography of Philo Studies, 1972–1973, Studia Philonica, 3 (1974–1975), 117–125; A Bibliography of Philo Studies, 1974–1975, Studia Philonica, 4 (1976–1977), 79–85; et sqq.; Bibliographia Philoniana 1935–1981, above in this same volume (ANRW II 21,1) 47–97. Among the general introductions to Philo, see J. Daniélou, Philon d'Alexandrie (Paris, 1958); E. R. Goodenough, An Introduction to Philo Judaeus (2nd ed.; Oxford, 1962); and S. Sandmel, Philo of Alexandria: An Introduction (New York, 1979).

forty books of his composition, and nearly half as many are known to have been lost. Consequently, the Philo scholar faces more than the commonplace, already overwhelming problems connected with the study of voluminous writers. These and other problems set forth below lie behind the often inconclusive and conflicting studies that comprise the bulk of our bibliographies.

Philo's two dialogues with his renegade nephew Alexander, better known as Tiberius Iulius Alexander[2], are among his least studied works. This state of Philo scholarship is due to several factors, not the least of which is the fact that there are no reliable translations of these works[3]. 'De Providentia' (Provid) I—II and 'De animalibus' (Anim), like most of the 'Quaestiones', are extant only in a 'classical' Armenian translation dating from the 6th century A.D.[4]. Of the original Greek, there are considerable fragments of Provid II and scant fragments of Anim[5]. The

---

[2] He was born probably early in the reign of Tiberius (ca. A.D. 15), after whom he was named. He seems to have taken part in the Alexandrian Jewish embassy to Gaius in A.D. 39/40 (Anim 54). Upon the accession of Claudius in A.D. 41, and possibly due to the mediation of Agrippa I, he entered Roman service and was known as Epistrategos of the Thebaid by A.D. 42. He became Procurator of Judaea under Claudius (ca. A.D. 46—48) and Prefect of Egypt under Nero (A.D. 66—70). He secured Alexandria for Vespasian (A.D. 69) and became Chief of Staff under Titus during the siege of Jerusalem (A.D. 70). There are a number of good studies on Alexander that deal with the passages in Josephus, the Egyptian inscriptions and papyri, and the Roman authorities. See A. STEIN, Iulius, n. 59, PW, XIX (1918), cols. 153—157 and ID., Die Präfekten von Ägypten in der römischen Kaiserzeit (Bern, 1950), pp. 37—38; A. LEPAPE, Tiberius Iulius Alexander, Préfet d'Alexandrie et d'Egypte, Bulletin de la Société Royale d'Archéologie d'Alexandrie, 8 (1934), 311—341; E. R. GOODENOUGH, The Politics of Philo Judaeus: Practice and Theory (New Haven, 1938), pp. 64—66; E. G. TURNER, Tiberius Iulius Alexander, The Journal of Roman Studies, 44 (1954), 54—64 (excellent discussion); V. BURR, Tiberius Iulius Alexander, Antiquitas: Abhandlungen zur alten Geschichte, 1 (Bonn, 1955) (excellent documentation); J. SCHWARTZ, Note sur la famille de Philon d'Alexandrie, Mélanges Isidore Lévy = Annuaire de l'institut de philologie et d'histoire orientales et slaves, 13 (Bruxelles, 1955), 591—602; and J. DANIÉLOU, Philon d'Alexandrie (Paris, 1958), pp. 11—39.

[3] J. B. AUCHER, Philonis Judaei sermones tres hactenus inediti: I et II de providentia et III de animalibus (Venice, 1822). No English translation of the Armenian text of Provid I—II was ever attempted. A recently completed study by the author, 'Philonis Alexandrini De Animalibus: The Armenian Text with an Introduction, Translation, and Commentary' (Diss. Basel, 1979), has just been published by the Philo Institute as: Studies in Hellenistic Judaism, Supplements to Studia Philonica, 1 (Chico, Calif., 1981). Translations of the Greek fragments of Provid II are readily available in translations of Eus. PE VII 21. 336b—337a (§§ 50—51); VII 14. 386—399 (§§ 3, 15—33a, 99—112). A translation of these fragments by F. H. COLSON is part of vol. IX of the LCL edition of Philo (Cambridge, Mass., 1941); a German version of the Latin translation of Provid I—II is found in: Philo von Alexandria, Die Werke in deutscher Übersetzung, VII, ed. W. THEILER (Berlin, 1964), translated by L. FRÜCHTEL; and a French translation basically of the Latin by M. HADAS-LEBEL, De Providentia I et II, constitutes vol. XXXV of 'Les œuvres de Philon d'Alexandrie' (Paris, 1973).

[4] H. LEWY, The Pseudo-Philonic De Jona. Part I: The Armenian Text with a Critical Introduction, Studies and Documents, 6 (London, 1936), 15—16.

[5] See especially the two recent editions cited above, n. 3.

Armenian translation, to be sure, is complete; however, the text[6] reflects occasional corruptions not only in its transmission but also in the lost Greek, such as the destroyed interlocutory setting throughout Provid I[7]. Moreover, the Armenian maintains the word order of the Greek, thus giving rise to syntactical difficulties that are not fully resolved in the Latin version rendered by J. B. AUCHER[8]. Consequently, his version has at times misled the few, more or less cautious translators who have relied on it.

It is regrettable that not all of Philo's works are extant. It is even more regrettable, because remediable, that the corpus of his extant works is not currently available in any modern language; indeed, not treated even in the two well-known indices to his works[9], which exclude not just the works that survive only in Armenian but even the Greek fragments of these works. The resulting partial study and use of Philo's works, coupled with the partial interest of those attracted to him, have left much to be desired in Philo scholarship. It is against such partial focusing on Philo that E. R. GOODENOUGH rightly warns, "We shall know Philo only when we accept him as a whole, and on his own terms," and goes on to add, "To do any special study of Philo without at least a sense of his writings as a whole is extremely dangerous"[10]. The lack of such an approach in Philo studies must have added to the neglect of the dialogues.

The dialogues were further neglected because of the unwarranted verdicts of those who declared them, along with the enigmatic Aet[11] and Quod Omn, 'youthful works', 'belonging to his early life'. Philo, they said, must have graduated from these 'purely philosophical', 'commonplace school exercises' into a theological maturity demonstrated in his exegetical works[12]. Thus, pro-

---

[6] No critical edition of the Armenian text as yet exists. For a catalogue of the Armenian MSS and their textual relationships, see the author's 'Philonis Alexandrini De Animalibus,' pp. 14–25.

[7] In its present form Provid I is not a dialogue but a sort of an exposition on the subject of providence. From its opening paragraphs H. DIELS, Doxographi Graeci (Berlin, 1879), p. 4, concluded that it must have been dialogical in form. This is further substantiated by the opening paragraphs of Provid II, as it is rightly observed by P. WENDLAND, Philos Schrift über die Vorsehung, ein Beitrag zur Geschichte der nacharistotelischen Philosophie (Berlin, 1892), pp. 38, 85.

[8] See above, n. 3; also Philonis Judaei paralipomena Armena: libri videlicet quatuor in Genesin, libri duo in Exodum, sermo unus de Sampsone, alter de Jona, tertius de tribus angelis Abraamo apparentibus (Venice, 1826), and the English translation by R. MARCUS in the LCL edition, Philo, Supplement I–II (Cambridge, Mass., 1953).

[9] H. LEISEGANG, Philonis Alexandrini opera quae supersunt, Indices, I–II (Berlin, 1926–1930) and G. MEYER, Index Philoneus (Berlin, 1974).

[10] An Introduction to Philo Judaeus, p. 19.

[11] For a survey of the questions surrounding this work, see the recent perceptive study by D. T. RUNIA, Philo's 'De aeternitate mundi': The Problem of Its Interpretation, Vigiliae Christianae, 35 (1981), 105–151.

[12] See, e.g., P. WENDLAND, Philos Schrift περὶ τοῦ πάντα σπουδαῖον . . . (Quod Omn), Archiv für Geschichte der Philosophie, 1 (1888), 509–517; L. COHN, Einteilung und Chronologie der Schriften Philos, Philologus Supplementband, 7 (1899), 389–391, 426; W. VON CHRIST, Geschichte der griechischen Litteratur II, Handbuch der klassischen Altertums-Wissenschaft, VII (6th ed.; Munich, 1920), 627–631. With the publication of

ponents of these views attempted to construct a chronological order of the works, dividing them basically into three groups: philosophical, exegetical, and historical or apologetic (the second and largest division in turn is subdivided into three groups or major commentaries on the Pentateuch)[13]. While this is not the place to discuss the chronological order of the works, suffice it to say that the divisions and subdivisions are acceptable, but their 'established' sequence and possibly the 'philosophical' designation are not[14].

In the course of a critical introduction to the dialogues, we shall provide synopses, survey the philosophical background, clarify the identity of the speakers, raise the question of authorship, and in discussing the date of composition we shall ascribe the dialogues to the closing years of the author's life. Moreover, by pointing to Philo's concurrent interest in philosophy and theology, the comparatively short period of his literary career, his tendency of gradual departure from the biblical text even in the commentaries on the Pentateuch, and the apologetic thrust of his works in general, we shall endeavor to show that the dialogues are more closely related to the rest of his works than is generally supposed.

I. Synopses

In Provid I—II Philo maintains belief in the providential sustenance of the world and his apostate nephew, Alexander, propounds disbelief. In Anim Alexander argues for the rationality of animals and Philo for their irrationality. Philo expresses displeasure with Alexander's philosophic position in both works.

Provid I lacks the interlocutory setting of Provid II. The book opens with a statement on the subject under consideration and an introduction to the syllogistic method employed in the reasoning (1—5). There follow three main discussions, each ending with a recapitulation of the workings of Providence. The first of these discussions is on the eternity of the world: its creation, governance, and

---

G. TAPPE's De Philonis libro qui inscribitur Ἀλέξανδρος ἢ περὶ τοῦ λόγον ἔχειν τὰ ἄλογα ζῷα quaestiones selectae (Diss. Göttingen, 1912), especially pp. 3—6, the placing of the dialogues at the very beginning of Philo's works tends to become customary. W. BOUSSET, Jüdisch-christlicher Schulbetrieb in Alexandria und Rom. Literarische Untersuchungen zu Philo und Clemens von Alexandria, Justin und Irenäus, Forschungen zur Religion und Literatur des Alten und Neuen Testaments, N.F. 6 (Göttingen, 1915), 137—148, ascribes the dialogues with Alexander to the days of Philo's philosophical training. H. LEISEGANG, Philon, PW, XXXIX (1941), cols. 6—8, likewise lists the dialogues first as does also A. LESKY, Geschichte der griechischen Literatur (Bern, 1957—1958), p. 729; et al.

[13] This was correctly perceived by H. EWALD, Geschichte des Volkes Israel, VI (3rd ed.; Göttingen, 1868), 257—312, as was also the correct order of the subdivisions.

[14] The author's reconstruction of the chronological order of Philo's works will appear in a forthcoming book: From Biblical Exposition to Apologetics: Literary Tendencies in Philo of Alexandria.

destruction (6–36); the second on the problems of natural catastrophies, protection, and retribution (37–76); and the last on the absurdities of astrological
fatalism (77–88). A summary of the arguments is given in conclusion (89–92).

Provid II maintains the form of a dialogue. It begins with Alexander's early
visit to Philo to resume the discussions of yesterday (1–2). Parts of the first two
discussions of Book I receive further consideration: the problem of retribution
(3–44) and that of the cosmos – its creation (45–58), governance (59–84), and
natural phenomena (85–112). In the epilogue Philo thinks he has given satis-
factory answers to Alexander's difficulties and goes on to invite further questions,
but Alexander politely declines (113–116).

Anim falls into two parts, each preceded by a short dialogue between Philo
and his interlocutor, Lysimachus (1–9, 72–76), a nephew of Alexander. Alexander's discourse on the rationality of animals, purportedly read in his presence,
comprises the first part (10–71) and Philo's refutation of Alexander's premise, the
second (77–100). Alexander begins his polemical discourse with sweeping
denunciations of man's appropriation of reason to himself (10–11). He attempts
to show among the brutes instances of the προφορικὸς λόγος, the reason which
finds utterance and expression (12–15). Then follows a lengthy argument for
their possession of the ἐνδιάθετος λόγος, the inner reason or thought (16–71).
Some talking and singing birds constitute the examples for the first kind of reason;
but the examples for the second kind of reason are far more numerous, including
not only such stock examples as spiders, bees, and swallows (16–22), but also
several performing animals (23–29) and a large number of others in whom
demonstrations of virtues and vices are postulated to exist (30–71). Philo,
haphazardly and with some lack of kindness to his opponent, argues that animals
do not possess reason. He ascribes the seemingly rational acts of animals to the
reasoning of nature (77–100). By emphasizing the rationality of animals, Alexander argues for a moral and juridical relationship between man and animals (10,
his opening remarks). This Philo rejects by insisting that there can be no equality
between man, who is privileged with reason, and animals devoid of it (100, his
concluding remarks).

II. The Philosophical Background

Platonism and Stoicism have long been regarded as being of major importance in moulding Philo's thought, which none the less remains excessively
religious in tone and determined by its Jewish outlook. The strength of the Stoic
influence is clearly seen in the responses to Alexander in Provid I–II and Anim[15].

---

[15] C. J. DE VOGEL, Greek Philosophy, III: The Hellenistic-Roman Period (Leiden, 1963),
81, finds in Provid II a systematic exposition of the objections against providence and their
refutation by the Stoics. The same could be said of Book I and Anim. On Philo's Stoicism,
see especially M. POHLENZ, Philon von Alexandreia, Nachrichten von der Gesellschaft der

While Philo's frequent use of Stoic terms with a meaning not at all Stoic may be true of several of his other works, it certainly is not true of these treatises, for there are major arguments as well as points of detail in which his thought, terminology, and phraseology are explicable by the Stoic background. Note that selections from about half of his responses to Alexander in these treatises are included in H. VON ARNIM's 'Stoicorum veterum fragmenta'[16]. Certainly, there seem to be more Stoic views expressed by Philo than VON ARNIM has admitted into his compilation.

Philo's cosmology in the dialogues owes not so much to Plato's 'Timaeus' as to a Stoic interpretation of that work. Likewise, his views on free will, deliberation, voluntary and involuntary acts, and responsibility for virtue and vice — views broadly developed in the dialogues — owe not so much to Aristotle's 'Ethica Nicomachea' as to Stoic ethical thought surrounding Aristotle's morals. Although like the Stoics Philo believed in a cosmic destiny which could override man's choice, his belief in a personal predestinating God differed sharply from the impersonal fatalism inherent in the Stoic doctrine of providence. And it is not that he is siding with the Stoics against Epicurean and Academic denial of providential care by the gods as perhaps arguing indirectly for a biblical understanding of Divine Providence[17].

The arguments attributed to Alexander in the dialogues were doubtless taken over by Philo from the arguments used by the opponents of the Stoics in the New Academy[18]. Chief among the opponents was Carneades of Cyrene, who flourished as head of the Academy in the middle of the 2nd century B.C. Like

Wissenschaften zu Göttingen, Philologisch-historische Klasse, N.F. 1, 5 (1942), 409—487. Numerous examples of Philo's supporting the Stoa against the New Academy can be cited throughout his responses to Alexander. In defending Divine Providence the distinction was made between God's primary works and the secondary or consequential effects (Provid II 100); e.g., eclipses are consequential effects, not God's primary intentions (79). Moreover, Philo is at one with the Stoics in the fundamental position that the irrational creation providentially exists for the sake of the rational (see below, nn. 23—24). In Provid I 22; II 48, 74 (SVF I, 85, 509, 548) he cites Zeno, Cleanthes, and Chrysippus by name. While no such names occur in Anim, two of the illustrations can be traced to Chrysippus (45—46, 84 [SVF II, 726], 88; see also SVF II, 1163, 1165; cf. 714—737). Much of the discussion in the latter treatise centers around uttered reason or speech (λόγος προφορικός) and mental reasoning or thought (λόγος ἐνδιάθετος). The distinction between these two kinds of reason, implied in Plato (Tht. 189E; Sph. 263E) and Aristotle (AP. 76b24), was emphasized by the Stoics in their debates with the New Academy: SVF II, 135, 233, etc.; for a fine discussion, see M. POHLENZ, Die Begründung der abendländischen Sprachlehre durch die Stoa, Nachrichten von der Gesellschaft der Wissenschaften zu Göttingen, Philologisch-historische Klasse, N.F. 1, 3 (Göttingen, 1939), 151—198. Subsequently, the distinction was employed by Philo (see especially Anim 12, 98—99 [SVF II, 734]; cf. Quod Det 40, 92, 129; Mut 69; Abr 83; Vita Mos II 127—130; Spec Leg IV 69) et al.; see M. MÜHL, Der λόγος ἐνδιάθετος und προφορικός in der älteren Stoa bis zur Synode von Sirmium 351, Archiv für Begriffsgeschichte, 7 (Bonn, 1962).

[16] 1—4 (Leipzig, 1903—1924).

[17] For a broader discussion of Philo's cosmology and theodicy in Provid I—II, see M. HADAS-LEBEL, De Providentia I—II, pp. 58—117, especially 90—91, 144—145 nn. 1—2.

[18] Cic. ND III 66—85; Fat. 11. 23—28; S.E.P. I 62—77.

Epicurus, Carneades insisted that the world's omnipresent imperfections militate against the Stoic belief in providential design in the world, the main example of which was claimed to be man himself — providentially endowed with reason and equipped for a virtuous life. Man's possession of reason, Carneades argued, speaks against providence rather than for it, since its actual use is determined by man's free will. And what about evidences of reason among the brutes as seen in their movements or actions? These and other questions raised by Carneades and his predecessor, Arcesilaus, greatly challenged the Stoic philosophers from Chrysippus to Posidonius — to whom the cumulative Stoic reply may be traced[19]. Like most other arguments, those against providence and the irrationality of animals led the Stoics to create an arsenal of counter arguments which Philo, like later Stoics and others, exploits[20]. His ingenuity in putting both the Academic criticism and the Stoic responses into good use appears in Provid I—II and Anim, where he reiterates the Stoic position against the Academic criticism he attributes to Alexander.

It is indeed difficult to discuss any aspect of Stoic doctrine without considering the interconnected mosaic of the whole philosophy — and that in the light of the fragmentary evidence. No doubt the questions of providence and the nature of man and animals and their relationship to the rest of nature are among the problems in Stoicism. In a broad sense, the workings of providence range throughout the universe: from the majestic cycles of heavenly bodies to the minutest anatomical details of insects[21]. In support of their doctrine of providence the Stoics brought forward evidences of design throughout nature. They attributed to the workings of providence not only cosmic phenomena but also the peculiar characteristics of the various creatures: their inclinations or dispositions to move in a particular direction or act in a certain way as a result of some inherent

[19] K. REINHARDT, Poseidonios (Munich, 1921), pp. 39—58, 124—127, 356—365. P. WEND-LAND, Philos Schrift über die Vorsehung (Berlin, 1892), pp. 83—84, identifies Posidonius as a primary source; cf. ID., Die philosophischen Quellen des Philo von Alexandria in seiner Schrift über die Vorsehung, Programm (Berlin, 1892) and M. APPELT, De rationibus quibusdam quae Philoni Alexandrino cum Posidonio intercedunt (Diss. Jena, 1906; Leipzig, 1907); so also M. POHLENZ, Tierische und menschliche Intelligenz bei Poseidonios, Hermes, 76 (1941), 1—13.

[20] Note that Chrysippus wrote 'On Providence' (Περὶ προνοίας, SVF III, App. II, p. 203) and Antipater of Tarsus wrote 'On Animals' (Περὶ ζῴων, SVF III, Ant. 48). Among later Stoics and others, note Cicero, in Book III of 'De finibus', which derives from traditional Stoic sources, and Book II of 'De natura deorum', which provides the closest parallels to Provid II; Seneca, in Book I of 'Dialogi', in the various 'Epistulae', and in the preface to 'Naturales quaestiones'; Epictetus in his 'Dissertationes'; Pliny in Books VIII and IX of his 'Naturalis historia'; Plutarch in three of his works 'De sollertia animalium' (Mor. 959 A—985 C), 'Bruta animalia ratione uti' (985 D—992 E), and 'De esu carnium' I—II (993 A—999 B); Aelian in 'De natura animalium'; Oppian in 'Cynegetica'; Origenes in 'Contra Celsum' (especially Book IV); Porphyry in 'De abstinentia' (especially Book III); in certain of the extant works of the Peripatetic Alexander of Aphrodisias: Περὶ ψυχῆς I, Περὶ εἱμαρμένης; et al.

[21] Provid I 51—53; Epict. Diss. I 16. 1—8; Origenes Cels. IV 54; etc. See also M. HADAS-LEBEL, De Providentia I—II, p. 52.

quality or habit. They argued that the apparent evidences of reasoned action shown by animals are not due to reason but to their natural constitution; the universal, causal reason is at work and not that of the animal[22]. We regret that it is not possible to discuss briefly that broad conception of nature or universal reason inherent in the Stoic monism.

As to the relationship of animals to humans, the Stoics argued that the irrational creation providentially exists for the sake of the rational, that animals were created for the sake of humans — just as humans were created for the sake of the gods[23]. This anthropocentric teleology, which finds its strongest proponent in Chrysippus[24], characterizes the whole cosmology of the Stoics. It is well known that they studied the cosmos primarily to understand man's place in the realm of things[25]. They explained a creature's self-consciousness and relationship to its environment by formulating the doctrine of affinity or endearment (οἰκείωσις)[26], which was held as a natural principle of justice. Among animals this principle is seen in their longing for self-preservation, in their love for offspring, and even in the association of different species for their mutual advantage; moreover, it is attested through its opposite, the natural aversion or antipathy (ἀλλοτρίωσις) between certain species[27]. With humans, however, this relationship is so intimate and peculiar that it would be unjust to extend it to lower animals. The Stoics explained man's self-consciousness in terms of his rationality and his affective relationships, beginning, naturally, with relations according to propinquity and moving on to the rest of mankind[28]. To this fraternity of rationals as a *civitas*

---

[22] SVF II, 714–737, 988; on the totalizing value given to nature, see 1106–1186. For a good discussion see J. CHRISTENSEN, An Essay on the Unity of Stoic Philosophy (Copenhagen, 1962).

[23] SVF II, 1152–1167; cf. the selections from Provid II in 1141–1150.

[24] Chrysippus went so far as to say that the pig was made more fecund than other animals in order to be a fitting food for man or a convenient sacrifice to the gods, horses assist man in fighting, wild animals exercise man's courage; the peacock is created for his tail and the peahen for accompanying symmetry, the flea is useful to prevent oversleeping, and the mouse to prevent carelessness in leaving the cheese about (Porph. Abst. III 20 [SVF II, 1152]; Plu. Mor. 1044 C–D [SVF II, 1163]; Porphyry adds that Chrysippus' views were criticized by Carneades [ibid.]; Plutarch reiterates similar views in 1065 B [SVF II, 1181]: the serpent's venom and the hyena's bile are useful in medicine). Philo reflects similar views (Provid II 84 [SVF II, 149], 91–92, 103; cf. Vita Mos I 60–62; Spec Leg IV 119–121). M. POHLENZ thinks such anthropocentrism is alien to Greek thought and hence must be of Semitic origin: Die Stoa. Geschichte einer geistigen Bewegung, I (Göttingen, 1964), 100.

[25] D.L. VII 88; cf. M. Ant. IV 23; X 6.

[26] S. G. PEMBROKE, Oikeiōsis, in: Problems in Stoicism, ed. A. A. LONG (London, 1971), pp. 114–149.

[27] See the passages cited under 'De primo appetitu et prima conciliatione' in: SVF III, 178–189.

[28] In addition to the Ciceronian passages in the reference above, see the numerous other references in S. G. PEMBROKE's excellent article, Oikeiōsis, especially pp. 121–132; cf. Mut 226; Vita Cont 70.

deorum atque hominum lower animals do not belong, for they are unequal in that they do not possess reason. Therefore, the Stoics maintained, there is no such thing as a justice which can obtain between humans and animals. Man cannot be charged with injustice when he makes unilateral use of animals, for it is to this end that animals are providentially made or naturally equipped[29].

The Stoa became vulnerable to the attacks of the New Academy for cherishing these and other views, particularly those on the role of sense-perception — which is also shared by creatures without reason — in the acquisition of knowledge[30]. The Academics seem to have argued that animals cannot make use of sense-perception without some knowledge or understanding[31]. But it was not so much improvidence and the rationality of animals that the opponents of the Stoics wanted to emphasize as man's free will and the denial of the possibility of knowledge or the existence of any positive proof or criterion for truth. They wanted to maintain an attitude of suspended judgment and thus utilized among other arguments the questions of improvidence in the world and evidences of rationality among the brutes[32]. To support their major arguments they often made use of material gathered by the Stoics themselves. Philo uses these arguments and counter-arguments systematically, placing them in a dialogical setting[33].

III. The Speakers

With regard to the speakers in the dialogues, there can be no doubt about the identity of Philo and his apostate nephew; however, the identity of Philo's interlocutor in Anim, Lysimachus, has been confused. The confusion arises from certain parts of the introductory and transitory dialogues between Philo (1, 75) and Lysimachus (72), where both of them refer to Alexander as "our nephew". This common reference to Alexander by Philo and Lysimachus led to an erroneous identification of Lysimachus as a brother of Philo, taking him to be either Alexander the Alabarch, Philo's notoriously wealthy brother and father of Tiberius Iulius Alexander[34], or another younger brother[35].

---

[29] See the passages cited under 'Iuris communionem non pertinere ad bruta animalia' in: SVF III, 367–376, and those cited under 'Animalia (et plantas) propter hominum utilitatem facta esse' in: SVF II, 1152–1167.

[30] Ibid.

[31] Plu. Mor. 960D–961B.

[32] M. POHLENZ, Die Stoa, I, 37–63, 98–101; II, 21–36, 55–58; F. H. SANDBACH, Phantasia Kataleptike, in: Problems in Stoicism, ed. A. A. LONG (London, 1971), pp. 9–21.

[33] For a discussion on the use of sources, see M. HADAS-LEBEL, De Providentia I–II, pp. 65–67 and the author's 'Philonis Alexandrini De Animalibus,' pp. 53–56.

[34] It is to be suspected that from a mistaken interpretation of these passages, the name Lysimachus has been added to the name of Alexander the Alabarch in the 11th century

Such an identification of Lysimachus distorts his true identity clearly stated in § 2, where, speaking of Alexander, he says: "He is my uncle (lit., mother's brother) and my father-in-law as well. As you are not unaware, his daughter is engaged (lit., promised by an [betrothal] agreement) to be my wife". J. B. AUCHER translates these lines correctly: „*Avunculus enim est, ac simul socer: quoniam non es nescius, quod filia eius mihi juxta suam etiam promissionem desponsata uxor est*". However, being puzzled by Philo's and Lysimachus' calling Alexander "our nephew", he leaves the question of relation unresolved[36]. G. TAPPE, who insists that Lysimachus is a brother of Philo and of the Alabarch, on the authority of a certain ANDREAS declares the text of this passage to be corrupt and goes on to provide the following translation: „*Avunculus enim sum ac simul socer: quoniam non es nescius quod filia mea ei iuxta meam etiam promissionem desponsata uxor est*"[37]. There is no basis for these forced emendations. Moreover, if Lysimachus is a brother of Philo and of the Alabarch (Alexander's father) and at the same time Alexander's "mother's brother", then the Alabarch would have married his own sister.

The absolutely clear relationship indicated in § 2 must stand and the references to Alexander as "our nephew" by Philo (1, 75) and Lysimachus (72) must be explained — especially the latter. Two possible solutions are proposed: (1) Just as Philo in §§ 1 and 75 refers to Alexander as "our nephew", using a plural of modesty, likewise Lysimachus in § 72 refers to Alexander as "our nephew" out of respect to his interlocutor, Philo. Note that Lysimachus' reference to "Alexander, our nephew" comes immediately after addressing Philo as "honorable" (ὦ τίμιε Φίλων), an address used earlier in § 2. (2) A possible corruption of "your nephew" to "our nephew", either in the Greek ὁ ἀδελφιδοῦς ὑμῶν to ὁ ἀδελφιδοῦς ἡμῶν or in the Armenian *եղբաւրորդին ձեր* to *եղբաւրորդին մեր*, may be suspected in § 72 (the possibly confused letters are underlined)[38].

The genealogical table below is based on Anim 1–2, 72, 75, and the passages in Josephus[39].

Ambrosian MS of Josephus (AJ XIX 276; cf. XVIII 159–160, 259–260; XX 100–103; BJ V 205); see M. POHLENZ, Philon von Alexandreia, p. 413. A. SCHALIT notes: „*Der zweite Name* Λυσίμαχος *in A 19 276 ist zweifelhaft*". K. H. RENGSTORF (ed.) s. v. Ἀλέξανδρος (no. 7) [Λυσίμαχος] Alabarch von Alexandrien, in: Namenwörterbuch zu Flavius Josephus. A Complete Concordance to Flavius Josephus, Supplement I (Leiden, 1968), 8. This erroneous association of the names is quite common.

[35] G. TAPPE, Ἀλέξανδρος, pp. 4–5. This equally misleading identification has influenced a host of scholars (including P. WENDLAND, TAPPE's major professor, and his associates) down to the present.

[36] Sermones tres, p. xi, n. 1.

[37] Ἀλέξανδρος, pp. 4–5.

[38] The confusion of the Armenian letters in these pronouns is as common as those in the Greek pronouns.

[39] AJ XVIII 159–160, 259–260; XIX 276–277; XX 100–103; BJ V 205 (cf. 44–46; II 220, 223, 309. 492–498; VI 236–243, on Alexander's career in Roman service).

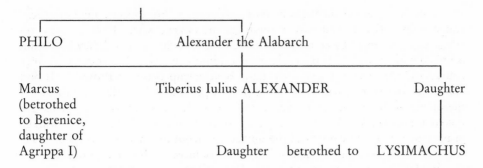

Considering the social status of the family of Lysimachus and his relation to Alexander, it is very likely that he too pursued a political career. He might be the same Iulius Lysimachus mentioned in 'Publications de la Sociéte Fouad I de Papyrologie', éd. par O. Guéraud et al., Cairo, 1939, III, 21, 8, whose three representatives appear among the nine magistrates with Tuscus the Prefect at the tribunal in the Great Atrium to hear grievances from veterans (dated Sebastos 7 of Nero's 10th year [September 5, A. D. 63])[40].

IV. The Question of Authorship

P. Wendland gives overwhelming evidence of the genuineness of Provid I—II by showing philosophical, linguistic, and stylistic affinities between these books and the rest of the works of Philo[41]. Likewise, the numerous parallels between Anim and the Philonic passages cited in a recently published commentary by the author, suggest more than just a common literary heritage or use of sources[42]. The Jewish authorship is clearly indicated in Provid I 22, 84; II 106—107[43]. While no such indication is found in Anim, its authorship can hardly be considered apart from that of Provid I—II.

[40] E. Balogh and H. G. Pflaum, Le 'concilium' du Préfet d'Égypte. Sa composition, Revue historique de droit français et étranger, 30 (1952), 123, identified with Alexander the Alabarch; E. G. Turner, Tiberius Iulius Alexander, p. 56, n. 17, suggests that he might be the nephew of Alexander. For the contents of the papyrus, see U. Wilcken, ed., Archiv für Papyrusforschung und verwandte Gebiete, 14 (1941), 174—175; W. L. Westermann, Tuscus the Prefect and the Veterans in Egypt (P. Yale Inv. 1528 and P. Fouad I, 21), Classical Philology, 36 (1941), 21—29.

[41] 'Philos Schrift über die Vorsehung,' written primarily in response to L. Massebieau, who doubted the Philonic authorship of Provid I: Le classement des œuvres de Philon, Bibliothèque de l'école des hautes études, Sciences religieuses, 1 (Paris, 1889), 87—90. See also M. Hadas-Lebel, De Providentia I et II, pp. 26—28, 357—361.

[42] See above, n. 3.

[43] F. H. Colson wrongly observes: "There are no allusions to the O. T., and no mention of Moses; the one and only fact which suggests that the writer is a Jew is the personal allusion to his visit to Jerusalem via Ascalon (§ 64) [II 106—107]". Philo, LCL IX, 448.

Philo's opponent throughout these dialogues is his apostate nephew Alexander. Provid II is linked with Provid I at the outset, where Philo remarks on Alexander's coming "to go over what is left on Providence" (1). Likewise, Anim is linked with Provid I—II by a reference to Philo's rejecting Alexander's "former courtesies" (3). There is also a thematic relationship between Provid I—II and Anim: the latter deals with a certain aspect of providence and thus complements the theme of the former (providence and the question of animal intelligence are linked in Provid I 51—53; cf. II 91—92, 103—108). In a broad sense, the workings of providence range throughout the universe — from the majestic cycles of heavenly bodies to the minutest anatomical details of insects. Moreover, both treatises are developed with a wealth of stock illustrations commonplace in Academic-Stoic controversies regarding divine providence and the rationality of animals. In both works Philo systematically supports the Stoic position against the Academic criticism which he attributes to Alexander. The Alexandrian origin of both treatises is certain: Provid II 55 and Anim 13 and 28 refer to Alexandria in Egypt, and Anim 7 alludes to a mixed assembly of Romans and Alexandrians. Besides, both titles have the testimony of Eusebius who cites them conjointly in his list of Philo's works[44].

The parody of an opponent's imagined speech is a common literary device. Interestingly enough, a selection of Alexander's arguments (Provid II 3) is introduced by Eusebius as a statement by Philo himself of the objections which opponents might adduce[45]. There can be little doubt about Alexander's cherishing the Academic questions attributed to him in Provid I—II and Anim. In answering him Philo, like the Stoics before him, finds himself in a predicament and, in search for answers, sometimes contradicts himself (cf. Provid II 32 and 102; 105 and 110). Some of the questions purportedly raised by Alexander in these dialogues are not even dealt with in Philo's replies. The composition of the treatises, however, may be taken with fair certainty to be Philo's. F. H. COLSON makes this observation on Provid I—II, "Philo was able to manipulate, even if he did not entirely invent, the part which Alexander plays and he does not seem to have treated his opponent fairly"[46].

H. DIELS was the first to suspect a tampering with Provid I[47]. He based his doubts about the originality of this book on two observations: its form differs from that of Provid II and the list of philosophical opinions in it corresponds with that in the 'De placitis epitome', a work which was once attributed to Plutarch but now to Aëtius, and which must be at least a hundred years later than Philo. DIELS' valid observations, however, led to erroneous conclusions, especially his thought that the present form of Provid I follows the pseudo-Plutarchian 'Placita'. The

---

[44] HE II 18.1—6; cf. Jerome De viris illustribus 11. For more on the preceding points, see above, Part II, p. 278 ff.

[45] PE VIII 14. 386, Ταῦτα εἰς ἀνασκευὴν καὶ μυρία ἄλλα πλείω τούτων εἰπών, ἑξῆς ἐπιλύεται τὰς ἀντιθέσεις διὰ τούτων. "After stating these and a host of others on the negative side he [Philo] next proceeds to refute the objections as follows".

[46] Philo, LCL IX, 449.

[47] Doxographi Graeci (Berlin, 1879), pp. 1—4.

differences between Provid I and II and the similarities between Provid I and the 'Placita' call for another, perhaps more accurate, interpretation. First, the composition of Provid I–II does not necessarily require an identical form throughout. Philo could have followed different forms in each of the two books, just as he did follow still another form in Anim. Examples of different forms even within single books abound in classical literature. Second, Philo and Aëtius after him must have made use of the same Peripatetic source which is found also in Stobaeus' 'Eclogae' and which may be traced ultimately to Theophrastus' Περὶ φυσικῶν δοξῶν.

The single authorship of Anim may be demonstrated through its structure, patterned after the first part of Plato's 'Phaedrus' (227 A – 237 A). Moreover, there seems to be further reliance on Plato's thought as expressed in the 'Phaedrus'. Since the Greek of Anim no longer exists, the following parallels between the introductory and transitory dialogues preceding and following Alexander's discourse in Anim (1–9, 72–76) and the introductory and transitory dialogues preceding and following Lysias' discourse in the 'Phaedrus' (227A–230E, 234D–237A) are most conveniently given in English translation[48]:

Philo's 'De animalibus'

"(1) PHILO: You remember the recent arguments, Lysimachus, which Alexander, our nephew, cited in this regard, that not only men but also dumb animals possess reason.

(2) LYSIMACHUS: Admittedly, honorable Philo, some differing opinions have been amicably presented to the speaker three times since then, for he is my uncle, and my father-in-law as well. As you are not unaware, his daughter is engaged to be my wife. Let us resume the discussion of this long, difficult, and wearisome subject and its absurd interpretation which does not appeal to me since it affects the clear light by distorting the obvious evidence.

(3) PHILO: With regard to clever sophistries, it is agreed that one ought to listen to them carefully, for nothing else seems to be so helpful to good

Plato's 'Phaedrus'

"And meeting the man who is sick with the love of discourse, he was glad when he saw him, because he would have someone to share his revel (228 B).

He said the same thing two or three times, as if he did not find it easy to say many things about one subject, or perhaps he did not care about such a detail (235 A).

Well then, my dearest, what the subject is, about which we are to take counsel, has been said and defined, and now let us continue keeping our attention fixed upon that definition (238 D).

---

[48] The translation of Plato's 'Phaedrus' is that of H. N. FOWLER, LCL I (Cambridge, Mass., 1914), 412–449, including the Greek text en face.

learning as to critically examine what the propagator is declaring. Had he truly wished to continue learning, he would not have allowed himself to become occupied with other concerns. Tell me, why would he leave his other affairs and come merely to entertain a relative with useless words designed to tickle the ears? Such an action would be considered neither kind nor appropriate by that person who has already rejected his former courtesies. Therefore do not anticipate receiving a particularly significant response to your request. You will not get very far with your request.

What was your conversation? But it is obvious that Lysias entertained you with his speeches (227 B).

Believe this of me, that I am very fond of you, but when Lysias is here I have not the slightest intention of lending you my ears to practice on (228 E).

But when the lover of discourse asked him to speak, he feigned coyness, as if he did not yearn to speak; at last, however, even if no one would listen willingly, he was bound to speak whether or no (228 C).

(4) LYSIMACHUS: Is not his want of leisure, Philo, the reason? You are not unaware of how many things are involved given relatives and social and community affairs at home.

What Lysias, the cleverest writer of our day, composed at his leisure and took a long time for (228 A).

(5) PHILO: Since I know that you are interested, indeed that you are always eager to hear new things, I shall begin to speak if you will keep quiet and not always interrupt my speech by making forceful remarks on the same matter.

(6) LYSIMACHUS: Such a restrictive order is unreasonable. But since it is expedient to seek and to ask for instruction, your order must be complied with. So here I sit quietly, modestly, and with restored humility as is proper for a student; and here you are seated in front of me on a platform, looking dignified, respectable, and erudite, ready to begin to teach your teachings.

I concede your point, for I think what you say is reasonable. So I will make this concession: I will allow you to begin (236 A).

So now that I have come here, I intend to lie down, and do you choose the position in which you think you can read most easily, and read (230 E).

(7) PHILO: I shall begin to interpret, but I will not teach, since I am an

I know very well that I have never invented these things myself, so the

interpreter and not a teacher. Those who teach impart their own knowledge to others, but those who interpret present from others information through accurate recall. And they do not do this just to a few Alexandrians and Romans — the eminent or the excellent, the privileged, the elite of the upper class, and those distinguished in music and other learning — gathered at a given place.

(8) The young man entered in a respectful manner, without that overconfident bearing that some have nowadays, but with a modest self-reliance that becomes a freeman — even a descendant of freemen. He sat down partly for his own instruction and partly because of his father's continuous, insistent urging.

(9) Eventually one of the slaves, who was sent to a place nearby, brought the manuscripts. Philo took them and was about to read.
(The MS of Alexander's discourse is brought forth and read [§§ 10—71]).

(72) LYSIMACHUS: These are the matters, honorable Philo, that Alexander, our nephew, presented and discussed when he came in.

(73) PHILO: Wonderful Lysimachus; time is longer than life! These matters may interest not only the peasants, but also those trained in philosophy. Now it is not as though I was not taught the things referred to; in fact I was nurtured with such instructions throughout childhood, on account of their certainty, intriguing names, and easy comprehension. And it is not that I studied them thoroughly, but surely I do know them well. Nor are you ignorant, as expressed by the tone of your

only alternative is that I have been filled through the ears, like a pitcher, from the well springs of another (235 C–D).

I know very well that when listening to Lysias he did not hear once only, but often urged him to repeat; and he gladly obeyed (228 A).

At last he borrowed the book and read what he especially wished (228 B).

(The MS of Lysias' discourse is brought forth and read [230 E–234 C]).

What do you think of the discourse . . . (234 C)?

Is it not wonderful . . .? More than that . . . (234 D).

I have not at all learned the words by heart; but I will repeat the general sense of the whole . . . in summary (228 D).

Now I am conscious of my own ignorance (235 C).

voice and indicated by the constant nodding of your head. Since you were listening to what was being read, what else would you need? You seemed to be absorbed like bacchanals and corybants, whose self-proclaimed revelations are not consistent with the reports of researchers and interpreters. On the one hand, there is a diction which results from the up and down movements of the tongue and terminates at the edges of the mouth; on the other hand, there is that which stems from the sovereign part of the soul and, through the marvelous employment of the vocal organ, makes sensible utterances.

As I looked at you, I saw that you were delighted by the speech as you read. So, thinking that you know more than I about such matters, I followed in your train and joined you in the divine frenzy (234 D).

(74) The affection of a father or of a mother for their children is unequaled. Even honest, wise, and knowledgeable parents blend with their words an indescribable affection when they relate their experiences to those who listen. They add quite a few nouns and verbs. That is fine and appropriate, you say. But from the interpreter's point of view, I admire your method. You appeared to present the subject much as the author himself would have presented it by reading. It seems to me that you have not omitted anything.

He has omitted none of the points that belong to the subject, so that nobody could ever speak about it more exhaustively or worthily than he has done (235 B).

(75) As for the recent questions which the young man raised, the new and diverse sophistries, and the terms used to delineate everything that is being disclosed, I am not persuaded by them as the fickleminded, whose habit is to be easily attracted by any fascinating thing. But I will thoroughly examine the truth, as one accustomed to do so, and will make it known to everyone after analyzing it critically. I must not always be impressionable to persuasive argumentation; otherwise

He appeared to me in youthful fashion to be exhibiting his ability (235 A).

what our nephew has already written, which is contrary to sound learning, would be readily believed. If you want to concern yourself with these matters, I will discuss them right now; but if you want to wait, let us agree to defer them to some other time.

You shall hear, if you have leisure to walk along and listen (227 B).

(76) LYSIMACHUS: Do you not realize Philo, that I hold in low esteem all other duties for the sake of my love for learning and hunger for truth? If you wish to teach these matters now, I would be most pleased."

Don't you believe that I consider hearing your conversation with Lysias 'a greater thing even than business', as Pindar says [I. i. 2] (227 B)?"

(Clearing of conscience at the beginning and at the end of the refutation [§§ 77, 100]).

(Clearing of conscience at the end of the refutation [242 C−243 E]).

V. The Date of Composition

Adding to the confusion that led to the traditional view of ascribing the dialogues to Philo's early life are the references to Alexander as "the young man" (ὁ νήπιος, Anim 8, 75). These are not to be taken literally as denoting age but rather, metaphorically or derogatorily, denoting inexperience or ignorance[49]. After all, time must be allowed for Alexander's maturity and familiarity with the authorities and the arguments he is made to cite in Provid I−II and Anim. Note that in Provid II he is referred to as ὁ ἀνήρ (1) and addressed as ὦ γεννα̃ιε (31, 62), ὦ θαυμάσιε (55), ὦ φίλε (56), etc.

There are two datable events recorded in Anim (27, 54). The celebrations spoken of in § 27 were given by Germanicus Iulius Caesar probably in A.D. 12, when he entered on his first term of consulship. The account, however, is taken from a literary source used also by Pliny (NH VIII 4) and Aelian (NA II 11). Some time, therefore, must be allowed for the period between the event and its literary description on the one hand and for the period between that literary composition and its use by Philo on the other hand. The embassy to Rome spoken of in § 54 is presumably the Alexandrian Jewish embassy to Gaius Caligula in A.D. 39/40. This delegation of five was headed by Philo himself and

---

[49] Numerous examples of the metaphorical use of the term can be cited from classical and biblical literatures.

probably included his brother, Alexander the Alabarch[50]. It now seems that Tiberius Iulius Alexander accompanied his uncle and, perhaps, his father on this delicate mission described in Philo's Gaium and Josephus' AJ, XVIII 257–260. The second of these two datable events is to be taken as determining the *terminus post quem* and not the first as is generally supposed. Thus, the *terminus post quem* of Anim has to be advanced by about thirty years.

Two other accounts in Anim (13, 58) can be dated by way of their datable parallels in Pliny. J. SCHWARTZ sees certain similarities between Anim 13 and NH X 120–121[51], where Pliny tells of a raven taught to salute by name first Tiberius, then Germanicus and Drusus, the sons of Tiberius – the first adopted – and that a talking thrush, a starling, and nightingales were owned by Agrippina, Claudius' fourth wife and niece, and the young princes: Britannicus, his son from previous marriage, and Nero, her son from previous marriage. SCHWARTZ goes on to suggest *"un nouveau* terminus post quem *de toute façon encore fort étoigné de la vraie date"*. His observation seems to indicate a post A.D. 48 date for the composition of Anim – after Claudius took Agrippina as his fourth wife. The horse-race account in Anim 58 is found also in Pliny NH VIII 160–161, where the event is said to have occurred during the secular games of Claudius Caesar, i.e. in A.D. 47[52].

Several other internal evidences indicate a late date for Anim. The introductory and transitory dialogues (1–9, 72–76) portray an old man conversing with a young relative, Lysimachus (see the genealogical table above), who twice addresses Philo as "honorable" (ὦ τίμιε Φίλων, 2, 72). Alexander had a daughter, probably in her teens, betrothed to her cousin, Lysimachus (2). Granting that Alexander was born early in the reign of Tiberius (ca. A.D. 15), whose *nomen* and *praenomen* he bears, was married in ca. A.D. 35 at the age of twenty, he would by ca. A.D. 50 have been in his mid-thirties, with a teenage daughter. Moreover, Alexander seems to have held some public office (3–4) and, probably, was beyond Philo's reach[53]. His apostasy, spoken of by Josephus in AJ XX 100, that "he did not persevere in his ancestral practices" (τοῖς πατρίοις οὐ διέμεινεν ἔθεσιν), is clearly reflected in the citation of oysters as fit for food – contrary to Jewish dietary laws (31; cf. Provid II 92).

The following life sketch of Alexander should prove to be of some help in establishing the tentatively drawn dates for his birth, marriage, and betrothal of his teenage daughter[54]. The events mentioned in Anim 54 and 2 are underscored.

---

[50] He was imprisoned on Gaius' orders and later released by Claudius. Jos. AJ XIX 276 suggests, though it does not positively require, the arrest to have taken place in Rome.

[51] Note sur la famille de Philon d'Alexandrie, p. 595, n. 1.

[52] C. H. RACKHAM's note, Pliny, LCL III (Cambridge, Mass., 1940), 112. It may be that in both cases Pliny has adapted the same source(s) used also by Philo. On such tendencies see the author's 'Philonis Alexandrini De Animalibus', pp. 53–56.

[53] Cf. Provid II 1; see also Y. AMIR, Philo Judaeus, Encyclopaedia Judaica, 13 (1971), cols. 410–411.

[54] See the authorities cited above, n. 2, especially E. G. TURNER's article.

Date	Event	Approx. Age
ca. A.D. 15	was born	—
ca. A.D. 35	was married	20
A.D. 39/40	participated in the Alexandrian Jewish embassy to Rome	25
A.D. 41	entered Roman service	26
A.D. 42	Epistrategos of the Thebaid	27
A.D. 46—48	Procurator of Judaea	31—33
ca. A.D. 50	daughter betrothed to Lysimachus	35
A.D. 66—70	Prefect of Egypt	51—55
A.D. 69	proclaimed Vespasian Emperor before the Alexandrian troops	54
A.D. 70	Chief of Staff under Titus during the siege of Jerusalem	55

The only and indirect reference to Alexander's age is found in BJ V 46, where Josephus remarks on Alexander as a counselor in the exigencies of war (σύμβουλος ταῖς τοῦ πολέμου χρείαις)[55] during the siege of Jerusalem by Titus in A.D. 70: "he was well qualified both by age and experience". When Josephus' AJ appeared in about A.D. 93/94 with the offensive remark on Alexander's renegadism (XX 100), Alexander might have been either dead or politically inactive.

In Provid II we find three indications suggestive of a late date for the dialogues: a possible allusion to Philo's failing eyesight (1); another clear indication of Alexander's apostasy (92), where, contrary to Jewish dietary laws, he is made to cite the hare with animals fit for food (cf. Anim 31); and a reference to one of Philo's pilgrimages to Jerusalem (107).

The internal evidence for a late date for the composition of the dialogues is overwhelming indeed. Consequently, they are to be ascribed to the closing years of the author's life (ca. A.D. 50) and placed at the end of the corpus of his works[56].

---

[55] Elsewhere Josephus describes Alexander's position as πάντων τῶν στρατευμάτων ἄρχων κριθείς and πάντων τῶν στρατευμάτων ἐπάρχοντος (BJ V 46; VI 237). For the rest of Josephus' references to Alexander, see above, n. 39.

[56] Among others who have challenged the arguments for the traditionally held view that Philo wrote the philosophical works Aet (as that is indeed Philonic), Quod Omn, Provid I—II and Anim before he undertook the expository works on the Pentateuch, see E. SCHÜRER, who observes that Anim belongs to Philo's later works, the embassy to Rome being already contemplated: Geschichte des jüdischen Volkes im Zeitalter Jesu Christi, III (4th ed.; Leipzig, 1909), 685; H. LEISEGANG, Philons Schrift über die Ewigkeit der Welt, Philologus, 92 (1937), 156—176, argues against P. WENDLAND that Aet belongs to the later years of Philo's life, to the time when he defended the Stoics on the notion of divine providence. Now that the Philonic authorship of Aet is certain, most of LEISEGANG's arguments could be claimed for Provid I—II and Anim, which he elsewhere (see above, n. 12) places at the beginning of Philo's works. After establishing the identity of the

VI. The Implications of the Dialogues for the Exegetical Works

The often quoted passage seemingly favoring the traditional view of Philo's growing out of philosophical writings into theological maturity and exegetical writings, Congr 73—80, has been misconstrued[57]. The passage, rightly understood, shows Philo's concurrent interest in philosophy and theology. Although philosophy is presented as the servant of wisdom (i.e. the Torah, the mistress), it is not so much the subordination of one to the other that is emphasized as the constant relationship of one with the other. Commenting on this and other related passages, D. WINSTON observes, "far from subordinating philosophy to Scripture, Philo is rather identifying the Mosaic Law with the summit of philosophical achievement"[58].

Philo's concurrent interest in philosophy and theology may be seen in his dialogues. In a passage never before considered, Provid II 115, Philo speaks of philosophy as his life interest (in response to Alexander's asking for time to hear more from Philo): "I always have time to philosophize, to which field of knowledge I have devoted my life; however, many and diverse yet delightful duties that would not be fair to neglect summon me". This conflict between political duties and personal endeavors expressed at the end of a philosophical treatise is reminiscent of that expressed at the beginning of an exegetical treatise, Spec Leg III 1—6. E. R. GOODENOUGH in his brilliant interpretation of the latter passage shows that "Philo's literary career as an interpreter of the Bible was a function of his life after he had gone into political affairs, carried on as a hobby or escape from politics"[59]. In due consideration of Provid II 115 and the date we have ascribed to the dialogues, we may add that Philo never fully retired from political life. We may also add that his concurrent interest in philosophy and theology and the interrelation of his works as a whole suggest that his works were written at the end of his political career and over a comparatively short period of time. The bulk of his writings does not make this supposition impossible[60].

speakers and the right date of Anim, M. POHLENZ argues that both the philosophical and the exegetical works belong to the same period, to the closing years of Philo's life, Philon von Alexandreia, pp. 412—415; E. G. TURNER, Tiberius Iulius Alexander, p. 56, in due consideration of the events of Alexander's life, observes, "Philo cannot have written these dialogues before A. D. 40—50".

[57] See, e.g., H. WOLFSON, Philo: Foundations of Religious Philosophy in Judaism, Christianity and Islam, I (rev. ed.; Cambridge, Mass., 1948), 149—150.

[58] Was Philo a Mystic? Society of Biblical Literature 1978 Seminar Papers, ed. P. J. ACHTEMEIER, I (Missoula, Montana, 1978), 164. In the same volume, see the author's article 'The Implications of Philo's Dialogues for His Exegetical Works', p. 184, where a similar understanding of the passage is arrived at independently.

[59] The Politics of Philo Judaeus, pp. 66—68; cf. F. H. COLSON's comment in: Philo, LCL VII (Cambridge, Mass., 1937), 631—632.

[60] M. HADAS-LEBEL cites the example of Cicero (De Providentia I et II, p. 39); one may also cite the example of Plotinus.

In the introductory and transitory dialogues in Anim, thought to be 'a purely philosophical work', he calls himself "an interpreter" (ἑρμηνεύς, 7, 74) – if by that he is to be understood as an interpreter of Scripture. We must note that no direct use is made of Scripture in either of the two dialogues; instead, the arguments appear within the context of Academic-Stoic polemics. This, however, does not rule out the existence of a possible biblical background. H. LEISE-GANG observes that by arguing for the rationality of animals Alexander is opposing not only the Stoic but also the Judaeo-biblical doctrine that only man is endowed with the rational spirit[61]. We may add that by emphasizing the irrationality of animals and thereby sanctioning their unilateral use by humans, Philo is perhaps defending the anthropocentric view of the cosmos reflected in Gen 1:26–28; 2:19–20; 9:2 – man's dominion over the irrational creation. We may likewise observe that in Provid I–II, Philo is perhaps defending the biblical view of teleology, including the necessity of evil for the ultimate good – as found in numerous accounts in Genesis and Exodus[62]. In view of these observations, the dialogues with Alexander may be treated as apologetic literature; indeed, the apologetic thrust of Provid II seems to have been recognized by Eusebius[63]. Philo's dialogues thus seem to fall in line with the rest of his works which are more or less colored by an apologetic overtone; moreover, they may have influenced Christian apologists in the manner of responding to pagan opponents, as seen in the appeal to Stoic philosophy rather than to Scripture[64].

We may cite for example Philo's Quod Omn, another of his mostly philosophical and more apologetic works, wrongly ascribed to his youth and thought to show by its numerous secular illustrations the truth of the Stoic paradox that the wise man alone is free[65]. In contrast, there are but five allusions to or quotations from the Pentateuch (29, 43, 57, 68–69 – all in the first half of the treatise); yet more than defending the Stoic paradox in this treatise Philo stresses that true freedom lies in following God (19–20, 160). Interestingly enough, Ambrose in his 37th letter, which to a large extent is a paraphrase of Quod Omn, observes after noting § 19 that David and Job said the same thing before Sophocles; after noting §§ 38–40, that masters, like purchasers of lions, become enslaved by their slaves, Ambrose cites Proverbs 17:2 (LXX); and after noting §§ 92–97, the story of the Indian Calanus and his firm resistance to Alexander, he points out that the Indian's heroism is surpassed by the Three Young Men and the Maccabean martyrs. Ambrose's awareness of Philo's apologetic concern in Quod Omn is all too obvious[66]. This concern, reflected

---

[61] Philon, col. 7.

[62] Cf. A. A. LONG, The Stoic Concept of Evil, Philosophical Quarterly, 18 (1968), 329–343.

[63] PE VIII 14. 386, quoted above, n. 45 (see its context).

[64] See M. HADAS-LEBEL, De Providentia I et II, p. 75; for a full discussion, see M. SPANNEUT, Le Stoïcisme des pères de l'Église de Clément de Rome à Clément d'Alexandrie, Patristica Sorbonensia, 1 (Paris, 1957).

[65] Quod Omn and the lost twin treatise mentioned in § 1, 'Every Bad Man Is a Slave', are generally believed to be from Philo's youthful days. See F. H. COLSON's introduction, Philo, LCL IX, 2–9.

[66] I owe much of this observation to F. H. COLSON, ibid., 5–6, n. c.

throughout the treatise, becomes all the more obvious in the treatment of the Essenes in §§ 75–91.

In an earlier treatise, 'De nobilitate' (Virt 187–227), Philo stresses not so much the Stoic paradox that the virtuous man alone is noble[67] as the biblical doctrine that everyone is to be judged by his conduct and not by his descent (226–227). However, unlike his marked departure into more apologetic thrust in Quod Omn and more so in the dialogues, Philo illustrates this doctrine entirely from the Pentateuch – more in keeping with his tendency in the exposition of the Law or the third commentary on the Pentateuch of which 'De nobilitate' seems to be an integral part[68].

To add to the validity of the foregoing observations, we shall revive a meritorious thesis put forward by M. ADLER, who observes in Philo's works comprising the allegorical commentary a gradual departure from the biblical text: whereas the earlier works (Leg All I–III, Cher, Sacr, Quod Det, Post, Gig, Quod Deus, Agr, Plant, Ebr) show close attachment to the text, gradually breaking into free composition, the later works (Sobr, Conf, Migr, Heres, Congr, Fuga, Mut, Somn I–II) are almost altogether free from such attachment and more philosophical[69]. Following ADLER's thesis on Philo's method, one is compelled to conclude that the more philosophical writings are of later development. Such a conclusion can in turn be substantiated by our demonstration of the late date of the dialogues and strengthened by our elaborations on LEISEGANG's observations noted above.

The view that Philo's more philosophical works are of later development gains added support from a forthcoming study where we shall demonstrate through internal evidence the primacy of the 'Quaestiones' among the allegorical commentaries on the Pentateuch[70]. We may note in passing that in the 'Quaestiones' Philo manifests his closest attachment to the frequently cited biblical text, from which midrashic form of exposition he clearly moves to a more artistic expression and a more Hellenized presentation of biblical philosophy.

Having demonstrated that the dialogues with Alexander belong to the closing years of Philo's life and that his philosophical interest concurs with his theological interest, we are led to conclude that perhaps most of Philo's literary career belongs to the closing years of his life, to the period following the political turmoils described in Flacc and Gaium. Moreover, his works, written over a comparatively short period of time, seem to be carefully structured compositions that progress not from philosophical into more theological writing but rather from a midrashic type exposition into a more apologetic approach conceivably climaxed in his dialogues.

---

[67] Ibid., VIII (Cambridge, Mass., 1939), xvi–xvii.

[68] A discussion on how this treatise is related to the other three in Virt is not within the scope of this study. Suffice it to say that the four treatises comprising Virt were thus known to Clement of Alexandria (Strom. II 18) and that there is a thematic relationship between this fourth treatise and Praem ('On Rewards and Punishments'), the following and last treatise in the exposition of the Law.

[69] Studien zu Philon von Alexandreia (Breslau, 1929), pp. 66–67.

[70] This will appear in the author's forthcoming book cited above, n. 14.

Philo and Gnosticism

by BIRGER A. PEARSON, Santa Barbara, Calif.

Contents

I. Survey of Scholarship

The problem of the relationship between the religious philosophy of Philo Judaeus of Alexandria and Gnosticism has been posed in various ways, depending especially upon how the problem of Gnosticism itself is understood, its essence, its historical origins, and its geographical and historical parameters. Philo has been understood by some scholars as a Gnostic, indeed as the first Gnostic,[1] or at least heavily influenced by Gnosticism. Alternatively, he has been taken as representing a stage in the development of Gnosticism, or even as a formative factor in certain mythico-philosophical systems of second-century Gnosticism. In general, more recent scholarship has tended toward the latter alternative, preferring to view Philo as representing a kind of 'pre-Gnostic' pattern of religious thought rather than a full-blown Gnosticism.[2]

---

[1] H. GRAETZ, Gnosticismus und Judenthum, Krotoschin, 1846, p. 5. In GRAETZ' view, Philo's speculative system of thought, embracing Jewish, Platonic, and near-eastern theosophical elements, was the chief representative of that 'Alexandrinismus' out of which Gnosticism developed.

[2] On the terms 'pre-gnostic' and 'proto-gnostic,' and definitional distinctions between 'Gnosticism' and 'Gnosis,' see the Final Document of the Colloquium on the Origins of Gnosticism held at Messina in 1966, published in U. BIANCHI, ed., Le origini dello gnosticismo,

That some relationship exists between Gnosticism and the religious philosophy of Philo can hardly be doubted. Nevertheless discussions of this problem tend to be concentrated in studies focused upon Gnosticism, whereas the major monographs and articles devoted exclusively to Philo frequently omit to treat his importance in connection with the development of Gnosticism, concentrating instead on Philo's debt to Greek philosophy and/or to his Jewish heritage,[3] or on the 'mystery' character of his religion,[4] or on his originality as a thinker and his formative influence on the history of philosophy,[5] or on other aspects of his life and thought.

In this survey of scholarship I shall concentrate mainly on work done in the past two decades, but I shall also have to discuss at some length two earlier works of exceptional importance, because of their relevance in current scholarly discussion. I refer to the now-classic opus of H. JONAS, 'Gnosis und spätantiker Geist',[6] and to that capstone of 19th-century research on Gnosticism, M. FRIEDLÄNDER's 'Der vorchristliche jüdische Gnosticismus'.[7]

1. FRIEDLÄNDER, JONAS, WLOSOK and WILSON

FRIEDLÄNDER's views on Gnosticism developed out of an attempt to identify the *minim* ("heretics") denounced so vigorously by the rabbis in the Talmud.[8] He found the answer in the writings of Philo, especially in those passages in which Philo polemicizes against 'allegorizing' opponents. The similarity in the arguments used by Philo against the 'allegorists' and by the rabbis against the *minim*

Colloquio di Messina 13—18 Aprile 1966, Studies in the History of Religions (Supplements to Numen) 12, Leiden, 1967, xx—xxiii (Italian version), xxiii—xxvi (French version), xxvi—xxix (English version), xxix—xxxii (German version). On the Messina Colloquium see further below.

[3] E.g. I. HEINEMANN, Philons griechische und jüdische Bildung, 2 vols., Breslau, 1921, 1928, r.p. Hildesheim, 1962; W. VÖLKER, Fortschritt und Vollendung bei Philo von Alexandrien: eine Studie zur Geschichte der Frömmigkeit, TU 49, Leipzig, 1938.

[4] E.g. J. PASCHER, Η ΒΑΣΙΛΙΚΗ ΟΔΟΣ: Der Königsweg zu Wiedergeburt und Vergottung bei Philo von Alexandreia, Paderborn, 1931; E. R. GOODENOUGH, By Light, Light: The Mystic Gospel of Hellenistic Judaism, New Haven, 1935, r.p. Amsterdam, 1969. It is interesting to note GOODENOUGH's one and only reference to Gnosticism (p. 119): "If . . . Philo is primarily religious rather than philosophical in his writings, he could yet have had no sympathy with that travesty of philosophy, the type of mythological presentation to which we give the collective name of Gnosticism. For all his Hermetic and Isiac roots, he is closer to Plotinus than to any mythological conception of Deity."

[5] H. WOLFSON, Philo: Foundations of Religious Philosophy in Judaism, Christianity and Islam, 2 vols., Cambridge, Mass., 1948.

[6] H. JONAS, Gnosis und spätantiker Geist, 1: Die mythologische Gnosis, FRLANT N.F. 33, Göttingen, 1934, 1964³, 2/1: Von der Mythologie zur mystischen Philosophie, FRLANT N.F. 45, Göttingen, 1954.

[7] M. FRIEDLÄNDER, Der vorchristliche jüdische Gnosticismus, Göttingen, 1898, r.p. Farnborough, 1972. Cf. B. PEARSON, Friedländer Revisited: Alexandrian Judaism and Gnostic Origins, Studia Philonica 2, 1973, pp. 23—39.

[8] E.g. b Shab 116a, with which FRIEDLÄNDER begins, p. iii.

made it unlikely that the rabbis were attacking Christian opponents. Gnosticism provides the answer for FRIEDLÄNDER as to the identity of both groups attacked, and he looks to Alexandria as the place where Gnosticism originated.

FRIEDLÄNDER begins his discussion with reference to the cultural and religious situation in the Jewish Diaspora prior to the time of Jesus, especially the Jewish community of Alexandria. The 'new wine' of Hellenistic culture and philosophy was being put into the 'old wineskins' of the Jewish religion. One of the manifestations of this process was the allegorical method of interpreting scripture. The Mosaic Law was interpreted as a 'revelation' of 'divine philosophy' (meaning the eclectic Platonism of the time), and a concomitant of this view was the apologetic argument that the Greek philosophers had learned their philosophy from Moses. Philo is himself a prime example of this trend, but he had forerunners, such as Aristobulus, Ps.-Aristeas, and Ps.-Solomon (pp. 1—3).

The allegorical interpretation of the Law led to divisions in Diaspora Judaism between the 'conservative' Jews who observed the letter of the Law, and 'radical' Jews who regarded the letter of the Law as peripheral (pp. 3—4).

Philo's writings provide clear evidence of such divisions according to FRIEDLÄNDER, and the *locus classicus* is Migr 86—93, in which Philo comments on Gen 12:2, "I will make your name great." FRIEDLÄNDER quotes the text in full (pp. 4—5):[9]

> "The meaning of this appears to me to be as follows. As it is an advantage to be good and morally noble, so is it to be reputed such. And, while the reality is better than the reputation, happiness comes of having both. For very many, after coming to Virtue's feet with no counterfeit or unreal homage and with their eyes open to her genuine loveliness, through paying no regard to the general opinion have become objects of hostility, just because they were held to be bad, when they were really good. It is true that there is no good in being thought to be this or that, unless you are so long before you are thought to be so. It is naturally so in the case of our bodies. Were all the world to suppose the sickly man to be healthy, or the healthy man to be sickly, the general opinion by itself will produce neither sickness nor health. But he on whom God has bestowed both gifts, both to be morally noble and good and to have a reputation of being so, this man is really happy and his name is great in very deed. We should take thought for fair fame as a great matter and one of much advantage to the life which we live in the body. And this fair fame is won as a rule by all who cheerfully take things as they find them and interfere with no established customs, but maintain with care the constitution of their country. There are some who, regarding laws in their literal sense in the light of symbols of matters belonging to the intellect, are

---

[9] Abbreviations of Philo's works in this article are those suggested by the editors of Studia Philonica (SP), 1, 1972, p. 92; other abbreviations used will follow the suggestions there set forth, pp. 92—96. References to Philo in this article are cited according to the Loeb Classical Library edition of Philo, and unless otherwise indicated, texts and translations are quoted from that edition. FRIEDLÄNDER's own references to Philo are to the MANGEY edition of 1742.

overpunctilious about the latter, while treating the former with easy-going neglect. Such men I for my part should blame for handling the matter in too easy and off-hand a manner: they ought to have given careful attention to both aims, to a more full and exact investigation of what is not seen and in what is seen to be stewards without reproach. As it is, as though they were living alone by themselves in a wilderness, or as though they had become disembodied souls, and knew neither city nor village nor household nor any company of human beings at all, overlooking all that the mass of men regard, they explore reality in its naked absoluteness. These men are taught by the sacred word to have thought for good repute, and to let go nothing that is part of the customs fixed by divinely empowered men greater than those of our time. It is quite true that the Seventh Day is meant to teach the power of the Unoriginate and the non-action of created beings. But let us not for this reason abrogate the laws laid down for its observance, and light fires or till the ground or carry loads or institute proceedings in court or act as jurors or demand the restoration of deposits or recover loans, or do all else that we are permitted to do as well on days that are not festival seasons. It is true also that the Feast is a symbol of gladness of soul and of thankfulness to God, but we should not for this reason turn our backs on the general gatherings of the year's seasons. It is true that receiving circumcision does indeed portray the excision of pleasure and all passions, and the putting away of the impious conceit, under which the mind supposed that it was capable of begetting by its own power: but let us not on this account repeal the law laid down for circumcising. Why, we shall be ignoring the sanctity of the Temple and a thousand other things, if we are going to pay heed to nothing except what is shewn us by the inner meaning of things. Nay, we should look on all these outward observances as resembling the body, and their inner meanings as resembling the soul. It follows that, exactly as we have to take thought for the body, because it is the abode of the soul, so we must pay heed to the letter of the laws. It we keep and observe these, we shall gain a clearer conception of those things of which these are the symbols; and besides that we shall not incur the censure of the many and the charges they are sure to bring against us."[10]

---

[10] Text: τὸ δέ ἐστιν, ὥς γ᾽ ἐμοὶ φαίνεται, τοιόνδε· ὥσπερ τὸ ἀγαθὸν εἶναι καὶ καλόν, οὕτω καὶ τὸ δοκεῖν εἶναι λυσιτελές. καὶ ἀμείνων μὲν δόξης ἀλήθεια, εὔδαιμον δὲ τὸ ἐξ ἀμφοῖν· μυρίοι γὰρ ἀνόθως καὶ ἀκολακεύτως προσελθόντες ἀρετῇ καὶ τὸ γνήσιον αὐτῆς ἐναυγασάμενοι κάλλος, τῆς παρὰ τοῖς πολλοῖς φήμης οὐ φροντίσαντες ἐπεβουλεύθησαν, κακοὶ νομισθέντες οἱ πρὸς ἀλήθειαν ἀγαθοί. (87) καὶ μὴν οὐδὲ τοῦ δοκεῖν ὄφελος μὴ πολὺ πρότερον τοῦ εἶναι προσόντος, ὥσπερ ἐπὶ σωμάτων πέφυκεν ἔχειν· εἰ γὰρ πάντες ἄνθρωποι τὸν νοσοῦντα ὑγιαίνειν ἢ τὸν ὑγιαίνοντα νοσεῖν ὑπολάβοιεν, ἡ δόξα καθ᾽ αὑτὴν οὔτε νόσον οὔτε ὑγείαν ἐργάσεται. (88) ᾧ δὲ ἀμφότερα δεδώρηται ὁ θεός, καὶ τὸ εἶναι καλῷ καὶ ἀγαθῷ καὶ τὸ δοκεῖν εἶναι, οὗτος πρὸς ἀλήθειαν εὐδαίμων καὶ τῷ ὄντι μεγαλώνυμος. προνοητέον δ᾽ ὡς μεγάλου πράγματος καὶ πολλὰ τὸν μετὰ σώματος βίον ὠφελοῦντος εὐφημίας. περιγίνεται δ᾽ αὕτη σχεδὸν ἅπασιν, ὅσοι χαίροντες σὺν ἀσμενισμῷ μηδὲν κινοῦσι τῶν καθεστηκότων νομίμων, ἀλλὰ τὴν πάτριον πολιτείαν οὐκ ἀμελῶς φυλάττουσιν.

In this text, FRIEDLÄNDER argues, we find reflected a fully-developed schism in Diaspora Judaism. An 'antinomian' party of Jews is referred to here, and these Jews differ from others such as the Therapeutae, the Palestinian Essenes, and Philo himself, not in their use of allegory *per se*, but precisely in their antinomian tendencies (pp. 4–9).

All of this accords very well with what the historical sources tell us about pre-Christian Jewish sects, he argues (pp. 9–17), but one can go further and identify such 'Christian' heresies as the Ophites, Cainites, Sethians, and Melchizedekians as the spiritual progeny – secondarily 'Christianized' – of the radical antinomians opposed by Philo (pp. 17–19).

The 'Cainite' sect (cf. Irenaeus Haer I.31; Ps.-Tertullian Haer 2.5 [CC 2, pp. 1399–1420]; Filastrius 2; Epiphanus Haer 37; Theodoret Haer 1.15; Augustine Haer 18) is a good example. They reputedly venerated Cain as the divine Dynamis, rejected all moral conventions, and rejected the Law and the God of the Law. This sect was already well-known to Philo (pp. 19–21), and as proof FRIEDLÄNDER quotes Post 52–53 (pp. 21–22):

"Now every city needs for its existence buildings, and inhabitants, and laws. Cain's buildings are demonstrative arguments. With these, though fighting from a city-wall, he repels the assaults of his adversaries, by forging plausible inventions contrary to the truth. His inhabitants are the wise in their own conceit, devotees of impiety, godlessness, self-love, arrogance, false opinion, men ignorant of real wisdom, who have reduced to an organized system ignorance, lack of learning and of culture, and other pestilential things akin to these. His laws are various forms of lawlessness and injustice, unfairness, licentiousness, audacity, senselessness, self-will, immoderate indulgence in

(89) Εἰσὶ γάρ τινες οἳ τοὺς ῥητοὺς νόμους σύμβολα νοητῶν πραγμάτων ὑπολαμβάνοντες τὰ μὲν ἄγαν ἠκρίβωσαν, τῶν δὲ ῥαθύμως ὠλιγώρησαν· οὓς μεμψαίμην ἂν ἔγωγε τῆς εὐχερείας· ἔδει γὰρ ἀμφοτέρων ἐπιμεληθῆναι, ζητήσεώς τε τῶν ἀφανῶν ἀκριβεστέρας καὶ ταμείας τῶν φανερῶν ἀνεπιλήπτου. (90) νυνὶ δ' ὥσπερ ἐν ἐρημίᾳ καθ' ἑαυτοὺς μόνοι ζῶντες ἢ ἀσώματοι ψυχαὶ γεγονότες καὶ μήτε πόλιν μήτε κώμην μήτ' οἰκίαν μήτε συνόλως θίασον ἀνθρώπων εἰδότες, τὰ δοκοῦντα τοῖς πολλοῖς ὑπερκύψαντες τὴν ἀλήθειαν γυμνὴν αὐτὴν ἐφ' ἑαυτῆς ἐρευνῶσιν· οὓς ὁ ἱερὸς λόγος διδάσκει χρηστῆς ὑπολήψεως πεφροντικέναι καὶ μηδὲν τῶν ἐν τοῖς ἔθεσι λύειν, ἃ θεσπέσιοι καὶ μείζους ἄνδρες ἢ καθ' ἡμᾶς ὥρισαν. (91) μὴ γὰρ ὅτι ἡ ἑβδόμη δυνάμεως μὲν τῆς περὶ τὸ ἀγένητον, ἀπραξίας δὲ τῆς περὶ τὸ γενητὸν δίδαγμά ἐστι, τὰ ἐπ' αὐτῇ νομοθετηθέντα λύωμεν, ὡς πῦρ ἐναύειν ἢ γεωπονεῖν ἢ ἀχθοφορεῖν ἢ ἐγκαλεῖν ἢ δικάζειν ἢ παρακαταθήκας ἀπαιτεῖν ἢ δάνεια ἀναπράττειν ἢ τὰ ἄλλα ποιεῖν, ὅσα κἂν τοῖς μὴ ἑορτώδεσι καιροῖς ἐφεῖται· (92) μηδ' ὅτι ἡ ἑορτὴ σύμβολον ψυχικῆς εὐφροσύνης ἐστὶ καὶ τῆς πρὸς θεὸν εὐχαριστίας, ἀποταξώμεθα ταῖς κατὰ τὰς ἐτησίους ὥρας πανηγύρεσι·μηδ' ὅτι τὸ περιτέμνεσθαι ἡδονῆς καὶ παθῶν πάντων ἐκτομὴν καὶ δόξης ἀναίρεσιν ἀσεβοῦς ἐμφαίνει, καθ' ἣν ὑπέλαβεν ὁ νοῦς ἱκανὸς εἶναι γεννᾶν δι' ἑαυτοῦ, ἀνέλωμεν τὸν ἐπὶ τῇ περιτομῇ τεθέντα νόμον· ἐπεὶ καὶ τῆς περὶ τὸ ἱερὸν ἁγιστείας καὶ μυρίων ἄλλων ἀμελήσομεν, εἰ μόνοις προσέξομεν τοῖς δι' ὑπονοιῶν δηλουμένοις. (93) ἀλλὰ χρὴ ταῦτα μὲν σώματι ἐοικέναι νομίζειν, ψυχῇ δὲ ἐκεῖνα· ὥσπερ οὖν σώματος, ἐπειδὴ ψυχή ἐστιν οἶκος, προνοητέον, οὕτω καὶ τῶν ῥητῶν νόμων ἐπιμελητέον· φυλαττομένων γὰρ τούτων ἀριδηλότερον κἀκεῖνα γνωρισθήσεται, ὧν εἰσιν οὗτοι σύμβολα, πρὸς τῷ καὶ τὰς ἀπὸ τῶν πολλῶν μέμψεις καὶ κατηγορίας ἀποδιδράσκειν.

pleasures, unnatural lusts that may not be named. Of such a city every
impious man is found to be an architect in his own miserable soul, until such
time as God takes counsel (Gen 11:6), and brings upon their sophistic
devices a great and complete confusion. This time will come when they are
building, not a city only, but a tower as well whose top shall reach to heaven
(Gen 11:4)."[11]

In this text 'Cain' is a symbol of heresy, and the specifics of the heresy
described by Philo are such as to suggest that he is arguing against a philosophiz-
ing sect which is characterized not only by constructing myths contrary to the
truth (κατὰ τῆς ἀληθείας μυθοπλαστῶν) but also by gross antinomianism. Philo
speaks against these heretics precisely as Irenaeus speaks against the Gnostics (cf.
Haer II.30.1—2). Thus, FRIEDLÄNDER concludes, there can be no doubt but that
the heretics combatted by Philo are the forerunners of the 'Christian' Gnostics
later opposed by the church Fathers (pp. 19—27).

The 'Melchizedekian' sect is of special interest to FRIEDLÄNDER. This group
regarded Melchizedek (cf. Gen 14; Ps 110:4) as a 'great Power' (Epiphanius Haer
55; Ps.-Tertullian Haer 8.3; Theodoret Haer 2.6; Augustine Haer 34; Filastrius
52), a 'Son of God' higher than the Messsiah. The Melchizedekian sect is pre-
Christian in origin, and when Jesus was later incorporated into the sect's system
of belief, he was ranked below Melchizedek, as the patristic references all indicate
(pp. 28—30).[12]

FRIEDLÄNDER argues that the Melchizedekian sect originated before Christianity in Diaspora Judaism, and quotes Philo, Leg All III.78—82 (pp. 31—32):

"Thus to those who ask what the origin of creation is the right answer would
be, that it is the goodness and grace of God, which He bestowed on the race
that stands next after Him. For all things in the world and the world itself is a
free gift and act of kindness and grace on God's part. Melchizedek, too, has
God made both king of peace, for that is the meaning of 'Salem,' and His
own priest (Gen 14:18). He has not fashioned beforehand any deed of his,
but produces him to begin with as such a king, peaceable and worthy of His
own priesthood. For he is entitled 'the righteous king,' and a 'king' is a thing

---

[11] Text: Ἐπειδὴ τοίνυν πᾶσα πόλις ἐξ οἰκοδομημάτων καὶ οἰκητόρων καὶ νόμων συν-
έστηκε, τὰ μὲν οἰκοδομήματά ἐστιν αὐτῷ λόγοι οἱ ἀποδεικνύντες, οἷς καθάπερ ἀπὸ
τείχους πρὸς τὰς τῶν ἐναντίων ἀπομάχεται προσβολὰς πιθανὰς εὑρέσεις κατὰ τῆς
ἀληθείας μυθοπλαστῶν, οἰκήτορες δὲ οἱ ἀσεβείας, ἀθεότητος, φιλαυτίας, μεγαλαυχίας,
ψευδοῦς δόξης ἑταῖροι δοκησίσοφοι, τὸ πρὸς ἀλήθειαν σοφὸν οὐκ εἰδότες, ἄγνοιαν
καὶ ἀπαιδευσίαν καὶ ἀμαθίαν καὶ τὰς ἄλλας ἀδελφὰς καὶ συγγενεῖς κῆρας συγκεκρο-
τηκότες, νόμοι δὲ ἀνομίαι, ἀδικίαι, τὸ ἄνισον, τὸ ἀκόλαστον, θρασύτης, ἀπόνοια,
αὐθάδεια, ἡδονῶν ἀμετρίαι, τῶν παρὰ φύσιν ἄλεκτοι ἐπιθυμίαι. (53) τοιαύτης πόλεως
ἕκαστος τῶν ἀσεβῶν ἐν ἑαυτοῦ τῇ παναθλίᾳ ψυχῇ δημιουργὸς εὑρίσκεται, μέχρις ἂν ὁ
θεὸς βουλευθεὶς ταῖς σοφιστικαῖς αὐτῶν τέχναις ἀθρόαν καὶ μεγάλην ἐργάσηται
σύγχυσιν. τοῦτο δ' ἔσται, ὅταν μὴ μόνον πόλιν, ⟨ἀλλὰ⟩ καὶ πύργον οἰκοδομῶσιν, οὗ ἡ
κεφαλὴ εἰς οὐρανὸν ἀφίξεται.

[12] Cf. also FRIEDLÄNDER, La secte de Melchisédec et l'épître aux Hébreux, REJ 5, 1882,
pp. 1—26; pp. 188—198; and 6, 1883, pp. 187—199.

at enmity with a despot, the one being the author of laws, the other of lawlessness. So mind, the despot, decrees for both soul and body harsh and
hurtful decrees working grievous woes, conduct, I mean, such as wickedness
prompts, and free indulgence of the passions. But the king in the first place
resorts to persuasion rather than decrees, and in the next place issues directions such as to enable a vessel, the living being I mean, to make life's voyage
successfully, piloted by the good pilot, who is right principle. Let the
despot's title therefore be ruler of war, the king's prince of peace, of Salem,
and let him offer to the soul food full of joy and gladness; for he brings bread
and wine, things which Ammonites and Moabites refused to supply to the
seeing one, on which account they are excluded from the divine congregation and assembly. These characters, Ammonites deriving their nature from
sense-perception their mother, and Moabites deriving theirs from mind their
father, who hold that all things owe their coherence to these two things,
mind and sense-perception, and take no thought of God, "shall not enter,"
saith Moses, "into the congregation of the Lord, because they did not meet
us with bread and water" (Deut 23:3f.) when we came out from the
passions of Egypt. But let Melchizedek instead of water offer wine, and give
to souls strong drink, that they may be seized by a divine intoxication, more
sober than sobriety itself. For he is a priest, even Reason, having as his
portion Him that IS, and all his thoughts of God are high and vast and
sublime: for he is priest of the Most High (Gen 14:18), not that there is any
other not Most High — for God being One "is in heaven above and on earth
beneath, and there is none beside Him" (Deut 4:39) — but to conceive of
God not in low earthbound ways but in lofty terms, such as transcend all
other greatness and all else that is free from matter, calls up in us a picture of
the Most High."[13]

---

[13] Text: τοῖς γοῦν ζητοῦσι, τίς ἀρχὴ γενέσεως, ὀρθότατα ἄν τις ἀποκρίνοιτο, ὅτι ἀγαθότης καὶ χάρις τοῦ θεοῦ, ἣν ἐχαρίσατο τῷ μετ' αὐτὸν γένει· δωρεὰ γὰρ καὶ εὐεργεσία
καὶ χάρισμα θεοῦ τὰ πάντα ὅσα ἐν κόσμῳ καὶ αὐτὸς ὁ κόσμος ἐστί. (79) Καὶ Μελχισεδὲκ βασιλέα τε τῆς εἰρήνης — Σαλὴμ τοῦτο γὰρ ἑρμηνεύεται — ⟨καὶ⟩ ἱερέα
ἑαυτοῦ πεποίηκεν ὁ θεός, οὐδὲν ἔργον αὐτοῦ προδιατυπώσας, ἀλλὰ τοιοῦτον ἐργα-
σάμενος βασιλέα καὶ εἰρηναῖον καὶ ἱερωσύνης ἄξιον τῆς ἑαυτοῦ πρῶτον· καλεῖται
γὰρ βασιλεὺς δίκαιος, βασιλεὺς δὲ ἐχθρὸν τυράννῳ, ὅτι ὁ μὲν νόμων, ὁ δὲ ἀνομίας
ἐστὶν εἰσηγητής. (80) ὁ μὲν οὖν τύραννος νοῦς ἐπιτάγματα ἐπιτάττει τῇ τε ψυχῇ καὶ
τῷ σώματι βίαια καὶ βλαβερὰ καὶ σφοδρὰς λύπας ἐργαζόμενα, τὰς κατὰ κακίαν λέγω
πράξεις καὶ τὰς τῶν παθῶν ἀπολαύσεις· ὁ δὲ [δεύτερος] βασιλεὺς πρῶτον μὲν [οὖν]
οὐκ ἐπιτάττει μᾶλλον ἢ πείθει, ἔπειτα τοιαῦτα παραγγέλλει, δι' ὧν ὥσπερ σκάφος τὸ
ζῷον εὐπλοίᾳ τῇ τοῦ βίου χρήσεται κυβερνώμενον ὑπὸ τοῦ ἀγαθοῦ [καὶ τεχνίτου] κυ-
βερνήτου, οὗτος δέ ἐστιν ὁ ὀρθὸς λόγος. (81) καλείσθω οὖν ὁ μὲν τύραννος ἄρχων
πολέμου, ὁ δὲ βασιλεὺς ἡγεμὼν εἰρήνης, Σαλήμ, καὶ προσφερέτω τῇ ψυχῇ τροφὰς εὐφροσύνης καὶ χαρᾶς πλήρεις· ἄρτους γὰρ καὶ οἶνον προσφέρει, ἅπερ Ἀμμανῖται καὶ
Μωαβῖται τῷ βλέποντι παρασχεῖν οὐκ ἠθέλησαν, οὗ χάριν ἐκκλησίας εἴργονται καὶ
συλλόγου θείου· Ἀμμανῖται γὰρ οἱ ἐκ τῆς μητρὸς αἰσθήσεως καὶ Μωαβῖται οἱ ἐκ τοῦ
πατρὸς νοῦ φύντες τρόποι δύο ταῦτα τῶν ὄντων συνεκτικὰ νομίζοντες νοῦν καὶ αἴσθησιν, θεοῦ δὲ μὴ λαμβάνοντες ἔννοιαν, "οὐκ εἰσελεύσονται" φησὶ Μωυσῆς ⟨εἰς ἐκκλη-
σίαν⟩ κυρίου, ... παρὰ τὸ μὴ συναντῆσαι αὐτοὺς ἡμῖν μετ' ἄρτων καὶ ὕδατος" ἐξ-

FRIEDLÄNDER concludes from the way in which Philo presents the Melchizedek mystery that antinomian heretics are here referred to. This is indicated in the stress that Philo puts on the oneness of God and the reference to 'Ammonites' and 'Moabites' who are excluded from the divine congregation (pp. 30—33).

FRIEDLÄNDER distinguishes the Melchizedekians from the Ophites and Cainites, arguing that the 'antinomianism' of the former was not as radical as that of the other Gnostics. He also suggests that Melchizedekianism is the one form of pre-Christian Gnosticism which qualifies best as the point of departure for Christian Gnosticism (pp. 33—39).

FRIEDLÄNDER summarizes his position on the origins of Gnosticism by stating that it began with the "Hellenization of Judaism in the Diaspora" (p. 44). Gnosticism served as the medium by which Judaism should become a world religion. It remained orthodox so long as the Law was observed — as is the case with Philo — and became heretical when the letter of the Law was rejected (pp. 40—45).

It was from „jüdische Alexandrinismus" that Palestinian Gnosticism (minuth = Gnostic heresy) derived, providing the occasion for the various attacks of the rabbis. The main features of the heretical Jewish Gnosis of Palestine were cosmogonic and theosophical teachings contradicting the unity of God, and antinomian behavior (pp. 45—116).[14]

FRIEDLÄNDER makes some important comments on Gnostic ethics at the end of his monograph, with reference especially to Philo. The Alexandrian Jewish tendency towards mortification of the flesh in the interests of a higher *gnosis*, he says, could lead either to asceticism or to libertinism. Whereas Philo has very clear ascetic tendencies, as can be seen in his instructions in Leg All III.151 ff., there were others, such as the 'Cainites,' who taught that bodily nature could be destroyed only by partaking of the passions of the flesh (pp. 116—119). Philo attacks such, according to FRIEDLÄNDER, in Leg All III.160 (quoted on p. 119):

> "There is an excellent point in the next words too: "Thou shalt go upon thy breast and thy belly" (Gen 3:14). For pleasure does not belong to the category of things becalmed and stationary, but to that of things moving and full of turmoil. For as the flame is in movement, so, not unlike a blazing thing, passion moving in the soul does not suffer it to be calm."[15]

ιοῦσιν ἐκ τῶν παθῶν Αἰγύπτου. (82) ἀλλ' ὁ μὲν Μελχισεδὲκ ἀντὶ ὕδατος οἶνον προσφερέτω καὶ ποτιζέτω καὶ ἀκρατιζέτω ψυχάς, ἵνα κατάσχετοι γένωνται θεία μέθῃ νηφαλεωτέρᾳ νήψεως αὐτῆς· ἱερεὺς γάρ ἐστι λόγος κλῆρον ἔχων τὸν ὄντα καὶ ὑψηλῶς περὶ αὐτοῦ καὶ ὑπερόγκως καὶ μεγαλοπρεπῶς λογιζόμενος· τοῦ γὰρ ὑψίστου ἐστὶν ἱερεύς, οὐχ ὅτι ἐστί τις ἄλλος οὐχ ὕψιστος — ὁ γὰρ θεὸς εἷς ὢν "ἐν τῷ οὐρανῷ ἄνω ἐστὶ καὶ ἐπὶ τῆς γῆς κάτω, καὶ οὐκ ἔστιν ἔτι πλὴν αὐτοῦ" —, ἀλλὰ τὸ μὴ ταπεινῶς καὶ χαμαιζήλως ὑπερμεγέθως δὲ καὶ ὑπεραύλως καὶ ὑψηλῶς νοεῖν περὶ θεοῦ ἔμφασιν τοῦ ὑψίστου κινεῖ.

[14] I omit further discussion of this section of FRIEDLÄNDER's monograph, important as it is, because Philo does not figure prominently in the discussion. But see my article, op. cit. n. 7, pp. 27—29.

[15] Text: Εὖ μέντοι καὶ τὸ προσθεῖναι· "πορεύσῃ ἐπὶ τῷ στήθει καὶ τῇ κοιλίᾳ"· ἡ γὰρ ἡδονὴ οὐκ ἔστι τῶν ἠρεμούντων καὶ ἱσταμένων, ἀλλὰ τῶν κινουμένων καὶ ταραχῆς

Similar Gnostics were found in Palestine, it is argued.[16] Those whom Philo encountered in Alexandria in his time were the 'fathers and grandfathers' of the Cainites denounced by Irenaeus (p. 119).

FRIEDLÄNDER's work is characterized by a critical analysis and interpretation of a rather narrow range of Greek and Hebrew texts, for the purpose of making a set of historical judgments as to the origin and development of Gnosticism. He had, of course, inherited from his scholarly predecessors certain assumptions regarding the nature of Gnosticism; in any case he does not indicate that he regarded as in any way problematical the question of its 'essence' or 'definition.' As a historian he was interested merely in tracing origins and lines of development.[17]

The work of H. JONAS[18] provides an interesting contrast. JONAS is more a philosopher than a historian (though his knowledge of the history of late antiquity is impressive indeed!). Under the influence of HEIDEGGER, JONAS makes an existentialist analysis of the main spiritual currents of late antiquity, seeing in Gnosticism the culminating point of Hellenistic religious syncretism with its acosmic tendencies. At the same time he attempts to arrive at an interpretation of the essence of Gnosticism, and to adumbrate its salient features. In doing so he includes in his purview such diverse currents as the Hermetic literature, the literature of the Mysteries, the magical papyri, Christian literature from St. Paul to Dionysius the Areopagite, Mandaeism, Manichaeism, Neopythagorean and Neoplatonic philosophy — including Philo of Alexandria. He sees a development in the Gnostic movement from 'mythological' Gnosis to 'mystical philosophy,' and devotes the first volume of his study to the former, and the second volume (Part 1)[19] to the latter.

JONAS understands Gnosticism (he uses the term 'Gnosis') as a development of late antiquity arising out of the clash and melding of Eastern and Western religious cross-currents in the Hellenistic period. Basically a syncretistic and eclectic phenomenon, 'Gnosis' can best be described as an "understanding of existence" (Daseinshaltung). Gnosticism cannot, therefore, be explained simply by tracing the history of the various concepts and traditions utilized, nor is it sufficient to trace the 'origins' of Gnosticism to a particular culture-area, such as

γεμόντων· ὥσπερ γὰρ ἡ φλὸξ ἐν κινήσει, οὕτως φλογμοῦ τινα τρόπον τὸ πάθος ἐν τῇ ψυχῇ κινούμενον ἠρεμεῖν αὐτὴν οὐκ ἐᾷ.

16 E.g. the famous Elisha ben Abuya. Cf. his discussion of Palestinian antinomians, pp. 76ff., and pp. 108f. (the latter with special reference to Elisha).

17 For further discussion and criticism of FRIEDLÄNDER's work, see below.

18 Op. cit. n. 6.

19 Part 2 of the second volume, intended to be devoted to Plotinus, has not been written. See his latest comment on this in the Introduction to his Philosophical Essays, Englewood Cliffs, N.J., 1974, p. xi: "I had committed myself to a comprehensive, perhaps over-ambitious analytic and synthetic task which was destined never to be completed (not to this day, anyway) in its initially conceived scope." Cf. also JONAS' other work on Gnosticism: The Gnostic Religion: The Message of the Alien God and the Beginnings of Christianity, Boston, 1958, 1963². The latter work is more restricted in its purview, and it might be argued that this very restrictiveness is methodologically more sound. See further on this question below.

Babylonia, Iran, ancient Greece, Egypt, etc. The Gnostics have in common a
basic Gnostic experience, as well as a common understanding of 'Knowledge'
(γνῶσις) itself (1, p. 80). Basic to the Gnostic experience are the consciousness of
alienation from the world and all its powers including the world-creator(s), the
need for liberation of the divine self (νοῦς, πνεῦμα) from the shackles of material
existence, the unique understanding of *gnosis* as a saving event, and a basically
revolutionary stance vis-à-vis older traditions and current systems of morality (1,
pp. 92–255).

JONAS describes the various systems of "mythological Gnosis" in volume 1
(pp. 255–424). His main discussion of Philo is found in volume 2 (pp. 70–121,
cf. pp. 38–43), wherein he traces the development from "mythological gnosis" to
"mystical philosophy." He confines his analysis of Philo essentially to the
problem of γνῶσις θεοῦ, entitling his chapter on Philo, 'Gotteserkenntnis, Schau
und Vollendung bei Philo von Alexandrien.'

He begins his discussion (p. 70) with some observations on a basic 'contradiction' in Philo: God is "incomprehensible" (ἀκατάληπτος), indeed not even
comprehensible by the mind (οὐδὲ τῷ νῷ καταληπτός, Quod Deus 62; cf. Quaes
Ex II.45: οὐδὲ τῆς καθαρωτάτης διανοίας). On the other hand, one finds in
Philo the exact opposite statement, i.e. that God is "comprehensible only to the
mind" (μόνῃ διανοίᾳ καταληπτός, Spec Leg I.20), and the adjective νοητός is
used frequently in Philo as a predicate of God. Similar problems occur in Philo
regarding the possibility of attaining a "vision" (ὅρασις) of God. To get at the
fundamental ideas of Philo on the problem of the knowledge of God, JONAS
divides the problem into two aspects: "theoretical knowledge of God" („Theoretische Gotteserkenntnis," pp. 74–99) and "mystical knowledge of God" (pp.
99–121).

JONAS interprets Philo's basic stress on the transcendence of God as a unique
product of his Platonic and Jewish backgrounds, and argues that insofar as God,
for Philo, is ἄγνωστος, we have to do with a basic category of Gnosticism.[20]
Philo resolves the problem of the theoretical knowledge of God by holding that
God's essence (οὐσία) is not accessible to man, but his existence (ὕπαρξις), that
he is, can be known. JONAS quotes Post 168f. in this connection (p. 81), wherein
Philo comments on Deut 32:39, "See, see that I AM":

> "When we say that the Existent One is visible, we are not using words in
> their literal sense, but it is an irregular use of the word by which it is referred
> to each one of His powers. In the passage just quoted He does not say "See
> Me," for it is impossible that the God who IS should be perceived at all by
> created beings. What he says is "See that I AM," that is "Behold My
> subsistence." For it is quite enough for a man's reasoning faculty to advance
> as far as to learn that the Cause of the Universe is and subsists. To be anxious
> to continue his course yet further, and inquire about essence or quality in

---

[20] Cf. JONAS' concluding statement on the 'Unknown God' of Gnosticism, in: The Gnostic
Religion, pp. 288f. It might be observed, however, that Philo does not use the term
ἄγνωστος. But cf. Josephus Ap. II.167. Josephus can hardly be called a 'Gnostic'!

God, is a folly fit for the world's childhood. Not even to Moses, the all-wise, did God accord this, albeit he had made countless requests, but a divine communication was issued to him, "Thou shalt behold that which is behind Me, but My Face thou shalt not see" (Exod 33:23). This meant, that all that follows in the wake of God is within the good man's apprehension, while He Himself alone is beyond it, beyond, that is, in the line of straight and direct approach, a mode of approach by which (had it been possible) His quality would have been made known, but brought within ken by the powers that follow and attend Him; for these make evident not His essence but His subsistence from the things which He accomplishes."[21]

But Philo does not confine himself to the 'natural' or 'cosmological' knowledge of God; he can speak also of an 'unmediated' experience of God. In this connection JONAS quotes and discusses Leg All III 99, Abr 119ff., and Praem 43—46 (pp. 85—87). The latter passage is especially important:

"These[22] no doubt are truly admirable persons and superior to the other classes.[23] They have as I said advanced from down to up by a sort of heavenly ladder and by reason and reflection happily inferred the Creator from His works. But those, if such there be, who have had the power to apprehend Him through Himself without the co-operation of any reasoning process to lead them to the sight, must be recorded as holy and genuine worshippers and friends of God in very truth. In their company is he who in the Hebrew is called Israel but in our tongue the God-seer who sees not His real nature, for that, as I said, is impossible — but that He IS. And this knowledge he has gained not from any other source, not from things on earth or things in Heaven, not from the elements or combinations of elements mortal or immortal, but at the summons of Him alone who has willed to reveal His existence as a person to the suppliant. How this access has been obtained may be well seen through an illustration. Do we behold the sun which sense perceives by any other thing than the sun, or the stars by any others than the stars, and in general is not light seen by light? In the same way God too is

---

[21] Text: τὸ δ' ὁρατὸν εἶναι τὸ ὂν οὐ κυριολογεῖται, κατάχρησις δ' ἐστὶν ἐφ' ἑκάστην αὑτοῦ τῶν δυνάμεων ἀναφερομένου. καὶ γὰρ νῦν οὔ φησιν· ἴδετε ἐμέ – ἀμήχανον γὰρ τὸν κατὰ τὸ εἶναι θεὸν ὑπὸ γενέσεως τὸ παράπαν κατανοηθῆναι – ἀλλ' ὅτι ἐγώ εἰμι ἴδετε, τουτέστι τὴν ἐμὴν ὕπαρξιν θεάσασθε. ἀνθρώπου γὰρ ἐξαρκεῖ λογισμῷ μέχρι τοῦ καταμαθεῖν ὅτι ἔστι τε καὶ ὑπάρχει τὸ τῶν ὅλων αἴτιον προελθεῖν· περαιτέρω δὲ σπουδάζειν τρέπεσθαι, ὡς περὶ οὐσίας ἢ ποιότητος ζητεῖν, ὠγύγιός τις ἠλιθιότης. (169) οὐδὲ γὰρ Μωυσῇ τῷ πανσόφῳ κατένευσεν ὁ θεὸς τοῦτό γε, καίτοι γε μυρίας ποιησαμένῳ δεήσεις, ἀλλὰ χρησμὸς ἐξέπεσεν αὐτῷ, ὅτι "τὰ μὲν ὀπίσω θεάσῃ, τὸ δὲ πρόσωπον οὐκ ὄψει" τοῦτο δ' ἦν· πάνθ' ὅσα μετὰ τὸν θεὸν τῷ σπουδαίῳ καταληπτά, αὐτὸς δὲ μόνος ἀκατάληπτος· ἀκατάληπτός γε ἐκ τῆς ἀντικρὺς καὶ κατ' εὐθυωρίαν προσβολῆς – διὰ γὰρ ταύτης οἷος ἦν ἐμηνύετ' ἄν – ἐκ δὲ τῶν ἑπομένων καὶ ἀκολούθων δυνάμεων ⟨καταληπτός⟩· αὗται γὰρ οὐ τὴν οὐσίαν, τὴν δ' ὕπαρξιν ἐκ τῶν ἀποτελουμένων αὐτῷ παριστᾶσι.

[22] The Stoics, according to JONAS.

[23] Those discussed in 40, who either deny the Godhead or take an agnostic position.

His own brightness and is discerned through Himself alone, without anything co-operating or being able to co-operate in giving a perfect apprehension of His existence. They then do but make a happy guess, who are at
pains to discern the Uncreated, and Creator of all from His creation, and are
on the same footing as those who try to trace the nature of the monad from
the dyad, whereas observation of the dyad should begin with the monad
which is the starting-point. The seekers for truth are those who envisage
God through God, light through light."[24]

Jonas takes this statement to be an authentic expression of Gnosticism.
Though acknowledging that Philo does not give expression to a strict dualistic
„Akosmismus," he nevertheless argues that the claim to an unmediated access to
God through Himself above and beyond the world and its way of knowledge is
essentially 'Gnostic' (p. 87, cf. p. 98).

In his discussion of the 'mystical' knowledge of God in Philo (pp. 99ff.)
Jonas begins with Philo's treatment of prophetic ecstasy. He quotes and discusses
the well-known passage in Heres 263—265 (p. 100), wherein Philo interprets the
experience of Abraham in Gen 15:12, "about sunset there fell on him an ecstasy":

"He refers to our mind under the symbol "sun." For what the mind is in us,
the sun is in the world, for each is a light-bearer, the one sending forth to the
whole world a sense-perceptible beam, the other sending forth to us by
means of its apprehensions mental rays. So long as the mind surrounds us
with its illumination, pouring forth as it were a noon-time beam into the
whole soul, we remain in ourselves and are not possessed. But when it comes
to its setting there falls upon us in all likelihood an ecstasy, a divine possession, a madness. For when the divine light shines, the human light sets; and
when the former sets the latter rises and dawns. This is what regularly

---

[24] This famous passage provides the title (φωτὶ φῶς) and starting point for E. R. Goodenough's important and controversial book, 'By Light, Light' (op. cit. n. 4). Text: ἀλλ'
οὗτοί γε οἱ θεσπέσιοι καὶ τῶν ἄλλων διενηνοχότες, ὅπερ ἔφην, κάτωθεν ἄνω προ-
ῆλθον οἷα διά τινος οὐρανίου κλίμακος, ἀπὸ τῶν ἔργων εἰκότι λογισμῷ στοχασάμενοι
τὸν δημιουργόν. εἰ δέ τινες ἐδυνήθησαν αὐτὸν ἐξ ἑαυτοῦ καταλαβεῖν ἑτέρῳ μηδενὶ
χρησάμενοι λογισμῷ συνεργῷ πρὸς τὴν θέαν, ἐν ὁσίοις καὶ γνησίοις θεραπευταῖς καὶ
θεοφιλέσιν ὡς ἀληθῶς ἀναγραφέσθωσαν. (44) τούτων ἐστὶν ὁ Χαλδαϊστὶ μὲν προσ-
αγορευόμενος Ἰσραήλ, Ἑλληνιστὶ δὲ ὁρῶν θεόν, οὐχ οἷός ἐστιν ὁ θεός — τοῦτο γὰρ
ἀμήχανον, ὡς ἔφην —, ἀλλ' ὅτι ἔστιν, οὐ παρ' ἑτέρου τινὸς μαθών, οὐχὶ τῶν κατὰ γῆν,
οὐχὶ τῶν κατ' οὐρανόν, οὐχὶ τῶν ὅσα στοιχεῖα ἢ συγκρίματα θνητά τε αὖ καὶ ἀθάνατα,
ἀλλὰ παρ' αὐτοῦ μόνου μετακληθεὶς τὴν ἰδίαν ὕπαρξιν ἀναφῆναι θελήσαντος ἱκέτη.
(45) πῶς δ' ἡ προσβολὴ γέγονεν, ἄξιον διά τινος εἰκόνος ἰδεῖν. τὸν αἰσθητὸν τοῦτον
ἥλιον μὴ ἑτέρῳ τινὶ θεωροῦμεν ἢ ἡλίῳ; τὰ δὲ ἄστρα μή τισιν ἄλλοις ἢ ἄστροις θεωροῦμεν; καὶ συνόλως τὸ φῶς ἆρ' οὐ φωτὶ βλέπεται; τὸν αὐτὸν δὴ τρόπον καὶ ὁ θεὸς ἑαυτοῦ
φέγγος ὢν δι' αὐτοῦ μόνου θεωρεῖται, μηδενὸς ἄλλου συνεργοῦντος ἢ δυναμένου συν-
εργῆσαι πρὸς τὴν εἰλικρινῆ κατάληψιν τῆς ὑπάρξεως αὐτοῦ. (46) στοχασταὶ μὲν οὖν οἱ
ἀπὸ τῶν γεγονότων τὸν ἀγένητον καὶ γεννητὴν τῶν ὅλων σπεύδοντες θεωρεῖν, ὅμοιόν τι
δρῶντες τοῖς ἀπὸ δυάδος μονάδος φύσιν ἐρευνῶσι, δέον ἔμπαλιν ἀπὸ μονάδος — ἀρχὴ
γὰρ αὕτη — δυάδα σκοπεῖν· ἀλήθειαν δὲ μέτιασιν οἱ τὸν θεὸν θεῷ φαντασιωθέντες,
φωτὶ φῶς.

happens to the race of prophets, for the mind is evicted from us at the arrival of the divine Spirit, but at its departure the mind enters once again. Mortal may not cohabit with immortal. Therefore the setting of the mind and the darkness around it produce ecstasy and divinely inspired madness."[25]

Here Philo no longer speaks of 'seeing' God, but uses categories common to the mystery-religions of late antiquity, especially the well-known analogy of ecstasy (and initiation) and death, though Philo shrinks from using the mystery-religions' category of deification which, for him, is theologically impossible (p. 101, cf. p. 110).

The experience of the 'setting' of the human light and the 'rising' of the divine — coupled with a characteristically 'Gnostic' depreciation of bodily existence — has practical consequences, too, in the realm of ethics. JONAS quotes Heres 69 in this connection (p. 103):

"Therefore, my soul, if thou feelest any yearning to inherit the good things of God, leave not only thy land, that is the body, thy kinsfolk, that is the senses, thy father's house, that is speech, but be a fugitive from thyself also and issue forth from thyself. Like persons possessed and corybants, be filled with inspired frenzy, even as the prophets are inspired."[26]

Philo's emphasis on the 'nothingness' of man before God leads ethically to self-denial and asceticism, and mystically to a knowledge and experience of God. Indeed for Philo γιγνώσκειν θεόν and ἀπογιγνώσκειν ἑαυτόν are correlates, as is shown by Somn I.60 (quoted on p. 106):

"For when he most knew,[27] then he most renounced[27] himself, in order that he might come to an accurate knowledge of him who really IS. Thus it naturally is, that he who thoroughly comprehends himself thoroughly re-

---

[25] My translation. Text: ἥλιον διὰ συμβόλου του ἡμέτερον καλῶν νοῦν· ὅπερ γὰρ ἐν ἡμῖν λογισμός, τοῦτο ἐν κόσμῳ ἥλιος, ἐπειδὴ φωσφορεῖ ἑκάτερος, ὁ μὲν τῷ παντὶ φέγγος αἰσθητὸν ἐκπέμπων, ὁ δὲ ἡμῖν αὐτοῖς τὰς νοητὰς διὰ τῶν καταλήψεων αὐγάς. (264) ἕως μὲν οὖν ἔτι περιλάμπει καὶ περιπολεῖ ἡμῶν ὁ νοῦς μεσημβρινὸν οἷα φέγγος εἰς πᾶσαν τὴν ψυχὴν ἀναχέων, ἐν ἑαυτοῖς ὄντες οὐ κατεχόμεθα· ἐπειδὰν δὲ πρὸς δυσμὰς γένηται, κατὰ τὸ εἰκὸς ἔκστασις καὶ ἡ ἔνθεος ἐπιπίπτει κατοκωχή τε καὶ μανία. ὅταν μὲν γὰρ φῶς τὸ θεῖον ἐπιλάμψῃ, δύεται τὸ ἀνθρώπινον, ὅταν δ' ἐκεῖνο δύηται, τοῦτ' ἀνίσχει καὶ ἀνατέλλει. (265) τῷ δὲ προφητικῷ γένει φιλεῖ τοῦτο συμβαίνειν· ἐξοικίζεται μὲν γὰρ ἐν ἡμῖν ὁ νοῦς κατὰ τὴν τοῦ θείου πνεύματος ἄφιξιν, κατὰ δὲ τὴν μετανάστασιν αὐτοῦ πάλιν εἰσοικίζεται· θέμις γὰρ οὐκ ἔστι θνητὸν ἀθανάτῳ συνοικῆσαι. διὰ τοῦτο ἡ δύσις τοῦ λογισμοῦ καὶ τὸ περὶ αὐτὸν σκότος ἔκστασιν καὶ θεοφόρητον μανίαν ἐγέννησε.

[26] Text: πόθος οὖν εἴ τις εἰσέρχεταί σε, ψυχή, τῶν θείων ἀγαθῶν κληρονομῆσαι, μὴ μόνον "γῆν," τὸ σῶμα, καὶ "συγγένειαν," ⟨τὴν⟩ αἴσθησιν, καὶ "οἶκον πατρός," τὸν λόγον, καταλίπῃς, ἀλλὰ καὶ σαυτὴν ἀπόδραθι καὶ ἔκστηθι σεαυτῆς, ὥσπερ οἱ κατεχόμενοι καὶ κορυβαντιῶντες βακχευθεῖσα καὶ θεοφορηθεῖσα κατά τινα προφητικὸν ἐπιθειασμόν·

[27] The word-play, ἔγνω – ἀπέγνω, is impossible to render adequately either in English or in German.

nounces himself, perceiving clearly the absolute nothingness of that which
has been created. He who renounces himself knows the One who IS."[28]

Thus, for Philo, self-knowledge is knowledge of one's own nothingness.[29]
JONAS understands this expression of the opposition between God and man (*"jen-
seitigem Gott und diesseitigem Mensch,"* p. 107) to be just another expression of
the basic Gnostic opposition between 'God' and 'world' (cf. also pp. 38 and 117).

Another indication of the 'Gnostic' tendency of Philo's religion, according
to JONAS, is his classification of mankind into three categories, corresponding to
the familiar Gnostic categories of 'Sarkics,' 'Psychics,' and 'Pneumatics'.[30] In this
connection he refers to Gig 60f. (p. 113, referring also to Cher 7—9 and Leg All
III.244f.) wherein Philo shows that some men are "of earth," some "of heaven,"
and others "of God":

"The earth-born are those who take the pleasures of the body for their
quarry, who make it their practice to indulge in them and enjoy them and
provide the means by which each of them may be promoted. The heaven-
born are the votaries of the arts and of knowledge, the lovers of learning. For
the heavenly element in us is the mind, as the heavenly beings are each of
them a mind. And it is the mind which pursues the learning of the schools
and the other arts one and all, which sharpens and whets itself, aye and trains
and drills itself solid in the contemplation of what is intelligible by mind. But
the men of God are priests and prophets who have refused to accept membership in the commonwealth of the world and to become citizens therein,
but have risen wholly above the sphere of sense-perception and have been
translated into the world of the intelligible and dwell there registered as
freemen of the commonwealth of Ideas, which are imperishable and incorporeal."[31]

---

[28] My translation. Text: ὅτε γὰρ μάλιστα ἔγνω, τότε μάλιστα ἀπέγνω ἑαυτόν, ἵνα τοῦ πρὸς
ἀλήθειαν ὄντος εἰς ἀκριβῆ γνῶσιν ἔλθῃ. καὶ πέφυκεν οὕτως ἔχειν· ὁ λίαν καταλαβὼν
ἑαυτὸν λίαν ἀπέγνωκε τὴν ἐν πᾶσι τοῦ γενητοῦ σαφῶς προλαβὼν οὐδένειαν, ὁ δ᾽
ἀπογνοὺς ἑαυτὸν γινώσκει τὸν ὄντα.

[29] Cf. JONAS' remarks in: The Gnostic Religion, p. 280, contrasting the Hellenic way to God
with the Philonic: "But to Philo self-knowledge means 'to know the nothingness of the
mortal race' (Mut 54), and through this knowledge one attains to the knowledge of God:
'for then is the time for the creature to encounter the Creator, when it has recognized its
own nothingness' (Heres 30)." Cf. also Gnosis 1, pp. 38—43.

[30] Cf. his discussion of *"anthropologische Zwei- und Dreistufigkeit"* in 1, pp. 212—214.

[31] Text: γῆς μὲν οἱ θηρευτικοὶ τῶν σώματος ἡδονῶν ἀπόλαυσίν τε καὶ χρῆσιν ἐπιτηδεύ-
οντες αὐτῶν καὶ πορισταὶ τῶν συντεινόντων εἰς ἑκάστην, οὐρανοῦ δὲ ὅσοι τεχνῖται καὶ
ἐπιστήμονες καὶ φιλομαθεῖς — τὸ γὰρ οὐράνιον τῶν ἐν ἡμῖν ὁ νοῦς (νοῦς δὲ καὶ τῶν
κατ᾽ οὐρανὸν ἕκαστον) τὰ ἐγκύκλια καὶ τὰς ἄλλας ἅπαξ ἁπάσας ἐπιτηδεύει τέχνας,
παραθήγων καὶ ἀκονῶν ἔτι τε γυμνάζων καὶ συγκροτῶν ἐν τοῖς νοητοῖς αὐτὸν — (61)
θεοῦ δὲ ἄνθρωποι ἱερεῖς καὶ προφῆται, οἵτινες οὐκ ἠξίωσαν πολιτείας τῆς παρὰ τῷ
κόσμῳ τυχεῖν καὶ κοσμοπολῖται γενέσθαι, τὸ δὲ αἰσθητὸν πᾶν ὑπερκύψαντες εἰς τὸν
νοητὸν κόσμον μετανέστησαν κἀκεῖθι ᾤκησαν ἐγγραφέντες ἀφθάρτων ⟨καὶ⟩ ἀσωμά-
των ἰδεῶν πολιτείᾳ.

JONAS sums up his discussion of Philo by stressing that the manifold ways in which γνῶσις θεοῦ functions in Philonic religion all develop from a common root, which in fact is the most original element of Philonic religion but also finally a Gnostic one: „die Überzeugung von dem radikalen, fast feindlichen Gegensatz zwischen menschlich-irdisch-kosmischem ('psychischem') und göttlich transzendentem ('pneumatischem') Sein, und davon, daß jenes sich preisgeben muß, damit dieses anwesend sein kann" (p. 120).

As we have seen, JONAS includes Philo in the 'Gnostic' stream of the religion of late antiquity, though he is frequently forced to admit that Philo's religion is not so radically dualist as that of the ('mythological') Gnostic systems he so brilliantly analyzes in his first volume. Perhaps, then, we might raise the question as to whether Philo's religion should be characterized as 'Gnostic' at all. That Philo shares and reflects the 'spirit of late antiquity' is, of course, clear. But is this 'spirit of late antiquity' to be defined, simply, as 'Gnosis' or 'Gnosticism'?[32]

In this connection we should take up for discussion the important monograph of A. WLOSOK, 'Laktanz und die philosophische Gnosis'.[33] In this work the author traces the history of the motif of the upright posture (rectus status) of man and his contemplation of heaven (contemplatio caeli) from Plato (Pol IX.585 B– 586 B; Tim 9 A–D) to Lactantius, showing how the philosophical anthropology of Plato develops in Hellenistic times into religious speculation. The product of this development she calls „philosophische Gnosis." Whereas Plato interpreted the upright posture of man, and his contemplation of heaven, as a symbol for his natural disposition toward knowledge and worship of God, in later syncretistic Platonism, partly in reaction to the agnosticism of the Academy's Skeptic phase, the knowledge of God becomes a religious mystery. Inasmuch as Alexandria was the major metropolis of Hellenistic religious speculation, it was natural that the union of philosophy and 'mystery theology' should occur here (cf. pp. 48ff.). This syncretistic process affected pagan, Jewish, and Christian religions. The basic premise shared by all is that the natural kinship with God has been disturbed, and man has lost some of his divinity. God is understood as basically unknowable, and knowledge of God and union with him depends on a mystery of salvation through which the broken relationship with God is restored.

It should be noted that whereas WLOSOK characterizes this Hellenistic religious philosophy as "philosophical Gnosis," she purposely avoids any attempt to define what she calls „mythologische Gnosis," and does not deal at all with the various religious systems more commonly referred to under the designations 'Gnostic' and 'Gnosticism.'[34]

---

[32] For further discussion of this basic problem of definition, see below.

[33] A. WLOSOK, Laktanz und die philosophische Gnosis: Untersuchungen zu Geschichte und Terminologie der gnostischen Erlösungsvorstellung, Abh. Heidelb. Ak. Wiss., Phil.-hist. Kl., Heidelberg, 1960.

[34] Cf. Laktanz, p. 6, n. 10. She expresses the hope that study of the Nag Hammadi texts will lead to scholarly clarity on the problem of the unity and parameters of the Gnostic movement.

As can be expected, Philo occupies an important role in WLOSOK's treatment of „*die religiöse Umdeutung der philosophischen Anthropologie in der hellenistischen Religionsspekulation.*"[35] WLOSOK argues that (at the latest) by the time of the beginning of the Empire, there existed a Platonizing pagan mystery-theology in which cult-myths and mystery-rites were interpreted allegorically, in the light of a Platonism colored by Neo-Pythagoreanism. This kind of allegory was especially useful for Jewish-Hellenistic scripture-interpretation and the combination of biblical ideas of revelation with Platonic notions of the transcendent God. Philo is a product of this development and its most important representative. Philo interprets the various narratives of the Pentateuch under the influence of syncretistic Platonism as examples of the union of man with God (cf. esp. pp. 58—60).

The starting-point for WLOSOK's discussion of Philonic philosophical Gnosis is Philo's interpretation of the traditional Platonic anthropology in the light of the biblical doctrine of man as the 'image of God,' as found in Plant 16 ff. I quote here the most important section of the passage 16—22 (WLOSOK quotes and discusses Plant 16—27, pp. 60—69):

"Furthermore, while He fashioned the plants head downwards, fixing their heads in the portions of the earth where the soil lay deepest, He raised from the earth the heads of the animals that are without reason and set them on the top of a long neck, placing the fore feet as a support for the neck. But the build allotted to man was distinguished above that of other living creatures. For by turning the eyes of the others downwards He made them incline to the earth beneath them. The eyes of man, on the contrary, He set high up, that he might gaze on heaven, for man, as the old saying is, is a plant not earthly but heavenly. Now while others, by asserting that our human mind is a particle of the ethereal substance, have claimed for man a kinship with the upper air, our great Moses likened the fashion of the reasonable soul to no created thing, but averred it to be a genuine coinage of that dread Spirit, the Divine and Invisible One, signed and impressed by the seal of God, the stamp of which is the Eternal Word. His words are "God inbreathed into his face a breath of Life" (Gen 2:7); so that it cannot but be that he that receives is made in the likeness of Him Who sends forth the breath. Accordingly we also read that man has been made after the Image of God (Gen 1:27), not however after the image of anything created. It followed then, as a natural consequence of man's soul having been made after the image of the Archetype, the Word of the First Cause, that his body also was made erect, and could lift up its eyes to heaven, the purest portion of our universe, that by means of that which he could see man might clearly apprehend that which he could not see. Since, then, it was impossible for any to discern how the understanding tends towards the Existent One, save those only who had been drawn by Him — for each one of us knows what he has himself ex-

---

[35] The title of part 2 of her book (pp. 48—179). In this section she treats Philo (pp. 50—114), the Hermetica (pp. 115—142), and Clement of Alexandria (pp. 143—179).

perienced as no other can know it — He endows the bodily eyes with the power of taking the direction of the upper air, and so makes them a distinct representation of the invisible eye. For, seeing that the eyes formed out of perishable matter obtained so great reach as to travel from the earthly region to heaven, that is so far away, and to touch its bounds, how vast must we deem the flight in all directions of the eyes of the soul? The strong yearning to perceive the Existent One gives them wings to attain not only to the furthest region of the upper air, but to overpass the very bounds of the entire universe and speed away toward the Uncreate."[36]

In this passage Philo starts with the anthropological tradition of Platonism, but as a 'corrective' he brings in the biblical doctrine of the 'image of God', which he interprets along Platonic lines. In doing so he also rejects Stoic views on the soul as an ethereal substance. He treats the upright posture of man and his ability to "lift his eyes to heaven" as a symbol of the soul's tending towards the transcendent God. In close dependence upon Plato's description of the flight of the soul (Phaedrus 247Bff.), Philo replaces Plato's statements on the soul's vision of the noetic cosmos with a claim that the soul's goal is a vision of God himself. But this flight of the soul to God is presented by Philo as a mystery-ascent, made possible by the special grace of God and his divine call:

"This is why those who crave for wisdom and knowledge with insatiable persistence are said in the Sacred Oracles to have been called upwards; for it

---

[36] Text: καὶ μὴν τὰ μὲν φυτὰ κατωκάρα ἀπειργάζετο τὰς κεφαλὰς αὐτῶν ἐν τοῖς βαθυ-γειοτάτοις γῆς μέρεσι πήξας, ζῴων δὲ τῶν ἀλόγων τὰς κεφαλὰς ἀνελκύσας ἀπὸ γῆς ἐπὶ προμήκους αὐχένος ἄκρας ἡρμόζετο τῷ αὐχένι ὥσπερ ἐπίβασιν τοὺς ἐμπροσθίους πόδας θείς. (17) ἐξαιρέτου δὲ τῆς κατασκευῆς ἔλαχεν ἄνθρωπος· τῶν μὲν γὰρ ἄλλων τὰς ὄψεις περιήγαγε κάτω κάμψας, διὸ νένευκε πρὸς χέρσον, ἀνθρώπου δὲ ἔμπαλιν ἀνώρθωσεν, ἵνα τὸν οὐρανὸν καταθεᾶται, φυτὸν οὐκ ἐπίγειον ἀλλ' οὐράνιον, ὡς ὁ παλαιὸς λόγος, ὑπάρχων. (18) ἀλλ' οἱ μὲν ἄλλοι τῆς αἰθερίου φύσεως τὸν ἡμέτερον νοῦν μοῖραν εἰπόντες εἶναι συγγένειαν ἀνθρώπῳ πρὸς αἰθέρα συνῆψαν. ὁ δὲ μέγας Μωυσῆς οὐδενὶ τῶν γεγονότων τῆς λογικῆς ψυχῆς τὸ εἶδος ὡμοίωσεν, ἀλλ' εἶπεν αὐτὴν τοῦ θείου καὶ ἀοράτου πνεύματος ἐκείνου δόκιμον εἶναι νόμισμα σημειωθὲν καὶ τυπω-θὲν σφραγῖδι θεοῦ, ἧς ὁ χαρακτήρ ἐστιν ὁ ἀίδιος λόγος· (19) "ἐνέπνευσε" γάρ φησιν " ὁ θεὸς εἰς τὸ πρόσωπον αὐτοῦ πνοὴν ζωῆς," ὥστε ἀνάγκη πρὸς τὸν ἐκπέμποντα τὸν δεχό-μενον ἀπεικονίσθαι· διὸ καὶ λέγεται κατ' εἰκόνα θεοῦ τὸν ἄνθρωπον γεγενῆσθαι, οὐ μὴν κατ' εἰκόνα τινὸς τῶν γεγονότων. (20) ἀκόλουθον οὖν ἦν τῆς ἀνθρώπου ψυχῆς κατὰ τὸν ἀρχέτυπον τοῦ αἰτίου λόγον ἀπεικονισθείσης καὶ τὸ σῶμα ἀνεγερθὲν πρὸς τὴν καθα-ρωτάτην τοῦ παντὸς μοῖραν, οὐρανόν, τὰς ὄψεις ἀνατεῖναι, ἵνα τῷ φανερῷ τὸ ἀφανὲς ἐκδήλως καταλαμβάνηται. (21) ἐπειδὴ τοίνυν τὴν πρὸς τὸ ὂν διανοίας ὁλκὴν ἀμήχανον ἦν ἰδεῖν ὅτι μὴ τοὺς ἀχθέντας πρὸς αὐτοῦ μόνους — ὃ γὰρ πέπονθεν ἕκαστος, αὐτὸς ἐξαιρέτως οἶδεν —, εἴδωλον ἐναργὲς ἀειδοῦς ὄμματος τὰ τοῦ σώματος ποιεῖ δυνάμενα πρὸς αἰθέρα ἀπονεύειν. (22) ὁπότε γὰρ οἱ ἐκ φθαρτῆς παγέντες ὕλης ὀφθαλμοὶ τοσοῦ-τον ἐπέβησαν, ὡς ἀπὸ τοῦ τῆς γῆς χωρίου πρὸς τὸν μακρὰν οὕτως ἀφεστῶτα ἀνα-τρέχειν οὐρανὸν καὶ ψαύειν τῶν περάτων αὐτοῦ, πόσον τινὰ χρὴ νομίσαι τὸν πάντῃ δρόμον τῶν ψυχῆς ὀμμάτων; ἅπερ ὑπὸ πολλοῦ τοῦ τὸ ὂν κατιδεῖν τηλαυγῶς ἱμέρου πτερωθέντα οὐ μόνον πρὸς τὸν ἔσχατον αἰθέρα τείνεται, παραμειψάμενα δὲ καὶ παντὸς τοῦ κόσμου τοὺς ὅρους ἐπείγεται πρὸς τὸν ἀγένητον.

accords with God's ways that those who have received His down-breathing should be called up to Him (Plant 23)."[37]

Wlosok concludes, „*Das höchste Ziel des Menschen ist nun die geistge-wirkte Gottesschau, die ihm nur noch als Gnadengeschenk zuteil wird*" (p. 69).

In describing the Philonic ascent of the soul as culminating in a „*Gottes-schau*" or a „*Lichtschau*,"[38] involving an „*Offenbarungsmysterium*" (p. 68), Wlosok does not take account of the fact that, for Philo, no ultimate access to God is possible. Philo says in the passage quoted above only that the soul ascends toward the Existent One, and the eye of the soul has a "yearning" (ἵμερος) to see the Existent One. In this connection we should recall Jonas' interpretation of Post 168f.[39]

Wlosok proceeds to interpret, in a similar vein, Leg All III. 96, 100–102; Vita Mos II. 69f.; Mut 54–56; and Somn II. 226 (pp. 69–76).

Her discussion of „*Aufrichtung und Himmelsschau*" (pp. 60–76) is fol-lowed by a second major section on „*Erleuchtung und Weisheitseinstrom*" (pp. 76–107). She argues that Philo knew of, and used, a mystical theory of enlight-enment current in Alexandria, such as was also adopted and reworked in Her-metic religion and later Christian theology. It builds especially on Platonic episte-mology and serves to 'spiritualize' the various conceptions belonging to the mystery cults. In the resulting 'philosophical Gnosis' human ignorance was underscored on the one hand, and a solution to the problem of religious know-ledge was advanced on the other. Philo is part and parcel of this philosophical Gnosis, with his theory of human ignorance (Ebr 265ff., treated pp. 77–81), his allegories of the biblical patriarchs and of Moses as examples of an „*Aufstiegs-mysterium zur Gottesschau*" (cf. p. 81), his various statements on divine light and religious enlightenment, and his presentation of 'Israel' (the Jewish community, according to Wlosok, cf. pp. 97ff.) as the "gnostic race" travelling the "royal way" of wisdom, virtue and γνῶσις θεοῦ (see esp. Quod Deus 142–144, 155f., 160f., 180; cf. pp. 102–107).

Thus, for Wlosok, Philo is representative of a "philosophical Gnosis" in which the major conceptions of the mystery cults are reinterpreted philosoph-ically and thereby 'spiritualized,' and in which philosophical traditions are given a religious and 'mystical' interpretation (cf. p. 111). Philo represents, too, an important step in the development of Christian theology (p. 113f.).

Whereas Wlosok eschews any discussion of what she (and Jonas) calls "mythological Gnosis," and thus leaves completely unanswered the problem of the relationship between Philo and 'Gnosticism' as more commonly conceived,

---

[37] Text: διὰ τοῦτο ἐν τοῖς χρησμοῖς οἱ σοφίας καὶ ἐπιστήμης ἄπληστοι διατελοῦντες ἀνα-κεκλῆσθαι λέγονται· πρὸς γὰρ τὸ θεῖον ἄνω καλεῖσθαι θέμις τοὺς ὑπ'αὐτοῦ καταπνευ-σθέντας. This is developed by Philo in what follows, with reference to Bezalel and Moses.

[38] Wlosok quotes in a note (p. 68, n. 22) a parallel passage, Op 69–71, wherein, however, the eye of the soul is blinded by a blazing light-stream before gaining access to God him-self!

[39] See above, pp. 304–305.

R. M. WILSON devotes an entire monograph to the problem of the relationship between Diaspora Judaism (especially Philo) and what he calls "the Gnosticism of the second century" (essentially = the „mythologische Gnosis" of JONAS and WLOSOK). Acutely aware of the controversies and problems involved in delineating the Gnostic movement, and especially in tracing its origins, he calls his book 'The Gnostic Problem.'[40]

After a chapter devoted to "the Judaism of the Dispersion" (ch. 1, pp. 1–29), WILSON devotes a lengthy chapter to "Alexandrian Judaism and Philo" (ch. 2, pp. 30–63), choosing to stress those aspects of Philo's writings which represent a link between Greek/Jewish speculation and Christian/Gnostic thought. He argues that Philo is not atypical of the main intellectual and religious currents of Alexandrian Judaism. Although Philo and others in Alexandria accommodated their Jewish faith to Greek ideas, Philo was and remained a Jew, and "his chief delight was in the faith of his fathers" (p. 48).

Philo occupies a prominent place in WILSON's third chapter, 'Gnosticism and Christianity in New Testament Times' (pp. 64–96), in which he takes up the controversial problem of the nature and origins of the Gnostic movement, stressing that "the question is complicated by problems of terminology" (p. 65). For his part WILSON wishes to limit the term 'Gnostic' to the kind of religion exemplified by the Gnostic systems of the second century described by Irenaeus and Hippolytus. "It must be admitted that there was a good deal of 'gnosticizing' thought in the early years of the Christian era, for example in Philo, but this is not yet definitely 'Gnostic' in the full sense. It would therefore seem advisable to adopt the narrower definition, recognizing the affinities with Gnosticism of such as Philo on the one hand, and Mandaeism and Manichaeism on the other, but reserving the term 'Gnostic' with DODD[41] as 'a label for a large and somewhat amorphous group of religious systems described by Irenaeus and Hippolytus in their works against Heresy, and similar systems known from other sources'" (pp. 67–68). WILSON states that the earliest documentary evidence goes back to the middle of the first century, and "it may be that 'Gnosticism' in the full sense is even older, but so far as can be seen at present it is more or less contemporary with Christianity" (p. 68).

According to WILSON, therefore, Philo cannot be regarded as a 'Gnostic.' The supposed 'Gnostic' traits in Philo are the product of his Hellenistic environment: the condemnation of the sensible world as a prison, the assumption of a kinship between the human soul and the heavenly world, his stress on the transcendence of God, the yearning of the soul for release and union with God, etc. But Philo's dualism is not so sharp as the Gnostic, "and in this and other respects he presents a less developed form of the scheme" (p. 72). Thus, although Philo has "certain Gnostic tendencies", he is nevertheless "far removed from the

---

[40] R. M. WILSON, The Gnostic Problem: A Study of the Relations between Hellenistic Judaism and the Gnostic Heresy, London, 1958. Cf. also Gnostic Origins, VC 9, 1955, pp. 193–211; and Gnostic Origins Again, VC 11, 1957, pp. 93–110.

[41] He quotes from C. H. DODD, The Interpretation of the Fourth Gospel, Cambridge, 1953, p. 97.

elaborate and detailed schemes of the later thinkers"; he cannot, therefore, be called a Gnostic (p. 73).

WILSON devotes the next two chapters to discussion of "the earlier Gnostic sects" (ch. 4, pp. 97–115) and "later Gnosticism and Christian philosophers" (ch. 5, pp. 116–148), using as his basic sources the (polemical) descriptions of the early church Fathers. In these chapters he finds some specific points of comparison with Philo: E.g. some points in Saturninus' system[42] "recall the writings of Philo,[43] such as the account of the creation of earthly man, although this seems more closely connected with Stoic doctrine" (p. 103); Basilides'[44] doctrine of the πνεῦμα shows affinities with the Platonizing views of Philo[45] (pp. 125 and 141, n. 81). But his conclusions regarding the relationship between Gnosticism and Judaism (including Philo) are reserved for his last two chapters (ch. 7, 'Judaism and Gnosticism,' pp. 172–255; ch. 8, 'Diaspora, Syncretism, and Gnosticism,' pp. 256–265). His basic conclusion is that "Judaism was a contributory source to the origin and development of Gnosticism" (p. 173), more specifically Diaspora Judaism (cf. p. 176). Nevertheless a full assessment of the relationship of Diaspora Judaism to Gnosticism is difficult, due to the paucity of sources. Philo "represents at most only Alexandria, and probably one aspect of Alexandria at that" (p. 179). He takes issue with FRIEDLÄNDER's theory of pre-Christian antinomian Gnostic sects, claiming that FRIEDLÄNDER "seems to read too much into his sources"; yet, on the other hand, he suggests that FRIEDLÄNDER's view, "while hardly applicable to the Diaspora as a whole, may well hold good for Jews on the fringe of Judaism or for apostates" (p. 181).

WILSON then proceeds to assess the relation of Judaism to Gnosticism under 1) the idea of God (pp. 183–202); 2) the nature of the world and creation (pp. 202–207); 3) anthropology (pp. 207–211); 4) salvation (pp. 211–218) and 5) the Redeemer (pp. 218–228). Philo occupies an important part of this discussion. Philo shares with Gnosticism the idea of the transcendence of God (pp. 183 and 185 f.), but Philo does not distinguish between the highest God and lower demiurge (p. 188). There are notable points of contact between Philo and the Gnostics in their doctrine of Sophia (pp. 195–199) and other cosmic powers (pp. 199–202), but whereas "Philo shows the tendency of the time towards mythological expression," the Gnostics "carry the hypostatization of divine attributes and abstract ideas to a further degree," under the basic impulse of "a wrong attitude towards God and towards the world" (p. 202).

Philo and Gnosticism share the basic assumption that man belongs to a higher, heavenly world, but this doctrine, going back to Plato and before, is a "commonplace in the Hellenistic Age" (p. 207). Philo interprets the biblical story of the Fall as a fall into matter[46] and equates the divine seed or spark with the

---

[42] Iren. Haer I.24.
[43] He refers to Op 69 ff., a text which will be treated below.
[44] Hippolytus Ref VII.20–27.
[45] He cites Gig 13.
[46] Op 151 ff. and Leg All II are cited.

divine inbreathing.[47] Man is viewed as ignorant of his true glory, needing to be roused out of his sleep and to strive up the path to his true abode. Such ideas are shared by the Gnostics; indeed Philo and the Gnostics share such specific ideas as the interpretation of the "coats of skin" in Genesis as referring to the earthly body (pp. 209f.).[48] With regard to salvation, too, "Philo has something of the Gnostic idea of the acquisition of ἀφθαρσία through γνῶσις, and, as at other points, is closer to Gnosticism than either Christianity or philosophy, but this is due to his assimilation of pagan ideas" (p. 216). Nevertheless there does not appear to be a "redeemer myth" in Philo such as one finds in Gnosticism (p. 221).

To sum up: whereas "Philo could in a sense be called a Gnostic, much as Paul or Clement of Alexandria, . . . in the narrower sense adopted in this study he is not a Gnostic" (p. 261).

It is clear that WILSON's book contains some important insights concerning the contribution of Hellenistic Judaism to the development of Gnosticism. Yet it lacks precision on the problem of the delineation and definition of Gnosticism, and therefore fails to distinguish clearly enough in what sense Philo is, or is not, 'Gnostic.'[49] When WILSON is finally satisfied with concluding that "Gnosticism is an atmosphere, not a system" (p. 261), we are left with something no less amorphous than JONAS' „spätantiker Geist."[50]

2. The Messina Colloquium and Recent Scholarship

WILSON's book appeared at a time when the now-famous Coptic Gnostic codices[51] discovered near Nag Hammadi, Egypt (ancient Chenoboskion), were still largely inaccessible to scholarly scrutiny. To be sure, he was able to devote a chapter to a consideration of two important Coptic texts (ch. 7),[52] but the vast

---

[47] Op 134ff. is cited. Cf. Gen 2:7, and further discussion below.

[48] Cf. Gen 3:21; Philo: Leg All III.69; Post 137; Conf 55; Valentinian Gnosticism: Clem. Alex. Exc Theod 55; Iren. Haer I.5.5; Hermetica: C.H. 7.2.

[49] Cf. the criticisms of K. RUDOLPH, Gnosis und Gnostizismus, ein Forschungsbericht, TR 36, 1971, pp. 105–108.

[50] WILSON's later book, Gnosis and the New Testament, Philadelphia, 1968, does not materially advance the discussion of the relationship of Philo to Gnosticism. He suggests the category 'pre-gnosis' for certain phenomena occurring in Philo, the Dead Sea Scrolls, and parts of the New Testament (p. 23), and finally also suggests that the earliest beginnings of the Gnostic movement "are to be sought in Jewish circles, probably in Palestine or Syria rather than Alexandria, for there are Jewish elements in Gnosticism of which there is no trace in Philo" (p. 144).

[51] A one-volume English translation of all of the tractates contained in the Nag Hammadi Codices is now available: J. M. ROBINSON and M. MEYER, ed., The Nag Hammadi Library in English, San Francisco and Leiden, 1977. For particulars on the discovery of the Nag Hammadi Codices see ROBINSON's introduction to this volume, and ROBINSON, The Discovery of the Nag Hammadi Codices, Biblical Archeologist 42 (1979), 206–224.

[52] Two Original Gnostic Documents: Apocryphon Johannis and Evangelium Veritatis. He used the version of the 'Apocryphon of John' found in the Berlin Gnostic Codex, a Coptic codex which was acquired by the Berlin Museum in 1896 but was first published only in

majority of the Coptic documents were still unpublished. Meanwhile, the reports that were circulated concerning these important documents, and especially the book by J. DORESSE, 'The Secret Books of the Egyptian Gnostics',[53] sparked an enormous interest in the phenomenon of Gnosticism in scholarly circles. In April, 1966, an international colloquium was held in Messina, Italy, organized by U. BIANCHI under the auspices of the International Association for the History of Religions, which was devoted to the problem of the origins and definition of Gnosticism. The published volume of essays from that colloquium[54] has had an extraordinary influence in scholarly circles, and represents a watershed in the recent history of scholarship on Gnosticism.

One of the most important results of this colloquium was a "proposal for a terminological and conceptual agreement with regard to the theme of the colloquium," prepared by an ad hoc committee[55] and agreed to by a majority of the 69 scholars participating in the colloquium.[56] The Messina statement suggests that the terms *gnosis* and 'Gnosticism' should be differentiated, and identifies the latter

---

1955: W. TILL, Die Gnostischen Schriften des koptischen Papyrus Berolinensis 8502, TU 60, Berlin, 1955; 2nd ed. by H.-M. SCHENKE, Berlin, 1972. The Gospel of Truth, tractate 3 of Codex I (the Jung Codex), was the first of the Nag Hammadi tractates to be published: M. MALININE, H.-C. PUECH, G. QUISPEL, Evangelium Veritatis: Codex Jung f. VIII^V−XVI^V (p. 16−32) / f. XIX^r−XXII^r (p. 37−43), Zürich, 1956. Cf. M. MALININE et al., Evangelium Veritatis (Supplementum): Codex Jung f. XVII^r−f. XVIII^V (p. 33−36), Zürich, 1961.

[53] J. DORESSE, Les livres secrets des Gnostiques d'Égypte, Paris, 1958, trans. P. MAIRET, The Secret Books of the Egyptian Gnostics, London, 1960. DORESSE was the first western scholar to study the Nag Hammadi Codices. In this book he gives a summary of the contents of the entire library, on the basis of a first-hand examination of the manuscripts, and also discusses the problem of Gnosticism. He mentions Philo briefly (Secret Books, p. 11) as an example of a philosopher influenced by Oriental mysticism. According to DORESSE, "Philo does not yet know the anxiety which will underlie the speculations of the Gnostics," but he does represent several themes that they later developed, such as "the notion of a transcendent deity," and "the idea that not only the earth but the heavens above it are in darkness" (ibid.).

[54] Op. cit. n. 2.

[55] The committee consisted of G. WIDENGREN, H. JONAS, J. DANIÉLOU, C. COLPE, and U. BIANCHI. It is evident that H. JONAS' views had a large impact on the document that resulted. See his important essay, 'Delimitation of the Gnostic Phenomenon − Typological and Historical', in: Le origini, pp. 90−108, r. p. under the title, 'The Gnostic Syndrome: Typology of Its Thought, Imagination, and Mood', in: H. JONAS, Philosophical Essays: From Ancient Creed to Technological Man, Englewood Cliffs, 1974, pp. 263−276.

[56] Another important event of the Colloquium was an appeal to UNESCO to complete a project begun in 1961 to photograph the entire Nag Hammadi Library for a facsimile edition, and thus make the manuscripts available for scholarly study. This appeal was formulated by a committee consisting of T. SÄVE-SÖDERBERGH, M. KRAUSE, and J. M. ROBINSON, and authorized by the entire Colloquium. The text of this appeal is published in: J. M. ROBINSON, The Coptic Gnostic Library Today, NTS 14, 1967−1968, p. 363, n. 1. All of the manuscripts have now been published in: The Facsimile Edition of the Nag Hammadi Codices, 11 volumes, Leiden, 1972−1979. A final volume, containing a full introduction by J. M. ROBINSON, with *addenda et corrigenda* to the other volumes, is at this writing still in preparation.

historically and typologically as "a concrete fact" of history, "beginning meth-odologically with a certain group of systems of the Second Century A.D. which everyone agrees are to be designated with this term." 'Gnosticism' is under-stood to involve "a coherent series of characteristics that can be summarized in the idea of a divine spark in man, deriving from the divine realm, fallen into this world of fate, birth, and death, and needing to be awakened by the divine counterpart of the self in order to be finally reintegrated." The Gnostic idea of the "'devolution' of the divine"[57] is seen to be "based ontologically on the concep-tion of a downward movement of the divine whose periphery (often called Sophia or Ennoia) had to submit to the fate of entering into a crisis and producing – even if only indirectly – this world, upon which it cannot turn its back, since it is necessary for it to recover the *pneuma* – a dualistic conception on a monistic background, expressed in a double movement of devolution and reintegration" (pp. xxvi—xxvii).

In contrast to the narrower definition of 'Gnosticism' proposed by the Messina colloquium, the term *gnosis* is given a broad definition, as "knowledge of the divine mysteries reserved for an elite" (p. xxvi). The specific *gnosis* of Gnos-ticism "involves the divine identity of the k n o w e r (the Gnostic), the k n o w n (the divine substance of one's transcendent self), and the m e a n s b y w h i c h o n e k n o w s (*gnosis* as an implicit divine faculty is to be awakened and actualized. This *gnosis* is a revelation-tradition of a different type from the Biblical and Islamic revelation-tradition)" (p. xxvii).

The Messina statement also distinguishes between 'proto-Gnosticism' and 'pre-Gnosticism.' The latter involves the "preexistence of different themes and motifs found in the later Gnosticism;" the former involves a discovery of "the essence of Gnosticism" in the centuries preceding the Second Century (p. xxvii).

Whether or not the terminology employed in the Messina statement is completely acceptable[58] – I find the term 'proto-Gnosticism' to be essentially meaningless – it is clear that this statement and especially JONAS' lucid article in the Messina volume (pp. 90—108)[59] present much greater clarity in defining the Gnostic phenomenon than was achieved before, even by JONAS himself with his interpretation of „spätantiker Geist."

Thus R. M. WILSON[60] now uses the definition proposed by the Messina Colloquium in developing his earlier work on the problem of the relation of Philo to Gnosticism. He states that Philo "belongs at most to Gnosis, not to Gnosti-cism" (p. 215). "Indeed the case of Philo is one of the best examples of the value of this distinction" (ibid.).

---

[57] Cf. JONAS' article in: Le origini, p. 92.

[58] Cf. K. RUDOLPH, Randerscheinungen des Judentums und das Problem der Entstehung des Gnostizismus, Kairos 9, 1967, pp. 106 f., but cf. also his more positive reaction in: Gnosis und Gnostizismus, ein Forschungsbericht, TR 36, 1971, pp. 13—15. See now also the im-portant book by K. RUDOLPH, Die Gnosis, Leipzig and Göttingen, 1977. This book should now be regarded as the standard treatment of Gnosticism.

[59] Op. cit. n. 55.

[60] R. M. WILSON, Philo of Alexandria and Gnosticism, Kairos 14, 1972, pp. 213—219.

One of the papers presented to the Messina Colloquium is devoted entirely
to the problem of "Gnostic elements in Philo," by one of the members of the ad
hoc committee that formulated the Messina statement, M. SIMON.[61] Beginning
with BRÉHIER's observation that Philo's point of departure for his religious
philosophy was not Greek philosophy *per se*, but *« cette théologie alexandrine qui
devait produire les systèmes gnostiques et la littérature hermétique »* (p. 359),[62]
SIMON takes up two basic questions: 1) Do the writings of Philo provide indications that Gnosticism existed in Jewish Alexandria in his day? 2) Are there
'Gnostic' or 'gnosticizing' elements in Philo's thought? (p. 360). In connection
with the first question he takes up the theses of FRIEDLÄNDER discussed above,
and concludes that one cannot find in Philo's writings evidence that the Gnostic
sects described by FRIEDLÄNDER actually existed (pp. 360—363).[63] As to the
second question, SIMON states that any *« 'gnosticisme' philonien »* is necessarily
limited by the biblical and Platonic affirmation that the world and its Creator are
good (p. 363, with reference to Op 21). It is true that Philo 'compromises' the
unity of God with his doctrine of intermediary powers (pp. 364—366), that he
holds to a dualistic anthropology (pp. 366—371), and that he even has a kind of
predestination doctrine akin to that of the Qumran scrolls (pp. 371 f.), but despite
the apparent Gnostic 'resonances' or 'affinities' in Philo's thought, one can find
no Gnosticism in the pure sense, whether 'Iranian' or 'Syro-Egyptian'[64] in Philo
(pp. 373 f.).[65]

Several other of the papers presented at Messina touch on Philo and his relation to Gnosticism. R. M. GRANT[66] claims that it is impossible to find in Jewish
literature the idea that the world has been created by angelic powers. Even if Philo
assigns the creation of the body and the irrational soul of man to the angels, he
does not say that they took part in the creation of the world (pp. 148 f.); Philo is
therefore representative of orthodox Judaism rather than Gnosticism. J. ZANDEE[67]
understands Philo's doctrine of Sophia — built upon Jewish Wisdom traditions
under the influence of Stoic and Platonic conceptions — as a forerunner of the
Gnostic Sophia doctrine, and argues that the Gnostic figure of Sophia developed
in Alexandria *„in einem vorchristlichen jüdischen Gnostizismus oder Protognosti-*

---

[61] M. SIMON, Eléments gnostiques chez Philon, in: Le origini, pp. 359—376.

[62] Cf. E. BRÉHIER, Les idées philosophiques et religieuses de Philon d'Alexandrie, Paris,
1950³, p. 317.

[63] Cf. also H.-F. WEISS, Einige Randbemerkungen zum Problem des Verhältnisses von
'Judentum' und 'Gnosis,' OLZ 64, 1969, p. 548.

[64] These are basic types of Gnostic dualism in JONAS' treatment; cf. Gnosis und spätantiker
Geist 1, pp. 284 ff., and pp. 328 ff.; also: The Gnostic Religion, pp. 236 f.

[65] In the discussion that followed SIMON's presentation, printed in: Le origini, pp. 374—376,
H. JONAS suggested that Philo's orthodox Jewish restraint against Gnosticism does not
operate in the case of his concepts of virtue and *gnosis theou* (cf. my discussion, above). J.
DANIÉLOU, on the other hand, noted that Philo's dualism stands within the tradition of
Platonic philosophy, and, against JONAS, noted the importance of *charis* in Philo's thought.

[66] R. M. GRANT, Les êtres intermédiaires dans le judaïsme tardif, in: Le origini, pp. 141—157.

[67] J. ZANDEE, Die Person der Sophia in der vierten Schrift des Codex Jung, in: Le origini,
pp. 203—214.

zismus" (pp. 210–212). P. BOYANCÉ shows that Philo interprets Gen 1:26 in such a way that he represents God addressing his 'powers' (especially in Op 74) in a manner reminiscent of the Demiurge's address to the younger gods in Plato's Timaeus 41 (pp. 349f.).[68] With this and other examples BOYANCÉ succeeds in showing that whereas other scholars have posited a Gnostic influence in Philo, it is sufficient instead to note the influence of Platonism (pp. 348–356).[69] C. COLPE[70] locates Philo's doctrine of the soul's heavenly ascent in the context of Middle-Platonism rather than Gnosticism (p. 437). R. M. WILSON[71] presents his theories concerning the Gnostic 'affinities' or 'anticipations' in Philo (p. 512) and his 'gnosticizing' tendencies (p. 596), but denies that there was a full-blown Gnosticism in New Testament times. At the same time he posits a specifically Jewish origin for Gnosticism (especially pp. 691ff. and 702). G. QUISPEL[72] interprets the prince's garment in the 'Hymn of the Pearl' as reflecting not a Gnostic but a Greek (Platonic) background, referring to Philo's interpretation of the "coats of skin" in Gen 3:21 (pp. 633f.).

It is apparent from the results of the Messina Colloquium that a general consensus is emerging with regard to Philo's relation to Gnosticism, viz. that he represents a 'pre-Gnostic' stage in the development of Gnosticism. This consensus is being maintained in studies that have appeared subsequent to the Messina Colloquium. Thus J.-E. MÉNARD, in an important study entitled 'Le mythe de Dionysos Zagreus chez Philon,'[73] comes to the conclusion that Philo is an excellent example of 'pre-Gnosticism' (p. 345).[74] He discusses Philo's psychological interpretation of the myth of Dionysus and the Titans (Quaes Gen II.82), placing it in a Middle-Platonic context,[75] and showing how it influenced subsequent Gnostic writers. A. WEDDERBURN, in a lengthy study of the Philonic conception of the

---

[68] P. BOYANCÉ, Dieu cosmique et dualisme: Les archontes et Platon, in: Le origini, pp. 340–356.

[69] Cf. also J. DANIÉLOU, Le mauvais gouvernement du monde d'après le gnosticisme, in: Le origini, pp. 448–459, esp. p. 454. S. PÉTREMENT refers to the same tradition in Philo, but does not mention Plato; instead she posits a Christian stage in the development of the specifically Gnostic myth of the seven creator-archons. See: Le mythe des sept archontes créateurs peut-il s'expliquer à partir du christianisme?, in: Le origini, pp. 460–487, esp. pp. 470, 481, and 486.

[70] C. COLPE, Die 'Himmelreise der Seele' außerhalb und innerhalb der Gnosis, in: Le origini, pp. 429–447.

[71] R. M. WILSON, Gnosis, Gnosticism and the New Testament, in: Le origini, pp. 511–527, and ID., Addenda et Postscripta, in: Le origini, pp. 691–702.

[72] G. QUISPEL, Makarius und das Lied von der Perle, in: Le origini, pp. 625–644.

[73] J.-E. MÉNARD, Le mythe de Dionysos Zagreus chez Philon, RevScRel 42, 1968, pp. 339–345.

[74] Cf. also J. MÉNARD, La 'Connaissance' dans l'Evangile de Vérité, RevScRel 41, 1967, pp. 1–28, esp. pp. 14ff., and ID., Les origines de la Gnose, RevScRel 43, 1969, pp. 24–38, esp. pp. 37f., where he appraises the results of the Messina Colloquium.

[75] Cf. also P. BOYANCÉ, Echo des exégèses de la mythologie grecque chez Philon, in: Philon d'Alexandrie, Lyon 11–15 Septembre 1966, Colloques Nationaux du Centre National de la Recherche Scientifique, Paris, 1967, pp. 169–186.

'Heavenly Man,'[76] concludes that those who try to explain Philo's exegesis of Gen 1:26f. and 2:7 in terms of a Gnostic myth are "putting the cart before the horse" (p. 324). Rather we find in Philo's exegesis "the fore-shadowing of later gnostic exegesis" (p. 325).[77] R. BAER, in an important study of Philo's use of the categories 'male' and 'female,'[78] relates Philo's use of the male-female categories to that of various Gnostic documents (pp. 66—76). Whereas certain Gnostics describe the fallible, erring part of the Godhead as female, for Philo God is asexual, and the categories of male and female function only within the created order. BAER, however, does not attempt to draw any lines of development from Philo to Gnosticism or *vice versa*. His study does, nevertheless, suggest the possibility of drawing such lines, most definitely in the direction from Philo and the Hellenized Judaism he represents to Gnosticism. G. C. STEAD[79] shows how the Valentinian Gnostic myth of Sophia could develop out of a "Hellenistic Judaism akin to Philo's" (p. 92),[80] indeed how most of the presuppositions of Valentinus can be reconstructed "merely by rearranging Philo's mental furniture" (p. 90).[81] And F. FALLON[82] discusses the Valentinian Gnostic Letter of Ptolemy to Flora, showing how Ptolemy's categories of legislation in scripture are foreshadowed by the distinctions that Philo makes in his interpretation of the Pentateuch. He concludes that "the Hellenized Judaism of a Diaspora Jew such as Philo has prepared the way for Ptolemy" (p. 51).

If one can now speak of a scholarly consensus to the effect that Philo represents, at most, a 'pre-Gnostic' stage in the development of Gnosticism, it is nevertheless not necessarily the case that the 'pre-Gnosticism' of Philo rules out the possibility that a fully developed Gnosticism existed already in Philo's time. After all, Simon Magus, the traditional 'founder' of the Gnostic heresy,[83] was a younger contemporary of Philo, is even supposed to have spent some time in Alexandria,[84] and is held by some modern scholars to represent a full-blown Gnosticism.[85] In the absence of any written source certainly datable to the early first century or before, the problem of determining the *terminus a quo* for Gnosticism is a difficult one, and can only be done, if at all, by careful traditions-analysis

---

[76] A. WEDDERBURN, Philo's 'Heavenly Man,' NT 15, 1973, pp. 301—326.

[77] See further on this below.

[78] R. BAER, JR., Philo's Use of the Categories Male and Female, ALGHJ 3, Leiden, 1970.

[79] G. C. STEAD, The Valentinian Myth of Sophia, JTS n.s. 20, 1969, pp. 75—104.

[80] For the definitive statement on the Jewish origins of the Gnostic Sophia myth(s), see G. W. MacRAE, The Jewish Background of the Gnostic Sophia Myth, NT 12, 1970, pp. 86—101.

[81] It has been argued that Valentinus knew and used the works of Philo. On this see G. QUISPEL, Philo und die altchristliche Häresie, TZ 5, 1949, pp. 429—436; and more recently H. CHADWICK, St. Paul and Philo of Alexandria, BJRL 48, 1965/66, p. 305.

[82] F. FALLON, The Law in Philo and Ptolemy: A Note on the Letter to Flora, VC 30, 1976, pp. 45—51.

[83] Iren. Haer I.23.4.

[84] Ps.-Clem. Hom 2.22 and 24.

[85] See e.g. H. JONAS, The Gnostic Religion, pp. 103—111; E. HAENCHEN, Gab es eine vorchristliche Gnosis?, ZTK 49, 1952, pp. 316—349; W. FOERSTER, Die 'ersten Gnostiker' Simon und Menander, in: Le origini, pp. 190—196. See now also RUDOLPH, Die Gnosis, op.cit. n. 58, pp. 312—316.

of the (later) Gnostic writings we now have, and/or by an analysis of the polemical arguments used by possible opponents of Gnosticism. The latter method has been tried with the Apostle Paul in the New Testament,[86] and, as we have seen, with Philo.

This brings us full circle, back to FRIEDLÄNDER, and my own recent attempt to assess the possibility of carrying further FRIEDLÄNDER's approach and insights, while hopefully avoiding the excesses of his argumentation. In my article, 'Friedländer Revisited,'[87] I discuss FRIEDLÄNDER's main arguments (pp. 23—30) and suggest some additional passages in Philo that may reflect an anti-Gnostic polemic (Conf 2f.; Dec 63; and Spec Leg I.54, quoted and discussed pp. 30—32). The latter passage, with its statement about those of the Jewish nation who "betray the honor due to the One," is reminiscent of the anti-Gnostic statement in the Mishnah (Ḥag 2.1): "And whosoever has no regard for the honour of his Creator, it were better for him had he not come into the world."[88] Although FRIEDLÄNDER's attempts to find the Gnostic sects of the Cainites, Ophites, and Melchizedekians in Philo may be said to have failed, his basic insight concerning the Jewish origins of Gnosticism is correct. Furthermore, that there were 'antinomian'[89] Gnostic groups in Alexandria in Philo's day remains a distinct possibility (pp. 32—35).[90]

One of the most controverted issues in the scholarly study of Philo and his relation to Gnosticism has to do with his interpretation of Gen 1:26f. and 2:7, the creation of man. Some scholars (e.g. E. KÄSEMANN,[91] E. BRANDENBURGER,[92] J. JERVELL,[93] L. SCHOTTROFF[94]) argue that Philo was influenced by a Gnostic

---

[86] See especially W. SCHMITHALS, Die Gnosis in Korinth, FRLANT 66, Göttingen, 1969³, and ID., Paulus und die Gnostiker, TF 35, Hamburg, 1965; and U. WILCKENS, Weisheit und Torheit, BHT 26, Tübingen, 1959. I have tried to show that these efforts are unsuccessful; see B. PEARSON, The Pneumatikos-Psychikos Terminology in 1 Corinthians: A Study in the Theology of the Corinthian Opponents of Paul and Its Relation to Gnosticism, SBLDS 12, Missoula, 1973.

[87] Op. cit. n. 7.

[88] P. BLACKMAN, ed., Mishnayot, New York, 1963, vol. 2, p. 494.

[89] Cf. H. JONAS' perceptive remarks on the 'revolutionary' character of Gnosticism, Delimitation of the Gnostic Phenomenon, op. cit. n. 55, p. 100; cf. The Gnostic Religion, pp. 92ff., and Gnosis und spätantiker Geist 1, pp. 214ff.

[90] So also P. POKORNÝ, Der soziale Hintergrund der Gnosis, in: K. W. TRÖGER, ed., Gnosis und Neues Testament, Berlin, 1973, pp. 77—87, especially p. 81, with reference to Spec Leg I.319 and 323. Cf. also E. BRANDENBURGER, Adam und Christus: Exegetisch-religionsgeschichtliche Untersuchung zu Römer 5, 12—21, WMANT 7, Neukirchen, 1962, p. 130, n. 1.

[91] E. KÄSEMANN, Das wandernde Gottesvolk: Eine Untersuchung zum Hebräerbrief, FRLANT 37, Göttingen, 1959³, pp. 65ff. and 133f.

[92] E. BRANDENBURGER, op. cit. n. 90, pp. 117—131; cf. also: Fleisch und Geist: Paulus und die dualistische Weisheit, WMANT 29, Neukirchen, 1968, p. 149.

[93] J. JERVELL, Imago Dei: Gen. 1, 26f. im Spätjudentum, in der Gnosis und in den paulinischen Briefen, FRLANT 85, Göttingen, 1960, pp. 55—62.

[94] L. SCHOTTROFF, Der Glaubende und die feindliche Welt: Beobachtungen zum gnostischen Dualismus und seiner Bedeutung für Paulus und das Johannesevangelium, WMANT 37, Neukirchen, 1970, pp. 127—131.

'Anthropos' myth.[95] Others (e.g. H.-M. SCHENKE,[96] U. FRÜCHTEL,[97] B. PEAR-
SON,[98] A. WEDDERBURN,[99] K.-G. SANDELIN[100]) deny this, and argue, instead,
that at best Philo's exegesis of Genesis represents a preliminary step in the development of Gnostic mythology.

Thus in what follows it may be useful to examine some representative
passages in Philo and in Gnostic literature bearing on this question, and seek to
establish the essential points of similarity and difference. In doing so we shall also
have to take up briefly the basic views of Philo and the Gnostics on the issue of
man's salvation.

II. Man and Salvation in Philo and Gnosticism

The place to begin a discussion of Philo's doctrine of man is certainly his
great treatise 'On the Creation of the World,' a document which belongs to a group
of writings addressed to a general audience, 'The Exposition of the Law.'[101] This
treatise is intended to serve as a commentary on the cosmology of Genesis (chs.
1—3), but it is important to note that it shows throughout a very heavy debt to
Plato's 'Timaeus,'[102] and perhaps also to current philosophical commentaries
thereon.[103] The focus, of course, is on the text of scripture, and, as we shall see,

---

[95] Cf. R. HAMERTON-KELLY, Pre-Existence, Wisdom and the Son of Man: A Study of the
Idea of Pre-Existence in the New Testament, SNTSMS 21, Cambridge, 1973, pp. 138—
142, where Philo is represented as utilizing a "'gnosticizing' tradition."

[96] H.-M. SCHENKE, Der Gott 'Mensch' in der Gnosis; Ein religionsgeschichtlicher Beitrag
zur Diskussion über die paulinische Anschauung von der Kirche als Leib Christi, Göttingen, 1962, pp. 121—124.

[97] U. FRÜCHTEL, Die kosmologischen Vorstellungen bei Philo von Alexandrien: Ein Beitrag
zur Geschichte der Genesisexegese, ALGHJ 2, Leiden, 1968, pp. 30—40.

[98] Op. cit. n. 86, pp. 17—21, 96.

[99] Op. cit. n. 76.

[100] K.-G. SANDELIN, Spiritus Vivificans: Traditions of Interpreting Genesis 2:7, in: G.
LINDESKOG, ed., Opuscula exegetica Aboensia in honorem Rafael Gyllenberg octogenarii,
Acta Ac. Ab. Ser. A, Humaniora 45:1, Åbo, 1973, p. 71.

[101] See E. R. GOODENOUGH, Philo's Exposition of the Law and his de vita Mosis, HTR 27,
1933, pp. 109—125; cf. also his book: An Introduction to Philo Judaeus, Oxford, 1962²,
pp. 35 ff.

[102] Cf. E. BRÉHIER, Les idées philosophiques, op. cit. n. 62, p. 78: « Presque tous les passages
importants du 'Timée', depuis le chapitre V (27c), jusqu'au chapitre XIV (41a) . . . se
retrouvent, plus ou moins altérés, dans l'œuvre de Philon.» He provides a list of passages
in n. 2, pp. 78f.

[103] E.g. a commentary by Posidonius? Cf. K. GRONAU, Poseidonios und die jüdisch-christ-
liche Genesisexegese, Leipzig, 1914, p. 2. It might be pointed out here that Eudorus, a
first century B.C. Alexandrian Platonist, also commented on the 'Timaeus', according to
Plutarch De an pr 3, 1013 B; 16, 1019 E; 1020 C. A. WLOSOK mentions Eudorus as a
Platonist influenced by Pythagoreanism, but does not mention his commentary on the
'Timaeus'; see: Laktanz, p. 52. In any case, it is clear that Philo must have been in contact

the scriptural text (i.e. the LXX, which Philo held to be divinely-inspired word for word[104]) sometimes causes Philo to modify his Platonic-Stoic terminology.[105]

The starting point for Philo is the proposition that the cosmos is in harmony with the Law of God (Op 3), that the Maker and Father (ποιητὴς καὶ πατήρ, cf. Tim 27 C) of the world is the perfect Mind (νοῦς) of the universe, who transcends the Good itself (αὐτὸ τὸ ἀγαθόν) and the Beautiful itself (αὐτὸ τὸ καλόν, Op 8), and that the Father and Maker cares for (ἐπιμελεῖσθαι) the world because he is good (Op 21, cf. Tim 29 A, E). He concludes his exordium with the statement (Op 24—25) that the κόσμος νοητός is the Logos of God, that Logos which is the Image (εἰκών) and archetypal seal (ἀρχέτυπος σφραγίς) according to which man was created (Gen 1:27).[106]

The verse-by-verse commentary on Gen 1—3 runs from 26—169. Philo's comments on Gen 1 culminate in a lengthy account of the creation of man. In this account he emphasizes the mind (νοῦς), the higher part of the soul, which God bestows upon man (νοῦν ἐξαίρετον ἐδωρεῖτο, ψυχῆς τινα ψυχήν, Op 66), and which for Philo is that which constitutes man's true humanity. Indeed "it is in respect of the mind, the sovereign element of ths soul that the word 'image' is used" in Gen 1:26f. (ἡ δὲ εἰκὼν λέλεκται κατὰ τὸν τῆς ψυχῆς ἡγεμόνα νοῦν, Op 69). This coheres logically with Philo's use of the term νοῦς of God himself (Op 8).

Especially interesting is Philo's exegesis of Gen 1:26 and the use of the plural in the expression, "Let us make man." He suggests that the words of the text refer to several creators rather than one (Op 72), God taking with him "others as fellow-workers" (Op 75). The reason for this is that man is "of a mixed nature" (Op 73), participating in both good and evil. Since the Father cannot be the cause of evil to his offspring, he used others to help him (Op 75). This is put very succinctly in Fug 68—70;[107] wherein we are also informed who the "others" are (the "powers" = angels) and what part of man the father created himself (man's higher rational self = νοῦς):

> "For this reason,[108] I think, when philosophizing on the creation of the world, after having said that all other things come into being by the agency of God, he (Moses) pointed out that man alone was fashioned with the coopera-

with other Alexandrian Platonists, and probably knew of the commentaries on the 'Timaeus' as well as the 'Timaeus' itself.

[104] See his remarkable account of the translation of the Law from 'Chaldaean' into Greek, in Vita Mos II. 31—44.

[105] We must of course also assume that he was in close contact with other Jewish interpreters of scripture.

[106] Philo also states here that the αἰσθητὸς κόσμος is a μίμημα of the divine εἰκών (the Logos), an εἰκὼν εἰκόνος. This can be said to be a 'Platonic' understanding of Gen 1:27: God is the Archetype of the Logos/Anthropos/Noetic world; the latter is the archetype of the sense-perceptible world, which is, therefore, an "image of an image." Plato, however, uses the term εἰκών only of the αἰσθητὸς κόσμος, Tim 92 C.

[107] Cf. also Conf 168f.

[108] The context is an observation, commenting on Gen 48:15, that God takes charge of the more important things for the soul while leaving the less important to a ministering angel.

tion of fellow-workers. For he says, "God said, 'Let us make man according to our image,'" the words "let us make" indicating many. Thus the Father of all things converses with his powers, to whom he assigned the fashioning of the mortal part of our soul by imitating his own craftsmanship when he formed the rational part in us. He thought it proper that the sovereign part in the soul should be created by the Sovereign, but the subject part by subjects. And he employed the powers that are with him not only for the reason mentioned, but because only the soul of man would receive conceptions of evil things as well as good, and would use one or the other, if it is not possible to use both. Therefore he (God) thought it necessary to assign the origin of evil things to other creators, but to reserve the origin of good things to himself alone."[109]

The inspiration for this explanation of Gen 1:26 is, of course, Plato's Timaeus 41 A–42 B. Plato has his Creator (the 'Demiurge')[110] fashion with his own hands the immortal part of man, but relegates to the lesser gods man's mortal nature, his body and lower soul. Plato's 'gods' become Philo's 'powers' or 'angels,' and the immortal part of man is equated (at least in some texts) with the εἰκών of God, and, as we shall see, with the divine inbreathing of Gen 2:7. It is also worthy of note that Philo does not ascribe the fashioning of man's body to the 'powers,' only the mortal part of the soul. In this departure from Plato's formulation, he is doubtless constrained by the text of Genesis, which plainly states that it was God himself who fashioned man's body out of the dust of the earth (Gen 2:7).

Although Philo interprets Gen 1:26f. in Op 69ff. as referring to empirical man (ἐμφερέστερον γὰρ οὐδὲν γηγενὲς ἀνθρώπου θεῷ, Op 69) he suddenly contradicts himself and suggests in Op 76 that the text is really referring to the genus (γένος) 'man' and distinguishing the species (τὰ εἴδη), 'male and female,' the individual members (τὰ ἐν μέρει) not yet having taken shape. This prepares us for his discussion of the second account of the creation of man, Genesis 2:7.

Philo's commentary on Gen 2:7 begins as follows (Op 134f.):

"After this he says that "God formed man by taking clay from the earth, and breathed into his face the breath of life" (Gen 2:7). By this also he shows

---

[109] My translation. Text: διὰ τοῦτ', οἶμαι, καὶ ἡνίκα τὰ τῆς κοσμοποιίας ἐφιλοσόφει, πάντα τἆλλα εἰπὼν ὑπὸ θεοῦ γενέσθαι μόνον τὸν ἄνθρωπον ὡς ἂν μετὰ συνεργῶν ἑτέρων ἐδήλωσε διαπλασθέντα. "εἶπε" γάρ φησιν "ὁ θεός· ποιήσωμεν ἄνθρωπον κατ' εἰκόνα ἡμετέραν," πλήθους διὰ τοῦ "ποιήσωμεν" ἐμφαινομένου. (69) διαλέγεται μὲν οὖν ὁ τῶν ὅλων πατὴρ ταῖς ἑαυτοῦ δυνάμεσιν, αἷς τὸ θνητὸν ἡμῶν τῆς ψυχῆς μέρος ἔδωκε διαπλάττειν μιμουμέναις τὴν αὐτοῦ τέχνην, ἡνίκα τὸ λογικὸν ἐν ἡμῖν ἐμόρφου, δικαιῶν ὑπὸ μὲν ἡγεμόνος τὸ ἡγεμονεῦον ἐν ψυχῇ, τὸ δ' ὑπήκοον πρὸς ὑπηκόων δημιουργεῖσθαι. (70) κατεχρήσατο ⟨δὲ⟩ καὶ ταῖς μεθ' ἑαυτοῦ δυνάμεσιν οὐ διὰ τὸ λεχθὲν μόνον, ἀλλ' ὅτι ἔμελλεν ἡ ἀνθρώπου ψυχὴ μόνη κακῶν καὶ ἀγαθῶν ἐννοίας λαμβάνειν καὶ χρῆσθαι ταῖς ἑτέραις, εἰ μὴ δυνατὸν ἀμφοτέραις. ἀναγκαῖον οὖν ἡγήσατο τὴν κακῶν γένεσιν ἑτέροις ἀπονεῖμαι δημιουργοῖς, τὴν δὲ τῶν ἀγαθῶν ἑαυτῷ μόνῳ.

[110] Philo uses this Platonic term for the Creator, δημιουργός, in numerous passages. See e.g. Op 36, 68, 138, 139, 146, 171.

very clearly that there is a vast difference between the man thus formed and the man that came into existence earlier after the image of God: for the man so formed is an object of sense-perception, partaking already of such or such quality, consisting of body and soul, man or woman, by nature mortal; while he that was after the (Divine) image was an idea or type or seal, an object of thought (only), incorporeal, neither male nor female, by nature incorruptible. It says, however, that the formation of the individual man, the object of sense, is a composite one made up of earthly substance and of Divine breath: for it says that the body was made through the Artificer taking clay and moulding out of it a human form, but that the soul was originated from nothing created whatever, but from the Father and Ruler of all: for that which He breathed in was nothing else than a Divine breath that migrated hither from that blissful and happy existence for the benefit of our race, to the end that, even if it is mortal in respect of its visible part, it may in respect of the part that is invisible be rendered immortal. Hence it may with propriety be said that man is the borderland between mortal and immortal nature, partaking of each so far as is needful, and that he was created at once mortal and immortal, mortal in respect of the body, but in respect of the mind immortal."[111]

In this passage we see that Philo distinguishes the 'man' of Gen 1:27 from the man referred to in Gen 2:7: the former is an ideal type (ἰδέα τις ἢ γένος κτλ.) while the latter is empirical man, consisting of both mortal and immortal parts. The immortal part is a "divine breath" (πνεῦμα θεῖον) from heaven, a conclusion suggested by the LXX text of Gen 2:7: ἔπλασεν ὁ θεὸς τὸν ἄνθρωπον ... καὶ ἐνεφύσησεν εἰς τὸ πρόσωπον αὐτοῦ πνοὴν ζωῆς. The statement that God sent down his divine breath "for the benefit of our race" is reminiscent of Plato's account of the Demiurge's address to the gods (Tim 41 B–D) stating why he has "sown" (σπείρας) the immortal element from himself (the νοῦς), as a kind of seed, into the mortal elements constructed by the gods in imitation of his own power (μιμούμενοι τὴν ἐμὴν δύναμιν), viz. that the universe might be perfect

---

[111] Text: Μετὰ δὲ ταῦτά φησιν ὅτι "ἔπλασεν ὁ θεὸς τὸν ἄνθρωπον χοῦν λαβὼν ἀπὸ τῆς γῆς, καὶ ἐνεφύσησεν εἰς τὸ πρόσωπον αὐτοῦ πνοὴν ζωῆς". ἐναργέστατα καὶ διὰ τούτου παρίστησιν ὅτι διαφορὰ παμμεγέθης ἐστὶ τοῦ τε νῦν πλασθέντος ἀνθρώπου καὶ τοῦ κατὰ τὴν εἰκόνα θεοῦ γεγονότος πρότερον· ὁ μὲν γὰρ διαπλασθεὶς αἰσθητὸς ἤδη μετέχων ποιότητος, ἐκ σώματος καὶ ψυχῆς συνεστώς, ἀνὴρ ἢ γυνή, φύσει θνητός· ὁ δὲ κατὰ τὴν εἰκόνα ἰδέα τις ἢ γένος ἢ σφραγίς, νοητός, ἀσώματος, οὔτ' ἄρρεν οὔτε θῆλυ, ἄφθαρτος φύσει. (135) τοῦ δ' αἰσθητοῦ καὶ ἐπὶ μέρους ἀνθρώπου τὴν κατασκευὴν σύνθετον εἶναί φησιν ἔκ τε γεώδους οὐσίας καὶ πνεύματος θείου· γεγενῆσθαι γὰρ τὸ μὲν σῶμα, χοῦν τοῦ τεχνίτου λαβόντος καὶ μορφὴν ἀνθρωπίνην ἐξ αὐτοῦ διαπλάσαντος, τὴν δὲ ψυχὴν ἀπ' οὐδενὸς γενητοῦ τὸ παράπαν, ἀλλ' ἐκ τοῦ πατρὸς καὶ ἡγεμόνος τῶν πάντων· ὁ γὰρ ἐνεφύσησεν, οὐδὲν ἦν ἕτερον ἢ πνεῦμα θεῖον, ἀπὸ τῆς μακαρίας καὶ εὐδαίμονος φύσεως ἐκείνης ἀποικίαν τὴν ἐνθάδε στειλάμενον ἐπ' ὠφελείᾳ τοῦ γένους ἡμῶν, ἵν' εἰ καὶ θνητόν ἐστι κατὰ τὴν ὁρατὴν μερίδα, κατὰ γοῦν τὴν ἀόρατον ἀθανατίζηται. διὸ καὶ κυρίως ἄν τις εἴποι τὸν ἄνθρωπον θνητῆς καὶ ἀθανάτου φύσεως εἶναι μεθόριον, ἑκατέρας ὅσον ἀναγκαῖόν ἐστι μετέχοντα, καὶ γεγενῆσθαι θνητὸν ὁμοῦ καὶ ἀθάνατον, θνητὸν μὲν κατὰ τὸ σῶμα, κατὰ δὲ τὴν διάνοιαν ἀθάνατον.

(τέλεος). Philo, as Plato, is emphasizing the providence of the Creator in speaking of God's purpose in sending down his 'breath' or 'spirit.'

Philo goes on to characterize the "first man" (πρῶτος ἄνθρωπος = Adam) in terms reminiscent of the ideal 'sage' of the Stoa (Op 136—144).[112] But here he seems, again, to reverse himself in his interpretation of Gen 1:27: the Creator using his own Logos as a παράδειγμα, "man was made a likeness and imitation (of the Logos) when the divine breath was breathed into his face" (ἀπεικόνισμα καὶ μίμημα γεγενῆσθαι τούτου τὸν ἄνθρωπον ἐμπνευσθέντα εἰς τὸ πρόσωπον). Thus Gen 1:27 and 2:7 are tied together to refer to empirical man. The first man was "closely related" (συγγενής τε καὶ ἀγχίσπορος) to God the Sovereign (ἡγεμών),[113] by virtue of the inbreathing of the "divine spirit" (πνεῦμα θεῖον, Gen 2:7 — Op 144). Even though the first man's descendants have fallen short of the perfection of their ancestor, they nevertheless preserve marks of their kinship with their first father, in that "every man in respect to his mind is allied to the divine Logos, having come into being as a copy or fragment or ray of that blessed nature" (πᾶς ἄνθρωπος κατὰ μὲν τὴν διάνοιαν ᾠκείωται λόγῳ θείῳ, τῆς μακαρίας φύσεως ἐκμαγεῖον ἢ ἀπόσπασμα ἢ ἀπαύγασμα γεγονώς, Op 146).[114] On this basis man can draw near to God by following the path of virtue and holding up as a goal "full conformity" (ἐξομοίωσιν) with God.[115]

Thus even within the one treatise Philo presents different interpretations of Gen 1:27 and 2:7, and the matter becomes even more complicated when we look at his other treatises, wherein we see a bewildering variety of terms used to distinguish man's higher nature from his lower nature.[116] Philo has two basic interpretations of Gen 1:27, one using the text to refer to an ideal type (as Op 76 and 134 cited above), and the other relating the text to the higher 'pneumatic' element of man referred to in Gen 2:7.[117]

Especially of interest to us for the purpose of this investigation is Philo's use of the term πνεῦμα to refer to man's higher nature (Plato's νοῦς, a term which Philo also frequently uses). Philo uses this terminology in another part of his general 'Exposition of the Law,'[118] Spec Leg IV.123. Commenting on the Mosaic prohibition of blood (Lev 3:17), Philo says,

---

[112] Cf. J. GIBLET, L'homme image de dieu dans les commentaires littéraux de Philon d'Alexandrie, in: L. CERFAUX and W. PEREMANS, ed., Studia Hellenistica 5, Universitas Catholica Lovaniensis, Louvain, 1948, p. 99.

[113] On the function of the term ἡγεμών in the Philonic creation account, see C. KANNENGIESSER, Philon et les pères sur la double création de l'homme, in: Philon d'Alexandrie, Lyon 11—15 Septembre 1966, Colloques Nationaux du Centre National de la Recherche Scientifique, Paris, 1967, pp. 284ff.

[114] On the Stoic terminology employed here see J. GIBLET, op.cit. n. 11, pp. 100f.

[115] This dynamic use of the term ἐξομοίωσις is reminiscent of the Platonic goal, ὁμοίωσις θεῷ (Theaet. 176B). Cf. U. FRÜCHTEL, Die kosmologischen Vorstellungen, p. 35.

[116] Cf. the very useful chart in R. BAER, Philo's Use of the Categories Male and Female, pp. 15f.

[117] Cf. J. JERVELL, Imago Dei, p. 53. The latter interpretation I would call 'Stoicizing.' Certainly one cannot, contra JERVELL, speak here of 'Gnostic' influence.

[118] Cf. n. 101 above. Most of the other Philonic texts cited in this study are from his "Allegory," addressed to a Jewish in-group; cf. GOODENOUGH, Introduction, p. 46.

"Blood is prohibited for the reason which I have mentioned, that it is the essence of the soul,[119] not of the intelligent and reasonable soul, but of that which operates through the senses, the soul that gives the life which we and the irrational animals possess in common. For the essence or substance of that other soul[120] is divine spirit, a truth vouched for by Moses especially, who in his story of the creation says that God breathed a breath of life upon the first-man, the founder of our race, into the lordliest part of his body, the face, where the senses are stationed like bodyguards to the great king, the mind. And clearly what was then thus breathed was ethereal spirit, or something if such there be better than ethereal spirit, even an effulgence of the blessed, thrice-blessed nature of the Godhead."[121]

The use of the term πνεῦμα as an interpretive equivalent of the word πνοή in Gen 2:7 is natural for a student of the LXX, for πνεῦμα is a term regularly used both of God and of man in the Greek Bible.[122] Indeed in Gen 6:17 and 7:15, passages which allude back to Gen 2:7, the word πνεῦμα is used instead of πνοή. Thus Philo can substitute πνεῦμα for πνοή in quotations of Gen 2:7, as in Leg All III.161 and Det 80. In Det 83 he refers to the πνεῦμα of man itself as the "image of God," rather than that which was created "according to" the image:[123]

"That faculty which we have in common with the irrational animals has blood as its essence, but the faculty which streams forth from the rational fountain is the spirit, not moving air, but a kind of impression stamped by divine power, to which Moses gives the proper designation, "image," indicating that God is the Archetype of rational nature, and man is a copy and likeness."[124]

---

[119] In the previous section he had alluded to the statement in Lev 17:11 and 14 (LXX): ἡ γὰρ ψυχὴ πάσης σαρκὸς αἷμα αὐτοῦ ἐστι.

[120] Cf. also Heres 55.

[121] Text: τὸ μὲν αἷμα δι' ἣν εἶπον αἰτίαν ὅτι οὐσία ψυχῆς ἐστίν — οὐχὶ τῆς νοερᾶς καὶ λογικῆς ἀλλὰ τῆς αἰσθητικῆς, καθ' ἣν ἡμῖν τε καὶ τοῖς ἀλόγοις κοινὸν τὸ ζῆν συμβέβηκεν. ἐκείνης γὰρ οὐσία πνεῦμα θεῖον καὶ μάλιστα κατὰ Μωυσῆν, ὃς ἐν τῇ κοσμοποιΐᾳ φησὶν ἀνθρώπῳ τῷ πρώτῳ καὶ ἀρχηγέτῃ τοῦ γένους ἡμῶν ἐμφυσῆσαι πνοὴν ζωῆς τὸν θεὸν εἰς τὸ τοῦ σώματος ἡγεμονικώτατον, τὸ πρόσωπον, ἔνθα αἱ δορυφόροι τοῦ νοῦ καθάπερ μεγάλου βασιλέως αἰσθήσεις παρίδρυνται· τὸ δ' ἐμφυσώμενον δῆλον ὡς αἰθέριον ἦν πνεῦμα καὶ εἰ δή τι αἰθερίου πνεύματος κρεῖσσον, ἅτε τῆς μακαρίας καὶ τρισμακαρίας φύσεως ἀπαύγασμα.

[122] It translates both רוּחַ and נְשָׁמָ֫ה, the latter used in the Hebrew text of Gen 2:7 (LXX πνοή). It has been observed that there are no Greek parallels to the doctrine of the superiority of πνεῦμα over ψυχή; this is originally a Jewish idea. See E. SCHWEIZER, art. πνεῦμα in TWNT VI, p. 394 = TDNT VI, p. 396.

[123] Contrast Heres 231: οὐχὶ εἰκόνα θεοῦ ἀλλὰ κατ' εἰκόνα. Cf. also Somn I.73f. and Dec 134 for a teaching similar to that of Det 83.

[124] My translation. Text: ἡ μὲν οὖν κοινὴ πρὸς τὰ ἄλογα δύναμις οὐσίαν ἔλαχεν αἷμα, ἡ δὲ ἐκ τῆς λογικῆς ἀπορρυεῖσα πηγῆς τὸ πνεῦμα, οὐκ ἀέρα κινούμενον, ἀλλὰ τύπον τινὰ καὶ χαρακτῆρα θείας δυνάμεως, ἣν ὀνόματι κυρίῳ Μωυσῆς εἰκόνα καλεῖ, δηλῶν ὅτι ἀρχέτυπον μὲν φύσεως λογικῆς ὁ θεός ἐστι, μίμημα δὲ καὶ ἀπεικόνισμα ἄνθρωπος.

Philo goes on to refer to man as a φυτὸν οὐράνιον (Det 85), recalling a famous statement from Plato's Timaeus.[125]

Thus far we have concentrated on Philo's doctrine of man's higher nature, derived from his interpretation of Gen 1:27 and 2:7. But we should also note what he says about man's body, for this, too, is relevant for our present purpose. Here, again, we observe certain contradictions in Philo's statements.

In Op 136ff., in the context of his commentary on Gen 2:7, he says that the earth-born (γηγενής) first man was made "most excellent in each part of his being in both soul and body," and that he was truly καλὸς καὶ ἀγαθός. That the body of the first man was "of fair form" (εὐμορφίαν) is proved on three grounds: 1) The material (ὕλη) of the newly-formed earth was pure and unalloyed; 2) God took the very best clay for forming man's body, for it was to be "a sacred dwelling place or shrine" (οἶκός τις ἢ νεὼς ἱερός) for the "reasonable soul" (ψυχῆς λογικῆς); and 3) thanks to his great skill the Creator "fashioned for the body goodly flesh and adorned it with a good complexion" (εὐσαρκίαν προσανέπλαττε καὶ εὔχροιαν ἠνθογράφει), that the first man might be "as beautiful as possible to look at" (κάλλιστον ὀφθῆναι).

In Leg All I.31f. Philo interprets Gen 2:7 in such a way as to emphasize the contrast between man's earthly and corruptible nature on the one hand, and his heavenly and incorruptible nature on the other. Earthly man is an "earthly formation of his Maker, not his offspring" (γήϊνον πλάσμα, ἀλλ' οὐ γέννημα ... τοῦ τεχνίτου). Here Philo does not speak of the fair form or the beauty of the body, as he did in Op of the first man, but rather emphasizes its "earthly" and corruptible nature. He even uses the noun πλάσμα (cf. Gen 2:7, ἔπλασεν), a noun which carries a negative connotation.[126]

Of course Philo can also use the common-place philosophical deprecations of the body, derived largely from Plato (who presumably derived them from 'Orphic' or Pythagorean sources).[127] Thus in Leg All I.105ff., commenting on Gen 2:17, Philo distinguishes two kinds of death, one of the body (which is really a deliverance), and the other of the soul, in which the soul becomes "entombed in passions and wickedness of all kinds" (ψυχῆς ἐντυμβευομένης πάθεσι καὶ κακίαις ἁπάσαις, Leg All I.106).

> "And this death is practically the antithesis of the death which awaits us all. The latter is a separation of combatants that have been pitted against one another, body and soul, to wit. The former, on the other hand, is a meeting of the two in conflict. And in this conflict the worse, the body, overcomes, and the better, the soul, is overcome. But observe that wherever Moses speaks of "dying the death," he means the penalty-death, not that which takes place in the course of nature. That one is in the course of nature in

---

[125] Timaeus 90A: φυτὸν οὐκ ἔγγειον ἀλλὰ οὐράνιον. Cf. Plant 17, quoted above in the context of our discussion of WLOSOK's work. Gen 1:27 and 2:7 are quoted in Plant 19.

[126] Cf. also Heres 57: πλάσμα γῆς.

[127] For a survey of the texts see P. COURCELLE, Le corps-tombeau, REA 63, 1966, pp. 101–122, esp. pp. 101–105. Cf. also E. R. GOODENOUGH, Philo on Immortality, HTR 39, 1946, pp. 85–108.

which soul is parted from body;[128] but the penalty-death takes place when
the soul dies to the life of virtue, and is alive only to that of wickedness. That
is an excellent saying of Heracleitus,[129] who on this point followed Moses'
teaching, "We live," he says, "their death, and are dead to their life." He
means that now, when we are living, the soul is dead and has been entombed
in the body as in a sepulchre;[130] whereas, should we die, the soul lives forthwith its own proper life, and is released from the body, the baneful corpse[131]
to which it was tied."[132]

And in Virt 76 Philo comments on the death of Moses as follows:

"When he had ended his anthems,[133] a blend we may call them of religion
and humanity, he began to pass over from mortal existence to life immortal
and gradually became conscious of the disuniting of the elements of which he
was composed. The body, the shell-like growth which encased him,[134] was
being stripped away and the soul laid bare and yearning for its natural
removal hence."[135]

In summary, we have observed a number of ways in which Philo brings to
bear upon his interpretation of scripture categories and terms derived from Platonism and Stoicism. We have also seen that he modifies his philosophical traditions when the text of scripture demands it, as was the case in his interpretations
of Gen 1:26f. and 2:7.[136] The variety of interpretations we find in Philo is probably due to his use of various traditions of exegesis.

[128] Cf. Plato, Phaedo 64 C.
[129] Cf. Sextus Empiricus, Hypotyposes III. 230.
[130] Cf. Plato, Gorgias 493 A; Cratylus 400 BC.
[131] Cf. Aristotle, Protr (ed. ROSE, fr. 59—61).
[132] Leg All I.106—108. Text: καὶ σχεδὸν οὗτος ὁ θάνατος μάχεται ἐκείνῳ· ἐκεῖνος μὲν
γὰρ διάκρισίς ἐστι τῶν συγκριθέντων σώματός τε καὶ ψυχῆς, οὗτος δὲ τοὐναντίον σύνοδος ἀμφοῖν, κρατοῦντος μὲν τοῦ χείρονος σώματος, κρατουμένου δὲ τοῦ κρείττονος
ψυχῆς. (107) ὅπου δ᾽ ἂν λέγῃ "θανάτῳ ἀποθανεῖν," παρατήρει ὅτι θάνατον τὸν ἐπὶ
τιμωρίᾳ παραλαμβάνει, οὐ τὸν φύσει γινόμενον· φύσει μὲν οὖν ἐστι, καθ᾽ ὃν χωρίζεται
ψυχὴ ἀπὸ σώματος, ὁ δὲ ἐπὶ τιμωρίᾳ συνίσταται, ὅταν ἡ ψυχὴ τὸν ἀρετῆς βίον θνῄσκῃ,
τὸν δὲ κακίας ζῇ μόνον. (108) εὖ καὶ ὁ Ἡράκλειτος κατὰ τοῦτο Μωυσέως ἀκολου-
θήσας τῷ δόγματι, φησὶ γάρ· "Ζῶμεν τὸν ἐκείνων θάνατον, τεθνήκαμεν δὲ τὸν ἐκείνων
βίον," ὡς νῦν μέν, ὅτε ζῶμεν, τεθνηκυίας τῆς ψυχῆς καὶ ὡς ἂν ἐν σήματι τῷ σώματι
ἐντετυμβευμένης, εἰ δὲ ἀποθάνοιμεν, τῆς ψυχῆς ζώσης τὸν ἴδιον βίον καὶ ἀπηλλαγμένης
κακοῦ καὶ νεκροῦ συνδέτου τοῦ σώματος. Cf. also Leg All III.69f.; Gig 15; Spec Leg
IV.188; Quaes Gen I.70; II.69; Quod Deus 150; Somn I.139.
[133] He refers to the Song of Moses, Deut 32.
[134] Cf. Plato, Phaedrus 250 C.
[135] Text: Ὡς δ᾽ ἐτέλεσε τὰς χορείας ὁσιότητι καὶ φιλανθρωπίᾳ τρόπον τινὰ συνυφασ-
μένας, ἤρξατο μεταβάλλειν ἐκ θνητῆς ζωῆς εἰς ἀθάνατον βίον κἀκ τοῦ κατ᾽ ὀλίγον
συνῃσθάνετο τῆς τῶν ἐξ ὧν συνεκέκρατο διαζεύξεως, τοῦ μὲν σώματος ὀστρέου δίκην
⟨περιπεφυκότος⟩ περιαιρουμένου, τῆς δὲ ψυχῆς ἀπογυμνουμένης καὶ τὴν κατὰ φύσιν
ἐνθένδε ποθούσης μετανάστασιν. Cf. also Jos 71, which is also the editor's source for the
emendation in the text of Virt 76.
[136] For other examples of Philo's interpretation of Gen 1:27 and 2:7, in addition to the texts
cited or quoted here, see the following. For Gen 1:27: Leg All I. 31—42, 53—55, 88—94;

That Philo represents at crucial points a wider Hellenistic-Jewish exegetical tradition seems clear, as e. g. in his differentiation of man's higher πνεῦμα from his lower ψυχή, based on a Platonic-Stoic reading of Gen 2:7,[137] his equation of man's higher self (Gen 2:7) with the 'man'created according to the image of God (Gen 1:27),[138] and his interpretation of Gen 1:26 to refer to the angels or 'powers' employed by God in creating man's lower nature.[139] And the general tendency of the Hellenistic era to depreciate the body and material existence in general is certainly not limited among Jews to Philo.[140]

As we shall see, it is precisely these Hellenistic-Jewish traditions of scripture-exegesis which form some of the most important building blocks for the fabrication of the Gnostic anthropogony.

One of the best and most complete examples we have of the Gnostic anthropogonic myth is that which is found in the 'Apocryphon of John' (Ap. John),[141] extant in Coptic but undoubtedly written originally in Greek. This is a document which is now extant in four Coptic versions: it is found in BG and in NHC II, III, and IV. Its multiple attestation suggests that it was an important text in Gnostic circles. Moreover it is an important text for scholarship in the history of Gnosticism, not only because of its contents but also because it is clearly a composite document representing various stages of development. In form[142] it consists of a religio-philosophical tract embodying a running commentary (a 'midrash')[143] on Genesis 1−8, set within the framework, probably secondary, of an

II. 4, 13; III. 96; Plant 44; Conf 146; Heres 56f., 164; Fug 71f.; Spec Leg I. 81, 171; III. 83; Quaes Gen I. 4, 8, 93; II. 56; IV.164; Quaes Ex II. 46. For Gen 2:7: Leg All I. 53−55, 88−95; II. 4−13, 19, 71−73; Congr 90; Somn I. 34; Quaes Gen I. 4−5, 28, 51, 87; II.17, 56, 66; IV.164; Quaes Ex II. 46.

[137] Josephus appears to read Gen 2:7 as referring to a trichotomy of body, soul, and spirit; see Ant I. 34. The Hellenistic-Jewish distinction between the higher πνεῦμα and the lower ψυχή is one of the bases of the discussion between Paul and his Corinthian opponents in 1 Cor 2 and 15; see B. PEARSON, The Pneumatikos-Psychikos Terminology, op. cit. n. 86.

[138] Cf. Wis 2:2f. and 23.

[139] This is known to Justin Martyr as a Jewish interpretation of Gen 1:26; see Dial 62. That God addressed the angels when he said, "Let us make man," is also a view found in Palestinian Jewish texts. See e.g. Tg. Ps-J. Gen 1:26.

[140] Cf. Wis 9:15.

[141] For abbreviations of the tractates of the Nag Hammadi Codices see now the 'Instructions for Contributors' published in JBL 95, 1976, p. 338; this system of abbreviations will be used here. The 13 codices themselves have been designated CG = (Codex) Cairensis Gnosticus, or NHC = Nag Hammadi Codex; the latter designation will be used here since it appears to be gaining currency. Cf. also BG = (Codex) Berolinensis Gnosticus 8502, another important Coptic Gnostic codex, on which see above, n. 52.

[142] The best treatment of the form and composition of 'Ap. John' is that of A. KRAGERUD, Apocryphon Johannis. En formanalyse, NorTT 66, 1965, pp. 15−38. On the Genesis-commentary in 'Ap. John,' see also S. GIVERSEN, The Apocryphon of John and Genesis, ST 17, 1963, pp. 60−76.

[143] For a similar kind of 'midrash' embodied in another Nag Hammadi tractate, and the terminology, 'Gnostic midrash,' see B. PEARSON, Jewish Haggadic Traditions in The Testimony of Truth from Nag Hammadi (CG IX,3), in: C. BLEEKER et al., ed., Ex Orbe Religionum: Studia Geo Widengren, vol. 1, Studies in the History of Religions (Supple-

apocalypse given by the resurrected Jesus Christ to his disciple John.[144] The framework, along with redactional elements within the larger text, represents a secondary 'Christianization' of an originally non-Christian ('pre-Christian'?) Gnostic system.[145]

Since the anthropogony in Ap. John is so representative of the basic Gnostic views concerning man and his creation, and since it shows a number of points of comparison and contrast with Philo, I shall restrict my discussion largely to this document. And since the text[146] of the version in NHC II tends to agree with that of NHC IV (fragmentary), and that of NHC III (fragmentary) with that of BG, I shall restrict my discussion to the versions in NHC II and BG, using the former as our basic reference.[147]

In the context preceding our focal passage, the highest God is mentioned, eternal and indescribable, whose mystical name is 'Man' (Anthropos),[148] from whom emanate the various beings that populate the heavenly world. The lowest of these divine emanations, 'Wisdom' (Sophia),[149] produces an ugly abortion

ments to Numen) 21; Leiden, 1972, pp. 457—470, esp. p. 461. This article is reprinted, with revisions, in: B. PEARSON, ed., Religious Syncretism in Antiquity: Essays in Conversation with Geo Widengren, American Academy of Religion and the Institute of Religious Studies, University of California, Santa Barbara, 'Series on Formative Thinkers' 1, Missoula, Mont., 1975, pp. 205—222.

[144] Part of what is now known as 'Ap. John' is found in Irenaeus' description of the teachings of the 'Barbelo-Gnostics,' Haer I.29. Irenaeus does not seem to know that this teaching is represented as a revelation of Jesus Christ to John, suggesting that Irenaeus knew the text without its framework.

[145] For a similar case, see NHC III,4: 'Soph. Jes. Chr.', a document which expands the basic (non-Christian) system expounded in NHC III,3 and V,1: Eugnostos, into a discourse of Jesus with his disciples. On 'Soph. Jes. Chr.' as an example of the 'Christianization' of Gnostic texts, see D. PARROTT, Evidence of Religious Syncretism in Gnostic Texts from Nag Hammadi, in B. PEARSON, ed., Religious Syncretism in Antiquity, op. cit. n. 142, pp. 173—189, and additional literature cited there.

[146] For Coptic text and German translation of the versions in NHC II, III, and IV, see M. KRAUSE and P. LABIB, Die drei Versionen des Apokryphon des Johannes im koptischen Museum zu Alt-Kairo, ADAIK, Kopt. Reihe 1, Wiesbaden, 1962. For Coptic text and an English translation of the version in NHC II, see S. GIVERSEN, Apocryphon Johannis, ATD 5, Copenhagen, 1963. For the facsimile edition of the version in NHC II, see The Facsimile Edition of the Nag Hammadi Codices, Codex II, Leiden, 1974, plates 11—42. For Coptic text and German translation of the version in BG, see TILL-SCHENKE, op. cit. n. 52. For this article I have used the KRAUSE and TILL-SCHENKE editions and the Facsimile Edition. The passages quoted are my own translation.

[147] Cf. B. PEARSON, Biblical Exegesis in Gnostic Literature, in M. STONE, ed., Armenian and Biblical Studies, Supplementary Volume 1 to Sion, Journal of the Armenian Patriarchate of Jerusalem, Jerusalem, 1976, pp. 70—80, where I treat extensively 'Ap. John', using the BG text as the basic reference.

[148] This idea is read out of Gen 1:26f. See H.-M. SCHENKE, Der Gott 'Mensch' in der Gnosis, op. cit. n. 96.

[149] On the Gnostic figure of Sophia and her relationship to the Jewish 'Wisdom' figure, see G. MACRAE, op. cit. n. 80. For the mythological background of the Jewish 'Wisdom' figure, see especially the important monograph by B. MACK, Logos und Sophia: Untersuchungen zur Weisheitstheologie im hellenistischen Judentum, SUNT 10, Göttingen, 1973.

called 'Yaldabaoth,'[150] 'Saclas,'[151] and 'Samael.'[152] He is chief of seven 'Archons,' and produces the other angelic beings and the lower world. Yaldabaoth declares in his ignorance, "I am a jealous god, and there is no other god beside me!" (NHC II, 13,8f.; BG 44,14f.; cf. Exod 20:5; Isa 45:5,6; 46:9). Sophia, the 'Mother,' realizes her own defect and the ignorance of her son, and repents. A heavenly voice comes to her, "Man exists and the Son of Man" (NHC II, 14,14f. = BG 47,15f.). Thereupon Yaldabaoth and his fellow Archons see in the waters of chaos (cf. Gen 1:2) the reflection of the image of God. The passage of interest to us now follows, and I quote from the text in NHC II:

> "And he (Yaldabaoth) said to the Authorities (ἐξουσία)[153] who were with him, "Come, let us create a man according to the image (εἰκών) of God, and according to our likeness (ⲈⲒⲚⲈ= ὁμοίωσις), in order that his image might become a light for us."[154] And they created from each others' powers, according to the signs which they had been given. And each one of the Authorities (ἐξουσία) provided a feature in the form (τύπος) of the image (εἰκών) which he had seen within his soul (ψυχική = ψυχή); he created a being (ὑπόστασις)[155] according to the likeness of the First Perfect Man. And they said, "Let us call him 'Adam,' in order that his name might become a power of light for us.""[156] (NHC II, 15, 1–13)

This passage is a mythopoetic expansion of Gen 1:26f. The εἰκών according to which the Creator and his archontic henchmen create a man is that of the highest God himself ('Man'), but it is noteworthy that the NHC II version illogically preserves the plural 'our' from Gen 1:26 in the case of the second term, 'likeness.' The 'image' is represented as a source of divine 'light,' as is the 'name' (Heb.

---

[150] 'Yaldabaoth' is the most frequent name used in Ap. John for the Gnostic Demiurge, but in NHC II,11,16ff. all three names occur together. The name 'Yaldabaoth' has often been taken to reflect an Aramaic etymology, ילדא בהות, "child of chaos." Cf. B. PEARSON, Jewish Haggadic Traditions, op. cit. n. 143, p. 467, n. 1, where it is noted that references to 'chaos' in the contexts where the name occurs tend to support the etymology. But see now also G. SCHOLEM, Yaldabaoth Reconsidered, in: Mélanges d'Histoire des Religions offerts à H.-C. Puech, Paris, 1974, pp. 405–421. SCHOLEM interprets the element *yald* as the "begetter" (not "begotten" or "child"), and the element *abaoth* as a shortened form of 'Sabaoth.'

[151] 'Saclas' is derived from Aramaic סכלא, "fool." Cf. B. PEARSON, Jewish Haggadic Traditions, p. 467, n. 7.

[152] Samael is the angel of death or the devil in Jewish sources. In Gnostic literature the name 'Samael' is explained as "the blind god." We have, again, an Aramaic etymology: סמא, "blind," and אל, "god."

[153] I shall note in parentheses only those Greek 'loan-words' that are important for our purposes to notice.

[154] In the BG version, the Authorities say to one another, "Let us create a man according to the image and likeness of God" – BG 48, 11–14.

[155] In the BG version they form (πλάσσειν) a formation (πλάσμα) from themselves, which is described as a "soul" (ψυχή) – BG 48, 14 – 49, 2.

[156] The BG version reads, "Let us call him 'Adam' that the name of that (Being) and his power might become light for us" – BG 49, 6–9.

'Adam' = Gr. 'Anthropos') given to their creation. That the Authorities see in the εἰκών a source of light (cf. φῶς, Gen 1:3) implies that they themselves are in a state of chaotic darkness (cf. σκότος, Gen 1:2).

In the case of the BG version it is especially clear that this passage reflects a conflation of Gen 1:26f. with 2:7, in the use of the verb πλάσσειν and the noun πλάσμα (Gen 2:7: ἔπλασεν), as well as the term "soul" (ψυχή). That what is being created by the Authorities is a 'soul' is made clear in what follows:

> "And the Powers (δύναμις) began. The first, Goodness, created a soul of bone;[157] the second, Forethought, created a soul of sinew; the third, Deity, created a soul of flesh; the fourth, Lordship, created a soul of marrow; the fifth is Kingdom, who created a soul of blood; the sixth is Zeal, who created a soul of skin; the seventh is Understanding, who created a soul of hair. And the multitude of angels stood up before it. They received from the Authorities the seven psychic hypostases in order to make the joining of the limbs and the joining of the trunk and the position (σύνθεσις) of the order of each one of the members.[158] . . . This is the number of the angels altogether; they are 365. They all worked on him until there was finished by them, limb for limb, the psychic (ψυχικόν) and the material (ὑλικόν) body (σῶμα). For there are others over the remaining passions (πάθος) which I have not told you. But if you wish to know them, it is written in the Book of Zoroaster.[159] And all the angels and demons worked until they had put in order the psychic (ψυχικόν) body (σῶμα), but their entire work was inert and motionless for a long time." (NHC II, 15,13−29; 19,2−14)

We are presented here with an elaborate myth of the creation of the soul of man, or his 'psychic body.' The mention of 'material body' (19,6) is an inconsistency, for as we shall see, the material body is not created until later in our narrative. In any case, this passage, with its reference to man's 'psychic body' is to be understood as a commentary on Gen 2:7, and probably reflects an earlier form of the Gnostic myth in which the creation of the body by the Archons is the main point.[160]

---

[157] In the BG version, each of the Powers is called a soul, and they work together to create a 'body,' assisted by 360 angels − BG 49, 9−51,1.

[158] At this point there occurs a very long passage describing how each of the 365 angels contributed a part to the 'psychic body' of man, as well as his various passions. The angels are given various names, consisting of *nomina barbara*. This section of the text comprises NHC II,15, 29−19, 2. The BG text, with its reference to 360 angels, reflects a knowledge of something like the passage from Codex II, but (mercifully!) does not provide the details.

[159] Porphyry, Vit Plot 16, includes an 'Apocalypse of Zoroaster' among the (Gnostic) books known to the circle of Plotinus. He also adds, "I, Porphyry, wrote a considerable number of refutations of the book of Zoroaster, which I showed to be entirely spurious and modern, made up by the sectarians to convey the impression that the doctrines which they had chosen to hold in honour were those of the ancient Zoroaster." Trans. A. H. ARMSTRONG, in Plotinus, vol 1, LCL ed., London, 1965. Of course, we are not certain that the book referred to in 'Ap. John' is the same as that refuted by Porphyry.

[160] Cf. e.g. Saturninus' version of the myth, as reported by Irenaeus, Haer I.24.1.

That Gen 2:7 is in the background here is confirmed by the following passage, which focuses upon the origin of man's 'spirit,' building upon the clauses (Gen 2:7bc), καὶ ἐνεφύσησεν εἰς τὸ πρόσωπον αὐτοῦ πνοὴν ζωῆς, καὶ ἐγένετο ὁ ἄνθρωπος εἰς ψυχὴν ζῶσαν:

> "But when the Mother (i.e. Sophia) wished to get (back) the power which she had given to the First Archon (i.e. Yaldabaoth), she prayed to the Father (μητροπάτωρ, lit. "mother-father") of the All, the One of great mercy, and he sent down the five luminaries[161] by the holy decree to the place[162] of the angels of the First Archon. They advised him with the purpose of bringing out the power of the Mother. And they said to Yaldabaoth, "Breathe into his face from your spirit (πνεῦμα), and his body (σῶμα) will arise." And he breathed into his face his spirit (πνεῦμα), which is the power of his Mother. He did not know, for he was in ignorance. And the power of the Mother went out of Yaldabaoth and into the psychic (ψυχικός) body (σῶμα) which they had made according to the likeness of the One who exists from the beginning. The body moved, and received strength, and it shone." (NHC II, 19,14−33)

In this commentary on Gen 2:7 we see that the doctrine of the "image" in Gen 1:27 is also connected to the narrative, tying the two creation texts together. However, we do not find here that the εἰκών of Gen 1:27 is equated with the πνεῦμα of Gen 2:7. Rather, the Powers had created the psychic body "according to" the image they had seen in the waters. But this psychic body can only receive true life by gaining heavenly spirit. The πνεῦμα breathed into man is the last remnant of heavenly substance or "power" (δύναμις, cf. NHC II, 10,21) received by Yaldabaoth from his errant mother, Sophia. By breathing this spirit into man the Creator himself is now bereft of it. On the other hand, we also understand that the heavenly πνεῦμα is now imprisoned in the 'psychic body' of man − and, as we see in the next episode, his 'material body' as well:

> "And the rest of the powers (δύναμις) immediately became jealous, for he had come into being through all of them, and they had given the man their strength,[163] and his understanding became stronger than those who had created him, and stronger than the First Archon. But when they realized that he was light, and that he thought more than they[164] and was free (lit.

---

[161] The BG version has "the Self-Born (αὐτογενής) and the four lights" − BG 51, 9−10. The *autogenes* is the divine Son in the Gnostic triad of Father, Mother, and Son. Cf. BG 35, 19. It is the Father who sends the lights, according to BG 41,5. The word μητροπάτωρ is used of the Father also at NHC II,20,9f. Cf. BG 52,18. But cf. NHC II,5,6f. and 6, 16, where μητροπάτωρ is an epithet that is used of Barbelo, the Mother of the Gnostic triad.

[162] It is probable that τόπος in the text is a corruption of τύπος and that the original version read, "in the form of the angels." This is what we find in the parallel text, BG 51,10f.: 2Ⲙ ⲠⲈⲤⲘⲞⲦ ⲚⲚⲀⲄⲄⲈⲖⲞⲤ. Cf. on this S. Giversen, Apocryphon Johannis, p. 255.

[163] The BG text adds, "and he had taken (φορεῖν) the souls of the seven Authorities (ἐξουσία) and their powers" − BG 52, 6−8.

[164] BG 52, 13f.: "he was wiser than they."

"stripped naked") from evil, they took him and threw him down to the nether region of complete materiality (ὕλη)." (NHC II, 19,34–20,9)

The πνεῦμα received by man thus makes him superior to his Creators, who thereupon become jealous of him and imprison him in the basest matter.

Curiously, this is all repeated in the following lengthy passage, which expands upon the meaning of Gen 2:7 and the myth built upon it with reference to texts which originally have to do with the creation of woman, Gen 2:18,20 and 3:20. The imprisonment of man in base matter by the Archons is also repeated, again with reference to Gen 2:7:

"But the Blessed Father (μητροπάτωρ), the merciful Beneficent One, took pity on the power (δύναμις) of the Mother which had been brought out of the First-Archon for the purpose of giving strength to the psychic (ψυχικόν) and sense-perceptible (αἰσθητόν) body (σῶμα). He sent forth through his beneficent and exceedingly merciful Spirit a helper (βοηθός) for Adam, a thought (ἐπίνοια) of Light, who is from him and who is called 'Life' (ζωή). And she assists (ὑπουργεῖν) the entire creation (κτίσις = mankind), suffering with him and leading him into his Fullness (πλήρωμα) and teaching him about his descent with the seed, teaching him about the way of ascent, the way whence he came. And the Thought of Light is hidden in Adam, that the Archons (ἄρχων) might not know it, but that the Thought (ἐπίνοια) (of Light) might be a correction for the defect of the Mother.[165] And the man became visible because of the shadow of the light which was in him. And his thought was exalted above all those who had created him. When they gazed upward, they saw him, that his thought was exalted. And they took counsel with the Archons (ἀρχοντική) and all the angels (ἀγγελική). They took fire and earth and water, and mixed them with each other and with the four fiery winds, and they beat them together and made a great turmoil. They brought him (Adam) into the shadow of death, in order that they might form (πλάσσειν) him again,[166] out of earth, water, fire, and wind (πνεῦμα), out of matter (ὕλη) which is the ignorance of darkness and desire (ἐπιθυμία) and their counterfeit (ⲈⲦⲰⲂⲂⲒⲀⲈⲒⲦ = ἀντίμιμον) spirit (πνεῦμα), which is the tomb (σπήλαιον, lit. "grotto")[167] of the remoulding (ἀνάπλασις)[168] of the body (σῶμα) which the robbers (λῃστής = the Creator Archons) had put on the man, the fetter of oblivion; and this one became a mortal man." (NHC II, 20,9–21,13)

In this remarkable passage we are taught that man has been given, along with his 'spirit' and 'power' of life — or rather, as an aspect of his 'spirit' — an intellectual capacity (ἐπίνοια) for salvation, i.e. the possibility of returning to his heavenly origins. This capacity for life is itself called 'Life,' (ζωή), the name given

---

[165] The BG version reads here, "our sister [Sophia]," (the text restored with the aid of the parallel in NHC III,25,20) — BG 54,1.

[166] The BG version reads, "They made another formation (πλάσις)" — BG 55,3.

[167] BG 55,10: ⲠⲘ̄ⳒⲀⲞⳛ = μνημεῖον or τάφος.

[168] BG 55,10: πλάσμα.

to the woman presented to Adam as a 'helper' in the text of Genesis (Gen 3:20; 2:18,20) which is here being interpreted allegorically. Thus the living spirit of man, his capacity for salvation, is identified as a feminine aspect of his self.[169] It is this aspect of the self that teaches mankind (κτίσις here should be interpreted to mean mankind) about his origins (his descent) and his destiny (his ascent = salvation).

The spiritual, heavenly part of man — which should rather be called the 'essential man'[170] — is encapsulated, as we have seen, in a 'soul' or 'psychic body.' But worse than that, it is imprisoned in a material (ὑλικόν) body as well. The text we have just quoted expands on the previous passage, referring to man's having been 'thrown' (his *Geworfenheit*)[171] into base matter, by describing mythically how the Creator-Archons, the "robbers,"[172] formed (πλάσσειν, cf. Gen 2:7) his body out of the four elements of matter (ὕλη), fire, earth, water, and air (or "wind"). This material body becomes a "tomb," a "fetter" in which essential man is imprisoned, and which is the occasion for his sleep of "oblivion" (ᛒⲰⲈ = λήθη) or "forgetfulness," his natural condition in this world. The NHC II version sums up the results of the activity of the Creator-Archons with a play on the text of Gen 2:7c: "and this one became a m o r t a l m a n," a statement expressing the very opposite of what "Moses said":[173] "and man became a living soul."

Yet in this seemingly hopeless condition, there is — this, indeed, is the basic Gnostic 'gospel' — a hope for salvation: to be awakened by *gnosis* out of 'sleep' and spiritual 'death.' The focus of salvation is upon the spiritual power "breathed into" (Gen 2:7) man by the Creator God (Yaldabaoth) as a ruse perpetrated by the highest God. As part of this spiritual inbreathing, man has, as we have seen, a 'Thought of Light' which provides for the possibility of man's (and 'Man's,' i.e. God's) salvation.

The term 'Thought (ἐπίνοια) of Light,' used of man's spiritual capacity for salvation, is utilized in a number of other contexts in Ap. John which shed light on its proper interpretation in the passage quoted above. Thus in the passage immediately following (II, 21,14f.), the Thought of Light "awakened his (Adam's) thought;" this is an allegorical interpretation of Gen 2:21f.[174] The

---

[169] Cf. the Valentinian Gnostic conception of man, wherein the spiritual seed in man's soul is feminine, and his heavenly counterpart (his 'angel') is masculine. On this see G. QUISPEL, La conception de l'homme dans la gnose Valentinienne, in his: Gnostic Studies, vol. 1, Istanbul, 1974, p. 52. We are also reminded in this connection of the Jungian concept of man's *anima*.

[170] Cf. C. H. I. (Poimandres) 15: οὐσιώδης ἄνθρωπος.

[171] A Heideggerian term used by H. JONAS, Gnosis und spätantiker Geist 1, pp. 106–109, to describe the Gnostic experience of having been 'thrown' into the material world. Cf. the phrase, "wherein we have been thrown," from the Valentinian formula quoted below, n. 178.

[172] This epithet is used of the Creator-Archons in the anthropogonic myth which occurs in 'Soph. Jes. Chr.' (NHC III,4 = BG 3).

[173] Cf. the recurring refrain in 'Ap. John', "not as Moses said": NHC II,13,19f.; 22,22f.; 23,3; 29,6.

[174] In the 'Hyp. Arch.' (NHC II,4), this entity is called the "spiritual woman" — II,89,11.

Thought of Light is also equated with the "tree of the knowledge of good and evil" (Gen 2:17; cf. 3:5), of which the Savior (here = Jesus Christ)[175] caused Adam and Eve to eat (II, 22,5—9). It is also that part of Adam from which the woman was created (II, 22, 28ff., another allegory on Gen 2:21f.). When Adam saw the woman that was brought to him, "the Thought of Light revealed herself and uncovered the veil that was over his mind. He became sober from the drunkenness of darkness, and he came to know his likeness" (NHC II, 23,4—9).[176] The Thought of Light is the instrument ("an eagle on the tree of knowledge") through which the Savior awakens Adam and Eve from their fall into sleep (NHC II, 23,26—35, with reference to Gen 3:7ab). When Yaldabaoth saw the Thought of Light revealed in Zoe (i. e. Eve), he carried her off and raped her (NHC II, 24,11—25).[177] And the Thought of Light is that which awakens "the seed (σπέρμα) of the perfect (τέλειος) generation (γενεά)," i. e. the Gnostics (NHC II, 28,1—4). In short, the Thought of Light hidden in man is the instrument and occasion for salvation, even the *gnosis* itself, by which man comes to know himself, his origin, and his destiny.[178]

When we compare this Gnostic myth[179] with Philo's doctrine of man, as revealed in the texts we have treated above, a number of significant similarities emerge. Both Philo and the Gnostics utilize as their basic source for their anthropology the text of Genesis, and both center their respective teachings on the key texts, Gen 1:26f. and 2:7. Both tend to conflate Gen 1:27 with 2:7, although Ap. John does not, as Philo (in some passages), equate the πνεῦμα of Gen 2:7 with the εἰκών of Gen 1:27.[180] Both derive from the text of Gen 2:7 a differentiation

---

[175] It is probable that in an earlier ('pre-Christian') form of the myth, this 'Savior' figure was the serpent of Gen 3:1ff. On the serpent-redeemer in (Ophite) Gnosticism, see B. PEARSON, Jewish Haggadic Traditions, op. cit. n. 143, pp. 461—465.

[176] In what follows, Gen 2:23a, 24, and 3:20 are paraphrased.

[177] In what follows the two sons born to Eve, Cain and Abel, are given the allegorical names Yawe (= יהוה) and Eloim! The myth of the rape of Eve is based on a Jewish haggada on Gen 4:1, teaching that Cain was the product of a liaison between Eve and the Devil, Samael. See Tg. Ps.-J. Gen 4:1; Yebamot 103b, 'Abod. Zar. 22b; Šabbat 146a; Pirqe R. El. 21; 2 Enoch 31:6.

[178] Cf. the well-known Gnostic formula found in Clement of Alexandria's Exc Theod 78.2: "What saves is the knowledge of who we were, what we became; where we were, wherein we have been thrown; whereto we speed, wherefrom we are redeemed; what birth is, and what rebirth" (my translation).

[179] For other Gnostic anthropogonic myths closely related to that of 'Ap. John', see Iren. Haer I.24.1 (Saturninus); I.30 ('Sethian-Ophites'); I.5.5—6 (Valentinians = Exc Theod 50—55; Hippolytus Ref VI.34); Mandaean Ginza R (LIDZBARSKI, trans., pp. 107ff.); NHC III,4: 'Soph. Jes. Chr.' = BG, 3; NHC II,4: 'Hyp. Arch.'; and NHC II,5: 'Orig. World'. For a survey of these and other Gnostic anthropogonic texts see B. PEARSON, The Pneumatikos-Psychikos Terminology, op. cit. n. 86, ch. 6, Genesis 2:7 in Gnostic Exegesis. Cf. also the important articles by K. RUDOLPH, Ein Grundtyp gnostischer Urmensch-Adam-Spekulation, ZRGG 9, 1957, pp. 1—20 and G. QUISPEL, Der gnostische Anthropos und die jüdische Tradition, in his: Gnostic Studies, vol. 1, Istanbul, 1974, pp. 173—195.

[180] For a Gnostic example of such an equation see the Simonian 'Megale Apophasis,' as reported by Hippolytus, Ref VI.9—18. On this text see K.-G. SANDELIN, Spiritus Vivificans, op. cit. n. 100, pp. 63f.

between man's higher πνεῦμα and his lower ψυχή. Both regard the πνεῦμα of man as of divine, heavenly origin, and that which is the focus of salvation. There is some similarity, also, between the ἐπίνοια of Ap. John and the διάνοια of Philo (Op 135), in that the ἐπίνοια/διάνοια represents for both the possibility of salvation. Philo and the Gnostics share the interpretation of Gen 1:26 which attributes the responsibility for the creation of man's lower soul to the angels or 'Powers' (this specific term being used by both). Both Philo and the Gnostics agree that man's earthly body is a πλάσμα of matter (ὕλη), consisting of the four basic elements of fire, earth, water, and air (cf. Philo, Op 136, 146). Both look upon the material body of man as a baneful 'tomb' and 'prison.' Both look upon the πνεῦμα of man as that part of man (the essential man) which is saved; for both the release of the heavenly spirit from the body and its ascent to its heavenly origins is basic to salvation. And, of course, both use the allegorical method of interpreting scripture.[181]

How are we to account for these similarities? Philo can certainly not be said to depend on Gnostic sources. If there is any literary dependence at all, the only possibility is that Philo is a source of the Gnostic anthropogony. Yet I do not see that a literary dependence of Ap. John upon Philo can be demonstrated. The most plausible solution is that Ap. John (and other Gnostic anthropogonies of a similar sort)[182] and Philo share common traditions, consisting not only of the LXX text of Genesis, but also of Hellenistic-Jewish traditions of Genesis-exegesis. A common Middle-Platonic milieu may also be posited for the negative way in which the material body is viewed by both.[183]

But what of the differences! For Philo, the biblical text (especially the Penta-teuch) is divine revelation which must be interpreted with careful attention to the meaning of each word (whether Philo is free of 'eisegesis' or not is beside the point). For the Gnostics the revelation consists of the myth which is constructed from the biblical text with the use of previously-existing traditions of interpreta-tion thereof. The myth is constructed with an attitude of absolute sovereignty over the biblical text, to the point of explicitly refuting it where it is useful to do so.[184] The text and the various (Jewish!) traditions of exegesis[185] are

---

[181] For an interesting example of how the same (allegorical) method of interpreting scripture can be employed with widely differing results, compare Ap. John's interpretation of the βοηθός of Gen 2:18,20 in the passage quoted above with Philo's interpretation in Leg All II.24: the "helper" of the mind (νοῦς) is sense-perception (αἴσθησις)! This coheres with Philo's general tendency to identify the mind (νοῦς) symbolically as masculine, and the whole realm of sense-perception as feminine. Cf. on this R. BAER, Philo's Use of the Cate-gories Male and Female, pp. 38–44.

[182] Cf. n. 179.

[183] Cf. the references in nn. 128 and 130, and the discussion above.

[184] Cf. n. 173, above, on the phrase, "not as Moses said."

[185] It should be pointed out that 'Ap. John' reflects the use of a number of Jewish traditions which have not been mentioned because of their absence in Philo. E. g. the inert state of the Powers' creation reflects the Palestinian Jewish tradition of the golem, where Gen 2:7 is interpreted with reference to the Hebrew text of Ps 139:16; cf. Midr. Gen. Rab. 14.8. The activity of the angels in creating the 'passions' of man reflect a doctrine found in T. Reub. 2f. that seven 'spirits of error' were given to man in creation. The 'counterfeit

re-interpreted with a revolutionary abandon[186] which reflects utmost contempt for the Biblical Creator and all his works and ways.

Thus, whereas for Philo the Biblical God is the One transcendent God, Creator and Preserver of the universe and the only Savior,[187] for the Gnostics God is split into a transcendent Deity ('Man'!) and a lower Creator who is described as an ignorant and malicious being and is given all the attributes of the Devil! Whereas for Philo man is the crown of God's creation and a "citizen" of God's world (κοσμοπολίτης, cf. Op 143 et passim), for the Gnostics man is utterly alien to the world. Both Philo and the Gnostics have a transcendent, basically 'unknowable' God; but Philo adheres to the Biblical view of the 'otherness' of God,[188] whereas God is, for the Gnostics, 'Man' — which is to say that man himself is God! Thus for the Gnostics the beginning of salvation is *gnosis*, a "knowledge" of God which is ultimately s e l f - k n o w l e d g e. For Philo, on the other hand, the beginning of salvation is self-renunciation[189] and trust in the grace of God.[190]

III. Conclusions

From this case study on the interpretation of Gen 1:26f. and 2:7 in Philo and Gnosticism, together with the survey of recent scholarship on the relationship between Philo and Gnosticism, the following conclusions emerge:

spirit' (ἀντίμιμον πνεῦμα) in 'Ap. John' may reflect a doctrine found in the Qumran scrolls concerning two opposing 'spirits' in man; cf. 1 QS iii, 18ff. on the "spirit of truth" and the "spirit of falsehood." In this case we do find a similar idea in Philo, in Quaes Ex I.23, on which see WLOSOK, Laktanz, pp. 107—111. The jealousy expressed by the Powers against Adam in 'Ap. John' reflects the envy against Adam attributed to the Devil in Vit. Ad. 12ff. Cf. B. PEARSON, Biblical Exegesis, op. cit. n. 147.

[186] On the revolutionary thrust of Gnosticism, see H. JONAS, opera cit. n. 89.

[187] Philo knows of no other "Savior" (σωτήρ) than God himself. Cf. e.g. Op 169: God is σωτήρ and εὐεργέτης. For other references, cf. the Index prepared by J. LEISEGANG as vol. 7 of the COHN-WENDLAND edition of Philo's works, Berlin, 1926.

[188] See e.g. Hos 11:9, "I am God and not man." Cf. Deut 4:39, "there is none beside Him," which Philo discusses in Leg All III.4,82; Migr 182f.

[189] Cf. the discussion above of JONAS' treatment of Philo's correlation between knowledge of God and self-renunciation. I can hardly think of any aspect of Philo's thought that is less 'Gnostic' than Philo's doctrine of ἀπογιγνώσκειν ἑαυτόν, JONAS to the contrary notwithstanding!

[190] To treat Philo's soteriology adequately would require an entire monograph, for soteriology is a major concern with Philo. But see the books by GOODENOUGH and PASCHER, opera cit. n. 4, as well as the treatment by WLOSOK discussed above. In connection with GOODENOUGH's book, one should also consult his important article, 'Literal Mystery in Hellenistic Judaism', in R. P. CASEY et al., Quantulacumque: Studies Presented to Kirsopp Lake by Pupils, Colleagues, and Friends, London, 1937, pp. 227—241. See also the article by A. JAUBERT, Le thème du 'Reste Sauveur' chez Philon d'Alexandrie, Lyon 11—15 Septembre 1966, Colloques Nationaux du Centre National de la Recherche Scientifique, Paris, 1967, pp. 243—254.

1. Philo cannot be described as a 'Gnostic' in the technical sense of the word. If, however, we use the designation 'philosophical *gnosis*' for that development in the history of Graeco-Roman philosophy wherein philosophy becomes oriented to religion and metaphysics (WLOSOK), we may include Philo's thought in that category. In any case, he does stand squarely within the Platonic tradition, more specifically in that development in the history of Platonism known as 'Middle Platonism.'[191] He is at the same time a Jew and has as his central concern the interpretation of the Pentateuch. These two factors — his Platonism and his Jewishness — make Philo an especially important figure to use as a focal point for drawing comparisons with the Gnostics, whose writings also reflect the influences of Judaism and popular Platonism.[192]

2. Philo is not dependent upon, or influenced by, Gnosticism. Rather, the earliest Gnostic writings show a clear dependence upon Jewish sources, not only the Old Testament, but also Jewish traditions of exegesis and Jewish haggadic and apocryphal traditions. Indeed the Jewish element in Gnosticism — which at the same time is anti-Jewish in its thrust — is so prominent as to suggest that Gnosticism originated within Judaism as a revolutionary protest movement against traditional Jewish religion. Philo is an important source for some (not all) of the Hellenistic Jewish elements borrowed by the Gnostics.

3. Philo can therefore be placed in the category of 'pre-Gnosticism,' as defined by the Messina Colloquium. Nevertheless this term can be misleading if we think strictly in terms of chronological development. For example, when scholars such as WILSON use expressions like 'not yet' or 'less developed' in connection with Philo, as compared to Gnosticism, the suggestion seems to be made that Philo's religious philosophy lies in a trajectory that logically and chronologically issues in Gnosticism. But to draw such a conclusion would clearly be wrong, for that would entail a misappraisal of the respective intentionalities of Philo and the Gnostics. Such a conclusion would also fail to take into account the possibility that a full-blown Gnosticism may, indeed, have existed already in Alexandria and elsewhere in Philo's time.

One of the most challenging tasks facing historians of religion is that of placing the Gnostic movement in a social context.[193] Here, too, Philo is an exceptionally important figure to use for comparative purposes, just because we

---

[191] See e.g. H. J. KRÄMER, Der Ursprung der Geistmetaphysik: Untersuchungen zur Geschichte des Platonismus zwischen Platon und Plotin, Amsterdam, 1964, pp. 266—281. Philo is called "the oldest preserved 'Neoplatonist'" in H. LEWY, Chaldaean Oracles and Theurgy: Mysticism, Magic and Platonism in the Later Roman Empire, Publications de l'Institut français d'archéologie orientale, Recherches d'archéologie, de philologie et d'histoire, vol. 13, Cairo, 1956, p. 315. LEWY's discussion of Middle Platonism and the Platonic elements in the Chaldaean Oracles is especially acute, and mentions Philo in a number of important contexts; see pp. 311—398.

[192] For this point see A. D. NOCK, The Milieu of Gnosticism (a review of JONAS' 'Gnosis und spätantiker Geist, 1'), and ID. Gnosticism, in his: Essays on Religion and the Ancient World, ed. Z. STEWART, Cambridge, Mass., 1972, pp. 444—451 and 940—959.

[193] Cf. E. MENDELSON, Some Notes on a Sociological Approach to Gnosticism, in: Le origini, pp. 668—675; and H. KIPPENBERG, Versuch einer soziologischen Verortung des antiken Gnostizismus, Numen 17, 1970, pp. 211—231.

know so much about his social milieu in the Alexandrian Jewish community.[194] Surely some conclusions ought to be possible concerning a hypothetical group of Gnostics in Alexandria (assuming that one or more Gnostic documents can be placed in Alexandria), just from what their writings tell us about their hatred of the Jewish Law, the Biblical Creator God, and the 'Authorities' who hold mankind in thrall, conclusions regarding their social class and, most importantly, their relationship to the powerful Jewish *politeuma* of Alexandria.[195] But that problem cannot be taken up here.

In conclusion, the religious intentionality of the Gnostics on the one hand, and Philo on the other, can be seen in stark contrast in the following summary statements:

From the Gnostics:[196]

"This, therefore, is the true testimony: When man knows himself and God who is over the truth, he will be saved."

From Philo:[197]

"He that has begun by learning these things with his understanding rather than with his hearing, and has stamped on his soul impressions of truths so marvellous and priceless, both that God is and is from eternity, and that He that really IS is One, and that He has made the world and has made it one world, unique as Himself is unique, and that He ever exercises forethought for His creation, will lead a life of bliss and blessedness, because he has a character moulded by the truths that piety and holiness enforce."[198]

---

[194] This point is made forcefully by W. MEEKS, who uses Philo as a point of comparison with the Fourth Gospel for the purpose of gaining some insights concerning its social milieu, in: The Divine Agent and His Counterfeit in Philo and the Fourth Gospel, in E. SCHÜSSLER FIORENZA, ed., Aspects of Religious Propaganda in Judaism and Early Christianity, University of Notre Dame Center for the Study of Judaism and Christianity in Antiquity, 2, Notre Dame, 1976, pp. 43–67.

[195] In my opinion it is not enough merely to deduce from the Gnostic sources a revolutionary hatred of the Roman imperial power, as KIPPENBERG does (op. cit. n. 193). Something must be made of the violent anti-Jewish thrust of much of the Gnostic literature, especially in the earliest sources.

[196] NHC IX, 3: The Testimony of Truth, 44,30–45,4. See The Nag Hammadi Library in English, op. cit. n. 51, p. 411. The Coptic text, with English translation, is now available in a complete critical edition: B. PEARSON, ed., Nag Hammadi Codices IX and X, Nag Hammadi Studies 15, Leiden, 1981.

[197] Philo concludes his treatise 'On the Creation of the World' with what has been called "the first creed of history" (GOODENOUGH, Introduction, p. 37), setting forth a five-fold statement on God and the world (Op 170–172). He summarizes this creed in his concluding paragraph, quoted here (Op 172).

[198] Text: ὁ δὴ ταῦτα μὴ ἀκοῇ μᾶλλον ἢ διανοίᾳ προμαθὼν καὶ ἐν τῇ αὑτοῦ ψυχῇ σφραγισάμενος θαυμάσια καὶ περιμάχητα εἴδη, καὶ ὅτι ἔστι καὶ ὑπάρχει θεὸς καὶ ὅτι εἷς ὁ ὢν ὄντως ἐστὶ καὶ ὅτι πεποίηκε τὸν κόσμον καὶ πεποίηκεν ἕνα, ὡς ἐλέχθη, κατὰ τὴν μόνωσιν ἐξομοιώσας ἑαυτῷ, καὶ ὅτι ἀεὶ προνοεῖ τοῦ γεγονότος, μακαρίαν καὶ εὐδαίμονα ζωὴν βιώσεται, δόγμασιν εὐσεβείας καὶ ὁσιότητος χαραχθείς.

Epilogue

This article was completed in 1976. Since that time a number of important works have appeared bearing on our subject, but the press of other duties has prevented me from taking them into account in the *Forschungsbericht* presented in part I. Nevertheless I am confident that the issues as defined in this article are still the pertinent ones, and the conclusions drawn still valid. I should add that part II of this article, in substantially the same form, was presented to the 29th Colloquy of the Center for Hermeneutical Studies in Hellenistic and Modern Culture, in Berkeley, California, on 17 April, 1977. The Protocol of this colloquy, containing my paper, responses by T. Conley, J. Dillon, B. L. Mack, D. Winston, A. Wire, and E. N. Lee, and minutes of the discussions, are published under the title 'Philo and the Gnostics on Man and Salvation,' ed. W. Wuellner, Berkeley, 1977. I am grateful to the editors of ANRW for permission to present in advance this portion of my ANRW article to my Berkeley colleagues, and for permission to publish it in the Colloquy series of the Center for Hermeneutical Studies in Berkeley.

Bibliography

1. Bibliographies on Philo:

Goodhart, H. L., and E. R. Goodenough, A General Bibliography of Philo Judaeus, in: E. R. Goodenough, The Politics of Philo Judaeus: Practice and Theory, New Haven, 1938, r.p. Hildesheim, 1967, pp. 125–321.
Feldman, L. H., Studies in Judaica: Scholarship on Philo and Josephus (1937–1962), New York, 1963.
Hilgert, E., Bibliographia Philoniana 1935–1981, published in this same volume (ANRW II, 21,1), pp. 47–97.

2. Bibliographies on Gnosticism:

Scholer, D. M., Nag Hammadi Bibliography 1948–1969, Nag Hammadi Studies 1, Leiden, 1971.
Id., Bibliographia Gnostica, Supplementa 1–11, in: Novum Testamentum 13 (1971), pp. 322–336; 14 (1972), pp. 312–331; 15 (1973), pp. 327–345; 16 (1974), pp. 316–336; 17 (1975), pp. 305–336; 19 (1977), pp. 293–336; 20 (1978), pp. 300–331; 21 (1979), pp. 357–382; 22 (1980), pp. 352–384; 23 (1981), pp. 361–380; and 24 (1982), pp. 340–368.

Philo's Rhetoric:
Argumentation and Style

by Thomas M. Conley, Urbana, Ill.

Contents

Introduction

For over fifty years now, scarcely any attention has been paid to Philo's style. In the first place, most scholars have seen their primary task as one of understanding Philo's philosophical position; and in the second, Philo's style has never been particularly well thought of by Hellenists. The first view seems to have resulted in the determination, to paraphrase Bishop BERKELEY, "to lay aside the words as much as possible and consider the bare notions themselves"; and the second has resulted in a tendency to bypass Philo's style on aesthetic grounds which find him pedantic, stilted, and perhaps frigid[1].

---

[1] In the view of most scholars Philo was a conscious but not always successful 'Atticizer' who wrote quite well by Attic standards considering the time and place in which he worked. As COHN remarked in the preface to his edition of the 'De opificio mundi' (p. xlii, see below, note 4 for complete reference): „sed etiamsi Philonis sermo non is est, qui cum Platonis elegantia vere comparari possit, laudem tamen boni et elegantis pro suo tempore scriptoris iure adeptus est." By the same token, however, WILAMOWITZ once complained

Nevertheless, another look at the matter is long overdue. Fifty years is a long time[2]. More importantly, many of the assumptions of a century ago about the relevance of the Attic ideal to Hellenistic Greek and about Philo's *Sitz im Leben* have been called into question during the past half-century. Indeed, many of the basic critical and hermeneutical assumptions shared by philologists who have made pronouncements on Philo's style have been criticized — though seldom directly — by writers in various disciplines, notably by proponents of the 'New Rhetoric'[3].

These recent developments suggest that it is time to attempt a fresh look at Philo's style and that an interdisciplinary approach might be most fruitful. Such an interdisciplinary approach, in this case inspired by the work of some of the New Rhetoricians, is the aim of the present study.

My central concern is with the question of how 'stylistic' features of Philo's works operate in relation to the persuasive designs Philo had on his audience. When I speak of 'persuasive designs', I do not envision a stark adversary situation wherein one party seeks to impress his opinions on another 'by any means necessary' and thereby win the day. The occasions for and ends of persuasion are not limited to such situations, but extend to any attempt by a speaker to increase an audience's adherence to the theses

---

of the labyrinthine periods to be found in Philo (cf. U. v. WILAMOWITZ-MOELLENDORFF, Commentariolum grammaticum 3 [Greifswald, 1889] = ID., Kleine Schriften 4 [Berlin, 1962], p. 642f.). COLSON complains that Philo is "an inveterate rambler" and that, as a writer, "he has many faults". Cf. the General Introduction in Vol. 1 of the Loeb Edition of Philo (Cambridge, Mass., 1961), p. x. He is "sometimes painfully pedantic", as well (ibid. p. xxii).

[2] Fifty years is in fact a very charitable figure, as the Bibliography appended to this study will show. It might almost be fair to say "one hundred years".

[3] Much has been said to suggest that Hellenistic style is a much more complex matter than W. SCHMID allowed for. The work of A. WIFSTRAND, for instance, is indispensible. See his brief but important article 'Stylistic Problems in the Epistles of James and Peter', Studia Theologica 1 (Lund, 1947/48), pp. 170—182. The complaints against the Attic 'Establishment' by M. HIGGINS (see below, note 5) have not gone unheard, despite vigorous reactions. On the *Sitz im Leben* of Philo's works: scholars now agree that the setting in the Alexandrian synagogue is an extremely important factor. See, especially, H. THYEN's 'Der Stil der jüdisch-hellenistischen Homilie' (Forschungen zur Religion und Literatur des Alten und Neuen Testaments 65; Göttingen, 1955). The relationship between Hellenism and Judaism in Philo's time has also received considerable attention, and it is clear that the matter is far more complicated than it was once thought to be. See esp. M. HENGEL, Judentum und Hellenismus. Studien zu ihrer Begegnung unter besonderer Berücksichtigung Palästinas bis zur Mitte des 2. Jhs. v. Chr. (Wissenschaftliche Untersuchungen zum Neuen Testament 10; Tübingen, ²1973).
For a review of some recent criticisms of traditional assumptions about style in general, see, e.g., B. GRAY, Style: The Problem and the Solution (Paris/The Hague, 1969). On the theory of style among proponents of the New Rhetoric, cf., e.g., I. A. RICHARDS, The Philosophy of Rhetoric (New York, 1936); K. BURKE, Counterstatement (Berkeley/London, 1968) and ID., A Rhetoric of Motives (New York, 1950); W. J. BRANDT, The Rhetoric of Argumentation (New York, 1970); and CH. PERELMAN and L. OLBRECHTS-TYTECA, Traité de l'Argumentation (Editions de l'Institut de Sociologie; Brussels, ²1970), English translation by J. WILKINSON and P. WEAVER, The New Rhetoric (Notre Dame, 1969), further cited as TA and NR respectively.

presented for its assent. Rhetoricians, after all, are not concerned exclusively with verbal coercion, but characteristically seek to establish or reinforce consensus as well. In attempting to do this, a rhetorician uses style as more than a mere embellishment. His style is the very agency of his attempt to gain or increase the agreement of his audience. I intend, therefore, to examine some of the stylistic phenomena in Philo as rhetorical phenomena, not as mere ornament; and as deliberate and intentional aspects of his argumentation, not simply as matters of habitual or idiosyncratic usage. Thus I have called this study 'Philo's Rhetoric', although most of it is taken up with subjects traditionally associated with style alone.

In the first section, we shall survey some aspects of Philo's style which have to do with syntax and usage. After that we shall look at Philo's use of figures, particularly the so-called 'figures of thought'. I have selected figures of thought for particular scrutiny because they bring out an important aspect of Philo's style which most discussions leave out, viz., what Philo's style shows us about his attempts to establish a particular relationship with his audience. After the survey, we shall take a look at an entire treatise, the 'De Cherubim', and watch Philo use those constructions and figures in an argumentative context.

I. 'Grammatical' Aspects of Philo's Rhetoric

In the prefaces to their editions of Philo's works and in chapters devoted to the subject, considerable space was given by SIEGFRIED, COHN, CUMONT, and others, to pecularities of phonology, accidence, syntax, word formation, and diction as well as to matters of style[4]. Here we shall concentrate on just

---

[4] The need felt in the mid-Nineteenth Century for a new edition of Philo resulted in most of what has been written specifically on his style. The important discussions are (cf. Bibliography for full references): C. SIEGFRIED (1875), pp. 31ff.; J. JESSEN (1889); L. COHN (1889), pp. xliff.; F. CUMONT (1891), pp. xviff.; P. WENDLAND (1892), pp. 100ff.; F. C. CONYBEARE (1895), pp. 354ff.; E. KRELL (1896), pp. 7ff. Scattered comments on Philo's style can be found in the notes to the Loeb edition of F. H. COLSON and G. H. WHITAKER. It should be recognized that although the observations made by these scholars were of utility to future editors and of interest to students of the history of the Greek language (e.g., JANNARIS, REIK, and ANLAUF — cf. below, note 5), the material to be found in the works cited above is restricted to such matters as Philo's avoidance of hiatus (e.g., JESSEN), peculiar diction and neologisms (SIEGFRIED, WENDLAND), and odd constructions (e.g., COHN). A. W. DE GROOT gives some statistics on Philo's clausulae in his 'Handbook of Antique Prose Rhythm' (Groningen, 1919), pp. 178ff. and 195ff.; and A. Q. MORTON and J. McLEMAN (Paul, the Man and the Myth. A Study in the Authorship of Greek Prose, London, 1966) offer some statistics on Philo's sentence length (cf. ibid. Table 6). Both may be useful for stylometric purposes, but probably for little else. No attempt has been made to provide a comprehensive study on the order of, e.g., J. PALM's excellent 'Über Sprache und Stil des Diodorus von Sizilien' (Diss. Lund, 1955).
I have not seen: L. TREITEL, De Philonis sermone (Breslau, 1870) or E. F. TRISOGLIO, Apostrofi, parenesi, e preghiere in Filone, Rivista Lasalliana (Torino) 31 (1964), pp.

three aspects of Philo's usage: a) his use of the optative, b) his use of verbal adjectives in -*teos*, and c) his management of first person pronouns.

1. Optative use

One of the grammatical aspects of Philo's style which has attracted much attention — perhaps more than it really deserves — is his use of the optative mood, which had become uncommon, if not more or less 'mummified', by Philo's time. There are still some aspects of Philo's optatives, however, which deserve to be considered[5].

KARL REIK was correct to point out that Philo frequently used the optative where Attic usage would lead us to expect a different construction and sometimes failed to use it where Attic usage would demand it. He was, however, too hasty in labelling Philo's *Optativgebrauch* 'artificial' and 'affected'. In calling attention to the rhetorical effect of the 'unnecessary' and unexpected optatives in Philo, REIK tends to confound rhetoric with artificiality. At Post. 7, for instance, Philo says,

(εἰ) . . . ἀδύνατον δ' ἐστὶν ὥσπερ ἐκ πόλεως τοῦδε τοῦ κόσμου μετα-
ναστῆναί τι μέρος αὐτοῦ μηδενὸς ἀπολειφθέντος ἔξω, λοιπὸν ἂν εἴη
λογισαμένους ὅτι . . .

REIK complains that here, as elsewhere in Philo (cp. Aet. 87), the optative is „*eine leere Form*". But Philo is not just being vain. Surely the effect of the optative here is to convey the impression that if it is impossible, then the only thing that could possibly be left for us to do is turn to an allegorical interpretation of Gen. iv. 16, the text being commented upon. The under-statement only strengthens this sense of inevitability. Similarly, at ibid. 4 the negation (οὐδ' ἂν ἔχοι) virtually guarantees that it could not con-ceivably be otherwise[6]. That these eventualities might have been expressed

357—410; 32 (1965), pp. 39—79, both of which look as though they might be relevant to our subject.

[5] The recognized definitive study on Philo's use of the optative is KARL REIK's 'Der Optativ bei Polybius und Philo von Alexandria' (Leipzig, 1907). ISAK UNNA had made some observations on the matter in his 'Über den Gebrauch der Absichtssätze bei Philo von Alexandrien' (Diss. Würzburg, 1895), passim. The conclusions of REIK's study (which was dedicated to W. SCHMID) were questioned by M. HIGGINS in: Why Another Optative Dissertation?, Byzantion 15 (1940/41), pp. 443ff. and subsequently defended vigorously by G. ANLAUF in his 'Standard Late Greek oder Atticismus?' (Diss. Köln, 1961). It seems incontestable that Philo was an "Atticizer"; but it is unclear to me how that fact justifies studiously biassed studies of his "Atticizing" by REIK et al. However tenuous his case for the dialectal survival of the optative, HIGGINS is surely correct in insisting that scholars try to see what Philo was trying to do, not what he failed to do, when he used an optative (cf. op. cit., p. 448).

[6] As J. CARRIÈRE explains it, this kind of construction expresses «*hors de toute hypothèse circonstanciée, la probabilité, la présomption suffisamment fondée en raison ou en expérience*». Cf. Stylistique grecque (Tradition de l'humanisme 6; Paris, 1967), p. 108.

in another construction is undeniable; but what Philo clearly wants to do in these passages is to emphasize the inevitable eventuality of what he says will happen (or not) without making an overt prediction.

On the other hand, in the almost formulaic εἴποι τις ἄν . . .[7] we are given a sense of the tentative, but far from impossible, likelihood of someone's making an objection or taking a different position on the subject[8]. In most cases Philo treats these possibilities seriously, sometimes taking scrupulous care to refute even an unlikely objection, sometimes working around one by means of a series of rhetorical questions. Since it is implied by the mood itself of the verb that the objection is only within the realm of (perhaps unlikely) possibility and not an actual objection, the credibility of the objection is diminished. Moreover, the apparent fact that Philo has given careful consideration to the matter being discussed and foresees even such remotely possible objections enhances his rhetorical *ethos*. There are, in short, definite rhetorical advantages to using the optative where, strictly speaking, another construction would do; and not all of them stem from mere affectation.

Philo often uses the optative where another construction might be more consistent with good Attic usage in order to suggest humility on his part — as when he says at Opif. 87 (after a thoroughly amplified analogy):

πολλὰ δ' ἂν ἔχοι τις λέγειν ἕτερα, βουλόμενος ἀπομηκύνειν, εἰς ἔνδειξιν τοῦ μηδὲν ἀπελευθεριάζειν ὑπεξῃρημένον τῆς ἀνθρώπου ἡγεμονίας.

Again, he uses the optative to achieve a measure of "understatement" when he concludes a learned mathematical disquisition with νομίζοιτ' ἂν εἰκότως ἥδε (sc. ἡ τῆς ἑβδομάδος οὐσία) πηγὴ παντὸς σχήματος καὶ πάσης ποιότητος (Opif. 97). It is also as a form of understatement that we must understand the substitution of an optative for a more clearly imperative expression at, e.g., Post. 9: καὶ ὅσοι μὲν ἐξ ἀνάγκης τοῦτο ὑπέμειναν . . . πιεσθέντες, ἐλέου μᾶλλον ἢ μίσους τυγχάνοιεν ἂν . . . κτλ.

All these examples suggest that REIK was perhaps too strict when he called Philo's optatives 'vain'. Philo's use of the mood seems largely governed by argumentative needs and intentions. Indeed, there is evidence that such usage was not only approved of by Philo's contemporaries as polite language, but expected of him[9]. One of the themes which runs through his use of the

---

[7] For examples of the use of this expression, cf. e.g., Sac. 99, Det. 74, Mut. 181, Heres 90, 101, etc. Cf. also, e.g., Conf. 142 (ἴσως δ' ἂν εἴποιέν τινες . . .), LA III.241 (φαίη τις ἄν . . .), etc.

[8] The use of the 'formula' is generally 'proleptic'. Cf. below, p. 352f. on prolepsis. By *ethos* here I mean the character of the speaker as it comes out *in the speech*. Cf. Aristotle, Rhetoric I.2, 1356 a 3ff.

[9] Speaking of the retention of the optative by some authors in a time when the optative was dying out, N. TURNER remarks, "the retention of the optatives . . . need not surprise us in view of their value for the liturgy, Jewish and Christian". Cf. MOULTON's 'Grammar of New Testament Greek', Vol. 3 (Edinburgh, 1963), p. 133. However, he has just referred

optative is that of understatement, particularly in the "imperative" use of the mood. By using such a construction, Philo puts himself in a different relationship with his audience than he would have by using, e.g., the imperative itself. Philo was not interested in hectoring his audience. The optative is not simply an elegant mode of expression but a form, we might say, of verbal litotes, of understatement meant to be seen as such[10].

2. Verbal adjectives in -teos

Understatement of imperative force is also achieved by the use of verbal adjectives in -teos, one of Philo's favorite ways of communicating obligation 'impersonally', i.e., not as deriving from the authority of Philo himself but purely as "what there is to be done"[11]. There are more than seventy-five such adjectives in Philo, many of them appearing only once (e.g., ἀναιρετέον, ἀπογνωστέον, ἐπιτολμητέον, παραστατέον) and others more often (ὑπολειπτέον (10), ἐρευνητέα (9), προνοητέον (4), etc.). Constructions using λεκτέον appear much more often than any of the others[12], most often in passages where Philo is offering a λύσις: e.g., LA I.48: ζητήσειε δ' ἄν τις, διὰ τί ... λεκτέον οὖν ... (cf. also LA II.103; Sac. 128; Agr. 94; Plant. 113; Ebr. 68; Conf. 170; Heres 101; Cong. 73, 88; Mut. 83, etc.). λεκτέον often appears as part of a rhetorical question. In every case it is more or less imperative in force[13].

When one begins to examine the ways in which Philo directs the attention of his audience, holding up and recommending to them a course of action, the vast range of his imperative techniques becomes evident. The vast majority of these are polite (unlike those of, e.g., Epictetus, whose

(loc. cit.) to their incidence in "the pompous and stereotyped jargon of devotion" (sic), so it is clear that he, too, considers the optative a „leere Form", despite its obvious place in the literature. Philo, on the other hand, may have seen things differently.

[10] On the imperative, see PERELMAN, TA 213 (NR 158): «La modalité injonctive s'exprime, dans nos langues, par l'impératif. Contrairement aux apparances, elle n'a pas de force persuasive: tout son pouvoir vient de l'emprise de la personne qui ordonne sur celle qui exécute: c'est un rapport de forces n'impliquant aucune adhésion. Quand la force réelle est absente ou que l'on n'envisage pas son utilisation, l'impératif prend l'accent d'une prière». On the care with which Attic orators handled the imperative, cf. C. W. E. MILLER, The Limitations of the Imperative in the Attic Orators, American Journal of Philology 13 (1892), pp. 399—436. Most instances of the actual imperative are virtually formulaic (e.g., ἰδού, ὅρα, etc.).

[11] In every case where Philo uses a verbal adjective in -teos, he might 'more naturally' have used δεῖ ... (which he does more than 200 times), προσήκει ... (110+), or χρή ... (165+). Figures are from G. MAYER, Index Philoneus (Berlin/New York, 1974).

[12] λεκτέον occurs 93 times.

[13] In rhetorical questions, e.g., τί οὖν λεκτέον; see the passage at LA I.90: ποίῳ ... διαπορητέον → (91): ζητητέον δὲ διὰ τί ... τί οὖν λεκτέον; (there follows a series of questions) → (92): εἰκότως οὖν ὁ Ἀδάμ ... Cp. LA I.33—35. For clearer imperative force, cf., e.g., Cher. 91, Agr. 39, Plant. 147, 167 (first person), Ebr. 17, 154, Fug. 94, 197, Spec. I. 168, 198, etc.

subtlest device seems to be the 'ironic imperative'), 'objective', and oblique; and thus Philo generally gives the impression that he is not demanding obedience but seeking in his audience a sense of communal dedication to the 'right' actions.

3. First person pronouns

This sense of communal bond which Philo attempts to create in and with his audience is also evident in his use of pronouns, as THYEN has done so much to demonstrate. Philo makes use of the personal ἐγώ mainly in passages which are almost diffident in tone[14]. He often extends the *egō* to include his listeners as well, as at Som. I.177:

> ἐάν τε γὰρ ὁ ἐν ἐμοὶ νοῦς ἀρετῇ τελείᾳ καθαρθῇ, καὶ αἱ τοῦ περὶ ἐμὲ γεώ-
> δους φυλαὶ συγκαθαίρονται, ἃς ἔλαχον αἱ αἰσθήσεις καὶ ἡ μεγίστη δεξα-
> μενή, τὸ σῶμα . . . κτλ.

— where ἐμοί and ἐμέ apparently refer not as much to Philo personally as to anyone and everyone (τις). Similarly, the ἐγώ in LA III. 156 is not to be taken as a personal ἐγώ — Philo is not being autobiographical here — but as a 'Universal I'.

At LA II.68f., Philo emphasizes the bond between himself and his audience when he employs, in turn, generalized first person, literal second person, and first person plural pronouns:

> μὰ τὸν ἀληθῆ μόνον θεὸν οὐδὲν οὕτως αἰσχρὸν ἡγοῦμαι ὡς τὸ ὑπολαμ-
> βάνειν ὅτι νοῶ ἢ ὅτι αἰσθάνομαι. ὁ ἐμὸς νοῦς αἴτιος τοῦ νοεῖν; πόθεν;
> . . . ἡ δὲ αἴσθησις αἰτία τοῦ αἰσθάνεσθαι; πῶς ἂν λέγοιτο . . . ; οὐχ
> ὁρᾷς . . . ; ὁρῶντες ἔστιν ὅτε οὐχ ὁρῶμεν καὶ ἀκούοντες οὐκ ἀκούομεν . . .
> κτλ.

At Sac. 124f., Philo does not address the audience directly, but he clearly invites them to identify with him[16].

---

[14] Cf. THYEN, op. cit., pp. 88ff., 101ff. Expressions like ὡς ἔμοιγε φαίνεται at, e.g., Cher. 55, Post. 39, Migr. 89, Immut. 128, etc., are "formulaic", and do not imply any claims to personal authority.

[15] Compare LA II, 32, 68 (where Philo immediately shifts into second-person address) and Cher. 113ff., a meditation for all present to participate in. See also Decal. 31ff., 41ff. It goes without saying that Philo's use of first person pronouns should be handled carefully. At Cong. 156f., for instance, Philo seems to speak in the first person, but the passage is also an instance of prosopopoeia (see below, p. 355f.). The *egō* at Cong. 6 is part of Philo's amplification on the etymology of Σάρα in Gen. xvi, 1. Cf. THYEN, loc. cit., and note 18 below.

[16] The ὁρῶ δ' ἔγωγε at Sac. 136 seems to be a parenthesis or 'footnote'. In περὶ ὧν κατ' ἰδίαν λέξομεν, we can see a rare intrusion of the personal Philo.

The exceptions to the observations made above on the 'diffidence' of Philo's ἐγώ (and of his first person constructions in general) are interesting. The opening sections of Mos. I, for instance, are solidly in the first person:

(1) Μωυσέως . . . τὸν βίον ἀναγράψαι διενοήθην . . . κτλ.

(2—3) (Greek writers have refused to recognize Moses.)

(4) ἀλλ' ἔγωγε τὴν τούτων βασκανίαν ὑπερβὰς τὰ περὶ τὸν ἄνδρα μηνύσω . . .
     . . . καὶ . . . ἔδοξα μᾶλλον ἑτέρων τὰ περὶ τὸν βίον ἀκριβῶσαι.

(5) Ἄρξομαι δ' . . . κτλ.

Two other instances are not nearly as 'ego-centered', but they do not fall into the 'diffident' category either: Decal. 75, ἀλλ' ἔγωγε νομίζω ταῦτα . . . ; Spec. I. 281, ἔγωγε οὐκ οἶδα . . . It should be recalled that all of these are from Philo's exposition of the Law, which had a different audience from that of the Allegory[17]. In the Exposition, Philo tends to speak with more personal authority[18].

In these brief observations on 'grammatical' phenomena in Philo I have tried to show that a purely grammatical analysis of his usage fails to get to the heart of the matter. Before deciding that Philo's optatives are affected or 'urbane', one should try to bear in mind that Philo was addressing an audience which had definite expectations of style and definite limits to their tolerance (especially under the circumstances) of rhetorical affectation. It may be that, had Philo succeeded in his supposed attempts to write Attic Greek, he would have failed with his audience. Before remarking on the prevalence of gerundives in -teos, again, one should consider the special requirements of Philo's rhetorical situation. The style proper to preaching in a synagogue is not the style of philosophical or quasi-philosophical argumentation — a point which will emerge more clearly, I hope, after we have examined the rhetoric of 'De Cherubim'.

---

[17] Cf., e.g., E. GOODENOUGH, Philo's Exposition of the Law and his De Vita Mosis, The Harvard Theological Review 26 (1933), esp. at p. 124ff.; and ID., An Introduction to Philo Judaeus (New Haven, 1940), Ch. 2 passim.

[18] The instances of ἔγωγε are interesting for what they may show about Philo's rhetoric. In all of Philo, there are only 18 occurrences of ἔγωγε/ἔμοιγε. In only two instances (Post. 120 and Fug. 3, which begins a long expeditio: see below, p. 352) can we describe Philo as assertive. At Post. 39, the ἔμοιγε comes naturally in the antithesis. For the rest, except that at Leg. 53, see the comments above in notes 15 and 16. A quick check of PREUSS's index to Demosthenes gives more than 135 instances of ἔγωγε/ἔμοιγε. One must, of course, take into consideration the differences in genre — and that is precisely the point, for differences in genre are indicative of differences in appropriate ethos. I have not looked into ἐγὼ αὐτός or other expressions which may have a bearing on this question. On the 'rhetoric of pronouns' see the comments of TH. M. CONLEY, in: Protocols of the Colloquies of the Center for Hermeneutical Studies 5 (Berkeley, 1975), pp. 14—22.

II. Figures and tropes

What makes style interesting from a rhetorical point of view is what it reveals about an author's intentions to relate stylistic resources to effects he wishes to produce in his audience. We have seen a few examples of how Philo's grammatical usages may indicate something about the relationship he sought to establish with his audience, a fundamental aspect of the rhetoric of his works. We turn now to the other 'parts' of Philo's style, his use of tropes and figures — primarily figures of thought — with a view toward seeing how, and in what measure, his use of particular figures is explainable not only by a desire for ornamentation but also by the requirements of argumentation[19].

There are distinct advantages to looking at tropes and figures as they relate to argumentation. In the first place, they become more interesting. As CH. PERELMAN has remarked, the study of figures is a useless pastime once their argumentative role is disregarded[20]. It would not be too much to say that it was precisely the loss of a sense of the argumentative situation in which argumentation takes place which led to the pointless and apparently endless proliferation of lists of figures and tropes wherein the only interest seems to have been in taxonomy and organization. It is no wonder that even Quintilian complains that the subject has been overdone[21].

The second advantage to looking at figures this way is that they become more susceptible to intelligent organization. The organization of the discussion which follows is not the traditional order to be found in, e.g., the 'Ad Herennium' or in LAUSBERG's exhaustive 'Handbuch'[22]. Since we are not interested in the extent to which Philo used tropes and figures but in their rhetorical functions and possibilities, we shall try to organize our observations around three general effects which the various figures are regularly employed to achieve in rhetorical discourse.

These three effects we shall call 'focus', which the orator seeks to achieve by directing his audience's attention to specific aspects of his subject matter; 'presence', by which a speaker makes the subject more important

---

[19] I intend to examine another important aspect of Philo's style — his construction of periods — in a separate study. It is too large a subject to treat adequately here.

[20] Cf. CH. PERELMAN, The New Rhetoric, in: Great Ideas Today for 1970 (Chicago, 1970), p. 289.

[21] Cf., e.g., Quintilian IX.i.22 and iii.99: *nam eos quidem auctores, qui nullum prope finem fecerunt exquirendis nominibus, praeteribo, qui etiam, quae sunt argumentorum, figuris ascripserunt.*

[22] H. LAUSBERG, Handbuch der Literarischen Rhetorik, 2 vols. (Munich, 1960; 2nd ed. 1973). J. MARTIN, Antike Rhetorik: Technik und Methode (Handbuch der Altertums-wissenschaft 2, 3; Munich, 1974) supersedes LAUSBERG in many important respects and is generally more useful to the student of Classical rhetoric.

to his audience; and 'communion', which refers to the bond a speaker seeks to establish between himself and his audience[23].

1. 'Focus'

The speaker's control over the perceptions and expectations of his audience is particularly apparent in the traditional figures of *distributio*, *expeditio*, *prolepsis*, and *praeteritio*. In some cases, *distributio*[24] may be effective as a dialectical division designed to restrict the range of discussion on or interpretation of the subject. Thus, at the beginning of 'De Fuga et Inventione', Philo distinguishes,

Αἰτίας οὖν ἔγωγε τρεῖς εἶναι νομίζω φυγῆς, μῖσος, φόβον, αἰδῶ. μίσει μὲν οὖν καὶ γυναῖκες ἄνδρας καὶ ἄνδρες γυναῖκας ἀπολείπουσι, φόβῳ δὲ τοὺς γονεῖς παῖδες καὶ δεσπότας οἰκέται, αἰδοῖ δὲ τοὺς ἑταίρους ... κτλ.

This distribution serves as a structuring principle for the next twenty sections or so. Another use of distribution is apparent in the presentation of several possible choices, the elimination of all but one, and the presentation of the final choice as the only reasonable one. This is, of course, the *expeditio* of the traditional lists of figures.[25] A good example can be found in the sections of 'De Cherubim' which deal with the meaning of the Cherubim in the account in 'Genesis' (Cher. 21—29). These sections may be outlined as follows:

(21) Τίνα δέ ἐστιν ἃ διὰ τῶν Χερουβὶμ ... νῦν ἐπισκεπτέον. μήποτε οὖν ...

(25) τὰ μὲν δὴ Χερουβὶμ καθ' ἕνα τρόπον οὕτως ἀλληγορεῖται ... μήποτε δὲ καθ' ἑτέραν ἐκδοχὴν ...

(27) Ἤκουσα δέ ποτε καὶ σπουδαιοτέρου λόγου παρὰ ψυχῆς ἐμῆς .. ἔλεγε δέ μοι ...

(29) Ἑκατέρου δὴ τῶν Χερουβίμ, ὦ διάνοια, δέξαι τύπον ἀκιβδήλευτον ...

Prolepsis[26] consists of taking up an anticipated or possible objection and disposing of it. A speaker will never, of course, take into consideration

---

[23] In what follows, I shall give a few references to traditional treatments (chiefly from the 'Ad Herennium' and Quintilian) along with references to PERELMAN's observations in 'Traité de l'Argumentation' where appropriate. Both PERELMAN and BRANDT (op. cit., note 3 above) provide valuable insights into the argumentative functions of figures and tropes.

[24] Traditionally, a division of a concept and apportioning of its parts. A structural *distributio* is one by which the structure of the argument which follows is controlled. See AdH IV. xxv.47; Q IV.v.18, VII.i.11, etc. At TA 668f. (NR 504f.), PERELMAN discusses the utility of *distributio* in providing to the audience a schema of reference.

[25] Cf., e.g., AdH IV.xxix.40: *expeditio est cum rationibus conpluribus enumeratis quibus aliqua res confieri potuerit, ceterae tolluntur, una reliquitur quam nos intendimus* ... See also Q IX.iii.99 and V.x.66ff., where *e.* is discussed as a line of argument.

[26] See, e.g., Q IX.ii.16f. (and with it VI.iii.100). Cf. MARTIN, op. cit., pp. 277—279 for further

all possible objections, but will concentrate on those which either present the greatest threat to his own interpretation or make his own interpretation easier to present as the reasonable one. Philo's works abound in *prolepsis*, and the introduction of possible objections is usually in the form of formulaic phrases like ἴσως ἄν τις εἴποι . . . or φαίη τις ἄν . . . "Rhetorical questions" may also serve to introduce possible objections. Philo's anticipations of actual objections which are part of a continuing controversy (e.g., between himself and the 'literalists') are often — at least on stylistic grounds — difficult to distinguish from his proleptic feints[27].

There are other means of achieving focus at the disposal of a speaker which usually operate on a smaller scale. Synonymity, for instance, may belong more properly to our category of 'presence'; but an apparent synonymy may often be a mild form of *correctio* or a way of emphasizing one specific aspect of the subject under discussion[28]. Similarly, some of the figures which are usually classified as ornamental — antitheses and parallelism, for instance — may develop into something more than mere ornaments of periodic construction when they are used to bring home to the listener an evaluation or revaluation of the matter being discussed[29]. Finally, it should be noted that similes, analogies, metaphors, and metonymies — all usually thought of as largely ornamental — can also be used by the speaker to turn his audience's attention to a particular quality possessed by the subject[30].

2. Presence

The devices by which a speaker renders something more 'present' to his audience may be divided into three main classes: 1) those which are

---

references. PERELMAN discusses *prolepsis* at TA 228f. (NR 169f.) and TA 663 (NR 501). Immut. 21 and 52, Som. II.201f. are reasonably good examples in Philo.

[27] On *praeteritio*, cf. AdH IV.xxvii.37; Q IX.ii.75, iii.98. *Pr.* is discussed by PERELMAN as one means for offsetting the dangers of argumentative 'amplitude', which may explain its virtual absence from Philo's works. One might add to the figures related to 'focus' *definitio* in cases where the function is not to clarify the 'objective' meaning of a term but to stress aspects of it which will produce the persuasive effect sought by the speaker. See TA 233f. (NR 172f.), TA 289 (NR 215).

[28] On apparent tautology in the use of synonyms, see TA 292f. (NR 216f.) and TA 588f. (NR 443f.). Among many examples of 'corrective' synonymy, see, e.g., LA I.6 (ἵσταται καὶ μένει) and Spec. II.196 (λιτὰς καὶ ἱκεσίας).

[29] Cf., e.g., Det. 49: ὁ μὲν δὴ σοφὸς τεθνηκέναι δοκῶν τὸν φθαρτὸν βίον ζῇ τὸν ἄφθαρτον, ὁ δὲ φαῦλος ζῶν τὸν ἐν κακίᾳ τέθνηκε τὸν εὐδαίμονα; and Som. II.302: οὐδὲ γὰρ περὶ ποταμῶν ἐστιν ἱστορίας ἡ παροῦσα σπονδή, περὶ δὲ βίων τῶν εἰκαζομένων ποταμίοις ῥεύμασιν, ἐναντιουμένων ἀλλήλοις.

[30] On the use of metaphors and similes in focussing attention on a particular aspect of the subject of discussion, often with evaluative undertones, see PERELMAN TA 506f. (NR 376f.), 534ff. (NR 398ff.). Aristotle discusses this use of metaphor and simile at Rhet. III.ii. 1405 a 10ff.

chiefly 'grammatical' (asyndeton, polysyndeton, etc.); 2) those which work on the principle of repetition and variation on a single theme (synonymity, anaphora, *gradatio*, etc.); and 3) those which actually 'dramatize' a subject (personification, prosopopeia, dialogue, etc.). Let us survey some examples of these.

Asyndeton/polysyndeton: Numerous examples of these have been noted by Philo's editors, so there is no need to attempt a listing here. And since the impression they make on a listener is quite evident[31], a few examples will suffice.

Sac. 101:

> ἀφελεῖς οὖν, ὦ ψυχή, πᾶν γενητὸν θνητὸν μεταβλητὸν βέβηλον ἀπὸ ἐννοίας τῆς περὶ θεοῦ τοῦ ἀγενήτου καὶ ἀφθάρτου καὶ ἀτρέπτου καὶ ἁγίου καὶ μόνου μακαρίου.

Along with the terminal assonance in both members, the alternation here is worth noticing. Such deliberate design should be carefully distinguished from what occurs in passages such as Opif. 62:

> πενταχῆ δὲ τμητὸν αἴσθησις, εἰς ὅρασιν, εἰς ἀκοήν, εἰς γεῦσιν, εἰς ὄσφρησιν, εἰς ἀφήν . . .

where no particular effect is being sought after, only a quick enumeration[32].

Opif. 22: Philo gives a most impressive display of balanced asyndeton here:

> ἦν μὲν γὰρ ἐξ αὐτῆς ἄτακτος, ἄποιος, ἄψυχος, ⟨ἀνόμοιος⟩, ἑτεροιότητος, ἀναρμοστίας, ἀσυμφωνίας μεστή· τροπὴν δὲ καὶ μεταβολὴν ἐδέχετο τὴν εἰς τἀναντία καὶ τὰ βέλτιστα, τάξιν, ποιότητα, ἐμψυχίαν, ὁμοιότητα, ταυτότητα, τὸ εὐάρμοστον, τὸ σύμφωνον . . . κτλ.

Spec. IV.187: This is an equally impressive use of polysyndeton:

> τάξιν ἐξ ἀταξίας καὶ ἐξ ἀποίων ποιότητας καὶ ἐξ ἀνομοίων ὁμοιότητας καὶ ἐξ ἑτεροιοτήτων ταυτότητας καὶ ἐξ ἀκοινωνήτων καὶ ἀναρμόστων κοινωνίας καὶ ἁρμονίας . . . κτλ.

Repetition: By far the most basic, and most complex, means of giving emphasis, creating presence, and making vivid are those which operate

---

[31] Cf. AdH IV.xxx.41: *Hoc genus et acrimoniam habet in se et vehentissimum est et ad brevitatem accomodatum.* DENNISTON's discussions of both asyndeton and polysyndeton are well worth consulting; see 'The Greek Particles' (Oxford, 1934), pp. xliiiff. and lxiiff.

[32] Compare, e.g., Cont. 18: . . . καταλιπόντες ἀδελφούς, τέκνα, γυναῖκας, γονεῖς, πολυανθρώπους συγγενείας, φιλικὰς ἑταιρείας κτλ. — which sound almost like a formulaic or commonplace list. Cf. also, e.g., Ebr. 195.

on the principle of repetition in its various forms. These include not only synonymity, which we mentioned before in another connection, but structural devices such as anaphora, parallelism, etc.[33] An excellent example of repetition with anaphora is to be found at Praem. 11:

> ταύτης δ' ὁ πρῶτος σπόρος ἐστὶν ἐλπίς . . .
>   ἐλπίδι μὲν γὰρ κέρδους ὁ χρηματιστὴς . . .
>   ἐλπίδι δ' ὁ ναύκληρος . . .
>   ἐλπίδι δόξης καὶ ὁ φιλότιμος . . .
>   δι' ἐλπίδα βραβείων . . .
>   ἐλπὶς εὐδαιμονίας . . . κτλ.[34]

At Opif. 79, we have anaphora and epiphora together:

> τουτὶ δὲ συμβήσεται, ἐὰν
>   μήτε αἱ ἄλογοι ἡδοναὶ ψυχῆς δυναστεύωσι . . .
>   μήτε αἱ δόξης . . . ἐπιθυμίαι τὸ τοῦ βίου κράτος ἀνάψωνται,
>   μήτε στείλωσι καὶ κάμψωσι διάνοιαν αἱ λῦπαι,
>   μήθ' ὁ κακὸς . . . ἀναχαιτίσῃ
>   μήτ' ἀφροσύνη καὶ δειλία . . . πλῆθος ἐπιθῆται.

Such extended repetitions are to be found often in Philo's works.

Lending themselves to an even more dramatic impressiveness are 'speaking in character' (prosopopoeia)[35] and 'dialogue' (sermocinatio)[36], two of the most obvious 'dramatic' devices Philo uses to achieve a sense of presence. Examples of prosopopoeia in Philo range in length and complexity from, on the one hand, short passages like Det. 78 to, on the other, the long harangue by 'Virtue' which occupies Sac. 28—45. Philo's dialogues are scattered throughout his works and perform various tasks. At Det. 150ff., for instance, Philo's sermocinatio works closely with prosopopoeia: 'Cain' is speaking in 150—158, and Philo responds at 158ff. At Conf. 116ff., Philo addresses those who would say "Let us make our own name", haranguing

---

[33] The author of the 'Ad Herennium' worked out a rather complete theory of repetition in his treatments of *gradatio*, anaphora, antistrophe (epiphora), *complexio*, *traductio*, and antanaklasis (IV.xiii.19—xiv.21). For PERELMAN's treatment, cf. TA 654, 667 (NR 494, 504) on *gradatio*; pp. 236f. (NR 175f.) on anaphora; pp. 294 (NR 218) on antanaklasis. On repetition generally, cf. also TA 544f., 606, 633, 667 (NR 406, 457, 478, 504). The psychological basis of *repetitio* may be hinted at by J. PIAGET's observation that the thing which is best or most often seen is, by that very fact, overestimated. Cf. Introduction à l'épistémologie génétique 1 (Paris, 1950), pp. 174ff.

[34] Compare, e.g., Som. I.192: ἀνίδρυτοι μὲν γὰρ οἱ λογισμοί, . . . ἀνίδρυτον δὲ καὶ τὸ σῶμα, . . . κτλ.
   At Hypothetica VIII.vii.5, we have a case of repetition used to achieve a sense of climax; compare the repetitions of εἴτε and καί in Opif. 140—142. Ebr. 106 mixes repetition, *expeditio*, and chiasm to produce a period — too long to be quoted here — of almost stupifying power.

[35] Cf. AdH IV.liii.66; TA 445 (NR 331).

[36] AdH IV.lii.65; TA 238 (NR 176). Quintilian (IX.ii.29ff.) holds *sermocinatio* and prosopopoeia to be inseparable.

them. At Heres 81, we have what could only be described as a 'proleptic dialogue':

συντείνει δὲ πρὸς ἠθοποιίαν καὶ τὸ "ἐξήγαγεν αὐτὸν ἔξω", ὅ τινες εἰώθασιν ὑπ' ἀμουσίας ἤθους γελᾶν φάσκοντες· εἴσω γάρ τις ἐξάγεται, ἢ ἔμπαλιν εἰσέρχεται ἔξω; ναί, φαίην ἄν, ὦ καταγέλαστοι καὶ λίαν εὐχερεῖς· ψυχῆς γὰρ τρόπους ἰχνηλατεῖν οὐκ ἐμάθετε . . . κτλ.

The devices productive of 'presence', a sense of dramatic and psychological immediacy, are various and cover an enormous range. All of them, it should be noted, are in some degree argumentative, not merely ornamental. With the last figures discussed above, prosopopoeia and dialogue, we get close to our last category of effects, that of 'communion'.

3. Communion

The forms in which subjects are presented may be used to establish communion between a speaker and his audience. In our observations on Philo's grammatical usage and in those on 'focussing' devices, we noted the effects on the audience's perception of the speaker's *ethos*. Devices intended to achieve a sense of presence can also create a feeling of immediacy between speaker and audience. In our last category of figures, however, we have those whose main purpose seems to be the strengthening of the bond between speaker and audience.

Among these figures of communion, *sententia* must surely be included. Maxims, apophthegmata, and quotations from Scripture do more than display Philo's erudition. In his use of these we can see Philo appealing to shared convictions and common knowledge of the texts upon which those convictions rest in his attempts to establish a bond of community between himself and his audience[37].

Prayers and some instances of apostrophe should also be taken into consideration[38]. The bonding force of prayer is obvious. A call to prayer is frequently an overt invitation to the audience to identify with the speaker and with the beliefs of the speaker. Thus, at Det. 146, after a long run of rhetorical questions (which also serve to produce communion, as we shall see) in which Philo alternates 'you' and 'we' constructions, Philo calls out,

Ἱκετεύωμεν οὖν τὸν θεὸν οἱ συνειδήσει τῶν οἰκείων ἀδικημάτων ἐλεγχόμενοι . . . κτλ.

---

[37] See the important discussion, '*Formes du discours et communion avec l'auditoire*', in TA 220—225 (NR 163—167). Cf. also ibid. 657 (NR 496): «*l'allusion à un fait de culture commun, une citation bien choisie suffiront à susciter la confiance, en montrant qu'il y a entre orateur et auditoires une communauté de valeurs*». And cf. pp. 68—72 (NR 51—56), '*Education et propaganda*'.

[38] On apostrophe, THYEN's discussion, op. cit., pp. 91ff., should be consulted.

At Ebr. 125f., Philo actually enjoins his audience to pray:

εὔχου δὴ τῷ θεῷ μηδέποτε ἔξαρχος οἴνου γενέσθαι, τουτέστι μηδέποτε ἑκὼν ἀφηγήσασθαι τῆς εἰς ἀπαιδευσίαν καὶ ἀφροσύνην ἀγούσης ὁδοῦ . . . κτλ.[39]

This injunction is part of Philo's effort to get his listeners to identify themselves as a group set apart from the wicked, "those whose voices show the deliberate madness of evil".

Apostrophe in Philo is a fairly complex matter. There are many 'apostrophic' passages in Philo, but not all of them work in the same way, nor do all of them indicate the same relationships between speaker and audience. As a 'figure of diction', apostrophe was traditionally associated with outbursts of indignation or grief and frequently confounded with *exclamatio*[40]. Such a description holds true for expressions like Cicero's *O tempora, o mores!* but it does not accurately describe, e.g., prayers addressed to God, which are in a sense apostrophic, nor does it reveal the full significance of a speaker's addressing an absent person in 'dialogue'. Moreover, the 'apostrophe' at, e.g., Mig. 169f. is spoken 'in character', a complication of figures apparently not contemplated by the ancient taxonomists.

Nor is the most frequent form of apostrophe in Philo, the address to the soul or to the mind, one which fits easily into the traditional definition. These instances of apostrophic address are, as THYEN has shown, instances of audience address as well, and paraenetic in intention.

Philo also uses the rhetorical question to bring himself close to his audience. Not every question in Philo is designed to create a sense of communion, to be sure; yet the use of *interrogatio* to that end is quite common in his works. The questions we are chiefly interested in are those by which he seeks to get his audience to participate "actively" in his exposition. Philo sometimes does this by posing the kind of question that requires no answer since the answer is so obvious, as at, e.g., Som. II. 145f.:

τίς γὰρ εἰς τὸν ἀγῶνα τοῦ βίου παρελθὼν ἄπτωτος ἔμεινε; τίς δ' οὐχ ὑπεσκελίσθη; . . . τίνι δ' οὐκ ἐφήδρευεν; . . . κτλ.

At Det. 142f., Philo helps a little by implicitly supplying the answers.

πότε γὰρ εἴποις . . . ;	ἆρ' οὐχ ὅταν . . . ;
πότε δὲ τὸν ἀμαθῆ . . . ;	οὐχ ὅταν ἀπόλειψιν . . . ;
πότε δὲ τοὺς ἄφρονας . . . ;	οὐχ ὅταν φρόνησις . . . ;
πότε δὲ τοὺς ἀκολάστους . . . ;	οὐκ ἐπειδὰν σωφροσύνη . . . ;
πότε δὲ τοὺς ἀσεβεῖς;	οὐχ ὅταν εὐσέβεια . . . ;

Philo thus carries his audience along with him; and by the time we get to διό μοι δοκοῦσιν . . . in 144, we can be sure that his audience will concur

[39] Cp., e.g., Sac. 224, Det. 146.
[40] Cf. Quintilian IX.ii.37f.; AdH IV.xv.22; and the comments of PERELMAN at TA 240, 445 (NR 178, 331).

with him. In a similar passage we have perhaps an even better example of *hypophora*:[41]

τίς γὰρ ἔδωκε . . . τὸ λευκόν; οὐχ ἡ ὄψις;
τίς δὲ τὴν φωνήν; οὐχ ἡ ἀκοή;
τίς δὲ τὸν ἀτμόν; οὐχ ἡ ὄσφρησις;
τίς δὲ τὸν χυλόν; οὐχ ἡ γεῦσις;
τίς δὲ τὸ τραχὺ . . . ; οὐχ ἡ ἀφή;

Philo poses questions at Det. 58ff. in such a way as to create a sense of expectation in his audience and then fulfill that expectation, a strategy very like a playwright's in its handling of the audience:[42]

(58) τί οὖν καὶ ἀποκρίσεως ὄφελος . . . ;
  ἀλλὰ ῥητέον, ὅτι τοιαῦτα . . .
τίνος οὖν ἕνεκα, φήσει τις ἴσως, λέγεται τοιαῦτα;
  ἵν' ἡ μέλλουσα τὰς ἀποκρίσεις . . .
(59) τί οὖν τὸ ἐκ ἀποκρίσεως ἐπαινετόν;
  ἰδοὺ τὴν ἀρετήν, φησίν . . . κτλ.

Finally, Philo sometimes uses a series of questions as an armature for amplified treatment of a subject. At Cher. 114 Philo amplifies along the lines of classical treatment 'by attributes', as described by Cicero, for instance, in his 'De Inventione':[43]

ποῦ γάρ μου τὸ σῶμα πρὸ γενέσεως ἦν;
ποῖ δὲ καὶ χωρήσει . . . ;
. . . πόθεν δὲ ἦλθεν ἡ ψυχή, ποῖ δὲ χωρήσει, πόσον δὲ χρόνον . . . ;
τίς δέ ἐστιν τὴν οὐσίαν ἔχομεν εἰπεῖν;
πότε δὲ καὶ ἐκτησάμεθα αὐτήν;

In these last examples of Philo's use of questions, we can begin to see why Quintilian refused to include *interrogatio* and *ratiocinatio* in the category of figures of diction (where they are placed by the Auctor ad Herennium, for instance) and hesitated to count many of the so-called figures of thought as figures at all, but assigned them to *inventio*[44]. That the line between figures and argumentation becomes vague in such instances suggests again that the distinction between invention and ornament is not as firm as many traditional accounts have tried to make it.

---

[41] MARTIN's discussion, op. cit., pp. 286ff., should be consulted. Hypophora in AdH is *subiectio* (IV.xxiii.33).

[42] On the relationship between form, expectation, and fulfillment, see the illuminating discussions by K. BURKE in 'Counterstatement' on 'The Psychology of Form' (pp. 29—44) and the remarks in the section entitled 'Lexicon Rhetoricae' (esp. at pp. 124ff.).

[43] Cf., under the heading "attributes of action", De Inv. I.xxvi.38—xxvii.42, II.xii.38—40.

[44] Quintilian IX.ii.100—107, dealing mainly with the lists of figures drawn up by Celsus and Rutilius; and iii.99, cited above, note 21.

III. The Rhetoric of 'De Cherubim'

Our way of handling Philo's use of figures and tropes has pointed to some weaknesses in the notion that forms of expression can profitably be detached from their contexts and implied that it would be more advantageous to look at Philo's language from a point of view which stresses the rhetorical functions of the figures he uses. Since the rhetorical function of a part of a given work can be seen only in light of the intention of the entire piece, I propose an examination of an entire work by Philo. I have chosen 'De Cherubim' chiefly because it is relatively brief, but also because I believe it brings out with particular clarity some of Philo's strategies of persuasion.

In examining this work I shall consequently try to restrict myself to the rhetoric of the piece, concentrating on the parts played in it by some of the usages and figures we looked at in the preceding sections of this study[45].

The first two sections (1—10 and 11—20) extract from the first few words chosen for commentary a set of coordinate themes, true vs. false knowledge and hostility vs. intimacy. Both of these themes will reappear later in the treatise. The style of 1—10 is consistent with an intention to lay down a brief foundation. All of the information is compressed into one long 'paratactic' summary period which is permeated by the language of the texts he is drawing upon from Gen. xvi and xxi, except in the parenthetical explanation of the meaning of 'Sarah', where Philo works in the distinction between *doxa* and *sophia*. After the very brief statement on the meaning of the story of Hagar, Philo hastens to the conclusion he has been moving towards, that it is entirely reasonable that Adam should have been 'cast out' of Eden. Τί οὖν θαυμάζομεν; he asks.

In the commentary on ἀντικρύ (11—20), Philo is more methodical and works his way through an *expeditio* to get to the true meaning of 'over against' in Gen. iii. 24. He also works into this discussion another key point of the treatise, the distinction between τὸ θεῖον ἄτρεπτον and τὸ μεταβλητόν. The discovery in Gen. xviii. 22 of the third (and correct) sense of 'over against' provides Philo with an opportunity to introduce

---

[45] This means that I will be skirting a number of problems which students of Philo have raised both about 'Cherubim' and about Philo's works in general. I will not concern myself with possible influences on Philo, for instance. I should, however, address one problem here, and that is whether 'Cherubim' as it is usually printed is, in fact, a single treatise. Many have argued that it is not, asserting that there is no real connection between the first thirty-nine paragraphs and the rest of the work; and some have speculated that 1—39 belong to a lost fourth book of the 'Legum Allegoriae'. See M. ADLER's discussion of this question in his 'Studien zu Philon von Alexandreia' (Breslau, 1929), pp. 24ff. Rhetorical analysis suggests, however, that there is enough argumentative unity in the work as printed to warrant the belief that Philo intended the commentaries on Gen. iii.24 and iv.1 to be taken together. I hope to be able to display some of that unity in the following commentary.

yet another contrast, that between those who desire estrangement and those who seek intimacy, and to add the thought that "to stand fast and acquire an unswerving mind is to step close to the power of God". The last and correct sense of 'over against', then, is that of 'intimacy'.

Philo now turns his audience's attention to what is symbolized by the Cherubim themselves: Τίνα δὲ . . . αἰνίττεται, νῦν ἐπισκεπτέον. Perhaps the author (Moses) means them as allegorical figures of the heavenly revolutions, Philo suggests: μήποτε οὖν τὴν τοῦ παντὸς οὐρανοῦ φορὰν δι' ὑπονοιῶν εἰσάγει· κίνησιν γὰρ αἱ κατ' οὐρανὸν σφαῖραι τὴν ἐναντίαν ἔλαχον ἀλλήλαις, κτλ.

There follows a complex explanation of this allegory which takes us up to 25, where Philo breaks off, saying that this is one explanation. But perhaps also (μήποτε δὲ . . .) there is another, viz., that the Cherubim represent the two hemispheres of heaven. After elaborating on these two possible explanations, however, Philo says at 27,

Ἤκουσα δέ ποτε καὶ σπουδαιοτέρου λόγου παρὰ ψυχῆς ἐμῆς εἰωθυίας τὰ πολλὰ θεολειπτεῖσθαι καὶ περὶ ὧν οὐκ οἶδε μαντεύεσθαι . . . κτλ.

— which effectively puts the previous two interpretations out of the picture. What Philo has done in this section is clearly the same thing he did with 'over against': in 20—27, that is, we see Philo working through another *expeditio*. As we see him propose and reject successive opinions and arrive finally at the one he wants to promote, we are left with the impression that the last is in fact the only genuine possibility, since the other two have been eliminated.

Moreover, the *logos* which follows is from a voice in Philo's soul, so it must, obviously, have authority. This 'very ardent' (σπουδαιότερος) *logos* is that, while God is really one, He has two potencies: ἀγαθότης and ἐξουσία, 'goodness' and 'sovereignty', of which the Cherubim are symbols (σύμβολα, 28). Through His goodness He came to create all that is, and through His sovereignty He rules what He has created. 'Between the two' is a third power which unites them, Reason (Λόγος); for it is through Reason that God is both Ruler and Good. The symbol for Reason is the fiery sword (τὴν φλογίνην ῥομφαίαν) of the passage.

After this revelation, Philo apostrophizes διάνοια, calling upon it to admit the image (τύπος) of the Cherubim and thereby reap the fruits of a happy lot. It is worth noting here that at first Philo addresses διάνοια; but as the apostrophe continues, the object of address looks, more and more, as if it were the audience, not his own mind. In the course of this apostrophic passage, Philo once again appeals to the audience's knowledge of Scripture as he introduces the contrast between Abraham the wise (ὁ σοφός) and Balaam — 'foolish people'. The energy of Philo's delivery begins to accumulate considerably in his amplification on Balaam's foolishness, and at 35 Philo enters into a dialogue with Balaam, taking the part of the pursuits which the foolish man blames for his misfortunes. At 39, he drops the persona (cf. Διὰ τούτων οὖν ἁπάντων ἱκανῶς οἶμαι δεδηλῶσθαι) and concludes that only the man who can use Reason rightly can be happy[46].

In two balanced sections (1—20 and 21—39) Philo has established a connection between intimacy with God, true knowledge and the right use of Reason, and happiness. This is clearly the connection he was interested in establishing from the beginning. Very little is contributed to this point by the explication itself of the symbolism of the Cherubim; and *exousia* and *agathotēs* were quickly passed by to get to Reason. As we shall see, the themes of God's power and goodness will play important parts later in the treatise; but the present subject of Philo's discourse is the nature and status of true knowledge.

So far it is clear that Philo is speaking on rather intimate terms with his audience. The extensive use of Scriptural quotation and allusion, the appeal to symbols, the sense of obligation to examine and speak on the passage from Genesis, and the stance toward those matters which Philo is maneuvering his audience into taking are all signs of a collective purpose and identity shared between speaker and audience[47].

The transition at 40 is abrupt, but not unusually so for Philo. When he has finished with one verse in a segment of Scripture he is commenting on, Philo often goes on to the next without warning[48]. Here, too, he simply picks up the discussion with a quotation of Gen. iv. 1: Ἀδὰμ δὲ ἔγνω τὴν γυναῖκα αὐτοῦ . . . In beginning to comment on this passage, Philo continues to speak as one of the community. The symbolism he reviews is common property: when he says φαμὲν εἶναι γυναῖκα τροπικῶς αἴσθησιν, he is not speaking just for himself. The first person plural is communicative here. Further, to speak thus is to speak μήποτ᾽ εἰκότως, and that could not be if no one but Philo were alert to the symbolic significances he refers to.

Philo intensifies the sense of communal identity in the next section (42—53). "In order that we may speak of the conception and birthpangs of the virtues", he says, "let those who are superstitious about such matters

---

[46] This is of course what Philo set out to show at § 30.

[47] We should recall the uses of the 'collective' or 'communicative' "We" and the indirect paraenetic effect of Philo's prosopopoeia at 29 ff. Cf. also the 'thanksgiving' at 32 (καὶ μεγίστη χάρις τῷ τεχνίτῃ . . .) and the implicit identification of the audience with those who are not among the unpurified at 33. As we shall see, Philo continually stresses his audience's identity as 'us' as against 'them'. For a discussion of 'identity' and 'identification' as central concepts in rhetoric, see K. BURKE, Rhetoric of Motives, pp. 19 ff. and pp. 55 ff. BURKE elsewhere explains: "The term 'identification' can be applied in at least three ways. The first . . . flowers in such usages as that of a politician who, though rich, tells humble constituents of his humble origins. The second kind of identification involves the workings of antithesis, as when allies . . . join forces against a common enemy. . . . But the major power of 'identification' derives from situations in which it goes unnoticed. My prime example is the word 'we', as when the statement that 'we' are at war includes under the same head soldiers who are getting killed and speculators who hope to make a killing in war stocks." (Dramatism and Development [Barre, Mass., 1972], p. 29). Our present use of the term is, of course, more benevolent.

[48] Compare, e.g., LA I.16, 19, 31, 43; II.40, 53; III.49, 59, 65; Sac. 11, 52; Post. 75; Det. 69; Gig. 6, 58. Note that they are all from the earlier parts of the 'Allegory'.

close their ears and depart". The effect of this is clearly to get the audience to identify with the initiated, who are worthy, and set themselves apart from "those who have no standards for measuring what is pure but their barren words and phrases and their vain usages and rituals"(42). We can, at any rate, hardly imagine anyone getting up and leaving at this point.

The 'secret instruction' (which Philo begins with ἀρκτέον οὖν τῆς τελετῆς ὧδε)[49] explains that virtues receive the seed of generation from God himself. As guarantor for this Philo offers Moses himself, who shows Sarah conceiving at the time when God visited her in solitude (Gen. xxi. 1). Even clearer is the case of Leah (cf. Gen. ix. 31), and there are also the examples of Rebecca (Gen. xxv. 21) and Zipporah (at Exod. ii. 22) to be taken into account. All of these are wives of men to whose virtue Moses has testified; and their examples show that lovers of wisdom reject, rather than choose, sense (i.e., women). For none of the husbands in the instance cited from Scripture is represented as knowing his wife. Adam, by contrast, speaks of knowing his.

This lesson, Philo reminds his audience, is a message for the initiated, those who practice piety without vanity. It is, of course, as initiates that Philo addresses his audience at this point (ὦ μύσται, 48), and it is as one of the initiated that he himself speaks (καὶ γὰρ ἐγὼ . . . , 49). Philo augments his previous argument from examples with a personal testimony, his own understanding of the χρησμός spoken ἐκ προσώπου τοῦ θεοῦ which he perceived in the words in 'Jeremiah' (iii. 4). From that "oracle" it is clear that God's way is not like ours. When God comes to consort with the soul, "He plants the native growth of implanted virtues" — or, rather, sows "ideas of virgin virtues in virginity" itself which, unlike the wives, never changes into woman (sense), as do the wives of humans (cf. 50).

Having related the testimony of Moses and his own vision and what he came to know from it, Philo apostrophizes the soul:

τί οὖν, ὦ ψυχή, δέον ἐκ οἴκῳ θεοῦ παρθενεύεσθαι καὶ ἐπιστήμης περι-
έχεσθαι, τούτων μὲν ἀποστατεῖς, αἴσθησιν δὲ ἀσπάζῃ τὴν ἐκθηλύνουσάν
σε καὶ μιαίνουσαν;

And with this he rounds off the discussion which began at 41, posing an apparently apostrophic question and warning the soul (which, at this point, may stand for the audience) that by cleaving to αἴσθησις it may, like Adam, beget a γέννημα πάμφυρτον καὶ πανώλεθρον who is also ἀδελφοκτόνον καὶ ἐπάρατον — a Cain. In short, it is altogether unreasonable for the soul to cling to sense; and yet, it is implied, the soul continues to do so, even at the risk of begetting another Cain[50].

---

[49] Compare the use of this expression at e.g. Mos. II.117 or Abr. 119, where Philo announces that he is moving from a literal to an allegorical exposition.

[50] Here Philo changes his stance toward his audience momentarily. Up to this point his main concern has been to establish a sense of audience identity; but beginning with his testimony at 49 and at 52, he establishes his own authority and uses it to call the soul to account and

The explication of the meaning of 'Cain' is introduced proleptically: "Someone might wonder (θαυμάσειε) about the form of expression here . . ." Whether or not there really is someone who might question the words of Moses, Philo makes a strong case for the difficulty of the problem. It looks as though Moses has indeed departed, in this passage, from his usual practice, Philo says, and the problem might bear some looking at (σκεπτέον ἂν εἴη . . . , 55). He then offers a 'guess' (cf. ὡς ἔμοιγε στοχαζομένῳ καταφαίνεται) at what Moses is telling us in the passage.

The 'guess' leads into a skillfully framed argument[51] supporting his contention that the mind deceives itself if it imagines that it gains possession of knowledge on its own, particularly if that knowledge is gained through sense. Demonstration of this is not simply an item on Philo's agenda for instruction in epistemology, but a proof of how foolish the soul addressed in 52 really is for clinging to the senses.

This is not very clear at first, for Philo occupies himself for some time (from 57—63) with an explanation of why the Mind is, οὐκ ἀλόγως (58), inclined to cling to sense. But at 63, Philo draws the parallel between the Mind and Alexander, who foolishly thought he possessed all he could see around him.

The explication of the Mind's comparable foolishness at 65f. leads directly into the second part of the argument, the dialogue with Laban at 68ff. Since Philo clearly has his audience on his side when he begins the interrogation of Laban, his purpose might seem to be to re-establish the kind of opposition between 'us' and 'them' which we saw at 42ff. But Philo does something quite different. He addresses someone in the second person throughout. At first, this 'you' is obviously Laban; but it gradually becomes unclear who 'you' refers to: is it Laban or, by insinuation, the members of the audience? To be sure, Philo would not risk alienating his audience by taking them to task as severely as he does the foolish Laban. Yet everything he says to Laban is applicable to those in the audience, too[52]. The insinuation here, as at 52, is that the members of Philo's audience, since they too are human, are liable to the same interrogation and implicated in the same kind of foolishness — a matter for blushing rather than boasting, Philo reminds us (70).

Philo then moves to the third part of his development of the theme of the alleged 'possessions' of the mind, taking up the example of Pharaoh

---

to issue a clear warning to his audience. He never berates his audience (recall what we said earlier about the persuasive force of the imperative), but the thrust of his remarks is quite evident.

[51] The argument might be re-written in the form *modus tollens*; but to do so would be to deprive it of its rhetorical significance.

[52] The second person verbs in 68ff. (e.g., ἔχεις, πέφυκας, τολμᾷς, etc.) are apparently directed to 'Laban'; but at 71, μεταβάλῃς, μοιραθῇς etc. refer to the audience. The parenthetical explanations in 68, 69, and 70 bring out the fact that Laban's claims might be made by any member of the audience.

familiar to his listeners from 'Exodus'. To him, Philo might say (εἴποιμ' ἄν), "O fool! Is it hidden from you that every created being who thinks he pursues is in fact pursued (διώκειν διώκεται)?" It seems reasonable to expect that any member of the audience who has been able to follow the argument might ask the same thing. And Pharaoh is, as Philo reminds his audience, an enemy both of reason and of nature itself (76). There could in fact be no deadlier enemy to the soul than one whose vanity leads him to claim for himself what belongs to God: τίς οὖν ἂν γένοιτο δυσμενέστερος ψυχῇ πολέμιος τοῦ διὰ μεγαλαυχίας τὸ ἴδιον θεοῦ προσκληροῦντος ἑαυτῷ; ἴδιον μὲν δὴ θεοῦ τὸ ποιεῖν . . . (77). What belongs to the created, on the contrary, is τὸ πάσχειν, to suffer.

In his explanation of what this means, Philo begins to re-establish the sense of community with his audience which we expected back at 76f. First, he constructs a rather elaborate antithesis between the lot of those who accept τὸ πάσχειν and that of those who do not. Any one who thinks it alien to himself to be passive is bound "to suffer the tortures of Sisyphus and endure the sufferings of an ignoble and unmanly soul." One should rather take his place firmly in 'the opposing ranks' and, "with the mightiest of virtues, patience and endurance, fortify his resolution and close the gates against the foe".

Then he makes a *distributio:* there are two kinds of passiveness. One is sheeplike and slavish, impotent and inert. The other is like the 'passiveness' of the man being barbered or of the boxer taking a blow in that both accommodate themselves to the action and thus combine the passive with the active (cf. ἀνακιρνᾶς τῷ πάσχειν τὸ ποιεῖν in 79).

And finally, at 82, he exhorts his hearers to avoid the slavish passiveness. By making his exhortation in first-person plural terms, he brings his audience, as it were, back into the fold:

τοῦτο μὲν οὖν τὸ πάθος μήτε σώματι μήτε πολὺ μᾶλλον ψυχῇ δεξώμεθά ποτε, τὸ δ' ἀντιπεπονθὸς ἐκεῖνο . . . ἵνα μὴ καθάπερ οἱ θηλυδρίαι κεκλασμένοι καὶ παρειμένοι καὶ προσαναπίπτοντες μετ' ἐκλύσεως ψυχικῶν δυνάμεων ἐξασθενῶμεν, ἀλλ' ἐρρωμένοι τοῖς διανοίας τόνοις ἐπελαφρίζειν καπικουφίζειν ἰσχύωμεν τὴν φορὰν τῶν ἐπαρτωμένων δεινῶν.

Now that it has been demonstrated to the satisfaction of reason that God alone can claim all things as his possessions, Philo moves into his next section with καὶ ὡς μεγαλοπρεπῶς ἅμα καὶ θεοπρεπῶς διεξέρχεται περὶ τούτων, κατανοήσωμεν — retaining the communal 'we' of 82. This begins a new phase in the argument of 'Cherubim'. We shall see that, from this point on, Philo is less interested in establishing agreement on the issues being discussed and even more concerned to reinforce the sense of commitment and community he has been striving to arouse in his audience.

When, in Philo's version of it, God says "All things are Mine: bounties and gifts and fruits which you shall observe and offer at My feasts to Me", He is laying down a *dogma* irrefutable in the eyes of "those who belong to the company of wisdom-lovers (τοῖς φιλοσοφίας θιασώταις⁵³, 85)''. Philo's explanation of the *dogma* is more than a straightforward account of what it means. He is speaking now to an audience which, by this point, identifies with the 'purified' in opposition to the 'unpurified', yet he hammers away at the fact that 'keeping festival' belongs to God alone:

μόνος ὁ θεὸς ἀψευδῶς ἑορτάζει· καὶ γὰρ μόνος γήθει καὶ μόνος χαίρει καὶ μόνος εὐφραίνεται καὶ μόνῳ τὴν ἀμιγῆ πολέμου συμβέβηκεν εἰρήνην ἄγειν . . .

To the repetition, variation, and polysyndeton here he adds alliteration and asyndeton in the second member:

ἄλυπός ἐστι καὶ ἄφοβος καὶ ἀκοινώνητος κακῶν, ἀνένδοτος, ἀνώδυνος, ἀκμής, εὐδαιμονίας ἀκράτου μεστός . . .

In the third, he continues with a *correctio*, which allows for even more amplification; and in the fourth, Philo recites a virtual litany, praising God as ἀρχέτυπον τὸ πρὸς ἀλήθειαν καλὸν τὸ ἀγένητον καὶ μακάριον καὶ ἄφθαρτον. What began rather dispassionately at 83 develops in the course of a few periods into something a good deal more 'feverish' by the end of 86. Indeed, from this point on we shall find Philo's expression more passionate than in earlier sections.

Philo is still rather agitated when he introduces the discussion of Exod. xx.10 et al. at 87, the point of which is to re-state the contrast between God, who is unchanging, and created things. Before he is able to get on the main track of what he wants to say, however, he must make up for the abruptness of the introduction of the phrase σάββατον θεοῦ. Thus, the opening of 87 contains two parentheses and a correction (ἀνάπαυλαν δὲ οὐ τὴν ἀπραξίαν καλῶν . . .)⁵⁴. In 88, the style becomes more even and carries on in a rather straightforward manner with some cataloguing. But Philo breaks off impatiently at 89 (εὔηθες δ' ἐστὶ . . .) because he needs to get to his point, that οἰκειότατον μόνῳ θεῷ τὸ ἀναπαύεσθαι.

Now that it has been shown that keeping festival pertains to God alone, says Philo, let us look at the other side: ἴθι γὰρ, εἰ θέλεις, συνεπίσκεψαι . . ., i.e., at the festivals of men, which are so vain and empty that ''a whole life would not be enough to relate in detail the follies inherent in them''. Nevertheless, a few words should be said (ὀλίγα . . . λεκτέον, 91). These 'few words' constitute a lengthy and spirited denunciation of the vanity and sinfulness of human festivals. Philo's indignation comes out

---

⁵³ I do not think very much importance should be attached to θιασώταις here. The word does not always refer to a religious cult association but is used for various types of groups — dining clubs, subdivisions of a phratry, etc. See the remarks of A. D. Nock, Essays on Religion and the Ancient World 2 (Cambridge, Mass., 1972), pp. 896f. (reprint of Nock's review of Goodenough, Jewish Symbols in the Greco-Roman Period 5—6, in: Gnomon 29 [1957] 524ff.).

⁵⁴ These show that Philo is eager to make sure the audience understands what Moses meant.

strongly in the asyndeton, correction, and paradox of the passage[55]. We are, of course, ready for this. Philo has been building up to this level of emotion for some time already. It might also be noted that Philo is again arousing the indignation of his audience toward 'them', thus intensifying the audience's awareness of its identity as a special group once more.

The chief failure of the heathens is that they do not understand the vast gulf between the created world and the uncreated, whose nature is grasped by mind alone (97). By this time, Philo has said enough on this subject to assume that his audience has some understanding of what that difference is. Thus he is in a position to concentrate on the exhortation of the initiated to practice the true piety, as it was defined back in sections 20, 29, and 43. There may be more instruction to come, but Philo's interest is in paraenesis at this point. The 'instructional' passages are used mainly for recapitulating and elaborating themes which have already been spoken on extensively.

The paraenesis in sections 98—101 is primarily in terms of what we should do:

(98) παρασκευάζωμεν τὸν τόπον ἐκεῖνον (sc., the Mind) ὡς ἔνεστι κάλλιστον . . .

(99) εἰ γὰρ βασιλεῖς ὑποδέχεσθαι μέλλοντες λαμπροτέρας κατασκευάζομεν . . . μηδενὸς τῶν εἰς κόσμον ὀλιγωροῦντες, ἀλλὰ πᾶσιν . . . χρώμενοι . . . (καὶ) . . . στοχαζόμενοι . . . κτλ.

(101) οἶκον οὖν ἐπίγειον τὴν ἀόρατον ψυχὴν τοῦ ἀοράτου θεοῦ λέγοντες ἐνδίκως καὶ κατὰ νόμον φήσομεν.

To a listener, the period beginning εἰ γὰρ βασιλεῖς . . . begins as a statement, gets complicated by the list of divine attributes triggered by τῷ βασιλέων βασιλεῖ, and ends as a question at ποδαπὸν οἶκον ἄρα χρὴ κατασκευάζεσθαι. But we must not imagine that Philo has lost the thread of his meaning here. He rather shows himself coming to the realization, as he speaks, that it is the coming of God Himself which we are to prepare for. Hence the question at 100 (λίθων μὲν ἢ ξυλίνης ὕλης;) can be dismissed as blasphemous, for the proper lodging place of God is the soul: ἀξιόχρεως μέντοι γε οἶκος ψυχὴ ἐπιτήδειος.

This lodging place in the invisible soul must have foundations in εὐφυΐα καὶ διδασκαλία if it is to be strong. Upon these foundations should

---

[55] The entire passage (92—97) builds up to a crescendo. 92 begins with a 'run' of single words (ἄδεια ἄνεσις ἐκεχειρία μέθη παροινία . . .), continues with modified nouns, and ends with longer phrases and a full clause (at ὕπνος ἐν ἡμέρᾳ . . .). The inconsistencies in the heathens' behavior are developed in a series of balanced clauses (e.g., at τότε τὰ μὲν πρακτέα ἄτιμα, τὰ δὲ μὴ πρακτέα ἐπίτιμα . . ., where emphasis is achieved by deliberate hiatus). Philo is at first ironic in 94, but then becomes more indignant than before, scoring the contradictions of the unpurified with a climactic ὡς ἀπεργάσασθαι θυσίας ἀνιέρους, ἱερεῖα ἄθυτα, εὐχὰς ἀτελεῖς, ἀμυήτους μυήσεις, ἀνοργιάστους τελετάς, νόθον εὐσέβειαν, κεκιβδηλευμένην ὁσιότητα . . . κτλ. The *correctio* comes in 96 (μᾶλλον ⟨δέ⟩). Philo carries on at this level down to 97.

be raised "virtues along with noble actions." The decorations of the *oikos* will consist of ἡ ἀνάληψις τῶν ἐγκυκλίων προπαιδευμάτων. Philo then surveys in some detail the powers and skills which stem from εὐφυΐα and the disciplines which belong to the correct διδασκαλία[56], elaborating somewhat the image of the house and its ornaments. "If this sort of house (τοιούτου . . . οἴκου) be raised", he says χρηστῶν ἐλπίδων τἀπίγεια πάντα ἀναπλησθήσεται κάθοδον δυνάμεως θεοῦ προσδοκήσαντα (106). The soul which fits itself out properly for God's coming, therefore, will achieve happiness (τὸ εὔδαιμον).

"The purified mind", he goes on at 107, "accepts the lord of all as its master (δεσπότης) and rejoices in being a slave to God":

τὸ γὰρ δουλεύειν θεῷ μέγιστον αὔχημα καὶ οὐ μόνον ἐλευθερίας ἀλλὰ καὶ πλούτου καὶ ἀρχῆς καὶ πάντων ὅσα τὸ θνητὸν ἀσπάζεται γένος τιμιώτερον.

Much of Philo's development of the themes of possession and divine sovereignty in 106—119 is recapitulatory, restating themes he has been elaborating since the beginning[57]. The rhetorical intensity of this section is remarkable. Philo reaches in it an emotional climax, using all the devices traditionally recommended to orators who want, in their perorations, to move their audiences deeply[58]. Philo begins to build at 108, where he quotes Leviticus xxv. 23 and asks:

ἆρ' οὐκ ἐναργέστατα παρίστησιν, ὅτι κτήσει μὲν τὰ πάντα θεοῦ, χρήσει δὲ μόνον γενέσεώς ἐστι;

βεβαίως, he replies himself, and there follows a virtual explosion of emotion. His treatment at 110f. of the theme of reciprocity is powerful:

οὕτως . . . ἔμελλεν, ἀντίδοσίν τινα καὶ ἀντέκτισιν πάντα διὰ πάντων ὑπομένοντα πρὸς τὴν τοῦ κόσμου παντὸς ἐκπλήρωσιν· ταύτῃ καὶ ἄψυχα ἐμψύχων καὶ ἄλογα λογικῶν καὶ δένδρα ἀνθρώπων καὶ ἄνθρωποι φυτῶν καὶ ἡμέρων ἀτίθασα καὶ ἀγρίων χειροήθη καὶ ἄρρεν θήλεος καὶ θῆλυ ἄρρενος καὶ συνελόντι φράσαι χερσαῖα ἐνύδρων καὶ ἔνυδρα ἀεροπόρων καὶ πτηνὰ τῶν προειρημένων καὶ προσέτι γῆς μὲν οὐρανός, οὐρανοῦ δὲ γῆ, ἀὴρ δὲ ὕδατος, ὕδωρ δὲ πνεύματος, καὶ πάλιν αἱ μεταξὺ φύσεις ἀλλήλων τε καὶ τῶν ἄκρων καὶ αἱ ἄκραι τῶν μέσων καὶ ἑαυτῶν ἐρῶσι·

---

[56] These disciplines are those of the traditional ἐγκύκλιος παιδεία. On this subject, see TH. M. CONLEY, 'General Education' in Philo of Alexandria, Protocols of the Colloquies of The Center for Hermeneutical Studies 15 (Berkeley, 1975), pp. 1—11.

[57] The idea of 107, for instance, is the same as that of 39. For that matter, it might be argued that the discussion of the *enkyklia* and the connection between true knowledge and happiness takes us back to the opening sections of the treatise. The theme of possession has, of course, received a great deal of attention. The question at 109 would be intelligible only in the context of what has come before it.

[58] Cf., e.g., Cicero, Part. xv.52ff. J. MARTIN's discussion at op. cit. pp. 153ff. should be consulted.

χειμών γε μὴν θέρους καὶ θέρος χειμῶνος καὶ ἔαρ ἀμφοῖν καὶ μετόπωρον ἔαρος καὶ ἕκαστον ἑκάστου . . . κτλ.

No doubt this theme lends itself to particular rhetorical treatment: when one is discussing oppositions, antithesis and some forms of word play are almost unavoidable. But *repetitio*, polysyndeton, *gradatio*, and anaphora are the results of stylistic effort. In 113f. Philo begins another series of questions, speaking first in the singular and then in the plural first person:

ἐγὼ γοῦν ἐκ ψυχῆς καὶ σώματος συνεστώς, νοῦν λόγον αἴσθησιν ἔχειν δοκῶν, οὐδὲν αὐτῶν ἴδιον εὑρίσκω· ποῦ γάρ μου τὸ σῶμα πρὸ γενέσεως ἦν; . . . τίς δέ ἐστιν τὴν οὐσίαν ἔχομεν εἰπεῖν; πότε δὲ καὶ ἐκτησάμεθα αὐτήν; . . . ἀλλὰ νῦν ὅτε ζῶμεν κρατούμεθα μᾶλλον ἢ ἄρχομεν καὶ γνωριζόμεθα μᾶλλον ἢ γνωρίζομεν . . .

He is no less intense in the questions at 116f., which are strongly marked by asyndeton and anaphora:

. . . ᾗ ἂν ἄγῃ, πρὸς χρώματα, πρὸς σχήματα, πρὸς φωνάς, πρὸς ὀσμάς, πρὸς χυλούς, πρὸς τὰ ἄλλα σώματα.

In the midst of these, he sums up, first at 117 and then again at 119:

γίνεται οὖν οὐ μόνον ἀληθὲς ἀλλὰ καὶ τῶν μάλιστα συντεινόντων εἰς παρηγορίαν τὸ τὸν κόσμον καὶ τὰ ἐν κόσμῳ τοῦ γεννήσαντος ἔργα τε εἶναι καὶ κτήματα.

If the mode of argument in the earlier parts of 'Cherubim' may be said to have progressed 'syllogistically' — from A to D through B and C — the form of argumentation here, in these late sections, may be said to progress 'repetitively'. And what holds for repetition as a figure holds as well for repetition as a structural principle. By maintaining the same truths and presenting them under different guises, Philo leads his audience almost to feel the principles underlying the different manifestations[59].

At 124 Philo seems to be ready to bring his discourse to a conclusion (πάντων οὖν ἀνωμολογημένων . . .). But instead he brings us back to the text he began discussing back at 40, pointing out another error on Adam's part. This is quickly finished with (after an *expeditio* which explains why God must be the cause and not the instrument), and Philo directs his audience to the point: true lovers of knowledge make the correct distinction, recognizing God as cause, not instrument, whereas those who are foolish enough to think they possess something through God are mistaken.

At the end of the treatise, Philo simply states what must be done by those who are among the purified and know the path of true piety. The

---

[59] Cf. pp. 354ff. above. On the significance of 'syllogistic form' and 'repetitive form' see K. BURKE, Counterstatement, pp. 123—126.

parallelism and anaphora of 129 are points of style that should be noted, but it would be hard to argue that here, at the end, Philo is interested in rallying his audience by arousing their emotions. Rather, he cites another passage from Scripture, once again drawing attention to the fact that it is not he, but Moses himself, who exhorts those who live by the Law:

στῆτε καὶ ὁρᾶτε τὴν σωτηρίαν τὴν παρὰ τοῦ κυρίου, ἣν ποιήσει ὑμῖν.

What has Philo been trying to do in the treatise we have just looked at? Someone approaching 'Cherubim' with the expectation of finding in it a philosophical exposition would probably conclude that, whatever Philo was trying to do, he did not do it very coherently[60]. That, however, is perhaps to expect something quite alien to Philo's intentions. Philo argues the emptiness of mere ritual practices and literal agreement with the surface meaning of Scripture without inner purity and true understanding. But if the above sketch of some of the rhetorical features of 'Cherubim' has suggested anything, it is that Philo was not primarily interested in instructing his audience to that effect. He spends most of his time and energy establishing and reinforcing a sense of community or solidarity both in and with his audience, a relationship fundamental to conviction and consensus as to that inner purity.

The implications of a reading such as the one we have just seen can be drawn in different directions. Some may construe Philo's call for 'inner purity' as a sign of the influence of Hellenistic mysteries, others as consistent with his commitment to the Torah. A rhetorical analysis is not sufficient to allow us to decide which, if either, of these interpretations is correct. The preceding observations, however, suggest that there is more in store for a student of Philo who is willing to look at his techniques of argumentation and presentation than a mere catalogue of 'unusual expressions'.

Bibliography

A. Philo: Texts cited from Philo I—X, ed. F. H. COLSON and G. H. WHITAKER (The Loeb Classical Library), Cambridge, Mass., 1929—1962.

B. Works referred to:

ADLER, MAXIMILIAN, Studien zu Philon von Alexandreia, Breslau, 1929.
ANLAUF, G., 'Standard Late Greek' oder Atticismus? Eine Studie zum Optativgebrauch im nachklassischen Griechisch, Diss. Köln, 1961.

---

[60] There is, I trust, no need to recite the litany of complaints against Philo on this score. Cf. H. A. WOLFSON, Philo. Foundations of Religious Philosophy in Judaism, Christianity, and Islam, 2 vols. (Structure and Growth of Philosophic Systems from Plato to Spinoza 2; Cambridge, Mass., ²1962), Vol. 1, pp. 98ff., and H. THYEN, Die Probleme der neueren Philo-Forschung, Theologische Rundschau N.F. 23 (1955), pp. 230ff.

BRANDT, W. J., The Rhetoric of Argumentation, New York, 1970.

BURKE, KENNETH, Counterstatement, Berkeley/London, 1968 (originally published New York, 1931).

ID., A Rhetoric of Motives, Berkeley/London, 1969 (originally published New York, 1950).

ID., Dramatism and Development (Heinz Werner Lecture Series 6), Barre, Mass., 1972.

CARRIÈRE, J., Stylistique grecque (Tradition de l'humanisme 6), Paris, 1967.

Cicero, De inventione, ed. H. M. HUBBELL (The Loeb Classical Library), Cambridge, Mass., 1949.

ID., Partitiones oratoriae, ed. H. RACKHAM (The Loeb Classical Library), Cambridge, Mass., 1942.

ID., Rhetorica ad Herennium, ed. HARRY CAPLAN, (The Loeb Classical Library), Cambridge, Mass., 1954.

COHN, L., Philonis Alexandrini libellus de opificio mundi, Breslau, 1889.

CONLEY, T. M., 'General Education' in Philo of Alexandria (Protocols of the Colloquies of The Center for Hermeneutical Studies 15), Berkeley, 1975, pp. 1—11.

CONYBEARE, F. C., Philo About the Contemplative Life, Oxford, 1895.

CUMONT, F., Philonis de aeternitate mundi, Berlin, 1891.

DE GROOT, A. W., A Handbook of Antique Prose Rhythm, I: Greek Prose Meter, Groningen, 1919.

DENNISTON, J. D., The Greek Particles, Oxford, 1934.

GOODENOUGH, E. R., Philo's Exposition of the Law and his De Vita Mosis, The Harvard Theological Review 26 (1933), pp. 109—125.

ID., An Introduction to Philo Judaeus, New Haven, 1940.

GRAY, B., Style: The Problem and its Solution (De proprietatibus litterarum, Series Maior 3), Paris/The Hague, 1969.

HENGEL, M., Judentum und Hellenismus. Studien zu ihrer Begegnung unter besonderer Berücksichtigung Palästinas bis zur Mitte des 2. Jhs. v. Chr. (Wissenschaftliche Untersuchungen zum Neuen Testament 10), Tübingen, ²1973.

HIGGINS, M. J., Why Another Optative Dissertation ?, Byzantion 15 (1940/41), pp. 443—8.

JESSEN, J., De elocutione Philonis Alexandrini (Philologorum nestori Hermanno Sauppe), Hamburg, 1889, pp. 1—12.

KRELL, E., Philo περὶ τοῦ πάντα σπουδαῖον εἶναι ἐλεύθερον, die Echtheitsfrage, Progr. Augsburg, 1896.

LAUSBERG, H., Handbuch der Literarischen Rhetorik, 2 vols., Munich, 1960 (2nd ed. 1973).

LEEMAN, A. D., Orationis Ratio: The Stylistic Theories and Practice of the Roman Orators, Historians, and Philosophers, 2 vols., Amsterdam, 1963.

MARTIN, J., Antike Rhetorik: Technik und Methode (Handbuch der Altertumswissenschaft 2, 3), Munich, 1974.

MILLER, C. W. E., The Limitations of the Imperative in the Attic Orators, American Journal of Philology 13 (1892), pp. 399—436.

NOCK, A. D., Essays on Religion and the Ancient World (ed. Z. STEWART), Cambridge, Mass., 1972.

PALM, J., Über Sprache und Stil des Diodoros von Sizilien. Ein Beitrag zur Beleuchtung der hellenistischen Prosa, Diss. Lund, 1955.

PERELMAN, CH., and OLBRECHTS-TYTECA, L., Traité de l'Argumentation: la nouvelle rhétorique (Editions de l'Institut de Sociologie), Brussels, ²1970.

ID., The New Rhetoric, Great Ideas Today for 1970, Chicago, 1970, pp. 273—309.

PIAGET, J., Introduction à l'Épistémologie génétique, 2 vols., Paris, 1950.

Quintilian, Institutio Oratoria, ed. H. BUTLER (The Loeb Classical Library), Cambridge, Mass., 1966.

REIK, KARL, Der Optativ bei Polybius und Philo von Alexandria, Leipzig, 1907.

RICHARDS, I. A., The Philosophy of Rhetoric, Oxford, 1936.

SIEGFRIED, C., Philo von Alexandria als Ausleger des alten Testaments, Jena, 1875.

THYEN, H., Der Stil der jüdisch-hellenistischen Homilie (Forschungen zur Religion und Literatur des Alten und Neuen Testaments 65), Göttingen, 1955.

TURNER, N., Syntax (Vol. III of J. H. MOULTON, A Grammar of New Testament Greek), Edinburgh, 1963.

UNNA, I., Über den Gebrauch der Absichtssätze bei Philo von Alexandrien, Diss. Würzburg, 1895.

WENDLAND, P., Philos Schrift über die Vorsehung: Ein Beitrag zur Geschichte der nach-aristotelischen Philosophie, Berlin, 1892.

WOLFSON, H. A., Philo. Foundations of Religious Philosophy in Judaism, Christianity, and Islam (Structure and Growth of Philosophic Systems from Plato to Spinoza 2), 2 vols., Cambridge, Mass., ²1962.

Philo's Ethical Theory

by DAVID WINSTON, Berkeley, Calif.

Contents

Introduction

The ethical theory of Philo is firmly rooted in his overpowering conception of God as the supremely transcendent Reality whose pervasive immanence controls and directs every aspect of cosmic activity. This notion of transcendent immanence which, unlike its Stoic counterpart, insists on the utter unknowability of the Supreme Principle as it is in itself and the incorporeal nature of its primal manifestation as Logos, converges nevertheless with the Stoic view in its depiction of the Logos' all-traversing cosmic course and its omnipresent vitality which holds together and administers the entire chain of creation (Mos. 2.134; Her. 188). Its highest terrestrial manifestation, however, is the intuitive intellect of man, envisaged by Philo as an inseparable portion of the Divine Mind (Det. 90; cf. Op.

Abbreviations:

b.   Babylonian Talmud
B.R.   Bereshit Rabbah
CAH   Cambridge Ancient History. 12 vols. 1923–39
HTR   Harvard Theological Review
HUCA   Hebrew Union College Annual
IDB   Interpreter's Dictionary of the Bible. 4 vols. Nashville, 1962
JQR   Jewish Quarterly Review

46).[1] Man is thus akin to the Divine and has unbroken access to it from within. Only his "unnatural use of himself"[2] obstructs his vision of the ever-present Deity, and Philo summons man to make his soul a house of God (Somn. 1.149).[3] Similarly, Epictetus chides his readers: "Why do you not know the source from which you have sprung? . . . It is within yourself that you bear Him, and do not perceive that you are defiling Him with impure thoughts and filthy actions" (2.8.14).[4] Manilius gave the Stoic view poetic expression: "Who can doubt that a link exists between heaven and man, to whom, in its desire for earth to rise to the stars, gifts outstanding did nature give and the power of speech and breadth of understanding and a wing-swift mind, and into whom alone indeed had God come down and dwells, and seeks himself in man's seeking of him? . . . Who could know heaven save by heaven's gift and discover God save one who shares himself in the divine?" (Astronomica 2.105–116).[5] Philo's sentiments are identical: "The invisible Deity stamped on the invisible soul the impression of itself, to the end that not even the terrestrial region should be without a share in an image of God" (Det. 68; cf. LA 1.38).

LCL	Loeb Classical Library
Lyon	Les Œuvres de Philon d'Alexandrie publiées sous le patronage de l'Université de Lyon, par R. ARNALDEZ, J. POUILLOUX, C. MONDÉSERT. Paris, 1961ff., vols. 1–34ᴬ, and 35
M.	Mishnah
MGWJ	Monatsschrift für Geschichte und Wissenschaft des Judentums
PAL	Philon d'Alexandrie, Lyon 11–15 Septembre 1966: colloque. Paris: Editions du Centre national de la recherche scientifique, 1967
RAC	Reallexikon für Antike und Christentum
REG	Revue des Études Grecques
SP	Studia Philonica
y.	Palestinian Talmud

[1] Cf. Plato Tim. 90C; Ps-Plato Axiochus 370B; Plotinus 6.9.9.7; 6.9.8.29; D.L. 7.143; Cicero ND 1.27; Posidonius F187, 6–7 KIDD; Epictetus 3.13.14; Diogenes of Apollonia DK A.19.

[2] This is the expression used by the Cambridge Platonist BENJAMIN WHICHCOTE, Discourses (Aberdeen, 1751) 3.102.

[3] Cf. QE 2.51; Virt. 188; Sob. 62; Somn. 2.251; Fug. 117; Praem. 123.

[4] Cf. Epictetus 1.3 and 1.9; Seneca Ep. 82.6; Plotinus 5.1.1; Gospel of Truth 22.13; Gospel of Thomas 55.

[5]
> quis dubitet post haec hominem coniungere caelo,
> cui cupiens terras ad sidera surgere, munus
> eximium natura dedit linguamque capaxque
> ingenium volucremque animum, quem denique in unum
> descendit deus atque habitat seque ipse requirit? . . .
> quis caelum posset nisi caeli munere nosse,
> et reperire deum, nisi qui pars ipse deorum est?

Cf. Astronomica 4.915–35; and Philo Det. 90 with Astronomica 2.117–27. See also Plotinus 5.1.10.5–6; Cicero Leg. 1.24–25: "Hence we are justified in saying that there is a blood relationship between ourselves and the celestial beings . . . Thus it is clear that man recognizes God because, in a way, he remembers and recognizes the source from which he sprang."

In correlation with his doctrine of the various levels of human spiritual attainment, Philo describes two sharply divergent paths through which men achieve knowledge of the existence of the utterly transcendent yet supremely immanent God. To the mind as yet uninitiated into the highest mysteries and still unable to apprehend the Existent by itself alone, but only through its actions as either creative or ruling, God appears as a triad constituted by himself and his two potencies, the Creative and the Regent. To the purified mind which has passed on beyond the dyad, God appears as one (Abr. 119–123). Philo thus distinguishes between the mind that apprehends God through his creation, and the mind that elevates itself beyond the physical universe and perceives the Uncreated One through a clear, unmediated vision. At Praem. 40 he speaks of those who have apprehended God through his works as advancing from down to up by a sort of heavenly ladder[6] and conjecturing his existence through plausible inference. "But the genuine worshippers and true friends of God are those who apprehend him through himself without the cooperation of reasoned inference, as light is seen by light." This formula is precisely that of Plotinus, who speaks of "seeing the Supreme by the Supreme and not by the light of any other principle . . . just as it is by the sun's light that we see the sun" (5.3.17.34–37; cf. 5.3.8.21).[7]

Philo, as in his wont, does not further explicate his "light by light / God through God" formula, doubtlessly relying on the fact that his audience would immediately recognize it as part of a well-known Greek philosophical tradition. The formula was apparently so widely known that it appears even in a work like the 'Apocalypse of Abraham'.[8] Its appearance both in Philo and Plotinus clearly indicates that it must have been already well established in Middle Platonism. Plotinus' version is especially close to Philo's, since both made precisely the same distinction between the existence of God which is knowable and his essence which is unknowable (5.5.6.20–21; cf. Philo Post. 169), and both adduced the same reason for man's inability to cognize the divine essence.[9] Since Plotinus

---

[6] For the history of this image in medieval Arabic and Jewish philosophy, see A. ALTMANN, Studies in Religious Philosophy and Mysticism (London, 1969) 41–72; B. ZAK, R. Solomon Alkabetz' Attitude Towards Philosophic Studies (Hebrew), in: Eshel Beer-Sheva (Beer-Sheva, 1976) 288–306. Isaac b. Latif speaks in his 'Ginze Ha-Melekh' of seven rungs of the ladder of human knowledge. Naḥmanides sees the value of all sciences in their function as a "ladder" to the knowledge of God. Yoḥanan Allemano calls geometry and astronomy a "ladder by which to ascend to heaven", an obvious allusion to the Ikhwan's saying: "Ptolemy loved astronomy; he made mathematics into a ladder by which he ascended to heaven."

[7] ἐφάψασθαι φωτὸς ἐκείνου καὶ αὐτῷ αὐτὸ θεάσασθαι, οὐκ ἄλλῳ φωτί, ἀλλ' αὐτό, δι' οὗ καὶ ὁρᾷ . . . οὐδὲ γὰρ ἥλιον διὰ φωτὸς ἄλλου. Both Philo and Plotinus are undoubtedly dependent for their sun image on Plato Rep. 507C–509B.

[8] Apocalypse of Abraham, chap. 7: "Yet may God reveal himself to us through himself." The formula is used here in the wake of an analysis which indicates that none of the parts of the universe could be a primary archē, but it is then followed by a direct divine revelation. Cf. SPINOZA, Short Treatise 1.1.10: "God, however, the first cause of all things, and even the cause of himself, manifests himself through himself."

[9] See Plotinus 5.5.10.6–7; Philo, frag. from QE, LCL, supp. 2, p. 250, lines 9–10: "in order for one to be able to comprehend Deity, it is first necessary to become Deity — the

asserts that we are taught by the intellect (*nous*) that the One exists, he undoubtedly deployed some form of the ontological argument, which, unlike the cosmological proof for God's existence which is based on deductive reasoning, constitutes an analytical truth[10] whose function is to clarify what is already implied by our definitions. The Platonists, however, had no monopoly on this form of argument, since the Stoics had also produced a version of it which clearly anticipated St. Anselm's famous *aliquid quo nihil maius cogitari potest* (Proslogion, chapters 2 and 3). They pointed out that not only does nothing exist that is superior to the world, but nothing superior can even be conceived (*ne cogitari quidem quicquam melius potest*: Cicero N.D. 2.18; cf. 2.46; Seneca NQ 1. pref. 13). The human mind thus possesses the notion of a being of the highest power or perfection, and may therefore be said to have the existence of God engraved within.[11]

Following Plato's lead (Phaedr. 249 CD), Philo indicates that the intuitive vision through which man knows God directly may at times be accompanied by a Bacchic frenzy, an ecstatic condition which shakes the soul to its very foundations. This mystic experience he describes as "seeing and being seen," as drawing near to God who has drawn the mind to himself (Somn. 2.226; Plant. 64; cf. Galat. 4:9; b. Sanhedrin 4b), and he often refers to it as a state of sober intoxication, which escorts the soul to the uppermost vault of the Intelligible World or Logos.[12] If we were now to fix our attention on the fact that for Philo the intuitive

---

very thing which is impossible" (θεὸν γενέσθαι δεῖ πρότερον – ὅπερ οὐδὲ οἱόν τε – ἵνα θεὸν ἰσχύσῃ τις καταλαβεῖν).

[10] It is interesting to find Al-Farabi and Samuel b. Tibbon using the image of ascending and descending the ladder of the sciences to designate the synthetic and analytic methods respectively. "In his *Ma'amar Yikawwu Ha-Mayim*, [Ibn Tibbon] initiated the interpretation of Jacob's dream as a prophetic vision on a par with the celestial visions of Ezekiel and Isaiah. In his view, all three 'allegorized the way by which man's intellect attained to its ultimate perfection.'. . . [He] interprets the difference between the visions of Isaiah and Jacob as one of method. Isaiah described the ultimate and perfect knowledge, viz. that of God and the angelic hierarchies, first, and then went down to the lower levels. Jacob, on the other hand, started from the bottom and worked his way upward. In more technical language, Isaiah chose as it were the 'analytical method' (*derekh ha-hatakhā we-ha-hataqā*), while Jacob employed the 'synthetical method' (*derekh ha-harkabā*) . . . This ingenious, yet far-fetched exegesis has no doubt for its source a passage in al-Fārābī's *The Harmony between Plato and Aristotle* (see F. Dieterici, *Alfarabi's Philosophische Abhandlungen* [Leiden, 1892] 13–14) which reads as follows: '. . . Plato thinks that a complete definition is obtainable only by the method of analysis, while Aristotle holds that a complete definition can be formed solely by the method of demonstration and synthesis. One should, however, know that questions like these may be compared to *a ladder on which one ascends and descends*. The distance is the same; the only difference is between the two who use the ladder in going up or down.'" (Altmann [cited n. 6] 59–61).

[11] For a more detailed discussion see D. Winston, Philo of Alexandria (New York, 1981) 26–30.

[12] The best known passage is at Op. 70. Cf. LA 3.82; Ebr. 147 ff.; Fug. 166; Praem. 122; Cont. 85; Prob. 13; QG 2.68; QE 2.15. See Hans Lewy, Sobria Ebrietas (Giessen, 1929). Lewy believes that Philo originated the expression himself, but this seems to me unlikely. In any case, he has failed to note the closest parallel, A.P. 9.752, which explains the contradiction in Cleopatra's ring which bore a figure of the goddess Drunkenness (*Methē*)

vision of God depends on the divine initiative (Somn. 1.71), and that the state of
sober intoxication belongs to the nature of the self-taught, which is "superior to
reasoning and truly divine, taking shape not through human design but through
God-inspired frenzy" (Fug. 168),[13] we should very likely conclude that here
indeed we have a head-on confrontation between the powers of autonomous
human reason and the supreme power of the Deity, with the latter totally eclip-
sing the former. It is at this very point, however, that Philo's bipolar perspective
comes into full play. In virtually all of his writings, we find at the center of Philo's
concern the issue of man's ultimate spiritual goal, which involves his escape from
the material world of contingent reality and his mystical attachment to God. The
male/female polarity is employed by Philo as a symbol of the dichotomy between
the rational and the eternal on the one hand, and the irrational and perishable, on
the other. The pejorative use of female terminology to describe the latter is found
throughout Philo's works.[14] Man's progress in the moral and religious life involves forsaking the realm of the female and "becoming male" (QE 1.8; QG 1.
49). The term 'female' in this context, as BAER (:48—49) has correctly noted,
refers to the material realm, which includes the male/female polarity, whereas
male refers to the realm, which is intrinsically asexual, the sphere of Logos and
God himself. A second way in which Philo describes forsaking the realm of sense-
perception is in terms of changing from duality to unity or 'becoming one' (cf.
Epinomis 992 B). He "who is resolved into the nature of unity, is changed into the
divine" (QE 2.29). A third way in which Philo describes the abandonment of the
sensible is in terms of changing from a woman into a virgin or 'becoming a virgin'. "When God begins to consort with the soul, he makes what before was a
woman into a virgin again, for he takes away the degenerate and emasculate passions which made it womanish and plants instead the native growth of unpolluted
virtues" (Cher. 50; cf. QE 2.3).[15]

It is significant that in those passages where Philo speaks of becoming male,
the focus is not upon God's activity and gifts of grace, but upon man's own effort.
In the struggle for moral progress, passively waiting for God's help is a vice, and
askēsis is the key to ethical achievement. In those passages, however, where Philo
speaks of becoming one or becoming a virgin, the emphasis is upon God's activity.
Man is to cease from striving and come to realize that all true virtue is ultimately

---

engraved on an amethyst, the stone of sobriety. See W. W. TARN, in: Cambridge Ancient
History (Cambridge, 1934) 10.38—39, and WINSTON (cited n. 11) 358, n. 341. Cf. H.
CHADWICK, in: Cambridge History of Later Greek and Early Medieval Philosophy (Cambridge, 1967) 150, n. 4. For a detailed analysis of Philo's mysticism, see WINSTON (cited
n. 11) 21—35.

[13] καινὸν γὰρ καὶ κρεῖττον λόγου καὶ θεῖον ὄντως τὸ αὐτομαθὲς γένος, οὐκ ἀνθρω-
πίναις ἐπινοίαις, ἀλλ' ἐνθέῳ μανίᾳ συνιστάμενον.

[14] See R. A. BAER, Philo's Use of the Categories Male and Female, Arbeiten zur Literatur
und Geschichte des hellenistischen Judentums 3 (Leiden, 1970).

[15] ὅταν δὲ ὁμιλεῖν ἄρξηται ψυχῇ θεός, πρότερον αὐτὴν οὖσαν γυναῖκα παρθένον αὖθις
ἀποδείκνυσιν, ἐπειδὴ τὰς ἀγεννεῖς καὶ ἀνάνδρους ἐπιθυμίας, αἷς ἐθηλύνετο, ἐκποδὼν
ἀνελὼν τὰς αὐθιγενεῖς καὶ ἀκηράτους ἀρετὰς ἀντεισάγει.

God's doing.[16] Moreover, in Her. 264 the mind is described as mortal and as surrounded by darkness and is sharply contrasted with the divine reality, thus reflecting a concept of mind not easily reconciled with Philo's description of mind as a "divine fragment."[17] The resolution of these apparent contradictions lies, I believe, in Philo's bifocal view of reality. From the human viewpoint, mind is a portion of the divine, radiant and immortal, but from the eternal perspective of God, it is but a minute fragment of Divinity, enveloped in darkness and mortality. Similarly, the passages employing the image of becoming male, where the emphasis is on man's effort, reflect the human perspective, whereas those passages employing the virgin image, where the emphasis is on God's activity and man's nothingness, reflect the eternal perspective of God.[18]

In sum, the human intellect, which is but an inseparable fragment of the Divine Mind, may be described in two diverse and apparently contradictory ways. Insofar as it is a human intellect, man may well take pride in it as his own personal possession, as an independent capacity which he controls and activates at will. To the extent, however, that it forms but a portion of the Logos from which it ultimately draws all its energy, it can no longer be described accurately as a human capacity at all, but rather as a particular activation of the Divine Mind.[19] It is the context which ultimately determines the semantic alternative to be employed by the author, in accordance with that aspect of reality which requires special emphasis, the eternal or the finite and contingent.

I. Freedom and Determinism

Philo's theory of free will can best be understood in the light of the double perspective sketched above. It can readily be seen that, from the eternal perspective of his mystical monism, human activity could well be described as totally passive and even as non-action, whereas in the light of his need to emphasize human moral responsibility, in his role as ethical instructor, man's limited freedom could equally well be magnified and ascribed to his relatively

---

[16] Plotinus, similarly, urges us not to pursue the vision, but to await its arrival quietly and prepare oneself, "just as the eye awaits the rising sun" (5.5.8.3—5).

[17] See BAER (cited n. 14) 55—56.

[18] Cf. J. M. RIST, Plotinus, The Road to Reality (Cambridge, 1967) 201: "The comparison of man to a puppet at Laws 644 DE, however, is introduced by a 'let us suppose.' In 803 C, though Plato alludes to the earlier passage, the 'let us suppose' is dropped, while in 804 B the comparison is defended — in reply to the objection of Megillus that the Athenian has a very low opinion of the human race — by the remark that 'when I said that, I had my mind on God.' Clearly, compared with God, Plato means to tell us, man will often seem of little significance." Cf. Pindar Nem. 6.1—4.

[19] The paradoxes which result from this double conception are elegantly exemplified by the Persian mystic Bayazid of Bistam: "I went from God to God, until they cried from me in me, 'O thou I.'" See R. A. NICHOLSON, The Mystics of Islam (London, 1963) 17.

lofty station in the hierarchy of being. We thus find the theme of man's nothing-ness and utter passivity running through much of Philo's writing. "So long as the mind supposes itself to be the author of anything", he writes, "it is far away from making room for God and from confessing or making acknowledgment to him. For we must take note that the very confession of praise itself is the work not of the soul but of God who gives it thankfulness" (LA 1.82).[20] In the following passage Philo's words have an unmistakably Stoic ring to them: "For we are the instruments, now tensed now slackened, through which particular actions take place, and it is the Artificer who effects the percussion of both our bodily and psychic powers, he by whom all things are moved" (Cher. 128; cf. Ebr. 107).[21] The Stoics similarly say, "The movements of our minds are nothing more than instruments for carrying out determined decisions since it is necessary that they be performed through us by the agency of Fate" (SVF 2.943).[22] In a fragment from the lost fourth book of the 'Legum Allegoriae' Philo reveals the full depth of this conviction that it is God alone who is active within all of creation in the precise sense of that term:

> "For strictly speaking, the human mind does not choose the good through itself, but in accordance with the thoughtfulness of God, since he bestows the fairest things upon the worthy. For two main principles are with the Lawgiver, namely, that on the one hand God does not govern all things as a man and that on the other hand he trains and educates us as a man [cf. Somn. 1.237; Deus 52ff.]. Accordingly, when he maintains the second principle, namely, that God acts as a man, he introduces that which is in our power as the competence to know something, will, choose, and avoid. But when he affirms the first and better principle, namely, that God acts not as man, he ascribes the powers and causes of all things to God, leaving no work for created being but showing it to be inactive and passive . . . But if selections and rejections are in strictness made by the one cause, why do you advise me, legislator, to choose life or death, as though we were autocrats of our choice?[23] But he would answer: Of such things hear thou a rather elementary explanation, namely, such things are said to those who have not yet been initiated in the great mysteries about the sovereignty and authority of the Uncreated and the exceeding nothingness of the created."[24]

---

[20] Cf. Somn. 2.224; LA 2.32, 46; 1.48; 3.136; Her. 120; Cher. 64, 71, 40–52, 77; Praem. 32–35.

[21] ὄργανα γὰρ ἡμεῖς, δι' ὧν αἱ κατὰ μέρος ἐνέργειαι, ἐπιτεινόμενα καὶ ἀνιέμενα, τεχνίτης δὲ ὁ τὴν πλῆξιν ἐργαζόμενος τῶν σώματός τε καὶ ψυχῆς δυνάμεων, ὑφ' οὗ πάντα κινεῖται (translation my own).

[22] *Animorum vero nostrorum motus nihil aliud esse, quam ministeria decretorum fatalium, siquidem necesse sit agi per nos agente fato* (translation by A. A. LONG).

[23] Cf. Plato Laws 860E: "If this is the state of the case, stranger (i. e., that all bad men are in all respects unwillingly bad), what counsel do you give us in regard to legislating for the Magnesian State? Shall we legislate or shall we not? 'Legislate by all means,' I shall reply."

[24] οὐδὲ γὰρ κυρίως ἀνθρώπινος νοῦς αἱρεῖται δι' ἑαυτοῦ τὸ ἀγαθόν, ἀλλὰ κατ' ἐπιφρο-σύνην θεοῦ δωρουμένου τοῖς ἀξίοις τὰ κάλλιστα· δυοῖν γὰρ ὄντων κεφαλαίων παρὰ τῷ

Wolfson has indeed attempted virtually to transform the simple meaning of the Philonic fragment quoted above, in his effort to attribute to Philo an absolute free will doctrine. He argues that "when Philo says that God gave to the human mind a portion 'of that free will which is his most peculiar possession and most worthy of his majesty' and that by this gift of free will the human mind 'in this respect has been made to resemble him',[25] it is quite evident that by man's free will Philo means an absolutely undetermined freedom like that enjoyed by God, who by his power to work miracles can upset the laws of nature and the laws of causality which he himself has established." The fact is, however, that Philo is only adapting here for his own use a characteristically Stoic notion. Epictetus, for example, writes:

νομοθέτῃ, τοῦ μὲν ὅτι οὐχ ὡς ἄνθρωπος ἡνιοχεῖ τὰ πάντα ὁ θεός, τοῦ δὲ ὅτι ὡς ἄνθρωπος παιδεύει καὶ σωφρονίζει, ὅτ' ἂν μὲν τὸ δεύτερον κατασκευάζῃ, τὸ ὡς ἄνθρωπος καὶ τὸ ἐφ' ἡμῖν εἰσάγῃ ὡς ἱκανὸς καὶ γνῶναί τι καὶ βούλεσθαι καὶ ἑλέσθαι καὶ φυγεῖν· ὅτ' ἂν δὲ τὸ πρῶτον καὶ ἄμεινον, ὅτι οὐχ ὡς ἄνθρωπος τὰς πάντων δυνάμεις καὶ αἰτίας ἀνάψῃ θεῷ μηδὲν ὑπολειπόμενος ἔργον τῷ γενομένῳ ἀλλὰ δείξας ἄπρακτον αὐτὸ καὶ πάσχον . . . εἰ δε ἐκλογαί τε καὶ ἀπεκλογαὶ κυρίως ὑπὸ τοῦ ἑνὸς αἰτίου γίνονται, τί μοι παραινεῖς ὦ νομοθέτα τὴν ζωὴν καὶ τὸν θάνατον αἱρεῖσθαι ὡς τῆς αἱρέσεως αὐτοκράτορι; ἀλλ' εἴποι ἄν, τῶν τοιούτων εἰσαγωγικώτερον ἄκουε· λέγεται γὰρ ταῦτα τοῖς μήπω τὰ μεγάλα μεμυημένοις μυστήρια περί τε ἀρχῆς καὶ ἐξουσίας τοῦ ἀγενήτου καὶ περὶ ἄγαν οὐδενείας τοῦ γενητοῦ. (See J. R. Harris, ed., Fragments of Philo Judaeus [Cambridge, 1886] 8. I have quoted the Drummond-Wolfson translation, but have made a number of modifications.) Cf. Her. 121, 124; Mut. 141, 155; Fug. 46; Op. 117; QE 3.48; Plato Laws 44DE.

A similar position to that of Philo was taken by the Jewish mystic Mordechai Yosef Leiner of Izbica (1802—54), who wrote that the signal characteristic of the future world is that in it the illusion of free choice will vanish, and that acts will no longer be ascribed to their human agents but to God, their true author. It is in the light of this view that he interprets the following passage from b. Pesaḥim 50a: "The future world is unlike our present world, for in our present world I [God] am written as YHWH but am called Adonai, but in the future world, I shall both be written as YHWH and be called YHWH." Like Philo, too, he admonishes his readers "to know and understand that everything you do is from God and save for him, no one may lift hand or foot to do aught, and you should not boast about your actions . . . for all the good which you do you may refer to God, but all the evil you must attribute to yourselves." (Mei Ha-Shiloaḥ, part 1:14b, 55b). See Joseph Weiss, The Religious Determinism of Yosef Mordechai Lerner [sic] of Izbica (Hebrew), in: Sefer Yovel le-Yitzhak Baer (Jerusalem, 1960) 447—53.

25 Wolfson is referring to Deus 47—48: "For it is the mind alone that the Father who begat it deemed worthy of freedom, and loosening the bonds of necessity, allowed it to range free, and of that power of volition which constitutes his most intimate and fitting possession presented it with such a portion as it was capable of receiving . . . But man who is possessed of spontaneous and self-determined judgment and performs for the most part activities deliberately chosen is rightly blamed for what he does with premeditation, praised when he acts correctly of his own will . . . But the soul of man alone has received from God the faculty of voluntary movement, and in this way especially is assimilated to him, and thus being liberated, as far as possible, from that hard and grievous mistress Necessity may suitably be charged with guilt, in that he does not honor its Liberator" (translation my own). See H. A. Wolfson, Philo (Cambridge, 1948) 1.436.

"But what says Zeus? 'Epictetus, had it been possible I should have made
both this paltry body and this small state of thine free and unhampered . . .
Yet since I could not give thee this, we have given thee a certain portion of
ourself, this faculty of choice and refusal.'" [1.1.10; cf. 2.8.11][26]

Now, the Stoics held a relative free will theory of the causal type, and all they
meant by saying that God has given us a portion of himself thereby enabling us to
make choices, is that (as A. A. LONG has neatly put it) "the Logos, the causal
principle, is inside the individual man as well as being an external force constrain-
ing him . . . this is but a fragment of the whole, however, and its powers are
naturally weak, so weak that 'following' rather than 'initiating' events is stressed
as its proper function."[27] For the Stoics, man is not a mechanical link in the causal
chain, but an active though subordinate partner of God. It is this which allows
them to shift the responsibility for evil from God to man.[28] Philo's meaning,
then, is that insofar as man shares in God's Logos, he shares to some extent in
God's freedom. That this is only a relative freedom is actually emphasized by him
when he says that God gave man such a portion of his freedom "as man was
capable of receiving" and that he was liberated "as far as might be" (Deus 47–48;
cf. Her. 186; Somn. 2.253). Yet this relative freedom, in Philo's view, is sufficient
for placing the onus of moral responsibility on man and clearing God from any
blame for man's sins (Fug. 79–80; Op. 149).

[26] Ἀλλὰ τί λέγει ὁ Ζεύς; "Ἐπίκτητε, εἰ οἷόν τε ἦν, καὶ τὸ σωμάτιον ἄν σου καὶ τὸ κτησί-
διον ἐποίησα ἐλεύθερον καὶ ἀπαραπόδιστον . . . ἐπεὶ δὲ τοῦτο οὐκ ἠδυνάμην ἐδώκαμέν
σοι μέρος τι ἡμέτερον, τὴν δύναμιν ταύτην τὴν ὁρμητικήν τε καὶ ἀφορμητικὴν . . ."
[27] A. A. LONG, Freedom and Determinism in the Stoic Theory of Human Action, in:
Problems in Stoicism, ed. A. A. LONG (London, 1971). See SVF 1.527; 2.975; 3.191;
Epict. 2.10; 3.5.8ff.; 4.1.89ff; 4.7.19ff; M. Aurelius 5.8; 4.34; 6.39; 3.16, 7.57; 12.1; 4.23;
Seneca Provid. 5.4ff.; Ep. 66.40; 76.16.
[28] Cf. Cleanthes' 'Hymn to Zeus':

> "Nothing occurs on the earth apart from you, O God,
> nor in the heavenly regions nor on the sea,
> except what bad men do in their folly;
> but you know how to make the odd even,
> and to harmonize what is dissonant; to you the alien is akin.
> And so you have wrought together into one all things that are good and bad,
> So that there arises one eternal 'logos' of all things . . ."

The translation is that of A. A. LONG in his 'Hellenistic Philosophy' (London, 1974) 181.
SVF 1.537, 11–17:

> οὐδέ τι γίγνεται ἔργον ἐπὶ χθονὶ σοῦ δίχα, δαῖμον,
> οὔτε κατ' αἰθέριον θεῖον πόλον οὔτ' ἐνὶ πόντῳ,
> πλὴν ὁπόσα ῥέζουσι κακοὶ σφετέραισιν ἀνοίαις·
> ἀλλὰ σὺ καὶ τὰ περισσὰ ἐπίστασαι ἄρτια θεῖναι,
> καὶ κοσμεῖν τἄκοσμα καὶ οὐ φίλα σοὶ φίλα ἐστίν.
> ὧδε γὰρ εἰς ἓν πάντα συνήρμοκας ἐσθλὰ κακοῖσιν,
> ὥσθ' ἕνα γίγνεσθαι πάντων λόγον αἰὲν ἐόντα.

For a detailed discussion, see A. J. FESTUGIÈRE, La Révélation d'Hermès Trismégiste
(Paris, 1949) 2.310–30.

Philo's deterministic scheme is further exemplified by his ideas concerning the soul's preexistence. Those of the purest type (called angels in Scripture), he tells us, have never come down from the heavenly region (Plant. 12; Somn. 1.140; Gig. 6), whereas others, having earthward tendencies, descend into mortal bodies. Among the latter, some (the souls of philosophers) come only as sojourners in order to expand their horizons and presently escape to their native habitat never to return, whereas others, possessed by a nostalgic longing for their mortal experiences, come running back for more (Conf. 77; QG 3.10, 45; Somn. 1.138), in accordance with a law of necessity (QG 4.74).[29]

II. Natural Law

In Philo's view the Mosaic Law is no arbitrary set of decrees handed down from on high, but rather the truest reflection of the Logos which is embodied in the physical universe and constitutes its immanent natural law. It will therefore be useful to survey the Greek philosophical tradition in which Philo's concept of natural law lies embedded. Anaximander had already intimated that human justice is rooted in the very structure of the cosmos, by correlating *dikē* with the cosmic order: "Things must render each other *dikē* and requital for their *adikia*, according to the ordering of time" (D-K B.1).[30] Heraclitus, however, is the first to state explicitly that the underlying and controlling unity of the universe is a divine Logos, to which human action must conform if it is to be a product of wisdom: "The wise is one, knowing the plan by which it steers all things through all" (D-K B.41). This is more clearly elaborated in fr. 114: "Speaking with understanding (*nous*) they must hold fast to what is shared by all, as a city holds to its

---

[29] For a detailed discussion of Philo's reasons for the soul's descent see D. WINSTON, Wisdom of Solomon (New York, 1979) 27–28; and for fuller discussion of Philo's doctrine of Free will, see D. WINSTON, Freedom and Determinism in Philo of Alexandria, SP (1974–75) 47–70.

[30] Hesiod had already regarded *dikē* as a quality shared by all humanity: "For the son of Kronos fixed this law for men, that fish and beasts and birds should devour one another, since there is no *dikē* in them; but to men he gave *dikē*, which is far the best" (Works and Days 276–280). We may compare the Vedic concept of *ṛta*, originally the ordered course of nature, but already signifying in the Mantras also the moral order (See M.HIRIYANNA, Outlines of Indian Philosophy [London, 1932] 33); and the Egyptian concept of *maat*, right order in nature and society, established by the primordial god Atum at the creation. "*Maat* is a basic value, not an explicit law. Thus the laws of Egypt are not divine injunctions but edicts which the king issues from time to time 'in the exercise of his supreme power, but by virtue of his insight into the nature of *maat*'" (S. MORENZ, Egyptian Religion [London, 1973] 118–119). WILSON has pointed out that "since the Pharaoh was himself a god, he was the earthly interpreter of *maat*, and the authority of codified law would have competed with his personal authority. Hence there was no continuing body of law in Egypt until Persian and Greek times" (J. WILSON, Culture of Ancient Egypt [Chicago, 1951] 50).

law, and even more firmly. For all human laws are nourished by a divine one. It prevails as it will and suffices for all and is more than enough.''[31] Similarly, according to Aristotle, Empedocles said in regard to not killing that which has life that "it is not right for some and wrong for others, 'But a universal precept, which extends without a break throughout the wide-ruling air and the boundless light'" (DK B.135; cf. 115).[32] Finally, although Plato does not offer an explicit formulation of the concept of natural law, it is clearly implied in his metaphysical theory. It is his view in the 'Timaeus' (41 AD) that the immortal part of the human soul, the *logistikon*, fashioned by the Demiurge himself is composed of what was left of the original ingredients used to compound the World-Soul (though these ingredients are of a lesser degree of purity than the original mixture). Hence man's reason is akin to the divine reason governing the cosmos as an immanent principle, and the moral precepts which it fashions are therefore cosmic or natural laws. Thus, in Rep. 6 (500 Cff.), the happy state is designed by artists who imitate the heavenly pattern, while in the 'Laws' (890 D) it is stated more explicitly that the lawgiver must defend law as something "which exists by nature."[33]

[31] The texts and translations of Heraclitus are from C. H. KAHN, The Art and Thought of Heraclitus (Cambridge, 1979) pp. 55 and 43. See also KAHN's discussion on pp. 14—15, 117—118, 170—172. Fr. B. 41: ἓν τὸ σοφόν· ἐπίστασθαι γνώμην ὅκη †κυβερνῆσαι† πάντα διὰ πάντων. Fr. 114: ξὺν νόῳ λέγοντας ἰσχυρίζεσθαι χρὴ τῷ ξυνῷ πάντων, ὅκωσπερ νόμῳ πόλις καὶ πολὺ ἰσχυροτέρως· τρέφονται γὰρ πάντες οἱ ἀνθρώπειοι νόμοι ὑπὸ ἑνὸς τοῦ θείου· κρατεῖ γὰρ τοσοῦτον ὁκόσον ἐθέλει καὶ ἐξαρκεῖ πᾶσι καὶ περιγίνεται.

[32] In Xenophon's Mem. 4.414, the Sophist Hippias speaks of unwritten laws as those which are observed in every country, and since all who observe them cannot possibly have met, they must have been made by the gods. In his famous funeral oration, Pericles praises observance of both the positive and unwritten laws (Thucydides 2.37.3), and speaking of the propriety of punishing deliberate crime but not involuntary error, Demosthenes says (De Cor. 275): "Not only will this be found in the [positive] law, but nature itself has decreed it in the unwritten laws and in the hearts of men." According to Antisthenes (fr. 101), the wise man acts not according to the established laws but in accordance with the laws of virtue. In the tragic poets the unwritten laws are unequivocally of divine origin (Sophocles Antig. 450ff.; Oed. Tyr. 863ff.; Euripides Ion 440ff.; Bacch. 895—896).

[33] Cf. Laws 714A: τὴν τοῦ νοῦ διανομὴν ἐπονομάζοντας νόμον. Gorg. 508 A: "And wise men tell us, Callicles, that heaven and earth and gods and men are held together by communion and friendship, by orderliness, self-control and justice; and that is the reason, my friend, why they call the whole of this world by the name of order." The 'wise men' here, as has often been observed, are probably the Pythagoreans. On the inevitable shortcomings of conventional written laws, which may be dispensed with if true knowledge and reason are present, see Laws 875 CD; Polit. 293 Eff. Yet even in the 'Politicus', as MORROW has pointed out, Plato maintains that in the present state of human affairs it is better that rulers should be bound by law, since our rulers do not possess the royal science and cannot be expected to acquire it. Moreover, even a ruler possessing political *technē* would find it necessary to rule by laws (294 C—295 B), so that law becomes a necessary ingredient in the ideal. All states other than that in which the scientific statesman is supreme are either more perfect copies of it or grosser and less adequate imitations. The latter owe their preservation to their following the code of laws enacted for the ideal state (297 D). Here we have, then, the recognition of a higher law, a *nomos* which belongs to the intelligible order and therefore exists by nature. In Laws 957 C Plato says of his ideal law that it is divine.

With Aristotle we enter the domain of systematic classification and are thus provided with a clear-cut definition and delineation of natural law:

"Now there are two kinds of laws, particular and general. By particular laws I mean those established by each people in reference to themselves, which again are divided into written and unwritten; by general laws I mean those based upon nature. In fact there is a general idea of just and unjust in accordance with nature, as all wise men in a manner divine, even if there is neither communication nor agreement between them." [Rhet. 1.13.1373b].

In the 'Nicomachean Ethics' he explains his own view on natural law:

"A rule of justice is natural that has the same validity everywhere, and does not depend on our accepting it or not. A rule is conventional (nomikon) that in the first instance may be settled in one way or the other indifferently, though having once been settled it is not indifferent . . . Some people think that all rules of justice are merely conventional, because whereas a law of nature is immutable and has the same validity everywhere, as fire burns both here and in Persia, rules of justice are seen to vary."

Aristotle then grants that

"in our world, although there is such a thing as natural law, yet everything is capable of change; and although it is thus difficult to determine which variables are as they are by nature and which are merely conventional, nevertheless some things are ordained by nature and others not." [EN 1134b 20].

Although Aristotles's approach is in some ways similar to that of Plato, in other respects it sharply diverges from it. "Now our treatment of this science [politics] will be adequate," says Aristotle, "if it achieves that amount of precision which belongs to its subject matter. The same exactness must not be expected in all departments of philosophy alike . . . It is the mark of an educated man to seek precision in each kind of inquiry just so far as the nature of the subject permits. It is as inappropriate to demand demonstration from an orator as it is to allow a mathematician to use merely probable arguments" (EN 1094b 13−23).[34] This is in stark contrast to Plato, for whom mathematical certainty served as the standard which the statesman should try to attain in ethical and political matters. Although

---

See G. R. Morrow, Plato and the Law of Nature, in: Essays in Political Theory presented to G. H. Sabine (New York, 1947) 17−44; also J. P. Maguire, Plato's Theory of Natural Law, Yale Class. St. 10 (1947) 151−178; F. Solmsen, The Theology of Plato (Ithaca, 1942) 161−174.

[34] Λέγοιτο δ' ἂν ἱκανῶς εἰ κατὰ τὴν ὑποκειμένην ὕλην διασαφηθείη· τὸ γὰρ ἀκριβὲς οὐχ ὁμοίως ἐν ἅπασι τοῖς λόγοις ἐπιζητητέον ... πεπαιδευμένου γάρ ἐστιν ἐπὶ τοσοῦτον τἀκριβὲς ἐπιζητεῖν καθ' ἕκαστον γένος ἐφ' ὅσον ἡ τοῦ πράγματος φύσις ἐπιδέχεται· παραπλήσιον γὰρ φαίνεται μαθηματικοῦ τε πιθανολογοῦντος ἀποδέχεσθαι καὶ ῥητορικὸν ἀποδείξεις ἀπαιτεῖν.

the distinction between right and wrong is a natural one, and generalizations are possible on moral questions, they are nevertheless true only for the most part.

It is in Stoicism, however, that we find the most elaborate formulations of natural law. Nature or God is for the Stoics a perfect being, and all value derives from it. Ethical values are clearly deduced from the first principles of nature governing all animal life. "The first thing which is dear to every animal is its own constitution and awareness of this . . . thus it is that the animal rejects what is harmful and pursues what is suitable (or akin) to itself" (D.L. 7.85–86).[35] Chrysippus thus held that "justice, as well as law and right reason, exists by nature and not by convention" (D.L. 7.128; Cicero Fin. 3.67; SVF 3.314).[36] In view of the fact that no complete work of the Early or Middle Stoa has survived, it is not surprising that the fullest statement of the Stoic conception of natural law should be found in Cicero's writings. The most representative passage comes from Rep. 3.33:

"True law is right reason in agreement with nature; it is of universal application, unchanging and everlasting . . . it is a sin to try to alter this law, nor is it allowable to attempt to repeal any part of it, and it is impossible to abolish it entirely . . . And there will not be different laws in Rome and at Athens, or different laws now and in the future, but one eternal and unchangeable law will be valid for all nations and all times, and there will be one master and ruler, that is God, over us all, for he is the author of this law, its promulgator and its enforcing judge. Whoever is disobedient is fleeing from himself and denying his human nature, and by reason of this very fact he will suffer the worst penalties, even if he escapes what is commonly considered punishment."[37]

---

[35] Cf. the fuller statement in Cicero Fin. 3.20–21.

[36] φύσει τε τὸ δίκαιον εἶναι καὶ μὴ θέσει, ὡς καὶ τὸν νόμον καὶ τὸν ὀρθὸν λόγον, καθά φησι Χρύσιππος ἐν τῷ Περὶ τοῦ καλοῦ.

[37] R. Reitzenstein, Drei Vermutungen zur Geschichte der römischen Literatur, in: Festschrift für Th. Mommsen (Marburg, 1893), and W. Theiler, Die Vorbereitung des Neuplatonismus, Problemata 1 (Berlin, 1930; repr. Berlin–Zürich, 1964) 44–50, argue for Antiochus of Ascalon, a stoicizing Platonist, as the source of Cicero's formulation of the natural law. See also J. Dillon, The Middle Platonists (London, 1977) 80–81, and R. A. Horsley, The Law of Nature in Philo and Cicero, HTR 71 (1978) 35–59. Horsley believes that Cicero's use of the term 'the divine mind' (mens divina) in Leg. 1.23 indicates Platonic influence. He asserts that "although our sources are fragmentary, it is apparent that the early Stoics rarely used the term 'mind' (nous), and that the more prominent use of the term 'mind' by late Stoics has probably been influenced by Posidonius' and others' rediscovery of Plato" (p. 41). There is inadequate warrant, however, for such a conclusion. There are sufficient indications that both Zeno and Chrysippus had already identified the terms God, Nous, Fate, and Zeus, and there is no reason to believe that this usage was rare (D.L. 7.135–136; cf. 7.138; SVF 1.157, 158, 146; 2.1027). Horsley notes correctly, however, that Philo and Dio Chrysostom frequently use the term thesmos, ordinance, as a synonym for nomos and orthos logos (SVF 3.335, 337), in which usage he sees a Platonic influence (Phaedr. 248C; Laws 957C). Most significant, however, in his view, is that Cicero's (Rep. 3.33) and Philo's (Mos. 2.48) texts clearly distinguish God from the law, making him the founder of the universal law of nature,

Elsewhere Cicero asserts that "the Law is the primal and ultimate mind of God, whose reason directs all things either by compulsion or restraint" (Leg. 2.8).[38] Finally, in the writings of Epictetus, we find the natural law grounded in the *prolēpseis*, or preconceptions which the Stoics believed were common to all men:

> "For who among us does not assume that the good is profitable and something to be chosen, and that in every circumstance we ought to seek and pursue it? . . . When then does contradiction arise? It arises in the application (*epharmogē*) of our preconceptions to the particular cases, when one person says, 'He did nobly, he is brave'; another, 'no, but he is out of his mind'. Hence arises the conflict of men with one another. This is the conflict between Jews and Syrians and Egyptians and Romans, not over the question whether holiness should be put before everything else . . . but whether the particular act of eating swine's flesh is holy or unholy." [1.22.1; cf. 2.11; 4. 1.41].[39]

whereas Stoic doctrine had identified God with law as well as with reason (D.L. 7.88, 134). This conception, he continues, again reveals Platonic influence on the natural law argument, probably from such texts as Tim. 41 E; Laws 720 E, 715 E–716 A. Although this argument is plausible, it remains indecisive, since it is very likely that the Stoics, in their continuous attempt to reconcile their views with the religious tradition (see, for example, Plato Laws 624 A; Minos 320 B), may very well have referred to God or Zeus as the founder of the law. It remains likely nevertheless, that the discussion of natural law in Cicero is basically Antiochian, since "it contains the characteristic mark of Antiochus' presence, a survey of the doctrines of the Old Academy, and of Zeno's agreement with it, and the doctrine is precisely what we should expect Antiochus to hold" (DILLON, p. 80).

[38] Cf. Leg. 1.33; 1.6; 2.10; N.D. 1.36; Inv. 2.160; Pro Milone 4.10; Ps-Aristotle De Mundo 400 b 28; Plutarch Moral. 601 AB; 329 B; Ps-Cicero Ad Herennium 2.10.14; 2.13.19; Quintilian 7.1.49. The Stoic doctrine of the *logos orthos* and *physis* as a standard for human morals occurs frequently in Clement of Alexandria (Paed. 2.87.2; 3.99.1; 3.100.2; Strom. 1.182.1; 2.18.4; 3.72.3). Mention should also be made of a passage in Cicero (Off. 3.50), from which we learn that the Stoic Antipater of Tarsus argued that everything known to the seller of an article must be known to the buyer also, on the philosophical supposition that a man had an obligation to consider the interests of others, beause of the natural society prevailing among all men. Diogenes of Babylon, on the other hand, took the opposite position. The concept of natural law is found at Rome as early as 167 B.C.E. in Cato's speech on behalf of Rhodes (Gellius 6.3.45), and Q. Mucius Scaevola, who considered an agreement between partners that one of them should have a larger share in profits than in losses (*ut quis maiorem partem lucretur, minorem damni praestet*) to be against the nature of partnership (*contra naturam societatis*) (Gaius 3.149; Dig. 17.2.30). Cf. b. Baba Meṣi'a' 70a, where such an arrangement is branded by the rabbis as wicked (I owe this reference to Prof. S. LIEBERMAN); Gellius 6.3.45: *Ac primum ea incallide conquisivit, quae non iure naturae aut iure gentium fieri prohibentur.*

[39] It would appear (although this would require extended treatment elsewhere) that in their conception of *koinai ennoiai* the Stoics were adapting in their own way Aristotle's notion of common sensibles and were thinking of ideas which the mind cannot help but form whenever it cognizes *sensibilia* by virtue of its internal structure. In the physical realm, these would be notions such as magnitude, shape, motion, and rest, and in the moral realm, the notions of good and evil (i.e., it perceives objects as either advantageous or disadvantageous for man in his drive to persevere in his own being). Although the soul, according to the Stoics, is at birth a blank sheet inasmuch as it is only with sense-

We may conclude this brief survey by summing up the characteristics of natural law according to our Greek sources. There is substantial agreement that natural law is cosmic or divine, and that it is consequently imprinted in human reason or in the hearts of men. Rooted in nature, its scope is clearly universal, and with the apparent exception of Aristotle,[40] its character is undoubtedly held to be unchangeable. There is some disagreement, however, as to the deductions that may be drawn from the basic norms of natural law. Whereas Aristotle would not allow the certainty of mathematical precision in the interpretation and detailed formulation of natural law, the Stoic position seems to converge in this instance with that of Plato. Alongside the latter's supreme confidence in the master dialectician's ability to correlate unerringly his contemplation of the eternal "Forms" with the moral demands of the social and political arena, we must place the equally confident assumption of the Stoics that their ideal sage could infallibly apply his moral preconceptions under all circumstances (D.L. 7.122; 125).[41]

Turning back to Philo, we find in his writings, too, a clearly articulated doctrine of natural law. It has been pointed out that there are at least thirty occurrences of the expression *nomos physeōs* in the works of Philo, in addition to numerous equivalent formulations.[42] Moreover, there are numerous occasions where Philo's discourse about nature passes over almost imperceptibly into speaking about God, a usage virtually equivalent to SPINOZA's famous locution: *Deus sive natura.*[43] Furthermore, not only does Philo take over the well-known Greek contrast between conventional and natural law,[44] but he explicitly asserts that the Torah is in conformity with the latter:

experience that the mind begins to function, its mode of functioning is predetermined and involves the formulation of certain fundamental notions which are universal to the operations of human reason. For a different interpretation, see F. H. SANDBACH, Ennoia and Prolepsis, in: Problems in Stoicism, ed. A. A. LONG (London, 1971) 22—37.

[40] Aristotle would probably agree that the basic principles of natural law are unchanging, and that it is only in the realm of their application that variations take place.

[41] For Plotinus, too, not only does the highest, unfallen level of soul remain unclouded by error, but, at least according to some passages, even the middle, rational level is not subject to error (1.1.9; 4.4.17; 6.4.15).

[42] See H. KOESTER, Nomos Physeos, in: Religions in Antiquity, ed. J. NEUSNER, Studies in the History of Religions 14 (Leiden, 1968) 521—541. KOESTER believes, however, that it is not possible to posit a Greek background for Philo's frequent use of the term 'law of nature', that it seems more advisable to understand this term as a fruit of Philo's efforts to unite basic elements of Jewish tradition with the inheritance of Greek Thought, and that the new term was designed to express a new concept which did not exist before in the Hellenistic world, i.e., "that the Father and Maker of the world was in the truest sense also its Lawgiver" (Mos. 2.48). His arguments, however, are unconvincing. For a good corrective, see HORSLEY (cited n. 37).

[43] See, for example, Sac. 98ff.; Mig. 128. See E. R. GOODENOUGH, By Light Light. The Mystic Gospel of Hellenistic Judaism (New Haven, 1935; repr., Amsterdam, 1969) 51; F. GEIGER, Philon von Alexandreia als sozialer Denker (Stuttgart, 1932) 12.

[44] Cf. Jos. 28—31; Ebr. 37, 47; QG 4.90, 184; Prob. 37, 46. For the Cynic influence here on Philo, see E. BRÉHIER, Les Idées Philosophiques et Religieuses de Philon d'Alexandrie (Paris, 1950) 14—17.

"His exordium is, as I have said, most admirable, since it encompassed the creation of the world, in order to indicate that the world and the Law are in mutual accord, and that a man who is law-abiding is thereby immediately constituted a world citizen, guiding his actions aright according to nature's intent, in conformity with which the entire universe is administered." [Op. 1–3].[45]

But according to Philo, even before the Mosaic Law was promulgated, the Patriarchs had already embodied these laws in their very life styles, thus constituting, as it were, *nomoi empsychoi* (Abr. 3–6, 34, 61, 275–276; Prob. 62; Virt. 194).[46] WOLFSON[47] has correctly pointed out that some of the elements in Philo's conception of natural law may be found in rabbinic literature as well. The rabbis, for example, speak of the seven Noachian laws, four of which are also described by Philo as natural laws.[48] Although the rabbis homiletically derive all seven from Scripture, with the exception of two of them, they assert that "even had they not been written in the Law, they ought to have been written" (Sifra, Aḥare 13.10; cf. b. Yoma 76b). Moreover, M. Kiddushin 4.14 states that "Abraham had fulfilled the whole Law before it was given," and although the version in the Tosefta says that the teachings of both the Written and the Oral Law were revealed to him, we are told in Bereshit Rabba 61.1 that "The Holy One blessed be He made his two kidneys serve like two teachers, and these welled truth and taught him wisdom." The implication of this image is that God inspired Abraham's mind so that he could gain a knowledge of the Law through his own reasoning. R. Levi is later even more explicit: "Abraham learned the Torah from himself, for it said, 'and a good man shall be satisfied from himself' (B.R. 95.3).[49] More significant, how-

---

[45] Cf. Op. 143; Ebr. 34, 142; Det. 52; Agr. 66; Plant. 49; Mig. 128; Somn. 2.174; Abr. 16, 60; Mos. 2.47–52, 181, 211; Decal. 32; Spec. 1.31, 155; 2.13; 3.32, 46–47; 4.20,203–206, 212; Virt. 132; Prob. 37, 62, 160; QG 1.27; 4.90, 184; QE 2.1; y.Kil'ayim 1.7; b. Kiddushin 39a. See I. HEINEMANN, Die Lehre vom ungeschriebenen Gesetz im jüdischen Schrifttum, HUCA 2 (1927) 149–171.

[46] Moses is himself also said to have become through the providence of God a *nomos empsychos* long before he actually became a legislator (Mos. 1.162; cf. 2.11). Cf. Aristotle EN 1128a31: "A cultivated and free man, then, will have this kind of attitude, being, as it were, a law unto himself (οἷον νόμος ὤν ἑαυτῷ)", and the dictum cited by Moses Ḥayyim Ephraim of Sudilkov in his 'Degel Maḥaneh 'Efrayim' (Korets, 1868) 4a: "The Zaddik himself is Law and Commandment" (E. URBACH, The Sages [Jerusalem, 1975] 438, n. 20 [Hebrew]). Similarly, St. Francis of Assisi said: "I am your breviary, I am breviary." For the Hellenistic doctrine of *nomos empsychos* see E. R. GOODENOUGH, The Political Philosophy of Hellenistic Kingship, Yale Classical Studies 1 (1928) 55–102.

[47] WOLFSON, Philo (cited n. 25) 1.182–187.

[48] Tosefta Aboda Zara 8.4–6; b. Sanhedrin 56a–b; B.R. 16; Jub. 7.20. In the latter two sources, only six commandments are promised as well as enumerated, whereas in the Tosefta, seven are promised and only six are enumerated. See L. FINKELSTEIN, The Book of Jubilees and The Rabbinic Halaka, HTR 16 (1923) 39–61. H. ALBECK, however, denied that Jubilees is referring to the Noahide laws (Das Buch Jubilaen und die Halacha [Berlin, 1930] 34; 59, n. 231).

[49] See the detailed discussion in URBACH (cited n. 46) 281–284. Although some of his strictures are well taken, he seems to be pressing the texts too hard in the opposite direc-

ever, is the well-known midrash in B.R. 1.1. in the name of the Palestinian
Amora of the third century, R. Hoshaya of Caesarea, which states that the Torah
served as God's paradigm in his creation of the world. It was long ago suggested
by J. Freudentahl[50] that Philo (Op. 16—20) was very likely the rabbi's source
for this Platonic concept.[51] In any case, if taken seriously, this midrash implies
the Philonic notion of the Torah as natural law, since the laws of nature in this
view are correlative with the laws of the Torah. There is no indication, however,
that such an inference was actually drawn by the rabbis. On the other hand, the
Philonic view is clearly reflected in Jewish Hellenistic literature. Josephus (Ant.
1.24) tells us that everything in the Torah "is set forth in keeping with the nature
of the universe." A similar view is taken by the author of 4 Maccabees (1:16—17):
"Wisdom is a knowledge of things divine and human and of their causes . . . This
wisdom is the education given by the Law." The commandments, moreover, are
in accordance with human nature: "We know also that the Creator of the World,
as a Lawgiver, feels for us according to our nature" (5:25). Considerably earlier,
the author of Aristeas to Philocrates (161) had already indicated a similar view in
his statement: "The legislation was not laid down at random or by some caprice of
the mind, but with a view to truth and as a token of right reason."[52]

tion. In later midrashim, as Urbach concedes, Abraham's autonomy is clearly emphasized
(Pesik. Rab. 33, 150a: Bemid. R. 14.2; Seder Eliahu R. 7). See also b. Erubin 100b: "If the
Torah had not been given we could have learned modesty from the cat, not to rob from
the ant, chastity from the dove, considerate behavior to our wives from the rooster" (cf.
Digest 1.1.1; Institutes 1.2.1: "Natural law is that which nature has taught all animals";
Cicero Off. 3.5 [Theft prohibited by natural law]). R. Ḥiyya connects this thought with
Elihu's reference (in Job 35:11) to God as the one "who teaches us by example of the
beasts of the earth, and instructs us by the fowls of heaven" (ibid.). For the idea of natural
law underlying a legal decision, see M. Gittin 4.5; 'Eduyot 1.13 (B. Cohen, Jewish and
Roman Law [New York, 1966] 1.26—28; 386, n. 41a). See also A. Lichtenstein, Does
Jewish Tradition Recognize an Ethic Independent of Halakha?, in: Modern Jewish Ethics,
ed. M. Fox (Ohio State University Press, 1975) 62—88. For a contrary view see M. Fox,
Maimonides and Aquinas on Natural Law, Diné Israel 3 (1972) 5—36.

[50] J. Freudenthal, Hellenistische Studien (Breslau, 1875) 1.73. In 1881 Grätz (MGWJ)
had suggested that Origen, who had settled in Caesarea in 231, may have been R.
Hoshaya's intermediate source. See also Bacher, JQR 3 (1891) 357—360. Urbach has
correctly noted that Philo's emphasis on the location of the Intelligible World in the mind
of God is missing in the midrash. Cf. also M. Abot 3.23: "R. Akiba said, Beloved are Israel
to whom was given a precious instrument wherewith the world was created"; Sifre Deut.
48; b. Nedarim 62a.

[51] A faint echo of Philo's notion of the Logos as an image of God, of which the Torah is in
turn a further image, may be seen in Rav Avin's statement that the Torah is an incomplete
form (nôbelet), i.e., only an image, of the supernal wisdom (B.R. 44.12).

[52] οὐ γὰρ εἰκῇ καὶ κατὰ τὸ ἐμπεσὸν εἰς ψυχὴν νενομοθέτηται, πρὸς δ᾽ ἀλήθειαν καὶ ση-
μείωσιν ὀρθοῦ λόγου.

III. Conscience

Closely linked with Philo's concept of natural law is his notion of conscience.[53] The metaphor of conscience as an internal judge or prosecutor was current in Hellenistic thought, although Philo's use of the term *elegchos* in addition to *syneidos* does not appear to be found in precisely this sense before him.[54] A considerably more important innovation in Philo's doctrine, however, would be the notion of conscience as a transcendent gift from God. The most emphatic affirmation of the immanence of the Elenchos comes at Decal. 87, where it is described as "every soul's birth fellow and house-mate."[55] In several passages it is clearly indentified with man's reasoning or as the true man within the soul (Deus 50; Post. 59; Det. 23; Fug. 131). Some scholars, however, are impressed by the many passages where the transcendence of the conscience is apparently upheld. Most emphatic is Deus 135—138 where conscience, identified with the High Priest, is described in quasi mystical terms as entering the soul like a pure ray of light, to reveal our hidden sins in order to purify and heal us. If their interpretation should be correct, it would mean that for Philo, man's immanent powers of reasoning are ultimately inadequate for applying ethical norms and that without the timely invasions of God's transcendent gift man would be morally adrift. Natural law, in short, must be supplemented by special divine aid. The fact is, however, that the language used by Philo is not at all unparalleled in Late Stoics like M. Aurelius and Seneca, and it can, I think, be demonstrated that Philo's doctrine of conscience does not outdistance the Stoic view which is shaped by their bifocal perspective and their conception of relative transcendence. I should like to cite a well-known passage from Seneca (Ep. 41.1—2, 4—5) dealing with conscience which I believe will illuminate Philo's own teaching on this matter. Seneca begins by saying that "it is foolish to pray for sound understanding when you can acquire it from yourself . . . God is near you, he is with you, he is within you . . . A holy spirit indwells within us, one who marks our good and bad deeds, and is our guardian. As we treat this spirit, so are we treated by it. Indeed, no man can be good without the help of God." Within the briefest compass, however, the

---

[53] See Op. 128; Ebr. 125, 149; Det. 22—23, 146; Jos. 47—48; Virt. 206; Fug. 5—6, 117—118, 151, 203; Deus 126, 135—138, 182—183; Decal. 87; QG 4.62; QE 2.13; See V. NIKIPRO-WETZKY, La Doctrine de l'Elenchos chez Philon in: PAL (colloque) 255—273; BRÉHIER (cited n. 44) 295ff.; R. T. WALLIS, The Idea of Conscience in Philo of Alexandria, SP 3 (1974—75) 27—40; D. E. MARIETTA, Conscience in Greek Stoicism, Numen 17 (1970) 176—187; W. D. DAVIES, art. Conscience, IDB, A—D (1962) 671—676; C. MAURER, art. synoida, syneidēsis, TDNT 7 (1971) 898—919.

[54] Cf. Euripides Or. 396; Menander Monost. 654, frs. 145, 522, 531; Terence Eun. 119, Adelph. 348; Plautus Most. 544; Cicero Cluent. 159; N.D. 3.85; Tusc. 4.45; Lucretius 3. 1011ff.; Seneca Ep. 97.15; 105.7; De Ira 3; Polybius 18.43.13; C.H., Poimandres, chap. 22; Kleis, chaps. 19—21.

[55] ὁ γὰρ ἑκάστῃ ψυχῇ συμπεφυκὼς καὶ συνοικῶν ἔλεγχος.

language of immanence suddenly shifts almost imperceptibly to that of transcendence.

"If you see a man who is unterrified in the midst of dangers, untouched by
desires, happy in adversity, peaceful amid the storm . . . will not a feeling of
reverence for him steal over you? Will you not say: 'This quality is too great
and too lofty to be regarded as resembling this petty body in which it dwells?
A divine power has descended upon that man.' When a soul rises superior to
other souls . . . it is stirred by a force from heaven. A thing like this cannot
stand upright unless it be propped by the divine. Therefore a greater part of
it abides in that place from whence it came down to earth. Just as the rays of
the sun do indeed touch the earth, but still abide at the source from which
they are sent, even so the great and hallowed soul, which has come down in
order that we may have a nearer knowledge of divinity, does indeed associate
with us, but still cleaves to its origin; on that source it depends, thither it
turns its gaze and strives to go, and it concerns itself with our doings only as
a being superior to ourselves."[56]

"Here," writes DODDS, "we have *in nuce* the Neoplatonic doctrine that within
the so-called process of emanation, in giving rise to the effect the cause remains
undiminished and unaltered.[57] The Platonic text on which Plotinus (5.4.2) and
Proclus (*Th. Plat.* 5.18.283) base it is *Tim.* 42 E, but it seems to be a product of
the Middle Stoa, and to have originated in the attempt to give God a real place in
the Stoic system over against the cosmos."[58] Our soul, then, according to Seneca,
is both immanent and transcendent, so that both forms of description are easily
interchanged depending on the focus which the philosopher has momentarily
adopted.[59]

---

[56] *Si hominem videris interritum periculis, intactum cupiditatibus, inter adversa felicem, in
mediis tempestatibus placidum . . . non subibit te veneratio eius? Non dices: „Ista res maior
est altiorque quam ut credi similis huic, in quo est, corpusculo possit? Vis ista divina descendit.“ Animum excellentem . . . caelestis potentia agitat. Non potest res tanta sine admini-
culo numinis stare. Itaque maiore sui parte illic est, unde descendit. Quemadmodum radii
solis contingunt quidem terram, sed ibi sunt, unde mittuntur; sic animus magnus ac sacer et
in hoc demissus, ut propius divina nossemus, conversatur quidem nobiscum, sed haeret
origini suae; illinc pendet, illuc spectat ac nititur, nostris tamquam melior interest.*

[57] See Plotinus 3.8.10; 4.8.6; 5.1.3 and 6; 5.2.1; Proclus Elements, props. 26—27; C.H. 12.1.

[58] E. R. DODDS, Proclus, The Elements of Theology (Oxford, 1963) 214. Cf. Wisd. 7:27;
LA 1.5; Det. 90; Conf. 136; Gig. 27; Ps-Aristotle De mundo 6.7 and 13; M. Aurelius 8.
57; 7.59; Numenius, ap. Eusebius Pr. Ev. 11.18; Cant. R. on Cant. 3:10; Augustine Conf.
9.5.1; b. Sanhedrin 39 a; B.R. 68.9; Tanḥuma, Behaʿalotka: "To what was Moses like? To
a burning candle; all kindle light from it, yet its light is undiminished;" Plato Parmen.
131 B; Heraclitus DK B. 114.

[59] Cf. M. POHLENZ, Die Stoa. Geschichte einer geistigen Bewegung (Göttingen, 2nd. ed.,
1959) 1.320—321, where the suggestion is made that it was the Pythagoreans who influenced Seneca's emphasis on conscience.

But what of those passages in which Philo speaks explicitly of conscience or the *theios logos* as entering and withdrawing from the soul?[60] Once more we are confronted by the bifocal view, this time in in the form of a principle which is but a corollary of the law of undiminished giving discussed above. It is concisely expressed later by Proclus (Elements, prop. 142):

"The gods are present alike to all things; not all things, however, are present alike to the gods, but each order has a share in their presence proportional to its station and capacity, some things receiving them as unities and others as manifolds, some perpetually and others for a time, some incorporeally and others through the body."[61]

Proclus' conception, according to DODDS, "reflects a general Hellenistic tradition which is common to pagan, Jewish, and Christian writers."[62] Speaking, then, from the human viewpoint, the *theios logos* enters man and departs; from the eternal perspective of God, however, the Logos is ever present to man, but its consummation in any particular case is conditioned by the fitness of the recipient.

IV. Philanthrōpia

The special kinship between God and man based on the notion of a Divine Logos at once immanent and transcendent, led inevitably to the concept of the unity of man. The Stoics had already spoken of the common community of gods and men: "The world is as it were the common house of gods and men, or the city belonging to both; for they alone make use of reason and live according to right

---

[60] Cf. Seneca Ep. 83: "Nothing is shut off from the sight of God. He is witness of our souls, and comes into the very midst of our thoughts – comes into them, I say, as one who may at any time depart."

[61] Cf. Wisd. 6:16; Philo Op. 23; C.H. 10.4; Plutarch Moral. 589 B; Plotinus 6.5.11 fin.; 6.9. 8: "Thus the Supreme as containing no otherness is ever present with us, we with it when we put otherness away"; M. Aurelius 8.54; Ps-Dionysius Div. Nom. 3.1; Musonius Rufus: "Cut off the dead part of your soul and you will recognize the presence of God" (fr. 53, LUTZ 145). There is a passage in Plato's 'Republic' (7.518 E) which already points in this direction: "But the excellence of thought, it seems, is certainly of a more divine quality, a thing that never loses its potency, but according to the direction of its conversion, becomes useful and beneficent, or again, useless and harmful." This was also the teaching of many Hasidic masters. "Where is the dwelling of God?", asked the Rabbi of Kotzk, and answering his own question, he said: "Wherever man lets him in." See M. BUBER, Hasidism and Modern Man (New York, 1958) 175–176 (cf. Maimonides Guide 2.12). DODDS notes that his was a favorite doctrine of the Cambridge Platonists, e.g., BENJAMIN WHICHCOTE (cited n. 2): "It is the incapacity of the subject, where God is not . . . for God doth not withdraw himself from us, unless we first leave Him: The distance is occasioned through our unnatural use of ourselves."

[62] DODDS (cited n. 58) 273.

and law" (Cicero N.D. 2.154; SVF 2.527–528).[63] The early Stoics, however, still emphasized the dichotomy between the wise and the foolish, and Zeno insisted that only the wise are capable of concord and unity (D.L. 7.32–33; SVF 3. 672, 674, 725).[63a] The Cynics had gone so far as to say that the non-wise are not men (D.L. 6.41, 60). It was only in the Middle Stoa, in the writings of Panaetius and Antiochus, through a fusion of the Stoic notion of *oikeiōisis* and the Peripatetic doctrine of *oikeiotēs*,[64] that an all-embracing doctrine of human unity took shape. Panaetius focussed his attention on the ordinary man, and thus produced an ethical ideal suited to the capacity of all (Seneca Ep. 116.5; Cicero Off. 1.46, 99). Going beyond the negative formulation of justice which forbids one man to injure another, he advances the positive definition of it as an active beneficence, which forms the bond of society (Cicero Off. 1.20).

> "While all that is created on the earth is made for the use of man, men were brought into being for the sake of men, so that they could be of value to each other. In this, therefore, we should follow nature's lead and contribute to the common welfare by an exchange of services, by giving and receiving, and we should use our skill, our hard work and our talents to strengthen the bonds of fellowship between men." [Off. 1.22].[65]

If men are thus born for mutual aid, peace must be superior to war, and when the latter does occur, brutality must be avoided:

> "There are two ways of deciding a conflict — by discussion, which is characteristic of men, and by violence the way of beasts; and we should resort to violence only if discussion is impossible. Therefore the only reason for going to war is to ensure that we can live in peace unharmed; and after victory those who have not been brutal or bloodthirsty in warfare should be spared." [ibid. 34–35].[66]

Justice must also be shown by the individual to his slave and towards those whose fortune places them in the lowest level of society. "The most humble lot and position is that of slaves, and we are well advised by those who tell us to treat

---

[63] Cf. Theophrastus, who is quoted by Porphyry as describing the world as "the common home of gods and men" (De Abst. 2.162.6); M. Aurelius 4.4.

[63a] Cf. J. RIST, The Stoic Concept of Detachment, in: The Stoics, ed. J. M. RIST (Berkeley–Los Angeles–London, 1978) 261–266.

[64] See the illuminating discussion of H. C. BALDRY, The Unity of Mankind in Greek Thought (Cambridghe, 1965) 177–203.

[65] *Quae in terris gignantur, ad usum hominum omnia creari, homines autem hominum causa esse generatos, ut ipsi inter se aliis alii prodesse possent, in hoc naturam debemus ducem sequi, communes utilitates in medium afferre mutatione officiorum, dando accipiendo, tum artibus, tum opera, tum facultatibus devincire hominum inter homines societatem.*

[66] *Nam cum sint duo genera decertandi, unum per disceptationem, alterum per vim, cumque illud proprium sit hominis, hoc beluarum, confugiendum est ad posterius, si uti non licet superiore. Quare suscipienda quidem bella sunt ob eam causam, ut sine iniuria in pace vivatur, parta autem victoria conservandi ii, qui non crudeles in bello, non immanes fuerunt.*

slaves like hired workers [the reference is to Chrysippus' definition, SVF 3.351]: labor must be required from them, but they must be given their dues." (ibid. 1. 41).[67] The fundamental principles on which all this is based are then elucidated.

> "We must go more deeply into the basic principles of fellowship and association set up by nature among men. The first is to be found in the association that links together the entire human race, and the bond that creates this is reason and speech, which by teaching and learning, by communication, discussion and decision brings men into agreement with each other and joins them in a kind of natural fellowship." [ibid. 1.50].[68]

Similarly, according to Antiochus, friendship is seen extending outwards from the family until it includes even the gods (Augustine C.D. 19.3).

> "In the whole realm of moral excellence there is nothing finer, nothing with wider implications, than the interrelationship of men with each other — the fellowship, as it were, that exists between them, their exchange of services, and indeed the affection which unites mankind. This affection comes into being right from our birth, in that children are loved by their parents and the whole family is held together by the bonds of marriage and parenthood. From there it gradually spreads beyond the home, first through ties of blood, then through marital relationships, then through friendships, later by association with neighbors, afterwards to fellow-citizens and to partners and friends in public life, and finally by embracing the entire human race." [Cicero Fin. 5.65].[69]

This human fellowship is identified with *iustitia*, and "linked with it are sense of duty, kindliness, liberality, benevolence, friendliness, and the other qualities of the same sort which are particularly related fo justice" (ibid., cf. Cicero Leg. 1. 22–39).

If we turn to Philo, we shall find virtually the same conceptual development just sketched for the Middle Stoa. "All we men", writes Philo, "are kinsmen and brothers, being related by the possession of an ancient kinship, since we receive the lot of the rational nature from one mother." (QG 2.60; cf. Decal, 41; Det. 164; Spec. 4.14). Moreover, "nature, who created man the most civilized of

---

[67] Musonius Rufus also insisted that masters respect the essential human rights of their slaves. See C. E. Lutz, Musonius Rufus 'The Roman Socrates', Yale Class. Studies 10 (1947) 3. 147; see also Seneca De Clement. 1.18.

[68] *Sed, quae naturae principia sint communitatis et societatis humanae, repetendum videtur altius; est enim primum quod cernitur in universi generis humani societate. Eius autem vinculum est ratio et oratio, quae docendo, discendo, communicando, disceptando, iudicando conciliat inter se homines coniungitque naturali quadam societate.*

[69] *In omni autem honesto de quo loquimur nihil est tam illustre nec quod latius pateat quam coniunctio inter homines hominum et quasi quaedam societas et communicatio utilitatum et ipsa caritas generis humani, quae nata a primo satu, quod a procreatoribus nati diliguntur et tota domus coniugio et stirpe coniungitur, serpit sensim foras, cognationibus primum tum affinitatibus, deinde amicitiis, post vicinitatibus, tum civibus et iis qui publice socii atque amici sunt, deinde totius complexu gentis humanae.*

animals to be gregarious and sociable, has called him to show fellowship and a spirit of partnership by endowing him with reason, the bond which leads to harmony and blending of characteristics." (Decal. 132–134;[70] cf. Praem. 92; Spec. 1. 317). Following Panaetius, Philo, too, emphasizes the positive aspect of justice as an active beneficence:

"Many persons try to do to others the opposite of the good which they have experienced . . . Rather should the wise man, as far as possible, impart to his neighbors his sagacity, the continent his temperance, the valiant his gallantry, the just his justice, and in general the good his goodness . . . For the gifts of the Chief Ruler are of universal benefit, given to some, not to be hidden by them when received, nor misused to harm others, but thrown into the common stock." [Virt. 166, 169].[71]

This quality of active beneficence is encapsuled by Philo in the word *philanthrōpia* (humanity or benevolence), a term which apparently came into philosophical prominence in the writings of Panaetius and Antiochus, and later in those of Epictetus' teacher Musonius Rufus, and with especial emphasis in those of Plutarch.[72] In a section of his essay 'On the Virtues' devoted to *philanthrōpia* (51–174), Philo points out that it has *eusebeia* or piety as its sister and twin,[73] for

---

[70] ἀγελαστικὸν γὰρ καὶ σύννομον ζῷον τὸ ἡμερώτατον ἄνθρωπον ἡ φύσις γεννήσασα πρὸς ὁμόνοιαν καὶ κοινωνίαν ἐκάλεσε, λόγον δοῦσα συναγωγὸν εἰς ἁρμονίαν καὶ κρᾶσιν ἠθῶν.

[71] πολλοὶ τὰ ἐναντία ὧν εὖ πεπόνθασι δρᾶν ἐπιχειροῦσιν . . . χρὴ δὲ καὶ τὸν φρόνιμον ἀγχίνους, ὡς ἔνι μάλιστα, τοὺς πλησιάζοντας κατασκευάζειν καὶ τὸν σώφρονα ἐγκρατεῖς καὶ γενναίους τὸν ἀνδρεῖον καὶ τὸν δίκαιον δικαίους καὶ συνόλως ἀγαθοὺς τὸν ἀγαθόν . . . κοινωφελεῖς γὰρ αἱ τοῦ πρώτου ἡγεμόνος δωρεαί, ἃς δίδωσιν ἐνίοις, οὐχ ἵν' ἐκεῖνοι λαβόντες ἀποκρύψωσιν ἢ καταχρήσωνται πρὸς ζημίαν ἑτέρων, ἀλλ' ἵν' εἰς μέσον προενεγκόντες . . .

[72] See LUTZ (cited n. 67) 92; R. HIRZEL, Plutarch (Leipzig, 1912) 23–32. HIRZEL states that Plutarch did not learn this concept from the Stoics. He has, however, overlooked the new development that took place in the writings of Panaetius, Antiochus, and Musonius Rufus. Cf. also Aristeas to Philocrates 208, 257, 290 (where the king feels *philanthrōpia* for his people). Cf. Wisd. 7:22; 3 Macc. 3:15; Plutarch Moral. 824D; SVF 2.1115 (where Chrysippus refers to the gods as *euergetikoi, philanthrōpoi*); Aeschylus Prom. 28; Demosthenes Or. 8.70; 21.49; Plato, Laws 713D; D.L. 3.9.8; Ps-Plato Def. 412E; SVF 3.292. An inscription of the third century C.E. praises *philanthrōpia* as divine (DITTENBERGER, Syll. 418, 104). With Plutarch's use of *synanthrōpein* (Moral. 823B), cf. Philo's use of *anthrōpopathein* (Decal. 43). Cicero's term *humanitas* clearly includes *philanthrōpia* whatever else it may imply, and the terms *benignitas, beneficentia*, and *benevolentia* all render aspects of *philanthrōpia*. The wise man, says Scipio in the 'De Republica', believes that while others may be called men, only those really are men who are accomplished in the arts characteristic of *humanitas*" (1.28). Cf. Decal. 110; Hypoth. 632; Cicero Rep. 2.48. See also C. J. DE VOGEL, Greek Philosophy (Leiden, 1959) 3.240. Among the Cynics, Crates especially seems to have archieved a reputation for *philanthrōpia*, in spite of the general Cynic contempt for the mob (see D. DUDLEY, A History of Cynicism [London, 1937] 43).

[73] *adelphēn kai didymon*; cf. Congr. 18. See GEIGER (cited n. 43) 4–17.

the love of God involves the love of man,[74] inasmuch as man, "the best of living creatures, through that higher part of his being, namely, the soul, is most nearly akin to heaven, the purest thing in all that exists, and, as most admit, also to the Father of the world, possessing in his mind a closer likeness and copy than anything else on earth of the eternal and blessed Archetype" (Decal. 134).[75] Following the pattern of the ten commandments, which are equally divided into two sets of five, the former comprising duties to God or piety, and the other duties to men, or justice (Her. 168; Spec. 2.63; cf. M. Yoma 8.9), Philo is fond of structuring his lives of the Patriarchs in a similar manner by first narrating examples of their piety, immediately followed by examples of their justice.[76] Although both piety and justice are in reality inseparable, Philo gives the chief place to piety or holiness,[77] since the love of God is primary and our highest good, all else being derivative from it. He also speaks loosely of the incompleteness of those who choose but one side of the coin:

"Some indeed have heretofore attached themselves to one portion of the commandments while appearing to neglect the other. They have taken their fill of the pure wine of piety and, completely renouncing all other affairs, devoted their personal lives entirely to the service of God. Others, surmising that there is no good outside one's duties to men, have espoused nothing but companionship with their fellows. In their desire for solidarity they provide the good things of life for all to use equally and deem it right to alleviate their straitened conditions as far as possible. These may justly be called lovers of men, the former lovers of God. Both are imcomplete in virtue, for only they who are highly esteemed in both spheres have it entire. But those who are neither counted among men by rejoicing with them at goods shared and grieving with them at their opposite nor hold fast to piety and holiness would seem to have been changed into the nature of beasts." [Decal. 108—110].[78]

---

[74] Cf. Plotinus 6.8.15: The individual soul will love all things, in so far as all things contain the principle of unity, for the One loves itself both in itself and in the rest of the cosmos; Seneca Ep. 90.3: colere divina, humana diligere.

[75] Cf. QG 3.42; Abr. 208.

[76] See Bréhier (cited n. 44) 27—28.

[77] Spec. 4.97, 135, 147; Decal. 119; Virt. 95; Praem. 53; cf. Plato Euthy. 12 Cff.; Protag. 330 B; Laches 119 D; Aristotle EN 1129 b, 27—28; 1249 b, 20; Ps-Aristotle Virtut. et vit. 1250 b, 23—24; Ps-Plato Def. 412—415; D.L. 3.83; SVF 2.1017 (ἔστι γὰρ εὐσέβεια ἐπιστήμη θεῶν θεραπείας ... ἡ ὁσιότης, δικαιοσύνη τις οὖσα πρὸς θεούς); SVF 3.660; b. Baba Batra 9 a; Aristeas to Philocrates 131. Philo accepts the doctrine of the mutual implication (antakolouthia) of the virtues, which in the wise man cannot be separated from one another (Mos. 2.7; Sac. 84; Virt. 181; cf. SVF 1.199; 3.295 ff.; Plato Protag. 329 E; Aristotle EN 1145 a 2—3; Cicero Fin. 5.67; Orat. 1.18.83; Albinus Did. 183.2—3; Apuleius De Plat. 2.228). Cf. however, H. J. Horn, Antakoluthie der Tugenden und Einheit Gottes, Jahrbuch für Antike und Christentum 13 (1970) 5—28.

[78] ἤδη μὲν οὖν τινες τῇ ἑτέρᾳ μερίδι προσκληρώσαντες ἑαυτοὺς ἔδοξαν τῆς ἑτέρας ὀλιγωρεῖν· ἄκρατον γὰρ ἐμφορησάμενοι τὸν εὐσεβείας πόθον, πολλὰ χαίρειν φράσαντες ταῖς ἄλλαις πραγματείαις ὅλον ἀνέθεσαν τὸν οἰκεῖον βίον θεραπείᾳ θεοῦ. οἱ δ' οὐδὲν ἔξω

What Philo seems to be saying is that one should serve both men and God through rational emotions (*eupatheiai*) rather than as a result of passions. One who seizes upon but one side of the coin, however, has obviously done so as a result of passion, whereas he who acts out of rational emotions would clearly be a lover both of God and of men. On the other hand, he who loves neither, i.e., neither practices love through rational emotions, nor through irrational ones, is nothing but a beast.[79]

Philanthrōpia, as we have seen, requires a benign attitude towards slaves, and Philo's position in this matter is essentially in line with that of the Stoa, though his own formulations are more explicit than theirs.[80] "Servants rank lower in fortune," he writes, "but in nature can claim equality with their masters, and in the law of God the standard of justice is adjusted to nature and not to fortune. And therefore the masters should not make excessive use of their authority over slaves by showing arrogance and contempt and savage cruelty." (Spec. 3.137).[81] Although in Spec. 2.123, he naturally reproduces the Biblical injunction which permits the acquisition of slaves from other nations and does his best to explain the necessity for it, his true sentiments are nevertheless revealed in the passage in Cont. 70, where he speaks with the greatest admiration of the attitude of the Therapeutae towards slavery:

τῶν πρὸς ἀνθρώπους δικαιωμάτων ἀγαθὸν ὑποτοπήσαντες εἶναι μόνην τὴν πρὸς ἀνθρώπους ὁμιλίαν ἠσπάσαντο ... τούτους μὲν οὖν φιλανθρώπους, τοὺς δὲ προτέρους φιλοθέους ἐνδίκως ἂν εἴποι τις, ἡμιτελεῖς τὴν ἀρετήν· ὁλόκληροι γὰρ οἱ παρ' ἀμφοτέροις εὐδοκιμοῦντες. ὅσοι δὲ μήτ' ἐν τοῖς πρὸς ἀνθρώπους ἐξετάζονται, συνηδόμενοι μὲν ἐπὶ τοῖς κοινοῖς ἀγαθοῖς, συναλγοῦντες δ' ἐπὶ τοῖς ἐναντίοις, μήτ' εὐσεβείας καὶ ὁσιότητος περιέχονται, μεταβεβληκέναι δόξειεν ἂν εἰς θηρίων φύσιν (translation my own).

[79] Very similar to Philo's view here is that of SPINOZA, who, in condemning pity as a passion, yet insists that he is "speaking expressly of a man who lives under the guidance of reason. For he who is moved neither by reason nor pity to help others is rightly called inhuman, for he seems to be dissimilar to man" (Ethics 4.50). Similarly, in his 'Tractatus Theologico-Politicus', chap 5, SPINOZA points out that he who is ignorant of Scripture and nevertheless knows by natural reason that God exists and has a true plan of life, is more blessed than the common herd of believers. But "he who is ignorant of Scripture and knows nothing by the light of reason is less than human and almost brutal, having nothing of God's gifts" (ELWES [New York, 1951] 78). (At Mut. 225, Philo alludes to the *prokoptōn* who, unlike the *sophos*, is unable to achieve that state in which all the virtues are automatically adhered to and all *pathē* have been converted into *eupatheiai* and bids him be content to "consort with one of the specific virtues" in lieu of living "amid the collected body of the many virtues.")

[80] See SVF 3.349—366. Chrysippus' definition of the slave as "a permanent hireling", distinguishable from the free laborer not by nature, but only by length of service, was no condemnation of slavery, as BALDRY has correctly pointed out (cited n. 64), but at least a rejection of the 'natural slave' of Aristotle (Polit. 1.2; EN 1161b 2—8). Several isolated earlier statements were more explicit than those of the Stoics: e.g., the Sophist Alcidamas' well-known statement that "God has left all men free; nature has made no man a slave" (Aristotle Rhet. 1373b 18), and the line of Philemon (a contemporary of Menander): "No man was ever born a slave by nature" (fr. 39, MEINEKE).

[81] Cf. Spec. 2.89 and 69; 2.81 (where he echoes Chrysippus' notion of the slave as a hired person); Prob. 19.

"They use no slaves to minister to their needs, since they consider the possession of servants to be entirely contrary to nature. For nature has created all men free, but the acts of injustice and greed of some who have energetically pursued inequality, the beginning of mischief, harnessed the power over the weaker and fastened it on the stronger."[82]

Philo's attitude toward war is also very similar so that of the Middle Stoa. The injunctions concerning war in Deut. 20:10ff., he conveniently limits to war against those who revolt from an alliance, in the conviction, as COLSON has remarked,[83] that "the Law could never have intended to sanction wars of conquest or aggression." Against these revolting allies

"your well-armed fighting force should advance with its armaments and encamp around them, then wait for a time, not letting anger have free play at the expense of reason . . . They must therefore at once send heralds to propose terms of agreement and at the same time point out the military efficiency of the besieging power. And if their opponents repent of their rebellious conduct and give way and show an inclination to peace, the others must accept and welcome the treaty, for peace, even if it involves great sacrifices, is more advantageous than war."

If the adversaries persist, then the attack must be pursued by troops "having in the justice of their cause an invincible ally." Moreover, women married and unmarried must be spared, "for to breathe slaughter against all, even those who have done very little or nothing amiss, shows what I should call a savage and brutal soul." "Indeed, so great a love for justice does the law instill into those who live under its constitution that it does not even permit the fertile soil of a hostile city to be outraged by devastation or by cutting down trees to destroy the fruits" (Spec. 4. 219–229).[84]

---

[82] διακονοῦνται δὲ οὐχ ὑπ' ἀνδραπόδων, ἡγούμενοι συνόλως τὴν θεραπόντων κτῆσιν εἶναι παρὰ φύσιν· ἡ μὲν γὰρ ἐλευθέρους ἅπαντας γεγέννηκεν, αἱ δέ τινων ἀδικίαι καὶ πλεονεξίαι ζηλωσάντων τὴν ἀρχέκακον ἀνισότητα καταζεύξασαι τὸ ἐπὶ τοῖς ἀσθενεστέροις κράτος τοῖς δυνατωτέροις ἀνῆψαν (translation my own).

[83] LCL, Philo 8.144, note b. Cf. Mos. 1.307, where he carefully justifies the war against the Midianites as one in defense of piety and holiness, and not to win domination nor appropriate the possessions of others; and Hypoth. 356, where he sheepishly suggests that perhaps the Israelites were "unwarlike and feeble, quite few in numbers and destitute of warlike equipment, but won the respect of their opponents who voluntarily surrendered their land to them."

[84] ἡ ὑμετέρα νεότης εὐοπλοῦσα μετὰ τῶν εἰς πόλεμον παρασκευῶν ἐπίτω καὶ στρατόπεδον ἐν κύκλῳ βαλλομένη καραδοκείτω μηδὲν ὀργῇ πρὸ λογισμοῦ χαριζομένη . . . εὐθὺς οὖν πεμπέτω κήρυκας τοὺς προκαλεσομένους εἰς συμβάσεις καὶ ἅμα τὸ ἀξιόμαχον τῆς παριδρυμένης δυνάμεως δηλώσοντας· καὶ ἐὰν μὲν ἐφ' οἷς ἐνεωτέρισαν μετανοήσαντες ὑπείκωσι πρὸς τὸ εἰρηναῖον τραπόμενοι, δεχέσθωσαν ἄσμενοι τὰς σπονδάς. 226: τοσοῦτον δ' ἔρωτα δικαιοσύνης ἐνεργάζεται τοῖς κατ' αὐτὸν πολιτευομένοις, ὥστ' οὐδὲ πόλεως ἐχθρᾶς τὴν ἀρετῶσαν γῆν ἐφίησι λυμαίνεσθαι δῃοῦντας ἢ δενδροτομοῦντας ἐπὶ φθορᾷ καρπῶν.

Finally, Philo points out that in practicing *philanthrōpia*, man is imitating God. "For what one of the men of old aptly said is true, that in no other action does man so much resemble God as in showing kindness, and what greater good can there be than that they should imitate God, they the created, Him the eternal?" (Spec. 4.73; cf. Spec. 1.294; Congr. 171).[85] Here, indeed, we touch upon the formula which for Philo constitutes the best way to describe the *telos* of man's life, *homoiōsis theōi*, and in adopting this Platonic goal he was following in the footsteps of Eudorus of Alexandria.[86]

We may conclude our discussion of Philo's ideal of *philanthrōpia* by considering its implications for the Biblical doctrine of Israel's election. Rooted as that ideal was in a universalistic conception of man, it necessarily entailed a reformulation of the latter. At every possible opportunity, Philo emphasizes the universal aspects of Jewish particularism. The Jews are indeed "the nation dearest of all to God", but it "has received the gift of priesthood and prophecy on behalf of all mankind." (Abr. 98; cf. Spec. 1.168; QE 1.10). "Out of the whole human race God chose Israel and called them to his service", but it is only because they are "in a true sense men" (Spec. 1.303).[87] Israel's function is "to offer prayers on behalf of the human race that it may be delivered from evil" (Mos. 1.49; cf. Spec. 2.162), and the High Priest makes prayers and gives thanks not only on behalf of the whole human race but also for the parts of nature, for he holds the world to be his country (Spec. 1.96—97; cf. QE 2.107; Mos. 2.135; Josephus Ant. 3.159). The Sabbath becomes for Philo "a festival of the universe" and belongs to all

---

[85] Cf. Aelian, Var. Hist. 12.59: "Pythagoras said that the two best gifts of the gods to men were speaking the truth and showing kindness, and that he added that both resembled the works of the gods"; Arsenius, Violarium 189: "Demosthenes, being asked what man has like God, said 'showing kindness and speaking the truth'." A. MOSÈS writes: "*L'attribution de la sentence à Démosthène par Arsenios De Malvasia* (Violetum, 1.189, WALZ) *semble être le résultat d'une erreur, puisque le même Arsenios* (p. 421, WALZ) *donne une partie de cette maxime sous le nom de Pythagore*" (Lyon 25.242). See HEINEMANN's and COLSON's notes ad loc., cf. Longinus 1.2; Strabo 10.3.9.

[86] See Fug. 63, where he quotes Plato's Theaet. 176 AB; Op. 144; Virt. 8, 168, 204—205; Spec. 4.188; Decal. 73; LA 2.4; cf. Plato, Tim. 90A ff.; Laws 716B. For Eudorus, see J. DILLON (cited n. 37) 114—135; and W. THEILER, Untersuchungen zur antiken Literatur (Berlin, 1970) 494—498. Since, as we have already seen, Philo's discourse on Nature often passes over imperceptibly into speaking about God, he could hold on equally well to the Stoic *telos* formula of consonance with nature. Cf. Mig. 128; Praem. 11—14. J. RIST writes: "The precise equation of the two expressions and outlooks (*homoiōsis theōi* and *homologoumenōs tēi physei zēn*) was probably made by Posidonius, and is found in Cicero, Seneca, and succeeding writers in their accounts of Stoicism" (Eros and Psyche [Toronto, 1964] 162). The idea of *imitatio Dei* was, of course, also distinctively Jewish. Cf. Mekilta, Beshalaḥ 3; b. Shabbat 133b; Sotah 14a. See A. MARMORSTEIN, The Imitation of God in the Haggadah, in: Studies in Jewish Theology, ed. J. RABBINOWITZ and M. LOEW (London, 1950) 106—121; S. SCHECHTER, Some Aspects of Rabbinic Theology (New York, 1909) 199ff.

[87] Abr. 98: καὶ ἐθνῶν τὸ θεοφιλέστατον, ὅ μοι δοκεῖ τὴν ὑπὲρ παντὸς ἀνθρώπων γένους ἱερωσύνην καὶ προφητείαν λαχεῖν.
Spec. 1.303: ἀλλ' ὅμως καὶ ἐξ ἅπαντος ἀνθρώπων γένους τοὺς πρὸς ἀλήθειαν ἀνθρώπους ἀριστίνδην ἐπιλέξαι εἵλετο καὶ προνομίας ἠξίωσε τῆς πάσης.

people as the birthday of the world (Op. 89). Passover, too, has a universal significance "in agreement with the general cosmic order" (Spec. 2.150), and 'Rosh Ha-Shanah' has in addition to its national significance also a universal one (Spec. 2.188).[88] Israel stands out as a model for all other peoples, "not for its own glory, but rather for the benefit of the beholders. For to gaze continuously upon noble models imprints their likeness in souls which are not entirely hardened and stony" (Praem. 114[89]; cf. QE 2.42, where Israel's Law is described "as a law for the world, for the chosen race is a likeness of the world").[90] In the light of this reading of the Jewish doctrine of election, Philo is no longer able to contain his own perplexity at the hostility that that doctrine had engendered within the pagan world in his own day. "I am astounded that some dare to accuse of inhumanity the nation that has shown such an extravagant sense of fellowship and goodwill to all men everywhere, that it has discharged its prayers and festivals and first fruit offerings on behalf of the human race in general" (Spec. 2.167).[91] Through proselytism, moreover, Philo sees the possibility of the participation of all nations in the universal religion of Judaism "as pilgrims to truth" who have abandoned the "mythical fables and multiplicity of sovereigns" to honor the "One who alone is worthy of honor" (Spec. 4.178; 1.309; 1.51−52; Mos. 2.44).[92] In a flash of enthusiasm, Philo actually envisages the advent of a messianic era of universal peace:

"This is what our most holy prophet through all his regulations especially desires to create, unanimity, neighborliness, fellowship, reciprocity of feeling, whereby houses and cities and nations and countries and the whole human race may advance to supreme happiness. Hitherto, indeed, these things live only in our prayers, but they will, I am convinced, become facts beyond all dispute, if God, even as he gives the yearly fruits, grants that the virtues should bear abundantly." [Virt. 119−120].[93]

---

[88] See S. BELKIN, Philo and the Oral Law (Cambridge, 1940) 192−218.

[89] οὐχ ὑπὲρ εὐδοξίας μᾶλλον ἢ τῆς τῶν ὁρώντων ὠφελείας· αἱ γὰρ συνεχεῖς τῶν καλῶν παραδειγμάτων φαντασίαι παραπλησίας εἰκόνας ἐγχαράττουσι ταῖς μὴ πάνυ σκληραῖς καὶ ἀποκρότοις ψυχαῖς.

[90] Cf. Wisd. 18:4; Test. Levi 14.4 (Jn 1.9); 4 Ezra 7.20; 2 Bar. 48.40; Mekilta, Baḥodesh 5.65, 100; b. Aboda Zara 2b.

[91] διὸ καὶ θαυμάζειν ἐπέρχεταί μοι, πῶς τολμῶσί τινες ἀπανθρωπίαν τοῦ ἔθνους κατηγορεῖν, ὃ τοσαύτῃ κέχρηται κοινωνίας καὶ εὐνοίας τῆς πρὸς ⟨τοὺς⟩ πανταχοῦ πάντας ὑπερβολῇ, ὡς τάς τε εὐχὰς καὶ ἑορτὰς καὶ ἀπαρχὰς ὑπὲρ τοῦ κοινοῦ γένους τῶν ἀνθρώπων ἐπιτελεῖν (translation my own).

[92] Cf. Spec. 2.73, where Philo points out that the distinction between Jew and alien is not an absolute one: "Those who are not of the same nation he describes as aliens, reasonably enough, and the condition of the alien excludes any idea of partnership, unless indeed by a transcending of virtues he converts even it into a tie of kinship, since it is a general truth that common citizenship rests on virtues and laws which propound the morally beautiful as the sole good." Cf. also Spec. 1.317.

[93] Cf. Spec. 2.48, where a similar vision is posed in more hypothetical terms; and Praem. 87−93, where Philo longs for the day when the primary war between man and beast will be brought to an end. Man will then be shamed into a horror of war.

This eschatological vision of human unity was in a sense already intimated in more theoretical terms by Cicero:

> "That justice is based upon nature will be evident, if you fully realize man's fellowship and unity with his fellow men. No two things are so closely and exactly alike as all of us are to each other. If degeneration of habits and false opinions did not pervert the weakness of our minds and turn it aside in whatever direction it begins to stray, no one would be so like himself as all would be like all . . . Reason is certainly common to all men, variable in what it learns but equal for all in its power to learn . . . There is indeed no one of any race who, given a guide, cannot make his way to virtue." [Leg. 1.10.28–30].[94]

Philo's prophetic heritage readily transformed this theoretical possibility into a messianic vision.[95]

V. Apatheia / Eupatheia

Inasmuch as, according to Philo, God is completely *apathēs*,[96] his *homoiōsis theōi* formula clearly implies that man's highest ethical ideal is constituted by a state of *apatheia*.[97] Thus, in his depiction of Isaac and Moses, Philo introduces them as prototypes of a higher ethical level than that of the ordinary man. Although both Isaac and Moses exemplify soul-types which achieve perfect virtue without toil, Moses presumably represents for Philo a higher type than does Isaac, since he is ultimately translated to an even higher station than that of the latter by being placed beside God himself, above genus and species alike (Sac. 8)

---

[94] *id iam patebit, si hominum inter ipsos societatem coniunctionemque perspexeris. nihil est enim unum uni tam simile, tam par, quam omnes inter nosmet ipsos sumus. quodsi depravatio consuetudinum, si opinionum vanitas non inbecillitatem animorum torqueret et flecteret quocumque coepisset, sui nemo ipse tam similis esset quam omnes essent omnium. 30: etenim ratio . . . certe est communis, doctrina differens, discendi quidem facultate par . . . nec est quisquam gentis ullius, qui ducem nactus ad virtutem pervenire non possit.*

[95] It should be noted, however, that Zeno had already looked forward to a Cosmopolis in which every citizen would be wise (SVF 1.262).

[96] See Op. 8; LA 3.2, 81, 203; Cher. 44, 46, 86; Sac. 101; Det. 54–56; Post. 4; 28; Deus 7, 22, 52, 56; Plant. 35.

[97] The same combination of *apatheia* and *homoiōsis theōi* occurs also in Neoplatonism and in Clement of Alexandria (Plotinus 1.2.3; 1.2.6; Porphyry Sent. 22; De Abst. 2.43; Clement Strom. 2.101.1; 6.111.3; 6.74.1; 6.105.1; 6.109.3). The Old Academy, as well as Middle Platonism, adopted the goal of *metriopatheia*: Cicero Ac. Pr. 2.131; Plutarch Virt. m. 443C, 444B, 451C; Albinus, Did. 30.5–6, LOUIS; Taurus, ap. Gellius 1.26.11; Maximus of Tyre, Or. 1.19b; 27.116b; cf. Plotinus 1.2.2 and 1.2.7 (of the lower ethical stage). Apuleius seems to be the only exponent of Middle Platonism who has openly adopted *apatheia* instead of *metriopatheia*. See S. LILLA, Clement of Alexandria (Oxford, 1971) 60–117.

Isaac thus symbolizes the wise man whose psyche, being *apathēs*, generates only *eupatheiai* or rational emotions, and is thus analogous to the Stoic sage who acts out of a fixity of disposition, no longer having to struggle to make rational decisions.[98] Moses, on the other hand, would appear to symbolize the god-like man, "given as a loan to earthlings" (Sac. 8) (i.e., he belongs to that category of rational souls that ordinarily never leave the supernal spheres for embodiment below), who has achieved an absolute *apatheia* and is no longer affected in any way by human feelings, living as it were in the disembodied realm of pure *nous*.[99]

[98] The one apparent difference is that Isaac achieved this level without toil, being *automathēs* or self-taught, whereas the Stoic sage has had to struggle to attain it. This difference, however, is probably not very significant, since Seneca could say that some men are so blessed with *euphyia* that they seem to have attained wisdom virtually without effort (Ep. 95.36). On Moses see LA 3.128−134, 140−147; QG 4.177; QE 1.15. On Isaac: Abr. 201−204; Fug. 166−167; Somn 1.160; Sob. 8; Congr. 36; Det. 46; Mut. 1.
Philo's doctrine of the *pathē*, however, is not completely consistent with that of the Stoics. The latter, for example, placed pity (*eleos*) among the species of mental pain (*lypē*), thus classifying it as a *pathos* (SVF 1.213; 3.452; 433; Seneca Clement. 5), and undoubtedly had to defend this hard position against the frequent attacks of their opponents. Cf. Cicero Tusc. 4.26.56: "Why pity rather than give assistance if one can? Or are we unable to be open-handed without pity? We are able, for we ought not to share distress ourselves for the sake of others, but we ought to relieve others of their distress if we can." It is interesting to note that the Hasidic teaching with regard to pity resembles that of the Stoics and also that of SPINOZA (see n. 79 above). It was their view that one should help not out of pity but out of love. "Thus it is told of one zaddik that when a poor person had excited his pity, he provided first for all his pressing need, but then, when he looked inward and perceived that the wound of pity was healed, he plunged with great, restful and devoted love into the life and needs of the other, took hold of them as if they were his own life and needs and began in reality to help" (M. BUBER, Hasidism and Modern Man [New York, 1958] 120−121). Moreover, even Epictetus and Seneca are unable to maintain this lofty position with rigorous consistency, and occasionally slip into expressions which describe the wise man as indulging in this forbidden emotion (Epictetus 4.13.16; Seneca Beat. 24.1; Benefic. 6.29). It is therefore no wonder that Philo, under the further impetus of Jewish tradition, sometimes ascribes pity both to the wise man and to God (Sacr. 121; Deus 75−76; cf. Jos. 82; Virt. 144). Similarly, he speaks approvingly of righteous anger (*orgē dikaia*: Fug. 90; Somn. 1.91; 2.7; Spec. 4.14; Mos. 1.302; cf. Aristotle EN 1125b, 31−32) and hatred of evil (*misoponēria*: Mos. 2.9; Spec. 1.55; 4.170; cf. Ps-Aristotle Virtut. et Vit. 1250b, 23−24; Plutarch Stoic Repug. 25, where it is condemned by Chrysippus; D.L. 7.111, 113). It may be noted that *misoponēria* was a quality ascribed to kings in so many inscriptions and papyri that it may be said to be a commonplace in official Ptolemaic literature; cf. Aristeas to Philocrates 280, 292. Finally, although he awards it only the second prize and recognizes the bitterness attached to it (QE 1.15), he nevertheless places repentance among the virtues and considers it the mark of a man of wisdom (Virt. 177; Abr. 26; Somn. 1.91; Spec. 1.103 ["in the souls of the repentant there remain in spite of all, the scars and prints of their old misdeeds"]; cf. Plato Gorg. 524E; Seneca De Ira 1.16.7; b. Yoma 86a); QE 1.82; Praem. 163). It is revealing, however, that he casually refers to repentance in another context as an irrational emotion (Aet. 40). For the Stoic attitude, see SVF 3.548; cf. Aristotle EN 1166b, 24−25.

[99] This seems to be the conclusion that must be drawn from Mig. 67, where it appears that Moses' excision of *epithymia* and *thymos* signifies his excision of all desire and the entire

He is thus contrasted with Aaron, the man still making moral progress, who practices only *metriopatheia*, or moderation of passion (LA 3.129).[100] The Stoic doctrine of *apatheia*, however, has been widely misunderstood both in ancient and in modern scholarship,[101] and we must therefore provide further amplification of this concept. The *apatheia* of the Stoic sage did not signify the elimination of all emotion, but rather only of *pathē*, defined by the Stoics as diseased or irrational emotions (in SPINOZA's terminology: "passive emotions", the result of "inadequate" ideas). The sage, who is guided only by an *orthos logos*, experiences only *eupatheiai* or rational emotions (in SPINOZA's terminology: "active emotions", the result of "adequate" ideas).[102] The distinction

range of spirited feelings, with the result that his *logistikon* operates in a sort of emotional vacuum. For a detailed analysis of the Philonic depiction of Moses, see my forthcoming study on this topic.

[100] See SVF 3.443ff.: D. L. 5.31; cf. Aristeas to Philocrates 256; 4 Macc. 3.2—5. Although Philo describes Abraham as practicing *metriopatheia* at his wife's death (Abr. 257), he should in all strictness have described Abraham's grief and tears in this instance as a sort of "sting and minor soul contractions" (*morsus et contractiunculae quaedam animi*: Cicero, Tusc. 3.82), as he does, for example, in QG 4.73; Gr. frag., LCL, suppl. 2 Marcus, p. 220, where we are told that Abraham experienced not a *pathos* but a *propatheia*. Cf. Aristotle De Motu Anim. 703b5.20; De Anima 3.9. For a full discussion of this question, see D. WINSTON, Philo of Alexandria (New York, 1981) 377—378, n. 531, and my forthcoming study of 'Philo's Doctrine of the Nature of God'.

[101] See L. EDELSTEIN, The Meaning of Stoicism (Cambridge, 1966) 2—4; J. RIST, Stoic Philosophy (Cambridge, 1969) 24—27; A. BONHÖFFER, Epictet und die Stoa (Stuttgart, 1890) 284ff.; F. H. SANDBACH, The Stoics (London, 1975) 59—68. WOLFSON believes that Philo, considering *eupatheiai* as virtues, is using that term in a sense which differs from the usage of the Stoics, since the latter, he claims, refused to identify them as virtues, reserving that designation only for a state of complete *apatheia* (WOLFSON [cited n. 25] 2.274—276). Such an interpretation, however, would render the Stoic position essentiallly incoherent, and although some of the ancient authors wrote "as if the *eupatheiai* were identifiable with correct impulses towards or from morally indifferent objects" (Plutarch Moralia 149A; Cicero Tusc. 4.12—14; Lactantius Div. Inst. 6.15), we should probably attribute this, as SANDBACH has suggested, to their misunderstanding of the Stoic theory. Moreover, as SANDBACH had pointed out, Andronicus of Rhodes, listing Stoic definitions of virtues and vices, *pathē* and *eupatheiai*, explained two kinds of joy as due to the presence of truly good things and caution as the avoidance of immoral acts (SVF 3.432). Similarly, Seneca defined joy as the mental elation of a man who trusts in his own goods and truths (Ep. 59); see SANDBACH (cited n. 101) 67—68. (In Det. 120, however, Philo's use of the term *eupatheia* differs from the strict Stoic usage; see COLSON and WHITTAKER ad loc. [LCL 2.495].) In short, *apatheia* was not conceived by the Stoics in a merely negative manner, but also positively as a state in which the *pathē* have been replaced by *eupatheiai*. It was their critics who sought to brand the Stoic sage as not only passionless, but also as a completely unfeeling and bloodless automaton of reason.

[102] There were four generic kinds of *pathē*: fear (*phobos*), lust (*epithymia*), mental pain (*lypē*), mental pleasure (*hēdonē*). The three *eupatheiai* (in Latin *constantiae*) were: wish or well-reasoned appetite (*boulēsis*), caution or well-reasoned avoidance (*eulabeia*), joy or well-reasoned elation (*chara*) (Cicero Tusc. 4.14; D. L. 7.116; Virgil Aen. 6.733). See especially SANDBACH's excellent analysis (cited n. 101).

between the Stoic and Peripatetic position has been described by SANDBACH[103] as follows:

> "This aim of being without passions was contrasted with the ideal of moderation in passion (*metriopatheia*) adopted by Peripatetics in dependence on Aristotle, who had held that it was wrong to feel either too little or too much fear, anger, or other emotion. The distinction although justified, can be exaggerated. The Stoic passion is an excessive uncontrolled drive, due to an overestimation of indifferent things, but there is also a correct drive towards these same things. The moderate passion of the Peripatetic is a correct feeling, and so could perhaps not be regarded by a Stoic as passion at all. But members of the two schools would be likely to differ over what was correct. What a Peripatetic would regard as a correct amount of anger or of fear would seem excessive to a Stoic."

This description is, in my view, inaccurate. The Peripatetic ideal did not involve complete elimination of irrational emotions, but only their moderation and control. The moderate passion of the Peripatetic would thus in no way be equivalent to the Stoic *eupatheia*, which is a completely rational feeling from the very first and requires no moderation. The Stoic sage, guided by an infallible process of reasoning, engenders within his psyche only rational emotions, since they are the result of perfectly rational ideas as to what is best for the human organism in its drive to increase its power to persevere in its own existence. The Peripatetic man of practical wisdom (the *sōphrōn*) would always feel the correct amount of fear or grief, whereas the Stoic wise man would never experience fear in the first place, since for him there is no correct amount of this emotion, but only a completely rational feeling of caution or wariness which constitutes its rational equivalent. Grief, on the other hand, which according to the Stoics has no rational equivalent, he would never be subject to in any form, experiencing at the most a mental sting or minor soul contractions, which are morally neutral and betray not the slightest trace of irrationality. Their Peripatetic opponents undoubtedly argued that such a psychic state was an impossible ideal and untrue to the human condition, but in any case, the chasm dividing the two schools was a deep one and due to substantive pilosophical differences.

That Philo was not insensitive to the Peripatetic criticism may be seen from a passage such as the following:

> "For the present we will follow the oracle and say that wisdom is indeed something existent, and so too the lover of wisdom, the wise man, but though he exists he is concealed from us who are evil, for good is unwilling to associate with bad."[104]

---

[103] SANDBACH (cited n. 101) 63—64; cf. RIST (cited n. 101) 24—27, who suggests that the difference between the Stoics and Peripatetics may have been only a semantic one.

[104] Cf. LA 1.102; Virt. 10; Gig. 2; Prob. 72; Mut. 213, 225; Praem. 26; Somn. 2.145; Mos. 2.147; Fug. 104; Spec. 1.252. The Stoics themselves were willing to admit the extreme rarity of the wise man. Cf. Seneca Ep. 42.1: The wise man, like the phoenix, appears once in five hundred years; Tranq. An. 7.4; SVF 3.545: "Wherefore on account of their

Moreover, Philo devoted much energy to the elucidation of the various stages on
the road to perfect wisdom. Only soul types endowed with the most extraordinary natural talents, symbolized for Philo by Isaac, Moses, and Melchizedek,
could achieve ethical perfection with little or no effort. The great patriarch
Abraham himself had to travel a difficult road before he could leave the level of
the heaven-born (who reach only as high as God's two Powers) and achieve citizenship among the God-born (who reach the One Logos), freemen of the commonwealth of Ideas (Gig. 60; cf. Her. 45). Although even the earth-born, or men of
blood, who are devoted to the pleasures of the body, enjoy occasional flashes of
higher truth, they are nevertheless unable to perceive the intelligible realities with
any degree of continuity (Gig. 20; 60; Her. 57). The heaven-born, for their part,
seize only one side of the divine polarity, either love or fear, and therefore worship God only through either one of those two modes, thus honoring him for
their own sakes (Deus 60—69; Gig. 47; Fug. 97; Plant. 90). Although not rejected
by the all-giving deity who begrudges no approach towards him, however imperfect, they carry off only the second prize, the first being reserved for the God-
born, who honor God for his sake alone (Abr. 124—130).[105] The latter have
grasped the divine polarity entire, and for them the deity is both God and Lord
(κύριος ὁμοῦ καὶ θεός: Mut. 19). This double aspect of the Logos is described by
Philo in a passage which reaches a high pitch of religious emotion:

> "He who says, 'Master, what will you give me?' virtually says the following:
> 'I am not unaware of your surpassing power, I know the fearfulness of your
> lordship; I approach you in fear and trembling, and yet again I am confident.
> For it was you who made known to me that I should have no fear; you have
> "given me an instructed tongue that I should know when to speak" (Isa. 50:
> 4), my mouth that was sewed up you have unraveled, and having opened it
> you rendered it more articulate; you have taught me to say what should be
> said, confirming the oracle "I will open your mouth, and teach you what
> you shall speak" (Exord. 4:12). For who was I that you should give me a share
> in speech, that you should promise me a "reward," a more perfect good than
> "grace" or "gift." Am I not a migrant from my country; was I not expelled
> from my kinsfolk; was I not alienated from my father's house? Do not all
> men call me disinherited, fugitive, desolate, disfranchised? You, Master, are
> my country, my kinsfolk, my paternal hearth, my franchise, my free
> speech, my great and glorious and inalienable wealth. Why then shall I not
> fearlessly speak my mind? . . . Yet I who assert my confidence concede in
> turn my feelings of terror and fear, though the fear and confidence do not
> wage irreconcilable war within me, as one might suppose, but constitute a

extreme magnitude and beauty we seem to be stating things which are like fictions and not
in accordance with man or human nature." See also the fascinating account of the Jewish
and Muslim legends of hidden righteous ones by G. Scholem, Die 36 verborgenen Ge-
rechten in der jüdischen Tradition, in: Idem, Judaica (Frankfurt am Main, 1963) 216—225;
cf. R. F. Nicholson, The Mystics of Islam (London, 1914) 123 ff. (on the Muslim *walis*
or saints).

[105] See D. Winston (cited n. 100) 375, n. 500.

harmonious blend. I feast insatiably on this blend, which has persuaded me to be neither outspoken without caution, nor cautious without speaking freely. For I have learned to measure my own nothingness and to gaze in wonderment at the exceeding perfection of your loving-kindness. And when I perceive that I am "earth and ashes" or whatever is still more worthless, it is then that I have the courage to approach you, when I am humbled, relegated to dust, reduced to the elemental point which seems not even to exist.'" [Her. 24–291].[106]

We have thus found once again that emphatic Philonic distinction between the purely rational grasp of reality which characterizes the wise man and allows him to envision the cosmos as a unified organism and the ultimately irrational understanding of all other men in which being is fragmented as its fitful and fleeting images undergo multiple refraction. At the summit of intuitive knowledge, the polarities of being are merged in the unity of the Logos, image of the unknowable Divine Essence, and the sage is thus enabled to function in a realm unmarred by contradiction or one-sidedness.

VI. Asceticism

The rational state of *apatheia* characterizing the wise man is envisaged by Philo neither as easily accessible nor as frequently attained. No secluded intellectual himself living in splendid isolation (LA 3.155; Fug. 28; Prob. 141; 26), nor yet fully at home in the turmoil of the political and social arena (Spec. 3.1–6), his sharpsigthed analysis of what constitutes the surest path to wisdom and happiness reflects his own unruffled yet passionate nature. It is characteristic of all created things, says Philo, that they are incomplete in themselves and stand at all times in reciprocal relationships with each other. Love draws them all together, ultimately producing a single harmony of perfections from the rich diversity of all being (Cher. 109–112). Although among earth-dwellers it is man's peculiar prerogative to seek out the ultimate unity of being, he can never dispense with his somatic nature and its material connection with all things. Even when his audacious mind bravely speeds away from the world of time and becoming to the realm of naked truth and eternal being, some part of him remains rooted below in the sphere of gross materiality. His loftiest achievement consists at best in living simultaneously on two diverse and discrete levels of being, after having successfully acquired a largely unbroken inner illumination from the rare flights of sober ecstasy which momentarily dot his upward-striving existence. Thus, for example, Porphyry said of Plotinus that he was able to live with other people and with himself at the same time (V.P. 8), that is, the activities of his lower self did not

[106] See Y. AMIR, Philo's Derashot on Fear and Love and their Relationship to the Palestinian Midrashim (Hebrew), Zion 30 (1965) 47–60; URBACH (cited n. 46) 348–370.

distract his higher self from its intellectual contemplation.[107] This rare style of dichotomous behavior which apparently characterizes Philo's sage, results in similarly divided statements on the part of Philo as to what constitutes the proper attitude towards the human body and its needs. The latter is by no means to be neglected, nor is its well-being deliberately to be compromised in any way. Philo, indeed, praises the divine skill which brings mind and bodily sense together by means of the subtle serpent pleasure, since otherwise there could be no intellectual apprehension at all (LA 2.71–73). Virtue signifies man's power of action, both bodily and mental, at which "the man of worth will aim as being most akin to himself", whereas vice signifies "impotence and weakness which are alien to upright character" (Virt. 167).[108] Those who needlessly fast or refuse the bath and oil, or are careless about their clothing and lodging, thinking that they are thereby practising self-control, are to be pitied for their error. They are similar to those counterfeits who never cease making sacrificial and costly votive offerings in their mistaken belief that piety consists in ritual rather than holiness, and thus attempt to flatter One who cannot be flattered and who abhors all counterfeit approaches (Det. 19–21). Moreover, it is a false strategy to oppose irrational desires by taking off in the opposite direction and practising austerities, "for in this way you will rouse your adversary's spirit and stimulate a more dangerous foe to the contest against you" (Fug. 25). Better to indulge in the various pursuits for external goods, but to do so with skillful moderation and self-control.[109] Many of

---

[107] See especially Plotinus 4.4.44. There is no indication, however, in Philo, as there is in Plotinus (2.9.2; 4.3.12; 4.8.8; 5.1.10), that a part of the soul remains forever above in contemplation of the eternal Forms. V.P. 8.10: "Even if he was talking to someone, engaged in continuous conversation, he kept to his train of thought . . . 20: In this way he was present at once to himself and to others, and he never relaxed his self-turned attention except in sleep (Συνῆν οὖν καὶ ἑαυτῷ ἅμα καὶ τοῖς ἄλλοις, καὶ τήν γε πρὸς ἑαυτὸν προσοχὴν οὐκ ἄν ποτε ἐχάλασεν, ἢ μόνον ἐν τοῖς ὕπνοις)." This was also the teaching of some of the Hasidic masters. R. Meshullam Phoebus, for example, says of the sage that he is divided within himself, and though going through the physical motions of sexual activity or the taking of food, "he is within like an angel, completely withdrawn from the material, whereas externally he is in the eyes of the beholders like an animal" (Derek Emet 19a). Meshulam interprets the statement in b. Shabbat 13a concerning 'Ula (who had kissed his sisters on their breast): pĕlîge dîdêh 'adîdêh (i. e., his [action] was divided from his [teaching]) to mean that he was divided within himself "from himself to himself." See R. Shatz-Uffenheimer, Quietistic Elements in 18th Century Hasidic Thought (Jerusalem, 1968) 52 (Hebrew). Cf. Maimonides Guide 3.51. For Naḥmanides' definition of devekut (or communion with God) which involved a blend of action and contemplation, see G. Scholem, Devekut or Communion with God, in: Idem, The Messianic Idea in Judaism (New York, 1971) 203–227.

[108] Cf. Spinoza, Ethics 4. Def. 8: "By virtue and power I mean the same thing" (see also ibid. prop. 18, schol.).

[109] Cf. Spec. 4.102 ("Moses opened up a path midway between Spartan austerity and Sybarite luxury"); Deus 162–165 (where Philo espouses the Aristotelian mean [EN 2.6–7], identifying the mesē hodos with the basilikē hodos leading to God); Post. 101; Mig. 147. "The presence of this Aristotelian doctrine in Plutarch (Moral. 84A; 444CD), Albinus (Did. 184.13f.), and Apuleius (De Plat. 2.228)", writes Lilla, "is most probably due to the fact that Antiochus of Ascalon and Arius Didymus (Stobaeus 2.39.11ff.), who both

those who turn away from the practical side of life, pretending to have conceived a contempt for fame and pleasure, are in reality practising an imposture, and are quite incapable of deceiving the more sharp-sighted.

"First, then, practice and apply yourselves in the affairs of both private and public life; and when by means of the sister virtues, household management and statesmanship, you have become statesmen and managers, make your migration, amidst this state of luxury, to a different and better way of life. For before the contemplative life it is well to struggle through the practical life, as a sort of prelude to a more perfect contest . . . Moreover, it is essential that those who deem it right to lay claim to the obligations toward God should first fulfill those toward men; for it is sheer naiveté to assume that you will attain to the greater when you are unable to surmount the lesser." [Fug. 36–38].[110]

As a matter of fact, even the wise man will indulge in heavy drinking though in the more moderate manner of the ancients rather than in the style of the moderns who drink "till body and soul are unstrung." For:

"the nature of wisdom is not somber and severe, constricted by anxiety and gloom, but on the contrary cheerful and serene, full of joy and gladness, conditions that often induce a man to sport and jest not untastefully."[111]

Moses, holiest of men, has indicated that sport and merriment is the height of wisdom by designating Isaac, the self-learner, as laughter itself (Plant. 167–168).[112] Drunkenness, according to Philo, reduces the overstrain and undue in-

greatly influenced the growth of Middle Platonism, expounded it at some length in their works" (LILLA [cited n. 97] 65). Antiochus' position, however, on this matter is far from clear, see DILLON (cited n. 37) 77. Philo, however, frequently emphasizes the need to be content with little, for the less one needs the closer one is to God (Virt. 8–9); cf. Xenophon Mem. 1.6.10; Philo Somn. 1.97; QG 2.67; Praem. 99–100; Virt. 6 ("in the judgement of truth not a single one is in want, for his needs are supplied by the wealth of nature which cannot be taken from him"); Prob. 77; Ebr. 214–215; Cont. 37–39; Xenophon Mem. 1.3.5; Musonius (in Stobaeus 751; 526.16; 173). For a detailed analysis of this theme and the parallel Cynic and Stoic sources, see P. WENDLAND, Philo und die kynischstoische Diatribe (Berlin, 1895).

[110] Fug. 36: πρότερον οὖν ἐγγυμνάσασθε καὶ προεμμελετήσατε τοῖς τοῦ βίου πράγμασιν ἰδίοις τε καὶ κοινοῖς καὶ γενόμενοι πολιτικοί τε καὶ οἰκονομικοὶ δι' ἀδελφῶν ἀρετῶν, οἰκονομικῆς τε καὶ πολιτικῆς, κατὰ πολλὴν περιουσίαν τὴν εἰς ἕτερον καὶ ἀμείνω βίον ἀποικίαν στείλασθε· τὸν γὰρ πρακτικὸν τοῦ θεωρητικοῦ βίου, προάγωνά τινα ἀγῶνος τελειοτέρου, καλὸν πρότερον διαθλῆσαι. 38: καὶ ἄλλως ἀναγκαῖον, τοὺς τῶν θείων ἀξιοῦντας μεταποιεῖσθαι δικαίων τὰ ἀνθρώπεια πρότερον ἐκπληρῶσαι· πολλὴ γὰρ εὐήθεια τῶν μειζόνων ὑπολαμβάνειν ἐφίξεσθαι ἀδυνατοῦντας τῶν ἐλαττόνων περιγίγνεσθαι (translation my own).

[111] ὅτι οὐ σκυθρωπὸν καὶ αὐστηρὸν τὸ τῆς σοφίας εἶδος, ὑπὸ συννοίας καὶ κατηφείας ἐσταλμένον, ἀλλ' ἔμπαλιν ἱλαρὸν καὶ γαληνίζον, μεστὸν γηθοσύνης καὶ χαρᾶς· ὑφ' ὧν πολλάκις προήχθη τις οὐκ ἀμούσως παῖξαί τι καὶ χαριεντίσασθαι (translation my own).

[112] Cf. Det. 138: "he that is despondent is not man"; QG 4.188: "God continually rejoices in his life and plays and is joyful, finding pleasure in play which is in keeping with the divine."

tensity of body and mind, and thus only intensifies the wise man's *eupatheiai* (cf. Legat. 82; QG 2.68).[113]

If the body is thus not to be neglected or compromised in any way, neither is it to be allowed to become the central focus of human concern or to usurp the higher dignity reserved for the rational element. Pleasure, as we have already seen, plays a crucial role in the life of ensouled creatures, but it must be accepted for what it really is and not elevated into a self-validating principle motivating human behavior. Following the teaching of Aristotle and the Stoics, Philo insists that joy, as well as pleasure, has no intrinsic importance, but is purely adventitious, a supervening aftermath or by-product of virtue (Det. 124; LA 3.80).[114] Moreover, although *hēdonē* in the sense of agreeable physical feelings is permitted even to the wise man, this is not the case when it denotes that type of mental pleasure which is accounted a *pathos* by the Stoics, and is the result of a faulty judgment.[115] "The serpent, pleasure," writes Philo, "is bad of itself; and therefore it is not found at all in a good man, the bad man getting all the harm of it by himself. Quite appropriately therefore does God pronounce the curse without giving pleasure an opportunity of defending herself, since she has in her no seed from which virtue might spring, but is always and everywhere guilty and foul" (LA 3.68).[116]

The body is for Philo, at best, a necessary evil (LA 3.72—73; cf. Her. 272), for it is a corpse, a shell-like growth (cf. Plato Phaedr. 250 C), "the dwelling-place

---

[113] Cf. Diogenes of Babylon, according to whom music promoted the kind of drinking-party that could be approved: "No form of play and relaxation is more suitable for free men than that one should sing, another play the cithara, another dance . . ." (SVF 3. Diogenes Babylonius 79). See SANDBACH (cited n. 101) 116. For the Stoic debate on whether the wise man will get drunk, see the excellent discussion in RIST (cited n. 101) 18—19. Cf. also Clement Paed. 2.32, where he defends wine-drinking). In Cont. 73 and QG 2.67, however, Philo suggests that the use of wine is superfluous, and in Agr. 35; Mos. 2.211; and Legat. 42 he warns against effeminate music and the frantic excitement brought on by dancers and scandalous scenes of mimes.

[114] Cf. Aristotle EN 1147b 31—33; D.L. 7.94, 86 (= SVF 3.76, 178); Arius Didymus, ap. Stobaeus 2.53.18; Albinus Did. 32:7 LOUIS (ἐπιγεννηματικὴ τῇ φύσει ὑπάρχουσα καὶ οὐδὲ οὐσιῶδες) (cf. Plato Phileb. 53 C: ἀεὶ γένεσίς ἐστιν, οὐσία δὲ οὐκ ἔστιν τὸ παράπαν ἡδονῆς).

[115] See SANDBACH (cited n. 101) 62: "If the pleasantness of experience of touch, sight, taste, smell and hearing was thought to be good and important, a pleasure arose that was passionate and to be censured (Cicero Tusc. 4.20), but the agreeable feelings themselves were not condemned by any Stoic, although there was no agreement on their exact status. Cleanthes denied that they were 'in accord with nature' or had any value in life, Archedemus thought that they were natural but without value, like the hairs in the armpit, while Panaetius believed some to be natural and others not." See Sextus Math. 11.73; and cf. E. ZELLER, The Stoics, Epicureans and Sceptics, transl. by O. J. REICHEL (London, 1892; repr. New York, 1962) 237—238.

[116] Cf. LA 3.107 (where *hēdonē* is considered the passion par excellence); Op. 160—161 (where the Epicureans are attacked as defenders of pleasure); Spec. 4.84 (where *epithymia*, an animal insatiable and incontinent [cf. Plato Tim. 70 E], is designated the fountain of all evils).

of endless calamities" (Conf. 177), wicked by nature and a plotter against the soul (LA 3.69). It is the source of both *agnoia* and *amathia*.[117]

> "For souls that are free from flesh and body spend their days in the theatre of the universe and with a joy that none can hinder see and hear things divine, which they have desired with love insatiable. But those which bear the burden of the flesh, oppressed by the grievous load, cannot look up to the heavens as they revolve, but with necks bowed downwards are constrained to stand rooted to the ground like four-footed beasts." [Gig. 29–31].[118]

Philo quotes with approval Heraclitus' saying 'we live their death, and are dead to their life'. "He means", explains Philo, "that now, when we are living, the soul is dead and has been entombed in the body as in a sepulchre; whereas should we die, the soul lives forthwith its own proper life, and is released from the body, the baneful corpse to which it was tied" (LA 1.108).[119] The soul that loves God will therefore disrobe itself of the body and the objects dear to it (LA 2.55);[120] it will kill the body and its senses (Ebr. 69–70), and devoting itself to genuine philosophy will "from first to last study to die to the life in the body" (Gig. 14).[121]

The three major roads to this higher life Philo represents by two triads of biblical figures, the first (Enosh, Enoch, Noah) symbolizing the beginning of man's striving toward perfection, and the second (Abraham, Isaac, and Jacob) its culmination. The latter are in reality:

> "soul types, all of them virtuous, one that aims at the good through teaching, one through nature and one through practice . . . But we must not fail to recognize that each of the three lays claim to the three qualities, but received his name from that which greatly predominated in him; for teaching

---

[117] Plato had already made a sharp distinction between *agnoia* and *amathia*. The former designates a lack of *epistēmē*, "a kind of emptiness (*kenotēs*) of habit of the soul" (Rep. 585 B; cf. Her. 297), which can be filled by *nous* and *trophē* (reason and training). The latter, on the other hand, is a condition of fundamental ignorance (cf. Ebr. 162: ἀλλὰ καὶ οἴηται εἰδέναι ἃ μηδαμῶς οἶδε δόξῃ ψευδεῖ σοφίας ἐπαιρόμενος) produced by *apaideutos trophē* or improper training, and a πονηρὰν ἕξιν τοῦ σώματος or a faulty habit of body due to a physiological defect (Tim. 86 B ff.; cf. also Sophist 228 ff.).

[118] Gig. 31: ψυχαὶ μὲν γὰρ ἄσαρκοι καὶ ἀσώματοι ἐν τῷ τοῦ παντὸς θεάτρῳ διημερεύουσαι θεαμάτων καὶ ἀκουσμάτων θείων, ὧν ἄπληστος αὐτὰς εἰσελήλυθεν ἔρως, μηδενὸς κωλυσιεργοῦντος ἀπολαύσουσιν. ὅσαι δὲ τὸν σαρκῶν φόρτον ἀχθοφοροῦσι, βαρυνόμεναι καὶ πιεζόμεναι ἄνω μὲν βλέπειν εἰς τὰς οὐρανίους περιόδους ἀδυνατοῦσι, κάτω δὲ ἑλκυσθεῖσαι τὸν αὐχένα βιαίως δίκην τετραπόδων γῇ προσερρίζωνται (translation my own). Cf. Wisd. 9:15, and my Anchor commentary ad loc.; Plant. 16–27; QG 4.46; Plato Tim. 90 A.

[119] Cf. Plato Gorg. 493 A; Craty. 400 B. There is a veiled reference here to that unpleasant story about the Etruscans, that they tied live men to corpses as a punishment (Aristotle Protr., fr. 10·b Ross) — an exemplum which had plainly by this time become a Sophistic commonplace. See LEISEGANG, note on Gig. 15, and DILLON (cited n. 37) 149.

[120] Isaac does not indeed become naked, but is always naked and without body (LA 2.59).

[121] Cf. Plato Phaedo 67 E, 64 A; Her. 239–240, 292; Cont. 34; Conf. 106; Mig. 9, 16, 204; Deus 2; Fug. 91; LA 1.103.

cannot be consummated without nature or practice, nor is nature capable of reaching its end without learning or practice, nor practice either unless there was the prior foundation of nature and teaching." [Abr. 52–53].[122]

It is clear, however, from many passages, that the superior gift is that of the privileged few who are so naturally endowed that they achieve wisdom virtually without effort.[123] It is evident from the passages already quoted, that for the average man it is necessary first to train within the sphere of everyday practical life before attempting loftier heights. The practisers, however, go continually up and down, and as mere *prokoptontes* (who are still in the region between the living and the dead: Somn. 2.234) are liable to reverse course and slip back into their former habits. "For many, after beginning to practise virtue, have changed at the last: but on the man to whom God affords secure knowledge, he bestows both advantages, both that of tilling the virtues, and also that of never desisting from them" (LA 1. 89;[124] cf. Gig. 48). There is yet a more subtle stage, in which the individual has already laid aside all passions and vices, but his assurance has not yet been tested. He can no longer slip back into the faults from which he has escaped, but he is not yet aware of this fact. Such a one has not yet attained wisdom, says Seneca, but has already gained a place nearby (Ep. 75.9).[125] It would appear that it is to this stage that Philo is alluding when he says that "the destruction and removal of passion is a good, yet it is not a perfect good, but the discovery of wisdom is a thing of transcendent excellence" (Somn. 2.270).[126]

---

[122] Cf. Plato Meno 70 A; Isocrates Antid. 186–188; Aristotle Polit. 1332a 38; EN 1103a 14; 1170a 11–12; D.L. 5.18; SVF 3.214; Antiochus of Ascalon (Cicero Ac. Post. 1.20, 38); Arius Didymus (Stobaeus 2.38.3; 2.51.5); Ps-Plutarch De lib. ed. 2A–B, 3A; Plutarch Moral. 554C; Albinus Did. 182.3–5; Apuleius de Plat. 2.222–223; Maximus of Tyre Or. 1.5d; 1.4d; Clement Strom. 1.31.5; 1.34.1. Plato seems to have limited the role of training to ordinary moral virtue. The intellectual virtues cannot be taught (Rep. 7. 518D, and SHOREY's note ad loc. in LCL Phaedo 82 AB 3). On the need for *euphyia* and *didaskalia*, see Cher. 101–105; cf. Mut. 211–213; 219; Deus 93; Sac. 113–117 (where Philo makes one exception to the rule that all effort is useless when ability is wanting, i.e., in the case of moral effort); Somn. 2.37 (where Philo defines *euphyia* as consisting of quickness of apprehension, persistence and goodness of memory).

[123] See Congr. 34–36; Mut. 256; QG 1.8; Sac. 64, 78; Deus 92–93; LA 3.125; Mig. 167, and COLSON's note ad loc.; cf. however, Post. 95, and COLSON and WHITTAKER's note ad loc.

[124] πολλοὶ γὰρ ἀσκηταὶ γενόμενοι τῆς ἀρετῆς ἐπὶ τοῦ τέλους μετέβαλον· ᾧ δὲ παρέχει ὁ θεὸς ἐπιστήμην βεβαίαν, τούτῳ δίδωσιν ἀμφότερα, ἐργάζεσθαί τε τὰς ἀρετὰς καὶ μηδέποτε αὐτῶν ἀφίστασθαι.

[125] According to the Stoics the wise man will not notice that he has actually become wise (SVF 3.539–542). Chrysippus, who speaks only of two classes (as Epictetus 4.2, but unlike Seneca, who repeats a threefold classification) says of the man who has advanced to the point where he only just falls short of wisdom or perfection: "He fulfills all appropriate actions in all respects and omits none; but his life is not yet in a state of well-being. This supervenes when these intermediate actions acquire the additional property of firmness (*to bebaion*), consistency (or habituation: *hektikon*), and their own proper coordination (or fixity: *idian pēxin*)" (SVF 3.510; Epictetus Ench. 48; cf. 3.657–670). Philo similarly uses the word *pēxis* at Agr. 160, where he reproduces Seneca's threefold classification.

[126] At Agr. 161, Philo refers explicitly to those who have reached this stage, using the Stoic expression διαλεληθότες σοφοί (unwitting wise men; see SVF 3.539–540).

Philo warns, however, against the danger of prolonging the training stage beyond its proper bounds,

> "since he who was a fighter by nature and had never become the slave of passions, but was constantly struggling with each of them, is not permitted to continue his wrestlings to the end, lest by his uninterrupted meeting with them he take on a serious blemish . . . Make an end now of your love of contentiousness, so that you may not be forever toiling, but have the capacity to benefit from your efforts. This you will never find if you remain here, dwelling still among the objects of sense, and spending your time amid corporeal qualities." [Mig. 26–28].[127]

The *prokoptōn* must presently take flight from the sense-perceptible realm, leaving behind not only the passions but external goods too, though not through faint-heartedness or inexperience of them, but rather under the guidance of right reason (Deus 150–153). "Great ventures such as these betoken a celestial and heavenly soul, which has left the region of the earth, has been drawn upwards, and dwells with divine natures" (ibid. 151). Such a mind, says Philo in connection with Moses, "has learned to gaze upward and frequent the heights, and as it ever haunts the upper atmosphere and closely examines the divine loveliness, it scoffs at earthly things, considering them to be mere child's play" (Mos. 1.190).[128] At Spec. 2.44–46, he describes the wise men as avoiding the gatherings of busybodies, such as law-courts, council-chambers, markets, congregations and in general any assemblage of careless men.[129] The former are the superb observers of nature, who,

> "while their bodies are fixed upon the earth, give wings to their souls, so that treading the ether they may fully inspect the powers residing in it, as behooves those who have become cosmopolitans, and have recognized the world to be a city whose citizens are the associates of wisdom, registered as such by virtue, to whom is entrusted the governing of the universal commonwealth. Filled with nobility and accustomed to having no regard for bodily or external ills, practiced in showing utter indifference to things in-

---

[127] ὁπότε καὶ τὸν ἀγωνιστὴν φύσει καὶ μηδέποτε παθῶν δοῦλον γεγενημένον, ἀεὶ δὲ ἀθλοῦντα τοὺς πρὸς ἕκαστον αὐτῶν ἄθλους, οὐκ ἐᾷ μέχρι παντὸς τοῖς παλαίσμασι χρήσασθαι, μή ποτε τῷ συνεχεῖ τῆς εἰς ταὐτὸ συνόδου χαλεπὴν ἀπ' ἐκείνων κῆρα ἀναμάξηται (translation my own). Cf. Det. 64–65.

[128] ἄνω γὰρ μεμάθηκε βλέπειν τε καὶ φοιτᾶν καὶ μετεωροπολοῦσα ἀεὶ καὶ τὰ θεῖα διερευνωμένη κάλλη χλεύην τίθεται τὰ ἐπίγεια, ταῦτα μὲν παιδιάν, ἐκεῖνα δὲ σπουδὴν ὡς ἀληθῶς νομίζουσα. See E. R. DODDS, Pagan and Christian in an Age of Anxiety (Cambridge, 1965) 7–10: "In the recurrent *topos* of the flight of the soul through the universe . . . we can trace a growing contempt for all that may be done and suffered beneath the moon" (Cicero Somn. Scip. 3.16; Seneca N.Q. 1, praef. 8; Ps-Aristotle De Mundo 8, 391a 18ff.). To Gregory of Nyssa, human affairs are but the play of children building sand castles which are promptly washed away. See also FESTUGIÈRE (cited n. 28) 2.449ff.

[129] Cf. SVF 3.703: "I think that the wise man does not meddle in the affairs of government, is of a retiring nature, and attends to his own affairs." For the ambivalence of both Philo and the Stoics in this matter, see my forthcoming study on this question.

different . . . unbowed by fortune's assaults through advance calculations
of its onsets, since the heaviest adversities are lightened by anticipation,
when the mind no longer finds anything novel in the events and apprehends
them but dully as if they were déjà vu and stale – such men naturally rejoice
in virtue and make their whole life a feast." [Spec. 2.45–46].[130]

The Stoic sage, similarly, never aims at things which he cannot achieve, subordinating his individual needs whenever they conflict with the universal plan.
According to Seneca, "the wise man comes to everything with the proviso 'if
nothing happens to prevent it'; therefore we say that he succeeds in everything
and nothing happens contrary to his expectation, because he presupposes that
something can intervene to prevent his design" (Benef. 4.34.4; cf. Tranq. An. 13.
2–3; SVF 3.482 and Cicero Tusc. 3.24–34, where it is represented as a Cyrenaic
view).[131]

We must now take a closer look at Philo's insistence that, in order to achieve
perfect wisdom, the *prokoptōn* must reject external goods under the guidance of
right reason. The Stoics had placed special stress on the notion that virtue is self-
sufficient for happiness (*autarkēs pros eudaimonian*) and the only good properly
speaking (*monon to kalon agathon*).[132] The Peripatetic view of the triple good

---

[130] τὰ μὲν σώματα κάτω πρὸς χέρσον ἱδρυμένοι, τὰς δὲ ψυχὰς ὑποπτέρους κατασκευά-
ζοντες, ὅπως αἰθεροβατοῦντες τὰς ἐκεῖ δυνάμεις περιαθρῶσιν, οἷα χρὴ τοὺς τῷ ὄντι
κοσμοπολίτας γενομένους, οἳ τὸν μὲν κόσμον ἐνόμισαν εἶναι πόλιν, πολίτας δὲ τοὺς
σοφίας ὁμιλητάς, ἀρετῆς ἐγγραφούσης, ᾗ πεπίστευται τὸ κοινὸν πολίτευμα πρυτα-
νεύειν. γέμοντες οὖν καλοκαγαθίας καὶ τῶν περὶ σῶμα κακῶν καὶ τῶν ἐκτὸς ἀλογεῖν
ἐθιζόμενοι καὶ ἐξαδιαφορεῖν τὰ ἀδιάφορα μελετῶντες . . . καὶ ταῖς τῆς τύχης μὴ
καμπτόμενοι προσβολαῖς διὰ τὸ προεκλελογίσθαι τὰς ἐπιθέσεις αὐτῆς – ἐπικουφίζει
γὰρ καὶ τὰ βαρύτατα τῶν ἀβουλήτων ἡ πρόληψις, καινὸν οὐδὲν ἔτι τῆς διανοίας τῶν
συμβαινόντων ὑπολαμβανούσης, ἀλλ' ὡς ἐπὶ παλαιοῖς καὶ ἑώλοις ἀμαυρὰν τὴν ἀν-
τίληψιν ποιουμένης –, εἰκότως ἐνευφραινόμενοι ταῖς ἀρεταῖς ἅπαντά γε τὸν βίον
ἑορτὴν ἄγουσιν (translation my own).
For the Stoic category of *adiaphora* see SVF 1.195; 3.117, 145–146. For the life of the wise
man as a feast, see Plutarch Moral. 20, and 4; I. HEINEMANN, Philons griechische und
jüdische Bildung (Breslau, 1930; repr. Hildesheim, 1962) 106–109. On the value of
prolēpsis (*praemeditatio*) as alleviating *lypē*, see the discussion in Cicero Tusc. 3.24–34 and
52 ff. and SVF 3.482.

[131] *ceterum ad omnia cum exceptione venit: „Si nihil inciderit, quod impediat." Ideo omnia illi
succedere dicimus et nihil contra opinionem accidere, quia praesumit animo posse aliquid
intervenire, quod destinata prohibeat.*

[132] See SVF 1.187; 3.29–45, 49–67; D.L. 7.101. Cf. Plato Rep. 387 DE; 385 D 11; Antiochus
of Ascalon, in Cicero Ac. Post. 1.22–23; Plutarch Virt. et Vit. 100 CD; Maximus of Tyre
Or. 12.62 b; Albinus Did. 180.33–35; 181.5 ff.; Apuleius De Plat. 2.238. According to
Cicero (Tusc. 5.29), the Old Academy in general, Speusippus, Xenocrates, and Polemon,
were united with Aristotle and Theophrastus in allowing that a modicum of physical and
external goods were essential to complete happiness. Eudorus, Atticus, and Hierax openly
criticize the Peripatetic view which regards happiness as dependent also on external goods
(Eudorus, ap. Arius Didymus in Stobaeus 2.42.7 ff.; Atticus and Hierax: Eusebius Pr.
Ev. 15.4.2 and 11; Stobaeus 4.31.92). Cf. also Plotinus 1.44; Justin Apol. 2.11; Clement Strom. 4.52.1–2; 5.96.5; 5.97.6. Antipater composed three books to prove against
Carneades that according to Plato *monon to kalon agathon* (SVF 3.56). "Albinus", writes

(Aristotle EN 1089 b; cf. SVF 3.136) is explicitly attacked by Philo. Joseph's coat of many colors, he says, indicates this tangled position. Joseph is

"one who molds his theories with an eye to statecraft rather than to truth. This appears in his treatment of the three kinds of good things, those pertaining to the outside world, to the body, and to the soul . . . He argues that each of the three classes mentioned has the character of a part or element and that it is only when they are all taken together in the aggregate that they produce happiness. In order, then, that he may be taught better ideas than these, he is sent to men who hold that nothing is a good thing but what has true beauty, and that this is a property belonging to the soul as soul."[Det. 7–9].[133]

In Her. 285–286, however, Philo seems to follow the compromise adopted by Antiochus of Ascalon, who distinguished the *vita beata*, which depends only on virtue, from the *vita beatissima*, which requires also the possibility of using external goods (Cicero Ac. Post. 1.22; 2.22; 1.134).[134] When will a man, asks Philo, have attained to a life of true bliss and happiness? "When there is welfare outside us, welfare in the body, welfare in the soul, the first bringing ease of circumstance and good repute, the second health and strength, the third delight in virtues."[135]

WITT, "states that the external goods are sometimes called by Plato *thnēta agatha*, a statement for which there is apparently no justification. The only verbal parallel I can discover is in Philo *Deus* 152." (R. E. WITT, Albinus and the History of Middle Platonism [Cambridge, 1937] 88). See, however, Laws 631 B, where Plato distinguishes between *anthrōpina* and *theia agatha*.

[133] πρὸς γὰρ πολιτείαν μᾶλλον ἢ πρὸς ἀλήθειαν φιλοσοφῶν τὰ τρία γένη τῶν ἀγαθῶν, τά τε ἐκτὸς καὶ περὶ σῶμα καὶ ψυχήν . . . τῶν γὰρ εἰρημένων ἕκαστον μερῶν τινα καὶ στοιχείων λόγον ἔχειν, ἀλλὰ κατὰ τὸ ἐκ πάντων ἄθροισμα. ταύτην οὖν τὴν δόξαν πέμπεται μεταδιδαχθησόμενος πρὸς ἄνδρας μόνον τὸ καλὸν ἀγαθὸν νομίζοντας, ὃ ψυχῆς ὡς ψυχῆς ἐστιν ἴδιον. Cf. Post. 95, 133; Spec. 2.48, 73; Deus 150–151; Ebr. 75; Virt. 5–6; Sob. 67–68; LA 2.17; Det. 122; QG 4.167.

[134] See A. LUEDER Die philosophische Persönlichkeit des Antiochos von Askalon (Göttingen, 1940) 56. In Ebr. 200–202, Philo uses the problem of the three-fold good as an example of the hopeless divisions of opinion among the philosophers.

[135] In QG 3.16, he writes that "felicity is the fulfillment of three perfections (or a prefection arising from three goods: MARCUS in note ad loc.), of spiritual goods, of corporeal goods, and of those which are external (cf. Clement of Alexandria Strom. 2.21.128, 5: συμπληροῦσθαι τοίνυν τὴν εὐδαιμονίαν ἐκ τῆς τριγενείας τῶν ἀγαθῶν). This doctrine was praised by some of the philosophers who came afterward, (such as) Aristotle and the Peripatetics. Moreover, this is said to have been also the legislation of Pythagoras . . . For in the end things happen to the soul which we manage to approach with difficulty, but first one must pass and run through the bodily and external goods, health and keenness of sense and beauty and strength, which are wont to flourish and grow and be attained in youth. And similarly those things which pertain to profit and selling, (such as) piloting and agriculture and trade. For all (this) is proper to youth." Here, however, Philo seems only to imply that external goods belong to the early stages of one's progress towards perfection; cf. QG 4.215; Seneca Ep. 92,1; Plato Laws 870 B. For the question of Philo's attitude toward external goods, see A. MICHEL, Quelques Aspects de la rhétorique chez

The rejection of external goods, however, must be, as we have seen, under the guidance of right reason. Improper intention or motivation can never yield virtuous action. According to the Stoics, to act appropriately is not in itself either good or bad in the sense of being morally good or bad. Accordingly, appropriate actions (*kathēkonta*) are designated as 'intermediate' (*mesa*). It is only when the latter are performed by a wise man that they become 'correct' or absolutely appropriate actions (*katorthōmata*) (SVF 3.516—517; cf. LA 1.56). Those who perform "any right action", says Philo, "without the assent of their judgement or will, but by doing violence to their inclination, do not achieve righteousness, but are wounded and chased by their inward feelings" (Deus 100). Similarly, "there is not a single bad man who really performs a sacrificial act, even though he lead to the altar in unceasing procession ten thousand bullocks every day; for in his case the mind, the most essential victim, is a blemished thing, and no blemish may come into contact with an altar" (Plant. 164).[136]

In sum, the ascetic strain in Philo's thought must be seen in its distinctive philosophical context to be adequately understood. Like any good Platonist, Philo would much prefer to dispense with material reality and the human body which constitutes an inseparable part of it. As a pilosophical realist, however, he accepts it and, like Plato and Plotinus justifies its existence within the divine scheme of things. He consequently never loses track of the body's legitimate needs and functions, though he is keenly aware of its capacity to entrap and entice the higher self. He believes that most men must wean themselves away from the physical aspect of things only very gradually and with the expenditure of much effort and toil, though he is aware of the psychological contamination which may result from too extended an exposure to bodily concerns.[137] He is convinced, however, that some, though not many, may ultimately succeed in focusing their minds much of the time on the eternal realities, while yet going through the motions of somatic activity which will have finally faded away into insignificance.

Philon, in: PAL (colloque) 97—99; and DILLON (cited n. 37) 146—148. Cf. WOLFSON (cited n. 25) 2.297—303.

[136] Cf. LA 1.99; 3.210; Cher. 14; Decal. 177. This was precisely the attitude of the Sufis. "A man who had just returned from the pilgrimage came to Junayd. Junayd said: 'From the hour when you first journeyed from your home have you also been journeying away from all sins?' He said, 'No!' 'Then,' said Junayd, 'you have made no journey.' When you reached the slaughter-place and offered sacrifice, did you sacrifice the objects of worldly desire'? He said: 'No!' 'Then,' said Junayd, 'you have not sacrificed.'" See NICHOLSON (cited n. 104) 91—92.

[137] Cf. Cont. 18—20; Praem. 17—19: "For if a man has really come to despise pleasures and desires and resolved in all sincerity to take his stand above the passions, he must prepare for a change of abode and flee from home and country and kinsfolk and friends without a backward glance. For great is the attraction of familiarity." (See also Maimonides M. T. Hilkhot Teshuvah 2.4) Philo's attitude is perhaps best exemplified by what he says in QG 4.47: "There are three ways of life which are well known: the contemplative, the active and the pleasurable. Great and excellent is the contemplative; slight and unbeautiful is the pleasureable; small and not small is the middle one, which touches on, and adheres to, both of them. It is small by reason of the fact that it is a close neighbor to pleasure; but it is great because of its nearness and also its kinship to contemplation."

Selected Bibliography

R. ARNALDEZ, La Dialectique des Sentiments chez Philon, in: PAL – colloque (see list of abbreviations, above p. 373) 299–330.

Y. BAER, The Early Hasidim in Philo's Works and in Hebrew Tradition (Hebrew), Zion 18 (1953) 91–108.

A. BENGIO, La dialectique de Dieu et de l'homme chez Platon et chez Philon d'Alexandrie: une approche du concept d'ἀρετή chez Philon, Mémoire de maîtrise. University of Paris IV, 1971 (Paris, 1971).

T. BILLINGS, The Platonism of Philo Judaeus (Chicago, 1919) 47–87.

E. BRÉHIER, Les Idées philosophiques et religieuses de Philon d'Alexandrie, Études de Philosophie médiévale 8 (Paris, 1950) 250–310.

P. COURCELLE, Philon d'Alexandrie et le précepte delphique, in: Philomathés. Studies and Essays in Memory of Philip Merlan, ed. R. B. PALMER and R. HAMERTON-KELLY (The Hague, 1971) 245–250.

J. DANIÉLOU, Philon d'Alexandrie (Paris, 1958) 143–181.

A. DIHLE, art. Ethik, RAC 6 (1966) 698–701.

O. DREYER, Untersuchung zum Begriff des Gottgeziemenden in der Antike. Mit besonderer Berücksichtigung Philos von Alexandrien, Spudasmata 24 (Hildesheim–New York, 1970).

M. FIEDLER, Δικαιοσύνη in der diaspora-jüdischen und intertestamentlichen Literatur, Journal for the Study of Judaism 1 (1970) 120–143.

Z. FRÄNKEL, Zur Ethik der jüdischen alexandrinischen Philosophie, MGWJ 16 (1867) 241–252; 281–297.

F. GEIGER, Philo von Alexandreia als sozialer Denker, Tübinger Beiträge zur Altertumswissenshaft 14 (Stuttgart, 1932).

A. GUILLAUMONT, Philon et les Origines du Monachisme, in: PAL – colloque (see list of abbreviations, above p. 373) 361–374.

M. HARL, Adam et les deux arbres du Paradis chez Philon d'Alexandrie. Pour une histoire de la doctrine du libre-arbitre, Recherches de Science Religieuse 50 (1962) 321–388.

I. HEINEMANN, Philons griechische und jüdische Bildung, Bericht des jüdisch-theologischen Seminars Fränckelscher Stiftung 1929 (Breslau, 1930; repr. Hildesheim, 1962).

IDEM, Philo's Lehre vom Eid, in: Judaica. Festschrift für H. Cohen (Berlin, 1912) 109–113.

W. KNUTH, Der Begriff der Sünde bei Philon von Alexandria (Diss., Würzburg, 1934).

J. LAPORTE, La doctrine eucharistique chez Philon d'Alexandrie, Théologie historique 16 (Paris, 1972) 191–246.

A. LEVI, Il problema dell'errore in Filone d'Alessandria, Rivista critica di storia della Filosofia 5 (1950) 281–294.

A. MADDALENA, Filone Alessandrino, Biblioteca di Filosofia Saggi 2 (Milan, 1970).

J. MILGROM, On the Origins of Philo's Doctrine of Conscience, SP 3 (1974–75) 41–45.

A. V. NAZZARO, Il γνῶθι σαυτόν nell'epistemologia filoniana, Annali della Facoltà di lettere e filosofia dell'Università di Napoli 12 (1969–70) 49–86.

V. NIKIPROWETZKY, La Doctrine de l'elenchos chez Philon, in: PAL – colloque (see list of abbreviations, above p. 373) 255–274.

E. A. PANTASOPULOS, Die Lehre vom natürlichen und positiven Rechte bei Philo Judaeus (Munich, 1893).

A. PELLETIER, Les passions à l'assaut de l'âme d'après Philon, REG 78 (1965) 52–60.

S. Sandmel, The Confrontation of Greek and Jewish Ethics: Philo, De Decalogo, in: Judaism and Ethics, ed. D. J. Silver (New York, 1970) 163—176.

G. Segalla, Il problema della volontà libera in Filone Alessandrino, Studia Patavina 12 (1965) 3—31.

S. Titkin, Die Lehre von den Tugenden und Pflichten bei Philo von Alexandrien (Diss., Breslau, 1895).

E. Turowski, Die Widerspiegelung des stoischen Systems bei Philon von Alexandreia (Diss., Berne, 1927).

W. Völker, Fortschritt und Vollendung bei Philo von Alexandrien (Leipzig, 1938).

R. T. Wallis, The Idea of Conscience in Philo of Alexandria, SP 3 (1974—75) 27—40.

W. Warnach, Selbstliebe und Gottesliebe im Denken Philons von Alexandrien, in: Wort Gottes in der Zeit. Festschrift Karl Schelkle, ed. H. Feld, J. Nolte (Düsseldorf, 1973) 189—214.

P. Wendland, Philo und die kynisch-stoische Diatribe (Beiträge zur Geschichte der griechischen Philosophie) (Berlin, 1895).

Idem, Die Therapeuten und die philonische Schrift vom beschaulichen Leben (Leipzig, 1896).

H. Windisch, Die Frömmigkeit Philons und ihre Bedeutung für das Christentum (Leipzig, 1909).

D. Winston, Freedom and Determinism in Philo of Alexandria, SP 3 (1974—75) 47—70.

M. Wolff, Die philonische Ethik in ihren wesentlichen Punkten, Philosophische Monatshefte 15 (1879) 333—350.

H. A. Wolfson, Philo (Cambridge, 1974) 2.165—321.

Translations from Philo, unless otherwise noted, are from the Loeb translation of Colson and Whittaker, with occasional modifications. References to Albinus, Apuleius, Clement of Alexandria, Maximus of Tyre, Stobaeus, and the 'Excerpta ex Theodoto' are, unless otherwise stated, to the following editions:

Albinus, ed. C. F. Hermann, Platonis dialogi secundum Thrasylli tetralogias dispositi, vol. 6 (Leipzig, 1884).

Apuleius, De Platone et eius Dogmate, ed. P. Thomas (Leipzig, 1908).
—, Apologia, ed. R. Helm (Leipzig, 1963).

Clement of Alexandria, ed. O. Stählin, 3 vols., ed. L. Früchtel (vol. 1, 2nd ed., Leipzig, 1963; vol. 2, 3rd ed., Berlin, 1960; vol. 3, Leipzig, 1909).

The Excerpta ex Theodoto of Clement of Alexandria, ed. and trans. R. P. Casey (London, 1934).

Maximus of Tyre, Philosophumena, ed. H. Hobein (Leipzig, 1910).

Stobaeus, Anthologium, ed. C. Wachsmuth and C. Hense, vols. 1—4 (Berlin, 1881—1912).

All the references in the notes to my forthcoming studies on various Philonic themes are to parts of an extensive paper entitled: 'The Limits of Jewish Piety and Greek Philosophy in Philo's Thought: A Study in the Fusion and Coextension of Ideas' (to be published in 'Jewish and Christian Self-Definition, vol. 3: Hellenistic Judaism in the Diaspora', as part of the McMaster University Project on Judaism and Christianity in the Greco-Roman Period: The Process of Achieving Normative Self-Definition).

Philo's Politics. Roman Rule and Hellenistic Judaism

by RAY BARRACLOUGH, Brisbane, Queensland (Australia)

Contents

Introduction

Philo's legacy was not a long-lasting one within Judaism. In subsequent history his form of Judaistic belief was to be eclipsed in the Diaspora by the Pharisaism which dominated Judaism after the failure of the Bar Kochba revolt. It was the Pharisee Yohanan ben Zakkai[1] and neither Philo nor any Zealot-like leader who was the precursor of the subsequent development of Judaism. Yet Philo was still an important figure. He was involved in a most significant effort to present the rights of Jews to the emperor Gaius, heading an embassy from Alexandrian Jewry for that purpose. He was a voluminous writer well acquainted with Judaistic and Hellenistic forms of thought.

Philo's writings are a collection of philosophical treatises, expositions using literal and allegorical exegesis, polemics, and passages explicatory of Jewish ways and the rights and treatment of Jews in the Roman empire. The 'Legatio ad Gaium' and 'In Flaccum' come nearest to being direct sources on the history of Philo's time and especially of his community in Alexandria; the accounts of the patriarchs and Moses which fill his other writings, though following the Scriptural narrative, are written primarily to point to a way of life Philo had espoused through his amalgam of Jewish and Hellenistic ideas. From such an assortment of writings I have sought to gauge Philo's attitude to Roman rule as well as his ideas on politics in general.

Philo's world-view emerges from the incorporation of Hellenistic philosophic ideas drawn especially from Platonism, Stoicism, and Pythagoreanism, into his estimate of the teaching of Moses' law. Though at times this amalgam of ideas does not cohere, it can be said that Philo looks to the past for the realisation of his political ideals, turning his gaze back pre-eminently to Moses. The hope of future

---

[1] JACOB NEUSNER, A Life of Rabbi Yohanan Ben Zakkai, Studia Post-Biblica, VI (Leiden, 1962).

glory for Israel, though present, occupies only a brief space in his writings. The Jewish scriptural perspective is not lacking in Philo's writings, but there it becomes the starting point for his overriding interest in the mastery of the soul over the body, the mind over the passions, in the individual person. He regards the ruler-and-ruled relationship primarily as analogous to the soul-body distinction.

Broadly speaking this thesis deals with ideas, yet it is not a history of ideas in the sense that it traces the development of Philo's thought.[2] Since there is no sustained writing from Philo directly on my theme (though he comes close to it in 'Legatio ad Gaium', 'In Flaccum' and 'De Iosepho') the method of selection is important. The nature of the thesis topic does not artificially create it, for selectivity "is the pre-condition for achieving any knowledge at all, whether it be scientific, historical or common sense".[3] The examination of the primary sources was commenced under three headings:

(i)   the writer's basic view of the world, including man, God, and social relationships;

(ii)   direct teaching on incidents involving rulers, citizenship, and attitudes towards Roman rule;

(iii) indirect or illustrative references in the documents to rulers generally, and to the Romans.

Attention has been concentrated on the second with due consideration of the other two.[4]

The task of ascertaining why authors in the past wrote as they did is never straightforward for the historian of ideas, and Q. SKINNER's[5] critique of methodology in pursuing the history of ideas is worth noting. Relevant to this study is his warning against "converting some scattered or quite incidental remarks by a classic theorist into his 'doctrine'"[6] whereby the author being studied has his ideas distorted, or at least adapted, to fit the themes the modern student is investigating. In our study of Philo his scattered remarks have been considered together with his more direct writings, for example on the ideal ruler or the dangers of "ochlocracy". When the author's doctrine is constructed only from scattered remarks, then tentative conclusions only can be presented, but when the remarks are consistent in the attitudes they convey, then a firmer assessment of these brief statements found in one's text can be essayed.

---

2 The difficulty in dating his writings overall, despite ERWIN R. GOODENOUGH's confidence on this point (An Introduction to Philo Judaeus [Oxford, 1962], pp. 30—51), precludes that.

3 V. A. HARVEY, The Historian and the Believer (London, 1967), p. 211; cf. W. H. WALSH, An Introduction to Philosophy of History (London, 1967), p. 178.

4 After setting out on this approach I found a similar plan suggested by C. E. B. CRANFIELD, The Christian's Political Responsibility According to the New Testament, SJT., XV (1962), p. 176—192.

5 Q. SKINNER, Meaning and Understanding in the History of Ideas, HT., VIII (1968), pp. 3—53. For a good critique of the details of SKINNER's arguments and his own suggested methodology see BHIKKU PAREKH and R. N. BERKI, The History of Political Ideas, JHI., XXXIV (1973), pp. 163—184.

6 SKINNER, Meaning and Understanding, pp. 7—10, 46.

The second caution is related to the former and deals with the student's expectation that the author was writing systematically on his subject, and was not influenced by fluctuations of mood, ideas or circumstances which might alter and even reverse the presentation of ideas in his work. In this approach contradictions and ambiguities tend to be minimised in the desire to grasp "the coherence" of the writer's thinking.[7] We know so little of Philo's life and personal circumstances, that the attempt to trace the fluctuations in his circumstances and beliefs is largely an exercise in conjecture. GOODENOUGH's[8] suggested chronology for Philo's writings is an attempt to grapple with this issue, but the complexity and inadequacy of the evidence leads one either not to attempt such an exercise or else like GOODENOUGH to search for a "coherent" pattern of development.

Thirdly, SKINNER[9] considers the "contextual" study of authors, commending the practice of setting the author in his philosophical and political context.[10] I have sought to do that in looking at Philo's background in Alexandria. The danger of such a method is "its proneness to distortion in a determinist direction"[11] and one has to weigh how much, for example, can be designated as Philo's own contribution and how much as simply the reflection of the philosophic ideas current in intellectual discussion in Alexandria. Sometimes this is impossible to ascertain.

There is another consideration pertinent to the assessment of Philo's ideas. ROBERT HAMERTON-KELLY notes that

"there is hardly any exposition more difficult to make or follow in modern scholarship than one in Philo's thought".[12]

That is to overstate the difficulty but he links this observation with his concern at the neglect of individual treatises in attempts made to gauge Philo's ideas and concepts. This present work falls within the scope of that criticism for it lacks a study of the compositional patterns of the voluminous writings extant from Philo's hand. While consideration is given to the motivation, style and audience in mind for the writing of 'Legatio ad Gaium' and 'In Flaccum', the other treatises from which I draw evidence of Philo's political ideas are not so scrutinized. Does that negate this effort? I do not believe so. Doubtless the conclusions I reach must be re-assessed by the long term study of Philo's writings with the tools of source, form, and redaction criticism. If the history of New Testament studies over the last century is any guide that will be a long process. As well, though it will sharpen our understanding of Philo's writings it will not necessarily lead to agreement as regards the conclusions scholars reach. Yet such study will help us in our understanding of Philo. Commentaries on Philo's expositions will be valuable assets.

---

[7] Ibid., pp. 16—20, 30.

[8] GOODENOUGH, op. cit.

[9] SKINNER, Meaning and Understanding, pp. 39—43.

[10] On the difficulty of setting limits to this approach see PAREKH and BERKI, History, p. 177—80.

[11] Ibid.

[12] ROBERT G. HAMERTON-KELLY, Sources and Traditions in Philo Judaeus: Prolegomena to an Analysis of His Writings, SP., I (1972), p. 3.

In defence of the present study of his ideas I assert that the distinctive and consistent lines of political thought that continually emerge in Philo's writings cannot be ignored or put to one side until detailed textual and compositional study of his works has been completed. The writings which are the major source of Philo's estimate of both Roman and ideal rule — 'Legatio ad Gaium', 'In Flaccum', 'De Iosepho' and 'De Vita Mosis' — have been well served with able commentators. Indeed, the only sustained studies of Philo's political ideas are those contained in the commentaries by HERBERT BOX,[13] E. MARY SMALLWOOD[14] and ERWIN GOODENOUGH.[15] My study leads me to propose significant alternatives to several of GOODENOUGH's major conclusions. I refer particularly to Philo's attitude to Roman rule and the extent of his antipathy to ochlocracy.

The repeated expression of the main forms of general political ideas throughout Philo's writings is a factor worth noting. These ideas occur in many contexts. They are threads interwoven into his expositions of scripture, whether expressed in literal or allegorical form. At other times they occur as illustrations or as anecdotes within his writings. Though through critical study of the text we will be able to find the threads of his various sources and we will discern how he varied his exposition in accord with contemporary practices or the needs of his readers, yet the main patterns of Philo's political ideas can already be gathered together. To pursue the image a little further, we can liken Philo's writings to a substantial but still incomplete tapestry. The interweaving of various colours in it is analogous to the amalgam of different sources with Philo's own views. A sweeping view of the tapestry shows firmer lines, consciously woven, while scattered about are threads that reflect in smaller scope the pattern as a whole. I have sought to detect both the firmer lines and the scattered threads of pattern in Philo's political thought. In examining the tapestry I hope that I have added some clues in the quest for Philo's understanding of life, especially in its political dimensions.

Part One:

Philo and the Roman World

I. The Political Situation in Alexandria

1. The Jewish Community

Josephus claimed[16] that right from the founding of Alexandria there was a Jewish community settled in that Greek city. The other notable groups resident

---

13 HERBERT BOX, Philonis Alexandrini — In Flaccum (London, 1939).

14 E. MARY SMALLWOOD, Philonis Alexandrini — Legatio ad Gaium (Leiden, 1961).

15 ERWIN R. GOODENOUGH, The Politics of Philo Judaeus. Practice and Theory (New Haven, 1938; repr. Hildesheim, 1967).

16 Ap. ii:35. Cf. BJ. ii:488.

there were the Greek and Macedonian soldiers, Alexander's camp-followers and the native Egyptians of Rhacotis, a village incorporated into the western part of the city. In Philo's time not only Alexandria but other major cities in the Roman Empire, including Rome itself,[17] had sizeable Jewish groups within their confines. Josephus' writings contain testimony from Strabo[18] and from himself[19] of the extensive dispersion of this people both in and beyond the Empire.

As an Alexandrian Jew Philo belonged to a group in the Empire who, though they might be regarded as odd with their stubborn monotheism and strange dietary customs, could not be ignored. Estimates vary as to their number at this time in history. Philo declares that in his day there were a million Jews living in Egypt.[20] It is difficult to estimate confidently Alexandria's population in A.D. 38 but a figure of two hundred and fifty thousand in a population approaching six hundred thousand would be a fair estimate.[21] Scholars differ also over the number of Jews in the empire, with estimates of six to seven million by JUSTER or four million by LIETZMANN and HARNACK, out of an approximate total of sixty million. Whatever figures are accepted it still remains that the Jews were a closely-knit, widely-spread and important minority group,[22] and the Jews of Alexandria were a significant community both in the world of Jewry and in that city.

The Jews had been granted political rights in Alexandria either when the city was founded in 331 B.C.[23] or else when Ptolemy I ruled.[24] As regards relations with the Romans, the Jews had experienced a much more amicable relationship than had the Greeks of that city. With the coming of Roman rule the Greeks resented not only the diminution in importance of their city but also the Jews' desertion of "the national dynasty on the arrival of the Romans and (their) reward in the confirmation of their privileges and in the special favour of the Emperors".[25]

---

[17] Leg. 155–8. See SMALLWOOD, Legatio, pp. 233–40.

[18] AJ. xiv:114–8.

[19] AJ. xi:133; xviii:310–79; BJ. ii:398; vii:43.

[20] Flacc. 43.

[21] Josephus (AJ. xii:11) relates that in the time of Ptolemy II there were 120,000 Jews in Alexandria. In recounting the suffering of the Jews in that city he estimated that the Roman attack on them in A.D. 66 claimed some 50,000 of their number and those who perished before the fury of the Alexandrians in A.D. 70 exceeded 60,000. One cannot verify Josephus' figures though his figure of seven and a half million for Egypt's population, excluding Alexandria, in his own time resembles the figure of seven million which Diodorus Siculus (i:31) gave for the population of Egypt some seventy years earlier. SMALLWOOD (Legatio, p. 215) estimates that the Jews made up thirty to forty per cent of Alexandria's population. M. ROSTOVTZEFF's suggestion of one million seems far too high (The Social and Economic History of the Hellenistic World [Oxford, 1967], II, pp. 1138–1139). For other estimates cf. Box, In Flaccum, p. 94; SALO WITTMAYER BARON, A Social and Religious History of the Jews (New York, 1952), I, p. 371.

[22] Leg. 215. GOODENOUGH (Politics, p. 20) comments that Philo referred to the Jews' numbers as an indirect warning to Claudius not to provoke them to revolt; cf. Dio x:6.4.

[23] BJ. ii:487–8; Ap. ii:35.

[24] AJ. xii:8.

[25] Jews and Christians in Egypt, ed. H. IDRIS BELL (London, 1924), p. 11.

The Jews had supported Gabinius[26] in 55 B.C. and later Caesar[27] in 48–47 B.C. when he was besieged in Alexandria. Upon Octavian's defeat of Antony and Cleopatra,[28] Alexandria came under his control. It was no longer a capital city but became a grain port for imperial benefit, and one of the three legions stationed in Egypt resided in the city. The emperor, and not the Senate, appointed the prefect[29] to administer the province and though depriving the Alexandrians of self-government,[30] he permitted the Jewish residents the privileges they had enjoyed under the Ptolemies.

There were other grounds for hostility between the Greek citizens and the Jews, namely economic and religious factors. The Jews were particularly active in commerce and were also employed as "tax farmers or farmers of the royal domains".[31] Whether many of them were persons of great wealth cannot be proved. To cite the example of the rich Alabarchs[32] is an inadequate statistic, though the Greeks may well have been convinced of the grand and hoarded wealth of those whom they despised.[33]

The discontent arising from the Jews' special religious ways and privileges is well summed up by BELL:

> "Precluded by their religion from sharing in many of the activities of their fellow-townsmen, to whom the πόλις was above all things a religious community united by the common service of the ancestral gods, and yet enjoying special privileges of their own and favoured, not by the Ptolemies only but by many of the Hellenistic monarchs, as later by the Romans, the Jews were naturally objects of suspicion and dislike".[34]

Resentment was felt towards both the Romans and the Jews. This is clearly expressed in the 'Acts of the Pagan Martyrs', a work designed for the Greeks of Alexandria, which records their laudable political actions. What emerges from

---

[26] AJ. xiv:99; BJ. i:175.

[27] AJ. xiv:127–36; 193; BJ. i:187–92; Ap. ii:61.

[28] Plut. Vit. Ant. 69, 71, 75–80.

[29] Strabo mentions some of the officials appointed under the prefect in Egypt – xvii:1.12–13.

[30] "The Alexandrians (were) no longer the privileged citizens of the capital of an independent kingdom, but the incipiently rebellious subjects of a foreign Empire" – JOHN MARLOWE, The Golden Age of Alexandria (London, 1971), p. 209.

[31] BELL, Jews and Christians, p. 11.

[32] The ἀλαβάρχης was the head official of the Jews in Alexandria during the Ptolemaic period. Philo records that his power was given to a Jewish γερουσία by Augustus. He was responsible for collection of taxes and, if ἐθνάρχης (Flacc. 10; AJ. xiv:117) refers to the same office, he was governor of the Jewish community. The three Alabarchs known by name, Alexander Lysimachus, Julius Alexander Lysimachus and Tiberius Julius Alexander, were all men of wealth.

[33] TCHERIKOVER and FUKS, commenting on Flacc. 57, consider that the Jewish community was made up of rich merchants, artisans, and the poor majority. They contend that Philo was linked to the interests of the wealthy and not sympathetic to the more nationalistic political interests of the Jewish poor – Corpus Papyrorum Judaicarum, eds. VICTOR A. TCHERIKOVER and ALEXANDER FUKS (Cambridge, Massachusetts, 1957), pp. 48–50, 67.

[34] BELL, Jews and Christians, p. 11.

these documents are three features which characterised the Greek populace of Alexandria – pride in their culture and Alexandrian citizenship, restlessness under Roman rule and their anti-Semitism.[35] The Alexandrians were known for their turbulent behaviour.[36] Though the writings range over the first two centuries A.D. they provide an insight into the Greek neighbours of Philo, amongst whom there circulated also more direct anti-Jewish writings. Apion, against whose works Josephus took up the pen, was an Alexandrian, as were such other anti-Semitic authors as Manetho, Chaeremon, and Lysimachus.[37] The attitude of disdain was reciprocated as, for example, in Philo's description of the religion of the Alexandrian Greeks in terms of the native Egyptian animal worship.[38] Alexandria then was a city acquainted with communal tension.[39]

Jewish claims to citizenship worsened the situation. It is now generally accepted by scholars that there were various levels of citizenship in Alexandria in Philo's time. It was a Greek city whose citizens were largely drawn from the Greek community, but, as SMALLWOOD[40] notes, a few Jews were citizens, such as the Alabarchs, Alexander (Philo's brother), and Demetrius.[41] These citizens were participants in the public religious observances and had entered the ἐφηβία which chiefly involved Greek athletic training. Pliny in his correspondence with Trajan referred to this Alexandrian citizenship, and distinguished it from the Roman form.[42] Both privileges were granted by the Romans in this case for

> "Alexandria lacked any civil body with the power to make decisions of this kind . . . such matters were under the administrative control of the Prefect to whom Trajan sends his recommendation for implementation".[43]

Trajan, following his predecessors as he says, was "extremely cautious in granting the freedom of the city of Alexandria".[44]

Making up the rest of the city's population were other ethnic groups, as well as the native Egyptians. The former were usually organised as πολιτεύματα and thus could be said to have had citizen rights. They were citizens of their own

---

[35] RAMSAY MACMULLEN, Enemies of the Roman Order – Treason, Unrest and Alienation in the Empire (Cambridge, 1967), p. 85; A. N. SHERWIN-WHITE, Racial Prejudice in Imperial Rome (Cambridge, 1970), pp. 86–7, 89–90, 93.

[36] Cf. Strabo xvii:1.12; Dio Chrys. Or. xxxii:41–3, 50–1, 69–74, 86–7.

[37] Josephus refers to these writers in his treatise Ap. i:227ff., 288–306; ii:1ff. See SMALLWOOD, Legatio, p. 248.

[38] Leg. 138–9, 163, 166.

[39] H. I. BELL, Anti-Semitism in Alexandria, JRS., XXXI (1941), pp. 4–5. On the relations existing amongst the various ethnic groups in Alexandria see P. M. FRASER, Ptolemaic Alexandria (Oxford, 1972), I, pp. 38–62 and on Greek antagonism in Alexandria towards the Jews dating at least from the time of Ptolemy Alexander, OSWYN MURRAY, Aristeas and Ptolemaic Kingship, JTS., XVII (1967), pp. 363–4.

[40] SMALLWOOD, Legatio, p. 4.

[41] AJ. xx:147.

[42] *admonitus sum a peritioribus debuisse me ante ei Alexandrinam civitatem impetrare, deinde Romanam, quoniam esset Aegyptius* – Pliny, Ep. x:6.1.

[43] A. N. SHERWIN-WHITE, The Letters of Pliny (Oxford, 1966), p. 570.

[44] Pliny, Ep. x:7.

ethnic community which had its distinctive customs and body of officials.[45] Thus the claim to have citizen-rights (πολιτεία) may well be linked to the existence of these πολιτεύματα and not to the higher status of Alexandrian citizenship. So also the term "Alexandrian"[46] with reference to Jews did not denote Alexandrian citizenship.[47] This is the explanation of those passages written by Josephus[48] and Philo[49] which suggest that the Jews possessed such citizenship. It would tally too with 2 Macc. 2:28, where the Jews were threatened by Ptolemy Philadelphus with a reduction of status to become merely λαοί, i.e. on a par with the native Egyptians.

Within their πολίτευμα the Jews had a council (γερουσία)[50] and law-courts. According to Philo the council of elders had been set up by Augustus after the death of their γενάρχης,[51] and its existence no doubt rankled with the Alexandrian Greeks who had no such body.[52] On the question of the law-courts GOODENOUGH has argued that in writing 'De Specialibus Legibus' Philo was:

". . . driven to make Jewish law conform to the various elements of jurisprudence in Alexandria in his day by a practical necessity, and we find that the Jewish courts of his day must have been under precisely the same necessity".[53]

His conclusion that Philo was describing a system of law which was actually operative in the contemporary Jewish courts in his city[54] has been criticised, notably by HEINEMANN[55] and MARCUS.[56] Certainly 'De Specialibus Legibus' shows acquaintance with Greek and Roman law, and the Jewish courts were ultimately answerable to the Roman authorities, even though, as Strabo noted[57] two generations before Philo's time, their institutions functioned with a fair degree of independence.

---

[45] βουλή or γερουσία.
[46] Leg. 194.
[47] AJ. xix:281, cf. SMALLWOOD, Legatio, p. 255.
[48] AJ. xii:121; BJ. ii:487—8; Ap. ii:38.
[49] Flacc. 8, 53; Leg. 44, 194, 349.
[50] Box, In Flaccum, pp. xxv—xxviii.
[51] Flacc. 10. Noting Philo's awareness of, and sensitivity to, the terms for different political offices DAVID SOLOMON contends that the term γενάρχης is the correct reading and that it refers to the traditional fatherly figurehead as distinct from the "clear cut politically—limmed personage represented by the ethnarch" (Philo's use of γενάρχης in 'In Flaccum', JQR., LXI [1970], pp. 128—31).
[52] H. I. BELL, Egypt under the Early Principate, in: CAH., X (Cambridge, 1934), p. 296.
[53] ERWIN R. GOODENOUGH, The Jurisprudence of the Jewish Courts in Egypt (Amsterdam, 1968), p. 22.
[54] Ibid., pp. 22—3.
[55] HEINEMANN's criticism is noted in an article by R. MARCUS, Recent Literature on Philo — 1924—1934, in: Jewish Studies in Memory of George Kohut, eds. S. W. BARON and A. MARX (New York, 1935), p. 472.
[56] Ibid.
[57] Josephus acknowledges Strabo as the source of this information — AJ. xiv:117.

The πολῖται of the Jewish community had a status somewhere between the Greek citizens (ἀστοί) and the native Egyptians called by Josephus and Strabo οἱ ἐπιχώριοι.[58] Both WOLFSON[59] and SMALLWOOD[60] contend that in V. Mos. 1:35,[61] which dealt with the status of the Jews in Egypt before their enslavement, Philo wrote of distinctions which referred to the Alexandrian situation. However, though the passage states that οἱ ξένοι considered themselves πολῖται and worthy to be received by the ἀστοί, it would seem unlikely that Philo would use the term ξένοι to denote the Jews in Alexandria and also argue that they differed little from the original inhabitants (αὐτόχθονες), i.e. the Egyptians. Elsewhere in his writings Philo associates Egyptians with ὁ ἄθεος ... τρόπος,[62] a description with which he would not wish to identify his fellow Jews.

The status of Egyptians within the empire was certainly not an enviable one. Egypt was alone amongst the provinces in that "the vast mass of its inhabitants were not organised into self-governing *civitates stipendiariae* possessing a local citizenship".[63] Tacitus expressed conservative Roman opinion which moulded the policy towards the Egyptians when he wrote of the province of Egypt as:

> ... *superstitione ac lascivia discordem et mobilem, insciam legum ignaram magistratuum*[64]

As with the Greeks, so we might expect that the Jews of Alexandria looked down on this group which did not "share in any form of citizenship".[65]

The Jews desired to move up in status. Though DAVIS[66] may well be right in stating that right from the foundation of the city a good number of Jews were recognized as Alexandrian citizens, yet Claudius' reference to the rights usurped by the Jews in Alexandria indicates that by A.D. 41 either many Jews or an energetic group among them were pressing for equal rights with the Greeks. They were, says Claudius, "in a city not their own".[67] Noting the reference in 'In Flaccum' 172 to the Jews as κάτοικοι, i.e. as aliens with the right of residence, SMALLWOOD summarises the situation thus:

[58] Strabo xvii:1, 12, 198; BJ. ii:487.

[59] H. A. WOLFSON, Philo on Jewish Citizenship in Alexandria, JBL., LXIII (1944), pp. 165–8, noted in SMALLWOOD, Legatio, p. 9.

[60] SMALLWOOD, ibid., sim. TCHERIKOVER and FUKS, p. 63.

[61] οἱ γὰρ ξένοι παρ' ἐμοὶ κριτῇ τῶν ὑποδεξαμένων ἱκέται γραφέσθωσαν, μέτοικοι δὲ πρὸς ἱκέταις καὶ φίλοι, σπεύδοντες εἰς ἀστῶν ἰσοτιμίαν καὶ γειτνιῶντες ἤδη πολίταις, ὀλίγῳ τῶν αὐτοχθόνων διαφέροντες.

[62] Leg. Alleg. iii:212. Cf. Post. C. 2; Heres 203; V. Mos. ii:193, 196; Fuga 180 and Leg. 163.

[63] SHERWIN-WHITE, Pliny, p. 568.

[64] Hist. i:11.

[65] Ap. ii:41.

[66] SIMON DAVIS, Race Relations in Ancient Egypt: Greek, Egyptian, Hebrew (London, 1951), pp. 111–2.

[67] ἐν ἀλλοτρίᾳ πόλει; 'Letter of Claudius to Alexandria' included by E. MARY SMALLWOOD, Documents Illustrating the Principates of Gaius, Claudius and Nero (Cambridge, 1967), No. 370. 1.95.

"The Jews were κάτοικοι or metics vis-a-vis the Greeks. They were πολῖται only vis-a-vis each other. There were in fact in Alexandria two parallel citizenships, that of the Greeks and that of the Jews.[68] In prestige the former certainly ranked higher, but in the sum total of their rights there may well have been little difference between them. This is possibly the meaning of Claudius' statement that the Jews had ἴση πολιτεία[69] with the Alexandrians".[70]

Probably it was those Jews influenced by Hellenistic thought in Alexandria who were eager to join the most prestigious group. SMALLWOOD, I feel, is correct in arguing[71] that the stricter, orthodox Jews would have opposed pressing for Greek rights because of the likelihood of compromise with pagan ways. Even the "syncretists" may have wanted some of the practices, for example nudity in the athletic training of ἔφηβοι, waived in their case. Their claims, with special concessions requested or not, stirred up further animosity in the city.[72] Particular incidents, notably the mocking of Agrippa with impunity in A.D. 38,[73] sparked the fire, but Philo grew up and wrote against a background of political, social and religious divisions between the Jews and their neighbours in Alexandria. Both Greeks and Egyptians could be stirred to hostility against the Jews and this factor must be borne in mind when Philo's writings are assessed. The immediate political situation rather than the issue of Roman rule usually colours his views on government and citizenship.

In Philo's account the pogrom of A.D. 38 occurred when Greek demagogues, namely Dionysius, Lampo and Isidorus,[74] stirred up and led the antisemitic forces; these were moved by nationalistic fervour, hatred of Jewish wellbeing, and desire for disorder and plunder. Amongst the more intelligent opponents of the Jews it was the issue of citizenship which roused most passion and, three years after this rioting, conflict arose again over this question. This time the immediate cause was the news of Gaius' death. In his letter to the Alexandrians in A.D. 41 Claudius set down the causes of trouble and warned both groups against further communal fighting:

---

[68] The Macedonians like the Jewish community had a πολίτευμα.

[69] AJ. xix:281.

[70] SMALLWOOD, Legatio, p. 10.

[71] Ibid., p. 14; contra, BELL, Jews and Christians, p. 16 and BOX, In Flaccum, p. xix.

[72] On the importance of a gymnasium education for being regarded as Greek see TCHERIKOVER and FUKS, p. 59.

[73] Flacc. 40.

[74] Isidorus and Lampo were remembered by the Alexandrian Greeks as heroes who had experienced Roman persecution because of Agrippa's friendship with Claudius. At the arraignment of Isidorus by Agrippa before the emperor the Alexandrian is purported to have declared: "Against what you, Agrippa, declare . . . I accuse (the Jews) of wishing to stir up the whole world . . . They do not think the same way as the Alexandrians, but more like Egyptians" — Acta Isidori, Recension C. Col. ii.11.20–26, in: The Acts of the Pagan Martyrs, ed. H. A. MUSURILLO (Oxford, 1954), p. 23.

"Wherefore once again I conjure you that, on the one hand, the Alexandrians show themselves forbearing and kindly towards the Jews, who for many years have dwelt in the same city, and dishonour none of the rights observed by them in worship of their god but allow them to observe their customs as in the time of the deified Augustus, which customs I also, after hearing both sides, have confirmed. And, on the other hand, I explicitly order the Jews not to agitate for more privileges than they formerly possessed, and in the future not to send out a separate embassy as if they lived in a separate city — a thing unprecedented — and not to force their way into gymnasi-archic or cosmetic games, while enjoying their own privileges and sharing a great abundance of advantages in a city not their own, and not to bring in or admit Jews from Syria or those who sail down from Egypt, a proceeding which will compel me to conceive serious suspicions; otherwise I will by all means proceed against them as fomenters of what is a general plague of the whole world".[75]

This issue of citizenship was a primary cause of tension and it is a weakness in GOODENOUGH's assessment of Philo's politics that he does not give sufficient attention to this local and thus, to Philo, most important political issue. The repeated and passionate criticism of "ochlocracy" occurs too often in his writings to have come from general philosophic discussion even though the rule of the mob was deprecated in Hellenistic political theory.

Before I consider in detail the riots of A.D. 38, Claudius' warning against bringing in Syrian and Egyptian Jews deserves comment. The emperor wished to forestall any uprising by, or because of, a larger Jewish population in Alexandria and so avoid "that which is a general plague (νόσος) of the whole world", namely disorder and violence. Against this interpretation of νόσος it has been suggested that Claudius is here referring to the strife between Jews and Christians and appeal is made to Suetonius (Claudius 25. 4)[76] to support this contention. However it is by no means established that the latter's statement was referring to Jewish and Christian antagonism in Rome,[77] while to link Claudius' statement with Tacitus' Annals xvi:44[78] involves further strained interpretation. The Jew-Greek antagonism in Alexandria was a particular example of that malady which could infect not only a city but an empire.

Another objection is that at this time there was no widespread disorder in the Roman world. In reply we may note that Claudius' comment was a general one. He was not describing the contemporary condition of the empire but rather the end result of communal tension wherever it occurred. LEWIS and REINHOLD,

---

[75] 'Letter of Claudius to Alexandria', SMALLWOOD, Documents, No. 370. 11.82–100: trans. Roman Civilization, eds. NAPHTALI LEWIS and MEYER REINHOLD (New York, 1966), II, pp. 368–9.

[76] *Iudaeos impulsore Chresto assidue tumultuantis Roma expulit.*

[77] See E. A. JUDGE and G. S. R. THOMAS, The Origin of the Church at Rome: a New Solution, RTR., XXV (1966), p. 84ff.

[78] On Christianity: . . . *repressaque in praesens exitiabilis superstitio rursum erumpebat, non modo per Iudaeum, originem eius mali . . .*

commenting on the phrase, suggest that he was referring "to the agitation for special privileges by the Jews of the Diaspora, who had settled in many cities of the Empire".[79] Against this interpretation two points stand: firstly, the references to the privileges of Jews in the letter does not tally with the term νόσος if it is taken as referring to their aspirations; secondly, the sources to which they refer with one exception[80] do not contain Jewish agitation for special privileges. It is worthwhile to note that Philo used the word νόσος with reference to general strife amongst Ἕλληνες καὶ βάρβαροι[81] and commenting on this passage SMALLWOOD adduces a number of examples where νόσος and νοσεῖν refer to conflict, particularly civil conflict.[82]

2. The Riots of 38 A.D.

It is from Philo's own writings that we draw most of our information concerning the anti-Jewish riots in Alexandria when Aulus Avillius Flaccus[83] was prefect. According to Philo,[84] he had ruled well until the death of Tiberius, but the accession of Gaius meant that his future was insecure, for his supporters in Rome Gemellus[85] and Macro[86] were executed by the new emperor, and he himself had played a part in the banishment to Gaius' mother.[87] Also he had been a

---

[79] LEWIS and REINHOLD, p. 369.

[80] BJ. ii:348—61; AE. 1928 Nos. 1—2; Babylonian Talmud "Sabbath" 33b. The exception is the revolt recorded by Cassius Dio (lxix:12.1 — 14.1) arising from the Jews' opposition to Hadrian's settling of foreigners in Jerusalem and the encouragement of pagan rites there. This hardly ranks as a typical case of agitation for special privileges.

[81] Leg. 145.

[82] SMALLWOOD surveying a number of ancient authors, such as Herodotus, Euripides, Xenophon, Plato and Plutarch, who use νόσος with reference to turmoil, concludes that "νόσος and νοσεῖν are used of war, especially civil war (στάσις), and its evils" (Legatio, p. 228).

[83] Flaccus became prefect in either A.D. 32 or 33. What is known of his administrative policies comes from the hostile testimony of Philo. Arrested in October, 38, he went first to Rome and then was exiled to Andros. Philo recorded his existence on the island and his murder on the orders of Gaius (Flacc. 154—91).

[84] Ibid. 1—8.

[85] Our ancient sources (Tac. Ann. vi:46.1; Jopseph. AJ. xviii:211—24; Suet. Tib. 76 and Cass. Dio lix:1.1) do not present a completely coherent picture as regards Tiberius' intentions for his grandson in relation to the principate. Gaius, an adopted son but one conscious of his descent from Germanicus, was in a stronger position to assume ultimate power over the younger Gemellus. For a fuller treatment of Gemellus' career and death, see SMALLWOOD, ibid. pp. 169—72 and J. P. V. D. BALSDON, The Emperor Gaius (Oxford, 1934), pp. 16f., 32, 37.

[86] Macro rose to prominence while Tiberius was on Capri, being appointed praetorian prefect by the emperor to bring about Sejanus' fall from power. Philo relates (Leg. 32—8) that towards the end of Tiberius' rule a strong bond developed between Macro and Gaius, but whether he hastened Tiberius' end or not is debatable. He met his death at Gaius' order in A.D. 38 just after having been appointed successor to Flaccus in Egypt (Leg. 69).

[87] Flacc. 9, 158. BALSDON, Gaius, pp. 131—2.

friend of Tiberius,[88] which did not endear him to Gaius. Locally, Flaccus had been troubled by one of the Alexandrian Greek nationalists, Isidorus, whom he exiled. Yet the latter's influence over the prefect's fortunes was not removed, for it seems that he was involved in the fall of Macro[89] and SMALLWOOD contends that Flaccus, faced with the continuing hostility of Isidorus, who in seeking revenge was prepared to move in a similar fashion against the prefect, became preoccupied with personal anxieties and allowed his rule to deteriorate.[90]

On the other hand, SHERWIN-WHITE[91] argues that Philo, in accounting for Flaccus' failure to halt the anti-Jewish disturbances of A.D. 38, offered anachronistic explanations drawn from the charges levelled at the prefect at his trial, and also from the bases for Gaius' purge of suspected opponents in A.D. 39−40. He contends that Flaccus' friendship with Tiberius was a "remote affair" by A.D. 38, that his support for Gemellus was not an issue when Flaccus had last been in Rome, and that Gaius "did not regard all the 'friends of Tiberius' . . . as his enemies after the fall of Macro".[92] Also only in A.D. 39 did the emperor act against Agrippina's accusers.

Thus this scholar argues that Flaccus' agreement with *agents provocateurs* in Alexandria was due not to fear of the emperor's wrath over his past friendships[93] but to Flaccus' desire

"to conciliate the most dangerous of his local enemies in order to forestall a malicious prosecution for maladministration".[94]

---

[88] Ibid. 9.

[89] Ibid. 10−16; SMALLWOOD, Legatio, p. 186.

[90] SMALLWOOD, Legatio, p. 15. However it was probably anti-Jewish sentiment (Flacc. 97−103) rather than neglect that caused the Jewish dedication to Gaius on his accession to remain in Flaccus' hands. Philo condemned him for failing to transmit the message to Gaius, alleging that Flaccus had "been seeking to utilize the emperor to supplement his own efforts to injure us" (ibid. 97). The arrival of Agrippa was sufficient for the resolution to be sent on with apologies and explanation to the emperor.

[91] A. N. SHERWIN-WHITE, Philo and Avillius Flaccus: a Conundrum, Latomus, XXXI (1972), pp. 820−8.

[92] He refers to the fate of such army commanders as Lentulus Gaetulicus, L. Apronius and Calvisius Sabinus, as illustrating his point that Gaius' displeasure was not felt until A.D. 39. He also points out that Aemilius Lepidus was a more powerful protector of Flaccus than Macro had been (Conundrum, p. 824).

[93] Philo declared that Dionysius, Lampo and Isidorus offered to back Flaccus' tenuous position with the support of the Alexandrian Greeks and asked in return "no greater benefaction than (the) surrendering and sacrificing (of) the Jews" (Flacc. 23). The prefect, needing support before Gaius, agreed to the suggestions of those whom Philo describes as "sedition-makers and enemies of the Commonwealth" (Ibid. 24). However as SHERWIN-WHITE pertinently comments: "Against a charge of *maiestas*, based on the Macro−Gemellus−Agrippina insinuations, the support of the public opinion of Alexandria was worthless" (ibid., p. 825). Contra: TCHERIKOVER and FUKS, p. 65.

[94] Ibid. He notes Flaccus' antagonism to this group during the good years of his prefecture (Flacc. 128−45).

Flaccus' arrest then is to be regarded as the start of Gaius' new policy of attacking the supposed enemies of his house and his power.[95]

The question is raised why Philo would explain Flaccus' behaviour in terms which would be considered creditable by his Roman readers and yet was silent on the motive that SHERWIN-WHITE suggests. In reply the latter contends that the Alexandrians were not well acquainted with indictment procedure. However Philo wanted to take another direction in interpreting the prefect's action, and who is to say that he was mistaken in alleging that Flaccus' espousal of Alexandrian Greek support was in part based on animosity towards the Jews? Hoping to safeguard his record as prefect, as SHERWIN-WHITE well argues, he joined forces with those most likely to challenge his administrative achievements and whose dislike for Alexandrian Jewry would be a certain bond linking the two parties.

At first Flaccus exhibited the new direction of policy by disregarding justice in law-cases involving Jews and Alexandrians, favouring the latter with his attention and turning away when the former gave their defence.[96] Such an attitude would soon be common knowledge in the city and it was but a matter of time before serious disturbances arose between the Jews and their antagonists. It is hard to see why, as SMALLWOOD suggests, "physical assault and religious persecution were (not) in the Greeks' minds when they made their agreement with Flaccus"[97] for the friction over citizenship as well as the other factors noted earlier were longstanding. The bargain made on their part with the prefect indicated more than just a desire to forestall Jewish ambitions, even admitting that in postulating the motives of the Alexandrians Philo wrote after the events.

The arrival of Agrippa[98] and the mockery directed at him were the sparks which ignited the situation. Agrippa, imprisoned by Tiberius for expressing the wish that Gaius would soon rule,[99] was on friendly terms with the new emperor and had been appointed by him to be king over the regions which Philip had

---

[95] Ibid., p. 826.

[96] Flacc. 24.

[97] SMALLWOOD, Legatio, p. 16.

[98] Julius Agrippa was more Idumaean than Jewish. His mother Berenice was descended from Idumaean nobility (Herod the Great being her uncle) (AJ. xv:253–8; xvi:11; xviii:133; BJ. i:552). His father Aristobulus was descended through his mother, Mariamme, from Hyrcanus, the last Hasmonean king (AJ. xiv:300; BJ. i:241). "He owed the name Julius (IG. iii:556) to his great-grandfather Antipater, who was given Roman citizenship by Julius Caesar (AJ. xiv:137; BJ. i:194), and Agrippa presumably to his grandfather's friendship with M. Vipsanius Agrippa (AJ. xvi:12–62). He spent his childhood and early manhood in Rome, until in A.D. 23 he went back to Judaea, where he led a varied, impecunious, and somewhat disreputable life for about twelve years. When he returned to the imperial court, probably early in 36, he was bidden by Tiberius to attend on Gemellus but thought it more to his advantage to cultivate Gaius, and despite a difference of over twenty years in age the two rapidly became friends" (SMALLWOOD, Legatio, p. 251).

[99] AJ. xviii:168, 187. BJ. ii:176–80. Gaius on his accession made him king of the region comprising Auranitis, Batanaea, Gaulanitis, Paneas and Trachonitis and Galilee was added in 39 A.D. He was also voted the rank of praetor by the senate. After some delay Agrippa set out in 38 A.D. to claim his kingdom and at Gaius' request passed through Alexandria.

governed as tetrarch.[100] On reaching Alexandria, Agrippa desired to enter the city quietly at night,[101] but his presence became known and this stirred the Alexandrian advisors of Flaccus to greater efforts. Harping on the slight to the prefect's prestige in having a king call unnecessarily at the city, resentful that a Jew had been crowned a king, and abetting the lazy and unoccupied mob in the city, who spoke slanderously of Agrippa, the anti-Jewish forces sought to make capital from the king's arrival. The crowning insult occurred with the setting up of a local lunatic named Carabas in royal robes flanked by a mock bodyguard in the gymnasium. Some fell before him to salute the "king", others to seek justice from him or for consultation with him. Finally, the mob crowding the spectacle acclaimed Carabas

> "as Marin which is said to be the name for 'lord' in Syria. For they knew that Agrippa was both a Syrian by birth and had a great tract of Syria over which he was king."[102]

Unchecked and unpunished by Flaccus, the crowd clamoured in the theatre in the early morning for the installation of images in the Jewish synagogues. It seems more likely that the crowd was propelled by its own recklessness and desire to insult the Jews as openly as possible, rather than by the desire to ingratiate itself with Gaius and avoid punishment from him for insulting Agrippa. Philo writes that they used the name of Caesar as a screen[103] in their resolve to further discomfort the Jews by placing images of the emperor in the syngogues. Though Philo blamed Flaccus,[104] it would seem that the Alexandrians had taken the power to themselves[105] to harm the Jewish residents of their city. Synagogues were seized and burnt. Pressured by the powerful crowd no doubt, Flaccus

> "issued a proclamation in which he denounced us as foreigners (ξένους) and aliens (ἐπήλυδας) and gave us no right of pleading our case but condemned us unjudged".[106]

The wording of this edict cannot be ascertained but its terms may not have been as severe as Philo maintained. Claudius, in his letter, referred to the Jews as "living in a city not their own". They were as we saw κάτοικοι. Possibly they were now relegated to the status of ξένοι as SMALLWOOD suggests.[107] This attack on the Jewish πολίτευμα meant that their numbers were legally eligible to reside

---

[100] BJ. ii:181. Tetrarch was the title used in Thessaly to describe the overseer of one quarter of the province. In the Roman empire this title was held by those governing portions of provinces and the position ranked below an Ethnarch.

[101] Flacc. 28.

[102] Ibid. 39.

[103] Flacc. 42.

[104] Ibid. 173—4.

[105] Leg. 132.

[106] Flacc. 54, cf. 172.

[107] SMALLWOOD, Legatio, p. 20.

only in one sector of the city.[108] The second clause of the edict may have been related to the efforts by Jews to gain Alexandrian citizenship, but more likely it refers to their defence of their traditional rights. An edict aimed against the Jews at this time would have been interpreted by their opponents as having wider ramifications in the streets than in the law courts, and to the mob it was an incentive to more fierce action.[109] They began to implement the edict ruthlessly and the worst then followed.

The Jews were herded into part of one of the five quarters, their property was either pillaged, mocked at or burnt while some of the mob robbed those Jews unfortunate enough to sail into the harbour at that time.[110] For the Jews themselves, the treatment they received was that savage cruelty which an inflamed and bloodthirsty mob, moved by vicious hatred, so fearfully inflicts.[111] The final suffering was experienced by the Jewish γερουσία. They had been arrested, on what charge we do not know, though Philo declares that they were innocent.[112] They were paraded through the streets to the theatre and there tortured so severely that some died, while those who survived remained in prison.[113]

The pogrom subsided for in the autumn of A.D. 38 Bassus was sent from Italy by Gaius to arrest Flaccus.[114] The Jews, however, were so crushed by their recent experiences that they did not have the will to celebrate the Feast of Tabernacles[115] and at first could not believe the news of Flaccus' arrest. When they had established this latter fact they rejoiced:

"with hands outstretched to heaven they sang hymns and led songs of triumph to God who watches over human affairs".[116]

---

[108] Flacc. 55; Box, In Flaccum, p. 99; SMALLWOOD, Legatio, pp. 215—6. Probably this sector was called Δέλτα (BJ. ii:495). When Philo wrote of this in Leg. 124—5 it was the mob who caused it and not Flaccus.

[109] In Leg. 119—20 Philo lays the primary blame on Gaius. It was his abrogation of the laws regarding Jewish rights which is said to have moved the rabble to attack the Jews. The desire to blacken Gaius, rather than to describe the local situation accurately, seems to guide Philo in this instance. (Cf. Leg. 115 and SMALLWOOD, Legatio, pp. 216—7.) Later in 'Legatio ad Gaium' he censured Flaccus "who could have put an end to this mob-rule single-handed in an hour had he chosen to" (132, cf. Flacc. 44, 53). But SMALLWOOD comments well that "the Greek mob was clearly out of control at this stage, and the restoration of order would have required the intervention of the Roman troops stationed in Egypt" (ibid., p. 220).

[110] Caesar wrote (B.Civ. iii:112) of the Alexandrians in the tower Pharos who plundered ships waylaid there by bad weather.

[111] Flacc. 56—72. Leg. 120—131. SMALLWOOD notes that there is some exaggeration in Philo's description (ibid., p. 218).

[112] Flacc. 77—82.

[113] Ibid. 73—85.

[114] Ibid. 109, 114.

[115] Ibid. 116.

[116] Ibid. 121.

Two of Flaccus' accusers before Gaius were Isidorus and Lampo.[117] It is not certain whether he was charged with general maladministration and failure to exercise control over the riots, or whether he was summoned because of his association with Macro and Gemellus, or as a result of Agrippa's letter concerning the suppression of the Jews' message of goodwill. Whatever the charges were, he was found guilty and exiled to Andros where he was eventually murdered.

Meanwhile in Alexandria one can only assume that the immediate circumstances of the Jews improved. By the next year they were able to offer a hecatomb[118] for sacrifice for Gaius' expected victory in Germany, thus reflecting some measure of prosperity. Presumably they moved out from the confines of the one quarter into which they had been forced, while the repair and use of the synagogues seem also to have followed.

Both the Jews and their adversaries in Alexandria were determined to present their accounts of the disturbances to the emperor. For the Jews it was important to seek vindication of their former position and to secure redress for the suffering they had endured. For their opponents it was important to avoid censure for the turmoil (passing the blame on to the Jews and Flaccus), and to prevent the Jews from gaining the privileged citizenship rights they sought. Philo led the Jewish embassy, while the redoubtable Isidorus as well as Apion and possibly Lampo were amongst those representing the Greeks.[119] The contents of the Jewish petition are only hinted at in Philo's reference to its "containing a summary of our sufferings and of our claims".[120] The sufferings referred of course to the pogrom; the claims involved the redress for property and goods and the return to the status cancelled by Flaccus' edict.[121]

When in Rome the embassy was thrown into consternation on receiving the news that Gaius intended to set up an image of himself in the Jerusalem temple. Philo recorded with all the tense detail felt by an eye-witness the difficulties they encountered in presenting their case to the emperor, and the crafty insinuations of their opponents. Contrary to their fears the Jews did not lose the case, nor, it would appear, did they win it. Rather, Gaius, after questioning them off-handedly in the gardens of Maecenas and Lamia[122] concerning their privileges and identity, (namely, Jewish exemption from the imperial cult), their political rights in Alexandria and their laws as regards abstinence from pork,[123] dismissed the delegates concluding that

---

[117] Ibid. 125—7. MARLOWE (p. 210) claims that Agrippa secured Flaccus' dismissal but there is no direct indication of this in our sources.

[118] Leg. 356. The hecatomb, the offering of one hundred beasts, presumably was sacrificed at Jerusalem (SMALLWOOD, Legatio, pp. 320—1).

[119] On the members of the embassies, SMALLWOOD, ibid., pp. 248—9, 320—1; on the date, P. J. SIJPESTEIJN, The Legationes ad Gaium, JJS., XV (1964), p. 87—96.

[120] Leg. 179.

[121] It is not so likely that there was a request for full Greek citizenship rights for some, if not all, of the Jews.

[122] Leg. 351.

[123] Ibid. 355—64.

"these men are not so much criminals as lunatics in not believing that I have been given a divine nature".[124]

No final decision from the emperor is recorded for us. Possibly, as SMALLWOOD[125] suggests, he gave none, either having dismissed the case, or else being struck down by the assassins' blades before he officially announced it.

His death and the accession of Claudius saw fresh trouble arise in Alexandria. On this occasion the Jews took the initiative by attacking the Greeks. According to Josephus' account,[126] which understandably glosses over Jewish culpability, the turmoil was brought under control by the prefect and the new emperor issued an edict[127] giving back to the Jews the rights they held before Gaius ruled, reinstating the πολίτευμα and protecting the synagogues.[128] This was followed by an edict more general in destination which declared:

". . . Kings Agrippa and Herod, my dearest friends, having petitioned me to permit the same privileges to be maintained for the Jews throughout the empire as those in Alexandria enjoy, I very gladly consented".[129]

By far the most important source of information concerning the situation of the Jews in Alexandria in Claudius' time is his famous letter to that city. It was prompted by a dispute which had been brought before him[130] and he addressed himself to both the Greek and Jewish communities. The question has arisen as to whether there were two delegations to Claudius from the Jews of Alexandria, and if so what this would reflect as regards the composition of that community. WILLRICH[131] argued that there were two embassies, giving among his reasons:

(i) the reference to ἐν δυσεὶ πόλεσειν (1.90) and δύο πρεσβείας (1.91);
(ii) a division between Hellenistic-theatre-going Jews and those more orthodox in their practices.[132]

This led BELL to revise his opinion and accept WILLRICH's case.[133]

Was one delegation drawn from the orthodox Jews, as SMALLWOOD[134] suggests, who did not want further rights because of the pagan practices

---

[124] Ibid. 367.
[125] SMALLWOOD, Legatio, p. 27.
[126] AJ. xix:279.
[127] AJ. xix:280—5, esp. 285: "I desire that none of their rights should be lost to the Jews on account of the madness of Gaius, but that their former privileges also be preserved to them, while they abide by their own customs; and I enjoin upon both parties to . . . prevent any disturbance".
[128] SMALLWOOD, Legatio, p. 28.
[129] AJ. xix:286—8.
[130] 'Letter of Claudius to Alexandria', SMALLWOOD, Documents, No. 370, 11.87—8.
[131] H. WILLRICH, Zum Brief des Kaisers Claudius an die Alexandriner, Hermes, LX (1925), pp. 482—9.
[132] Less weighty is his reference to analogies with incidents described in Ac. 18:14; AJ. xx: 179—80; 1 Macc. 1:14; 2 Macc. 4:9—10.
[133] H. I. BELL, Juden und Griechen im Römischen Alexandreia (Leipzig, 1927), pp. 26—7; cf. Jews and Christians in Egypt, ed. H. I. BELL (London, 1924), p. 18.
[134] SMALLWOOD, Legatio, p. 29.

associated with them? Or were they complementary embassies seeking Greek citizenship for the Jewish community and drawn from those Jews who already held that right and those lacking it, as BALSDON[135] suggests? SMALLWOOD objects to this latter suggestion, arguing that the Jews who held the prized citizenship were neither numerous enough nor keen enough to advertise their Jewishness and would "have felt themselves adequately represented by the Greek delegation".[136] This assumes that they had little concern for the elevation of fellow-members of their race — true indeed for a Tiberius Alexander, but was it true for all? Also it means that on his important question they would cut all ties by opposing the Jewish embassy. We do not know how deeply the "modernist" and orthodox groups were divided. For the important embassy after the pogrom of A.D. 38 the more "modernist" Philo was chosen as head of a body representing the whole Jewish community. This consideration leads me to accept BALSDON's suggestion as more convincing even though it is uncertain, probably even unlikely, that Philo's delegation pressed claims for Greek citizenship.

In his letter Claudius confirmed the right of the Jews to their πολίτευμα. He chastised both ethnic groups for their share in the disturbances in the city and warned them to avoid provoking each other. The Jewish petition for equal citizenship rights with the Greeks was disallowed, but the privileges they had held in the time of Augustus were confirmed. We may assume that from Claudius' decision peace between the disputing parties came to Alexandria in Philo's last years.

II. The Cultural and Intellectual Environment in Alexandria

Philo was not the first Jew in Alexandria to be influenced by the Hellenistic culture around him. In that city Greek-speaking Jews before his day had sought to bridge the dichotomy between acceptance of the Jewish faith and espousal of the philosophies of the Greek world. This is seen in such writings as the Sibylline Oracles, the 'Wisdom of Solomon' and the 'Letter of Aristeas'. The Jewish writer Aristobulus[137] advocated the notion, which Philo also expressed, that Plato and the Pythagoreans drew their main ideas from the Jewish law. Philo purported to believe that it was in Alexandria that the Jewish scriptures were first completely translated into Greek under the sponsorship of Ptolemy Philadelphus.[138] In any case the translation of the Jewish scriptures into Greek was motivated by mis-

---

[135] BALSDON, Gaius, p. 144.

[136] SMALLWOOD, Legatio, p. 29.

[137] Aristobulus lived in Alexandria either in the third or second century B. C. Quotations from his writings are to be found in Eusebius' Praep. Ev. viii:10 and xiii:12. In the former passage he writes of poets and philosophers learning from Moses while in the latter passage he shows obvious acquaintance with, and attraction to, Stoic, Platonic and Pythagorean ideas.

[138] V. Mos. ii:30—35.

sionary aims, as well as to give a knowledge of the law to those many Jews who did not know the Hebrew language. Thus the Septuagint came into the hands of Greek-speaking Gentiles, some of whom were attracted by its high morality and monotheism while others were repelled by its contents. Therefore the Jews needed to explain and defend their writings.

This movement of ideas was not in one direction only, as Aristobulus' adoption of the Greek philosophers indicates. Platonic, Aristotelian, Stoic and Pythagorean ideas were incorporated into the liberal Alexandrian Jew's outlook. In their defence of the Jewish scriptures these ideas were expounded from the text[139] with the aid of allegorical interpretation. By this method Jews were able to appropriate Hellenistic views of life without conscious apostasy from Judaism. Yet it must not be thought that Judaism in Alexandria was totally syncretisic; there were orthodox Jews as well as those attracted by the more sophisticated thought of the Gentile world.

It is not possible to ascertain the strength of support for the various shades of Judaistic thought in Alexandria. Philo, obviously influenced by the Greek philosophers, was esteemed so highly as to be placed in charge of the embassy to Gaius. Was Alexandrian Jewry, then, an isolated pocket where Hellenised Jews were in the majority and held the positions of influence in their πολίτευμα?[140] As M. SIMON admits, the sources available to answer these questions are thin. He argues that though the temple and its 'liturgies sanglantes' were declining in importance in the estimation of those touched by Greek thought, yet the teaching of the Pharisees extended throughout the Dispersion and was agreeable in spirit to the openness of Alexandrian Judaism's response to its environment.[141]

Against this latter point one can object that the Pharisees were more conservative than, and not so eclectic as, SIMON portrays them.[142] Also it is striking from Philo's writings how high a place the temple held not only in his estimation but also in the eyes of a wider circle of Jews. Philo looked to the permanent existence and functions of the temple[143] and linked the fall of the Jewish people with its ruin[144] and the ruin of Jerusalem,[145] and his fellow-delegates in Rome expressed the same attachment to the temple. Though Philo did not share the strong messianic expectation of the Pharisees as depicted in Psalm of Solomon 17,

---

[139] E.g., according to the doctrine of creation in Wsd. 11:7 the world was said to be formed "out of shapeless matter" (ἐξ ἀμόρφου ὕλης). This writing was "a deeply felt call to traditional piety, and its easy use of the philosophic cliches is therefore the more significant" (MOSES HADAS, Hellenistic Culture [New York, 1963], p. 76).

[140] MARCEL SIMON, Situation du Judaisme Alexandrin dans la Diaspora, in: Philon d'Alexandrie, R. ARNALDEZ, C. MONDÉSERT and J. POUILLOUX, eds. (Paris, 1967), p. 18.

[141] « Je reste convaincu, tout bien pesé, que le judaisme alexandrin, comme celui de la Diaspora en général, avec les adaptations qu'exigeaient ses conditions particulières de vie, s'apparente étroitement à celui des Phariséens de Palestine » (ibid., p. 20).

[142] Cf. P. ACKROYD's case that too much emphasis is placed on the adoption of Iranian ideas (Exile and Retoration [London, 1968], pp. 9−12).

[143] Leg. 157.

[144] Ibid. 184, 193.

[145] Ibid. 281.

yet he looked forward to the rule of God's special man in fulfilment of Dt. 30:1–10 and Num. 24:7.[146] In 'Legatio ad Gaium' he emphasised Jerusalem's rank as μητρόπολις not only of Judaea but of other regions in which Jews had settled. The Alexandrian Jews were no isolated pocket of Jewry, and the evidence from Jewish burial sites to which SIMON appeals endorses this impression.

From Philo's writings one observes that he and similar expositors were under attack from the "literalists". The latter were the more conservative Jews who regarded the use of allegory as a vehicle for the introduction of pagan philosophical concepts. Certainly allegorical exposition was strongly associated with Stoic commentaries, but it was not foreign to Jewish expositors even in Palestine.[147] It was well established within the Jewish community in Alexandria.[148] To conclude then in general terms, the main features of Alexandrian Judaism could be found elsewhere in the Diaspora and even in Judaea.[149]

Turning to the non-Jewish culture of Aleazandria, we cannot speak with precision as regards the particular schools of philosophy ascendant in Philo's time. By the first century A.D. there had been a fusion of thought from the major philosophies of which we find ample evidence in Philo's own writings. Platonic, Aristotelian, Stoic, Epicurean, Pythagorean and other streams of ideas clashed or intermingled in this city, which at this time was « *d'un des centres intellectuels les plus vivants − le plus vivant sans doute et le plus considerable − de l'hellénisme* ».[150] Within its confines could also be found devotees of astrology and oriental religions, while native Egyptian beliefs were held by the indigenous peoples.

In appearance Alexandria was a splendid city.[151] Both the enthusiastic Achilles Tatius[152] and the more restrained Strabo[153] described its magnificence. The latter admired particularly the public places, royal palaces, the Museum, the famous tomb of Alexander, the harbour and the theatre above it. Amongst its cultural landmarks was the Μουσεῖον,[154] a philosophical school and library, which the first Ptolemy had founded. Its close attachment to the palace meant that its imported teachers and their successors never quite broke free to question and philosophize independently, and in both literature and art the Alexandrians came

---

[146] Praem. 95, but see pp. 480–1.

[147] HARALD RIESENFELD, The Gospel Tradition (Oxford, 1970), pp. 144–60; GEZA VERMES, "He is the Bread", in: Neotestamentica et Semitica, E. EARLE ELLIS and MAX WILCOX, eds. (Edinburgh, 1969), pp. 258–263. S. LIEBERMAN argues that the Palestinian Rabbinic circles were little touched by first-hand contact with Greek philosophy, but that contact with such ideas came through the Jews of Alexandria − How Much Greek in Jewish Palestine, in: Biblical and other Studies, A. ALTMAN, ed., Philip W. Lown Institute of Advanced Judaic Studies, Studies and Texts, I (Cambridge, Mass., 1963), pp. 123–41.

[148] DAVID M. HAY, Philo's References to Other Allegorists, SP., VI (1979–80), pp. 58–61.

[149] This would be true with the possible exception of the "radical allegorists" who dismissed any literal meaning. Philo's criticism of them shall be dealt with later, see pp. 448–9.

[150] SIMON, Situation, p. 21.

[151] E. A. PARSONS, The Alexandrian Library (New York, 1952), pp. 58–9.

[152] Achilles Tatius v: 1–2.

[153] Strab. xvii:1.8–10.

[154] Ibid. xvii:1.8.

to be noted for their style rather than their content.[155] However, this institution did come into a new lease of life with the coming of the Romans. Ptolemy Soter also erected the library at Alexandria which was to become famous throughout the ancient world. Its foundation was due to the inspiration of an Athenian thinker, Demetrios of Phaleron, and within its walls were numerous writings dealing with the knowledge and theories which had been accumulated by the Hellenic peoples.[156]

W. H. C. FREND suggests that Jewish efforts in proselytising, and the clash of cultures this action precipitated, were major factors behind the riots in Alexandria.[157] Certainly relations between the Greek and Egyptian cultures were more amiable and syncretism could proceed in peace, though Egyptian religion might be despised by educated Greeks for containing superstitious or undignified beliefs. The Serapeum witnessed to the intermingling of Greek and Egyptian religion and in the old Egyptian quarter stood the temple of Serapis[158] where

> "the Greco-Egyptian populace could worship at common altars, with a composite ritual, under an elaborate priesthood that could trace its spiritual succession from the old priests of Zeus and the more ancient hierarchies of Osiris".[159]

Into such a fusion of cultic activity the Jew could not enter, but in the world of philosophy there were not wanting ideas which could be accommodated by more liberal minded Judaists. For example, the Alexandrian philosopher named Eratosthenes had declared that the classification of men as Ἕλληνες and βάρβαροι ought to be replaced by their designation as either good or bad.[160]

For the Greeks of Alexandria the Gymnasium was another building which was integral to their identity and culture. Reckoned by Strabo[161] to be the most beautiful building in Alexandria, it was "the centre for the ἐφηβεία, and the phrase οἱ ἀπὸ τοῦ γυμνασίου[162] denoted the select class of Alexandrian citizens who had undergone ephebic training".[163] It was situated near the main Jewish community and was the scene both for the demonstration organised by Isidorus against Flaccus[164] and for the mocking mimicry of Agrippa using the dim-witted Carabas.[165]

---

[155] HADAS, Hellenistic Culture, p. 23.

[156] PARSONS, Library, p. 71.

[157] CR., XIII (1963), p. 62.

[158] Note the rather satirical description of the adoption of this god into the city given by CHARLES KINGSLEY, Alexandria and Her Schools (Cambridge, 1854), pp. 12—13.

[159] PARSONS, Library, p. 72.

[160] Strab. i:4.9.

[161] Strab. xvii:1.10.

[162] Appian, sentenced to death by Commodus, regards his position as a gymnasiarch as precious (Acta Appiani, P. Oxy. 33, col. iii: 11.60—69, MUSURILLO, pp. 66—7).

[163] SMALLWOOD, Legatio, p. 223.

[164] Flacc. 136—9.

[165] Ibid. 34—9.

This, then, was the city of Philo. As we turn to consider him and his ideas it will become evident that he was influenced by the political situation, the ethnic and cultural strands and the historical background of this prominent city in the Roman empire.

III. Philo – the Man and Philosopher

Philo was not only steeped in the religio-philosophical world of Alexandria, but as regards the Jewish community in that city he was also no novice in affairs related to law and government. His leadership of the embassy to Gaius reflects a considerable background of political experience amongst the Alexandrian Jews, and since he was an old man[166] at this time, no doubt his years of experience contributed to his being appointed as leader. It was a delicate mission – everything concerning the status of the Jews in Alexandria in the early Empire was delicate. Nor was it a routine mission. Much rested on the delegates' shoulders, and they were aware that at Rome they had to deal with an unknown quantity in the Emperor and to face a coterie of anti-Jewish flatterers in the rival deputation.

Josephus, who is virtually our only informant, records that Philo was a leading Jew in Alexandria, "a man held in the highest honour, brother of Alexander[167] the alabarch and no novice in philosophy".[168]

It is debatable whether the details JACQUES SCHWARTZ[169] claims to have discovered as regards Philo's family background can be established. SCHWARTZ suggests that Philo's grandfather as a supporter of Antipater gained Roman citizenship from Julius Caesar in Judea, that he was of Hasmonean descent, that Philo's father migrated to Egypt during Herod the Great's rule. Wealthy and

---

[166] Leg. 1. In terms of experience he considered himself better equipped than his fellow delegates (Leg. 182). If εὐλαβέστερος means "cautious" which fits the context then SMALL-WOOD's suggestion (Legatio, pp. 254–5) that he refers here to "the practical training given him by his previous political career" rather than his background of formal or philosophical education is probably correct.

[167] Alexander Lysimachus was noted amongst Jews for his ancestry and wealth (AJ. xx:100); on one occasion decorating the temple gates with gold and silver (BJ. v:205) and on another giving a large loan to Agrippa (AJ. xviii:163). He was imprisoned by Gaius but released by Claudius (AJ. xix:276). He was the father of Tiberius Julius Alexander but unlike his son he followed the practices of the Jews (AJ. xx:100). On the latter figure see E. G. TURNER, Tiberius Julius Alexander, JRS., XLIV (1954) pp. 54–64 and J. SCHWARTZ, L'Egypte de Philon, in: Philon d'Alexandrie, R. ARNALDEZ, C. MONDESERT and J. POUILLOUX, eds. (Paris, 1967), p. 35.

[168] AJ. xviii:259. Josephus states that there were three delegates in the Jewish embassy (xviii:257) but Philo, the participant, says that it numbered five (Leg. 370). Gaius heard Philo separately from the rest of the embassy (xviii:260).

[169] JACQUES SCHWARTZ, Note sur la famille de Philon d'Alexandrie, in: Mélanges Isidore Lévy. Annuaire de l'Institut de philologie et d'histoire orientales et slaves. Université libre de Bruxelles, XIII (1953), pp. 599–601.

well-placed, Philo's family would have had friendly contact with Gentiles in Alexandria. As well, SCHWARTZ contends that Philo was probably a member of the Jewish πολίτευμα and thus involved in political affairs, while also a possessor of Roman citizenship through inheritance.

If Philo shared his brother Alexander's prosperity then Philo was certainly affluent. That he served on the πολίτευμα is likely, considering his membership of the embassy to Gaius. However, as regards the other details marshalled by SCHWARTZ noted above S. STEPHAN FOSTER[170] contends that there is "no confirming documentation . . . no concrete evidence has been presented which either identifies Philo's forebears, or gives their citizenship status, or details their movement from place to place".[171]

From Philo's own writings we know that he was no recluse, being a participant in Alexandrian social functions, attending theatres, wrestling and chariot racing,[172] though in a noted passage[173] he yearns for the life unspoiled by the world's affairs. Within his writings there are passages[174] whose details indicate that he was engaged in civic business. GOODENOUGH, by comparing the legislation in 'De Specialibus Legibus' with Graeco-Roman law, has argued that Philo was for many years a political administrator of some kind,[175] that he served on the Jewish law-courts and was aware of how the Jewish law had to be administered in a community lacking full autonomy in the city and in the Empire. Philo therefore was not lacking in a keen awareness of the struggle for Jewish recognition against clever Greek leaders, a pagan though not unfriendly administration, and a hostile mob.

1. Philo's Debt to Greek Philosphy

The paramount influence over Philo from the Greek philosophies was that of Platonism.[176] On occasions he expressly acknowledges Plato's thoughts as, for example, in describing the earth as a mother "for as Plato says, earth does not

---

[170] AJ. xx:100.

[171] S. STEPHEN FOSTER, A Note on the 'Note' of J. Schwartz, SP., IV (1975), p. 27.

[172] H. CHADWICK, Philo, in: The Cambridge History of Later Greek and Early Medieval Philosophy, A. H. ARMSTRONG, ed. (Cambridge, 1970), p. 139. As examples he notes dinners (Leg. Alleg. iii:155—6; Fuga 28—9; Spec. Leg. iv:74—5), theatres (Prob. 141), pancratiasts (ibid. 26) and racing (frag. ap. Eus., P. E. viii:14.58). WOLFSON's contention that there was no cultural assimilation between the Jews and Gentiles in Alexandria cannot apply to Philo. Cf. ALAN MENDELSON, A Reappraisal of Wolfson's Method, SP., III (1974), pp. 14—16.

[173] Spec. Leg. iii:1—6.

[174] Ibid. iii:181—3; iv:55—78; iv:2.

[175] GOODENOUGH, Jurisprudence, pp. 2, 9—10, 13—20, 22, 77; HENRY CHADWICK, St. Paul and Philo of Alexandria, BJRL., XLVIII (1966), p. 291.

[176] Som. i:44, 188. On the pervasive influence of Greek thought on Philo's ideas see ISAAK HEINEMANN, Philons griechische und jüdische Bildung (Hildesheim, 1962, reprinting of ed. Breslau, 1932).

imitate woman, but woman earth".[177] The Platonic theory of ideas is found throughout Philo's philosophical writings, and he readily uses such terms as ἀρχέτυπος, παράδειγμα and ἰδέα.[178] He describes God's creative work, the guidance of the godly and the pursuit of the good life all in terms of the theory of 'ideas'.[179] The passions or desires of the flesh are seen as the besetting evils facing the godly, philosophic mind[180] and Philo, along with Plato, regards it as good that the prison-like body should not encumber the soul[181] which is set free to meditate on God.[182]

Philo's cosmology also embraces some of Plato's notions. So in his allegorical exposition of Gen. 4 he writes of the particles of the dead men being redistributed "to the various forces of the universe out of which they were constituted".[183] His description of souls descending "into the body as though into a stream"[184] and his whole section on the affinity amongst souls (ἄγγελοι and δαίμονες in the cosmos) reflects Plato's writings.[185] The division of the soul into λόγος, θυμός and ἐπιθυμία by Philo is inspired by the same source[186] as is his dictum that the suffering of wrong is not as grievous as the doing of it.[187]

Another major influence on Philo was Stoicism. Scattered through his philosophical writings are terms associated with Stoic views.[188] He writes favourably of the Stoic basis of schooling[189] and linked with it is his incorporation of the Stoic idea of philosophy.[190] His division of the soul[191] reflects its concepts. His views of the virtues, of the four passions,[192] of the sevenfold division of bodily functions[193] and of the fourfold classification of material things[194] are traceable to

---

[177] Opif. 133; cf. Pl. Menex. 238A; Ti. 51A. For other Platonic terms see Opif. 54; Mut. 212; Agr. 16; Heres 249–51; cf. Pl. Tht. 191C.

[178] Spec. Leg. i:48; cf. Leg. 1–5.

[179] Det. 34; Post. C. 135; V. Mos. ii:127.

[180] Sacr. 6.

[181] Som. i:43.

[182] Gig. 14–5. Those who follow the philosophic life which leads to fellowship with God are described as μελετῶντες ἀποθνῄσκειν (Post. C. 135), a phrase strongly reminiscent of Plato's (ἀποθνῄσκειν μελετῶσι) in Phd. 67E. Cf. also Gig. 14 with Phd. 64A.

[183] Post. C. 5; cf. Pl. Ti. 42E.

[184] Gig. 13.

[185] Pl. Phdr. 284C; Symp. 202E; Ti. 43A.

[186] Spec. Leg. iv:92; Leg. Alleg. i:70–3; iii:115; cf. Pl. Ti. 69E f.

[187] Jos. 20.

[188] E.g. πῆξις ("solidity") Agr. 160; cf. SVF. iii:510; and Agr. 161; cf. SVF. iii:539–40. Cf. David Winston, Freedom and Determinism in Philo of Alexandria, SP., III (1974), pp. 56–7; John Dillon and Abraham Terian, Philo and the Stoic Doctrine of Εὐπάθειαι, SP., IV (1975), pp. 17, 20.

[189] Congr. 71–157. After the tender food of instruction comes the stronger dish of philosophy – Prob. 160.

[190] "For philosophy is the practice or study of wisdom, and wisdom is the knowledge of things divine and human and their causes" – Congr. 79; cf. SVF. ii:36.

[191] Opif. 117.

[192] Leg. Alleg. ii:99; Decal. 142–53.

[193] Ibid., i:11.

[194] Ibid., ii:22–3.

the Stoic schools. The Stoic notion that the sage is a king he applies to Abraham. From this stream of thought comes the notion that such a man lives "according to nature".[195] So too does the aphorism that "every good man is free", on which Philo writes a separate work.

At the outset of one of his major works, Philo weaves into his presentation two distinctive Stoic concepts, namely citizenship of the world (κοσμοπολίτης) and living according to the will of nature (τὸ βούλημα τῆς φύσεως).[196] Yet he rejects the Stoic notion that heaven or God's dwelling is simply a void (κενός). Such a view, writes Philo, is put foward by "marvelmongers".[197] However, when he speaks of philosophic discussion amongst the ancients, he divides it into the same three categories, logical, ethical and physical, as did the Stoic schools, even using the same illustrations as utilised by Diogenes Laertius.[198] Philo suggests that the distinctive Stoic notion that "the morally beautiful alone is good" is drawn from the virtue commended in Moses' writings[199] and he can on occasions use the Stoic definition of good without any specific acknowledgement. However, this does not necessarily indicate that he is a convinced Stoic, but that such notions had become "common property" in the intellectual milieu of Alexandria of his day.

Philo was also influenced by Neo-Pythagoreanism with its discussion of numbers and numerical relationships in its account of reality.[200] Further, one notes his indebtedness to Aristotle. The four aspects of God's causative work[201] and the espousal of "the middle way"[202] are drawn from his thought,[203] while there are affinities between Aristotle's idea of the "educational trinity" and Philo's description of Isaac, Abraham and Jacob.[204] Philo as well draws upon a common source of Greek ideas and it is sometimes impossible to name a definite school. For example, the notion that "the stars are souls divine"[205] was believed by Plato, Aristotle and the Stoics as well as being a foundation of contemporary astrology. That the four elements out of which the universe was formed were earth, water, air and fire[206] had long been postulated in Greek philosophy. The virtues which figure prominently in Philo's concept of the good life had been enumerated by both Plato and the Stoics.

However Philo does not accept all Greek philosophical ideas uncritically. He consistently rejects Epicureanism and the popular understanding of it. He is

---

[195] Prob. 160; V. contempl. 64.
[196] Opif. 3, 142. V. Mos. ii:48 cf. Diog. Laert., vii:87 and SVF. i:262.
[197] Heres 228.
[198] Diog. Laert., vii:40 cf. Agr. 14.
[199] Post. C. 133.
[200] Opif. 89–111; Leg. Alleg. i:2–5; Plant. 120–5.
[201] Cher. 125.
[202] Immut. 162–5.
[203] Cf. Arist., Eth. Nic. ii:6, 7.
[204] Sacr. 5–7.
[205] Gig. 8; Plant. 12.
[206] Plant. 120.

critical of its tenets,[207] seeing in the serpent's human speech[208] the example of the champions of pleasure, while the Epicurean assertion of the plurality of worlds and the absence of providence he likewise denies.[209] Nor do other schools escape his critical notice. The Sceptics' doubts concerning God's existence he considers to be rebutted by the teaching of Moses.[210] The suggestion that the world is eternal, found for example in Aristotle, is also refuted.[211] The Stoic idea that God is "the soul of the cosmos" he rejects on several occasions,[212] though he does refer to God as "the mind of the universe".[213] Besides Philo regards Plato's approach to philosophy as wrongly oriented in comparison with Moses' foundation.[214] But this brief resumé of Philo's criticisms of Greek thought must not blind us to the fact that he was deeply influenced by Hellenistic ideas. It does indicate that he maintained a critical estimate of them and could judge them from Biblical stand-ards.

2. The Assessment of Philo's Contribution

Debate has raged over whether Philo is basically a Judaistic or a Hellenistic thinker and also over the sophistication and originality of his thought. At one extreme Philo's use of Pythagorean numerology, Stoic-Platonic ideas, allegorical exegesis and Jewish scriptures may be seen as a boring failure, so that W. L. KNOX can comment that "as a philosopher Philo is negligible; as a writer he achieved a dullness which is portentous".[215] On the other hand, H. A. WOLFSON[216] sees a well-controlled and harmonious system of thought emerge throughout Philo's writings. H. CHADWICK[217] regards Philo as a valid scriptural philosopher, and E. R. GOODENOUGH,[218] in a detailed study, seeks to establish him as a persuasive

---

[207] Opif. 160–2, 165–7.

[208] Qu. Gen. iii:1.

[209] Opif. 171–2. Epicureanism is attacked also in the allegorical exegesis of Ex. 2:12–5 in Fuga 147–8. Cf. also Som. ii:209, 283.

[210] Opif. 170.

[211] Ibid. 171.

[212] Aet. 84; Leg. Alleg. 197; Migr. 179–81.

[213] Som. i:2.

[214] Ibid. ii:49.

[215] WILFRED L. KNOX, Some Hellenistic Elements in Primitive Christianity (London, 1944), p. 34. F. H. COLSON and G. H. WHITAKER (Philo, I, pp. ix–xxii) describe Philo as an "eclectic" who could only interpret but not create, being "entirely devoid of creative genius" (pp. xvi–xvii).

[216] HARRY AUSTRYN WOLFSON, Philo, Foundations of Religious Philosophy in Judaism, Christianity and Islam, 2 vols. (Cambridge, Massachusetts, 1948). See also JACQUES CAZEAU, Système implicite dans l'exégèse de Philon. Un exemple: le De praemiis, SP., VI (1979–80), pp. 3, 5.

[217] HENRY CHADWICK, St. Paul and Philo of Alexandria, BJRL., XLVIII (1966), pp. 290–2.

[218] "Philo is the chief source for knowledge of the details of this (Hellenized-Judaistic) Mystery, but he does not stand alone . . . certainly it is in terms of the Mystery that Philo alone becomes intelligible, for all his writing is oriented about it, and directed toward its

purveyor of a Jewish mysticism. He argues that the Torah was not merged into
this mystery, but rather that Mosaic religion was seen as "the Greater Mystery"
within Philo's world.[219]

J. DRUMMOND regards Philo's purpose as the desire not

". . . to step into the arena as the champion of a new philosophy, but rather
to present an *apologia* for the teaching of Moses by showing that, even where
it appeared questionable or trifling, it was full of the highest philosophical
truth. His philosophy, therefore, only comes in by the way, and is guided
by the requirements of his biblical interpretation".[220]

He declares that Philo was following the Alexandrian tradition – a tradition of
eclecticism[221] – while still regarding himself as a devout orthodox Jew writing to
defend the Mosaic faith "not only against idolatrous superstition or atheistic
philosophy, but against the free-thinking tendencies among his own people".[222]
E. BRÉHIER sees Philo as greatly influenced by those eddies of thought at Alexandria[223] which later were to produce the various streams of Gnosticism.

Not surprisingly, explicit debate is found within the ranks of students of
Philo. W. L. KNOX criticizes the tidy system of thought which WOLFSON finds in
Philo's works. He contends that WOLFSON falls into wishful thinking in seeking
to use the "hypothetico-deductive method" (i:106) with which "to uncover
(Philo's) unuttered thoughts and to reconstruct the latent processes of Philo's
reasoning". KNOX also asserts that WOLFSON fails to assess "the importance of the
later Stoic-Platonism or Platonic Stoicism (with a dash of Pythagoreanism)" in
Philo's thought and thus fails to discuss adequately the Logos.[224] Both KNOX and
WOLFSON criticize GOODENOUGH's assessment of Philo's works. WOLFSON considers it was not Philo's aim to present Judaism as a "better mystery" than the
religions of his environment, while KNOX regards the effort to understand Philo's
thought in terms of a "Light-mystery" religion as a misconception of his aim.[225]
Rather, Philo's aim he believes

". . . was to justify Judaism in terms of contemporary thought, and to read
into it as much of the conventional theology of the Hellenistic world as he
could drag in by hook or by crook. His desire was partly due to the need of
countering anti-Semitic propaganda; but it was enhanced by the fact that

---

explanation". – E. R. GOODENOUGH, By Light, Light. The Mystic Gospel of Hellenistic
Judaism (New Haven, 1935), p. 8.

[219] Ibid., pp. 95–99, 102, 115.
[220] JAMES DRUMMOND, Philo Judaeus or The Jewish Alexandrian Philosophy in its Development and Completion (London, 1888), I, p. 1.
[221] Ibid., pp. 2–3.
[222] Ibid., p. 13.
[223] ÉMILE BRÉHIER, Les Idées Philosophiques et Religieuses de Philon d'Alexandrie, Études
de Philosophie médiévale, VIII (Paris, 1925), pp. 316–7.
[224] WILFRED L. KNOX reviewing WOLFSON, Philo: JTS., XLIX (1948), pp. 210–4.
[225] W. L. KNOX, St. Paul and the Church of the Gentiles (Cambridge, 1961), p. ix.

Judaism was far more of a missionary religion than most contemporary cults".[226]

Our difficulty is the lack of any attempt by Philo to set out a completed system of thought.[227] His primary material was drawn from the Jewish Pentateuch and he wrote as a member of the Jewish πολίτευμα[228] in Alexandria yet the features of Platonic, Stoic and neo-Pythagorean ideas can be readily seen interwoven into his thought.[229] The debate, it seems, will continue for some time whether Philo was a Jewish thinker overmastered by a Greek education, or a Greek philosopher anchored at heart to a Jewish identity. However SANDMEL's basic assessment is sound that

". . . the little or greatly hellenized Philo is in his own light a loyal Jew and that the philosophy . . . he used in his writings seemed to him either congruent with his Judaism or even derived from it . . ."[230]

That scholar concludes that within the wider stream of Judaism "Philo reflects Hellenized Judaism but at the same time he is in many ways unique within that entity we can call Hellenistic Judaism . . . It is not wrong to regard Philo as representing a marginal *viewpoint*. But I have seen no evidence that Philo speaks for a segment of Jewry large enough to be called a *marginal Judaism*."[231]

A further important question to ask is, for whom were his political writings intended? 'Legatio ad Gaium' and 'In Flaccum' were written mainly for Gentiles and sought to show both the folly of persecuting Jews and that a just ruler need have no fear of doubting their genuine allegiance. 'De Iosepho' and 'De Vita Mosis' were written for those Jews facing the temptation to abandon their links with Judaism through the attraction of Hellenistic thought. Both of these political writings show that the ideal ruler described in Greek philosophy is to be found within the ranks of Judaism in the persons of Moses and Joseph. I cannot agree with GOODENOUGH who, in accordance with his theory that Philo was writing at times "in code" for his readers, considers that 'De Specialibus Legibus' was

---

[226] Ibid., p. x.

[227] DRUMMOND, Philo Judaeus, I, p. 257.

[228] H. STUART JONES, Claudius and the Jewish Question at Alexandria, JRS., XVI (1926), p. 27–29.

[229] For a discussion of Pythagorean influence on Philo's thought on kingship, see GOODENOUGH, Politics, pp. 94–6 and for Stoic-Platonic influence on his ideas, ID., Light, pp. 4, 20–1, 55–6, 81, 121–4, 137–8, 374–8. Cf. HEINEMANN, Philons Bildung, pp. 183, 542–3.

[230] SAMUEL SANDMEL, Philo's Place in Judaism: A Study of Conceptions of Abraham in Jewish Literature, HUCA., XXV (1954), p. 213. However the Gentile influence upon him produced more than just a "veneer of Hellenistic philosophy" – contra: C. A. PIERCE, Conscience in the New Testament (London, 1958), p. 41. CHADWICK (Philo, p. 137) comments on V. Mos. i:23 that "it reflects Philo's own experience when he credits Moses with Greek tutors".

[231] SAMUEL SANDMEL, Philo of Alexandria – an Introduction (Oxford, 1979), p. 147.

intended for the Alexandrian Jews,[232] and 'De Iosepho' for Gentile readers. In the latter Philo argued "by innuendo" that Joseph provided the ideal for any Roman prefect ruling over Egypt. This conclusion is linked with his assessment of the political feelings hidden in Philo's allegorical writings, namely resentment towards the Romans.[233] Judging from the history of Jewish relationships with Roman rule in Alexandria this seems unlikely, and GOODENOUGH has himself to resort to allegorizing[234] to present a tidy system of political thought propagated either "direct", "in code" or "by innuendo" in Philo's writings. Also, as A. H. M. JONES notes, GOODENOUGH presents

> "a mechanical and schematic picture of Jew versus Roman. The true position was far more complicated. The Alexandrians were . . . bitterly hostile to the imperial government . . . In contrast the privileges of the Jewish community had been, if not enlarged, steadily maintained . . . In these circumstances Professor Goodenough's picture of Philo as a bitter opponent of Rome would, if true, prove him to have been a senseless fanatic".[235]

A more straightforward explanation would be to take Philo's allegorical writings as the systematic collection of philosophical-expository material from his synagogue addresses — what COLSON calls "a mosaic of sermonettes".[236] Filled out by Philo's expansions on his sources they are the sustained work of this expositor of the Sabbath lection[237] in an Alexandrian synagogue. This understanding would fit well Philo's self-defence against two other hermeneutical methods likely to be found amongst other expositors which he regarded as inadequate. On the one side were those whom he called the "literalists", i.e. "those who are used to discussing in details the literal and outward interpretation of the laws".[238] Philo's purpose was wider, so that he could "in obedience to the suggestions of right reason expound in full the inward interpretation".[239] This

---

[232] GOODENOUGH, Politics, pp. 31–32.

[233] Ibid., pp. 6–7.

[234] Ibid., pp. 5–8.

[235] A. H. M. JONES in his review of GOODENOUGH's 'Politics' in: JTS., XL (1939), p. 183.

[236] COLSON and WHITAKER, Philo, I, p. xiv. In a personal discussion Dr. CHADWICK doubted my point. However WOLFSON (I, p. 96) refers to Philo's writing having "the form of sermons or homilies" and P. BORGEN (Bread from Heaven: An Exegetical Study of the Concept of Manna in the Gospel of John and the Writings of Philo, Novum Testamentum, Suppl. X [Leiden, 1965] pp. 46–51) detects in Philo's work a homiletic pattern similar to that found in John. RICHARD D. HECHT goes further and describes Philo's exposition of the Law as a "rewritten Bible" (Patterns of Exegesis in Philo's Interpretation of Leviticus, SP., VI [1979–80], p. 135).

[237] Though JAMES R. ROYSE makes this point only in relation to Philo's 'Questions and answers on Genesis and Exodus' (The Original Structure of Philo's Quaestiones, SP., IV [1975], pp. 62–3) I consider that it has wider application. Cf. BURTON L. MACK who in 'Exegetical Traditions in Alexandrian Judaism', SP., III (1974), pp. 71–109 indicates and begins the work that needs to be done on this question.

[238] Sobr. 33.

[239] Ibid.

latter course involved, as Philo admitted, "resorting to allegory".[240] He often extolled the allegorical method of exposition:[241]

> . . . allegory, that wise master builder[242] . . .
> . . . the scientific mode of interpretation[243]. . .
> . . . words in their plain sense are symbols of things latent and obscure.[244]

Philo did not consider that the other group's knowledge was erroneous. Rather it was inadequate. They had not recognized "that the letter is to the oracle but as the shadow to the substance".[244a] He did not reject the literal sense (which would be held by the conservative Jews in Alexandria), especially over such an important matter as, for example, circumcision.[244b] He discussed its literal and allegorical interpretations and likened them to the body and the soul. As care had to be taken for the body so one "must pay heed to the letter of the laws". By incorporating the literal sense into their understanding Philo assured his readers that they "would not incur the censure of the majority and the charges they are sure to bring against us".[244c] Thus there was a division between the "modernists", a minority,[245] and the "conservatives", a majority, in Alexandrian Jewry.

On Philo's other flank there were what GOODENOUGH calls the "radical allegorists"[246] who dismissed the worth of any literal interpretation of the Scriptures. These expositors were strongly influenced by the surrounding Gentile philosophies, more so than Philo, though, as noted earlier, one must not regard allegorical interpretation as foreign to the expository methods of conservative Judaism.[247] As HAY notes Philo's criticism of them occurs only in one passage — Migr. 88—93. In jettisoning any literal understanding of the scriptural text they were cutting themselves off from an adequate expression of Jewish identity lived out in obedience to the Mosaic law. Pertinent to this study is HAY's suggestion that such allegorists were likely to be "disengaged politically"[248] from the defence of the Jewish ἔθνος and their "established customs" in Alexandria. Philo, while supportive of their philosophy, urges them to remain within the dimensions of Jewish practice.

---

[240] Agr. 27.
[241] Philo's references to other allegorists are numerous. For the listing of passages see HAY, Philo's References, pp. 42—3. On the contrast with the literalists: ibid. pp. 45—6.
[242] Som. ii:8.
[243] Fuga 108.
[244] Spec. Leg. i:200; Conf. 14, 143.
[244a] Conf. 190.
[244b] Migr. 93.
[244c] Ibid. 92—3.
[245] HAY, Philo's References, p. 45.
[246] GOODENOUGH, Light, pp. 254, 295, 301.
[247] Cf. n. 147. On Philo's relation to Gentile allegorism: JESSE SCOTT BOUGHTON, The Idea of Progress in Philo Judaeus (New York, 1932), pp. 35—54; BRÉHIER, Idées philosophiques, pp. 37—61.
[248] HAY, Philo's References, p. 48.

Philo's remarks on both schools[249] appear to be most appropriately addressed to an audience of Jews and Gentile proselytes who were being wooed by these
differing expository methods and the teachings associated with them. He took a
mediating position, commencing from the Jewish Scriptures, open to a literal
meaning but influenced in his exposition by Hellenistic ideas. To say that he drew
from these differing sources does not mean that he merely produced a "scissors
and paste" commentary on the Scriptures. Certainly his finished product was not
a tidily wrapped philosophical parcel (pace WOLFSON) but as CHADWICK rightly
concludes, "there at least emerges a coherent pattern of attitudes, a religious and
philosophical climate".[250] With this background to Philo in mind we can turn to
his political ideas.

IV. Philo's Attitude to Roman Rule

1. In 'Legatio ad Gaium' and 'In Flaccum'

Before examining 'Legatio ad Gaium' and 'In Flaccum' it is necessary to
ascertain the purposes and audiences Philo had in mind in writing the documents.[251] COLSON[252] and SCHÜRER[253] argue that the former was basically "an
invective against Gaius"[254] and that the information concerning the embassy
merely illustrated this theme. Eusebius regarded the title Περὶ Ἀρετῶν as an
ironical comment on Gaius' vices. SMALLWOOD[255] notes other suggestions, stating that the majority of scholars favour the rendering of Ἀρετῶν in the sense of
Θεία Δύναμις; the contents thus demonstrating God's just and powerful care for
his people. Such a purpose would parallel that of 'In Flaccum'.[256]

The 'Legatio ad Gaium' was written after the death of Gaius and the accession of Claudius[257] while the brief comment in Leg. 3 indicates Philo's appreciation of the stable rule subsequently exercised by the imperial authorities, which
demonstrated to his readers, he trusts, the sure providence of God. GOOD-
ENOUGH[258] contends that he was writing to Claudius, giving advice on the qual-

---

[249] BRÉHIER, Idées philosophiques, p. 62—6.

[250] CHADWICK, Philo, pp. 138, 140—1.

[251] The question of the relation of 'Legatio ad Gaium' to the five books of Philo mentioned by
  Eusebius (Hist. Eccl. ii:5) is not relevant here; for a discussion see SMALLWOOD, Legatio,
  pp. 37—43.

[252] COLSON, Philo, X, pp. xvi—xxvi.

[253] EMIL SCHÜRER, Geschichte des Jüdischen Volkes im Zeitalter Jesu Christi (Leipzig,
  1909), III, pp. 677—81.

[254] Hist. Eccl. ii:18, 8.

[255] Ibid., pp. 39—40.

[256] Flacc. 189—91; cf. Leg. 3, 293, 347—8; SMALLWOOD, Legatio, p. 325.

[257] Leg. 107, 206.

[258] Politics, pp. 19—20, 103—5; cf. SMALLWOOD, Legatio, p. 182.

ities of leaders through the mouth of Macro and idealizing the presentation of the rule of Augustus and Tiberius. He noted Philo's references to the numerous Jewish communities in the empire[259] and sees it as an indirect warning to the new emperor of the need to appreciate carefully their strength and support. From a study of the contents the following possibilities arise: it was written for Jews wavering from the moral monotheism central to their faith, for Gentiles to demonstrate the action of the true God, for the Roman authorities and in particular Claudius.

There are indications in favour of all three and a combination of audiences may have been in view. Sometimes anomalous features appear as regards their identity. Philo's introduction to his treatise may have been meant to reassure Jews, but they are spoken of in terms seemingly intended for Gentile readers.[260] The reference to Roman law[261] was possibly meant for Jewish ears, and the Jews are portrayed as standing alone in the dark years of Gaius' rule, opposing his claims to deification.[262] The work may thus have been written to Jews in Alexandria[263] who were disappointed with the limited success of the embassy,[264] or who needed assurance for their monotheistic belief.

The suggestions of a wide Gentile audience are more general than particular — Leg. 3 has been noted, and 118, 210—2 appear to be explanations of Jewish belief. These factors may point to a narrower audience, the most powerful Gentile, Claudius, and his assistants. More particular pointers to this latter grouping can be found in the glowing description of the Roman world,[265] the mention of the regard Julia Augusta had for the protection of Judaism,[266] and above all the deliberate references to the praiseworthy and just policies carried out by Augustus and Tiberius towards the Jews as well as towards their subjects generally in the empire.[267] Before Gaius' rule was distorted by his madness he too, in Philo's view, had ruled wisely after the same pattern.

As if writing to one with considerable power in the empire, Philo drew attention to the number of the Jews and their strength,[268] allied with their love of peace,[269] their respect for the emperor,[270] and their reasonable requests.[271] Even

---

[259] Ibid., p. 20; Leg. 215, 281—2.

[260] Leg. 3.

[261] Ibid. 28—9. SMALLWOOD, Legatio, p. 176.

[262] Ibid. 6—116, 133, 162, 180—3, 190, 198, 204, 268, 335—7, 339—50, 359; cf. SMALLWOOD, ibid., p. 210.

[263] Though Alexandria was praised highly (173 cf. 338), Philo was critical of the Alexandrians (119—20, 162—72).

[264] Ibid. 3, 193—7, 370—1. Was it the extreme allegorists who held little regard for the Temple (212)?

[265] Ibid. 8—13.

[266] Ibid. 310—332.

[267] Ibid. 140—161, 167. He records Tiberius' rebuke of Pilate for the latter's anti-Jewish policy (303—5).

[268] Ibid. 215—7, 226, 281—3.

[269] Leg. 233, 236, 279—80.

[270] Ibid. 301, 356.

[271] Ibid. 243.

with the surprising omission of Claudius as a likely claimant to power in Leg. 32,[272] the terse description of Claudius' punishment of Helicon,[273] and the account of Roman law-court procedure,[274] the other features indicate that he at least was in mind as a recipient of Philo's writing. The evidence points to the work having a dual purpose — to persuade Claudius to look favourably on the Jews,[275] and to convince those among the latter who were wavering in their faith over the events in Alexandria that their God was still sovereign over the affairs of mankind.

To turn to Philo's other overt political treatise, if the καὶ of Flacc. 191 is translated as "also", then, as COLSON[276] suggests, this account may have followed that dealing with Sejanus' anti-Jewish policy and the judgment he received. GOODENOUGH,[277] considering that the contents give the only indication of its purpose and audience, regards this writing as the "second treatise" to which Eusebius referred[278] which describes in greater and separate detail the pogrom in Alexandria. He considers it to be written for Gentile readers, "probably a Roman audience", unacquainted with the city.[279] Narrowing the time and audience even further, he claims that the intended recipient was the new prefect appointed after Gaius' assassination. This was a time of renewed Jewish power in Alexandria because not only did the Jews turn in force upon their Alexandrian persecutors but Claudius had Isidorus and Lampo condemned to death and in his letter to Alexandria, though he rebuked the Jews, he established their right to live peace-fully in the city.[280] 'In Flaccum' is not anti-Roman in tone,[281] but contains a "bold warning that any prefect (will) bring himself to the gutter if he (deals) unfavourably with God's chosen people",[282] while the moral to the account (191) would have encouraged Jewish readers, especially those in Alexandria.

In considering Philo's attitude to Roman rule, at the outset one notes that he believed that Roman power was encompassed by the mightier force of God. Assuring his readers of the reality of God's providential care for mankind, and

---

[272] "Although Philo is writing under Claudius, who, as the events of January, 41, showed, could be a rallying point if necessary, he completely overlooks him here" (SMALLWOOD, Legatio, p. 177).

[273] Ibid. 206.

[274] Ibid. 350. J. A. CROOK (Consilium Principis. Imperial Councils and Counsellors from Augustus to Diocletian [Cambridge, 1955], p. 40) considers Philo was contrasting Gaius' practice with what he knew to be Claudius'. The procedure is described in detail to emphasize the record of Gaius' injustice towards this loyal and peace-loving group in the empire.

[275] The readers were also to perceive clearly the prefect's guilt in acting against the Jews (ibid. 132).

[276] F. H. COLSON, Philo, IX, p. 295 n.a. Eusebius states that Philo wrote of Sejanus' anti-Jewish policy (Hist. Eccl. ii:5.6).

[277] GOODENOUGH, Politics, pp. 9—10. SMALLWOOD notes the similar conclusion reached by MASSEBIEAU and COHN (Legatio, p. 41).

[278] Hist. Eccl. ii:5.6 — δεύτερον σύγγραμμα.

[279] Flacc. 45, 55, 74, 78—80, 89, 91, 116.

[280] GOODENOUGH, Politics, p. 11.

[281] Cf. BALSDON (Gaius, p. 221) who considers it "more spiteful in tone than the Legatio".

[282] GOODENOUGH, Politics, p. 10.

especially for His people, he intimated that "the present critical time and the many important questions now being settled"[283] under Claudius indicated God's control over the political and social order. Granted that Philo wrote too extravagantly of the peaceful state of the Roman empire before Gaius' madness,[284] I cannot agree with GOODENOUGH[285] that Philo did not appreciate the benefits of Roman rule. His emphasis on peace, law and harmony[286] in describing the Roman order was in accord with the conditions he considered most desirable in a state. Philo was not alone in his respect for Roman rule. Though the contents of Agrippa's letter are probably Philo's handiwork,[287] Agrippa's friendship with Gaius and later Claudius as well as Josephus' views[288] indicate a respect wider than Philo's circle. Paul the Pharisee based his exhortation about respect for the Roman authorities on sound Jewish monotheism.[289]

In 'In Flaccum' also Philo wrote favourably of imperial rule, pointing again to the excellencies of Augustus' and Tiberius' administrations. Presuming that this treatise was written for the eyes of the new prefect, as well perhaps as for Claudius himself, one can allow for hyperbole in the description of the early emperors in comparison with Gaius and his prefect Flaccus. Nevertheless Philo was not being hypocritical in commending features of Roman rule. In seeking to highlight the Jewish embassy's anxious audience with Gaius, where the latter's advisers and his own whims are painted in such critical colours, Philo described earlier imperial hearings in glowing terms stating that when cities sent embassies these were duly heard and their evidence weighed impartially.[290] The contrasting comparison with Gaius' procedure would have been acceptable to those acquainted with the latter's judicial proceedings,[291] though the memory of Tiberius' record in the latter years of his rule would have set him with and not against Gaius.[292]

---

[283] Leg. 3. SMALLWOOD suggests that he is referring to Claudius' efforts to deal with the Alexandrian situation in the first year of his principate. "The present participle παρών and the phrase κατ' αὐτόν suggest that Philo was writing while tension was still high, perhaps before Claudius' final decision was made known by his *Letter* in November, 41" (Legatio, p. 152).

[284] In exalting the rule of Augustus and Tiberius certainly Philo was aiming to underline the havoc wrought by Gaius. It meant that he presented a consciously over-optimistic picture of peace in Tiberius' reign, omitting reference to the troubles in Germany, Africa, Gaul and Thrace of which it is not too bold to assume he must have known some details.

[285] Politics, pp. 40–41, cf. SMALLWOOD, Legatio, p. 158.

[286] Leg. 141.

[287] SOLOMON ZEITLIN, Did Agrippa write a letter to Gaius Caligula?, JQR., LVI (1965), pp. 27–31.

[288] E.g. Agrippa's words in BJ. ii:350–4, 390, 401, represent Josephus' sentiments.

[289] Ro. 13:1–7; S.B. III, pp. 303–5; cf. H. LOEWE, Render unto Caesar (Cambridge, 1940), pp. 28–9.

[290] Flacc. 105–6. For officials having to render an account cf. I.G. 1². 91.25,27 – λόγον διδόντων (rendering of account), εὐθύνας διδόντων (conduct of official); cf. 105.

[291] Cf. Suet. Calig. 38.

[292] ROBIN SEAGER, Tiberius (London, 1972), pp. 226–40.

a) Augustus

The occasion for Philo's praise of Augustus was the contrast between his rule and that of Gaius. It must be remembered that he was writing a polemic and not a calm discussion of the merits and demerits of the emperors. Thus the superlatives used must be tempered by his other views on ideal rule and the lessons he wished to impress on his reader in 'Legatio ad Gaium'. One must admit that there was a security and a ready appeal to law enjoyed by the Jews in the early Roman empire which could not be ignored by Philo. His praise of Roman government was exaggerated for the purpose of this treatise, but it was not hypocritical.

The features of Augustus' rule to which Philo drew particular attention were the protection of Jewish religious freedom,[293] the provision of peace on land and sea,[294] and government with order.[295] What was particularly appreciated was Augustus' policy of non-interference with Jewish customs,[296] and Philo recounted his unprecedented action in safeguarding Jewish welfare in Rome by arranging alternative corn-distribution for the Jews when observance of the sabbath precluded them from receiving it.[297] So eager was Philo to appeal to imperial favour that he contended that Augustus' awareness of the value of the Jews[298] (rather than the precedents set by Julius Caesar[299]) shaped his policy.[300] Our information from Suetonius[301] leads us to doubt Philo's rosy estimate of Augustus' thinking, but it does indicate his determination to link together Augustus' consideration of Jewish welfare with his efficient administration of the Roman empire. Where Philo levelled criticism against maladministration, it was against Flaccus who had failed to exercise his power to protect Jewish rights.[302]

The contents of Philo's passage have led some to doubt whether all that refers to Augustus comes from his hand. It is questioned whether Philo the Jew would, as the climax of his description, recount the voting of divine honours to Augustus by all the civilised world and also write so proudly of the Σεβαστεῖον in Alexandria.[303] Rather it is suggested that Philo had incorporated a local Gentile writing into his own. It is important to observe that the polytheistic elements noted above were written in the third person. It is likely that he drew upon

---

[293] Leg. 153—9, 311—8.

[294] Ibid. 144—6, 309. On the suppression of piracy, see SMALLWOOD, Legatio, p. 229.

[295] Ibid. 147.

[296] Ibid. 153—5. SMALLWOOD, ibid. p. 240.

[297] Leg. 153—161. SMALLWOOD, Legatio, p. 242.

[298] Leg. 156.

[299] AJ. xiv:190—216.

[300] In Leg. 240 there is brief mention of the interest of M. Vipsanius Agrippa, Gaius' grandfather, in maintaining Jewish religious liberty, but Philo omits, probably deliberately, to allude to Pompey's entry into the holy of holies contrary to Jewish wishes (292, 300; cf. BJ. i:152).

[301] According to Suetonius (Aug. 93), who wrote on Augustus' attitude to foreign rites, he praised Gaius for not offering prayers at Jerusalem.

[302] Leg. 132.

[303] So W. L. KNOX, Some Hellenistic Elements in Primitive Christianity (London, 1944), pp. 48—9.

contemporary eulogies for his terminology and reproduced their inflated terms of praise.[304] Philo is not presenting his own confession of belief. This is clear on examining Leg. 154 where he noted that Augustus did not accept the significance of these honours and refused to be regarded as a god. Whether the emperor went so far as to "approve" the Jews who refrained from accepting him as a god is extremely doubtful, though he was aware of the sizable Jewish community in Rome, on one occasion having been petitioned by a deputation of over eight thousand Jews in that city.[305] He did permit the Jews to offer sacrifices to their God on his behalf rather than to his "genius", the latter cultic action being contrary to their beliefs.

Philo extracted all that he could from Augustus' official policy towards the Jews. He read into his awareness of their sacrifices the belief that

> "it was essential for a special place consecrated to the invisible God be set apart in the earthly regions, and for it to contain no visible representation to help people to share in fair hopes and enjoy perfect blessings".[306]

It is unlikely either that Augustus had special regards for the Temple[307] or was noted as a philosopher as Philo asserted.[308] One can see the latter point in the portrayal of him as a sage-king, but it seems to be flattery rather than a conscious reference to his fulfilling the ideal Philo enunciated elsewhere in Platonic-Stoic terms. To heighten Gaius' ignorance and ungodliness Philo was prepared to be extravagant in praise towards his predecessors, and these passages were intended for an emperor claiming a much closer relationship with Augustus and Tiberius than with Gaius.

b) Tiberius

As with Philo's treatment of Augustus, the strong points of Tiberius' rule are accentuated and the troubles either ignored or minimized. He also is presented primarily in terms of the contrast between his rule and that of Gaius. Thus he is said to have bequeathed to his successor prosperity, peace, harmony and good laws so that people marvelled at the nature of the Empire.[309] Our other sources[310] confirm Tiberius' interest and accomplishments in learning,[311] and his capable administration of the Empire's economy, though Philo describes the wealth he ac-

---

[304] GERHARD DELLING, Philons Enkomion auf Augustus, Klio, LIV (1972), pp. 175—87.

[305] BJ. ii:80; AJ. xvii:300.

[306] Leg. 318. SMALLWOOD's translation (Legatio, p. 132).

[307] The usual offering to pagan gods would have aroused Jewish feeling, thus Augustus accommodated the custom to a special people in the empire.

[308] Suetonius (Aug. 75, 79) refers to his philosophical reading and writings but they seem not to have been a substantial feature of his activities.

[309] Leg. 8.

[310] Suet., Tib. 70; Tac., Ann. iv:58.1.

[311] Leg. 142.

cumulated for the state in order to heighten Gaius' extravagance.[312] Philo is silent on the mutinies on the Rhine and Danube which broke out on Augustus' death. This was not quite the contrast Philo was looking for in comparison with Gaius' promising accession. That Gaius came to rule Philo explains as the work of fate, for Tiberius was wary of his ambitions.[313] This explanation differs from the account in 'In Flaccum' of Gaius' seizure of sole imperial power. There Tiberius is held to be in part responsible for not acting on his negative assessment of Gaius, having been deceived according to Philo by a cunning adviser, Macro.[314]

Philo idealizes the rule of Tiberius. It was inaccurate, and Philo would have known it, to write that

> "he held sway over land and sea and did not let the smallest spark of war smoulder in Greece or the world outside Greece, and to the very end of his life provided peace and the blessings of peace . . ."[315]

Germanicus' campaigns alone would have been known in Alexandria without too great a delay, even if the troubles in Africa, Gaul and Thrace were not widely known. Similarly Philo does not refer to Tiberius' expulsion of the Jews recorded in other ancient sources.[316] Any anti-Jewish action was due to Sejanus, argues Philo, and the emperor's expulsion of the Jews is not mentioned. Philo reverses the picture further by portraying Tiberius as filled with righteous indignation at Sejanus' "slanderous" attack on the Jews and as seeking to reassure them of their rights, "since they are of a peaceful disposition", and of their Laws "since they are conducive to public order".[317] In Leg. 160—1 he lauds the loyalty of his countrymen and Tiberius' acknowledgement of their value to the empire. It is the interest of his fellow Jews that is paramount, not accuracy, and the praise of Tiberius is decidedly for imperial consumption.[318] Even the glowing description of his manner reads like that of a doting friend,[319] and not fair comment, if we are to give some credence to the predominant picture of Tiberius' dourness.[320]

As regards 'In Flaccum', Philo has little to say of the individual emperors. Augustus is not mentioned separately, and Tiberius appears only in connection with Macro's defence of Gaius. Philo states that the emperor, on a number of occasions, had resolved to be rid of Gaius[321] because the latter was "a reprobate naturally unfitted for authority" and because he feared for Gemellus' safety after Gaius' accession.[322] Whether there was any substance in this account of Tiberius'

---

[312] Ibid. 9. Tiberius' accumulation of wealth is noted elsewhere; cf. Suet., Calig. 37; Dio lix:2.5—6.
[313] Ibid. 24.
[314] Flacc. 11—13.
[315] Leg. 141.
[316] Tac., Ann. ii:85.5; Suet., Tib. 36; Dio lvii:18.5a; Joseph., AJ. xviii:81—5.
[317] Ibid. 161.
[318] Cf. SMALLWOOD, Legatio, p. 244.
[319] Ibid. 167.
[320] ROBIN SEAGER, Tiberius (London, 1972), pp. 56—7, 118, 144.
[321] Leg. 41, 58. BALSDON (Gaius, p. 21) is sceptical of the report.
[322] Flacc. 12.

estimate seems very doubtful,[323] but that Tiberius was fooled by Macro's defence of Gaius does not speak highly for the emperor whom Philo is praising in contrast to his successor.

c) Gaius

Not only is there a contrast drawn between Gaius and the earlier emperors, but, as with Philo's presentation of Flaccus, his villainy is heightened by the contrast between the populace's joyous expectations at his accession and the later injustice of his rule. The Jews shared in the celebrations, offering a hecatomb at his accession.[324] Despite Philo's emphasis on the festivities, the description in Leg. 12 may not be exaggerated.[325] However to describe the social conditions in such terms as

> "the rich had no precedence over the poor, nor the distinguished over the obscure, creditors were not above debtors, nor masters above slaves, the times giving equality before the law"[326]

was pretentious.[327]

A change for the worse occured in Gaius' behaviour as a consequence of his serious illness. This was all good dramatic effect for Philo's purpose, but contradicts the suggestion of his unsuitability for ruling which, according to Philo, Tiberius earlier had detected so accurately.[328] That Gaius was not of sound health is well attested though the debate still continues as to the nature of his illness.[329] Philo refers to it to accentuate this unhealthy condition as a significant cause of Gaius' hostility to the Jews. It arose out of sickness not reason, out of delusions of self-grandeur and a refusal to acknowledge the benefits which the Jews contributed to the empire. Consequent upon the change Gaius epitomized all that was to be rejected by the ideal ruler. Instead of σωφροσύνη there was now ἀκρασία; instead of a yearning for the pursuits of the mind the emperor's attention was captured by bodily pleasure, food, drink and unrestrained eating, practices which Philo elsewhere condemns in rulers.[330] Finally, instead of purity

---

[323] SMALLWOOD, Legatio, pp. 172–3.

[324] Leg. 231, 356. The daily offerings for the emperor are mentioned in 157.

[325] Cf. SMALLWOOD, Legatio, pp. 161–2.

[326] Leg. 13.

[327] The phrases were probably drawn from the purple passages of accession rhetoric. SMALLWOOD (Legatio, pp. 163–4) points out similarities with various Utopias described by Aratus, Iambulus and the prophecy of material prosperity and social concord in Oracula Sibyllina iii:367–80.

[328] Flacc. 12; Leg. 34; cf. Suet., Calig. 11.

[329] Suggestions are that Gaius had a nervous breakdown (BALSDON, Gaius, p. 36) or was an alcoholic or a neurotic (M. CARY, A History of Rome down to the Reign of Constantine [London, 1957], n. 2). More recent suggestions are that he had an overactive thyroid gland (ROBERT S. KATZ, The Illness of Caligula, CW., LXV [1972], pp. 223–4) or that he was a manic (VIN MASSARO and IAIN MONTGOMERY, Gaius – Mad, Bad, Ill, or all Three?, Latomus, XXXVII [1978], pp. 908–9).

[330] See pp. 492–3.

which Moses pre-eminently displayed[331] and which marked Joseph's treatment of Potiphar's wife,[332] Gaius practiced sexual immorality, "that destroyer of soul and body".[333] Philo implied that Gaius had not previously indulged in these activities because of Tiberius' presence.[334]

Certainly he is not averse to creating a contrast between the behaviour of Gaius and his predecessor but as SMALLWOOD comments, "if Philo had been able to represent his enemy Gaius as leading a thoroughly disreputable life before as well as after his accession, he would hardly have failed to do so".[335] The likely picture is that the tendencies of which Philo disapproves were present earlier but the sickness caused them to come to full expression.[336]

From Gaius' removal of his rivals Philo adduces the first clear manifestation of that brutal cunning which he sees as a feature of his rule.[337] To worsen the comparison with the early promise of that rule Philo states that the mastery of his passions over his policies grew rather than abated with time.[338] Again Philo's words do not quite agree with our other sources. For example, he states that Gemellus was a "closer heir" than Gaius and that the former was killed on a trumped-up charge of conspiracy. SMALLWOOD[339] contends that Philo is viewing the matter from the viewpoint of Gemellus' supporters and oversimplifying the situation. As Flaccus probably held that view, Philo may have been simply reproducing what was current in Alexandria. Gaius had good grounds for expecting the chief inheritance.[340] Nor was it surprising that he had Gemellus removed, for his supporters could well have given cause for suspicion. His ambition to be rid of Gemellus, whether the latter was guilty or not, cannot be dismissed as Philo's creation.

---

[331] V. Mos. i:1.25–33.

[332] Jos. 41–8.

[333] Leg. 14, cf. Suet., Calig. 36.

[334] CAH., X, pp. 638–9; SEAGER, Tiberius, p. 202.

[335] SMALLWOOD, Legatio, p. 164. Was Philo aware of the incident reported by Tacitus (Ann. vi:9) of which he would have disapproved but over which the contemporary world would not have been duly concerned?

[336] Leg. 14, 22, 34, 59; Suet., Calig. 10; Tac., Ann. vi:9; 20.1.

[337] Leg. 22.

[338] Flacc. 182. ANDRÉ PELLETIER (in editing 'In Flaccum' [Paris, 1967], p. 16) makes the plausible suggestion that Philo was influenced in his presentation by such narratives as Esth. 5:13–10:3 and 2 Macc. 5:15–6; 7:47–9; 8:16–9:13 which contained similar themes of persecution, divine intervention to rescue God's people and the punishment of the villain.

[339] SMALLWOOD, Legatio, p. 171.

[340] According to Suetonius (Tib. 76) and Dio (lix:1.1) Tiberius divided his inheritance equally between Gaius and Gemellus. Suetonius recorded a rumour that at one time to free himself of succession worries Tiberius would have killed both (Tib. 72). Tacitus (Ann. vi:46), Suetonius (Calig. 19) and Josephus (AJ. xvii:211) testify to the emperor's greater affection for Gemellus. Josephus records an incident whereby Tiberius was reluctantly persuaded that the gods had chosen Gaius and so commissioned him to rule (AJ. xviii:211–4, 219–24). If Tacitus is to be believed he foresaw Gemellus' death at Gaius' instigation; cf. Suet., Calig. 13.3; BALSDON, Gaius, pp. 17–18; SMALLWOOD, Legatio, pp. 169–71.

There are times however, when Philo presents what appear to be deliberate misrepresentations of Gaius,[341] for example, in charging that he bore ill-will towards the Claudian house. The written sources, the coins and the calender evidence gathered by SMALLWOOD[342] fly in the face of this opinion and though the imperial audience knew otherwise, Claudius' estimate of his predecessor could have encouraged Philo to be daring on this point.[343] Another example is the depiction of Gaius' rule as inspiring upheaval throughout the empire.[344] Except for the riot at Alexandria and possibly Aedemon's rebellion in Mauretania[345] the empire was relatively peaceful. In contrasting Gaius with mythological heroes who brought peace Philo allows himself poetic licence.

It is Gaius the person, not Gaius the emperor, whom Philo attacks, for it was to his character and not his official acts that the attack on the Jews could be traced. They were persecuted not because they were anti-Roman but because they emerged as those most openly opposed to Gaius. In a striking passage,[346] Gaius is clearly distinguished from his predecessors in that he sought war with the Jewish people, whereas Augustus and Tiberius had upheld their rights. He regarded his subjects as slaves, flouted the law, and ruled as a tyrant.[347] Later Philo illustrates the avarice[348] and the caprice of Gaius,[349] noting practices which we find alleged against Gaius in other sources.[350] Even if he is not substantially correct, that such criticisms were commonly associated with Gaius' misrule would have added force to Philo's polemic. His work is sprinkled with descriptions of Gaius as "quarrelsome and cantankerous",[351] having an "unsociable and uncooperative disposition and inconsistency of character",[352] "deceptive and false in character",[353] "an iron-hearted and pitiless creature",[354] "an ignoble wretch and utter coward".[355] With biting sarcasm he writes of Gaius' close advisers who taught him the important duties of joking and singing to divert his attention from the pre-

---

[341] λυμεών in Leg. 92 does not necessarily indicate sexual irregularity and it seems unlikely that that is its sense here, else Philo would have enlarged on such an offence.

[342] SMALLWOOD, Legatio, pp. 178—9.

[343] BALSDON, Gaius, pp. 95, 143, 175.

[344] Leg. 90, 104.

[345] SMALLWOOD (Legatio, p. 199) doubts that Philo would have known of the latter disturbance.

[346] Ibid. 119.

[347] The phrase τοῦ ἄρχοντος τρέποντος εἰς δεσπότην indicates such a gradation. Though used elsewhere to denote "master" (SMALLWOOD, Legatio, p. 213), δεσπότης here has the stronger sense of "tyrant". It is probably so used also in 208; cf. 286.

[348] Leg. 343—5.

[349] Ibid., p. 339—42.

[350] Suet., Calig. 27—34; Dio lix:18.1—5.

[351] Leg. 52.

[352] Ibid. 34.

[353] Ibid. 59.

[354] Ibid. 87.

[355] Ibid. 90.

servation of peace in the empire.[356] Even his appearance was displeasing – his body and mind were effeminate and weakened.[357]

It was his ambition for absolute power which led him to overthrow the three restraining forces upon an emperor – the senatorial and equestrian orders, and his family.[358] Here Philo differs from Suetonius. According to the latter Gaius could claim the support of the equestrian order against the Senate almost to the time before his death[359] and certainly so after Macro's removal. Where they do agree is in reporting that the possession of wealth, not criminal offences, marked out some of Gaius' victims.[360] To Philo, his greatest villainy, the blasphemous[361] step of self-deification, was the clearest confirmation of his "mental derangement".[362]

With regard to the Alexandrian situation, Philo does not present a consistent picture of Gaius' role. In his other work 'In Flaccum', the blame for the tragedy is attributed to Flaccus and the anti-Jewish Alexandrian demagogues, whereas in Leg. 115 Philo states that Gaius was already suspicious of the Jews in the Empire as the only group who frowned on his claim to deification. Though the conservative Senatorial families of Rome also found the idea unpalatable, Philo classes all others besides the Jews as agreeable to this blasphemy, some even offering προσκύνησις to the emperor.[363] Having over-simplified the opposition to the emperor, Philo can thus accentuate Gaius' resolve to attack the Jewish people; a resolve of which the Alexandrian mob took advantage.[364] Here one suspects is a fabrication of Gaius' motives which could be woven into a work condemning his injustice towards the Jews. A more accurate estimate is that Gaius first became actively concerned with the attitude of the Jews only after the initial disturbances in Alexandria. As noted earlier[365] the trouble for the Jews in that city arose out of the local situation and the signal for upheaval was not any knowledge of Gaius' attitudes but the arrival of Agrippa. In fact the crowd in mocking him was running a serious risk by insulting the king who was a friend of the emperor from

---

[356] Ibid. 203–4.
[357] Ibid. 110; cf. Suetonius' description of the women's clothing he sometimes wore and his unattractive appearance (Calig. 50, 52).
[358] Leg. 74. According to Dio (lix:16.1–9) his conflict with the Senate did not commence until 37 A.D. but Philo interprets his removal of Silanus and Macro as vicarious defeats of the senators and *equites* respectively (Leg. 75).
[359] Suet., Calig. 49.
[360] Ibid. 38–41; Leg. 98, 105, 108; cf. Dio lix:14–5; 21; 22.3–4; 28.8–11.
[361] On ἀθεωτάτης (Leg. 77) see SMALLWOOD, Legatio, p. 193.
[362] Leg. 75–6.
[363] Leg. 116, cf. 118. On προσκύνησις see E. BARKER, Alexander to Constantine (Oxford, 1959), pp. 11–4. Philo and his embassy did obeisance to Gaius (Leg. 352) but this, though a flattering gesture, was not worship (cf. Dio lix:24.4). Worship was accorded Gaius and one of Claudius' acts soon after becoming emperor was to forbid the worship (προσκυνεῖν) of himself (Dio lx:5.4).
[364] Ibid. 119–20; cf. the account of the disturbance at Jamnia (201) where the Gentile inhabitants presumably could count on the tacit support of the procurator Capito. However one doubts that Gaius displayed anti-Jewish action at this period.
[365] See pp. 422–4.

whose presence he had only recently come. Gaius' animosity to the Jews must be dated after this incident; it was certainly not a cause of it.[366]

Gaius, though not well disposed towards the embassy led by Philo, did not reject their case.[367] Even though Philo suspected a sinister motive in his handling of the case and refers to him not as their judge but as their accuser,[368] his readiness to ask questions (admittedly with some levity)[369] if not to hear all the answers,[370] indicated that he was not as implacable an enemy as Philo makes out.[371]

But the time came when both Gaius and his impious advisers were no more. The emperor who had mocked the Jews, even committing the extreme sin in Jewish eyes of uttering the name of Yahweh,[372] was now succeeded by Claudius, who set about to undo his unjust acts.[373] Apelles and Helicon, the malicious advisers who had counselled Gaius concerning the Jamnia incident, "received the wages of their sacrilege", the former being tortured by Gaius and the latter executed as a criminal by Claudius.[374]

Philo's purpose in 'Legatio ad Gaium' is to plead a cause, to propagate an exaggerated picture of Gaius' inhuman rule which was inseparably linked with his attitude towards the Jews in the empire. Given this aim the differences between this account and that in 'In Flaccum', where Flaccus and the Alexandrian mob occupy the centre stage, are understandable.

Even when allowance is made for the propagandist purpose of 'In Flaccum', there is ample evidence in it of Philo's feelings towards Gaius. There is not the detail found in 'Legatio ad Gaium', but the same picture emerges of a ruler who changed from being "reasonable and amenable"[375] to one who deliberately set about ridding himself of any rival or conscientious adviser.[376] The damning description of Gaius the judge which Philo presents in his account of the embassy's hearing is paralleled by his narration of Gaius' control over the judicial proceedings against Flaccus. According to Philo, animosity had swamped any desire on the emperor's part for justice and the judge had already decided against the defendant.[377] In agreement with Suetonius' description of Gaius, Philo relates that even after passing judgment he was not content but, being "of a savage

---

[366] Philo's purpose overcame his concern for accuracy as we note in the exaggerated description of Gaius' actions in Leg. 346; cf. SMALLWOOD, Legatio, p. 207. He emphasizes how Gaius answered Petronius' letter with duplicity "concealing his wrath until a suitable time" (Leg. 260) and was deceptive towards Agrippa (333). As regards the first charge we can only compare Philo's view with that of Josephus, who stated that he did not hide his anger in his reply to Petronius (AJ. xviii:304–10; BJ. ii:203).

[367] Leg. 181.

[368] Ibid. 180, 349.

[369] Ibid. 363.

[370] Ibid. 363–4, 367.

[371] SMALLWOOD, Legatio, pp. 254–5.

[372] Leg. 353.

[373] Dio lx:5.1.

[374] Ibid. 206.

[375] Flacc. 14.

[376] Ibid. 13.

[377] Flacc. 126; cf. Leg. 349–50.

disposition and insatiable in penalties",[378] he caused further hardship to fall on those whom he disliked; as, for example, in ordering the murder of those exiles whom he considered to be living in comfort.[379] At the head of one list Gaius put Flaccus' name.[380] This placing could be Philo's invention to underscore the moral of his work that God brought full retribution upon the ruler who persecuted the Jews.[381]

d) Roman Administrators

Philo's attitude to Roman rule is conveyed not only in his comments on the emperors, but also in his assessment of less powerful administrators within the empire: Flaccus, Pilate, Macro, Petronius and Sejanus.

α) Flaccus

In 'Legatio ad Gaium' Philo places the blame for the pogrom in Alexandria antecedently on Gaius. However in the 'In Flaccum' the prefect becomes the main villain and his guilt is heightened by a contrast with the early years of his administration. This theme is expressed at the outset when Philo claims that he praises Flaccus' meritorious acts "not because it is right to praise an enemy but to present his villainy more conspicuously".[382] Flaccus' guilt as a bad ruler was thus compounded by his obvious capacity to rule well.[383] One suspects that this contrast was largely of Philo's making, but the lack of information from any other source on the nature of Flaccus' rule prevents us from reaching a final verdict.

The introduction leaves us in no doubt as to Philo's attitude to this Roman prefect. He portrays him as determinedly anti-Jewish, cunning in his methods and tyrannical by nature.[384] However his early career in Alexandria had been marked by a remarkable grasp of the local situation and indications of wise and fair administration,[385] including the following of precedent with regard to the punishment of Jewish offenders.[386] Philo commends him in particular for re-sisting pressure from the arrogant,[387] and for suppressing the "sodalities and

---

[378] Ibid. 182; cf. Suet., Calig. 27−32.

[379] Ibid. 183−4.

[380] Ibid. 185.

[381] Ibid. 191. One may ask why Philo then did not write of Gaius' assassination to make the same point in 'Legatio ad Gaium'. Presumably such a lesson was given in the "counter-story" (παλινῳδία) to which he refers the reader in Leg. 373.

[382] Flacc. 7.

[383] "To a man who goes astray through ignorance of the better course pardon is granted, but he who knowingly commits wrong has not a defence and is already condemned in the court of his conscience". Ibid., cf. 145. On Philo's understanding of conscience, see pp. 542−4; Box, In Flaccum, pp. 76−7.

[384] Ibid. 1.

[385] Flacc. 2−3.

[386] Ibid. 79.

[387] Ibid. 4.

clubs" with their drunken participants.[388] Philo is doubtless exaggerating the coarseness of these social activities in the light of his views on gluttony and drunkenness,[389] but such clubs could cause strife.[390] All in all, Flaccus established εὐνομία,[391] that condition necessary to a peaceful society.

To maintain that peace he personally ensured that the force at his disposal was well drilled and satisfactorily paid,[392] thus guaranteeing its readiness to assist him in his administration and allaying the need for its members to plunder the possessions of his subjects. So well did he govern in the first five years of his prefecture, Philo reports, that he surpassed his predecessors.[393] This early promise of a just rule, described in such glowing colours by Philo,[394] became the ground for condemnation of Flaccus' later injustices against the Alexandrian Jews. The crime was the more serious because it was wilfully committed and Philo, claiming a vision of the prefect's soul, declares that Flaccus' own conscience condemned him.[395] That Philo is inflating Flaccus' good qualities for the purposes of dramatic contrast appears from his praise of the prefect's grasp of fiscal matters,[396] in contrast to his later statement that no governor could hope to be familiar with the intricate details of the economy, as well as judicial matters.[397] Box contends that Flaccus was guilty of over-exaction[398] but whether this was a feature of the whole of his prefecture or only of the early period cannot be established.

As noted earlier,[399] Philo attributes the content of the charges raised later against Flaccus at his trial as the cause of the prefect's anxiety,[400] leading him to consort with the mob and its demagogues in opposition to the Jews. So duplicity dominated Flaccus' attitude towards them and his earlier cordiality is not on Philo's reckoning to be regarded as genuine but was a cloak to cover the anti-

---

[388] The use of ἀφηνιάζειν suggests that Flaccus also wished to curtail any possible political disturbance which might arise from their drunkenness. Cf. COLSON's translation of the phrase depicting their activities as "political intrigue".

[389] Ebr. 4, 15—29.

[390] Box (In Flaccum, p. 73) refers to the descriptions found in Juvenal xv:33—92 but being a satirist he is not our best source. From Pliny's correspondence (Ep. x:96.7) we know that Trajan had ordered the cessation of similar assemblies in Bithynia.

[391] Flacc. 5.

[392] Ibid. "The presence of an army of occupation in a city the inhabitants of which mostly resented the domination of Rome required the most rigid discipline. To prevent outbreaks and fracas it was essential to keep the soldiery as far as possible out of the social and political life of the country" (Box, In Flaccum, p. 75).

[393] Flacc. 8.

[394] He does the same in describing Gaius' rule. See Leg. 8—13 where the first seven months are described in terms of a "golden age".

[395] Ibid. 7.

[396] Ibid. 4.

[397] Ibid. 133.

[398] Box, In Flaccum, p. 70.

[399] See pp. 429—31.

[400] He depicts Flaccus as despairing for his future at Gaius' accession because of his friendship with Tiberius, Gemellus and Macro and his opposition to Agrippina, Gaius' mother (Flacc. 8—12).

Jewish frame of mind which was his from the outset.[401] Philo thus avoids any suggestion of Jewish culpability for the troubles which were to follow. In this treatise, as in 'Legatio ad Gaium', the troublemakers were never amongst Philo's own people.

Philo seeks to illustrate Flaccus' duplicity by citing several incidents. Though outwardly cordial to Agrippa, he willingly[402] allowed him to be insulted by the Alexandrian crowd.[403] Philo astutely appeals to Agrippa's status in the Roman world in castigating Flaccus' encouragement of misrule and anarchy,[404] mindful of Agrippa's friendship with Claudius.[405] According to Philo, Flaccus was bribed by the mob by receiving honours which may be taken as testimonials given to the prefect for sanctioning their actions.[406] For such selfish disregard of public peace and order, he is regarded by Philo as servile (παλίμπρατος);[407] the mob wrought their evil work not in the absence of rule but with the ruler's favour.[408]

Philo ascribes to this situation the direst of consequences — the passing of rule from the prefect's hands into those of the Alexandrian leaders, Dionysius, Isidorus and Lampo.[409] He writes scathingly of these men and their accomplices who, though secretly Flaccus' foes, were accepted as counsellors and friends by him. (Flaccus had his reasons, however, as has been noted.) Philo calls the new advisers Egyptians, not Greeks or Alexandrians — an intended insult — and for the prefect to call upon such men was a departure from "reason" as, in order to accommodate them, he dismissed his former competent counsellors.

In his determination to condemn these Alexandrian leaders, Philo contradicts the picture of Flaccus drawn later in the treatise. Here, by dint of circumstances, Flaccus made a hazardous change of policy through which the vocal antagonists of the Alexandrian Jews were able to exert unrivalled influence. Elsewhere, however, Philo charges Flaccus with a prior determination to trouble the Jews. Doubtless the presentation of Flaccus is moulded by the conclusion Philo wishes to arrive at in this writing; whether the Greeks' anti-Jewish programme was as clearly formulated as Philo renders it or not, their presentation of it to Flaccus was purportedly based not on an appeal to any similar feeling on his part, but to

---

[401] Ibid. 1, 98—101.

[402] Philo emphasizes this (ibid. 35).

[403] Ibid. 33.

[404] Ibid. 35; cf. 40: "When Flaccus heard, or rather saw all this, it was his duty to take and keep the madman (Carabas) in charge, to prevent him from providing an occasion to the railers for insulting their betters and then to punish those who had arrayed him thus, because they had dared both in word and deed both openly and indirectly to insult a king, a friend of Caesar's, a person who had received Praetorian honours from the Roman Senate."

[405] Agrippa was a key supporter of Claudius at the latter's accession (BJ. ii:206—13; AJ. xix: 236—65; Dio lx:8.2) and was suitably rewarded (BJ. ii:215—7, 247; AJ. xix:274).

[406] Box, In Flaccum, p. xliv.

[407] Flacc. 41.

[408] Ibid. 44, 51; cf. Leg. 346 where the initiative in defiling the synagogues is attributed incorrectly to Gaius.

[409] Ibid. 20.

the support they could give him before Gaius.[410] One concludes that the ascription to Flaccus of premeditated anti-Jewish action is a reading back from the events, a product of Philo's polemic, though in all likelihood the prefect shared that general antipathy to Jewish ways which was the rule rather than the exception amongst Romans.[411]

Further blame is heaped upon Flaccus.[412] The seizure of the synagogues was followed by a harsher measure, namely, the removal of the Jews' citizenship rights.[413] As noted earlier, this was an attack on the Jewish πολίτευμα and, despite Philo's wording (μετουσίας πολιτικῶν δικαίων) not an attack on the Roman citizenship which only a minority of the Jews held.[414] Flaccus is said to have declared by an edict that the Jews were ξένοι καὶ ἐπήλυδες and to have worsened this ruling by refusing them the right of appeal. Flaccus now reached the limits of judicial injustice.

> "He became everything himself, accuser, enemy, witness, judge and the agent of punishment, and then to the first two wrongs he added a third by permitting those who wished to pillage the Jews as at the sacking of a city".[415]

The prefect is portrayed as a wilful antagonist who deprived the Jews of their rights and is to be numbered among the perpetrators of tyranny.[416] Roman rule was not immune elsewhere from tyrannical administration by provincial governors[417] and Philo lists the ugly features — bribery, plunder, the exile of innocent people and the execution of the "powerful without judicial sentence".[418] In the past such administrators had to answer to the emperors Augustus and Tiberius who are described most favourably by Philo as "impartial judges" influenced "neither by enmity nor by favour but by the nature of the truth".[419] As such they stood in sharp contrast to Flaccus.[420]

Philo takes pains to argue that the breakdown of rule had two causes: the malice of leading Alexandrian demagogues and their following mob against the Jews, and secondly, Flaccus' designs to secure his own safety. Though Philo

---

[410] Flacc. 21—3. On the exaggerated importance they are supposed to have given to Alexandria see Box, In Flaccum, pp. 81—2.
[411] Cf. Ac. 16:20—1. The Roman senatorial condescension towards Judaism was well expressed by Tacitus, Hist. v:4—5.
[412] Ibid. 116, 124.
[413] Flacc. 53.
[414] TCHERIKOVER and FUKS, pp. 61—7.
[415] Flacc. 54. The earlier attacks are recorded in 41 and 53.
[416] Ibid. 43—4, 54.
[417] P. A. BRUNT, Charges of Provincial Maladministration under the Early Principate, Historia, X (1961), pp. 189—223.
[418] Flacc. 105.
[419] Flacc. 106.
[420] Ibid. 24.

makes much of the failure to find arms amongst the Jews,[421] the disturbances caused by the latter as noted in Claudius' letter suggest that he intended to whitewash his fellow Jews from blame for any violence. He emphasizes the peacefulness of the Jews, who emerge as innocent victims[422] hounded by an arrogant prefect and a spiteful mob.

Box contends that the Jews did offer resistance which Philo astutely failed to record.[423] He discusses in particular[424] the reference to the search for arms, and he believes that the Jews had not hidden them, nor did they possess them in A.D. 38. That they used arms in A.D. 41 was probably due to the lesson they had learnt from their recent bitter experience of their vulnerability. His main point is that Philo was writing for Gentiles as well as Jews and among the former there would likely be Alexandrian citizens familiar with the events. Thus if the search for arms had been successful Philo's duplicity could easily have been exposed.[425] However in confused situations credible eyewitnesses could have been called for to support both positions. If arms had been found this embarrassing fact could have been deleted just as the charge of Jewish resistance at the synagogues could be denied. One may doubt the full assertions of Philo concerning the Jews' lack of arms,[426] but if completely misleading he could easily have been contradicted. Presumably the resistance was on a small scale,[427] giving a pretext for the mob the step up their destructive activity, but not sufficiently sustained to feature as a major incident in the pogrom.

As Philo's narrative proceeds the evidence condemning Flaccus' rule was in turn surpassed by the disclosure of harsher actions against the Jews. The attack on the synagogues was followed by the withdrawal of their political rights and of their communal security.[428] Box[429] discusses whether the phrase αὐτὸς γενόμενος τὰ πάντα κατήγορος is an anti-climax after τί ἂν εἴη τυραννίδος ἐπάγγελμα μεῖζον[430] but Philo indicates that this last act, the declaration of the Jews as aliens without right of appeal against his edict, was the worst by describing in horrific detail its sequel — the ferocious plundering of the Jews. That a prefect should have connived at this was to Philo the climax of his misrule. It is not clear that the permission to plunder is meant by Philo to be taken as an official edict. That he is not specific indicates that this was not the case, for Philo seeks to bring out any incriminating action he can to condemn the foolishness of Flaccus' anti-Jewish measures. The Alexandrians regarded the edict as providing them with an

---

[421] Ibid. 95. Philo reads more into the fruitless search for arms, seeing in Flaccus' actions the worst of intentions and regarding this act simply as an excuse to plant an armed force in the Jewish quarter (86).

[422] Ibid. 90–2, 48.

[423] Box, pp. lix–lx. Philo (ibid. 48) gives a hint of the expected Jewish response.

[424] Ibid. pp. lx–lxi.

[425] Cf. Box (In Flaccum, p. 101) on Flacc. 64.

[426] Ibid. 90–1, 94.

[427] Box (In Flaccum, p. lxi) suggests that the Jews did not use "regular weapons of war".

[428] Flacc. 53.

[429] Box, In Flaccum, p. 99.

[430] Flacc. 54.

opportunity to evict the Jews from all parts of the city except their one permitted quarter. Whether official or not, the resultant pogrom stemmed in Philo's eyes from Flaccus' malevolence.[431]

With regard to the forms of punishment, the prefect treated the Jewish council of elders as criminals of the Egyptian class.[432] To Philo, sensitive of the rights of Alexandrian Jews, this last act was the crown of Flaccus' barbarism. Firstly, his treatment stood in contrast to the honour Augustus had bestowed upon the council by appointing them to administer Jewish affairs after the death of the γενάρχης.[433] With an eye to Roman custom, Philo blames Flaccus also for failing to observe the practice of leniency associated with the festivals for the deified Augusti.[434] Flaccus is also said to have had them summarily arrested. Philo of course, speaks only of their great age and their innocence of any crime.[435] Perhaps the prefect had grounds for fearing Jewish resistance and sought to dissuade the leaders from supporting it. Thirty-eight members of the Sanhedrin, which numbered seventy-one, were arrested. This could indicate that the arrests were either based on valid charges, that this number were known, or suspected, to be implicated, or the only ones unable to avoid detection, or else that Flaccus was content to humiliate publicly only those who were easily found in their homes. Scourged before their adversaries, some of the elders died, while others suffered long from their ill- treatment. Insult was added to injury by the method of punishment – the elders being subjected to more degrading punishment than their Jewish inferiors.

The thrust of the treatise lay in describing Flaccus' fall from power, and Philo sees it as due to several forces ranged against him. Firstly God, taking pity on His people, brought Flaccus low.[436] Secondly, justice[437] entered the battle against him;[438] and thirdly, the rendering of an account of one's rule before the Roman emperors,[439] even under Gaius, spelt ruin for Flaccus.[440] Philo's comments about the general Roman administration in his two overtly political works are always commendatory and, even allowing for the possibility that this was written for the successor to Flaccus,[441] it tallies with the observations to be drawn from the wider range of his writings.

---

[431] Ibid. 73.

[432] Ibid. 75.

[433] Flacc. 74; AJ. xix:281–3.

[434] Ibid. 81.

[435] Ibid. 82.

[436] Flacc. 102–3.

[437] On Philo's concept of justice, see pp. 512–18.

[438] Ibid. 104–7.

[439] Ibid. 105–6.

[440] Philo reports that he was unmoved by the flattering communications by which Flaccus hoped to establish himself securely in the emperor's favour. If this were true, hatred of Flaccus and not praise of disinterested justice would be the explanation for Philo's relating such an anecdote concerning Gaius.

[441] GOODENOUGH, Politics, pp. 9–19.

Contrast heightens drama[442] and Philo's artistry embraces this device to round off the description of Flaccus' deserved punishment. Besides the contrast between his early and later rule, there was that between his treatment of the Jews and the injuries he subsequently suffered. Philo recounts these latter in relation to the prefect's persecution of the Jews and not to the formal charges of which he was found guilty. The lesson is spelt out repeatedly and then in conclusion —

> "Such also was the fate of Flaccus, who thereby became an indubitable proof that the help which God can give was not withdrawn from the nation of the Jews".[443]

Even in such an incidental event as Flaccus' winter voyage into exile Philo draws out a moral lesson. God let him experience the "terrors of the sea" in order to punish further this man who "had filled the elements of the universe with his impious deeds".[444]

Flaccus suffered the bitter experience of being accused by those who from the beginning had been his enemies.[445] Stripped of his wealth and property, which Philo indicates as quite substantial,[446] he was exiled to the island of Andros.[447] His journey to this lonely destination stood in stark contrast[448] to the time when as the appointed ἐπίτροπος of Egypt "the cities then beheld him puffed with pride, parading the grandeur of his good fortune".[449] Now, instead of respect he met mockery and pity.

The remainder of Philo's description of Flaccus' end is an artfully contrived picture[450] of his regretful and misanthropic utterances,[451] as one possessed with divine inspiration acknowledging the power of the true God, that is, the God of the Jews.[452] Flaccus is a pitiable figure and he who had been educated with Augustus' grandsons,[453] now in despair at his fate cried like a madman over his

---

[442] Ibid. 152−3, 170.

[443] Flacc. 191.

[444] Ibid. 125.

[445] Ibid. 146.

[446] Ibid. 148. Box (In Flaccum, p. 120) comments that Philo may have had Flaccus in mind in V. contempl. 48−56 but this is a general denunciation of Gentile feasting; cf. Juvenal x:27; xi:123−9.

[447] Ibid. 151.

[448] Ibid. 152, 154−6, 184, 173, cf. Leg. 324.

[449] Ibid. 152. Philo in making much use of contrast seems to have lengthened the voyage (Box, In Flaccum, pp. xlvii−xlviii).

[450] "Philo ascertained the general circumstances of the exile's habit of life and . . . upon some foundation of fact he built an edifice of psychological inferences" (Box, In Flaccum, p. xlviii). However he may have enquired more closely of Flaccus' last days to embellish his treatise than Box allows.

[451] Flacc. 159.

[452] Ibid. 169−75.

[453] Ibid. 158. The θυγατριδοῖ τοῦ Σεβαστοῦ who were fellow scholars with Flaccus were C. Caesar (20 B.C.−A.D. 4), L. Caesar (17 B.C.−A.D. 2) and Agrippa Postumus (12 B.C.− A.D. 14) (Box, In Flaccum, p. 122).

previous honours and power in Alexandria.[454] He stood as a warning of the danger of attacking God's people even when the latter appeared most helpless.[455] His end was remorseful, and it was ignominious — he was hacked to death. Even in that manner of execution Philo sees a link with his misrule in Alexandria, for the number of his wounds equalled the number of Jews who had been killed when he was prefect of Egypt.[456]

In 'Legatio ad Gaium' Flaccus is depicted as playing a negative role, allowing the rule of the city to pass by default to the mob,[457] but Philo's purpose in writing about the embassy accounts for this brief mention. Flaccus must not steal[458] the ignominy which is to be attributed to Gaius and the Alexandrian crowd. When he is brought on to the main stage in 'In Flaccum' his actions and fate signify the folly of any administrator defying God by ruling harshly over His people.[459]

β) Pilate

Pilate was appointed ἐπίτροπος[460] of Judaea (c. 26 A.D.) by Tiberius, and in accord with Philo's purpose of honouring that emperor, he emphasizes strongly that Pilate's unjust, anti-Jewish policy was carried out without Tiberius' knowledge and against his wishes. When the emperor eventually learnt of Pilate's action in setting up golden shields dedicated to Tiberius in Herod's palace in Jerusalem he immediately and severely reprimanded the prefect.[461] Pilate's action was a violation of Jewish customs which had been guaranteed by "kings and emperors",[462] and Philo alleges that Pilate feared as a consequence that the "venality, violence, theft and unnecessary cruelty"[463] associated with his rule would be revealed to Tiberius. Because of his hatred for the Jews, he had no redeeming feature in Philo's estimation, his character being marred by an "inflexible, stubborn and cruel disposition",[464] by obstinacy, spite and a quick temper, while his failure to comply with the Jews' requests indicated his cowardice.[465]

---

[454] Ibid. 163.

[455] Ibid. 169—78.

[456] Ibid. 188—90.

[457] Leg. 132. SMALLWOOD, Legatio, p. 219—220.

[458] In Leg. 114—122 the blame for the pogrom was laid primarily on Gaius and the Alexandrian mob but in Flacc. 53—4 the herding of the Jews into one quarter is seen as arising not from the mob's awareness of Gaius' hatred for the Jews but from their reaction to an edict by Flaccus depriving the latter of their rights as members of a πολίτευμα.

[459] Flacc. 191.

[460] "Prefect" is the better translation of this term, following the recent Latin inscription.

[461] Leg. 299—304.

[462] Leg. 300, cf. 305.

[463] Ibid. 302.

[464] Ibid. 301.

[465] Had he been there Philo (who on this matter spoke through Agrippa) would readily have appended his signature to the Jews' letter of complaint to Tiberius (ibid. 303).

Is Philo's assessment of Pilate valid? According to Josephus he had stirred Jewish animosity by bringing Roman military standards with the portraiture of Tiberius into Jerusalem, and by taking money from the Temple to build an aqueduct for the city.[466] Though forced to retract before the Jews' opposition over the standards, he severely crushed their protest against the aqueduct.[467] In a sensitive province such as Judaea these actions were unwise and endorse the impression gained from Philo, as do the gospel accounts which attest to his scorn of the Jews and his readiness to discomfort them.[468] Philo's account of the introduction of the aniconic shields into the city seems to refer to a different incident from that of the standards as he admits that the shields had no images traced on them,[469] though, as SMALLWOOD argues, the Jews may have felt that Pilate "might now be initiating another attack by a seemingly innocent action which was to be the forerunner of some definite contravention of the Law".[470] Certainly Philo, conscious of the sufferings of his fellow-Jews, had cause to write bitterly of Pilate's rule.

γ) Petronius

In contrast to Pilate stood another Roman official with responsibility for Judaea, Petronius,[471] who recognized Jewish firmness not as damnable obstinacy but as courage to maintain their precious laws whatever the cost.[472] He was by nature "kind and gentle",[473] moved by pity for the Jews' plight in the face of Gaius' provocative intention of erecting his statue in their temple. His delaying tactics against Gaius' impetuous plan and his fair treatment of the Jews are explained by Philo as springing from an acquaintance with Jewish philosophy and religion, and a disposition to seek after "things worthy of serious attention".[474] Clearly he was a man under God's hand.

Philo's high estimate of Petronius is based on his efforts to avoid conflict between his master and the Jews. For this he was rebuked in scathing terms by his emperor,[475] yet stood firm. (Josephus records that he was saved from death by

---

[466] BJ. ii:175—7.

[467] Ibid.

[468] Mk. 15:10—12; Lk. 13:1—5; J. 19:19—22.

[469] Leg. 299.

[470] SMALLWOOD, Legatio, p. 304.

[471] Petronius was *augur cooptatus* in A.D. 7, suffect consul in A.D. 19 and proconsul of Asia for six years under Tiberius (IGR. iv.1499). Mentioned by Tacitus (Ann. vi:45) as being in Rome in A.D. 36, assessing fire damage, he subsequently was legate of Syria for three years from A.D. 39 (SMALLWOOD, Legatio, p. 285).

[472] Leg. 209. So also AJ. xviii:269—72; BJ. ii:192—201.

[473] εὐμενὴς καὶ ἥμερος (ibid. 243). If ἐστι is the correct reading instead of ἦν (cf. SMALL-WOOD, Legatio, p. 279) then Petronius could have been still alive. Cf. AJ. xix:300—12.

[474] Leg. 245.

[475] "You concern yourself with the institutions of the Jews, the nation which is my worst enemy; you disregard the imperial commands of your sovereign . . . Oh but you had

receiving the news of Gaius' assassination.)[476] Philo's presentation of Petronius shows that the touchstone of his assessment of Roman officials was not their identification with Roman imperialism but their attitude and actions towards the Jews, who at this period were to be found from the Tiber to the Euphrates.

δ) Macro

Macro might seem to be an exception to this criterion but it is not fanciful to see in his advice to Gaius the potential prevention of the emperor's eventual clash with the Jews. Certainly Philo presents him favourably. His defence of Gaius in the presence of Tiberius was coupled with an earnest attempt to induce Gaius to control his inconsistent and alarmingly erratic way of life.[477] This account of Macro is closely parallel to that in 'In Flaccum', the latter giving a briefer picture of his changing relationship with Gaius up to Macro's death.[478] He emerges as a loyal adviser,[479] concerned over Gaius' lack of self-control and determined, rather pedantically, to reform Gaius to a reasonable (πειθαρχικός) way of life. Philo's favour for Macro is unmistakable; he absolves him from blame in his efforts to defend Gaius before Tiberius, because Macro was deceived by Gaius' earlier readiness to take admonition.[480] He is debited with neither cunning nor ambition in advancing Gaius' rise to power but his support was given out of "sincerity, zeal and ardour".[481] No blemish spots Philo's portrait of this man and though his wife's adultery with Gaius is mentioned Macro is portrayed as ignorant of the affair.[482] Macro became Philo's mouthpiece[483] in the counsel he tendered. His advice to Gaius covered good manners, public decorum and the goals of good government, and the virtues which Macro urged on the emperor — peace and the absence of envy — were the antithesis of what Philo saw in Gaius' principate when his animosity towards the Jews was revealed.

---

compassion! Then did pity weigh more than Gaius with you?" (ibid. 256—7). The dating of the correspondence is not relevant here. See the discussion in SMALLWOOD, Legatio, pp. 286—7.

[476] BJ. ii:203.

[477] Leg. 33—40.

[478] E.g. In Flacc. 14 Philo simply states that Macro admonished and exhorted Gaius while Leg. 43—51 gives us the details; cf. BOX, In Flaccum, p. 78.

[479] Flacc. 14.

[480] Ibid. He does not mention Gaius' illness in this writing, but summarily reports his changed behaviour.

[481] Leg. 60.

[482] Leg. 39—40. Tacitus (Ann. vi:45) and Dio (lviii:28; lix:10.6) both record that Macro knew of and agreed to the seduction of his wife, Ennia Thrasylla. Suetonius (Calig. 12.2) states that Macro was ignorant of the liaison and that Gaius had given her a written promise to marry him if he became emperor.

[483] SMALLWOOD, Legatio, p. 182. Philo too might well have been an "edifying bore" as BALSDON (Gaius, p. 38) describes Macro. He comments further (p. 21) that Macro "would scarcely have recognized himself in Philo's idealized picture of him".

ε) Sejanus

By the same criterion Sejanus was one Roman official who failed because, according to Philo,[484] he had accused the Jews in Rome before the emperor, as well as preparing an attack on them throughout the empire. The substance of the charges is not given, though Philo writes of them as aimed at the destruction of his race. One may be pardoned for questioning if not the attitude of Sejanus recorded here, at least the motive Philo ascribes to him; namely, his recognition of the Jews as the only group likely to oppose his evil actions.[485] Was Philo here referring to the expulsion of the Jews from Rome under Tiberius[486] which is dated by both Tacitus and Dio at A.D. 19?[487] Significantly Philo did not mention Tiberius' action for it would have contradicted his thesis that Gaius, the only evil emperor, was also the only one to oppose the Jews.[488] He did admit that some Jews were found guilty of criminal acts in the empire but their crimes were not connected with their Jewish identity and customs.[489] The action of A.D. 19 was ignored, while that taken against these Jews whom Philo mentioned was minimised, and any suggestion of Jewish disloyalty was to be regarded as initiated by the discredited Sejanus. Thus, in Philo's apology, the instruction sent out by Tiberius to punish only those Jews who had committed criminal acts and to assure the Jewish communities of their security was best understood against the background of this slander concerning the Jews in Rome.[490] Some had indeed been punished, but what was to be checked was the praetorian prefect's efforts to make the lot of the Jews most precarious in relation to the Roman authorities.[491] Consistent with this estimate of Sejanus is that presented in 'In Flaccum'. This confidant of Tiberius is said to have been openly opposed to the Jews and to have taken measures to persecute them. What Philo means by "the whole nation"[492] is presumably not that all Jews suffered but that, in the face of hostility and perhaps the actual persecution of some by Sejanus, they envisaged an ultimate threat

---

[484] Leg. 159—65. Cf. Flacc. 1 (Sejanus' "anti-Jewish" policy).

[485] Philo argues that rather than being those subjects in the empire whose loyalty was most to be doubted, their fidelity towards the good emperor would stand in contrast to the unprincipled flattery of Sejanus demonstrated by other groups (Leg. 155—6).

[486] Tac., Ann. ii:85.5; Suet., Tib. 36; Joseph., AJ. xviii:81—5; Dio lvii:18.5a.

[487] Josephus (AJ. xviii:65) places the account of the expulsion in his narration of Pilate's rule in Judaea.

[488] SMALLWOOD, Legatio, p. 244.

[489] Leg. 161. I cannot accept LÉON HERRMANN's contention that Philo was anti-Christian and blamed them for this uproar (Chrestos. Témoignages païens et juifs sur le christianisme du premier siècle, Coll. Latomus, CIX [Bruxelles, 1970], pp. 24—32). Philo's silence over them (pp. 23, 29) indicates rather that he does not concern himself with them.

[490] Leg. 160—1.

[491] If we regard the attack on the Roman Jews as separate from the expulsion of 19 A.D. it is possible that Sejanus was seeking to malign the Jews so that the earlier moderate measures of Tiberius would be sharpened against this group whose popularity with the Romans was by no means assured.

[492] σύμπαν ... τὸ ἔθνος (Flacc. 1).

against them all,[493] and the phrase is expressive of Philo's solidarity with his fellow-Jews.

As regards Sejanus' attitude to the Jews from our other sources, Tacitus notes his influence over Tiberius[494] and while he was an adviser to the emperor the latter acted to expel Jews as well as devotees of Isis from Rome.[495] It is significant that in Josephus' account of the affair Sejanus is not mentioned, and the key figure to tell Tiberius of the trouble was Saturninus, whose wife had been fleeced by clever Jewish embezzlers.[496] In the light of this omission it would seem that Philo exaggerated the danger posited to the Jews by Sejanus' close association with Tiberius. However, the evidence from coinage points to some anti-Jewish feeling on Sejanus' part.[497] Considering his fate, Philo was on safe ground in charging him and not Tiberius with the anti-Jewish action. To highlight the evil of Gaius a little white-washing of his predecessor was in order.

2. In Philo's other Writings

I have already criticized GOODENOUGH's contention that Philo had the same antipathy towards the Romans as the skipper of a small boat has towards a hurricane.[498] His estimate of Philo's other writings must now be examined in order to assess fully Philo's attitude to Roman rule.[499] GOODENOUGH claims to detect in the references to flamboyant festivals and drunken feasts in Som. ii:61—4 indications of anti-Roman jibes.[500] However Philo was plainly envisaging the general pagan world and not singling out the Romans for criticism. Similarly it would be difficult to designate the Romans as the only ones in view in Philo's contrast between those practising gluttony and drunkenness on the one hand, and those pursuing the virtue of ἐγκράτεια on the other.[501] In defending this virtue in his exposition of the sacrifices required by Moses' law, Philo again was considering Gentile society; he criticizes those who mocked such a virtue and who ran "in search of richly laden tables, miserable slaves to birds and fishes . . .

---

[493] Leg. 160. In 346 and Flacc. 44 Philo exaggerated the threat posed by Gaius' and Flaccus' actions respectively against the wider ranks of Jewry.

[494] . . . simul praetorii praefectus Aelius Seianus, collega Straboni patri suo datus, magna apud Tiberium auctoritate (Ann. i:24).

[495] Tacitus (Ann. ii:85) records it as a Senatorial decree.

[496] AJ. xviii:83.

[497] E. MARY SMALLWOOD, Some Notes on the Jews under Tiberius, Latomus, XV (1956), pp. 328—9.

[498] GOODENOUGH, Politics, p. 7.

[499] GOODENOUGH's exposition of 'De Iosepho', which he considers was written to show the Romans that the best ruler of Egypt had in fact been a Jew, will be discussed under Philo's portrait of the ideal statesman.

[500] GOODENOUGH, ibid., pp. 24—7, 31.

[501] Ebr. 20—2; cf. Spec. Leg. i:148—50.

unable even in their dreams to taste the flavour of true freedom".[502] Amongst the Alexandrian Greeks such a pattern of behaviour could well have been observed by critical Jewish eyes. Moses, having foreseen the evils attendant upon gluttony and greed, forbade his people to model their festivities on those of the Gentiles, and by observing this ordinance the Jews thus occupied themselves not with riotous feasting but with restraint and godliness.[503] Philo's view of Gentile eating habits was common to orthopraxic Jewry in the pagan world;[504] it did not indicate a specific anti-Roman sentiment.

GOODENOUGH detects a reaction also against Roman judicial practice in Philo's discussion as to whether capital punishment was to be inflicted on one who struck his parents. Philo castigates the "dignitaries and legislators"[505] who do not pass such a sentence as being swayed by the opinion of men and not by truth.[506] The term ἐυπάρυφοι is regarded by GOODENOUGH as a reference to Roman officials,[507] and in support he appeals to its occurrence in Leg. 344 and Spec. Leg. iv.63; but neither passage compels us to see in this term a particular reference to Roman rule. In the former Philo refers to rich dignitaries from whom Gaius gained wealth and in the second passage he is condemning magistrates who accepted bribes and this, as COLSON indicates, was inspired by Plato's writing on the issue.[508] As regards the term νομοθέτης it is unmistakably applied to Moses,[509] towards whom Philo certainly bore no antipathy. GOODENOUGH's case is tenuous and as well it assumes that the readers readily recalled Philo's use of ἐυπάρυφος in markedly different writings.

COLSON raises a strong objection to GOODENOUGH's other claim that the penalty of cutting off the hands rather than execution was a direct reference to Roman law as practised in Philo's time.[510] In this instance Philo lampoons such a punishment,[511] yet in the case when a woman is convicted of seizing the genitals of her husband's adversary that is the penalty Philo endorses,[512] though in the latter case he resorts to allegory to explain such a punishment. GOODENOUGH[513]

---

[502] Ibid. i:173—6.
[503] Ibid. i:193.
[504] WOLFSON, I, pp. 74—5. It is not necessary to regard this as Philo's defence of a Jewish mystery religion (as does GOODENOUGH, Jurisprudence, p. 40). The phrase ὀρθὸς λόγος τῆς φύσεως (Som. ii:95—7; cf. GOODENOUGH, Politics, pp. 27—31) had strong Stoic connotations and the passage parallels statements elsewhere which are simply contrasting Jewish and Gentile life-styles and not presenting features of a mystery religion (Spec. Leg. ii:193—4; cf. GOODENOUGH, Jurisprudence, pp. 66—7).
[505] ἐυπάρυφοι καὶ νομοθέται.
[506] Spec. Leg. ii:244.
[507] GOODENOUGH, Jurisprudence, pp. 74—5.
[508] COLSON, VIII, pp. 430—1. He refers to Leges xii:955 C—D and notes the use of ἡμιμόχθηροι in Resp. i:352.
[509] E.g. Spec. Leg. iii:102, 151.
[510] COLSON, VII, pp. 629—30.
[511] Spec. Leg. ii:145—7.
[512] Ibid. iii:174—7.
[513] Ibid., p. 241. He considers that this was a law still maintained in the πολίτευμα by the Jewish courts even though it was contrary to the principles of Greek legal procedure.

comments that to carry out the literal sentence was contrary to Greek and Roman law on ὕβρις and thus Philo interpreted the punishment allegorically conscious that his defence of the Jewish law would be regarded by the Greeks as "juristically weak". One cannot agree with his other conclusion that in both passages Philo was openly criticizing Roman law and administration of justice.[514] However he is correct in claiming that Philo, in his treatment of the fifth commandment had been markedly influenced by Roman law,[515] and he presents a strong case for Philo's incorporating Roman legal principles into his exegesis of the commandment against murder, writing "as though the Roman law were implicit in the Jewish".[516] In a later passage on capital punishment for murder, Philo is opposed to its evasion by means of ransom or banishment.[517] The latter practice was not unique to the Romans but was known also to be the Greek alternative to the death penalty.[518] Philo here is not specifically anti-Roman; he is anti-Gentile, defending the superlative laws of Moses.

He condemns the practice of augury,[519] but again such opposition need not be regarded as directed specifically against the Romans, though their observance of the custom is thus criticized. As GOODENOUGH[520] points out, the Septuagintal renderings of Jer. 27:9 and 36:8–9 contain a similar judgment, thus indicating this injunction's long history amongst Greek-speaking Jews. Philo also condemns magicians but in this matter he would have been in agreement with the public practice of Roman rulers.[521]

Philo does not deal with the payment of imperial tribute as do the synoptic evangelists.[522] However he does put forward several general principles regarding coinage in commenting on Dt. 23:18[523] with its reference to the rejection from the tabernacle of a prostitute's earnings given in payment of a vow. He observes that the coins are not evil in themselves but are tainted because of their owner and the way in which they were earned. If he regarded Roman rule as requiring that which contravened what was owed to God, as in the case of Gaius' order to the Jews, then Philo was ready to stand firm, but from what can be gauged elsewhere of his attitude towards Roman rule, it would seem that under normal circumstances he would not have been opposed to paying tribute to Caesar.

---

[514] GOODENOUGH, Jurisprudence, pp. 74–5.

[515] Ibid., pp. 67–72.

[516] Ibid., p. 108. Cf. pp. 100–8 for his commentary on Spec. Leg. iii:83–98.

[517] Spec. Leg. ii:150.

[518] GOODENOUGH, Jurisprudence, p. 133.

[519] Spec. Leg. iv:48.

[520] Ibid., pp. 186–7.

[521] Ibid. iv:50–1; Tac., Ann. ii:69; cf. Suet., Ner. 34.4; Tac., Hist. i:22. The early Christians shared Philo's view as, for example, when Paul opposed a certain μάγος at Paphos (Ac. 13:6–12), when books on magic were destroyed by converts in Ephesus (19:19) and in the condemnation of sorcery in Rv. 9:21 which was in agreement with Dt. 18:10 (which prohibited augury as well).

[522] Mt. 22:15–22; Mk. 12:13–7; Lk. 20:20–6.

[523] Spec. Leg. i:104.

The conclusion is that Philo's positive and specific estimates of Roman rule are not called into question by those passages which present a critical view of Gentile society. In so far as the Romans are criticized, it is because of their participation in pagan practices which Philo condemns and not because of distinctive evil on their part. This is the right understanding of his criticism of gluttonous feasting, drunkenness, lenient judiciaries and the practice of augury. He writes in the vein of an anti-Gentile Jew and not an anti-Roman patriot.

Philo's appreciation of Roman rule is genuine. The maintenance of peace experienced under the first two Roman emperors and restored in Alexandria under Claudius is seen as due to God's providential care of the world. Such stability Philo appreciates, not only because it guaranteed the Jews' physical safety but also because it enabled them to practise their customs unmolested. Philo prizes Roman non-interference in these customs, and he points to Augustus' policy as setting imperial precedent for this attitude. However, the positive contributions which both Augustus and Tiberius made are singled out largely in contrast to the effects of Gaius' misrule. As with his predecessor Tiberius punished those who ruled tyrannously in the provinces and in contrast with Gaius heard embassies justly, weighing evenly the evidence. The major disturbances under Tiberius are conveniently omitted except those involving the Jews, which are blamed on the discredited subordinates, Pilate and Sejanus.

Philo presents the early promise of Gaius' reign as shortlived, and terminated by two evils which to Philo are inseparable: Gaius' megalomania and his determination to persecute the Jews. Even a Roman emperor was not immune from the tyranny of passions and pleasure to the detriment of his rule, though Philo stresses that this instance was atypical. Gaius' response to the Jewish embassy from Alexandria indicated his disdain for justice, his voicing the forbidden name of Yahweh revealed an insensitivity to Jewish ways foreign to his predecessors, while his claim to deification was insane blasphemy. With regard to less powerful Romans, Petronius emerges positively in Philo's writings because of his respect for Jewish ways and his efforts to forestall Gaius' designs upon the Jerusalem temple. Philo describes Flaccus' early rule in Egypt in favourable terms, but this prefect joins Gaius, Sejanus and Pilate, whom Philo singles out for searing criticism, because of their opposition to the Jews.

While Philo's accounts oscillate between attaching more blame either to Flaccus or to the mob, his prefecture is roundly condemned. Philo, however, is criticizing the man and not his office; his ire is not directed against Roman rule. Two other Romans are also condemned by Philo. The one Sejanus was dead and his name in disgrace. Philo would not have had it otherwise because he presents him as determined to discomfort the Jews throughout the Empire. The other, Pilate, was the cause of turbulence in the province of Judaea and rightly received, if Philo is to be believed, Tiberius' censure.

Philo's apologetic purpose is thus clear — only bad Romans persecuted the Jews; the good acknowledged their rights and the benefits they contributed to the Empire. One detects in Philo's view a desire to restore the status quo for Jews as established in the earlier years of the Empire. His more theoretical ideas, which will be considered later, tally with this desire for peaceful, static conditions.

V. Philo and Jewish Nationalism[524]

Philo does not list Jewish rights in the Empire as extensively as does Josephus,[525] but he is minded to show that the privileges which contemporary Jews could claim rested on solid precedent. Under the Ptolemies the Alexandrian Jews had never been required to set up images or statues in their places of prayer,[526] and Gaius' grandfather and great-grandfather[527] had permitted them to retain their customs,[528] and paid honour to the temple and admired its splendour or its simplicity.[529] But in his appeal to precedent Philo looked largely to Augustus and Tiberius.[530]

Augustus is commended in two separate passages in 'Legatio ad Gaium' for his just treatment of the Jews. According to Philo he was familiar with the size and activities of the Jewish community in Rome,[531] even approving the Jews' refusal to call him a god[532] in contrast to others who so addressed him. (One suspects here a fabrication to support Philo's polemic against Gaius.[533]) Certainly the Jews were a sizable minority within the city, though their precise status was not clear.[534] It is possible that most were Roman citizens,[535] which is the impression Philo wishes to give.[536] He states that they were not forced to violate any of their national customs,[537] a valuable point to guarantee imperial precedent for the

---

[524] The term 'nationalism' here refers to that movement for independence from foreign rule which came to forceful expression in the Maccabean revolt against Antiochus Epiphanes. This independence movement continued on in spirit, if not in name, and led to the attempted rejection of Roman rule in the Jewish war of 66—70 A.D. and the Bar Kochba revolt in A.D. 132—5. The success of the Maccabeans was not repeated. See W. R. FARMER, Maccabees, Zealots and Josephus (Oxford, 1956).

[525] AJ. xiv:188—222; xvi:162—70.

[526] Leg. 137—8.

[527] Marcus Vipsanius Agrippa and Augustus respectively.

[528] Ibid. 240. Through the mouth of Agrippa Philo points to the notable privilege granted the Jews to hold assemblies in Asia when σύνοδοι had been banned (ibid. 137—8). Josephus refers to Agrippa's decrees to Ephesus and Cyrene (AJ. xvi:167—70) and that of Augustus protecting the Jews of Asia — xvi:162—6.

[529] Ibid. 291, 294—7, 310.

[530] Ibid. 156—7, 314—5; Flacc. 50; cf. AJ. xvi:163.

[531] Ibid. 155—6.

[532] Ibid. 154.

[533] Whether Philo was ignorant of, or chose to ignore, the official sanctioning of the ruler cult in parts of the West as well as the East is hard to determine. Though Augustus did not encourage it, yet he could discreetly use this exaltation of his person.

[534] Josephus refers to a large local Jewish deputation which laid charges against Archelaus before Augustus (BJ. ii:80—93). If the number of eight thousand is correct it indicated a considerable community in Rome. Cf. Dio lx:6.6.

[535] SMALLWOOD (Legatio, p. 235) observes on Leg. 158 that the Jews' reception of free corn suggested that many of them had gained full franchise by the time of Augustus.

[536] Leg. 155.

[537] Ibid. 157.

treatment that the Alexandrian Jews now desired from the Romans. He does not mention Julius Caesar's rulings as regards the Jews,[538] emphasizing rather the precedent set by the two emperors, but he does point out that Augustus had not disturbed the Jews' privileges which had been established under the Republic, namely, the right to meet in the synagogues and to send offerings to the temple.[539] Besides following precedent, Augustus ordered that the Jews, because of their observance of the sabbath, were not to be overlooked in the distribution of grain.[540]

There were two possible situations which could explain the case Philo puts forward here. Perhaps Claudius' impatience with the Jewish community in Rome was already discernible, and so Philo stresses the attitude of "the good emperors"[541] towards this minority group so that both precedent and law witnessed to the Jews' peaceable and honourable activities. In support of this is his silence as regards Tiberius' action against the Jews in Rome, concerning which Tacitus, Suetonius and Dio[542] supply information with which in most particulars Josephus[543] agrees except in its dating. Philo embarrassed by Tiberius' action omitted it, or else sought to associate it entirely with the discredited Sejanus.[544] The other possibility is that Philo was indicating the pattern for Claudius to follow in dealing with the Alexandrian situation. In favour of this view is the detailed concern for the synagogues.[545] However, the rights of the Jews as a πολίτευμα were not fully or precisely spelt out and this was the privilege the Alexandrian Jews were eager to establish, so presumably the first motive was at work. Proper treatment of the Jewish community at Rome, and thus of the Jews in the empire, was the criterion by which incidents were selected from the actions of the emperors because any anti-Jewish action could well encourage fiercer outbursts in the provinces.

Philo portrays Augustus' treatment of the Jews as a clear endorsement of the virtues of σωφροσύνη and δικαιοσύνη which were inculcated in their synagogues. Concomitant with it was his allowing them to send money or representatives to Jerusalem.[546] Augustus' order is not extant and it seems reasonable to conclude that Philo inflates the estimate of the Jews in it, though he declares that

---

[538] AJ. xiv:190−216; cf. Augustus' decree in xvi:162−5. Philo in stating that Augustus knew (Leg. 156) of the Jewish synagogues in Rome implies that their rights had been protected under the Republic (SMALLWOOD, ibid., p. 236).

[539] Ibid. 156.

[540] Leg. 158; SMALLWOOD, ibid., p. 242.

[541] Philo does not use the phrase but his case resembles Tertullian's test of the emperors (Apol. 5.1−8).

[542] Tac., Ann. ii:85; Suet., Tib. 37; Dio lvii:18; cf. ELMER TRUESDELL MERRILL, The Expulsion of the Jews from Rome under Tiberius, CPhil., XIV (1919), pp. 365−72.

[543] AJ. xviii:81−4; SMALLWOOD, Legatio, p. 243.

[544] Tiberius consistently opposed attacks on the Jews (Leg. 159−61, 303−5).

[545] Ibid. 346; cf. SMALLWOOD, Legatio, p. 240.

[546] Leg. 313.

he has reproduced the sense if not the words of the edict.[547] His other illustration of Augustus' goodwill was the provision in his will for burnt offerings to be offered daily to the ὕψιστος Θεός at his expense.[548] This was simply the continuation of existing policy, and in his lifetime Augustus had also contributed dedications. The posthumous burnt-offerings to be offered by the Jews were, according to Philo, a memorial "of a character truly imperial"[549] and Philo adorns Augustus' instruction with an explanation which parades the philosophical preeminence of Jewish monotheism in the ancient world.[550] Tiberius also allowed the temple to be used without any interference, as was clearly demonstrated in his censuring of Pilate over the shields' episode.[551]

The goodwill of both emperors was reciprocated, because in the synagogues tribute monies were dedicated in their honour while prayers, votive offerings and sacrifices were offered on their behalf.[552] Philo elsewhere, writing with exaggerated sentiments of loyalty, endeavours to portray the Jews as ardent supporters of Roman rule. Through the desecration of their synagogues, the Jews "by losing their meetinghouses were losing also what they would have valued as worth dying many thousand deaths, namely, their means of showing reverence to their benefactors, since they no longer had the sacred buildings where they could set forth their thankfulness".[553] He even goes so far as to say that "everywhere in the habitable world the religious veneration of the Jews for the Augustan house has its basis as all may see in the meeting-houses".[554] Contrast, not accuracy, is his purpose here. The Jews were compelled to forsake those places in which they wished to honour the emperor, whereas Flaccus' suppression of these peaceable subjects conferred no honour on his master.

At Gaius' accession the Jews of Alexandria had readily paid appropriate homage allowable within their law in presenting a resolution[555] to Flaccus for conveyance to the emperor. His failure to forward the document was brought to Agrippa's attention, in whose care, since he was a friend of Gaius, they knew their resolution was safe, while Philo adds that Agrippa himself testified to the loyalty of the Jews to the imperial house.[556] Also the Jews had closed their shops in mourning for the death of Drusilla, Gaius' sister.[557] Thus of their loyalty to

---

[547] He quotes the letter from Gaius Norbanus Flaccus to the magistrates at Ephesus which conveys the instructions but not the motives of Augustus (ibid. 315; cf. AJ. xvi:166, 171; SMALLWOOD, Legatio, pp. 309–10).

[548] Ibid. 317, 157.

[549] μνῆμα τρόπων ὄντως αὐτοκρατορικῶν (ibid. 157).

[550] Ibid. 318.

[551] Leg. 298–305.

[552] Ibid. 133, 280, 305; cf. Flacc. 48–9, 97.

[553] Flacc. 48; Box, In Flaccum, p. 97.

[554] Ibid., 49.

[555] The ψήφισμα (Flacc. 97) contained provisions of "prayers and dedications of houses of prayer and the setting up of inscribed metal objects therein on behalf of Gaius" (Box, In Flaccum, p. 110).

[556] Ibid. 103.

[557] These closed shops were plundered by the mob (ibid. 56).

their Roman rulers Philo presents no doubt. He writes a tidy apologetic which omits any reference to disturbances involving the Jews or to Augustus' sanctioning of the ruler-cult. Rather Jewish rights and loyalty are consistently upheld in his glowing account of the good emperors' attitudes towards the Jews.

Granted what has just been concluded, there are, however, assertions in Philo's writings in which he would seem to be sympathetic with those who desired the creation of a Jewish state, independent of Roman rule. He certainly regards Israel as the nation held dearest by God Who confers on it the office of priest and prophet for the sake of mankind.[558] So the high priest of the Jews is different from those of other nations because he intercedes for the whole creation,[559] and "the Jewish nation is to the whole inhabited world what the priest is to the State".[560] The Jewish people are qualified for that exalted position because they observe the divine laws which provide for the purification of body and soul. Philo is fond also of interpreting "Israel" as "the viewers of God"; to belong to the race named "Israel" is to possess vision,[561] to see God.[562] Though from Conf. 91 such a capacity would seem to be restricted only to Jews, in 92—95 the sense of vision is presented in the familiar philosophical form of the soul transcending the bodily limits, and this "God-beloved race"[563] symbolizes the minds of all men who are open to wisdom[564] and have forsaken bodily passions.

It would seem then that syncretism has triumphed in Philo's thought, but it can be argued that he takes the leading ideas of others and applies them only to the Jews. Thus he maintains that what is a commendable practice in other cultures had already been foreshadowed by Moses.[565] For example the Spartan practice of a dishonourable man not being allowed to introduce a matter to the Senate had as its guiding principle a truth taught by Moses.[566] Philo reassures his readers that the Stoic Zeno was indebted to Jewish law for his ideas on the freedom of the wise man[567] and that Heraclitus took his five views from Moses.[568] He suggests the possibility of Socrates having learned from Moses' law,[569] and also that Greek legislators copied from the same legislation in not admitting that evidence which had been only supposedly heard by the witness.[570]

---

[558] Abr. 98.

[559] Spec. Leg. i:97, 168; iii:131. They were appointed as intercessors for the human race for good not evil (V. Mos. i:149).

[560] Spec. Leg. ii:163. The Jews supplicate God out of goodwill for their fellow men (ii:167).

[561] Immut. 144; Conf. 148, cf. Gen. 32:38.

[562] Conf. 56; Migr. 54, 113; Qu. Gen. iii:49; iv:233; Qu. Ex. ii:43. Israel is "the soul which sees", just as Jacob is a type of hearing (Conf. 72, cf. Congr. 51).

[563] Heres 203.

[564] Ibid. 204. To Philo, Israel incorporates those whose minds contemplate God and the world (Som. i:172—3).

[565] Josephus similarly emphasizes the antiquity of the Jewish scriptures to demonstrate their superiority (Ap. i:6—9).

[566] Det. 134—5.

[567] Prob. 57.

[568] Qu. Gen. iv:152.

[569] Ibid. ii:6.

[570] Spec. Leg. iv:61; GOODENOUGH, Jurisprudence p. 13.

Philo expects Israel one day to be the prominent nation among all the peoples of the world,[571] but this is dependent on people displaying those virtues which reflect God's character.[572] In Virt. 75 and V. Mos. ii:288 he looks to the future fulfilment of the promises God had made through Moses to His people. In Praem. 88—90 he refers to the harmony yet to exist between the virtuous man and wild beasts in terms which seem to be drawn from the vision of Isaiah.[573] He lists the external blessings promised — "victories over enemies . . . establishments of peace and abundant supplies of the good things of peace, honours, offices and . . . eulogies".[574] In Praem. 169—71 one finds his most sustained description of the future restoration of Israel, of God's gathering them to enjoy prosperity as a nation; their previous adversity is regarded as for their own chastisement and not due to any virtue in their overlords. Yet this seemingly distinct national hope is largely removed to another plane by Philo, because the treatise ends by applying this promise to the budding of the soul to its full virtue.[575] Examining this passage Yehoshua Amir suggests that Philo has moulded traditional messianic expectations to be closer to his own outlook.

> "No doubt the popular source from which Philo drew identified the place of ingathering as the Holy Land, and the obscuring of its territorial identity is part of Philo's other-worldliness".[576]

Philo dehistorizes the coming events to the level of the individual soul and its virtues. Yet in this conclusion Philo uses terms which contain echoes of the political dimensions attached to the restoration of the Jews. From the virtue that grows in the soul states, nations and people reach their greatness. Philo holds both elements together, but in the wider compass of his writings the historical denouement is more on the fringe than at the centre of his interest.[577]

Messianic expectation features but little in Philo's thought, the personal Messiah being mentioned explicitly in only one passage.[578] Quoting from the Septuagintal sense of Num. 24:7[579] which speaks of a man coming to rule over

---

[571] Qu. Ex. ii:76.

[572] Praem. 126, 169—71. The change in the lives of the Jews should so strike their masters that they would be set free by those "ashamed to rule over men better than themselves" (164).

[573] Is. 11:6—9; COLSON, VI, pp. 455—6.

[574] Moving on to expound Dt. 7:12ff., he deals with the physical protection promised to them.

[575] Praem. 172.

[576] YEHOSHUA AMIR, The Messianic Idea in Hellenistic Judaism (English translation by CHANAH ARNON of הרציון המשיחי ביהדות ההלניסטית in: Machanayim, CXIV [Shevat 5730 = 1970], pp. 54—67), Immanuel, II (1973), p. 58.

[577] J. DE SAVIGNAC, Le Messianisme de Philon d'Alexandrie, NT., IV (1959), p. 319; AMIR p. 58—9.

[578] Praem. 95. So SAVIGNAC, Messianisme, p. 319, contra GEIGER, Philon von Alexandreia als sozialer Denker, Tübinger Beiträge zur Altertumswissenschaft, XIV (Stuttgart, 1932), p. 107.

[579] The Hebrew rendering is "Water shall flow from his buckets, and his seed shall be in many waters" of LXX "There shall come forth a man from his seed and shall rule over many nations." Obviously the translators sought to make better sense of the Hebrew rendering.

many nations, Philo does not dwell on the coming man's identity or character but simply on his function as victor in war over powerful and large nations. Rather than proceeding to describe the qualities of his rule, Philo refers generally to the rulers of God's people as exhibiting the three qualities required for good government – dignity, strictness, and benevolence.[580] J. SAVIGNAC has well argued that the one whose coming Philo mentions, and hopefully awaits, is the Logos.[581]

> « Philon aurait estimé que comme le Logos avait conduit le peuple dans son premier exode, semblablement il le dirigerait dans le second, conformément à cette représentation du messianisme populaire que fait de la béatitude de l'avenir le retour de l'âge d'or ou des temps glorieux du passé. »[582]

The Logos is poured out from God and brings order to the cosmos.[583] Yet when the Logos brings deliverance it is to be not the conquest of other nations through the leadership of a human warrior, but the deliverance of the soul, of the mind, which aspires heavenwards, redeemed by the "divine vision" sent by God.

In writing of the Jewish ἔθνος Philo likens it to an orphan in the world. It does not share in the customs of the outside family of mankind but is isolated in that it lives "under exceptional laws which are necessarily grave and severe, because they inculcate the highest standard of virtue".[584] Yet in relation to God it is not orphaned "because it has been set apart out of the whole human race as a kind of first fruits to the Maker and Father".[585] However the majority reject the Jewish ordinances, though they are the way to excellence and teach rulers what is required of them.[586] Despite this rejection arrogant Gentile rulers will one day submit their wretched rule to the scrutiny of God.[587]

Philo also contrasts the Jewish festivals with those of the barbaric and Greek nations.[588] His distinctions are Greek in spirit but his sentiments are Jewish. The Jewish sabbaths and festivals are held to honour God, the true Being, but the festivals of others arose out of fabricated myths. These festivities Philo abhors, marked as they are by reprobate practices, ineffectual sacrifices and the absence of σωφροσύνη.[589] They stand condemned before the searching gaze of God. Yet even in this stricture on Gentile ways Philo describes the Deity with epithets

---

[580] Praem. 97.
[581] He compares Praem. 95 with Conf. 62–3 and V. Mos. i:66, 166; ii:254 (SAVIGNAC, Messianisme, pp. 321 ff.).
[582] Ibid., p. 322.
[583] JOHN DILLON, Ganymede as the Logos: Traces of a Forgotten Allegorization in Philo, SP., VI (1979–80), pp. 37, 40.
[584] Spec. Leg. iv:179.
[585] Ibid. iv:180.
[586] Spec. Leg. iv:183.
[587] Ibid. iv:172–3.
[588] Cf. Agr. 267; Ro. 1:14–6.
[589] Cher. 92–6; Virt. 40.

drawn from the Hellenistic world.[590] Also when he enlarges on the Jewish festivals, the theme of God's election associated with these practices is blunted by his moral allegorizing. For example, the unleavened bread is a reminder not primarily of the exodus from Egypt but of the kneading of "savage untamed passion" with reason, and the Passover represents "the passage from the life of passions to the practice of virtue".[591] The Jewish festivals are therefore a bridge to Philo's syncretized world view and not a pointer to Judaism's particularity.

Those converted to Judaism have turned from ties of blood, customs, rites and idle fables to the "clear vision of the truth and the worship of the one and truly existing God",[592] and are to be accepted "as our dearest friends and closest kinsmen".[593] Philo thus links together as having a knowledge of "the highest . . . most ancient cause of all things" not only the Jews who gain this belief from their "customs and laws", but those others who have not wandered into polytheism but have become monotheists.[594] Polytheists are so foolish as to credit heaven with what Philo abhors on earth, ochlocracy.[595] On the other hand monotheists are lovers of virtue and take their lineage from ὀρθὸς λόγος.[596] They are lovers of peace in contrast to polytheists who, because of the division of loyalty to various gods, are makers of troubles and fill the world with wars.[597] So those who choose the true God and do not set up creatures as divine, join the Jewish nation.[598] This was not the outlook that was to be embraced later by the Palestinian Zealots. The knowledge of God seems for Philo to depend on insight, not on God's election and so one comes into a relationship with Him through the mind and not observance of the law and circumcision. Also this knowledge is expressed in terms of the Stoic-Platonic idea,[599] and not the Biblical call to right living before God and one's neighbour.

---

[590] "For the eye of the Absolutely Existent needs no other light to effect perception, but He Himself is the archetypal essence of which myriads of rays are the effluence, none visible to sense, all to the mind" (Cher. 97).

[591] Sacr. 63.

[592] Virt. 102, 178—9; cf. 1 Th. 1:19; Spec. Leg. ii:164—5.

[593] Virt. 179.

[594] Ibid. 65. He describes Aristotle's opposition to polytheism as "godly and devout" (Aet. 10, 16).

[595] Opif. 171; cf. Spec. Leg. i:331; Ebr. 42—5; Qu. Ex. i:20; ii:2. Polytheism banishes any thought of God from the soul and so it produces atheism (Ebr. 107—10). Philo declares dogmatically that polytheism and atheism are condemned by the law; however his scriptural basis is not the Shema but allegorical exegesis of Dt. 23:1—2. The hallmark of atheism is not defiance of the revealed God (cf. Ro. 1) but the barbaric quest for bodily pleasure as against the higher realm of the soul (Fuga 180; Leg. Alleg. iii:22—4; Cher. 9; cf. F. COPLESTON, A History of Philosophy, I: Greece and Rome, The Bellarmine Series, IX [London, 1951], p. 257).

[596] Conf. 43; cf. 147—8 where the Logos is the eldest born image of God.

[597] Ibid. 42.

[598] Virt. 166.

[599] Ibid. 170; cf. Spec. Leg. iii:167.

Though the foreigner is not a member of the nation, being excluded by kinship, he can gain that privilege by a "transcendancy of virtues". As the basis for such a conclusion Philo advances a principle strongly Stoic in nature.

"It is a general truth that common citizenship rests on virtues and laws which propound the morally beautiful as the sole good".[600]

Yet again even within the same writings one finds the contrary. Philo clearly warns against intermarriage with other nations because their customs will turn the Jew or at least the children of the marriage towards polytheism, "the worst of miseries".[601] Also the foreigner[602] is not to rule because Moses

"assumed . . . that one who was their fellow-tribesman and fellow-kinsman related to them by the tie which brings the highest kinship, the kinship of having one citizenship and the same law and one God who has taken all members of the nation for His portion, would never sin"[603]

by amassing wealth or compelling God's people to wander endlessly. Yet Philo notes that in the law itself it is stated that a brother or son or other relative can lead God's people astray[604] and so kinship, ties from ancestors and blood relationships or intermarriage are to be cast aside if they hinder the honour of God. Those who pursue God's glory will "receive in exchange kinships of greater dignity and sanctity".[605]

On the practical level, Philo defends Moses and his fellow Jews[606] against those who charged the Jews of his day[607] with being a troublesome community inspired by harmful laws emanating from a cunning and unscrupulous demagogue. His case is that Moses, who through his virtue retained the people's loyalty under the trying circumstances of the Exodus, could not have been a deceiver.[608] His human status is emphasized[609] not in order to rationalize[610] the account but rather

---

[600] Spec. Leg. ii:73. This seems to be the sense also of Qu. Gen. iii:62.

[601] Ibid. iii:29; cf. AJ. viii.191; cf. Dt. 17:16—7.

[602] Philo likens the Jews to clean and strong creatures and the Gentiles to asses who are unclean and weak. However he urges, having proselytes in view, that difference in race is not to be a basis of accusation (Virt. 146—7).

[603] Spec. Leg. iv:159; cf. his exegesis in Agr. 84—6 where the literal prohibition against possessing numerous horses is not acceptable to Philo, as obviously a ruler needs a substantial force of them.

[604] Ibid. i:316; Dt. 13:1—11.

[605] Ibid. i:317; Virt. 206—11; Abraham, the first monotheist, is the pattern of excellence for all proselytes who came from polytheism into "a commonwealth (πολιτεία) full of true life and vitality, with truth as its director and overseer (ἐπίσκοπος)" (ibid. 213, 216, 219).

[606] Hyp. 6.2.

[607] Considering the criticisms levelled against Moses by Apollonius Molon, Lysimachus and others (Ap. ii:145) it would seem that Philo is defending him against contemporary slander from some Greek authors possibly in Alexandria.

[608] COLSON, IX, p. 416 gives two other suggestions: (a) the docility of the people and (b) divine influence, but Philo's emphasis is on Moses' character.

[609] Hyp. 6.2.

[610] So COLSON, XI, p. 408.

to show the respect outsiders should have towards him, his laws and his followers. When Philo recounts the conquest of Palestine he takes pains to turn attention towards the exemplary lives of Joshua's band and away from the hostilities. He expressly urges his readers to look away from the historical narrative to the reasonable cause of their victory, namely the respect in which their enemies held them, despite their unwarlike and feeble condition.[611] God had been the active one in the great events of the Exodus and Philo speaks of "revelations from God through dreams and visions", not to reduce the supernatural content but to pass lightly over the distress and upheaval caused by God's powerful hand in Egypt in support of His people. No mention is made of the antagonism felt towards the Jews in Egypt. Rather their increasing numbers and their yearning[612] for their original homeland are given as the reasons for their departure. These explanations by Philo are understandable because he wishes to emphasize the peaceful life-style of the Jews, and the respect men of old had for them. So in his apologetic, Jewish laws and Jewish esteem for Moses are inextricably woven together to produce a pattern of lawful and just behaviour.[613]

In contrast to the ambiguity of Philo's views on Jewish national aspirations, he consistently interprets the nations mentioned in the scriptures in a derogatory vein. The Egyptians incessantly represent the bodily passions, the visionless community, those taken up with sense-perception, lovers of the body, and spurners of both virtue and God.[614] Egypt symbolizes atheism, because it feeds the body and does not care for the soul and worships the creature rather than the Creator.[615] The mind that seeks God separates itself also from Edom, that domain of earthly values,[616] and the Hittites, who symbolize "senselessness".[617] The Chaldeans stand in error by pursuing their study of astrology, bringing the heavens down to earthly existence, and making fate and necessity divine.[618] In their failure to acknowledge God's transcendance and His work as creator of the universe[619] these people typify the ungodly. Thus Abraham rightly left Chaldaea[620] "the tongue of sky-prating astrology" because in pursuing reason he espoused the worship of the first Cause of all things.[621]

[611] Hyp. 6.6.

[612] Ibid. 6.1.

[613] Hyp. 6.8—9.

[614] V. Mos. ii:161, 165, 168—9. (An exception is Virt. 106—7 where he endorses Moses' words on showing friendship to the Egyptian. There Egypt is not equated with passion.) Heres 316; Congr. 20—1, 83—4, 86, 163; Conf. 70, 81, 88, 91—5; Migr. 18, 20, 97, 151; Abr. 103.

[615] "The worst of evils". Spec. Leg. i:330; Fuga 180; Jos. 254; V. Mos. i:23; ii:193—5; 270.

[616] Migr. 146.

[617] Qu. Gen. iv:241.

[618] Migr. 179, 194.

[619] Congr. 49; Abr. 77—8. Instead they make gods out of the created world (Qu. Gen. iii:1).

[620] Som. i:161; Virt. 212—6. Moses, who is by γένος a Chaldaean (which means Hebrew — V. Mos. ii:26) also leaves that region (i:5). He has his ancestry traced back to Abraham (i:7) and as an infant is recognized as a Hebrew in appearance (i:15).

[621] Som. i:161; Abr. 69—70, 77—8.

The Canaanites symbolize vices,[622] Syria arrogance,[623], and Amalek passion.[624] However, several of these nations contributed to the education of that greatest of Hebrews, Moses, though he soon out-stripped his teachers. Distinctive features of Egyptian, Assyrian and Chaldaean cultures were taught to him, but he rose above these conflicting fields of learning and sought truth.[625] Philo is so determined to allot to Moses' education the riches of every major culture that he even includes Greek tutors amongst his mentors.[626] This anachronistic reference arises from his description solely in Hellenistic terms of Moses' educative process. By reason within him Moses grasped philosophical doctrines and, to use good Stoic terminology, pursued "nature's right reason"[627] which is the basis of virtue. Allied to this was his exemplary adoption of the Philonic virtues — σωφροσύνη and καρτερία.[628]

Though Philo espouses cosmopolitanism he is aware of divisions amongst men. Thus Greeks are distinguished from barbarians, Athenians from Lacedaemonians, Scythians from Egyptians, Europeans from Asiatics. He observes that no states or cultures incorporate the institutions of others into their laws[629] but rather at times deliberately show disrespect for others' ways.[630] However, Jewish ways attracted people everywhere[631] — a statement in contradiction to Philo's assertion elsewhere that the Jewish law was accepted by few.[632] Those who see the light, that is, those who honour virtue,[633] respect Jewish law. There are indeed virtuous men to be found everywhere.[634] He appeals to universal observance of the sabbath, the keeping of the Jewish passover and the wide respect for Jewish fasting. It is a grand appeal for the surpassing excellence of Jewish ways in the world of nations. This romance is continued, reaching its climax with the account of the writing of the Septuagint. The translation was produced, Philo claims, at the request of some who lamented that such treasures were available only to the "barbarians".[635] His account of the motives for the writing of the Septuagint bursts with pride over his Jewish heritage and he looks beyond his own time when the Jewish nation is weak to a new era when

---

[622] Congr. 83, 85.
[623] Ibid. 41.
[624] Ibid. 55.
[625] V. Mos. i:21−4.
[626] Ibid. i:21, 23.
[627] Ibid. i:48.
[628] Ibid. i:25.
[629] This is clearly an inaccurate generalisation.
[630] V. Mos. ii:19.
[631] Ibid. ii:20.
[632] Spec. Leg. iv:179.
[633] V. Mos. ii:17, 271; Virt. 179.
[634] Ibid. ii:20.
[635] Ibid. ii:27. The greatness of the laws is reflected in that the task of translation was not given to private individuals or magistrates but to kings. That Ptolemy Philadelphus was associated with this work made him literally the greatest of rulers (ii:29). This is to be seen as an isolated paean.

"each nation would abandon its peculiar ways, and throwing overboard their ancestral customs, turn to honouring our laws alone".[636]

This is amongst Philo's most eloquent expressions of Jewish uniqueness and is noticeably devoid of allegorical depths; yet one must regard it again only as a part of his world view in which Judaistic particularism struggles with universalism.

When Philo considers the response of Jews to Roman rule he takes pains to convince Claudius that both law and history bore testimony to their commendable activity in the Empire, and that both Augustus and Tiberius had sanctioned Jewish practices. The Jews responded by giving loyalty, and even in Gaius' reign they had shown full respect within their rights to the emperor. Admittedly Philo's pen on occasions writes exaggerated descriptions of Jewish loyalty while past imperial action against the Jews is passed over in silence. In Philo's reflective expositions on the destiny of Israel and the Jews he claims a special identity for his people, but also accepts all monotheists and lovers of virtue into their ranks. He attributes the riches of Gentile philosophical thought to Moses, and believes that Israel will one day be restored to power and rule preeminent, yet he in fact applies this promise to the realm of the soul attaining perfect virtue. So also the Jewish festivals, which Philo regards as superior to those of the Gentiles, signify the conquest of passion by virtue and the Gentile nations are presented unfavourably because of what they symbolize – atheism, passion, vice. In accord with this blunted nationalistic hope, messianic expectation is not prominent in Philo's thought and when the messiah is identified he is the Logos who will lead the souls of men to the contemplative vision of God. Philo's praise of Jewish ways is aimed not at deepening the nationalistic fervour of his people but at defending them before Gentile critics. Thus Philo emerges not as a nationalist but as holding an ambiguous position. His view of the political world around him is plainly one that supports the status quo, based on acceptance of the benefits of Roman rule. His zeal, inspired by philosophy, is not directed towards nationalist[637] aims but the fruits of contemplative world-citizenship.

Part Two:
Philo's Theory of Rule

The main sources for Philo's ideas on ideal rulers are 'De Vita Mosis' and 'De Iosepho'. While certainty is unattainable it seems likely that they were written to persuade Jewish readers to retain their links with Judaism.[638] In both works Philo

[636] V. Mos. ii:44.

[637] BRÉHIER, Idées philosophiques, p. 32.

[638] SANDMEL, Philo, p. 47. His suggestion (p. 64) that 'De Iosepho' came from Philo's old age is possible, though the strength of Philo's apologetic does not seem to indicate "a lack of zest".

seeks to show that the riches in Hellenistic political aspirations were attainable with the Judaistic heritage. Significantly 'De Iosepho' is subtitled ΒΙΟΣ ΠΟΛΙ-ΤΙΚΟΥ. It is a sustained treatise by Philo on the qualities of a true ruler in which Joseph is depicted, through literal and allegorical exposition, as an ideal statesman.

The contrary picture of Joseph sketched in 'De Somniis' can be explained as Philo's use of allegorical interpretation to suit a different purpose. In 'De Somniis' the emphasis is on the superiority of the soul over the body, a theme, interestingly enough, which is affirmed in 'De Iosepho'. However in 'De Somniis' the allegorical interpretation of Joseph's name and actions require him to be not an exemplar but a villain. The variableness of the allegorical glasses Philo wears is the explanation.

The major source for Philo's presentation of Moses as the ideal ruler comes from the sustained exposition in 'De Vita Mosis'. This treatise is supported by references eleswhere to Moses' political granduer whether in other expositions of 'Exodus' as in Sacr. 9 or in expansive descriptions of Moses as in Congr. 132 and Virt. 70. In Philo's writing on ideal rulers two figures from his Judaistic heritage stand on the centre stage.

I. Moses and Joseph — the Ideal of Statesmanship

1. Moses as Ruler and Philosopher-King

According to Philo, God had placed the mantle of ideal rule pre-eminently on Moses, though in Philo's tract on the model statesman Joseph wore it also. There is no question in Philo's mind but that Moses was the human ruler surpassing all others.[639] God had gifted him with no ordinary virtue such as that which kings and other rulers had,[640] and his elevation was not due to the use of force but was based on the "goodness, nobility of conduct and universal benevolence" which constantly stamped his life.[641] Being thus appointed king by God because of his virtue, and having rejected Egypt's rule because of his noble spirit and hatred of evil, he was made ruler over a nation more populous and greater than others, a nation which was the special supplicant to God for other nations to do right.[642]

Though Moses led a multitude of people out of Egypt,[643] he was established king by God not by a host in arms.[644] It was God who exercised sovereignty[645]

---

[639] Josephus held the same view (Ap. ii:158—160).
[640] Sacr. 9.
[641] V. Mos. i:148; cf. Leg. 50—1.
[642] V. Mos. i:149.
[643] Ibid. i:147.
[644] Praem. 54.
[645] Cf. Joseph., AJ. ii:165.

in the establishment of his rule and the people in turn responded to God's impulse.[646] Philo contrasts Moses' enlightened ways with the practices of those who had "thrust themselves into power" and had taken pains to exalt their own houses and promote their sons to great power.[647] Moses, for his part, decided neither to establish a dynasty nor to set up his family in positions of power, with the result that fratricide, a tragic feature with newly-risen kings, was not associated with his name.[648]

Philo approves of Plato's ideal[649] that states are best governed by philosopher-kings,[650] but even these rulers pale before the actual Moses who "combined in his single person not only these two faculties (i.e. ἡ βασιλικὴ καὶ φιλόσοφος) but also three others, legislative ability, the high-priestly office and prophecy".[651] Philo affixes these distinctly Hebraic additions to the qualities contained in the Platonic ideal. This is not simply mechanical eclecticism on his part, but springs from his belief that what is to be admired in the Greek ideals for rulers is present in Moses, and what the Jewish scriptures wrote of him complemented this Hellenic estimate of the ideal ruler.

Philo explains why the three qualities drawn from the scriptural record of Moses' life are essential capacities in the ideal ruler. With regard to legislative ability, it is

> "a king's duty to command what is right and forbid what is wrong. But to command what should be done and to forbid what should not be done is the peculiar function of law; so that it follows at once that the king is a living law (νόμος ἔμψυχος), and the law a just king."[652]

This concept was carried over from Pythagorean discourses on kingship into Platonic and Aristotelian thought, as GOODENOUGH points out.[653] Whereas according to Xenophon Socrates desired that the ruler be answerable to the laws of the city,[654] Plato seemed to approve of the good ruler as one who, from his own wisdom, sets laws for different situations.[655] However, Philo goes further in stating that the good king, in this cases Moses, is law[656] and seems thus to adopt the Pythagorean notion. Again, in detecting a Hellenic virtue in Moses' rule,

---

[646] Praem. 54.

[647] V. Mos. i:150.

[648] Spec. Leg. iii:18. Philo had the Persians in mind.

[649] Pl., Resp. v:473 D; vi:499 B; vii:540 D; Leges iv:711 D, 712 A, 713 E.

[650] V. Mos. ii:2. Along with Plato he envisaged guardians, but he had already allocated this role to the elders; those who had attained "wisdom through practice . . . well fitted to steer the course of earthly things" (ii:4).

[651] V. Mos. ii:2–7.

[652] Ibid. ii:4.

[653] GOODENOUGH, Hellenistic Kingship, pp. 61–3. He quotes the Pythagorean Archytas of Tarentum: "Every community consists of the ruling element, the ruled and a third element, the laws. Now laws are of two kinds, the animate (ἔμψυχος) law, which is the king, and the inanimate, the written law". Cf. HEINEMANN, Philons Bildung, p. 182.

[654] Ibid., p. 61; Xen. Mem. iv:6.12.

[655] Polit. 294a.

[656] Abraham is described by Philo as a νόμος and θεσμὸς ἄγραφος – Abr. 276.

Philo regards it as uniquely displayed in him; Moses was unsurpassed in the role of νόμος ἔμψυχος and mediator.[657]

In Plato's writing the legislator established the state and then framed laws in agreement with its continuing form and existence, but to Philo Moses wrote of the founding of the world in a different vein.

> "He considered that to begin his writings with the foundation of a man-made city was below the dignity of the laws, and, surveying the greatness and beauty of the whole code with the accurate discernment of his mind's eye, and thinking it too good and godlike to be confined within any earthly walls, he inserted the story of the genesis of the 'great City', holding that the laws were the most faithful picture of the world-polity".[658]

So Moses' law was in accord with natural law and by it the harmony of the universe was both discerned and maintained.[659] Again the uniqueness of Moses' rule is presented in terms indistinguishable from Greek descriptions of the ordering of the universe, which indicates how Philo can grasp the highest pagan thoughts and attribute them to Moses. That figure is not only "another Plato who contrives laws for an ideal community"[660] but one greater than Plato.[661]

As regards the two other Hebraic qualities which Philo attributes to Moses, the office of high priest was necessary because the competent ruler ought to apprehend divine as well as human affairs, "for without God's directing care the affairs of kings and subjects cannot go straight",[662] while the gift of prophecy was needed by the human ruler "in order that through the providence of God he might discover what by reasoning he could not grasp".[663] All of these virtues worked together in harmony and were to be found in Moses, the best of kings, lawgivers, priests and prophets.[664] Moses was selected as the bearer of God's legislation because he possessed the purest mind and by descent was attached to truth.[665] He was the greatest and most perfect of men[666] and this unsurpassed legislator was himself νόμος ἔμψυχος καὶ λογικός, not by his own attainment but by God's foreknowledge.[667] He possessed those four virtues which Greek thought held could only be found in the ideal legislator.

> "The legislative faculty had for its brothers and close kinsmen these four in particular: love of humanity, of justice, of goodness, and hatred of evil . . .

---

[657] V. Mos. i:155—62. See W. RICHARDSON, The Philonic Patriarchs as Νόμος Ἔμψυχος, St. Pat., I, p. 519.

[658] Ibid. ii:51.

[659] Ibid. ii:52.

[660] YEHOSHUA AMIR, Philo and the Bible, SP., II (1973), p. 4.

[661] V. Mos. ii:12.

[662] Ibid. ii:5.

[663] Ibid. ii:6, 187—90. One might see here a link with Joseph's capacity to interpret human life by interpreting dreams (Praem. 54—6).

[664] Ibid. i:334.

[665] Congr. 132.

[666] μέγιστος, τελειότοτος (V. Mos. i:1—2).

[667] Ibid. i:162.

By love of humanity he is bidden to produce for public use his thoughts for the common weal; by justice to honour equality and to render to every man his due; by love of goodness to approve of things naturally excellent, and to supply them without reserve to all who are worthy of them for their unstinted use; by hatred of evil to spurn the dishonourers of virtue, and frown upon them as the common enemies of the human race.

It is no small thing if it is given to anyone to acquire even one of these — a marvel surely that he should be able to grasp them all together. And to this Moses alone appears to have attained, who shows distinctly these aforesaid virtues in his ordinances".[668]

Moses was thus the example all rulers were to emulate[669] and Philo in his description of Moses' qualities[670] presents an unrestrained panegyric. In contrast to Philo's villains, Gaius, Flaccus and Sejanus, Moses' central aim was to benefit those over whom he ruled. Hence he did not (and here in Philo's eyes he was unique) feather his own nest[671] nor parade his majesty, but lived unassumingly, rejecting the arrogance commonly associated with human rule. Here indeed is a criticism of Roman practice, but it was the oriental rulers who delighted most in the trappings of power.[672] The treasures Moses had in abundance were not these externals but the qualities of a great king —

"the repeated exhibition of self restraint (ἐγκράτεια), continence, temperance (σωφροσύνη), shrewdness, good sense, knowledge, endurance of toil and hardships, contempt of pleasures, justice, advocacy of excellence, censure and chastisement according to law for wrongdoers, praise and honour for well-doers, again as the law directs".[673]

When he exhorted his people they listened, recognizing in the force of his words not those of a ruler lording it over his subjects,[674] but his concern for justice and equality amongst them.[675]

The figure of Moses begins eventually to take on supernatural dimensions. God gave him the wealth of the earth so thus he became "a partner of (God's)

---

[668] V. Mos. ii:9–10. Cf. Som. ii:243–4. Philo's elaboration of the four virtues was drawn from a cross-section of thought — Platonic (rendering one's due), Pythagorean (honouring equality), Stoic (approving the naturally excellent).

[669] He was their ἀρχέτυπος and παράδειγμα (Virt. 70, cf. V. Mos. i:158–9).

[670] V. Mos. i:151–8.

[671] Ibid. i:152–155.

[672] When GOODENOUGH discusses the passage on the beasts of burden (Politics, p. 7) and sees there a slight on the Romans he is partly correct, but more likely it is a criticism of pagan practices which Philo would have witnessed amongst the Greeks and Egyptians in Alexandria.

[673] V. Mos. i:154. The last two notions one finds clearly endorsed in Paul's and Peter's expectations of good rule (Ro. 13:3; 1 Pt. 2:14).

[674] Ibid. i:324.

[675] Ibid. i:328; cf. Leg. 47.

own possession",[676] God's heir (κληρονόμος).[677] All that Greek philosophy looked for in the ideal political man Moses embodied. As well as being a philosopher-king, he was the genuine κοσμοπολίτης and friend of God, the beholder of God's secret ways. Only he, and certainly not his opposite, Gaius, was rightly privileged to be called "god and king", the same title accorded to the Almighty.[678] Moses is depicted as the model (παράδειγμα) to be"imitated". BURTON MACK[679] contends that the paradigm is meant to confirm the Jews' corporate life and to undergird their claim to have found the true purpose of living.

Philo's assessment of Moses reflects the exclusive pride of Judaism in its major founder. Yet Hellenistic concepts are dominant in Philo's presentation.

". . . He takes for granted the Greek theory of revelation which is different from the theory of Jewish tradition. For the educated Greek the Godhead does not speak *to* man but *within* man . . . Philo is not at all offended by the statement that Moses is called God. For Philo something divine must be incorporated in Moses' personality in order to understand the Pentateuch as coming from his hand".[680]

The ideals of kingship − that the king embodies just law and knows the way of God − are realized in Moses, and no adequate comparison is possible with any known Gentile leader. The praise Philo bestows on Augustus and Tiberius is due largely to the desire to condemn Gaius (though he admires both rulers) and given the audience for those documents in which their praises are sung, it would have been imprudent to compare such emperors unfavourably with the greatest ruler, Moses.

2. Joseph as Statesman

Though there is no mistaking Philo's high estimate of Moses' political capacities, when he comes to write a sustained piece on the ideal statesman he selects for his source the Genesis account of Joseph's adventures.[681] The contradictions between the picture it presents of Joseph and that found for example in Som. ii: 90−109 has led GOODENOUGH to detect in the former work a message conveyed "by innuendo".[682] He contends that 'De Iosepho' was written as a cleverly concealed criticism of Roman rule. Thus he explains Philo's contradictory treatment of Joseph in this writing and in 'De Somniis' by arguing that in the former work

---

[676] Ibid. i:155.
[677] Ibid. i:156.
[678] V. Mos. i:158. ". . . the Hellenistic form of Isis mythology and of the kingship ideology in Egypt which was informed by that mythology is the sufficient source for the essential features of the cosmic logos-king of Israel" − BURTON L. MACK, Imitatio Mosis: Patterns of Cosmology and Soteriology in the Hellenistic Synagogue, SP., I (1972), p. 51.
[679] Ibid., pp. 38−41.
[680] YEHOSHUA AMIR, Philo and the Bible, SP., II (1973), p. 4.
[681] The subtitle of 'De Iosepho' is Βίος πολιτικοῦ.
[682] GOODENOUGH, Politics, chaps. II−III.

Joseph[683] was depicted as the desirable "type of the Roman prefect" in Egypt and that Philo wished by inference to "remind the Gentiles that Egypt had at least once been ideally governed — by a Jew".[684] He contends that in the latter work Philo wrote his barbed criticism of Roman rule "in code".[685] There is sufficient in Philo's account of Joseph's life in 'De Iosepho' to substantiate GOODENOUGH's contention that Joseph is intended to epitomize the qualities of the ideal statesman in Hellenistic political thought. On the other hand one must disagree with his conclusion that in this writing there is a skilful and well camouflaged anti-Roman thrust. Certainly at one point Philo views the Romans critically, but overall the barbs spring from anti-Gentile rather than anti-Roman feeling.

In Philo's presentation, Joseph from his youth had acquired or possessed the qualities commonly ascribed to the ideal king. (In the course of the narrative Philo refers to Joseph's capacity to interpret dreams as part of the capacity of the statesman.[686]) From this early age Joseph had been trained in kingship by being employed as a shepherd and that this was a preparation for rule Philo readily proves by reference to the Greek poets.[687] Joseph's father saw in the lad "a noble spirit which rose above ordinary conditions", which quality, as GOODENOUGH points out, was expected of great rulers in other Hellenistic writings on political leadership.[688]

It is from Philo's allegorical explanation of Joseph's name that the pronounced Hellenistic ideas of kingship emerge. Even the interpretation of Joseph's name as "an addition to the lord"[689] is expounded in political terms. Yet this different interpretation of the name found in Jos. 28—31 is linked with Mut. 89 where laws are regarded as an addition to nature. In Som. ii:47 Joseph symbolizes the addition of arrogance, that cardinal sin of rulers in Philo's eyes, but he also represents the additions of gluttony, flamboyant clothing, lavish buildings and beds.[690] Philo, interpreting the name allegorically, is at liberty to turn the meaning of Joseph's name according to his purpose. In this passage his express aim (ii.48) is to decry excess in accumulating the necessities of life. GOODENOUGH regards the passage as strongly anti-Roman in tone,[691] and undeniably the allusion to the wearing of golden wreaths in the market place by those who said that they were

---

[683] Ibid., p. 55.

[684] Ibid., p. 63.

[685] Ibid. chap. II.

[686] Jos. 125; contrast Som. ii:105—7 where his rejection of dreams is commended.

[687] τὸ ποιητικὸν γένος — Jos. 2. "Of course Joseph never became king, but Philo is thinking so closely in terms of the theory of kingship that the word has come in unawares." (GOODENOUGH, Politics, p. 46).

[688] Cf. Diotogenes: "And he will succeed (in being the statesman) if first he makes an impression of majesty by his appearance and utterances and by looking the part of the ruler" (Stob. iv:7.62, p. 267 HENSE). Jacob's fourth son, Judah, also could be considered an ideal ruler as he is described as "princely in nature" (Jos. 189).

[689] κυρίου πρόσθεσις — Jos. 28. VALENTIN NIKIPROWETZKY, Κυρίου πρόσθεσις. Note Critique sur Philon d'Alexandrie, De Iosepho, 28, REJ., CXXVII (1968), 389.

[690] Som. ii:48, 53, 55, 57.

[691] Politics, pp. 24—5.

"not only free men but . . . even rulers over many other people"[692] suggests Roman practice and claims. This may then be regarded as a rare instance when the Romans are clearly indicated in a context generally aimed at Gentile arrogance.

Philo discusses the customs and laws of states in a Stoic-Cynic vein,[693] regarding them as additions to the "law of nature",[694] and contrasting them with the law of Moses. In Jos. 29—36 this perspective is clearly evident when it is recalled that he regards Mosaic law as synonymous with natural law. The world is to be considered as the great city (μεγαλόπολις) and "it has a single πολιτεία and a single law; this is the law . . . of nature", which commands the right and forbids wrongdoing.[695] Philo permits no excuse for the setting up of local laws, laws which are "inventions and additions",[696] for behind such divisions amongst states lies the rejection of "the ordinances of nature". Just as man-made laws are an addition to the law of nature so "the politician is an addition to the man whose life accords with nature".[697] Such is the interpretation Philo gives of his translation of the name Joseph as "addition of a lord" (κυρίου πρόσθεσις).[698]

However the varied experience of the statesman is presented disimpassion-ately by Philo through his allegorization of Joseph's multicoloured coat.[699] In noting the diverse experiences of political life and the politician's response to them Philo writes in pragmatic vein. "There is no hint of bitterness . . . States take many different forms, vary widely in their laws and the *politicus* must take on the character of warrior or peaceful man, or what else, and use force or persuasion, as circumstances demand".[700] There is also the sober realisation that the states-man does not hold absolute power but is potentially a slave in that he is dependent upon the support of the crowd and can be despatched by them at whim,[701] while within he can be dominated by arrogance, which will lead him to ruin. This danger from arrogance is introduced through allegorization of the wild beasts which were reported to have killed Joseph.[702]

When Philo resumes the narrative, he portrays Joseph unmistakably as one rightly destined to rule. The disparaging terms to describe Joseph the politician are past, because his noble life now indicated that he was under God's care.[703] He

---

[692] Som. ii:62.
[693] L. COHN and P. WENDLAND, Philo von Alexandria (Berlin, 1962), I, p. 156.
[694] GOODENOUGH, Politics, p. 80.
[695] Jos. 29.
[696] Ibid. 29—30.
[697] Jos. 31.
[698] The Hebrew יסף means "to add" — προστιθέναι Gen. 30:24; cf. πρόσθεσις (Som. ii:47).
[699] Ibid. 32—6.
[700] GOODENOUGH, Politics, p. 48.
[701] Ibid. 35—36.
[702] Ibid. 36. As COLSON notes, "the fake statement . . . is treated as true for the purposes of allegory", Philo, VI, p. 160 n.a. In Som. ii:65—6 the wild beast is likened to the forces of this life which oppose men of virtue — "complexities, foolish fictions using covetousness and cunning".
[703] Jos. 37. GOODENOUGH comments on this phrase that "in all his actions and pronounce-ments he followed divine guidance and inspiration, or in other words he had the dis-position of the ideal Hellenistic king" (Politics, pp. 48—9).

was being prepared for rule by nature[704] (that is, his natural qualities) and the particular stage of preparation which Philo found in the sacred text, namely the management of a household, was a familiar analogy in Greek philosophic discussion of rule.[705] The similarity between Philo's statement and Plato's on the same theme[706] is too close to be explained as simply Philo's adoption of a mosaic of Greek ideas. Here he is directly dependent on Plato for the key notions he propounds on the preparation for, and the carrying out of, rule.

The third necessity for statecraft is self-mastery[707] — that virtue which Philo prizes so highly, as did sophisticated Hellenistic thought. This quality, in conjunction with Joseph's desire to be a faithful manager of Potiphar's household, is found readily enough in his refusal to commit adultery with his master's wife.[708] One significant addition to the Genesis account is Joseph's words that "we children of the Hebrews follow laws and customs which are especially our own".[709] GOODENOUGH contends that it was "a section obviously inserted as propaganda for the Gentile reader".[710] But it could well be meant for the committed Jews, reinforcing their adherence to Judaism,[711] or else as an indication that Philo, despite his espousal of Hellenistic ideas, in the daily areas of life which marked off Jewish culture is as orthopraxic[712] as the best.

The ruler is to exercise this quality of self-control especially in dealing with his sexual passions. Philo posits lack of restraint (ἀκρασία) as the cause of countless small as well as large conflicts amongst both the Greeks and barbarians,[713] because when a ruler is gripped by ἀκρασία it eventually provokes civil strife and wars. In strong contrast stand the fruits of self-control (σωφροσύνη): order (εὐστάθεια), peace (εἰρήνη) and full satisfaction of life's joys.[714] This was familiar to Hellenistic political theorists,[715] and Philo, in his Stoic-oriented treatise on the free man, says much the same in relation to the good ruler.

---

[704] Ibid. 38, 40.

[705] Pl., Polit. 259C; Arist., Pol. iii:10.2.

[706] Jos. 39, cf. Pl., Polit. 258 E ff.

[707] ἐγκράτεια (ibid. 54). The sentiment though not the term occurs in Pr. 16:32.

[708] Ibid. 40. Joseph's possession of σωφροσύνη was also demonstrated here.

[709] Ibid. 42–3; cf. Gen. 39:8–9.

[710] Politics, p. 50.

[711] GEORGE HOWARD (The 'Letter of Aristeas' and Diaspora Judaism, JTS., XXII [1971], p. 348) comments that the 'Letter of Aristeas' is "contrary to popular opinion, an apology to Palestinian Judaism rather than to the Gentile world". S. JELLICOE in reviewing PELLETIER's edition of 'Lettre d'Aristée à Philocrate' (JTS., XV [1964], p. 112) suggests that the audience was the Jewish community in Alexandria.

[712] "It has always been wrong to speak of Orthodox Judaism at any time in the history of Rabbinic Judaism. Orthodoxy there never was nor is there any; orthopraxis there once was, and is, though today the observance of full orthopraxis is hard indeed" (J. BOWMAN, Samaritan Studies, BJRL., XL [1957–8], p. 309). Cf. WOLFSON, Philo, I, p. 74. On prohibition of inter-marriage see Jos. 43; WOLFSON, ibid., I, pp. 74–5, nn.66–7.

[713] Jos. 56.

[714] Ibid. 57.

[715] GOODENOUGH, Politics, p. 50.

"For if the soul is driven by desire, or enticed by pleasure, or diverted from its course by fear, or shrunken by grief, or helpless in the grip of anger, it enslaves itself and makes him whose soul it is a slave to a host of masters. But if it vanquishes ignorance with good sense, incontinence with self control (σωφροσύνη), cowardice with courage and covetousness with justice, it gains not only freedom from slavery but the gift of ruling as well".[716]

If that passage was written in Philo's youth as COLSON suggests[717] then his Stoic undercutting of Jewish identity and claims for civic rights[718] was later tempered by a deeper commitment to the Jewish community.[719]

GOODENOUGH's desire to relate the contents of 'De Iosepho' to Philo's environment is commendable and one needs to remember Philo's experience as a member of the Jewish community in Alexandria. The harrassment of the Jews (climaxing in the pogrom under Flaccus) illustrated the necessity for good rule, otherwise the tyrannical mob, unchecked and unpunished, could wreak the savagery of its hate. Philo comments that

"the true statesman knows quite well that the people have the power of a master; yet he will not admit that he is a slave, but regards himself as a free man and shapes his activities to please his own soul . . . since the leadership and charge of the state is put into his hands, he will know how to hold it as a good guardian, or an affectionate father".[720]

The barren influence of the crowd is signified in the eunuch because, in contrast to the wise ruler, "the multitude is unproductive of wisdom though it seems to practise virtue".[721]

The marks and duties of the ideal ruler are these: that he does not dissemble in seeking to achieve his aims, that he is ready to die rather than be swayed by the wishes of the tyrannical mob,[722] that he governs and guides the crowd of subjects, as a tutor[723] or a father[724] giving to the people not what they demand but what

---

[716] Prob. 159.

[717] Philo, IX, p. 5.

[718] I.e. if Prob. 158 is to be taken at face value with its call to seek truth and its refusal "to ascribe citizenship or freedom to possessors of so-called civic rights or slavery to servants . . . but dismissing questions of race and certificates of ownership and bodily matters in general, study the nature of the soul".

[719] For example, it stood in contrast to the intense and presumably later pride he displayed over Jewish adherence for many centuries to Mosaic law even in the face of death (Hyp. 6.8–9). That claim is sounded in a work intended for Gentile readers (6.1).

[720] Jos. 67.

[721] Ibid. 59. The eunuch thus did not symbolize Roman power though he was Joseph's master. In Mut. 173 he represented indiscipline.

[722] Ibid. 68.

[723] So ἐπίτροπος is to be translated, contrary to the political interpretation GOODENOUGH attaches to it in Som. ii:43 (Politics, pp. 22–3).

[724] Ibid. 67.

will improve their condition.[725] He is to be a ruler free from selfish passions and partisan loyalties. The terms are drawn from Stoic thinking.

> "For, though the people be a master, I am not a slave, but as highly-born as any, one who claims enrollment among the citizens of that best and greatest state, this world. For when neither presents, nor appeals, nor craving for honours, nor desire for office, nor spirit of pretentiousness, nor longing for reputation, nor incontinence, nor unmanliness, nor injustice, nor any other creation of passion and vice can subdue me, what domination is still left for me to fear? Clearly, it can only be that of men, but men, while they assume the sovereignty of my body, are not sovereigns of the real I".[726]

> "For when a mixed crowd of heterogeneous persons comes together, it says what is right, but it thinks and does the opposite. It prefers the spurious to the genuine, because it is under the dominion of appearances and does not practise what is truly excellent".[727]

It is surely significant that Philo reserves his most vitriolic epithets for the mob, regarding it as the major force opposing the true statesmen and thus reinforcing the view that the Alexandrian anti-Jewish crowd and not the Roman government is the target for his ire. The crowd can not generate statesmen (though it can topple the good ruler);[728] it never attains wisdom; it knows what is right but can not do it. Its fault lies not in its Gentile idolatry but in its failure to attain the Hellenic virtues.

How is the good statesman, then, to respond to the crowd? GOODENOUGH sees as the direct background to this the manipulation of the prefect by the Alexandrian mob.[729] This seems overstrained and there is one omission from Philo's description which weakens his case. Philo is aware of the armed support on which the Roman ruler could call (cf. Flacc. 5) so that the Alexandrian mob was not invincible, yet in his account the mob is considered as having superior force, if not to kill the statesman then to punish him for his good acts.[730] GOODENOUGH relates this point also to the position of the Roman prefect in Alexandria,[731] and admittedly the exhortation to rulers takes on a deeper meaning when consideration is given to the mob's influence on Flaccus; but if this was written before that prefect's time, as is probable, Philo's words may have no particular person in mind. Obviously one can find advice here for the Alexandrian prefect as for any

---

[725] Ibid. 73—5.

[726] Jos. 69—71. If the soul is free of these, the ruler is free to rule well and the citizen is eager to assert justice whether as a jury member (72) or a councillor, or an elder in the assembly (73).

[727] Ibid. 59.

[728] There is not necessarily a contradiction involved here with Jos. 67. The crowd can not produce from its ranks the wise ruler but it can exert brute force to destroy such a man.

[729] Politics, p. 52.

[730] Jos. 79.

[731] "The passage is the subtlest kind of flattery. When it is recalled that the Alexandrian mob tended perennially to turn against the Jews, and that the only hope of the Jews lay in a strong, fearless and impartial prefect, the objective of Philo is obvious" (Politics, p. 52).

ruler of a city, but it is against mob-rule that Philo expressly writes. The Roman ruler who follows his advice, who is not swayed to revoke or ignore the old privileges accorded his subjects,[732] is acceptable to him. His dutiful ruler possesses those Stoic virtues enunciated in Prob. 24—5, and is not praised simply for his Jewish adherence. This weakens GOODENOUGH's point that in 'De Iosepho' Philo is skilfully demonstrating "that Egypt had at least once been ideally governed — by a Jew".[733]

Using the image of love-making, Philo reiterates that self-control should hold back the ruler from the crowd's allurement.[734] Expounding the theme allegorically, Philo represents the crowd as the obstacle facing the statesman in the exercise of good rule. Its influence is linked with that of the passions which will entice a man from the life of right and freedom. From it comes the pressure to rule unjustly and the allurement of bribery,[735] but the good ruler unflinchingly rejects such overtures. To submit would be a travesty of the proper submission of the crowd to the ruler.[736] In sketching the relationship of the ruler to the crowd Stoic terms[737] dominate, and reference to the Old Testament political imagery of God's relation to rulers and multitudes is lacking.[738] Though the statesman knows that the crowd has power over him yet he is determined to be free, and will not bind his soul to it. The crowd can harm the body but that is of little account.[739] On the surface this sounds much like the words of the Matthean Jesus (Mt. 10:28) but lying behind his saying is the perspective absent from Philo's Stoic-oriented treatment, namely the eschatological fear of God.

Philo also likens the statesman, Joseph, to a doctor[740] who cares for his patient whatever his social position. In tending a ruler or a despot, the doctor applies, "the fire or the knife, he the subject to his ruler".[741] Therefore, Philo concludes, the ruler is called "to attend . . . the whole state afflicted by the more powerful distempers" and is not to "sacrifice the future welfare of all and minister to the cares of this man and that man with flattery utterly slave-like . . . unworthy of the free".[742] Hence one of the signs of Joseph's good rule was his care for his

---

[732] Ibid. 64.

[733] Politics, pp. 62—3.

[734] Ibid. 64.

[735] Jos. 68—70.

[736] Ibid. 64, 79.

[737] E.g. his reference to "citizenship of the world" (ibid. 69).

[738] G. ERNEST WRIGHT, The Old Testament and Theology (New York, 1969), Ch. 4.

[739] Jos. 67, 71.

[740] Following the Septuagint's designation of Potiphar as a cook (Gen. 39:1), Philo wrests from this further proofs of the evil influence of the crowd in political life. His comparison of the cook with the physician is probably drawn from Plato (Grg. 464Dff., 500B and 501A) as there is no mention of a physician at this point in the Septuagint (cf. Jos. 75—7). In political life the physician is like the laws and rulers whose existence is for the welfare of society (cf. GOODENOUGH, Light, p. 144), while the cooks are "the swarming crowd of younger spirits" whose aim is pleasure and who delight in lawlessness (Jos. 63).

[741] Jos. 76.

[742] Ibid. 77.

subjects,[743] and while in prison he did not flatter the notable, but regarded all men alike.[744]

The ideal statesman draws back from the enticements of passion and pleasure,[745] after which the despotic mob hankers, and so it treats him as an enemy, whereas he is its friend and helper.[746] The mob will not submit and thus can not truly rule, for submission is part of the preparation for exercising authority. Aristotle's axiom is echoed elsewhere by Philo — "He who has learned to be ruled also learns at once how to rule".[747] One is not surprised to find that the ideal statesman is also an interpreter of dreams, Philo regarding the latter experiences as encompassing the whole of human life. In the rise and fall of states, the hopes and fears of all men — sailors, merchants, athletes and the rest — there was confusion and disorder, like the jumbling of dreams in a man's sleep. Into this world the statesman should come forward and exhort his people as he interpreted the experiences of life for them.[748]

Philo then proceeds to give precise examples of the ruler's art, drawing both from the Mosaic legislation and from Hellenistic thought. In sitting on a jury the statesman is to be swayed neither by partiality towards the rich nor by pity for the poor.[749] If acting as adviser or speaking in the public assembly, he is to aim at the general good,[750] and neither fear of consequences nor the use of flattery is to mar his actions. To sum up the ruler's virtues, Philo quotes not from the Jewish scriptures but from Euripides.[751] The good ruler is to rebuke, warn and correct foolish men and ideas, motivated not by presumption but by frankness.[752] Reverting to a Platonic image, Philo relates this to the doctor's art in effecting for the state that which will heal its diseases,[753] and in not being swayed from such a beneficial course by the master-servant relationship.[754] For its part the crowd has to respond rightly to its ideal ruler and it errs in attacking him who acts for its benefit, because in rejecting him it returns to its natural state, which is disorder and insubordination. Even the true ruler has first to learn to submit, but such an attitude the truculent crowd will not adopt, although it benefits most when it is guided by a wise ruler.[755]

---

[743] Ibid. 157.

[744] Ibid. 88.

[745] Compare Macro's effort to move Gaius to self-control (Leg. 43—6).

[746] Ibid. 79.

[747] Qu. Gen. iii:30. Jos. 38—9 indicates the influence of the Greek commonplace, that household management was a form of state management. By Philo's time it had become part of the common stream of political ideas.

[748] Jos. 135—47.

[749] Jos. 72—4; cf. Qu. Ex. ii:10.

[750] Ibid. 73. Philo appears to be opposed in theory to consultation and assumes that the free ideal ruler is infallible, knowing the right decision in the cases before him.

[751] Ibid. 78; Eur., Phoen. 521.

[752] νήφουσα παρρησία (Ibid. 73).

[753] Jos. 77; cf. the discussion of the term νόσος on pp. 428—9.

[754] Ibid. 76.

[755] Ibid. 67, 74.

As noted earlier,[756] GOODENOUGH sees in this exposition of the duties of the good ruler an allusion to the situation in Alexandria, but the duties are too general to be linked specifically to that milieu. The passage reads as a set piece rather than a covert reference to his immediate environment, for after its rounding off with a balanced conclusion[757] the narrative is resumed. The concept of the free man ruling his soul dominates the whole piece, and thus Joseph represents the Stoic ideal rather than Jewish leadership in Gentile territory. However, I am in agreement with GOODENOUGH's other conclusion, that in this presentation Joseph's qualities accord with the Hellenistic ideal of kingship. For example, he compares Philo's commendation of Joseph as ἀλεξίκακος[758] with the similar Greek praise of Zeus, Heracles and Hermes. Though this term is lacking in any direct reference here,[759] its use by Philo to describe Augustus' capacity to rule well[760] indicates that it was associated with ideal rule in his mind.[761] Also, GOODENOUGH, rightly sees in Joseph's reforming influence upon the hardened jailors and criminals[762] an exemplification of Diotogenes' description of the good king.[763] Philo goes on to recount that the jailors and prisoners were converted by Joseph's philosophy and manner of life.[764] GOODENOUGH concludes that he incorporates the Pythagorean understanding of the king's saving power,[765] and that his embellishments of the Genesis account, such as Pharoah's discernment of wisdom and a free and noble spirit in Joseph,[766] have as their rationale the portrayal of the ideal ruler.

However, GOODENOUGH is less plausible in his exposition of Jos. 117—9. He links the use of ἐπιμέλεια (with reference to Joseph's oversight of Pharaoh's household) with the office of ἐπιμελητής, a term used for a steward of the emperor who looked after his special interests.[767] Further he sees in Joseph's being appointed to the ἐπιτροπή . . . τῆς Αἰγύπτου πάσης an unmistakable allusion to the office of Roman prefect.[768] This interpretation is supposedly reinforced by the tradition that Joseph received from Pharaoh the actual rule even though Pharaoh retained the title of rule, thus making Joseph viceroy of the king-

---

[756] See pp. 491—2.

[757] Ibid. 79.

[758] Jos. 80.

[759] GOODENOUGH, Politics, p. 53.

[760] Leg. 144.

[761] GOODENOUGH, Politics, p. 53. D. R. DUDLEY, reviewing GOODENOUGH's book, rightly comments that this concept of the duties of kingship was ancient and well known (JRS., XXX [1940], p. 127).

[762] Jos. 81—7.

[763] Ibid. He points out how Philo altered the Genesis account by making Joseph rather than God the one who moved the jailor to show him special consideration.

[764] Note the singling out of σωφροσύνη amongst his virtues (ibid. 87).

[765] Politics, p. 54.

[766] Jos. 106—7.

[767] Politics, p. 55, n. 47.

[768] Ibid. p. 23 and n. 11. Philo uses ἐπίτροπος (Jos. 184, 196) interchangeably with ὕπαρχος (157) and ἡγεμών (193).

dom, yet in practice he had the power of king.[769] GOODENOUGH sums up his case
thus:

> "A more accurate definition of the office of the *praefectus Aegypti* could not
> be drawn up. For the ἐπίτροπος in Egypt was distinguished from the other
> ἐπίτροποι by the fact that he had been given by Augutus *imperium* on a par
> with the *proconsul*. So he came to be known as the governor with the *impe-
> rium*, the ἡγεμών, very possibly an abbreviation of ἐπίτροπος σὺν ἡγε-
> μονίᾳ, or some such title. When Philo adds the detail that Joseph's commis-
> sion included also the supervision of the household of Pharaoh he has com-
> pleted the essential characterisation of the prefect. For that officer functioned
> not only as the procurator with *imperium*, but he was also the steward of
> Egypt, since Egypt was a part of the personal estate of the emperor".[770]

This interpretation is questionable. In the first place, Philo's account of Joseph's
elevation follows closely the narrative source. There Pharaoh acknowledged that
the Spirit of God dwelt in Joseph and appointed him over his house and over the
people in general, reserving for himself the ascendancy of the throne.[771] Secondly,
it is by no means certain that Philo's use of terms indicates the prefect. R. MARCUS
notes that ἐπίτροπος is not necessarily used as a technical term when applied to
Flaccus.[772] He observes that Moses is so described[773] in a context which does not
convey the sense of "prefect", and Petronius is called ἐπίτροπος of Syria[774] by
Philo when his official position was *legatus*. M. RADIN agrees, contending that
the official title of the prefect was not ἐπίτροπος but rather ἔπαρχος and
ἡγεμών.[775] Ἐπίτροπος suggests rather the general sense of "administrator" and
if it designates a particular office, that would be the inferior position of procurator
and not prefect.[776] These objections on contextual and linguistic grounds are sufficient for the rejection of GOODENOUGH's case, and the passage is explicable
without resort to it.

There is a defensive note in Philo's introduction to the interpretation of
dreams (125–43) and he is at pains to support the notion that a great statesman
can also have this power.[777] As GOODENOUGH argues, this was not expected in
the ideal Hellenistic ruler and Philo allegorizes the gift in order to incorporate this
quality which was esteemed in the Jewish scriptures.[778] Possessing this gift, the
good ruler is able accurately to judge all the experiences in human life, for the

---

[769] Jos. 119.

[770] Politics, p. 55.

[771] Gen. 41:38–40, cf. Jos. 116.

[772] RALPH MARCUS, Review of E. R. GOODENOUGH's 'The Politics of Philo Judaeus', AJP., LX
(1939), pp. 485–6.

[773] V. Mos. i:114.

[774] Leg. 333.

[775] Som. ii:43.

[776] MAX RADIN, Review of E. R. GOODENOUGH's 'The Politics of Philo Judaeus', CPhil.,
XXXIV (1939), pp. 269–272, cf. p. 272.

[777] Jos. 125.

[778] Gen. 28:12–6; 37:5–11; 40 – 41:37; 1 Km. 28:6, 15; Da. 1:17; 2:1–45; 5:12.

transient events of nations are but as insubstantial as dreams.[779] For Philo, the interpreter of dreams is equivalent to the soul,[780] which rises above the experiences that overwhelm the senses and cause them to perceive only "confusion, inequality and irregularity".[781] Out of this disarray the great statesman brings order, explains through reason and truth the visions that come to his subjects, and exhorts the wealthy to be compassionate, the famous to be humble, and the poor to be not disconsolate.[782] It is noteworthy that confusion and disorder, the distinctive features of mob rule, are the conditions Philo emphasizes as excluded from the situation set in order by the ideal ruler.

Returning to his narrative, Philo comments that the statesman does not hold the office of king. He stands between the king and the citizens, and his task is to serve them both.[783] No doubt one is to understand the sense of this in terms of Philo's earlier passages on the relation of the physician to his master. The interpretation of the tokens of Joseph's prestigious position — chariot, ring and necklace — differs from that given in Som. ii:43–7. There Joseph's position as second-in-command is portrayed as "insignificant and absurd" and is compared with the "infliction of indignity and deceit".[784] He was overcome by conceit, busied himself in providing food for the body and neglected the soul.[785] The necklace signified a life moved by necessity and not by the order which reflected nature's way, while the ring was empty of any pledge. The very name "Joseph"[786] signified the arrogance of those who made additions to nature's laws. In 'De Iosepho' on the other hand, his position in the second chariot indicated the important role he played in handling affairs of state, and under God's hand he governed the crowd. The ring, rather than being devoid of meaning, was a genuine pledge of trust between ὁ βασιλεὺς δῆμος and ὁ πολιτικός. The necklace indicated not only the fame which came from the crowd's acclamation of good rule but also it signified punishment, for it could drag him down when he displeased his master.[787] In a following note Philo refers to the type of exposition given in 'De Somniis': he mentions a different allegorical interpretation adopted by some wherein the king was equivalent to the mind which ruled over the body, and the main servants of the king — the chief baker, butler and cook — catered for the sensual needs of the body.

How are we to explain these different interpretations? It may be that they reflect different times and purposes in writing. Thus while 'De Iosepho' represents his general understanding of the practice of political rule, 'De Somniis' contains the criticism of Flaccus that came to full expression in his express work on that

---

[779] Jos. 127–36, 140.

[780] Later the image is altered, in that sleep becomes equivalent to earthly existence and waking to heavenly existence (ibid. 147).

[781] Ibid. 142.

[782] Ibid. 143–4.

[783] Ibid. 148.

[784] Som. ii:43.

[785] Ibid. ii:46.

[786] See pp. 492–3.

[787] Jos. 150.

figure. That seems the likely possibility. Other explanations are that the different sources Philo uses for his different writings contain divergent allegorical expositions, or that for those of his writings meant for Gentiles his political ideas had to be presented more carefully. Yet if 'In Flaccum' was meant for Gentile readers, Philo presents his views in it quite strongly. To use allegorical interpretation opens a gate to varied expositions. Allegorization was a means Philo used to carry out his purposes in writing. The covering of the same material did not mean that his use of the method was to be the same.

After being appointed second in command, Joseph, so one reads from the Genesis narrative,[788] travelled throughout the land of Egypt. Philo mentions and enlarges upon this, describing Joseph's actions and how he impressed the people not only by the benefits he brought them but also by his striking appearance and attractive manner.[789] GOODENOUGH argues,[790] that by using the term ὕπαρχος Philo is thinking also of the Roman prefect, but such an interpretation again seems too strained. The scriptural account was sufficient for Philo to expand upon in order to convey what is required of the good ruler.[791] To link Philo's account with his commendation of Flaccus' early rule is to conjecture too precise a *Sitz-im-Leben*. The passage is for the benefit not particularly of the prefect of Egypt but of any ruler. Joseph displayed the virtues which Philo lauds on other occasions. His soul ruled his passions[792] and he desired to encourage men in their spirits as well as to feed their bodies.[793] Such attributes make the wise man a ruler whatever his position.

GOODENOUGH, in pursuing Philo's narrative, sees in Jos. 174 a reference to the king exercising divine authority. He refers to Reuben's words in which the eldest brother rebuked the rest for their evil action against Joseph.

> "We are reaping the rewards of our self-will and impiety. The plot we hatched for him is under inquisition, but the inquisitor is no man but God or the word or law of God".[794]

He detects in them a reference to Joseph

> "as being only the vehicle through whom logos or divine law operated. In his official capacity he was divinity, not humanity. This statement seems of great importance to me as marking Philo's ultimate concession to the current theory of kingship. Bitterly as he opposes any assumption of divinity on the part of the ruler himself, or any cult of the ruler, Philo is quite ready to admit that the good ruler is the mediator of divine rulership to men, and

---

[788] Gen. 41:46.

[789] Jos. 157.

[790] Politics, pp. 56—7.

[791] Gen. 42:6 refers to Joseph as ἄρχων τῆς γῆς (LXX).

[792] Jos. 166. The twin Greek virtues of ἐγκράτεια and σωφροσύνη were much prized by Philo. — Early Ideals of Righteousness by R. H. KENNETT, Mrs. ADAMS and H. M. GWATKIN (Edinburgh, 1910), pp. 59—60.

[793] Ibid. 162.

[794] Jos. 174; Gen. 42:22.

although the ruler must be regarded as a human being in nature, his royal, official, voice is the voice not only of logos and divine law, but of God".[795]

However, GOODENOUGH's exegesis is unconvincing on two counts. Firstly, the emphasis in the passage falls on the prospect of retribution, not on Joseph as the instrument of retribution, and Philo is simply enlarging on his source.[796] Secondly, Philo wishes to qualify the suggestion that God judges and so he adds ἢ λόγος ἢ νόμος θεῖος. In his exposition of God's ways with mankind, he takes pains to dissociate God from personally administering judgment, and though he is not always consistent on this point,[797] it is still an important element in Philo's theology, and it appears here at an appropriate place. Thus in this passage no reference is made to Joseph or any other human ruler.

That the brothers marvelled at the dining arrangements[798] provides Philo with an opportunity to present further qualities of Joseph's rule. His ways were exemplary for civilization[799] because he brought good order not only to the state, but also to such minor cultural affairs as the conduct of a feast. Joseph, the good ruler, considered the welfare of his country even in setting a banquet for his brothers. Philo elsewhere expresses his disfavour towards the intemperate feasts of the gluttonous. Here he endorses that view and, referring to the famine-stricken country of the time, he commends the mean which Joseph followed in the banquet[800] between uncontrolled feasting and depressing sombreness. The butt of his remarks is the general lack of restraint which he observes in Gentile feasts of his day; there is no particular anti-Roman element[801] in the biting attack on gluttonous and ostentatious feasting.[802]

Philo follows the Genesis narrative to its climax, describing the consternation over the cup being found in Benjamin's sack, the response by the brothers and Joseph to this incident, and Joseph's revelation of his identity to them. Admittedly Philo expands on his source, but again GOODENOUGH reads too much into the words when he detects in Joseph's response clear clues as to the identity of Philo's readers. He may well be correct in seeing in Joseph's words[803] a veiled criticism of Roman practice, especially in view of the contemporary instance cited in Spec. Leg. iii: 159–62.[804] However there is no indication that

"the reader is a person who knows Jewish legal customs, but not Jewish religious teaching or history, which would probably have described very well the Roman rulers of Egypt who had had practical experience with

---

[795] Politics, p. 58.

[796] Gen. 42:22.

[797] See p. 513.

[798] Gen. 43:33.

[799] The comparison is made with the uncivilized past (Jos. 204).

[800] Ibid. 204–5.

[801] Contra. GOODENOUGH, Politics, pp. 24–5 commenting on Som. ii:61–64.

[802] Jos. 206.

[803] "What good reason is there for including in the penalties those who had no share in the offence?" (Jos. 220).

[804] GOODENOUGH, Jurisprudence, pp. 134–50; 230–1.

Jewish legal processes, while they were indifferent to other aspects of Jewish life".[805]

Moreover Philo's paraphrase of Gen. 44:17,[806] with its reference to Joseph's threatening to punish by slavery, presents Joseph favourably, and GOODENOUGH's contention that "Philo did not want the prefect or the *iuridicus* to quote to them this Jewish precedent which gave slavery as the penalty",[807] is off the mark because the sentence of slavery is said to be "the moderate and more humane course",[808] and since Philo followed his source so closely it is more reasonable to suggest Jewish and sympathetic Gentile readers than Roman.

GOODENOUGH also relates Philo's omission of Gen. 47:13—26 to his theory that Philo was writing to counsel the Romans on ruling.

> "It is highly significant that he omits altogether the circumstantial account of how Joseph used the desperate poverty of the populace during the last years of the famine to destroy all freedom in the lower classes, and to make all Egyptians except the priests the personal slaves of Pharaoh, tilling land to which not they but Pharaoh held the title. Philo did not wish the Romans to know that for such highhandedness one of the great heroes of Jewish history offered an example and precedent".[809]

Yet Gen. 47:27 — 50:14 was also omitted, and if Philo had the Alexandrian or even Egyptian situation so particularly in view, 47:27 with its description of the Israelites' prosperity would have provided a fine opportunity to point out the benefits accruing from the sympathetic encouragement of Jewish communities.

Joseph's virtues continue to be enumerated as the narrative unfolds. He wished to be reconciled to his brothers, recognizing in all that had befallen him the purposes of God,[810] while, in a phrase reminiscent of Paul (Gal. 2:10), he declared his concern for all men but especially those of his own kin.[811] He sought to distribute food evenly throughout the nation,[812] and he acknowledged God as the source of his good fortune.[813] These qualities were reiterated by his brothers — his forgiving spirit, concern for his family, his wisdom and awareness of God's sovereignty and his perseverence ($\kappa\alpha\rho\tau\epsilon\rho\iota\alpha$) in the face of their ill-treatment and other trials.[814] He spurned arrogance and pride of position even when elevated by Pharaoh, and did not seek to reveal that he was of noble birth.[815] Philo has enlarged on his source in providing all these details, but it is sufficient to see here

[805] GOODENOUGH, Politics, p. 59.
[806] Joseph declares, "Only the man in whose hand the cup was found shall be my slave".
[807] Politics, pp. 59—60.
[808] Jos. 221.
[809] Politics, p. 61.
[810] Jos. 236, 240.
[811] Ibid. 241, cf. 244.
[812] Ibid. 243.
[813] Ibid. 244.
[814] Jos. 246.
[815] Ibid. 248—9.

the extended praise for a fellow Jew rather than agreement in every part with the theory of Hellenistic kingship, and to regard the virtues as rounding out by general examples Joseph's right to be considered the commendable practitioner of the βίος πολιτικός. The same may be said of his qualities described in Jos. 258–60. His honesty, linked with his self-restraint, forbade him to enrich himself at the country's expense. Philo expresses this attitude to wealth, one of the lesser goods according to Plato, in a phrase reminiscent of the 'Laws'.[816]

It is reading too much into the panegyric on Joseph to see imported there the concepts contained in the Pythagorean ideals of kingship. That Joseph was handsome Philo could deduce from his source.[817] That he created harmony out of disorder was certainly a quality of the ideal ruler found in Diotogenes' thought, though the comparison with the latter's writing on harmony is not very productive, for Diotogenes was discussing the harmonizing of the ruler into a deity.[818] In Joseph's response to the disruptive incidents in his life Philo has sufficient material to write on harmony and order. GOODENOUGH notes as the third royal virtue the "power of speech". Significantly Philo links Joseph's interpretation of dreams, which as GOODENOUGH himself admits did not arise in the Hellenistic ideal, with his capacity to move people by persuasion not by force,[819] the distinctive quality Moses also possessed. The ideal of eloquence was shared by various philosophies and one needs to be cautious in determining the intention of Philo in its use. For him Joseph the ruler is basically the good man. The final sentence of the treatise anchored to the Genesis narrative praises his virtue. It was this basis which provided the mainstay of Philo's account of the good statesman and not his effort to contrast Joseph with the contemporary Roman prefects of Egypt.[820]

Thus Moses and Joseph both embodied ideal rule. Their noble characters, their love of virtue, meant that subjects obeyed them through persuasion not force. For his part Moses was not only the philospher-king and νόμος ἔμψυχος but according to Philo's interpretation he possessed the greatest legislative ability, he rightly exercised a high-priestly office, and he exhibited prophetic power. He combined in himself the virtues sought by Hellenistic thought in the ideal ruler, and his rule was marked by justice, philanthropy, benefactions and goodness. Joseph as well is to be emulated because he too exhibited the virtues so much

---

[816] Leges i:631 C, cf. Jos. 258. To see in the words καθάπερ τε οἰκίαν μίαν Αἴγυπτον (259) a direct reference to Aristotle's thought is not required. It was a common image and in extolling Joseph's administration Philo could use it to describe his honest and efficient rule.

[817] The source indicated that Potiphar's wife was attracted to Joseph (Gen. 39:7).

[818] GOODENOUGH, Hellenistic Kingship, p. 68.

[819] Jos. 269.

[820] GOODENOUGH, Politics, p. 62. The comment on the fate of the Jews in Egypt in V. Mos. i:35 might be regarded as a reference to the position of Philo's contemporaries. "Strangers ought to be regarded as friends and settlers who are anxious to obtain equal rights with the burgesses and are near to being citizens because they differ little from the original inhabitants." Here may be a case for envisaging Gentile (or more precisely Alexandrian Greek) readers, except that the Jews of Alexandria tended to consider themselves present in Alexandria right from its founding.

prized by Philo, restraint and contempt of pleasures. He also had been trained as a shepherd, the basic foundation for any good leader. His manner of life revealed his ruling qualities; he did not fear the crowd but sought his subjects' improvement as a doctor did that of the body. He was not ruled by arrogance, nor did he seek fame and power but treasured the soul's rule over the passions, and in interpreting dreams he possessed the capacity to interpret life. Philo contrasts the rule of these two leaders not specifically with Roman but with Gentile practices in general, and in particular with the turmoil ochlocracy produced. Yet dominant in the portrayal of Moses and Joseph as ideal rulers is Philo's Greek heritage; though Jewish figures, their virtues are clearly presented in Hellenic dress.

II. Introduction of Chapters III–VI

The wide range of sources drawn upon in the following chapters touch upon significant aspects of Philo's political thought. The scattered but numerous references in Philo's works to law, justice, monarchy, democracy, ochlocracy, tyranny, citizenship, and the relative value of public life compared to the contemplative, indicate the pervasiveness of these ideas in his thinking. In the ensuing chapters one finds that the only writings which deal in a sustained way with any of these political ideas are 'De Specialibus Legibus' and 'De Vita Contemplativa'. However, it is significant that the wider ambit of references drawn from many of Philo's other works either underline or enlarge upon the political themes Philo affirms in these two writings.

The bulk of the references that are noted are drawn from his allegorical works. The interpretation through allegorical exposition of the inner meaning of the scriptural text was dear to Philo's heart. That such exposition is studded with political ideas that Philo either takes for granted or wishes to commend is worth noting. Also significant is the reasonable consistency of these ideas that Philo expresses in these various writings. While detailed study of the sources and exegetical traditions Philo uses will help to ascertain the scope of Philo's originality on these themes, their frequency of occurrence testify to their being well absorbed in his expression of political ideas and imagery.

III. Law and Justice

1. God as the Source of Law

To Philo legislation is an integral part of the ordering of society,[821] but what does "law" mean in his political thought? Does he regard the Mosaic law as the

---

[821] Qu. Ex. i:3.

only law for a civilized state? Considering his espousal of Hellenistic philosophy, one is not surprised to find him relating his understanding of Mosaic law in this regard to the notion of natural law.[822] Thus natural law preceded Moses' law because it produced the order essential for the functioning and beauty of the created world,[823] and this legislated order is grounded in the design of the Divine Reason.[824] The created world preceded man's institutions, and its order is that of "nature's right relation" functioning through divine law.[825] Shifting to a Platonic key, Philo asserts that its order is the reflection of God's excellent model already existing in the realm of ideas and when divorced from this model, earth becomes chaotic.[826] Thus the order of the created world is the prototype[827] for the order that is guaranteed in a city through its constitution and law.

God dispelled disorder in giving form to the world[828] and because He is good and His laws are perfect, the establishment of order through law is grounded in His very being. Nor is God beholden to any outside measure as is man, for all just law springs from His will and pleasure.[829] Since God is the source of law, the difficulties encountered in applying it were brought to Him by Moses,[830] because God alone can "distinguish by infallible and absolutely unerring tests the finest differences and thereby show His truth and justice".[831] Also inherent in the administration of law is the power to reward good and to punish evil.[832] Philo does not draw back, as on other occasions,[833] from directly apportioning the retributive responsibility to God who uses either unwitting agents[834] or, as in the case of Phinehas, zealously devout men[835] to punish evildoers.[836]

God's exercise of law is first seen in his framing of the world,[837] and thus it follows that the created world is not autonomous but that its harmony is God's doing.[838] Thus the human legislator is not immune in acting lawlessly[839] and will encouter God's retribution. Also the despot who spurns God's law, as did the

---

[822] ANDRÉ MYRE, La loi dans l'ordre cosmique selon Philon d'Alexandrie, Science et esprit, XXIV (1972), pp. 245—6.
[823] Opif. 28.
[824] Ibid. 20.
[825] τῆς φύσεως ὀρθὸς λόγος (ibid. 143).
[826] Leg. Alleg. iii:152; cf. Opif. 16—22.
[827] Spec. Leg. iv:187—8.
[828] Spec. Leg. iv:187; Qu. Gen. i:55. Order always overcomes disorder whether in the universe, in reason (Sacr. 82), or in the state (Qu. Gen. iv:12).
[829] Opif. 46; Sacr. 131; Spec. Leg. i:279; MYRE, La loi, p. 246.
[830] Num. 27:5.
[831] V. Mos. ii:237.
[832] Sacr. 132; cf. Ro. 13:3—4.
[833] See p. 513.
[834] Prov. 2.37.
[835] V. Mos. i:300—4.
[836] Congr. 179.
[837] Plant. 35; Som. i:241.
[838] Cher. 109—113; WOLFSON, I, pp. 337—9.
[839] Spec. Leg. iii:164—6. Philo has the principles of Mosaic Law in mind.

king of Egypt in regard to Sarah, will be punished by God.[840] For this reason, too, the machinations of Balak to corrupt God's people were thwarted.[841]

The pattern for God's rule in human society is to be found in the Mosaic regulations, obedience to which produces peace and harmony amongst households, cities and nations. God's law as found in the Mosaic decalogue is synonymous in Philo's thought with natural law,[842] and this summation of God's divine law is the fountain from which all other laws flowed.[843] The Mosaic law is superior to all other constitutions because it was given directly by God Who set His law within the universe, making the world both a great and lawful city.[844] Israel and its law are God's gift to the world, and just as the people of God epitomize the world, so Mosaic law epitomizes its laws.[845] Even in Hyp. 6.9, where Philo minimises the supernatural transmission of the Mosaic law[846] he indicates that code's superiority by pointing to the devotion given it by its adherents and their dedicated agreement not to alter one part of it.

The laws Moses heralded are so far superior to all others that not only Jews but members of Gentile nations respect them.[847] Philo exaggerates markedly, but he is striving to undergird his case that all other law-codes are marked by transience, whereas

"Moses is alone in this, that his laws, firm, unshaken, immovable, stamped . . . with the seals of nature herself, remain secure from the day when they were first enacted to now".[848]

In a passage very similar in style to that expressing Paul's wonderment at the power of Christ's love (Ro. 8:38−9), Philo climaxes his praise of Moses' law. All the obstacles encountered in life − famine, war, tyranny, rebellion of soul, body, passion or vice − will not overpower the law of Moses.[849]

---

[840] Abr. 94−6.

[841] V. Mos. i:300−5.

[842] So Abr. 5−7, 16, 60−1; Spec. Leg. ii:13. Philo holds that the Mosaic law, unwritten in the time of the patriarchs, was observed by them for they lived in accord with nature. Cf. John's statement that the Logos existed as God and became flesh in Jesus (J. 1:14, 17).

[843] Congr. 120.

[844] μεγαλόπολις . . . νόμιμος (Qu. Ex. ii:42).

[845] Ibid.

[846] In contrast for example to Qu. Ex. ii:42.

[847] V. Mos. ii:17−20.

[848] Ibid. ii:14.

[849] Ibid. ii:16. The law of Christ does not hold for Paul that strongly Stoic vein which runs through Philo's understanding of the law's purpose. Paul would not have disagreed with the first reason Philo gives for Moses' writing the law, namely that "the Father and Maker of the world was in the truest sense also its Lawgiver" (ibid. ii:48; cf. Ro. 1:18−32), but the concept of natural law found in Ro. 1 is surpassed by Philo's second reason: "that he who would observe the laws will accept gladly the duty of following nature and live in accordance with the ordering of the universe" (ibid.; Opif. 3).

2. The Observance of Law

Where law and justice are esteemed by both ruler and subject, then he who has authority rules well and his subjects benefit because they are ruled by reason.[850] When the disorder within a person which is caused by passion is subdued by reason's rule, then both individual man and society will experience peace and good order, "those perfect forms of the good".[851] So within a community even a small minority ruled by reason can maintain peace, even though every city has within it evil men[852] and thus the germs for disorder, what Philo terms the disease of civic life.[853] He who follows reason, who aspires to good order, is "a lover of peace"[854] and "a man of worth".[855] Such was Abraham who, though being stronger than Lot, did not grasp a privileged position.

> "He alone took for his ideal not the exercise of strength and self-aggrandizement but a life free from strife and so far as lay with him of tranquility and thereby he showed himself the most admirable of men".[856]

He typifies one who is obedient to God's law; the wise man whose citizenship is in heaven and whose soul is ruled according to Nature's Law.[857]

The good man is to live both a law-abiding life in society and one contemplative of nature, for this produces peace. The secondary requirement is "to abstain from sinfulness of word, either by lying or perjury or subtlety or calumny, and in general from aiming at the ruin of others".[858] This reads as a general proscription, and though with hindsight it may apply in Philo's situation to Dionysius and his fellow demagogues, it is straining the passage and its context to see here a specific reference to them. However, the fulfilment of one's obligations towards one's rulers is not the full expression of the good man's actions. So, for example, Philo condemns the quest for virtue in the political realm in order to gain a good position under one's ruler.[859]

What Philo desires is for men to reach beyond observance of the laws to the life contemplative of nature,[860] an experience which cuts across ethnic and cultural

---

[850] Som. ii:154.

[851] Qu. Gen. iv:95.

[852] Disorder is inherent in the evil man (ibid. iv:23) as, for example, in Esau who was "the enemy of intercourse, humaneness and community, leading an unsocial life" (ibid. iv:165).

[853] The Armenian version reads πολιτικὰς νόσους; cf. Cod. R. which reads πολεμικὰς νόσους.

[854] Som. ii:40; cf. Abr. 27.

[855] Abr. 225.

[856] Ibid. 216; cf. Ro. 12:18.

[857] Agr. 65–6. That is, ruled by ὁ ὀρθὸς λόγος for it is synonymous with true law (Ebr. 142; cf. SVF. iii:613).

[858] Mut. 240; cf. Js. 3:2–7.

[859] It is the ὀρθὸς λόγος which tests men's motives, to determine whether their searching after improvement is really a desire for virtue; for it is according to νόμος θεῖος that virtue is sought for its own sake (Leg. Alleg. iii:167–8).

[860] Spec. Leg. ii:45, 52.

divisions. Such men avoid tribunals not out of love for lawlessness but because a
public place provides a gathering point for irresponsible men.[861] Rather, their
souls aspire to heavenly realities and they abjure the sway of passions.[862] If cities
possess these aspirants to virtue then peace will be found in them.[863] Such an
aspirant was Moses who took Jethro in hand, a man consumed by changing
customs and opinions,[864] led him away from the strife of a citizen's lot and, as the
guardian of the law, instructed him aright.[865]

Law stands in the same contrast to lawlessness as does the rule of a king to
that of tyrant. Here the meaning of the name Melchizedek[866] occupies Philo's
attention. In expounding that name he presents the same contrast between the
rule of the king and the tyrant which one encounters in Plato's writings, namely,
tyrannical rule by compulsion and decree and kingly rule by persuasion and
principle.[867] To Philo the enaction of fierce laws leads only to evil and further
indulgence of the passions. Thus his theoretical response to problems of law and
order is not to recommend the imposition of more law but the improvement of
subjects by the example and admonitions given by the king.[868] Indeed the good
king is a living law.[869]

When either rulers or laws are banished from a city the result is anarchy, a
condition which Philo classifies as the worst of evils.[870] In a rhetorical list[871] he
spells out the patterns of behaviour present in that society which rejects the
restraint of law. The lawlessness referred to here and elsewhere in his writings[872]
is in contrast to the ways of the Jews who, following their laws so steeped in
virtue, live as citizens of a godly πολιτεία in which the evils of paganism are
excluded.[873] With the similes familiar from Platonic discussion he likens the fate

---

[861] Ibid. ii:44.

[862] Spec. Leg. ii:46.

[863] Ibid. ii:47—8.

[864] Ebr. 37; Agr. 43; Mut. 103.

[865] Sacr. 50.

[866] He is by translation of his name מלכיצדק (Gen. 14:18) βασιλεὺς δίκαιος (Leg. Alleg. iii:
79) or "prince of peace" (iii:81), in contrast to the tyrant who is a "ruler of war".

[867] Ibid. iii:80; Pl., Resp. ix:574C—576D, 587B—C; cf. viii:548B.

[868] These are particularly directed to subjects who live according to ὁ ὀρθὸς λόγος (Leg.
Alleg. iii:80). Phinehas is said to have conquered pleasure and established virtue by using
reason as his weapon (Post. C. 182, cf. Gig. 41). What the law requires (as Philo allegorically interprets it) is the rule of reason within man (iv:216) over those parts of man's life
which can not exercise freedom maturely.

[869] V. Mos. ii:4; Det. 141. Philo is indebted to Pythagorean thought (GOODENOUGH, Hellenistic Kingship, p. 64—5 notes Diotogenes' writings in Stob. iv:7.61) and that of Plato
(Grg. 484B) and Aristotle (Rh. iii:3).

[870] Qu. Ex. i:3.

[871] Post. C. 52. The long list of evils given in Sacr. 32 reflects Stoic interest in such categoriza-
tion. On the distinctive differences between Stoic and Pauline-Petrine tables of conduct see
JOHN HOWARD YODER, The Politics of Jesus (Grand Rapids, Mich., 1972), pp. 163—92.

[872] The linking of rejection of God's laws with rebellion against social responsibilities occurs
in Immut. 17; Qu. Gen. iv:65; Ebr. 143, 77—9; Mut. 150.

[873] Spec. Leg. i:314—9; iii:51, 167.

of a lawless city to that of a ship without a pilot, or a chariot without a rider,[874] or a sick man without a physician.[875] Yet worse than all defiance of order is the rejection of God's sacred ordinances[876] and it is the mark of Phinehas' high purpose that he sought what God delighted in: "the maintenance of a well-ordered state under good laws, in the abolishing of wars and factions . . . between cities . . . and in the soul".[877] Philo regards the ruler as in duty bound to punish evildoers. That affirmation is made within a passage describing the restraint demonstrated by the godly Israelites in not attacking one among them who broke the sabbath.

The experiences of Moses are the basis for enjoining on rulers the duty of sharing the burden of their rule with assistants, who are to be chosen to give judgement in law and to administer the state. The qualities desired are freedom from arrogance, concern for justice, reverence for God and capacity for the task.[878] The ruler is to submit to their care the less important details of administration, while those of greater moment are his concern. By the term "greater" Philo takes care to explain that he does not mean matters involving the rich and powerful, but rather those cases involving persons without distinction, wealth or honour, who have only the judge to defend their cause.[879] He has in mind the widow, the orphan and the stranger,[880] those whom the Mosaic Law compassionately considers because they lack helpers ready at hand.[881] The human monarch is to concern himself with these, because he stands before the Universal King who has not "spurned them from jurisdiction".[882]

Writing more generally, Philo observes that the commendable ruler (that is, the ruler who keeps the law) honours equality,[883] is free from bribery, judges justly, and is rewarded with long-lasting honour.[884] The reward of "long honour" does not necessarily mean a long term of rule, but "the law-abiding ruler, even when dead, lives an age-long life through the actions which he leaves behind him . . . monuments of high excellence which can never be destroyed".[885] The appeal to the lawful reigns of Augustus and Tiberius is in part a reflection of this principle, though motivated more by the desire to heighten the lawlessness of Gaius' rule. Those rightly exercising authority perform a useful function. Magistrates by their stern injunctions, and by the punishments they administer, raise the standard of conduct in those with whom they are dealing. In speaking

[874] Det. 141. In Mut. 149 using the same illustration, as well as the example of the farmer, he refers to the blessings of law introduced by virtue.
[875] Jos. 63; cf. Pl. Grg. 464Dff.; 500B–501A.
[876] Det. 142.
[877] Post. C. 184.
[878] Spec. Leg. iv:170.
[879] Ibid. iv:172.
[880] I.e. proselyte (ibid. iv:177–8).
[881] Qu. Ex. ii:3.
[882] Spec. Leg. iv:176; cf. i:308–10, ii:108, 218.
[883] On Philo's understanding of equality see pp. 522-3.
[884] Ibid. iv:165–9.
[885] Ibid. iv:169.

plainly and directly they are society's friends.[886] One might compare this section on magistrates with Ro. 13:1–7, noting the similarity in commending their role in dealing with the evildoer. The difference lay in that whereas Paul links their work directly with the purpose of God for society and enjoins obedience not just out of fear but for conscience sake aware of the rule of God, Philo urges that they be obeyed because such good conduct is a virtue.

3. God as the Source of Justice

Though Philo prizes justice highly,[887] it is its implementation in the soul[888] rather than in the state that grips his interest. Plato had spoken of three virtues in the soul; Philo adds justice as a fourth,[889] but he echoes Plato's chariot, rider, and horses imagery in his description of it.[890] However, when he comes to define justice he draws upon distinctly Stoic ideas,[891] regarding it as "the bar of nature".[892]

> "It is the function of justice to assign to each what he deserves, and justice sustains the part neither of prosecutor nor of defendant but of judge".[893]

Other philosophical strands are woven into Philo's concept of justice. For example, in describing equality, which he terms "the nurse or mother of justice",[894] though the Aristotelian mean is mentioned,[895] it is Philo's Pythagorean ideas which fill out his understanding of justice. He refers to what "the masters of natural philosophy" had taught, namely that "equality is the mother of righteousness".[896] As COLSON suggests, it would seem that the Pythagoreans are intended, especially as Philo goes on to link equality with the concept of proportion.[897]

---

[886] Migr. 116.

[887] In his usual style he calls it "the chief among the virtues" (Abr. 27), but a little later he posits piety as the "highest and greatest of virtues" (ibid. 60; cf. Plant. 122).

[888] E.g. as in Heres 243.

[889] Designated as the fourth virtue, justice occurs in the soul when self-assertion and desire are ruled by reason (Leg. Alleg. i:72). The other three virtues are prudence, courage and self-mastery (i:66–9).

[890] Pl. Phdr. 253–4.

[891] As COLSON notes (Philo, VI, p. 600f.) Philo's description of justice as "the assessor of God, justice who surveys all our doings" (Jos. 48; cf. V. Mos. ii:53, 200; Spec. Leg. iv: 201), bears strong resemblance to Seneca's words penned a generation later (Phd. 159–161).

[892] Conf. 126. Standing according to φύσις not τύχη is how God judges men in Moses' law. On that basis all men are equal, whether slave or master (Spec. Leg. iii:137). So Philo incorporates Stoic thought into his exposition.

[893] Leg. Alleg. i:87; cf. SVF. iii:262. On Plant. 122 he equates the relation of equality to justice with that of mother to child.

[894] V. Contempl. 17; Qu. Ex. ii:6; Spec. Leg. iv:231, 238.

[895] Qu. Ex. i:67.

[896] Spec. Leg. iv:231.

[897] Ibid. iv:232.

Philo declares that even the best courts and judges are fallible, but God never errs. Men perceive what is manifest and can be misled by delusory sensations, the moods of passion, or outright evil, but God is moved by justice and truth in his judgments.[898] God governs the world by justice just as the mind governs the body.[899] He observes and exposes all things,[900] punishing those who practise vice and injustice, the evils prompted by desire.[901] Because of God's relationship to the universe, being its husband, father, maker and ruler,[902] there is no possibility of flight from his scrutiny and assessment. Even to escape from a human king is difficult but to escape from God is impossible.[903]

God's kingly rule is that of just father,[904] and because He fights for justice Moses appealed to him to free the oppressed and to judge the oppressors.[905] Philo, however, takes pains on more than one occasion to dissociate God from the direct administration of just punishment. God gives benefits by his own hand but leaves the punishment of evil in the hands of his serving powers. Philo observes that this is the practice of monarchs who thus imitate the divine nature.[906] He is not asserting that human justice is the clear reflection of God's, but that the method of administration is similar. Elsewhere he gives reasons for this view, declaring that God wishes to encourage men to do good without brandishing possible punishment over them. In 'De Fuga et Inventione' he expounds this again, stating that it is not fitting for God to punish, being the "original and perfect lawgiver", but that he has given that responsibility to those of his servants who were associated with him in man's creation.[907]

Justice is personified[908] as one of the attendant powers who surveys human affairs and punishes those who set themselves against God's commandments.[909] She performs her task faithfully,[910] assists the innocent and will eventually bring down the plans of the guilty.[911] So Cain fleeing from God met "justice" avenging

---

[898] Prov. 2.36. The final justice, Philo even calls it "the only justice" is directed towards God because he deserves man's greatest response (Leg. Alleg. iii:910). So the godly, such as Isaac, seek after it (Qu. Gen. iv:194).

[899] Abr. 74—6.

[900] Spec. Leg. i:271—5; iii:19; Cher. 16—7; Migr. 115; V. Mos. i:55.

[901] Abr. 137—41; Decal. 173; Heres 271; Hyp. 7.9; Prov. 2.34.

[902] Det. 147, 153—5.

[903] The penalty for rebellion against God is banishment (Post. C. 8—9; Gig. 46—7; Fuga 84; Opif. 169; Immut. 73) and the greatest punishment is for the soul to be banished by God (Qu. Gen. iv:4, 8). Thus God had acted in the time of Noah (Abr. 60; V. Mos. ii:53).

[904] Abr. 232; Prov. 2.2—3.

[905] V. Mos. i:47, 72—3; cf. Ex. 2:23—5; 3:7—10; 7:16; 8:1—2, 20—1; 9:1—4; Ps. 78:12—6. As with Luke, Philo portrays God as taking vengeance on the persecutor of His people (Flacc. 191; cf. Ac. 12:1—3, 21—3).

[906] Abr. 144; cf. Det. 122.

[907] So Philo understands ποιήσωμεν in Gen. 1:26.

[908] E.g. V. Mos. ii:162; Decal. 177.

[909] Conf. 118, 120, 128.

[910] Decal. 177—8.

[911] Migr. 225. Although justice sometimes moves slowly yet it moves surely (V. Mos. i:326; Decal. 95).

the impious.[912] Desertion from her ranks means an encounter with the agents of God. He, having direct care of peace and goodness, deputes the juridical rule to these subordinates, yet in the last analysis He is the just sovereign of the world.[913] But Philo is not always consistent in maintaining this division between God's beneficial and retributive powers.[914] He recounts that in the dramatic events of the exodus it was God who, using the elements of the earth, brought chastisement on the Egyptians, though admittedly He used men to signal the oncoming judgments.[915]

Those situations in which it seems painfully obvious that God's justice has departed, namely the rule of a cruel tyrant or the occurrence of natural disasters, Philo reckons as still within God's just rule. The tyrant is raised up to purge evil cities of their violence, injustice and impiety. Having done his work he himself is destroyed because, though an agent of God, his own actions also call out for requital.[916] The natural calamities serve God's purpose in a similar fashion, directly punishing communities for their wickedness[917] because no evil can remain unpunished by God.[918]

Philo is confident that God will punish perjury,[919] which he associates with impiety. He states that when the perjurer is punished by men, it is the one who carries out the Mosaic penalty who is to be recognized as the pious administrator, whereas the Graeco-Roman penalty of scourging is administered by one whose feelings of indignation are not sufficiently stern. It may be that he is seeking to justify to Gentile readers the strong prohibition in the Decalogue against false witnessing, equating it with violation of the royal oath.[920] However, his last comment that "except to persons of a servile nature, a flogging is as severe a penalty as death" may be instead a justification to orthodox Jewish readers of the Jewish court's adoption of this Graeco-Roman practice in Alexandria.

4. The Practice of Justice

Philo brackets together concern for mankind (φιλανθρωπία) and justice as general duties;[921] on another occasion he defines justice as the care to see that no

---

[912] Post. C. 12.
[913] Spec. Leg. i:207.
[914] V. Mos. i:96—102, 119, 132; Spec. Leg. iii:121, 128. In Hyp. 7.9 Philo writes that men's evil deeds are avenged by God Himself. So God's wrath was directed against the first couple (Opif. 156; cf. Gig. 46—7; Migr. 115; Qu. Ex. i:22).
[915] V. Mos. i:107.
[916] Spec. Leg. ii:39—40.
[917] Ibid. ii:41; cf. Praem. 136.
[918] Qu. Gen. ii:54.
[919] Spec. Leg. ii:27—8; cf. ii:252—4.
[920] As GOODENOUGH argues (Jurisprudence, pp. 179—84).
[921] Spec. Leg. ii:63. On Moses as the great philanthropist see GEIGER, Philon von Alexandreia, pp. 96—101.

man suffers want.[922] Other examples of the practical requirements of justice Philo quotes from Mosaic law, notably that code's insistence on just scales and measurements.[923] To one who serves on a jury, justice consists in the handing down of an impartial and right decision, swayed neither by wealth nor by poverty.[924] Justice is to be untouched by "wealth, fame, official posts (and) honours",[925] because a judge is to be influenced by pure justice in reaching his verdicts.[926] GOOD-ENOUGH[927] examines Philo's more detailed account of his expectations of judges in Spec. Leg. iv:55—78. He argues convincingly that Philo is largely inspired by Greek notions of the ideal judge, notions which Philo adapts from "some current Greek treatise" to describe the Jewish judge.[928]

The judge is to "bear the impress of the operations of nature as from an original design, and thus imitate them",[929] while he will be more keen to dispense justice if he regards himself as on trial even as he presides.[930] He is to possess those virtues which make him alert to deceit and ready to respond according to a person's actions, unswayed by "supplication and lamentation".[931] He is not to be moved by polytheism and its long-winded defenders,[932] nor to accept gifts even if that leads him to judge justly because such actions still betray a "half depravity".[933] Plato acknowledged that even the unjust sometimes act justly to preserve themselves,[934] but Philo points to Moses' command for judges to pursue justice justly.[935] In obedience to Dt. 16:19[936] the judge is to consider the actions and not the persons brought before him.[937] Thus family affinity, or past enmity, or compassion for the poor[938] is not to influence his judgments. This last consideration, the presence of the poor, leads Philo to digress on the responsibilities of the rich under God's law. Moses' legislation is replete with warnings against the boastful and self-satisfied,[939] and with encouragement to those who distribute

---

[922] So Joseph ruled justly in distributing food evenly throughout Egypt (Jos. 258—60).

[923] Heres 162.

[924] Jos. 72.

[925] Det. 122; Conf. 126.

[926] Spec. Leg. iv:56. Moses appealed to God's true judgment (Immut. 18) in contrast to the shadowy decisions of men, to appoint a just ruler in his place over God's extraordinary nation (Virt. 58—65).

[927] Jurisprudence, pp. 189—206.

[928] Ibid., pp. 189—90.

[929] Spec. Leg. iv:55.

[930] Ibid. iv:57.

[931] Philo (ibid. iv:66) claims that some Greek lawmakers copied from Moses' law the safeguard against accepting only verbal evidence.

[932] Ibid. iv:59—60.

[933] ἡμιμόχθηρος (ibid. iv:62—5).

[934] "They did injustice only half-corrupted (ἡμιμόχθηροι)" (Resp. i:352 C; Leges xii:955 C—D).

[935] Ibid. iv:66; Cher. 13; Dt. 16:20.

[936] "You shall not pervert justice; you shall not show partiality; and you shall not take a bribe, for a bribe blinds the eyes of the wise and subverts the cause of the righteous."

[937] Ibid. iv:70—1.

[938] Ibid. iv:72; Ex. 23:3.

[939] Qu. Gen. ii:48.

their wealth to the needy because God has a special care for the poor.[940] However amongst judges, concern for justice and not compassion is to be the dominant spirit, and they are under obligation to discern closely the case before them because they are answerable as stewards to God.[941]

As the greatest of administrators Moses exemplified justice not only in his law but in his own actions. He protected and championed the cause of Jethro's daughters and the weak, oppressed Hebrews.[942] He inflicted on the Amalekites the cruel fate they had planned for others,[943] and he acted justly in his own estimation (and in Philo's) in killing the Egyptian who only lived to destroy men.[944] Defence of oneself against aggression is just[945] and Moses acted to defend himself and his oppressed people. Yet he could temper justice with mercy. Acknowledging the Hebrews' just indignation against the Edomites (Num. 22:14–21) he still counselled restraint out of regard for his kinsmen, both Hebrews and Edomites.[946] On the other hand, Philo lauds Phinehas' and his supporters' action in killing the idolaters in the camp as punishment for their crimes.[947] Yet even though the killing of one's enemies is justified, Philo declares that in a just execution some trace of blame remains on those ordering and executing it because dead and living share in the "primal common kinship of mankind".[948]

Because even legislators can judge unjustly and thus need direction for their juridical task, God's pattern for law is available in the Mosaic code. Philo relates Moses' injunction to pursue justice justly[949] to the need for instruction of judges lest in ignorance they do the opposite to what they intend.[950] He cites the case, from which culture is uncertain,[951] of the unjust execution of the relatives of a guilty tyrant[952] and argues that legislators in their concern for justice are to follow the Mosaic pattern in fixing penalties proportionate to the crime.[953] COLSON[954]

---

[940] Spec. Leg. iv:72–4; Qu. Ex. ii:99.

[941] Ibid. iv:71; Qu. Gen. ii:14, 16, 51; cf. J. 19:11.

[942] V. Mos. i:50, 54–6. They too experienced the strengthening arm of that irresistible ally, justice (i:142, 260).

[943] Philo refers to them as Phoenicians (ibid. i:218; cf. Prob. 89).

[944] Ibid. i:44.

[945] Virt. 109.

[946] V. Mos. i:241–9.

[947] V. Mos. i:301–3.

[948] Ibid. i:314.

[949] δικαίως τὸ δίκαιον διώκειν (Det. 18); cf. δικαίως τὸ δίκαιον διώξῃ (Dt. 16:20). In Cher. 14–7 he interprets it as the call to pursue what is another's due not just for show but sincerely.

[950] Heres 163.

[951] GOODENOUGH (Jurisprudence, p. 135) following HEINEMANN regards it as "an old Macedonian law against tyranny which had probably been retained in the Ptolemaic law" and the reference to it as an allusion by Philo "to the customs in vogue among his neighbours". COLSON (VII, pp. 629–30) considers the law was embodied in the code of Hammurabi but that neither it nor contemporary legislation prompted Philo's remarks.

[952] Spec. Leg. iii:164–6.

[953] Ibid. iii:181–3.

[954] COLSON, VII, p. 640.

suggests that Philo in criticising disproportionate punishment is not referring to any specific legislation. However the parallels with Greek law which GOOD-ENOUGH[955] adduces so closely fit Philo's words that, even granted that the likely penalty in Alexandrian courts for τραύματα καὶ πηρώσεις was banishment and not ἀτιμία, Philo's readers would not have found it difficult to identify the legislators he was criticizing.

Justice, equality, Mosaic law — all require the *lex talionis*. However, Philo admits special cases, some covered by Mosaic law, such as the striking of a father, or other offences committed in a profane or sacred place or on *dies fasti* or *dies nefasti*, in which this penalty can not be consistently applied. This qualification is not introduced as a rider to "a bit of musing on the philosophy of law and penalty"[956] but is an instance where Philo has to trim his sails in the face of Roman practice.[957] However, where possible, Philo endorses the penalties inscribed in the Mosaic law. Those who blame God for evil, for example, are blasphemous and deserve to be punished,[958] and Philo recounts with alacrity the mortal judgment on one who had mocked God and the law of Moses.[959] Man is not to oppose God's infallible judgment, because God is the measure of all things. In an indictment of the pagan law courts, Philo crisply exhorts:

"Let us never then prefer our own tribunal to that of God"[960]

where God's tribunal is reflected in the Mosaic law. However, within the same writing, he refers to this same infallible court as the assize of "nature",[961] thus illustrating again the fusion in his writings of Hellenistic and Hebraic thought.

Philo understands law and justice in terms steeped in Greek political theory — equality, proportion, natural law. He regards God as the perfect legislator meting out pure justice through natural law, which was His means of ordering the world, and through the Mosaic code which expresses that law in written form. Moses' law provides the pattern of divine rule and adherence to it leads to peace. It surpasses other systems of law not only in its content but also because it was given by God and cannot be weakened by time or catastrophe. However Philo, while asserting that the clear expression of God's justice is to be found in Moses' law, has to trim its requirements to accord with Roman judicial practice. As well, when he writes of what the law requires of judges, Hellenic ideas unmistakably dominate his thinking. Yet he contends that the just legislator is to follow Moses' example. He is to govern firmly but not harshly, to collect taxes fairly and not greedily, to rule restrainedly and not arrogantly, to promote equality and to rule honestly. The administration of the law is to be shared with those enamoured to justice, while the ruler is to concentrate on those matters in-

---

955 GOODENOUGH, Jurisprudence, p. 137.
956 GOODENOUGH, ibid., p. 139.
957 Spec. Leg. iii:183.
958 Fuga 84.
959 Mut. 61—2.
960 Prov. 2.36.
961 Ibid. 2.61; Spec. Leg. iii:121; cf. "divine court of justice" (Qu. Gen. ii:60).

volving the defenceless. In drawing together these ideas Philo is consistently bi-cultural, but one must conclude that Hellenistic political theory exerts a greater influence than does Judaism on his understanding of law and justice.

IV. The Four Forms of Rule

1. Monarchy

Despite Philo's regarding Moses as the ideal ruler, he is largely indebted to Hellenistic thought for his ideas on kingship. The kingly rule of such famous Jewish figures as David and Solomon is not mentioned. As well "in Philo's political theory, the role of the monarch in Judea in his own time and in the period immediately before him plays no role whatsoever".[962] It is personnel mentioned in Genesis and Exodus — Adam, Melchizedek, Abraham and Moses — who are the exemplars of true monarchy. They are presented as embodying the Stoic-Platonic virtues Philo expects to see in kings.

Philo is favourably disposed towards monarchy as a system of rule and associates with it men of quality.[963] Admittedly in scattered passages he notes that it tends to encourage prying spies,[964] and sanctions flatterers, "toadies who . . . batter to pieces and wear out the ears of those on whom they fawn".[965] But monarchy is a form of rule to be desired when based upon law because the law and the summary of it written by the ruler are the image of its archetype, the kingship of God.[966] Kingship, having been delegated by God, is to be patterned on His Hule and, applying the Stoic maxim, it is shared by those who are wise.[967]

Philo declares that the relationship between a king and his subjects is not unique. The same pattern can be observed in other social situations, such as the relationship of a headman to a village, a householder to a house, a physician to his patients, a general to an army or a pilot to the sailors.[968] Contrary to Aristotle he writes that "statecraft and household management are related virtues",[969] and so to benefit the state it may be necessary to dress as a commoner, just as it "becomes the master to dress as a slave to know the condition of his house".[970] Philo refers to the soul either entering into bondage through desire or gaining the gift of ruling

---

[962] SANDMEL, Philo, p. 103.

[963] Fuga 10—11.

[964] V. Mos. i:10; cf. Abr. 93.

[965] Abr. 111. They are especially condemned for their very existence depends on the utterance of falsehoods and thus in time they will oppose godly men (V. Mos. i:46).

[966] Spec. Leg. iv:160, 164. Like God, rulers have the power to do both good and evil but the good ruler, imitating God, wills only the good (iv:186—7).

[967] Prob. 117: HEINEMANN, Philons Bildung, pp. 183, 186—7.

[968] Spec. Leg. iv:186.

[969] Qu. Gen. iii:165; cf. Arist., Pol. i:1.2; i:2.3, 21.

[970] Spec. Leg. iv:206; cf. Qu. Gen. iv:206.

through knowledge as well as self-control, courage and justice.[971] If the soul is naked it needs philosophy to reach a life conducted agreeably to nature. All this was Zeno's goal, but Philo regards the inspiration as coming from a source "higher than Zeno", namely Moses.

As in both Hebrew[972] and Greek[973] thought shepherd imagery with reference to kingship is commonly found, so in Philo's thought God is regarded as the shepherd of his people. Just as the mind is shepherd over the body, so God rules over the soul.[974] In conjunction with "His true word and first-born Son" God rules the whole universe perfectly. He is the Shepherd over the four basic elements, land, water, air and fire, while plants, animals and the celestial bodies are led by His righteousness and law.[975] Thus the art of shepherding is a necessary skill in learning to be king.[976] By it Moses was equipped to command the flock of mankind[977] and Joseph too received this necessary preparation for ruling. Just as generals are to engage in "hunting", so a shepherd's supervision of tame animals is preparation for leading civilized subjects. Thus it is honourable for kings to be called shepherds of the people and Philo, speaking through Macro, describes the ruler as a shepherd who applies to himself the lessons he wishes his people to learn.[978]

Though the likening of an Israelite king to a shepherd is found in the Jewish scriptures, Philo acknowledges Homer as his source for the concept of the shepherd ruler.[979] However his ideas differ from Homer's in that he considers some rulers no more than sheep themselves. Those enticed by the senses to gluttony, wealth and glory are no longer leaders but led.[980] Only good kings can rightly be called shepherds and among that number Moses' position is unchallenged even though in the scriptures he is never called king.

Adam was the first human king, being appointed by God as ruler over all other creatures.[981] Melchizedek was also an example, his very name indicating royal rule and justice.[982] He was also a peacable king, being ruler of Salem,[983] and so stood in contrast to the war-mongering despot. As well, while the despot decrees for "both soul and body harsh and hurtful decrees",[984] the king, in this

---

[971] Prob. 160.
[972] Num. 27:16—17; 2 Km. 24:17; 3 Km. 22:17; 2 Ch. 18:16; Ps. 23:1; 80:1; Is. 40:11; Jer. 31: 10; Ezek. 34; Mi. 5:5; Zech. 11.
[973] Hom., Il. i:263; Xen., Symp. 4.6; Pl., Resp. i:343 B but cf. Pol. 267—75.
[974] Agr. 54, 64—6.
[975] Agr. 51—3.
[976] Note especially V. Mos. i:61—2.
[977] Ibid. i:60.
[978] Leg. 44, cf. 20, 76.
[979] Prob. 31; Hom. Il.ii:243. In Jos. 2—3 he acknowledges Greek poetic precedent for the idea.
[980] Prob. 31; cf. Agr. 47.
[981] Opif. 148.
[982] Leg. Alleg. iii:79.
[983] שלם means "peace".
[984] Ibid. iii:79—81. Philo allegorizes Gen. 14:18.

instance Melchizedek, resorts to persuasion and issues helpful directions rather than impose his will by arbitrary commands.[985]

Abraham too had the spirit of a king due to his faith in God, and accompanying this faith were all the other virtues so that he was esteemed a king by those around him.[986] His life, however, aspired to a realm not to be identified with his environment or his neighbours. His sovereignty was like that of Moses, not gained by armed might but by God's choice, because God favours virtue and rewards the pious with imperial powers (αὐτοκρατέσιν ἐξουσίαις) in order to benefit their fellow men.[987]

This pattern of commendable rule is best exemplified in Moses, ideal king and lawgiver. He was fitted for this office because he was able to apprehend both human and divine affairs by being appointed a priest and a prophet.[988] Like Melchizedek, he too fulfilled the Platonic ideal in his administration of the law, moving men by "suggestions and admonishments not by despotic ordering".[989]

Thus the rule of the good monarch reflects the rule of God, the supreme king who governs justly the universe. Reflecting Hellenistic thought Philo states that the true king rules like a shepherd over his people. Philo presents from the scriptures four men in whose lives clearly could be discerned this delegated rule of God. They are Adam, Melchizedek the peace-bringing king who like Moses ruled by persuasion not force, Abraham whose faith and virtue made his contemporaries esteem him a ruler, and finally Moses the greatest legislator, prophet, priest and leader. Though drawn from the Jewish scriptures these men are presented in terms of the Hellenistic ideal king.

2. Democracy

Because the Jews had never known democratic rule within their own communities, Philo's ideas on democracy are substantially, though not exclusively, inspired by Hellenistic thought. Various suggestions have been made as to the main influence on Philo's thinking on this matter. Socrates' teaching[990] has been seen as the source of Philo's use of the term "democracy". Others[991] contend that the Roman principate provided Philo's pattern. Though agreeing that his contemporary situation is important for understanding his concept of democracy, I consider that he is largely influenced both by Pythagorean ideas and by Jewish partisanship. The latter influence is expressed in his admiration for Moses and his briefly expressed hope that Israel would eventually rank first in the world.

---

[985] This distinction is not original to Philo but is to be found in Plato's thought.

[986] Virt. 216; cf. βασιλεὺς παρὰ θεοῦ εἶ σὺ ἐν ἡμῖν (Gen. 23:6).

[987] Ibid. 218.

[988] V. Mos. ii:66—7, 4—6.

[989] Ibid. ii:50—1.

[990] Notably Pl., Menex. 238 C. So E. LANGSTADT, Zu Philos Begriff der Demokratie, in: Occident and Orient, ed. BRUNO SCHINDLER (London, 1936), pp. 349—50.

[991] GOODENOUGH, Politics, pp. 88—90; COLSON, VIII, p. 437; cf. Dio lii:2—40.

Philo does not envisage democracy in terms of the rule of assembled citizens. The clearest hint as to what he understands by democracy occurs in a passage concerning the rise and fall of nations:

"For circlewise moves the revolution of that divine plan (λόγος ὁ θεῖος) which most call fortune (τύχη). Presently in its ceaseless flux it makes distribution city by city, nation by nation, country by country. What these had once, those have now. What all had, all have. Only from time to time is the ownership changed by its agency, to the end that (ἵνα) the whole of our world should be as a single state enjoying (ἄγεσθαι) that best of constitutions, democracy".[992]

COLSON[993] comments from this passage that in Philo's estimation "the democracy which the world enjoys consists in each getting its turn".[994] However if ἵνα is taken as purposive as in the translation above and ἄγεσθαι as having the middle sense of "take to oneself",[995] then Philo here may be speaking generally of that Jewish hope wherein the nations will eventually acknowledge the rule of God mediated through the same power which had led Moses. He does not state it outright, speaking of λόγος ὁ θεῖος as the commonly called τύχη. Yet God's purpose is that no city or nation will be permanently established, except that in the time ahead His nation will be established forever and Israel will attain its ascendancy when all the others have passed their prime.[996]

Democracy is to be found in the soul as well as in society, and there are two types of "soul-cities". The better, which adopts democracy in its constitution, honours equality and is ruled by law and justice; the worse, which is ruled by ochlocracy, is marked by inequality, lawlessness and injustice.[997] Philo urges the reader to seek the city of God[998] in the soul that has no "warring, faction or turmoil" and in the "vision-seeking mind". So democracy in its ideal form is the

---

[992] Immut. 176.

[993] He comments that Philo's concept of democracy does not tally with the ideas of Plato, or Aristotle, or the Stoics on this topic.

[994] COLSON and WHITAKER, III, p. 489. The possession of authority changes as Fortune transfers its influence from one group to the next. Thus the ebb and flow of power is man's lot (Immut. 172–8).

[995] LS., p. 18.

[996] Qu. Ex. iv:76.

[997] Conf. 108; Spec. Leg. i:308–10; ii:108, 218.

[998] The phrase in Conf. 108 is hard to reconstruct. COLSON (IV, pp. 68–9 n. 1) argues for the rendering θεοῦ δ' (ἐν) ὕμνο(ι)ς ἡ τοιάδε ᾄδεται which he interprets as "such a soul city or such a πολιτεία is called in the Psalms God's (city)", and he dismisses the reading θεοῦ δε ὕμνος ἡ τοιάδε as well as COHN and WENDLAND's suggestions of (i) εὐνομωτάτη δ', (ii) θεοῦ δ' ὄπαδος, (iii) εὐδόκιμος. He notes that the phrase ἐν ὕμνοις is used earlier in Conf. 52 (cf. Som. ii:242) with a quotation from the Psalms. Further force is given to his reading in Som. ii:246–51 where Ps. 46:4 is quoted with its reference to the city of God which Philo relates to the soul of the wise man.

submission to God's rule, and when democracy rules in the soul so too does reason the chastener.[999]

Philo singles out equality, law and justice[1000] as the marks of democracy. In commending equality he comprehends it as treatment for proportionate worth,[1001] pointing out that exactly equal payment for different work and different professions is equality only in name. The disturbances and factions which arise actually bring about inequality, because in the subsequent confusion, order, the prerequisite for maintaining equality, is jettisoned.[1002] He offers as a practical example of the implementation of equality the proportional payment of taxes.[1003] In this regard God's providential rule is again the pattern for human rule because under it equality is distributed in proportion to the state of the recipients.[1004]

Thus by democracy Philo means each group or part of society possessing its appropriate amount of power and through the establishment of proportionate equality true order is born.[1005] His concept of proportionate equality is evident in Jos. 9 where Jacob chides Joseph for desiring to gain dominion over his family which is displeasing to all who care for equality and justice between kinsfolk.[1006] In the passage following[1007] Jacob advises his sons that within a homogeneous group their equal rights should lead them to act together.[1008] This was the basis of Moses' exhortation to Ephraim and Manasseh because they shared equal rights with the Israelites — "one race, the same fathers, one house, the same customs, community of laws".[1009] Their offence lay in claiming a preference out of proportion to their position as equal sharers in Israel's life, and in tending towards arrogance. This is hated by God,[1010] the author of equality,[1011] for inherent in arrogance is man's selfish claim to greater honour and rights out of proportion to his station. These stations are to be respected; so to strike a father is more serious than to strike a stranger, and to abuse a ruler is worse than to abuse an ordinary citizen.[1012]

---

[999] Abr. 242−3.

[1000] Such qualities of rule had long been prized in Greek political thought. V. EHRENBERG, The Greek State (London, 1972), pp. 43, 49−52, 70, 80, 88−92, 94−5, 98−9, 177.

[1001] The advocacy of proportion in relation to equality is found not only in Pythagorean thought (Philo contends that the study of geometry would plant equality and justice in the soul − Congr. 16) but in Plato's (Resp. viii:558 C, Leges vi:757 C) and Aristotle's writings (Pol. 1280 a).

[1002] Spec. Leg. i:121; Virt. 180.

[1003] Heres 145.

[1004] Mut. 232; cf. Heres 60, 154, 163−5; Spec. Leg. iv:232−6,

[1005] Spec. Leg. iv:166; Abr. 242.

[1006] In Decal. 165−7 Philo strongly endorses the authority of parents over children, father over son.

[1007] Jos. 10.

[1008] Equals are not to be put together with unequals (Qu. Gen. iv:157).

[1009] V. Mos. i:324.

[1010] Spec. Leg. iv:165−6.

[1011] Ibid. i:265.

[1012] Ibid. iii:183.

These are instances in Philo's writings when ἰσότης clearly signifies "equality" as it is now popularly understood. In his discussion of vows he suggests that the inequalities between men, as for example between ruler and slave, do not count before God when each vows his vow. What is inequality in men's sight is equality in God's.[1013] Does not nature provide sustenance equally available for all?[1014] Pointing to the Spartans Philo ascribes the lack of luxury amongst their nobles as due to their regarding distinctions as contrary to nature, and he proceeds to explain.

> "For nature has borne all men to be free, but the wrongful and covetous acts of some who pursued that source of evil inequality have imposed their yoke and invested the stronger with power over the weaker".[1015]

Thus inequality between ruler and ruled is contrary to natural law.

Remembering that Philo equates natural law with the Mosaic code, it is not surprising that Moses is singled out as the one who best praised equality because he lauded justice and opposed injustice.[1016] The latter brings both foreign and civil wars but equality produces peace.[1017] Evidence of equality is to be found throughout the Mosaic legislation — equal tablets, equal sets of five commandments, equal sacrifices and so on.[1018] All point to equality's origin in God's ordering of the world and its application in Mosaic law. Yet, despite Philo's interest in the Jews' destiny noted earlier, he does not see this ascendancy of Jewish law in terms of national political supremacy. For example, in Qu. Gen. iv:216 the scriptural promise "The nations shall serve thee" (Gen. 27:29) is completely allegorized. Even in what Philo calls the literal interpretation, the ruler becomes the mind while the allegorical sense is that this ruler is the Logos ruling the irrational parts of the soul as signified by the nations.[1019]

To sum up, the pertinent features of Philo's understanding of democracy are threefold. Democracy is linked with the proportionate sharing of rule. The Jews have a right to receive respect because their law contains the final philosophy and it is this God-loving nation that can lay claim to equality and righteousness. Democracy is rule in proportion to the arrangement of groups in society; neither the majority nor the crowd exercise democratic rule, but those whose ideas espouse order and justice. In praising democracy and equality Philo draws upon Hellenistic ideas while retaining his Jewish identity and aspirations. He looks to the time when it will be the turn of the Jews finally to rule. However his messianic expectation is directed not towards a national leader but the coming rule of the Logos in men's souls.

[1013] Spec. Leg. ii:34.
[1014] V. Contempl. 17; Qu. Ex. ii:72.
[1015] V. Contempl. 70.
[1016] Heres 161.
[1017] Ibid. 161—2.
[1018] Ibid. 167—8, 174—206.
[1019] Qu. Ex. i:4.

3. Ochlocracy

Ochlocracy, in Philo's estimation, is the worst abuse of political power, and when he refers to the crowd, whether in using a political analogy or in his general exposition, in the majority of cases he is disdainful of its influence. He points to the mob's simplicity in being fooled by clever demogagues;[1020] it is "the vulgar herd"[1021] which knows not the life of virtue, and which cannot appreciate the satisfaction experienced in seeking divine wisdom.[1022] It yearns for desire not reason.[1023] If the multitude does have a mind then it is generally[1024] one that errs, that is "vanity-ridden . . . (clinging) to false opinion",[1025] and divorced from the mind of God. The crowd's lack of restraint means that its participation in power even through elections is not to be desired.[1026] Majority opinion is not necessarily right opinion, that is, opinion according to nature. It can well be the height of lawlessness, fluctuating and fixed by no standard.[1027] Particularly in his commentary on the law Philo warns against riotous assembly which "debases the long established sure coinage of civic life",[1028] and the crowd's rule represents all that is disorderly and discordant with nature – vice, ignorance, senselessness, incontinence, injustice.[1029]

The divisions within the soul, the conflict between the mind and senses, Philo describes vividly in terms of communal strife. As he notes elsewhere,[1030] peace in cities is but a copy of inward peace of man. The better soul-city is ruled by democracy, law and justice whereas the worse is governed by the "counterfeit" of rule, ochlocracy,

> "which takes inequality for its ideal and in it injustice and lawlessness are paramount . . . disorder rather than order, confusion rather than constancy and stability".[1031]

Erroneous philosophies also contribute to mob rule. Philo has in mind the Epicureans and Sceptics as he expounds men's rebellion in building the tower of

---

[1020] Heres 302–3.

[1021] Mut. 213.

[1022] Congr. 174.

[1023] V. Mos. i:26.

[1024] The terms πλῆθος and δῆμος are not always used disparagingly. When referring to the people of God (Praem. 76) or to a general peace-loving community (Flacc. 41) the terms are used favourably. When the crowd seeks to rule it merits the epithets noted above.

[1025] Ebr. 198; Conf. 106. Elsewhere he states that the crowd has no mind and soul, being ready to sell its voice to the highest bidder (Flacc. 138).

[1026] Spec. Leg. ii:231.

[1027] Ibid. iv:88; Leg. 67, cf. 149.

[1028] Ibid. iv:47.

[1029] Virt. 180–1; Praem. 20; Qu. Gen. iv:47; Flacc. 35, 41. Philo comments that in the pogrom at Alexandria the mob exceeded the armies of nations in the ravages it wrought (56–62).

[1030] Som. ii:147.

[1031] Conf. 108–9.

Babel. The Sceptics promote confusion because, in their arrogance, they declaire their disbelief both in God's existence and in his power over the world.[1032]

Philo develops the account of Babel along similar though more extensive lines in Som. ii:283—302. Here the builders are materialists, regarding the world as "uncreated, imperishable, without guardian, helmsman or protector".[1033] Their mocking of God's rule is fruitless, their efforts result in confusion — the meaning of "Babel" — and they create anarchy.[1034] All this comes from a seemingly harmless verse reading "All the earth was one lip" (Gen. 11:1)! Yet the reference has still more significance, for Philo has in view with these disparaging comments not just the builders of old but a community much nearer in time and space. Nor has he in mind only the sceptical teachers of his day who declare: "We are the leaders, we are potentates; all things are based on us. Who can cause good and its opposite save we?".[1035] In his commentary, he takes up the reference to "lip" and declares that Moses spoke only of Egypt's river as having lips and that there is no express reference to "lip" in regard to the other nations' rivers. Philo defends himself against the objection that he is splitting hairs in his exposition.

> "For the subject which now engages our researches is not the lore of rivers as such, but that of lives . . . compared to the currents of rivers and of opposite kinds. For the lives of the good and the bad are shewn; one in deeds, and the other in words and words belong to the tongue, mouth, lips . . ."[1036]

There our manuscript ends. Although elsewhere Egypt tends to be allegorized as "passion", the context of this whole passage suggests that it is in Philo's own environment that he sees as the forces of confusion the voices raised against the true God, notably the voices of the mob.[1037]

Σωφροσύνη and καρτερία[1038] are virtues much commended by Philo and regarded as directly opposed to that passion which seizes the uncontrolled mob.[1039] One might thus expect that the passionless eunuch will symbolize virtue, but he too is represented by the crowd.

> "How then does the multitude represent eunuchs? It is because the multitude is unproductive of wisdom,[1040] though it seems to practise virtue. For when a mixed crowd of heterogeneous persons comes together, it says what is right but thinks and does the opposite. It prefers the spurious to the

---

[1032] Ibid. 114; cf. Ebr. 199.

[1033] Ibid. ii:283.

[1034] Som. ii:286—7.

[1035] Ibid. ii:291, cf. 298. The whole of the quotation indicates that it is not distinctly an anti-Roman tirade but a criticism of the arrogant philosophers who refuse to acknowledge God's absolute power over their lives.

[1036] Ibid. ii:302.

[1037] Som. ii:294—5.

[1038] Moses while a youth displayed these virtues (V. Mos. i:25).

[1039] Jos. 57.

[1040] Spec. Leg. ii:31.

genuine because it is under the domination of appearances and does not practise what is truly excellent".[1041]

Philo at this point reproduces Plato's allegorical contrast between a cook and a
physician.[1042] The latter denotes beneficial laws and just rulers not swayed by
flattery while the cook symbolizes the swarming crowd of dissolute youth seeking
immediate pleasure.[1043] Such a mob should be dealt with in the same way as a
doctor treats the more powerful distempers.[1044]

In the story of Joseph, Potiphar's wife signifies the multitude's desire to
draw the statesman down to its own level. Though the people are masters the true
statesman is not to be their slave.[1045] This section[1046] may be regarded as a digression aimed at the evils of mob rule and the ideal ruler's response to the crowd's
power. Philo's main interest lies in Joseph's mastery over the multitude, a mastery
to which only the good ruler can attain. However Philo records that Joseph,
while taking his stand against passion and the despotic people, was not victorious
because the crowd took him and upbraided him though he was promoting their
best interest. The last sentence in the digression brings us back to Philo's chief
target — the unruly crowd which through its action

> "receives the greatest of punishments, indiscipline, whereby it fails to learn
> the lesson of submission to government".[1047]

The flouting of authority marks out the leaders who urged apostasy on the
people at Mount Sinai. That crowd, beset by the "miseries which anarchy creates"
and having lost control of themselves through the influence of drink, proceeded in
their madness to riot.[1048] Later Philo condemns revolution more precisely.
Referring to the priests and their more numerous assistants he regards the former
as established in a superior position of authority, while the latter represent the
multitude who do not possess the right to usurp that authority. When subjects
attack their rulers they destroy what is to Philo the "most excellent promoter of
the common wealth, order".[1049]

Whereas GOODENOUGH contends that Philo's writings contain sustained
criticism of Roman rule, I affirm that Philo's hatred of ochlocracy[1050] is a prime

---

[1041] Jos. 59; Prov. 2.31, cf. Leg. 1—6.
[1042] Grg. 464 Dff., 500 B, 501 A. There the physician represents justice and the cook the
flattery of rhetoric.
[1043] Jos. 62—3.
[1044] Ibid. 77.
[1045] Ibid. 67, 69.
[1046] Jos. 54—79.
[1047] Ibid. 79.
[1048] V. Mos. ii:161, 164, 169, cf. Praem. 75—6.
[1049] Ibid. ii:277.
[1050] GOODENOUGH does not discuss adequately this aspect of Philo's thought and, though he
notes GEIGER's study, he has only two references to ochlocracy (Politics, pp. 86, 90) in
his study of Philo's political ideas. GEIGER (Philon von Alexandreia, p. 53) sums up
Philo's attitude thus: „Für die Ochlokratie hat Philon nur Worte bitterster Verachtung
und Geringschätzung".

factor in his criticism of the misuse of political power. To take an example —
GOODENOUGH has argued that in his description of Jethro Philo is writing in code
about the arrogant Romans[1051] who do not respect true law. Undeniably Jethro is
presented unfavourably in Mut. 103—104; Sacr. 50; Agr. 43 and Ebr. 37. However in all but the first reference the indications are that Jethro signifies the unruly
mob rather than the Romans. For example, one reads in Ebr. 36 that

> "Jethro is a compound of vanity, closely corresponding with a city or com-
> monwealth peopled by a promiscuous horde, who swing to and fro as their
> idle opinions carry them".

Hence the meaning derived from Jethro's name, namely "uneven", is regarded by
Philo as expressive of his actions.[1052] He is the demagogue who stirs the
crowd,[1053] who leads astray the senses.[1054] After referring to Jethro as representing the force causing laws to vary from city to city,[1055] Philo immediately goes on
to link the reference to him in Ex. 3:1[1056] to mob rule. To experience ochlocracy
is to suffer the fate of shepherdless sheep.

> "So might mob-rule, the very worst of bad constitutions, the counterfeit of
> democracy . . . infect us, while we spend our days in ceaseless experience of
> disorders, tumults and intestine broils".[1057]

Anarchy he describes as the mother of mob rule[1058] and Jethro is one who when
unattended obeys that mother. Next Philo laments the rule of one who is too
gentle and so is overwhelmed by the crowd whom Philo designates as cattle.[1059] It
is best for Jethro to be shephered by Moses[1060] because Jethro signifies both the
weak ruler who gives way before the mob and the movement of the mob itself.

As regards the presentation of Jethro in Mut. 103—4, GOODENOUGH
sees in it a reference to the Roman *iuridicus* who occupied the office of the σύμβουλος. Though the precise title of those sent out to deal with the legal situations
of new provinces was δικαιοδότης he contends that the reader would understand
who is meant by σύμβουλος.[1061] Understood in this light the conversion of such
an adviser, noted in Mut. 105, indicates that some Roman officials supported the
Jews' adherence to Jewish laws.

[1051] Ibid., pp. 35—8.
[1052] Agr. 43—4.
[1053] Ebr. 37, cf. 45—6, Heres 302.
[1054] Ebr. 46.
[1055] Agr. 43.
[1056] "Moses was shepherding the sheep of Jethro".
[1057] Agr. 45.
[1058] Ibid. 46.
[1059] Ibid. 47—8; Prob. 30, cf. Som. ii:90—2; contra GOODENOUGH (Politics, p. 7) who interprets the beasts as the Romans.
[1060] Sacr. 50.
[1061] Namely the Roman *iuridici* (ibid., p. 36).

"Jethro, still the Roman *iuridicus*, is thus the prototype of those men who made the legal adjustment which recognized Jewish law in Alexandria . . . The Roman officials who made this concession were to Philo not 'arrogant men', but men who represented the 'pastoral care of God'".[1062]

But is not this interpretation too subtle? Philo delights to play on names and their significance[1063] and the allegorical nuances in a name sometimes carry him well beyond his original theme. How much Hebrew Philo knew, if any, is a debated question.[1064] Even if his kowledge was minimal, he seems to have had at his disposal a list of names and variant meanings stemming from Hebrew roots and the name יִתְרוֹ was associated with the root יתר which signifies "remainder" or "abundance", or "excess". Jethro's addition of what was superfluous[1065] to the Mosaic provision is the basis of Philo's estimate of him. He ignores some of the material in Exodus and takes Ex. 18:17[1066] as his major cue for his exposition.

If Philo's treatment of Jethro is meant to be political writing "in code", then it can be regarded as directed against both the Alexandrians and apostate Jews. The former required of those Jews wishing to be full citizens participation in the rites of citizenship, which rites were regarded as superfluous and harmful by devout Jews. Jethro as well represents those Jews, as for example Philo's nephew, who, having gained power in the wider community, seek to persuade their fellow Jews to compromise to gain greater rights.

What then is to be made of the change in interpretation so that "Jethro" no longer means "vanity" but "the espousal of the flock of God"?[1067] If this is a reference to the Roman legate or the local demagogue who became a "god-fearer" then Philo's use of term πολλάκις is patently inaccurate. No Jewish reader, in Alexandria at least, could believe that such conversions were frequent. However, if the apostate or compromising Jew being drawn away by Alexandrian Greek ways is in mind, it could perhaps be said that he was outside the flock of God. His conversion would mean a return and the instances of such changes of heart would be sufficient to merit the use of πολλάκις.

The uncontrolled mob is like the uncontrolled senses which bring havoc to the body.[1068] Mob rule is the absence of that rule which brings order to society

---

[1062] Sacr. 37.

[1063] E.g. מדינה equals "judgment", cf. Mut. 106; כללב equals "all heart" (ibid. 123).

[1064] J. A. EMERTON, Were Greek Transliterations of the Hebrew Old Testament used by Jews before the time of Origen?, JTS., XXI (1970), pp. 17–31.

[1065] Mut. 114.

[1066] Jethro declares to Moses as regards the latter's overburdened administrative duties: "What you are doing is not good".

[1067] Mut. 103–6. When Philo deals with Jethro as priest of Midian, the antithesis between sense perception and reason dominates his exposition. If there is any local political reference intended, then it entails criticism of Alexandrian demagogues, for the daughters of Jethro were troubled by "the comrades of envy and malice, the shepherds of an evil herd" (ibid. 114).

[1068] Sacr. 104–6. God prefers the few just to the multitude of the unjust, contrary to men's judgment (Migr. 60–1).

and expresses itself in anarchy which leads to disaster and ultimately death.[1069]
When Philo considers his Alexandrian environment, uppermost in his thinking is
not his response to the Romans but his abhorrence of the uncontrolled mob. This
does not mean that the references dealt with in this chapter were written subsequent to A.D. 38. The anti-Jewish feeling in Alexandria did not arise overnight
and the Jewish minority had already experienced,[1070] and certainly still feared,
outbreaks of mob hostility. This Alexandrian mob inflamed with anti-Jewish
feeling is the prime example of ochlocracy in action, and Philo's fierce antipathy
to ochlocracy is an essential element in his political thought.

4. Tyranny

Philo singles out other forms of rule which he considers undesirable besides
ochlocracy. He records that Moses' law forbids both dishonest and tyrannous
government[1071] because the ruler is to have a tender regard for his subjects so that
he can aptly be described as "a father over his children".[1072] On the other hand
those who use their authority to harm their subjects are to be called enemies not
rulers.[1073] In this regard Philo particularly abhors a tyrant, associating his rule
with lawlessness and contrasting it to the lawful rule of a king. Whereas a king
persuades his subjects to follow the right principle, a tyrant decrees what subjects
are to do.[1074] So Pharoah, in seeking to take Sarah, ignored the laws regarding the
treatment of strangers and is thus described as "a licentious and cruel-hearted
despot".[1075]

The tyrant, like the mob, is to be dreaded because he sets law aside. However in a piece of somewhat tortuous casuistry Philo can in a special case advocate
the restoration of a despot but only so as to harm or betray him.[1076] Yet there are
occasions when God raises up tyrants to punish or purge a people because of their
disobedience.[1077] Such a despot, equipped by nature to rule, is empowered by
God "when a dire famine and death of virtue takes possession of states . . . for
wickedness cannot be purged away without some ruthless soul to do it".[1078] So
the tyrant is likened to a public executioner, set up for a horrid but necessary task.

[1069] The lack of a ruler means that men soon occupy themselves with anarchy and its accompanying lawlessness (Det. 141; Qu. Gen. i:73).

[1070] Joseph. BJ. ii:487—9; cf. Ap. ii:68—72.

[1071] Philo applies the exhortation not to commit fraud among the people (Lev. 19:16) to rulers
in particular (Spec. Leg. iv:183). In his estimation Sejanus combined both evils, being
naturally tyrannical and powerful through cunning (Flacc. 1).

[1072] "Good rulers may be truly called the parents of states and nations in common, since they
show a fatherly affection" (ibid. iv:184, cf. Prov. 2.3).

[1073] Ibid. iv:185.

[1074] Leg. Alleg. iii:79; cf. V. Mos. i:39, 43. — HEINEMANN, Philons Bildung, p. 186.

[1075] Abr. 95 cf. V. Mos. i:36. Unless laws are adhered to by rulers then government whether
by one or by an oligarchy is enslavement (Prob. 45).

[1076] Cher. 14.

[1077] Prov. 2.37—40.

[1078] Ibid. 2.39.

Here is a perspective which will counsel endurance rather than revolution, arguing that the tyrant can even benefit the race, being raised up to purify it.

The tyrant himself is answerable to God who knows that his service is due to "an impious and ruthless soul" and so treats him as the worse offender.[1079] Yet following the spirit of the *lex talionis* Philo urges that at a tyrant's fall from power his family are not to be murdered.[1080] Such a despot, however, is not to be mourned and when Philo finds in his source lamentation for a tyrant's death, he ressorts to allegory to explain such a phenomenon. Pharoah, the tyrant in view, denotes man's tendency to seek after pleasure and to spurn self-control and the demise of such a ruler leads to lamentation over the way of life he has encouraged.[1081]

Philo advises the man who has acquired power to recognize that it is not his by capacity but through God's generosity, his abilities coming from God's hand.[1082] Having become rich he is not to impoverish others, nor having secured glory to seek to belittle and dishonour them. Nor is he to be moved by envy.[1083] He is to be favourable to others as God has been to him and to shun arrogance, because those filled with self-importance will face "the divine tribunal".[1084] Arrogance is the cardinal sin of a ruler and is the particular temptation facing a tyrant. It leads to unjust administration in any realm.[1085] It shows itself in ostentatious display, while foolish people worship the arrogant ruler giving him gold crowns, purple robes and a retinue of attendants. Is this the ascetic Philo writing, or is he more particularly criticizing Roman rule, or censuring the Alexandrian citizens for their propensity to elevate a popular leader beyond his worth?[1086] The latter group could well be in mind.

In 'De Somniis' he depicts Joseph as the example of one overruled by arrogance.[1087] Joseph's sheaf stood upright amongst the rest like frisky horses rearing their necks. The exposition is typical.

> "So all the followers of vainglory set themselves up above everything, above cities and laws and ancestral customs and the affairs of the several citizens. Then they proceed from the leadership of the people to dictatorship over the people".[1088]

[1079] Ibid. 2.40.

[1080] Spec. Leg. iii:164—5; cf. Prov. 2.55.

[1081] Det. 95.   [1082] Virt. 165.

[1083] Virt. 170.

[1084] Ibid. 171; cf. Praem. 94. The Mosaic law unmistakably condemns fraud (Spec. Leg. iv: 183).

[1085] V. Mos. i:324.

[1086] An example would be the excessive flattery the Alexandrians bestowed on Germanicus — 'Germanicus Papyrus', SB. 1911, p. 794ff., noted by BALSDON, Gaius, p. 7. Cf. Tac. Ann. ii:59.

[1087] Joseph is depicted as the blighting presence of arrogance and is rebuked for it in singularly Stoic terms by Jacob (Som. ii:134—6).

[1088] Ibid. ii:78—9. Philo's critical portrait of him changes when he recounts how Joseph weaned himself from his attachment to Egypt and reestablished his relationship with his father's people and with God.

Boastful rulers are only too ready to mock widows and orphans, in contrast to God who cares for these dependent members of society.[1089] Thus no tyrant is to contravene God's will by arrogantly despising those of low degree, because arrogance is condemned as contrary to reason, to God's law and to nature.[1090]

Arrogance is the source of many social evils[1091] and is to be found particularly in immature rulers. Such a one was Alexander the Great. Philo describes his proud claim to the control of Europe and Asia as the utterance of a childish soul, and his vain boast indicated that in his essential being he was a commoner and not a king.[1092] Associated with arrogance[1093] is covetousness, prohibited in Moses' law because it causes plundering, robbery, falsehoods, adulteries,[1094] or other crimes whether public or private. The robber who attains office disregards established law, robs whole cities, and under the cloak of administrative positions he feeds his ambition for power on the spoils of his rule.[1095] If men set their covetous eyes on ruling positions they are tending towards tyranny. They become

> "factious, inequitable, tyrannical in nature, cruel-hearted, foes of their country, merciless masters to those who are weaker, irreconcilable enemies of their equals in strength, and flatterers of their superiors in power as a preparation for their treacherous attack."[1096]

Philo considers that many are drawn on to this destructive path by the craze for power.[1097] They are apt to make their own might their God[1098] and thus despise both God and the rights of their fellow men.[1099]

Philo likens the abuse of political power to a master-slave relationship, a figure not similarly used by any New Testament writer.[1100] Just as masters are

---

[1089] V. Mos. ii:241; cf. Decal. 41.

[1090] Decal. 40–2.

[1091] Boastfulness, haughtiness, inequality – these are the sources of wars, both civil and foreign (Decal. 5).

[1092] Cher. 63.

[1093] It particularly besets rulers who are dominated by the desire for fame (Spec. Leg. iv: 84–8).

[1094] Commenting on the sixth commandment, Philo considers adultery weakens the State (Decal. 127). The offence is punishable by death because adulterers are "the common enemies of the whole human race" (ibid. iii:11).

[1095] "These are oligarchically-minded persons, ambitious for despotism or domination, who perpetrate thefts on a grand scale, disguising the real fact of robbery under the grand-sounding names of government and leadership" (Decal. 136).

[1096] Spec. Leg. iv:89.

[1097] Virt. 162.

[1098] Cf. 1 Qp. Hab. vi. Philo (Prov. 2.28, 30) records how Dionysius was "enamoured . . . of tyranny as something divine" and yet was not content because of his suspicions of designs against his power.

[1099] Qu. Gen. ii:24.

[1100] In the New Testament we find reference to the master-slave relationship, e.g. Eph. 6: 5–9; 1 Pt. 2:18–25, but the image is not used in relation to rulers and their subjects. The exception is Ro. 13:4 where the one in authority is a διάκονος of God.

duty bound to refrain from harsh treatment towards their slaves[1101] so rulers of cities are to restrain their desire to abuse their authority and to bring undue hardship on their subjects. He refers particularly to the ruler's collection of taxes which can injure not only victim but also spoiler in that his life is defiled by his greed.[1102] Governed by covetousness, such rulers choose tax-collectors whose main trait is ruthlessness and give to them authority to go beyond what is just. The result of such harsh appropriation of the people's goods is "universal chaos and confusion".[1103] Philo emphasizes the savagery of such misrule by referring to what apparently was a contemporary example of unimaginable cruelty, the mutilating of dead bodies of those whose relatives owed money, in order to move the latter to ransom the dead bodies.[1104] Such actions demonstrate that rulers neither practise what they teach as virtues, nor observe the rules they are appointed to administer.[1105]

When despotic power and hostility are combined then deeper tragedy for the oppressed follows. The description Philo gives of the latter's woes in Praem. 137–140 reads like a resumé of the Jews' experience in the harrowing period of Flaccus' prefecture, but the passage is set in a wider context[1106] of distress and punishment which are depicted as a commentary on Dt. 28 with its listing of blessings and curses upon Israel. Philo does cite from his own experience the arrogant claims of a despot who in ruling Egypt sought to deny the Jews several of their customs, especially sabbath observance. This despot tried both persuasion and compulsion,[1107] claiming for himself superhuman powers, the force of destiny and daring even to compare his "all miserable self" with God.[1108] It is not possible to ascertain whom Philo has in mind. Flaccus seems unlikely, as he brought in no restrictions against observance of the sabbath, so, if Philo is writing with any degree of accuracy, one of the prefect's predecessors had sought to pursue this policy. However, it was his actions, not his Roman authority, which manifested his vainglory. Anti-Jewish policy on the part of any ruler is the local and final example of arrogance which is part of the tyrant's villainy.

Arrogance is the basic cause of the boastful tyrant's misrule. It feeds his greed for more wealth and power, and needs to be checked by self-control and obedience to God's law. The ruler lacking self restraint promotes discord because he grasps after absolute power and sets himself above the law in seeking to be a

---

[1101] Spec. Leg. i:90. On treatment of slaves see ii:122–3 and on the law allowing the slave respite from a harsh master see iii:196–7, 201.

[1102] Ibid. ii:92; αὐτῶν refers to οἱ ἡγεμόνες rather than πόλεις. Luke records a similar warning to tax collectors (Lk. 3:13).

[1103] Spec. Leg. ii:94.

[1104] Ibid. ii:94–6; cf. iii:159–63 and GOODENOUGH, Jurisprudence, p. 134 and n. 156.

[1105] Ibid. ii:96.

[1106] Praem. 127–51.

[1107] Som. ii:123–4.

[1108] Som. ii:129. Such a policy finds support amongst "the rank and file" (ii:133) who devise evil against the disciples of virtue. If there is any hint to their identity the wrestling imagery which Philo employs (ii:134) may point to the members of the γυμνάσιον in Alexandria but this is only conjecture.

tyrant. Philo also condemns tyranny because a tyrant lacks that fatherly affection for his people which the good ruler displays. He rules by force rather than by example, going beyond the law. However Philo places the tyrant within the compass of God's power, because after he has been used by God to punish a people, he too will face God's judgment. Thus Platonic and Judaistic ideas are combined in Philo's understanding and condemnation of tyranny.

V. The Theory and Practice of Citizenship

1. The Duties of Citizens

Philo writes that according to the Mosaic law men have two fundamental duties to perform — that towards God in living lives of piety and holiness, and that towards men in showing humaneness and justice.[1109] While expounding the Mosaic obligation of children to honour their parents, he is prompted to see that this particular duty leads on to laws dealing with "subjects . . . obeying their rulers, . . . rulers . . . promoting the welfare of their subjects".[1110] In society he detects two orders, two estates: the superior class comprising seniors, parents, rulers, benefactors and masters, the lower class comprising children, subjects, receivers of benefits and slaves.[1111] Obedience towards one's superiors is to be rendered due to fear of the ruler's might, the desire to follow nature, and to please both God and man.[1112] This service to God is essential for citizenship, because the refusal to reverence God is accompanied by the refusal to honour one's parents, one's country and benefactors.[1113] Within a well-ordered state (and order is seen as an essential element in the functioning of a state[1114]) those possessing the "reasoning principle" turn away from self-seeking and shoulder their responsibilities in society.[1115] Their duties are:

> ". . . regard for the honouring . . . of parents, for the ordering of their children aright, for the safety of their country, for the maintenance of the laws, for the security of good customs, for the better conduct of things

---

[1109] Spec. Leg. ii:63. Philo does not enlarge here on what is involved in these duties for his comment comes in the midst of a discussion on the Sabbath.

[1110] Decal. 167.

[1111] Ibid. 166.

[1112] "For if you honour parents or show mercy for the poor or do kindness to your friends or defend your country or observe with care your duties to all men in general, you will surely be well-pleasing to all with whom you have to do, but also well-pleasing before God" (Mut. 40).

[1113] V. Mos. ii:198.

[1114] Post. C. 184—5.

[1115] The harmony and security of the state depends on the citizens as well as the ruler. "Therefore in a city good men (who are equivalent to reason's aspiration to wisdom) are the surest warrant of performance" (Sacr. 126).

private and public, for the sanctity of temples, for piety towards God,[1116] ... management of a house, leadership in a city, reverence towards elders, respect for the memory of the departed, fellowship with the living,[1117] ... to sacrifice life itself for any single one of these that I have named is honour and glory".[1118]

As regards the right attitude to rulers, Philo notes, in writing against drunkenness, that subjects are to approach their rulers soberly.[1119] Elsewhere in an illustration he observes that subjects are expected to "render due service",[1120] and that fear of the ruler's power ought to influence the citizen's behaviour.[1121] Commenting on Gen. 27:40,[1122] he draws together the familiar Hellenistic illustrations of the right response to rule to support his argument in favour of submission to those in authority. Sailors save their ship by obeying the pilot and a household is secure when slaves obey the master.[1123] Servitude itself is profitable especially when one has a virtuous master,[1124] because by it the foolish man's character will be improved[1125] for he will free himself from the bondage of passions, from arrogance and insolence,[1126] and will become a servant of him who practises σωφροσύνη.[1127]

So from his interpretations of scripture Philo concludes that "a state (is saved) when the inhabitants yield and submit to the magistrates, the young to their elders, and the unskilled to the skilled and informed".[1128] This last phrase is too brief for one to say that it came directly from Plato's concept of ruler and subject as outlined in the 'Republic', but it is likely that this belief of Philo's originated in Plato's philosophy rather than in the Jewish scriptures. The statesman or king, for his part, is to recognize that his sway is exercised under the hand of God who is the source of man's gifts of rule. Holding this perspective, even the weak member of society can thank God for the gifts he has received.[1129]

Philo declares that simply to recognize the common duty, or even to carry it out, is not to fulfill one's responsibilities. The proper motive is essential − right action should have "the assent of judgment".[1130] If its mainspring is sour, then

---

[1116] Immut. 17−8.

[1117] Post. C. 180−1.

[1118] Immut. 17−8. Also there is parental responsibility to offspring and Philo condemns the exposure of children (Spec. Leg. iii:110−5).

[1119] Ebr. 131.

[1120] Conf. 54.

[1121] Fuga 98.

[1122] "By your sword you shall live, and you shall serve your brother; but when you break loose you shall break his yoke from your neck".

[1123] His general theme is the need for the headstrong fool to submit to others.

[1124] Qu. Gen. iv:236.

[1125] Prob. 57. According to Philo Zeno gained this truth from Mosaic Law.

[1126] Leg. Alleg. iii:194.

[1127] Congr. 175−6.

[1128] Qu. Gen. iv:236.

[1129] Mut. 222.

[1130] Immut. 100.

the doers of the action are to be regarded as "bastard citizens", alien from that great commonwealth virtue.[1131] Yet he contends, when expounding on the actions allowable by the phrase "do justice justly",[1132] that there are instances when the end justifies the means. Thus sometimes what is contrary to duty can be done in the "spirit of duty", and the spirit is to take precedence over the letter. Such occasions are the doctor's withholding knowledge of a severe method of treatment, or, in the political realm, the giving of false information to an enemy in order to save one's own country.[1133] Philo was indebted to Plato for these illustrations.[1134]

In Is. 58:5 a cultic act, fasting, is regarded as fulfilled in compassionate and just social action, and Philo expresses a similar perspective when he refers to good civic behaviour as "the best purification".[1135] The behaviour he has in mind is living with one's fellow-citizens peaceably and lawfully, and abstaining from that abuse of the tongue which leads to slander and so ruins other members of society. He regards offences in speech as worse than those arising from wrong action, and if his observations are linked with his experiences in Alexandria, then the anti-Jewish slanders which led ultimately to the pogrom clearly exhibited in his view the absence of citizen-like qualities on the part of the Jews' adversaries.

Philo, in his exegesis of Gen. 16:12b[1136] in two separate works, denies the sophist's capacity to fulfill the duties of a citizen. The sophist likes disputation and disagreement and opposes "the representatives of the sciences".[1137] These attributes are placed in a political context in Philo's more explicit discussion of Ishmael who represents the sophist, being "wild in thought, while the wise man is civil (πολιτικός) and is suited to the state and to civilisation (πόλις καὶ πολιτεία); but the man of wild thought is from that very fact a lover of contention".[1138] Whereas the sophist will shake the existence of the state if given free rein, good men maintain civic stability.[1139] Such is the literal interpretation[1140] of Ex. 12: 17b[1141] and though secondary to the allegorical sense Philo gives that passage, he includes the pointed comment that as a community Israel occupies the position of good men. Discussing the meaning of "force" in the phrase "I will bring out your force from Egypt" Philo comments:

[1131] Ibid. 103.

[1132] Dt. 16:20.

[1133] Cher. 15.

[1134] The references to a physician (in terms less detailed than Philo's) and to deceptive information being given to an enemy occurs in that order in Resp. iii:389. Such deception towards enemies or citizens for the benefit of the State ought to be done by only the ruler; no subject is to do it (ibid. iii:389 C).

[1135] Mut. 240; cf. Hb. 13:8.

[1136] "His hands shall be against all men, and all men's hands against him".

[1137] Fuga 209–10. In Qu. Gen. iii:33 they are specified as Academics and Sceptics, following Marcus' rendering of σκεπτικοί (Supp. I, p. 221 n.c.).

[1138] Qu. Gen. iii:33.

[1139] Sacr. C. 126.

[1140] Qu. Ex. i:21.

[1141] ". . . for on this very day I brought your (force) out of the land of Egypt".

"Force is the godly piety of the seeing nation. Now, so long as those who have this force dwell in cities and villages, the cities and villages act well and properly, for they are adorned at least with the virtue of others if not with their own".[1142]

The wellbeing of Alexandria thus depended on that of the Jewish community. For them to be deprived of their rights or expelled from the city would spell ruin to the city. This is not Philo's explicit message here, but in his overall thinking, especially from the experiences narrated in 'Legatio ad Gaium', that is his claim.

Apart from 'In Flaccum' and 'De Legatione ad Gaium' are there any passages which indicate Philo's view on the attitude to be adopted towards contemporary rulers? GOODENOUGH sees as important in this regard the passage in 'De Somniis' calling for caution in choosing the best way to mitigate the effects of harsh rule. Those who display "untimely frankness" are likened to "lunatics and madmen" for they forget that they are like cattle in the hand of the ruler.[1143] GOODENOUGH couples Philo's illustration of the ship biding its time in a storm-sheltered bay[1144] with the reference to rulers and cattle in the market place,[1145] seeing in both instances a veiled reference to the Romans whom "Philo loved . . . no more than the skipper of a tiny boat loves a hurricane".[1146] However it would seem that here Philo is referring more generally to relationships with Gentile power groups. The passage commences with a caution addressed to those Jewish hot-heads who wished to fight without considering either the might of the forces against them or the repercussions for their fellow Jews.[1147]

Rather than conclude that Som. ii:83—92 refers to the Romans, three factors point to a different interpretation. All of the illustrations in the passage, with the exception of that indicating a ship, refer to a crowd; for example, brutes, scorpions, asps,[1148] men, sons of Cheth. The sons of Cheth are presented unfavourably as "enemies of reason who remove institutions", while in the final illustration, rulers are to be distinguished from the beasts, and respect is to be given to the former. So it is the Alexandrian Greeks and not the Romans who are in view. The Greeks' response to Roman-Jewish accord in Alexandria led Philo to refer to them as beasts who, though they could be fierce, feared Roman rule and so were restrained. If the Jews wished to gain greater rights, they were to avoid conflict and impress their Alexandrian neighbours by their reasonable and subservient lives, thus softening and taming their fierce opposition.[1149]

[1142] Ibid. i:21.

[1143] Som. ii:83—4.

[1144] Som. ii:85—6.

[1145] Ibid. ii:92.

[1146] Politics, p. 7.

[1147] Josephus levelled the same criticism against the Zealots (Vit. 17—9).

[1148] The reference to the scorpions and asps of Egypt may well be a thinly veiled reference to the Alexandrians.

[1149] Som. ii:90—2.

In other sections of Philo's writings there are further indications that he did not share the views of those who, like Judas of Galilee,[1150] revolted against Rome. Just as God has overlordship of the world, so kings have rights over the property of their kingdoms, even that property over which private citizens appear[1151] to have control.[1152] Philo would not quibble at taxes paid to Caesar. He likens those who attack legitimate rulers to "bad slaves[1153] . . . trusting to sedition and violence".[1154] Even in a legitimate cause sanctioned by the law of Moses, Philo contends that citizens are not to take the law into their own hands.[1155] They are not to be accomplices to a crime, and in support he cites Lev. 5:1,[1156] interpreting it as condemning perjury. For his part the true citizen is to be influenced by piety and not by shame or fear, so that he will not remain silent[1157] but bring the criminal to justice. As regards the Jews' response to the marks of idolatry in pagan society around them, both Philo and Josephus[1158] agree in enjoining restraint on the reaction against idolatrous practices. There is to be no reviling of θεοί because it will lead to an irreverent uttering of the singular θεός.[1159] Certainly those who believe in many gods are in error, but for the avoidance of conflict Philo recommends that their "gods" not be mocked.[1160] Such restraint was necessary for peace in Alexandria.

Following the injunction not to revile gods[1161] is the command in Ex. 22: 28b not to curse a ruler. Philo's first point in his exposition is rather strange considering his preceding paragraph because he writes that according to some poets rulers share a lineage with the gods.[1162] However he explains this in terms of ruler's possessing power in themselves to do good or evil. He contends, secondly, that abuse of a ruler is debarred because in response to such verbal opposition rulers deal harshly not only with the offender but with the wider community. Thirdly, though Philo does not quote the end of vs. 28b he takes up the phrase "rules of the people" and wrings from it a case for Jewish superiority as found in the ranks of Jewish rulers.

[1150] Judas refused to have his property registered by Quirinus in the census (BJ. ii:118; vii: 253) regarding it as the act of a slave and rebelled (AJ. xviii:1–5). In BJ. ii:117–8 Josephus also states that Judas had refused to pay the tribute to the Romans.

[1151] δοκεῖν.

[1152] Plant. 54–8.

[1153] Philo is not opposed to slavery and expresses the ancient world's fear of slave uprisings.

[1154] Abr. 228.

[1155] V. Mos. ii:214.

[1156] "If any one sins in that he hears a public adjuration to testify and though he is a witness, whether he has seen or come to know the matter, yet does not speak, he shall bear his iniquity."

[1157] Spec. Leg. ii:26.

[1158] AJ. iv:207; Ap. ii:237; cf. HEINEMANN, Philons Bildung, pp. 38–9.

[1159] V. Mos. ii:205; Spec. Leg. i:53.

[1160] Qu. Ex. ii:3.

[1161] The Septuagint at Ex. 22:27a reads θεοὺς οὐ κακολογήσεις.

[1162] Qu. Ex. ii:6.

35*

"In the third place (Scripture) does not seem to legislate about every ruler, but hints in many ways that he who is (ruler) of the whole people and belongs to the Hebrew nation has been appointed as a virtuous ruler and leader".[1163]

Philo warns against the uprooting of established customs.[1164] It is possible that lying behind this advice was the experience of the Alexandrian Jews, secure under the precedents of imperial favour before Gaius' rule yet aware of the feeling against their claims and privileges on the part of some of their fellow citizens.[1165] More likely Philo is writing for Jewish readers because the barbed words of Migr. 89–90 appear to be aimed at those Jews who completely rejected any literal force in the law, who brought criticism against existing society, who interfered with established customs and cared not about the constitution of their country. Philo's syncretism had not robbed him of his determination to maintain Jewish rights in a mixed community, and he warned these people, who restored only to allegorical or Hellenistic explanations of Judaism's heritage, not to neglect the customs "fixed by divinely empowered men greater than those of our time".[1166] Philo here is opposed to needless action against a tolerable political situation. Yet he is prepared to commend courage and boldness[1167] before rulers when such action is intended to challenge one's superiors to better actions and is thus beneficial to them.[1168] Moses displayed such virtue because he even dared to speak out to God whereas others would fear even to speak to human kings.[1169] Thus Moses again is the exemplar, this time of ideal citizenship.

2. Citizenship as an Ideal

When one examines Philo's ideas on ideal citizenship, the ambiguity detected in other areas of his thinking is found here also. Though at heart a Jew in his political theorizing he is a Greek. When he comes to consider citizenship he is influenced strongly by Stoic thought[1170] and relates the matter closely to current ideas on citizenship of the world. The notions override his particular Jewish spirit, so that he can describe his Jewish contemporaries who abide only by a literal interpretation of the law as "men of narrow citizenship" (μικροπολῖται). In interpreting Dt. 7:7–8 — a passage which unmistakably declares God's election of Israel by grace — Philo widens its scope, indicating that it includes those who are wise, those who are citizens of the world.[1171] It is these wise ones who

---

[1163] Qu. Ex. ii:6.
[1164] Migr. 88–90.
[1165] COLSON, VII, p. 631 n. 3.
[1166] Ibid. 90.
[1167] Heres 5, 19.
[1168] Ibid. 6.
[1169] Heres 20–21.
[1170] COLSON, VI, pp. 156 n.a.; 600 n. 28.
[1171] οἱ κοσμοπολῖται (Migr. 59–61).

are "the open-eyed contemplators of the world" and who thus share in its citizenship.[1172] In allegorizing[1173] Noah's genealogy he presents him as a sage whose primary attachment was to virtue and not to his family or national group.[1174] However when Philo describes Moses as the ruler of the world because of his relationship to God, it seems that Jewish particularity partly asserts itself, but he allows that the virtuous man also shares in God's possessions, he too being a world citizen.[1175] Moses then did not possess this privilege alone, though Philo contends that he alone among men rightly was called God and king.[1176] Amongst world-citizens Moses is ranked first.

The affirmation that God's people are pilgrims on earth is treated by Philo in regard to the soul's sojourn in the world of sense perception. In Platonic vein he speaks of the soul being freed one day from the body and returning to its mother-city (μητρόπολις). Philo elaborates on the nature of this city in Som. ii:250–4. It is not found as an earthly city – Jerusalem being allegorized[1177] – but in that soul where exists peace, contemplation or "the vision-seeking mind"[1178] which reaches out for the untreated. Because of God's transcendence, man's soul becomes this city,[1179] and those who, by nature or through instruction, seek after the one God join the "godly commonwealth", "the camp of piety", whose members are distinguished not by their circumcision,[1180] but by their monotheism.[1181]

Writing in Stoic terms, Philo refers to the world as the great city (μεγαλό-πολις)[1182] governed by natural law,[1183] and it was nature's order and constitutions established by God which made it a world-city.[1184] Adam was the first κοσ-μοπολίτης[1185] who lived according to τὸ βούλημα τῆς φύσεως because the world, being a well ordered state (εὔνομος πόλις) was in concert with universal

---

[1172] Som. i:39.

[1173] Jos. 28; cf. Decal. 1.

[1174] Abr. 31.

[1175] V. Mos. i:157; cf. Qu. Gen. iii:39 where Abraham, ὁ σπουδαῖος is a world-citizen. He who is σπουδαῖος can say that all the earth is his fatherland (Prob. 145).

[1176] BURTON L. MACK (Imitatio Mosis – Patterns of Cosmology and Soteriology in the Hellenistic Synagogue, SP., I [1972], p. 27) regards this as evidence that Philo believed Moses to be "the divine Man". A. J. M. WEDDERBURN (Philo's 'Heavenly Man', NT., XV [1973], p. 318) argues that Philo identifies the "heavenly man" with the Logos.

[1177] For example, in Qu. Gen. iii:10, men are said to be sojourners on God's earth and slaves to the body's passions.

[1178] Som. ii:251.

[1179] "Whosoever then has the strength to forsake war and fatality, creation and perishing, and cross over to the camp of the uncreated, of the imperishable, of free-will, of peace, may justly be called the dwelling-place and city of God" (Som. ii:253; cf. Decal. 45, 49).

[1180] Qu. Ex. ii:2.

[1181] Spec. leg. i:51; GOODENOUGH, Jurisprudence, p. 33 n. 5.

[1182] Jos. 29; cf. Spec. Leg. i:34; Qu. Ex. i:1.

[1183] The natural world conveys to the seeking mind the commandments of God, and it was by this means, according to Philo, that God spoke to Abraham (Abr. 60).

[1184] Ibid. 61.

[1185] Opif. 3, 142.

law.[1186] He fulfilled his citizenship by "conversing and consorting" with spiritual and divine natures, following after the path of virtue by which he served his Father and King, God.[1187] So too the wise man lives.[1188] However, Philo to some extent contradicts this concept of the wise man being a citizen of the world. Writing in 'De Cherubim' he depicts man in the world as in a foreign city (ζένη πόλις) and states that God alone can rightly claim the status of a citizen (πολίτης). To label man as a citizen is a misuse[1189] of the term, because the wise man is honoured by being called a sojourner and alien in the world, while the fool is an outcast from the city of God.[1190]

The contrast between the wise man's finding heaven as his fatherland and earth as a foreign country is not grounded by Philo in an eschatological or historical awareness[1191] of God's work, but is moulded by the Platonic view of mind and body. A striking comparison is found between Hb. 11 and similar passages in 'De Confusione Linguarum' and 'Quis Rarum Divinarum Heres Sit'. Both writers look back to the heroes of faith and both would have agreed that heaven is "where their citizenship lies",[1192] but Philo goes on to cite the cases of Abraham, Jacob and Job as signifying those who yearned to go from the region of the senses back to the realm of ἀρεταί, the realm of the "truly existent".[1193] Abraham in his wanderings was an outcast from all but God,[1194] and Philo explains Abraham's alienation allegorically: the land from which the patriarch departed symbolizes the body, while his kinsfolk and his father's house whom he left behind symbolize senses and speech respectively.[1195] It is God who is variously described as his "country . . . kinsfolk . . . paternal hearth . . . franchise . . . boldness . . . great and glorious and inalienable wealth".[1196]

The centres of power in the world — states and their laws — Philo considers in Stoic fashion as extraneous additions to nature's pattern.[1197] He regards cities as centres of evil and especially conducive to the display of arrogance,[1198] the vice

---

[1186] Ibid. 3; Agr. 66.

[1187] Opif. 144.

[1188] The evil man can not follow virtue and so is an exile (Leg. Alleg. iii:1—2).

[1189] κατάχρησις.

[1190] Cher. 121; cf. Gig. 66—7. His ways are banished ἐκ τῆς τοῦ κόσμου πολιτείας (Conf. 196). Banishment of the soul is a thing to be feared because the soul can then never return to its first dwelling (Det. 142—9).

[1191] The New Testament posits the distinction as between the shadow or type foreshadowing the reality, e.g. Hb. 9:1—24; 2 Cor. 3:7—18. Philo speaks of God as the guardian (κηδεμών) of the world (ἡ μεγαλόπολις) who watches over it to fulfil his purposes (Prov. 2. 39).

[1192] Conf. 78; cf. Hb. 11:13—6.

[1193] Heres 70.

[1194] Heres 26.

[1195] Ibid. 69.

[1196] Ibid. 27. These great ones of old are not colonists in their bodies but aliens (Conf. 78—82). The great example is Moses who is credited with a citizenship akin to Adam and whose goodness was recognized from the beginning of his life.

[1197] Jos. 29.

[1198] Decal. 2—4.

which he associates with the pomp that accompanied the prefect in Alexandria.[1199] Yet, as noted earlier, he describes the world as a μεγαλόπολις and a πόλις νόμιμος, and argues that it requires the best law of state to govern it.[1200] His explanation of that law illustrates well how Stoic and Jewish ideas jostled for supremacy in his mind:

"And it is fitting that it should have a worthy author of law and legislator, since among men (God) appointed the contemplative race (i.e. Israel) in the same manner (as the law) for the world. And rightly does he legislate for this race, also prescribing (its law) as a law for the world, for the chosen race is a likeness of the world, and its Law (is a likeness of the laws) of the world".[1201]

In a brief passage in 'De Somniis'[1202] he designates those who are excluded from citizenship of God's world. They are those who erect inscriptions, not to God, but to themselves, to the feeble creation. From this it would seem that they who erect monuments like Augustus' 'Res Gestae' are thus proclaimed to be foolish.[1203] On the other hand those described in terms befitting the κοσμοπολῖται amongst the individuals or groups who were Philo's contemporaries were a Jewish contemplative community, the Therapeutae. They excelled because of their dedication to monotheism,[1204] their yearning for a "vision of the Existent One",[1205] while their asceticism rose above the careless abandonment to philosophy displayed by Anaxageras and Democritus.[1206] One is not surprised to learn that this contemplative Jewish community interpreted their scriptures allegorically.[1207] They reflected Philo's own syncretism, and admiring his own world-view in theirs he extols them thus:

"(They) have taken to their hearts the contemplation of nature and what it has to teach, and have lived in the soul alone, citizens of Heaven and the world, presented to the Father and Maker of all by their faithful sponsor Virtue, who has procured for them God's friendship and added a gift going hand in hand with it, true excellence of life, a boon better than all good fortune and rising to the very summit of felicity".[1208]

Pursuit of virtues was the passport into world-citizenship, but when sides had to be taken on the issue of local citizenship, as in the tense Alexandrian situation during

---

[1199] Ibid. 4; cf. Flacc. 4.
[1200] The citizens of this state are the spiritual and divine natures, some invisible, others such as the stars quite visible (Opif. 144). They are to share with man in this perfect state whose laws existed before man because the world existed before him.
[1201] Qu. Ex. ii:42.
[1202] Som. i:243.
[1203] Ibid. i:244.
[1204] V. Contempl. 3–10.
[1205] Ibid. 11.
[1206] Ibid. 14.
[1207] Ibid. 29.
[1208] V. Contempl. 90.

and after the pogrom, Philo was a Jew of Alexandrian Jewry, proud of its identity, sensitive to scorn of its customs and ready to plead for its rights.[1209/10]

3. The Role of Conscience

Whereas Paul includes an appeal to conscience in his exhortation on the right attitude Roman Christians were to have to rulers, Philo does not refer to conscience in such a context. However, he has more to say on the understanding of conscience than any New Testament writer, and he gives it a higher value than does Paul as regards its capacity to be the internal judge of man's actions. He uses the concept largely in the sphere of the soul-passions conflict, and prominent in his thought is the negative connotation[1211] which C. PIERCE[1212] establishes in Paul's use of the term. Conscience is the scrutineer "established in the soul like a judge",[1213] which severely reproves and threatens against deliberate evil or gently admonishes when the soul stumbles into unintentional wrongdoing.[1214] However, it can also be a witness to worthy acts; so Joseph called on God to test his conscience.[1215] It can teach what is right.[1216] So Philo regards one valuable use of the Sabbath as a time for "the improvement of character and submission to the scrutiny of conscience".[1217]

Elsewhere Philo associates conscience with the essence of man, the "man within man". It is said to exercise various roles of authority over a person, ruling as "king and governor", judging and arbitrating life's contests, and acting also as a scrutinizer (ἔλεγχος) of one's actions. Philo's use of ἔλεγχος may have stemmed not from his original thought[1218] but from the influence of Leviticus 5:21—6.[1219] In Gen. 31:37, 42 the verb ἐλέγχω has the sense of "arbitrate" or "judge". Philo internalizes the function:

> "He assumes the part of witness or accuser, and all unseen, convicts us from within, not allowing us so much as to open our mouth, but holding in and curbing the tongue with the reins of conscience (συνειδότος), checks its wilful and rebellious course".[1220]

[1209/1210] Leg. 361—6; Flacc. 191.

[1211] E. g. Jos. 47—8, 214, 262.

[1212] C. A. PIERCE, Conscience in the New Testament (London 1958), pp. 60—4.

[1213] Opif. 128; cf. Spec. Leg. iii:54; iv:40.

[1214] Det. 146, Immut. 138, Opif. 128.

[1215] Jos. 265.

[1216] Dec. 87.

[1217] Opif. 128.

[1218] RICHARD T. WALLIS, The Idea of Conscience in Philo of Alexandria, SP., III (1974), pp. 29, 31.

[1219] JACOB MILGROM, On the Origins of Philo's Doctrine of Conscience, SP., III (1974), pp. 42—44.

[1220] Det. 23; cf. Heres 6—7 and PIERCE, Conscience, chaps. 1—2.

In Fuga 117–118 conscience is regarded as synonymous with the indwelling Logos. It is the λόγος θεῖος.[1221] Philo refers to a voice or prompter within which, even if the soul's sight is clouded, can guide one on the right paths.[1222] So in Som. ii:2 it is used to denote the suggestion God gives in the interpreting of dreams.[1223] Conscience works within every man, even the wicked, who are warned by it that their evil is not ignored by God. The convicting conscience is the flashing red light within them pointing to God's omniscience and their encounter with justice.[1224]

Philo has a higher view of conscience than does Paul[1225] as evinced in the definition he gives it – "an impartial scrutinizer (ὁ ἐλέγχων) unequalled in veracity"[1226] watching over men's actions and thoughts. The touchstone of judgment is ὁ ὀρθὸς λόγος and it is the role of ὁ ἔλεγχος to rebuke and reproach the soul for its foolish, undisciplined, unjust and stained behaviour.[1227] In Philo's thought submission to the passions is the transgression, and he who ignores ὁ ἔλεγχος faces destruction.[1228] The idea that the conscience can be corrupted (Tit. 1:15) is not countenanced by Philo for it is the one and only court which is never misled by oratorical artifices.[1229]

Basic to good citizenship is fear of God which Philo identifies with the obligation to follow nature's law, to heed reason. However obedience is to be rendered not only because of God's ordinance but out of fear for the ruler's power. It is especially profitable for a citizen to be governed by a virtuous and restrained ruler but when governed by an evil ruler Philo commends the boldness of those who challenge such a leader to improve his rule. On the other hand the citizen is to exercise restraint particularly over his tongue because slander destroys civil peace. In particular Philo spurns revolt and the uprooting of established customs and he criticizes those who attack rulers as being no more than slaves in their thinking, relying on violence not reason. Rather citizenship is to be fulfilled with the right motive, and by living in this way citizens secure peace, maintain law, order and

---

[1221] Immut. 182, cf. Det. 146.

[1222] Som. i:164; cf. Mut. 139; Jos. 110.

[1223] It is the "secret tenant" (Som. ii:252). The word is used in other senses: of the memories a student has of his teacher's words (Congr. 67), or of the enticing music of pleasure (Post. C. 155; cf. Congr. 67).

[1224] Conf. 119–21.

[1225] COLSON and WHITAKER (I, p. xx) suggest that his concept of conscience shows a great advance above his Stoic predecessors and a remarkable approximation to the Christian view; cf. A. A. KENNEDY, Philo's Contribution to Religion (London, 1919), pp. 53, 106–14. For key differences between Paul's and the Stoic Seneca's views on conscience see J. N. SEVENSTER, Paul and Seneca, Novum Testamentum, Suppl. IV (Leiden, 1961), pp. 84–102.

[1226] Post. C. 59. However in Conf. 124–7 Philo argues strongly that the mind can be deluded. In contrast to Philo's glowing definition of this ἔλεγχος, Paul does not regard the conscience as impartial. He speaks of "a seared conscience" (1 Ti. 4:2) and a "defiled conscience" – Tit. 1.15.

[1227] Immut. 126.

[1228] Ibid. 183.

[1229] Virt. 206.

piety and evince respect for elders, magistrates and other informed members of society. Moses of course was the ideal citizen as too was Adam, yet Philo adopts the familiar Stoic concept of κοσμοπολίτης in outlining the qualities contributing to the ideal. The one to be emulated is he who aspires after the realm of the soul and of virtue, who yearns to be free from the body and earthly confines, and who seeks the pure, perfect, spiritual Being, God. Philo does not expressly link the claims of conscience with the citizen's response to his ruler, though it is related to his vision of ideal citizenship in that the conscience infallibly condemns the quest for bodily pleasure. It acts as a restraining rather than initiating influence though God uses it to guide man, and so the citizen, on to the right path.

VI. The Superiority of the Contemplative Life

Philo devoted one whole work to a description of a contemplative community in the vicinity of Alexandria. The details of his description indicate that he had first hand contact with this group though his account tends to present them in ideal terms drawn as much from his aspirations as from his observations. The points pertinent to our study that he makes in 'De Vita Contemplativa' will be noted first. In the allusions to the wider range of his writings which will follow one finds that they tend to underline and enlarge upon the key ideas in 'De Vita Contemplativa'.

Philo describes the life of a contemplative community called the Therapeutae. He holds them in high esteem because they profess to cure both body and soul, because they worship God in the light of nature and the holy laws of Moses,[1230] and because they regard the nature of the soul as superior to the cares of the body.[1231] They gave practical expression to the third tenet by giving their property away to their relatives or friends. In this Philo commends them for their thoughtfulness in that rather than abandoning their possessions they sought to benefit others with their goods. Their action epitomized justice and equality for now they drew their wealth from nature and not the inequitable distribution found in normal society. Now they had time for reflection and the pursuit of wisdom in contrast to the anxious care over money-making and sustenance.[1232] The simplicity of their way of life, based on their ἐγκράτεια, commended the superior way that they had chosen.

Another sign of their wisdom was their use of allegorical interpretation in studying the holy scriptures. Such exposition occurred at their weekly meeting with the senior one among them giving instruction. Philo's description of the president's procedure reads like a summary of the bulk of his own writings:

[1230] V. contempl. 2, 64.
[1231] Ibid. 2, 10—11, 34, 78.
[1232] V. contempl. 16—7, 34—8, 67.

". . . amid this silence . . . he discusses some question arising in the Holy Scriptures or solves one that has been propounded by someone else . . . His instruction proceeds in a leisurely manner; he lingers over it and spins it out with repetitions . . . The exposition of the Sacred Scriptures treats the inner meaning conveyed in allegory".[1233]

The teaching deals with both the literal and the invisible or spiritual sense. The former applies to the body and the latter to the soul.

A further sign of their commendable ways was their observance of natural law in that, considering all humans to be free, they had no slaves. Thus, again, they reject inequality. Service is to be done willingly, not by compulsion. Philo concludes his description of this community by commending their experience of the riches of life. They are citizens both of heaven and of this world. They contemplate nature and live for it and for the soul. Virtue itself is the patron commending them to God. They experience true excellence of life which surpasses all other possessions and fortune.

What this community enjoyed Philo elsewhere individualizes in terms of the soul and the body. To him no ruling position in society can compare in value with that life in which the soul ruled supreme over the senses. To present this hierarchical estimate of human experience Philo favours the Stoic-Platonic contrast between ideal rule stemming from the well-directed soul and the actual rule found in society around him. This does not mean that Philo considers this Hellenized perspective as something separated from a Jewish view.[1234] In his allegorical exegesis of Gen. 25:23[1235] he regards the freedom-slavery alternatives facing the soul as reflecting the assessment by God of man's response to pleasure. So the Stoic epigram becomes a divine proposition.

"In God's judgment that which is base and irrational is by nature a slave, but that which is of fine character and endowed with reason is princely and free".[1236]

The possession of virtue, however slight, indicates not only freedom but the acquisition of leadership and sovereignty, while its absence leads to the subjugation of reason.

Greater than the possession of kingship is the quality of shepherding[1237] because to possess reason is to have the ability to shepherd the body, the senses and pleasures, and "to rule them with vigour and with a right strong yet even gentle hand".[1238] This capacity which equips man to govern not only his body but the state is implanted by Nature, and so the true ruler is not set up by human forces

---

[1233] Ibid. 75–8, 28, 30.

[1234] Qu. Gen. iv:235.

[1235] "And the Lord said to Rebekah, 'Two nations are in your womb, and two people born of you shall be divided; the one shall be stronger than the other, the elder shall serve the younger' ".

[1236] Leg. Alleg. iii:89. Cf. SVF. iii:617; Mut. 152; Sobr. 57; Migr. 197; Som. ii:244.

[1237] See p. 519.

[1238] Sacr. 49. Here also the image of the charioteer in relation to rule is used.

but rather recognized for who he is. It is on this basis that Philo is opposed to selection by lots[1239] or by votes. He praises the "rulers appointed for ever by Nature herself",[1240] and sees such a one in Abraham because his contemporaries detected his rulership qualities and were not swayed by his lack of wealth or wandering existence. Rather "they perceived the kingship in his mind" and the virtues of prudence, temperance, bravery and justice in his life.[1241]

More than once Philo contrasts the possession of earthly power and its trappings with the prize of immortal reality. He contrasts the transitoriness of high office, fame, honours, wealth and nobility of birth with the possession of hope in the eternal God.[1242] The prize for the "conquering" of pleasure is not the reception of earthly honours and riches,[1243] but it consists in doing "the good". In defeating powerful pleasure one gains "the noble and glorious crown, which no human assembly has ever bestowed".[1244]

In Stoic vein he regards the free man as the true ruler, however much he be dominated by a mortal tyrant.[1245] He who pursues reason, who is influenced by God's wisdom,[1246] is rightly regarded not only as a ruler but as a monarch, as a king of kings, who holds power from God.[1247] Here Philo has in mind the rule that is exercised over the senses and over irrational behaviour.[1248] So he who pursues virtue is in reality a king whatever his social position.[1249] Philo finds this teaching in Moses' writings by a dexterous combination of Gen. 2:10 and 33:6. The division of the river into four heads (2:10) means that the Word is "split up into four virtues, each of which is royal" and, having mentioned virtues, Philo then allegorizes 33:6 to indicate the Mosaic authorship of his doctrine:

> ". . . and when he points to the virtues (Moses) means thereby to declare that the Sage who possesses them is a king, a king appointed not by men but by nature, the infallible, the incorruptible, the only free elector. Thus it was said to Abraham by those who saw his worthiness: 'thou art a king from God with us' (Gen. 33:6). And thus they laid down the doctrine for the students of philosophy, that the Sage alone is a ruler and a king, and virtue is rule and a kingship whose authority is final".[1250]

[1239] Spec. Leg. iv:156−7. To decide by lot means that reason is not consulted (ii:231).

[1240] Mut. 151.

[1241] Ibid. 152−3; cf. Som. i:124.

[1242] Abr. 262−8; Qu. Gen. iv:149; Leg. Alleg. iii:107; cf. Jos. 131−141 where he mentions the transitory fame of Dionysius of Corinth and Croesus.

[1243] These are the weapons for wielding power gained through cunning (Leg. Alleg. ii:107; Det. 136).

[1244] Leg. Alleg. ii:108.

[1245] "Only the wise man is free and a ruler, even if he may have ten thousand masters of his body" (Post. C. 138; cf. Stob. Ecl. ii in SVF. iii:589).

[1246] Qu. Gen. iv:107−8.

[1247] He writes, as did Aristotle, of the kingly art (τέχνη τις βασιλική) amongst other arts which the wise man possesses (ibid. iv:76).

[1248] Ibid. iv:121.

[1249] Post. C. 128; Qu. Gen. iii:22; SVF. iii:295.

[1250] Som. ii:243−4; cf. Abr. 261; Mut. 152.

This true king rules over the irrational tendency which is within every man, and so looks to the realm of pure reason as his fatherland,[1251] for he is able to conquer every passion offered to the senses in the material world.[1252] One such good man in society can save a city or a nation from ruin,[1253] and he who is "law-abiding and obedient to God" is equal in worth to a city, a nation or even the world.[1254] Virtue is the source of good laws, good governments, good statesmen and so of well-ordered peace.[1255] Though the virtuous man turns away from luxurious living[1256] he is truly rich.[1257] The other Stoic paradox of the rich enslaved and the wise freed is presented in Prob. 125–136, where Philo affirms that natural freedom is not inferior to kingship and that the wise man will choose death rather than slavery.[1258] The alternative aphorism, namely that though the fool may rule as king he remains a fool, Philo finds in natural law, which he claims also to be the scriptural teaching. However his expression of it is so strongly Stoic in form that his philosophical milieu and not a scriptural passage[1259] is his inspiration:

> "And in the second place (scripture) lays down a most natural law . . . that not one of the foolish is a king, even though he should be master of all the land and sea, but only the wise and God-loving man, even if he is without the equipment and resources through which many obtain power with violence and force".[1260]

In one important sense, however, the wise man is a slave. Philo follows this thought in a direction mapped out by Jewish monotheism. The man who rules himself, his passions or desires, can still be a slave but a blessed one, for to be a slave of God surpasses not only freedom but the highest sovereignty.[1261] The wise man seeks after simplicity and quietness,[1262] with which no possession of royal power is comparable.[1263] He owes his loyalty to the virtues and not to any human authority; he is an exile in the company of men.[1264] Abraham exhibited such an

---

[1251] Agr. 41, 65; Plant. 52; Sobr. 57; cf. SVF. iii:617–9.

[1252] Plant. 145.

[1253] Migr. 119.

[1254] Decal. 37. Sim. Virt. 185–6; Qu. Gen. iii:44. In Praem. 113–4 the good man is considered to be greater than a city.

[1255] Mut. 149–50.

[1256] Som. i:121–6; ii:9.

[1257] Prob. 8–9.

[1258] He expands this in his treatment of the ideal statesman in Jos. 67–79.

[1259] E. g. "Better is a poor and wise youth than an old and foolish king who will no longer take advice" (Eccl. 4:13).

[1260] Qu. Gen. iv:76, 108, 230; iii:22. The fool is the slave to those who love virtue (Sobr. 69).

[1261] ἡ μεγίστη ἀρχή (Plant 53). As regards Heres 7 with its reference to a ruler of the world, it is unlikely that the Roman emperor is in mind; the picture is rather a general one; cf. also Qu. Ex. ii:105.

[1262] Som. ii:64; Abr. 22–3, 27, 30.

[1263] Abr. 24.

[1264] Ibid. 31.

attitude when he separated from Lot even though he possessed the superior strength because

> "he alone took for his ideal not the exercise of strength and self-aggrandizement but a life free from strife and so far as lay with him of tranquility, and thereby he showed himself the most admirable of men".[1265]

He who, like Abraham, is declared a friend of God (Gen. 18:17) receives from God sovereignty and freedom from arrogance,[1266] because Abraham, through faith in τὸ ὄν,[1267] was deemed a wise man, and the wise man rules like a pilot, or a general. Another wise man was Joseph who refused to hoard material wealth though having the political power to do so, because he sought the invisible riches — the virtues for which the godly yearn.[1268] Wealth and glory are not to be sought[1269] but if received by the wise man he is to use them "for improvement of life".[1270] Philo considers that in his time there were not a few who possessed wealth and political power who used both wisely, not being subservient to them, but living simply as the poor.[1271] Such rulers act rightly due to two factors: they possess the right nature and have received the correct training so that they put their responsibility to other men above that to themselves, and secondly, they are reminded of their partnership with their fellow men, and so drawn away from arrogance and the maintenance of inequality.[1272] Their rule benefits their cities with "plenty, abundance, order and peace", and they can indeed be called ideal rulers.[1273] In contrast stands the "nouveaux riches"[1274] who, blinded by the sensory riches which fortune has placed in their laps, do not seek the virtues which those who exercise authority should follow. They who determinedly seek glory and power infect philosophy with "the baseness of mere opinion",[1275] and abandon themselves to a soulless way of life, to bondage,[1276] and to the harm of their subjects.[1277] The tyrant is thus not to be envied but pitied,[1278] because

---

[1265] Ibid. 216.

[1266] Sobr. 57.

[1267] Abr. 270.

[1268] Jos. 258.

[1269] The wise one is not taken up with pursuing power; rather he dwells with ἡ θεία φύσις (Immut. 149—51, 116).

[1270] The contrast between the right and wrong use of wealth and glory is presented at length in Fuga 28—34.

[1271] Spec. Leg. ii:20.

[1272] Ibid. ii:21.

[1273] Ibid. ii:22.

[1274] Philo (ibid. i:25) warns against those who make wealth their god. The conclusion in i:23 may point in this instance to the Jews led away from their faith by their luxury. On Philo's own substantial financial position cf. Simon p. 43, and his possible sympathy with the established wealthy Jews cf. TCHERIKOVER, p. 67.

[1275] Gig. 39.

[1276] Immut. 115.

[1277] Sobr. 42; cf. Flacc. 1.

[1278] Cf. Ling. 164 with Plato's discussion of the tyrannical man in Resp. xi:573 B—580 C, esp. 579 C—E.

though he seems to hold absolute power his life is bereft of any virtue,[1279] and beyond the grasping after human rule lies the barrenness of separation from God.[1280]

The attraction of wealth, glory, honour and rule in themselves is really a temptation which can overpower the senses and lead men to desert their souls even in the midst of their lauding the contemplative and obscure life.[1281] However, distaste for wealth, honour and political tasks does not necessarily indicate a soul attuned to God because this attitude can spring from the avoidance of responsibility. Philo's advice to those who seek satisfaction by forsaking public duty in order to contemplate God is that they ought first to learn how to fulfill their responsibilities with a proper pursuit of virtue.[1282] The tasks of managing a house and ruling a state are not to be despised, because the practical precedes the contemplative way of life.[1283] Philo thus values the possession of political power when it is regarded as a lesser but still commendable pursuit carried out by the lover of virtue.[1284] But to pursue office for its own sake is to exchange the shadow for the reality,[1285] because noble birth and honours though useful in God's service are external objects.[1286]

Those who pride themselves on their power are trusting in outward, perishable objects. It is these as well as those consumed by greed who provoke turmoil and wars because

"the greatest quarrels both of men . . . and of states have arisen . . . to gain advantages pertaining to the body and outward things. But for the sake of culture and virtue, which are goods of the mind, the noblest part of our being, no war either foreign or civil has ever yet broken out".[1287]

Philo can sound the jarring note of judgment which hangs over powerful rulers, and there is no mistaking that the Romans are intended to come within its compass,[1288] but he is not basically anti-Roman. For example, the outburst in Post. C.

[1279] Ling. 164–7.

[1280] Ling. 166–7. For the proper exercise of rule it is essential to know God, but to endorse this view Philo quotes from Plato: Tht. 176a (Fuga 82).

[1281] Ebr. 57–9, 63; BORGEN pp. 122–6; SIMON pp. 80–4. These honours cannot compare with the benefit of sobriety in the soul (Sobr. 2–4). Strong drink, wealth and fame rightly used by the good man enhance his virtues but for the man ruled by them they parade his foolishness (Plant. 171).

[1282] "When engaged in business, were you determined to be just . . . when you held posts of honour, did you practise simplicity? State business is an object of ridicule to you people. Perhaps you have never discovered how serviceable a thing it is" (Fuga 35).

[1283] Ibid. 36, 38.

[1284] Mut. 80. According to Philo Moses regarded governments (ἀρχάς), together with first fruits and passover, as things of special excellence (Congr. 89). The mention of "rule" in relation to the number ten (Ibid. 92, 110) suggests that ἀρχάς rather than εὐχάς is the preferred reading (COLSON and WHITAKER, IV, p. 503, n. 4).

[1285] Post. C. 113.

[1286] Qu. Gen. iv:215–6.

[1287] Post. C. 117–8.

[1288] Plant. 66–7.

112—123 against ambition for political office is inspired not by ardent Jewish patriotism but by his Hellenic philosophical tenets. These tenets dominate his assessment of the value of political power. Power is not to be despised, but the practical life is to give way to the contemplative life in which the soul seeks virtue and spurns the trappings of earthly power. In aspiring after God man learns to rule himself and to be truly a king.

VII. Summary

Philo's political ideas are neither accessibly compact nor always consistent. However there is basic agreement between his theoretical ideas concerning political power and his practical response to Roman rule. Philo is concerned for a life of contemplation for the individual, stability for society and the *status quo* for the Jews in the Roman Empire. The contemplative life surpasses but does not contradict the political life, the stability of society is lauded again and again in Philo's allegorical exegesis of the Jewish scriptures, and the recognition of the value and the rights of the Jews in the Empire is the yardstick by which Roman rulers are to be judged.

The static, rather than dynamic, nature of Philo's political thought is illustrated even in that action which would seem to indicate political initiative on his part — his leadership of the embassy representing the Alexandrian Jews before Gaius. However, the embassy goes in reaction to misrule which threatens the status of this Jewish community. Its dispatch under Philo's leadership is a defensive measure seeking to regain the lost ground. Philo, by no means a modest man, cannot disguise the fact that the embassy was on the defensive throughout the time it pleaded its case before Gaius. In accord with Philo's static political attitudes is his selection of Roman rulers whose administrations he condemns. Gaius, Flaccus, Pilate and Sejanus were all disgraced figures and could safely be condemned, especially when Philo takes care to laud the overall benefits of Roman rule.

The benefits which Philo sees Augustus and Tiberius conferring on the world are those which promote stability and the opportunity to pursue the contemplative life. Peace, harmony, justice — these are the virtues Philo prizes. The occasion for his extolling them is his reading of the Jewish scriptures, but these virtues are realized in the pursuit of the ideal political life that Philo portrays in an eclectic absorption of various strands of Hellenistic political thought. This does not mean that his consciousness of being a Jew is submerged, but his mind is in large part captured by Hellenistic ideas.

There are occasions when antinomies occur within his thought, when Judaistic and Hellenistic ideas jostle together or co-exist within his treatment of a political subject. For example Moses and Joseph, great figures in Judaism, are singled out particularly as the exemplars of ideal rule and yet Philo's understanding of that ideal is an amalgam of Pythagorean, Stoic and Platonic ideas. So too

Philo writes of Israel as a distinct race, but its ranks are swelled by all those who aspire to contemplate the Divine and whose hearts yearn for the virtues prized in Hellenistic thought. Adam, Melchizedek, Abraham and Moses possess citizenship in God's world, but world-citizenship, a strongly Stoic concept, is also possessed by those who aspire after virtue and seek beyond to God.

Philo's special interest in political matters lay positively in his concern for jurisprudence and negatively in his abhorrence of ochlocracy. The Mosaic code provides ample material for exposition on juridical matters and Philo's writings in 'De Specialibus Legibus' are largely devoid of allegorization and are his most sustained defence for the practice of Jewish customs within the Roman Empire. However, in accord with his generally pacific political response to Roman rule he is prepared at times to trim the enforcement of Moses' code to Graeco-Roman practice, though he is not afraid to level criticism at it. Philo's abhorrence of ochlocracy tallies with the threefold strand noted above in his thought. It rejected contemplation, destroyed stability and threatened Jewish rights. These rights came under most serious attack from anti-Jewish mobs and Philo's hatred of the Alexandrian mob is writ large in his work.

One final but essential point needs to be noted. Though Philo's political ideas are abstracted from the experiences of major figures in Hebrew history, and major events in that movement of history, his own ideas are devoid of movement. True, there are glimmers as in his messianic hope and his understanding of democracy, but the impetus of *Heilsgeschichte* escapes his ken. His static view of history undergirds his static political ideals.

Abbreviations

Sources

1 Qp. Hab	Qumran Commentary on Habakkuk
M. Pol.	The Martyrdom of Polycarp
Philo	Philo
Abr.	De Abrahamo
Aet.	De Aeternitate Mundi
Agr.	De Agricultura
Cher.	De Cherubim
Conf.	De Confusione Linguarum
Congr.	De Congressu quaerendae Eruditionis gratia
Decal.	De Decalogo
Det.	Quod Deterius Potiori insidiari solet
Ebr.	De Ebrietate
Flacc.	In Flaccum
Fuga	De Fuga et Inventione
Gig.	De Gigantibus
Heres	Quis Rerum Divinarum Heres
Hyp.	Hypothetica
Immut.	Quod Deus immutabilis sit
Jos.	De Iosepho
Leg.	De Legatione ad Gaium

Leg. Alleg.	Legum Allegoriae
Migr.	De Migratione Abrahami
Mut.	De Mutatione Nominum
Opif.	De Opificio Mundi
Plant.	De Plantatione
Post. C.	De Posteritate Caini
Praem.	De Praemiis et Poenis
Prob.	Quod Omnis Probus Liber sit
Prov.	De Providentia
Qu. Ex.	Quaestiones et Solutiones in Exodum
Qu. Gen.	Quaestiones et Solutiones in Genesin
Sacr. C.	De Sacrificiis Abelis et Caini
Sobr.	De Sobrietate
Som.	De Somniis
Spec. Leg.	De Specialibus Legibus
V. contempl.	De Vita Contemplativa
Virt.	De Virtutibus
V. Mos.	De Vita Mosis

Reference Works

AE.	L'Annee Epigraphique (Paris, 1888ff.).
CAH.	The Cambridge Ancient History, 12 vols., J. B. BURY, S. A. COOK, F. E. ADCOCK, and M. P. CHARLESWORTH, eds. (Cambridge, 1923–53).
GT.	A Greek-English Lexicon of the New Testament, C. L. WILIBALD GRIMM and JOSEPH HENRY THAYER, eds. (Edinburgh, 1908, reprint of 4th ed.).
IG.	Inscriptiones Graecae, 14 vols., pub. under auspices of the Berlin Academy (Berlin, 1873ff.).
IGR.	Inscriptiones Graecae ad Res Romanas Pertinentes, 4 vols., R. CAGNAT, ed. (Paris, 1906–27).
JE.	The Jewish Encyclopedia, 12 vols, ISIDORE SINGER, ed. (New York, 1901–1906).
LS.	Greek-English Lexicon, compiled by HENRY GEORGE LIDDELL and ROBERT SCOTT, eds., revised by HENRY STUART JONES and RODERICK MACKENZIE (Oxford, 1953).
MG.	A Concordance to the Greek Testament, W. F. MOULTON and A. S. GEDEN, eds. (Edinburgh, 1967, reprint of 4th ed.).
SB.	Kommentar zum Neuen Testament aus Talmud und Midrasch, H. L. STRACK and P. BILLERBECK, eds. (München, 1922–28).
SIG.	Sylloge Inscriptionum Graecarum, W. DITTENBERGER, ed. (Leipzig, 1915–24).
SVF.	Stoicorum Veterum Fragmenta, 4 vols., H. VON ARNIM, ed. (Berlin, 1903–1924).
St. Ev.	Studia Evangelica, 6 vols., F. L. CROSS, ed. (Berlin, 1956).
St. Pat.	Studia Patristica, 5 vols., F. L. CROSS, ed. (Berlin, 1957).
TDNT.	Theological Dictionary of the New Testament, 9 vols. (Grand Rapids, 1964–75), trans. by G. W. BROMILEY of: Theologisches Wörterbuch zum neuen Testament, G. KITTEL and G. FRIEDRICH, eds. (Stuttgart, 1933–70).

Journals

AJP.	American Journal of Philology.
BJRL.	Bulletin of the John Rylands Library.
CPhil.	Classical Philology.

CR.	Classical Review.
ET.	The Expository Times.
HT.	History and Theory.
HTR.	Havard Theological Review.
HUCA.	Hebrew Union College Annual.
JBL.	Journal of Biblical Literature.
JEH.	Journal of Ecclesiastical History.
JES.	Journal of Ecumenical Studies.
JHI.	Journal of the History of Ideas.
JJS.	Journal of Jewish Studies.
JQR.	Jewish Quarterly Review.
JRS.	Journal of Roman Studies.
JSS.	Journal of Semitic Studies.
JTS.	Journal of Theological Studies.
NT.	Novum Testamentum.
REJ.	Revue des Études Juives.
RQ.	Revue de Qumran.
RTR.	Reformed Theological Review.
SJT.	Scottish Journal of Theology.
SP.	Studia Philonica.
YCS.	Yale Classical Studies.
ZNW.	Zeitschrift für die Neutestamentliche Wissenschaft.

I rapporti tra l'impero romano e il mondo ebraico al tempo di Caligola secondo la 'Legatio ad Gaium' di Filone Alessandrino

di Clara Kraus Reggiani, Roma

Sommario

I. Il momento storico nella produzione filosofica di Filone

1. Interdipendenza dell''In Flaccum' e della 'Legatio ad Gaium'

Quando un filosofo di evidente orientamento mistico come Filone abbandona, in età ormai avanzata[1], il campo della metafisica, dell'etica pura, dell'allegoria biblica per avventurarsi sul terreno degli eventi storici e porsi di fronte a problemi politici di attualità, la forma del racconto e il modo dell'indagine non possono che recare viva l'impronta della sua forte e singolare personalità. Le conclusioni raggiunte rientrano in sede concettuale nel contesto di tutta la sua speculazione, che viene sempre più rivalutata dalla critica moderna delle più opposte tendenze, attraverso il riscatto da un ingiustificato isolamento: al pensatore di Alessandria spetta un posto ben preciso nell'ambito della grecità post-classica, perché è suo il merito di aver ideato quella filosofia d'ispirazione religiosa che, ben lungi dall'essere un tentativo marginale ed episodico di conciliazione dei concetti elaborati dai filosofi greci più vicini al problema del divino con i principi contenuti nel pensiero mosaico, determinò invece nella storia dello spirito il momento di frattura con il mondo del paganesimo greco-romano e il conseguente passaggio ad una speculazione nuova, che aveva il suo fulcro nel monoteismo puro di una religione rivelata.

Filone affrontò appunto con animo insieme di filosofo e di credente la realtà di un evento cruciale per il suo popolo, che nell'estate del 38 d. C. subì in Alessandria d'Egitto il primo pogrom di cui esista memoria storica[2]. Nella vicenda egli fu coinvolto di persona — prima come testimone oculare dei fatti, poi in qualità di membro o capo dell'ambasceria[3] inviata subito dopo a Caligola per rivendicare i diritti degli Ebrei alessandrini — e dei

---

[1] È ignota la data di composizione della 'Legatio ad Gaium' (quanto quella dell''In Flaccum'), ma in Leg. 1 e 182 F. dice di se stesso che era ormai vecchio all'epoca dell'ambasceria (40 d. C.); si deve dunque immaginare che fosse nato qualche decennio prima di Cristo. F. DELAUNAY, Philon d'Alexandrie, Parigi 1867, 1870², p. 12, fa risalire la nascita al 30 a. C. circa, O. STÄHLIN, Gesch. der griech. Literatur, II 1, Monaco 1920, p. 625, al 20 a. C., E. R. GOODENOUGH, An Introduction to Philo Judaeus, Yale Univ. Press 1940 e Oxford 1962², p. 2, propende per il 25 a. C., A. NAZZARO, Il problema cronologico della nascita di Filone Alessandrino, Rend. Acc. di Arch., Lett. e Belle Arti di Napoli XXXVIII, 1963, pp. 129—138, per il 15—10 a. C.

[2] L'anno del pogrom è indicato in Fl. 56, dove F. precisa che la plebaglia di Alessandria saccheggiò le merci degli Ebrei irrompendo nelle loro botteghe chiuse in segno di lutto per la morte di Drusilla, sorella di Caligola, avvenuta il 10 giugno del 38 d. C. (cfr. D. C. LIX,11,1 e CIL XIV Suppl. 4535 r. 29). Il periodo di lutto pare fosse prolungato in Alessandria fino ad agosto, perché dal racconto di F. (Fl. 26) risulta che l'aggressione agli Ebrei ebbe luogo dopo l'arrivo di Agrippa, il quale avendo atteso i venti etesii, per consiglio di Gaio, non poteva essere partito da Pozzuoli che circa trenta giorni dopo il solstizio d'estate, ossia verso il 20 luglio.

[3] Si deve a Giuseppe Flavio, AJ XVIII, 25, la notizia che F. fosse capo dell'ambasceria; l'autore allude a sé come al più anziano dei cinque delegati (Leg. 182).

particolari del pogrom diede una duplice versione: la più estesa nell' 'In Flaccum', la più concisa nella 'Legatio ad Gaium', di diversa lunghezza ma di uguale intensità drammatica, per il crudo realismo descrittivo cui fa da contrappunto un accorato commento. Due versioni dunque di una medesima testimonianza, di tanto più preziosa in quanto unica e certamente attendibile. Con la pregevolezza di tale unicità documentaria contrasta tuttavia, almeno all'apparenza, un dato paradossale: che nell' 'In Flaccum' la responsabilità dell'atto persecutorio è addossata al governatore di Alessandria, Avillio Flacco, nella 'Legatio' invece allo stesso imperatore Caligola. Lo sconcertante mutamento di visuale ha dato luogo a ipotesi interpretative più o meno plausibili[4]. L'atteggiamento di Filone non si presta in effetti ad alcuna spiegazione univoca e definitiva: le due tesi contrastanti sono sostenute con lo stesso fervore, ma in veste del tutto autonoma, senza il minimo accenno all' 'In Flaccum' nella 'Legatio' né viceversa. Data l'indubbia paternità filoniana di ambedue gli scritti, le radici di una contraddizione tanto palese vanno ricercate in motivazioni che non possono essere né di ordine storico né di natura politica. Uno scrittore di storia o un uomo politico avrebbero evitato di smentirsi così clamorosamente per non compromettere la propria attendibilità o la propria influenza. Ma l'interesse di Filone era rivolto altrove.

Si sarebbe tentati di immaginare — postulata, come sembra facilmente accertabile, l'anteriorità dell' 'In Flaccum' rispetto alla 'Legatio'[5] e con essa la completa indipendenza di uno scritto dall'altro[6] — che il filosofo, al tempo in cui stendeva la prima opera, pur conoscendo e condannando la crudeltà d'animo di Caligola, ignorasse la posizione ostile da lui assunta nei confronti degli Ebrei di Palestina, che è invece il motivo dominante dell'opera maggiore; in questo caso, solo più tardi, all'epoca dell'ambasceria a Roma, egli avrebbe collegato i fatti di Alessandria con quelli di Palestina, riconoscendo in Caligola il vero responsabile del pogrom e in Flacco, cui allude senza farne

---

[4] Limitando l'indicazione bibliografica a due casi-limite, ricorderemo che A. MOMIGLIANO, Aspetti dell'antisemitismo alessandrino in due opere di Filone, La Rassegna mensile di Israel, V 5—6, 1930, pp. 275—286, trovò nei particolari descrittivi e nel tono generale delle due versioni del pogrom lo spunto per datare le due opere — rispettivamente al 41 d. C. la 'Legatio' e al 53 d. C. l' 'In Flaccum' — non solo ponendo un forte stacco nei tempi di composizione, ma invertendone anche l'ordine, di contro all'opinione corrente, secondo la quale l' 'In Flaccum' precede la 'Legatio', e che il GOODENOUGH, Politics of Philo Judaeus, New Haven e Londra 1938, p. 7ss. e ID., Introduction cit., pp. 72—76, partendo da un'interpretazione in chiave strettamente politica riteneva che le due opposte visuali fossero ammissibili solo in quanto si trattava di due pamphlets polemici e occasionali.

[5] Ambedue gli scritti sono posteriori alla morte di Caligola, come si deduce dal tempo passato con cui F. si riferisce all'imperatore in Fl. 180 e dal modo scoperto di denunciare i suoi delitti in Fl. 10—15 e in Leg. 22—65. Un'aperta allusione alla sua morte (avvenuta il 24 gennaio 41, cfr. Suet. Cal. 59, 1) si legge in Leg. 107, mentre di un'esecuzione avvenuta durante il suo regno è data notizia in Leg. 206. — Per l'anteriorità dell' 'In Flaccum' rispetto alla 'Legatio' cfr. C. KRAUS, Filone Alessandrino e un'ora tragica della storia ebraica, Napoli 1967, p. 130s.

[6] Cfr. più avanti p. 574.

il nome, un connivente di secondo piano. Sennonché, nel caso di un tale ravvedimento, Filone non avrebbe avuto motivo di tacerlo; semmai, sarebbe stato indice di coerenza da parte sua denunciare apertamente, nella 'Legatio', la rettifica di visuale circa il vero responsabile del pogrom, con la stessa schiettezza con la quale dichiarava che le rivendicazioni degli Ebrei di Alessandria, dopo la tragedia del pogrom, perdevano ogni loro importanza di fronte al pericolo incombente sull'ebraismo nella sua totalità a seguito della politica di Gaio Caligola[7]. Il silenzio di Filone rimane un enigma insoluto e insolubile, quasi emblematico indizio della fluidità che la dimensione storica degli eventi assumeva nella sua visuale di assiduo ricercatore dei valori dello spirito e insieme concreta dimostrazione di quanto ambigui fossero, fin dal tempo del primo pogrom, il movente e il fine della persecuzione ebraica. Nel caso specifico, alla mente del filosofo appariva valido un solo postulato: che l'ideatore della persecuzione, in quanto irrazionale e inumana, doveva essere stato un uomo dalla mente sconvolta, fosse la sua follìa temporanea e fortuita (come nel caso di Flacco) oppure profonda e congenita (come nel caso di Caligola).

Proprio per l'insolubilità del quesito fin qui discusso è impossibile ignorare del tutto l''In Flaccum' quando si voglia comprendere a fondo la 'Legatio'. Ad un'attenta analisi, l''In Flaccum' risulta essere un vero e proprio trattato a tesi, ispirato al medesimo concetto che costituirà molto più tardi l'ossatura del 'De mortibus persecutorum' di Lattanzio: alla minuziosa descrizione del pogrom, che occupa quasi tutta la prima parte dello scritto (Fl. 21—103), è contrapposta nella seconda parte (Fl. 104—191) una descrizione altrettanto puntuale della morte di Flacco, che ha permesso o provocato la persecuzione. Il persecutore, sul quale si abbatte l'odio di Caligola per ragioni affatto estranee alla questione ebraica[8], soccombe alle stesse torture da lui lasciate infliggere ai perseguitati: la legge del contrappasso per analogia è incisivamente scandita dall'autore, nel corso di un racconto costruito secondo uno schema di rigida simmetria. La punizione di Flacco si attua in un modo idoneo ad avvalorare la tesi biblica che la provvidenza divina sta dalla parte del popolo di Israele.

2. Impostazione e contenuto della 'Legatio ad Gaium'

Del tutto diversa è l'impostazione della 'Legatio'[9], opera di carattere essenzialmente narrativo, che di contro alla brevità e alla linearità dell''In

---

[7] Leg. 193s.

[8] Aulo Avillio Flacco, nominato prefetto d'Egitto da Tiberio nel 32 d. C., era amico del prefetto del pretorio Macrone (cfr. n. 18) e sostenitore di Tiberio Gemello nella successione all'impero (cfr. n. 17). Cadde dunque vittima dell'odio di Caligola, al pari di Macrone (Fl. 13—16 e Leg. 32—62) e di Tiberio Gemello (Leg. 22—31), come oppositore del suo potere, a un anno di distanza dai primi due, nel 38 d. C., in seguito alla commutazione dell'esilio nell'isola di Andros in condanna a morte (Fl. 51 e 180—185).

[9] L'ediz. critica fondamentale del testo greco della 'Legatio' rimane tuttora quella di COHN—WENDLAND—REITER, Philonis Alexandrini opera quae supersunt, Berlino 1896

Flaccum' presenta un'estensione doppia (373 paragrafi) e un estremo disordine strutturale. Prima di accedere alla complessa problematica che lo scritto propone, è necessario esaminarne il contenuto, secondo la suddivisione da noi già altrove prospettata[10]. Nella 'Legatio' si intrecciano quattro tematiche: 1. la delineazione del carattere di Caligola; 2. il pogrom di Alessandria d'Egitto e la situazione della diaspora alessandrina; 3. i fatti di Palestina e il problema ebraico in senso lato; 4. i particolari relativi all'ambasceria, che non rientrano in un settore specifico dell'opera, ma affiorano lungo tutto il contesto, costituendo sul piano psicologico l'elemento di raccordo delle altre parti.

In un breve proemio (§§ 1—7) Filone enuncia una tesi di carattere generale, muovendo dalla constatazione che le creature umane, nella loro cecità, sarebbero irrimediabilmente sommerse dal caos degli eventi legati al caso (τύχη) senza l'intervento provvidenziale dell'Essere supremo (πρόνοια θεοῦ). Scaturisce di qui la più ispirata esaltazione di Dio che Filone abbia mai scritto e che trova riscontro solo in analoghe esaltazioni della letteratura liturgica. Lo scetticismo di coloro che ancora si agitano nel dubbio sarà vinto — egli dice — dalla testimonianza del popolo ebraico che attraverso la propria esperienza mistica ha avuto il privilegio di „vedere Dio" e ne gode la protezione[11]. Infine, trasferendo alla sfera del divino un'argomentazione applicata da Platone al campo della giustizia umana, nel passo del Protagora (232D—324C) in cui sostiene il fine benefico e paradigmatico delle punizioni inflitte al reo di una qualunque colpa, Filone afferma che Dio, in quanto si identifica con il sommo bene, non può largire che il bene ed esplica quindi a fine benefico anche i suoi poteri punitivi. L'umanità comune, cui è preclusa la facoltà di distinguere il contingente dall'essenziale nella sua vicenda terrena, tanto meno sa riconoscere il bene nel male quando è sottoposta a prove che sembrano insostenibili e tali sono per chi non le accetta e le supera confidando in quel bene supremo cui esse sono tramite e delle quali Dio si serve come di uno strumento di salvezza.

—1930, 7 voll. (nel vol. VI a cura di COHN—REITER, 1915). Il testo con traduz. tedesca rientra nell'ediz. di COHN—HEINEMANN—ADLER—THEILER, Die Werke Philos von Alexandria, Breslavia 1909—1964, 7 voll.; con traduz. inglese nell'ediz. del COLSON, Philo, Londra 1937—1943, 10 voll.; con traduz. francese nel vol. 32, a cura di A. PELLETIER (1973), nella collana diretta da ARNALDEZ—POUILLOUX—MONDÉSERT per le Édit. du Cerf di Parigi. Quest'ultima ediz. è concepita in forma monografica, con ampio comm. introduttivo e ricche appendici, ma ha il suo precedente nel lavoro di E. MARY SMALLWOOD, Legatio ad Gaium, Leida 1961, che — in parallelo con l'ediz. altrettanto fondamentale dell'In Flaccum', dovuta a H. BOX (Oxford 1939) — fu la prima a pubblicare l'opera corredandola, oltre che della traduz. inglese, di un'introduzione storica di gran pregio e di un commento di non comune dottrina, ricco di precisazioni linguistiche, filologiche, storico-cronologiche, epigrafiche ecc., tanto esauriente in ogni senso da essere strumento prezioso per lo studio della 'Legatio', da qualsiasi punto di vista la si voglia considerare. Meno approfondito l'esame della personalità di F., che la studiosa pospone ai suoi interessi di ricercatrice storica, erudita e profonda.

[10] C. KRAUS, op. cit., p. 61.

[11] Per la falsa etimologia del nome 'Israele' cfr. l'ampia e documentata spiegazione della SMALLWOOD, Legatio, pp. 153—155.

Il tema della provvidenza ricorre nella 'Legatio' solo entro le parti auto-
biografiche relative all'ambasceria e forse era teoricamente sviluppato nella
sezione finale mancante dell'opera; ma tutto il racconto storico dei fatti si
snoda sopra un unico motivo di fondo: la lotta inerme della pietà umana e
religiosa del popolo ebraico contro l'empietà disumana e profanatrice di
Caligola.

II. Un'interpretazione significativa della figura di Caligola

1. La tradizione storica su Caligola

Dal proemio di ispirazione religiosa si passa bruscamente a una prima
lunga sezione (§§ 8—113), nella quale Filone analizza in modo aspramente
polemico la personalità dell'imperatore Gaio Caligola (38—41 d. C.), met-
tendone in luce quegli aspetti negativi che servono ad illustrare le ragioni
della sua politica antiebraica, nelle due fasi successive del pogrom di Alessandria e della tentata violazione del Tempio di Gerusalemme. Per quanto lo
spunto sia dei più particolaristici, il ritratto di Caligola che emerge da questa
singolare analisi acquista valore documentario di grande rilievo, quando se
ne consideri l'unicità rispetto al resto della tradizione storica. L'urto tra
Caligola e l'ebraismo poteva interessare soltanto gli scrittori ebrei oppure un
nemico giurato del mondo giudaico quale fu Tacito. Ma sventuratamente la
testimonianza tacitiana è andata perduta con il naufragio della parte degli
'Annales' concernente Caligola (libri VII—X, perché nella sezione mutila
del l. XI la narrazione riprende dall'anno 47 d. C.), nella quale — a giudicare
dall'allusione ai fatti di Palestina in un passo delle 'Historiae'[12] — è lecito
supporre che l'argomento fosse trattato diffusamente. Nulla di apprezzabile
circa la figura dell'imperatore si legge nelle 'Antiquitates Judaicae' di Giuseppe Flavio, l'unica fonte ebraica parallela a Filone, dove c'è un'ampia
relazione sui fatti di Palestina (AJ XVIII, 261—309), ma appena un fugace
accenno al pogrom di Alessandria (ibid. 257—260), in quanto causa occasionale dell'invio a Gaio delle due opposte ambascerie, greca ed ebraica.
Nessuna allusione all'odio di Caligola per gli Ebrei nella vita suetoniana e
nel lacunoso libro LIX di Dione Cassio, le due sole fonti pagane superstiti,
utili alla ricostruzione del breve principato di Gaio. Da esse si ricava tuttavia
una sicura testimonianza circa la follìa e l'efferatezza del giovane principe,
confermate peraltro entrambe anche da Seneca[13], che ebbe a farne esperienza
diretta, e dallo stesso Tacito[14], in una frase breve ma significativa. Filone,

---

[12] Tac., Hist. V, 9: *Dein iussi a C. Caesare effigiem eius in templo locare arma potius sumpsere,
quem motum Caesaris mors diremit.*

[13] Sen., Cons. ad Helv. 10: *C. Caesar, quem mihi videtur rerum natura edidisse ut ostenderet
quid summa vitia in summa fortuna possent.* Cfr. anche De ira I, 20; III, 18—20, 22.

[14] Tac., Ann. VI, 20: *immanem animum subdola modestia tegens.*

come Seneca, aveva conosciuto Caligola di persona e durante il soggiorno in
Italia aveva raccolto tutte le voci che correvano sul suo conto, certo ingi-
gantite dagli informatori, i quali dovevano essere stati in gran parte Ebrei
di Roma. Nessuno meglio di loro, cultori del monoteismo, avrebbe potuto
cogliere l'aspetto sacrilego della pretesa di Gaio alla deificazione in vita,
nessuno meglio di Filone sarebbe stato in grado di dare un volto e una fisionomia precisa all'imperiale dissacratore della divinità. Se si ritengono, per
esempio, storicamente validi i contorni che la figura di Traiano presenta nel
'Panegirico' di Plinio il Giovane, in vista della circostanza che l'imperatore
in questione era degno delle lodi a lui tributate, e non si riconosce quindi
nella veste encomiastica un motivo di pregiudizio all'attendibilità della fonte,
altrettanto deve valere in senso opposto per la veste fortemente sarcastica
dell'invettiva filoniana, nei confronti di un imperatore la cui crudeltà mentale trova esplicita conferma nelle fonti sopra citate, immuni da ogni sospetto
di tendenziosità.

2. La follìa di Caligola e la sua pretesa alla deificazione in vita

All'invettiva vera e propria Filone premette il racconto delle vicende di
Caligola, dal momento della sua salita al potere. È un periodo di speciale
floridezza dell'impero e i sudditi accolgono con entusiasmo il nuovo principe;
ma la loro gioia sarà di breve durata, perché all'ottavo mese di regno Gaio
è colpito da grave malattia, in conseguenza della vita dissoluta che conduce
da quando è scomparso Tiberio[15]. Poi, sembra riprendersi dal male: una
ripresa effimera, che deluderà ben presto la speranza di un ritorno alla nor-
malità (§§ 8—21). In effetti, Gaio è radicalmente trasformato: la sua natura
crudele esplode trovando sfogo nell'eliminazione delle persone a lui più vicine.
La sua follìa miete tre vittime, costrette una dopo l'altra al suicidio per
motivi speciosi[16], nelle persone del cugino adolescente, Tiberio Gemello,
designato da Tiberio a suo coerede dell'impero (§§ 22—31)[17], del prefetto
del pretorio Macrone, che lo ha aiutato ad assicurarsi il principato (§§ 32—

---

[15] In pieno contrasto con F., secondo il quale Tiberio avrebbe esercitato su Gaio un'azione
di freno (Leg. 14), Suetonio afferma che il futuro imperatore indulgeva ad ogni sorta di
vizi, ancor vivo Tiberio (Cal. 11).

[16] La successione delle morti (che non si può ricostruire da Suetonio) è in Dione Cassio diversa: i suicidi di Tiberio Gemello e di Silano sono posti alla fine del 37 (LIX, 8, 1 e 4), quello
di Macrone, che nell'ordine viene ad essere il terzo anziché il secondo come in F., doveva
essere avvenuto nella prima metà del 38, a poca distanza dei due precedenti (LIX, 10, 6).

[17] Mentre l'imperatore eletto, Gaio Cesare Caligola, era erede in linea indiretta, in quanto
figlio di Germanico Cesare (a sua volta figlio di Druso maggiore, fratello di Tiberio), Tiberio
Gemello, nato nel 19 d. C., era erede diretto, in quanto figlio di Druso minore (figlio di
Tiberio) e fratello gemello di Germanico, morto nel 23 d. C. La designazione esplicita di
Tiberio Gemello a coerede dell'impero si ritrova solo in D. C. LIX, 1, 2—3, mentre è
ambigua la versione dei fatti data da Suet., Tib. 76 e Cal. 14, 1. Per il controverso problema
circa la successione di Tiberio cfr. SMALLWOOD, Legatio, pp. 169—171.

42)[18], del padre della moglie defunta, Silano (§§ 62—65)[19]. Tuttavia, l'ascendente di Gaio sull'opinione pubblica non subisce scosse; anzi, ognuno dei tre crimini è giustificato come atto di legittima difesa della dignità imperiale.

Eliminati gli oppositori del dispotismo, l'imperatore avanza la sua pretesa alla deificazione in vita[20], e per impressionare la fantasia dei sudditi ricorre agli accorgimenti più stravaganti, come quello di travestirsi, indossando di volta in volta gli abbigliamenti dei semidei e delle divinità con cui intende di essere identificato, e sfoggiandone i simboli. Di queste sue esibizioni istrionesche parla anche Dione Cassio (LIX, 26, 5—10), il quale tuttavia non vi scorge altro che una delle tante estrosità del principe maniaco, fissato nell'idea di avere una natura „più che umana". Filone invece ravvisa nelle farse inscenate da Gaio la sacrilega profanazione di quei valori assoluti del divino che la sua anima religiosa rispetta finanche nelle forme della simbologia pagana. Diversa è nei due autori anche la struttura della narrazione, che in Dione Cassio non segue alcun ordine preciso e occupa poco spazio, mentre in Filone ha uno sviluppo ampio e si svolge secondo una schema retorico, elaborato fino alla minuzia. Vi si trova applicata in maniera singolare la tecnica del simbolismo, che è la stessa dei trattati filoniani dell'allegoria biblica. Così risponde ad un metodo preciso il ritmo triadico delle argomentazioni: tre sono state le vittime di Gaio (Tiberio Gemello, Macrone, Silano), tre le parti vitali dello stato che essi simboleggiavano (la famiglia imperiale, il senato, l'ordine equestre), tre saranno i semidei (Eracle, Dioniso, i Dioscuri), tre le divinità (Ermes, Apollo, Ares) cui Gaio pretenderà di uguagliarsi.

Dei tre semidei sono analizzate le virtù secondo l'ordine dato (§§ 78—85), mentre il confronto con i vizi opposti di Gaio viene fatto in ordine inverso rispetto ai Dioscuri, a Dioniso, a Eracle (§§ 86—92): all'amore fraterno, di

---

[18] Per Macrone cfr. E. STEIN, RE XVI, 2, 1935, col. 1565ss., s. v. Naevius. Il nome completo è Q. Naevius Sutorius Macro, prefetto del pretorio dal 31 d. C. dopo la morte di Seiano, da lui stesso catturato per ordine di Tiberio il 18 ottobre di quell'anno (D. C. LXIII, 10). È descritto da Tacito (Ann. VI, 29) come uomo privo di scrupoli, non meno di Seiano sospettato da Tiberio di connivenza con Gaio Caligola (Ann. VI, 48). La caratterizzazione del personaggio in F. si discosta dalle altre fonti, mentre non differiscono sostanzialmente da esse i particolari storici (cfr. D. C. LVIII, 9—10 e Suet. Cal. 12, 3—4 e 26,1).

[19] Per M. Junius Silanus cfr. E. HOHL, RE X 1, 1917, coll. 1097—1098, s. v. Junius. Silano, che fu consul suffectus nel 15 d. C., aveva goduto di grande autorità sotto Tiberio (D. C. LIX, 8, 5; Tac., Ann. V, 10) e, secondo tutte le fonti, fu costretto al suicidio da Caligola (Suet., Cal. 23, 3; D. C. LIX, 4, 5). La figlia Giunia Claudia (Tac., Ann. VI, 20) o Claudilla (Suet., Cal. 12, 1—2), mai citata per nome né da F. né da Dione Cassio, sposò Caligola presumibilmente nel 33 d. C. (Tac., l. cit.) e morì, sembra di parto (Suet., Cal. 12, 2; Tac., Ann. VI, 45) prima che Caligola assumesse l'impero.

[20] Nota la SMALLWOOD (Legatio, pp. 191—192) che F. ha volutamente anticipato alla prima metà del 38 d. C. la pretesa di Caligola alla deificazione, per poter riferire ad essa i disordini di Alessandria. Giuseppe Flavio (AJ XVIII, 256) fissa l'epoca al 39, dopo ben due anni di buon governo; Dione Cassio (LIX, 26, 5—28, 8) la sposta al 40, rilevando però che l'idea risaliva a un periodo anteriore (ibid. 26, 5). Oltre a Dione Cassio, che ne parla diffusamente, qualche accenno alla deificazione si trova in Sen., De ira III, 30, 8—9; 32; 52, in Jos., AJ XVIII, 256; XIX, 4 e 11; Suet., Cal. 22, 3; 33, 1; 52, 2 e in Aur. Victor., Liber de Caesar. 3, 10.

cui sono emblema i Dioscuri, è contrapposto l'odio del principe per i propri
congiunti, alla mitezza di Dioniso la sua crudeltà, ai benefici largiti da
Eracle agli uomini la sua sete insaziata di devastare il mondo intero. L'analisi
delle virtù di Ermes Apollo e Ares e dei vizi contrari di Gaio avviene invece
secondo una linea parallela: prima il confronto con Ermes (§§ 99—102), poi
con Apollo (§§ 103—110), infine con Ares (§§ 111—113). Ermes è messaggero
veloce di liete novelle, Gaio propagatore solerte di notizie funeste; Apollo è la
luce, Gaio la tenebra; Ares la forza che allontana il male, Gaio la quintes-
senza della depravazione.

Per quanto pazzo e mitomane, Gaio è consapevole della resistenza che
gli Ebrei opporranno alla sua pretesa di ottenere culto divino da tutti i
sudditi dell'impero; anzi, proprio in quanto conosce il loro attaccamento
alle tradizioni avite, egli scatenerà contro l'ebraismo la guerra più spietata
(§§ 114—119).

3. Il pogrom del 38 d. C. ad Alessandria d'Egitto

Si innesta qui, con logica coerente al contesto, la descrizione del pogrom (§§ 120—131), che è poco estesa ma corrisponde, a grandi linee, all'altra più particolareggiata dell''In Flaccum'. Prevenendo le intenzioni di
Caligola, la plebaglia di Alessandria attacca gli Ebrei, con il duplice scopo
di sfogare l'odio che nutre nei loro confronti e di ingraziarsi l'imperatore.
Dunque, la presupposizione non espressa è che l'iniziativa della massa ano-
nima abbia il suo movente in un atteggiamento antiebraico del principe di
cui sia giunta in Egitto sicura notizia. Gli Ebrei sono cacciati dalle loro case
e assistono al saccheggio dei propri averi, messi in vendita sulle piazze, alla
luce del sole. Spinti a migliaia in uno spazio ristrettissimo, essi rischiano di
morire soffocati a cielo scoperto, a causa dell'aria ammorbata dal loro stesso
respiro. Si riversano allora sulle spiagge e nei cimiteri, mentre gruppi di
altri, catturati prima o giunti dopo dalla campagna, vengono uccisi a sassa-
te o a percosse. Chiunque cerchi di evadere è arso vivo oppure trascinato per
le caviglie lungo le vie della città, fino a ridursi ad una massa informe. L'ar-
dimento degli aggressori è alimentato dall'indifferenza del prefetto romano
che non interviene; e comincia l'assalto alle sinagoghe. Nel corso delle deva-
stazioni e degli incendi vanno distrutti gli oggetti dedicati agli imperatori
e le case adiacenti. Le sinagoghe superstiti vengono profanate: in ognuna si
collocano statue di Gaio, nella maggiore e più venerata si trasporta dal
ginnasio una sua effigie in bronzo posta sopra una vecchia quadriga.

4. I predecessori di Caligola, con una delineazione in chiave etica del prin-
cipato augusteo

Quest'ultimo particolare, in sé di ben scarso rilievo, dà l'avvio ad una
lunga digressione (§§ 138—160), nel corso della quale l'autore ribadisce insi-

stentemente il concetto di quanto indegno sia Gaio del culto che pretende gli venga tributato in vita, dimostrandolo attraverso una serie di confronti. Nessuno dei Tolomei — egli rileva — in trecento anni di regno ha mai accampato diritti su simili onoranze, che pure sarebbe stato facile ottenere da un popolo come l'egiziano, abituato a rendere culto persino agli animali. La stessa considerazione vale per Tiberio e per Augusto, dei quali Filone tesse un elogio. L'accenno ai meriti di Tiberio è molto conciso: in sostanza, il defunto imperatore è chiamato in causa solo in quanto si presta ad essere contrapposto a Gaio, per il suo amore della pace, per la saggezza e la serietà del carattere (§§ 140—142). Molto più esteso e soprattutto molto più interessante sotto il profilo storico il giudizio su Augusto. Indubbiamente l'autore, nel delineare il carattere e l'azione politica dei tre imperatori di casa Giulio-Claudia, durante il principato dei quali si svolse l'arco della sua vita, è mosso da spirito di parte: il suo metro di valutazione, infatti, è commisurato sempre e soltanto all'atteggiamento assunto da ciascuno dei tre principi nei confronti dell'ebraismo. Tuttavia da quello che può definirsi un vero e proprio panegirico di Augusto (§§ 143—158) si raccolgono alcune indicazioni tutt'altro che prive d'interesse, che sono tenute in pochissimo conto quando si deplora la perdita dell'intera tradizione letteraria diretta, coeva al primo imperatore di Roma: nelle sporadiche citazioni che se ne fanno, esse occupano un posto del tutto marginale, in parallelo con qualche frase isolata del contemporaneo Strabone, a semplice conferma del fatto che l'opinione pubblica del tempo riconosceva la grandezza di Augusto e giudicava il suo un monarcato assoluto, ma utile e necessario in rapporto alla situazione interna ed esterna di Roma. Questo fu di certo il convincimento di Strabone, che definiva ,,assoluto" il potere di Augusto (VI, 4, 2 p. 288C), individuando in lui ,,un capo dell'impero con pieni poteri, arbitro a vita della guerra e della pace" (XVII, 3, 5 p. 840). L'idea fu condivisa del resto, anche da autori di età più tarda come Tacito (Hist. I, 1; Ann. I, 2), Suetonio (Aug. 28) e persino da Dione Cassio (LIII, 16, 1), il quale peraltro prospettò anche la tesi opposta — propugnata dallo stesso imperatore nelle sue 'Res gestae' — di una monarchia temperata e rispettosa delle libertà repubblicane. A tale alternativa fa capo il contrasto di opinioni circa il fondamento giuridico del principato augusteo che la storiografia moderna non ha mai cessato di dibattere. È evidente che la testimonianza filoniana non può portare un contributo tangibile al chiarimento della ,,questione augustea"; ma stupisce che studiosi come la SMALLWOOD e il PELLETIER, il quale ne cita il giudizio dichiarando di condividerlo, ritengano Filone ,,capace di riconoscere, a sessant'anni di distanza, la vera natura del monarcato costituzionale di Augusto"[21]. A nostro

---

21 SMALLWOOD, Legatio, p. 228; PELLETIER, Legatio, p. 168, n. 3. L'asserzione assiomatica della SMALLWOOD sembra voler assegnare a Filone un ruolo dirimente nella definizione dei caratteri singolari del principato augusteo. Ma, come cerchiamo di dimostrare nel contesto della nostra trattazione, i termini del problema non sono così semplici. Si è evitato di proposito, non essendo questo il nostro compito, di ripercorrere qui le lunghe e complesse diatribe moderne sulla 'questione augustea', che d'altronde si trovano già condensate nel sintetico e lucidissimo resoconto di S. MAZZARINO (Il pensiero storico classico, Roma

avviso, se c'era un aspetto del principato augusteo che non poteva interessare né colpire l'attenzione di Filone era proprio quello del fondamento giuridico su cui esso si basava. Nel formulare il suo giudizio su Augusto il filosofo oscillava, come in ogni altro tema da lui affrontato, tra due opposti poli, che lo portavano da un lato alla tensione verso l'astratto, dall'altro al senso pieno della concretezza. A chi esamini con occhio spassionato l'estesa esaltazione della pace augustea (§§ 143—149), non può sfuggire che sono ripresi in essa molti dei luoghi comuni divulgati dalla poesia celebrativa dell'epoca e che di filoniano c'è solo il climax degli spunti elogiativi, sottolineato da una certa ampollosità lessicale. Ma tipica di Filone è invece la strutturazione concettuale di fondo. La pace che Augusto ha assicurato all'impero va vista come il frutto della coesistenza in lui di due doti che, se riunite in un principe, rendono perfetto il suo governo: la dirittura morale (§ 143: καλοκἀγαθία) e l'acume politico (§ 149: ἡγεμονικὴ ἐπιστήμη). Secondo l'autore, lo stesso titolo di 'Augusto' è stato tributato all'imperatore in vista delle sue virtù morali eccedenti la normale misura umana, prima ancora che per il potere assoluto di cui dispone. Ancora una volta Filone ha

1968, III, p. 263ss.). Rimane comunque accertato che gli studiosi del nostro secolo hanno chiamato in causa Filone solo come fonte accessoria, con riferimento all'uso di certa terminologia che era di uso ufficiale ai suoi tempi o a notazioni isolate, senza approfondire la posizione altrettanto interessante quanto soggettiva da lui assunta sul tema. — In questa sede ci limitiamo a registrare alcune delle citazioni tratte dalla 'Legatio' e secondariamente dall'In Flaccum', presenti in scritti che hanno per oggetto Augusto e le perculiarità del governo da lui instaurato. — Accenna a Filone in quanto assertore di un potere assoluto assunto da Augusto N. A. MASCKIN (Il principato di Augusto, Roma 1956, II, p. 5), il quale sottolinea la coincidenza dell'opinione di un autore che parla dell'imperatore a una distanza relativamente breve dalla sua morte con quella di Strabone, suo contemporaneo. Allo stesso proposito tale coincidenza è messa in luce da P. DE FRANCISCI in 'Genesi e struttura del principato augusteo' (Atti della Reale Accademia d'Italia, Memorie della classe di scienze morali e storiche, Roma 1941, VII, 2,1). A p. 5 e p. 35 del suo ampio saggio il DE FRANCISCI riporta la motivazione dell'appellativo di 'Augusto' addotta da Filone in Leg. 143: ὁ διὰ μέγεθος ἡγεμονίας αὐτοκρατοῦς ὁμοῦ καὶ καλοκἀγαθίας πρῶτος ὀνομασθεὶς Σεβαστός, a comprova della tesi di una concentrazione di poteri assoluti nelle mani del principes, in parallelo con l'analoga testimonianza di Strabone (VI, 4, 2 p. 288 e XVII, 3, 25 p. 840) — tesi non condivisa dallo studioso che vede il principato augusteo come „un regime sostanzialmente monarchico innestato sulle istituzioni repubblicane formalmente conservate" (ibid., p. 7). È citato inoltre Fl. 105 a testimonianza dell'arbitrio e della corruzione di taluni governatori delle province all'epoca di Augusto e di Tiberio. — Sotto il profilo della terminologia e di alcuni concetti specifici Filone è citato da J. BÉRANGER in 'Recherches sur l'aspect idéologique du principat', Basel 1953. A p. 44 n. 73 c'è un richiamo a Leg. 19, 24, 44, 318 dove l'imperatore è designato con il nome di ἡγεμών = princeps, a dimostrazione del fatto che si tratta di un termine tecnico ricorrente in documenti epigrafici e in editti dell'età giulio-claudia, di cui è dato l'elenco. A p. 178 n. 53 è riportata l'espressione che si legge in Leg. 27: τὸ βάρος τῆς ἡγεμονίας = pondus o moles imperii, come corrispondente di Ovidio, Tristia II, 221 e Fasti VI, 645, di Tacito, Ann. I, 11, 1, di Plinio, Paneg. V, 6. A p. 182 i πόνοι del potere sono paragonati alle fatiche di Eracle, secondo Leg. 90. A p. 206 è riportata la frase: τὴν ἐπιμέλειαν καὶ προστασίαν εἰς δυναστείαν καὶ τυραννίδα μεθαρμοσάμενοι di Fl. 105, già citata dal DE FRANCISCI (v. sopra), a conferma della circostanza che la 'cura ac tutela rei publicae' poteva degenerare in tirannide, data l'impercettibilità del limite di trapasso dalla forma di governo migliore alla deteriore.

sostituito una motivazione di ordine etico-filosofico ad una argomentazione di ordine politico-costituzionale e ha dato quindi una propria interpretazione, sia pure poco realistica, del principato augusteo. Quanto peso abbia la componente etica nella valutazione complessiva è dimostrato da una correlazione quasi impercettibile; infatti, il concetto di καλοκἀγαθία dell'esordio è ripreso nella conclusione dell'elogio, dove al dato della dirittura morale legata alla persona si aggiunge quello della generosità nel senso più lato del termine: Augusto non fu soltanto καλὸς καὶ ἀγαθός per una spinta egocentrica, ma fu l'uomo che ,,durante la sua vita non tenne mai nascosta cosa che fosse nobile (καλόν) o buona (ἀγαθόν)'' (§ 147), in altre parole non fu solo il largitore di benefici materiali, bensì anche il maestro di principi etici. L'interpretazione in chiave moralistica di un personaggio che fu certamente dotato di inconsueta abilità politica acquisterebbe in originalità e in valore se non si scoprisse che essa serve da premessa ad un secondo elogio nel quale Filone esalta la tolleranza religiosa di Augusto nei confronti di tutti i popoli dell'impero e degli Ebrei in particolare. Per rispetto alle loro patrie tradizioni egli non ha mai fatto introdurre in alcuna sinagoga una statua che lo rappresentasse e ha concesso loro speciali privilegi. Tra l'altro ha riconosciuto agli Ebrei di Roma il diritto di godere della cittadinanza romana pur mantenendo anche quella ebraica ed ha arricchito di doni suoi personali il Tempio di Gerusalemme, oltre ad istituirvi sacrifici quotidiani e perpetui a proprie spese (§§ 153—158).

L'infondatezza di quest'ultima notizia[22] potrebbe coinvolgere, invalidandole, ognuna delle asserzioni precedenti; sennonché il ricorso all'iperbole non tanto ha lo scopo di sottolineare il pieno riconoscimento del culto ebraico da parte di Augusto, quanto piuttosto di approfondire ulteriormente il contrasto tra il suo atteggiamento filoebraico e la politica antiebraica di Caligola, e più ancora la contrapposizione dell'autocrazia liberale di Augusto al dispotismo schiavistico di quest'ultimo.

Sulla medesima linea della deformazione storica subordinata al fine di dimostrare come i predecessori di Caligola nutrissero simpatia per gli Ebrei si colloca la notizia relativa a Tiberio che segue nel testo (§§ 159—161): Filone accenna a provvedimenti presi dal successore di Augusto a danno degli Ebrei d'Italia e forse dell'intera diaspora per istigazione di Seiano, provvedimenti che però sarebbero stati revocati subito dopo la condanna a morte del prefetto del pretorio. L'iniziativa della persecuzione è dunque attribuita a Seiano, mentre a Tiberio viene assegnato il ruolo di vittima di un inganno[23].

---

[22] Il particolare è in effetti privo di fondamento storico. Giuseppe Flavio (c. Ap. II, 77) dice che i sacrifici quotidiani erano finanziati dall'intera comunità ebraica. Il Momigliano (CAH X, 329) ritiene che essi fossero istituiti da Erode il Grande e F. qui deformi la verità per dimostrare la completa adesione di Augusto al culto ebraico.

[23] Di una persecuzione ebraica architettata da Seiano non parla nessun autore all'infuori di F., il quale doveva invece avervi almeno accennato nella parte iniziale dell''In Flaccum' (ritenuto appunto uno scritto acefalo), a giudicare dalle parole con cui si apre l'opera nella forma in cui la possediamo: ,,Secondo dopo Seiano, quasi ne avesse raccolto l'eredità,

III. Le vicende dell'ambasceria ebraica a Roma in correlazione con i fatti di Palestina del 39/40 d. C.

1. Primi faticosi contatti degli ambasciatori ebrei con Caligola

Il racconto interrotto al § 119 riprende al § 162, con un rinnovato spostamento di scena da Alessandria a Roma. Qui, Caligola si va sempre più convincendo di essere veramente un dio, confortato nei suoi vaneggiamenti dalle lusinghe di uno stuolo di Egiziani, il cui capo — Elicone — è un personaggio astuto e losco, che funge da *longa manus* all'ambasceria dei Greci alessandrini, venuta per controbattere le richieste degli Ebrei. È questa la prima volta che Filone accenna alle due opposte ambascerie simultaneamente presenti a Roma (§§ 172—174), parlandone come di cosa già nota. Si svolge dietro alle quinte una serie di intrighi, fomentati da Elicone, che i Greci hanno corrotto con forti somme di danaro; ed ha inizio — con la descrizione degli inutili sforzi fatti dai delegati ebrei per sventare il complotto — la vera e propria 'Legatio', la quale si riduce a ben poca cosa, in quanto resoconto dell'ambasceria: tra il primo rapido incontro con Caligola (§§ 178—185) e l'unica, farsesca udienza (§§ 349—373) è inserito un racconto minuzioso dei fatti di Palestina[24], che in senso stretto sono un parallelo dei disordini di Alessandria, ma in senso lato ampliano la visuale, spostandola dai problemi locali alla questione ebraica nella sua totalità. Da questo momento Filone assume nella narrazione il ruolo di personaggio, in nome dell'ambasceria di cui fa parte, ricollegando di volta in volta le notizie provenienti dalla Palestina con le impressioni che esse suscitano in lui e negli altri quattro delegati.

Costretti dall'impossibilità di essere ricevuti da Caligola, gli ambasciatori ebrei gli fanno pervenire un memoriale, il cui contenuto rimane ignoto. Ha quindi luogo un breve incontro a distanza con l'imperatore, sulla riva

Avillio Flacco riprese il piano di aggressione contro gli Ebrei." L'unica ipotesi formulabile è che F. addossasse a Seiano — ingigantendo e deformando i fatti — la responsabilità di aver provocato a suo tempo le misure repressive prese da Tiberio nei confronti della diaspora ebraica, nel 19 d. C. Sulla natura di tali provvedimenti si ricavano dalle fonti notizie molto contrastanti (cfr. Tac., Ann. II, 85; Suet., Tib. 36; Jos., AJ XVIII, 81—84), ma dovette trattarsi di esportazioni e di minacce di espulsione. Per quanto concerne l'ipotetica persecuzione di Seiano cfr. E. M. SMALLWOOD, Some notes on the Jews under Tiberius, Latomus XV, 1956, pp. 322—329. Forse aveva già colto nel segno E. T. MERRILL, The Expulsion of Jews from Rome under Tiberius, Class. Philol. XIV, 1919, pp. 365—372, secondo il quale F. avrebbe attribuito a Seiano l'istigazione a perseguitare gli Ebrei per non smentire la sua tesi che prima di Caligola nessun imperatore era stato loro ostile.

[24] Il racconto dei fatti di Palestina occupa largo spazio (Leg. 199—348) ed è la parte documentata anche da Giuseppe Flavio (BJ II, 185—203; AJ XVIII, 261—309), ma in due versioni che non solo sono attinte da una fonte del tutto divergente da F., bensì risultano anche discordanti tra loro in molti particolari. Il raffronto dei due testi, filoniano e flaviano, pone quindi dei problemi più che risolvere le più gravi difficoltà.

destra del Tevere, nei giardini di Agrippina, che si risolve in un suo cenno
di benevolo saluto ai delegati e nella vaga promessa di un prossimo colloquio (§§ 180—183).

Per seguire Gaio, la delegazione si sposta a Pozzuoli dove apprende da
un anonimo personaggio ebreo i gravi avvenimenti di Palestina, attraverso
un racconto che ha tutte le caratteristiche di una ῥῆσις ἀγγελική da tragedia (§§ 184—260). A Gerusalemme si sta per commettere un sacrilegio
perché Gaio ha dato l'ordine di erigere nel Tempio una statua che lo rap-
presenti, sotto il nome di Zeus Epifane. La notizia provoca disperazione
nei delegati ebrei che si sentono oppressi in ugual misura dal peso della responsabilità implicita nella loro missione presso l'imperatore e dall'angoscioso
interrogativo di quale possa essere, nel disegno di Dio, il fine ultimo della
sciagura che incombe sul mondo ebraico. In forma dubitativa Filone esprime
quella che è la sua personale convinzione: forse quella sciagura è solo un male
apparente, mandato da Dio per mettere gli Ebrei alla prova e consentire
loro di ricavarne liberamente il bene — un bene che non è un dono gratuito,
bensì sofferta conquista (§ 196).

2. I disordini provocati in Palestina dalla pretesa di Caligola alla deificazione

In Palestina la popolazione è in rivolta, sia pure inerme. La causa reale
della minacciata profanazione del Tempio è la pretesa di Gaio alla deificazione in vita (§§ 197—198); la causa occasionale è stata offerta dall'episodio
di Iamnia in Giudea (§§ 199—202), che Filone ricostruisce sulla falsariga
dei disordini di Alessandria. La popolazione ebraica del luogo reagisce questa
volta violentemente a un atto provocatorio da parte dei non Ebrei; dell'in-
cidente viene inviata a Roma una relazione distorta, per mettere in cattiva
luce la parte ebraica agli occhi dell'imperatore, il quale fa pervenire a Petronio, governatore della Siria, una lettera con l'ordine di provvedere subito
alla collocazione della statua. La disposizione di Gaio mette in grave imbarazzo Petronio il quale da un lato conosce bene gli Ebrei e giudica addirittura una grave minaccia sul piano militare la loro entità numerica,
dall'altro valuta il rischio di un rifiuto opposto all'imperatore (§§ 213—219)[25].
Un suo tentativo di trovare una soluzione con l'aiuto dei sacerdoti e dei
magistrati ebrei fallisce e provoca anzi una reazione violenta da parte del
popolo, che si riversa in massa in Fenicia, dove risiede Petronio, per dare una
dimostrazione drammatica della propria ferma volontà di impedire la vio-

---

[25] A proposito di P. Petronio, governatore di Siria durante l'impero di Caligola, è particolarmente interessante notare la diversa interpretazione data del personaggio da F. e da
Giuseppe Flavio: mentre il filosofo gli attribuisce da un lato una certa conoscenza del
temperamento e dei costumi ebraici, ma dall'altro l'uso di una tattica diplomatica nei
confronti di Gaio, lo storico palestinese lo presenta invece addirittura in veste di eroico
propugnatore della causa ebraica, per la quale Petronio sarebbe stato pronto a morire
(cfr. AJ XVIII, 278).

lazione del Tempio, minacciando un suicidio collettivo in luogo di una reazione armata contro i Romani. Il governatore di Siria si lascia commuovere e risponde a Caligola in termini dilatori: adduce a pretesto il tempo necessario alla costruzione della statua e prospetta il pericolo che gli Ebrei, per ripicca, devastino il raccolto di cui si approssima il tempo, compromettendo gli approvvigionamenti necessari a preparare una degna accoglienza a Gaio e al suo seguito, la cui venuta in Asia Minore e in Siria è ormai imminente (§§ 220—253).

Gaio accusa il colpo infertogli dalla lettera di Petronio; ma a sua volta teme i governatori delle provincie e risponde diplomaticamente, con lodi per la premura dimostrata verso di lui, ma con la ripetuta richiesta di accelerare l'allestimento della statua (§§ 254—260).

3. L'intervento del re Agrippa e la sua lettera a Caligola

A Roma nel frattempo è arrivato il re Agrippa[26], che è all'oscuro di quanto sta succedendo il Palestina e dello scambio di missive intercorso tra Gaio e Petronio. Ad informarlo di ogni particolare sarà l'imperatore stesso, cui egli è legato da vecchia amicizia. Le notizie apprese fanno cadere Agrippa in istato di deliquio, ripresosi dal quale manda a Gaio una supplica scritta, perché desista dal suo proposito (§§ 261—275).

Nell'estesa lettera di Agrippa (§§ 276—329) sono riuniti e sistematicamente inquadrati tutti i punti della questione ebraica in rapporto all' impero di Roma, che altrove Filone tocca solo di sfuggita e discute separatamente. La storicità del documento non è dimostrabile: in Giuseppe Flavio si riscontra una versione dei fatti del tutto diversa[27], dalla quale è comunque

---

[26] La biografia di Agrippa I, nipote di Erode il Grande, è tracciata da Giuseppe Flavio in AJ XVIII, 133—354. Ebbe questi una giovinezza dissoluta, tanto che per pagare i debiti dovette recarsi ad Alessandria d'Egitto e chiedere un prestito di duecentomila dracme all'alabarca Alessandro, fratello di F. In Fl. 28 c'è un'allusione a questo suo primo viaggio in Egitto. Precedentemente Agrippa aveva già stretto amicizia a Roma con vari membri della famiglia imperiale e in particolare con Gaio; e a Roma ritornò subito dopo la sua visita ad Alessandria. Ma alla fine del 36, Tiberio lo fece mettere in carcere per un'osservazione indelicata nei suoi riguardi, ed egli vi rimase sei mesi, finché lo liberò Gaio, appena salito al potere. Dal nuovo imperatore Agrippa ricevette sotto forma di regno la tetrarchia comprendente la Galaunitide, la Traconitide, la Batanèa e Paniàs, di cui il suo defunto zio paterno, Filippo, aveva percepito le rendite (cfr. Fl. 25). Subito dopo il conferimento del regno, Agrippa riparte per la Palestina e sulla via del ritorno passa per Alessandria dove è in atto il fermento che porterà alle violenze del pogrom. La sua non è una visita ufficiale (Fl. 28), ma sarà lui ad incaricarsi di far pervenire a Gaio l'editto contenente gli onori decretati all'imperatore dagli Ebrei, al momento della sua assunzione all'impero, che il governatore Flacco si era rifiutato di inoltrare (Fl. 97—103).

[27] In AJ XVIII, 289—301 al posto della lettera c'è uno scambio di idee tra Agrippa e Caligola durante un banchetto offerto dal re ebreo all'imperatore. L'intera scena è evidentemente romanzata sulla falsariga del cap. VII del 'Libro di Ester': prima che Agrippa esponga le sue richieste, riguardanti le sorti degli Ebrei di Palestina, Caligola s'impegna ad esaudire

esclusa l'esistenza di una lettera. Di storicamente accertato vi è dunque solo l'intervento diretto del re ebreo: ma circa il modo di tale intervento non vi può essere certezza. In teoria, Filone,— contemporaneo agli avvenimenti e amico di Agrippa — doveva essere meglio informato di Guiseppe Flavio; in realtà appare più verosimile l'ipotesi che egli si servisse della finzione epistolare per accentuare l'effetto drammatico del racconto, attribuendo ad Agrippa quella che era la sua personale visione dei fatti[28].

Nell'esordio della lettera (§§ 276—293) Agrippa fa il punto della situazione, rammentando a Gaio da un lato la propria appartenenza al popolo ebraico, dall'altro le prove di devozione date dagli Ebrei alla casa dei Cesari senza venir meno per questo al loro culto tradizionale. Quanto a Gerusalemme, cui il re ebreo si dichiara legato da vincoli indissolubili, essa non è più soltanto la patria degli Ebrei di Palestina, bensì dell'intera diaspora, ormai estesa a tutto l'impero: il che significa che un beneficio concesso a Gerusalemme torna a vantaggio dell'ebraismo intero. Infine è posto l'accento sul rispetto dimostrato anche dai nemici più acerrimi nei confronti del Tempio, nel quale nessuno mai ha osato collocare immagini fatte da mano umana per timore di commettere un sacrilegio inespiabile.

Nella parte centrale della lettera (§§ 294—320) ricorre un ripetuto elogio di Tiberio e di Augusto. In questa occasione viene esplicitamente lodato il rispetto di Tiberio per le tradizioni ebraiche, motivato con il merito di essere intervenuto a favore dei Giudei al tempo di Ponzio Pilato[29] revocando un ordine del governatore di Giudea che, a scopo esclusivamente vessatorio, aveva disposto la collocazione di certi scudi d'oro nella reggia di Erode il Grande[30]. Un provvedimento, insomma, che andava al di là del rispetto per il Tempio e non aveva rapporto con l'introduzione di una statua pagana nella cella più interna di esso, dove persino il sommo sacerdote metteva piede una sola volta all'anno, nel giorno del Digiuno.

L'encomio di Augusto che segue (§§ 309—319) ricalca quasi testualmente l'altro, già esaminato, dei §§ 143—158, con l'aggiunta di qualche variante.

qualunque suo desiderio e poi mantiene la promessa, mandando a Petronio un contrordine circa la statua.

[28] Dell'autenticità della lettera si è sempre discusso; lo studio più recente del problema si deve a S. ZEITLIN, Did Agrippa write a letter to Gaius Caligula?, Jew. Quart. Rev. LVI, 1965/66, pp. 22—31.

[29] Ponzio Pilato tenne probabilmente il governo della Giudea dal 26 al 36/37 d. C. (cfr. E. M. SMALLWOOD, The Date of the Dismissal of Pontius Pilate from Judaea, Journ. Jew. Stud. V, 1954, pp. 12—21).

[30] L'episodio di una tentata violazione del costume ebraico da parte di Ponzio Pilato compare anche in una duplice versione di Giuseppe Flavio (BJ II, 169—174 e AJ XVIII, 55—59), in cui però si parla dell'introduzione in Gerusalemme di alcune immagini di Tiberio, subito dopo ritirate dallo stesso governatore. Si tratta di un episodio che non ha nulla in comune con quello riferito da F.; l'equivoco che ha portato a voler identificare i due racconti (come fa il COLSON, Philo X, pp. XIX—XX) deriva dalla confusione creata da Eusebio, il quale cita due volte F. (HE II, 5, 7 e Dem. Ev. VIII, 2, 123) e due volte Giuseppe (Chron. a. XIX di Tiberio e Dem. Ev. VIII, 3, 111) sempre a conferma di una profanazione del Tempio di Gerusalemme attuata da Pilato, che viceversa non compare affatto in nessuna delle due fonti ebraiche.

A conferma della disposizione data ai governatori delle provincie asiatiche di consentire ai soli Ebrei i raduni nelle sinagoghe (laddove ogni altra riunione era vietata perché politicamente sospetta) e di non impedire l'invio di contributi in danaro, portati a Gerusalemme a mezzo di legazioni sacre, è riprodotto il testo di una lettera del proconsole Gaio Norbano ai magistrati di Efeso, contenente gli ordini relativi di Augusto (§§ 314—315). Questo è un dato concreto e storicamente documentato[31]; ma l'adesione di Augusto al culto del Tempio, per avere autentico valore secondo le intenzioni di Filone, deve essere soprattutto di ordine spirituale e viene infatti spiegata con il presupposto di una sua ,,profonda preparazione filososofica" (§ 310). Si arriva così addirittura all'individuazione in Augusto della figura di ,,un imperatore-filosofo non secondo a nessuno" (§ 318), con un deciso sconfinamento nel campo della fantasia, subordinato al consueto scopo di mostrare a Caligola quanto più illuminati di lui fossero stati i suoi predecessori nel rapporto con gli Ebrei. Infatti, la lettera di Agrippa si chiude con un'esortazione a seguire il loro esempio e con una calorosa perorazione della causa ebraica (§§ 312—329).

Gaio non rimane insensibile alle parole del re amico e invia un contrordine a Petronio. Ma la doppiezza del carattere continua ad avere in lui il sopravvento: la lettera al governatore di Siria porta in chiusa minacce di severa repressione in caso di manchevolezze anche lievi da parte degli Ebrei di Palestina e, quanto alla statua, il principe ne fa costruire una di nascosto, con il proposito di portarla personalmente in Giudea (§§ 330—338.)

4. Fallimento della missione ebraica presso Caligola

Una parentesi digressiva, nella quale sono condensate le critiche alla falsità di Gaio e alla protervia della sua politica antiebraica (§§ 346—348), serve di passaggio all'ultima sezione dell'opera (§§ 349—372), che si riallaccia nel tono all'invettiva iniziale. Ricompare bruscamente la vicenda dell'ambasceria e si parla del vero e proprio processo cui essa sarà sottoposta, ma in modo del tutto irregolare: una questione importante come la posizione giuridica di un gruppo etnico in seno alla città di Alessandria, non verrà dibattuta attraverso discorsi d'accusa e di difesa nell'aula di un tribunale, con la serietà voluta dalla prassi, bensì nei giardini di Mecenate e di Lamia sull'Esquilino. Qui Gaio ha fatto aprire le porte di una serie di padiglioni allestiti per una festa e li visita, passando dall'uno all'altro. Gli ambasciatori ebrei, ammessi alla sua presenza, si genuflettono adattandosi all'uso della prosternazione introdotto di recente a corte. Gaio li accoglie con risa sgangherate e chiede se siano loro quelli che, unici tra i suoi sudditi, si rifiutano di riconoscere in lui un dio. La domanda provoca gli applausi gioiosi dell'op-

---

[31] Una lettera analoga, inviata da G. Norbanus Flaccus, proconsole d'Asia, a Sardi e una versione abbreviata degli ordini impartiti da Augusto si trova in Jos. AJ XVI, 166 e 171. Per Norbano Flacco cfr. SMALLWOOD, Legatio, p. 309s.

posta ambasceria greca, un membro della quale accusa apertamente gli Ebrei di non aver reso a Gaio gli onori dovuti. Protestano questi ultimi, ricordando i sacrifici fatti al momento della sua successione, della sua guarigione e in propiziazione della campagna germanica. È vero, ribadisce Caligola: hanno sacrificato, ma non *a* lui, bensì *per* lui ad un altro Dio. Il tutto si svolge mentre l'imperatore entra in un padiglione e ne esce per ispezionarne un altro, impartendo ordini pratici di vario genere. I delegati ebrei lo inseguono da un punto all'altro, bersagliati dai motti schernevoli degli avversari greci: una scena pietosamente farsesca (§ 359). Caligola rivolge loro una seconda domanda: per quale motivo gli Ebrei non mangino carne di maiale. In ossequio alla tradizione dei padri, sarà l'ovvia risposta. La terza domanda, l'unica importante e pertinente, su quali siano i diritti di cittadinanza vantati dagli Ebrei, sarà formulata dall'imperatore in modo da precludere ai presunti interlocutori qualsiasi possibilità di spiegazione. I delegati si dispongono infatti ad illustrare dettagliatamente le proprie ragioni, ma Caligola scompare nel padiglione maggiore, dal quale esce solo per entrare in un altro. Ridotti alla disperazione, al punto da temere per la propria vita, Filone e i suoi compagni si rifugiano nella preghiera. Quando Caligola riappare all'aperto, non fa che congedarli con una battuta di scherno: in fondo è povera gente, più stolta che malvagia nel rifiutarsi di crederlo un dio (367). La minaccia di morte si dilegua; ma gravemente compromessa risulta la causa ebraica, quasi che dal fallimento dell'ambasceria dipendessero le sorti dell'intera diaspora, in stretto rapporto con il senso di responsabilità collettiva già denunciato altrove (§ 192).

Caligola, dunque, odia gli Ebrei perché non si piegano a riconoscere in lui la personificazione di una divinità. Ora, dice l'autore, bisogna dire la 'palinodia'. E l'opera s'interrompe con questa enigmatica espressione.

IV. Problemi di composizione e di struttura inerenti alla 'Legatio ad Gaium'

1. La testimonianza di Eusebio di Cesarea

L'analisi dettagliata del contenuto della 'Legatio' fornisce lo strumento idoneo a valutare l'inorganicità dello scritto ed è premessa necessaria allo studio dei problemi di carattere compositivo e strutturale che esso implica.

Alla sola 'Legatio' sembra riferirsi un passo della 'Historia Ecclesiastica' di Eusebio di Cesarea (HE II, 5, 1): ,,Filone racconta in cinque libri le vicende degli Ebrei durante l'impero di Gaio, trattando nella stessa opera: della pazzia di Gaio che si era proclamato un dio e aveva commesso durante il suo impero un numero incalcolabile di atti violenti; delle tribolazioni sofferte dagli Ebrei del suo tempo; dell'ambasceria inviata a Roma di cui lui stesso fu membro, in rappresentanza dei suoi connazionali di Alessandria, e di come, presentatosi a Gaio per difendere le tradizioni avite, riportò come unico

risultato scherno e dileggio, e poco mancò che ci rimettesse la vita". Se
Eusebio non avesse aggiunto altro, si potrebbe concludere con relativa facilità che i cinque libri di cui l'autore parla, senza citare il titolo dell'opera,
corrispondano approssimativamente ad altrettante sezioni individuabili al-
l'interno della 'Legatio'. Sennonché nel seguito del contesto, dopo una breve
parentesi nella quale è riportato il breve passo di Giuseppe Flavio relativo
all'episodio dell'ambasceria (HE II, 5, 2—5 = AJ XVIII, 257—260), Eusebio ritorna a Filone e questa volta nomina la 'Legatio': ,,Anche Filone
stesso nella Legatio da lui scritta (ἐν ᾗ συνέγραψε πρεσβείᾳ) racconta con
esattezza i particolari di ciò che fece in quell'occasione. Ma io ometterò tutto
il resto della narrazione, limitandomi a riferire la parti da cui risulteranno
chiare al lettore le sciagure conseguenti a quanto gli Ebrei osarono contro
Cristo e che essi subirono contemporaneamente e subito dopo" (HE II, 5, 6).
La congettura più lineare è che Eusebio si riferisca ripetutamente alla medesima opera: una prima volta per riassumerne a grandi linee il contenuto, una
seconda volta per estrarne alcune notizie particolari, utili a confermare la
sua tesi che la causa delle persecuzioni subìte dagli Ebrei è di ordine religioso,
dovendo essi espiare la colpa di aver voluto la condanna di Cristo. Eusebio,
del resto, denuncia a chiare note il criterio che intende adottare e il suo punto
di vista non può che essere diametralmente opposto a quello del filosofo
ebreo, il quale di contro vede nell'ingiustizia umana la causa degli atti persecutori e nella provvidenza divina il mezzo di salvazione. Nel testo eusebiano,
all'enunciato preliminare segue l'elenco delle persecuzioni ebraiche ri-
cordate nel testo di Filone, secondo il criterio cronologico preannun-
ciato: sono stati contemporanei alla crocifissione di Cristo il progetto di
sterminio del popolo ebraico attribuito a Seiano e il tentativo di profanazione del Tempio da parte di Pilato (HE II, 5, 7); immediatamente successiva è stata la persecuzione di Caligola (HE II, 6, 1), ad illustrare la quale
l'autore riporta testualmente il passo della 'Legatio' in cui i fatti di Alessandria e quelli di Palestina sono riassunti e collegati tra loro (HE II, 6, 2 =
Leg. 346). Ma, superata una difficoltà, se ne presenta subito un'altra: a
questo punto Eusebio ricorda ancora una volta, ma in maniera più incisiva
e precisa, il pogrom del 38 d. C. cui ha già alluso vagamente in HE II, 5, 1:
,,Nel secondo libro intitolato 'Sulle virtù', lo stesso Filone racconta di in-
numerevoli altre atrocità toccate agli Ebrei di Alessandria, che vanno al di
là di ogni descrizione" (HE II, 6, 3). Ora si sa bene che Filone descrisse il
pogrom due volte, in due scritti diversi nello spirito e nella forma; tuttavia
ci sono motivate ragioni per credere che l'autore intenda riferirsi alla versione della 'Legatio'. L'imbarazzo maggiore è creato da quel titolo 'Sulle
virtù'; ma in HE II, 18, 8, a conclusione di un lungo e confuso elenco dei
trattati filoniani, Eusebio afferma che fu proprio Filone a intitolare περὶ
ἀρετῶν l'opera comunemente nota con il nome di 'Legatio' (πρεσβεία) e per
di più spiega quello che, secondo lui, era stato il motivo della scelta: ,,Si
dice che sotto l'impero di Claudio, Filone — che era già stato a Roma al
tempo di Gaio — leggesse dinanzi al senato romano, raccolto in riunione plena-
ria, le cose da lui scritte sull'empietà di Gaio, che con icastica e sottile ironia

(μετὰ ἤθους καὶ εἰρωνείας) aveva intitolato 'Sulle virtù'. L'opera, così pare, riscosse tanto successo che la si considerò degna di essere accolta nelle pubbliche biblioteche". Eplicitamente alla 'Legatio' riporta infine una nota del 'Chronicon' (a. XXI di Tiberio), nella quale si parla di Seiano come dell'istigatore di Tiberio allo sterminio degli Ebrei, secondo quanto avrebbe scritto Filone *in libro legationis secundo*[32]. L'alternanza dei due titoli — περὶ ἀρετῶν e πρεσβεία — attribuiti alla medesima opera è comprovata dalla tradizione manoscritta; ma mentre nel caso di πρεσβεία (Legatio) l'assunzione del termine a titolo dell'intera opera è pienamente giustificabile, la soluzione si presenta problematica per l'altro titolo, περὶ ἀρετῶν. Secondo Eusebio le ἀρεταί si riferiscono per antifrasi ai vizi di Caligola, e Filone avrebbe scelto il titolo μετὰ ἤθους καὶ εἰρωνείας, espressione di senso oscuro, che ha il suono di uno stravagante ossimoro. L'interpretazione di Eusebio è respinta da alcuni studiosi moderni come un banale fraintendimento[33], mentre altri la accettano integralmente[34] oppure la giudicano ingenua ma non del tutto inverosimile[35]. In sostanza, Eusebio non avrebbe potuto né voluto ammettere che le ἀρεταί si riferissero — come sembra più vicino al vero — alle virtù che il popolo ebraico doveva possedere per affrontare le prove mandategli da Dio: secondo Filone, il suo popolo era eletto alla sofferenza sulla via che lo portava al perfezionamento di se stesso, per Eusebio invece esso, come si è visto, era condannato a espiare una colpa insanabile. È questo l'equivoco che va chiarito: voler intuire le intenzioni di Filone attraverso il giudizio di Eusebio, significa cadere nel medesimo errore metodologico che si commette ogniqualvolta si stralci una citazione di contenuto concettuale e non meramente informativo dal contesto cui appartiene.

Nella 'Legatio' il termine ἀρετή compare ripetutamente, con riferimenti diversi: di conseguenza, le ipotesi circa il significato del titolo περὶ ἀρετῶν sono condizionate tutte, nella loro molteplicità, al maggior rilievo dato ad una tematica piuttosto che ad un'altra[36]. Ma questo è soltanto uno dei problemi irrisolti che l'opera obbliga ad affrontare.

---

[32] Il testo è tratto dalla rielaborazione geronimiana dei 'Chronici Canones' di Eusebio (ed· I. K. FOTHERINGHAM, Londra 1923, p. 258).

[33] DELAUNAY, op. cit., p. 88; S. REITER, Ἀρετή und der Titel von Philos Legatio, Ἐπιτύμβιον H. Swoboda dargebracht, Reichenberg 1927, p. 228; SMALLWOOD, Legatio, p. 39.

[34] M. L. MASSEBIEAU, Le classement des œuvres de Philon, Bibl. de l'Éc. des Hautes Étud. Sciences relig. I, 1889, p. 77, n. 2; H. LEISEGANG, Philon, RE XX 1, 1941, coll. 48—49; C.—H.—A.—TH. VII, p. 167.

[35] COLSON, Philo X, p. XIVs.

[36] Citiamo solo alcune tra le molte interpretazioni proposte: il DELAUNAY (op. cit., p. 88) scorgeva nel titolo un riferimento al coraggio dimostrato dagli Ebrei nell'avversare la pretesa di Gaio alla deificazione, E. SCHÜRER, Gesch. des jüd. Volkes im Zeitalter Jesu Christi, Lipsia 1909, III[4], p. 682, un generico accenno al trionfo della virtù sull'empietà, il MASSEBIEAU (op. cit., p. 77) un'allusione sarcastica alle virtù degli dei con cui Gaio voleva identificarsi. Del tutto diversa l'opinione di W. WEBER, Eine Gerichtsverhandlung vor Kaiser Traian, Hermes L, 1915, p. 75, secondo il quale le ἀρεταί sono l'intervento miracoloso di Dio in favore dell'ambasceria; tale tesi fu accolta e giustificata con la presunta caduta nei mss. del nome di Dio — ΘΥ — dal REITER (art. cit., pp. 228—237), che considera la 'Legatio' una aretalogia, una „*Wundererzählung ad maiorem Dei gloriam*".

Trascurando i più marginali, sono quattro i quesiti che non si possono ignorare: il primo investe la struttura dello scritto, il secondo si riferisce al problema della mancante 'palinodia', il terzo alla precisazione dell'anno dell'ambasceria, il quarto alla posizione giuridica degli Ebrei alessandrini.

2. La struttura della 'Legatio' nelle interpretazioni moderne

Circa il primo quesito, che ha la sua radice nei 'cinque libri' cui Eusebio accenna in HE II, 5, 1 cit., la critica moderna si è divisa in due opposte correnti: la prima, che fa capo allo SCHÜRER[37], sostiene la tesi unitaria, secondo la quale l''In Flaccum' e la 'Legatio' avrebbero fatto parte di un'unica opera molto voluminosa dal titolo Περὶ ἀρετῶν, di cui tre libri su cinque si suppongono perduti e che sarebbero stati distribuiti a un di presso così: l. I introduzione; l. II persecuzioni di Seiano e di Pilato; l. III l''In Flaccum'; l. IV la 'Legatio'; l. V la 'palinodia'. La teoria dello SCHÜRER ebbe scarso seguito[38] e fu ben presto soppiantata dall'opposta tesi separatista — considerata a tutt'oggi l'unica valida — di cui fu propugnatore il MASSEBIEAU[39]. La sua teoria (nota con il nome di MASSEBIEAU-COHN, per l'adesione quasi integrale ad essa del secondo studioso[40]) si impernia sulla netta convinzione dell'indipendenza di uno scritto dall'altro: una convinzione basata su dati concreti quali il riferimento ad altre fonti antiche in aggiunta ai passi eusebiani[41], la distinzione dei titoli nei mss.[42], l'esame interno dei testi. Nella sola 'Legatio' si individuano, dunque, altrettante sezioni corrispondenti ai 'cinque libri' di Eusebio. Il COLSON[43], cui si deve il ritocco più recente alla teoria MASSEBIEAU-COHN (da lui peraltro accettata appieno

---

L'interpretazione di WEBER e REITER fu accolta dal COLSON (Philo X, p. XIVss.), sia pure con qualche riserva, e respinta invece dal LEISEGANG (art. cit., col. 49), che ritorna più o meno alla teoria del DELAUNAY.

[37] Op. cit., III[4], pp. 677—683.

[38] Aderirono alla tesi: H. I. BELL, Jews and Christians in Egypt, Londra 1924, p. 22; H. S. JONES, Claudius and the Jewish Question at Alexandria, JRS XVI, 1926, p. 22; A. MOMIGLIANO, Rass. di Israel, cit., pp. 276s. (ma con molta riserva); H. LEWY, Philon von Alexandrien, Berlino 1935, p. 7. La SMALLWOOD sembra propendere per la teoria dello SCHÜRER, ma in sostanza, dopo aver esposto tutte le tesi esistenti (Legatio, pp. 37—43) non prende posizione per nessuna.

[39] Le classement, cit., pp. 65—78.

[40] L. COHN, Einleitung und Chronologie der Schriften Philos, Philol. Supplbd. VII, 1899, pp. 421—424.

[41] Alla testimonianza di Eusebio si aggiunge qualche citazione più tarda: Fozio (Bibl., cod. 105) ricorda un λόγος οὗ ἐπιγραφὴ Γάϊος ψεγόμενος καὶ Φλάκκος ἢ Φλάκκων ψεγόμενος, cioè due scritti distinti che, stando, al titolo, erano considerati due invettive. Giovanni Damasceno nei 'Sacra parallela' cita passi tratti da opere intitolate rispettivamente τὰ κατὰ (ο πρὸς) Φλάκκον e τὸ (ο τὰ) πρὸς Γάϊον oppure ἡ πρὸς Γάϊον πρεσβεία.

[42] Per la distinzione dei due titoli nei mss. e le varianti di essi cfr. C.—W.—R., vol. VI, proleg. II, p. XLVIIss.

[43] Op. cit., pp. XVI—XXVI.

nella sostanza), si limita ad escludere del tutto la presenza nella 'Legatio' di lacune più o meno vaste postulate dal MASSEBIEAU, e propone di considerare l'opera così suddivisa: l. I introduzione e storia di Gaio (§§ 1—113); l. II il pogrom di Alessandria e una digressione sul migliore trattamento goduto dagli Ebrei sotto Augusto e Tiberio (§§ 114—161); l. III avvenimenti esterni all'Egitto e tentata violazione del Tempio di Gerusalemme (§§ 162—348); l. IV la seconda udienza (§§ 349—373); l. V la palinodia (mancante). Apprezzabile, in questa ricostruzione, il particolare che nel libro II rientrino insieme i fatti citati da Eusebio come appartenenti al libro II della 'Legatio' (Chron., a. XXI di Tiberio) e quelli attribuiti al libro II del περὶ ἀρετῶν (HE II, 6, 3), un accostamento che risolve la più grave delle incongruenze che infirmavano la tesi unitaria. D'altra parte l'esclusione di qualsiasi lacuna all'interno dell'opera pecca per eccesso non meno della presupposizione del MASSEBIEAU, che parla addirittura di mutilazioni, oltre che di sicure lacune. Ma sono semplici varianti sullo stesso tema di fondo dal quale non si evade neppure qualora si immagini che il disordine strutturale della 'Legatio' e la mancanza della parte conclusiva siano dovute a carenza di elaborazione e che quindi lo scritto sia incompiuto piuttosto che gravemente o parzialmente mutilo.

3. Il problema della *palinodia*

Più che mai affidato alla congettura è il secondo quesito, relativo al presumibile contenuto della 'palinodia' preannunciata in Leg. 373. Il termine significa „ritrattazione" di un'idea prima sostenuta e si sa che fu applicato per la prima volta alla ritrattazione poetica di Stesicoro nei confronti di Elena[44]; ma l'espressione ricorre anche ad altro proposito, seppure sporadicamente[45]. La palinodia filoniana ha dato adito alle elucubrazioni più disparate. Secondo alcuni studiosi la sezione mancante avrebbe avuto carattere storico-narrativo: lo SCHÜRER[46], postulando un perfetto parallelismo strutturale tra l''In Flaccum' e la 'Legatio', vi immaginava contenuta una descrizione della morte di Caligola, punito anche lui con l'assassinio del male fatto agli Ebrei; il THEILER[47], capovolgendo i termini, dava il nome di 'palinodia' ai discorsi posti in bocca al governatore di Alessandria nella seconda parte dell''In Flaccum' (quando questi ravvisava nelle torture cui era sottoposto la punizione delle vessazioni inflitte agli Ebrei) e postulava l'esistenza di un analogo discorso fatto pronunciare a Caligola alla fine della 'Legatio'. Il MASSEBIEAU[48] intendeva 'palinodia' nel senso di „contro-

---

[44] Plat., Ep. III, 319e, Phaedr. 243b; Isocr., Hel. 64.
[45] Plat., Phaedr. 257a; Cic., ad Att. IV, 5, 1; Plut., Alex. 53, 4: Luc., Apol. 708.
[46] Op. cit. I⁴, p. 501, n. 174; III⁴, p. 679.
[47] COHN—HEINEMANN—ADLER—THEILER, vol. VII, p. 169s.
[48] Le classement cit., p. 72.

partita" e riteneva che alla fine fossero raccontati il castigo di Gaio e la vittoria degli Ebrei, una realtà storicamente confermata, a suo avviso, dalla riabilitazione loro concessa da Claudio. Sostanzialmente antitetica l'opinione del LEISEGANG[49], secondo il quale la parte conclusiva era occupata da una disquisizione etico-religiosa: Filone, nella palinodia, avrebbe ripreso in esame l'intera politica antiebraica di Caligola per additare in essa una delle prove mandate da Dio al fine di offrire agli Ebrei l'occasione di esercitare e di far conoscere le proprie virtù, riallacciandosi al principio enunciato in Leg. 196. Lo studioso formula tale ipotesi in base all'identificazione della palinodia filoniana con quella platonica, che egli riunisce in una definizione unica: si tratterebbe della riparazione all'offesa recata a un dio con l'elogio di quanto prima si è criticato. La definizione è esatta per quanto riguarda il Fedro platonico e l'elogio di Eros che Socrate pronuncia per prevenire la vendetta del dio, irritato dal suo precedente discorso[50]; meno esatta risulta a proposito di Filone e solo il confronto del significato che il filosofo annette altrove al medesimo termine aiuta a chiarire una divergenza che il LEISEGANG non rileva.

Nel 'De somniis' (II, 292) sono chiamate ἱεραὶ παλινῳδίαι le ritrattazioni dell'uomo superbo che, acquistata chiara coscienza del torto commesso nel credersi onnipotente, implora e ottiene il perdono di Dio ,,ascoltando la voce del pentimento (μετάνοια)". Ancora, nel 'De posteritate Caini' (§ 179) sono accostati due passi della Genesi (XXX, 2 e 24): nel primo, alla richiesta di Rachele a Giacobbe di darle dei figli, questi risponde: ,,Posso io sostituirmi a Dio?", nel secondo, dopo la nascita di Giuseppe, Rachele rivolge direttamente a Dio la sua preghiera: ,,Mi conceda Iddio un secondo figlio". In sede allegorica Filone ravvisa nel mutato atteggiamento di Rachele una prova del suo pentimento e definisce la sua preghiera a Dio una παλινῳδία ἱερωτάτη. Vi è dunque nella palinodia filoniana un elemento sostanzialmente nuovo rispetto a quella platonica, ossia la μετάνοια, il pentimento, che a sua volta presuppone il senso di colpa, ignoti al paganesimo greco-romano.

Bisogna ritenere che la palinodia prevista alla fine della 'Legatio' avesse lo stesso carattere di sacralità che le è attribuito nei trattati allegorici. A pronunciarla non poteva essere stato — così ci sembra — altri che lo stesso Filone; e non a titolo personale, bensì in nome del popolo ebraico divenuto cosciente della volontà provvidenziale celata nella persecuzione. Si tornerebbe così, con piena coerenza ma in maniera più chiaramente filoniana di quanto vuole il LEISEGANG alla tesi del proemio: ammesso che il filosofo ravvisasse nella morte violenta e improvvisa di Caligola l'intervento di un aiuto soprannaturale a favore degli Ebrei, il suo fine ultimo era — presumibilmente — di dimostrare come gli increduli abbiano bisogno di prove concrete per acquisire una certezza che il saggio raggiunge attraverso la contemplazione e la fede.

---

[49] Journ. of Bibl. Liter. LVII, 1938, p. 408ss. e ID., RE XX 1, 1941, col. 47s.
[50] Plat., Phaedr. 243a.

4. Il problema della cronologia

Il terzo quesito sposta la ricerca dal piano concettuale a quello storico-erudito della cronologia: mentre da accenni indiretti ma precisi dell''In Flaccum' l'epoca del pogrom si può datare con certezza all'agosto del 38 d. C.[51], nella 'Legatio' manca ogni indicazione utile a fissare la data d'invio dell'ambasceria a Roma. Dal testo si ricava soltanto che la seconda udienza ebbe luogo nel 40 d. C.[52]; quanto alla partenza degli ambasciatori, essa avvenne nel cuore dell'inverno (Leg. 190), ma è impossibile stabilire se Filone si riferisca all'inverno del 38/39 o del 39/40. La questione è stata ampiamente e variamente dibattuta, senza che si sia potuta raggiungere una risposta definitiva, perché manca un'esatta cronologia tanto della storia di Caligola per il biennio 38/39—39/40[53], quanto dei contemporanei fatti di Palestina[54], cui la datazione dell'ambasceria è strettamente legata. La SMALLWOOD, che dà le spiegazioni più esaurienti, conclude per la seconda datazione; ed è questa l'ipotesi che appare più plausibile[55].

5. Il problema dello *status civitatis* degli Ebrei di Alessandria e la 'Lettera' di Claudio agli Alessandrini

Quarto nell'ordine da noi prefissato, ma d'importanza primaria sotto il profilo storico, è il quesito circa la posizione giuridica degli Ebrei di Alessandria, considerato in se stesso e nel quadro più ampio dei rapporti tra l'ebraismo e l'impero di Roma. Nell'annosa diatriba insorta tra i sostenitori della tesi che gli Ebrei avessero la cittadinanza di pieno diritto e i propugnatori

---

[51] Cfr. sopra n. 2.

[52] Nel corso della seconda udienza viene ricordato l'olocausto propiziatorio offerto dagli Ebrei κατὰ τὴν ἐλπίδα τῆς Γερμανικῆς νίκης (Leg. 356), frase che a nostro avviso si riferisce ad un'impresa già compiuta (cfr. C. KRAUS, op. cit., p. 118); l'udienza stessa non poté quindi aver luogo che nel 40, dopo il rientro dell'imperatore in Italia, documentato dagli AFA (CIL VI, 32347, 15), dai quali risulta che egli fu presente ai sacrifici degli Arvali il 29 maggio e il 1° giugno del 40, ossia che si trovava nei pressi di Roma fin dalla tarda primavera di quell'anno.

[53] Oltre all'approssimazione degli estremi cronologici della campagna germanica — il cui inizio si suppone risalisse all'estate del 39 in base all'interpretazione congetturale di un passo di Dione Cassio (LIX, 17, 1) — ne rimane nebuloso anche lo svolgimento: da alcuni accenni sparsi dello stesso Dione (LIX, 21, 3; 22—24; 25, 2ss.) e di Suetonio (Cal. 17, 1 e 3) si ricava che la cosiddetta „campagna", dopo una rapidissima puntata al di là del Reno, si ridusse ad una manovra fittizia e servì solo da pretesto per un prolungato soggiorno a Lione, dove l'imperatore ebbe modo di continuare la sua vita dissoluta.

[54] Data la completa discordanza tra F. e Giuseppe Flavio, di cui si è detto alla n. 24, il problema della ricostruzione cronologica dei fatti di Palestina ha dato luogo ad una lunga serie di congetture da parte degli studiosi. Si veda in proposito l'articolo della SMALLWOOD, The Chronology of Gaius' Attempt to Desecrate the Temple, Latomus XVI, 1957, pp. 3—17, nel quale i dati forniti da F. sono integrati con quelle desunti da Giuseppe.

[55] Cfr. assieme all'art. sopra citato, SMALLWOOD, Legatio, pp. 47—50 e per la rimanente bibliografia C. KRAUS, op. cit., p. 75, n. 47.

della tesi opposta, secondo la quale essi non godevano che della *civitas minor*, implicante il possesso dei diritti civili con l'esclusione di quelli politici, sembrano ormai aver prevalso i secondi. Alla tesi più restrittiva aderisce la SMALLWOOD, che espone in lucida sintesi gli estremi del problema e le soluzioni proposte, concludendo che presumibilmente gli Ebrei erano considerati stranieri aventi diritto di soggiorno ad Alessandria, ma al tempo stesso anche cittadini, in quanto membri di uno dei πολιτεύματα costituitisi in seno alla πόλις greco-macedone al tempo dei Tolomei[56]. In tale formula conciliativa, che la studiosa subordina peraltro all'insolubilità tuttora attuale del problema, risulta sovrapposto alla realtà di un'organizzazione politica promossa dai monarchi ellenistici il punto di vista romano, quale emerge — come vedremo — dalla 'Lettera agli Alessandrini' di Claudio.

L'ambiguità del problema (che in questa sede può essere appena sfiorato) nasce essenzialmente dal fatto che la natura concreta dei 'diritti', per la rivendicazione dei quali furono mandate non una ma più ambascerie a Roma, non è specificata in alcuna delle fonti storiche o pseudostoriche di cui disponiamo, perché all'epoca i termini della questione dovevano essere ben noti o almeno erano dati per tali. La testimonianza di Filone avrebbe potuto dissipare, essa sola, ogni dubbio, se il filosofo vi avesse incluso un'esplicita definizione dello *status civitatis* dei suoi correligionari di Alessandria. Ma sappiamo ormai che sarebbe vano cercare una qualsiasi indicazione tra le righe della 'Legatio'; e lo stesso vale per l''In Flaccum', dove pure il tema della 'cittadinanza' degli Ebrei è toccato più da vicino, ma sempre in maniera allusiva e comunque estranea all'ambito strettamente giuridico. Si è cercato di trovare un chiarimento agli sparsi accenni di Filone negli indizi desumibili da documenti di dubbia autenticità storica come gli 'Acta Martyrum Paganorum'[57] e da un documento ufficiale come la 'Lettera' di Claudio: le conclusioni sono rimaste alla fase dell'ipotesi, perchè anche in queste fonti non-ebraiche i δίκαια sono un sottinteso e non costituiscono

---

[56] SMALLWOOD, Legatio, p. 10 e per un'esauriente bibliografia degli studi concernenti lo *status civitatis* degli Ebrei d'Alessandria cfr. ibid. p. 7, nn. 1 e 2.

[57] Gli 'Acta Martyrum Paganorum' (ediz. crit. in H. A. MUSURILLO, The Acts of the Pagan Martyrs, Acta Alexandrinorum, Oxford 1954 e Acta Alexandrinorum, Lipsia 1961; ediz. crit. e commentata in V. A. TCHERIKOVER, CPJ II, 1960, pp. 55—107) sono frammenti papiracei di una produzione che è qualcosa di mezzo tra la storia romanzata e il resoconto protocollare (l'epoca della composizione o della trascrizione si fa risalire all'inizio del III sec. d. C.). Si tratta in prevalenza della ricostruzione di processi intentati dai Romani ai Greci di Alessandria per l'opposizione fatta al governo centrale sotto l'impero di Claudio, Traiano, Adriano e Commodo. Gli 'Acta' contengono evidenti spunti antisemitici, che rivelano meglio di ogni altra fonte i soprusi sofferti dagli Ebrei in Alessandria e i metodi usati dai Greci alessandrini, i quali cercavano in un presunto filosemitismo degli imperatori il mezzo adatto a svolgere la loro propaganda antiromana. L'espressione *martiri pagani* fu coniata da A. BAUER, Heidnische Märtyrerakten, Arch. f. Papyr. I, 1901, p. 30, 1, in parallelo con *martiri cristiani*, pur non trattandosi affatto di una persecuzione religiosa, probabilmente per le condanne a morte inflitte agli imputati e per qualche altra affinità esteriore. — Spetta al MOMIGLIANO (Rass. di Israel, cit., p. 282) il merito di aver richiamato l'attenzione sul fatto che era più logico ricorrere ai dati forniti dagli 'Acta' per chiarire F., che non adoperare le opere filoniane a chiarimento di questi frammenti papiracei.

quindi argomento di definizione o di discussione. Di contro alla reticenza di Filone sta la dichiarata certezza di Giuseppe Flavio, che è quanto mai sospetta perché invalidata da un equivoco di base: lo storico ebreo vuol far credere ad una totale parità di diritti tra Ebrei e Greci in Alessandria d'Egitto, secondo lui stabilita da Alessandro Magno (BJ II, 487: ἰσομοιρία e c. Ap. II, 35: ἴση τιμή), confermata da Giulio Cesare (AJ XIV, 188) e riconosciuta da Claudio (AJ XIX, 281: ἴση πολιτεία). Non è difficile rilevare che l'aggettivo ἴσος, ricorrente in ognuna delle formule usate, è di significato ambiguo in quanto può riferirsi a identità o a equivalenza, e — ammessa l'esistenza di un πολίτευμα ebraico entro la πόλις greca[58] — e molto più verosimile che si trattasse di equivalenza piuttosto che di identità. Quanto poco fondata fosse la sua certezza di un riconoscimento dei diritti politici degli Ebrei da parte dell'imperatore Claudio, si ricava dal confronto con il testo degli editti che, stando alla sua versione, questi avrebbe emanato nei primi mesi del 41 d. C. subito dopo la successione all'impero[59], e la sezione riguardante gli Ebrei (rr. 72—104) della 'Lettera' di Claudio, più volte citata, la cui scoperta e la cui pubblicazione[60] hanno portato alla luce la fonte più importante per la storia degli Ebrei in Egitto durante il periodo romano. Il documento, che risale alla fine del primo anno del regno di Claudio[61], vale a chiarire da un lato i punti deboli della presunta certezza storica di Giuseppe Flavio, dall'altro l'utopistica e antistorica visuale di Filone. Dopo un accenno al contrattacco scatenato in Alessandria dagli Ebrei contro i Greci dopo la morte di Caligola (rr. 73—77), Claudio minaccia di prendere provvedimenti contro i responsabili del pogrom, che di proposito ha rinunciato ad individuare, ed esorta gli Alessandrini ad una pacifica convivenza con gli Ebrei che da lungo tempo dimorano nella loro stessa città (rr. 77—84). Sul piano pratico l'unica ingiunzione fatta agli Alessandrini è il rispetto delle tradizioni religiose ebraiche, già decretato da Augusto e da lui, Claudio, confermato dopo aver sentito le due parti avverse (rr. 85—88). Il seguito è tutto un elenco dei divieti posti agli Ebrei, ai quali si ordina: di non pretendere privilegi maggiori di quelli goduti prima (rr. 89—90), di non mandare più due ambascerie, cosa mai successa in passato, come se abitassero in due città diverse (rr. 90—92), di non intromettersi negli agoni presieduti da ginnasiarchi o cosmeti, spingendosi in tal modo al di là delle libertà già eccessive loro concesse ἐν ἀλλοτρίᾳ πόλει, in una città che non è la loro (rr. 92—95), di arrestare l'immigrazione in Alessandria di Ebrei provenienti dalla Palestina o dal resto dell'Egitto (rr. 96—98). In chiusa all'elenco dei

---

[58] Al πολίτευμα ebraico si riferisce esplicitamente (due secoli prima di F.) lo Ps.-Aristea (Lettera a Filocrate, 310) e vi allude con la definizione di πολιτεία αὐτοτελής Strabone (ap. Jos. AJ XIV, 117). È probabile che equivalga nel senso a πολίτευμα il termine πολιτεία usato da F. in Fl. 53 e in Leg. 349 e 363.

[59] Jos. AJ XIX, 280—285 e 287—291.

[60] Pap. Lond. 1912, pubblicato per la prima volta da H. I. BELL, op. cit., Londra 1924, pp. 1—37. L'ediz. più recente è di V.A. TCHERIKOVER (CPJ II, 1960, pp. 36—60).

[61] La data della 'Lettera' si deduce dal breve editto che la precede (rr. 1—13), recante il nome del prefetto L. Aemilius Rectus, il quale ne ordinò la pubblicazione il 10 novembre del 41 d. C.,

divieti c'è un'aperta minaccia: in caso di inossequenza da parte degli Ebrei, Claudio li perseguiterà con ogni mezzo ,,come provocatori di un morbo comune a tutto il mondo abitato" (rr. 99—100). Dunque, gli Ebrei, definiti prima ,,antichi coabitatori" dei Greci in Alessandria, sono poi diffidati dall'assumere atteggiamenti inopportuni in quanto ospiti di una città che non è la loro; si parla di privilegi in loro godimento senz'altra precisazione; si apprende che l'afflusso di Ebrei ad Alessandria è continuo e del tutto sgradito e che, d'altra parte, vi è scissione all'interno del loro stesso gruppo etnico, se vengono inviate a Roma due ambascerie (una verosimilmente di Ebrei ortodossi, l'altra di Ebrei ellenizzati)[62]. Dall'insieme non risulta quale fosse in concreto la posizione giuridica degli Ebrei nella città ,,ospitante", ma nella sostanza essa è prospettata come una posizione ambigua e tenuta sotto controllo sia dalla popolazione greca del luogo che dal governo di Roma; a tutto questo si aggiunge un dissidio tra gli stessi Ebrei, più o meno assimilati. L'ebraismo è visto con occhio tutt'altro che benevolo, fino al punto di essere considerato un pericolo per l'impero. Nell'unico dato positivo — la restituzione della libertà di culto — non si può riconoscere altro che un atto di diplomazia da parte del nuovo imperatore, il quale percepisce l'urgenza di eliminare o prevenire ogni causa di disordine nelle provincie, ma soprattutto vuole che sia divulgato il suo proposito di ripristinare la linea politica di Augusto.

Anche la 'Lettera' di Claudio, per la parte concernente gli Ebrei, è stata oggetto delle interpretazioni più contrastanti. Nell'ambito della critica più recente, la SMALLWOOD vede in essa gli estremi di una soluzione politica imparziale e prudente, intesa a riportare pace tra Greci ed Ebrei; il TCHERIKOVER, al contrario, scorge nell'atteggiamento di Claudio il ripetersi della posizione antisemitica che aveva ispirato l'editto di Flacco, in cui gli Ebrei di Alessandria sono definiti ξένοι καὶ ἐπήλυδες, stranieri e immigrati (Fl. 54), il che corrisponde in sostanza al concetto espresso nella 'Lettera' che essi godessero benefici esorbitanti la giusta misura ,,in una città non loro" (rr. 94—95)[64]. A nostro avviso, è quest'ultima l'interpretazione più veridica, come si è cercato di dimostrare con l'esame analitico del testo. La lettura del documento in chiave negativa avvalora la nostra tesi dell'er-

---

[62] È questa l'ipotesi circa le due ambascerie contemporaneamente presenti alla corte di Claudio nel suo primo anno di regno — il cui invio fu conseguente ad un'insurrezione armata degli Ebrei contro i Greci di Alessandria, documentata da Giuseppe Flavio (AJ XIX, 278) — sostenuta ragionevolmente da H. WILLRICH, Zum Brief des Kaisers Claudius an die Alexandriner, Hermes LX, 1925, pp. 482—489, e pienamente accolta dalla SMALLWOOD (Legatio, p. 29, n. 2), in quanto appunto costituisce una conferma del dissidio esistente in Alessandria tra gli Ebrei assimilati che aspiravano alla cittadinanza di pieno diritto e gli ortodossi che invece non avevano tale mira, in quanto l'appartenenza a una πόλις greca implicava obblighi inaccettabili per un religioso, quali la frequenza del teatro, la partecipazione alle attività del ginnasio e il rispetto del culto pagano. Cfr. in proposito anche JONES, JRS XVI, 1926, p. 30s. e MOMIGLIANO, L'opera dell'imperatore Claudio, Firenze 1932, p. 63ss.
[63] SMALLWOOD, Legatio, p. 30s.
[64] CPJ I, p. 74.

rore di valutazione storica commesso da Giuseppe Flavio, quando attribuiva a Claudio una condotta favorevole agli Ebrei, in base al tono dei
due primi editti da lui emessi, nei quali peraltro era dato maggiore risalto al
fattore religioso che non a quello politico.

Quanto a Filone, tutto nella 'Legatio' fa supporre che egli non conoscesse
la 'Lettera'; ma è una semplice supposizione che diverrebbe certezza se si
potesse assegnare una data alla composizione dell'opera, che per certo si sa
soltanto essere stata scritta dopo la morte di Caligola[65]. Sempre sul piano delle
ipotesi immaginose, si potrebbero invertire i termini e dare per indubitato
che Filone ignorasse l'esistenza del documento: in tal caso, si acquisirebbe
un elemento assai utile a fissare la datazione della 'Legatio' a un periodo
anteriore all'autunno del 41 a. C. Ma il terreno è ancora una volta infido: è
bensì inammissibile che a Filone, se conosceva la 'Lettera', sfuggisse il mala-
nimo di Claudio verso gli Ebrei alessandrini; d'altro canto però non è possibile escludere che, in ossequio al principio di scindere sempre l'essenziale dal
secondario, la 'questione ebraica' fosse legata, nella sua ideologia, ad una
prospettiva eccedente in assoluto i confini di specifiche rivendicazioni citta-
dine. Ne abbiamo due prove: da un lato il suo silenzio sulla natura dei
'diritti' politici tanto discussi, dall'altra l'esplicita e ribadita insistenza sul
rifiuto degli Ebrei ad accettare qualsiasi innovazione che intaccasse la loro
osservanza di precise norme etico-religiose, non contaminate da interessi
pratici e degne, nella loro sacralità, di essere difese anche con il sacrificio
della vita.

All'apparenza, Claudio soddisfaceva appieno a quella che Filone denun-
ciava come l'istanza di maggior peso e, concedendo agli Ebrei di esercitare
liberamente il proprio culto riparava alle falle create da Caligola nei rapporti
tra Roma e il mondo ebraico per un suo folle vaneggiamento. Ma nella realtà
politica, la sua era una manovra prudenziale ispirata a tutt'altro che a simpatia verso gli Ebrei. La minaccia di repressioni violente, nel caso di un loro
concentramento numericamente eccessivo in una sola città, tradiva insieme
prevenzione e timore in vista della potenziale capacità di corrosione della
compagine imperiale romana da parte di un nucleo ebraico troppo forte.
Sotto la maschera del munifico restauratore della tolleranza religiosa, Claudio
non faceva che deformare a strumento specioso una delle componenti della
politica provinciale cui Augusto era ricorso come a mezzo autentico di paci-
ficazione, e gettava il seme di quella azione distruttiva che avrebbe portato
all'attrito definitivo tra Ebrei e Gentili, determinando la catastrofe degli
anni 66—70 e, con la distruzione del Tempio di Gerusalemme ad opera di
Tito, alla scomparsa di Israele dalla scena della storia.

Di tutto questo non c'è nella 'Legatio' di Filone il minimo sospetto.
Una frase posta all'inizio dell'opera suscita il ricorso alla mente del *nunc
demum redit animus* di Tacito (Agr. 3): il filosofo proclama che ,,la circostanza attuale e le molte importanti questioni definitesi nel corso di essa
varranno a convincere anche gli increduli, che non ammettono esista una

---

[65] Cfr. sopra n. 5.

provvidenza divina nei confronti dell'umanità e in particolare del popolo supplice" (Leg. 3). Non è appurabile a quale circostanza Filone si riferisca, ma il suo modo di esprimersi rivela che egli si sente al sicuro, protetto da un nuovo stato di cose, favorevole alla causa abraica.

V. Ipotesi interpretative

1. La presunta posizione politica di Filone

Alla luce di tutte queste considerazioni, appare più che mai inaccettabile l'interpretazione data della 'Legatio' dal GOODENOUGH il quale, studiando quest'opera insieme all''In Flaccum', definisce i due scritti due pamphlets politici indirizzati rispettivamente al nuovo imperatore e al nuovo prefetto di Alessandria, a scopo intimidatorio, con il meditato proposito di prospettare loro il pericolo cui si espongono i persecutori dell'ebraismo[66]. Alla base di una simile tesi, sospetta in se stessa per il rigido parallelismo dell'impostazione, sta un capovolgimento di fondo che non può essere accettato: partendo dalla giusta premessa che non esiste soluzione di continuità tra i trattati filosofico-allegorici di Filone e i suoi due scritti relativi alla persecuzione, il GOODE-NOUGH, anziché verificare tale continuità nel sostrato speculativo di questi due ultimi scritti, capovolge nettamente i termini e pretende di scoprire nei primi l'elaborazione di determinati principi politici, che il filosofo avrebbe nascosto sotto il velo dell'allegoria biblica e applicato in seguito ad una realtà effettiva infierendo, sotto la spinta del pogrom, contro personaggi romani ormai defunti. In funzione della sua complessa teoria, lo studioso americano — profondo conoscitore della produzione filoniana — postula che Filone in alcune delle opere aventi per tema l'esegesi allegorica del Pentateuco (in particolare nel 'De somniis') si rivolgesse ad un ristretto numero di Ebrei iniziati al metodo dell'allegoria biblica, per denunciare i difetti capitali dei Romani e l'oppressività del loro governo[67], e in una delle opere riservate all'esegesi delle leggi mosaiche (il 'De Josepho') parlasse invece ad un pubblico di Gentili interessati all'ebraismo, per dimostrare che gli Ebrei avevano idee ben chiare sulla figura del *politicus* per eccellenza[68]. L'intera disquisizione, dottissima e ampiamente documentata, ha i caratteri di un vero e proprio paralogismo per l'infondatezza delle postulazioni di fondo, proposte come altrettanti dati obiettivi, laddove sono il frutto di una lettura in chiave politica strettamente personale.

---

[66] Politics cit., p. 7ss.; Introduction cit., p. 72ss. — La tesi del GOODENOUGH fu accolta da J. DANIÉLOU, Philon d'Alexandrie, Parigi 1958, p. 75s., ed è citata senza commento dal TCHERIKOVER (CPJ I, p. 63, n. 31).

[67] Politics, pp. 21—41.

[68] Ibid., pp. 42—63.

Al Goodenough bisogna tuttavia riconoscere il merito di essere stato l'unico dopo il Momigliano, a porsi in concreto il problema di come si giustificasse la duplice versione del pogrom data da Filone e il cambiamento di visuale implicito in tale duplicità. Del resto, che la sua tesi fosse adattabile con qualche forzatura all''In Flaccum', ma risultasse priva di consistenza rispetto alla 'Legatio' fu forse lo stesso Goodenough a constatarlo. Infatti, mentre nei 'Politics' trascura di proposito tutto il sostrato etico-religioso dell'opera, che a suo avviso ha sapore di posticcio in quanto strumento di sottile fine politico, trova fuori posto che Filone nel capitolo introduttivo della 'Legatio' ,,apra al lettore la visuale del Mistero"[69] e altrove definisce opera di ,,pura teoria" l'intera 'Legatio'[70], presentata prima come uno scritto propagandistico, con fini eminentemente politici. Un altro palese contrasto si riscontra tra l'affermazione che Filone avesse assunto un atteggiamento antiromano in un momento impreciso, ma comunque anteriore al pogrom e viceversa avesse additato in Augusto e Tiberio due esempi di principi perfetti secondo l'ideale ellenistico, in cui si contemperavano il principio di sovranità e il rispetto delle libertà democratiche[71]. Su quest'ultima affermazione si possono avanzare non poche riserve, specialmente riguardo ad Augusto, nel quale Filone riconobbe bensì una personalità di eccezione e un equo pacificatore dell'impero, ma in quanto ricollegava i due dati dell'innato prestigio personale e dell'azione politica pacificatrice ad un accentramento di poteri, che il principe avrebbe attuato con la sostituzione della ,,monarchia" alla ,,poliarchia" (Leg. 149), comprovando l'opportunità di tale innovazione con i risultati ottenuti.

2. Echi in Filone di formulazioni teoriche sul principato romano

In aggiunta a quanto si è detto sopra, bisogna qui rilevare che, spiegando una seconda volta la ragione del conferimento al principe dell'appellativo di ,,Augusto" (Leg. 309), Filone usa termini che richiamano alla mente il binomio liviano *virtus ac fortuna*: Cesare Ottaviano avrebbe avuto per primo quel titolo ἀρετῆς ἕνεκα καὶ τύχης. La coincidenza è troppo evidente per essere casuale, tanto più se si consideri che nel linguaggio filoniano τύχη significa normalmente ,,caso" è non già ,,fortuna" nell'accezione latina positiva del termine. Sarebbe del tutto arbitrario postulare che Filone attingesse alla fonte liviana; non lo è altrettanto il supporre che Livio avesse associato Augusto alle altre figure di uomini grandi cui i Romani dovevano l'acquisto della propria potenza e che ciascuno singolarmente — come Camillo, come Scipione — erano stati da lui presentati in una luce particolare proprio in quanto a loro azione aveva avuto esito felice *virtute ac fortuna*, cioè grazie al concorso di una loro dote personale e del destino di Roma. La concezione storica di Livio dovette avere indubbia risonanza presso i suoi contemporanei

[69] Ibid., p. 12.
[70] Ibid., p. 110.
[71] Ibid., p. 88.

forse al punto di divenire voce corrente. Ora, c'è motivo di credere che Filone si basasse su dati di fatto, a lui noti o appresi da una tradizione diffusa, assai più che su premesse teoriche, almeno quando parlava della realtà di Roma. Se ne può trovare una conferma: in Leg. 43—51 è posto in bocca a Macrone, une delle tre vittime di Caligola, un discorso che presumibilmente corrisponde in proporzioni minime al tipo dei περὶ βασιλείας ellenistici di cui si conosce l'esistenza e si deplora la perdita. Tale discorso ha per tema la definizione del principe perfetto; ma la figura di principe che Macrone esalta e propone a modello di rettitudine e composta serietà al dissoluto Caligola, più che essere costruita sulla falsariga di una filosofia politica, ricalca i contorni di quel tipo di ,,monarca" che ha già avuto la sua realizzazione storica in Augusto: l'intero discorso suona, in sostanza, come una esortazione al ripristino della politica augustea, disgiunta da qualsiasi intento teorico.

VI. L'umanesimo di Filone

1. La filosofia filoniana della storia

I limiti e i difetti della rievocazione storica di Filone, subordinata com'è alla difesa di una causa particolare, non si possono né si devono disconoscere. Eppure i suoi giudizi hanno un fondo di verità che merita di essere scoperto e valutato senza prevenzioni e che si può recepire se si cerchi di sciogliere il groviglio di componenti eterogenee, che la coincidenza o la divergenza di passione e ragione rendono di volta in volta perspicue o impenetrabili. La 'Legatio', in effetti, è ravvivata per tutta la sua estensione da un monologo interiore del filosofo, che ha bensì abbandonato la storia sacra per la storia presente, ma che nell'attualità del suo tempo ricerca la verifica di certi principi ideologici, irrinunciabili e irreversibili, che in parte gli sono congeniali e congeniti, in parte costituiscono il risultato della meditazione di una intera vita. Nei suoi enunciati — che si tratti di Romani, di Greci o di Ebrei, di teoria o di pratica, di utopia o di realtà — si avverte di continuo la presenza di una controllata dismisura, che in tanto è controllata in quanto permette alla ragione di moderare il raptus passionale e in tanto eccede la misura comune in quanto apre la via a intuizioni, la cui validità supera i limiti del tempo.

Un'accurata analisi del sostrato speculativo della 'Legatio' — che peraltro è ormai apprezzata anche come fonte storica di informazione documentaria[72] — porta a concludere che Filone ha gettato le basi di una filosofia

---

[72] L'importanza della 'Legatio' come fonte storica è rilevata da A. NAZZARO, Recenti studi filoniani (1963—1970), Napoli 1973, p. 19, n. 47, che cita due studi cui F. è servito come fonte di chiarificazione, rispettivamente circa Tiberio e Ponzio Pilato: F. DE FISCHER, La politique dynastique sous le règne de Tibère, Synteleia V. Arangio Ruiz, Napoli 1964, pp. 54—65, e A. BAJŠIĆ, Pilatus, Jesus und Barabbas, Biblica XLVIII, 1967, pp. 7—28.

della storia, improntata a un carattere nuovo rispetto a tutta la precedente storiografia greca: nella sua visione il mondo non è più dominato dall'invidia di una divinità gelosa dei propri privilegi, come voleva Erodoto, né dalla ferrea legge di necessità e di forza di cui era arbitro l'uomo, come riteneva Tucidide né dal capriccio del caso, secondo la visione di Polibio. Per Filone il mondo è governato benevolmente dalla provvidenza del Dio unico dell'Antico Testamento, che si identifica con il bene supremo; e la πρόνοια θεοῦ, che nell' 'In Flaccum' appare come beneficio esclusivo del popolo ebraico, si estende nello spirito della 'Legatio' all'umanità intera. La vicenda del „popolo supplice" di Israele, scampato con le sole armi della fede e della preghiera alla minaccia di una profanazione del tempio di Gerusalemme, per la morte improvvisa di Caligola, è solo un esempio di come la provvidenza divina protegga, con il suo vigile intervento chi cade vittima della violenza umana; la posizione di privilegio di questo popolo non è che un riflesso del suo particolare patrimonio teologico, l'unica vera e spirituale richezza di cui esso si senta depositario e mediatore al resto dell'umanità. Il concetto della 'mediazione' di Israele è implicito nella μετάνοια, in virtù della quale diviene partecipe della πρόνοια θεοῦ chiunque, ebreo o non — ebreo, faccia atto di contrizione e attraverso il pentimento riconosca la propria impotenza umana.

Era questo un messaggio di pace, ma troppo arcano nella sua formulazione insieme umana e metafisica; e rimase quindi senza eco. Anzi, per un loro oscuro presentimento, i successivi imperatori di Roma avrebbero avvertito sempre di più nelle forze inermi di una credenza mistica quel pericolo che non avvertivano da parte di una qualsiasi forza militarmente armata. Filone, a sua volta, non sospettò in alcun modo l'imminente rovina del proprio popolo né poteva immaginare che sarebbe stato raso al suolo, dopo pochi decenni, quel Tempio che egli paventava venisse profanato con l'introduzione in esso di una statua pagana. Mancò dunque al filosofo la percezione del seguito che gli eventi da lui vissuti avrebbero avuto nell'immediato futuro. In compenso, egli fu il primo a indicare i valori potenzialmente universali contenuti nel pensiero ebraico, gettando le basi di una linea di pensiero che avrebbe avuto il suo sviluppo nel corso dei secoli e fu il primo ad individuare un fenomeno nato con la diaspora e perpetuatosi con essa, che con termine moderno si può chiamare della 'doppia nazionalità'.

2. La 'doppia nazionalità' degli Ebrei della diaspora

Filone ne parla come di una realtà di fatto nell' 'In Flaccum' (§ 46), dove si sofferma appunto sull'origine e sull'espansione della diaspora e dice degli Ebrei che „essi considerano loro città madre la Città Santa, nella quale sorge il Tempio consacrato all'Altissimo, ma tengono in conto di patria le città in cui abitano per eredità trasmessa loro dai padri, dai nonni, dai bisnonni e da antenati ancor più lontani, le città in cui sono nati e sono stati allevati". Nella 'Legatio' (§ 157) è sottolineata come indice della larghezza di vedute di Augusto la particolare circostanza che egli non togliesse agli Ebrei abitanti a Roma la cittadinanza romana ,,per il solo fatto che non dimenticavano la loro appartenenza a quella ebraica ('Ιουδαϊκὴ πολιτεία)". Ed è ancora questo l'argomento chiave della lettera di Agricola a Gaio: ,,Gerusalemme è la mia patria ed è la città madre non della sola Giudea, ma anche della maggior parte degli altri paesi, a causa delle colonie che essa ha mandato in epoche diverse nelle terre confinanti . . . e in terre lontane" (Leg. 281 s.). Gerusalemme, dunque, è il centro ideale verso il quale una forza centipetra fa convergere spiritualmente gli Ebrei dislocati nei punti più eccentrici dell'ecumène: se un punto della diaspora è colpito, ne risentono tutti gli altri, ma se è colpita Gerusalemme le ripercussioni sull'intera cosmopoli d'Israele sono di una gravità infinitamente maggiore. Sul piano storico, il legame che unisce l'ebraismo palestinese all'ebraismo disperso non è agli occhi di Filone un rapporto di filiazione, bensì di reciproca responsabilità e di reciproca influenza, in quanto ogni membro della diaspora appartiene a due patrie, quasi allegoricamente rappresentate come due genitori, esplicanti l'una il ruolo di madre (Gerusalemme, la ,,metropoli"), l'altra il ruolo di padre (la ,,patria" d'adozione, lontana da Gerusalemme). Ma sul piano ideologico, il vincolo materno ha peso qualitativamente molto maggiore di quello paterno, e lo si scopre in un passo altrettanto significatico quanto parentetico all'apparenza. In Leg. 193 s. Filone si chiede se abbia un senso o se sia lecito alla luce della legge divina e umana (ὅσιον ἢ θεμιτόν) sostenere i diritti politici (πολιτεία) di un nucleo della diaspora quando Caligola intende minare alle basi l'intero edificio dell'ebraismo nelle sue strutture ideali, mettendo in pericolo la cittadinanza ,,più universale" degli Ebrei (καθολικωτέρα πολιτεία). L'enunciazione, che questa volta esce dalla sfera concreta per evadere in quella delle formulazioni di principio, non lascia dubbi: nella visuale filoniana, la cittadinanza ideale, la καθολικωτέρα πολιτεία che lega l'ebreo disperso al Tempio di Gerusalemme, simbolo e fulcro dell'ebraismo, assolve rispetto alla πολιτεία più ristretta, in forza della quale si è cittadini di una qualche città, lo stesso ruolo che lo spirito assolve rispetto alla materia, sulla quale domina e prevale. Gli Ebrei della diaspora amano entrambe le loro patrie, ma di un amore diverso: il godimento dei diritti politici è subordinato al rispetto dei patrii costumi.

Sarebbe errore grave scambiare un simile atteggiamento per fanatica difesa dell'ortodossia religiosa: in netta opposizione al mondo pagano, Filone non difende l'osservanza di un culto, ma prospetta agli uomini del suo tempo e del tempo avvenire — e non ai propri correligionari soltanto — l'esistenza di una *civitas* spirituale, che trascende ogni interesse terreno. Da un riscontro con i trattati si ricava la certezza che la καθολικωτέρα πολιτεία è molto più che non il semplice simbolo della solidarietà ebraica: essa coincide, in effetti, con la φιλόθεος πολιτεία, la *civitas* cara a Dio, in cui Mosè (Spec. I,51) accoglie, senza distinzione di appartenenza o non appartenenza all'ebraismo, ogni uomo dotato di virtù, che sia tale per nascita o che tale diventi per fermo proposito.

Filone alessandrino e l'esegesi cristiana.
Contributo alla conoscenza dell'influsso esercitato da Filone sul IV secolo, specificatamente in Gregorio di Nazianzo

di Francesco Trisoglio, Torino

Sommario

I. Influsso di Filone sull'esegesi cristiana dei primi quattro secoli

Fozio (Cod. 105, MG. CIII, col. 373 A) espresse l'opinione che l'interpretazione allegorica della Bibbia, diffusa nella Chiesa, abbia avuto il suo principio in Filone e non è raro trovare in dotti moderni l'asserzione, variamente formulata, che la storia della teologia cristiana abbia mosso i primi passi partendo dalla speculazione dell'esegeta alessandrino. Bastano rilievi di questo genere per giustificare il profondo interesse che gli studiosi della cultura occidentale hanno dedicato e più ancora stanno dedicando alla complessa figura di Filone.

Egli si trovò infatti a vivere in un'epoca ed in un ambiente che furono direttamente investiti da una delle più radicali crisi che si riscontrino nella serie dei secoli. La civiltà ebraica, portatrice di un messaggio unico per purezza di concezione religiosa e per capacità di concentrare tutta la vita nell'idea divina, si sentiva pervasa da un'intima inquietudine. Proprio nel momento in cui stava per sublimarsi in quel cristianesimo che l'avrebbe insieme consacrata ed accantonata, percepiva l'ombra di una minaccia più grave e decisiva di quelle passate: i remoti antenati avevano dovuto lottare contro la forza delle armi nemiche, contro il malo esempio dell'idolatria circostante, contro l'eterno impulso delle passioni sregolate; ora invece bisognava resistere al fascino sottile di una civiltà smagliante nella sua raffinatezza formale, allettante nella sua ricchezza concettuale, incantevole nella sua acutezza psicologica, ammirevole nella sua sapienza civile. L'ellenismo che era giunto ad un palmo dal travolgere, con le sue ondate dovunque dilaganti, la rocca di Gerusalemme, estremo atollo nel quale si era raccolto l'ebraismo, era stato rintuzzato dalla reazione dei Maccabei al tempo di Antioco IV Epifane (166—160 a. C.), però la lotta non si presentava come conclusa. E poi non si trattava di uno scontro di eserciti, ma di idee: i primi si possono anche distruggere per intero, le seconde invece possono unicamente morire; ma muoiono solo quando sono soverchiate da altre, che il più delle volte superano le antagoniste assorbendo quanto esse hanno di vitale e di dinamico. Il giudaismo allora, sotto lo stimolo del pericolo ed anche sotto il pungolo dell'orgoglio, invece di trincerarsi in una difensiva sicuramente destinata alla catastrofe, si lanciò in un'offensiva che fondeva in unità apologetica e propaganda. I più svariati generi letterari furono fatti scendere in lizza: la storia e la cronologia con lo Pseudo-Ecateo, con Demetrio ed Eupolemo, con Artabano, con Cleodemo, con Giasone di Cirene, con Tallo, con Giusto di Tiberiade, con Flavio Giuseppe; la filosofia con Aristobulo e con il Quarto Libro dei Maccabei; l'epica con Teodoto e con Filone l'Antico; la tragedia con Ezechiele; l'esegesi biblica con Filone.

Quest'ultimo che aveva osservato l'apostasia insinuarsi non solo nella diaspora della sua città ma addirittura nella cerchia della sua famiglia — il nipote T. Giulio Alessandro aveva abiurato, abbracciando un credo filosofico assolutamente incompatibile con la rivelazione biblica — si era ben presto convinto che l'unico mezzo per salvare la tradizione ebraica, nella quale credeva con tutta l'anima, consisteva nel ripensarla secondo le categorie della filosofia greca, che egli si era intimamente assimilata, e di presentarla secondo il suo linguaggio, che era diventato il contrassegno ufficiale di tutte le persone culturalmente superiori. Nella sua missione di salvataggio, che aveva un po' la risolutezza d'una crociata, puntò direttamente su quello che gli sembrò il cuore del patrimonio biblico e che identificò nella legge: su di essa focalizzò la sua attenzione ed alla sua rilettura in senso moderno consacrò i suoi tre grandi commenti: la 'Spiegazione delle Leggi', l' 'Allegoria delle Leggi' e le 'Quaestiones'. L'indiscussa venerazione per la parola di Dio ed il culto per la sua stessa formulazione, che costituivano una componente irrinunciabile della sua mentalità ebraica, gli imponevano l'accettazione del senso letterale che egli non pensò mai a rigettare, specie in sede programmatica, però come strumento della sua rinnovazione del testo sacro scelse l'allegoria, la quale, soprattutto per merito degli stoici, aveva acquisito un incontrastato diritto di cittadinanza nell'interpretazione letteraria. La classicità, con tale accorgimento, aveva elevato Omero al di sopra delle contestazioni che la sensibilità morale, via via più scaltrita, aveva incominciato ad opporgli: Filone si propose di raggiungere gli stessi risultati riguardo alla Scrittura, che rappresentava per il suo popolo un elemento vitale assai più assoluto di quanto fosse Omero per i Greci.

All'impiego dell'allegoria come metodo ermeneutico[1] egli fu dunque
mosso: a) dalla necessità di conciliare l'ispirazione divina con le apparenti

[1] Sui caratteri dell'esegesi filoniana vedi: Z. FRANKEL, Über den Einfluß der palästinischen
Exegese auf die alexandrinische Hermeneutik, Leipzig, 1851, pp. X-354; C. G. A. SIEG-
FRIED, Die hebräischen Worterklärungen des Philo und die Spuren ihrer Einwirkung auf
die Kirchenväter, Magdeburg—Berlin, 1863, pp. 37; ID., Philo von Alexandria als Ausleger des alten Testaments, Jena, 1875, pp. VI-418 (influssi filoniani sulla successiva esegesi biblica giudaica: pp. 278—302, e su quella cristiana: pp. 303—399); S. KARPPE,
Philon et le Zohar, deux expressions analogues de l'allégorisme, in: Étude sur les origines
et la nature du Zohar, précédée d'une étude sur l'histoire de la Kabbale, Paris, 1901,
pp. 527—581; J. Z. LAUTERBACH, The Ancient Jewish Allegorists in Talmud and Midrash,
in: The Jewish Quarterly Review, N. S. I (1910—1911), pp. 291—333; 503—531; W.
BOUSSET, Jüdisch-christlicher Schulbetrieb in Alexandria und Rom. Literarische Untersuchungen zu Philo und Clemens von Alexandria, Justin und Irenäus, Göttingen, 1915,
pp. 319 (su Filone pp. 8—154); J. TREITEL, Philonische Studien, hrsg. von M. BRANN,
Breslau, 1915, pp. VI-130 (ripubblicazione di articoli sulle feste giudaiche, pp. 1—5 e
6—65; sulla posizione religiosa e culturale di Filone, pp. 66—84; sull'haggada in Filone,
pp. 85—113; sull'origine, il significato e l'ambito dell'esegesi allegorica, pp. 114—122;
sulla dottrina degli intermediari e delle potenze divine, pp. 123—130); E. STEIN, Die
allegorische Exegese des Philo aus Alexandreia (Beihefte zur Zeitschrift für die alttestamentliche Wissenschaft, n. 51), Gießen, 1929, pp. V-61; ID., Alttestamentliche
Bibelkritik in der späthellenistischen Literatur, Lwów, 1935, pp. 48; J. HEINEMANN,
Altjüdische Allegoristik, Breslau, 1936, pp. 88 (trattazione generale con scarsi riferimenti
diretti a Filone); M. J. SHROYER, Alexandrian Jewish Literalists, in: Journal of Biblical
Literature, LV (1936), pp. 261—284; S. SANDMEL, Philo's Environment and Philo's
Exegesis, in: Journal of Bible and Religion, XXII (1954), pp. 248—253; G. DELLING,
Wunder, Allegorie, Mythus bei Philon von Alexandrien, in: Wissenschaftliche Zeitschrift der M.-Luther-Univ. Halle, VI (1956—57), pp. 713—739; stesso autore e
stesso titolo in: Festschrift O. Eissfeldt, Berlin, 1959, pp. 42—68; J. PÉPIN, Mythe
et allégorie. Les origines grecques et les contestations judéo-chrétiennes, Paris, 1958,
pp. 231—242; J. POUILLOUX, Philon d'Alexandrie: recherches et points de vue
nouveaux, in: Revue de l'Histoire des Religions, CLXI (1962), pp. 135—137;
V. HARRIS, Allegory to Analogy in the Interpretation of Scriptures, in: Philological
Quarterly, XLV (1966), pp. 1—23; J. PÉPIN, Remarques sur la théorie de l'exégèse allégorique chez Philon, in: Philon d'Alexandrie. Colloque Lyon 11—15 Septembre 1966, Paris,
1967, pp. 131—167; K. OTTE, Das Sprachverständnis bei Philo von Alexandrien. Sprache
als Mittel der Hermeneutik (Beiträge zur Geschichte der biblischen Exegese, n. 7),
Tübingen, 1968, pp. VIII-162; R. MAYER, Geschichtserfahrung und Schriftauslegung.
Zur Hermeneutik des frühen Judentums, in: Die hermeneutische Frage in der Theologie
(Schriften zum Weltgespräch, n. 3), Freiburg i. Br., 1968, pp. 290—355; J. CHRISTIANSEN,
Die Technik der allegorischen Auslegungswissenschaft bei Philon von Alexandrien (Bei-
träge zur Geschichte der biblischen Hermeneutik, n. 7), Tübingen, 1969, pp. 191; A. V.
NAZZARO, Realtà e linguaggio in Filone d'Alessandria, in: Le Parole e le Idee, XI (1969),
pp. 339—346 (in connessione con l'opera dell'OTTE); J. AMIR, The Relations between
Philo's and the Homeric Allegory, in: Eškolot, VI (1971), pp. 35—46 (in ebraico);
J. GRIBOMONT, s. v. Isaac, in: Dictionnaire de Spiritualité, VII, 1971, col. 1990; S. SAND-
MEL, Philo's Place in Judaism. A Study of the Conception of Abraham in Jewish Literature,
2nd ed. rev., New York, 1971, pp. XXIX-232; J. VIDAL, Le thème d'Adam chez Philon
d'Alexandrie, Mémoire de Maîtrise, Paris, 1971, pp. 143; C. GNILKA, Aetas spiritalis.
Die Überwindung der natürlichen Altersstufen als Ideal frühchristlichen Lebens (Theophaneia, n. 24), Bonn, 1972 (nella sezione C, cap. I tratta dell'esegesi allegorica in Filone
[pp. 75—87] e negli esegeti cristiani [pp. 87—115]); J. C. H. LEBRAM, Eine stoische Auslegung von Ex. 3,2 bei Philo, in: Das Institutum Judaicum der Univ. Tübingen 1971—72,
Tübingen, 1972, pp. 30—34; T. C. G. THORNTON, Trees, Gibbets and Crosses, in: Journal
of Theological Studies, XXIII (1972), pp. 130—131 (cfr. Deut. 21, 22—23 con De spec.

aporie di cui vedeva costellato il testo rivelato preso nella sua accezione immediata; b) dalla teoria dell'esemplarismo che lo induceva a cercare

Leg. III 152); J. Amir, Philo and the Bible, in: Studia Philonica, II (1973), pp. 1—8; J. Cazeaux, Aspects de l'exégèse philonienne, in: Revue des Sciences Religieuses, XLVII (1973), pp. 262—269; A. Myre, La loi et le Pentateuque selon Philon d'Alexandrie, in: Science et Esprit (Montréal), XXV (1973), pp. 209—225; V. Nikiprowetzky, L'exégèse de Philon d'Alexandrie, in: Revue d'Histoire et de Philosophie Religieuses, LIII (1973), pp. 309—329; E. Starobinski-Safran, Significations des noms divins — d'après Ex. 3 — dans la tradition rabbinique et chez Philon d'Alexandrie, in: Revue de Théologie et de Philosophie, CVI (1973), pp. 426—435 e, in italiano, in: Rassegna mensile d'Israele (Roma), XLI (1975), pp. 546—556; A. J. M. Wedderburn, Philo's "heavenly man", in: Novum Testamentum, XV (1973), pp. 301—326 (Filone interpreta in vari testi Gen. 1, 26 segg. come creazione di un ,,uomo celeste" in opposizione a quello creato in Gen. 2, 7 formato di corpo e d'anima); H. Dörrie, Zur Methodik antiker Exegese, in: Zeitschrift für die Neutestamentliche Wissenschaft, LXV (1974), pp. 121—138 (al par. 8 pp. 133—134 esamina in Filone la sua tesi che l'antica esegesi, più che al testo, aderiva all'eredità culturale consolidata dai secoli); M. Petit, Les songes dans l'œuvre de Philon d'Alexandrie, in: Mélanges H.-Ch. Puech, Paris, 1974, pp. 151—159; B. L. Mack, Exegetical Traditions in Alexandrian Judaism. A program for the analysis of the Philonic corpus, in: Studia Philonica, III (1974—75), pp. 71—112 (per capire Filone è necessario comprendere la tradizione esegetica giudaica di Alessandria ed il giudaismo ellenistico in generale); F. Bolgiani, L'ascesi di Noè. A proposito di Theoph. ad Autol. III, 19, in: Studi in onore di M. Pellegrino, Torino, 1975, pp. 295—333 (alle pp. 322—327 presenta l'interpretazione filoniana di Noè come ,,eunuco"); C. del Valle, Aproximaciones al método alégorico de Filón de Alejandría, in: Helmantica, XXVI (1975), pp. 561—577 (l'interpretazione allegorica di Filone ha la sua origine nel giudaismo palestinese ed ellenistico); negli: Studies on the Testament of Joseph, ed. G. W. E. Nickelsburg Jr. (Society of Biblical Literature, Septuaginta and Cognate Studies, n. 5), Missoula, 1975, pp. VII-153, il primo degli ultimi quattro contributi, i quali confrontano il Giuseppe del Testamento con i ritratti che ne fanno altri scrittori giudaici, è di D. J. Harrington, che prende in considerazione il Filone spurio e quello autentico; A. Myre, Les caractéristiques de la loi mosaïque selon Philon d'Alexandrie, in: Science et Esprit, XXVII (1975), pp. 35—69; E. Starobinski-Safran, Sabbats, années sabbatiques et jubilés. Réflexions sur l'exégèse juive et chrétienne de Lévitique 25, in: Mélanges E. Bréguet, Genève, 1975, pp. 37—45 (interpretazione anche di Filone su queste istituzioni); V. Nikiprowetzky, Rébecca, Vertue de Constance et Constance de Vertu chez Philon d'Alexandrie, in: Semitica, XXVI (1976), pp. 109—136; M. Petit, À propos d'une traversée exemplaire du désert du Sinaï selon Philon (Hypothetica VI, 2—3, 8): texte biblique et apologétique concernant Moïse chez quelques écrivains juifs, ibidem, pp. 137—142; E. Starobinski-Safran, La lettre et l'esprit chez Philon d'Alexandrie, in: Rencontre Chrétiens et Juifs, X (1976), pp. 43—51; P. Borgen—R. Skarsten, Quaestiones et solutiones: some observations on the form of Philo's Exegesis, in: Studia Philonica, IV (1976—77), pp. 1—15; D. Jobling, "And Have Dominion ...". The interpretation of Genesis 1, 28 in Philo Judaeus, in: Journal for the Study of Judaism, VIII (1977), pp. 50—82 (basandosi su fonti soprattutto stoiche e platoniche intende la signoria umana nel senso delle attività culturali); J. P. Martín, El texto y la interpretación. La exégesis según Filón de Alejandría, in: Revista Bíblica (Buenos Aires), XXXIX (1977), pp. 211—222; V. Nikiprowetzky, Le commentaire de l'Écriture chez Philon d'Alexandrie. Son caractère et sa portée. Observations philologiques (Arbeiten zur Literatur und Geschichte des hellenistischen Judentums, n. 11), Leiden, 1977, pp. X-293. — Programmaticamente, qui come in seguito, non vengono segnalati gli studi rimasti manoscritti o dattiloscritti. — Nel presente volume (ANRW II 21,1) vedi J. Cazeaux, Philon d'Alexandrie, exégète, pp. 156—226 e B. L. Mack, Philo Judaeus and Exegetical Traditions in Alexandria, pp. 227—271.

dietro alle cose gli archetipi razionali che ne avevano prodotto la forma;
c) dalla dottrina platonica dell'analogia tra gli αἰσθητά ed i νοητά all'interno del cosmo; d) dal dogma stoico della solidarietà di tutti gli esseri
che si risolveva in una simpatia universale; e) dall'opinione vulgata che la
natura amasse dissimularsi; f) dalla prassi che era invalsa, nelle scuole da
lui frequentate, ad opera dei grammatici alessandrini; g) dalla passione di
dimostrare all'intellettualità pagana che la sua fede non cedeva, in razionalità speculativa, alle loro correnti filosofiche. Sebbene del metodo allegorico
non fosse l'inventore, ne divenne tuttavia il partigiano più convinto e
l'applicatore più tenace. Per lui ne erano suscettibili quasi tutti i passi e
molti andavano con esso obbligatoriamente trattati: erano quelli che
sminuivano la santità del messaggio biblico con sconcezze, ne mettevano
in dubbio la sapienza con assurdità, contraddizioni, vaniloquii, ne abbassa-
vano l'altezza con l'ingenuità degli antropopatismi divini, ne minavano la
serietà con inesattezze e con favole corrispondenti ai miti pagani. L'avver-
tenza di precisare che l'interpretazione traslata era sottratta al capriccio
soggettivo dell'esegeta, in quanto tacitamente segnalata dallo stesso scrittore sacro, non era certo superflua come non era sufficiente. Già la molteplicità delle interpretazioni parallele, per quanto parzialmente resa più
agevole da qualcuna delle motivazioni che lo avevano indotto ad abbrac-
ciarle, se apriva all'esegeta una pluralità di campi in cui spaziare, poteva
ingenerare nel lettore il sospetto di una certa gratuità. Perciò Filone cercò
di imporsi una qualche disciplina, di perseguire una coerenza, almeno per
sommi capi e nella maggioranza dei casi, che ovviasse alla possibile accusa
di equivocità nella rivelazione o di divagazione nel chiosatore. Non si
ridusse invece a contenere in un numero rigorosamente ristretto i tipi dei
sensi allegorici; egli infatti ammise: a) quello cosmologico (come quando
sull'albero della vita seguì certi suoi innominati predecessori che vi avevano
visto il sole; nella scala di Giacobbe scorse un emblema dell'atmosfera; nei
padri di Abramo interpretò il sole, la luna ed altre stelle; nell'abito del
sommo sacerdote ravvisò un simbolo dell'universo e delle sue parti; nella
spada dei Cherubini trovò un richiamo al sole); b) quello antropologico (per
cui, ad esempio, considerò l'albero della vita come figura del nous o del
cuore, la scala di Giacobbe come schermo dell'anima umana, il campo ed
il cielo di Gen. 2,19 come allusione alla mente, il sale dei sacrifici come
parallelo dell'anima vivificatrice del corpo); c) quello pneumatico (in forza
del quale nei padri di Abramo avvertì una rappresentazione delle idee
archetipe verso le quali il sapiente deve ritornare e negli alberi non frutti-
feri un adombramento della logica); d) quello morale (di cui abbiamo dei
casi esemplari nell'Abramo dell'Her., che diventa il tipo ideale del servo
di Dio, del fedele, del profeta, nella scala di Giacobbe, che risulta l'immagine dell'asceta il quale sale o scende nella virtù e nei valori dello spirito,
nelle pinne e nelle squame, che Mosè menziona come proprie dei pesci, le
quali alludono alla saldezza ed alla sobrietà che mettono l'anima in condizione di vincere tutte le fatiche, nell'agricoltura che si dimostra come
trasposizione della vita dello spirito); e) quello anagogico — che conduce

direttamente alla divinità — (di cui ci diede uno specimen quando affermò che i cherubini posti ad oriente dell'Eden ed armati di spade fiammeggianti erano la bontà e la sovranità le quali costituiscono le principali potenze divine, e quando invitò a riconoscere nel pastore di greggi Dio che regge l'universo); f) quello sapienziale — che illustra le leggi che regolano la natura umana nel suo agire — (di cui può essere raffigurazione la scala di Giacobbe quale riferimento ai successi ed agli insuccessi degli affari umani); g) quello politico (a cui si attenne quando spiegò il pastore come personificazione della regalità e l'allevatore di bestiame come emblema dell'oclocrazia e della tirannide).

È facile notare che enorme ampiezza di prospettive fornisse questo metodo esegetico; in pratica qualunque campo nel quale la nostra intelligenza potesse avventurarsi veniva di diritto acquisito alla Bibbia; qualsiasi progresso realizzato da qualsiasi scienza era immediatamente recepibile dalla Sacra Scrittura. Il pericolo di una fossilizzazione della parola di Dio era sventato e veniva dissipato quell'uggioso senso del 'superato' che poteva mettere a disagio molti credenti colti e diventare un'*humus* propizia per eventuali defezioni. La Bibbia da libro di un'epoca diventava libro di tutte, da vettrice di fatti si trasformava in suggeritrice di modelli, da storia passava a filosofia, soprattutto morale. Si trattava di un arricchimento grandioso: la Genesi non era più solo la lontana storia di tutta l'umanità ma la biografia spirituale, drammaticamente calda, di ogni singolo individuo; la Legge si spogliava di ogni arcaicità per rispondere a tutte le ansie ed a tutte le domande della persona nel suo perenne divenire e nel suo incessante espandersi. A tali pregi non mancava ovviamente una contropartita negativa: la Scrittura universalizzata veniva sottratta ad ogni sospetto di inadeguatezza, ma veniva anche spogliata di quella concretezza storica che le conferiva un'autenticità estremamente preziosa. Filone s'accorse naturalmente del rischio e cercò di pararlo insistendo sulla veracità del senso letterale: era una posizione saggia ed era un'acuta percezione che tutto il suo superbo edificio sarebbe crollato qualora gli fosse stato incrinato il fondamento della storicità. Non si poteva presentare una parola di Dio senza presupporre che Dio avesse — in un determinato tempo ed in un determinato luogo — parlato; non si poteva fare dei patriarchi gli archetipi perfetti delle virtù umane qualora non fossero esistiti: sarebbero stati sviliti a fantasmi. Tutto questo non sfuggì a Filone, ma rimase, appunto, allo stato di presupposto. La storicità egli l'affermò, ma la superò troppo in fretta; la credette sufficientemente, ma sufficientemente non la sentì. La legge mosaica fu quindi sottoposta alla tendenza a slittare da esplicita rivelazione, dovuta ad un intervento positivo di Dio, a comunicazione implicita contenuta nell'azione creativa. Identificata con la legge naturale perdeva in maestà ed in sacralità quanto acquistava in universalità.

Coerente con questa spersonalizzazione degli avvenimenti storici era la decisa diluizione dell'idea messianica. Tutto teso all'elevazione del singolo individuo considerato nella sua ecumenicità, non nutriva più molto interesse alle sorti specifiche del popolo ebraico come tale: se si appassionava ardentemente ed agiva per la sorte dei suoi concittadini perseguitati, non trepidava per i destini, astrattamente intesi, dell'ebraismo. Per lui il Messia non era più il liberatore d'Israele che sarebbe apparso nel καιρός fissato dall'imperscrutabile piano divino, era l'effetto liberante esercitato dalla legge mosaica qualora fosse stata illuminatamente capita e fedelmente seguita. Il Logos per Filone fu un'entità sfuggente ed oscillante: divino senz'essere Dio, dotato di un'esistenza incerta tra l'indipendenza di una persona autonoma e la relatività di una semplice forza divina, intermediario tra Dio ed il mondo in quanto agente nella creazione ed intercessore che aiuta l'intelligenza umana a salire, legge e destino dell'universo, fu un concetto continuamente sollecitato in ogni direzione da ogni sorta di personificazioni e di metafore. Per il Nuovo Testamento il Logos era invece una Persona trinitaria perfettamente caratterizzata, era Dio fattosi uomo in esecuzione di un piano eterno; l'Incarnazione diventava l'inserimento dell'assoluto nella storia, la quale veniva quindi riaffermata. Il messianismo cristiano salvava perciò l'universalità filoniana ma ne ricuperava anche la storicità. Era una diversità teologica che produceva un riflesso diretto nell'esegesi: per l'Alessandrino l'Antico Testamento da solo, mancando di un punto di riferimento, non poteva trovare nessuna spiegazione tropologica se non nella rassomiglianza delle nature dalla quale scaturiva l'allegoria; per i cristiani invece, oltre all'Antico, esisteva il Nuovo Testamento, fatto che creava un rapporto bilaterale il quale sfociava naturalmente nella tipologia: l'Antico Testamento, stimato come parte integrante nell'unità del piano soteriologico divino, veniva giudicato come il momento dialetticamente propedeutico alla conquista della verità totale: era la lettera contrapposta allo spirito del Nuovo, l'ombra contrapposta alla realtà, il provvisorio contrapposto al definitivo; eventi, persone, oggetti dell'Antico diventavano quindi prefigurazioni di corrispondenti eventi, persone, oggetti del Nuovo Testamento. La tipologia, stabilendo una relazione che pareva emergere dagli avvenimenti ed esigere dall'esegeta solo il riconoscimento successivo, lasciava l'impressione di assidersi su basi più obiettivamente solide dell'allegoria, aperta ad una polivalenza simbologica, la quale nel critico sembrava trovare non tanto lo scopritore quanto il creatore. Probabile frutto inconscio di questa differenza di posizioni fu il diverso atteggiamento psicologico di fronte alla Bibbia: Filone ebbe infatti prevalenti preoccupazioni apologetiche, i cristiani predominanti aspirazioni missionarie. La sicurezza di Cristo, che insegnava con autorità, si trasmise in qualche modo anche ai suoi discepoli: essi pensavano più a mostrare che a dimostrare, più a rivelare che a giustificare.

Se di fronte a questa vasta impresa di aggiornamento e di universalizzazione della Scrittura era naturale che reagissero con un dispettoso ostracismo tanto i sadducei, attaccati al testo biblico nella sua immobilità, quanto i farisei, che lo interpretavano in funzione antiellenistica e nazionalistica canonizzando le tradizioni dei padri, che essi tendevano a rendere anguste con la loro normativa soffocante piuttosto che ad aprire verso nuove concezioni, era altrettanto naturale che si rivolgessero con un notevole interesse i cristiani. Anch'essi credevano nella santità della parola di Dio ed anch'essi, che adoravano il Verbo incarnato, erano persuasi che la parola pronunciata dovesse, essa pure, incarnarsi nelle culture via via successive. L'ellenismo appariva quindi a loro, come a Filone, un campo fertile nel quale seminare il grano divino in vista di una moltiplicazione sempre rinnovata. Spinti dall'investitura di predicare la verità a tutte le genti, capirono che la brillante civiltà ellenistica poteva convertirsi in tramite eccellente e nel suo sfruttamento trovarono la via parzialmente aperta dall'opera di Filone. Se ne servirono, ovviamente con criteri attentamente selettivi. La rivelazione neotestamentaria segnava delle linee discriminative precise ed indiscutibili; il gusto dei singoli, integrato dall'esperienza individuale, completava per ciascuno le direttrici di marcia. L'attività di cernita era poi facilitata, e quasi suggerita, dal carattere stesso dell'opera filoniana: luminosa eppure monotona, acuta e pure spesso artificiale, multiforme e, non soltanto per questo, frammentaria. La sua qualità di scolio più che di trattato, togliendole anche l'aspetto di una sistematicità fortemente concatenata, invitava ad una scelta di materiali che si presentavano già quasi come disarticolati per ulteriori costruzioni.

Più saldamente ancorati alla storia, i cristiani non si lasciarono molto attrarre dalle speculazioni cosmologiche, solo mediocremente da quelle antropologiche, molto invece da quelle teologiche e morali: la Bibbia diventava una lezione sempre attuale ed una fonte sempre fluente di illuminazioni e di stimoli. L'allegoria si prestava eccellentemente a scartare aporie, a sopprimere motivi di scandalo, a portare il suggello biblico su specifiche esigenze pastorali che nascevano da particolari situazioni ambientali. Di norma i cristiani furono più sobrii nell'uso di questo strumento, efficace ma anche fin troppo facile ed esposto al rischio di sorvolare sulle difficoltà in luogo di risolverle. Alcuni dei Padri quindi lo usarono, avvalendosi delle sue indubbie capacità mistiche, altri invece lo riguardarono con diffidenza preferendo un esame del sacro testo più scientificamente obiettivo e quindi atto a dimostrazioni più sicuramente cogenti. Ne vennero così le due scuole più importanti: a) quella alessandrina, che soprattutto con Clemente ed Origene portò l'allegorismo al massimo fulgore e che ebbe come rappresentanti Didimo il Cieco, S. Cirillo d'Alessandria, S. Ippolito, S. Ilario di Poitiers S. Ambrogio e come simpatizzanti i tre Cappadoci (dei quali S. Basilio fu più vicino agli Antiocheni, il Nisseno agli Alessandrini, il Nazianzeno equidistante in posizione centrale) e pur con molta moderazione S. Agostino; b) quella antiochena, che all'allegoria sostituì la 'teoria', intesa come più piena comprensione del senso storico, e che ebbe come favoreggiatori S. Metodio e S. Epifanio e come più autorevoli corifei Diodoro di Tarso, Teodoro di Mopsuestia, S. Giovanni Crisostomo e l'Ambrosiaster. Su di una posizione eclettica si attestò S. Girolamo. In un'area, come questa, per sua natura sottratta a confini precisi la realtà si colorò evidentemente di tutte le sfumature, per cui l'abbozzo or ora tracciato rappresenta soltanto uno schema scheletrico e puramente orientativo. In pratica ogni spiccata personalità cristiana assunse un proprio atteggiamento nel quale, il più delle volte, entrava come ingrediente almeno minoritario, anche l'allegoria. L'influsso filoniano fu dunque di rilevantissima importanza: nell'ardua opera di tradurre la rivelazione in teologia i Padri della Chiesa misero spesso a profitto le speculazioni del pensatore egiziano rielaborandole nei modi più vari. Si comprende pertanto come questo fatto abbia attirato gli sguardi degli studiosi del cristianesimo e della civiltà occidentale nel suo complesso. Finora sono state discretamente numerose le indagini che hanno mirato a porre in chiaro di quale genere e di quale intensità siano state le relazioni che collegarono gli scrittori cristiani a Filone: quasi tutti gli esponenti ragguardevoli della patristica greca ed alcuni anche di quella latina sono stati affrontati con lui; tra le poche eccezioni la più sorprendente è quella che concerne S. Gregorio di Nazianzo[2]. Scopo della presente disamina sarebbe

---

[2] Negli studi filoniani il Nazianzeno sembra essere così 'fuori di mano' che persino uno studioso specializzato come H. Pinault, Le Platonisme de Saint Grégoire di Nazianze. Essai sur les relations du Christianisme et de l'Hellénisme dans son œuvre théologique, La Roche-sur-Yon, 1925, pp. XII-244, nonostante che l'argomento lo invitasse abbastanza esplicitamente a considerare come testimone anche colui di cui si disse che o Filone platonizza o Platone filonizza (S. Girolamo, De vir. ill. 11), si limita — tranne un paio di casi, a p. 91 ed a p. 98 — a pochi e generici richiami. A documentare quest'esclusione può essere utile un prospetto essenziale delle ricerche esperite a questo riguardo. Segnaliamo pertanto: C. G. A. Siegfried, Die hebräischen Worterklärungen des Philo . . . (per questo lavoro e per quello seguente cfr. la nota 1) (di carattere generale); Idem, Philo von Alexandria als Ausleger des alten Testaments . . ., il quale nello 'Zweiter Theil, zweiter Abschnitt: Philo's Einfluß auf die christliche Schriftauslegung', nel secondo capitolo considera i Padri Greci: Barnaba (pp. 330—332), gli antichi apologisti (pp. 332—340), Clemente Alessandrino (pp. 343—351), Origene (pp. 351—362), Eusebio di Cesarea (pp. 362—364), altri scrittori e specialmente Efrem Siro (pp. 364—371); nel terzo capitolo pòi indaga sui Padri Latini: Ambrogio (pp. 371—391), Girolamo ed altri (pp. 391—398); T. Förster, Ambrosius, Bischof von Mailand. Eine Darstellung seines Lebens und Wirkens, Halle a. S., 1884, pp. 102—112; L. S. Potwin, Philo and the Διδαχή, in: The Bibliotheca Sacra, XLIII (1886), pp. 174—176; M. Ihm, Philon und Ambrosius, in: Neue Jahrbücher für Philologie und Paedagogik (Jahrbücher für classische Philologie), CXLI (1890), pp. 282—288; P. Wendland, Neu entdeckte Fragmente Philos, Berlin, 1891, pp. 109—114: Philo und Origenes; Id., Philo und Clemens Alexandrinus, in: Hermes, XXXI (1896), pp. 435—456; S. Karppe, Philon et la Patristique, in: Id., Essais de critique et d'histoire de philosophie (Bibliothèque de philosophie contemporaine), Paris, 1902, pp. 1—33 (trattazione generale assai superficiale); A. Pelli, Studi su Filone Giudeo, Bologna, 1906, pp. 19—24 (di nessuna importanza); J. Geffcken, Zwei griechische Apologeten, Leipzig—Berlin, 1907, pp. XLIII-333 (Aristide ed Atenagora); J. Martin, Philon, Paris, 1907, il quale alle pp. 283—286 fa qualche osservazione generale sui Padri che si servirono di Filone, tacendo completamente di Gregorio; P. Heinisch, Der Einfluß Philos auf die älteste christliche Exegese (Barnabas, Justin und Clemens von Alexandria). Ein Beitrag zur Geschichte der allegorisch-mystischen Schriftauslegung im christlichen Altertum (Alttestamentliche Abhandlungen, n. 1, 1/2), Münster i. W., 1908, pp. 296; H. Windisch, Die Frömmigkeit Philos und ihre Bedeutung für das Christentum. Eine religionsgeschichtliche Studie, Leipzig, 1909 (cfr. a pp. 123—124 accenni a Clemente Alessandrino, Origene ed Agostino e qualche altro richiamo qua e là); I. M. Pfättisch, Der Einfluß Platos auf die Theologie Justins des Märtyrers (Forschungen zur Christlichen Literatur- und Dogmengeschichte, n. X,1), Paderborn, 1910, pp. 55—57; H. Lesêtre, Philon, in: F. Vigouroux, Dictionnaire de la Bible, vol. V, Paris, 1912, coll. 310—311 (sulla sua influenza in genere); W. Bousset, Jüdisch-christlicher Schulbetrieb in Alexandria und Rom (cfr. nota 1); W. Christ—W. Schmid—O. Stählin, Geschichte der

(Proseguimento della nota 2)

griechischen Literatur, II. Teil, 1. Hälfte, 6. Aufl., München, 1920, Nachdruck 1959, p. 659 (influsso di Filone su Clemente Alessandrino ed Origene); E. R. GOODENOUGH, The Theology of Justin Martyr, Jena, 1923, pp. 320 (particolarmente pp. 44—45; 125—134; 141—175; 189—205; 221—223; 229; 293—294); H. LEISEGANG, Der Ursprung der Lehre Augustins von der Civitas Dei, in: Archiv für Kulturgeschichte, XVI (1926), pp. 127—158 (dove sostiene che Agostino conobbe Filone tramite Ambrogio); J. LEBRETON, Histoire du dogme de la Trinité, t. II⁵, Paris, 1928, pp. 663—677 (su Giustino); W. VÖLKER, Das Abraham-Bild bei Philo, Origenes und Ambrosius, in: Studien und Kritiken zur Theologie. Festgabe F. Kattenbusch, Gotha, 1931, pp. 199—207; H. LEWY, Neue Philontexte in der Überarbeitung des Ambrosius. Mit einem Anhang: Neu gefundene griechische Philonfragmente, in: Sitzungsberichte der preußischen Akad. d. Wissenschaften, Philos.-histor. Klasse, IV, Berlin, 1932, pp. 23—84; W. KNUTH, Der Begriff der Sünde bei Philon von Alexandria, Würzburg, 1934, pp. 82—85: Historische Perspektive: Philons Sündenbegriff bei Augustin; H. L. GOODHART and E. R. GOODENOUGH, A General Bibliography of Philo Judaeus, New Haven, 1938 (nelle pp. 298—301 rimandano alle note delle edizioni delle opere di Clemente Romano, Barnaba, Aristide, Giustino Martire, Taziano, Atenagora, Teofilo d'Antiochia, Clemente Alessandrino, Ireneo, Origene, Pseudo-Giustino, Eusebio, Epifanio, Costituzioni Apostoliche, Basilio Magno, Eusebio, Girolamo, Ambrogio); J. QUASTEN, Der Gute Hirt in hellenistischer und frühchristlicher Logostheorie, in: Heilige Überlieferung. Festschrift I. Herwegen, Münster, 1938, pp. 51—58 (influenza della figura filoniana del Logos-pastore su Clemente Alessandrino); B. ALTANER, Augustinus und Philon von Alexandrien: eine quellenkritische Untersuchung, in: Zeitschrift für katholische Theologie, LXV (1941), pp. 81—90; M. W. BLOOMFIELD, A Source of Prudentius' Psychomachia, in: Speculum, XVIII (1943), pp. 87—90 (dove sostiene che l'allegoria che Prudenzio, nella prefazione della sua opera, trae dalla storia di Bera, re di Sodoma, risale a Filone, De Abrahamo: 225—244); C. MONDÉSERT, Clément et Philon, in: Clément d'Alexandrie: Introduction à l'étude de sa pensée religieuse à partir de l'Écriture (Théologie, n. 4), Paris, 1944, pp. 163—183; J. DANIÉLOU, La typologie d'Isaac dans le christianisme primitif, in: Biblica, XXVIII (1947), pp. 363—393 (dove paragona l'interpretazione di Isacco in Filone, Clemente Alessandrino, Origene, Ambrogio); M. HERMANIUK, La Parabole Évangélique. Enquête exégétique et critique (Univ. Catholica Lovaniensis, Dissertationes, n. II 38), Bruges–Paris–Louvain, 1947, pp. 493 (pp. 411—420: rapporti Clemente Alessandrino — Filone); W. VÖLKER, Die Vollkommenheitslehre des Clemens Alexandrinus in ihren geschichtlichen Zusammenhängen, in: Theologische Zeitschrift, III (1947), pp. 15—40 (per l'influsso di Filone su Clemente cfr. le pp. 22—29 e per quello di Filone su Clemente e su Origene le pp. 29—39); S. CARAMELLA, I neoplatonici nelle Confessioni di S. Agostino, in: Nuovo Didaskaleion, I (1947), pp. 49—54 (relazioni con le 'Quaestiones in Genesim' di Filone); J. DANIÉLOU, L'incompréhensibilité de Dieu d'après saint Jean Chrysostome, in: Recherches de Science Religieuse, XXXVII (1950), pp. 176—194 (dove il tema viene trattato, dalla sua origine in Filone, lungo tutta la letteratura cristiana); H. DE LUBAC, Histoire et esprit. L'intelligence de l'Écriture d'après Origène (Théologie, n. 16), Paris, 1950 (cfr. pp. 150—166: La part de Philon); K. L. SCHMIDT, Jerusalem als Urbild und Abbild, in: Eranos-Jahrbuch, XVIII (1950), Sonderband für C. G. Jung, pp. 207—248 (dove sostiene l'influenza di Filone sull'idea della Gerusalemme celeste dei Padri della Chiesa); H. A. WOLFSON, The Veracity of Scripture in Philo, Halevi, Maimonides and Spinoza, in: S. LIEBERMAN, Alexander Marx Jub., Vol. I, New York, 1950, pp. 603—630 (dove afferma, tra l'altro, che i quattro tipi di argomenti usati da Filone per stabilire la divina origine della Torà e dei Profeti sono impiegati anche da Giustino); J. PÉPIN, Recherches sur le sens et les origines de l'expression caelum caeli dans le livre XII des Confessions de saint Augustin, in: Archivum Latinitatis Medii Aevi, XXIII (1953), pp. 185—274 (dove sostiene che per l'esegesi di questa forma, tratta dai Salmi, Agostino è tributario anche di Filone); H. CROUZEL, Théologie de l'Image de Dieu chez Origène, (Théologie, n. 34), Paris, 1956 (per Filone vedi le pp. 52—57; 148—153 e passim); J. DANIÉLOU, Théologie du Judéo-Christianisme. Histoire des doctrines chrétiennes avant Nicée, Vol. I, Tournai–Paris–Rome, 1958 (dove osserva la dipendenza da Filone di

(Proseguimento della nota 2)

Giustino: pp. 182—183; Origene: pp. 188—189; Clemente Alessandrino: pp. 225—226); P. SMULDERS, A Quotation of Philo in Irenaeus, in: Vigiliae Christianae, XII (1958), pp. 154—156; G. J. M. BARTELINK, Μισόκαλος, épithète du diable, ibid., pp. 37—44 (per questa locuzione probabile influsso di Filone su Eusebio di Cesarea); H. CORNÉLIS, Les fondements cosmologiques de l'eschatologie d'Origène, in: Revue des Sciences Philoso-phiques et Théologiques, XLIII (1959), pp. 32—80 e 201—247; W. JAEGER, Echo eines unerkannten Tragikerfragments in Clemens' Brief an die Korinther, in: Rheinisches Mu-seum, CII (1959), pp. 330—340 (specialmente pp. 335—340, dove si opera un accostamento con Filone); G. B. LADNER, Eikon, in: Reallexikon für Antike und Christentum, IV, (1959), pp. 771—786 (dove si studia la traslazione del concetto dal sensibile allo spirituale, da Platone a Filone, a S. Paolo, ai Padri della Chiesa); H. DE LUBAC, Exégèse Médiévale. Des quatre sens de l'Écriture, I (Théologie, n. 41), Paris, 1959 (su Filone cfr. pp. 203—208 e 376—380); A. WLOSOK, Laktanz und die philosophische Gnosis. Untersuchungen zu Geschichte und Terminologie der gnostischen Erlösungsvorstellung, in: Abhandlungen der Heidelberger Akad. d. Wissenschaften, Philos.-histor. Klasse, 1960, 2, Heidelberg, 1960, pp. XX-272 (dove le pp. 50—114 concernono Filone, 143—179 Clemente Alessandrino e 180—231 Lattanzio); P. COURCELLE, Saint Augustin a-t-il lu Philon d'Alexandrie ?, in: Revue des Études Anciennes, LXIII (1961), pp. 78—85; J. DANIÉLOU, il quale, recensendo H. CROUZEL, Origène et la connaissance mystique (Museum Lessianum. Section théologique), Paris, 1961, pp. 633, in: Recherches de Science Religieuse, XLIX (1961) a p. 613, osserva che una certa trasposizione del platonismo costituisce il legame di Filone, di Clemente, di Origene, di Gregorio di Nissa, d'Evagrio, dello Pseudo-Dionigi, i quali formano una corrente ben definita, una 'scuola'; U. TREU, Etymologie und Allegorie bei Klemens von Alexandrien, in: Studia Patristica, IV, Berlin, 1961, pp. 191—211; S. LILLA, Middle Platonism, Neoplatonism and Jewish-Alexandrian Philosophy in the Terminology of Clement of Alexandria's Ethics, in: Archivio Italiano per la Storia della Pietà (Roma, Edizioni di Storia e Letteratura), III (1962), pp. 1—36; J. C. M. VAN WINDEN, In the Beginning. Some Observations on the Patristic Interpretation of Genesis 1,1, in: Vigiliae Christianae, XVII (1963), pp. 105—121 (su Ambrogio); H. A. WOLFSON, The Philo-sophy of the Church Fathers. I: Faith, Trinity, Incarnation, Second Edition, Cambridge, Mass., 1964, pp. 635 (dove cita numerosi esempi dell'influenza filoniana sui Padri della Chiesa in generale); J. H. WASZINK, Bemerkungen zu Justins Lehre vom Logos spermati-kos, in: Mullus. Festschr. Th. Klauser, Münster, 1964, pp. 380—390; H. RONDET, Le péché originel dans la tradition. Tertullien, Clément, Origène, in: Bulletin de Littérature Ecclésiastique, LXVII (1966), pp. 115—148 (influsso di Filone su Clemente); J. DANIÉLOU, Philon et Grégoire de Nysse, in: Philon d'Alexandrie. Colloque Lyon 11—15 Septembre 1966, Paris, 1967, pp. 333—346 (F. fu certo nella biblioteca di Greg. di Nissa, ma fu solo una delle sue fonti); F. SZABÓ, Le Christ et le monde selon saint Ambroise, in: Augusti-nianum, VIII (1968), pp. 325—360; B. MONDIN, Filone e Clemente. Saggio sulle origini della filosofia religiosa, Torino, 1968, pp. 141 (passim somiglianze e discordanze tra i due); A. HENRICHS, Philosophy, the Handmaiden of Theology, in: Greek, Roman and Byzantine Studies, IX (1968), pp. 437—450 (trapasso della valutazione della filosofia come subordinata alla teologia da Filone a Clemente Alessandrino, ad Origene, a Didimo il Cieco); J. RAASCH, The Monastic Concept of Purity of Heart and its Sources, III: Philo, Clement of Alexandria and Origen, in: Studia Monastica, X (1968), pp. 7—55; H. CHADWICK, Philo and the Beginnings of Christian Thought, in: Cambridge History of Later Greek and Early Medieval Philosophy, ed. by A. H. ARMSTRONG, Cambridge, 1970, pp. 133—192; J. SCHWARTZ, Philon et l'apologétique chrétienne du second siècle, in: Mélanges A. Dupont-Sommer, Paris, 1971, pp. 497—507; J. M. FORD, The Ray, the Root and the River. A Note on the Jewish Origin of Trinitarian Images, in: Studia Patristica, XI (Texte und Untersuchungen, n. 108), Berlin, 1972, 158—165; P. COURCELLE, Ambroise de Milan dévot de la monade, in: Revue des Études Grecques, LXXXVII (1974), pp. 144—154 (Ambrogio conobbe la concezione teologica della monade, di origine pitagorica, attraverso Filone); E. LANNE, La «xeniteia» d'Abraham dans l'œuvre d'Irénée. Aux origines du thème monastique de la «peregrinatio», in: Irenikon, XLVII (1974), pp. 163—187 (Filone

appunto di fare per il Nazianzeno quello che è già stato effettuato per la grande maggioranza degli altri autori greci cristiani.

Allo scopo di non gonfiare a dimensioni eccessive il lavoro, si è proceduto con il metodo di un saggio condotto su di una sola orazione. A questo fine è stata scelta la XIV, sull'amore dei poveri, che sembra offrire requisiti soddisfacenti: è abbastanza lunga per fornire una base adatta a riscontri ed a giudizi sufficientemente indicativi; tocca un argomento alieno da qualsiasi tecnicismo che imprigioni lo scrittore in un ordine obbligato di concetti e che lo costringa entro le strettoie di un linguaggio speciale; svolge un tema che non fu mai neppure sfiorato da Filone, allontanando quindi ogni pericolo di confondere collusioni dovute unicamente alla materia con accostamenti intenzionali, ed infine presenta una scena di così umana drammaticità da commuovere fortemente l'animo dell'autore e da spingerlo a considerazioni

viene richiamato passim e soprattutto alle pp. 183—186); G. Madec, Saint Ambroise et la Philosophie, Paris, 1974 (alle pp. 52—60 illustra Ambrogio come ,,*Philo Christianus*''); L. F. Pizzolato, La coppia umana in sant'Ambrogio, Milano, 1974, pp. 34 (Filone passim); S. Sagot, La triple sagesse dans le *De Isaac vel anima*. Essai des procédés de composition de saint Ambroise, in: Ambroise de Milan. XVIᵉ Centenaire de son élection épiscopale, Paris, 1974, pp. 77—114; H. Savon, Saint Ambroise critique de Philon dans le De Cain et Abel, in: Studia Patristica, XIII (Texte und Untersuchungen, n. 116), Berlin, 1975, pp. 273—279; A. De Vivo, Nota ad Ambrogio, 'De Abraham' I, 2, 4, in: Ambrosius Episcopus. Atti del Congresso internazionale di studi ambrosiani nel XVI centenario della elevazione di sant'Ambrogio alla cattedra episcopale, vol. II (Studia Patristica Mediolanensia, n. 7), Milano, 1976, pp. 233—242 (Ambrogio e Filone); E. Lucchesi, Un trait platonicien commun à Virgile et Philon d'Alexandrie, in: Revue des Études Grecques, LXXXIX (1976), pp. 615—618 (connessione con Ambrogio, De Abraham II, 1, 4); R. J. Daly, The Soteriological Significance of the Sacrifice of Isaac, in: Catholic Biblical Quarterly, XXXIX (1977), pp. 45—75 (interpretazione filoniana e suo influsso sugli scrittori cristiani a partire dal secondo secolo); J. D. B. Hamilton, The Church and the Language of Mystery. The First Four Centuries, in: Ephemerides Theologicae Lovanienses, LIII (1977), pp. 479—494 (il linguaggio della Chiesa attinse *mysterion* dal Medio Platonismo: sviluppo partendo da Filone e poi risalendo attraverso Giustino, Clemente Alessandrino, Origene, i Cappadoci, Tertulliano); E. Lucchesi, L'usage de Philon dans l'œuvre exégétique de saint Ambroise. Une «Quellenforschung» relative aux commentaires d'Ambroise sur la Genèse (Arbeiten zur Literatur und Geschichte des hellenistischen Judentums, n. 11), Leiden, 1977, pp. 140; H. Savon, Saint Ambroise devant l'exégèse de Philon le Juif, Paris, 1977: Tome I: Texte, pp. 392; Tome II: Notes, pp. 221; L. F. Pizzolato, La dottrina esegetica di S. Ambrogio (Studia Patristica Mediolanensia, n. 9), Milano, 1978, pp. XXII-360; J. C. M. van Winden, Quotations from Philo in Clement of Alexandria's Protrepticus, in: Vigiliae Christianae, XXXII (1978), pp. 208—213. — Da questa rassegna appare evidente che quanti hanno trattato dei rapporti tra Filone ed un Padre della Chiesa sono stati piuttosto succinti e superficiali, mentre quanti lo hanno considerato nell'ambito di temi particolari sono stati necessariamente delimitati dal loro stesso programma. In complesso pare che si possa ancora ripetere quanto già disse W. Völker, Fortschritt und Vollendung bei Philo von Alexandrien. Eine Studie zur Geschichte der Frömmigkeit (T. U., 49, 1), Leipzig, 1938, a p. 42, dove mentre ribadiva l'utilità di indagini sul tema 'Filone e la Patristica', dichiarava anche che i lavori fino ad allora presentati testimoniavano che ci si trovava soltanto all'inizio della ricerca. A lui faceva eco, circa trent'anni dopo, il voto espresso al colloquio filoniano di Lione nel 1966 che si insistesse sulle analisi che documentassero la presenza dello scrittore alessandrino tra i padri greci (cfr. p. 375 del citato volume degli atti).

fervide e patetiche, per la loro stessa natura refrattarie a lavori d'intarsio. Quest'orazione delimita il nostro campo visivo, porgendo il quadro preciso dei motivi sui quali si è concentrato l'esame; però questi motivi sono stati riscontrati anche in tutta la rimanente produzione di Gregorio: abbiamo infatti creduto indispensabile tenere sempre dinanzi agli occhi l'orizzonte completo, per poter valutare con sicurezza il peso dei singoli raffronti, giacchè è ben diverso il significato di un'asserzione o di una formulazione a seconda che sia presente solo nella nostra orazione oppure ritorni, più o meno spesso, altrove. Per interpretare con maggiore obiettività le somiglianze ed evitare l'equivoco di attribuire ad influsso filoniano ciò che potrebbe invece avere altra provenienza, abbiamo anche indicato i passi, sia biblici sia classici, che potrebbero aver esercitato una qualche azione sul pensiero o sulla forma di Gregorio.

Considerato il carattere parziale della nostra ricerca — anche se crediamo che un allargamento di area finirebbe essenzialmente con l'accumulare più numerosi esempi e con l'ampliare il numero dei contatti, ma non con il mutare le conclusioni ultime — ci è parso opportuno di segnalare anche fatti in se stessi limitatamente rappresentativi, ma che, addizionati ad altri risultanti da un'estensione dell'esame, potrebbero assumere una nuova e più significativa importanza: quindi mentre siamo d'avviso che la presente disamina possa autorizzare già di per sè deduzioni valevoli, l'abbiamo anche condotta in modo che possa integrarsi facilmente con altre eventuali. Le affinità rilevate sono state ordinate seguendo lo sviluppo dell'orazione gregoriana.

II. Filone e Gregorio: concomitanze concettuali

Cap. I, MG col. 857—860 A:

Gregorio scrive: ,,Siamo tutti quanti poveri e bisognosi della grazia divina, anche se, misurato con piccole misure, uno sembra essere da più di un altro." E Filone, Spec. I 293 p. V 70, 18—20: ,,Guardando alla grandezza di Dio ognuno deve prendere coscienza della propria debolezza di creatura, anche se differisce per benessere da altri[3]." I due pensieri sono

---

[3] Le citazioni vengono eseguite indicando volume, pagina e linee dell'edizione COHN—WENDLAND—REITER che viene normalmente seguita. Le abbreviazioni sono quelle adottate nell'edizione delle 'Sources Chrétiennes'. — Per i frammenti sono stati utilizzati: Fragments of Philo Judaeus, newly ed. by J. RENDEL HARRIS, Cambridge, 1886, pp. XXIII-110; Neu entdeckte Fragmente Philos, nebst einer Untersuchung über die ursprüngliche Gestalt der Schrift 'De Sacrificiis Abelis et Caini' von P. WENDLAND, Berlin, 1891, pp. XI-152; K. PRAECHTER, Unbeachtete Philon-Fragmente, in: Archiv für Geschichte der Philosophie, IX (1896), pp. 415—426; H .LEWY, Neue Philontexte in der Überarbeitung des Ambrosius. Mit einem Anhang: Neu gefundene griechische Philonfragmente, in: Sitzungsberichte der preuß. Akad. d. Wiss., Philos.-hist. Klasse, IV, Berlin, 1932, pp. 23—84; F. PETIT,

analoghi, ma si svolgono su due piani differenti. Gregorio, come cristiano e come vescovo, tende a collocarsi nell'ordine soprannaturale ed a considerare i vari oggetti dal punto di vista della grazia; Filone invece, nella sua qualità di filosofo, inclina a porsi nell'ordine naturale ed a riguardare in quest'ambito anche l'azione divina. È questa un'osservazione che va tenuta pure presente per alcuni rilievi seguenti.

Cap. I, col. 860 A:

Gregorio nel suo esordio invita gli ascoltatori a pregare: συνεύξασθε δὲ καὶ ἡμᾶς πλουσίως τοῦτον ὑμῖν χορηγῆσαι, καὶ θρέψαι τῷ λόγῳ τὰς ὑμετέρας ψυχάς, καὶ διαθρύψαι πεινῶσι τὸν πνευματικὸν ἄρτον· εἴτε ἀπ' οὐρανοῦ τροφὴν ὕοντας, καθάπερ Μωϋσῆς ὁ παλαιὸς ἐκεῖνος. L'interpretazione della manna caduta dal cielo come di un cibo spirituale per l'anima, si trova già in Leg. III 162 p. I 148, 17—19. Poco oltre — par. 173 p. 151, 16—19 — Fil. presenta Mosè (Ex. 16, 15) nell'atto di dire: ,,οὗτός ἐστιν ὁ ἄρτος'', ἡ τροφή, ἣν δέδωκεν ὁ θεὸς τῇ ψυχῇ, προσενέγκασθαι τὸ ἑαυτοῦ ῥῆμα καὶ τὸν ἑαυτοῦ λόγον· οὗτος γὰρ ὁ ἄρτος, ὃν δέδωκεν ἡμῖν φαγεῖν, ,,τοῦτο τὸ ῥῆμα''. Anche in Her. 79 p. III 19, 2—3, Fil. partendo dalla manna[4], considera il λόγον

Les fragments grecs du livre VI des Questions sur la Genèse de Philon d'Alexandrie. Édition critique, in: Le Muséon, LXXXIV (1971), pp. 93—150 (27 paragrafi). I 7 frammenti del Pap. P. 17027 dei Berliner Staatl. Museen pubbl. da K. STAHLSCHMIDT, Eine unbekannte Schrift Philons von Alexandrien (oder eines ihm nahestehenden Verfassers), in: Aegyptus, XXII (1942), pp. 161—176 non presentano nessun interesse per i nostri raffronti. Per le opere di Filone esistenti solo nella traduzione armena si cita la versione latina di G. B. AUCHER seguita dall'indicazione della pag. ed inoltre vol. e pag. della riedizione nella 'Bibliotheca sacra Patrum Ecclesiae Graecorum. Pars II Philonis Judaei operum omnium', Tom. VI, 1829; VII, 1830; VIII, 1830, Lipsiae, alquanto più facile da reperire. Per le 'Quaestiones in Genesim' e 'in Exodum' si riporta la vers. di R. MARCUS: Philo Supplement I: Questions and Answers on Genesis, transl. from the anc. Armenian version, London—Cambridge, Mass., 1961; II: Questions and Answers on Exodus, ibid., 1961, solo dove qualche particolare ragione lo consiglia. Il medesimo criterio è stato applicato per l'edizione di F. PETIT, L'ancienne version latine des Questions sur la Genèse de Philon d'Alexandrie, I: Édition critique, II: Commentaire (Texte und Untersuchungen, nn. 113—114), Berlin, 1973, pp. 102 e 192. L'autore non ha potuto servirsi di G. MAYER, Index Philoneus, Berlin—New York, 1974, pp. X-312, perchè uscito quando ormai il presente lavoro era già stato consegnato al Comitato editoriale, dove rimase a lungo nello stato di bozze che successivamente non permisero che integrazioni di carattere bibliografico. Per questo motivo anche le nuove ricche 'Œuvres de Philon d'Alexandrie' delle Éditions du Cerf furono adoperate solo a controllo successivo ed in quelle opere che giunsero al pubblico in epoca anteriore alla stesura definitiva della presente ricerca. Per panorami bibliografici sull'epoca più recente, vedi in questo medesimo volume (ANRW II, 21,1) E. HILGERT, Bibliographia Philoniana 1935—1981, pp. 47—97 e P. BORGEN, Philo of Alexandria. A critical and synthetical survey of research since World War II, pp. 98—154.

[4] È questo un ricordo a cui pure Gregorio ritorna volentieri, sia nelle orazioni che nelle poesie, giocando anche spesso sulle medesime parole che si trovano in questo passo. — Per un'ampia indagine sui valori traslati di quest'espressione cfr. P. BORGEN, Bread from Heaven. An Exegetical Study of the Concept of Manna in the Gospel of John and the Writings of Philo (Supplem. to Novum Testamentum, n. 10), Leiden, 1965, pp. X-217. Vedi anche P. BEAUCHAMP ... (1967) in nota 310 e B. J. MALINA, The Palestinian Manna Tradition. The Manna Tradition in the Palestinian Targums and Its Relationship to

che Dio rivolge agli uomini come un cibo celeste dell'anima. Va notato che mentre Ex. 16, 4 ha ἄρτος tanto Filone che Gregorio recano anche τροφή: è probabile che l'uso di questo termine sia dovuto alla sua maggior facilità ad essere trasferito al senso figurato. Infatti entrambi lo intendono come una metafora per designare la sapienza che nutre lo spirito[5]: in Gregorio manca il termine σοφία, ma ne è chiaramente espresso il concetto; in Filone invece ricorrono spesso tanto il vocabolo che l'idea[6].

L'unione di χορηγεῖν con la τροφή costituita dalla manna piovuta dal cielo, in Filone si trova in Mos. II [III] 266 p. IV 263, 11. Per una variazione sul medesimo atteggiamento, cfr. Her. 76 p. III 18, 9—10 e per χορηγεῖν collegato con ammonimenti di sapienza, cfr. Spec. II 29 p. V 92, 19[7]. Il nesso πλουσίως . . . χορηγεῖν che in Gregorio è usato per il nutrimento dello spirito, ricorre anche in Filone per designare concetti analoghi: cfr. Contempl. 35 p. VI 55, 7—8. Per una frase parallela cfr. Decal. 178 p. IV 307, 18—19. È inoltre opportuno notare che il verbo χορηγεῖν, che non ricorre mai nel Pentateuco, anche nei 18 casi nei quali è usato nel resto del VT.[8] e nei 2 in cui è impiegato nel N. non designa mai il sostentamento spirituale dell' anima.

Cap. I, col. 860 A:

Gregorio ricordando il precedente di Gesù, si augura di poter nutrire abbondantemente la folla dei suoi ascoltatori: ἄρτοις ὀλίγοις ἐν ἐρημίᾳ τρέφοντας μέχρι κόρου καὶ μυριάδας. Filone, alludendo al nutrimento fornito da Dio agli Ebrei nei quarant'anni di peregrinazioni nel deserto — episodio biblico a cui Gregorio si era richiamato immediatamente prima — in Spec. II 199 p. V 135, 17—19 dice: τοὺς ἡμετέρους προγόνους μυριάσι πολλαῖς ἐρήμην . . . διεξιόντας . . . διέθρεψεν[9]. Per quanto concerne la formulazione, Gregorio è assai più vicino a Fil. che non a Matth. 14, 15—21;

New Testament Writings (Arbeiten zur Geschichte des Spätjudentums und Urchristentums, n. 7), Leiden, 1968, pp. XV-111.

[5] L'interpretazione dell'ammaestramento come di un banchetto si trova più volte nelle orazioni di Gregorio.

[6] Per la presenza dell'aggettivo, riferito però non ad ἄρτος nè a τροφή ma a βρῶμα, cfr. I Cor. 10, 3.

[7] Cfr. anche Gregorio, or. 7,3 col. 757 C e 34,2 col. 241 B. Le citazioni delle opere del Nazianzeno vengono fatte sulla PG del MIGNE rinviando alla colonna. Per brevità si omette l'indicazione del vol. per il quale basta specificare ora che le orazioni 1—26 si trovano nel vol. XXXV; le orazioni 27—45 nel vol. XXXVI; le epistole e le poesie nel vol. XXXVII; gli epitaffi e gli epigrammi nel vol. XXXVIII. — Per le epistole va ora usata l'edizione di P. GALLAY (Collection des Universités de France), vol. I (1964), epp. 1—100; vol. II (1967), epp. 103—249. Per le epistole teologiche (nn. 101; 102; 202) vedi l'edizione GALLAY-JOURJON (Sources Chrétiennes, n. 208), Paris, 1974.

[8] Le citaz. della Bibbia che non contengano particolari precisazioni si riferiscono al testo dei LXX nell'ediz. di A. RAHLFS[6], Stuttgart, s. d.

[9] Per altre espressioni di Gregorio assai simili a questa cfr. or. 38,16 col. 329 C e poem. I 2,3,90 col. 639. — Minute precisazioni sui valori semantici di τρέφω nei suoi tempi e nelle sue composizioni ci vengono offerte da CL. MOUSSY, Recherches sur ΤΡΕΦΩ et les verbes grecs signifiant «nourrir» (Études et Commentaires, n. 70), Paris, 1969, pp. 37—89.

Marc. 6, 34—44; Luc. 9, 11—17; Ioann. 6, 5—13 che narrano la moltiplicazione dei pani.

Cap. I, col. 860 A:

Gregorio definisce Gesù come τῆς ἀληθινῆς ζωῆς αἴτιος. Filone in Leg. I 32 p. I 69, 9 dichiara che la nostra mente è terrestre e corruttibile, a meno che ὁ θεὸς ἐμπνεύσειεν αὐτῷ δύναμιν ἀληθινῆς ζωῆς e vedi anche par. 35 p. 70, 3[10]. Questa formula non ricorre nè nell'AT. nè nel N.; una certa somiglianza esteriore, accompagnata però da una sostanziale diversità di significato, si trova in I Thess. 1, 9: θεῷ ζῶντι καὶ ἀληθινῷ[11].

Cap. I, col. 860 A:

Gregorio paragona le singole virtù ai molteplici fiori di un prato ricco di corolle profumate. Filone in Plant. 37 p. II 141, 7 dice che Dio pianta nell'anima un παράδεισον ἀρετῶν e poco oltre — par. 43 p. 142, 13 — sostiene che l'arca di Noè era simbolo delle passioni e dei vizi, mentre il giardino lo era delle virtù: cfr. anche ibid. 46 p. 143, 5. Questo traslato fu caro a Filone: cfr. Leg. I 45 p. I 72, 12—13; ibid. I 54 p. 74, 3; Opif. 153 p. I 53, 20.

Cap. II, col. 860 B:

Gregorio cita Enos come campione della speranza: τῆς ἐλπίδος, Ἐνώς, ὃς πρῶτος ἤλπισεν ἐπικαλεῖσθαι τὸν Κύριον. — La Gen. 4, 26 dice di Enos: οὗτος ἤλπισεν ἐπικαλεῖσθαι τὸ ὄνομα κυρίου τοῦ θεοῦ. Il Nazianzeno ha attinto evidentemente dalla fonte biblica, ma vi ha inserito πρῶτος; ora, tanto questa determinazione, quanto il particolare rilievo che fa di Enos il campione della speranza, si trovano già in Filone: cfr. Abr. 7—8 p. IV 3, 3—5: τὸν πρῶτον ἐλπίδος ἐραστὴν προσεῖπεν „ἄνθρωπον" τὸ κοινὸν τοῦ γένους ὄνομα ... δωρησάμενος αὐτῷ. Χαλδαῖοι γὰρ τὸν ἄνθρωπον Ἐνὼς καλοῦσιν[12].

Cap. II, col. 860 C:

Gregorio insegna che Dio unì alla creta del nostro corpo lo spirito quale ὁδηγὸν τῶν καλλίστων. Per Filone, Sacrif. 51 p. I 222, 11 la retta ragione (ὀρθὸς λόγος) è la guida verso i beni: ὑφηγητὴς τῶν καλῶν.

Cap. III, col. 861 A:

Gregorio, commentando lo zelo di Finees, dice che egli uccise la Madianita e l'Israelita che avevano ostentatamente peccato, „per scacciare la vergogna dai figli d'Israele". Filone, Mos. I 303 p. IV 192, 9 osserva che

---

[10] Per un'altra concordanza su questo tema cfr. or. 38,13 col. 325 B (or. 45,9 col. 633 C) dove Cristo è considerato come ἡ πηγὴ τῆς ζωῆς e Filone, Fug. 198 p. III 152,24—26 dove di Dio si dice che ζωῆς ἐστιν ... ἡ πηγή. Entrambi alludono alla vita dello spirito.

[11] La formula ἡ ἀληθινὴ ζωή è presente ancora sia in Gregorio, or. 18,42 col. 1041 B che in Filone, Leg. III 52 p. I 124,21.

[12] Su questo merito di Enos cfr. anche or. 28,18 col. 49 A e 43,70 col. 592 A.

sull'esempio di Finees anche altri uccisero i colpevoli „purificando via così la contaminazione dal popolo". Questo rilievo che ricorre, se non con esatta identità di vocaboli certo con precisa corrispondenza di senso, nei due scrittori, non c'è in Num. 25, 6—15 dov'è referito l'episodio di Finees[13].

Cap. III, col. 861 B:

Gregorio nota come S. Paolo esercitasse sul suo corpo una severa disciplina e come colpisse di un salutare timore τοὺς . . . ἐφιέντας τῷ σώματι. Filone, Mutat. 174 p. III 186, 21—22 osserva: σώματος ἀγαθὸν οὐ προσ-ιέμεθα οἱ τὰ ψυχῆς ἰδόντες. La locuzione ἐφίημι τῷ σώματι è estranea tanto all'A. che al NT.

Cap. IV, col. 861 C:

Gregorio scrive: καλὸν ἐρημία, vedendovi un ambiente particolarmente propizio allo sviluppo della vita divina, della quale cita come più perfetti cultori Elia, Giovanni Battista e soprattutto Gesù. Anche Filone vede nel-l'ἐρημία un ambiente assai favorevole all'acquisto della sapienza divina: cfr. Her. 127 p. III 30, 4—5: φιλέρημος μὲν γὰρ ἡ θεία σοφία e ibid. 234 p. 53, 2: ὁ γὰρ θεοῦ λόγος φιλέρημος καὶ μονωτικός. Quest'ultimo termine equivale all' ἑαυτῷ συγγινόμενος di Gregorio[14].

Cap. IV, col. 864 A:

A sintesi del lungo elenco di virtù che ha celebrate, Gregorio pone una formula con la quale approva sia l'attività pratica che quella contemplativa: καλὸν θεωρία καὶ καλὸν πρᾶξις[15]. Anche Filone divide ogni possibile impegno umano in queste due vocazioni fondamentali: sappiamo inoltre come que-st'alternativa si sia presentata in maniera acuta alla coscienza di entrambi gli scrittori e come abbia segnato di una nota drammatica la loro esistenza. Anche Filone dichiara l'alto merito che risiede in tutti e due questi stati di vita: cfr. Leg. I 57—58 p. I 75, 13 e 17; Mos. I 48 p. IV, 131, 8—9; Decal. 101 p. IV 292, 7—8; Spec. II 64 p. V 102, 15—16; Praem. 11 p. V 338, 18—20; Framm. p. II 670 MANGEY e p. 95 R.H. Cfr. anche Fug. 36—37 p. III 118, 4—10 e Contempl. 1 p. VI 46, 1—3. Nel Praem. 51 p. V 347, 7—11

[13] Questo personaggio ritorna relativamente spesso in Gregorio: cfr. or. 16,20 col. 961 C; ep. 77,7 GALLAY p. 96; poem. II 1,15,22—23 col. 1252. Su di lui, nella Bibbia ed in Filone, vedi J.-A. MORIN, Les deux derniers des douze: Simon le zélote et Judas Iskariôth, in: Revue Bibliquè, LXXX (1973), alle pp. 338—342.

[14] L'esaltazione dell' ἐρημία ed il suo amore per essa sono come un sospiro che esce spesso dal cuore di Gregorio: cfr. poem. I 2,17, 1 col. 781; or. 3,1 col. 517 A; 42,24 col. 488 B; 21,19 coll. 1101 D—1104 A.

[15] Per una più ampia presentazione di questo problema nella classicità vedi A. GRILLI, Il problema della vita contemplativa nel mondo greco-romano, Milano—Roma 1953, pp. 364; G. REDLOW, Theoria. Theoretische und praktische Lebensauffassung im philosophischen Denken der Antike, Berlin, 1966, pp. 166; R. MÜLLER, Βίος θεωρητικός bei Antiochos von Askalon und Cicero, in: Helikon, VIII (1968), pp. 222—237. — Per quanto concerne diret-tamente Gregorio cfr. il recentissimo M. KERTSCH, Gregor von Nazianz' Stellung zu Theoria und Praxis aus der Sicht seiner Reden, in: Byzantion, XLIV (1974), pp. 282—289.

(cfr. Framm. p. 96 R.H.) Fil. distribuisce cronologicamente i due generi di vita, assegnandone uno alla giovinezza e l'altro alla vecchiaia; un analogo concetto è espresso in Quaest. in Exod. II 31 p. 490 A. e VII 300. In Praem. 51 p. V 347, 7—11 Fil., pure in un equo riconoscimento di ambedue, sembra attribuire una certa preminenza alla vita contemplativa; tale propensione si manifesta anche altrove: cfr. Migr. 47 p. II 277, 13—14 e Contempl. 67 p. VI 64, 3—4. Però egli afferma anche chiaramente l'importanza sostanziale della pratica: cfr. Congr. 46 p. III 81, 9—10. Stesso equilibrio e stessa sottile preferenza in Gregorio[16].

Il Nazianzeno considera la contemplazione come elevazione della mente verso la divinità: ἡ μέν, ἐντεῦθεν ἐπανιστᾶσα, καὶ εἰς τὰ Ἅγια τῶν ἁγίων χωροῦσα, καὶ τὸν νοῦν ἡμῶν πρὸς τὸ συγγενὲς ἐπανάγουσα; per Filone la contemplazione del cielo induce la mente ad amare gli oggetti celesti, intesi non nella loro concretezza astronomica ma nel loro valore traslato di cose divine: cfr. Opif. 77 p. I 26, 6—8: ἡ θεωρία τῶν κατ' οὐρανόν, ἀφ' ἧς πληχθεὶς ὁ νοῦς ἔρωτα καὶ πόθον ἔσχε τῆς τούτων ἐπιστήμης[17].

Cap. IV, col. 864 A:

Gregorio considera la contemplazione come τὸν νοῦν ἡμῶν πρὸς τὸ συγγενὲς ἐπανάγουσα: questo συγγενές è Dio, il quale è diventato nostro parente essenzialmente mediante la creazione della notra anima fatta a sua immagine e somiglianza[18]. Tale συγγένεια con Dio costituisce pure uno degli elementi fondamentali della concezione antropologica di Filone: cfr. Opif. 77 p. I 26, 1—2: τῆς αὐτοῦ συγγενείας μεταδοὺς ὁ θεὸς ἀνθρώπῳ τῆς λογικῆς, ἥτις ἀρίστη δωρεῶν ἦν e cfr. anche poco sopra, 74 p. 25, 8—10; Abr. 41 p. IV 10, 4—5, dove è detto che Iddio si irritò perchè τὸ ζῷον τὸ ἄριστον εἶναι δοκοῦν καὶ συγγενείας ἀξιωθὲν τῆς πρὸς αὐτὸν ἕνεκα τῆς ἐν τῷ λόγῳ κοινωνίας invece di darsi alla virtù fece il male; Decal. 134 p. IV 299, 1—5: ἄνθρωπος ... συγγενέστατος ... τῷ τοῦ κόσμου πατρί, τῶν

---

[16] Cfr. Congr. 46 p. III 81,9—10: „La pura contemplazione senza la pratica non reca nessun giovamento" e Gregorio, or. 4,73 col. 597 B, il quale esalta la „conoscenza che si esprime nella pratica".

[17] Il binomio θεωρία—πρᾶξις è fondamentale nel pensiero e nella vita di Gregorio: per una breve definizione dei due termini cfr. poem. I 2,34,130—131 col. 955. La posizione rispettiva dei due elementi è spiegata in or. 4,113 coll. 649 B—652 A e cfr. anche poem. I 2,33, 1—4 col. 928. I richiami ora più insistiti ora più fuggevoli sono poi frequentissimi; basti rinviare al breve dibattito sulla loro utilità in poem. II 1,11,302—311 coll. 1050—1051. — Può infine essere interessante notare che tutti e due gli scrittori ebbero nella loro vita parentesi dedite alla contemplazione: per Gregorio basta ricordare Arianzo, Annesi, Seleucia d'Isauria e poi di nuovo Arianzo; per Fil. cfr. Leg. II 85 p. I 107,14—15: „Spesse volte io, abbandonati i parenti, gli amici e la mia patria, καὶ εἰς ἐρημίαν ἐλθών, ἵνα τι τῶν θέας ἀξίων κατανοήσω ... Cfr. anche Contempl. 18—20 p. VI 51,1—12.

[18] E. Des Places, La syngeneia chrétienne, in: Biblica, XLIV (1963), pp. 304—332 offre un rapido sguardo su questo tema della parentela dell'uomo con Dio dal NT. a S. Cirillo di Alessandria. La trattazione è stata ampliata dal medesimo autore in: Syngeneia. La parenté de l'homme avec Dieu, d'Homère à la Patristique (Études et Commentaires, n. 51), Paris, 1964, pp. 223. — Vedi Platone, Republ. X p. 611 E; Leg. X p. 899 D.

ἐπὶ γῆς ἁπάντων οἰκειότατον[19] ἀπεικόνισμα καὶ μίμημα τῆς ἀιδίου καὶ εὐδαίμονος ἰδέας τὸν νοῦν λαβών. Cfr. anche Opif. 144 p. I 50, 20—21. Il pensiero
non varia sostanzialmente quando Filone afferma la συγγένεια invece che
con Dio con il Logos divino; si tratta solo di una variazione espressiva, come
testimoniano i raffronti con le citazioni precedenti; infatti in Exsecr.
163 p. V 374, 15—18 sostiene che coloro i quali si pentono delle loro colpe
troveranno in Dio la misericordia e la salvezza, poichè egli diede τῷ γένει
τῶν ἀνθρώπων ἐξαίρετον . . . καὶ μεγίστην δωρεάν, τὴν πρὸς τὸν αὐτοῦ
λόγον συγγένειαν, ἀφ' οὗ καθάπερ ἀρχετύπου γέγονεν ὁ ἀνθρώπινος νοῦς.

Cap. IV, col. 864 A:

Gregorio vede nella contemplazione un'elevazione della mente umana
fino alla natura divina e nella pratica una testimonianza concreta, mediante
le azioni, dell' amore per Cristo. Identico è l'atteggiamento di Filone:
in Abr. 88—89 p. IV 21, 14—18 egli parla della mente dell'uomo la quale
„con il suo pensiero si sollevò in alto e contemplò un'altra natura spirituale
migliore di quella visibile e colui che è insieme il creatore ed il dominatore
di entrambe" e subito dopo prosegue: „Questo è il primo atteggiamento di coloro che amano Dio: ad esso seguono poi delle azioni tutt'altro che spregevoli".

Cap. V, col. 864 A:

Gregorio afferma che ognuna delle virtù è μία τις σωτηρίας ὁδός, la
quale conduce alle dimore celesti. Filone, Opif. 144 p. I 50, 22—23 asserisce
che l'uomo segue Dio sulle vie aperte dalle virtù. Cfr. anche Quaest. in Exod.
II 65 p. 513 A. e VII 320, dove Marcus, p. 111, riporta anche il framm.
greco. La congiunzione dei concetti di ὁδός e di ἀρετή con vari intendimenti
è frequente in Fil.

Cap. V, col. 864 B:

Gregorio parla di una via che conduce alle eterne e beate dimore, che
naturalmente sono immaginate in cielo, e Filone scrive: Poster. 31 p. II 8, 4:
τὴν εἰς οὐρανὸν ἄγουσαν ὁδόν; ibid. 101 p. 22, 3: ἡ πρὸς αὐτὸν (scil. θεόν)
ἄγουσα ὁδός. Cfr. pure Framm. Ex. XXIII 33 p. 58 R. H.; ibid. XXV 20
p. 65; Quaest. Ex. II 26 p. 486 A. e VII 297 (Marcus p. 67 fr. gr.); ibid. II
29 p. 488 A. e VII 298—299; Mos. II [III] 189 p. IV 244, 17; Spec. I 300 p.
V 72, 14—15; Virt. 51 p. V 280, 1—2. Quanto all'espressione σωτηρίας
ὁδός oltre ad Act. 16, 17, cfr. Ios. 183 p. IV 100, 21 e Migr. 26 p. II 273,
26—27 e per Gregorio, or. 24, 8 col. 1177 A e 43, 63 col. 580 A.

---

[19] Per οἰκεῖος in questo senso pregnante cfr. Gregorio, or. 28,17 col. 48 C. Sulla forte
caratterizzazione stoica che questo concetto ebbe nella sua ascendenza precristiana vedi
S. G. Pembroke, Oikeiōsis, in: Problems in Stoicism, ed. by A. A. Long, London, 1971,
pp. 114—149.

Cap. V, col. 864 B:

Gregorio sostiene che ci sono διάφοροι βίων αἱρέσεις e Filone, Sacrif. 11 p. I 206, 15 menziona τὴν τῶν βίων προαίρεσιν e in Exsecr. 142 p. V 369,'13—14 ricorda come esistano βίων ἰδέαι μυρίων. È puramente esteriore il richiamo a Diogene Laerzio VII 130.

Cap. V, col. 864 B:

Gregorio, dopo aver esaminato quanto siano numerose e varie le virtù, esorta: καὶ ὁ μὲν τήνδε κατορθούτω τὴν ἀρετήν, ὁ δὲ τήνδε, ὁ δὲ πλείους, ὁ δὲ τὰς πάσας, εἰ οἷόν τε. Filone in Abr. 34 p. IV 8, 18—19, parlando di Noè, dice: οὐ μίαν ἀρετὴν ἀλλὰ πάσας ἐκτήσατο καὶ κτησάμενος ἑκάστη κατὰ τὸ ἐπιβάλλον χρώμενος διετέλεσεν e in Mutat. 225 p. III 195, 23—196, 2 osserva: ,,Sarebbe desiderabile danzare con il coro completo delle virtù; ma se questo supera le capacità della natura umana, accontentiamoci se ad uno riesce di raggiungere una sola delle singole virtù, il dominio di sè o la fortezza o la giustizia o l'amore del prossimo. Purchè[20] l'anima porti e partorisca un qualche bene . . ."[21].

Cap. V, col. 864 B:

Gregorio invita ciascuno a camminare nella via dello spirito: ὁδευέτω καὶ ἐφιέσθω τοῦ πρόσω[22] e Filone in Decal. 50 p. IV 280, 5—7 nota che i comandamenti offrono εὐρείας ὁδοὺς . . . πρὸς ἄπταιστον ψυχῆς ἐφιεμένης ἀεὶ τοῦ βελτίστου πορείαν[23].

Cap. V, col. 864 B:

Gregorio incita ognuno a percorrere il suo cammino avendo Dio come guida: ἑπέσθω τῷ καλῶς ὁδηγοῦντι καὶ κατευθύνοντι καὶ διὰ τῆς στενῆς ὁδοῦ . . . ἄγοντι. Filone in Deter. 29 p. I 264, 24 menziona chi conversa τῷ συνοδοιπόρῳ καὶ ἡγεμόνι τῆς τε ὁδοῦ καὶ τῆς ψυχῆς θεῷ ed in Prob. 62 p. VI 18, 12—13 rileva che anticamente ci furono uomini che eccellevano in virtù ἡγεμόνι μόνῳ θεῷ χρώμενοι[24]. Tanto in Gregorio che in Filone l'accenno

---

[20] È lo stesso movimento di Gregorio: μόνον . . .

[21] Gregorio in poem. Ι 2,17,33—35 col. 784, dopo aver indicato varie virtù, soggiunge: ,,Tra queste percorri la strada che vuoi. Se tutte, meglio; se poche, ti metti in secondo ordine; se una sola, ma bene, sarà lo stesso una cosa gradita." Cfr. anche or. 21,1 col. 1081 A; ibid. 4 col. 1085 B; 43,76 col. 597 C; epitaph. 73 col. 49; poem. II 2,1,210 col. 1466.

[22] Con altre parole, ma con uguale intento, S. Paolo Phil. 3, 13 si era già rappresentato come τοῖς δὲ ἔμπροσθεν ἐπεκτεινόμενος.

[23] Anche nell'or. 4, 124 col. 664 BC Gregorio esprime l'obbligo di progredire sempre nella virtù e di tendere continuamente in avanti. Vedi pure or. 28, 24 col. 60 B.

[24] È un'immagine che in Gregorio ricorre anche altrove: nell'or. 15, 11 col. 932 A dice dei Maccabei che θεὸς ἦν ὁδηγὸς τῶν τοιούτων ἄθλων e nell'or. 34, 7 col. 248 C complimenta gli Egiziani che vennero alla chiesa cattolica καλῶς ὁδηγηθέντες ὑπὸ τοῦ Πνεύματος, mentre nell'or. 4, 44 col. 569 A deplora l'errore dei filosofi pagani che si servirono ὡς ὁδηγῷ λόγῳ καὶ μὴ θεῷ. — Vedi anche Apoc. 7, 17 e l'assai incerta tradizione manoscritta di Ioann. 16, 13. Per un'ampia ricerca su di un tema che si affianca a questi in un significato spesso sinonimico vedi P. G. MUELLER, Χριστὸς ἀρχηγός.

alla pratica della virtù è seguito dal richiamo all'ossequenza alla guida divina. Cfr. anche Decal. 81 p. IV 287, 10—11.

Cap. V, col. 864 C:

Gregorio inculcando fortemente la misericordia, dice che essa costituisce il più puro atto di culto verso Dio, che nessun attributo gli è più congenito, e che pertanto ῷ (scil. θεῷ) προσοιστέον τὸν ἔλεον πρὸ τῆς κρίσεως. Questo passo, che non è biblico, se può essere in qualche modo collegato con Iac. 2, 13: κατακαυχᾶται ἔλεος κρίσεως (cfr. anche Os. 6, 6), richiama anche Deus 76 p. II 73, 12—16: ,,Perchè il nostro genere sopravviva . . . (Iddio) introduce in più la misericordia . . . καὶ οὐ μόνον δικάσας ἐλεεῖ, ἀλλὰ καὶ ἐλεήσας δικάζει· πρεσβύτερος γὰρ δίκης ὁ ἔλεος παρ' αὐτῷ ἐστιν ἅτε τὸν κολάσεως ἄξιον οὐ μετὰ τὴν δίκην, ἀλλὰ πρὸ δίκης εἰδότι.

Cap. V, col. 864 C:

Gregorio dichiara: φιλανθρωπίᾳ τὸ φιλάνθρωπον ἀντιδίδοται[25]. Lo stesso atteggiamento di pensiero e la stessa costruzione stilistica (anche se spostati su di un settore parallelo, in quanto Gregorio parla della carità verso il prossimo, mentre Filone tratta del perdono) ricorrono in Filone Framm. p. II 670 MANGEY: ἀφέσει ἀντιδίδοται ἄφεσις. Questa sentenza potè inoltre impressionare notevolmente Greg. anche perchè segue immediatamente ad un'esortazione che ha un così profondo sapore evangelico: συγγνώμην αἰτούμενος ἁμαρτημάτων, συγγίνωσκε καὶ αὐτὸς τοῖς εἴς σε πλημμελοῦσιν: cfr. Matth. 6, 12, 14 e 15; 18, 32—35; Marc. 11, 25—26; Luc. 11, 4.

Cap. VI, col. 864 C:

Gregorio, pensando πᾶσι . . . πτωχοῖς, dichiara: προεισενεκτέον ἀνθρώπους ὄντας ἀνθρώποις τὸν ἔρανον τῆς χρηστότητος, alludendo, più che ad una vaga benevolenza, all'aiuto effettivo. Cfr. Filone, Congr. 29 p. III 116, 18: σὺ δὲ ἔρανον παρέξεις πένησι φίλων e Agric. 90 p. II 113, 16 dove menziona un ἔρανον εἰς ἐπανόρθωσιν ἐνδείας[26]. Vedi anche Hypoth. in Eusebio, Praep. Evang. VIII 7, 6 p. I 430, 20, 21 MRAS in G.C.S. Per la locuzione cfr. Ebr. 23 p. II 174, 19[27] e ibid. 20 e 23 p. 174, 1 e 14. Quanto all'idea di aiuto vicendevole accompagnata dal poliptoto con homo in accus.-dat. vedi Quaest. Gen. I 23 p. 17 A. e VI 262.

Cap. VI, col. 864 C:

Gregorio invita a soccorrere coloro che furono rovinati a causa della φορολόγων ἀπανθρωπία e Filone in Spec. II 92 p. V 109, 1—2 invita οἱ τῶν πόλεων ἡγεμόνες (Greg. immediatamente prima ha nominato gli ἄρχον-

---

Der religionsgeschichtliche und theologische Hintergrund einer neutestamentlichen Christusprädikation (Europäische Hochschulschriften), Bern, 1973, pp. 432.

[25] Concetto e poliptoto appaiono anche in or. 43,36 col. 545 A; 44,7 col. 616 A; poem. I 2,33, 160 col. 939. Per il pensiero cfr. poem. I 2,17,29 col. 783.

[26] Senso ed espressione molto simili in or. 2,27 col. 436 B.

[27] Per un identico modulo espressivo cfr. or. 7,18 col. 777 C.

τες) a cessare di rovinare i loro sudditi φόροις καὶ δασμοῖς συνεχέσι καὶ μεγάλοις.

Cap. VI, col. 865 A:

Gregorio, dopo aver considerato il nostro corpo come un elemento meschino, infido e causa di angosce, afferma malinconicamente: ᾧ πῶς συνεζύγην, οὐκ οἶδα. Cfr. Filone, Her. 92 p. III 20, 25: τὸ θνητὸν ᾧ συνεζεύγμεθα; Poster. 60 p. I 13, 17: ψυχῆς ... σώματι συνεζευγμένης. Per συζεύγνυμι riferito al collegamento dell'anima e del corpo cfr. anche Aet. 59 p. VI 91, 9[28].

Cap. VI, col. 865 A:

Gregorio di fronte al mistero della connessióne, in unità di persona, di due entità così contrastanti, come l'anima ed il corpo, esce in un interrogativo che denota l'intensità con cui sente il problema e che ripropone uno dei temi che caratterizzano la sua spiritualità: πῶς εἰκών τέ εἰμι θεοῦ, καὶ τῷ πηλῷ συμφύρομαι? Il concetto dell'εἰκὼν θεοῦ è uno dei cardini su cui ruota tutto il suo sistema ascetico e mistico. In quest'orazione l'εἰκών è considerata: 1°) come qui, quale elemento della drammatica antinomia che rende difficile un equilibrio nel composto umano; 2°) come fattore che ci conferisce una nobiltà la quale ci potrebbe anche elevare in superbia e che pertanto viene controbilanciata dalla presenza del fango corporeo: cap. VII, col. 865 C: ἵν᾽ ὅταν ἐπαιρώμεθα διὰ τὴν εἰκόνα, διὰ τὸν χοῦν συστελλώμεθα; 3°) come partecipazione alla vita divina, che va conservata con la nostra responsabile corrispondenza: cap. XIV, col. 876 A: οἱ τὸ κατ᾽ εἰκόνα καὶ λαχόντες ὁμοίως ἡμῖν, καὶ φυλάσσοντες ἴσως ὑπὲρ ἡμᾶς; 4°) come forza che ci guida alle cose più belle e che ci eleva dalla terra al cielo: cap. II, col. 860 C: τὴν εἰκόνα τῷ χοῖ συζεύξας (scil. Gesù) ὁδηγὸν τῶν καλλίστων e cap. XX, col. 884 B, dove dice che noi crediamo κατ᾽ εἰκόνα θεοῦ γεγονέναι ... τὴν ἄνω τε οὖσαν καὶ πρὸς ἑαυτὴν ἕλκουσαν. — Anche per Filone l'εἰκὼν θεοῦ[29] è un concetto assai familiare, solo che egli lo considera più sotto l'aspetto ontologico che non sotto quello psicologico-morale. Dice infatti: — 1°) che la nostra mente è stata creata κατὰ τὴν εἰκόνα di Dio: cfr. Leg. I 42 p. I 71, 13—14 e Her. 56 p. III 14, 6—7; che l'anima umana è θεία εἰκών e che è θεοειδὴς ὁ ἀνθρώπινος νοῦς cfr. Spec.

---

[28] In Greg. συνεζύγην è riferito all'unione dell'anima con il corpo in poem. II 1,88,78 col. 1438; cfr. anche in quest'orazione il cap. VII col. 865 C.

[29] La bibliografia su questo tema è ricca di molte decine di titoli. Per brevità citiamo solo, come più vicini a Filone: H. WILLMS, Εἰκών. Eine begriffsgeschichtliche Untersuchung zum Platonismus ... (1935) in nota 310; J. GIBLET, L'Homme image de Dieu dans les Commentaires ... (1948) in nota 310; H. MERKI, ὉΜΟΙΩΣΙΣ ΘΕΩ. Von der platonischen Angleichung an Gott ... (1952) in nota 310; D. M. CRESSAN, Imago Dei. A Study in Philo and St. Paul ... (1959) in nota 324; H. WILDBERGER, Das Abbild Gottes ... (1965) in nota 310; A. ALTMANN, Homo imago Dei in Jewish and Christian Theology, in: Journal of Religion, XLVIII (1968), pp. 235—259; P. SCHWANZ, Imago Dei als christologisch-anthropologisches Problem in der Geschichte der Alten Kirche von Paulus bis Clemens von Alexandrien (Arbeiten zur Kirchengeschichte und Religionswissenschaft, n. 2), Halle, 1970, p. 248.

III 207 p. V 207, 16—17; che lo spirito è un'impronta della potenza divina ἣν ... Μουσῆς εἰκόνα καλεῖ, δηλῶν ὅτι ἀρχέτυπον μὲν φύσεως λογικῆς ὁ θεός ἐστι, μίμημα δὲ καὶ ἀπεικόνισμα ἄνθρωπος, cfr. Deter. 83 p. I 277, 7—9; che la ψυχὴ λογική dell'uomo è la più rassomigliante a Dio delle immagini divine, cfr. Opif. 137 p. I 48, 5. Vedi anche Spec. I 171 p. V 41, 23—42, 1 e Decal. 134 p. IV 299, 4—5. — 2⁰) che la nostra anima è stata plasmata sul modello del Logos divino: cfr. Spec. I 81 p. V 21, 9; Confus. 147 (cfr. fine 146) p. II 257, 8—9 (cfr. lin. 4—5); Opif. 139 p. I 48, 14—15. Particolarmente esplicito è in Her. 231 p. III 52, 7—13. — 3⁰) che la somiglianza si limita all'intelletto e non al corpo: cfr. Opif. 69 p. I 23, 4—6. — 4⁰) che il νοῦς, il quale realizza in sè l'εἰκών, è l'elemento direttivo della nostra coscienza: cfr. Opif. 69 p. I 23, 6—7. In Virt. 205 p. V 329, 10—13 osserva che il primo uomo ebbe come padre direttamente Dio, del quale γενόμενος εἰκὼν κατὰ τὸν ἡγεμόνα νοῦν ἐν ψυχῇ, avrebbe dovuto mantenere l'immagine pura da ogni macchia (ἀκηλίδωτον τὴν εἰκόνα φυλάξαι), seguendo, per quanto gli fosse possibile, le virtù di chi lo aveva generato. — 5⁰) che intercorre una distinzione fondamentale tra τὸν κατὰ τὴν εἰκόνα τυπωθέντα ἄνθρωπον e τὸν πεπλασμένον: il primo è uguale all'albero che produce la vita immortale ... il secondo invece è fatto di un corpo composto e terrestre che non partecipa della natura non plasmata e semplice: cfr. Plant. 44 p. II 142, 14—15. In Opif. 134 p. I 46, 14—19, commentando Gen. 2, 7, osserva: ,,(Mosè) fa vedere con la massima chiarezza la differenza totale che c'è tra l'uomo ora plasmato e quello che era stato precedentemente generato ad immagine di Dio; questo che è stato plasmato è sensibile ed ormai partecipa alla qualità, è composto di corpo e d'anima, è uomo o donna, è mortale per natura: l'altro invece fatto ad immagine di Dio, è un'idea, un genere o un sigillo; è intelligibile, incorporale, nè maschio nè femmina, incorruttibile per natura." Queste distinzioni vengono espresse anche in Leg. I 53 e 54 p. I 74, 6—17; ibid. I 88 p. I 84, 11—14; ibid. I 90 p. I 85, 1—3: quando senti nominare Adamo γήϊνον καὶ φθαρτὸν νοῦν εἶναι νόμιζε· ὁ γὰρ κατ' εἰκόνα οὐ γήϊνος, ἀλλ' οὐράνιος; cfr. anche ibid. II 4 p. I 90, 20.

Il raffronto tra le posizioni di Gregorio e quelle di Filone mostra che, pur attraverso a due mentalità notevolmente differenti, ci sono rilevanti punti d'incontro: 1⁰) entrambi dànno questa verità come un fatto indiscutibile e fondamentale e la pongono al centro della loro speculazione; 2⁰) Filone lega strettamente l'εἰκών al Logos e Gregorio ce la fa dare da Gesù che è il Logos di Dio; 3⁰) entrambi sottolineano nell'εἰκών un elemento antitetico al corpo; 4⁰) entrambi la considerano come il principio direttivo della nostra vita spirituale; 5⁰) entrambi la vedono come un dono divino che va conservato (φυλάσσοντες — φυλάξαι) puro da macchie; 6⁰) in entrambi questo concetto richiama l'opposizione dell'uomo terrestre e di quello celeste, di quello corruttibile e mortale e di quello incorruttibile ed immortale[30].

---

[30] L'accostamento esteso a tutte le oraz. di Greg. conferma nelle linee essenziali questi rilievi; infatti: 1⁰) entrambi considerano l'immagine come l'elemento che collega direttamente

Cap. VI, col. 865 A:

Gregorio deplora che il corpo, quando sta bene, faccia guerra all'anima: ὃ καὶ εὐεκτοῦν πολεμεῖ. In Leg. III 46 p. I 123, 10—11 Filone immagina che Aronne paragoni il corpo ad una παρεμβολῇ, ad uno στρατοπέδῳ πολέμων καὶ κακῶν ὅσα πόλεμος ἐργάζεται πλήρει, μετουσίαν εἰρήνης οὐκ ἔχοντι. Quanto ad εὐεκτεῖν riferito alla salute fisica — che in questa sola orazione ritorna ancora tre volte: cap. XVIII col. 880 C, XX col. 881 D e XXVIII col. 896 AB — vedi Mutat. 215 p. III 193, 18: τῷ τὸ μὲν σῶμα εὐεκτοῦντι[31].

Cap. VI, col. 865 A:

Gregorio, parlando del proprio corpo dal punto di vista dell'anima, dice: ὃ καὶ ὡς σύνδουλον ἀγαπῶ. Filone in Prov. II 22 p. 59 A. e VIII 56 parla di medici che guariscono τὸ δοῦλον ψυχῆς σῶμα. Cfr. anche Eusebio, Praep. evang. VIII 14, 17 p. I 466, 13 Mras. In Leg. I 33 p. I 69, 13 menziona un φιλοσώματον νοῦν: qui però Fil. non intende tanto l'anima in senso assoluto, quanto l'intelligenza nel momento in cui sta per introdursi nel corpo. Cfr. ibid. 32 p. 69, 6—8.

Cap. VI, col. 865 A:

Gregorio, sempre parlando come anima, dice del corpo: ὃ καὶ ὡς δεσμὸν φεύγω. Filone in Leg. II 57 p. I 101, 22 a proposito di Nadab e Abiud (Lev. 10, 1) dice: πάντα δεσμὸν . . . σωματικῆς ἀνάγκης διαρρήξαντες ed in Deter. 158 p. I 294, 7—8: λυθεὶς γὰρ τῶν ἀρρήκτων σώματος καὶ περὶ σῶμα δεσμῶν[32]. Per la designazione del corpo come di un δεσμωτήριον cfr. Ebr. 101 p. II 189, 25; Her. 85 p. III 20, 11—12 e Gregorio, ep. 195, 3 Gallay II, 86; vedi anche epigr. 24, 3—4 col. 96. Di contestata autenticità Virt. 78 p. V 287, 8—9 assai vicino a Gregorio.

l'uomo a Dio; 2[0]) ne fanno il principio normativo della vita dello spirito; 3[0]) insistono sulla necessità di mantenerla esente da macchie. Questo riscontro ribadisce però che, sull'unità sostanziale di concezione, si sviluppano interessi distinti: Fil. si attiene preferibilmente ad un punto di vista ontologico-antropologico inclinando ad una certa astrattezza filosofica, consona con la sua posizione di pensatore privato; Greg. invece immette nella sua speculazione il fervore che nasce dalla considerazione che il Verbo si è fatto carne proprio per sanare quest'elemento deturpato dalla colpa e si lascia guidare dallo zelo pastorale il quale non si limita a svelare la verità, ma mira soprattutto a farla vivere in mezzo alle tentazioni della vita quotidiana.

[31] Per idee ed espressioni analoghe cfr. or. 12,3 col. 845 B; 2,91 col. 493 B; poem. I 2,14,60 col. 760; ibid. v. 68; I 2,15,149—152 col. 777; II 1,44,9—10 col. 1350; ibid. 45,114 col. 1361 e or. 45,30 col. 664 B.

[32] È una valutazione alla quale Gregorio ritorna volentieri: cfr. or. 43,2 col. 497 A; poem. II 1,46,9 col. 1378; ibid. 49,7 col. 1385 e 50,88 col. 1391. Si tratta comunque di una concezione platonica: cfr. Phaid. p. 67 D. Un inquadramento più ampio in P. Courcelle, Gefängnis (der Seele), übers. von H. J. Horn, in: Reallexikon für Antike und Christentum, IX, 1976, coll. 294—318 (per Filone cfr. le coll. 299—300).

Cap. VI, col. 865 B:

Gregorio dichiara: all'infuori del corpo οὐκ ἔχω τίνι συνεργῷ πρὸς τὰ κάλλιστα χρήσωμαι[33]. Filone in Leg. I 103 p. I 88, 6—7, si pone di fronte alla medesima relazione, anche se poi la risolve con una valutazione opposta, dicendo che per l'acquisto della virtù basta l'intelletto: τὸ δὲ σῶμα οὐχ οἷον οὐ συνεργεῖ πρὸς τοῦτο, ἀλλὰ καὶ κωλυσιεργεῖ. Per l'espressione cfr. Fug. 21 p. III 114, 15; ibid. 168 p. 147, 2—3; Confus. 110 p. II 250, 5—6 e altrove.

Cap. VI, col. 865 B:

Gregorio asserisce: δεῖ με πρὸς Θεὸν ἀναβῆναι διὰ τῶν πράξεων e Filone, Confus. 95 p. II 247, 9—10 rileva che coloro i quali rendono il loro culto a Dio hanno come caratteristica di ἀναβαίνειν δὲ τοῖς λογισμοῖς πρὸς αἰθέριον ὕψος: quest'ultima locuzione non è altro che una delle varianti delle quali i Giudei si servivano volontieri per fare da schermo alla divinità: è una designazione che diventa generica per desiderio di essere rispettosa.

Cap. VII, col. 865 B:

Gregorio, parlando delle ribellioni del corpo contro l'anima, scrive: οὐκ ἔχω πῶς φύγω τὴν ἐπανάστασιν. Filone nell'Her. 284 p. III 65, 7 ricorda le χαλεπαὶ καὶ βαρύταται (cfr. Gregorio appena sotto βαρηθείς) ἐπαναστάσεις delle passioni che tormentano l'anima; in Mos. II 16 p. IV 204, 4 menziona la σώματος ... ἐπανάστασις. Vedi anche Congr. 59—60 p. III 84, 6—9: „Il corpo è il luogo dei piaceri e delle passioni ... L'anima viene meno e perde di vigore sotto l'azione della passione (τῷ πάθει: cfr. Gregorio, cap. VIII, col. 868 A: διὰ τὸ πάθος) quando il corpo l'assale con grandi e burrascose ondate[34]."

Cap. VII, col. 865 B:

Gregorio teme di essere aggravato (βαρηθείς) dalle pastoie del corpo che lo tirano in basso o lo trattengono a terra. Cfr. Filone, Spec. IV 114 p. V 235, 9—11: „Il corpo, che è greve di propria natura, opprime e trascina in giù con sè gli spiriti deboli, soffocandoli ed appesantendoli con la massa della sua carne" e Opif. 158 p. I 55, 6—8: „(L'uomo che ama il piacere) a stento riesce a tenere il capo eretto, aggravato (βαρυνόμενος) e trascinato giù, dato che l'intemperanza gli dà lo sgambetto e lo fa rovinare a terra."

---

[33] Anche se J. GIBLET, L'homme image de Dieu ... (1948) in nota 310 sostiene, tra l'altro, che secondo Filone il corpo è uno strumento necessario nel nostro viaggio verso Dio, è però innegabile che il suo atteggiamento più comune verso il corpo è di una radicata diffidenza. Cfr. al riguardo anche F. WAGNER, Geschichte des Sittlichkeitsbegriffes. Erst. Bd.: Sittlichkeitsbegriff in der antiken Ethik (Münsterische Beiträge zur Theologie, n. 14), Münster i. W., 1928, pp. 170—177.

[34] Cfr. anche l'or. V 35 col. 709 B dove il Naz. dichiara che la mensa eucaristica serve a placare πᾶσαν παθῶν ἐπανάστασιν; poem. II 1, 28, 8 col. 1288 e ibid. 45, 40 col. 1356 dove parla della σὰρξ ἐπανισταμένη.

Sulle ἡδοναὶ καὶ ἐπιθυμίαι . . . βαρύνασαι καὶ πιέσασαι τὴν ὅλην ψυχήν cfr. Deter. 16 p. I 262, 4—5[35].

Cap. VII, col. 865 B:

Gregorio sostiene che il corpo ἐχθρός ἐστιν εὐμενής, καὶ φίλος ἐπίβουλος. Filone, Leg. III 69 p. I 127, 30—31 considera ἡμῶν τὸ σῶμα come πονηρόν τε καὶ ἐπίβουλον τῆς ψυχῆς, espressione che ripete pressocchè alla lettera poco sotto, § 71 p. I 128, 6—7; appena oltre — p. 128, 9—11 — afferma che „quando l'intelligenza si innalza e si consacra ai misteri del Signore, giudica il corpo πονηρὸν καὶ δυσμενές; quando invece essa si allontana dalla ricerca delle cose divine, lo stima φίλον αὐτῷ (riferito a νοῦς) καὶ συγγενὲς καὶ ἀδελφόν[36]. L'angolo visuale tra Filone e Gregorio è evidentemente diverso, però interpreta un medesimo dato di fatto e lo esprime in maniera analoga. È inoltre opportuno notare che — di fronte allo stesso problema — Gregorio presenta delle reazioni assai più controllate; infatti egli si tiene attentamente lontano dal reciso pessimismo filoniano nei riguardi del corpo. Vedi a questo proposito Leg. III 72. Che il corpo sia un νεκρός è reiteratamente asserito da Filone: cfr. anche § 69 p. 127, 31 e 32; § 70 p. 128, 6; § 74 p. 128, 25 e 129, 5[37]. In Confus. 177 p. II 263, 14—15 il corpo viene

---

[35] Il motivo della carne che ci appesantisce e ci aggrava verso terra è ripetutamente toccato dal Nazianzeno: cfr. or. XVI 15 col. 953 C; poem. I 2, 9, 26—27 col. 669; ibid. 10, 66—67 col. 685; II 1, 1, 33—36 col. 972; ibid. 34, 171—172 col. 1319; ibid. 45, 37 col. 1356. Anche la metafora qui usata delle πέδαι che avvincono al basso non è un accenno passeggero ed isolato: cfr. poem. II 1, 46, 7 col. 1378 dove la σάρξ è definita ἰλυόεσσα πέδη, βρίθουσα μολυβδίς (ricorda or. XXXVII 16 col. 301 B); vedi inoltre poem. I 2, 10, 20 col. 682; ibid. 10, 602 col. 724; ibid. 14, 65 col. 760; II 1, 49, 1—4 coll. 1384—1385.

[36] Greg. in poem. I 2, 14, 59—60 col. 760 denomina la carne εὐμενὴς ἐχθρός; appena sotto (v. 62) dichiara dubbio che essa gli sia mai stata εὐμενής ed in poem. II 1, 46, 5 col. 1378 scrive: σάρξ ἐχθρὴ φιλίη τε, γλυκὺς μόθος, ἐσθλὸν ἄπιστον. Con altra immagine, ma con uguale intendimento, in poem. I 2, 14, 61 col. 760 rappresenta l'elemento corporeo come θὴρ πικρὸν σαίνων. Per singole indagini che forniscano indicazioni utili ad un inquadramento e ad un approfondimento di questo tema cfr. W. Schauf, Sarx. Der Begriff 'Fleisch' beim Apostel Paulus unter besonderer Berücksichtigung seiner Erlösungslehre (Neutestamentliche Abhandlungen, n. 11, 1.—2. Heft), Münster i. W., 1924, pp. XVI-208; K. G. Kuhn, Πειρασμός—ἁμαρτία—σάρξ im NT und die damit zusammenhängenden Vorstellungen, in: Zeitschrift für Katholische Theologie, CLIX (1952), pp. 200 segg.; E. Schweizer, Die hellenistische Komponente im neutestamentlichen σάρξ-Begriff, in: Zeitschrift für die neutestamentliche Wissenschaft, XLVIII (1957), pp. 237—253; W. Seibel, Fleisch und Geist beim heiligen Ambrosius (Münchener Theologische Studien, II. System. Abt., 14. Bd.), München, 1958, pp. XIV-206; Schweizer, s. v. σάρξ, in: Filone, pp. 121—122, nel 'Theologisches Wörterbuch zum Neuen Testament' di G. Kittel, VII, 1964; A. Sandt, Der Begriff 'Fleisch' in den paulinischen Briefen (Biblische Untersuchungen, n. 2), Regensburg, 1967, pp. X-335; E. Brandenburger, Fleisch und Geist. Paulus und die dualistische Weisheit (Wissenschaftliche Monographien zum Alten und Neuen Testament, n. 29), Neukirchen, 1968, pp. 244; N. Lazure, La convoitise de la chair en I Jean II, 16, in: Revue Biblique, LXXVI (1969), pp. 161—205.

[37] Questa concezione, quantunque assai rara, non è però estranea del tutto a Gregorio: cfr. poem. I 2, 14, 64—65 col. 760 dove chiede alla sua anima: τίς δέ σε νεκροφόρον θήκατο ?

definito come „roccaforte di ogni sorta di calamità" per l'anima. Gli aggettivi ἐχθρός ed ἐπίβουλος sono accostati in Contempl. 37 p. VI 56, 3—4.

Cap. VII, col. 865 B:

A proposito di questa unione contrastata tra corpo ed anima, Gregorio esclama: ὦ τῆς συζυγίας καὶ τῆς ἀλλοτριώσεως! Filone a sua volta in Plant. 25 p. II 139, 1 parla della διάζευξις καὶ ἀλλοτρίωσις del corpo e dello spirito. Cfr. anche Decal. 124 p. IV 297, 12.

Cap. VII, col. 865 B:

Gregorio afferma che noi, in quanto anima, siamo una parte, un frammento di Dio: μοῖραν ἡμᾶς ὄντας Θεοῦ. Filone, Leg. III 161 p. I 148, 7—12 scrive: τὸ μὲν οὖν σῶμα ἐκ γῆς δεδημιούργηται, ἡ δὲ ψυχὴ αἰθέρος ἐστίν, ἀπόσπασμα θεῖον . . . ἡ δὲ αἰθερίου φύσεως μοῖρα οὖσα ψυχὴ (ἔχει τροφὰς) πάλιν αἰθερίους καὶ θείας. L'espressione di entrambi proviene dalla grande fonte platonica: cfr. infatti Crizia p. 121 A dove il filosofo ateniese parla di ἡ τοῦ θεοῦ μοῖρα che noi avemmo e che andò progressivamente inquinandosi a contatto con l'elemento mortale che è proprio della nostra natura[38].

Il nesso αἰθερίου φύσεως μοῖρα è equivalente al μοῖρα . . . Θεοῦ di Gregorio: si tratta di una delle solite perifrasi per evitare il nome di Dio; lo dimostra anche la coppia di aggettivi αἰθερίους καὶ θείας che immediatamente seguono e che sono certo sinonimi. Il contrapposto, che qui troviamo, tra l'anima celeste e divina ed il corpo fatto di terra è stato anche sottolineato da Gregorio poche righe sopra: cfr. cap. VI, col. 865 A: εἰκών τέ εἰμι Θεοῦ, καὶ τῷ πηλῷ συμφύρομαι.

In Deter. 90 p. I 278, 26—29 si domanda come la mente umana così piccola potrebbe contenere la grandezza del cielo e del mondo se non fosse τῆς θείας καὶ εὐδαίμονος ψυχῆς ἐκείνης ἀπόσπασμα; in Opif. 146 p. I 51, 6—7 afferma: „Ogni uomo è imparentato, mediante la sua intelligenza, con il logos divino, poichè egli è τῆς μακαρίας φύσεως . . . ἀπόσπασμα; in Somn. I 34 p. III 212, 7 dice del νοῦς umano che è ἀπόσπασμα θεῖον ed in Mutat. 223 p. III 195, 16—19 esclama: „Ragione, breve parola ma cosa totalmente perfetta e divina, frammento (ἀπόσπασμα) dell'anima universale o, come è più pio dire per quelli che seguono la filosofia di Mosè, copia somigliante dell'immagine divina (εἰκόνος θείας)." È di alto interesse la specificazione filoniana dell'equivalenza tra l'ἀπόσπασμα stoico e la εἰκὼν θεοῦ biblica. Anche accettando più volte la terminologia filosofica corrente, Filone tiene a sottrarre l'anima a qualunque possibile identificazione con la natura del cielo, per ricollegarla direttamente all'origine divina: in Plant. 18 p. II 137, 8—13 scrive che gli altri filosofi hanno detto che il nostro spirito era una particella della natura eterea (τῆς αἰθερίου φύσεως . . . μοῖραν), mentre invece il grande Mosè non assimilò la forma dell'anima ragionevole ad alcuno degli esseri soggetti al divenire, ma disse che era un esemplare auten-

---

[38] Gregorio in poem. I 2, 10, 135 col. 690 parla di chi osserva la legge di Dio ed onora l'anima, cioè Θεοῦ τε μοῖραν ἣν ἔχει; cfr. anche ibid. 9, 131 col. 678.

tico del soffio invisibile di Dio, segnato e plasmato dal sigillo di Dio, il cui tipo è il Logos eterno. Cfr. anche Her. 231 p. III 52, 4—8 e Deter. 83 p. I, 277, 6—10. In Opif. 135 p. I 47, 4—7 ricorre all'immagine abbastanza peregrina della colonia (ἀποικία) inviata quaggiù da Dio, affinchè, se l'uomo è mortale nella sua parte visibile, sia almeno immortale in quella invisibile[39].

Cap. VII, col. 865 B:

Gregorio parla di noi, in quanto anima, come ἄνωθεν ῥεύσαντας. Per Filone, Her. 184 p. III 42, 12 il νοῦς, la parte più pura dell'anima umana, è, ontologicamente, ἀπ' οὐρανοῦ καταπνευσθεὶς ἄνωθεν. Filone preferisce la metafora del soffio, mentre Gregorio sceglie quella del flusso: l'analogia dei due traslati e l'identità di significato logico collegano strettamente le due formulazioni[40].

Cap. VII, col. 865 C:

Gregorio sostiene che il dissidio tra l'anima ed il corpo è disposto da Dio per insegnarci a ricorrere a lui: ἐν τῇ πρὸς τὸ σῶμα πάλῃ καὶ μάχῃ πρὸς αὐτὸν ἀεὶ βλέπειν. Filone, Leg. III 190 p. I 155, 24—25 menziona la πάλην δ' οὐ τὴν σώματος ἀλλ' ἣν παλαίει ψυχὴ πρὸς τοὺς ἀνταγωνιστὰς τρόπους αὐτῆς πάθεσι καὶ κακίαις μαχομένη[41] ed in Deter. 9 p. I 260, 16—19 asserisce: ,,Coloro che amano la virtù sopportano un grandissimo peso (cfr. Gregorio βαρηθείς), la lotta contro il corpo ed i piaceri del corpo . . . .'' — Sull'imperfezione delle cose come stimolo per rivolgerci a Dio, in Cher. 109 p. I 196, 9—12 scrive: ,,Dio non fece nessuna delle cose particolari perfetta . . . affinchè nella sua brama di raggiungere ciò di cui era priva, fosse obbligata ad accostarsi a colui che era in grado di darglielo'': il concetto di Filone è generale, quello di Gregorio ne è una singola applicazione; però entrambi esprimono il medesimo piano della Provvidenza e lo valutano esattamente nella stessa maniera. — Cfr. anche Gregorio in quest'or. § 20, col. 884 A B.

Cap. VII, col. 865 C:

Continuando il suo pensiero Gregorio dichiara che la nostra debolezza congenita è stata disposta dalla Provvidenza come un correttivo alla nostra dignità, che avrebbe potuto elevarci in superbia. Filone, Praem. 119 p. V 363, 19—22 afferma che coloro i quali si sforzano di praticare la virtù e di conformare la loro vita alle sacre leggi eviteranno le malattie ,,ed anche se avvenisse loro qualche indisposizione, ciò non accadrebbe per fare loro

---

[39] Per questo contrasto vedi subito sotto Gregorio.

[40] L'immagine di un flusso sceso in noi dall'alto è frequente in Gregorio: cfr. or. II 91 col. 493 B; poem. I 2,10,60—61 col. 685; vedi anche poem. I 2,8,15 col. 650 e per altra espressione equivalente or. XXI 2 col. 1084 C e poem. II 1,28,6 col. 1288. Sulla provenienza da Dio dell'anima umana cfr. or. II 17 col. 425 BC.

[41] Gregorio in poem. I 2,10,123 col. 689 afferma che l'uomo, nella vita morale, riporta la corona ἐκ μάχης τε καὶ πάλης. Vedi anche epist. 32,2 GALLAY I p. 40; poem. I 2,3,17 col. 634; II 1,33,2 col. 1305.

del male, ma per ricordare alla creatura mortale che è mortale, per disperdere l'orgoglio esageratamente superbo e per il miglioramento dei costumi".

Cap. VII, col. 865 C:

Gregorio, pensando alla dignità dell'anima, proclama che noi uomini siamo μέγιστοι e Filone, Decal. 134 p. IV 299, 1—2 scrive: ἄνθρωπος δέ, ζῷον ἄριστον κατὰ τὸ κρεῖττον τῶν ἐν αὐτῷ, τὴν ψυχήν.

Cap. VII, col. 865 C:

Gregorio insegna che noi uomini siamo ἐπίγειοι καὶ οὐράνιοι. Il contrapposto è già neotestamentario ma in senso completamente diverso: o indica cose celesti e terrestri (Ioann. 3, 12; I Cor. 15, 40) o gli abitanti del cielo e della terra (Phil. 2, 10). In Filone non ricorre mai l'antitesi precisa come è posta da Gregorio, però ci sono formulazioni che nella sostanza le equivalgono e che nella forma presentano notevoli concomitanze: in Deter. 85 p. I 277, 16—17 Filone scrive: μόνον γὰρ δὴ τῶν ἐπὶ γῆς φυτὸν οὐράνιον ὁ θεὸς ἄνθρωπον εἰργάσατο; in Plant. 17 p. II 137, 7—8 nota che il creatore fece l'uomo eretto ,,affinchè contemplasse il cielo, essendo egli una creatura celeste e non terrestre (φυτὸν οὐκ ἐπίγειον ἀλλ' οὐράνιον)"; cfr. anche Leg. III 162 p. I 148, 13—14; Her. 88 p. III 21, 4—5. Più carico di preoccupazioni filosofico-teologiche, e quindi più teso nella forma, ma nella sostanza parallelo all' intendimento di Gregorio è Leg. I 31 p. I 68, 27—69, 6. Vedi inoltre Somn. I 146 p. III 236, 8—10; Leg. I 43 p. I 71, 21—23; I 45 p. I 72, 8—9 e 11—12. Questi due aggettivi sono messi a fronte come neutri sostantivati in Abr. 69 p. IV 17, 6—7; Ios. 147 p. IV 92, 1—2.

Cap. VII, col. 865 C:

Gregorio, nella sua sintesi della nostra natura, fa seguire un'altra antinomia: noi uomini siamo πρόσκαιροι καὶ ἀθάνατοι. Anche Filone, Confus. 149 p. II 257, 17—18 sottolinea il contrapposto tra 'anime immortali' e 'corpi corruttibili'[42].

Cap. VII, col. 865 C:

Gregorio, pensando all'anima ed al corpo di cui siamo composti, esclama: τοιοῦτον τὸ κρᾶμα ἡμῶν. Vedi Filone, Mutat. 184 p. III 188, 10: ἡμεῖς γεγόναμεν κράματα, θείου καὶ θνητοῦ συγκερασθέντων; Ebr. 101 p. II 189, 22: (ὁ ἄνθρωπος) τὸ ψυχῆς καὶ σώματος . . . κρᾶμα[43]. Cfr. inoltre Spec. I 1, 66 p. V 17, 5—6.

---

[42] Per quest'antitesi cfr. Gregorio, or. II 75 col. 481 C; VII 23 col. 785 B; XXXVIII 11 col. 324 A (= XLV 7 col. 632 B). Nell'or. XXVIII 22 col. 56 A si pone il quesito come mai in noi τὸ ἀθάνατον τῷ θνητῷ συνεκράθη. Vedi anche poco sotto, col. 56 B.

[43] Per κρᾶμα relativo al composto umano cfr. or. XX 11 col. 1077 C; XXVII 7 col. 20 C; XXXII 9 col. 184 C.

Cap. VII, col. 865 C:

Gregorio afferma che la strana mescolanza di anima e corpo che costituisce la nostra natura è stata disposta dalla Provvidenza a questo scopo, ἵν' ὅταν ἐπαιρώμεθα διὰ τὴν εἰκόνα, διὰ τὸν χοῦν συστελλώμεθα. In un frammento — p. II 673 M. — Filone per inculcare la dolcezza di tratto con il prossimo si avvale della medesima considerazione di cui si serve Gregorio: (il re) εἰ γὰρ καὶ εἰκόνι θεϊκῇ τετίμηται, ἀλλὰ καὶ κόνει χοϊκῇ συμπέπλεκται[44]. Inoltre in Spec. I 263—265 p. V 64, 5—16 invita a conoscere la sostanza del nostro corpo che consta di terra e di acqua; questa scoperta ci libererà dalla superbia e ci farà piacere a Dio che odia l'orgoglio. In questo passo si possono segnalare anche alcune concomitanze verbali: βούλεται Filone, § 263 lin. 5 e Gregorio, cap. 7 lin. 9; συνεκράθη Filone, § 264 lin. 11 e κρᾶμα Gregorio, cap. 7 lin. 18; ἐπίβουλος Filone, § 265 lin. 12 e Gregorio, cap. 7 lin. 4. Un identico concetto è espresso in Somn. I 211 p. III 250, 18—22. Vedi inoltre Opif. 135 p. I 46, 20—47, 1; Her. 29 p. III 8, 11[45].

Cap. VIII, col. 868 A:

Gregorio dice che il corpo è συγγενές dell'anima e subito dopo lo dichiara a lei φίλον, nonostante i pericoli di cui è causa. Filone, Fug. 90 p. III 129, 5 asserisce: ἀδελφὸν μὲν ψυχῆς τὸ σῶμα (cfr. anche poco sotto, § 91).

Cap. VIII, col. 868 A:

Gregorio afferma che, se accusa il corpo come nemico a causa delle passioni, lo abbraccia però come amico διὰ τὸν συνδήσαντα. L'uso di συνδέω per significare la connessione dell'anima e del corpo è familiare a Filone: cfr. Leg. I 108 p. I 89, 11 dove parla dell'anima liberata συνδέτου τοῦ σώματος; ibid. III 72 p. I 128, 17 dove ammonisce che l'anima non abbia da fallire il suo destino sotto l'azione del συνδέτου (scil. σώματος: l'ellissi dimostra come il verbo sia ormai diventato così tecnico da risultare autosufficiente); inoltre Deter. 48 p. I 269, 15; Somn. I 46 p. III 215, 1; ibid. I 110 p. III 228, 19[46]. Poco oltre — I 111 p. III 228, 21 — dice del logos (la ragione) che è per noi un amico, anzi è ἐνδεδεμένος[47].

Cap. VIII, col. 868 A:

Gregorio esorta ad amare il prossimo sofferente e ad essere ὅπερ ἐστὶν ἀλλήλοις τὰ μέλη, τοῦτο ἕκαστος ἑκάστῳ: nell'immagine delle membra è

---

[44] I due sostantivi di così pregnante significato sono accostati, quantunque con altro intendimento, anche nell'or. XXXVII 6 col. 289 BC. Per χοϊκός vedi E. SCHWEIZER, in: Theologisches Wörterbuch zum Neuen Testament, IX, 1973, pp. 460—468.

[45] Che la carne sia per noi un mezzo per tenerci umili è detto anche in Gregorio, or. XXXVIII 11 col. 324 A (= XLV 7 col. 632 B).

[46] Riguardo a Dio, considerato come creatore dell'anima e del corpo cfr. or. XXXVIII 11 col. 324 AB (= XLV 7 col. 632 B). Per συνδέω in quest'accezione vedi anche or. II 3 col. 409 C; ibid. 17 col. 425 C; ibid. 23 col. 433 A; VII 21 col. 781 B; poem. I 2, 3, 16 col. 634.

[47] Cfr. anche Platone, Timeo 73 B: τῆς ψυχῆς τῷ σώματι συνδουμένης.

evidente la suggestione paolina[48], ma si può anche ricordare che prima ancora, Filone, Virt. 103 p. V 296, 2—3 aveva invitato ad amare gli estranei, condividendone pene e dolori, ὡς ἐν διαιρετοῖς μέρεσιν ἓν εἶναι ζῷον δοκεῖν[49].

Cap. IX, col. 868 B:

Gregorio, contemplando lo stato miserando dei lebbrosi, osserva come essi soffrano non solo della povertà, male comune ad altri indigenti, ma anche di una seconda disgrazia, costituita dalla malattia: τοῖς μὲν ἄλλοις ἓν μόνον ἐλεεινόν, τὸ τῆς ἀπορίας· . . . τοῖς δὲ τοῦτο . . . καὶ μᾶλλον . . . εἰς τὰ ἀναγκαῖα μετὰ τῶν σαρκῶν ἀφήρηνται . . . Πρὸς δὲ τῇ πενίᾳ, καὶ ἡ νόσος κακὸν δεύτερον, καὶ κακῶν τὸ ἀπευκτότατον καὶ βαρύτατον καὶ εἰς κατάραν τοῖς πολλοῖς προχειρότατον. Filone, Praem. 127 p. V 365, 18—19 e 143 p. V 369, 18 stabilisce la medesima gradazione, separando però i due momenti con una trattazione sulla servitù, i cui limiti d'inizio e di termine non sono, ad ogni modo, espressamente segnati; scrive infatti: πρώτην ἀράν, ὡς κουφότατον κακόν, ἀναγράφει πενίαν καὶ ἔνδειαν καὶ σπάνιν τῶν ἀναγκαίων καὶ μετουσίαν παντελοῦς ἀπορίας . . . καὶ πρὸς τούτοις αἱ σωματικαὶ νόσοι. Oltre al movimento generale del pensiero sono visibili anche significative analogie di forma: ἀπορίας — ἀπορίας; τὰ ἀναγκαῖα — τῶν ἀναγκαίων; πρὸς δὲ τῇ πενίᾳ — πρὸς τούτοις; πενίᾳ — πενίαν; νόσος — νόσοι; κακὸν δεύτερον . . . καὶ βαρύτατον — κουφότατον κακόν; κατάραν — ἀράν.

Cap. IX, col. 868 BC:

Gregorio osserva che i lebbrosi sono ridotti ad una tale miseria ὥστε μικρὸν γοῦν τε βοηθεῖσθαι παρὰ τῆς ἐλπίδος, ἢ μόνον τοῖς ἀτυχοῦσίν ἐστι φάρμακον. Filone, Ios. 20 p. IV 65, 15—16 dichiara che chi subisce un danno ingiustamente δυσὶ βοηθεῖται τοῖς μεγίστοις, ἐλέῳ καὶ ἐλπίδι. Inoltre in un frammento — p. II 673 M. — Filone chiama la speranza παραμύθιον delle sventure: al riguardo va notato che Gregorio al cap. XII, col. 872 C usa παραμυθία come sinonimo figurato di φάρμακον: παραμυθίαν τοῖς ἕλκεσι; cfr. anche cap. XXVI, col. 892 B. Per la medesima idea espressa con altre immagini cfr. Praem. 10 p. V 338, 11; Deter. 120 p. I 285, 22; Ios. 113 p. IV 85, 3; Abr. 7 p. IV 3, 1[50].

Cap. X, col. 869 A:

Gregorio vede nei lebbrosi degli ἄνθρωποι νεκροὶ καὶ ζῶντες, osservando il progressivo smantellamento dell'organismo operato dalla malattia. In Filone non manca un caso di analogo ossimoro che trae ugualmente lo spunto dalla considerazione dei lebbrosi: commentando una prescrizione del

---

[48] Cfr. Rom. 12, 4—5; I Cor. 12, 12—27; Ephes. 4, 25.
[49] Per la concezione del prossimo come nostro membro vedi anche or. XXXIII 2 col. 216 C e XXXVII 18 col. 304 B.
[50] Su questo tema vedi or. VI 19 col. 748 A; XVII 2 col. 965 C; XVIII 43 col. 1041 B.

Levitico (13, 14) che ha un aspetto paradossale, in Deus 124 p. II 82, 23—25 nota che, secondo la comune opinione, sono le carni malate che corrompono le sane, quelle morte che distruggono le vive: οἱ ἄνθρωποι τὰ νοσοῦντα φθορὰς τῶν ὑγιαινόντων καὶ τὰ νεκρὰ τῶν ζώντων . . . νομίζουσι. In Fug. 55 p. III 122, 8 si allude a quanti vivono a lungo ma male ed ai buoni che muoiono presto: ζῶντες ἔνιοι τεθνήκασι καὶ τεθνηκότες ζῶσι. In Praem. 70 p. VI 351, 19 afferma che Caino meritava una punizione di nuovo genere: ζῆν ἀποθνήσκοντα ἀεί[51].

Cap. X, col. 869 A:

Gregorio rappresenta i lebbrosi come ἠκρωτηριασμένοι τοῖς πλείστοις τοῦ σώματος μέρεσι[52]. Filone richiama più volte macabri spettacoli di questo genere: in Somn. II 168 p. III 285, 23—24 presenta un gruppo di ubriachi ἀκρωτηριαζόντων ὦτα καὶ ῥῖνας καὶ ἅπερ ἂν τύχῃ τοῦ σώματος ⟨μέρη καὶ μέλη⟩; in Contempl. 44 p. VI 58, 1 parla di risse sanguinose scoppiate in banchetti pagani: τὰ σώματα ἠκρωτηριασμένοι. Vedi anche Spec. III 179 p. V 200, 8: οὐχ ὅπως ἀκρωτηριάζηται τὸ σῶμα στερόμενον ἀναγκαιοτάτου μέρους e ibid. I 80 p. V 21, 2—3 e I 3 p. V 1, 18—2, 1.

Cap. X, col. 869 A:

Gregorio ritrae i lebbrosi così deformati dalla malattia da essere diventati irriconoscibili e riferisce che essi citavano i loro padri, madri, fratelli come elementi di identificazione. Filone, Confus. 183 p. II 264, 18—19 — naturalmente in altra situazione, non essendosi mai specificatamente occupato di lebbrosi — scrive: „Spesso degli individui che prima non conoscevamo, li abbiamo identificati mediante i loro parenti.“

---

[51] L'ossimoro vivo—morto si presta in Gregorio a utilizzazioni molteplici: in or. XXI 15 col. 1097 B egli se ne serve contro gli ariani che avevano calunniato Atanasio di aver ucciso un certo Arsenio che poi si presentò vivo e vegeto; in poem. II 1, 75, 2 col. 1422 lo usa per indicare di sentirsi vicino a morte; in poem. II 1, 11, 1919 col. 1163 dice di sè dopo l'abdicazione di Costantinopoli: πάρειμι νεκρὸς ἔμπνοος; in poem. II 1, 1, 203 col. 985 presentandosi come morto al mondo afferma: νέκυς ἔμπνοός εἰμι; in poem. I 2, 9, 104 col. 675 dichiara che senza Cristo siamo dei νέκυες ζώοντες. Per quest'antitesi in senso morale cfr. poem. II 2, 5, 142 col. 1532 ed in senso ascetico poem. II 1, 48 col. 1384 e 50, 55 col. 1389.

[52] In Gregorio e Filone queste menomazioni fisiche sono deplorate o riprovate; invece in IV Macc. 10, 20 sono esaltate come il supremo trionfo di un martire: ὑπὲρ τοῦ Θεοῦ τὰ τοῦ σώματος μέλη ἀκρωτηριαζόμεθα. — Per recentissime trattazioni sulla lebbra nel mondo biblico ed in quello protocristiano cfr. L. DEROUSSEAUX—J. COUDERT, Lèpre, in: Catholicisme, VII, 29, Paris, 1972, pp. 411—421; S. G. BROWNE, Leprosy in the Bible, London, 1974, pp. 24; I. SIMON, La dermatologie hébraïque dans l'antiquité et au moyen âge (Périodes biblique, talmudique et rabbinique), in: Revue de l'histoire de la Médecine Hébraïque, CX (1974), pp. 149—154; CXI (1975), pp. 7—14; E. V. HULSE, The Nature of Biblical 'Leprosy' and the Use of Alternative Medical Terms in Modern Translations of the Bible, in: The Palestine Exploration Quarterly, CVII (1975), pp. 87—105; A. STETTLER, Lepra und Pest in der Antike, in: Antike Welt, VIII, 4 (1977), pp. 42—44; J. WILKINSON, Leprosy and Leviticus. The Problem of Description and Identification, in: Scottish Journal of Theology, XXX (1977), pp. 153—169.

Cap. X, col. 869 B:

Gregorio osserva che i nostri spiriti sono avvolti da un misero corpo: τὸ σῶμα . . . περικείμενοι. Filone, Migr. 193 p. II 306, 6—8 usando un verbo che ha un significato affine e che suggerisce la stessa immagine, scrive: (ὁ ἡμέτερος νοῦς) περιέχεται ὡς ἐν ἀγγείῳ τῷ σώματι.

Cap. XI, col. 869 C:

Per sottolineare lo strazio di un padre che deve scacciare il figlio perchè lebbroso, Gregorio si chiede: τί πατρὸς γνησιώτερον? e Filone, Congr. 177 p. III 109, 7—8 si chiede parimenti: τί γὰρ οἰκειότερον υἱῷ πατρὸς ἢ υἱοῦ πατρί? Per la locuzione πατὴρ γνήσιος cfr. Somn. II 273 p. III 302, 14; Aet. 83 p. VI 98, 18; Legat. 62 p. VI 167, 10; ibid. 71 p. VI 169, 2[53].

Cap. XI, col. 869 C:

Gregorio rappresenta l'angoscia di una madre costretta ad allontanare da sè il figlio colpito dalla lebbra: προθεῖσα θρηνεῖ, καθάπερ τεθνηκότα τὸν ζῶντα. Filone, Somn. II 66 p. III 269, 15—16 dice che per i viziosi ἔτι ζῶσιν αὐτοῖς ὡς νεκροῖς προτεθήσεται πένθος, ἀξίαν . . . θρήνων καρπουμένοις ζωήν e subito dopo — lin. 16—17 — richiama il fatto da cui ha prima tratto l'allegoria: ἐπεὶ καὶ Ἰακὼβ τὸν Ἰωσὴφ ἔτι ζῶντα πενθεῖ. Cfr. Ios. 189 p. IV 102, 7.

Cap. XI, col. 872 A:

Nel lamento che mette sulle labbra della madre del lebbroso, Gregorio afferma che era meglio morire bambino ἀθλίως ζήσεσθαι μέλλοντι καὶ ζωὴν θανάτου χαλεπωτέραν. Sono espressioni frequenti in Filone: Deter. 62 p. I 272, 16—17 (ἀθλίως ἔμελλε βιώσεσθαι); Congr. 174 p. III 108, 17—18 (ἀθλίως καὶ ταλαιπώρως ζῆν); Decal. 68 p. IV 284, 14; Prob. 8 p. VI 3, 6; Legat. 31 p. VI 161, 18; Flacc. 159 p. VI 149, 15; ibid. 179 p. VI 152, 13; Her. 113 p. III 26, 20—21; framm. p. II 669 M.

In Opif. 164 p. I 57, 10 Filone asserisce che la mollezza dei costumi suole produrre θανάτου χαλεπωτέραν ζωήν. Per formulazioni analoghe vedi: Spec. III 154 p. V 193, 14—15; Flacc. 129 p. VI 143, 29; ibid. 132 p. 144, 13; Aet. 74 p. VI 96, 3—4; Prob. 114 p. VI 32, 19—33, 1. L'unione delle due frasi di Gregorio ricorre anche in Filone: vedi Spec. IV 91 p. V 229, 22—23: τὴν ἀθλίαν . . . συμβαίνει ζωὴν ἀποτελεῖσθαι, παντὸς ἀργαλεωτέραν θανάτου[54].

---

[53] Cfr. Ps.-Luciano, Amores 19 e Platone Comico (KOCK, Plat. 192 vol. I p. 655; EDMONDS, Plat. 192 vol. I p. 552).

[54] Cfr. Filemone (Stobeo, Anthol. IV 53,8 WACHSMUTH-HENSE vol. V p. 1100; MEINEKE 121,8 vol. IV p. 114; KOCK, Fil. 203 vol. II p. 532; EDMONDS, Fil. 203 vol. III A p. 86): θανεῖν κράτιστόν ἐστιν ἢ ζῆν ἀθλίως; Gnomai monost. 296 (EDMONDS vol. III B p. 926): κρεῖττον τὸ μὴ ζῆν ἐστιν ἢ ζῆν ἀθλίως.

Cap. XI, col. 872 A:

La madre nell'accommiatarsi dal figlio ἐπαφίησι πηγὰς δακρύων. La locuzione non certo peregrina di πηγὴ δακρύων nella Bibbia ricorre solo in Ier. 8, 23 o 9, 1, nei tragici è più volte documentata[55] ed è presente anche in Filone: cfr. Ios. 23 p. IV 66, 3—4 (πηγὴν δακρύων ἀνιείς); ibid. 238 p. IV 111, 21[56].

Cap. XI, col. 872 B:

Gregorio lamenta che si sia più disposti a convivere con un φονεύς, un μοιχός ed un ἱερόσυλος (citandoli come i delinquenti per antonomasia) che non con un lebbroso che non ha fatto nulla di male. Filone, Ios. 84 p. IV 79, 4 nello stendere un elenco di individui che commisero gravissimi crimini si richiama ad ἀνδροφόνοις, μοιχοῖς, ἱεροσύλοις.

Cap. XI, col. 872 B:

Gregorio deplora che siamo più benevoli verso un delinquente che non verso uno sventurato καὶ τὸ μὲν ἀπάνθρωπον ὡς ἐλευθέριον ἠσπασάμεθα. Filone, Mos. I 95 p. IV 141, 15—16 rileva che non proviamo compassione di quelli che furono ridotti ingiustamente in ischiavitù, τῆς αὐτῆς ἀπανθρωπίας . . . ὥσπερ ἀγαθοῦ τινος ἐπειλημμένοι βεβαιοτάτου.

Cap. XII, col. 872 B:

Gregorio osserva che i lebbrosi ἀπελαύνονται πόλεων, ἀπελαύνονται οἰκιῶν e da tutte le riunioni pubbliche. Cfr. Filone, Leg. III 1—2 p. I 113, 4—5 e 9—10: ἀπελήλαται πόλεως . . . ἄπολις καὶ ἄοικος ὁ φαῦλός ἐστι; Sacrif. 32 p. I 215, 1[57]. In Flacc. 123 p. VI 142, 23—26 gli Ebrei ricordano le vessazioni ricevute dal governatore: ἐληλαμένοι καὶ στερόμενοι πόλεως καὶ τῶν ἐν πόλει δημοσίων καὶ ἰδιωτικῶν περιβόλων, ἀπόλιδες καὶ ἀνέστιοι μόνοι . . . γενόμενοι; vedi anche Migr. 90 p. II 286, 2—3[58].

Cap. XII, col. 873 B:

Gregorio ritrae i lebbrosi nell'atto in cui si gettano in mezzo alla folla ἵνα βραχέα ζωῆς ἐφόδια παρὰ τῶν τρυφώντων συλλέξωνται. Filone in un

---

[55] Vedi Sofocle, Antig. 803; Trach. 852; Euripide, Eracle 429—430; cfr. anche Eschilo, Agam. 887—888; Prom. 401; Euripide, Alc. 1067—1068; Eracle 98—99; 1354—1355.

[56] Per altri luoghi di Gregorio nei quali ricorre quest'espressione cfr. or. II 67 col. 477 A; V 26 col. 696 A; VIII 14 col. 805 B; XXV 12 col. 1216 B (bis); XXXII 19 col. 196 C; poem. I 2,1,358 col. 549; II 1,17,88 col. 1268; ibid. 45,2 col. 1353; ibid. 46,27 col. 1379; II 2,1,238 col. 1468; epitaph. 116,1 col. 71. Nell'or. XVII 1 col. 965 B collega questa locuzione con Geremia 8,23 e nella XXII 8 col. 1140 BC la introduce a commento di una frase che egli cita dalle Lamentazioni 1,15. Nell'epist. 40,3 GALLAY p. I 50 dice δακρύων ἀφῆκα πηγάς riecheggiando Fil. Ios.

[57] Ricorda il verso di un poeta comico non identificato (cfr. Giuliano, or. VI p. 195 B; KOCK, framm. 127 adesp., vol. III p. 432; EDMONDS, adesp. 1204 A vol. III A p. 498): ἄπολις, ἄοικος, πατρίδος ἐστερημένος.

[58] Cfr. or. V 18 col. 688 A dove Gregorio ricorda che l'Apostata prima della spedizione ἠλαύνετο δήμοις καὶ πόλεσι.

framm. riferito da Eusebio, Praepar. Evang. VIII 14 MG XXI, col. 656 CD e GCS Mras I 465, 8—10 contrappone il τὶς βραχείας ποτὲ τροφῆς ἄσμενος ai τοῖς τῆς φύσεως ἀγαθοῖς ἐντρυφῶντες.

Cap. XIII, col. 873 C:

Gregorio osserva il contrasto che la solennità religiosa produce: all'interno della chiesa melodie sacre, al di fuori nenie e lamenti di lebbrosi che piangono la loro miseria: ἀντᾴδει δὲ τοῖς ἱεροῖς ἔνδον μέλεσιν ὁ τῶν αἰτήσεων ὀδυρμός. Per un contrapposto identico seppure espresso con diverso intento cfr. Spec. III 125 p. V 185, 14—15: ἐπετέλουν σὺν ᾠδαῖς καὶ ὕμνοις ἀντὶ θρήνων[59].

Cap. XIII, col. 873 D:

Gregorio asserisce che esiste γέλωτος οὐ καλοῦ δάκρυον ἐπαινούμενον e Filone, Migr. 157 p. II 299, 14—15 afferma che il nutrimento dello spirito è fornito da lacrime che manifestano la nobile gioia dell'intimo: τὰ τοῦ ἐνδιαθέτου καὶ σπουδαίου γέλωτος ἐμφανῆ δάκρυα.

Cap. XIV, col. 876 A:

Gregorio proclama che non è giusto trascurare i lebbrosi, i quali sono uomini come noi, hanno la nostra stessa natura e sono stati compaginati con gli stessi elementi fisici: οἱ τὴν αὐτὴν ἡμῖν λαχόντες φύσιν . . . Il concetto di una solidarietà di natura che stringe tutti gli uomini al di sopra delle classi sociali e della fortuna è una delle convinzioni basilari che hanno animato il pensiero di Gregorio. In questa sola orazione vi ritorna ripetutamente: cfr. il συγγενές di cap. V col. 864 B; VIII col. 868 A; X col. 869 B; XXIII col. 888 B e τό τε τῆς φύσεως ὁμότιμον di cap. XXV col. 889 C. Filone in Quaest. Ex. II 12 p. 475 A. e VII 288 si chiede: *Quis enim quemquam ex hominibus, quorum una est cognatio naturae, praetermittet . . . ?*[60] In Spec. I 294 p. V 71, 4—5 invita a venire in soccorso πρὸς ἀνθρώπους τοὺς φύσει συγγενεῖς καὶ ἀπὸ τῶν αὐτῶν στοιχείων σπαρέντων. Gregorio sviluppa più ampiamente questo spunto e lo approfondisce con apporti cristiani. Un altro passo che merita di essere riferito perchè consuona particolarmente con Gregorio sia nell'orientamento generale del pensiero che per richiami minuti è Decal. 41 p. IV 278, 6—8 dove è detto: Non è giusto inorgoglirsi e gonfiarsi di fronte ai nostri simili οἳ τύχαις μὲν ἀνίσοις ἴσῃ δὲ καὶ ὁμοίᾳ συγγενείᾳ κέχρηνται μίαν ἐπιγραψάμενοι μητέρα τὴν κοινὴν ἁπάντων ἀνθρώπων φύσιν. Ora Gregorio: 1°) al cap. XXXVI col. 905 C dichiara che i poveri sono creature di Dio ὁμοίως che i ricchi, anche se τὰ ἔξωθεν ἄνισα; 2°) ribatte con insistenza sulla συγγένεια che tutti ci lega: oltre i passi citati cfr. cap. XXIII col. 888 C; XXV col. 892 A; XXVI col. 892 B; 3°) al

---

[59] Nell'or. VI 18 col. 745 A Gregorio rievoca·i θρῆνοι τοῖς ὕμνοις ἀντεγειρόμενοι all'epoca della schiavitù babilonica. Vedi anche or. XVIII 28 col. 1020 B.

[60] Cfr. Marcus p. 47: ,,*for who would disregard any human being, with whom he has a single natural kinship* (μία συγγένεια φύσεως) . . .?''

cap. VIII col. 868 AB osserva come sia κοινή la nostra fragilità di uomini ed al cap. XV col. 876 C ricorda come sia πρὸς τῆς ἀνθρωπίνης φύσεως il comprenderci ed amarci a vicenda, anche in considerazione τῆς ἴσης ἀσθενείας; 4°) φύσις viene inoltre usato nel senso pregnante di un legame che ci unisce in una solidarietà non rinnegabile: cfr. cap. XVIII col. 880 C; XXV col. 889 C; XXVI col. 892 B (bis). — Sull'identità di natura come argomento per un trattamento giusto verso tutti cfr. Spec. III 14 p. V 212, 19—22.

Cap. XIV, col. 876 B:

Gregorio asserisce che i lebbrosi sono συγκληρονόμοι τῆς ἄνω ζωῆς, καὶ εἰ παραπολὺ τῆς ἐνταῦθα διήμαρτον. Filone, Fug. 59 p. III 123, 1—3 scrive: „I sacerdoti Nadab e Abiud per vivere muoiono, permutando l'esistenza mortale con la vita incorruttibile e si trasferiscono dal mondo generato a quello ingenito[61]." Cfr. anche Gregorio, cap. XXI di quest'orazione, col. 884 D.

Cap. XV, col. 876 C:

Gregorio parla di Cristo, τοῦ ἀγαθοῦ ποιμένος: evidentemente ha presente Ioann. 10, 11—14, che però usa tre volte καλός e mai ἀγαθός, il quale invece ricorre in Agric. 49 p. II 105, 11—12 dove è detto che l'anima trova (τυχεῖν) in Dio un pastore irreprensibile ed assolutamente buono: ἀνυπαιτίου καὶ πάντα ἀγαθοῦ ποιμένος[62]. Questa metafora viene poi sviluppata nelle righe seguenti, dove Dio è presentato come supremo pastore (49—53

---

[61] Per qualche indagine sul concetto mistico-spirituale di vita cfr. F. MUSSNER, ZΩH. Die Anschauung vom 'Leben' im vierten Evangelium, unter Berücksichtigung der Johannesbriefe (Münchener Theologische Studien, I. Hist. Abt., 5. Band), München, 1952, pp. XV-190 (cfr. pp. 32—35: Die griechische Metamorphose des jüdischen Lebensbegriffs bei Philo von Alexandria); G. GRUBER, ZΩH. Wesen, Stufen und Mitteilung des wahren Lebens bei Origenes (Münchener Theologische Studien, II. System. Abt., 23. Band), München, 1962, pp. XXIII-342; G. PH. KOSTARAS, Der Begriff des Lebens bei Plotin, Hamburg, 1969, pp. 147; J. CAMPOS, El 'Libro de la Vida', I: En la Sagrada Biblia; II: En la tradición patrística, in: Helmantica, XXI (1970), pp. 115—147 e 249—302 (analisi dei 22 passi dell'A. e del NT. che contengono quest'espressione e descrizione del suo sviluppo semantico fino al termine del secolo VIII); A. ORBE, El dilema entre la vida y la muerte. Exégesis prenicena de Deut. 30,15—19, in: Gregorianum, LI (1970), pp. 305—365 e 509—536 (va dagli autori giudaici a Metodio d'Olimpo; per Filone cfr. le pagg. 309—315); G. CROCETTI, Le linee fondamentali del concetto di vita in Jo 6,57, in: Rivista Biblica Italiana, XIX (1971), pp. 375—394; P. GRELOT, De la mort à la vie éternelle (Lectio divina, II. 67), Paris, 1971, pp. 276; R. SCHNACKENBURG, Das Johannesevangelium. II .Teil: Kommentar zu Kap. 5—12 (Herders Theologische Komment. zum Neuen Testament, IV, 2), Freiburg i. Br., 1971 (Excursus su ζωή: pp. 434—435); S. ZAÑARTU, El concepto ZΩH en Ignacio de Antioquía (Publicaciones de la Universidad Pontificia Comillas, Madrid, Serie I, Estudios 7; Teología I, 4), Madrid, 1977, pp. 296.

[62] Greg. in or. I 6 col. 400 B; XVIII 4 col. 989 A; XXXVIII 14 col. 328 A (= XLV 26 col. 657 D) usa invece ὁ ποιμὴν ὁ καλός. La locuzione ἀγαθὸς ποιμήν ricorre poi anche nell'or. II 34 col. 441 C, riferita al vescovo. — Per quest'immagine nell'antico Oriente, in Grecia e nel Nuovo Testamento vedi M. VERENO, Die Symbolik des Hirten, in: Antaios, XII (1971), pp. 575—589.

p. II 105, 9—106, 12); ciò costituisce una novità rispetto alla Bibbia, la quale, pur esprimendo talora i rapporti tra Dio ed il suo popolo con traslati pastorali[63], non gli attribuisce direttamente l'epiteto di ποιμήν[64].

Cap. XV, col. 876 C:

Gregorio dichiara che la noncuranza verso i miseri non è πρὸς τῆς ἀνθρωπίνης φύσεως la quale impone la comprensione ἐκ τῆς ἴσης ἀσθενείας μαθοῦσα τὸ εὐσεβὲς καὶ φιλάνθρωπον ed insiste anche altrove sulla comune ἀσθένεια: cfr. cap. VIII col. 868 AB e XII col. 873 A. Filone, Mutat. 197 p. III 190, 17—18 asserisce: οἰκειότατον ἀνθρώπου φύσει τὸ εὖ καὶ βουλεύεσθαι καὶ πράττειν καὶ λέγειν. In Spec. IV 201 p. V 255, 11 deplora vivamente coloro che, nella loro fortuna, ,,si credono superiori τῆς φυσικῆς ἀνθρώπων ἀσθενείας ed in Abr. 208 p. IV 46, 12—13 afferma: τῆς γὰρ αὐτῆς φύσεώς ἐστιν εὐσεβῆ τε εἶναι καὶ φιλάνθρωπον. — Per l'associazione di queste due virtù vedi anche Virt. 95 p. V 293, 10—11: εὐσεβείᾳ καὶ φιλανθρωπίᾳ ταῖς ἀρετῶν ἡγεμονίσιν ἐπικοσμῶνται; Spec. IV 97 p. V 230, 23—24; Virt. 51 p. V 279, 19—20. — Al cap. XXIX col. 897 A Gregorio ottiene un duro effetto sarcastico contrapponendo le due radici ironicamente capovolte.

Cap. XVI, col. 876 D:

Gregorio rileva il contrasto tra i lebbrosi che ὕπαιθροι ταλαιπωρήσουσιν ed i ricchi che abitano in lussuose dimore; al cap. XXXIV col. 904 B menziona il povero il quale ταλαιπωρῇ νυκτὸς καὶ ἡμέρας αἴθριος. Per rappresentazioni analoghe cfr. Filone, Spec. III 17 p. V 154, 22—23: πλείω χρόνον . . . ἐν ὑπαίθρῳ ταλαιπωροῦντας ἢ ἐν ταῖς πόλεσιν οἰκοῦντας[65]; Aet. 4 p. VI 73, 10—11: (Anassagora) ταλαιπωρεῖται διανυκτερεύων ὕπαιθρος; Spec. I 301 p. V 73, 5; II 206 p. V 137, 20—21[66].

Cap. XVI, col. 877 A:

Di fronte ai lebbrosi che dimorano all'aperto stanno i ricchi con le loro sontuose abitazioni: ἡμεῖς δὲ οἰκήσομεν οἰκίας ὑπερλάμπρους, λίθοις παντοίοις διηνθισμένας . . . καὶ ψηφῖδος λεπτῆς διαθέσει καὶ ποικιλίᾳ γραφῆς, ὀφθαλμῶν ἀπατηλοῖς δελεάσμασι[67]. Filone, Cher. 104 p. I 195, 7—10 scrive: γραφαὶ καὶ πινάκια καὶ λίθων πολυτελῶν διαθέσεις, αἷς οὐ μόνον τοίχους ἀλλὰ καὶ

---

[63] Cfr. ad es. II Sam. 7, 7; I Chron. 11, 2; 17, 6; Ps. 22 (23), 1; 27 (28), 9; 36 (37), 3; 77 (78), 52 e 71—72; 79 (80), 2; Os. 13, 5; Mich. 2, 12; 5, 3; 7, 14; Zacch. 11 passim; Ier. 23, 1—2; Ezech. cap. 34. Vedi anche P. DE ROBERT, Le Berger d'Israël. Essai sur le thème pastoral dans l'Ancien Testament (Cahiers Théologiques, n. 57), Neuchâtel—Paris, 1968, pp. 103.

[64] Qualche volta tale qualifica gli è applicata, ma soltanto attraverso ad una similitudine: cfr. Eccli 18, 13; Is. 40, 11; Ezech. 34, 12.

[65] Cfr. or. XXV 9 col. 1209 C.

[66] Cfr. Tucidide I 134, 1: ἵνα μὴ ὑπαίθριος ταλαιπωροίη e Orazio, Carm. II 3, 22—23.

[67] Per identità di fondo ed analogie di forma cfr. poem. I 2,8,134—139 coll. 658—659 e II 1,88,141—143 coll. 1440—1441.

τὰ ἐδάφη ποικίλλουσι ... τέρψιν δὲ περιποιεῖ μόνον τοῖς ἐνοικοῦσιν; nel Prob.
66 p. VI 20, 1—2 dice che la vana gloria trovò λίθων ποικίλων καὶ πολυτελῶν ... ἰδέας e che le pregiò come ὄψεως ἀπάτην (quanto a πολυτελής
viene usato da Gregorio poco oltre, cap. XVII col. 877 C); nel Deter. 157
p. I 293, 22—23 rammenta che, tra quelli che consideriamo beni autentici,
poniamo ποικιλίαις χρωμάτων δι' ὄψεως ἡσθῆναι. Cfr. anche Contempl. 49
p. VI 59, 1—2.

Filone, Sacrif. 21 p. I 210, 8 dice che l'ἡδονή veste πολυτελεῖς ἐσθῆτας
ἐπηνθισμένας. È una frase di cui troviamo precisi echi nella col. 877 di
Gregorio; anch'egli deplora che i ricchi si effeminino con ἐσθῆτι molle e
fluente (lin. 12), che vivano in case διηνθισμένας (lin. 2) d'ogni lusso, che
usino profumi πολυτελεστάτοις (lin. 4 dal fondo).

Cap. XVI, col. 877 AB:

Gregorio, di fronte alla miseria dei lebbrosi, condanna il lusso dei
ricchi: ,,Noi ci effemineremo in abiti molli e fluenti, in finissimi tessuti di
lino e di seta; in alcuni faremo piuttosto brutta che bella figura (οὕτω γὰρ
ἐγὼ καλῶ πᾶν τὸ περιττὸν καὶ περίεργον) ... .'' Filone, Somn. I 124 p. III
231, 22—24 afferma che i ricercatori delle sacre verità ,,amano le cose
usuali ed a buon prezzo, tanto che non si vergognerebbero mai di un man-
tello di scarso valore, anzi al contrario considererebbero come una vergogna
ed una grave disavventura per loro dei vestiti preziosi''. In Praem. 99
p. V 358, 18 riferendosi ai vestiti, biasima τὴν περίεργον καὶ περιττὴν ...
πολυτέλειαν[68].

Cap. XVI, col. 877 B:

Gregorio osserva che i lebbrosi οὐδὲ τῆς ἀναγκαίας τροφῆς εὐπορήσου-
σιν (cfr. cap. XII col. 872 C). Filone, Spec. II 85 p. V 107, 9—10, mentre
descrive la miseria di chi è tormentato dalla fame e dal bisogno, ricorda
che è necessario rendere il povero τῶν εἰς τἀναγκαῖα ἀφορμῶν εὐπορηκώς
(anche in Gregorio ricorre subito dopo il termine ἀφορμαί). Vedi anche
Opif. 79 p. I 27, 10—11: ἐν ... τῶν ἀναγκαίων εὐπορίᾳ διάξουσιν; Spec. II
185 p. V 132, 3: εὐπορίᾳ ... τῶν ἀναγκαίων.

Cap. XVI, col. 877 B:

Gregorio rileva che i lebbrosi giudicano la loro cecità, che in sè sarebbe
il più grave dei mali, come il più leggero, perchè almeno così non scorgono
tutta la loro miseria: τὸ βαρύτατον τῶν κακῶν κουφότατον κρίνοντες[69]. Cfr.
Filone, Sobr. 4 p. II 216, 4—5: ,,Gli occhi del corpo e la luce sensibile sono
stimati in maniera eccezionale da noi tutti, e molti di coloro che hanno
perso gli occhi hanno fatto getto volontariamente anche della vita, κουφότερον κακὸν πηρώσεως θάνατον εἶναι δικάσαντες; Abr. 57 p. IV 14, 3—4;

---

[68] Per questa coppia di aggettivi vedi anche or. XXVII 1 col. 12 A; XXVIII 20 col. 52 C.
[69] Per questa contrapposizione cfr. epist. 24,2 GALLAY p. 32; 197,4 p. II, 88. Nell'or. XXI 7
col. 1089 A sono messi a fronte i due positivi.

ibid. 154 p. IV 35, 15—16. — Per l'accostamento della cecità e dei βαρύτερα κακά cfr. Praem. 143 p. V 369, 24—370, 2. Per l'espressione cfr. il βαρύτατον κακῶν di Confus. 22 p. II 234, 3 ed il κακῶν τὸ βαρύτατον di Prob. 139 p. VI 39, 15; — 2°) il τὸ κουφότατον ... τῶν κακῶν di Praem. 136 p. V 368, 1; — 3°) il βαρύτατον κακόν di Sacrif. 16 p. I 208, 2 (Fug. 190 p. III 151, 17); — 4°) il κουφότατον κακόν di Praem. 127 p. V 365, 18; — 5°) il βαρύτερον κακόν di Legat. 119 p. VI 177, 12; — 6°) il κουφότερον κακόν di Migr. 161 p. II 300, 8; Somn. II 150 p. III 283, 4; Ios. 15 p. IV 64, 17; ibid. 25 p. IV 66, 14; Virt. 124 p. V 303, 2; Flacc. 128 p. VI 143, 20; ibid. 162 p. VI 149, 26.

Cap. XVII, col. 877 C:

Gregorio vede in quella profusione di fiori olezzanti e di profumi squisiti un mezzo per effeminarsi (ἵνα καὶ μᾶλλον ἐκθηλυνώμεθα), denuncia poi l'immoralità delle leccornie di cui i cuochi fanno sfoggio e deplora l'abuso dei vini (col. 880 A e B). Filone, Plant. 158—159 p. II 165, 3—13 ritrae l'effeminatezza (ἐξεθήλυναν) che proviene soprattutto dalle raffinatezze dei cuochi e dei profumieri e poi insiste sugli eccessi del vino[70].

Cap. XVII, col. 877 C—880 A:

Così Gregorio descrive la mollezza di un banchetto di certi raffinati suoi contemporanei: oltre allo sfoggio di tappeti preziosi, di fiori esotici e di profumi costosissimi, παῖδας δὲ παρεστάναι, τοὺς μὲν ἐν κόσμῳ καὶ ἐφεξῆς, ἀνέτους τὰς κόμας καὶ θηλυδρίας, καὶ τῇ κατὰ πρόσωπον κουρᾷ περιειργασμένους, πλεῖον ἢ ὅσον συμφέρει λίχνοις ὀφθαλμοῖς κεκοσμημένους· τοὺς δὲ τὰς κύλικας ἐπ' ἄκρων δακτύλων ἔχοντας, ὡς οἷόν τε εὐπρεπέστατά τε ὁμοῦ καὶ ἀσφαλέστατα· τοὺς δὲ ὑπὲρ κεφαλῆς ἄνεμον ταῖς ῥιπῖσι σοφιζομένους, καὶ ταῖς ἐκ χειρῶν αὔραις τὸ πλῆθος τῶν σαρκῶν ἀναψύχοντας· καὶ τὰ ἐπὶ τούτοις, πλήθειν μὲν κρεῶν τὴν τράπεζαν, πάντων χορηγούντων ἡμῖν τῶν στοιχείων πλουσίως, ἀέρος, γῆς, ὕδατος· καὶ στενοχωρεῖσθαι τοῖς μαγείροις καὶ ὀψοποιῶν μαγγανεύμασιν, ἀγῶνα δὲ εἶναι πᾶσιν, ὅστις ὡς μάλιστα τὴν λίχνην ἡμῖν καὶ ἀχάριστον κολακεύσει γαστέρα ....

Per un quadro che presenti notevoli concomitanze con questo cfr. Contempl. 50—51 p. VI 59, 5—11: „Fanno da camerieri degli schiavi così graziosi e così belli che sembrano giunti non per compiere il servizio, ma piuttosto per compiacere l'occhio dei riguardanti[71] con la loro stessa presenza. Di questi alcuni, che sono ancora ragazzi (παῖδες), versano il vino, mentre porgono l'acqua degli adolescenti ben lavati e depilati, dal volto imbellettato, dagli occhi tinteggiati e dalle chiome accuratamente pettinate

---

[70] Gregorio ribadisce ripetutamente l'azione effeminante dei profumi: cfr. or. XXIV 3 col. 1173 A; XXXVIII 5 col. 316 B; XL 38 col. 413 B; XLIV 6 col. 613 B; poem. II 1, 1, 70 col. 975.

[71] Gregorio nell'or. XXIV 9 col. 1180 A mette in guardia contro i funesti effetti degli ὀφθαλμοὶ λίχνοι; nell'or. VIII 10 col. 800 C condanna coloro che con i cosmetici deturpano la bellezza data da Dio facendone un idolo λίχνοις ὄμμασιν.

e strette in trecce; portano infatti i capelli lunghi ... " e continua descrivendone gli abiti eleganti e studiati con cura speciale, poi prosegue (§ 52, p. VI 59, 17—19): ,,Altri stanno sullo sfondo in attesa del loro turno, e sono giovanetti o adolescenti che fioriscono della prima lanugine, che fino a poco prima sono stati trastullo dei pederasti e che poi sono stati con molta accuratezza addestrati ai compiti più gravosi" (la stessa cosa sembra suggerire Gregorio quando ce li presenta nell'atto di reggere coppe sulla punta delle dita ὡς οἷόν τε εὐπρεπέστατά τε ὁμοῦ καὶ ἀσφαλέστατα[72]). In seguito — § 53, p. VI 60, 1 — ricorda le svariate vivande περὶ ἃ σιτοπόνοι καὶ ὀψαρτυταὶ πονοῦνται; rappresenta quei convitati che volgono avidamente gli occhi in giro (τοῖς ὀφθαλμοῖς ... περιλιχνεύουσι: § 53, p. 60, 3—4. Cfr. la nota n. 71) ed infine — § 54, p. 60, 8—9 — nota espressamente come ci siano τράπεζαι πλήρεις ἁπάντων ὅσα γῆ τε καὶ θάλαττα καὶ ποταμοὶ καὶ ἀὴρ φέρουσιν ἔκλογα πάντα καὶ εὔσαρκα[73].

Stretta consonanza di motivi, e spesso anche di vocaboli, riscontriamo pure in Spec. III 37 p. V 160, 13—20 dove, di coloro che si dànno alla pederastia, dice: ,,Ormai abituati ad essere affetti dalla malattia dell'effeminatezza (νόσον θήλειαν) si snervano nell'anima e nel corpo non lasciando più ardere nessuna scintilla della loro virilità; con i capelli del capo vistosamente acconciati (περιφανῶς ... τὰς τῆς κεφαλῆς τρίχας ἀναπλεκόμενοι), tutti ben ornati (διακοσμούμενοι), con gli occhi spalmati e dipinti con cerussa, belletti e cose del genere, copiosamente unti di profumi olezzanti (εὐώδεσι μύροις) — infatti in tutti coloro che si ornano per allettare (εἰς εὐκοσμίαν) il profumo (τὸ εὐῶδες) è quello che esercita l'attrattiva maggiore — non arrossiscono di usare perfide arti per mutare in femminile (εἰς θήλειαν) la natura maschile[74]." Appena prima Filone aveva affermato che queste pratiche oscene erano addirittura oggetto di vanto, cosa che, nel suo campo, dirà appena dopo anche Gregorio: ,,Bisogna infatti che noi o siamo o ci facciamo credere effeminati e più dispendiosi di quanto sia necessario, come se ci vergognassimo se non siamo stimati corrotti ...[75]". In Spec. I 176 p. V 43, 4—6 Filone rivolge il suo sarcasmo su ,,coloro che si dànno da fare attorno a simposi ed a banchetti, che vanno alla caccia di tavole preziosamente imbandite e che sono miseri schiavi dei volatili, dei pesci e delle carni." Anche qui si notano alcuni punti d'incontro con Gregorio: 1º) Quell' affaccendarsi attorno a lauti pranzi ci richiama gli 'incanti' dei cuochi che vanno a gara a chi aduli di più il ventre (col. 880, lin. 9—11); — 2º) le

---

[72] Per i vari tipi di servi nelle case sfarzose cfr. poem. I 2, 8, 144—148 col. 659.

[73] Per tavole, cuochi e cibi forniti all'umana golosità dai tre elementi cfr. anche poem. II 1, 12, 614—616 coll. 1210—1211; ibid. 32, 24 col. 1302; II 2, 3, 140—142 col. 1490. Vedi inoltre or. VI 15 col. 741 B. — Per l'abbozzo di un festino voluttuosamente sontuoso cfr. poem. II 1, 88, 84—92 col. 1438.

[74] Il richiamo a servi dall'aspetto femmineo ricorre anche in poem. I 2, 28, 92 col. 863 ed il termine θηλυδρίαι in poem. II 1, 12, 425 col. 1197 e nel carme II 2, 8, 93 col. 1383 che appartiene ad Anfilochio d'Iconio. Vedi l'or. XXXV 4 col. 261 A (che è spuria) e poem. II 2, 4, 158 col. 1517 (dove l'autore parla di ἀνδρῶν θηλυτέρων).

[75] Cfr. la fine del cap. XVII col. 880 B.

πολυτελεῖς τραπέζας (stessa formula in Congr. 31 p. III 117, 1) hanno notevole somiglianza sia verbale che concettuale con τὴν τράπεζαν κατερράνθαι μύροις . . . πολυτελεστάτοις (col. 877, cap. XVII lin. 6—8); — 3⁰) la precisa determinazione delle vivande che consistono in ,,uccelli, pesci, carni" trova riscontro in Gregorio dove dice che al lussuoso convito ,,hanno generosamente contribuito tutti gli elementi: l'aria, la terra, l'acqua" (col. 880 lin. 7—8); — 4⁰) la specifica menzione di κρεῶν corrisponde a πλήθειν μὲν κρεῶν τὴν τράπεζαν (col. 880 lin. 6—7); — 5⁰) i δοῦλοι della golosità coincidono con i δοῦλοι γαστρός della fine del cap. XVII (col. 880 B).

Quanto alla frase τὰς κύλικας ἐπ' ἄκρων δακτύλων ἔχοντας (col. 880 lin. 2), si può notare che Filone usa due volte — Deus 168 p. II 91, 14—15; Somn. II 70 p. III 270, 12—13 — ἄκρῳ δακτύλῳ ψαύειν indicandolo come un proverbio ed interpretandolo in maniera traslata.

Gregorio — col. 880 lin. 5 — considera τὸ πλῆθος τῶν σαρκῶν e Filone, Spec. IV 114 p. V 235, 10—11, quantunque in altro senso, parla di τῷ πλήθει τῶν σαρκῶν.

Per quanto concerne la specificata denominazione dei tre elementi come fornitori di cibi agli uomini — πάντων χορηγούντων ἡμῖν τῶν στοιχείων πλουσίως, ἀέρος, γῆς, ὕδατος (col. 880 A) — c'è da osservare che si tratta di un atteggiamento abituale a Filone: cfr. Agric. 24 p. II 100, 1—5; Confus. 154 p. II 258, 14—15; Opif. 78 p. I 26, 17—18; ibid. 84 p. I 29, 12—13; Cher. 62 p. I 185, 15. Per l'elencazione dei tre elementi in cui vivono gli esseri animati cfr. Mos. II [III] 121 p. IV 228, 11; ibid. 126 p. IV 229, 19; Spec. IV 118 p. V 235, 24; Aet. 131 p. VI, 113, 4.

Gregorio sottolinea il rapporto tra il banchetto ed il ventre insaziabile, ed anche Filone, Spec. I 174 p. V 42, 15—19, insiste sullo stesso tema: entrambi rilevano l'impegno solerte dei cuochi, la servilità della gola e del ventre (Gregorio alla fine del cap., col. 880 B), le malattie fisiche e spirituali che ne provengono (cfr. Gregorio all'inizio del cap. XVIII, col. 880 B). Il nesso stabilito da Gregorio tra le raffinatezze dei cibi, l'abbondanza e la squisitezza dei vini, le brame del ventre e quelle sessuali, è già proclamato in questo stesso trattato da Filone — I 192 p. V 46, 19—21 —: ,,Il vino puro ed il mangiare ghiottonerie in istato di ubriachezza (ricorda Gregorio: ἡμῖν δὲ καὶ μέχρι μέθης οἱ τοῦ οἴνου κρατῆρες, μᾶλλον δὲ καὶ ὑπὲρ τὴν μέθην: col. 880 AB), attizzando le insaziabili cupidigie del ventre, coinvolgono nell'incendio anche le bramosie τὰς ὑπὸ γαστέρα". Ibid. IV 113 p. V 234, 25—235, 2 Filone ritorna sull'argomento e ritrae coloro che ,,introducono nel loro misero ventre ininterrottamente dei tributi di vino, di manicaretti, di pesci, insomma tutto ciò che creano le raffinate e minuziose cure di pasticceri e di cuochi i quali confezionano ogni sorta di ghiottonerie e rianimano e rinfocolano (ἀναρριπίζουσαι) le brame cupide ed insaziabili (τὰς ἀπλήστους καὶ ἀκορέστους ἐπιθυμίας)"; Filone ricorda poi coloro che sono ,,poveri schiavi non solo della concupiscenza, ma di tutte le passioni". Anche qui, oltre alle concordanze nello spirito e nei particolari della scena, vanno notate alcune singole concomitanze, come ἀπλήστους—ἀπλη-

στότατον; ἀκορέστους—κόρος e la tipica presenza di ἀναρριπίζουσαι in
Filone e di ταῖς ῥιπῖσι in Gregorio: sono elementi caratteristici anche se
adoperati tecnicamente in maniera diversa. Vedi anche Aet. 125 p. VI
110, 19: εἰ μὴ πρὸς ἀνέμων ῥιπίζοιτο.

Quanto ai caratteri dell'espressione va osservato che Gregorio parla
delle arti μαγείρων καὶ ὀψοποιῶν ed è interessante notare che in questi
casi anche Filone ricorre ad un binomio di sostantivi: oltre a Spec. I 174 e
IV 113 testè citati, vedi: Prob. 31 p. VI 9, 15—16: τὰ μαγείρων καὶ σιτοποιῶν ἡδύσματα; Confus. 95 p. II 247, 8: σιτοποιῶν ἢ μαγείρων ἔργα[76].
Cfr. anche Deter. 26 p. I 264, 3; Prob. 156 p. VI 44, 5—6 (anche l'inquadramento è esattamente gregoriano); Opif. 158 p. I 55, 13—14.

Gregorio definisce poi il ventre: 1º) come τὸ βαρὺ φορτίον καὶ ἀρχέκακον e Filone è perfettamente sulla medesima linea quando in Spec. IV 85
p. V 228, 20—21 asserisce τὸ ... ἀρχέκακον[77] πάθος ἐστὶν ἐπιθυμία: per il
concetto, ma non per la forma e le immagini cfr. Contempl. 37 p. VI 56,
3—4; — 2º) come τὸ ἀπληστότατον θηρίον ed anche qui Filone è in pieno
accordo, infatti in Comtempl. 74 p. VI 66, 1 dice che il vino ed i cibi raffinati
eccitano τὸ θρεμμάτων ἀπληστότατον, cioè τὴν ἐπιθυμίαν; in Somn. II 147
p. III 282, 19 afferma di conoscere individui che naufragarono περὶ γαστέρα
ἄπληστον[78]. Vedi inoltre Ebr. 22 p. II 174, 8; Ios. 93 p. IV 81, 3; Virt. 163
p. V 317, 11—12.

Gregorio infine proclama il ventre come καταργουμένην αὐτίκα σὺν
τοῖς καταργουμένοις βρώμασι: la fonte è I Cor. 6, 13: τὰ βρώματα τῇ κοιλίᾳ,
καὶ ἡ κοιλία τοῖς βρώμασιν· ὁ δὲ θεὸς καὶ ταύτην καὶ ταῦτα καταργήσει,
però il nerbo stilistico ed il particolare tipo di poliptoto indurrebbero anche
a pensare a Opif. 119 p. I 42, 1—2: φθαρτοῦ σώματος φθαρταὶ τροφαί[79].

Cap. XVII, col. 880 A:

Gregorio stabilisce la contrapposizione tra quelli che stentano a trovare
acqua da bere (κόρος καὶ ὕδατος) e quelli che dispongono di vino fino ad
ubriacarsi (μέχρι μέθης); anche Filone, Spec. I 249 p. V 60, 19 pone il contrasto tra il bere ὕδωρ e la μέθη.

Cap. XVII, col. 880 B:

Gregorio con un vivace estro satirico ed una fantasia lucida ritrae la
posa piena di sufficienza dei convitati sazi e schifiltosi: τὸν μὲν ἀποπεμ-
ψόμεθα τῶν οἴνων, τὸν δὲ ἐγκρινοῦμεν ὡς ἀνθοσμίαν, περὶ δὲ τοῦ φιλοσοφή-
σομεν. Filone, Contempl. 55 p. VI 60, 13—16 osserva uno spettacolo analogo:
(τράπεζαι) αἱ μὲν ἐκκομίζονται κεναὶ διὰ τὴν τῶν παρόντων ἀπληστίαν ...

---

[76] Cfr. or. XLIII 63 col. 580 C e poem. I 2, 8, 123—126 col. 658.
[77] Per ἀρχέκακος riferito al ventre cfr. poem. I 2, 1, 44 col. 525; II 1, 1, 283 col. 991;
II 2, 1, 216—217 col. 1467. Vedi un'espressione sinonimica in or. IV 123 col. 664 A.
[78] Sull'insaziabilità del ventre cfr. poem. I 2, 10, 593 col. 723; II 1, 1, 66 col. 975; II
2, 3, 277 col. 1500.
[79] La ripresa in participio dell'affermazione paolina avviene anche in or. XXVI 6 col. 1236 A
e XL 39 col. 416 A.

τὰς δὲ λωβήσαντες καὶ σπαράξαντες ἡμιβρώτους ἐῶσιν. L'atteggiamento gregoriano sui vini assaggiati e respinti per assumere il tono d'intenditore e creare un' atmosfera di lusso e di abbondanza richiama quello parallelo filoniano sui cibi che per sazietà e, anche, per boria, vengono assaggiati e poi sdegnati. Anche il particolare sottolineato da Gregorio delle dissertazioni che s'imbandiscono sulle portate è stato colto da Filone, Agric. 36 p. II 102, 10—12.

Cap. XVII, col. 880 B:

Gregorio presenta certi ghiottoni come schiavi γαστρὸς καὶ τῶν ὑπὸ γαστέρα. Quest' espressione, sotto diverse forme, è frequentissima in Filone: per l'uso di ὑπὸ vedi Deus 15 p. II 59, 13—14; Spec. I 192 p. V 46, 19—21[80]. Assai più comune è la costruzione con μετά: Sacrif. 49 p. I 221, 19—20: γαστρὸς καὶ τῶν μετὰ γαστέρα ἡδονῶν; Deter. 157 p. I 293, 24—25; Fug. 35 p. III 117, 23—24; Cher. 93 p. I 193, 1; Spec. II 195 p. V 134, 16; ibid. III 43 p. V 162, 6—7; Virt. 208 p. V 330, 17—18; ibid. 182 p. V 323, 9; Mos. I 160 p. IV 158, 20—159, 1; Poster. 155 p. II 34, 15; framm. p. 108 R. H. In Leg. III 114 p. I 138, 24—25 γαστήρ la seconda volta è sostituito dal pronome: vedi anche ibid. III 139 p. I 143, 19—20 e III 141 p. 144, 6. Più volte in seconda sede invece di γαστήρ usa ὑπογάστριος cfr. Opif. 158 p. I 55, 10—13[81]; Mos. II 23 p. IV 205, 13—16: in entrambi i casi il pensiero combacia perfettamente con quello di Gregorio; vedi inoltre Somn. II 147 p. III 282, 19—20; Spec. II 163 p. V 125, 17. Nelle opere che non ci sono giunte nell'originale greco troviamo: Quaest. Gen. I 12 p. 10 A. e VI 256: *in cibis elaboret et potibus, atque ventris, eorumque quae sunt sub ventre, voluptates operetur*[82]; cfr. ibid. II 59 p. 143 A. e VI 354 (MARCUS p. 146); Quaest. Ex. II 100 p. 532 A. e VII 336 (MARCUS p. 147).

In Gig. 18 p. II 45, 16 Filone contrappone i due membri di questo binomio che in genere considera unitamente: cfr. anche Deter. 113 p. I 284, 1—3; Congr. 80 p. III 88, 4—5[83]. Talora usa solo la seconda metà di questa coppia: vedi Leg. III 157 p. I 147, 11—12; Spec. I 166 p. V 40, 18; Somn. I 122 p. III 231, 7—8. In Agric. 37 p. II 102, 16—17 dichiara che „alla golosità tiene dietro come seguace naturale il piacere sessuale" e subito dopo — 38 p. 102, 22—24 — fornisce la spiegazione logica della disposizione fisiologica del ventre e degli ὑπογάστρια . . . ὄργανα[84].

---

[80] La formula ritorna ancora nell'or. XXVII 3 col. 16 A.

[81] Quest'ultimo comma è riportato dai mss. ma espunto da WENDLAND a cui aderisce COHN.

[82] MARCUS p. 8: "*it labours with regard to food and drink, and produces the various pleasures of the belly and those parts which are below the belly.*"

[83] Nell' epigr. 27,5 col. 97 Gregorio proscrive i cultori del ventre ed in poem. II 2,6,69 col. 1547 osserva che un ventre morigerato è freno alle passioni.

[84] Vedi Clemente, Strom. II 20, 106, 2: γαστρὸς καὶ τῶν ὑπὸ γαστέρα κρατητέον; Basilio, Hom. in illud Attende tibi ipsi 8 MG. XXXI col. 216 C: μὴ σχολάζειν γαστρί, μηδὲ τοῖς ὑπὸ γαστέρα πάθεσιν; cfr. Gregorio Niss., De Beatitud. or. IV MG. XLIV col. 1244 B; De virgin. 4 MG. XLVI col. 344 A.

Per quanto concerne la schiavitù nella quale il piacere riduce, cfr. anche Leg. II 29 p. I 96, 16—18: „Quando nella mollezza e nella raffinatezza dei conviti l'intelligenza si dimentica di se stessa, vinta da tutto ciò che conduce al piacere, noi siamo resi schiavi e mostriamo apertamente la nostra immondezza"[85].

Cap. XVIII, col. 880 BC:

Gregorio, di fronte ai danni arrecati dai vizi della gola e della lussuria, chiede a sè ed ai suoi ascoltatori: τί νοσοῦμεν καὶ αὐτοὶ τὰς ψυχὰς νόσον πολὺ τῆς τῶν σωμάτων χαλεπωτέραν? Sulla figura etimologica applicata all'anima, cfr. Spec. III 11 p. V 153, 5: ἀνίατον νόσον ψυχῆς νοσοῦντας[86].

Sull'affermazione che le malattie dell'anima sono più pericolose di quelle del corpo vedi: Spec. I 239 p. V 58, 15[87]; ibid. III 99 p. V 177, 22—178, 1; Virt. 26 p. V 273, 3—4; ibid. 13 p. 269, 19; Deus 66 p. II 71, 12—13[88].

Per un parallelo tra le malattie del corpo e dell'anima cfr. il framm. di Hypoth. riferito da Eusebio, Praepar. Evang. VIII 11, 11 MG. XXI col. 641 D e GCS Mras p. I 456, 9; framm. p. II 674 M. e p. 77 R.H.; Contempl. 2 p. VI 47, 3; Prob. 12 p. VI 4, 1—5. — Vedi anche ARNIM, Stoic. Vet. Fragm. III p. 120 n. 471.

Sull'aggettivo χαλεπός attribuito alle malattie dell'anima o del corpo cfr. Leg. III 36 p. I 121, 6—7; ibid. III 124 p. I 140, 24—25; Cher. 68 p. I 187, 1—2; ibid. 96 p. I 193, 17; Poster. 47 p. II 10, 25; Decal. 142 p. IV 301, 4; Spec. I 4 p. V 2, 3; ibid. I 24 p. V 6, 9—10; ibid. I 239 p. V 58, 15; ibid. III 99 p. V 177, 22[89].

Filone menziona ancora le malattie dell'anima in Leg. I 45 p. I 72, 11; Cher. 69 p. I 187, 9; Deter. 44 p. I 268, 13—14; ibid. 123 p. I 286, 7—8; Deus 67 p. II 71, 16—17; Plant. 114 p. II 156, 12; Her. 284 p. III 65, 6; Congr. 18 p. III 75, 18; Ios. 10 p. IV 63, 15; ibid. 87 p. IV 79, 18; Spec. II 157 p. V 124, 6; ibid. III 11 p. V 153, 5; Prob. 76 p. VI 22, 8.

Cap. XVIII, col. 880 C:

Gregorio riguardando alla malattia dei lebbrosi ed alla crapula dei ricchi, dice che questa è una malattia spirituale assai più grave di quella fisica, in quanto l'una è involontaria mentre l'altra viene per propria scelta. Identico contrapposto in Filone, Sacrif. 48 p. I 221, 8—10.

---

[85] Luciano(?), Epigr. 64 ed. Iacobitz fa dire ad un cinico μὴ δεῖν δουλεύειν γαστρὶ ... ἀρετήν e Seneca, Epist. 123,3 scrive: *magna pars libertatis est bene moratus venter et contumeliae patiens.*

[86] Cfr. or. XX 5 col. 1072 A: τὴν ... νόσον νοσήσωμεν.

[87] Cfr. Gnomai monost. 75 (Edmonds vol. III B p. 908): βέλτιόν ἐστι σῶμά γ' ἢ ψυχὴν νοσεῖν.

[88] Sulla maggior gravità delle malattie spirituali rispetto a quelle fisiche cfr. anche epist. 34,6 Gallay p. I 45.

[89] Per νόσος χαλεπή cfr. anche Menandro (Kock, Men. 535 vol. III p. 159; Edmonds, Men. 535 vol. III B p. 776) e Teocrito II 95; XXX 1.

Cap. XVIII, col. 880 C:

Gregorio, commosso dallo strazio dei lebbrosi, prorompe in un'imprecazione: che io non abbia di che coprirmi sofficientemente (μὴ σκέπης [μοὶ γένοιτο ἱκανῶς ἔχειν]) se non offrissi loro un vestito ([εἰ μὴ] μεταδοίην ἐσθῆτος). Anche Filone presenta l'alternanza sinonimica ἐσθής—σκέπη: cfr. Spec. I 165 p. V 40, 7—8; Decal. 77 p. IV 286, 12—13. Vedi Deter. 19 p. I 262, 24.

Cap. XVIII, col. 880 C:

Gregorio invita a staccarci dai beni terrestri per seguire sinceramente Cristo καὶ ἀναπτῶμεν ὡς κοῦφοι πρὸς τὸν ἄνω κόσμον. Filone, Somn. I 139 p. III 235, 6 parla di anime ἄνω κούφοις πτεροῖς πρὸς αἰθέρα ἐξαρθεῖσαι[90]; in Spec. I 207 p. V 50, 1—3 insegna che ἡ . . . τοῦ φιλοθέου ψυχὴ πρὸς ἀλήθειαν ἀπὸ γῆς ἄνω πρὸς οὐρανὸν πηδᾷ καὶ πτερωθεῖσα μετεωροπολεῖ; cfr. anche Opif. 70 p. I 23, 15—16; Spec. II 45 p. V 97, 15—16[91].

Filone, Spec. IV 72 p. V 225, 20 osserva che la Sacra Scrittura promette ricompense ,,a coloro che considerano i loro beni non come possessi personali, ma come proprietà comune dei bisognosi". Gregorio cap. XVIII col. 880 D—881 A dichiara che il possesso dei beni viene santificato dalla partecipazione che se ne fa ai bisognosi ed all'inizio del cap. XXIV col. 889 A esorta a ,,non essere cattivi amministratori dei beni ricevuti", tanto più che ,,si posseggono dei beni altrui", ma a darne generosamente ,,a coloro che sono tormentati dall'indigenza". Il passo di Gregorio 880 D—881 A trova un riscontro in Spec. II 107 p. V 111, 24.

Cap. XIX, col. 881 A:

Gregorio, per invitare alla saggezza della vita, domanda ai suoi ascoltatori: οὐ τὰ ἀνθρώπινα λογιούμεθα? e Filone, Spec. II 21 p. V 90, 22 dice che la buona educazione ὑπομιμνήσκει τῆς ἀνθρωπότητος: il significato di entrambi è vicino, anche se Gregorio lo sposta più verso il destino delle cose umane, mentre Filone ha maggiormente l'occhio ai sentimenti ed ai doveri umani.

---

[90] Platone, Fedro p. 249 D (e cfr. p. 246 D) proclama che, quando uno vedendo la bellezza di quaggiù si rammenta della vera bellezza, allora πτερῶται e ἀναπτερούμενός τε καὶ προθυμούμενος cerca di ἀναπτέσθαι . . . βλέπων ἄνω τῶν κάτω δὲ ἀμελῶν. Lo slancio alato dell'uomo verso l'alto è espresso anche nel Teeteto p. 173 E. — P. COURCELLE, Tradition néo-platonicienne et tradition chrétienne des ailes de l'âme, in: Plotino e il Neoplatonismo in Oriente e in Occidente. Atti del Convegno internazionale di Roma, 5—9 ottobre 1970 (Accademia nazionale dei Lincei, Quaderno, n° 198), Roma, 1974, pp. 265—325 studia lo sviluppo dei miti delle ali dell'anima resi immortali da Platone in Phaidr. 246 A—256 E e l'immagine applicata da Filone ai testi biblici che ne erano suscettibili e poi passata nell'ambiente cristiano come risalite dell'anima verso Dio dopo le cadute nel peccato (per Filone cfr. pp. 269—71 e richiami passim, e per Gregorio di Nazianzo pp. 287—88).

[91] Per il volo dell'anima verso Dio cfr. or. II 22 col. 432 B; XXVI 13 col. 1245 A; XXVIII 28 col. 65 B; XXXVII 16 col. 301 B; poem. I 2, 1, 6 col. 522; II 1, 45, 279—280 col. 1373.

Cap. XIX, col. 881 AB:

Gregorio si chiede ancora: οὐκ ἐν τοῖς ἑτέρων κακοῖς τὰ ἡμέτερα εὖ θησόμεθα? e Filone esprime lo stesso concetto in Spec. IV 223 p. V 261, 16—262, 1: τοῖς ἑτέρων πάθεσιν ἄνθρωποι διδάσκονται σωφρονεῖν[92].

Cap. XIX, col. 881 B:

Gregorio proclama l'instabilità delle cose umane: φύσει μὲν γὰρ οὐδὲν τῶν ἀνθρωπίνων βέβαιον, οὐδὲ ὁμαλόν, οὐδὲ αὔταρκες, οὐδὲ ἐπὶ τῶν αὐτῶν ἱστάμενον· ἀλλὰ κύκλος τις τῶν ἡμετέρων περιτρέχει πραγμάτων[93], ἄλλοτε ἄλλας ἐπὶ μιᾶς ἡμέρας πολλάκις, ἔστι δ' ὅτε καὶ ὥρας, φέρων μεταβολάς. Vedi Fil. Spec. I 27 p. V 7, 3—5 (cfr. poem. II 1, 77, 3 col. 1424); framm. p. 6 R. H.; Somn. I 156 p. III 238, 7—10 (e poco prima 153 p. 237, 20—21); Ios. 136 p. IV 89, 11—12; Spec. II 67 p. V 103, 7—8; ibid. I 277 p. V 67, 5; Mos. I 31 p. IV 127, 7—9 (allusione al framm. di Euripide 420 NAUCK[2] riferito testualmente in Somn. I 154 p. III 237, 21—238, 1); Ios. 131 p. IV 88, 13—14; ibid. 134 p. IV 89, 1—3; ibid. 136 p. 89, 11—12; ibid. 141 p. 90, 7; Gig. 28 p. II 47, 15—17 (cfr. or. XVIII 42 coll. 1040 C—1041 A); Spec. II 67 p. V 103, 6—8; Ios. 144 p. IV 91, 11. In Somn. I 153—156 p. III 237, 20—238, 10 esprime lo stesso concetto di Greg., ma siccome sta commentando la scala di Giacobbe, quest' immagine gli è imposta dall'argomento. In tutti questi passi, oltre all'accordo del pensiero, si possono rilevare numerosi e significativi incontri di vocaboli e di espressioni.

Anche il κύκλος di Gregorio[94] ha il suo riscontro nel vortice circolare di Filone Somn. I 153—156: la stessa metafora mira a rendere la medesima concezione della realtà ma attraverso a rappresentazioni diverse. Cfr. anche Quaest. Ex. II 55 p. 509 A. e VII 316 (MARCUS p. 104).

Cap. XIX, col. 881 B:

Per indicare intuitivamente la fragilità della nostra fortuna, Gregorio usa un'iperbole efficace anche se assai vulgata, dicendo che è meglio

---

[92] Gregorio nell'or. XVI 19 col. 961 B raccomanda διὰ τῶν ἀλλοτρίων κακῶν τὰ οἰκεῖα εὖ τίθεσθαι.

[93] Per l'idea di κύκλος in Gregorio cfr. anche or. IV 12 col. 541 C; poem. I 2, 16, 25 col. 780; ibid. 8, 71 col. 654. Tutto questo tema è poi più ampiamente sviluppato nell'or. XVII 4 coll. 969 B—972 A dove ritornano immagini e vocaboli. — Quanto all' ἄλλοτε ἄλλας, che immediatamente segue, ne ha illustrato lo schema stilistico e soprattutto la portata concettuale J. KRAUSE, Ἄλλοτε ἄλλος. Untersuchungen zum Motiv des Schicksalswechsels in der griechischen Dichtung bis Euripides, Diss. München 1975 (Tuduv-Studien, Reihe Kulturwiss., n. 4), München, 1976, pp. 304 più l'indice.

[94] Cfr. Erodoto I 207, 2: μάθε ὡς κύκλος τῶν ἀνθρωπηίων ἐστὶ πρηγμάτων, περιφερόμενος e Aristotele, Fisica IV 14 p. 223 B 24: φασὶ γὰρ κύκλον εἶναι τὰ ἀνθρώπινα πράγματα. Lo Ps.-Aristotele di Problem. XVII 3 p. 916 A 28 dopo aver detto che, come nel movimento del cielo e di ognuno degli astri c'è un κύκλος, così è probabile che anche la nascita e la morte delle cose caduche siano dello stesso genere, conclude osservando: καθάπερ καὶ φασι κύκλον εἶναι τὰ ἀνθρώπινα. Doveva quindi essere un detto proverbiale, quantunque LEUTSCH—SCHNEIDEWIN, Corpus Paroem. Graec. II p. 492 non rechi altra testimonianza che la presente. Lo Ps.-Focilide, Sentent. 27 nota a sua volta: ὁ βίος τροχός· ἄστατος ὄλβος.

prestare fede νυκτὸς ἀπατηλοῖς ὀνείρασιν che non ad essa. Vedi Filone, Ios. 130 p. IV 88, 8—10⁹⁵.

Cap. XIX, col. 881 B e C:

Gregorio per indurre i suoi ascoltatori ad assistere con i loro aiuti i lebbrosi, ricorre anche ad argomenti non molto spiritualmente elevati, ma che hanno il pregio di toccarli nel loro stesso interesse personale. Suggerisce infatti loro che debbono offrire una parte della loro abbondanza: 1⁰) o perchè non abbiano mai da cadere nella disgrazia, poichè Dio spesso concede ai buoni anche i beni (χρηστοῖς) di questo mondo χρηστότητι τὸ συμπαθὲς προκαλούμενον; 2⁰) o perchè possano avere in se stessi una piena sicurezza (παρρησίαν) nei riguardi di Dio, che essi soffrono non per la loro malvagità ma per un particolare piano di Dio; 3⁰) o per poter chiedere ai benestanti, come dovuta, quell'umana assistenza (φιλανθρωπίαν) che essi, quando stavano bene, usarono verso gli altri.

Ora 1⁰) Filone Spec. I 283 p. V 68, 14—16 elenca tra i motivi per i quali si offrono sacrifici a Dio ,,il perdurare dei beni presenti, l'acquisto di quelli futuri, l'allontanamento dei mali presenti od attesi" ed in Leg. I 34 p. I 69, 18—20 dichiara che,, Dio nella sua generosità favorisce i beni a tutti ... stimolandoli (προκαλούμενος) alla brama ed al possesso della virtù." L'uso di προκαλέω in quest'accezione è abbastanza congeniale a Filone: vedi Decal. 162 p. IV 304, 22—23; Spec. II 96 p. V 109, 24; ibid. II 234 p. V 144, 6; ibid. II 71 p. V 104, 8—9.

2⁰) In Her. 19 p. III 5, 18—20 dichiara: ,,Il giusto possiede una tale sicurezza (παρρησία⁹⁶, scil. nei confronti di Dio) che non solo ha il coraggio di parlargli e di gridare, ma addirittura di rivolgergli dei rimproveri."

---

⁹⁵ Gli accenti e le immagini usati in questo passo da Gregorio ritornano, variamente combinati, in parecchi altri luoghi: cfr. or. VII 19 col. 777 CD; XVIII 42 col. 1041 B; XLII 6 col. 465 B; poem. I 2,1,371—373 col. 550; I 2,16,22—24 col. 780; II 1,1,89—95 coll. 976—977; ibid. 88,53—55 col. 1437. — Questo passo dell'or. XIV ha uno sviluppo parallelo nell'epist. 29,1—2 GALLAY I pp. 35—36.

⁹⁶ Gregorio in epist. 42,5 GALLAY I p. 54 scrive: se faremo eleggere Basilio μεγάλην παρρησίαν πρὸς τὸν Θεὸν κτησόμεθα. Il termine παρρησία per ricchezza di sviluppo storico e densità originale di contenuto è uno di quelli più caratteristici di tutta la grecità: per indagini che lo lumeggino adeguatamente cfr. E. PETERSON, Zur Bedeutungsgeschichte von παρρησία, in: Reinhold-Seeberg-Festschrift, I, Leipzig, 1929, pp. 283—297; SCHLIER, s. v., in: KITTEL, Theol. Wört., V, 1954, pp. 869—884; H. JAEGER, Παρρησία et fiducia (Étude spirituelle des mots), in: Studia Patristica, I (T.U., n. 63), Berlin, 1957, pp. 221—239; W. C. VAN UNNIK, Παρρησία in the 'Catechetical Homilies' of Theodore of Mopsuestia, in: Mél. Chr. Mohrmann, Utrecht-Anvers, 1963, pp. 12—22; J. GAMBIER, La liberté chrétienne selon saint Paul, in: Stud. Evang. II (T.U., n. 87), Berlin, 1964, pp. 330—331; G. SCARPAT, 'Parrhesia'. Storia del termine e delle sue traduzioni in latino, Brescia, 1964, pp. 145; L. ENGELS, Fiducia dans la Vulgate. Le problème de traduction παρρησία—fiducia (Graecitas et Latinitas Christianorum Primaeva, Suppl. I), Nijmegen, 1964, pp. 97—141; M. GIGANTE, Philodème: Sur la liberté de parole, in: Actes du VIIIᵉ Congrès de l'Association G. Budé, Paris 5—10 avril 1968, Paris, 1969, pp. 196—217; G. J. M. BARTELINK, Quelques observations sur παρρησία dans la littérature paléo-chrétienne, in: Graecitas et Latinitas Christianorum Primaeva, Supplem. III, Nijmegen, 1970, pp. 5—57; R. G. COQUIN, Le thème de la παρρησία et ses expressions symboliques dans les rites d'initiation

3⁰) In Spec. II 78 p. V 105, 19—106, 2 Filone invita a non esigere interessi per i capitali prestati: ,,A loro volta, quando capiterà l'occasione, ricambieranno ai loro creditori il medesimo beneficio, ricompensando con uguali aiuti coloro che furono i primi a prestare il favore." Poco prima — 71 p. V 104, 8—12 — aveva scritto un altro passo in cui, oltre a puntualizzare con esattezza lo stesso concetto, aveva sintetizzato parecchi spunti toccati da Gregorio in questo capitolo; dice infatti: (l'anno sabatico) ,,stimola (προκαλούμενος) i ricchi alla φιλανθρωπίαν affinchè dando una parte dei proprii beni (χρηστά) ai bisognosi, possano aspettarsi dei beni anche per se stessi, se capitasse loro qualche rovescio[97]; svariati sono infatti i destini umani (τὰ ἀνθρώπινα) e la vita non sta mai ancorata sui medesimi, ma a guisa di un vento instabile[98], muta verso posizioni contarie[99].''

Cap. XX, col. 881 C e D:

Gregorio esorta: Μὴ καυχάσθω, φησίν, ὁ σοφὸς ἐν τῇ σοφίᾳ αὐτοῦ, μηδὲ ὁ πλούσιος ἐν τῷ πλούτῳ αὐτοῦ, μηδὲ ὁ δυνατὸς ἐν τῇ ἰσχύϊ αὐτοῦ[100]· κἂν εἰς τὸ ἄκρον ὦσιν ἐληλακότες, ὁ μὲν σοφίας, ὁ δὲ περιουσίας, ὁ δὲ δυνάμεως. Filone, Spec. IV 74—75 p. V 226, 1—12 scrive: ,,Il ricco non monti la guardia ai suoi tesori dopo aver raccolto in casa una grande quantità di argento e d'oro, ma li metta a disposizione di tutti, per migliorare il duro tenore di vita dei bisognosi con delle cordiali elargizioni (ἱλαραῖς μεταδόσεσι); se uno è diventato famoso, non si levi in superbia vantandosene orgogliosamente, ma onorando l'uguaglianza (ἰσότητα τιμήσας) conceda libertà di parola a coloro che sono oscuri; chi possiede la forza del corpo si faccia sostegno dei più deboli ... e si faccia un motivo di vanto di mettere la propria forza a disposizione di coloro che non possono aiutarsi da sè. Quanti infatti hanno attinto alle fonti della sapienza ... anche senza invito, di propria iniziativa, si accingono a soddisfare l'utilità del prossimo versando il flusso del loro pensiero nelle anime altrui attraverso alle orecchie, affinchè anche gli altri partecipino alla medesima scienza." Gregorio cita Geremia e tale passo pare anche essere lo sfondo della rielaborazione filoniana: però mentre il profeta si riferisce soprattutto alla conoscenza di Dio, Filone e Gregorio lo inseriscono in un contesto che inculca la comprensione e la carità verso il prossimo. Lo sviluppo di Filone è inoltre tutto disseminato di spunti che avranno la loro eco in Gregorio: infatti (1⁰) Filone osserva il ricco nell'atto di ammassare in casa sua cumuli d'oro e d'argento, e Gregorio — cap. XVI col. 877 A — contempla le οἰκίας ... χρυσῷ καὶ ἀργύρῳ καταστρα-

---

à Antioche, in: Proche-Orient Chrétien, XX (1970), pp. 3—19; A. MOMIGLIANO, La libertà di parola nel mondo antico, in: Rivista Storica Italiana, LXXXIII (1971), pp. 499—524.

[97] Vedi or. XVII 10 col. 977 A; poem. I 2, 30, 6 col. 909.

[98] Gregorio ha testè affermato che è meglio fidarsi αὔραις ... οὐχ ἱσταμέναις piuttosto che dell'umana prosperità.

[99] Il concetto che i giusti possano essere afflitti da sventure οὐ διὰ κακίαν ἀλλὰ διά τινα οἰκονομίαν divina, è già di origine stoica, cfr. Plutarco, De Stoicorum repugnantiis 35 p. 1050 E e Crisippo in ARNIM, Stoic. Vet. Fragm. II n. 1176 p. 338.

[100] Vedi Ier. 9, 22 e cfr. anche I Sam. 2, 10.

πτούσας.   2⁰) Filone esorta: μήτ' οὖν ... θησαυροφυλακείτω e Gregorio —
cap. XVIII col. 881 A — riprende la condanna evangelica del θησαυρίζειν
(cfr. Luc. 12, 16—21).   3⁰) Filone raccomanda di dare ἱλαραῖς μεταδόσεσι
e Greg. — cap. XXXVIII col. 908 C — ricorda Rom. 12, 8 dove si ammonisce di porgere al prossimo il nostro aiuto ἐν ἱλαρότητι.   4⁰) Filone subito
dopo consiglia: μεταδιδότω ... τοῖς ἀδόξοις e poco oltre τῆς ἰδίας ἰσχύος
μεταδιδόναι τοῖς ἐξ ἑαυτῶν ἀπειρηκόσιν e Gregorio usa μεταδίδωμι per le
sue esortazioni in favore dei poveri: cfr. cap. XVIII col. 880 C: μεταδοίην
ἐσθῆτος e XXII col. 885 B: μεταδῶμεν τῶν ὄντων τοῖς πένησιν (cfr. però
anche Luc. 3, 11; Ephes. 4, 28).   5⁰) Filone prosegue: μήτ', εἴ τις ἔνδοξος, ὑψηλὸν
αἴρων αὑτὸν αὐχείτω φρυαττόμενος. Quest' intimazione non c'è in Geremia:
è introdotta da Filone e ritorna come una dichiarata inserzione anche in
Gregorio: ἐγὼ δὲ προσθήσω ... μηδὲ ὁ περίβλεπτος ἐν τῇ δόξῃ (καυχάσθω).
6⁰) Lo ὑψηλὸν αἴρων αὑτὸν αὐχείτω di Filone potrebbe quasi sembrare
condensato nel τῶν ὑψαυχενούντων di Gregorio cap. XVIII col. 896 B.
7⁰) Filone esorta: chi è forte ἔρεισμα τῶν ἀσθενεστέρων ἔστω e Gregorio —
cap. XV col. 876 C — presenta Cristo come ὁ ... τὸ ἀσθενὲς ἐνισχύων ed
il diavolo — cap. XXVI col. 892 B — come colui che spinge τοῖς ἀσθενεστέροις τοὺς θρασυτέρους.   8⁰) Filone invita a trasmettere al prossimo la
propria sapienza e Gregorio — cap. XXVII col. 893 B — esorta a praticare
con i derelitti principalmente le opere di misericordia spirituale (οἷς εὐερ-
γετεῖται ψυχή), parlando loro in modo da trarne un abbondante frutto di
dottrina e di pietà e ragionando con loro sulla tolleranza delle sofferenze.
9⁰) Filone vuole che l'aiuto sia ,,anche senza invito, di propria iniziativa"
e Gregorio — cap. XXVII col. 893 B — formula la norma: ,,Innanzi
tutto e sopra tutto dà a chi ti chiede, ed anche prima che ti chieda."

Per quanto concerne l'ultima parte del passo gregoriano, in Filone
abbiamo espressioni che anticipano quelle del Cappadoce con un'esattezza
talora quasi assoluta: cfr. Mos. II 58 p. IV 213, 20: καίτοι γ' οὐκ ἐπ' ἄκρον
ἦλθε σοφίας[101]; Agric. 161 p. II 127, 24: τοὺς γὰρ ἄχρι σοφίας ἄκρας ἐλη-
λακότας; Opif. 8 p. I 2, 16; Somn. II 221 p. III 294, 8; Ios. 268 p. IV 118, 7;
Leg. II 86 p. I 107, 24; Poster. 174 p. II 38, 28; Deus 110 p. II 80, 2; Migr.
175 p. II 302, 23—24; Abr. 58 p. IV 14, 10; Mos. II [III] 151 p. IV 235, 14;
Contempl. 72 p. VI 65, 11; ibid. 90 p. 71, 2; framm. Gen. XIX 14 p. 33 R.H.
e Gen. XXVI 32 p. 43 R.H.

Cap. XX, col. 881 D:

Dopo l'esortazione a non vantarci della sapienza, della ricchezza e
della potenza terrene, Gregorio aggiunge altre doti che non ci debbono
indurre in orgoglio: Μηδὲ ὁ περίβλεπτος ἐν τῇ δόξῃ, μηδὲ ὁ εὐεκτῶν ἐν τῇ
ὑγιείᾳ, μηδὲ ὁ καλὸς ἐν τῇ ὥρᾳ, μηδὲ ὁ νέος ἐν τῇ νεότητι, μηδὲ ἐν ἄλλῳ
μηδενὶ τῶν ἐνταῦθα ἐπαινουμένων ... ὁ ὑπὸ τούτου φυσώμενος· ἀλλ' ἢ ἐν
τούτῳ καυχάσθω ὁ καυχώμενος μόνον, ἐν τῷ συνιεῖν καὶ ἐκζητεῖν τὸ Θεόν ...

---

[101] Cfr. anche or. XLII 6 col. 465 B: εἰς ἄκρον προελθεῖν λαμπρότητος; poem. II 1, 1, 179
col. 983; or. XXXVIII 9 col. 320 C (= XLV 5 col. 629 A).

Τὰ μὲν γάρ ἐστι ῥευστὰ καὶ πρόσκαιρα e continua insistendo sulla fuggevolezza di questi possessi. Anche Filone, Spec. I 311 p. V 75, 2—8 svolge
gli stessi concetti, procedendo con un parallelismo che, se non si estende
alla disposizione delle singole parti, investe però la sostanza del pensiero:
ἔστω δή, φησί, μόνος θεὸς αὔχημά σου καὶ μέγιστον κλέος, καὶ μήτ' ἐπὶ
πλούτῳ μήτε δόξῃ μήτε ἡγεμονίᾳ μήτε σώματος εὐμορφίᾳ μήτε ῥώμῃ μήτε
τοῖς παραπλησίοις, ἐφ' οἷς εἰώθασιν οἱ κενοὶ φρενῶν ἐπαίρεσθαι, σεμνυνθῇς,
λογισάμενος ὅτι πρῶτον μὲν ἀμέτοχα ταῦτ' ἐστὶ τῆς ⟨τοῦ⟩ ἀγαθοῦ φύσεως,
ἔπειτα δ' ὅτι καιρὸν ὀξὺν ἔχει τῆς μεταβολῆς, μαραινόμενα τρόπον τινά, πρὶν
ἀνθῆσαι βεβαίως. L'elaborazione è personale dei due scrittori, in quanto lo
spunto iniziale di Deuter. 10, 21 si limita a dire di essere fieri di Dio. Da
notare, l'esatta corrispondenza nei seguenti binomi, nei quali il primo
membro è di Filone ed il secondo di Gregorio: πλοῦτος — πλοῦτος; δόξα —
δόξα; ἡγεμονία — δύναμις; σώματος εὐμορφία — ὥρα e νεότης; ῥώμη —
ἰσχύς; entrambi chiudono poi il loro elenco con un'indicazione generica
riassuntiva: ,,e tutte le altre cose di questo tipo di cui si suole andare
fieri".

Cap. XX, col. 884 A:

Gregorio esorta ad aiutare i poveri, giacchè ciò è un πρὸς τὸ μέλλον
ἑαυτῷ τι χρηστὸν ἀποτίτεσθαι e Filone, Mos. I 199 p. IV 168, 3 dichiara
che Iddio invitava a sopportare pazientemente le avversità χρηστὰ περὶ
τῶν μελλόντων προσδοκῶντες.

Cap. XX, col. 884 A:

Gregorio dichiara che tutti i beni umani sono fugaci e che ,,come nel
gioco degli scacchi, vengono rimescolati e trasferiti una volta dagli uni ed
un'altra dagli altri (ὥσπερ ἐν παιδιᾷ ψήφων, ἄλλοτε εἰς ἄλλους μεταρριπτού-
μενα καὶ μετατιθέμενα)" e Filone, Mos. I 31 p. IV 127, 6—7 sostiene che ,,non
c'è nulla di più instabile della fortuna, la quale gioca a scacchi, in su ed
in giù, i destini umani (τύχης γὰρ ἀσταθμητότερον οὐδὲν ἄνω καὶ κάτω τὰ
ἀνθρώπεια πεττευούσης)" e in Ios. 136 p. IV 89, 11—12 menziona ,,gli
stravolgimenti delle cose umane e gli spostamenti in su ed in giù come in
una partita a scacchi (καὶ τὰς ἄνω καὶ κάτω πεττείας)"[102].

Cap. XX, col. 884 A:

Gregorio insegna che nel mondo tutto è disposto τῇ πάντα νοῦν ὑπερ-
εχούσῃ Σοφίᾳ[103] e Filone, Spec. I 263 p. V 64, 7 con una struttura stilistica
ed un atteggiamento mentale analogo nomina la πανθ' ὑπερβάλλουσαν
θεοῦ δύναμιν.

---

[102] In poem. II 1, 85, 11—12 col. 1432 afferma: πάντα χρόνος πεσσοῖσιν ὁμοίϊα τῇδε
κυλίνδοι, κάλλος . . . ; cfr. anche or. XXXIV 4 col. 244 C; epist. 204, 6 GALLAY II p. 96.
[103] Con diverso intento ma con formula parzialmente uguale S. Paolo, Phil. 4, 7 dice: ,,La
pace di Dio ἡ ὑπερέχουσα πάντα νοῦν custodirà i vostri cuori."

Cap. XX, col. 884 AB:

Gregorio osserva che noi siamo delusi dai beni visibili μεταβαλλομένοις καὶ μεταβάλλουσι, καὶ ἄνω καὶ κάτω φερομένοις τε καὶ περιτρεπομένοις. L'uso delle radici di μεταβάλλω e περιτρέπω accoppiate per rendere la fuggevolezza del mondo, è ben documentato in Filone: cfr. Opif. 151 p. I 52, 22—23: οὐδὲν τῶν ἐν γενέσει βέβαιον, τροπὰς δὲ καὶ μεταβολὰς ἀναγκαίως τὰ θνητὰ δέχεται[104]; Spec. I 26 p. V 6, 20—21 dove si afferma l'instabilità delle ricchezze terrestri: φέρεται γὰρ πνεύματος τρόπον ἀστάτου τροπὰς καὶ μεταβολὰς παντοίας ἐνδεχόμενα[105]; Mos. II [III] 121 p. IV 228, 14; Congr. 104 p. III 93, 9. Per questo binomio vedi ancora: Opif. 22 p. I 6, 19—20; Her. 247 p. III 56, 9; Mutat. 57 p. III 167, 11—12; ibid. 243 p. III 199, 3; Decal. 104 p. IV 292, 26—27; Spec. II 143 p. V 120, 8—9; ibid. III 178 p. V 200, 5; ibid. IV 144 p. V 241, 18; ibid. IV 235 p. V 264, 6—7; Aet. 59 p. VI 91, 9—10. Sembra però che questa coppia verbale avesse già una lunga tradizione nel linguaggio filosofico, essendo stata usata, talora in combinazione con altri vocaboli, dai seguaci di Talete e di Pitagora, da Eraclito e dagli Stoici[106].

Per l'uso di ἄνω καὶ κάτω riferito alla mutevolezza delle condizioni umane cfr. Ios. 136 p. IV 89, 11—12; Mos. I 31 p. IV 127, 7[107].

Per l'impiego di questa coppia di avverbi insieme a μεταβολή cfr. Aet. 109 p. VI 106, 6—9 e per la presenza di questa locuzione comunque adoperata vedi Ios. 16 p. IV 64, 20—21; Decal. 57 p. IV 281, 18—21 (ter); Flacc. 120 p. VI 142, 7; ibid. 131 p. 144, 9; ibid. 162 p. 149, 29; Legat. 359 p. VI 221, 4—5.

Cap. XX, col. 884 B:

Gregorio illustra il piano provvidenziale per cui dall'instabilità dei beni terrestri siamo spinti a quelli autentici riserbatici da Dio: πρὸς τὸ μέλλον μεθορμησώμεθα. Filone, Congr. 108 p. III 94, 7 parla dell'anima che si libera dalle colpe passate e si trasferisce verso la natura che non erra: πρὸς τὴν ἀπλανῆ φύσιν μεθορμιζομένης.

Cap. XX, col. 884 B:

Gregorio osserva: ἡμᾶς ἡ περὶ τοῦτο (scil. il benessere temporale) ἡδονὴ καὶ ἀπάτη ἔχει δουλώσασα[108]. Anche Filone insiste reiteratamente sulla schiavitù nella quale il piacere riduce l'uomo; vedi: Leg. II 107 p. I 111, 30—

---

[104] Trasportandosi su di un piano ontologico-morale, Filone spiega così l'ineluttabilità della caduta di Adamo: cfr. anche M. HARL, Adam et les deux Arbres du Paradis (Gen. II—III) chez Philon d'Alexandrie, in: Recherches de Science Religieuse, L (1962), p. 356.

[105] Da notare la presenza di φέρομαι, di ἄστατος che in Gregorio compare nella riga seguente, di πνεῦμα che corrisponde ai venti instabili richiamati da Gregorio nel capitolo precedente, col. 881 B.

[106] Cfr. ARNIM, Stoic. Vet. Fragm. II n. 324 p. 116,20—23 e n. 572 p. 178,44.

[107] Vedi al riguardo anche or. XVIII 3 col. 988 C e poem. II 1,77,2 col. 1424.

[108] Cfr. S. Paolo, Tit. 3, 3 che rappresenta certi cristiani prima della conversione come δουλεύοντες . . . ἡδοναῖς ποικίλαις.

112, 1: πάντα ἡδονῆς δοῦλα καὶ ὁ βίος ὁ τῶν φαύλων δεσπόζεται ὑφ᾽ ἡδονῆς[109]; Opif. 165 p. I 58, 4 dove è detto che l'uomo sedotto dall'ἡδονή
divenne ὑπήκοος ἀνθ᾽ ἡγεμόνος καὶ δοῦλος ἀντὶ δεσπότου; Mos. I 299 p. IV
191, 7 (per l'equivalenza di πάθος ad ἡδονή cfr. § 295, p. 190, 12); Opif. 167
p. I 58, 14—15; Virt. 36 p. V 276, 8[110].

Per uno stretto collegamento dei concetti di ἡδονή e di ἀπάτη vedi:
Opif. 165 p. I 57, 12—13 dove è detto che τὰς . . . ἀπάτας αὐτῆς ἡδονή non
le rivolse all'uomo ma alla donna; Leg. III 66 p. I 127, 16; framm. p. II
678 M.; Sacrif. 26 p. I 212, 5—7.

Cap. XX, col. 884 B:

Gregorio proclama che noi siamo stati creati κατ᾽ εἰκόνα Θεοῦ . . . τὴν
ἄνω τε οὖσαν καὶ πρὸς ἑαυτὴν ἕλκουσαν ed alla fine del cap. seg. presenta
il Salvatore come ἀεὶ καὶ πάντας τοὺς ἑαυτοῦ μαθητὰς ἀπὸ γῆς καὶ τῶν περὶ
γῆν εἰς οὐρανοὺς ἕλκων καὶ τὰ οὐράνια.

Questo cammino ascensionale dell'anima, dalla terra al cielo, è anche
uno dei motivi sui quali Filone insiste più volentieri. In Her. 70 p. III
16, 20—21 parla della nostra anima (διανοίας) . . . ὑπὸ τοῦ ὄντως ὄντος
ἡγμένης καὶ ἄνω πρὸς αὐτὸ εἱλκυσμένης[111]. Vedi anche Sacrif. 8 p. I 205,

---

[109] Vedi or. XV 10 col. 929 B dove proclama che i Maccabei non erano ταῖς ἡδοναῖς
δουλεύσαντες.

[110] Verso la fine del secondo sec. d. C. Sesto, Sentent. 574, ritoccando un noto aforisma
evangelico (Matth. 6, 24; Luc. 16, 13), scriveva: οὐκ ἔστιν ἅμα δουλεύειν ἡδονῇ καὶ θεῷ.
La locuzione del resto non era nuova: Senofonte, Memor. I 5, 5 aveva asserito che ταῖς
ἡδοναῖς δουλεύων uno corrompe il corpo e lo spirito (cfr. anche ibid. I 6, 8) e nell'Apol.
16 fa dire a Socrate: chi conoscete meno di me δουλεύοντα ταῖς τοῦ σώματος ἐπιθυμίαις?
Platone, Phaidr. p. 238 E aveva parlato della necessità che vengano ricercate le
soddisfazioni da τῷ δὴ ὑπὸ ἐπιθυμίας ἀρχομένῳ δουλεύοντί τε ἡδονῇ; Isocrate, Ad
Nicocl. 29 p. 20 D aveva espresso l'avviso che fosse la cosa più degna di un re ἂν
μηδεμιᾷ δουλεύῃς τῶν ἡδονῶν; Anassandrida (Stobeo, Anthol. III 6,6 WACHSMUTH—
HENSE vol. III p. 281; MEINEKE 6,23 vol. I p. 148; KOCK, Anass. 60 vol. II p. 161;
EDMONDS, Anass. 60 vol. II p. 78) ammonisce: μηδέποτε δοῦλον ἡδονῆς σαυτὸν ποίει
e Menandro sentenzia: ἅπανθ᾽ ὅσα ζῇ . . . δοῦλα ταῦτ᾽ ἔσθ᾽ ἡδονῆς guadagnandosi il
rimprovero di Plutarco, De audiendis poet. p. 21 C (cfr. KOCK, Men. 611 vol. III
p. 184; EDMONDS, Men. 611 vol. III B p. 804); Polibio XVIII 15, 16 menziona degli
animali ταῖς τοῦ σώματος ἐπιθυμίαις αὐταῖς δουλεύοντα (cfr. anche IV 3, 1), ed Ero-
diano, Ab excessu divi Marci I 17, 9 presenta Commodo come ἐπαλλήλοις καὶ διαφόροις
συνεχόμενος ἡδοναῖς, αἷς . . . καὶ ἄκων ἐδούλευεν.

[111] Nell'or. XVI 15 col. 953 C Gregorio parla della ,,mente che tende all'alto, o almeno è
stata creata per tendere all'alto". L'atteggiamento dell'uomo che guarda al cielo è
stato richiamato più volte da Gregorio, cfr. poem. I 2, 10, 16 col. 682; ibid. 13, 12 col.
755; II 1, 1, 43 col. 973; ibid. 12, 638 col. 1212 ed 804 col. 1225; ibid. 45, 38 col. 1356;
ibid. 78, 13 col. 1426; ibid. 81, 1 col. 1427; II 2, 5, 150 col. 1532. Per l'uso di ἕλκω
detto di Cristo che ci tira verso il cielo cfr. or. V 27 col. 697 BC; XVII 12 col. 980 B;
XL 31 col. 404 A; poem. II 1, 1, 76 col. 975; II 2, 3, 101 col. 1487. Sul cammino del-
l'uomo dalla terra al cielo cfr. poem. I 2, 9, 137 col. 678; ibid. 10, 64 col. 685, 75 col.
686, 139 col. 690 e 903 col. 745; ibid. 34, 221 col. 961; — II 1, 1, 122 col. 979; ibid.
17, 58 col. 1266; ibid. 23, 13—14 col. 1283; ibid. 32, 55 col. 1304; ibid. 34, 173—174
col. 1319; ibid. 45, 10 col. 1354, 34 col. 1356 e 261 col. 1371; ibid. 47, 36 col. 1384;
ibid. 86, 5—7 col. 1433; ibid. 88, 69—75 col. 1438; — II 2, 7, 118 col. 1560.

12—13; Fug. 62 p. III 123, 18—20; Spec. IV 115 p. V 235, 11—14; Deter. 88 p. I 278, 12; Cher. 41 p. I 180, 12—13; Spec. I 207 p. V 50, 1—2; Leg. I 38 p. I 70, 19—20; Plant. 23—24 p. II 138, 13—15 e 20—23 cfr. 21 p. 138, 3; Her. 239 p. III 54, 3—4[112]; Deter. 114 p. I 284, 12.

Cap. XXI, col. 884 C:

Gregorio, alludendo alla provvisorietà della nostra vita terrestre ed alla perennità di quella celeste, si chiede: chi distinguerà παροικίαν καὶ κατοικίαν[113]? Questo contrasto, espresso in questi medesimi termini, è assai caro a Filone. In Gen. 47, 4 i fratelli di Giuseppe dicono al Faraone: παροικεῖν ἐν τῇ γῇ ἥκαμεν ... νῦν οὖν κατοικήσομεν ... ἐν γῇ Γεσέμ: però i due verbi sono usati nel loro senso reale e la contrapposizione non sembra nemmeno percepita. Filone, Agric. 65 p. II 108, 16—19 dopo aver riferito questo passo schematizzandolo all'estremo („παροικεῖν, οὐ κατοικεῖν ἤλθομεν": anche l'antitesi è ormai chiaramente segnata e consapevole), subito continua: τῷ γὰρ ὄντι πᾶσα ψηχὴ σοφοῦ πατρίδα μὲν οὐρανόν, ξένην δὲ γῆν ἔλαχε, καὶ νομίζει τὸν μὲν σοφίας οἶκον ἴδιον, τὸν δὲ σώματος ὀθνεῖον, ᾧ καὶ παρεπιδημεῖν οἴεται. In Confus. 76 p. II 244, 3—4, parlando degli Egiziani, dice: εὑρόντες τὸ πεδίον κατῴκησαν ὡς ἐν πατρίδι, οὐχ ὡς ἐπὶ ξένης παρῴκησαν: anche questa volta l'opposizione tra questi due verbi si trova già in Gen. 26, 2—3 che Filone commenta appena dopo (§ 80): però anche qui nella Bibbia i verbi hanno il loro valore proprio senza implicazioni metafisiche, che vengono invece loro conferite dall'esegeta: vedi infatti § 78 p. 244, 13—14 e 81 p. 244, 25—245, 2. Per una forte sottolineatura di questi concetti espressi con questi verbi cfr. Her. 267 p. III 61, 8—12; Quaest. Gen. III 45 pp. 216—217 A. e VII 42 (MARCUS p. 240); ibid. IV 74 p. 103 A. e VII 109 (MARCUS p. 352); III 10 p. 182 A. e VII 14 (MARCUS p. 192—193); ibid. II framm. 8 LEWY p. 77; Sobr. 68 p. II 228, 19—21. Per altri casi vedi Cher. 120 p. I 198, 20—22; 121 p. 198, 23—25 (cfr. anche p. 199, 1); Sacrif. 44 p. I 220, 3—4; Congr. 23 p. III 76, 23—24[114].

Cap. XXI, col. 884 C:

Nell'ansia di allontanare gli uomini dai godimenti terreni per avviarli ai valori spirituali, Gregorio si chiede: τίς (διαιρήσει) σκότος ἀπὸ τοῦ φωτός? Filone, Spec. I 54 p. V 13, 17—20 condanna coloro che abbandonano il vero Dio σκότος αἱρούμενοι πρὸ αὐγοειδεστάτου φωτός; cfr. anche

---

[112] Filone parla di „anime che, purificate, hanno la forza di salire in alto scambiando il cielo con la terra e l'immortalità con la distruzione". Gregorio in questo stesso passo si chiede chi distinguerà la tenda terrestre dalla città celeste e l'ombra di morte dalla vita eterna.

[113] Queste due radici sono accostate, ma non contrapposte in Hebr. 11, 9.

[114] Per l'uso di questa paronomasia cfr. anche or. VII 4 col. 760 B; VIII 23 col. 816 D; XVIII 3 col. 988 D. I due termini, per quanto correlativi, sono più volte usati anche isolatamente: cfr. or. VI 21 col. 749 A; XXXIII 12 col. 229 AB; XXXIX 11 col. 345 C; XL 31 col. 404 A (cfr. Salmo 86, 7); XLIV 7 col. 616 A; poem. I 2, 2, 149 col. 590.

Somn. II 39 p. III 265, 8; II 106 p. III 275, 29—276, 1; Spec. IV 166 p. V 247, 3—5[115].

[115] La contrapposizione, in senso traslato, tra luce e tenebre, è una di quelle metafore intuitive che la natura stessa sembra proporre. Nell'AT però essa tende ad arrestarsi nelle regioni esteriori della vita, designando più le conseguenze pratiche della moralità che non le sue intime radici che penetrano nella coscienza illuminata; questo aspetto è invece più volte messo in evidenza nel NT. — Oltre all'accezione citata la terminologia luminosa adempie spesso nei due scrittori ad usi assai simili: 1°) Gregorio ritrae, con una frequenza che sembra quasi diventare regola, la divinità con epiteti di luce: segnaliamo tra i casi più interessanti e meno stereotipi: or. II 76 col. 484 AB; VI 12 col. 737 B (Dio è τὸ πρῶτον φῶς: cfr. or. XL 10 col. 372 B e 37 col. 412 C); XXI 2 col. 1084 C e 3 col. 1085 AB (il Battista e Cristo); poem. I 1, 38, 6 col. 522; I 2, 9, 27—29 col. 669; II 1, 38, 5—6 coll. 1325—1326; ibid. 46, 49 col. 1381. Filone, Somn. I 75 p. III 221, 3—6 insegna che πρῶτον μὲν ὁ θεὸς φῶς ἐστι; cfr. anche ibid. I 72 p. 220, 16—17; Praem. 46 p. V 346, 14; Spec. I 42 p. V 11, 4—6; Cher. 96 p. I 193, 23—24; Deus 58 p. II 69, 20—21; Fug. 136 p. III 138, 19—20. — 2°) Gregorio in poem. I 1, 9, 93 col. 464 presenta Cristo come 'datore', in poem. I 1, 32, 7—9 col. 512 come 'creatore', in poem. II 1, 23, 20 col. 1284 come 'fonte della luce'. Filone, Ebr. 44 p. II 178, 25 attribuisce a Dio l'epiteto di φωσφόρος. — 3°) Gregorio in poem. I 1, 4, 26—27 col. 417, polemizzando con Mani, afferma che se c'era la tenebra non c'era Dio. Filone, Virt. 164 p. V 317, 16—17 sostiene che quando Dio risplende nell'anima „si dissipa la tenebra delle passioni e delle malvagità". — 4°) Gregorio in or. VI 12 col. 737 B insegna che le potenze angeliche „sono luce ed irraggiamento della luce perfetta" e Filone, Deus 78 p. II 74, 4 parla delle potenze ingenerate „le quali sono attorno a Dio ed irraggiano una luce splendidissima". — 5°) Gregorio nell'or. XVI 9 col. 945 C proclama che gli eletti „saranno accolti dalla luce ineffabile e dalla visione della Trinità risplendente" e nell'or. XI 6 col. 840 B scrive che „noi saremo avvolti dallo splendore della luce della Trinità". Filone, Confus. 61 p. II 241, 12 afferma che Dio fece crescere le virtù celesti „dall'incorporea luce che emana da lui stesso" ed in Her. 264 p. III 60, 15—16 afferma che „quando la luce divina brilla penetra nell'umanità". — 6°) Gregorio nell'or. II 7 col. 416 A a sintesi del suo sogno di vita perfetta dice che vuole fare di sè „uno che aggiunge luce a luce" ed in poem. II 2, 4, 79 col. 1511 esprime come suo programma quello di progredire sempre verso la luce, giacchè come luce egli concepisce la vita dello spirito (cfr. poem. II 1, 1, 552—555 col. 1011) e crede che il bene fondamentale della vita sia il Θεοῦ φάος (cfr. poem. I 2, 14, 95 col. 763). Anche Filone presenta la luce divina come meta dell'umana perfettibilità: in Opif. 71 p. I 24, 6—7 pensa che l'uomo, penetrato da un amore più alto, venga come portato alla presenza del gran re ed allora „nella sua brama di vedere, i raggi assolutamente puri di una luce concentrata si riverseranno in lui a guisa di un torrente, fino al punto di causare le vertigini, con i loro barbagli, agli occhi dell'anima". — 7°) Gregorio in or. VIII 23 col. 816 C presenta la beatitudine del paradiso come dominata dal fulgore divino (προσαστραπτούσης ταῖς ἡμετέραις ψυχαῖς ὅλῳ τῷ φωτὶ τῆς θεότητος) ed in poem. I 2, 10, 82 col. 686 dichiara che l'anima giunta alla vista di Dio sarà φωτὸς κορεσθεῖσα. Filone, Somn. II 74 p. III 271, 3 osserva l'anima θείῳ φωτὶ χαίρουσαν. — 8°) Gregorio definisce la colpa (poem. I 2, 9, 25 col. 669) come ἡμετέρη νύξ ed in or. XVIII 28 col. 1017 D menziona τὸ σκότος τῆς ἁμαρτίας; cfr. anche or. VI 13 col. 737 D; IX 3 col. 824 A; poem. II 1, 54, 3 col. 1398. Filone, Somn. II 140 p. III 281, 12—13 asserisce: βαθὺ μὲν σκότος κακοῖς, τηλαυγὲς δὲ φῶς ἀγαθοῖς; cfr. anche Spec. I 288 p. V 69, 15—16. — 9°) Per l'espressione τέλειον φῶς cfr. Gregorio, or. VI 12 col. 737 B e Filone, Leg. I 18 p. I 65, 14. — Per studi che affrontino questo tema in più ampi orizzonti cfr. A. M. GIERLICH, Der Lichtgedanke in den Psalmen. Eine terminologisch-exegetische Studie (Freiburger Theol. Stud., n. 56), Freiburg i. Br., 1940, pp. 206; R. BULTMANN, Zur Geschichte der Lichtsymbolik im Altertum, in: Philologus, XCVII (1948), pp. 1—36 poi riportato in: Exegetica, Tübingen, 1967, pp. 323—355 e nella stessa opera, Torino, 1971,

Cap. XXI, col. 884 C:

Gregorio si domanda: τίς τῷ ῥέοντι πλούτῳ τὸν μὴ λυόμενον (ὠνήσεται)? ed al cap. XXXIV col. 904 B esorterà: μήτε πλούτῳ ῥέοντι προστιθώμεθα καρδίᾳ. Sulla fuggevolezza delle cose, in quest'orazione, cfr. cap. XIX col. 881 B; XX col. 884 A (i nostri beni sono ῥευστά); XXX col. 897 B (la ὕλη porta in se stessa τὸ ἄτακτον, ὥσπερ ἐν ῥεύματι). Anche Filone indugia su questa rappresentazione delle cose della terra: cfr. Spec. I 27 p. V 7, 3—5 dove trasferisce sul piano sociologico della ricchezza la nota reminiscenza eraclitea che stabiliva il fluire delle cose sul piano ontologico. In Mutat. 214 p. III 193, 15 esprime la sua ammirazione per chi sa πλούτῳ πολλῷ ῥέοντι ἀντισχεῖν[116]; cfr. anche Ios. 131 p. IV 88, 13—14; Congr. 159 p. III 105, 16.

Cap. XXI, col. 884 C:

Gregorio proclama beato chi διαιρῶν τῇ τομῇ τοῦ Λόγου τῇ διαιρούσῃ τὸ κρεῖττον ἀπὸ τοῦ χείρονος[117] innalza il suo cuore verso l'alto. Sullo sfondo della mente dello scrittore ci fu certo Hebr. 4, 12 dov'è detto che ὁ λόγος τοῦ Θεοῦ è τομώτερος ὑπὲρ πᾶσαν μάχαιραν δίστομον, però va

---

pp. 69—107; S. AALEN, Die Begriffe 'Licht' und 'Finsternis' im Alten Testament, im Spätjudentum und im Rabbinismus (Skrift. Norske Vidensk.-Akad. i Oslo II. Hist.-Filos. Klasse 1951, No. 1), Oslo, 1951, pp. 351; A. WLOSOK, Laktanz und die philosophische Gnosis (Abhandl. der Heidelberger Akad. der Wiss., Philos.-hist. Klasse, Jahrgang 1960, 2. Abhandl.), Heidelberg, 1960, pp. 50—114: Philo von Alexandrien; L. R. STACHOWIAK, Die Antithese Licht—Finsternis — ein Thema der paulinischen Paränese, in: Theologische Quartalschrift, CXLIII (1963), pp. 385—421; F. N. KLEIN, Die Lichtterminologie bei Philon von Alexandrien und in den hermetischen Schriften. Untersuchungen zur Struktur der religiösen Sprache der hellenistischen Mystik, Leyde, 1962, pp. X-232; M. MARTÍ-NEZ, Teología de la luz en Orígenes, in: Misc. Comillas, XXXVIII (1962), pp. 5—120; A. F. LOSEV, Évolution de la notion de nuit dans le mythe et la philosophie grecque, in: Meander, XXIV (1969), pp. 103—115 (in polacco: concerne soprattutto i discepoli di Plotino); J. CHMIEL, Lumière et charité d'après la Première Épître de saint Jean, Préface du P. D. MOLLAT (Studia Ecclesiastica, n. 10; Biblica, n. 2; Dissertationes, n. 9), Rome, 1971, pp. XLVIII-267; S. AGRELO, Algunos precedentes culturales de la simbología cristiana de la luz, in: Antonianum, XLVII (1972), pp. 96—121; H. CONZELMANN, s. v. φῶς, in: Theologisches Wörterbuch zum Neuen Testament, IX, 1973, pp. 302—349 (per Filone pp. 322—324); M. MARTÍNEZ PASTOR, La simbolología y su desarrollo en el campo semántico de 'lux' en Orígenes-Rufino, in: Emerita, XLI (1973), pp. 183—208; D. BREMER, Licht als universales Darstellungsmedium. Materialien und Bibliographie, in: Archiv für Begriffsgeschichte, XVIII (1974), pp. 185—206; M. G. CIANI, ΦΑΟΣ e termini affini nella poesia greca. Introduzione a una fenomenologia della luce (Università di Padova: Pubblicazioni della Facoltà di Lettere e Filosofia, n. 51), Firenze, 1974, pp. 190; S. AGRELO, El tema bíblico de la luz, in: Antonianum, L (1975), pp. 353—417; D. BREMER, Licht und Dunkel in der frühgriechischen Dichtung. Interpretationen zur Vorgeschichte der Lichtmetaphysik (Archiv für Begriffsgeschichte, Suppl. 1), Bonn, 1976, pp. X-446; J. J. ENZ, Origin of the Dualism Expressed by 'Sons of Light' and 'Sons of Darkness', in: Biblical Research, XXI (1976), pp. 15—18.

[116] Per il πλοῦτος ῥέων cfr. anche l'or. XXXIII 7 col. 224 B e poem. I 2, 10, 443 col. 712. Vedi inoltre or. I 4 col. 397 B.

[117] Per riprese di questa formula cfr. or. XXXVII 4 col. 288 A; XXXIX 15 col. 352 D; poem. I 2, 25, 10 col. 814.

anche tenuto presente Filone, Her. 130 p. III 30, 20—21 dove dice che Dio divide la natura dei corpi e delle cose τῷ τομεῖ τῶν συμπάντων ἑαυτοῦ λόγῳ, ὃς εἰς τὴν ὀξυτάτην ἀκονηθεὶς ἀκμὴν διαιρῶν οὐδέποτε λήγει. Infatti Filone e Gregorio a differenza di Hebr. si riferiscono alle cose del mondo ed usano quel διαιρέω che manca nella lettera. Vedi anche Spec. I 209 p. V 50, 14—15.

Cap. XXI, col. 885 A:

Gregorio invita a non attaccarsi troppo ai beni corruttibili e a non πᾶσαν τὴν ἐντεῦθεν εὐδαιμονίαν ὑπολαμβάνειν. Analogamente Filone, Spec. I 25 p. V 6, 17—18 deplora che la maggioranza vada dietro all'oro ed all'argento τὰ τοῦ . . . πλούτου μόνα ἢ μάλιστα εὐδαιμονίας αἴτια νομίζοντες.

Cap. XXII, col. 885 BC:

Gregorio esorta alla generosità verso i poveri con questa icastica immagine: ἀπόθου μακρὰν ἀπὸ τῆς κάτω νεμομένης φλογός. Filone, Fug. 158 p. III 144, 8—9 parla di τῆς φλογός . . . καταδραμούσης καὶ ὅλην ψυχὴν ἐπινεμηθείσης e in Decal. 173 p. IV 306, 20—21 paragona l'ἐπιθυμία ad una fiamma che tutto consuma e distrugge.

Cap. XXII, col. 885 C:

Con un fervido empito oratorio Gregorio invita a soccorrere i poveri come unico modo per dare a quel Dio da cui abbiamo tutto ricevuto: δὸς ὀλίγον, παρ' οὗ τὸ πλεῖον ἔχεις· δὸς καὶ τὸ πᾶν, τῷ τὰ πάντα χαρισαμένῳ. Οὐδέποτε νικήσεις μεγαλοδωρεὰν Θεοῦ, κἂν πάντα προῇ τὰ ὄντα, κἂν τοῖς οὖσι σεαυτὸν προσθῇς. Καὶ τοῦτο γάρ ἐστι λαβεῖν, τὸ τῷ Θεῷ δοθῆναι . . . καὶ οὐδὲν δώσεις ἴδιον, ὅτι τὰ πάντα παρὰ Θεοῦ. E poche righe dopo (col. 888 A) continua: (non è possibile) οἷς δίδομεν νικῆσαι Θεόν. Οὐ γὰρ ἔξω τι τῶν αὐτοῦ δίδομεν, οὐδὲ ὑπὲρ τὴν ἐκείνου φιλοτιμίαν. Anche questa è una delle concezioni che Filone ha più profondamente e costantemente sentite[118]. Gregorio celebra la μεγαλοδωρεὰν Θεοῦ e Filone, Congr. 171 p. III 108, 3—4 usa questa medesima qualificazione come culmine di una *climax* appassionatamente ascendente: Dio gli appare infatti come ἀγαθός . . . καὶ ἀγαθῶν αἴτιος, εὐεργέτης, σωτήρ, τροφεύς, πλουτοφόρος, μεγαλόδωρος[119]. Talora parrebbe quasi richiamare questo vocabolo composto mediante una *iunctura* che dica ancora di più: infatti in Spec. I 298 p. V 72, 1 mette in evidenza τοῦ φιλοδώρου θεοῦ μεγάλην ἐπικουρίαν e in Cher. 29 p. I 177, 13

---

[118] Il motivo d'altronde era già stato saldamente messo in chiaro dalla speculazione filosofica classica che aveva volentieri considerato il mondo e tutto quanto esso reca di buono, di utile e di bello come un dono della magnificenza divina. Lo Ps.-Aristotele di De mundo 6 p. 397 B 13—14 scrive infatti: „È una convinzione antica e tradizionale presso tutti gli uomini che tutte le cose ci sono giunte da Dio e per mezzo di Dio."

[119] In or. VII 24 col. 785 B Gregorio scrive: μεγάλη θεοῦ τοῦ μεγαλοδώρου φιλανθρωπία· ὃς μικρὰ αἰτῶν, μεγάλα χαρίζεται. Su Dio μεγαλόδωρος cfr. or. XIII 2 col. 853 C; XL 27 col. 397 C. Sulla liberalità con cui Dio ricompensa ciò che diamo a lui cfr. anche or. XVII 10 col. 977 B.

fa menzione τοῦ μεγάλου καὶ φιλοδώρου θεοῦ[120]. Φιλόδωρος diventa per Filone uno degli attributi più essenziali ed evidenti di Dio; lo designa infatti così in Fug. 62 p. III 123, 19; ibid. 66 p. 124, 12—13; Mutat. 46 p. III 165, 3; Leg. I 34 p. I 69, 18; ibid. III 40 p. 121, 24; ibid. III 166 p. 149, 17; Cher. 20 p. I 174, 23; Deter. 138 p. I 289, 19; Poster. 26 p. II 7, 3; Agric. 173 p. II 130, 12; Plant. 37 p. II 141, 6; ibid. 88 p. 150, 25; ibid. 91 p. 151, 11; Ebr. 82 p. II 185, 9; Confus. 182 p. II 264, 12; Migr. 30 p. II 274, 22; Her. 31 p. III 8, 19; Abr. 254 p. IV 56, 3; Spec. I 221 p. V 54, 5; Praem. 126 p. V 365, 14.

Per Gregorio Dio è ὁ πάντα χαρισάμενος (cfr. anche cap. XXV col. 889 C: τὰς πρώτας τοῦ ζῆν ἀφορμὰς ἀφθόνους ἅπασιν ἐχαρίσατο e ibid. col. 892 A). Filone in Agric. 53 p. II 106, 11—12 presenta Dio come colui che ha voluto πλήρη καὶ τέλεια τἀγαθὰ τοῖς οὖσιν ἅπασιν ... χαρίζεσθαι[121]; in Leg. I 34 p. I 69, 18—19 proclama: φιλόδωρος ὢν ὁ θεὸς χαρίζεται τὰ ἀγαθὰ πᾶσι ed in Plant. 88—89 p. II 150, 25—151, 3 leva un inno alla sua inesausta liberalità. Sul concetto che Dio χαρίζεται (cfr. Leg. III 196 p. I 156, 30) e che tutto è χάρις di Dio, Filone ha usato alcune formule mirabili per limpidezza, vigore, nettezza: cfr. Leg. III 78 p. I 129, 27 e poco oltre p. 130, 4—5; Deus 107 p. II 79, 11—12 (cfr. ibid. 5 p. II 57, 14—15); Mutat. 58 p. III 167, 17—18; ibid. 155 p. 183, 7; Spec. I 285 p. V 69, 3—4; ibid. II 53 p. V 99, 21; ibid. II 180 p. 130, 20; ibid. II 204 p. 137, 12; Confus. 127 p. II 253, 14—15; ibid. 181 p. 264, 6—7; ibid. 182 p. 264, 15; Cher. 123 p. I 199, 15; Opif. 23 p. I 7, 3—5; ibid. 168 p. 59, 6; Plant. 89 p. II 150, 27—151, 3 e 91—93 specie p. 151, 11 e 21; framm. p. 11 R.H. e pp. 80 e 84 ibid.

Gregorio ribadisce che tutto è possesso di Dio: ὁ πάντα χαρισάμενος; τὰ πάντα παρὰ Θεοῦ; οὐ γὰρ ἔξω τι τῶν αὐτοῦ δίδομεν. Filone insiste sulla stessa concezione: cfr. Spec. I 271 p. V 65, 21; ibid. II 180 p. V 130, 17—18; Leg. III 78 p. I 130, 1; Mos. I 157 p. IV 157, 23; Quaest. Gen. III 10 p. 182 A. e VII 14 (MARCUS p. 192).

Gregorio, in conseguenza di quest'impostazione, afferma: οὐδὲν δώσεις ἴδιον, ὅτι τὰ πάντα παρὰ Θεοῦ. In perfetto accordo è Filone: cfr. Her. 103 p. III 24, 3—5: ἴδιον ... οὐδὲν ἔχεις ἀγαθόν, ἀλλ' ὅ τι ἂν νομίσῃς ἔχειν, ἕτερος παρέσχηκεν. ἐξ οὗ συνάγεται ὅτι θεοῦ τοῦ διδόντος κτήματα πάντα; Spec. II 180 p. V 130, 17—18 dove scrive che, per quanto offriamo a Dio le decime sui prodotti della terra, non gli diamo nulla del nostro: διδόντας μὲν οὐδέν, αὐτοῦ γὰρ τὰ πάντα καὶ κτήματα καὶ δωρεαί. Vedi anche Deus 5 p. II 57, 14—15.

Gregorio proclama: „Non vincerai mai la magnanimità di Dio, anche se ti privassi di tutti i tuoi beni, anche se ai tuoi beni aggiungessi te stesso. Καὶ τοῦτο γάρ ἐστι λαβεῖν, τὸ τῷ Θεῷ δοθῆναι; per quanto tu porti a lui,

---

[120] In or. XVIII 12 col. 1000 A Greg. ricorda τοῦ Θεοῦ τὸ φιλόδωρον.
[121] Sul concetto che tutti i beni che abbiamo sono un dono di Dio cfr. inoltre or. II 95 col. 497 B; VII 1 col. 756 B; XVI 18 col. 957 CD; XIX 8 col. 1052 C; XL 25 col. 393 C; poem. I 2, 28, 84 col. 863. Sull' universale padronanza di Dio cfr. or. XXXIX 13 col. 348 D e poem. II 2, 3, 255 col. 1498.

te ne rimarrà sempre la parte maggiore." Filone, Spec. I 144 p. V 35, 8 dichiara che gli Israeliti pagano volentieri i contributi per i sacerdoti, λαμβάνειν ἀλλ᾽ οὐ διδόναι νομίζοντες e in Mutat. 25 p. III 161, 14—16 a proposito di Mosè esclama: ὢ παγκάλης ... ἀντιδόσεως ἀξιωθείς, θείας προνοίας ἀντιδοῦναι ἑαυτόν[122]. Vedi anche Leg. III 10 p. I 115, 14.

Cap. XXII, col. 885 C—888 A:

Per dimostrare che è impossibile vincere la magnanimità di Dio, Gregorio ricorre ad una originale analogia: οὐδὲ ὑπὲρ τὴν κεφαλὴν γενέσθαι σώματος μέγεθος ὑπερκειμένην ἀεὶ τοῦ σώματος. La medesima contrapposizione tra κεφαλή e σῶμα ricorre in Praem. 114 p. V 362, 13: Filone dice che quell'ἔθνος che si comporterà onestamente ἐπιβήσεται πᾶσιν ἔθνεσιν ὥσπερ κεφαλὴ σώματι. Cfr. anche ibid. 125 p. V 365, 10—11.

Cap. XXIII, col. 888 A:

Per mettere in luce la generosità divina, Gregorio esorta: γνῶθι πόθεν σοι τὸ εἶναι, τὸ ἀναπνεῖν[123], τὸ φρονεῖν[124] e Filone, Congr. 96—97 p. III 91, 13—14 e 20 afferma: ἡ γὰρ ζωὴ καὶ διαμονὴ καὶ αὔξησις καὶ ὑγίεια αὐτῷ (scil. τῷ σώματι) θεία γίνεται χάριτι e soggiunge che non dobbiamo lodare Dio solo per questo, ma καὶ ἐπὶ τῷ νῷ.

Cap. XXIII, col. 888 A:

Gregorio asserisce: τὸ μέγιστον, τὸ γινώσκειν Θεόν. Vedi Filone, Cher. 48 p. I 181, 22—24: τῶν ὄντων κτημάτων τὸ καλλιστεῦον, ἡ περὶ τοῦ αἰτίου (della causa, cioè di Dio) ... ἐπιστήμη; Decal. 81 p. IV 287, 11—12: τὸ ἄριστον ... τέλος, ἐπιστήμην τοῦ ὄντως ὄντος (cfr. Gregorio τῆς ὄντως Σοφίας: cap. XXXII col. 901 A); Spec. I 345 p. V 84, 4—5; Deter. 86 p. I 277, 28—278, 1; Legat. 4 p. VI 156, 5[125].

---

[122] Greg. riprende alquanto più analiticamente questo concetto in or. XL 40 col. 417 A: ὅλους διδόντες ἡμᾶς αὐτούς, ὅλους ἀντιλαμβάνωμεν· ἐπειδὴ τοῦτό ἐστι λαβεῖν καθαρῶς, τὸ τῷ Θεῷ δοθῆναι ed in poem. I 2, 10, 177—178 col. 693 lo parafrasa specificandolo: δεῦρό μοι σαυτὸν δίδου, / δός, καὶ Θεῷ δώσωμεν, ὃν λήψῃ δοθείς.

[123] Lo spunto deriva probabilmente da Act. 17, 25 dove S. Paolo dice di Dio: αὐτὸς διδοὺς πᾶσι ζωὴν καὶ πνοήν.

[124] Sull' importanza di conoscere la nostra origine cfr. or. XVIII 8 col. 993 C; poem. I 2, 31, 7. col. 911.

[125] Sulla grandezza della conoscenza di Dio cfr. or. XVII 9 col. 976 C; XIX 8 col. 1052 CD; XXIII 11 col. 64 B; XXXII 23 col. 201 A; XXXVIII 11 col. 324 A; poem. I 1,30,10—11 col. 509; I 2,10,931 col. 747. — Sul problema della conoscenza di Dio cfr. A. WAIBEL, Die natürliche Gotteserkenntnis in der apologetischen Litteratur des zweiten Jahrhunderts, Kempten–München, 1916, pp. 140; E. PRUCKER, Γνῶσις Θεοῦ. Untersuchungen zur Bedeutung eines religiösen Begriffs beim Apostel Paulus und bei seiner Umwelt (Cassiciacum, n. 4), Würzburg, 1937, pp. 141 (nelle pp. 48—55 studia la γνῶσις θεοῦ nel giudaismo ed in Filone); U. WILCKENS, Weisheit und Torheit. Eine exegetisch-religionsgeschichtliche Untersuchung zu I Kor. 1 und 2 (Beiträge zur historischen Theologie, n. 26), Tübingen, 1959 (su Filone cfr. le pp. 139—159); F. GABORIAU, Le thème biblique de la connaissance. Étude d'une racine, Paris, 1969, pp. 94; W. VANDERMARCK, Natural

Cap. XXIII, col. 888 A:

Gregorio insegna che l'uomo possiede l'ἀγγέλων ἰσοτιμίαν[126] e Filone, Sacrif. 5 p. I 204, 6 proclama che Abramo era ἴσος ἀγγέλοις γεγονώς[127].

Cap. XXIII, col. 888 AB:

Gregorio, pensando ai benefici naturali e soprannaturali concessi da Dio agli uomini, chiede ai suoi ascoltatori: ,,Donde ti derivano tutti questi beni e chi te li ha forniti?'' Poi il suo sguardo si allarga al mondo e contempla il cielo (κάλλος οὐρανοῦ), il sole (ἡλίου δρόμον), la luna (σελήνης κύκλον), le stelle nella loro perfetta armonia (ἀστέρων πλῆθος, καὶ τὴν ἐν τούτοις πᾶσιν, ὥσπερ ἐν λύρᾳ, εὐαρμοστίαν καὶ τάξιν ὡσαύτως ἔχουσαν); osserva l'alternanza delle stagioni (ὡρῶν ἀλλαγάς, μεταβολὰς καιρῶν), degli anni (ἐνιαυτῶν περιόδους), dei giorni e delle notti (ἡμέρας καὶ νυκτὸς ἰσομοιρίαν); considera i prodotti della terra (γῆς ἐκφύσεις), la distesa dell'aria (ἀέρος χύσιν), l'ampiezza del mare (πλάτη θαλάττης λελυμένης καὶ ἰσταμένης), la profondità dei fiumi (βάθη ποταμῶν), i soffi dei venti (ἀνέμων ῥεύματα): e tutto vede come opera di Dio.

Si tratta di un tema caro allo stoicismo[128] e caro a Filone che lo trovò consono alla mentalità biblica. In Deus 107 p. II 79, 10—12 afferma che il saggio scopre χάριν ὄντα θεοῦ τὰ πάντα, γῆν, ὕδωρ, ἀέρα, πῦρ, ἥλιον, ἀστέρας, οὐρανόν, ζῷα καὶ φυτὰ σύμπαντα ed in Agric. 51 p. II 105, 22—25 dichiara che γῆν καὶ ὕδωρ καὶ ἀέρα καὶ πῦρ καὶ ὅσα ἐν τούτοις φυτά τε αὖ καὶ ζῷα ... ἔτι δὲ οὐρανοῦ φύσιν καὶ ἡλίου καὶ σελήνης περιόδους καὶ τῶν ἄλλων ἀστέρων τροπάς τε αὖ καὶ χορείας ἐναρμονίους ὁ ποιμὴν καὶ βασιλεὺς θεὸς ἄγει.

Gregorio domanda: τίς ἔδωκέ σοι κάλλος οὐρανοῦ βλέπειν e continua sottintendendo il medesimo interrogativo ad ognuno dei grandi spettacoli cosmici che costituiscono i momenti della sua meditazione. Un identico atteggiamento adotta Filone, Prov. II 40 p. 75 A. e VIII 66 quando dice che non dobbiamo guardare alle quisquilie della terra, ma *caeli naturam contemplari, solis circuitus, lunae formas in crescendo, maris extensiones, elationes fluminum, aeris mutationes, annuas tempestatum vicissitudines, generationes animalium, plantarum proprietates, fructuum proventum aliaque quam plurima, quorum unum quodque divina factum arte mire pulcherrimum*

Knowledge of God in Romans. Patristic and Medieval Interpretation, in: Theological Studies, XXXIV (1973), pp. 36—52.

[126] In Ps. 8, 6 si dice che l'uomo è appena inferiore agli angeli; in Luc. 20, 36 si dichiara che nel regno dei cieli tutti sono ἰσάγγελοι (cfr. Matth. 22, 30 e Marc. 12, 25); S. Paolo poi in I Cor. 6, 3 esalta il cristiano addirittura al disopra degli angeli. L'espressione gregoriana non si trova però nè nell'A. nè nel N. Testamento.

[127] L'accostamento dell'uomo e dell'angelo è abbastanza frequente in Gregorio che in varie circostanze tende ad equipararli in valore: cfr. or. XXXVIII 11 col. 324 A (XLV 7 col. 632 A); XL 26 col. 396 B; XLIII 62 col. 576 C; poem. I 2,3,6 col. 633; ibid. 7,3—4 col. 648; ibid. 10, 625 col. 725 e 892 col. 744; II 1,38,25—26 col. 1327; ibid. 45, 21 col. 1355.

[128] Cfr. ARNIM, Stoic. Vet. Fragm. I n. 528 p. 119,22—26 e 30—31.

est. Vedi anche Spec. II 45 p. V 97, 12—14; Mos. I 212 p. IV 171, 6—16. Quanto all'alzare gli occhi verso il cielo cfr. Plant. 20 p. II 138, 1—2.

La locuzione κάλλος οὐρανοῦ — presente in Eccli 43, 9 — è anche documentata in Filone, Abr. 159 p. IV 36, 21—22[129].

Gregorio nomina l'ἡλίου δρόμον e l'ἡλίου δρόμον richiama anche Filone, Aet. 88 p. VI 100, 8; cfr. però Esdr. I 4, 34: ταχὺς τῷ δρόμῳ ὁ ἥλιος.

Gregorio ricorda il σελήνης κύκλον che, per quanto si possa interpretare nel senso di 'disco, sfera', è più plausibile intendere come 'orbita', data la vicinanza di δρόμον per il sole e l'accenno alla τάξις che governa tutti gli astri. Per questa medesima accezione di κύκλος della luna cfr. Spec. II 142 p. V 119, 19; invece in Somn. I 134 p. III 234, 5—6 usa il vocabolo in riferimento alla forma. Per l'espressione comunque[130] vedi anche Mos. II [III] 224 p. IV 252, 12; Spec. I 177 p. V 43, 13; ibid. II 57 p. V 101, 3[131].

Per l'ἀστέρων πλῆθος[132] di Gregorio si può ricordare Congr. 133 p. III 99, 14: ἀστέρων πλῆθος; Opif. 56 p. I 18, 22: τῷ πλήθει τῶν ἄλλων ἀστέρων ed un passo filoniano indebitamente trasferito in Spec. I 300 p. V 72, 20. Cfr. Her. 86 p. III 20, 18[133].

Gregorio richiama quindi all'armonia che connette i singoli astri nelle loro vicendevoli relazioni: τὴν ἐν τούτοις πᾶσιν, ὥσπερ ἐν λύρᾳ, εὐαρμοστίαν καὶ τάξιν ὡσαύτως ἔχουσαν. Filone, Opif. 126 p. I 43, 9—10 scrive: λύρα μὲν γὰρ ἡ ἑπτάχορδος ἀναλογοῦσα τῇ τῶν πλανήτων χορείᾳ τὰς ἐλλογίμους ἁρμονίας ἀποτελεῖ. Vedi inoltre Confus. 56 p. II 240, 14; Opif. 70 p. I 23, 16—18; Somn. I 37 p. III 212, 22; framm. Gen. VIII, 6 pp. 22—23 R. H. — Quanto al binomio εὐαρμοστίαν καὶ τάξιν rammenta Opif. 22 p. I 6, 20—7, 1 dove è detto che Dio creatore introdusse nel disordine della materia originaria la τάξιν e τὸ εὐάρμοστον[134].

Gregorio osserva le ὡρῶν ἀλλαγάς, μεταβολὰς καιρῶν e Filone, Poster. 113 p. II 25, 2 parla di καιρῶν . . . μεταβολαῖς ed in Congr. 133 p. III 99, 13 e Abr. 69 p. IV 17, 6 menziona le ὡρῶν μεταβολαί[135].

---

[129] Per altri impieghi e variazioni di questa formula vedi or. IV 96 col. 629 C; XII 4 col. 848 B; XL 41 col. 417 B. Per la bellezza del cielo considerata nei suoi riflessi religiosi cfr. anche poem. I 1,9,14—15 coll. 457—458.

[130] Ricorda Euripide, Iphig. Aul. 717; Ion. 1115: κύκλος πανσέληνος; Erodoto VI 106: κύκλος (scil. τῆς σελήνης).

[131] Vedi anche or. XLIV 10 col. 617 C: σελήνης κύκλος.

[132] Cfr. Ps. 146, 4: πλήθη ἄστρων.

[133] Per la locuzione cfr. or. VI 15 col. 741 A. Per l'elevazione dagli astri a Dio cfr. anche or. XXVIII 29 col. 68 BC; poem. I 1, 30, 7—15 col. 509; II 1, 38, 12—22 coll. 1326—1327.

[134] Nell' or. VII, 7 col. 761 C Greg. afferma che il fratello Cesario sapeva ἐκ τῆς τῶν οὐρανίων εὐαρμοστίας καὶ τάξεως τὸν δημιουργὸν θαυμάσαι; cfr. or. XXVIII 6 col. 32 C. Sull'εὐαρμοστία καὶ συμφωνία dell'universo cfr. or. XXXVIII 10 col. 321 B = XLV 6 col. 629 C. Per un inno alla τάξις che regna nel mondo cfr. or. XXXII 8—10 coll. 181—185 e vedi anche or. XVI 5 col. 940 C.

[135] Cfr. Sap. 7, 18: μεταβολὰς καιρῶν. Su καιρός e sinonimi vedi J. BARR, Biblical Words for Time (Studies in Biblical Theology, n. I, 33), London, 1969, pp. 221.

Gregorio introduce nell'argomentazione le ἐνιαυτῶν περιόδους[136]: la stessa locuzione ricorre in Mos. II [III] 222 p. IV 252, 2; Aet. 52 p. VI 89, 3—4; ibid. 71 p. 95, 7; 109 p. 106, 5—6; 123 p. 110, 7; 146 p. 117, 20[137].

Gregorio cita poi, come opera mirabile, la ἡμέρας καὶ νυκτὸς ἰσομοιρίαν. Filone, Her. 163 p. III 38, 3—4 mette in evidenza la ἰσότης divina: ἡμέραν γὰρ καὶ νύκτα καὶ φῶς καὶ σκότος ἰσότης ἔταξε τοῖς οὖσι[138]; in Fug. 184 p. III 150, 12—14 nota: ,,(Il sole) in dodici mesi compie il proprio giro e gli uomini nei mesi dell'anno compiono un ugual numero di ore di giorno e di notte"; in Spec. IV 232 p. V 263, 17—19 domanda: ,,Chi non sa che il sole ha misurato i giorni in rapporto alle notti e le notti in rapporto ai giorni con uguali spazi corrispettivi?" In Her. 148—150 p. III 34, 15—35, 9 indugia in un'attenta analisi su questo problema.

Gregorio considera la ἀέρος χύσιν e Filone, Leg. III 99 p. I 135, 7—8 enumera le ὕδατός τε καὶ ἀέρος χύσεις tra i particolari di un'ampia contemplazione dell'universo che mira a dimostrare che autore di tutto quanto esiste è Dio[139].

Cap. XXIII, col. 888 B:

Gregorio perora: ,,Chi, o uomo, ti diede le piogge, l'agricoltura, i cibi . . . ? Chi ha disposto che gli animali fossero al tuo servizio e che tu fossi il re di tutto quanto c'è sulla terra? Non è forse quel Dio che ora ti chiede, per tutti questi benefici, che tu ti dimostri amorevole verso il tuo prossimo? Sarebbe davvero vergognoso se, dopo aver ricevuto tanto, non gli dessimo in cambio neppure quest'unica cosa, l'amore verso il prossimo. Dio ci separò dagli animali donando a noi soli la ragione, e noi ci imbestialiremo al punto da crederci superiori agli altri perchè siamo più ricchi?" Filone, Spec. II 172—174 p. V 128, 5—21 svolge un'argomentazione analoga: ,,Chi ti diede, o uomo, tutti i beni della terra? Chi ti innalzò sopra tutti gli altri animali fornendoti la ragione? Dio! Dobbiamo quindi essergli riconoscenti come verso un benefattore: ma si dimostra grato verso Dio, che non ha bisogno di nulla, chi mantiene lo stesso atteggiamento verso gli uomini che hanno bisogno di tante cose[140]."

Cap. XXIII, col. 888 B:

Gregorio chiede all'uomo: Chi ti diede . . . γεωργίαν, cibi (τροφάς), arti, abitazioni, leggi, costituzioni civili, βίον ἥμερον? Anche Filone, Her. 137 p. III 32, 7—9 mette in stretta relazione l'agricoltura e la vita civile del-

---

[136] Cfr. Platone, Tim. p. 47 A: ἡμέρα τε καὶ νὺξ . . . καὶ ἐνιαυτῶν περίοδοι καὶ ἰσημερίαι e Plutarco, Def. orac. 19 p. 420 B: ἐτῶν περίοδοι.

[137] Cfr. Greg. or. VIII 21 col. 813 B: ἐτῶν περιόδους.

[138] Quest' equilibrio del giorno e della notte è richiamato anche in or. VI 15 col. 741 A e XLIV 3 col. 609 B.

[139] Cfr. or. IV 96 col. 629 C: ἀέρος χύσις e XXVIII 28 col. 65 B dove, dimostrando l'esistenza di Dio, si chiede: τίς ὁ χέας ἀέρα?

[140] Per uno svolgimento consimile in termini consimili, usato per affermare l'uguaglianza di tutti gli uomini, cfr. or. XXXIII 9 col. 225 B.

l'uomo: infatti la γεωργία produce dei frutti che servono τῷ πάντων ἡμερωτάτῳ ζῴων ... ἀνθρώπῳ. C'è un medesimo sviluppo di pensiero.

Gregorio inoltre considera il βίον ἥμερον come uno dei doni precipui da Dio fatti agli uomini[141] e Filone insiste significativamente nel qualificare l'uomo come ἥμερον ζῷον, usando volentieri il superlativo: cfr. Decal. 115 p. IV 295, 11; ibid. 132 p. 298, 16; Spec. I 295 p. V 71, 10; Praem. 92 p. V 357, 1; Aet. 68 p. VI 94, 3. In Decal. 160 p. IV 304, 13—14 Filone — come Gregorio — presenta come dono divino la ἥμερος τροφή e richiama l'ἥμερον ζῷον; cfr. § 162 p. 304, 22.

Cap. XXIII, col. 888 B:

Gregorio interroga ancora: πόθεν σοι τῶν ζῴων τὰ μὲν ἡμέρωται καὶ ὑπέζευκται, τὰ δὲ τροφῇ παραδέδοται; τίς σε κύριον καὶ βασιλέα πάντων κατέστησε τῶν ἐπὶ τῆς γῆς? Filone, Deus 47 p. II 66, 18—20 dichiara: τὰ μὲν γὰρ ἄλλα ζῷα ... καταζευχθέντα καὶ ἐγχαλινωθέντα πρὸς ὑπηρεσίαν ἀνθρώποις παραδέδοται ὥσπερ οἰκέται δεσπόταις. Per il concetto che Dio abbia creato gli animali per gli usi dell'uomo che ne è signore cfr. anche Spec. II 69 p. V 103, 20—21 (vedi subito dopo § 70 p. 104, 1—4 e framm. Gen. VI 7 p. 18 e VI 17 p. 20 R.H.); Opif. 83 p. I 29, 3—6 (πάντα ... ἡμερώθη) e poco oltre 85 p. 30, 2—9; 87 p. 30, 17; 88 p. 31, 5—7; Mos. II 22 p. IV 205, 6—7; Abr. 45 p. IV 11, 5—8; Aet. 65 p. VI 93, 5—6; Quaest. Gen. II 9 p. 88 A. e VI 314 (MARCUS p. 82); ibid. II 58 p. 141 A. e VI 353 (MARCUS p. 144); Leg. II 9 p. I 92, 12—13; Virt. 154 p. V 314, 16—17; Deus 107 p. II 79, 10—12; Opif. 77 p. I 26, 3—5 e accenni successivi[142]. — Quanto alla regalità dell'uomo sulla natura e su tutti gli esseri viventi che essa contiene cfr. Opif. 84 p. I 29, 9—13 (cfr. anche §§ 85—86 p. 29, 19—30, 15; 88 p. 31, 4—7; 142 p. 50, 8; 148 p. 51, 24—25); Prov. I 70 p. 33 A. e VIII 35; Agric. 8 p. II 96, 23—24; framm. Gen. II 19 p. 12 R.H.; Mutat. 63 p. III 168, 11—13; Spec. IV 14 p. V 212, 16—18.

Cap. XXIII, col. 888 BC:

Gregorio inculca la riconoscenza a Dio per i beni già ricevuti e per quelli sperati: τοσαῦτα παρ' αὐτοῦ, τὰ μὲν λαβόντες, τὰ δὲ ἐλπίζοντες. Anche Filone, Spec. II 187 p. V 132, 9—11 asserisce che dobbiamo ringraziare Dio per i beni ricevuti in passato e per quelli che speriamo in futuro; ibid. I 138 p. V 34, 4 rammenta i χαριστήρια ... εὐγονίας οὔσης τε καὶ ἐλπιζομένης[143]. Per questo binomio contrapposto cfr. Spec. II 12 p. V 88, 11;

---

[141] Non è questo un tema caro alla speculazione classica; le quattro grandi scuole filosofiche antiche tendevano ad accantonarlo. Per rapidi accenni all'uomo considerato come ἥμερον ζῷον cfr. Platone, Sophist. p. 222 B e C; Leg. VI p. 766 A; Phaidr. p. 230 A.

[142] Va inoltre tenuta presente l'investitura dell'uomo sopra tutti gli esseri viventi espressa in Gen. 1, 26 e 28. Va però notato che i LXX usano ἄρχω e κατακυριεύω, ma non il sostantivo βασιλεύς impiegato da Gregorio e da Filone, Opif. 86 p. I 30, 9; Virt. 154 p. V 314, 17 ecc.

[143] Per un contrasto analogo cfr. epist. 223,9 GALLAY II p. 116; or. XIX 4 col. 1048 B.

Leg. III 87 p. I 132, 16—17; Somn. I 91 p. III 224, 8—9; Fug. 145 p. III 141, 9—10; Praem. 102 p. V 359, 10; Mutat. 222 p. III 195, 11—15.

Cap. XXIII, col. 888 C:

Gregorio, di fronte ai ricchi insensibili alle miserie dei poveri, si abbandona ad un'aspra rampogna: (Dio) τῶν θηρίων ἡμᾶς ἐχώρισε, καὶ λόγῳ μόνους τῶν ἐπὶ γῆς ἐτίμησεν· ἡμεῖς δὲ ἡμᾶς αὐτοὺς θηριώσομεν, καὶ τοσοῦτον ... διεφθάρμεθα ἢ μεμήναμεν, ἤ, οὐκ ἔχω τί λέγειν, ὥστε ... ? Filone, Prob. 8 p. VI 3, 3 dinanzi a situazioni e ad usi che gli paiono assurdi, si chiede indignato: non sono forse cose παράλογα καὶ γέμοντα πολλῆς ἀναισχυντίας ἢ μανίας ἢ οὐκ ἔχω τί λέγω ... [144]? In Aet. 68 p. VI 94, 3—4 stabilisce — come Gregorio — uno stretto legame tra il dono della ragione ed il nostro superamento della crudeltà ferina: λόγον δωρησαμένης φύσεως αὐτῷ (scil. τῷ ἀνθρώπῳ) γέρας, ᾧ καὶ τὰ ἐξηγριωμένα πάθη κατεπᾴδεται καὶ τιθασεύεται; in Decal. 115 p. IV 295, 10—11 contrappone all'uomo, τὸ ἡμερώτατον ζῷον, la violenza θηρίων; in Praem. 91 p. V 356, 18 dice che, in seguito alla cupidigia, gli uomini diventano ,,più feroci degli animali privi di ragione".

La frase di Gregorio ἡμεῖς δὲ ἡμᾶς αὐτοὺς θηριώσομεν richiama Ps.-Filone, De Iona 31 p. 596 A. e VII 394: *ante omnia cum hanc a deo gratiam susceperimus, humanae naturae nos participes fieri, statim postquam nati sumus, bestiis invidimus; et rationales conditi, in brutorum naturam reversi sumus.*

Anche l'uso di διαφθείρω riferito alla natura razionale dell'uomo, è precorso da Filone, Her. 302 p. III 68, 25.

Cap. XXIII, col. 888 C:

Dopo aver lungamente illustrato gl'immensi benefici che la bontà di Dio fece agli uomini, Gregorio conclude con una domanda grave e densa: Dio οὐκ αἰσχύνεται Πατὴρ ἡμῶν καλεῖσθαι, Θεὸς ὢν καὶ Δεσπότης· ἡμεῖς δὲ καὶ τὸ συγγενὲς ἀρνησόμεθα? Filone, Spec. I 294 p. V 70, 22—71, 5 imposta un'argomentazione analoga: ,,Se il fondatore e creatore di tutte le cose, che non ha bisogno di niente di quanto produsse, guardando, non all'immensa grandezza della sua potenza e della sua signoria, ma alla tua debolezza, ti fa partecipe della ricchezza della sua bontà soddisfacendo ai bisogni che provi, che cosa non si conviene dunque che tu faccia verso gli uomini che ti sono imparentati per natura (πρὸς ἀνθρώπους τοὺς φύσει συγγενεῖς) e che sono formati degli stessi tuoi elementi (ἀπὸ τῶν αὐτῶν στοιχείων σπαρέντας: per questi rilievi cfr. Gregorio, cap. XIV, col. 876 A)?" Per altri passi di quest'oraz. in cui Gregorio richiama la comune συγγένεια cfr. cap. V col. 864 B; X col. 869 B; XXIII col. 888 B; XXV, col. 892 A; XXVI, col. 892 B.

---

[144] Cfr. or. XVIII 39 col. 1037 C: οὐκ ἔχω λέγειν (non però come qui a conclusione di una *climax* progressiva).

Cap. XXIV, col. 889 B:

Gregorio deplora che i ricchi sogliano μόσχοις τε ἁπαλοῖς ἐκ βουκολίων
... πιαίνεσθαι. Si tratta di una libera citazione da Amos 6, 4. In Abr. 108
p. IV 25, 14—15 Filone scrive: αὐτὸς δὲ εἰς τὰ βουκόλια συντείνας, ἁπαλὸν
καὶ εὔσαρκον ἀγαγὼν μόσχον ... C' è da notare che ἁπαλός in Amos non
appare e che invece con μόσχος è comune ai nostri due scrittori. Non è
neppure presente nell'Antico Testamento[145] nè nel Nuovo.

Cap. XXV, col. 889 C:

Gregorio afferma che Dio mise tutta la natura, senza nessuna restri-
zione, a disposizione degli animali che vivono sulla terra, nell'acqua e
nell'aria: γῆν δὲ χερσαίοις πᾶσιν ἥπλωσεν ... καὶ ποταμοὺς ... ἀέρα δὲ
πτηναῖς φύσεσι, καὶ ὕδωρ ὅσοις ὁ βίος ἔνυδρος. Filone, Somn. I 135 p. III
234, 10—11 nota che Iddio γῆ μὲν τὰ χερσαῖα ἐγκατεσκεύαζε, θαλάτταις δὲ
καὶ ποταμοῖς τὰ ἔνυδρα: il fatto osservato è il medesimo, quantunque
l'angolo visuale, e quindi l'accento, siano diversi: Fil. rileva che tutte le
parti dell'universo sono popolate, Greg. che le parti dell'universo sono
abitate senza delimitazioni di particolari diritti e privilegi.

Riguardo all'espressione cfr. Spec. IV 100 p. V 231, 11—12: ὅσα τῶν
χερσαίων ἢ ἐνύδρων ἢ πτηνῶν ἐστιν εὐσαρκότατα (cfr. Gregorio cap. XVII,
col. 880 A); Confus. 6 p. II 231, 3: ὅσα ζῷα χερσαῖα καὶ ἔνυδρα καὶ πτη-
νά: questo formulario ritorna pressochè identico in Spec. III 8 p. V 152,
7—8; ibid. IV 116 p. 235, 16—18; ibid. 118 p. 235, 24—25. Vedi inoltre
Opif. 147 p. I 51, 14—15.

Per la locuzione πτηναὶ φύσεις usata a designare gli uccelli, vedi Mos. I
218 p. IV 173, 1; Sacrif. 66 p. I 229, 8; Mutat. 178 p. III 187, 11; Decal.
115 p. IV 295, 11—12; cfr. anche Somn. II 213 p. III 292, 27—28.

Cap. XXV, col. 889 C:

Gregorio mette in evidenza la liberale magnificenza divina: Iddio τὰς
πρώτας τοῦ ζῆν ἀφορμὰς ἀφθόνους ἅπασιν ἐχαρίσατο ... κοινὰς τὰς αὐτὰς
καὶ πλουσίας ... προέθηκεν[146]. La stessa cosa e quasi con gli stessi termini
aveva detta Filone in Decal. 17 p. IV 272, 9—10: Iddio γὰρ πρὸς τὸ ζῆν
ἀφθονίαν δοὺς καὶ τὰς πρὸς τὸ εὖ ζῆν ἀφορμὰς ἐδωρεῖτο.

Quanto all'espressione ricorda anche Spec. I 156 p. V 37, 23: τοσαύτας
προσόδων ἀφορμὰς χαρισάμενος τοῖς ἱερεῦσιν. Per un accostamento di
ἄφθονος e di πλούσιος vedi Fug. 102 p. III 132, 16 e per un richiamo alla
grandezza del dono divino (δωρεάν: cfr. appena sotto Gregorio: ἰσότητι
τῆς δωρεᾶς τιμῶν) costituito dalla generosità (ἀφθονίαν) con cui ci nutre
cfr. Spec. II 180 p. V 130, 15.

---

[145] Nell' AT solo in Gen. 18, 7 con μοσχάριον e cfr. Levit. 9, 2 cod. Vat.¹.

[146] Altre considerazioni sull'infinita generosità divina verso tutti gli esseri, le quali con-
suonino con queste anche per notevoli analogie verbali, si trovano nell'or. XXVIII 28
col. 65 B. Sull'argomento vedi W. C. van Unnik, Ἀφθόνως μεταδίδωμι, Bruxelles, 1971,
pp. 70.

Cap. XXV, col. 889 C:

Gregorio specifica: τὰς . . . τοῦ ζῆν ἀφορμὰς ἀφθόνους ἅπασιν ἐχαρίσατο . . . οὐ νόμῳ περιγραφομένας, οὐχ ὁρίοις διειργομένας . . . ἀλλὰ πλουσίας . . . δεικνὺς τὸν πλοῦτον τῆς ἑαυτοῦ χρηστότητος. Filone, Her. 31 p. III 8, 19 — 20 rivolgendosi a Dio esclama: ἄφθονοι μέν, ὦ φιλόδωρε, αἱ σαὶ χάριτες καὶ ἀπερίγραφοι καὶ ὅρον . . . οὐκ ἔχουσαι; in Sacrif. 124 p. I 252, 8—9 dichiara: τοῦ θεοῦ τὸν ἀπεριόριστον καὶ ἀπερίγραφον πλοῦτον αὐτοῦ . . . καὶ τοῖς ἀναξίοις δωρουμένου (anche Gregorio, richiamando Matth. 5, 45, aveva appena sopra affermato che il Signore dispensa i suoi benefici tanto sui buoni quanto sui peccatori); in Poster. 174 p. II 38, 23—25 esorta: σκόπει . . . τὸν ἀπερίγραφον τοῦ θεοῦ πλοῦτον ed in Opif. 23 p. I 7, 6 insegna che le grazie con le quali Dio ci benefica sono ἀπερίγραφοι. Quest' aggettivo è caro a Filone che lo usa volentieri: cfr. Sacrif. 59 p. I 226, 3—4: ἀπερίγραφος γὰρ ὁ θεός, ἀπερίγραφοι δὲ καὶ αἱ δυνάμεις αὐτοῦ[147]; Poster. 151 p. II 33, 23—24; Her. 190 p. III 44, 2—3.

Cap. XXV, col. 889 C:

Gregorio, sostenendo l'uguaglianza di tutti gli uomini, presenta Dio come τό τε τῆς φύσεως ὁμότιμον ἰσότητι τῆς δωρεᾶς τιμῶν. Filone, Spec. II 34 p. V 94, 2—3 afferma: παρὰ μὲν ἡμῖν ἀνισότης, ἰσότης δὲ παρὰ θεῷ τίμιον. Sul concetto di ἰσότης in Filone — che significa tanto 'uguaglianza' quanto 'equità' — vedi Spec. IV 231—238 p. V 263, 12—265, 6 e per la sua celebrazione cfr. anche l'ampio passo di Her. 141—206 pp. III 32, 21—47, 13. In Spec. II 21 p. V 90, 23 Filone afferma che la παιδεία ὀρθή induce illustri personaggi a collocarsi al livello comune: τὸ ἄνισον ἰσότητι θεραπεύουσα. Vedi anche ibid. II 68 p. V 103, 16; Prob. 79 p. VI 23, 4—9[148]. Greg. al cap. XXXVI col. 905 C sostiene che ricchi e poveri sono entrambi creature di Dio καὶ εἰ τὰ ἔξωθεν ἄνισα.

Cap. XXV, col. 889 C:

Gregorio deplora i ricchi χρυσὸν καὶ ἄργυρον . . . καὶ τῶν λίθων τοὺς διαυγεῖς κατορύξαντες. In Filone Decal. 133 p. IV 298, 21—299, 1 χρυσὸς μὲν καὶ ἄργυρος καὶ λίθοι πολυτελεῖς vengono citati come κόσμος οἰκοδομημάτων (cfr. Gregorio cap. XVI col. 877 A: ἡμεῖς δὲ οἰκήσομεν οἰκίας . . . λίθοις παντοίοις διηνθισμένας καὶ χρυσῷ καὶ ἀργύρῳ καταστραπτούσας). In Virt. 85

---

[147] In or. XXVIII 7 col. 33 C Gregorio insegna che attributo essenziale di Dio è di non essere περιγραπτός. — I due scrittori sostengono che, secondo l'originario intendimento divino, non esistettero all'inizio confini che determinassero possessi privati della terra: sulla loro successiva comparsa, sul loro significato e sugli aspetti cultuali e giuridici che li concernevano cfr. G. PICCALUGA, I segni di confine nella religione romana (Quaderni di 'Storia e materiali di Storia Rel.', n. 9), Roma, 1974, pp. 352.

[148] Nell' or. XVI 5 col. 940 C Greg. sostiene che la creazione fu un oggetto di godimento comune ed a pari diritti (ἰσότιμον); in XVIII 20 col. 1008 C lamenta che i poveri siano la parte più disprezzata τῆς ὁμοτίμου φύσεως ed in XIX 13 col. 1060 A proclama che Cristo introdusse nel mondo τὴν συμπάθειαν καὶ τὸ ὁμότιμον.

p. V 289, 4—5 è menzionato ὁ πλοῦτος ἄψυχος ἐν ταμείοις καὶ μυχοῖς γῆς κατορωρυγμένος[149].

Cap. XXV, col. 889 CD:

Gregorio considera χρυσὸν καὶ ἄργυρον... καὶ τῶν λίθων τοὺς διαυγεῖς... e τι ἄλλο τοιοῦτον come πολέμου καὶ στάσεως ... γνωρίσματα[150]. Filone, Prov. II 18 p. 57 A. e VIII 54—55 in Eusebio, Praepar. Evang. VIII 14, 12 GCS Mras p. I 465, 11—14 dichiara che a causa delle ἀργύρου τε καὶ χρυσοῦ κτήσεις e della φιλαργυρία si è prodotto ἐκ μὲν εἰρήνης συνεχὴς καὶ ἀδιάστατος πόλεμος; in Poster. 117 p. II 25, 25 a proposito dei φιλοσώματοι, dei φιλάργυροι e dei φιλόδοξοι dice: δημιουργοὶ δ' εἰσὶ πάντες οὗτοι πολέμου; in Decal. 153 p. IV 303, 3—7 asserisce: ,,Tutte le guerre tragicamente famose[151] che furono combattute da Greci e barbari ... sono derivate da un'unica fonte, dalla cupidigia delle ricchezze o della gloria o del piacere; queste sono le cose per le quali il genere umano si inquieta"[152].

Per l'uso di γνώρισμα nell'accezione attiva di 'elemento rivelatore', cfr. Spec. I 42 p. V 11, 5 dove è detto che la luce è ἑαυτοῦ γνώρισμα.

Cap. XXV, col. 892 A:

Gregorio considera le disuguaglianze sociali come delle ,,malattie comuni che si abbatterono sull'umanità insieme alla malvagità (κακία) e che da essa furono escogitate". Anche Filone Cher. 96 p. I 193, 17—18 è convinto che nei malvagi la κακία generi delle malattie: ... νοσημάτων χαλεπῶν, ἃ κακίας ἀμήχανος δύναμις προσέβαλε.

Cap. XXV, col. 892 A:

Gregorio definisce la servitù come uno degli ἀρρωστήματα κοινά τινα τῇ κακίᾳ συνεισπεσόντα, κἀκείνης ὄντα ἐπινοήματα. Che le passioni rendano

---

[149] È questo un uso pratico ed un atteggiamento letterario ampiamente documentato: cfr. Erodoto VIII 36; Platone, Euthyd. p. 288 E; Aristotele, framm. 248 p. 1524 A 2; Demostene, Contr. Aphob. I 53 p. 830 5 e III 49 p. 859,9—10; Menandro, Dyscol. 812 ed. Gallavotti; Plauto, Aulul. 667—681 e 701—712; Orazio, Sat. I 1,41—42.

[150] Anche questo motivo non è certo nuovo: cfr. Platone, Phaid. p. 66 C: διὰ γὰρ τὴν τῶν χρημάτων κτῆσιν πάντες οἱ πόλεμοι γίγνονται; Aristotele, Pol. V 2 p. 1302 A 32 dice che i motivi per i quali gli uomini στασιάζουσιν, ἐστὶ κέρδος καὶ τιμή; Ps.-Focilide, Sentent. dopo aver apostrofato l'oro come κακῶν ἀρχηγέ (v. 44; cfr. anche framm. adesp. 129 Nauck²: ὦ χρυσέ ... πάντων κρατιστεύων τύραννε), continua (vv. 46—47) affermando che l'oro è la causa delle battaglie, degli esili, delle uccisioni...; Tacito, Hist. IV 74 asserisce: *aurum et opes, praecipuae bellorum causae*; Seneca, Epist. 94,57 nota: *(natura) aurum quidem et argentum et propter ista numquam pacem agens ferrum, quasi male nobis committerentur, abscondit. Nos in lucem propter quae pugnaremus, extulimus, nos et causas periculorum nostrorum et instrumenta ... eruimus.* Tucidide I 83,2, anticipando un famoso aforisma moderno, già osservava: ἔστιν ὁ πόλεμος οὐχ ὅπλων τὸ πλέον, ἀλλὰ δαπάνης. Cfr. anche Sofocle, Antig. 295—297.

[151] τραγῳδηθέντες: cfr. Gregorio cap. XIII col. 873 C: ἐκτραγῳδοίην.

[152] Cfr. anche or. XIX 14 col. 1061 A; XXXIV 4 col. 244 C; poem. I 2, 8, 103 col. 656; II 1, 11, 870—871 col. 1089; II 2, 80, 3 col. 122 epigr.

schiava l'anima è un tema sviluppato da Filone in Her. 268—273 p. III 61, 12—62, 14: cfr. particolarmente 271 p. III 62, 2—3: αἰ... ἡγεμονίαι παθῶν βαρεῖαν τοῖς ἀρχομένοις ἐπάγουσι δουλείαν. In Prob. 17 p. VI 5, 3 dichiara che c'è una schiavitù delle anime ed una dei corpi: padroni dei corpi sono uomini, ψυχῶν δὲ κακίαι καὶ πάθη e ibid. 159 p. VI 44, 17—22 afferma: ,,(L'anima) se si abbandona alle passioni, se si lascia adescare dal piacere, se si svia per il timore, se si arresta davanti al dolore, se si lascia vincere dall'ira, asservisce se stessa e si rende schiava e soggetta ad infiniti padroni; se invece abbatte la stoltezza con la saggezza, la sfrenatezza con il controllo di se stessa ... aggiunge alla libertà anche l'attitudine al comando". Cfr. inoltre Contempl. 70 p. VI 65, 2—4.

Cap. XXV, col. 892 A:

Gregorio, nella sua impugnazione delle distinzioni sociali, afferma che schiavitù e libertà non esistettero all'inizio dell'umanità, ma che ὁ πλάσας ἀπ' ἀρχῆς τὸν ἄνθρωπον, ἐλεύθερον ἀφῆκε καὶ αὐτεξούσιον[153]. Filone, Deus 49 p. II 67, 12—13 dichiara che Dio fece τὸν ἄνθρωπον ἄφετον καὶ ἐλεύθερον; appena prima (47 p. 66, 15—18), parlando del nostro spirito, aveva asserito: ,,Il Padre Creatore lo degnò, esso solo, della libertà (ἐλευθερίας); lo lasciò libero (ἄφετον) sciogliendogli le catene della necessità, e gli donò quella parte che fu in grado di ricevere della disponibilità del volere, la qual cosa costituisce il bene più conveniente e più proprio" ed in Fug. 212 p. III 155, 8—9 presenta il Creatore come un essere libero, produttore di altri esseri liberi[154]: in entrambi i casi Filone parla di una libertà morale di fronte al bene ed al male e non di una libertà giuridica; mentre Gregorio le affianca entrambe. Anche Filone però sostiene spesso la libertà giuridica dell'uomo all'atto della creazione in perfetta sintonia con Gregorio, usando solo φύσις in luogo di πλάσας: cfr. Spec. II 69 p. V 103, 19—21; ibid. 84 p. 107,

---

[153] Per una più precisa valutazione dei termini cfr. M. HARL, Adam et les deux Arbres du Paradis (Gen. II—III) chez Philon d'Alexandrie, in: Recherches de Science Religieuse, L (1962), pp. 376—377: ,,Notiamo: il termine αὐτεξούσιος che presso i cristiani designerà il libero arbitrio, non è mai impiegato da Filone per qualificare l'uomo. Questo aggettivo che in lui è all'incirca sinonimo di αὐτοκράτωρ e che significa che uno 'dispone di se stesso', può qualificare soltanto Dio; fu l'errore dei cattivi, come Caino, quello di credersi autonomi. Filone impiega parecchi altri termini per nominare il libero movimento dell'uomo, la sua capacità di volere il bene: αὐτοκίνητος, ἑκούσιος, ἐθελουργός, ἐθελούσιος, αὐτοκέλευστος, προαιρετικός sono gli epiteti di κίνησις, γνώμη; sono i termini della volontà secondo Aristotele. Quando dice anche che l'uomo è ἄφετος ὁ ἐλεύθερος allora indica, in termini stoici, che il saggio può liberare l'intelletto dalle imposizioni del corpo e della necessità. Ma nè la volontà nè la liberazione sono l'equivalente dell'autonomia."

[154] In poem. I 2, 1, 158 col. 534 Gregorio afferma che Adamo prima del peccato era libero ed in poem. I 2, 33, 133—134 coll. 937—938 impugna come iniqua la distinzione tra servi e padroni in nome dell'identità del creatore, della legge e del destino. — Per creare uno sfondo a queste affermazioni sarà utile leggere i capp. 3° (stoicismo), 5° (patristica fino al III secolo) e 6° (patristica del IV—V secolo) di P. A. MILANI, La schiavitù nel pensiero politico. Dai Greci al Basso Medio Evo, Milano, 1972, pp. 402.

4; ibid. 122 p. 115, 9—10; ibid. III 137 p. 189, 2—3; IV 14 p. 212, 19—22; ibid. 18 p. 213, 21—22; Contempl. 70 p. VI 65, 2—4. Esplicito ed interessante è poi Filone, Spec. II 82 p. V 106, 14—15 dove dichiara: μισθωτός ἐστιν, ὦ ἄνθρωπε, ὁ λεγόμενος δοῦλος, καὶ αὐτὸς ἄνθρωπος ὤν, ἔχων πρὸς σὲ τὴν ἀνωτάτω συγγένειαν; qui affiorano alcuni punti di contatto con Gregorio: 1⁰) al λεγόμενος filoniano fa eco il τὰ τοιαῦτα τῶν ὀνομάτων di lin. 6 col. 892 A e l'εἰς ὀνομάτων ἀλλοτριότητας di lin. 4 cap. XXVI col. 892 B; — 2⁰) l'appello alla dignità dell'ἄνθρωπος, su cui insiste anche Gregorio, ricordando i benefici divini di cui fu oggetto; — 3⁰) il richiamo alla comune parentela, che anche Gregorio rammenta lin. 1 col. 892 e lin. 4 cap. XXVI; — 4⁰) anche questo particolare tipo di poliptoto con ἄνθρωπος è familiare a Gregorio: infatti al cap. VI col. 864 C ed al cap. XII col. 873 A lo ritroviamo con ἄνθρωπος accompagnato, come qui, dal part. pres. di εἰμί, ed al cap. XXVIII col. 896 B con l'uso, come qui, del vocativo.

Cap. XXV, col. 892 A:

Gregorio, dopo aver affermato che Dio creò l'uomo libero, continua: τοῦτο καὶ τῷ λοιπῷ γένει τῶν ἀνθρώπων βουληθείς τε καὶ χαρισάμενος δι' ἑνὸς τοῦ πρώτου σπέρματος. Filone, Opif. 145 p. I 51, 3—5 sostiene che la bellezza dell'anima e del corpo che Dio concesse al primo uomo prosegue, anche se attenuata, nei suoi discendenti, in forza della loro parentela con il primo padre, e poco oltre (148 p. 52, 4—7) asserisce che il primo uomo ottenne da Dio la regalità sugli animali e che i suoi discendenti, pure attraverso a tante generazioni, hanno conservato questo dominio che fu loro trasmesso dal capostipite.

Cap. XXV, col. 892 AB:

Gregorio, per stabilire l'autentico senso della libertà e della ricchezza e quello della schiavitù e della povertà, conia un lucido aforisma: ἐλευθερία δὲ καὶ πλοῦτος, ἡ τῆς ἐντολῆς μόνη τήρησις ἦν· πενία δὲ ἀληθὴς καὶ δουλεία, ἡ ταύτης παράβασις. Questo concetto che la genuina libertà consista nell'ubbidire ai comandamenti di Dio e che la vera schiavitù risieda invece nella loro trasgressione, costituisce una delle convinzioni basilari anche di Filone. Vedi Sacrif. 127 p. I 253, 9—10; Prob. 20 p. VI 5, 17; ibid. 45 p. 13, 13—15; ibid. 62 p. 18, 12—14. — Quando Gregorio — 3 righe sopra — afferma che l'uomo è νόμῳ τῷ τῆς ἐντολῆς μόνῳ κρατούμενος si riferisce ovviamente alla legge divina, ed anche Filone, Prob. 46 p. VI 13, 17—18 specifica che il νόμος che rende liberi non è quello mortale, ma quello incorruttibile plasmato dalla natura immortale. Più volte poi Filone, invece di dire che la libertà consiste nell'ossequenza ai comandamenti di Dio, ricorre a formule equivalenti: cfr. Prob. 42 p. VI 12, 12; ibid. 52 p. 15, 5; ibid. 60 p. 17, 7; ibid. 136 p. 39, 4; ibid. 159 p. 44, 17—22. Infine, in alcuni casi, invece di coordinare su di uno stesso piano i due concetti di libertà e di ubbidienza a Dio, mette in forte evidenza il secondo sovraordinandolo al primo: cfr. Cher. 107 p. I 196, 1—3; Spec. I 57 p. V 14, 21—15, 1; Somn. II 100 p. III

275, 7—9; Plant. 53 p. II 144, 14—15; framm. in Giovanni Damasceno, Sacra Parall. p. 775 p. II 657 M. e VI 215 Schw.[155].

Cap. XXVI, col. 892 B:

Tra le cause delle ingiuste disuguaglianze sociali Gregorio nomina ἡ δολερὰ τοῦ ὄφεως τυραννὶς, ἀεὶ τῷ λίχνῳ τῆς ἡδονῆς ὑποσύρουσα. Anche Filone stabilisce uno stretto legame tra il serpente biblico ed il piacere che travia: cfr. Agric. 97 p. II 114, 28—30: τὸν μὲν οὖν τῆς γυναικὸς ὄφιν ... ἡδονὴν εἶναί φαμεν; ibid. 108 p. 116, 25: (ὁ ὄφις) τῆς Εὔας ἡδονῆς ὢν σύμβου-λον; Opif. 157 p. I 55, 2; ibid. 164 p. 57, 5—7; ibid. 165 p. 57, 12—13; Leg. II 72 p. I 104, 23—24; ibid. 74—79 particolarmente pp. 104, 30—105, 1; ibid. 105 p. 111, 25; ibid. 106 p. 111, 28—30; ibid. III 66 p. 127, 16; ibid. 75 p. 129, 6; ibid. 76 p. 129, 14—15; ibid. 246 p. 167, 23; Quaest. Gen. I 31 p. 22 A. e VI 266 (Marcus pp. 18—19); ibid. I 47 p. 31 A. e VI 273 (Marcus p. 27); ibid. I 48 p. 31 A. e VI 273 (Marcus p. 27).

Quanto all'uso di τυραννίς con una passione cfr. Confus. 197 p. II 267, 7. Ibid. 113 p. 250, 21 parla di costruire un baluardo inespugnabile τῇ τυράννῳ κακίᾳ.

Per la formula gregoriana τῷ λίχνῳ τῆς ἡδονῆς si può ricordare quella filoniana di Migr. 143 p. II 296, 3—4 dove parla di un uomo πεινῶντος ἡδονῆς καὶ λίχνου παθῶν.

Sui composti di σύρω per rendere lo sviamento dello spirito allettato da subdole influenze vedi in Gregorio ὑποσύρω ed in Filone κατασύρω: Leg. 73 p. I 80, 15; Somn. I 44 p. III 214, 11; ibid. II 237 p. 296, 26; παρασύρω: Spec. I 30 p. V 8, 4[156].

Per l'idea del piacere come principio di ingiustizie cfr. Opif. 152 p. I 53, 9—10: (ἡδονὴν) ἥτις ἐστὶν ἀδικημάτων καὶ παρανομημάτων ἀρχή.

Cap. XXVI, col. 892 B:

Gregorio dichiara che la tirannia del serpente servendosi dell'attrattiva del piacere spinse τοῖς ἀσθενεστέροις τοὺς θρασυτέρους. Filone, Contempl. 70 p. VI 65, 2—4 cercando una spiegazione etiologica dell'uso dei Terapeuti

---

[155] Vedi un bello sviluppo su questo tema in or. XXXIV 8 coll. 248 D—249 A ed altri accenni interessanti in or. XXIII 11 col. 1164 A; XXV 17 col. 1224 A; XLI 7 col. 437 C; XLIV 8 col. 616 B; poem. I 2,26,27—29 col. 853; I 2,33,139 col. 938. — Anche se nel NT non ci sono asserzioni che siano la radice immediata della teoria gregoriana ci sono però degli spunti che la coonestano e la sostengono: cfr. Ioann. 8,32—36; II Petr. 2,19 e vedi anche Rom. 6,16—20; 8,2 e 21; II Cor. 3,17; Gal. 5,1. — Per un prospetto della concezione filoniana su quest'argomento vedi F. Geiger, Philon von Alexandreia als sozialer Denker, (Tübinger Beiträge zur Altertumswissenschaft, n. 14), Stuttgart, 1932, pp. 65—81. — Utilissimi inquadramenti ci offrono anche D. Nestle, Eleutheria. Studien zum Wesen der Freiheit bei den Griechen und im Neuen Testament, I: Die Griechen (Hermen. Untersuchungen zur Theologie), Tübingen, 1967, pp. 164; A. Guëmes Villanueva, La libertad en S. Pablo. Un estudio sobre ἐλευθερία paulina, Pamplona, 1971, pp. 263.

[156] Per l'uso in Gregorio di composti di σύρω in un significato morale parallelo a quello presente cfr. παρασύρω in or. XXI 21 col. 1105 BC; XXV 4 col. 1204 A; XXVI 9 col. 1240 A; XXX 1 col. 104 D; epist. 7, 4 Gallay I p. 9 e κατασύρω in XXVII 5 col. 17 A.

di non farsi servire da schiavi nel banchetto sacro, ma solo da liberi che
attendessero di loro spontanea volontà a quest' incombenza, stende un periodo che può sembrare la sintesi di alcune tra le convinzioni più accette a
Gregorio: (ἡ φύσις) μὲν γὰρ ἐλευθέρους ἅπαντας γεγέννηκεν, αἱ δέ τινων
ἀδικίαι καὶ πλεονεξίαι (Gregorio nella riga seguente dichiara la πλεονεξία
colpevole della stessa ingiustizia) ζηλωσάντων τὴν ἀρχέκακον ἀνισότητα
καταζεύξασαι τὸ ἐπὶ τοῖς ἀσθενεστέροις κράτος τοῖς δυνατωτέροις ἀνῆψαν.

Cap. XXVI, col. 892 B:

Gregorio sostiene che in grazia delle umane cupidigie ἐρράγη τὸ συγγενὲς εἰς ὀνομάτων ἀλλοτριότητας, καὶ τὸ τῆς φύσεως εὐγενὲς πλεονεξία
κατέτεμε. In Prob. 79 p. VI 23, 4—9 Filone ci comunica che gli Esseni
condannavano i padroni di schiavi non solo come ingiusti, in quanto pro-
fanavano l'ἰσότητα, ma anche come empi, in quanto distruggevano il
θεσμὸν φύσεως ... ἢ πάντας ὁμοίως γεννήσασα καὶ θρεψαμένη μητρὸς δίκην
ἀδελφοὺς γνησίους ... ἀπειργάσατο· ὧν τὴν συγγένειαν ἡ ἐπίβουλος πλεονεξία ... διέσεισεν, ἀντ' οἰκειότητος ἀλλοτριότητα ... ἐργασαμένη[157]. È
una trattazione analoga a quella di Gregorio, il quale, in una traccia sostanzialmente identica, inserisce anche altre più fitte considerazioni. Il raffronto
rivela che: 1º) entrambi richiamano le ἀφορμάς: Filone — § 78 p. 23, 2 —
per condannare quelle viziose; Gregorio — cap. XXV col. 889 C — per appro-
vare quelle legittime; — 2º) Filone sottolinea l'attività nutritrice che la
natura esplica verso tutti gli uomini e Gregorio — cap. XXV col. 889 C —
presenta il mondo come aperto a soddisfare abbondantemente le esigenze
di tutti gli esseri viventi; — 3º) entrambi parlano di ἰσότης e di φύσις:
Filone per condannare coloro che calpestano queste norme fondamentali di
vita e Gregorio per affermare che Dio onorò τὸ ... τῆς φύσεως ὁμότιμον
ἰσότητι τῆς δωρεᾶς; — 4º) Filone presenta la natura come πάντας ὁμοίως
γεννήσασα e Gregorio insiste due volte a breve distanza (lin. 1 col. 892 e
lin. 4 cap. XXVI) sul fatto che tutta l'umanità è συγγενής, incontrandosi
perfettamente con Filone che proprio ora ne testifica la συγγένεια; — 5º)
Filone dichiara che la natura è una madre che generò tutti come ἀδελφοὺς
γνησίους e Gregorio — cap. XXV col. 892 A — insegna che Dio beneficò
tutti ugualmente δι' ἑνὸς τοῦ πρώτου σπέρματος; — 6º) Filone dice che la
ἐπίβουλος πλεονεξία scrollò il legame di parentela che intercorre tra gli
uomini e Gregorio che τὸ τῆς φύσεως εὐγενὲς πλεονεξία κατέτεμε, conferendo
al verbo un più crudo vigore; — 7º) finalmente Filone asserisce che la πλεονεξία produsse ἀντ' οἰκειότητος ἀλλοτριότητα e Gregorio che in causa della
πλεονεξία e delle passioni ad essa collegate ἐρράγη τὸ συγγενὲς εἰς ὀνομάτων
ἀλλοτριότητας. Per un concetto analogo cfr. Spec. IV 14 p. V 212, 19—22.
Per la locuzione τὸ τῆς φύσεως εὐγενές cfr. Agric. 59 p. II 107, 18—19:
τὸ τῆς φύσεως ἐλεύθερόν τε καὶ εὐγενές ... ἐπιδειξάμενοι e Prob. 123 p. VI 35,
11—12: τῆς ψυχῆς τὸ ἐλεύθερον καὶ εὐγενὲς καὶ φύσει βασιλικὸν ὑπηχούσης.

[157] Vedi poem. II 1, 1, 77—82 col. 976.

In questi esempi Filone stringe ἐλεύθερον ed εὐγενές in una coppia fissa e Gregorio considera appunto l'ἐλεύθερον come τὸ τῆς φύσεως εὐγενές.

Cap. XXVI, col. 892 B:

Gregorio propugna la tesi che la cupidigia dei più potenti abbia spezzato la nobiltà della natura umana προσλαβοῦσα καὶ νόμον, τῆς δυναστείας ἐπίκουρον. Filone, Confus. 112 p. II 250, 18—20 in una prosopopea immagina che la mente dei malvagi dica dinanzi alla calca delle passioni: ,,Promulghiamo delle leggi che rassodino il vantaggio del più forte per coloro che sono capaci di accaparrarsi sempre più beni che non gli altri''[158].

Cap. XXVI, col. 892 B:

Gregorio esorta: ,,Guarda alla primitiva uguaglianza, non alla distinzione che ne venne alla fine, alla legge del creatore, non a quella del dominatore.'' Nello stesso spirito Filone, Spec. II 21 p. V 90, 20—21 loda quei signori che inclinano ,,a stimare la dignità umana più delle loro posizioni di preminenza''.

Capp. XXVI—XXVII, col. 892 C—893 A:

Gregorio invita: γενοῦ τῷ ἀτυχοῦντι θεός, τὸν ἔλεον Θεοῦ μιμησάμενος. Οὐδὲν γὰρ οὕτως, ὡς τὸ εὖ ποιεῖν, ἄνθρωπος ἔχει Θεοῦ· κἂν ὁ μὲν μείζω, καὶ ὁ δὲ ἐλάττω εὐεργετῇ, ἑκάτερος, οἶμαι, κατὰ τὴν ἑαυτοῦ δύναμιν. Filone, Spec. IV 186—187 p. V 252, 1—3 asserisce: ,,Il bene consiste non nel danneggiare, ma nell'aiutare tutti quelli che è possibile. Infatti il seguire Dio risiede proprio in questo, poichè anch'egli ha la possibilità di fare del bene e del male, ma vuole solo il bene''; in framm. p. 84 R.H. proclama: πέφυκεν ὁ θεὸς εὖ ποιεῖν; in Spec. IV 73—74 p. V 225, 21—226, 1 cita il detto di un antico il quale afferma: ,,Gli uomini non fanno nulla di simile a Dio se non quando fanno del bene''[159] e subito commenta: ,,Qual bene infatti più grande potrebbe esistere per degli esseri mortali che imitare Iddio[160]?'' In Mutat. 129 p. III 178, 27—28 dichiara che il beneficare è l'attributo proprio di Dio.

---

[158] Per dei precedenti nel mondo culturale greco cfr. Platone, Republ. pp. 338 C—339 A; Protag. p. 337 CD. L'opposizione tra legge e natura era un tema familiare alla sofistica cfr. Gorgia p. 482 E.

[159] L. COHN in questo passo della sua edizione cita VAHLEN³ che collega questa sentenza con περὶ ὕψους p. 2, 16 e poi, per conto suo, aggiunge Cicerone, Lig. 38. I. HEINEMANN, Philo von Alexandria. Die Werke in deutscher Übersetzung, Band II, 2. Aufl., Berlin, 1962, loc. cit. p. 269 afferma che questa massima, frequentemente citata, fu attribuita a Pitagora e a Demostene. Cfr. però L. STERNBACH, De gnomologio Vaticano inedito, in: Wiener Studien, IX (1887), p. 199 n. 53: Ἀριστοτέλης ἐρωτηθεὶς ὑπό τινος, τί ἄνθρωπος ἴσον ἔχει Θεῷ, εἶπε ,,τὸ εὐεργετεῖν''.

[160] A questo proposito cfr. or. XVII 9 col. 976 D; poem. I 2,30,5 col. 909; ibid. 33,221—224 col. 944 ed anche poem. I 2,17,7—8 col. 782. Per l'imitazione di Dio nel concetto filoniano cfr. A. HEITMANN, Imitatio Dei. Die ethische Nachahmung Gottes nach der Väterlehre der zwei ersten Jahrhunderte (Studia Anselmiana, n. 10), Roma, 1940, pp. 47—64 e H. MERKI, ΟΜΟΙΩΣΙΣ ΘΕΩ̣. Von der platonischen Angleichung an Gott zur Gottähnlichkeit bei Gregor von Nyssa (Paradosis, n. 7), Freiburg i. d. Schweiz, 1952, pp. 35—44.

Cap. XXVII, col. 893 A:

Gregorio elenca tra i benefici che Dio ci ha concessi τὸν φυσικὸν νόμον ἄγραφον[161]. Filone, Abr. 16 p. IV 4, 22—24 parla di un ἄγραφος νόμος ... ὃν ἡ φύσις ἔθηκε. Per l'espressione νόμος φύσεως[162] cfr. Opif. 13 p. I 4, 4—5; ibid. 171 p. 60, 7—8; Poster. 185 p. II 41, 6; Agric. 31 p. II 101, 8; ibid. 66 p. 108, 20; Plant. 132 p. II 159, 21; Sobr. 25 p. II 220, 27; Abr. 135 p. IV 31, 4; ibid. 249 p. 55, 8—9; Mos. II 7 p. IV 202, 2; ibid. II [III] 245 p. 257, 20; Spec. I 306 p. V 74, 6—7; ibid. III 32 p. 158, 19; ibid. III 189 p. 203, 11; ibid. IV 204 p. 257, 3; Praem. 42 p. V 345, 17; ibid. 108 p. 361, 2—3; Prob. 30 p. VI 9, 7; Contempl. 59 p. VI 61, 16; Quaest. Gen. IV 157 p. 366 A. e VII 162; cfr. ibid. 205 p. 408 A. e VII 189[163]. C'è però da notare che nell'identità di questa formula, che ricorre frequentemente anche al plurale, sono racchiusi contenuti concettuali diversi: talvolta infatti indica la norma morale, talaltra invece il limite della natura, la sua disposizione, il suo impulso o il logico significato delle cose.

Quanto al νόμος ἄγραφος[164] cfr. Abr. 5 p. IV 2, 11—12; ibid. 276 p. IV 60, 17; Legat. 115 p. VI 176, 18—19; Her. 295 p. III 67, 12—13; Spec. IV 149 p. V 242, 18 (cfr. ibid. lin. 25); Decal. 1 p. IV 269, 5; Virt. 194 p. V 326, 16—17[165].

[161] Si tratta di un'idea che era già stata ampiamente dibattuta nella cultura classica e che aveva avuto una sistemazione ben consapevole soprattutto dalla scuola stoica; per taluni rinvii cfr. le mie Reminiscenze e consonanze classiche nella XIV orazione di San Gregorio Nazianzeno, in: Atti Accad. d. Scienze di Torino, XCIX (1964—1965), pp. 178—179.

[162] Per il νόμος φύσεως in Gregorio ricorda or. XXXII 7 col. 181 B; epist. 32, 3 GALLAY I p. 40. — Sulla legge e sulla natura che le fa da supporto cfr. M. OSTWALD, Nomos and the Beginnings of the Athenian Democracy, Oxford, 1969, pp. XIV-228; M. SPANNEUT, La notion de nature des Stoïciens aux Pères de l'Église, in: Recherches de Théologie ancienne et médiévale, XXXVII (1970), pp. 165—173; J. DE ROMILLY, La loi dans la pensée grecque des origines à Aristote (Collection d'Études anciennes), Paris, 1971, pp. 269; L. MONSENGWO PASINYA, La notion de nomos dans le Pentateuque grec (Analecta Biblica, n. 52), Roma, 1973, pp. 246 (viene tenuto presente Filone nei capp. 5° e 6°); A. MYRE, La loi de la nature et la loi mosaïque selon Philon d'Alexandrie, in: Science et Esprit, XXVIII (1976), pp. 163—181; V. NIKIPROWETZKY, Le commentaire de l'Écriture chez Philon d'Alexandrie ... (1977) (cfr. nota 1), al cap. 5°.

[163] Cfr. anche H. LEWY, Neue Philontexte ... (Sitzungsber. d. preuß. Akad. d. Wiss., Philos.-histor. Klasse, IV), Berlin, 1932, p. 83 n. 27. — Ricorda inoltre ARNIM, Stoic. Vet. Fragm., I, p. 42, 35—39.

[164] In or. IV 93 col. 625 C Greg. ironeggia mordacemente contro il livore di Giuliano verso i Cristiani, definendo ἄγραφος νόμος i suoi tirannici procedimenti verso di loro.

[165] Che quando Filone parla di ἄγραφος νόμος non intenda la legge orale talmudica e le tradizioni giudaiche che interpretavano il Pentateuco, ma la legge naturale non scritta degli Stoici, cfr. R. HIRZEL, Ἄγραφος νόμος, in: Abh. Sächs. Ges. d. Wiss. Philol.-histor. Classe, XX, 1, Leipzig, 1900, p. 98; I. HEINEMANN, Die Lehre vom ungeschriebenen Gesetz im jüdischen Schrifttum, in: Hebrew Union College Annual, IV (1927), pp. 149—171 (specialm. pp. 152—159); S. SANDMEL, Parallelomania, in: Journal of Biblical Literature, LXXXI (1962), pp. 1—13; J. M. BAUMGARTEN, The Unwritten Law in the Pre-Rabbinic Period, in: Journal for the Studies of Judaism (Leiden), III (1972—73), pp. 7—29.

Cap. XXVII, col. 893 A:

Gregorio insegna che Dio ci concesse di vincere il demonio che ci aveva vinti con il peccato originale. Per un analogo ossimoro sul concetto di vittoria cfr. Leg. II 108 p. I 112, 6—7: σπούδασον στεφανωθῆναι κατὰ τῆς τοὺς ἄλλους ἅπαντας νικώσης ἡδονῆς e Mos. I 295 p. IV 190, 9—10: πρὸς . . . ἧτταν τῶν ἀεὶ νικᾶν δυναμένων[166].

Cap. XXVII, col. 893 B:

Gregorio invita a tenere al prossimo sofferente delle conversazioni formatrici, che producano dei frutti di dottrina e di pietà paragonabili agli interessi di un capitale[167]. Filone, Spec. IV 75 p. V 226, 13—17 esorta a formare i giovani nella sapienza dello spirito in modo che portino frutti di nobiltà morale a guisa di un campo ben coltivato: il medesimo traslato è appoggiato a due paragoni, differenti in sè, ma identici nel loro significato.

Cap. XXVII, col. 893 C:

Gregorio si rivolge al 'servo di Cristo' e lo apostrofa: ὦ . . . καὶ φιλόθεε καὶ φιλάνθρωπε. Filone, Decal. 110 p. IV 294, 1—2 sembra contrapporre queste due determinazioni: infatti parlando di coloro che sono inclini a trascurare gli uomini per curare solo i doveri verso Dio, e di coloro che tendono a trascurare Dio per attendere solo agli obblighi verso gli uomini, dice τούτους μὲν οὖν φιλανθρώπους, τοὺς δὲ προτέρους φιλοθέους ἐνδίκως ἄν εἴποι τις; però in Prob. 83 p. VI 24, 5 le unisce strettamente: χρώμενοι τῷ τε φιλοθέῳ[168] καὶ φιλαρέτῳ καὶ φιλανθρώπῳ[169]. In Quaest. Gen. III 42 p. 211 A. e VII 37 (MARCUS p. 232) dichiara l'interdipendenza di questi due amori: solet enim dei amator illico etiam hominum amator esse; cfr. anche ibid. IV 29 p. 269 A. e VII 82 (MARCUS p. 305)[170].

Cap. XXVII, col. 893 C:

Gregorio esorta a superare il timore che si ha per il possibile contagio ed a curare i lebbrosi in nome dell'εὐσέβεια. Anche Filone, Spec. II 26 p. V 92, 2 pone in evidenza il contrasto tra timore e pietà nell'adempimento del proprio dovere: φόβῳ διδοὺς πλέον ἢ εὐσεβείᾳ.

---

[166] Nell'or. II 24 col. 433 B Gregorio considera Cristo, nella sua vittoria sul demonio, come νικῶν τὸν νικήσαντα. Il medesimo ossimoro, ma stavolta scherzosamente, viene usato per indicare l'assenso di Gregorio ad alcuni amici che gli domandavano un discorso: or. XIX 4 col. 1048 A.

[167] La stessa metafora ricorre anche nell'or. XXVI 5 col. 1233 B.

[168] Per una più sicura comprensione di questo concetto cfr. F. DIRLMEIER, ΘΕΟΦΙΛΙΑ—ΦΙΛΟΘΕΙΑ, in: Philologus, XC (1935), pp. 57—77 e 176—193; M. VIDAL, La Theophilia dans la pensée religieuse des Grecs, in: Recherches de Science Religieuse, XLVII (1959), pp. 161—184.

[169] Isocrate, Evag. 43 p. 197 adopera già un simile binomio: θεοφιλῶς καὶ φιλανθρώπως.

[170] Nell'or. XXXVIII 17 col. 332 B è detto che le virtù sono φιλάνθρωποι καὶ φιλόθεοι.

Cap. XXVIII, col. 896 A:

Gregorio osserva: πᾶς ὁ πλέων ἐγγύς ἐστι τοῦ ναυαγίου, καὶ τόσῳ μᾶλλον, ὅσῳπερ ἂν τολμηρότερον πλέῃ. Per l'allegoria della navigazione orgogliosa che, a causa dell'eccessiva sicurezza, si conclude con un naufragio, cfr. Mutat. 215 p. III 193, 20—194, 1; sulla navigazione prospera (cfr. Gregorio poche righe sotto: ἕως πλεῖς ἐξ οὐρίας) che termina inaspettatamente anch'essa in un naufragio cfr. Ios. 139 p. IV 89, 19—20. Sull'uso traslato di ναυαγέω vedi anche Somn. II 147 p. III 282, 19.

Cap. XXVIII, col. 896 A:

Gregorio cerca di inculcare la comprensione verso i diseredati e sofferenti, rammentando ai ricchi la precarietà della salute fisica: πᾶς ὁ σῶμα περικείμενος ἐγγύς ἐστι τῶν τοῦ σώματος κακῶν. Anche Filone rampogna i ricchi che si dimostrano crudeli verso i poveri, ammonendoli come siano essi pure soggetti alle malattie ed alle disgrazie dei derelitti, in quanto anch'essi rivestono un corpo fragile: Spec. IV 200 p. V 255, 12—13: σῶμα μὲν πάσαις ἁλωτὸν νόσοις περιφέροντες. Appena sotto poi — § 201 p. 255, 18—19 — inserisce la similitudine del navigante il quale, dopo aver lungamente goduto di una favorevole traversata, viene fatto naufragare dalla fortuna quando è ormai quasi giunto nel porto della felicità. Questa stessa similitudine introduce e conclude il richiamo di Gregorio alla instabilità del nostro vigore fisico.

Cap. XXVIII, col. 896 B:

Gregorio, riprendendo uno spunto già prima toccato (cfr. cap. XIX col. 881 AB: οὐκ ἐν τοῖς ἑτέρων κακοῖς τὰ ἡμέτερα εὖ θησόμεθα?) esorta: ἐν ἀλλοτρίαις συμφοραῖς ταῦτα παιδεύθητι[171]. Filone, Mos. I 325 p. IV 197, 16—17 dichiara: ἔδει μὲν ὑμᾶς ταῖς ἑτέρων πληγαῖς πεπαιδεῦσθαι[172].

Cap. XXVIII, col. 896 B:

Gregorio stimola ad aiutare i poveri con contribuzioni materiali commisurate alle proprie possibilità economiche, ma soprattutto insiste perché si porti loro il sostegno della nostra solidarietà spirituale, in quanto la partecipazione alla loro sofferenza ne costituisce il più efficace sollievo. Filone, Virt. 103 p. V 295, 16—296, 2 riferisce che Mosè ordina di amare i forestieri sia per quanto concerne il corpo, mediante gli aiuti possibili, sia per quanto riguarda lo spirito, dividendone dolori e gioie[173].

Cap. XXVIII, col. 896 BC:

Gregorio richiama la prescrizione di Deuter. 22, 1—4 la quale comanda che qualora uno veda il giovenco o la pecora altrui smarriti, non se ne

---

[171] Cfr. Gnomai monost. 651: βλέπων πεπαίδευμ' εἰς τὰ τῶν ἄλλων κακά.

[172] Gregorio or. XVII 5 col. 972 B afferma che sono saggi coloro i quali παιδεύονται ταῖς συμφοραῖς.

[173] Per consonanze classiche su questo tema cfr. Euripide, framm. 119 (Andromeda) NAUCK²; Ps.-Demostene, Epitaph. 35 p. 1400,7.

disinteressi, ma li riconduca al loro proprietario e, similmente, quando uno vedesse l'asino od il giovenco altrui caduti lungo la via non faccia finta di niente, ma aiuti a rialzarli insieme al padrone. Da questo precetto deduce poi l'obbligo tanto più stringente di soccorrere i nostri fratelli[174], se la legge divina ci impone l'obbligo di aiutare perfino gli animali privi di ragione[175]. Filone, Quaest. Ex. II 12 p. 475 A. e VII 288 (MARCUS pp. 46—47) commentando Ex. 23, 5 (Se tu vedessi il giumento del tuo vicino caduto sotto il suo carico, non passerai oltre, ma aiuterai a rimetterlo in piedi) scrive: *humanitatis familiaritatisque nimiam abundantiam hic ostendit, eo quod non tantum hortetur inimicis quoque prodesse, verum etiam gravitatem oneris animalium brutorum sublevare maxime iam cadentium ob depressionem ingentis ponderis. Quis enim quemquam ex hominibus, quorum una est cognatio naturae, praetermittet, edoctus a divina lege ac solitus nec iumenta etiam praeterire?* Gregorio rivolge la medesima domanda in termini equivalenti: πόση γὰρ ὀφείλεται τοῖς ὁμοφύλοις καὶ ὁμοτίμοις ἡ καὶ μέχρι τῶν ἀλόγων ἀπαιτουμένη? Identico concetto in Virt. 139—140 p. V 308, 12—309, 4; ibid. 160 p. 316, 10—13; Spec. I 260 p. V 63, 9—13; ibid. II 89 p. 108, 9—12; ibid. IV 203 p. 256, 17—18. L'idea che il trattamento verso gli animali debba costituire come una specie di prova *in corpore vili* di quello che deve essere praticato con i nostri simili è espressa in Mos. I 62 p. IV 134, 11—13 dove Filone sostiene che può diventare un perfetto re soltanto chi possiede l'arte di guidare il gregge, ἐν ἐλάττοσι ζῴοις παιδευθεὶς τὰ τῶν κρειττόνων· ἀμήχανον γὰρ τὰ μεγάλα πρὸ τῶν μικρῶν τελεσθῆναι; Gregorio stabilisce lo stesso rapporto vedendo nel rispetto verso gli animali un allenamento verso un amore più alto: γυμνάζων ἡμᾶς ἀπὸ τῆς εἰς τὰ μικρὰ φιλανθρωπίας, ἐπὶ τὴν τελειοτέραν καὶ μείζονα[176].

Cap. XXVIII, col. 896 C:

A proposito dei misteri dell'ermeneutica biblica Gregorio dichiara: οὐκ ἐμὸν τοῦτο εἰδέναι ἀλλὰ τοῦ πάντα ἐρευνῶντος καὶ γινώσκοντος Πνεύματος[177]· ὃ δ' οὖν ἐγὼ καταλαμβάνω, καὶ ὅσον εἰς τὸν ἐμὸν ἥκει λόγον ... [178].

---

[174] In Luc. 14,5 abbiamo uno spunto soltanto implicito ed in I Cor. 9,9—10 l'allegoria si volge in altra direzione.

[175] Per un'analoga interpretazione di questa disposizione biblica cfr. or. XXXVIII 14 col. 328 C (XLV 26 col. 660 B).

[176] Una rapida ma interessante indagine che può inquadrare il problema qui trattato è contenuta in M.-L. HENRY, Das Tier im religiösen Bewußtsein des alttestamentlichen Menschen (Sammlung gemeinverständlicher Vorträge und Schriften aus dem Gebiet der Theologie und Religionsgeschichte, nn. 220/221), Tübingen, 1958, pp. 52. Vedi anche U. DIERAUER, Tier und Mensch im Denken der Antike. Ideengeschichtliche Studien zur Tierpsychologie, Anthropologie und Ethik (Studien zur antiken Philosophie, n. 6), Amsterdam, 1977, pp. XVII-320. — Quanto all'idea che il rispetto inculcato dalla Bibbia per gli animali sia un'allusione a quello che essa intende ispirare verso gli uomini cfr. H. A. WOLFSON, The Philosophy of the Church Fathers, Vol. I: Faith, Trinity, Incarnation, 2nd edit., Cambridge, Mass., 1964, pp. 43—72 dove si ha onnipresente Filone.

[177] Questa frase è un adattamento di I Cor. 2,10.

[178] Per una mossa dialettica consimile cfr. or. II 17 col. 425 C; XXVIII 12 col. 40 C. Per una

Per un atteggiamento mentale perfettamente corrispondente cfr. Opif. 72 p. I 24, 18—21 dove scrive: Quando Dio creò l'uomo parlò in plurale (ποιή-σωμεν ...): avrebbe forse bisogno di qualche collaboratore? creò il cielo e la terra da solo, e l'uomo non era capace di metterlo su senza aiuti? ,,La causa in tutta la sua verità è necessario che Iddio solo la conosca, ma quella che, stando ad una congettura probabile, appare persuasiva e ragionevole, non deve essere nascosta ed è questa .... .'' Anche Filone: 1⁰) si trova alle prese con un passo scritturale di difficile interpretazione; — 2⁰) afferma che Dio solo ne conosce il senso autentico; — 3⁰) proclama chiaramente che la sua spiegazione è solo una congettura personale; — 4⁰) esprime il proprio parere. Vedi anche ibid. 61 p. I 20, 6.

Cap. XXIX, col. 896 C:

Gregorio afferma che per i galantuomini περισπουδαστότερος κέρδους ἔλεος. Filone, Legat. 242 p. VI 200, 15 sostiene che presso gli Ebrei οὐχ ὑπὲρ κέρδους ἀλλ' ὑπὲρ εὐσεβείας ἐστὶν ἡ σπουδή: il concetto di σπουδή è in entrambi gli scrittori il perno centrale che raffronta e contrappone il κέρδος ed il culto verso Dio; infatti l'ἔλεος di Gregorio equivale all'εὐσέβεια di Filone, in quanto Gregorio dichiara — cap. V col. 864 BC — che l'ἔλεος è la migliore θεραπεία verso Dio.

Cap. XXIX, col. 896 CD:

Gregorio a proposito dei filosofi pagani dice: οἱ συνηγόρους τοῖς πάθεσι θεοὺς εὑρίσκοντες... Filone, Somn. II 276 p. III 302, 22—24 parlando anch'egli dei filosofi pagani scrive: οἱ μὲν ἐπὶ συνηγορίαν ἡδονῆς καὶ ἐπιθυμίας ... ἐτράποντο[179], contrapponendo il πάθος al λογισμῷ; poco oltre — II 278 p. 303, 8—9 — invece dice del saggio che δυνήσεται τὰς συνηγορούσας τῷ πάθει πιθανότητας ἀνατρέψαι.

Cap. XXIX, col. 897 A:

Gregorio commentando i sacrifici umani di certi popoli dice καὶ μέρος εὐσεβείας αὐτοῖς ἡ ἀπανθρωπία[180]. Anche Filone ne parla in termini ana-loghi: cfr. Spec. I 312 p. V 75, 10—12: μήτε ... ζηλώσωμεν τὰς ἐκείνων ἐν αἷς εὐσεβεῖν δοκοῦσιν ἀσεβείας. Cfr. anche Abr. 181 p. IV 41, 2—3.

Cap. XXX, col. 897 B e C:

Gregorio sostiene che la fortuna del malvagio può essere una condanna di Dio affinché la caduta sia più rovinosa e la punizione più grave e giusta.

---

dichiarazione di incompetenza di fronte au misteri della Sacra Scrittura cfr. poem. II 1,1,378—379 col. 998.

[179] Greg. nell'or. XXVII 6 col. 20 A si domanda: i pagani non prenderanno le nostre dispute teologiche come συνήγορον τῶν οἰκείων θεῶν καὶ παθῶν?

[180] Il germe del concetto c'è anche in Ioann. 16,2 ma in altro contesto e con tutt'altra formulazione.

Cfr. Filone, Spec. I 314 p. V 75, 19—21: „Per molti le fortune momentanee diventano un'insidia in quanto sono un'esca di mali violenti ed incurabili"; cfr. anche Confus. 164 p. II 260, 25—261, 2. Nelle sventure che colpiscono i buoni Gregorio vede un modo per distruggere quel po' di colpevolezza che anche i migliori hanno ed una purificazione come l'oro nella fornace: assai vicino è Filone, Deter. 146 p. I 291, 16—21.

Cap. XXX, col. 900 A:

Gregorio invita a non indugiare sul δυστέκμαρτον della sapienza divina e dichiara che essa è ἀνέφικτος per qualsiasi saggio. Filone, Migr. 195 p. II 306, 22 nota il desiderio di τὸν ... δυστέκμαρτον πατέρα τῶν ὅλων κατανοῆσαι[181] ed in Spec. I 44 p. V 11, 14—15 consiglia: μηδέ σε τῶν ἀνεφίκτων ἔρως αἱρέτω. Sull'incomprensibilità divina cfr. le righe che precedono immediatamente quest'ultima citazione: p. 11, 12—13 e vedi anche ibid. 49 p. 12, 13—14.

Cap. XXXI, col. 900 B:

Gregorio, pur respingendo l'opinione di quanti vedono nelle sofferenze un castigo divino delle colpe, non esclude che ciò effettivamente talvolta possa avvenire, o per frenare il vizio con le sventure dei malvagi[182] o per aprire la strada alla virtù con la felicità dei buoni: ἀρετῆς ὁδοποιουμένης εὐπαθείᾳ τῶν βελτιόνων. L'accostamento di ἀρετή e di εὐπάθεια è abbastanza comune in Filone: cfr. Leg. I 45 p. I 72, 14: ἀρετῇ δὲ ἁρμόττον εἰρήνη καὶ εὐπάθεια; Deter. 120 p. I 285, 19—20; Mutat. 167 p. III 185, 4[183]. In Cher. 12 p. I 173, 1—2 a proposito di Gen. 4, 16, in cui è detto che Caino andò ad abitare a Naid di fronte ad Eden, commenta: „Naid viene interpretato come 'scuotimento' e Eden come 'delizia', τὸ μὲν κακίας κλονούσης ψυχὴν σύμβολον, τὸ δὲ ἀρετῆς εὐπάθειαν αὐτῇ περιποιούσης": da notare anche i due cola paralleli e contrapposti, il primo dominato da κακίας ed il secondo da ἀρετῆς, come in Gregorio.

Per la locuzione εὐπάθεια καὶ ἀρετή cfr. Sacrif. 103 p. I 244, 7 e cfr. anche Execr. 160 p. V 373, 22. Per ἀρετή combinato con εὐπάθεια e contrapposto a κακία vedi Leg. III 22 p. I 118, 12—13; Migr. 219 p. II 312, 12—14; Abr. 204 p. IV 45, 18—19.

In Her. 241 p. III 54, 10—11 Filone dice che i pensieri i quali tendono all'alto appartengono alla classe migliore, poiché la virtù li accompagna: συνοδοιπορούσης ἀρετῆς: qui è la virtù che contribuisce ad aprire la via ai buoni, in Gregorio è la prosperità dei buoni che contribuisce ad aprire la via alla virtù.

---

[181] Cfr. or. XXVIII 21 col. 53 A.

[182] Questa fu già una posizione di Crisippo, cfr. Plutarco, Stoic. repugn. 15 p. 1040 C, in: ARNIM, Stoic. Vet. Fragm. II n. 1175 p. 337, 39—41.

[183] Nell'or. XVII 10 col. 977 B Gregorio insegna: „Dio talora ripaga anche con i beni di quaggiù, perchè crediamo a quelli futuri."

Cap. XXXI, col. 900 B:

Gregorio afferma che nell'altra vita οἱ μὲν τὰ τῆς ἀρετῆς ἆθλα, οἱ δὲ τὰ τῆς κακίας ἐπιτίμια δέξονται. Filone, Praem. 3 p. V 337, 1—2 asserisce: μέτειμι . . . ἐπὶ τὰ προτεθέντα καὶ τοῖς ἀγαθοῖς ἆθλα καὶ τοῖς πονηροῖς ἐπιτίμια. Analoga alternativa con analogo ritmo in Spec. III 62 p. V 167, 11—12.

Cap. XXXI, col. 900 B:

Gregorio dichiara τὸ κάλλος τῇ πρὸς ἄλληλα σχέσει συνιστάμενον. Filone, Quaest. Gen. IV 99 p. 323 A. e VII 126 (MARCUS pp. 382—383) presenta una *pulchritudinem corporis . . . iuxta illam formositatem nominatam, quae ex symmetria partium decoreque formae constat.*

Cap. XXXI, col. 900 C:

Gregorio, parlando di Dio come dell'ordinatore del mondo, dichiara: οὔτε ἐκεῖνος ἄτεχνος ᾖ, ὡς ἡμεῖς, οὔτε ταῦτα διοικεῖται ἀτάκτως, ὅτι μὴ καὶ ἡμῖν ὁ λόγος γνώριμος[184]. Filone, Her. 157 p. III 36, 15—16 afferma che Dio dispone con perfetta esattezza e giustizia tutte le cose ,,e non diminuì la sua abilità di artefice (τὶ τοῦ τεχνικοῦ) a causa della scarsa chiarezza della materia''. In un framm. — p. II 661 M. e p. 81 R. H. — osserva: οὐ πάντα τῷ θνητῷ γένει γνώριμα e a p. II 662 M. aggiunge: ,,Infinite cose, non dico delle più necessarie, ma anche di quelle che sembrano essere più piccole, sfuggono alla mente dell'uomo.''

Cap. XXXII, col. 900 C:

Gregorio afferma che coloro i quali non scorgono l'azione della Provvidenza nel mondo, rassomigliano a coloro che sono colti dal mal di mare e dalle vertigini: οὐ πόρρω τῶν ναυτιώντων ἐσμὲν καὶ ἰλιγγιώντων e poco sotto: ἂν . . . ἰλιγγιάσωσιν. Per Filone, Opif. 71 p. I 24, 7 l'uomo che, passando attraverso a gradi sempre più alti, giunge all'intelligibile, può contemplare gli esemplari e le idee delle cose sensibili che vedeva quaggiù: viene allora pervaso da una specie di ebbrezza astemia[185] ed invasato da un trasporto divino simile a quello dei coribanti; in uno slancio che lo solleva ancora, egli arriva ad essere investito da puri raggi d'una luce concentrata, finché ,,l'occhio dell'intelligenza cade in preda alle vertigini''. In Filone sono le vertigini di chi tocca l'ineffabile, in Gregorio quelle di chi

---

[184] Per passi che toccano questo tema vedi or. XLII 18 col. 480 A; poem. I 1,6,34 col. 432; II 1,42,18—21 col. 1345.

[185] L'idea della sobria ebbrezza era assai radicata nei filoni mistici. Cfr. H. LEWY, Sobria ebrietas. Untersuchungen zur Geschichte der antiken Mystik (Beih. z. Zeitsch. f. d. neutestam. Wiss., n. 9), Gießen, 1929, pp. 175; A. CHASTAGNOL, Autour de la sobre ivresse de Bonosus, in: Bonner Historia-Augusta-Colloquium 1972—74 (Antiquitas, R. 4. Beiträge zur Historia-Augusta-Forschung, n. 12), Bonn, 1976, pp. 91—112 (considera anche in generale Filone ed i Padri).

rifiuta di incominciare il cammino[186]. In Ios. 142 p. IV 90, 16—17 nota che di fronte ai grandi problemi dell'ordinamento dell'universo noi restiamo smarriti; è un complesso di quesiti che ci fa venire le vertigini: σκοτοδινιᾶν ἀναγκάζει καὶ πολὺν ἐμποιεῖ ἴλιγγον. Cfr. anche framm. Dam. Par. 748 p. 73 R. H.[187].

Cap. XXXII, col. 900 D:

Gregorio ironizza su coloro che, non ammettendo la Provvidenza, non riconoscono che Iddio sia più sapiente di loro: οὐ γὰρ ἀνέχονται σοφώτερον αὐτῶν εἶναι τὸν Θεόν e poco oltre — col. 901 A — osserva che negando la ragionevolezza dell'universo perché non ne scorgono la ragione εἰσὶ δι' ἀπαιδευσίαν σοφοὶ ἢ διὰ σοφίαν ... τὴν περιττήν, ἄσοφοι καὶ ἀσύνετοι. Filone, Prov. I 57 p. 27 A. e VIII 30 si chiede ironicamente: *ecquis providentia ipsa sapientior est, ut vituperet quae ab ea fiunt?* ed alcune pagine dopo, sempre a proposito dei negatori della Provvidenza, esclama — ibid. I 71 p. 33 A. e VIII 36 —: *Sed vae huiusmodi hominibus tam audaci praesumptione occupatis! qui tam amenter se ingratos providentiae praebent; quippe qui sibi ipsis immerito sapientes videantur;* e tosto — ibid. I 73 p. 34 A. e VIII 36 — li condanna recisamente: *malus autem homo stulte nimis sibi persuadet non esse providentiam.*

Quanto all'ossimoro ottenuto con la paronomasia di σοφία e di radici equivalenti — proprio in riferimento al tema della Provvidenza — cfr. Prov. I 2 p. 2 A. e VIII 9: *Quomodo ergo is, qui providentia destitutus est, providentiam accusare poterit, quum ipse careat providentia? Fieri enim nequit, ut legitimas accusationes proferat, quum prius eruditus atque intelligentia boni instructus ipse non sit;* e ibid. I 26 p. 13 A. e VIII 18: *ceterum quomodo erit quis providus sine providentia aut sapiens sine sapientia?* ed anche in I 91 p. 43 A. e VIII 44 parla di *sapiens sine sapientia.* Per un analogo atteggiamento stilistico: cfr. Confus. 150 p. II 257, 25—26; framm. p. 49 R. H.

Cap. XXXII, col. 901 A:

Gregorio, dinanzi ai negatori della Provvidenza, propone tre metodi per arrivare alla scoperta di quella verità che essi non riescono a raggiungere: a) καμεῖν περὶ τὸν λόγον ..., ὡς τάχ᾽ ἂν τῇ φιλοπονίᾳ δοθησομένης τῆς ἀληθείας; b) σοφωτέροις ἑαυτῶν ταῦτα συμφιλοσοφεῖν καὶ πνευματικω-

---

[186] L'espressione di Greg. si collega probabilmente con una fonte demostenica. Infatti abbiamo testimonianza che lo scoliaste anonimo alla Retorica di Aristotele III 4 p. 1407 A 5 attribuì a Demostene un frammento che egli cita e nel quale, dopo aver richiamato la situazione dei passeggeri colti dal mal di mare su di una nave agitata dalla tempesta, chiosa: οὕτω καὶ ὁ δῆμος ναυτιᾷ καὶ ἰλιγγιᾷ ἀφορῶν πρὸς τὰ πράγματα: Cfr. Anonymi et Stephani in Artem Rhetoricam commentaria, ed. RABE, Berolini, 1896, p. 179, 9—10.

[187] Per queste metafore cfr. XXXII 29 col. 208 B; XXXVI 7 col. 273 C; poem. I 2, 2, 506 col. 618. Il verbo ἰλιγγιάω è usato anche per indicare la difficoltà nella comprensione di alti problemi metafisici (or. XXVIII 21 col. 53 B e 31 col. 72 AB), per esprimere lo smarrimento dinanzi all'indirizzo da conferire alla propria vita (or. XXVI 9 col. 1240 A) e per rendere il pervertimento di giudizio a cui ci spinge la nostra passionalità (or. XXII 6 col. 1137 B).

τέροις e sottolinea che questa è una via opportuna in quanto la γνῶσις è un χάρισμα, un dono divino, e solo pochi lo posseggono; c) valendosi dell'esplicazione antecedente come di un'introduzione, afferma che bisogna procacciarsela con la purezza della vita e παρὰ τῆς ὄντως Σοφίας σοφίαν ἐπιζητεῖν. Le tre vie sono dunque: a) impegnarsi in un faticoso sforzo di ricerca; b) frequentare maestri qualificati che trasmettano quanto hanno acquisito; c) ottenerla per dono divino, meritandola con la purezza della vita.

Ora è noto che uno dei cardini su cui ruota la concezione filoniana della vita spirituale è quello della triplice distinzione della conoscenza e dell'ἀρετή: a) quella ἀσκητική, personificata in Giacobbe; b) quella διδακτική, rappresentata da Abramo; c) quella αὐτοδίδακτος e αὐτομαθής, simboleggiata in Isacco. Cfr. Mutat. 88 p. III 172, 14—18; ibid. 263 p. 202, 3—5; Somn. I 68 p. III 219, 21—24; Poster. 78 p. II 17, 10—14. In Sobr. 38 p. II 223, 9—11 sostiene che coloro i quali posseggono le virtù cardinali, le hanno acquistate φύσεως μὲν εὐμοιρίᾳ, νομίμοις δ' ὑφηγήσεσι, πόνοις δ' ἀηττήτοις καὶ ἀοκνοτάτοις χρησάμενοι: vediamo nettamente distinti i tre tipi: quello ascetico che richiede i πόνοι[188] invincibili ed instancabili; quello didattico che viene impartito, invece che da uomini, dalle prescrizioni legali; quello innato e naturale indicato dalla φύσεως εὐμοιρίᾳ, sebbene l'espressione lasci piuttosto implicito che si tratta di un dono di Dio. Questo viene invece apertamente dichiarato in Congr. 35—36 p. III 79, 6—16 dove, dopo le solite tre distinzioni, dell'αὐτομαθὲς γένος di cui è figura Isacco, è detto — § 36 p. 79, 15—16 —: θεοῦ γὰρ τὸ αὐτομαθὲς καὶ αὐτοδίδακτον ἄνωθεν ἀπ' οὐρανοῦ καλὸν ὀμβρήσαντος. Per questi tre tipi e per considerazioni al riguardo cfr. anche Abr. 52 p. IV 13, 3—18; Sacrif. 5—7 p. I 204, 5—205, 4.

Per quanto concerne il metodo ἀσκητικός vedi inoltre: Mutat. 84 p. III 171, 25—26: οὗτοι περὶ τὴν ἄσκησιν[189] καμόντες; ibid. 86 p. 172, 3—5: ὁ μὲν γὰρ χρῆται διδασκάλῳ ἑτέρῳ, ὁ δ' ἐξ ἑαυτοῦ ζητεῖ τε καὶ σκέπτεται καὶ πολυπραγμονεῖ, μετὰ σπουδῆς ἐρευνῶν τὰ φύσεως, ἀδιαστάτῳ χρώμενος καὶ συνεχεῖ πόνῳ. Cfr. anche Sacrif. 41 p. I 219, 1—2 ed un framm. conservato in Giovanni Damasceno, Sacra Parall. p. 405 D; II 650 M. e VI 205 Schw. (cfr. p. 69 R.H.).

Per quanto si riferisce al metodo διδακτικός vedi Mutat. 86 p. III 172, 3 testé citato; Prob. 12 p. VI 4, 3—4 dove asserisce che le persone le

---

[188] La necessità della φιλοπονία per conseguire la verità e la visione delle cose divine, nonchè della cultura in genere, è più volte esplicitamente ribadita da Greg.: cfr. or. II 48 col. 457 A; VII 17 col. 776 C; XX 12 col. 1080 C; XXVIII 12 col. 41 A; XXXIV 13 col. 253 A; XXXVII 7 col. 292 A; XLIII 13 col. 512 A; epist. 6,4 Gallay I p. 7; 51,8 ibid. p. 68.

[189] Sul valore e sul significato dell'ascesi in Filone cfr. W. Völker, Fortschritt und Vollendung bei Philo von Alexandrien. Eine Studie zur Geschichte der Frömmigkeit (T.U., n. 49, 1), Leipzig, 1938, pp. 198—239: Die ἄσκησις als Weg zur Vollkommenheit. Vedi anche E. Bréhier, Les idées philosophiques et religieuses de Philon d'Alexandrie (Études de Philos. Médiév., n. 8), 2e éd., Paris, 1925, pp. 272—295.

quali agiscono rettamente devono ἀπαιδευσίαν[190] ἀπώσασθαι, γενόμενοι σοφῶν ἀνδρῶν ὁμιληταί; framm. II 667 M. e p. 70 R.H.; Virt. 215 p. V 332, 6—10; framm. su Ex. XXIII 20 p. 52 R.H. In Sacrif. 7 p. I 204, 14—205, 4 dichiara: ,,Non è piccolo il numero di coloro che hanno imparato ἐξ ἀκοῆς καὶ ὑφηγήσεως . . . coloro poi che hanno rinunciato alle ὑφηγήσεις degli uomini, μαθηταὶ δὲ εὐφυεῖς θεοῦ γεγονότες, τὴν ἄπονον ἐπιστήμην ἀνειληφότες, passano nel genere incorruttibile e perfettissimo ottenendo una sorte migliore di quella dei precedenti e come membro del loro gruppo è stato ammesso Isacco." Questo passo ci introduce nella terza categoria, alla sapienza concessa direttamente da Dio che ne è il supremo possessore e come la personificazione perfetta. Vedi Deter. 30 p. I 265, 2: τὸν τῆς σοφίας ἡγεμόνα θεόν; Sacrif. 64 p. I 228, 13: ἡ πηγὴ τῆς σοφίας ὁ θεός; Fug. 97 p. III 131, 1: (λόγος θεῖος) ὃς σοφίας ἐστὶ πηγή; ibid. 137 p. 139, 4; Poster. 151 p. II 33, 21—22; ibid. 153 p. 34, 5; Her. 19 p. III 5, 15—16[191]; ibid. 127 p. III 30, 5.

Quanto alla purezza di vita necessaria per raggiungere la sapienza cfr. Prob. 3 p. VI 2, 3—4[192].

Cap. XXXII, col. 901 A:

Gregorio sostiene che bisogna καθάρσει βίου ταύτην (scil. γνῶσιν) θηρεύειν[193]. In Somn. I 251 p. III 257, 19—20 troviamo la stessa metafora per un pensiero analogo: ὁ πρὸς τὴν τῶν καλῶν ἐπιτηδευμάτων ὡρμημένος θήραν[194].

Cap. XXXII, col. 901 A:

Gregorio invita παρὰ τῆς ὄντως Σοφίας σοφίαν ἐπιζητεῖν. Per l'espressione in poliptoto del concetto che l'uomo attinge la sua sapienza da quella divina cfr. Leg. II 87 p. I 108, 3—5: οὗτος δὲ ὑπὸ τοῦ θεοῦ ποτίζεται κάλλι-

---

[190] Vocabolo che subito sotto ritornerà due volte in Gregorio.

[191] Qui sono specificati, come in Gregorio, i due possibili insegnanti: Dio e gli uomini saggi.

[192] La necessità della purezza dell'anima per raggiungere la conoscenza di Dio è, nella scia dell'insegnamento evangelico — cfr. Matth. 5,8 — una delle convinzioni basilari di Gregorio il quale ama ribadirla ogniqualvolta se ne presenti l'occasione. Eccone una documentazione essenziale: or. II 39 col. 448 A; XI 4 col. 836 C; XX 12 col. 1080 B; XXIII 11 col. 1161 C; XXVII 3 coll. 13 D—16 A; XXVIII 1 col. 25 C; ibid. 2 col. 28 B; XXIX 11 coll. 88 D—89 A; XXXII 15 col. 192 A; ibid. 16 col. 193 A; XXXIX 8—9 col. 344 A—C; XL 5 col. 364 B; ibid. 45 col. 424 C; XLV 11 col. 637 BC; poem. I 2,10,630 col. 725 e vv. 972—975 col. 750; ibid. 16,36—37 col. 781; II 1,1,631 col. 1017; ibid. 45,196 col. 1376.

[193] Per la formulazione ricorda: Antifonte, Cor. 18 p. 102 Blass²: ἀνάγκη . . . τὴν διάγνωσιν . . . θηρεύειν; Platone, che usa due volte una locuzione vicinissima a quella gregoriana: Polit. p. 264 A: ἣν . . . θηρεύομεν ἐπιστήμην; Theait. p. 198 A: ἣν ἂν βούληται τῶν ἐπιστημῶν θηρεύειν; Aristotele, Anal. poster. 14 p. 79 A 25; Rhet. 21 p. 1395 B 4; Metaph. XX 6 p. 1063 A 14. Per un analogo uso traslato di θηρεύω riferito ad alti valori spirituali, cfr. Euripide, Iphig. Aul. 568. Vedi inoltre Ps.-Demostene, Erot. 21 p. 1407, 16.

[194] Questa metafora così plastica, anche se forse attenuata dalla consuetudine, ricorre anche altrove in Greg.: cfr. or. XXVIII 21 col. 53 A; XLII 13 col. 473 A; poem. I 2,10,291—292 col. 701.

στον ποτὸν σοφίαν ἐκ τῆς πηγῆς, ἣν αὐτὸς ἐξήγαγεν ἀπὸ τῆς ἑαυτοῦ σοφίας. Per un altro poliptoto con σοφία cfr. Migr. 39 p. II 276, 7[195].

Cap. XXXII, col. 901 A:

Gregorio dichiara affetti da ἀπαιδευσία coloro che, negando la Provvidenza, ἀλογίαν τοῦ παντὸς καταψεύδονται. Filone, Opif. 45 p. I 14, 17 afferma che una delle cause per le quali taluni negano la Provvidenza è l'ἀμαθία ὑπερβάλλουσα. Quanto alla forma cfr. ibid. 7 p. 2, 12—14 dove scrive che certuni τοῦ . . . θεοῦ πολλὴν ἀπραξίαν ἀνάγνως κατεψεύσαντο[196].

Cap. XXXII, col. 901 A:

Gregorio riferisce, tra le varie opinioni aberranti sulla Provvidenza, anche i sostenitori del caso: οἱ μὲν τύχην καὶ τὸ αὐτόματον[197] ἐδογμάτισαν, ὄντως αὐτόματα καὶ ὡς ἔτυχεν ἀναπλασθέντα ἐπινοήματα. L'oratore impugna le posizioni degli avversari riprendendo ironicamente le parole di cui essi si servivano. Un identico atteggiamento di pensiero e di stile troviamo in Opif. 171 p. I 60, 4—6: εἰσὶ γὰρ οἱ πλείους ὑπολαμβάνοντες εἶναι κόσμους, οἱ δὲ καὶ ἀπείρους, ἄπειροι καὶ ἀνεπιστήμονες αὐτοὶ . . . ὄντες[198].

Cap. XXXII, col. 901 AB:

Tra i negatori della Provvidenza Gregorio elenca coloro che ,,ammettono un potere irrazionale ed indissolubile delle stelle, le quali intrecciano i nostri destini come vogliono, o meglio, sono costrette ad operare questi intrecci; essi accampano inoltre confluenze e recessioni di pianeti e di stelle

---

[195] Sul concetto di σοφία in chiave religiosa cfr. U. WILCKENS, Weisheit und Torheit. Eine exegetisch-religionsgeschichtliche Untersuchung zu I. Kor. 1 und 2 (Beitr. z. hist. Theol., n. 26), Tübingen, 1959: pp. 97—213: Der religionsgeschichtliche Hintergrund des Sophia-Begriffes (le pp. 139—159 sono dedicate a Filone); B. L. MACK, Logos und Sophia. Untersuchungen zur Weisheitstheologie im hellenistischen Judentum (Studien zur Umwelt des Neuen Testaments, n. 10), Göttingen, 1973, pp. 220 (a Filone è consacrata tutta la seconda parte: pp. 108—184). Dei sette studi raccolti in: Aspects of Wisdom in Judaism and Early Christianity, ed. R. L. WILKEN, University of Notre Dame, Notre Dame—London, 1975, pp. 218, il primo di J. M. ROBINSON tratta di Gesù come σοφός e σοφία ed il quinto di J. LAPORTE esamina Filone nella tradizione della letteratura biblica sapienziale. — Vedi anche F. CHRIST, Jesus Sophia. Die Sophia-Christologie bei den Synoptikern (Abhandlungen zur Theologie des Alten und Neuen Testaments, n. 57), Zürich, 1970, pp. 196; J. MARBÖCK, Weisheit im Wandel. Untersuchungen zur Weisheitstheologie bei Ben Sira (Bonner Biblische Beiträge, n. 37), Bonn, 1971, pp. XXVII-192.

[196] Per καταψεύδομαι in identica accezione cfr. or. V 5 col. 669 B.

[197] Sulla natura e sull'azione della τύχη e dell'αὐτόματον cfr. specialmente Aristotele, Phys. II 4 p. 195 B 31—36; II 5 p. 197 A 32; ibid. 196 B 10—16; Gener. et corrupt. II 6 p. 333 B 6; Cael. I 12 p. 283 A 32; ibid. II 5 p. 287 B 25; Metaph. X 8 p. 1065 B 3. Cfr. anche Menandro, Suppos. (Stobeo, Eclog. I 6,1 WACHSMUTH—HENSE vol. I p. 84; MEINEKE vol. I p. 50; KOCK, Men. 482—483 vol. III p. 139; EDMONDS, Men. 482—483 vol. III B p. 742) che sottopone tutte le cose al dominio della fortuna. Per un ampio panorama di opinioni antiche sul tema περὶ τύχης καὶ τοῦ αὐτομάτου vedi Stobeo, Anthol. I 6 WACHSMUTH—HENSE vol. I pp. 83—90.

[198] Contro i sostenitori del caso cfr. anche or. IV 44 col. 568 BC; V 2 col. 665 C.

fisse". Per la condanna di qualsiasi determinismo astrologico cfr. Opif. 45 p. I 14, 8—17 dove Filone asserisce che Dio non volle che gli uomini attribuissero la causa di tutto ciò che nasce e germina sulla terra alla rivoluzione delle stelle in cielo; e subito dopo — 46 p. 15, 5 — nega che le creature celesti (e pensa chiaramente agli astri) siano αὐτοκρατεῖς. Cfr. anche Migr. 179 p. II 303, 14—16; Abr. 69 p. IV 16, 21—17, 7; Spec. I 13 p. V 3, 18—19; Quaest. Gen. I 100 p. 72 A. e VI 304[199]. L'argomento viene naturalmente affrontato con maggior impegno ed ampiezza in Prov.: per concordanze con Gregorio cfr. i §§ I 77 (p. 36 A. e VIII 38); 79; 81; 82; 84.

Quanto alla δυναστείαν . . . ἄλυτον delle stelle cfr. Prov. I 87 p. 40 A. e VIII 41: *ubi est natalitiorum nomen immutabile?*

Per il binomio πλανητοί — ἀπλανεῖς[200] cfr. Filone, Opif. 31 p. I 10, 1; ibid. 70 p. 23, 16—17; ibid. 113 p. 39, 22—40, 1; ibid. 147 p. 51, 22; Leg. III 99 p. I 135, 5; Plant. 12 p. II 136, 2—3; Abr. 69 p. IV 17, 5; 158 p. 36, 14; Mos. I 212 p. IV 171, 9; Decal. 53 p. IV 281, 2; Spec. I 13 p. V 4, 3; ibid. 34 p. 9, 12; ibid. 210 p. 50, 23; ibid. II 45 p. 97, 14; ibid. 151 p. 122, 14; ibid. 255 p. 148, 13; III 187 p. 202, 13; Praem. 41 p. V 345, 11; Contempl. 5 p. VI 47, 17; Aet. 10 p. VI 76, 7; ibid. 46 p. 87, 2—3.

Per σύνοδος riferita agli astri cfr. Spec. III 188 p. V 202, 16[201].

Cap. XXXII, col. 901 B:

Tra i nemici della Provvidenza Gregorio annovera coloro che sostengono κυρίαν τοῦ παντὸς κίνησιν[202]. Tale teoria è sconfessata anche da Filone, Confus. 98 p. II 247, 21—22: οὐδ' ὁ κόσμος ἅπας ἀφέτῳ καὶ ἀπελευθεριαζούσῃ κινήσει κέχρηται; Poster. 23 p. II 6, 5—6: τὸ μὲν οὖν ἀκλινῶς ἑστὼς ὁ θεός ἐστι, τὸ δὲ κινητὸν ἡ γένεσις; ibid. 29 p. II 7, 20—21; Ebr. 199 p. II 209, 1—2 dove, riferendo le opinioni contrastanti dei filosofi, dice: „Taluni, senza pensare ad un sovrintendente e ad un capo, collegano il mondo ad un moto irrazionale ed automatico."

---

[199] Contro l'astrologia ed il potere delle stelle sulla nostra vita cfr. or. XXV 6 col. 1205 C; XXVIII 14 col. 44 C; poem. I 1,5,15—71 coll. 425—429; ibid. 6,10—23 col. 430—431; I 2,10,190—192 col. 694; II 1,11,1158 col. 1108.

[200] Cfr. epist. 81, 2 GALLAY I p. 104: τῶν ἀστέρων τοὺς ἀπλανεῖς . . . τοὺς πλάνητας.

[201] Per l'opinione di Fil. sul potere delle stelle cfr. A. MEYER, Vorsehungsglaube und Schicksalidee in ihrem Verhältnis bei Philo von Alexandria, Würzburg–Aumühle, 1939, pp. 63—67. — U. TODINI, La cosmologia pitagorica e le muse enniane, in: Rivista di cultura classica e medioevale, XIII (1971), pp. 21—38, osservando che Virgilio, Aen. X, 215—216 deriva da Ennio, sposta il terminus ante quem dell'identificazione degli astri e delle Muse da Filone ad Ennio. — Per una recente storia dell'astrologia puoi consultare W. KNAPPICH, Geschichte der Astrologie, Frankfurt, 1967, pp. XII—369 con illustrazioni.

[202] La speculazione filosofica greca presenta alcune formulazioni alle quali Greg. potrebbe riferirsi: Crisippo — cfr. Galeno, Defin. Med. 95 vol. XIX p. 371 K., in: ARNIM, Stoic. Vet. Fragm. II n. 1133 p. 328, 19—20 — pensava che la φύσις ἐστὶ πῦρ τεχνικὸν . . . ἐξ ἑαυτοῦ ἐνεργητικῶς κινούμενον. Ma già ben prima Anassimandro era d'avviso che all'inizio delle cose ci fosse un'ἀΐδιος κίνησις, cfr. DIELS, Fragm. d. Vorsokrat. I 12 A: 9 lin. 12; 11 lin. 5; 12 lin. 23; 17 lin. 24.

Cap. XXXII, col. 901 B:

Gregorio combatte coloro che πενίαν πολλὴν τῆς Προνοίας κατέγνωσαν. Filone, Opif. 7 p. I 2, 13—14, già citato, deplora coloro che τοῦ ... θεοῦ πολλὴν ἀπραξίαν ἀνάγνως κατεψεύσαντο ed appena oltre — fine § 9 — difende espressamente τὴν πρόνοιαν[203]. Per altri suoi interventi su questa verità cfr. ibid. 10 p. I 3, 7—10; Praem. 23 p. V 340, 21—341, 1; Quaest. Gen. IV 87 p. 312 A. e VII 117[204].

Cap. XXXII, col. 901 B:

Gregorio beffeggia coloro i quali escludono il mondo umano dal raggio di azione della Provvidenza[205], ὥσπερ δεδοικότες μὴ τῷ πλείονας εὐεργετεῖσθαι, ἀγαθώτερον ἀποφήνωσι τὸν εὐεργέτην, ἢ ἀποκάμνοι αὐτοῖς ὁ Θεὸς εὖ ποιῶν πλείονας[206]. Sull'attributo divino della 'beneficenza' Filone ritorna ripetutamente con nettezza e vigore. Vedi Deus 108 p. II 79, 16—17 dove afferma che Dio prodigò infiniti doni all'universo ἀπιδὼν εἰς τὴν ἀίδιον ἀγαθότητα καὶ νομίσας ἐπιβάλλον τῇ μακαρίᾳ καὶ εὐδαίμονι φύσει ἑαυτοῦ τὸ εὐεργετεῖν; Spec. I 169 p. V 41, 14—15; ibid. 209 p. 50, 17; ibid. 221 p. 54, 5; ibid. 272 p. 65, 26; ibid. 300 p. 72, 13; Opif. 23 p. I 7, 3; Poster. 154 p. II 34, 9—10; Plant. 89 p. II 150, 28—151, 3; Mutat. 129 p. III 178, 27—28; framm. Gen. VI 1 p. 18 R. H.[207].

Per quanto concerne la ridicola ipotesi che Dio si stanchi nel governo del mondo, vedi Sacrif. 40 p. I 218, 10—14, dove, come in Gregorio, il concetto di infaticabilità divina[208] è strettamente connesso con quello di

---

[203] In or. XXVII 10 col. 24 C tra le altre posizioni inaccettabili sostenute da filosofi classici Gregorio condanna 'Αριστοτέλους τὴν μικρολόγον Πρόνοιαν.

[204] Sui fondamenti e sulle caratteristiche del concetto di Provvidenza in Filone cfr. A. Meyer, op. cit. pp. 14—42. S. Sowers, On the Reinterpretation of Biblical History in Hellenistic Judaism, in: Oikonomia. Heilsgeschichte als Thema der Theologie. O. Cullmann ... gewidmet, Hamburg, 1967, pp. 18—25 nota che πρόνοια e δίκη sono i due concetti in funzione dei quali particolarmente Giuseppe e Filone interpretano la storia. — Vedi anche C. Parma, Pronoia und Prouidentia. Der Vorsehungsbegriff Plotins und Augustins (Studien zur Problemgeschichte der antiken und mittelalterlichen Philosophie, n. 6), Leiden, 1971, pp. VIII—168.

[205] Al riguardo vedi in Filone, Confus. 121 p. II 252,13—14; framm. p. 70 R.H.

[206] Ricorda, a questo proposito, lo Ps.-Aristotele, De mundo, 6 p. 400 B 5 segg.: ,,Ciò che è il pilota sulla nave, l'auriga sul cocchio, il corifeo nel coro, il legislatore nella città, il generale nell'esercito, la stessa cosa è Dio nel mondo, ma con questa diversità: che per essi il comandare è causa di fatica, di agitazione e di preoccupazioni, mentre per lui è privo di qualsiasi pena, stanchezza e spossatezza fisica; egli, dimorando nell'immobilità, muove e guida tutte le cose dove e come vuole, nelle loro varie forme e nature, proprio come la legge dello stato, pur rimanendo immota nella mente di coloro che la accettano, amministra tutte le attività che concernono il governo."

[207] Su ciò cfr. Greg. or. XXVIII 26 col. 61 C; XXXII 26 col. 204 B; XXXVIII 9 col. 320 C (=XLV 5 col. 629 A); XL 27 col. 397 C. Sulla generosità di Dio e sulla sua azione di benefattore verso gli uomini cfr. H. Neumark, Die Verwendung griechischer und jüdischer Motive in den Gedanken Philons über die Stellung Gottes zu seinen Freunden, Würzburg, 1937, pp. 17—49 e particolarmente 49—62.

[208] Anche qui si può scoprire in entrambi gli scrittori una eco stoica; cfr. Eustazio, In Hom. p. 1389, 55, in: Arnim, Stoic. Vet. Fragm. I n. 549 p. 125, 1 dove si menziona τὴν ἀκάματον καὶ ἀκοπίατον πρόνοιαν e Cicerone, Nat. deor. III 92 ibid. II n. 1107 p. 322, 7—10.

Provvidenza: ὁ μὲν γὰρ τοῦ σύμπαντος ἡγεμὼν οὐρανοῦ τε καὶ κόσμου . . . τὸν τοσοῦτον κόσμον ἄνευ πόνων πάλαι μὲν εἰργάζετο, νυνὶ δὲ καὶ εἰσαεὶ συνέχων οὐδέποτε λήγει — θεῷ γὰρ τὸ ἀκάματον ἁρμοδιώτατον[209].

Cap. XXXIII, col. 901 C:

Gregorio contrappone la realtà effettiva della Provvidenza ai μῦθοι dei negatori. Cfr. Praem. 162 p. V 374, 8—9: τοὺς ἄπλαστον ἀλήθειαν ἀντὶ πεπλασμένων μύθων μεταδιώκοντας[210].

Cap. XXXIII, col. 901 C:

Gregorio invita a respingere le negazioni della Provvidenza εἴπερ τι μέλει τοῦ λόγου λογικοῖς οὖσιν ἡμῖν καὶ λόγου θεραπευταῖς[211]. Anche Filone, Prov. I 2 p. 2 A. e VIII 9 ne mette in rilievo il carattere di razionalità: *Providentia irrationalisne est, an rationalis? Rationalis utique.*

Cap. XXXIII, col. 901 C:

Gregorio invita i suoi ascoltatori a non prestare fede a quanti impugnano la Provvidenza κἂν εὐδρομῶσι τὴν γλῶτταν ἐν τοῖς ἀτόποις λόγοις καὶ δόγμασι. Filone, Prov. I 17 p. 9 A. e VIII 14—15 dice: *Ne ergo quis ab aliis sophistis* (Gregorio poche righe sopra: φάσκοντες εἶναι σοφοί) *illusus aliter sentiat* . . . ed afferma legittima la propria concezione *quamvis artificiosis verbis ab illis undique impediatur.* Ibid. I 69 p. 32 A. e VIII 35 nuova condanna delle parole capziose con le quali gli avversari cercavano di attaccare questo dogma: *commentitia astruens verba atque artificiosa, adversus providentiam vis armari, ut tollas de mundo sapientissimam providentiam.* Sull'impudente loquacità degli empi cfr. Decal. 63 p. IV 283, 3—6; Spec. II 6 p. V 86, 16—87, 2; Mos. II [III] 198 p. IV 246, 13—14; Confus. 34 p. II 236, 4—5[212].

Quanto alla formulazione cfr. Deter. 23 p. I 263, 20—21: τὸν αὐθάδη . . . δρόμον γλώττης ἐπέσχεν. Positivo invece l'εὔτροχον στόμα di Mos. I 84 p. IV 139, 11.

Il binomio λόγοι καὶ δόγματα è abbastanza abituale a Filone: cfr. Opif. 158 p. I 55, 9; Confus. 36 p. II 236, 13; Ios. 86 p. IV 79, 14; Spec. II

---

[209] In poem. I 2, 10, 189 col. 694 Greg. proclama stolti coloro che limitano la Provvidenza μὴ κάμοι σώζων Θεός.

[210] Su μῦθος usato nell'accezione di 'fandonie' ed esplicitamente contrapposto alla verità cfr. Isocrate, Evag. 66 p. 202: εἰ τοὺς μύθους ἀφέντες τὴν ἀλήθειαν σκοποῖμεν.

[211] Sull'uso particolare di λόγος e di λογικός cfr. R. BERNARD, L'image de Dieu d'après Saint Athanase (Théologie, n. 25), Paris, 1952 a p. 42: Le rapprochement λόγος—λογικός est-il un jeu de mots?; C. MONDÉSERT, Vocabulaire de Clément d'Alexandrie: le mot λογικός, in: Recherches de Science Religieuse, XLII (1954), pp. 258—265; G. J. M. BARTELINK, Jeux de mots autour de λόγος, de ses composés et dérivés chez les auteurs chrétiens, in: Mél. Chr. Mohrmann, Utrecht—Anvers, 1963, pp. 23—37.

[212] Sulla mania ciarliera degli eretici cfr. or. XXXVIII 2 col. 313 BC. In or. XVI 2 col. 956 D Gregorio contrappone la sapienza cristiana alla vuota verbosità dei retori: ὅστις γλῶσσαν μὲν εὔστροφον ἔχει.

61 p. V 101, 22; ibid. II 63 p. 102, 7; ibid. III 1 p. 150, 8; ibid. IV 140 p. 240, 17; Prob. 3 p. VI 2, 3²¹³.

Per la locuzione τοῖς ἀτόποις λόγοις cfr. Poster. 87 p. II 19, 3: ἔργοις δὲ ἀτόποις καὶ λόγοις χρῆσθαι.

Cap. XXXIII, col. 901 C:

Gregorio invita a credere Θεὸν εἶναι τὸν πάντων ποιητὴν καὶ δημιουργόν. Filone, Mutat. 29 p. III 162, 1—2 spiega che τὸ „ἐγώ εἰμι θεὸς σὸς" ἴσον ἐστὶ τῷ ἐγώ εἰμι ποιητὴς καὶ δημιουργός. Sul binomio ποιητὴς καὶ δημιουργός riferito a Dio cfr. Aet. 15 p. VI 77, 11. Su Dio δημιουργός di tutte le cose cfr. Leg. III 99 p. I 135, 10—11: ἔστιν ὁ τοῦδε τοῦ παντὸς δημιουργὸς ὁ θεός²¹⁴; Spec. I 20 p. V 5, 9—10: θεὸς ... πάντων δημιουργός; ibid. I 265 p. 64, 15—16; ibid. II 165 p. 126, 9—10.

Cap. XXXIII, col. 901 D:

Gregorio considera la Provvidenza come τὴν τοῦδε τοῦ παντὸς συνεκτικήν τε καὶ συνδετικήν. L'idea che l'azione di Dio sul mondo si manifesti essenzialmente nel „tenerlo unito insieme e concatenato" è fondamentale in Filone. I due concetti sono spesso collegati: cfr. Her. 23 p. III 7, 8—9: (ὁ θεὸς) τῶν ὅλων δεσμός ἐστι συνέχων αὐτὰ ἄλυτα καὶ σφίγγων διαλυτὰ ὄντα ἐξ ἑαυτῶν; ibid. 188 p. 43, 16—17; ibid. 246 p. 56, 1—2; Fug. 112 p. III 133, 26—134, 2; Aet. 36 p. VI 84, 11; ibid. 75 p. 96, 15—16; ibid. 137 p. 114, 16—19; Opif. 131 p. I 45, 11—12; Plant. 9 p. II 135, 4—7; Confus. 166 p. II 261, 11. Per l'idea di Dio συνέχων il mondo cfr. Sacrif. 40 p. I 218, 13—14; Mos. II [III] 133 p. IV 231, 13; ibid. 238 p. 256, 1—3; Abr. 74 p. IV 18, 16—18; Migr. 181 p. II 303, 25; Spec. III 190 p. V 203, 14²¹⁵. I vocaboli συνέχειν e συνεκτικός riferiti all'azione divina nel mondo, sono di tradizione stoica²¹⁶.

Cap. XXXIII, coll. 901 D—904 A:

Gregorio con un ragionamento pieno di evidenza afferma: προνοητὴν εἶναι τούτων, ὧν ποιητὴν εἶναι ἀναγκαῖον. Vedi Filone, Opif. 171 p. I 60,

---

213 Per la coppia λόγοι καὶ δόγματα cfr. epist. 19, 6 GALLAY I p. 27.

214 Nell'or. IV 78 col. 604 B Gregorio considera il Verbo come ὁ τοῦδε τοῦ παντὸς δημιουργός e nella XIX 12 col. 1057 B come ὁ πάντων δημιουργὸς καὶ δεσπότης. — Per un approfondimento teologico recente su questo tema vedi W. BEINERT, Christus und der Kosmos. Perspektiven zu einer Theologie der Schöpfung, Freiburg, 1974, pp. 128.

215 Questi due attributi dell'azione divina sono richiamati anche altrove da Gregorio: cfr. or. II 35 col. 444 A; VI 14 col. 740 C; XXII 14 col. 1148 B; XXVIII 6 col. 32 C; XXXII 8 col. 184 B. Vedi anche or. XVI 5 col. 940 B. — Sull'azione ordinatrice, equilibratrice ed armonizzatrice di Dio sul mondo vedi ANITA FANTONI, L'unità del cosmo nei 'discorsi' di Gregorio Nazianzeno, in: Studia Patavina, XXV (1978), pp. 295—305.

216 Cfr. ARNIM, Stoic. Vet. Fragm. II n. 346 p. 119,45 e 120,2; n. 348 p. 120,42; n. 351 p. 121, 24,25,27,36,38; n. 352 p. 122,4; n. 354 p. 122,19; n. 356 p. 122,37,39,40; n. 439 p. 144,24, 25,26,27,28; n. 440 p. 144,31,35,36 e p. 145,2,3,4,5,12; n. 441 p. 145,16,21; n. 447 p. 147, 28,29; n. 448 p. 147,34—36; n. 449 p. 147,40,41; n. 716 p. 205,20—21; n. 1132 p. 328, 14,16. Per l'unione delle due radici vedi ibid. n. 441 p. 145,25 e p. 145,32—34.

6—8: προνοεῖ τοῦ κόσμου ὁ θεός· ἐπιμελεῖσθαι γὰρ ἀεὶ τὸ πεποιηκὸς τοῦ γενομένου ... ἀναγκαῖον e cfr. § 172 p. 60, 13; Spec. I 209 p. V 50, 16—17: ὁ γὰρ θεὸς ἀγαθός τέ ἐστι καὶ ποιητὴς καὶ γεννητὴς τῶν ὅλων καὶ προνοητικὸς ὢν ἐγέννησε; ibid. III 189 p. 203, 10—12: ὁ γεννήσας πατὴρ (ed intende Dio) νόμῳ φύσεως ἐπιμελεῖται τοῦ γενομένου, προνοούμενος καὶ τοῦ ὅλου καὶ τῶν μερῶν; Prov. I 26 p. 13 A. e VIII 18: *oportet ut creator provide curam habeat rerum ab ipso creatarum*; ibid. II 49 p. 80 A. e VIII 70; Virt. 216 p. V 332, 12—13[217].

Cap. XXXIII, col. 904 A:

Gregorio, dopo aver dichiarato che la creazione del mondo ne implica la provvidenza, continua: εἰ μὴ μέλλοι τὸ πᾶν τῷ αὐτομάτῳ φερόμενον, ὥσπερ ὑπὸ λαίλαπος ναῦς, αὐτίκα λυθήσεσθαί τε καὶ διασπασθήσεσθαι διὰ τὴν ἀταξίαν τῆς ὕλης, καὶ πρὸς τὴν ἀρχαίαν σύγχυσίν τε καὶ ἀκοσμίαν ἐπαναχθήσεσθαι. Anche Filone contrappone più volte l'idea del 'caso' a quella di una 'guida' che regga il mondo: cfr. Praem. 42 p. V 345, 14—17[218]; Leg. III 30 p. I 119, 26—28; framm. p. II 666 M. e p. 23 R.H.; p. II 669 M. e p. 70 R.H.

Gregorio, dicendo che l'universo in balia del caso è come una nave in balia della tempesta, sottintende abbastanza esplicitamente la metafora di Dio come timoniere e pilota del mondo. Anche quest' immagine è abituale a Filone: cfr. Somn. I 157 p. III 238, 12—13; II 283 p. 304, 3; Virt. 36 p. I 179, 3—4; Confus. 98 p. II 247, 22—23; Her. 228 p. III 51, 23; ibid. 301 p. 68, 20; Aet. 83 p. VI 98, 19; Ps.-Filone, De Iona 35 p. 599 A. e VII 396[219]. Tale traslato è più volte usato proprio in connessione con l'affermazione della Provvidenza divina: cfr. Opif. 46 p. I 15, 5; Confus. 114—115 p. II 250, 28—251, 1; Prov. I 72 p. 34 A. e VIII 36; ibid. I 75 p. 35 A. e VIII 37.

Gregorio collega la mancanza di un pilota con il disastro della nave e dell'universo. Lo stesso pensiero è presente in Filone sia nella forma positiva, che Dio è la salvezza del mondo, sia in quella negativa, che la sua assenza ne causerebbe lo sfacelo: cfr. 1°) Abr. 70 p. IV 17, 12—13 dove dice che Abramo vide τοῦ κόσμου τινὰ ... κυβερνήτην ἐφεστῶτα καὶ σωτηρίως εὐθύνοντα τὸ οἰκεῖον ἔργον; Quaest. Gen. IV 88 p. 314 A. e VII 118 (MARCUS p. 368); Ebr. 199 p. II 209, 1—5; — 2°) Deter. 141 p. I 290, 15—16; Poster. 145 p. II 32, 16—18.

Gregorio dichiara che senza la Provvidenza l'universo διασπασθήσεσθαι διὰ τὴν ἀταξίαν τῆς ὕλης, καὶ πρὸς τὴν ἀρχαίαν σύγχυσίν τε καὶ ἀκοσμίαν ἐπαναχθήσεσθαι. Anche Filone insiste ripetutamente sull'opera divina che condusse la materia dal disordine originario all'ordine successivo: cfr. Plant. 3 p. II 133, 12—13: ,,L'ordinatore del mondo τὴν οὐσίαν ἄτακτον

---

[217] Cfr. poem. I 1,6,16 col. 431: ,,Se si toglie la Provvidenza si toglie anche Dio."
[218] Cfr. or. V 24 col. 693 B; XXVIII 16 col. 48 B.
[219] Per il traslato che interpreta Dio come timoniere dell'universo cfr. or. XXVIII 16 col. 45 D; poem. I 1,5,11—14 col. 425; II 1,78,10 col. 1425; II 2,7,302 col. 1574.

καὶ συγκεχυμένην οὖσαν ἐξ αὐτῆς εἰς τάξιν ἐξ ἀταξίας καὶ ἐκ συγχύσεως εἰς διάκρισιν ἄγων cominciò a darle una forma"; Somn. I 241 p. III 256, 9—10: Dio stabilì la natura delle cose τὴν ἀταξίαν καὶ ἀκοσμίαν εἰς κόσμον καὶ τάξιν ἀγαγών[220]; Spec. IV 187 p. V 252, 4—5; Aet. 106 p. VI 105, 13—15; Prov. I 7 p. 5 A. e VIII 11; Opif. 22 p. I 6, 18—7, 2; ibid. 28 p. 8, 17—9, 3[221].

Per l'ἀταξία τῆς ὕλης cfr. Spec. I 329 p. V 79, 19—20. Per altre combinazioni di ἀταξία e di σύγχυσις cfr. Praem. 76 p. V 353, 8—9; Legat. 94 p. VI 173, 3—4; per la coppia σύγχυσις καὶ ἀκοσμία cfr. Confus. 109 p. II 250, 4—5. Sull'ipotesi di un ritorno dell'universo alla caotica confusione primigenia cfr. Prov. I 35 pp. 16—17 A. e VIII 21. Per un movimento stilistico che richiami da vicino quello di Gregorio cfr. Spec. I 328 p. V 79, 13—14.

Cap. XXXIII, col. 904 A.:

Gregorio afferma che dobbiamo credere nella Provvidenza κἂν διὰ τῶν ἐναντίων ὁ βίος ἡμῖν διεξάγηται. Filone, Opif. 73 p. I 25, 5—6 presenta l'uomo come colui il quale ἐπιδέχεται τἀναντία. Cfr. Her. 311 p. III 70, 25; Mos. I 117 p. IV 147, 8—9[222].

Cap. XXXIII, col. 904 A.:

Gregorio afferma che gli aspetti misteriosi del dogma della Provvidenza sono opportuni in quanto noi tendiamo a disprezzare facilmente τὸ ῥᾳδίως ληπτόν[223], mentre ammiriamo tanto più ciò che è sopra di noi quanto più si dimostra irraggiungibile: καὶ γυμνάζει τὸν πόθον ἅπαν τὸ διαφεῦγον τὴν ἔφεσιν. La stessa notazione psicologica è rilevata in Filone il quale in Spec. I 45 p. V 11, 20—21 esprime la brama di conoscere le forze che servono Dio, ὧν διαφεύγουσα ἡ κατάληψις . . . ἐνεργάζεταί μοι πόθον τῆς διαγνώσεως[224].

Per πόθος riferito alla conoscenza di Dio cfr. Spec. I 50 p. V 12, 20 e Virt. 215 p. V 332, 6[225].

Cap. XXXIV, col. 904 B:

Gregorio invita a non attaccarsi troppo alle ricchezze passeggere (τῇ ῥοῇ) consumando insieme ad esse una parte dell'anima: τῆς ψυχῆς τι ταύτῃ προσαναλίσκοντες. Filone, Spec. IV 83 p. V 228, 13—15 scrive: ,,La

---

[220] L'ἀταξία nell'assenza divina è affermata in or. XXIX 2 col. 76 A. Per il binomio ἀταξία—σύγχυσις cfr. or. XXV 7 col. 1208 B e per quello ἀταξία—ἀκοσμία cfr. or. XLIII 26 col. 532 B e XLIV 3 col. 609 C. Ricorda il magnifico inno all'ordine in or. XXXII 8—9 coll. 181 C—184 B.

[221] Cfr. or. XVI 5 col. 940 B.

[222] Nell'or. IV 8 col. 540 A Greg. parla della Provvidenza ἐκ τῶν ἐναντίων πολλάκις τὰ βελτίω διοικουμένης, cfr. anche ibid. 12 col. 541 D; XXIV 13 col. 1184 C; epist. 34, 4 GALLAY I p. 45; poem. I 2, 8, 197—198 col. 663.

[223] Cfr. or. III 2 col. 520 A: οὕτως εὐκαταφρόνητον ἅπαν τὸ ῥᾳδίως νικώμενον e vedi anche or. IV 114 col. 652 B; XXVI 2 col. 1229 B; XXVIII 12 col. 40 D; XXXII 15 col. 192 A; XXXIX 10 col. 345 A; XL 13 col. 376 A; poem. II 2, 7, 142 col. 1562.

[224] Cfr. or. II 76 col. 484 B.

[225] Cfr. or. XXIV 17 col. 1189 C; XXXVIII 7 col. 317 C (=XLV 3 col. 628 A).

cupidigia, occupando tutta l'anima . . . la infiamma e la brucia, fino a quando l'abbia completamente divorata e consunta (ἐξαναλώσῃ)[226]."

Cap. XXXV, col. 905 A:

Gregorio fa notare che gli autori biblici, ispirati da Dio, non hanno parlato saltuariamente dell'obbligo di aiutare i bisognosi, ma ne hanno trattato tutti e con il massimo zelo, τοῦτο διακελευόμενοι, καὶ ποτὲ μὲν προτρέποντες, ποτὲ δὲ ἀπειλοῦντες, ποτὲ δὲ ὀνειδίζοντες· ἔστι δὲ ὅτε καὶ τοὺς κατορθοῦντας ἀποδεχόμενοι. Filone, Spec. IV 72 p. V 225, 16—19 dice di Mosè: ,,Egli ha pressochè riempito tutta la sua legislazione di precetti che spingono alla compassione ed all'amore vicendevole, ha lanciato gravi minacce contro i superbi e gli arroganti ed ha promesso grandi premi a quelli che cercano di portare un rimedio alle sventure del prossimo."

Cap. XXXVII, col. 908 A:

Gregorio invita: καθαρθῶμεν . . . ῥύψωμεν . . . τὰ τῶν ψυχῶν ῥύπη τε καὶ μολύσματα. Filone, Decal. 10 p. IV 270, 24—271, 2 dichiara parimenti: τὴν ψυχὴν ἀναγκαῖόν ἐστιν ἀπορρύψασθαι καὶ ἐκκαθήρασθαι τὰς δυσεκπλύτους κηλῖδας.

Cap. XXXVII, col. 908 AB:

Gregorio, parlando di malattie fisiche che trasferisce metaforicamente sul piano morale, osserva che queste μικρῶς μὲν ὁ νόμος ἐκάθηρεν, δεῖται δὲ Χριστοῦ θεραπεύοντος; ritorna poi sulla stessa immagine un po' più sotto quando considera la situazione di chi è così disperato ὡς μηδὲ τὴν θεραπείαν ἐπιζητεῖν ed esorta invece chi ha ancora speranze di ripresa: πρόσελθε τῷ θεραπευτῇ[227]. Per quanto concerne la legge è più che naturale uno spostamento di valutazione, se si tien conto della diversa posizione religiosa: cfr. comunque Deus 67 p. II 71, 16—17 dove Filone considera il legislatore biblico come τῶν τῆς ψυχῆς παθῶν καὶ νοσημάτων ἄριστος ἰατρός.

Sulla concezione di Dio come medico delle malattie spirituali[228] vedi Spec. II 17 p. V 89, 15—16; Leg. III 215 p. I 161, 9—11; Quaest. Gen. II

---

[226] Ricorda il famoso aforisma di Eraclito — 'Raccolta dei frammenti e traduzione italiana' di R. WALZER, Hildesheim, 1964, p. 120 n. 85 —: ,,Ardua cosa è combattere con la brama; ciò che vuole essa compra a prezzo dell'anima (θυμῷ μάχεσθαι χαλεπόν· ὃ γὰρ ἂν θέλῃ, ψυχῆς ὠνεῖται).

[227] Alla mente di Gregorio sono qui, con ogni probabilità, presenti gli spunti evangelici nei quali Cristo viene chiamato medico (cfr. Matth. 9,12; Marc. 2,17; Luc. 5,31) e viene ricordato nella sua attività di risanatore (cfr. Matth. 4,23 e 24; 8, 7 e 16; 9,27—33 e 35; 10,1 e 8; 11,5; 12,10—14,15,22; 14,14; 15,30; 17,18; 19,2; 20,30—34; 21,14; Marc. 1,34; 3,1—5, 10,15 ecc.).

[228] Per uno studio di ambito limitato ma utile su questo tema cfr. P. C. J. EIJKENBOOM, Het Christus-Medicusmotief in de preken van Sint Augustinus, Assen, 1960, pp. XXIII-237. Per testi dispersi e poco noti di apologisti, teologi, atti apocrifi su questo argomento, che nei Padri fu ampiamente insistito vedi G. DUMEIGE, Le Christ médecin dans la littérature chrétienne des premiers siècles, in: Rivista di archeologia cristiana, XLVIII (1972), pp. 115—141.

29 p. 110 A. e VI 330 (Marcus p. 108); ibid. III 51 p. 226 A. e VII 49[229];
Ps.-Filone, Orat. in Sampson 7 p. 553 A. e VII 354; De Iona 2 p. 579 A. e
VII 377. In Leg. III 177 p. I 152, 13—14 quest'azione risanatrice è attri-
buita al Logos e in Spec. II 31 p. V 93, 7 alla retta ragione.

Cap. XXXVII, col. 908 B:

Gregorio esorta chi ha delle colpe ad esercitare la carità verso il
prossimo sofferente, a sanare τὰ τραύματα διὰ τῶν τραυμάτων, κτῆσαι τῷ
ὁμοίῳ τὸ ὅμοιον. Filone in un frammento — p. II 672 M. e p. 104 R.H. —
afferma che Dio ci tratterà come noi avremo trattato il nostro prossimo, e
continua: προενέγκωμεν οὖν τοῦ ἐλέου τὸν ἔλεον, ἵνα τῷ ὁμοίῳ τὸ ὅμοιον
ἀντιλάβωμεν[230]: ad una piena concordanza concettuale si aggiunge una
notevolissima coincidenza espressiva. Per il medesimo poliptoto, ma in
senso diverso, cfr. un framm. in Eusebio, Praepar. Evang. VIII 14 GCS
Mras I 465, 17—18: τὸ γὰρ ὅμοιον χαίρει τῷ ὁμοίῳ[231]. Per un poliptoto
simile tra aggettivi sostantivati cfr. Her. 56 p. III 14, 3.

Cap. XXXVIII, col. 909 A:

Gregorio invita ad evitare nell'esercizio della beneficenza la δοκιμασία
e l'ἀμφιβολία cioè gl'inquieti esami e le dubbiosità sull'opportunità di un'elar-
gizione. Filone, Spec. II 84 p. V 107, 4—5, dopo aver consigliato un'opera
di generosità verso un derelitto, aggiunge: ,,E non essere dubbioso ... ma
concedi gioiosamente il tuo favore[232]."
Filone, Mos. II [III] 240 p. IV 256, 12—18, a commento della preghiera
delle figlie di Salpaad, a cui il Signore annuì, si sfoga in un'invettiva che è
tramata su motivi i quali ritorneranno pressochè tutti nell'orazione di
Gregorio. Dice infatti: ,,Venite dunque avanti ... voi che vi inorgoglite
della vostra fortuna (e Gregorio cita: ,,Non si glorii ... il ricco nella sua
ricchezza": cap. XX col. 881 C ed invita a non considerare come felicità la
sazietà di un cibo e di una bevanda corruttibili, cap. XXI col. 885 A. Per

---

[229] La denominazione metaforica di 'medico' viene da Gregorio attribuita sia a Dio — cfr.
or. VIII 18 col. 809 BC; XVIII 28 col. 1020 A — sia a Cristo — cfr. or. XX 4 col. 1069 A;
poem. I 1,2,61 col. 406; ibid. 9,37—39 col. 459; I 2,1,142—144 col. 533 (identico al prec.);
ibid. 15,109 col. 774. In poem. II 1,15,38 col. 1253 e ibid. 34, 205 col. 1322 Cristo è considerato come 'rimedio dei mortali' ed in II 1,89,5—6 col. 1443 come colui che conferisce
l'efficacia ai medicamenti.

[230] Sul piano gnoseologico-religioso cfr. F. N. Klein, Die Lichtterminologie bei Philon von
Alexandrien und in den hermetischen Schriften, Leiden, 1962, p. 213: Das Grund-
schema religiöser Erkenntnis und Heilsgewinnung: der ὅμοιον ὁμοίῳ—Gedanke. Per
un inquadramento generale vedi S. Maracchia, I contrari nell'antichità classica, in:
Cultura e scuola, n° 48 (1973), pp. 206—218.

[231] Per questo poliptoto in Gregorio cfr. XXXVIII 13 col. 325 B (= XVL 9 col. 633 CD);
epist. 101 col. 188 B e Gallay-Jourjon, Sources chrétiennes, n. 208, § 51 p. 58; 100
Gallay II p. 6. Per quello opposto (τῷ ἐναντίῳ τὸ ἐναντίον) cfr. or. VI 8 col. 732 B; XL
24 col. 392 B.

[232] Nell'or. XVIII 20 coll. 1008 C—1009 A Greg. enuclea i motivi che qui sono accennati,
ma che, per eccessiva concentrazione, sono anche diventati oscuri. Sullo sfondo è
presente Is. 58, 8—9.

il termine εὐπραγία cfr. Gregorio cap. XIX col. 881 B), voi che camminate con il capo più eretto di quanto abbia stabilito la natura (cfr. Gregorio cap. XXVIII col. 896 B, dove ritrae Dio in atto di alzare minacciosamente la mano κατὰ τῶν ὑψαυχενούντων καὶ παρατρεχόντων τοὺς πένητας), che aggrottate le sopracciglia (cfr. Gregorio cap. XXV col. 892 A che irride quanti αἴρουσι τὴν ὀφρύν), che deridete la vedovanza delle donne e che schernite quella lacrimevole sventura, ancora più lacrimevole della precedente, costituita dall'abbandono dei bambini orfani (cfr. Gregorio cap. VI col. 864 C che invita a soccorrere quanti hanno bisogno, soprattutto εἴτε διὰ χηρείαν ... εἴτε δι' ὀρφανίαν); badate che coloro i quali sembrano così miseri e così disgraziati non sono considerati da Dio come esseri spregevoli ed ignoti." Quest'ultimo pensiero è poi un po' come l'anima della concezione gregoriana dei poveri: egli rappresenta due volte (cap. XXVIII col. 896 B e XXXV col. 905 A) Iddio con la mano minacciosamente levata contro gli oppressori dei poveri; dichiara i miseri partecipi di tutti i carismi soprannaturali, redenti dalla morte di Cristo, coeredi della vita celeste, consepolti con Cristo per essere conglorificati con lui (cap. XIV col. 876 A e B); ritrae intenzionalmente Cristo mentre raccoglie la pecorella smarrita e spossata, che considera come emblema dei poveri (cap. XV col. 876 C); asserisce che dare ai poveri è un dare a Cristo e a Dio (cap. XVIII col. 880 D—881 A e XXXVI col. 905 C), che Dio ci offre i suoi doni per invitarci all'amorevolezza verso i bisognosi (cap. XIX col. 881 BC); proclama che Dio si irrita e punisce coloro che si abbandonano al lusso, ignorando le sofferenze dei derelitti (cap. XXIV col. 889 B), che le distinzioni sociali non furono introdotte da Dio, ma che si insinuarono in seguito all'umana malvagità (cap. XXV col. 892 A) e sferza duramente chi sostiene il contrario (capp. XXIX col. 897 AB, XXX col. 897 BC, XXXVI col. 905 BC); rileva che gli scrittori biblici, guidati dallo Spirito Santo, insistettero tutti e sempre sulla carità verso i sofferenti (cap. XXXV coll. 904 C—905 A); definisce i tribolati come membra di Cristo (cap. XXXVII col. 908 A); rammenta la dannazione da lui pronunciata contro coloro che non soccorrono alle necessità degli indigenti (cap. XXXIX col. 909 B); finalmente identifica i poveri con Cristo (cap. XL col. 909 B).

In Decal. 41 p. IV 277, 18—278, 8 Filone scrive: „Se l'increato ... colui che non ha bisogno di nulla, il creatore dell'universo, il benefattore (εὐεργέτης), il re dei re, il sommo Iddio non sopportò di trascurare neppure il più meschino, ma credette giusto di invitare anche costui al banchetto λογίων καὶ θεσμῶν ἱερῶν ... come potrebbe addirsi a me che sono mortale di ὑψαυχενεῖν καὶ πεφυσῆσθαι mostrandomi insolente πρὸς τοὺς ὁμοίους, οἳ τύχαις μὲν ἀνίσοις ἴσῃ δὲ καὶ ὁμοίᾳ συγγενείᾳ κέχρηνται μίαν ἐπιγραψάμενοι μητέρα τὴν κοινὴν ἁπάντων ἀνθρώπων φύσιν? In questo passo è facile scorgere un intreccio di concomitanze tra i due scrittori; infatti anche Gregorio: 1⁰) sottolinea come sia attributo essenziale di Dio quello di essere εὐεργέτης (cap. XXXII col. 901 B); — 2⁰) afferma che anche i derelitti sono stati chiamati, come noi, a parte νόμων, λογίων ... concessi da Dio per la salvezza spirituale degli uomini (cap. XIV col. 876 AB); — 3⁰) contrappone la condotta di Dio alla nostra, in quanto egli fornì loro tanti beni naturali e soprannaturali (cap. XIV col. 876 A e B) mentre noi li disprezziamo (cap. XV col. 876 C e XXIII col. 888 C); — 4º) usa il plastico verbo ὑψαυ-χενεῖν (cap. XXVIII col. 896 B); — 5º) adopera il verbo φυσᾶν (cap. XX col. 881 D); — 6º) al cap. XXXVI col. 905 C dichiara che, tanto ricchi che poveri, siamo tutti creature di Dio, anche se τὰ ἔξωθεν ἄνισα; — 7º) sulla συγγένεια che stringe tutti gli uomini ama frequentemente ritornare: cfr. capp. V col. 864 B; X col. 869 B; XXIII col. 888 B; ibid. col. 888 C; XXV col. 892 A; XXVI col. 892 B; — 8º) inoltre afferma che tutti abbiamo la stessa natura umana (cap. XIV col. 876 A), fa appello alla comune natura (capp. XV col. 876 C; XVIII col. 880 C; XXVI col. 892 B), irride a chi si crede per natura superiore ai più poveri (cap. XXIII col. 888 C) e proclama τὸ τῆς φύσεως ὁμότιμον (cap. XXV col. 889 C e cfr. anche cap. XXVI col. 892 B).

III. Filone e Gregorio: concomitanze lessicali

Finora abbiamo segnalato delle concomitanze che investono particolari aspetti del mondo teologico, filosofico, morale, psicologico e che attestano identità, o almeno somiglianze, di pensiero; esistono però anche altri raffronti di carattere essenzialmente lessicale e stilistico che si riferiscono al momento della formulazione del pensiero; non hanno quindi il valore indicativo dei primi, ma recano pure un loro contributo alla valutazione, in quanto testimoniano di propensioni del gusto e di abitudini mentali. Si incontrano infatti talora atteggiamenti retorici, schemi di frase, abbozzi d'immagini, *iuncturae*, composizioni verbali, delimitazioni o rinvigorimenti semantici di vocaboli i quali paiono sottrarsi al dominio dell'ovvio per denotare una scelta dello scrittore. Non sembra pertanto opportuno tralasciare questi elementi, anche se la loro efficacia dimostrativa va vista più nella loro frequenza e nella loro quantità globale che non in ogni singola presenza: ognuna in se stessa infatti si può spiegare come un incontro fortuito o come l'effetto di un influsso di chissà quale provenienza, mentre non è più facilmente postulabile l'azione del caso o di influenze disparate quando si riscontrano una medesima atmosfera linguistica ed un'identica tendenza a determinate soluzioni espressive. Meritano pertanto di essere segnalati i seguenti casi:

Cap. I, col. 857:

Gregorio chiama i suoi ascoltatori συμπένητες: egli ama i composti con σύν che indicano identità di stato o di funzione; tra gli altri vedi συλλειτουργός in epist. 183, 9 GALLAY II p. 74. Cfr. Filone, Spec. I 96 p. V 24, 5—6 dove, parlando del sommo sacerdote, dice ταῖς ἱερουργίαις συλλει-τουργῇ πᾶς ὁ κόσμος αὐτῷ[233].

---

[233] Tale tipo di composti non si riscontra nè nel NT nè nell'AT.

Cap. I, col. 860 A:

Gregorio afferma che non è facile τῶν ἀρετῶν τὴν νικῶσαν εὑρεῖν[234]. Filone, Spec. I 250 p. V 60, 24 ha νικώσης εὐσεβείας.

Cap. I, col. 860 A:

Gregorio parla di δοῦναι τὰ πρεσβεῖα. Cfr. Filone, Poster. 63 p. II 14, 9—10; Mos. I 242 p. IV 178, 12—13. Non è possibile stabilire un collegamento con Daniele — Teodozione, Sus. 50[235].

Cap. I, col. 860 A:

vedi (τῇ ἀρετῇ) δοῦναι . . . τὰ νικητήρια e Filone, Leg. III 74 p. I 129, 4—5; Spec. I 9 p. V 3, 2.

Capp. II—IV, coll. 860 B—864 A:

Gregorio imposta una lunga anafora su καλόν: le varie virtù ci sfilano dinanzi presentate da questa valutazione che le scandisce. Anche Filone usa ripetere καλόν in inizio di frase con un'intonazione analoga: cfr. Cher. 13 p. I 173, 5 (cfr. anche 9 p. 172, 7—8); Congr. 7 p. III 73, 17; Spec. I 55 p. V 13, 21; ibid. II 72 p. V 104, 12; Prob. 62 p. VI 18, 11[236].

Cap. II, col. 860 B e C:

Gregorio fa seguire alla sua affermazione dell'eccellenza di una virtù la documentazione oggettiva, basata sulla testimonianza di una grande figura: καὶ μάρτυς . . . Anche in Filone il termine μάρτυς (o μάρτυρες) a conferma di un'asserzione è frequente e può essere seguito: a) da un nome proprio di persona: cfr. Deter. 50 p. I 270, 2; ibid. 138 p. 289, 12—13; Migr. 3 p. II 269, 3; Her. 120 p. III 28, 11—12; — b) dal nome di Dio: cfr. Ebr. 139 p. II 197, 5; Ios. 265 p. IV 117, 16; Mos. II [III] 284 p. IV 267, 7; — c) da un nome comune che designa persone: cfr. Opif. 88 p. I 30, 19; Sacrif. 17 p. I 208, 4; Deter. 34 p. I 265, 23—24; ibid. 99 p. 280, 25; Poster. 57 p. II 13, 1; Abr. 64 p. IV 15, 15; Ios. 134 p. IV 88, 22; Spec. I 37 p. V 9, 22; Prob. 72 p. VI 21, 9; ibid. 92 p. 26, 10; ibid. 98 p. 28, 10—11; — d) da un nome comune che richiama indirettamente la persona umana: cfr. Abr. 29 p. IV 7, 19; — e) da un nome proprio geografico: Prob. 73 p. VI 21, 9; — f) da un nome di cosa: cfr. Cher. 108 p. I 196, 3; Poster. 121 p. II 26, 25; Confus. 157 p. II 259, 4; Fug. 13 p. III 112, 16; ibid. 184 p. 150, 10 e 11—12; Somn. II 220 p. III 294, 3; ibid. II 297 p. 306, 1; Mos. II [III] 120 p. IV 228, 4; Aet. 120 p. VI 109, 3.

---

[234] Cfr. or. XXI 10 col. 1092 C.

[235] Cfr. Platone, Gorg. p. 524 A dove però si allude essenzialmente al conferimento di un incarico.

[236] Per un' anafora dello stesso genere con καλόν cfr. or. XL 39 coll. 413 C e 416 A, seguita come qui al § 10 dalla ripresa con πείθω: cap. 39 col. 416 B: πείθει με τοῦτο Δαβίδ.

Cap. II, col. 861 A:

Gregorio per sottolineare la mitezza di Cristo lo ricorda durante la passione οὐδὲ . . . φωνὴν προϊέμενος. È evidente l'allusione ad Isaia 42, 2 e 53, 7, però in nessuno di questi luoghi ricorre l'espressione usata da Gregorio. La locuzione φωνὴν προίημι è invece abbastanza familiare a Filone: cfr. Opif. 160 p. I 56, 2; ibid. 163 p. 56, 21; Mutat. 242 p. III 198, 20; Decal. 32 p. IV 275, 22—276, 1. Nei LXX si trova solo in Prov. 8, 4.

Cap. V, col. 864 B:

Gregorio considera la carità come κεφάλαιον νόμου καὶ προφητῶν. L'espressione κεφάλαιον νόμου, sconosciuta sia nell'AT che nel NT, ricorre in Decal. 154 p. IV 303, 9; ibid. 175 p. 306, 26—307, 1; cfr. anche Deus 53 p. II 68, 15—16; Spec. II 1 p. V 85, 5—6; ibid. II 242 p. 145, 26; ibid. IV 41 p. 218, 13; Praem. 2 p. V 336, 12; Congr. 120 p. III 96, 18. Per l'accostamento di κεφάλαιον a νόμος ed a προφήτης vedi Decal. 19 p. IV 272, 20—21.

Cap. VII, col. 865 B:

Gregorio vede nella carne un pericolo μὴ ἀπὸ Θεοῦ πέσω. Cfr. Filone, Mutat. 175 p. III 186, 26: οὐκ ἀπὸ θεοῦ πεσών. L'espressione non appare nè nell'AT nè nel NT, nè nella forma semplice del verbo nè nei suoi composti[237].

Cap. VII, col. 865 C:

Gregorio pensa che forse senza corpo noi ci saremmo insuperbiti: ἐπαιρόμενοι καὶ μετεωριζόμενοι. Questi participi formano un binomio di radici verbali molto caro a Filone: cfr. Opif. 163 p. I 57, 4; Leg. III 186 p. I 154, 25—26; Deter. 152 p. I 292, 25; Ebr. 101 p. II 189, 22; Confus. 90 p. II 246, 12; Her. 241 p. III 54, 14—15; Fug. 45 p. III 119, 15; Mutat. 154 p. III 182, 31; Somn. I 211 p. III 250, 22; Ios. 149 p. IV 92, 14—15; Mos. I 31 p. IV 127, 8—9; ibid. I 177 p. 162, 15; ibid. I 218 p. 172, 24—173, 1; ibid. II [III] 90 p. 222, 4; ibid. II [III] 139 p. 232, 20; Decal. 143 p. IV 301, 10; Spec. I 37 p. V 10, 2—3; ibid. I 44 p. 11, 15; ibid. II 230 p. 142, 29; Virt. 173 p. V 320, 11—12; Contempl. 3 p. VI 47, 11; Aet. 86 p. VI 99, 17—18; ibid. 136 p. 114, 13—14[238].

Cap. VII, col. 865 C:

Gregorio conclude la digressione sul composto umano per tornare al suo tema: ταῦτα μὲν οὖν ὁ βουλόμενος φιλοσοφείτω, καὶ ἡμεῖς γε συμφιλοσο-

---

[237] Per πίπτω e composti usati per indicare il distacco da Dio e dalle cose divine o soprannaturali cfr. or. II 40 col. 449 A; XVI 15 col. 956 A; XXV 1 col. 1197 A; ibid. 5 col. 1204 C; XXVI 14 col. 1248 A; XXXI 12 col. 148 A (bis); XXXII 6 col. 180 C; ibid. 33 col. 212 B; XXXIX 6 col. 341 A; XL 19 col. 384 B; ibid. 46 col. 425 B; XLIII 69 col. 589 A; XLV 24 col. 656 C; poem. I 2, 10, 152 col. 691; ibid. 15, 138 col. 776; ibid. 34, 260 col. 964; II 2, 3, 291 col. 1501. Nell'or. XLIV 7 col. 613 C ἐκπίπτω viene usato assolutamente, per designare la caduta originale, che ci staccò da Dio.

[238] Cfr. Aristofane, Av. 1447—1448: ὑπὸ γὰρ λόγων ὁ νοῦς ⟨τε⟩ μετεωρίζεται ἐπαίρεταί τ' ἄνθρωπος (vedi anche Pax 80): dove però i vocaboli hanno il loro senso reale.

44*

φήσομεν εὐκαιρότερον. Νυνὶ δέ, ὅ μοι λέγειν ὁ λόγος ὥρμησε . . . Per delle preterizioni equivalenti in Filone, cfr. Mutat. 37 p. III 163, 3—4: „Se quanto abbiamo detto sia persuasivo, lo vedremo ἐν καιρῷ· νυνὶ . . . φήσαμεν; Deus 133 p. II 84, 22: „Lo vedranno coloro che sono soliti e che amano (indagare questi problemi)"; Prob. 20 p. VI 6, 2—3: „La trattazione . . . sia rimandata ad un altro momento più opportuno (εἰς καιρὸν ἐπιτηδειότερον)"[239].

Cap. VIII, col. 868 A:

Gregorio invita a curare il corpo che considera come τὸ συγγενὲς καὶ ὁμόδουλον dell'anima. Cfr. Abr. 116 p. IV 27, 2—3: τὸν ἑστιάτορα συγγενῆ καὶ ὁμόδουλον ἡγοῦντο.

Cap. X, col. 869 A:

σύ μοι φίλος ποτὲ καὶ γνώριμος. Per vari tipi di iuncturae con questi due aggettivi cfr. Somn. I 111 p. III 228, 20—21; Abr. 273 p. IV 60, 4; Spec. II 132 p. V 117, 11[240].

Cap. X, col. 869 B:

χρηστὸς καὶ φιλάνθρωπος. Questa coppia (che ritornerà al cap. XXXVII, col. 908 A) è cara anche a Filone: cfr. Fug. 96 p. III 130, 12; Abr. 203 p. IV 45, 11; Ios. 82 p. IV 78, 21; ibid. 176 p. 99, 5; ibid. 198 p. 103, 20; ibid. 264 p. 117, 9—10; Spec. II 75 p. V 105, 6—7; ibid. II 96 p. 110, 1—2; ibid. III 156 p. 194, 2—3; Virt. 97 p. V 294, 4; ibid. 101 p. 295, 8; Legat. 67 p. VI 168, 5[241]. Lo stesso binomio si riscontra anche nella forma di sostantivo: χρηστότης καὶ φιλανθρωπία[242] in Spec. II 141 p. V 119, 13—14; Legat. 73 p. VI 169, 12.

Cap. XII, col. 872 C:

Gregorio rileva l'incoerenza di un procedimento con l'inciso τὸ παραδοξότατον. Il τὸ παραδοξότατον parentetico-esclamativo è frequentissimo anche in Filone: cfr. Deter. 48 p. I 269, 11; ibid. 94 p. I 279, 18; Poster. 19 p. II 5, 6—7; Plant. 62 p. II 146, 6; Ebr. 66 p. II 182, 4; ibid. 178 p. 204, 18; Confus. 31 p. II 235, 24—25; ibid. 59 p. 240, 27; ibid. 132 p. 254, 5; Congr. 3 p. III 72, 9; Fug. 180 p. III 149, 21; Somn. II 23 p. III 263, 1; ibid. 185 p. 288, 20; Mos. II [III] 125 p. IV 229, 14; ibid. 213 p. 250, 1;

---

[239] Per un atteggiamento oratorio simile a questo cfr. or. XXXVIII 8 col. 320 B (=XLV 4 col. 628 C); XL 3 col. 361 B. Per il particolare aspetto di *praeteritio* che consiste nel sospendere l'argomento lasciandone l'ulteriore approfondimento a chi lo desidera cfr. or. XXVIII 12 col. 41 AB; XLI 2 col. 429 D. Per altri rinvii che aggiornano un tema a migliore occasione cfr. or. II 109 col. 508 C; XVI 9 col. 945 D; XVIII 8 col. 1008 A; XXVIII 5 col. 32 B; XLI 6 col. 437 B; XLII 18 col. 480 B.

[240] Cfr. or. V 20 col. 689 A; VII 14 col. 772 C.

[241] Per l'accostamento di questi due aggettivi cfr. anche or. XIX 15 col. 1061 B; ibid. 17 col. 1064 B; epist. 78, 6 GALLAY I p. 99.

[242] Vedi anche Tit. 3, 4: ἡ χρηστότης καὶ ἡ φιλανθρωπία ἐπεφάνη τοῦ σωτῆρος ἡμῶν θεοῦ.

Aet. 109 p. VI 106, 7. Questo superlativo può anche essere introdotto da una relativa (cfr. Mos. I 143 p. IV 154, 11—12; Legat. 80 p. VI 170, 24) o da una congiunzione (cfr. Opif. 124 p. I 43, 1—2)[243].

Cap. XIII, col. 873 C:

εἰ πάντα ἐκτραγῳδοίην; cfr. Mutat. 196 p. III 190, 7—8.

Cap. XV, col. 876 B:

Gregorio considera i cristiani come un λαὸς ... ἐξαίρετος. Questa locuzione, che non si trova nè nell'AT nè nel NT[244], è invece presente in Praem. 123 p. V 364, 18. In Virt. 199 p. V 327, 17—18 abbiamo γένος ἐξαίρετον ed in Legat. 117 p. VI 176, 25 ἔθνος ἐξαίρετον.

Cap. XV, col. 876 B:

Gregorio parla di Cristo come di τοῦ ταπεινώσαντος ἑαυτὸν μέχρι τοῦ ἡμετέρου φυράματος. L'inizio della frase si rifà a Phil. 2, 5—8 ma la fine non ha fondamento in nessuno dei due Testamenti e invece richiama Sacrif. 108 p. I 246, 4—5: τὸ τοίνυν φύραμα κυρίως ... ἡμεῖς ἐσμεν αὐτοί.

Cap. XV, col. 876 C:

Gregorio si domanda se si dovranno fuggire gli ammalati come ἑρπετῶν καὶ θηρίων τὰ πονηρότατα. Cfr. un enunciato simile nelle Quaest. Gen. I 36 p. 25 A. e VI 268: ex bestiarum et serpentum virulentissimo[245].

Cap. XVI, col. 877 B:

Gregorio parla di vestiti riposti negli armadi e destinati a diventare σητῶν δαπάνη καὶ χρόνου τοῦ τὰ πάντα καταναλίσκοντος[246]. Vedi Filone, Prob. 104 p. VI 30, 12: ὑπὸ σέων[247] ἢ χρόνου ... εἰς ἅπαν διαφθαρησόμενα.

Cap. XVI, col. 877 B:

Gregorio osserva che i lebbrosi, privi di mani, non hanno più nemmeno i mezzi fisici per chiedere l'elemosina: οὐδὲ τὰς πρὸς τὴν αἴτησιν ἀφορμὰς παρὰ τοῦ σώματος ἔχοντες. Quanto alla frase cfr. Prob. 71 p. VI 20, 21—21, 1: ἔχοντες οὖν τοιαύτας παρ' ἑαυτοῖς ἀφορμάς[248] e vedi anche ibid. 78

---

[243] Per questa locuzione cfr. anche or. III 1 col. 517 AB; VII 4 col. 760 A; XL 43 col. 421 A. Nell'or. XXI 32 col. 1120 D assume la forma del positivo in frase relativa.

[244] In Petr. I 2, 9 occorrono γένος ἐκλεκτόν e λαὸς εἰς περιποίησιν.

[245] Cfr. or. IV 20 col. 549 A; XXVIII 2 col. 28 B.

[246] Cfr. or. XVI 19 col. 960 CD; poem. I 2, 28, 69—70 col. 861; ibid. 31, 55 col. 915.

[247] Σέων è tema anteriore a cui succede poi σητῶν.

[248] Quanto all'espressione cfr. Zenone e seguaci (Stobeo, Ecl. II 7, 5ᵇ³ WACHSMUTH-HENSE vol. II p. 62, 9—11): ἔχειν γὰρ ἀφορμὰς παρὰ τῆς φύσεως ... πρὸς τὴν τοῦ καθήκοντος εὕρεσιν; Cleante (Stobeo, Ecl. II 7, 5ᵇ⁸ WACHSMUTH-HENSE vol. II p. 65, 8—10): πάντας γὰρ ἀνθρώπους ἀφορμὰς ἔχειν ἐκ φύσεως πρὸς ἀρετήν. Vedi anche Crisippo (Diogene Laerzio VII 76); Isocrate, Areop. 32 p. 146.

p. VI 23, 2; Flacc. 1 p. VI 120, 6; ibid. 102 p. 139, 5; Legat. 152 p. VI 183, 26; ibid. 248 p. 201, 21; ibid. 259 p. 203, 16.

Cap. XX, col. 884 A:

Gregorio riserva ai beni soprannaturali la qualifica di τὰ ἑστῶτα καὶ μένοντα e Filone, Somn. II 221 p. III 294, 6—7 presenta Dio come ἑστὼς ἐν ὁμοίῳ καὶ μένων[249].

Cap. XXV, col. 889 BC:

Gregorio richiama il νόμον Θεοῦ τὸν ἀνωτάτω καὶ πρῶτον. Per questa coppia di superlativi cfr. Spec. III 192 p. V 204, 6; Cher. 27 p. I 176, 19; Decal. 103 p. IV 292, 20; Leg. I 71 p. I 79, 21; Legat. 198 p. VI 192, 8. Parecchi sono inoltre in Filone i casi di ἀνωτάτω affiancato ad un altro superlativo equivalente a πρῶτος e di ἀνωτάτω riferito ad un sostantivo che regge il genitivo θεοῦ. Inoltre va notato che ἀνωτάτω in posizione attributiva è documentabile più volte in Gregorio[250] ed è tanto comune in Filone da costituire una delle più evidenti caratteristiche del suo modus scribendi.

Cap. XXVI, col. 892 C:

Gregorio invita il ricco a ringraziare Dio: ὅτι τῶν εὖ ποιεῖν δυναμένων ἐγένου, ἀλλ᾽ οὐ τῶν εὖ παθεῖν δεομένων. Per il contrasto tra εὖ ποιεῖν ed εὖ πάσχειν cfr. Opif. 23 p. I 7, 7—8.

Cap. XXVII, col. 893 B:

Gregorio menziona τὰ τῆς εὐσεβείας σπέρματα[251]. L'uso metaforico di σπέρμα accompagnato dal genitivo di un nome di virtù — sconosciuto sia all'A. che al NT. — è invece assai familiare a Filone.

Cap. XXVII, col. 893 C:

Gregorio per designare i 'medici' usa con puro valore pleonastico la circonlocuzione ἰατρῶν παῖδες. Questa perifrasi, che non si riscontra in nessuno dei due Testamenti, è abbastanza usuale in Filone: cfr. Plant. 173 p. II 168, 21; Confus. 151 p. II 258, 3; Somn. I 51 p. III 216, 2; Ios. 160 p. IV 95, 8—9; framm. p. II 674 M. e p. 102 R.H.; Quaest. Gen. IV 35 p. 272 A. e VII 84.

Cap. XXVII, col. 893 C:

Gregorio scongiura di non fuggire i lebbrosi ὡς ἄγος, ὡς μίασμα. Per la composizione di questi due sostantivi vedi Spec. III 42 p. V 161, 20—162, 1; ibid. III 127 p. 186, 9.

---

[249] Per questa coppia sinonimica cfr. or. III 7 col. 524 C; XLIII 13 col. 512 C. Invece i due participi tendono a contrapporsi alla fine di questo capitolo col. 884 B e in or. XVIII 3 col. 988 C.

[250] Cfr. or. VIII 23 col. 816 C; XX 1 col. 1065 A; XXIV 15 col. 1188 B; XXV 4 col. 1201 D; XXIX 2 col. 76 A; XXXI 10 col. 144 B; XXXIV 8 col. 248 D.

[251] Cfr. anche or. XXVI 19 col. 1224 C; XLII 4 col. 461 C.

Cap. XXVIII, col. 896 B:

Gregorio ammonisce che il Signore lancia le sue minacce κατὰ τῶν ὑψαυχενούντων verso i poveri. Questo verbo, che sbozza insieme un atteggiamento fisico ed una passione dell'anima, piacque a Filone che lo usò volentieri: cfr. Decal. 41 col. IV 278, 5; Mutat. 154 col. III 182, 31—183, 1; Fug. 44 p. III 119, 12—13; Leg. III 18 p. I 117, 12; Cher. 35 p. I 178, 19; ibid. 66 p. 186, 16; Agric. 106 p. II 116, 19; Congr. 127 p. III 98, 9; Spec. IV 120 p. V 236, 8[252].

Cap. XXVIII, col. 896 C:

τελειοτέραν καὶ μείζονα. Per l'accostamento di questi due comparativi cfr. Spec. II 128 p. V 116, 18; Mutat. 128 p. III 178, 20[253].

Cap. XXIX, col. 896 C:

Gregorio asserisce che convincono alla misericordia ὁ λόγος καὶ ὁ νόμος. Per l'avvicinamento immediato di λόγος e di νόμος cfr. Ebr. 142 p. II 197, 19; Ios. 174 p. IV 98, 12; Decal. 13 p. IV 271, 12—13 e vedi anche Deter. 13 p. I 261, 12; Migr. 130 p. II 293, 13 e 15—16[254].

Cap. XXIX, col. 897 A:

Gregorio accenna ad orecchie θείοις συνειθισμένας δόγμασι. Cfr. Filone, Spec. III 1 p. V 150, 8: θείοις ἀεὶ λόγοις συγγινόμενος καὶ δόγμασιν. Per la locuzione θεῖα δόγματα cfr. Deter. 133 p. I 288, 8—9; Confus. 51 p. II 239, 10; Migr. 131 p. II 294, 2; Mutat. 202 p. III 191, 17. L'espressione non è biblica.

Cap. XXXI, col. 900 B:

ἐχούσης ὁμαλόν τι . . . τῆς . . . ἀνωμαλίας. Per un esempio simile di ossimoro e di paronomasia cfr. Ios. 269 p. IV 118, 9—10: ἡ ἐν ταῖς . . . ἀνωμαλίαις ὁμαλότης.

Cap. XXXI, col. 900 C:

ἄτακτον καὶ ἀνώμαλον. Cfr. Opif. 97 p. I 33, 12: τὸ ἀνώμαλον καὶ ἄτακτον καὶ ἄνισον[255].

Cap. XXXIII, col. 901 C:

Gregorio usa τερατεύομαι per deplorare tutte le teorie negatrici della Provvidenza, tra le quali spicca quella astrologica (cap. XXXII, col. 901 A).

---

[252] Per l'impiego di questo verbo cfr. anche poem. II 1, 11, 1928 col. 1164; vedi inoltre ibid. 12, 572 col. 1207.

[253] Cfr. or. VIII 9 col. 800 A; XVII 8 col. 976 AB; ibid. 13 col. 980 C; XVIII 20 col. 1008 D; XL 19 col. 384 B; epist. 101 col. 185 A e GALLAY-JOURJON § 40 p. 54.

[254] Cfr. or. VII 22 col. 785 A; XVII 9 col. 976 C. — Vedi inoltre E. L. COPELAND, *Nomos as a Medium of Revelation* — Paralleling Logos — in Ante-Nicene Christianity, in: Studia Theologica, XXVII (1973), pp. 51—61.

[255] Cfr. or. XVIII 3 col. 988 C.

Filone, Her. 97 p. III 22, 21 usa questo medesimo verbo ugualmente in polemica contro l'astrologia[256]. Lo adopera poi ancora in Decal. 76 p. IV 286, 9 contro l'idolatria; in Praem. 8 p. V 338, 1 contro la mitologia pagana; in Aet. 48 p. VI 87, 18 contro opinioni filosofiche errate; ibid. 68 p. VI 93, 23 contro antiche leggende.

Cap. XXXIII, col. 904 A:

Gregorio si serve di ἐπιστατέω per indicare il governo divino delle cose create. Per quest'uso — che è sconosciuto sia all'Antico che al Nuovo Testamento — cfr. Agric. 53 p. II 106, 10—11; Her. 166 p. III 38, 17.

Cap. XXXIV, col. 904 B:

Gregorio parla della povertà come τῆς μισουμένης μερίδος. È abbastanza ampiamente documentabile in Filone un analogo atteggiamento mentale per cui egli inclina ad interpretare, come dialetticamente contrapposta, una situazione che si potrebbe anche considerare assolutamente in se stessa; in questi casi si serve volentieri del vocabolo μερίς: cfr. Deus 132 p. II 84, 20: τρέπεται δὲ πρὸς μερίδα τὴν χείρω; Deter. 140 p. I 290, 7—8: φαῦλοι . . . ἀργαλεωτάτην μερίδα καρπούσθωσαν; Praem. 63 p. V 350, 8—9: μακαρίας δὲ καὶ εὐδαίμονος ὅταν τύχῃ μερίδος e vedi anche Leg. III 131 p. I 142, 7; Sacrif. 119 p. I 250, 10; Deter. 140 p. I 290, 8; Poster. 87 p. II 19, 6; Deus 150 p. II 88, 14; Sobr. 67 p. II 228, 13; Confus. 111 p. II 250, 16; Decal. 108 p. IV 293, 16; ibid. 110 p. 294, 7—8; Prob. 105 p. VI 30, 17; Contempl. 82 p. VI 68, 14—15; Flacc. 9 p. VI 122, 8—9; framm. p. 95 R. H.[257].

Cap. XXXV, col. 905 B:

Gregorio scrive: ὀφθαλμοὶ . . . ἐπιβλέπουσιν (ὃ τοῦ βλεφάρου κρεῖττον καὶ κυριώτερον). Cfr. Filone, Her. 55 p. III 13, 18—19: ὀφθαλμὸς . . . τὸ κυριώτατον μέρος τὸ ᾧ βλέπομεν.

Cap. XXXVII, col. 908 B:

A proposito di quanti si sono lasciati irrimediabilmente ferire dal demonio, Gregorio esclama: φεῦ τῆς πληγῆς ὄντως. Per una simile, abbastanza abnorme, posizione predicativa di ὄντως dopo un sostantivo cfr. Flacc. 169 p. VI 151, 4 dove dice che il cielo stellato è il vero mondo nel

---

[256] Nota in entrambi i casi il rilievo dato a κίνησις.

[257] Gregorio dimostra una tendenza abbastanza spiccata a tradurre una determinazione qualificativa in una circonlocuzione, plasticamente assai più rilevata, con μερίς in genitivo: nell'or. XI 1 col. 832 C ricorda gli uomini ὑψηλοὺς καὶ τῆς ἄνω μερίδος; nell'or. XVI 15 col. 953 C dichiara che, dopo aver peccato, il convertirsi è proprio degli uomini probi καὶ τῆς σωζομένης μερίδος; nell'or. XIX 11 col. 1056 BC esorta: μὴ γενώμεθα τῆς τοῦ πλουσίου μερίδος; nell'or. XXXVI 2 col. 268 A proclama di non essere di quelli che hanno trasformato la Chiesa in un teatro a forza di complimenti: οὐ ταύτης ἡμεῖς τῆς μερίδος. Vedi anche XXXVIII 17 col. 332 A; epist. 10, 15 GALLAY I p. 16; 11, 10 p. 18; 16, 8 p. 24.

mondo: τὸν ἐν κόσμῳ κόσμον ὄντως; Prob. 6 p. VI 2, 12: θαύματ᾽ ὄντως. Vedi anche Spec. I 252 p. V 61, 6; Legat. 21 p. VI 159, 17—18. Per una simile costruzione con aggettivi vedi, ad es., Congr. 132 p. III 99, 7; Mutat. 193 p. III 189, 21; Contempl. 88 p. VI 70, 10.

IV. Filone e Gregorio: argomenti esterni

Per integrare l'efficacia dimostrativa degli accostamenti concettuali, stilistici e linguistici sopra stabiliti, è opportuno rilevare anche gli argomenti esterni che li possono convalidare.

Purtroppo la diffusa reticenza degli antichi a scendere a designazioni esplicite, che indusse Gregorio a non immettere nelle sue opere se non pochi nomi di classici[258], ci ha privati di una testimonianza che sarebbe stata decisiva per accertare la conoscenza diretta di Filone da parte di Gregorio. Bisogna però subito avvertire che, anche senza una tale avversione, ben difficilmente Gregorio avrebbe inserito il nome di Filone nei suoi scritti. Infatti, al di là di un'istintiva alterezza verso chi era pur sempre stato un estraneo, Gregorio non aveva motivo di nominare Filone. Sarebbe stato conveniente il chiamarlo esplicitamente in causa qualora si fossero riferiti — tanto a scopo polemico quanto a fine epidittico — dei suoi assiomi nettamente caratterizzati e dotati di una notevole importanza nella storia della cultura[259]: l'approfondimento teologico ne avrebbe guadagnato in

---

[258] L'esame dell'uso di Gregorio mostra che egli indulgeva alquanto più facilmente a formulare i nomi degli scrittori quando assumeva un tono amabilmente e briosamente scherzoso oppure vivacemente ironico: cfr. or. IV 100 col. 636 B (Pindaro); IV 115 col. 653 A (Orfeo); V 15 col. 684 A (Erodoto); or. XLIII 20 col. 521 B (Pindaro); epist. 9,1 GALLAY I p. 12 e 204,5 p. II 96 (Pindaro); or. XLIII 24 col. 529 B (Omero); epist. 5,1 p. I 5 (Omero); 11, 3 p. I 17 (Euripide); 12,6 p. I 19 (Lacone); 13,1 p. I 20 (Teognide); 24,4 p. I 32 (Platone); 30,2 p. I 38 e 230,2 p. II 121 (Omero); 70,4 p. I 90 (Omero); 71,5 p. I 91 (Omero); 156,2 p. II 47 (Omero); 166,2 p. II 57 (Omero); 173,4 p. II 62 (Pindaro); 180,2 p. II 70 (Dionisio d'Alicarnasso); 190,5 p. II 81 (Demostene e Omero); 195,1 p. II 85 (Esiodo). Nell'epist. 31,4 p. I 39 e nella 178,5 p. II 67 introduce Platone (nella seconda accenna anche fugacemente ad Aristofane: § 7) come punto di appoggio alla sua argomentazione nel corso di un colloquio intimo ed affettuoso. Tutte le volte invece che il richiamo ha un valore ufficialmente dimostrativo, il nome viene regolarmente taciuto: cfr. or. XXVIII 4 col. 29 C; ibid. 16 col. 48 A; ibid. 30 col. 69 A; XXIX 2 col. 76 C; XLIII 64 col. 581 B. Comunque si tratta sempre di inserzioni estremamente concise. Quando, in luogo di una citazione letteraria, se ne ha una storica che verte su fatti o qualità, virtù o vizi, o quando egli è indotto a formulare giudizi di merito, allora naturalmente i nomi vengono pronunciati: una loro omissione infatti avrebbe distrutto tutto il valore probativo o polemico dei passi.

[259] Sebbene, anche quando si verifichi questo caso, vediamo come la tradizione si mostri restia. Giustino, che pure lo conobbe, non lo nominò mai (cfr. A. HARNACK, Geschichte d. altchrist. Lit., 2. erweit. Aufl., I 2, riprod. fotost. Leipzig, 1958, p. 859); Clemente ed Origene che di Filone si servono con frequenza e per temi di profondo impegno, se stiamo ai 'Testimonia' raccolti dal COHN nella prefazione della sua edizione alle pagg. LXXXXV —LXXXXVII, lo nominarono in tutto solo quattro volte ciascuno (ed Origene in una di

sicurezza e chiarezza. Ma questo non è mai il caso di Gregorio: infatti egli
non ci lasciò saggi di esegesi sul Pentateuco dove avrebbe avuto occasione
di affiancarsi o di scontrarsi con Filone; non trattò mai i problemi dogma-
tici con intenti puramente storici, ma solo con propositi di un'esposizione
chiarificatrice davanti ad un pubblico disorientato dalle chiacchiere degli
eretici e dei teologi improvvisati; non divagò dalle esigenze fondamentali
del suo tempo che esigevano la lotta serrata e perspicua contro l'arianesimo
e l'apollinarismo, i quali non avevano rapporti sostanziali con le speculazioni filoniane.

L'indagine teologica, l'esortazione morale, la trattazione esegetica, la
notazione psicologica, lo sfogo del sentimento, la celebrazione delle persone
virtuose, l'attacco violento contro i nemici della Chiesa, le schermaglie
mordaci contro i suoi avversari personali, in Gregorio sono contrassegnati
dalla costante e vigile presenza della sua personalità: i materiali possono
essere di varia provenienza, però non sono mai accumulati grezzi, sono
sempre sottoposti ad un'elaborazione individuale che non ne distrugge la
natura, ma ne unifica la forma ed il tono; ci possono essere spunti, ma
non copiature — come pure certi suoi contemporanei facevano abbastanza
facilmente —; si può pensare donde sia provenuto un particolare elemento,
ma non è più possibile applicargli con certezza un'etichetta di proprietà
originaria. Questo stile del Nazianzeno, per cui si assimila intimamente il
suo cibo, mentre costituisce l'attestazione della sua ricchezza e probità di
scrittore, esclude da parte sua la citazione delle fonti: il mosaico gli appartiene senz'altro, le singole tessere, di ristrettissimo ambito, non possono
essere gravate di continui rinvii letterari[260].

Se noi non incontriamo il nome di Filone nella produzione superstite
di Gregorio, abbiamo però tutti i motivi di credere che Gregorio lo abbia
effettivamente incontrato lungo gli itinerari geografici e culturali della sua
vita. Infatti dopo una prima dirozzatura scolastica a Cesarea di Cappadocia, Gregorio sentendo in sè urgente la vocazione a diventare un grande
intellettuale cristiano, si recò a Cesarea di Palestina, che costituiva allora

---

queste — Comment. in Ev. Matth., XVII 17 t. IV p. 124 Lomm. — surrogò addirittura
il nome proprio con uno scoloritissimo τις appena determinato per i dotti dalla citazione
del titolo dell'opera); S. Basilio, nonostante che abbia ripetutamente Filone come sotto-
fondo, trova un solo posto nei 'Testimonia' (p. CIV) ed un posto solo trova pure S. Ambrogio
(ibid.) anche se al riguardo il Cohn potè scrivere: ,,Ambrosius vero Philonem in scriptis ad
Pentateuchum exegeticis praecipuum auctorem ac ducem ita sibi elegit, ut nonnullos libros
eius totos fere compilaret'' (ibid. p. I) e più oltre: ,,Maxime omnium scriptorum ecclesiasti-
corum Philonem usurpavit Ambrosius episcopus Mediolanensis, quem in scriptis quibusdam
quasi latinum Philonem esse dixeris'' (ibid. p. LXII). Il Nisseno non viene menzionato nei
'Testimonia', quantumque in qualche raro caso citi Filone espressamente: cfr. infatti
Contra Eunomium, lib. III tom. V 24 p. 159,9—10 ed. Jaeger, Pars altera, Berolini, 1921
(Lib. VII MG. XLV col. 748 C) e ibid. lib. III tom. VII 8 p. 206,18—30 (Lib. IX MG. XLV
col. 804 B e C), dove lo tratta con un'ironia più o meno sprezzante.

[260] Sarebbe ingenuo aspettarsi in Gregorio periodi trasportati di peso come avviene in
Ambrogio. Diversi erano i due scrittori e molto diverse le circostanze nelle quali vennero
a trovarsi i due vescovi. Uno studio sulle relazioni intellettuali di Gregorio va condotto
con una finezza enormemente maggiore.

uno dei vivai di studi più rinomati dell'Oriente. Celebri retori offrivano agli alunni, che accorrevano da ogni parte, la possibilità di dissetarsi a tutte le sorgenti della filosofia, della retorica e della poesia; però, per chi non avesse ristretto i proprii interessi alle cose del mondo, Cesarea offriva un'altra attrattiva: essa era la città nella quale avevano insegnato e studiato Origene, Panfilo ed Eusebio, i quali avevano fondato e fatto prosperare una scuola illustre, che poteva valersi di una biblioteca specializzata di oltre 30.000 volumi. Gregorio frequentò sicuramente con zelo le lezioni di metafisica, di teologia e di esegesi e potè documentarsi direttamente sulle fonti che venivano richiamate durante i corsi. Se si pensa a quanto Origene dedusse da Filone, alle ampie citazioni[261] che ne trasse Eusebio nella sua 'Praeparatio Evangelica' VIII 14 e XI 24 ed alla conoscenza che delle sue opere dimostrò nella Storia ecclesiastica[262] possiamo concludere che sugli scaffali della collezione Cesariense gli scritti di Filone dovevano certamente essere presenti in un corpus che comprendeva anche opere a noi giunte solo in traduzione[263].

Però, dopo qualche tempo, gl'inviti del fratello Cesario, che lo aveva preceduto ad Alessandria, e forse più ancora il richiamo di quella città che splendeva come il più luminoso faro di cultura ed il più dinamico centro religioso dell'Oriente, lo convinsero a trasferirvisi. Non forse casualmente Alessandria, patria di Filone, divenne anche culla della teologia cristiana: Clemente ed Origene vi rinnovarono la medesima impresa, cercando di esprimere e di sistemare il messaggio della Redenzione con l'apporto della speculazione classica. L'identità dell'esigenza di rivestire la parola di Dio, espressa in forme storiche e quindi soggetta ad obsolescenza, mediante un

---

[261] Cfr. C. G. A. SIEGDRIED, Philo von Alexandria als Ausleger des Alten Testaments, Jena, 1875, p. 362: „Eusebio di Cesarea conosceva con esattezza Filone."

[262] È suggestiva e convincente l'ipotesi del COHN, op. cit. p. IV, che l'elenco degli scritti filoniani trasmessoci da Eusebio (Hist. Eccl. II 18) non sia altro che il catalogo dei trattati dell'Alessandrino conservati nella Biblioteca di Cesarea.

[263] Questa supposizione è confermata da una prova documentaria di eccezionale evidenza. Infatti S. Girolamo nell'Epist. 34,1 e nel De vir. ill. 113 ci comunica che Euzoio, che da giovinetto aveva studiato alla scuola di Cesarea, quando poi divenne vescovo della stessa città, visto che il patrimonio librario raccolto da Origene e da Panfilo si stava deteriorandò, provvide — continuando l'opera di Acacio, suo predecessore sulla cattedra episcopale (338—365) — a farlo trascrivere su nuove pergamene (in membranis instaurare conatus est). Ora nel cod. Vindob. theol. gr. 29 in capo al libro di Filone, De opificio mundi, si leggono questo parole disposte a croce greca: Εὐζόιος ἐπίσκοπος ἐν σωματίοις ἀνενεώσατο dove l'espressione ἐν σωματίοις ἀνενεώσατο equivale al passo riferito di Girolamo (COHN, op. cit. p. III). Questo trattato filoniano era già dunque da lungo tempo a Cesarea, tanto che Euzoio durante il suo episcopato (366—379) si trovò costretto a farlo rinnovare; e se c'era questo — che Eusebio considerava come una parte delle 'Legum allegoriae' — è naturale che ci fossero anche gli altri. Da tale fortunata testimonianza possiamo anche trarre una conferma all'ipotesi — del resto ovvia — che Eusebio si servisse per le sue citazioni filoniane dei mss. cesariensi; infatti gli estratti che egli tolse dal 'De opificio mundi' (Praepar. Evang. VIII 14, Opif. §§ 7—12 e ibid. XI 24, Opif. §§ 24—27; 29—31; 35; 36) dimostrano un accordo tale con il 'cod. Vindob.' da indurci ad affermare che entrambi provennero dal medesimo apografo (cfr. COHN, op. cit. p. XXXVII). Per il 'De Providentia' e le 'Quaestiones in Genesim' e 'in Exodum' cfr. Eusebius, Hist. Eccl. II 18, 4—6.

sano eclettismo culturale che la modernizzasse e la rendesse più pregevole agli occhi dei dotti, postula almeno un medesimo clima spirituale e se non rende necessaria lascia almeno supporre come largamente possibile una suggestione dell'antico sui successori, posteriori solo di poche generazioni[264]. I due maggiori dottori del Didaskaleion conobbero infatti con notevole precisione l'opera del loro concittadino[265] e ne manifestarono il loro apprezzamento sia con le citazioni, numerose, anche se ordinariamente anonime, sia con l'accoglierne quelle tesi sostanziali che non fossero state superate dal cristianesimo. Se Filone fu sino dall'inizio uno dei pilastri della scuola alessandrina, lo dovette restare anche in seguito, dato che l'atmosfera non mutò sensibilmente: quando vi giunse Gregorio, direttore ed animatore ne era Didimo il cieco, il quale, pur con i temperamenti imposti dall'ortodossia, era un convinto origenista. Il Nazianzeno, entrando in questa temperie culturale[266], sviluppò quella sua intimità con Filone[267] che con ogni probabilità era già stata inaugurata a Cesarea di Palestina. Qui infatti aveva incontrato in Eusebio il più autorevole iniziatore a Filone: siccome non è immaginabile che un appassionato studioso quale egli era frequentasse la scuola ancora dominata dalla grande figura dello storico senza leggerne le opere, possiamo essere sicuri che Gregorio conobbe i passi nei quali Eusebio presentava con tanta ammirazione il pensatore giudaico: e si trattava di notizie atte a suscitare tutta la simpatia di un cristiano; sembrava un'autentica annessione alla Chiesa di una nobile personalità che ne fosse stata esclusa solo per un capriccio della sorte. Oltre ad inserirlo ufficialmente nel novero degli scrittori cristiani[268] Eusebio dà quasi per scontata la sua appartenenza ideale alla nuova fede, concentrando la sua attenzione nel sottolinearne l'eccellenza[269]; considera poi la sua ambasceria a Caligola come una generosa e pericolosa battaglia in favore della giustizia e della dignità umana[270]; interpreta la descrizione dei Terapeuti del 'De vita contemplativa' come la presentazione di una comunità monastica cristiana

---

[264] Sembra logico ricondurre l'allegorismo della scuola alessandrina a quello filoniano.

[265] Cfr. la nostra nota 2 e COHN, op. cit. p. LX: ,,*Clementem Alexandrinum inprimis in Stromatum libris Philonis verba saepius tacite exscripsisse vel in usum suum convertisse satis constat*''... e poco oltre: ,,*Clementis exemplum secutus Origenes, cum allegoricam Scripturae sacrae interpretationem vehementissime amplexus esset, in commentariis suis ad Philonem se proxime adiunxit, sed ut magis doctrina et sententiis eius quam verbis uteretur.*''

[266] Non sappiamo però se abbia seguito le lezioni di Didimo.

[267] Siccome è noto che l'eredità del Didaskaleion — attraverso ad un opportuno ed equilibrato processo di decantamento dagli eccessi che erano comprensibili nei pionieri, ma che andavano eliminati — passò ai Cappadoci, risulta coerente metterli in relazione immediata con tutta quella scuola, dai presupposti alle successive elaborazioni. — È assai verosimile che S. Girolamo abbia attinto alla sequela di Didimo la stima e la conoscenza che dimostra di possedere per l'opera filoniana.

[268] Cfr. Hist. Eccl. II 18, 1—8 dove ne inquadra l'elenco degli scritti con alte lodi.

[269] In Hist. Eccl. II 4, 2 giudica l'Alessandrino ἀνὴρ οὐ μόνον τῶν ἡμετέρων, ἀλλὰ καὶ τῶν ἀπὸ τῆς ἔξωθεν ὁρμωμένων παιδείας ἐπισημότατος ed appena dopo — II 4, 3 — proclama universalmente noto il contributo da lui portato περὶ ... τὰ θεῖα καὶ πατρία μαθήματα.

[270] Ibid. II 5, 1—7.

sorta ad Alessandria quale frutto della predicazione di S. Marco[271]; riferisce come una tradizione ormai diffusa che Filone, sotto il regno di Claudio, intrattenne relazioni con S. Pietro che evangelizzava Roma e dichiara il fatto non inverosimile, in quanto il 'De vita contemplativa', scritto in seguito, conterrebbe chiaramente le norme di vita della Chiesa quali erano ancora ai suoi tempi osservate[272]; afferma che quando Filone descrive nella maniera più esatta gli asceti cristiani[273] lascia chiaramente trasparire che non solo conosce, ma che approva e venera gli uomini apostolici della sua età[274]; fornisce quindi un riassunto e parecchi estratti del 'De vita contemplativa', dove l'ascetismo viene presentato e celebrato con sincero fervore[275]. Va inoltre notato che l'attribuzione eusebiana a Filone di una specie di criptocristianesimo non cadde nel vuoto, ma s'impose creando un'opinione che la accolse per canonica: infatti anche S. Girolamo[276] colloca Filone *inter scriptores ecclesiasticos* perché magnificò la comunità cristiana di Alessandria e la asserì sparsa in molte province, e ribadisce i colloqui romani con S. Pietro aggiungendovi di suo un'opinabile duratura amicizia; Anastasio Sinaita[277] lo include tra gli esegeti ecclesiastici; Fozio[278] continua a menzionare le relazioni tra Filone e Pietro e la stessa cosa fa Suda[279].

Un altro titolo — indebito, ma pur comunemente attribuitogli — doveva rendere Filone meritevole di molto rispetto presso qualsiasi cristiano che conoscesse almeno mediocremente la sua fede; egli fu cioè creduto l'autore della Sapienza di Salomone[280], entrando quindi nella lista degli

---

[271] Ibid. II 16, 2.

[272] Ibid. II 17, 1.

[273] Eusebio vede nei Terapeuti dei cristiani probabilmente di origine giudaica. Questa valutazione, grazie al prestigio dello storico, si trasmise anche ai posteri: cfr. S. Epifanio, Panarion haer. 29,5 GCS Holl I. Bd., Leipzig, 1915, p. 326; S. Girolamo, Vir. ill. 8 e 11; Cassiano, Instit. CSEL Petschenig, Prag–Wien–Leipzig, 1888, p. 20,25 segg.; Sozomeno, Hist. Eccl. I 12,9 GCS Hansen, Berlin, 1960, p. 26; Fozio, Bibl. cod. 105, anche se prima (cod. 104) li aveva presi per filosofi giudei; Suda, s. v. Φίλων.

[274] Hist. Eccl. II 17,2.

[275] Ibid. II 17,3—24.

[276] Vir. ill. 11.

[277] In Hexaem. VII MG. LXXXIX col. 961.

[278] Bibl. cod. 105.

[279] Cfr. voce Φίλων.

[280] Il Codice Muratoriano, il cui originale fu quasi certamente scritto in greco verso il 170—180 d. C., non elenca la Sapienza tra i libri del VT ma tra quelli del NT ed asserisce che sarebbe stata *ab amicis Salomonis in honorem ipsius scripta*. Ci si chiese chi fossero questi *amici* di Salomone ed apparve subito plausibile la congettura del Tregelles e del Fitzgerald i quali proposero che l'enunciato latino — che tradisce nel redattore un'evidente imperizia — fosse da ricondurre ad un testo greco il quale suonasse: ἡ σοφία Σαλωμῶνος (ὁ Σαλωμῶντος) ὑπὸ Φίλωνος εἰς δόξαν αὐτοῦ γεγραμμένη (ὁ εἰς τιμὴν αὐτοῦ συγγραφεῖσα). L'estensore del più antico ed autorevole canone scritturale della Chiesa di Roma attribuiva dunque la Sapienza a Filone, probabilmente in seguito alla fama di filocristiano e di uditore simpatizzante di S. Pietro che si era ormai diffusa. Ed anche questa non fu un'idea isolata e destinata a cadere senza risonanza, in quanto S. Girolamo, Praef. in libros Salomonis ML. XXVIII col. 1242 attestava che *nonnulli* credevano la Sapienza di Filone. Quest'opinione perdurava al tempo di Giuliano d'Eclana e di S. Agostino: cfr. Opus imperf. contr. Julianum IV 123 ML. XLV col. 1420. Su tale

autori ispirati che godevano di una grandissima autorità. Dice a questo proposito lo ZAHN: „Quanto alla forma letteraria Filone aveva scritto in onore di Salomone, quanto al contenuto della sua opera egli era un immediato precursore di Cristo, come nel suo genere Giovanni Battista[281]." Insomma Filone, un po' per quello che fu davvero e più ancora per quello che fu creduto, venne guardato con viva simpatia dai cristiani, i quali — di fronte all' ostilità rabbinica — presero sotto la loro protezione il suo patrimonio letterario. Scrive infatti il COHN: „*Philonis Alexandrini memoria a Judaeis non minus quam a paganis fere neglecta tota pendet ab ecclesia Christiana. Nam cum doctrina moralis et Testamenti Veteris interpretandi ratio Philonis cum sacris ecclesiae Christianae libris maxime conspirare viderentur, ab antiquis scriptoribus ecclesiasticis eius opera studiosissime lectitata atque usurpata sunt*"[282] e lo ZAHN parlando della Sapienza dice: „Come le rimanenti opere del Giudeo alessandrino, così anche questo suo preteso lavoro fu letto e diffuso non dai Giudei, ma dai Cristiani"[283].

Da quanto esposto appare chiaro che nei focolai di cultura cristiana ci dovevano essere le opere di Filone e che una larga parte degli intellettuali ecclesiastici di più notevole spicco le doveva avere tra le mani, chè altrimenti non si capirebbe in che cosa consistesse tale opera di apprezzamento e di tutela espletata dalla Chiesa greca. Non solo è dunque agevole ammettere che nuclei alacri, quali erano Cesarea di Palestina e soprattutto Alessandria, sua patria, facessero di Filone uno di quei classici che entrano nei programmi d'insegnamento, ma bisogna anche ritenere che città come Costantinopoli e Cesarea di Cappadocia ne fossero fornite e che probabilmente anche sedi episcopali minori, conventi e forse anche volonterosi studiosi privati lo possedessero nelle loro raccolte locali per l'uso immediato.

Che Basilio e Gregorio di Nissa, con i quali Gregorio visse in fraterna intimità, conoscessero Filone con rilevante ampiezza, è ormai indubitabilmente assodato: entrambi lo citano espressamente ed entrambi, e specialmente il secondo, ne fanno uno dei punti di riferimento della loro speculazione[284]. Tra i contemporanei di Gregorio S. Girolamo, discepolo ed amico

questione vedi soprattutto TH. ZAHN, Geschichte des Neutestamentlichen Kanons, II 1, Erlangen—Leipzig, 1890, pp. 95—105; B. MOTZO, Saggi di Storia e Letteratura Giudeo-Ellenistica, in: Contributi alla Scienza dell'Antichità, Firenze, 1924, pp. 32—34; L. BIGOT, Sagesse, in: Dict. Théol. Cath. XIV, 1, Paris, 1939, coll. 709; 722—723 e 744, e più recentemente P. KATZ, The Johannine Epistles in the Muratorian Canon, in: Journal of Theological Studies, VIII (1957), pp. 273—274 (che però non aggiunge nulla di nuovo); M. TREVES, Il libro della Sapienza, in: Parola del Passato, fasc. 84 (1962), pp. 192—201 (198—199).

[281] TH. ZAHN, op. cit. p. 104.

[282] L. COHN, op. cit. p. I.

[283] TH. ZAHN, op. cit. p. 104. Per altre affermazioni in questo medesimo senso cfr. A. HARNACK, op. cit. p. 858; W. CHRIST—W. SCHMID—O. STÄHLIN, Gesch. d. griech. Lit., II. Teil, I. Hälfte, 6. Aufl., München, 1920, Nachdruck 1959, pp. 655—656; E. SCHÜRER, Geschichte des jüdischen Volkes im Zeitalter Jesu Christi, 4. Aufl., III. Bd., Leipzig, 1909, p. 637; W. BOUSSET, Die Religion des Judentums im neutestamentlichen Zeitalter, 2. Aufl., Berlin, 1906, p. 505.

[284] Cfr. J. DANIÉLOU, Philon d'Alexandrie, Paris, 1958, p. 214.

di Gregorio, onorava ufficialmente Filone e S. Ambrogio lo adoperava senza misura: era ormai, almeno tacitamente, considerato come una 'Praeparatio Evangelica'[285] e addirittura come un Padre della Chiesa in partibus[286].

D'altronde Gregorio non aveva nessun motivo di essere ostile a Filone. Egli era uomo di larga serenità spirituale[287], nativamente incline ad attingere a tutte le fonti della cultura, propenso ad assimilarsi tutto ciò che potesse diventare mezzo di approfondimento e di elevazione dell'anima, persuaso che la verità cristiana fosse tanto forte da nutrirsi di quanto di positivo trovava attorno senza lasciarsene snaturare, conscio che l'ortodossia teologica non dipende dai libri che si leggono ma dalle convinzioni che si professano. Come non temette di allacciare cordiali amicizie con pagani e di studiare lungamente ed avidamente i classici, che pure erano spesso, sia dogmaticamente sia moralmente, agli antipodi del cristianesimo, così non si vede perchè avrebbe dovuto mostrare disdegno verso Filone. Anzi il personaggio sembrava fatto apposta per accattivarsene le simpatie: anch'egli era un innamorato della classicità, anch'egli era convinto che fosse possibile e legittimo valersi della civiltà greca per conferire maggior lustro e forza di penetrazione alla parola divina, anch'egli dovette lottare contro ostilità e resistenze. Entrambi sentirono la vocazione ad una vita contemplativa permeata di ascetismo e di studio, ed entrambi ne furono parzialmente distratti da difficili incombenze alle quali dovettero prestarsi per il bene dei loro fratelli di fede; tutti e due perseguirono come loro ideale l'accostamento a Dio mediante una progressiva spogliazione delle cupidige terrene e tutti e due consacrarono la loro penna soltanto ad argomenti

---

[285] F. J. FOAKES JACKSON, Philo and Alexandrian Judaism, in: A History of Church History. Studies of Some Historians of the Christian Church, Cambridge, 1939, p. 39—55 presenta Fil. come una 'Praeparatio Evangelica', che con la sua concezione spiritualizzata di Dio ed il suo concetto del Logos, aperse la via all'accettazione del cristianesimo. — Per quanto concerne i rapporti tra questi due Padri latini e Filone vedi, in questo medesimo volume (ANRW II 21,1), il solerte studio di H. SAVON, Saint Ambroise et saint Jérôme, lecteurs de Philon, pp. 731—759. In esso l'autore per Ambrogio conferma l'ampiezza delle corrispondenze filoniane, notandone però la libertà, in quanto il vescovo di Milano ne conservò spesso le formule mutandone tuttavia il contenuto, grazie ad una vigilanza costante e ad un senso sicuro della fede che, attraverso ad una rielaborazione talora spinta assai in profondità, gli fecero filtrare le proposte dell'Alessandrino, assumendone solo quanto era coerentemente integrabile con il cristianesimo. Per quanto riguarda Girolamo la sua conoscenza diretta di Filone sarebbe invece piuttosto scarsa o poco evidente: si tratterebbe più di menzioni elogiative che non di un effettivo interesse immediato.

[286] La definizione, felicemente epigrammatica, è di J. GEFFCKEN, Religiöse Strömungen im 1. Jahrhundert n. Chr. (Studien d. apologetischen Seminars in Wernigerode, n. 7), Gütersloh, 1922, p. 25. Al riguardo vedi anche J. E. BRUNS, Philo Christianus. The Debris of a Legend, in: Harvard Theological Review, LXVI (1973), pp. 141—145.

[287] Gregorio certo condivideva le alte e belle parole che Origene scriveva in risposta alle insinuazioni di Celso, quando presentava sè ed i cristiani dicendo: ἡμεῖς . . . οἱ μελετήσαντες μηδενὶ ἀπεχθάνεσθαι τῶν καλῶς λεγομένων, κἂν οἱ ἔξω τῆς πίστεως λέγωσι καλῶς, μὴ προσφιλονεικεῖν αὐτοῖς, μηδὲ ζητεῖν ἀνατρέπειν τὰ ὑγιῶς ἔχοντα: Contra Celsum VII 46 MG. XI col. 1488 BC; GCS KOETSCHAU II, Leipzig, 1899, p. 197, 14—17.

direttamente od indirettamente religiosi; entrambi fusero letteratura e Bibbia subordinando sempre le dottrine umane alla verità divina. D'altra parte non sarebbe stato questo il primo caso nel quale i cristiani si avvalessero di precedenti giudaici; sappiamo infatti come la prima apologetica cristiana si approvvigionasse piuttosto ampiamente presso quella ebraica[288], attingendovi alcune argomentazioni sulle quali amò maggiormente insistere e come questo fatto non destasse scandalo in nessuno. Inoltre Filone attirava quasi necessariamente l'attenzione di un teologo e di un esegeta, oltre che per il suo monumentale commento su importanti passi del Pentateuco, anche per altri due motivi: 1º) la presenza di vistose rassomiglianze con certi testi del NT, tra i quali spiccavano particolarmente il prologo giovanneo e l'epistola agli Ebrei: all'analisi le analogie potevano anche dimostrarsi illusorie o ridursi assai, ma per fare ciò era pur necessario un esame accurato; — 2º) l'offerta di un metodo interpretativo ben caratterizzato e consapevole, il quale, sebbene potesse rivelarsi difettoso e pericoloso, non poteva però venire preventivamente trascurato da chiunque sentisse una responsabilità di maestro. Per di più l'allegorismo si manifestava, fino dal primo sguardo, come un'arma che, se richiedeva prudenza nel maneggio, era però in grado di rendere eminenti servigi sia sul piano pastorale, per coonestare qualsiasi saggia norma morale che il momento richiedesse, sia su quello esegetico, per superare le tante aporie bibliche che eretici e pagani si compiacevano di mettere in risalto per confondere le coscienze.

L'intima coerenza dei fatti, dei luoghi, dei tempi, delle convenienze e delle esigenze interne ed esterne che caratterizzano gli eventi biografici di Gregorio ci determina a credere che il Nazianzeno abbia effettivamente incontrato l'Alessandrino e che il contatto non sia stato nè sterile nè superficiale[289]. Alla dimostrazione apoditticamente completa non manca che la

---

[288] J. GEFFCKEN, Zwei griechische Apologeten, Leipzig—Berlin, 1907, dopo aver tracciato un profilo dell'apologetica giudaica (pp. XXII—XXXI), soffermandosi particolarmente su Filone (pp. XXIV—XXIX), conclude dicendo: ,,L'erede dell'apologetica giudaica è in certo senso quella cristiana" (p. XXXII). Vedi anche M. PELLEGRINO, Gli Apologeti greci del II secolo, Roma, 1947, pp. 12—13.

[289] Questa conclusione apre però l'adito ad un altro quesito: Gregorio si familiarizzò con tutto Filone oppure ne conobbe solo alcuni trattati e quali? Alla domanda si può tentare una risposta solo se si pongono alcune precisazioni e cautele. Innanzi tutto in casi del genere contano molto gli elementi positivi e quasi nulla quelli negativi; una citazione — qualora sia testuale ed inequivocabile — indica con certezza la conoscenza di un'opera (salvo la possibilità di ricorso a florilegi), mentre il silenzio non autorizza ad arguirne l'ignoranza, perchè non è pensabile che uno scrittore faccia di una sua composizione la mostra completa della sua erudizione. In secondo luogo la base piuttosto ristretta sulla quale è stata costruita la nostra indagine invita alla prudenza: per la sua stessa natura essa impone una scelta di temi e quindi un'esclusione di altri che potrebbero — introducendo nuovi e diversi rapporti — mutare le valutazioni finali. Ciò però non invalida i risultati raggiunti, li dimostra solo suscettibili di integrazione da parte di altre ricerche che potranno aggiungere ulteriori addendi in vista di un totale sempre più esatto. Inoltre va tenuto presente che l'orizzonte dello studio è stato solo apparentemente circoscritto all'orazione XIV: infatti essa — per il suo carattere largamente umano e privo di tecnicismi — accoglie molte delle convinzioni

testimonianza autobiografica, ma sappiamo come non fossero questi i temi sui quali Gregorio, per quanto parlasse volentieri ed a lungo di sè, amava intrattenere i suoi ascoltatori; gli piaceva sfogarsi rievocando i suoi sogni solo in piccola parte realizzati, lamentando i suoi crucci ed i suoi molti dolori, deplorando gli amici ed i nemici che lo avevano indegnamente trattato. Quando rivolgeva indietro il suo sguardo, non lo fermava sulla biblioteca, che pure studiava ed aveva cara, ma sulla sua anima ipersensibile, che al tocco più leggero vibrava di gioia o di sofferenza; la sua confidenza

più care e dei sentimenti più vigorosamente vitali di Gregorio, i quali ritornano spesso in altri suoi scritti, come dimostrano le note di richiamo; l'area è quindi più ampia di quanto non faccia pensare la limitazione programmatica. Ma se il consuntivo — pur nella sua provvisorietà — risulta attendibile, esso non è però di agevole precisazione nelle sue componenti: la molteplicità delle opere filoniane, la relativa uniformità dei loro temi, la scarsa varietà d'interessi del loro autore, la sua tendenza a tutto riportare ai medesimi principi attraverso ai medesimi canoni ermeneutici, il suo patrimonio lessicale piuttosto ridotto, la sua disponibilità stilistica poco elastica, comportano frequentemente ripetizioni di concetti e di formule in mezzo a cui non è facile stabilire quale sia il punto di origine di un elemento che può scaturire, con ugale legittimità, da parecchie sorgenti. Anche la norma metodologica di raggruppare le concomitanze più generiche attorno a quelle più specifiche non può — per il molteplice ritornare anche di queste ultime — essere sempre decisiva. Tuttavia un esame che unisca la valutazione della tipicità degli accostamenti con la loro quantità permette di ⋅ redigere una tabella indicativa che scaglioni le opere filoniane secondo una progressiva vicinanza o lontananza dall'orazione di Gregorio. In base a questi criteri si sono divisi in cinque gruppi — che non intendono essere rigidi — gli scritti di Filone: nel primo sono collocati quelli che presentano un numero ed una nettezza tale di concordanze da farne dedurre la conoscenza pressochè sicura da parte di Gregorio; nel secondo quelli per i quali tale conoscenza riveste soltanto un ragguardevole grado di probabilità; nel terzo quelli che lasciano in una posizione di dubbio; nel quarto quelli che, in base ai raffronti riscontrati, concedono solo tenui possibilità di affermare un rapporto; nel quinto quelli in cui i fattori di collegamento sono scarsissimi e vaghi, tali che farebbero escludere la conoscenza gregoriana qualora essa fosse necessariamente legata a delle tracce esplicite. I gruppi sono pertanto i seguenti, avvertendo che anche nell'interno di ognuno di essi le opere sono disposte, per quanto è possibile, secondo la loro maggiore aderenza al gruppo precedente o seguente. — 1° gruppo: 'Quis rerum divinarum heres sit'; 'De decalogo'; 'De vita contemplativa'; 'De Providentia'; 'De opificio mundi'; 'De mutatione nominum'; 'De specialibus legibus'. Per quanto concerne quest'ultimo grande trattato bisogna notare che il libro più sfruttato è stato il II°, il quale nella sezione 'De septenario' offre una densità di rassomiglianze davvero eccezionale; viene poi il IV° in cui spicca particolarmente il 'De iudice', seguito dal 'De iustitia' e dal 'De concupiscentia'; succede quindi il I° nel quale si distingue il 'De victimis', seguito dal 'De sacrificantibus' e dal 'De sacerdotum honore'; ultimo è il libro III° piuttosto generico. — 2° gruppo: 'De fuga et inventione'; 'De somniis'; 'De Iosepho'; 'Quod omnis probus liber sit'; 'De praemiis et poenis' e 'De exsecrationibus'; 'De vita Mosis'; 'De aeternitate mundi'. — 3° gruppo: 'De confusione linguarum'; 'De Abrahamo'; 'De sacrificiis Abelis et Caini'; 'Quod deterius potiori insidiari soleat'; 'De agricultura'; 'De plantatione'. — 4° gruppo: 'De congressu eruditionis gratia'; 'Quaestiones in Exodum'; 'De Cherubim'; 'De posteritate Caini'; 'De ebrietate'; 'Quod deus sit immutabilis'; 'Legum allegoriae', il cui III° libro non è però privo di affinità meritevoli di considerazione. — 5° gruppo: 'De virtutibus', che solo nel 'De humanitate' presenta dei punti di contatto di qualche rilievo; 'Quaestiones in Genesim'; 'In Flaccum'; 'Legatio ad Gaium'; 'De sobrietate'; 'De migratione Abrahami'; 'De gigantibus'; 'Alexander'. — Per la sua qualità di frammento non è stato possibile elencare l''Apologia pro Iudaeis' ('Hypothetica').

non mirava ad appagare la curiosità altrui, ma a procurarsi un sollievo attraverso all'altrui compatimento. Egli pensava a comunicare i suoi sentimenti; l'elenco dei suoi libri, caso mai, lo avrebbero steso gli altri. E l'esame della sua voluminosa eredità letteraria, anche semplicemente attraverso allo spiraglio di una sola orazione, conferma che sulle pagine della guida ideale della diaspora alessandrina egli passò lungo tempo. La massa delle concomitanze segnalate, pur nella diversità di religione, di argomento e di età, non è ragionevolmente spiegabile in altra maniera; la percentuale ordinaria di formule e di atteggiamenti comuni che si possono considerare come risultato automatico del linguaggio qui è stata di gran lunga superata. Di fronte alla quasi sconfinata libertà che il pensiero e la lingua hanno davanti nell'atto di esprimersi, questo tenace parallelismo che appaia i due scrittori, interrompendosi pressochè unicamente dinanzi alle citazioni neotestamentarie del secondo, si rivela come un prodotto non del caso, ma dello studio. Gregorio si creò un patrimonio concettuale e linguistico assai riccamente composito; nella sua diuturna applicazione intellettuale egli attinse da tanti ingegni precedenti contributi che poi sintetizzò nella sua personalità vigorosamente originale: uno di questi ingegni fu Filone d'Alessandria.

V. Influsso filoniano sulla cultura cristiana greca del IV secolo

La scuola giudaica alessandrina trovò in Filone il suo culmine massimo ed il suo unico testimone. Tutto è andato smarrito di quell'animoso fervore letterario che contraddistinse la metropoli egiziana negli ultimi due secoli avanti Cristo e nella prima metà del primo della nostra era. Il tempo, pur con qualche vistosa eccezione, è buon giudice nel concedere il diritto di sopravvivenza alle opere dell'ingegno umano e quindi possiamo pensare che la loro perdita non sia stata meritevole di molto rimpianto; è inoltre certo che lo spirito, se non i contributi specifici, furono assunti e trasfusi nella meditazione filoniana[290]. In sostanza la pattuglia di letterati ebrei, sicuramente tanto appassionati nelle loro convinzioni quanto sprovveduti di doti artistiche, dovette elaborare il messaggio biblico e rivivere la storia del popolo che lo raccolse e tramandò operando nella luce della civiltà ellenistica contemporanea. Essi indicarono la via e probabilmente fornirono larga copia di materiali al ripensamento più fortunato del loro con-

---

[290] M. SIMON, Situation du judaïsme alexandrin dans la Diaspora, in: Philon d'Alexandrie, Colloque Lyon 11—15 Septembre 1966, Paris, 1967, pp. 17—31 conclude il suo contributo affermando che ,,il prestigio di Alessandria come focolare di cultura giudaica non sopravvisse a Filone". — Per qualche illuminazione specifica sull'ambiente culturale alessandrino e su talune concomitanze che vi si stabilirono tra filonismo e gnosticismo vedi J. ZANDEE, Les enseignements de Silvanos et Philon d'Alexandrie, in: Mélanges H.-Ch. Puech, Paris, 1974, pp. 337—345.

cittadino[291]. Che in Filone confluiscano infatti molteplici rivoli pare una cosa abbastanza evidente; egli stesso rinvia più volte a fonti generiche ma reali e la sua voce sembra di volta in volta colorarsi di echi di assai diversa provenienza solo parzialmente fusi in unità di tono e di ritmo. Questa situazione, che si intuisce senza poterla sempre dimostrare per la sparizione pressochè completa della documentazione relativa, viene confermata dall'analogia dei rapporti filoniani con la cultura greca che possiamo riscontrare grazie a quanto di essa ci è pervenuto[292].

[291] Sulla figura e sulla collocazione cronologica, ugualmente imprecisabili, di Aristobulo vedi gli studi di H. GRAETZ, Der angebliche judäische Peripatetiker Aristobulos und seine Schriften, in: Monatsschrift für Geschichte und Wissenschaft des Judenthums, XXVII (1878), pp. 49—60 e 97—109; M. JOËL, Aristobul, der sogenannte Peripatetiker, nei suoi 'Blicke in die Religionsgeschichte zu Anfang des 2. christlichen Jahrhunderts', I, Breslau, 1880, pp. 79—100; A. ELTER, De Gnomologiorum Graecorum historia atque origine commentatio, Bonn, 1893—1895, parti V—IX, coll. 149—254; P. WENDLAND, inserito nel testo dell'ELTER nella parte IX alle coll. 229—234; E. SCHÜRER, Aristobulos, nella sua 'Geschichte des jüdischen Volkes im Zeitalter Jesu Christi', III vol., 3ª edizione, Leipzig, 1898, pp. 384—392; E. BRÉHIER, Les idées philosophiques et religieuses de Philon d'Alexandrie, Paris, 2e éd., 1950, pp. 46—49; N. WALTER, Anfänge alexandrinisch-jüdischer Bibelauslegung bei Aristobulos, in: Helikon, III (1963), pp. 353—372; ID., Der Thoraausleger Aristobulos. Untersuchungen zu seinen Fragmenten und zu pseudepigraphischen Resten der jüdisch-hellenistischen Literatur (T. U., n. 86), Berlin, 1964, pp. XXI-283; A. NOMACHI, Aristobulos and Philo, with Special Reference to ἑβδομάς, in: Journal of Classical Studies (Kyôto), XV (1967), pp. 86—97 (in giapponese con riassunto in inglese); CL. KRAUS REGGIANI, Aristobulo e l'esegesi allegorica dell'Antico Testamento nell'ambito del giudaismo ellenistico, in: Rivista di Filologia e d'Istruzione Classica, CI (1973), pp. 162—185. L'anteriorità di Aristobulo rispetto a Filone non pare comunque contestabile. — Per le ultime pubblicazioni su altre figure di evanescenti scrittori giudaici cfr. M. HENGEL, Judentum und Hellenismus (Wissenschaftliche Untersuchungen zum Neuen Testament, n. 10), Tübingen, 1973, pp. 169—175: Eupolemo; B. Z. WACHOLDER, Eupolemus. A Study of Judaeo-Greek Literature (Monographs of the Hebrew Union College Annual, n. 3), Cincinnati—New York—Los Angeles—Jerusalem, 1974, pp. 332; N. WALTER nell'ultima parte delle 'Jüdische Schriften aus hellenistisch-römischer Zeit', Band III, 2, Gütersloh, 1975, pp. 167—299, presenta 'Fragmente jüdisch-hellenistischer Exegeten: Aristobulos, Demetrios, Aristeas'; il medesimo N. WALTER nella medesima collezione, Band I, 2 (1976), pp. 90—163, offre 'Fragmente jüdisch-hellenistischer Historiker', con introduzione e traduzione di Eupolemo, Teofilo, Filone il Vecchio, Cleodemo Malca, Artapano, Pseudo-Eupolemo, Pseudo-Ecateo I e II.

[292] Per quanto concerne le fonti di Filone si possono mettere a profitto: F. J. BIET, Quid in interpretatione Scripturae sacrae allegorica Philo Judaeus a graecis philosophis sumpserit, Diss., Sancti Clodoaldi, 1854, p. 95; M. JOËL, Über einige geschichtliche Beziehungen des philonischen Systems, in: Monatsschrift für Geschichte und Wissenschaft des Judenthums, XII (1863), pp. 19—31, rist. nei suoi 'Beiträge zur Geschichte der Philosophie', Breslau, 1876, I, App. pp. 53—67; H. VON ARNIM, Quellenstudien zu Philo von Alexandria (Philologische Untersuchungen, n. 11), Berlin, 1888, p. 142; O. HENSE, Bion bei Philon, in: Rheinisches Museum, XLVII (1892), pp. 219—240; A. SCHMEKEL, Die Philosophie der mittleren Stoa in ihrem geschichtlichen Zusammenhange dargestellt, Berlin, 1892, pp. 409—423 e 430—432; P. WENDLAND, Die philosophischen Quellen des Philo von Alexandria in seiner Schrift über die Vorsehung, in: Progr. des Köllnischen Gymn., Berlin, 1892, pp. 27, ripreso in: ID., Philos Schrift über die Vorsehung. Ein Beitrag zur Geschichte der nacharistotelischen Philosophie, Berlin, 1892, pp. 120; E. NORDEN, Über den Streit des Theophrast und Zeno bei Philo περὶ ἀφθαρσίας κόσμου, in: ID., Beiträge zur Geschichte der griechischen Philosophie, in: Jahrbücher für classische Philologie, Supplbd.

(Proseguimento della nota 292)

XIX (1893), pp. 440—452; Fr. C. Conybeare, Notes on the Philonean Reading of two
Passages in the Timaeus, 38 B and 28 B, in: The Journal of Philology, XXI (1893), pp.
71—72; P. Wendland, Philo und die kynisch-stoische Diatribe, in: P. Wendland und
O. Kern, Beiträge zur Geschichte der griechischen Philosophie und Religion, Berlin,
1895, pp. 119; P. Wendland, Eine doxographische Quelle Philo's, in: Sitzungsberichte
der K. Preußischen Akad. der Wissenschaften zu Berlin, Berlin, 1897, II, pp. 1074—1079;
J. Horovitz, Das platonische Νοητὸν Ζῷον und der philonische Κόσμος Νοητός, Diss.
Marburg, 1900, pp. XI-103; M. Apelt, De rationibus quibusdam quae Philoni Alexan-
drino cum Posidonio intercedunt (Commentationes Philologae Jenenses, n. 8, fasc. 1),
Leipzig, edid. Seminarii Philologorum Jenensis professores, 1907, pp. 89—141; G. R. S.
Mead, Philo von Alexandrien und die hellenistische Theologie, in: Vierteljahrsschrift für
Bibelkunde, III (1908), pp. 183—226; H. Leisegang, Die Raumtheorie im späteren Platonismus, insbesondere bei Philon und den Neuplatonikern, Diss. Straßburg, Weida i. Th.,
1911, pp. 93; K. Gronau, Poseidonios und die jüdisch-christliche Genesisexegese, Leipzig
und Berlin, 1914, pp. VIII-313; F. Cumont, Un mythe pythagoricien chez Posidonius
et Philon, in: Revue de Philologie, XLIII (1919), pp. 78—85; K. Reinhardt, Philo und
Boëthos, in: Kosmos und Sympathie. Neue Untersuchungen über Poseidonios, München,
1926, pp. 20—25; I. Heinemann, Die griechischen und die jüdischen Elemente in Philos
Stellung zu Tempel, Opfer und Eid, in: Festschrift zum 75jährigen Bestehen des jüdisch-
theologischen Seminars Fraenkelscher Stiftung, Breslau, 1929, pp. 3—96; E. R. Good-
enough, A Neo-Pythagorean Source in Philo Judaeus (Yale Classical Studies, n. 3), New
Haven, 1932, pp. 115—164; H. Neumark, Die Verwendung griechischer und jüdischer
Motive in den Gedanken Philons über die Stellung Gottes zu seinen Freunden, Diss.
Würzburg, Breslau, 1937, pp. 65; H. Fraenkel, Heraclitus on the Notion of a Generation
(Vorsokr. 22 A 19), in: American Journal of Philology, LIX (1938), pp. 89—91; J. P.
Maguire, The Sources of Pseudo-Aristotle De Mundo, in: Yale Classical Studies, VI
(1939), pp. 109—167 (l'autore sconosciuto e Filone si sarebbero attenuti ad una fonte
comune che probabilmente era neo-pitagorica); J. B. McDiarmid, Theophrastus on the
Eternity of the World, in: Transactions and Proceedings of the American Philological
Association, LXXI (1940), pp. 239—247 (Teofrasto fonte di Filone); W. Wiersma, Der
angebliche Streit des Zenon und Theophrast über die Ewigkeit der Welt, in: Mnemosyne,
Ser. III, VIII (1940), pp. 235—243; M. Muehl, Über die Herkunft des platonischen
Versöhnungsgedankens, Staat V 470 e, in: Philologische Wochenschrift, LXI (1941),
pp. 429—431 (fonte comune tra Platone e Filone potrebbe essere stato Biante); Id., Zu
Poseidonios und Philon, in: Wiener Studien, LX (1942), pp. 28—36; P. Boyancé, Les
Muses et l'harmonie des sphères, in: Mélanges F. Grat, I, Paris, 1946, pp. 3—16 (fondo
pitagorico della concezione filoniana della musica come imitazione di quella delle sfere);
P. Moraux, Une nouvelle trace de l'Aristote perdu, in: Les Études Classiques, XVI (1948),
pp. 89—91; L. Fruechtel, Zur Aesopfabel des Kallimachos, in: Gymnasium, LVII
(1950), pp. 123—124; W. Lameere, Sur un passage de Philon d'Alexandrie (De plantatione, 1—6), in: Mnemosyne, Ser. IV, IV (1951), pp. 73—80 (influsso peripatetico); L.
Alfonsi, Un nuovo frammento del Περὶ φιλοσοφίας aristotelico, in: Hermes, LXXXI
(1953), pp. 45—49; A. N. M. Rich, The Platonic Ideas as Thoughts of God, in: Mnemosyne, Ser. IV, VII (1954), pp. 123—133; L. Alfonsi, Il περὶ βίου θεωρητικοῦ di Filone
e la tradizione protrettica, in: Wiener Studien, LXX (1957) (Festschrift Mras), pp. 5—10;
M. Hadas, Plato in Hellenistic Fusion, in: Journal of the History of Ideas, XIX (1958),
pp. 3—18; A. F. J. Klijn, The Single One in the Gospel of Thomas, in: Journal of Biblical
Literature, LXXXI (1962), pp. 271—278 (Filone ed il vangelo secondo Tommaso derivano
dalle stesse fonti); L. Wächter, Der Einfluß platonischen Denkens auf rabbinische Schöp-
fungsspekulationen, in: Zeitschrift für Religions- und Geistesgeschichte, XIV (1962),
pp. 36—56; P. Boyancé, Note sur la φρουρά platonicienne, in: Revue de Philologie,
XXXVII (1963), pp. 7—11; Id., Sur l'exégèse hellénistique du Phèdre (Phèdre, p. 246 c),
in: Miscellanea Rostagni, Torino, 1963. pp. 45—53; P. M. Schuhl, Philon, les banquets
et le Séder pascal, in: Miscellanea Rostagni . . ., pp. 54—55; W. Theiler, Philon von
Alexandria und der Beginn des kaiserzeitlichen Platonismus, in: Festgabe für J. Hirsch-

Da quale sistema filosofico Filone attinse in maniera precipua per confezionare l'impalcatura logico-psicologica sulla quale stendere le sue convinzioni religiose? È un quesito che ha attirato studiosi validi e seri e che li ha sparpagliati ai quattro venti; i loro responsi sono stati sorprendentemente divergenti: infatti per T. H. BILLINGS[293] egli è intimamente platonico; per E. ZELLER[294] ondeggia tra platonismo, stoicismo e neopita-

berger, Frankfurt, 1965, pp. 199—218; I. LÉVY, Recherches esséniennes et pythagoriciennes, Genève–Paris, 1965 (pp. 37—50: Parabole d'Héraclide. Héraclide et Philon; pp. 51—56: Sur quelques points de contact entre le 'Contra Apionem' et l'œuvre de Philon d'Alexandrie); P. COURCELLE,. Le corps-tombeau, Platon, Gorgias 493 a, Cratyle 400 c, Phèdre 250 c, in: Revue des Études Anciennes, LXVIII (1966), pp. 101—122; A. MICHEL, Quelques aspects de la rhétorique chez Philon, in: Philon d'Alexandrie. Colloque Lyon 11—15 Septembre 1966, Paris, 1967, pp. 81—103; M. ALEXANDRE, La culture profane chez Philon, ibid. pp. 105—130; P. BOYANCÉ, Écho des exégèses de la mythologie grecque chez Philon, ibid. pp. 169—188; K. MARICKI-GADJANSKI, Heraclitus retractatus (in serbo con riassunto in inglese), in: Jahrbuch der Philosophischen Fak. in Novi Sad, XI (1968), pp. 25—43; F. W. KOHNKE, Das Bild der echten Münze bei Philo von Alexandria, in: Hermes, XCVI (1968—1969), pp. 583—590 (Filone deriva quest'immagine e molte altre idee da Eudoro di Alessandria); W. THEILER, Philo von Alexandria und der hellenisierte Timaeus, in: Philomathes. Studies Ph. Merlan, The Hague, 1971, pp. 25—35; R. G. HAMERTON-KELLY, Sources and Traditions in Philo Judaeus. Prolegomena to an Analysis of His Writing, in: Studia Philonica, I (1972), pp. 3—26; E. J. BARNES, Petronius, Philo and Stoic Rhetoric, in: Latomus, XXXII (1973), pp. 787—798 (influsso di Posidonio su Filone); A. H. CHROUST, Some Remarks about Philo of Alexandria, De aeternitate mundi V, 20—24. A fragment of Aristotle's On philosophy, in: Classical Folia (New York), XXVIII (1974), pp. 83—88; IDEM, A Fragment of Aristotle's On Philosophy. Some Remarks about Philo of Alexandria, De Aeternitate Mundi, 8, 41, in: Wiener Studien, N. F. VIII (1974), pp. 15—19; IDEM, A Fragment of Aristotle's On philosophy in Philo of Alexandria, De opificio mundi I, 7, in: Divus Thomas (Piacenza), LXXVII (1974), pp. 224—235; P. BOYANCÉ, Étymologie et théologie chez Varron, in: Revue des Études Latines, LIII (1975), pp. 99—115 (riconduce ad Antioco di Ascalona la concordanza tra Varrone e Filone che coincidono nello stabilire per ogni vocabolo quattro gradi di spiegazioni e nell'assegnare al „re" il quarto che costituisce il culmine); A. H. CHROUST, Lucretius, De rerum natura V. 110ff., a possible reference to Aristotle's On philosophy, in: Acta Classica (Cape Town), XVIII (1975), pp. 141—143 (Lucrezio si richiama ad Aristotele quale è riportato in Filone); IDEM, Some Comments on Philo of Alexandria, De aeternitate mundi, in: Laval Théologique et Philosophique, XXXI (1975), pp. 135—145 (De aeternitate mundi 5,20—24; 6,28—7,34; 8,39—43 sono autentici frammenti del 'De philosophia' di Aristotele, con solo qualche ritocco stilistico); J. M. DILLON, The Transcendence of God in Philo: Some Possible Sources, in: Center for Hermeneutical Studies, Protocol Series, XVI (1975), pp .1—8 (derivazioni da Speusippo e da taluni neopitagorici); O. SCHOENBERGER, Spiegelung eines alten Versus?, in: Rheinisches Museum, CXIX (1976), pp. 95—96 (un antico frammento poetico sarebbe alla base di De posteritate Caini 18); A. H. CHROUST, Aristotle's On philosophy and Plutarch's De facie in orbe lunae, in: Wiener Studien, N. F. XI (1977), pp. 69—75 (avvalendosi anche di Plutarco si mostra che il De aeternitate mundi 6,28—7,34 è un frammento del 'De philosophia' di Aristotele); B. A. PEARSON, Philo and the Gnostics on Man and Salvation, in: Center for Hermeneutical Studies, XXIX (1977), pp. 1—17 (sue fonti sarebbero il testo della Genesi dei LXX, tradizioni ellenistico-giudaiche, Medio platonismo); J. DILLON, Philo Judaeus and the Cratylus, in: Liverpool Classical Monthly, III (1978), pp. 37—42.
[293] The Platonism of Philo Judaeus, Diss. Chicago, 1919, pp. VIII-105.
[294] Die Philosophie der Griechen in ihrer geschichtlichen Entwicklung, III. Teil, II. Abt., 5. Aufl., Leipzig, 1923, pp. 385—467.

gorismo in un fondamentale dissidio; per E. Bréhier[295] dall'intreccio di
componenti svariate emerge la concezione stoica imbibita di apporti egiziani; per M. Heinze[296] hanno la preminenza le concomitanze stoiche,
seppure selettivamente filtrate; per M. Pohlenz[297] il sostrato concettuale
è di estrazione stoica orientata però in senso giudaico; per H. Leisegang[298]
ci troviamo di fronte ad un caso di stoicismo integrale; per E. Turowski[299]
si tratta di uno stoicismo di tipico stampo posidoniano; per K. Gronau[300]
e per M. Apelt[301] l'influsso posidoniano è in netta prevalenza; per F. Cumont[302] caratteristica del nostro scrittore è l'abbondanza di concetti ari-
stotelici; per W. L. Knox[303] Filone non è un pensatore originale ma un
compilatore; per H. Lewy[304] Filone non ha tanto una dottrina quanto una
specie di atmosfera che è il riflesso teoretico di una religione mistica; per
M.-J. Lagrange[305] quello filoniano è soprattutto un eclettismo strumentale
che lo induce a scegliersi di volta in volta gli alleati più adatti per le singole
battaglie che intende ingaggiare; A. J. Festugière[306] nega recisamente
che Filone possegga un qualsiasi sistema; infine H. A. Wolfson[307] respinge
il problema asserendo che Filone si propone unicamente di cogliere il senso
dei versetti biblici servendosi all'uopo delle formule filosofiche che gli
venivano più acconce, ma senza attribuire loro quello specifico significato
tecnico che possedevano nelle scuole che le avevano coniate: per quanto
infatti siano frequenti le espressioni stoiche egli critica sostanzialmente lo
stoicismo inclinando piuttosto verso Platone, di cui accetta però le singole
dottrine solo dopo severi esami[308].

---

[295] Les idées philosophiques et religieuses de Philon d'Alexandrie (Études de Philosophie
Médiévale, n. 8), 3e éd., Paris, 1950, pp. 336.
[296] Die Lehre vom Logos in der griechischen Philosophie, Oldenburg, 1872, pp. 204—298;
rist. Aalen, 1961.
[297] Philon von Alexandreia, in: Nachrichten . . . (1942), (cfr. nota 308), pp. 409—487 e: Die
Stoa. Geschichte einer geistigen Bewegung, Göttingen, 1948—1949, vol. I, pp. 369—378
e II, pp. 180—184; nella traduzione italiana, Firenze, 1967, cfr. vol. II, pp. 193—215.
[298] Philon. Nr. 41, in: RE., XX 1 (1941), coll. 1—50.
[299] Die Widerspiegelung des stoischen Systems bei Philon von Alexandreia, Borna–Leipzig,
1927, pp. V-58.
[300] Poseidonios und die jüdisch-christliche Genesisexegese, Leipzig–Berlin, 1914, pp. 1—2.
[301] De rationibus quibusdam quae Philoni Alexandrino cum Posidonio intercedunt . . . (1907),
cfr. nota 292.
[302] Philonis De aeternitate mundi edidit et prolegomenis instruxit F. C., Berolini, 1891, p. VI.
[303] Some Hellenistic Elements in Primitive Christianity, London, 1944, pp. 34—54. In una
nota alle pp. 47—54 sostiene che larghi tratti del De Opificio Mundi, 89—127, sono tramati
sulla cosmogonia posidoniana, fondata sul Timeo platonico.
[304] Introduzione al suo 'Philo, Philosophical Writings, Selections', Oxford, 1946.
[305] Le Judaïsme avant Jésus-Christ, 3e éd., Paris, 1931, pp. 542—586.
[306] La révélation d'Hermès Trismégiste, II: Le Dieu cosmique, Paris, 1949, pp. 519—572.
[307] Philo. Foundations of Religious Philosophy . . . (1962), (cfr. nota 308), vol. I, p. 97.
[308] Per trattazioni complessive sul pensiero e sull'opera di Filone puoi vedere I. A. Fabri-
cius, Bibliotheca Graeca, sive notitia scriptorum veterum Graecorum, 4a ed. G. Chr.
Harles, Hamburg, 1795, vol. IV, pp. 721—750; J. G. Buhle, Lehrbuch der Geschichte
der Philosophie und einer kritischen Literatur derselben, Göttingen, 1799, vol. IV, pp. 69
— 141; A. F. Dähne, Geschichtliche Darstellung der jüdisch-alexandrinischen Religions-

(Proseguimento della nota 308)

Philosophie, Halle, 1834—1835, 2 voll., pp. XX-497 e VIII-266; J. G. MÜLLER, Philo und die jüdisch-alexandrinische Religionsphilosophie, in: Real-Encyklopädie für protestantische Theologie und Kirche, 1. Aufl., Gotha, 1859, vol. XI, pp. 578—603; H. EWALD, Geschichte des Volkes Israel, 3. Aufl., Göttingen, 1868, vol. VI, pp. 257—312; A. HAUSRATH, Neutestamentliche Zeitgeschichte, Heidelberg, 1872, vol. II, pp. 126—179; J. DRUMMOND, Philo and the Principles of the Jewish-Alexandrine Philosophy, London and Manchester, 1877, pp. 28; M. NICOLAS, Études sur Philon d'Alexandrie, in: Revue de l'histoire des religions, V (1882), pp. 318—339; VII (1883), pp. 145—164; VIII (1883), pp. 468—488; 582—602; 756—772; O. HOLTZMANN, Philo von Alexandrien, in: B. STADE, Geschichte des Volkes Israel, Berlin, 1888, vol. II, pp. 521—551; J. DRUMMOND, Philo Judaeus or the Jewish-Alexandrian Philosophy in its Development and Completion, London, 1888, 2 voll., pp. VIII-359; 355; ristampato anastat. ad Amsterdam nel 1969; E. RENAN, Histoire du peuple d'Israel, Paris, 1893, vol. V, pp. 345—380; ID., Philon d'Alexandrie et son œuvre, in: Revue de Paris, I (1894), pp. 37—55; É. HERRIOT, Philon le Juif. Essai sur l'école juive d'Alexandrie, Paris, 1898, pp. XIX-366; J. MARTIN, Philon, Paris, 1907, p. 303; E. SCHÜRER, Philo der jüdische Philosoph, nella sua 'Geschichte des jüdischen Volkes im Zeitalter Jesu Christi', III⁴, Leipzig, 1909, pp. 633—716; N. BENTWICH, Philo Judaeus of Alexandria, Philadelphia, 1910, p. 273; M. LOUIS, Philon le Juif, estratto da 'Philosophes et Penseurs', Paris, 1911, pp. 62; J. HEINEMANN, Philons griechische und jüdische Bildung, in: Festschrift zum 75jährigen Bestehen des jüdisch-theologischen Seminars, Breslau, 1929, pp. 96; ID., Philons griechische und jüdische Bildung. Kulturvergleichende Untersuchungen zu Philons Darstellung der jüdischen Gesetze, Breslau, 1932, pp. 598, rist. Hildesheim, 1962, pp. 606; G. BARDY, Philon de Juif, in: Dictionnaire de Théologie Catholique, XII, Paris, 1933, coll. 1439—1456; E. STEIN, Filone d'Alessandria. Il dotto, le opere, la dottrina e la filosofia (in ebraico), Varsavia, 1937, pp. 309 (limita fortemente la conoscenza filoniana della lingua e della cultura ebraica); W. L. KNOX, Pharisaism and Hellenism, in: Judaism and Christianity, vol. II: H. LOEWE, The Contact of Pharisaism with Other Cultures, London—New York, 1937, pp. 61—111, ristampa New York, 1969; S. BELKIN, Philo and the Oral Law. The Philonic Interpretation of Biblical Law in Relation to the Palestinian Halakah, Cambridge, Mass., 1940, pp. XI-292; M. POHLENZ, Philon von Alexandreia, in: Nachrichten der Akad. der Wissenschaften in Göttingen, Phil.-hist. Klasse, 1942, n. 5, Göttingen, 1942, pp. 409—487, riportato in: ID., Kleine Schriften, Hildesheim, 1965, pp. 305—383; F. HEVESI, Gli antichi filosofi giudaici, Budapest, 1943, pp. 181—236 (in ungherese con riassunto in tedesco alle pp. 422—426); E. BRÉHIER, Les idées philosophiques et religieuses de Philon d'Alexandrie, cfr. nota 295; F. PROOST, Tussen twee werelden. Philo Judaeus, Arnhem, 1952, pp. 51; J. DANIÉLOU, Philon d'Alexandrie, Paris, 1958, pp. 220; E. R. GOODENOUGH presenta Filone in: S. NOVECK, Great Jewish Personalities in Ancient and Medieval Times, New York, 1959, pp. XVI-351 (pp. 97—119); R. ARNALDEZ, 'Introduction générale', all'edizione delle opere di Filone, Paris, 1961, pp. 17—112 premessa al 'De opificio mundi'; Jewish Philosophy and Philosophers, ed. by R. GOLDWATER, London, 1962, pp. 200, a cura di vari collaboratori, tra i quali R. LOEWE, Philo and Judaism in Alexandria; E. R. GOODENOUGH, An Introduction to Philo Judaeus, 2nd ed., Oxford, 1962, pp. 167; H. A. WOLFSON, Philo. Foundations of Religious Philosophy in Judaism, Christianity, and Islam, 3rd ed., Cambridge, Mass., 1962, 2 voll., pp. XVI-462; XIV-531; C. MONDÉSERT, R. CADIOU, J. E. MÉNARD, R. ARNALDEZ, A. FEUILLET, Philon d'Alexandrie, in: Dictionnaire de la Bible, Supplément VII, Paris, 1966, coll. 1288—1351 (nel 'Dictionnaire de la Bible' di F. VIGOUROUX, vol. V, Paris, 1912, coll. 300—312 la voce 'Philon' era stata redatta da H. LESÊTRE); A. MADDALENA, Filone Alessandrino, Milano, 1970, pp. 486; W. H. WAGNER, Philo and Paideia, in: Cithara (Essays in Judaeo-Christian Tradition, n. 10), St. Bonaventure, New York, 1971, pp. 53—64; E. R. GOODENOUGH, Philo von Alexandria, in: Große Gestalten des Judentums, hrsg. von S. NOVECK, I, Zürich, 1972, pp. 9—32; H. HEGERMANN, Griechisch-jüdisches Schrifttum, in: Literatur und Religion des Frühjudentums, Würzburg—Gütersloh, 1973, pp. 163—180 e 353—369; A. MENDELSON, A Reappraisal of Wolfson's Method, in: Studia Philonica, III (1974—75), pp. 11—26

Certo che il ridurre l'apparato filosofico ellenico che riscontriamo in Filone ad una specie di cava da cui estrarre ogni sorta di frasi, sconnesse ed avulse da una loro architettura logica, si presenta come una tesi audace, ma la stessa paradossalità della posizione ci riporta a quell'eclettismo che, sostenuto da molti studiosi, appare come la caratteristica più obiettiva della fisionomia culturale di Filone. E, in fondo, era naturale che egli adottasse un tale atteggiamento di fronte alla filosofia; non era infatti un filosofo ma un teologo, e suo scopo non era di offrire una spiegazione razionale del mondo ma di riesprimere in termini moderni la rivelazione mosaica[309]. La filosofia si riduceva quindi per lui ad ancella, o meglio ad interprete, della parola divina. Sarebbe pertanto stato senza senso il legarsi ad una scuola, che avrebbe fatalmente finito con il farlo deviare dal suo cammino, rinunciando ai contributi delle altre, che invece gli avrebbero potuto giovare in determinati frangenti. La rotazione delle speculazioni umane sarebbe stata una prova del suo sostanziale distacco da loro ed una garanzia che suo filo conduttore era l'insegnamento divino contenuto nella Bibbia[310].

(partecipazione di Filone alla cultura pagana e complessità del suo mondo); TH. CONLEY, 'General Education' in Philo of Alexandria, in: Center for Hermeneutical Studies, Protocol of the Fifteenth Colloquy ... 1975, Berkeley, 1975, pp. 44 (pp. 1—11); H. PARUZEL, Filono el Aleksandrio, in: Biblia Revuo (Ravenna), XII (1975), pp. 81—114. In questo volume (ANRW II 21,1) cfr. S. SANDMEL, Philo Judaeus: An Introduction to the Man, his Writings, and his Significance, pp. 3—46.

[309] E. R. GOODENOUGH, By Light, Light . . ., 1935, considerò Filone più ellenico che giudaico, ma fu una posizione errata che egli stesso ripudiò — in: Journal of Biblical Literature, LVIII (1939), pp. 57—58 — grazie alla solidità delle obiezioni del VÖLKER.

[310] Sulle convinzioni filosofiche, teologiche e mistiche di Filone vedi: I. B. CARPZOV, De λόγῳ Philonis, non Johanneo adversus Thomam Mangey, Helmstadt, 1749, pp. 44; E. H. STAHL, Versuch eines systematischen Entwurfs des Lehrbegriffs Philo's von Alexandrien, in: J. G. EICHHORN, Allgemeine Bibliothek der biblischen Litteratur, IV, 5, Leipzig, 1793, pp. 767—890; J. BRYANT, The Sentiments of Philo Judaeus Concerning the λόγος, or Word of God . . ., Cambridge, 1797, pp. VII-290; CHR. G. L. GROSSMANN, Quaestiones Philoneae, I. De theologiae Philonis fontibus et auctoritate; II. De λόγῳ Philonis, Leipzig, 1829—1830, pp. 65 e 70; A. H. SARAZIN, De philosophica Philonis Judaei doctrina, Strasbourg, 1835, pp. 39; H. DENZINGER, Dissertatio de Philonis philosophia et schola Judaeorum Alexandrina, Diss. inaug., Herbipoli, 1840, pp. 162; F. C. BAUR, Die christliche Lehre von der Dreieinigkeit und Menschwerdung Gottes in ihrer geschichtlichen Entwicklung, Tübingen, I, 1841, pp. 59—78 e 92—102; F. KEFERSTEIN, Philo's Lehre von den göttlichen Mittelwesen. Zugleich eine kurze Darstellung der Grundzüge des philonischen Systems, Leipzig, 1846, pp. VII-256; E. VACHEROT, Histoire de l'École d'Alexandrie, Tome premier, Paris, 1846, rist., Amsterdam, 1965, pp. 125—167; J. BUCHER, Philonische Studien. — Versuch, die Frage nach der persönlichen Hypostase des in den philonischen Schriften auftretenden Logos auf historisch-pragmatischem Wege zu lösen. Zugleich eine gedrängte Darlegung des philonischen Systems, Tübingen, 1848, pp. XII-44; L. NOACK, Der Jude Philon von Alexandrien und seine Weltansicht, in: Psyche, II (1851), pp. 4—7; J. A. B. LUTTERBECK, Der philonische Lehrbegriff, in: ID., Die Neutestamentlichen Lehrbegriffe, oder Untersuchungen über das Zeitalter der Religionswende, die Vorstufen des Christenthums und die erste Gestaltung desselben, Mainz, 1852, I, pp. 418—446; T. RUBINSOHN, Philo and his Opinions, in: The Christian Review, XVIII (1853), pp. 119—135; ANONIMO, Philo Judaeus and Alexandrian Jewish Theology, in: The Eclectic Review, N. S. X (1855), pp. 602—613; J. M. JOST, Geschichte des Judenthums und seiner Secten, Leipzig, I, 1857,

(Proseguimento della nota 310)

pp. 99—108; 344—361; 367—393; M. Wolff, Die Philonische Philosophie in ihren Haupt-momenten dargestellt, 2. verm. Aufl., Gothenburg, 1858, pp. X-61 (1. Aufl. Leipzig, 1849); Z. Frankel, Alexandrinische Messiashoffnungen, in: Monatsschrift für Geschichte und Wissenschaft des Judenthums, VIII (1859), pp. 241—261; 285—308; 321—330; J. G. Müller, Die messianischen Erwartungen des Juden Philo, Basel, 1870, pp. 25; L. Treitel, De Philonis Judaei sermone, Diss. inaug., Vratislaviae, 1872, pp. 29; J. Busch-mann, Eine exegetische Studie über den Logos des Philo, Progr. der Stiftsschule, IV, Aachen, 1872, pp. 26; M. Heinze, Die Lehre vom Logos in der griechischen Philosophie, Oldenburg, 1872, pp. 204—297; Rippner, Über die Ursprünge des philonischen Logos, in: Monats-schrift für Geschichte und Wissenschaft des Judenthums, XXI (1872), pp. 289—305; P. Paulidis, Ἡ περὶ θεοῦ διδασκαλία κατὰ Φίλωνα τὸν Ἰουδαῖον, in: Ἀθήναιον, I (1872), pp. 191—207; 328—353; J. Buschmann, Die Persönlichkeit des philonischen Λόγος. Eine exegetische Studie über Philo's Λόγος unter Zugrundlegung seiner eigenen Schriften, Aachen, 1873, pp. 65; H. Soulier, La doctrine du Logos chez Philon d'Alexandrie, Diss. inaug. Lipsiensis, Torino, 1876, pp. VIII-165; J. Réville, Le Logos d'après Philon d'Alexan-drie, Genève, 1877, pp. 94; H. Graetz, Das Korbfest der Erstlinge bei Philo, in: Monats-schrift für Geschichte und Wissenschaft des Judenthums, XXVI (1877), pp. 433—442; Fr. Klasen, Die alttestamentliche Weisheit und der Logos der jüdisch-alexandrinischen Philosophie auf historischer Grundlage in Vergleich gesetzt. Beitrag zur Christologie, Freiburg i. Br., 1878, pp. VI-87; A. Harnoch, De Philonis Judaei λόγῳ inquisitio, Regiomonti, 1879, pp. 38; J. Carvallo, Paragraphes du livre de la Création de Philon rela-tifs aux propriétés des nombres, in: Revue des Études Juives, VI (1882—1883), pp. 273—278; R. M. Wenley, Socrates and Christ. A Study in the Philosophy of Religion, Edin-burgh—London, 1889, pp. 274 (cap. VIII: Philo Judaeus and his significance: pp. 163—182); M. Freudenthal, Die Erkenntnislehre Philos von Alexandria, Inaug.-Diss. Greifswald, Berlin, 1891, pp. 77, stampato anche in: Berliner Studien für classische Philo-logie und Archaeologie, n. 13, Berlin, 1891, pp. 77; J.-E. Neel, Le philonisme avant Philon, in: Revue de Théologie et de Philosophie, XXV (1892), pp. 417—433; M. Dienst-fertig, Die Prophetologie in der Religionsphilosophie des ersten nachchristlichen Jahr-hunderts, unter besonderer Beachtung der Verschiedenheit in den Auffassungen des Philon von Alexandrien und des Flavius Josephus, Inaug.-Diss. von Erlangen, Breslau, 1892, pp. 33; E. Hoehne, Die Berührungspunkte zwischen Moses und Plato: das ist zwischen Altem Testament und platonischer Philosophie, zum Teil nach Philo, Leipzig, 1893, pp. 39; E. A. Pantasopulos, Die Lehre vom natürlichen und positiven Rechte bei Philo Judaeus, Inaug.-Diss. von Erlangen, München, 1893, pp. 28; K. Kiesewetter, Philo von Alexandria, nell'opera 'Der Occultismus des Altertums', II, Leipzig, 1896, pp. 693—737; A. Aall, Der Logos. Geschichte seiner Entwickelung in der griechischen Philosophie und der christlichen Litteratur, Leipzig, 1896, vol. I, pp. 184—231; J. Horo-vitz, Untersuchungen über Philons und Platons Lehre von der Weltschöpfung, Marburg, 1900, pp. XIII-127; L. H. Mills, Philo's δυνάμεις and the Amesha Spenta, in: The Journal of the R. Asiatic Society of Great Britain and Ireland, 1901, pp. 553—568; O. Pfleiderer, Das Urchristentum, seine Schriften und Lehren in geschichtlichem Zusammenhang beschrieben, 2. Aufl., Berlin, 1902, vol. II, pp. 1—16 e 25—54; L. Treitel, Der Nomos, insonderheit Sabbat und Feste, in philonischer Beleuchtung, an der Hand von Philos Schrift De Septenario, in: Monatsschrift für Geschichte und Wissenschaft des Judenthums, XLVII (1903), pp. 214—231; 317—321; 399—417; 490—514; L. H. Mills, The Philonian Logos, in: Zarathuštra, Philo, the Achaemenids and Israel . . ., Leipzig, 1903—1906, vol. I, pp. 136—208; E. Caird, The Philosophy and Theology of Philo, in: The Evolution of Theology in the Greek Philosophers, Glasgow, 1904, vol. II, pp. 184—209; L. Treitel, Die religions- und kulturgeschichtliche Stellung Philos, in: Theologische Studien und Kritiken, LXXVII (1904), pp. 380—401; A. S. Carman, Philo's Doctrine of the Divine Father and the Virgin Mother, in: The American Journal of Theology, IX (1905), pp. 491—518; P. Barth, Die stoische Theodizee bei Philo, in: Philosophische Abhandlungen M. Heinze gewidmet, Berlin, 1906, pp. 14—33; G. Falter, Beiträge zur Geschichte der Idee, Teil I: Philon und Plotin, Gießen, 1906, pp. 37—102; H. Guyot,

(Proseguimento della nota 310)

L'Infinité divine depuis Philon le Juif jusqu'à Plotin. Avec une introduction sur le même sujet dans la philosophie grecque avant Philon le Juif, Paris, 1906, pp. XII-260; K. S. L. GUTHRIE, The Message of Philo Judaeus of Alexandria, London, 1909, pp. 96; H. WINDISCH, Die Frömmigkeit Philos und ihre Bedeutung für das Christentum. Eine religionsgeschichtliche Studie, Leipzig, 1909, pp. 140; K. HERZOG, Spekulativ-psychologische Entwicklung der Grundlagen und Grundlinien des philonischen Systems, Inaug.-Diss., Nürnberg, 1911, pp. 127, ristamp. a Leipzig, 1911; O. HOLTZMANN, Zwei Stellen zum Gottesbegriff des Philon, in: Zeitschrift für die Neutestamentliche Wissenschaft, XIII (1912), pp. 270 —272; L. COHN, Zur Lehre vom Logos bei Philo, in: Judaica . . . H. Cohen, Berlin, 1912, pp. 303—331; L. TREITEL, Die alexandrinische Lehre von den Mittelwesen oder göttlichen Kräften, insbesondere bei Philo, geprüft auf die Frage, ob und welchen Einfluß sie auf das Mutterland Palästina gehabt, in: Judaica . . . H. Cohen, Berlin, 1912, pp. 177—184; BERGMANN, Die stoische Philosophie und die jüdische Frömmigkeit, in: Judaica . . ., pp. 145—166; H. LEISEGANG, Die Begriffe der Zeit und Ewigkeit bei Philon, in: Die Begriffe der Zeit und Ewigkeit im späteren Platonismus (Beiträge zur Geschichte der Philosophie des Mittelalters, n. XIII, 4), Münster i. W., 1913, pp. 10—14; N. BENTWICH, From Philo to Plotinus, in: The Jewish Quarterly Review, N.S. IV (1913—1914), pp. 1—21; H. STRATHMANN, Geschichte der frühchristlichen Askese bis zur Entstehung des Mönchtums, Leipzig, 1914, vol. I, pp. 83—157; B. KELLERMANN, Licht und Logos bei Philo, nella sua traduz. e commento dell'opera 'Die Kämpfe Gottes' di Lewi ben Gerson, Berlin, 1916, vol. II, pp. 307—336; F. H. COLSON, Philo on Education, in: The Journal of Theological Studies, XVIII (1916—1917), pp. 151—162; F. HEINEMANN, Philos Bedeutung für die abendländische Geistesgeschichte, in: Neue jüdische Monatshefte, III (1918—1919), pp. 424—430; H. A. A. KENNEDY, Philo's Contribution to Religion, London, 1919, pp. XI-245; O. CASEL, De philosophorum Graecorum silentio mystico (Religionsgeschichtliche Versuche und Vorarbeiten, n. XVI, 2), Gießen, 1919, pp. 72—86; I. HEINEMANN, Philons Lehre vom Heiligen Geist und der intuitiven Erkenntnis, in: Monatsschrift für Geschichte und Wissenschaft des Judenthums, LXIV (1920), pp. 8—29 e 101—122; L. TREITEL, Gesamte Theologie und Philosophie Philos von Alexandria, Berlin, 1923, pp. 150; M.-J. LAGRANGE, Le Logos de Philon, in: Revue Biblique, XXXII (1923), pp. 321—371; W. FAIRWEATHER, The Jewish Hellenist Philo of Alexandria, in: Jesus and the Greeks; or, Early Christianity in the Tideway of Hellenism, Edinburgh, 1924, pp. 159—216; H. LEISEGANG, Logos, in: RE XIII 1 (1926), coll. 1035—1081; ID., Sophia, ibid., III A 1 (1927), coll. 1019—1039; B. A. STEGMANN, Christ, the 'Man from Heaven'. A Study of I Cor. 15, 45—47 in the Light of the Anthropology of Philo Judaeus, Diss. Catholic University (The Catholic University of America New Testament Studies, n. 6), Washington, 1927, pp. XVI-104; J. LEBRETON, Histoire du dogme de la Trinité des origines jusqu'au Concile de Nicée, 8e édit., Paris, 1927, vol. I, pp. 178—251; R. B. HOYLE, Spirit in the Writings and Experience of Philo, in: The Biblical Review, XIII (1928), pp. 351—369; H. LEWY, Sobria Ebrietas. Untersuchungen zur Geschichte der antiken Mystik, Gießen, 1929, pp. 174; R. REITZENSTEIN, Philos Lehre von der Wiedergeburt, in: Die Vorgeschichte der christlichen Taufe, Leipzig—Berlin, 1929, pp. 103—126; H. R. WILLOUGHBY, The Mysticism of Philo, in: ID., Pagan Regeneration: A Study of Mystery Initiations in the Graeco-Roman World, Chicago, 1929, pp. 225—262; J. GROSS, Philons von Alexandreia Anschauungen über die Natur des Menschen, Diss., Tübingen, 1930, pp. 90; R. B. HOYLE, Philo on Inspiration, in: Biblical Review, XV (1930), pp. 23—39; J. S. BOUGHTON, Conscience and the Logos in Philo, in: The Lutheran Church Quarterly, IV (1931), pp. 121—133; J. PASCHER, Ἡ βασιλικὴ ὁδός. Der Königsweg zu Wiedergeburt und Vergottung bei Philon von Alexandreia (Studien zur Geschichte und Kultur des Altertums, n. XVII, 3—4), Paderborn, 1931, pp. 280; K. STAEHLE, Die Zahlenmystik bei Philon von Alexandreia, Leipzig—Berlin, 1931, pp. VI-92; F. E. ROBBINS, Arithmetic in Philo Judaeus, in: Classical Philology, XXVI (1931), pp. 345—361; M.-J. LAGRANGE, Le Judaïsme avant Jésus-Christ (Études Bibliques), 3e édit., Paris, 1931 (su Filone cap. XXI, pp. 542—586); A. MARMORSTEIN, Philo and the Names of God, in: The Jewish Quarterly Review, N.S. XXII (1931—1932), pp. 295—306; R. B. TOLLINTON, The Alexandrine

(Proseguimento della nota 310)

Teaching on the Universe. Four Lectures, London, 1932, pp. 181; F. GEIGER, Philon von Alexandreia als sozialer Denker (Tübinger Beiträge zur Altertumswissenschaft, n. 14), Stuttgart, 1932, pp. XI-118; J. S. BOUGHTON, The Idea of Progress in Philo Judaeus, Diss. Columbia University, New York, 1932, pp. IX-291; R. MARCUS, Divine Names and Attributes in Hellenistic Jewish Literature, Proceedings of the American Academy for Jewish Research, 1931—1932, Philadelphia, 1932, pp. 43—120; H. WENSCHKEWITZ, Philo von Alexandria, in: ID., Die Spiritualisierung der Kultusbegriffe Tempel, Priester und Opfer im Neuen Testament (Ἄγγελος. Archiv für neutestamentliche Zeitgeschichte und Kulturkunde, n. 4), Leipzig, 1932, pp. 67—87; R. MONDOLFO, L'infinità divina da Filone ai Neoplatonici e i suoi precedenti, in: Atene e Roma, (XXXV), N.S. I (1933), pp. 192—200; H.-C. PUECH, Μορμωτός. A propos de Lycophron, de Rab et de Philon d'Alexandrie, in: Revue des Études Grecques, XLVI (1933), pp. 311—333 (sull'estasi; su Filone pp. 324—333); H. SCHMIDT, Die Anthropologie Philons von Alexandreia, Diss. Leipzig, Würzburg, 1933, pp. VII-179; W. KNUTH, Der Begriff der Sünde bei Philon von Alexandria, Diss. Jena, Würzburg, 1934, pp. VI-85; E. R. GOODENOUGH, By Light, Light. The Mystic Gospel of Hellenistic Judaism, New Haven—London, 1935, pp. XV-436; H. WILLMS, Εἰκών. Eine begriffsgeschichtliche Untersuchung zum Platonismus. I. Teil: Philon von Alexandreia. Mit einer Einleitung über Platon und der Zwischenzeit, Münster i. W., 1935, pp. VII-121; W. L. KNOX, Abraham and the Quest for God, in: Harvard Theological Review, XXVIII (1935), pp. 55—60; F. GRÉGOIRE, Le Messie chez Philon d'Alexandrie, in: Ephemerides Theologicae Lovanienses, XII (1935), pp. 28—50; M. PEISKER, Der Glaubensbegriff bei Philo hauptsächlich dargestellt an Moses und Abraham, Inaug.-Diss. Breslau, Aue i. Sa., 1936, pp. 34; E. R. GOODENOUGH, Literal Mystery in Hellenistic Judaism, in: Quantulacumque. Studies presented to K. Lake, London, 1937, pp. 227—241 (Filone vede nell'Antico Testamento la verità che salva, come i filosofi l'avevano scorta nella filosofia, ma in più egli scopre nei riti un'efficacia sacramentale che eleva l'uomo alla vita immateriale); H. NEUMARK, Die Verwendung griechischer und jüdischer Motive in den Gedanken Philons über die Stellung Gottes zu seinen Freunden, Inaug.-Diss., Würzburg, 1937, pp. IX-65; W. VOELKER, Fortschritt und Vollendung bei Philo von Alexandrien (Texte und Untersuchungen zur Geschichte der altchristl. Lit., n. 49, 1), Leipzig, 1938, pp. 350; M. M. AHMAD, Die Verwirklichung des Summum bonum in der religiösen Erfahrung, München, 1939, pp. 157 (con un capitolo dedicato a Filone); A. MEYER, Vorsehungsglaube und Schicksalsidee in ihrem Verhältnis bei Philo von Alexandria, Würzburg–Aumühle, 1939, pp. 87; E. R. GOODENOUGH, Problems of Method in Studying Philo Judaeus, in: Journal of Biblical Literature, LVIII (1939), pp. 51—58; F. J. FOAKES JACKSON, Philo and Alexandrian Judaism . . ., vedi nota 285; F. V. COURNEEN, Philo Judaeus had the Concept of Creation, in: New Scholasticism, XV (1941), pp. 46—58; A. S. PEASE, Caeli enarrant, in: Harvard Theological Review, XXXIV (1941), pp. 163—200 (questo argomento teologico fu usato, tra gli altri, anche da Filone, pp. 189—190); H. A. WOLFSON, Philo on Free Will and the Historical Influence of his View, ibid., XXXV (1942), pp. 131—169; G. VERBEKE, L'évolution de la doctrine du Pneuma du stoïcisme à S. Augustin. Étude philosophique, Paris—Louvain, 1945 (su Filone pp. 236—260); M. PULVER, Das Erlebnis des pneuma bei Philon, in: Eranos-Jahrbuch, XIII (1945), pp. 111—132; E. R. GOODENOUGH, Philo on Immortality, in: Harvard Theological Review, XXXIX (1946), pp. 85—108; C. W. LARSON, Prayer of Petition in Philo, in: Journal of Biblical Literature, LXV (1946), pp. 185—203; R. M. GUASTALLA, Judaïsme et hellénisme. La leçon de Philon d'Alexandrie, in: Revue des Études Juives, VII (1946—1947), pp. 3—38 (insegnamenti moderni dai successi e dagli scacchi filoniani); E. VANDERLINDEN, Les divers modes de connaissance de Dieu selon Philon d'Alexandrie, in: Mélanges de Science Religieuse, IV (1947), pp. 285—304; J. DANIÉLOU, The Philosophy of Philo, in: Theological Studies, IX (1948), pp. 578—589; E. R. GOODENOUGH, Wolfson's Philo, in: Journal of Biblical Literature, LXVII (1948), pp. 87—109; J. GIBLET, L'homme image de Dieu dans les commentaires littéraux de Philon d'Alexandrie, in: Studia hellenistica, V, Leiden, 1948, pp. 93—118; R. MARCUS, Wolfson's Revaluation of Philo, in: The Review of Religion, XIII (1948—1949), pp. 368—381; L. ROBERTS, Wolf-

(Proseguimento della nota 310)

son's Monument to Philo, in: Isis, XL (1949), pp. 199—213; H. Jonas, The Problem of the Knowledge of God in the Teaching of Philo of Alexandria (in ebraico), in: Commentationes ... in memoriam I. Lewy, Jerusalem, 1949, pp. 65—84; I. Heinemann, Philo als Vater der mittelalterlichen Philosophie ?, in: Theologische Zeitschrift, VI (1950), pp. 99—116; A. Levi, Il problema dell'errore in Filone d'Alessandria, in: Rivista critica di Storia della Filosofia, V (1950), pp. 281—294; A. Laurentin, Le pneuma dans la doctrine de Philon, in: Ephemerides Theologicae Lovanienses, XXVII (1951), pp. 390—437; S. Sandmel, Abraham's Knowledge of the Existence of God, in: Harvard Theological Review, XLIV (1951), pp. 137—139; T. Verhoeven, Monarchia dans Tertullien, Adversus Praxean, in: Vigiliae Christianae, V (1951), pp. 43—48 (utilità dell'accezione filoniana del termine per capirne l'uso in Tertulliano); A. Levi, Il concetto del tempo nelle filosofie dell'età romana, in: Rivista critica di Storia della Filosofia, VII (1952), pp. 173—200; H. Merki, ΟΜΟΙΩΣΙΣ ΘΕΩ. Von der platonischen Angleichung an Gott . . ., vedi nota 160 (su Filone pp. 35—44 e 57—83); W. Dittmann, Die Auslegung der Urgeschichte im Neuen Testament, Göttingen, 1953, pp. XVI-258 (microfilm: sono considerati anche Filone e Giuseppe); H. Jonas, Gnosis und Spätantiker Geist, II, 1: Von der Mythologie zur mystischen Philosophie, Göttingen, 1954, pp. 70—121; S. Sandmel, Philo's Place in Judaism. A Study of the Conception of Abraham in Jewish Literature, in: The Hebrew Union College Annual, XXV (1954), pp. 209—237; XXVI (1955), pp. 151—332, pubblicato poi separatamente a Cincinnati nel 1956 (è una reazione a Wolfson; limita inoltre le sue rassomiglianze con il rabbinismo): di quest'opera è poi uscita un'edizione accresciuta, New York, 1972, pp. XXIX-232; A. W. Argyle, The Logos of Philo. Personal or Impersonal, in: Expository Times, LXVI (1954—1955), pp. 13—14; C. Spicq, Agapè. Prolégomènes à une étude de théologie néo-testamentaire, in: Studia Hellenistica, X, Leiden, 1955, pp. 171—183; J. Coste, Notion grecque et notion biblique de la souffrance éducatrice, in: Recherches de Science Religieuse, XLIII (1955), pp. 481—523; H. Rusche, Die Gestalt des Melchisedek, in: Münchener Theologische Zeitschrift, VI (1955), pp. 230—252 (anche in Filone e nei Padri); H. Tyen, Die Probleme der neueren Philo-Forschung, in: Theologische Rundschau, XXIII (1955), pp. 230—246; J. Héring, Eschatologie biblique et idéalisme platonicien, in: Studies in honor of C. H. Dodd, Cambridge, 1956, pp. 444—463 (pp. 446—450); A. Momigliano, Problemi di metodo nella interpretazione dei simboli giudeo-ellenistici, in: Athenaeum, XXXIV (1956), pp. 237—248 (relazione tra quei simboli ed il pensiero di Filone); W. Richardson, The Philonic Patriarchs as νόμος ἔμψυχος, in: Studia Patristica, I (T.U., n. 63), Berlin, 1957, pp. 515—525; H. Karpp, 'Prophet' oder 'Dolmetscher'? Die Geltung der Septuaginta in der Alten Kirche, in: Festschrift G. Dehn, Neukirchen—Moers, 1957, pp. 103—117 (Filone ed i Padri greci sull'ispirazione dei LXX); P. Kaufmann, Don, distance et passivité chez Philon d'Alexandrie, in: Revue de Métaphysique et de Morale, LXII (1957), pp. 37—56; G. M. Pozzo, Logos, Uomo e Dio in Filone Alessandrino, in: Humanitas, XII (1957), pp. 371—374; H. A. Wolfson, Negative Attributes in the Church Fathers and the Gnostic Basilides, in: Harvard Theological Review, L (1957), pp. 145—156 (esamina il metodo di Filone e quello di Albino e Plotino per sfruttare gli attributi negativi nella conoscenza di Dio e li raffronta con quelli usati dai Padri greci e da Basilide); S. Lauer, Philo's Concept of Time, in: Journal of Jewish Studies, IX (1958), pp. 39—46; G. B. Ladner, Eikon, in: Reallexikon für Antike und Christentum, IV, Lief. 29, 1959, coll. 771—786 (su Filone: A, II, coll. 773—774); J. K. Feibleman, Religious Platonism. The Influence of Religion on Plato and the Influence of Plato on Religion, London, 1959, pp. 236 (Philo's Philosophy of Religion, pp. 96—127; The Influence of Philo on Plotinus, pp. 131—134); V. Guazzoni Foà, Il concetto di provvidenza nel pensiero classico e in quello pagano, in: Giornale di Metafisica, XIV (1959), pp. 69—95; J. de Savignac, Le messianisme de Philon d'Alexandrie, in: Novum Testamentum, IV (1960), pp. 319—324; A. Wlosok, Laktanz und die philosophische Gnosis (1960), cfr. nota 2; S. Sandmel, Filón y sus discípulos, in: Davar (Buenos Aires), LXXXV (1960), pp. 3—19; H. A. Wolfson, The Philonic God of Revelation and his Latter-Day Deniers, in: Harvard Theological Review, LIII (1960), pp. 101—124, riportato in: H. A. Wolfson, Religious Philosophy, Cambridge, Mass., 1961, pp. 1—26; in quest'opera

(Proseguimento della nota 310)

il WOLFSON pubblica anche: 'The Veracity of Scripture from Philo to Spinoza. Spinoza and the Religion of the Past', pp. 217—269; H. HEGERMANN, Philo und sein Kreis, in: ID., Die Vorstellung vom Schöpfungsmittler im Hellenistischen Judentum und Urchristentum (T.U., n. 82), Berlin, 1961, pp. 6—87; M. HARL, Adam et les deux arbres du Paradis (Gen. II—III) ou l'homme milieu entre deux termes (μέσος—μεθόριος) chez Philon d'Alexandrie. Pour une histoire de la doctrine du libre arbitre, in: Recherches de Science Religieuse, L (1962), pp. 321—388; F. N. KLEIN, Die Lichtterminologie bei Philon von Alexandrien und in den hermetischen Schriften . . ., vedi nota 115 (su Filone·pp. 11—79); A. LUNEAU, Les âges du monde. État de la question à l'aurore de l'ère patristique, in: Studia Patristica, V (T.U., n. 80), Berlin, 1962, pp. 509—518 (testimonianza anche di Filone); S. MATUSZEWSKI, Philosophia Philonis Alexandrini eiusque influxus in pristinum christianismum (in polacco), Warszawa, 1962, pp. 197; K. PRUEMM, Reflexiones theologicae et historicae ad usum Paulinum termini εἰκών, in: Verbum Domini, XL (1962), pp. 232—257; P. BOYANCÉ, Études philoniennes, in: Revue des Études Grecques, LXXVI (1963), pp. 64—110; J. HAUSSLEITER, Erhebung des Herzens, in: Reallexikon für Antike und Christentum, VI, Lief. 41 (1964), coll. 1—22 (Filone: A, IV; coll. 10—11); H. JONAS, Heidegger and Theology, in: Review of Metaphysics, XVIII (1964), pp. 207—233 ed in tedesco: Heidegger und die Theologie, in: Evangelische Theologie, XXIV (1964), pp. 621—642; E. VANDERLINDEN, La foi de Virgile, in: Bulletin de l'Association G. Budé, Paris, 1964, pp. 448—458 (accostamenti della fede di Virgilio con quella di Filone); F. TRISOGLIO, Apostrofi, parenesi e preghiere in Filone d'Alessandria, in: Rivista Lasalliana, XXXI (1964), pp. 357—410; XXXII (1965), pp. 39—79; V. NIKIPROWETZKY, Problèmes du récit de la création chez Philon d'Alexandrie, in: Revue des Études Juives, IVe Sér., IV, (1965), pp. 271—306; G. PFEIFER, Zur Beurteilung Philons in der neueren Literatur, in: Zeitschrift für die Alttestamentliche Wissenschaft, LXXVII (1965), pp. 212—214; G. SEGALLA, Il problema della volontà libera in Filone Alessandrino, in: Studia Patavina, XII (1965), pp. 3—31; W. THEILER, Philo von Alexandria und der Beginn des kaiserzeitlichen Platonismus, in: Parusia . . . J. Hirschberger, Frankfurt a. M., 1965, pp. 199—218; L. M. DE REIK, Ἐγκύκλιος παιδεία. A Study of its Original Meaning, in: Vivarium, III (1965), pp. 24—95 (il § 8 è dedicato a Filone); H. WILDBERGER, Das Abbild Gottes. Gen. 1, 26—30, in: Theologische Zeitschrift, XXI (1965), pp. 245—259; 481—501 (studio del tema nell'antico oriente, nel giudaismo, in Filone e nel Nuovo Testamento); I. D. KARAVIDÓPOULOS, Ἡ περὶ Θεοῦ καὶ ἀνθρώπου διδασκαλία Φίλωνος τοῦ Ἀλεξανδρέως, in: Θεολογία (Atene), XXXVII (1966), pp. 72—86; 244—261; 372—389 e ediz. separata pp. 56; E. MÜHLENBERG, Die Unendlichkeit Gottes bei Gregor von Nyssa. Gregors Kritik am Gottesbegriff der klassischen Metaphysik (Forschungen zur Kirchen- und Dogmengeschichte, n. 16), Göttingen, 1966, pp. 215 (su Filone pp. 58—64); H. A. WOLFSON, Plato's Pre-existent Matter in Patristic Philosophy, in: Studies in honor of H. Caplan, Ithaca, 1966, pp. 409—420 (anche opinione filoniana); A. KROKIEWICZ, Sceptycyzm grecki. Od Filona do Sekstusa, Warszawa, 1966, pp. 316; R. M. GRANT, Early Christian and Pre-Socratic Philosophy, in: ID., After the New Testament. Studies on early Christian literature and theology, Philadelphia, 1967, pp. 85—112; M. HARL, Cosmologie grecque et représentations juives dans l'œuvre de Philon d'Alexandrie, in: Philon d'Alexandrie. Colloque Lyon 11—15 Septembre 1966, Paris, 1967, pp. 189—205; P. BEAUCHAMP, La cosmologie religieuse de Philon et la lecture de l'Exode par le livre de la sagesse: le thème de la manne, ibid., pp. 207—219; A. JAUBERT, Le thème du 'reste sauveur' chez Philon, ibid., pp. 243—254; V. NIKIPROWETZKY, La doctrine de l'élenchos chez Philon, ses résonances philosophiques et sa portée religieuse, ibid., pp. 255—275; CH. KANNENGIESSER, Philon et les Pères sur la double création de l'homme, ibid., pp. 277—297; R. ARNALDEZ, La dialectique des sentiments chez Philon, ibid., pp. 299—331; H. J. KRÄMER, Der Ursprung der Geistmetaphysik. Untersuchungen zur Geschichte des Platonismus zwischen Platon und Plotin, 2. Aufl , Amsterdam, 1967, pp. 480 (su Filone pp. 266—284 e passim); H. CHADWICK, Philo and the Beginnings of Christian Thought, in: The Cambridge history of later greek and early medieval philosophy, ed. by A. H. ARMSTRONG, Cambridge, 1967, pp. 133—192; R. M. GRANT, Les êtres intermédiaires dans le judaïsme

(Proseguimento della nota 310)

tardif, in: Studi e Materiali di Storia delle Religioni, XXXVIII (1967), pp. 245—259; B. MONDIN, Il problema dei rapporti tra fede e ragione in Platone e in Filone Alessandrino, in: Le Parole e le Idee, IX (1967), pp. 9—16; ID., Esistenza, natura, inconoscibilità e ineffabilità di Dio nel pensiero di Filone Alessandrino, in: Scuola Cattolica, XCV (1967), pp. 423—447; A. PELLETIER, Deux expressions de la notion de conscience dans le judaïsme hellénistique et le christianisme naissant, in: Revue des Études Grecques, LXXX (1967), pp. 363—371; S. SOWERS, On the Reinterpretation of Biblical History in Hellenistic Judaism, in: Oikonomia. Heilsgeschichte . . . O. Culmann, Hamburg, 1967, pp. 18—25, cfr. nota 204; V. NIKIPROWETZKY, La spiritualisation des sacrifices et le culte sacrificiel au temple de Jérusalem, chez Philon d'Alexandrie, in: Semitica, XVII (1967), pp. 97—116; O. ARNDT, Zahlenmystik bei Philo, Spielerei oder Schriftauslegung?, in: Zeitschrift für Religions- und Geistesgeschichte, XIX (1967), pp. 167—171; A. ALTMANN, Homo imago Dei in Jewish and Christian Theology, in: Journal of Religion, XLVIII (1968), pp. 235—259; U. FRÜCHTEL, Die kosmologischen Vorstellungen bei Philo von Alexandrien. Ein Beitrag zur Geschichte der Genesisexegese (Arbeiten zur Literatur und Geschichte des hellenistischen Judentums, n. 2), Leiden, 1968, pp. X-198; A. MADDALENA, L'ἔννοια e l'ἐπιστήμη θεοῦ in Filone ebreo, in: Rivista di Filologia e d'Istruzione Classica, XCVI (1968), pp. 5—27; J. E. MÉNARD, Le mythe de Dionysos Zagreus chez Philon, in: Revue des Sciences Religieuses, XLII (1968), pp. 339—345; B. MONDIN, L'universo filosofico di Filone Alessandrino, in: Scuola Cattolica, XCVI (1968), pp. 371—394; F. RICKEN, Gab es eine hellenistische Vorlage für Weisheit 13—15?, in: Biblica, XLIX (1968), pp. 54—86; H. DOERRIE, Präpositionen und Metaphysik. Wechselwirkung zweier Prinzipienreihen, in: Museum Helveticum, XXVI (1969), pp. 217—228; D. BAER, Incompréhensibilité de Dieu et théologie négative chez Philon d'Alexandrie, in: Présence Orthodoxe, VIII (1969), pp. 38—46; H. A. WOLFSON, Greek Philosophy in Philo and the Church Fathers, in: The Crucible of Christianity, ed. by A. TOYNBEE, London, 1969, pp. 309—316; C. COLPE, Der Begriff Menschensohn und die Methode der Erforschung messianischer Prototypen, in: Kairos, XI (1969), pp. 241—263; A. V. NAZZARO, Il ΓΝΩΘΙ ΣΑΥΤΟΝ nell'epistemologia filoniana, in: Annali della Facoltà di Lettere e Filosofia dell'Università di Napoli, XII (1969—1970), pp. 49—86; ID., Nota a Filone. De migratione Abrahami 8, in: Rivista di Filologia e d'Istruzione Classica, XCVIII (1970), pp. 188—193; J. AMIR, A Religious Interpretation of a Philosophical Term in Philo, in: Commentationes B. Katz, Tel Aviv, 1970, pp. 112—117 (su εὐστάθεια, dagli Stoici riferito all'uomo costante e da Filone riservato a Dio come solo che si opponga al mondo in perenne movimento); R. A. BAER, JR., Philo's Use of the Categories Male and Female (Arbeiten zur Literatur und Geschichte des Hellenistischen Judentums, n. 3), Leiden, 1970, pp. XII-116; J. LAPORTE, La chute chez Philon et Origène, in: Kyriakon. Festschrift J. Quasten, Münster/Westf., 1970, pp. 320—335; S. GIVERSEN, L'expérience mystique chez Philon, in: Mysticism. Based on papers read at the symposium on mysticism held at Åbo on the 7th—9th Sept., 1968 (Scripta Instituti Donneriani Aboensis, n. 5), Stockholm, 1970, pp. 91—98; O. DREYER, Untersuchung zum Begriff des Gottgeziemenden in der Antike, mit besonderer Berücksichtigung Philos von Alexandrien (Spudasmata, n. 24), Hildesheim–New York, 1970, pp. VIII-164; H. SÉROUYA, Les étapes de la philosophie juive. Antiquité hébraïque, Paris, 1970, pp. 480; H. J. HORN, Antakoluthie der Tugenden und Einheit Gottes, in: Jahrbuch für Antike und Christentum, XIII (1970), pp. 5—28 (per Filone pp. 22—24); H. BRAUN, Wie man über Gott nicht denken soll. Dargelegt an Gedankengängen Philons von Alexandria, Tübingen, 1971, pp. 128; J. WHITTAKER, God Time Being. Two Studies in the Transcendental Tradition in Greek Philosophy (uno di questi studi è: God and time in Philo of Alexandria), (Symbolae Osloenses, Suppl., n. 23), Oslo, 1971, pp. 66; P. COURCELLE, Philon d'Alexandrie et le précepte delphique, in: Philomathes. Studies . . . in memory of Ph. Merlan, The Hague, 1971, pp. 245—250; J. LAPORTE, La doctrine eucharistique chez Philon d'Alexandrie (Théologie historique, n. 16), Paris, 1972, pp. 276; A. MYRE, La loi dans l'ordre moral selon Philon d'Alexandrie, in: Science et Esprit, XXIV (1972), pp. 93—113; 217—247; H. HOMMEL, Kosmos und Menschenherz. Zur Interpretation und Geschichte religiöser Metaphern, in: Festschrift K. J. Merentitis, Athenai,

(Proseguimento della nota 310)

1972, pp. 147—169 (sul cuore dell'uomo pio come simulacrum Dei o altare: anche in Filone); D. DELASSUS, Le thème de la Pâque chez Philon d'Alexandrie, Mémoire de maîtrise, Lille, 1972, pp. 127; B. L. MACK, Imitatio Mosis. Patterns of cosmology and soteriology in the hellenistic synagogue, in: Studia Philonica, I (1972), pp. 27—55 (basandosi su De vita Mosis I, 158—159 nota in Filone un'interpretazione mistica dell' esperienza del Sinai ed una tendenza del giudaismo ellenistico a sviluppare un'interpretazione cosmica di se stesso); R. M. WILSON, Philo of Alexandria and Gnosticism, in: Kairos, XIV (1972), pp. 213—219; D. M. HAY, Philo's Treatise on the Logos-Cutter, in: Studia Philonica, II (1973), pp. 9—22 (rileva l'unicità dell'enfasi che nel 'Quis rerum divinarum heres' pone in risalto il compito del Logos come tagliatore nella creazione e nella redenzione); G. KAHN, «Connais-toi toi-même» à la manière de Philon, in: Revue d'Histoire et de Philosophie Religieuses, LIII (1973), pp. 293—308; E. MUEHLENBERG, Das Problem der Offenbarung in Philo von Alexandrien, in: Zeitschrift für die Neutestamentliche Wissenschaft, LXIV (1973), pp. 1—18 (Filone ammette insieme la necessità di un'autorivelazione divina e l'uomo come inizio della conoscenza); W. WARNACK, Selbstliebe und Gottesliebe im Denken Philons von Alexandria, in: Festschrift K. H. Schelkle, Düsseldorf, 1973, pp. 198—214; A. J. M. WEDDERBURN, Philo's 'Heavenly Man', in: Novum Testamentum, XV (1973), pp. 301—326; MARY J. WEAVER, Πνεῦμα in Philo of Alexandria, Diss. University of Notre Dame, 1973, pp. 308 (microfilm): cfr. Dissertation Abstracts, XXXIII (1973), 6445 A (il Pneuma come dono di Dio a tutti quelli che lo riconoscono ed amano); J. WHITTAKER, Neopythagoreanism and the Trascendent Absolute, in: Symbolae Osloenses, XLVIII (1973), pp. 77—86 (Filone fu il primo a rifiutare al principio supremo ogni determinazione positiva); P. BOYANCÉ, Le dieu très haut chez Philon, in: Mélanges H.-Ch. Puech, Paris, 1974, pp. 139—149; A. DESCAMPS, Pour une histoire du titre «Fils de Dieu». Les antécédents par rapport à Marc, in: Bibliotheca Ephemeridum Theologicarum Lovaniensium, XXXIV (1974), pp. 529—571 (il par. IV, 2 concerne Filone e Giuseppe); LAURA GAZZONI, L'„erede" nel Quis rerum divinarum heres sit di Filone Alessandrino, in: Rivista di Filologia e di Istruzione Classica, CII (1974), pp. 387—397; W. MAAS, Unveränderlichkeit Gottes. Zum Verhältnis von griechisch-philosophischer und christlicher Gotteslehre (Paderborner Theologische Studien, n. 1), München—Paderborn—Wien, 1974, pp. 211 (tra i testimoni più importanti è esaminato Filone); J. MILGROM, On the Origins of Philo's Doctrine of Conscience, in: Studia Philonica, III (1974—75), pp. 41—45; R. T. WALLIS, The Idea of Conscience in Philo of Alexandria. Protocol of the Thirteenth Colloquy: 12 January 1975, Berkeley, 1975, pp. IV-47 (al WALLIS che negò a Filone una coerente teoria metafisica sullo stato di coscienza risposero, oltre al MILGROM, J. M. DILLON, W. S. ANDERSON, S. SANDMEL, D. WINSTON, W. WUELLNER); P. COURCELLE, Le typhus, maladie de l'âme d'après Philon et d'après saint Augustin, in: Misc. E. Dekkers, Brugge, 1975, vol. I, pp. 245—288; J. EGAN, Gregory of Nazianzus and the Logos Doctrine, in: Essays D. M. Stanley, Willowdale, 1975, pp. 281—319 (il par. 4 concerne Filone); L. M. DE RIJK, Quaestio de ideis. Some notes on an important chapter of Platonism, in: Studies C. J. de Vogel, Assen, 1975, pp. 204—213 (sviluppa il tema da Platone al sec. XVI passando particolarmente per Filone, Plotino, S. Agostino); E. SCHWEIZER, Menschensohn und eschatologischer Mensch im Frühjudentum, in: Misc. A. Vögtle, Freiburg, 1975, pp. 100—116 (il secondo par. riguarda Filone); F. SICILIANO, Alla luce del Logos. Filone d'Alessandria, Cosenza, 1975, pp. VIII-79; C. H. TALBERT, The Concepts of Immortals in Mediterranean Antiquity, in: Journal of Biblical Literature, XCIV (1975), pp. 419—436 (come prototipo degli uomini immortali Filone esemplificò Mosè); M. Δραγωνα Μοναχου, Το προβλημα του κακου στο Φιλωνα τον 'Αλεζανδρεα με ειδικη αναφορα στο Περι προνοιας, in: Philosophia, V—VI (1975—76), pp. 306—352; G. D. FARANDOS, Kosmos und Logos nach Philon von Alexandria (Elementa, n. 4), Amsterdam, 1976, pp. III-319; W. KELBER, Die Logoslehre von Heraklit bis Origenes, Stuttgart, 1976, pp. 271; M. SIMON, Jupiter—Yahvé. Sur un essai de théologie pagano-juive, in: Numen, XXIII (1976), pp. 40—66 (fondandosi, per quanto concerne Filone, soprattutto sulla 'Legatio ad Gaium', illustra un tentativo sincretistico mirante ad attenuare l'incomprensione vicendevole che regnava tra il giudaismo ed il paganesimo greco-romano); J. DILLON—A. TERIAN, Philo

La forza propulsiva di Filone fu infatti una fede ardente. La sua originalità non consistette nel rinnovare la speculazione razionale antecedente ma nel fonderla con la fede in modo che la ragione umana e quella divina si unissero in una sintesi davvero universale. Il suo apporto individuale fu quindi quello di operare una simbiosi della mentalità ebraica e di quella greca, simbiosi da cui nacque la teologia. Filone di fronte alla filosofia non si comportò come uno scettico che l'adoperasse con il distacco con cui si maneggia uno strumento privo di vita; ne aveva percepito tutta la nobiltà e tutta la forza illuminatrice, aveva capito che essa poteva diventare una temibile avversaria come pure una preziosa alleata in grado di preparare nel modo migliore la mente umana al suo colloquio con la rivelazione divina. Nell'alternativa non aveva esitato: se l'era assunta come ausiliaria convinto che la religione non osteggiasse nessuno dei valori autentici, anzi li esigesse e sapesse sterilizzare quei fermenti pericolosi che alcune di queste teorie potessero portare commisti in se stesse. Della personalità di Filone si sono avanzate parecchie definizioni: il WOLFSON ne ha fatto un grande pensatore originale, il GOODENOUGH un benemerito trasmettitore della filosofia antica ed il rivelatore di un supposto mistero giudaico[311], il VÖLKER un esegeta privo di interessi speculativi ed animato da una spiritualità mistica di stampo giudaico, il DANIÉLOU l'autore del primo tentativo di spiegazione dei dati biblici giovandosi dei quadri della filosofia antica. Se il frammentarismo delle sue composizioni autorizza giudizi divergenti, l'impressione unitaria che ne emerge pare consuonare con le pacate opinioni del DANIÉLOU e del VÖLKER: Filone fu un'anima fervida di un'intensa e genuina aspirazione religiosa. Il razionalismo dominante in larghi strati della speculazione greca gli servì solo a formare il *crepidoma* sul quale innalzò il suo tempio alla divinità, guidato dalla fede ebraica[312] ed incorag-

---

and the Stoic Doctrine of εὐπάθειαι, in: Studia Philonica, IV (1976—77), pp. 17—24; J. DILLON, The Middle Platonists. A Study of Platonism 80 B.C. to A.D. 220, Ithaca, N.Y., London, 1977, pp. XVII-429 (esamina il medio platonismo alessandrino in Eudoro e Filone); J. AMIR, Die Begegnung des biblischen und des philosophischen Monotheismus als Grundthema des jüdischen Hellenismus, in: Evangelische Theologie, XXXVIII (1978), pp. 2—18 (presenta il monoteismo giudaico in Giuseppe e Filone e quello ellenistico in Posidonio); A. BROADIE—J. MACDONALD, The Concept of Cosmic Order in Ancient Egypt in Dynastic and Roman Times, in: L'Antiquité Classique, XLVII (1978), pp. 106—128 (sul termine filoniano di Logos riferito al concetto dell'ordine universale). — Nel presente volume (ANRW II 21,1) vedi il contributo di B. A. PEARSON, Philo and Gnosticism, pp. 295—342.

[311] Sul fantomatico mistero giudaico di cui Filone sarebbe il rivelatore cfr. P. ZIEGERT, Über die Ansätze zu einer Mysterienlehre, aufgebaut auf den antiken Mysterien bei Philo Judäus, in: Theologische Studien und Kritiken, LXVII (1894), pp. 706—732; L. CERFAUX, Influence des Mystères sur le Judaïsme alexandrin avant Philon, in: Le Muséon, XXXVII (1924), pp. 29—88; S. A. HORODETSKE, Filone ed il Mistero giudaico, in: Debir, II (1924), pp. 165—175 (in ebraico); E. R. GOODENOUGH, By Light, Light, New Haven, 1935, passim; ID., An Introduction to Philo Judaeus, 2nd edit., Oxford, 1962, pp. 138—158.

[312] Sui rapporti di Filone con la cultura giudaica e particolarmente con il midrasc, l'halakah, l'haggada vedi: B. RITTER, Philo und die Halacha. Eine vergleichende Studie unter steter Berücksichtigung des Josephus, Leipzig, 1879, pp. XI-139; A. EPSTEIN, Le livre des Jubilés, Philon et le Midrasch Tadsché, in: Revue des Études Juives, XXI (1890), pp. 80—97; XXII (1891), pp. 1—25; J. Z. LAUTERBACH, Philo Judaeus. His Relation to

giato da importanti correnti dello stesso pensiero classico. La mentalità ebraica lo sottrasse al rischio di qualsiasi dilettantismo religioso presentandogli la divinità come il centro vitale a cui tende la persona umana e la consuetudine con la civiltà ellenica gli tolse qualsiasi sentore di angusto. Sono molto più numerose e fondate le critiche che si possono muovere allo scrittore[313] che non quelle che si possono rivolgere all'uomo Filone.

the Halakah, in: The Jewish Encyclopedia, New York—London, X, 1905, pp. 15—18; L. Treitel, Agada bei Philo, in: Monatsschrift für Geschichte und Wissenschaft des Judentums, LIII (1909), pp. 28—45; 159—173; 286—291, ristampato in: Philonische Studien, hrsg. von M. Brann, Breslau, 1915, pp. 85—113; B. Revel, The Karaite Halakah, and its Relation to Sadducean, Samaritan and Philonian Halakah, Part I, Thesis, Philadelphia, 1913, pp. 88; Id., Philonian Halakah, in: The Jewish Forum, XI (1928), pp. 120—122; E. Stein, Philo und der Midrasch. Philos Schilderung der Gestalten des Pentateuch verglichen mit der des Midrasch (Beihefte zur Zeitschrift für die Alttestamentliche Wissenschaft, n. 57), Gießen, 1931, pp. 52; G. Allon, Studies in Philonian Halacha, in: Tarbiz, V (1933—1934), pp. 28—36; 241—246; VI (1934—1935), pp. 30—37; 452—459 (in ebraico); S. Belkin, The Alexandrian Halakah in Apologetic Literature of the First Century C. E., Philadelphia (1936), pp. 70; B. J. Bamberger, The Dating of Aggadic Materials, in: Journal of Biblical Literature, LXVIII (1949), pp. 115—123; D. Daube, Rabbinic Methods of Interpretation and Hellenistic Rhetoric, in: The Hebrew Union College Annual, XXII (1949), pp. 239—264; S. Belkin, L'interpretazione dei nomi in Filone, in: Horeb, XII (1956), pp. 3—61 (in ebraico, come i seguenti); Id., Filone e la tradizione midrascica della Palestina, ibid., XIII (1958—1959), pp. 1—60; Id., Le Domande e Risposte sulla Genesi e sull'Esodo di Filone di Alessandria ed il loro rapporto con il Midrash di Palestina, ibid., XIV—XV (1960), pp. 1—74; Id., L'esposizione filoniana della Torah alla luce degli antichi Midrasch rabbinici, in: Sura, IV (1960), pp. 1—68; A. G. Wright, The Literary Genre Midrash, in: Catholic Biblical Quarterly (Washington, D.C.), XXVIII (1966), pp. 105—138; 417—457; S. Daniel, La Halacha de Philon selon le premier livre des Lois spéciales, in: Philon d'Alexandrie. Colloque Lyon 11—15 Septembre 1966, Paris, 1967, pp. 221—241; F. Dexinger, Ein 'Messianisches Szenarium' als Gemeingut des Judentums in nachherodianischer Zeit?, in: Kairos, XVII (1975), pp. 249—278 (esamina Filone — soprattutto il 'De Praemiis' —, Giuseppe e le tradizioni dei rabbini vissuti nel primo secolo d. Cr.); R. G. Hamerton—Kelly, Some Techniques of Composition in Philo's Allegorical Commentary, with Special Reference to De Agricultura. A Study in the Hellenistic Midrash, in: Essays W. D. Davies, Leiden, 1976, pp. 45—46. — Sull'attività apologetica di Filone cfr. M. Friedländer, Geschichte der jüdischen Apologetik als Vorgeschichte des Christenthums, Zürich, 1903, pp. XV-499; P. Krüger, Philo und Josephus als Apologeten des Judentums, Leipzig, 1906, pp. IV-82. — Sulla possibile conoscenza della lingua ebraica da parte di Filone oltre a numerosi accenni in studi di vario genere ed a pubblicazioni specifiche scritte in ebraico e qui non riportate per difficoltà tipografiche cfr. il vecchio C. Siegfried, Die hebräischen Worterklärungen des Philo . . ., alla nota 1 ed i recenti A. Hanson, Philo's Etymologies, in: Journal of Theological Studies, XVIII (1967), pp. 128—139 (Filone avrebbe conosciuto un pochino l'ebraico); A. Nazzaro, Filone Alessandrino e l'ebraico, in: Rendiconti dell'Accademia di Archeologia, Lettere e Belle Arti di Napoli, XLII (1967), pp. 61—79 (ne avrebbe avuto una conoscenza approfondita); D. Rokeaḥ, A New Onomasticon Fragment from Oxyrhynchus and Philo's Etymologies, in: Journal of Theological Studies, XIX (1968), pp. 70—82 (non l'avrebbe conosciuto). È inoltre noto che furono per una risposta positiva H. A. Wolfson e S. Sandmel, dubbiosa S. Belkin e negativa H. Lewy; vedi anche la discussione seguita alla comunicazione della Daniel nel colloquio di Lione, p. 241.

[313] Per trattazioni sulle opere in generale o su singoli scritti vedi: A. F. Dähne, Einige Bemerkungen über die Schriften des Juden Philo, angeknüpft an eine Untersuchung über deren ursprüngliche Anordnung, in: Theologische Studien und Kritiken, VI (1833), pp. 984—1040; C. G. O. Grossmann, De Philonis Judaei operum continua serie et ordine chronologico

(Proseguimento della nota 313)

commentatio, Leipzig, 1841 e 1842, pp. 28 e 31; E. ZELLER, Der Streit Theophrasts gegen Zeno über die Ewigkeit der Welt, in: Hermes, XI (1876), pp. 422—429; F. BUECHELER, Philonea, in: Rheinisches Museum, XXXII (1877), pp. 433—444 (note critiche sul 'De aeternitate mundi'); E. ZELLER, Der pseudophilonische Bericht über Theophrast, in: Hermes, XV (1880), pp. 137—146; J. BERNAYS, Über die unter Philon's Werken stehende Schrift über die Unzerstörbarkeit des Weltalls, in: Abhandlungen der K. Akademie der Wissenschaften zu Berlin, aus dem Jahre 1882, Philosophisch-historische Klasse, III, Berlin, 1883, pp. 82 (questo ed i tre studi antecedenti concernono il 'De aeternitate mundi'); R. AUSFELD, De libro περὶ τοῦ πάντα σπουδαῖον εἶναι ἐλεύθερον qui inter Philonis Alexandrini opera fertur, Diss., Gottingae, 1887, pp. 58; P. WENDLAND, Philo's Schrift Περὶ τοῦ πάντα σπουδαῖον εἶναι ἐλεύθερον, in: Archiv für Geschichte der Philosophie, I (1888), pp. 509—517; L. MASSEBIEAU, Le classement des œuvres de Philon, in: Bibliothèque de l'École des Hautes Études. Sciences Religieuses, Paris, I (1889), pp. 1—91; P. WENDLAND, Neu entdeckte Fragmente Philos, nebst einer Untersuchung über die ursprüngliche Gestalt der Schrift De sacrificiis Abelis et Caini, Berlin, 1891, pp. 152 (contiene anche: III. Philo und Procopius von Gaza, pp. 29—105; IV. Die Quaestiones Philos und Theodoret, pp. 106—108; V. Philo und Origenes. Origenes und Procop, pp. 109—124); P. WENDLAND, Philos Schrift über die Vorsehung. Ein Beitrag zur Geschichte der nacharistotelischen Philosophie, Berlin, 1892, pp. VII-120; E. KRELL, Philo, Περὶ τοῦ πάντα σπουδαῖον εἶναι ἐλεύθερον, die Echtheitsfrage, Programm des Gymn. bei St. Anna, Augsburg, 1896, pp. 38; P. WENDLAND, Kritische und exegetische Bemerkungen zu Philo, in: Rheinisches Museum, LII (1897), pp. 465—504; LIII (1898), pp. 1—36; ID., Zu Philos Schrift de posteritate Caini (Nebst Bemerkungen zur Rekonstruktion der Septuaginta), in: Philologus, LVII (1898), pp. 248—288; L. COHN, Einteilung und Chronologie der Schriften Philos, in: Philologus, Supplbd. VII, 3 (1899), pp. 387—435, pubblicato anche separatamente, Leipzig, 1899, pp. 51; ID., Beiträge zur Textgeschichte und Kritik der Philonischen Schriften, in: Hermes, XXXVIII (1903), pp. 498—545; J. H. A. HART, Philo of Alexandria, in: The Jewish Quarterly Review, XVII (1904—1905), pp. 78—122; 726—746; XVIII (1905—1906), pp. 330—346; XX (1907—1908), pp. 294—329; L. MASSEBIEAU e É. BRÉHIER, Essai sur la chronologie de la vie et des œuvres de Philon, in: Revue de l'Histoire des Religions, LIII (1906), pp. 25—64; 164—185; 267—289, con tiratura a parte, Paris, 1906, pp. 84; L. COHN, Neue Beiträge zur Textgeschichte und Kritik der philonischen Schriften, in: Hermes, XLIII (1908), pp. 177—219; B. MOTZO, Un'opera perduta di Filone (περὶ βίου πρακτικοῦ ἢ Ἐσσαίων), in: Atti della R. Accademia delle Scienze di Torino, XLVI (1910—1911), pp. 860—880; ID., Le Ὑποθετικά di Filone, ibid., XLVII (1911—1912), pp. 556—573; H. J. LAWLOR, Eusebiana. Essays on the Ecclesiastical History of Eusebius Bishop of Caesarea, Oxford, 1912, pp. 138—145; G. TAPPE, De Philonis libro qui inscribitur Ἀλέξανδρος ἢ περὶ τοῦ λόγον ἔχειν τὰ ἄλογα ζῷα quaestiones selectae, Diss., Gottingae, 1912, pp. 80; M. ADLER, Bemerkungen zu Philos Schrift περὶ μέθης, in: Wiener Studien, XLIII (1922—1923), pp. 92—96; XLIV (1924—1925), pp. 220—223; XLV (1926—1927); pp. 117—120; 245—248; S. REITER, Ἀρετή und der Titel von Philos 'Legatio', in: Ἐπιτύμβιον H. Swoboda, Reichenberg, 1927, pp. 228—237; M. ADLER, Zu Philo Alexandrinus, ibid., pp. 15—17; ID., Studien zu Philon von Alexandreia, Breslau, 1929, pp. VII-102; R. MARCUS, The Armenian Translation of Philo's Quaestiones in Genesim et Exodum, in: Journal of Biblical Literature, XLIX (1930), pp. 61—64; A. KROKIEWICZ, De duobus Philonis libris Romae scriptis, in: Eos, XXXIII (1930—1931), pp. 395—410; G. TROTTI, Filone Alessandrino, Roma, 1932, pp. 58 (esame critico ed esegetico del 'De vita contemplativa' e del 'De aeternitate mundi' per confermarne l'autenticità); E. R. GOODENOUGH, Philo's Exposition of the Law and his De vita Mosis, in: The Harvard Theological Review, XXVI (1933), pp. 109—125; M. ADLER, Das philonische Fragment De deo, in: Monatsschrift für Geschichte und Wissenschaft des Judentums, LXXX (1936), pp. 163—170; H. LEISEGANG, Philons Schrift über die Ewigkeit der Welt, in: Philologus, XCII (1937), pp. 156—176; ID., Philons Schrift über die Gesandtschaft der alexandrinischen Juden an den Kaiser Gaius Caligula, in: Journal of Biblical Literature, LVII (1938), pp. 377—405; B. BOTTE, La vie de Moïse par Philon, in: Cahiers Sioniens, VIII (1954), pp. 173—180;

Questo infatti seppe ovviare all'inconveniente in cui urtano spesso i mistici, che è quello di tenere lo sguardo così teso verso l'assoluto da dimenticare il contingente, e di usare un linguaggio così concentrato sulle loro visioni interiori da diventare incomprensibile a quanti di quelle visioni non sono partecipi. Nel suo anelito a salire a Dio non dimenticò che suo punto di partenza era la terra; egli che sacrificò all'esigenza della perfezione individuale l'attenzione allo sviluppo storico dell'umanità, non dimenticò di essere cittadino di Alessandria e non disdegnò di prendere parte attiva sia alle manifestazioni che segnavano il normale svolgersi della vita civica

L. ALFONSI, Il περὶ βίου θεωρητικοῦ di Filone e la tradizione protrettica, in: Wiener Studien, LXX (1957: Festschrift Mras), pp. 5—16; Y. HIRAISHI, On Philo's Theory of Ideas, in: Journal of Classical Studies (Kyôto), XII (1964), pp. 1—12 (in giapponese con riassunto in inglese: su 'De opificio mundi' 16—25); A. MÉASSON, Le De Sacrificiis Abelis et Caini de Philon d'Alexandrie, in: Bulletin de l'Association G. Budé, Paris, 1966, pp. 309—316; G. BOLOGNESI, Note al testo del 'De providentia' di Filone, in: Armeniaca. Mélanges du 250ᵉ anniversaire..., Venise, 1969, pp. 190—200; D. HENNIG, Zu der alexandrinischen Märtyrerakte P. Oxy. 1089, in: Chiron, IV (1974), pp. 425—440 (in P. Oxy. 1089 si tratta anche dell'Avillio Flacco dell'In Flaccum di Filone); E. LUCCHESI, La division en six livres des Quaestiones in Genesim de Philon d'Alexandrie, in: Muséon, LXXXIX (1976), pp. 383—395 (varie divisioni dell'opera, nessuna delle quali risale a Filone); J. R. ROYSE, The Original Structure of Philo's Quaestiones, in: Studia Philonica, IV (1976—77), pp. 41—78. — Per commenti a singoli passi vedi: R. MARCUS, A Note on Philo's Quaestiones in Gen. II, 31, in: Classical Philology, XXXIX (1944), pp. 257—258; W. LAMEERE, Sur un passage de Philon d'Alexandrie (De plantatione, 1—6), in: Mnemosyne Ser. IV, IV (1951), pp. 73—80; J. POUILLOUX, Le calendrier et un passage de Philon d'Alexandrie, in: Revue des Études Anciennes, LXVI (1964), pp. 211—213 (su 'De decalogo' 96); V. NIKIPROWETZKY, Schadenfreude chez Philon d'Alexandrie? Note sur In Flaccum 121 sqq., in: Revue des Études Juives, CXXVII (1968), pp. 7—19; ID., Κυρίου πρόσθεσις. Note critique sur Philon d'Alexandrie, De Josepho 28, ibid., pp. 387—392; M. ZICÀRI, Nothus in Lucr. V 575 e in Cat. 34, 15, in: Studia Florentina A. Ronconi oblata, Roma, 1970, pp. 525—529 (richiamo di due passi filoniani); P. HENDRIX, Een paasvigilie in Philo's 'De Vita contemplativa', in: Nederlands Theologisch Tijdschrift, XXV (1971), pp. 393—397; M. PETIT, À propos d'une réminiscence probable d'Is. dans le Quod omnis probus liber sit, in: Mélanges A. Dupont-Sommer, Paris, 1971, pp. 491—495; J. CAZEAUX, Littérature ancienne et recherches des structures, in: Revue des Études Augustiniennes, XVIII (1972), pp. 287—292 (simmetrie tra il libro di Giona e il 'De fuga et inventione' 121—124); ID., Interpréter Philon d'Alexandrie, in: Revue des Études Grecques, LXXXV (1972), pp. 345—352 (commenta 'De Abrahamo' 61—84 rifacendosi all'interpretazione di S. SANDMEL, Philo's Place in Judaism. A Study of Conceptions of Abraham in Jewish Literature, Cincinnati, 1956, pp. 110—115 sui paragrafi 61—68; ma soprattutto vuole offrire una metodologia di lettura e di comprensione del pensiero filoniano); W. SCHWANZ, A Study in pre-Christian Symbolism. Philo, De somniis I, 216—218, and Plutarch, De Iside et Osiride 4 and 77, in: Bulletin of the Institute of Classical Studies of the University of London, XX (1973), pp. 104—117 (valori simbolici dei vestiti di lino e di lana e di quelli pluricolori o bianchi); R. CANTALAMESSA, Origene e Filone. A proposito di C. Celsum IV, 19, in: Aevum, XLVIII (1974), pp. 132—133 (coloro ai quali allude Origene nel C. Celsum IV, 19 debbono essere quanti condividevano l'opinione di Filone, De somniis I, 232 e 238). — Sono poi in generale da tenere presenti le introduzioni alle singole opere nell'edizione delle 'Sources Chrétiennes', quelle dei volumi VII (1937), VIII (1939), IX (1954), X (1962) curati da F. H. COLSON per la Loeb, e quelle di H. Box, In Flaccum, Oxford, 1939, pp. 129 e di E. M. SMALLWOOD, Legatio ad Gaium, 2ⁿᵈ edit., Leiden, 1970, pp. 3—50.

sia alle tempeste eccezionali che minacciavano di travolgerla. E. R. GOOD-
ENOUGH[314] ha il merito di aver sostenuto la tesi secondo cui Filone si occupò
con solerzia dell'amministrazione della società giudaica alessandrina e,
come introduzione a questo assunto, richiama alle testimonianze che egli
stesso ci lasciò di essere intervenuto alle espressioni più appariscenti della
vita urbana, quali conviti, rappresentazioni tragiche, gare atletiche, corse
dei cocchi[315]. Filone era dunque un mistico che non respingeva la monda-
nità e che sapeva alternare i soggiorni nei romitori dei Terapeuti[316] con

---

[314] The Jurisprudence of the Jewish Courts in Egypt. Legal Administration by the Jews
under the early Roman Empire as described by Philo Judaeus, New Haven, 1929,
pp. IX-268 (pp. 2—3). Vedi anche ID., Philo and the Public Life, in: The Journal of
Egyptian Archaeology, XII (1926), pp. 77—79; N. BENTWICH, Philo as Jurist, in:
Jewish Quarterly Review, XXI (1930—1931), pp. 151—161.

[315] Per il GOODENOUGH Filone nel 'De Specialibus Legibus' si ispira alla legge giudaica che
vigeva nella comunità ebraica di Alessandria, mentre per lo HEINEMANN, Philons griechische und jüdische Bildung . . ., egli, attingendo da concetti giuridici greci e romani, svolge
un tema teorico.

[316] Sui Terapeuti, sugli Esseni e sui movimenti ascetici del suo tempo vedi: B. DE MONT-
FAUCON e J. BOUHIER, Lettres pour et contre, sur la fameuse question, si les solitaires,
appelés Thérapeutes, dont a parlé Philon le Juif, étaient Chrétiens, Paris, 1712, pp. XII-
383; I. G. CARPZOV, De Essenis, in: Apparatus historico criticus antiquitatum sacri
codicis et gentis Hebraeae, Francofurthi, 1748, pp. 215—240; J. J. BELLERMANN, Geschichtliche Nachrichten aus den Alterthümern über Essäer und Therapeuten, Berlin,
1821, pp. VIII-180; CHR. G. L. GROSSMANN, De Ascetis Judaeorum veterum ex
Philone, Altenburgi (1833), pp. 26; T. DE QUINCY, On the Essenes, in: Blackwood's
Edinburgh Magazine, CCXCI (1840), pp. 105—116; 453—473; 639—649; A. RITSCHL,
Über die Essener, in: Theologische Jahrbücher, XIV (1855), pp. 315—356; C. D. GINS-
BURG, The Essenes. Their History and Doctrines. An Essay, reprinted from the 'Transactions of the Literary and Philosophical Society of Liverpool', London, 1864, pp. 82;
E. BENAMOZEGH, Storia degli Esseni, Firenze, 1865, pp. 552; K. TH. KEIM, Die jüdische Auf-
klärung. Philon der Alexandriner. Die Essäer, in: ID., Geschichte Jesu von Nazara in ihrer
Verkettung mit dem Gesammtleben seines Volkes, Zürich, 1867, vol. I, pp. 208—225;
282—306; G. CLEMENS, De Essenorum moribus et institutis, Diss., Königsberg, 1868,
pp. 32; B. TIDEMAN, Het Essenisme, Leiden, 1868, pp. V-115; W. CLEMENS, Die Quellen
für die Geschichte der Essener, in: Zeitschrift für wissenschaftliche Theologie, XII (1869),
pp. 328—352; F. DELAUNAY, Introduction au livre de Philon d'Alexandrie ayant pour
titre: De la vie contemplative, in: Revue Archéologique, N.S. XXII (1870—1871), pp.
268—282; B. TIDEMAN, Esseners en Therapeuten, in: Theologisch Tijdschrift, V (1871),
pp. 177—188; F. DELAUNAY, Sur l'authenticité du livre de Philon d'Alexandrie qui a pour
titre: De la vie contemplative, in: Revue Archéologique, N.S. XXVI (1873), pp. 12—22;
ID., Moines et sibylles dans l'antiquité judéo-grecque, 2e éd., Paris, 1874, pp. XIX-403;
P. E. LUCIUS, Die Therapeuten und ihre Stellung in der Geschichte der Askese. Eine
kritische Untersuchung der Schrift: De vita contemplativa, Straßburg, 1879, pp. 210;
A. HILGENFELD, Philo und die Therapeuten, in: Zeitschrift für wissenschaftliche Theologie,
XXIII (1880), pp. 423—440; DEMMLER, Christus und der Essenismus, in: Theologische
Studien aus Württemberg, I (1880), pp. 29—53; 122—149; P. E. LUCIUS, Der Essenismus in seinem Verhältniss zum Judenthum. Eine kritische Untersuchung, Straßburg,
1881, pp. 131; A. HILGENFELD, Die Essäer, in: Zeitschrift für wissenschaftliche Theologie,
XXV (1882), pp. 257—292; L. MASSEBIEAU, Le traité de la vie contemplative et la question des Thérapeutes, in: Revue de l'histoire des religions, XVI (1887), pp. 170—198;
284—319; R. OHLE, Die Essäer des Philo. Ein Beitrag zur Kirchengeschichte, in: Jahrbücher
für protestantische Theologie, XIII (1887), pp. 298—344; 376—394; ID., Die Essener. Eine
kritische Untersuchung der Angaben des Josephus, ibid., XIV (1888), pp. 221—274;

(Proseguimento della nota 316)

366—387; ID., Die pseudophilonischen Essäer und die Therapeuten (Beiträge zur Kirchengeschichte, n. 1), Berlin, 1888, pp. 79; ID., Über die Essäer in Quod omnis probus liber. Ein Nachtrag, in: Jahrbücher für protestantische Theologie, XIV (1888), pp. 314—320; A. HILGENFELD, Die Essäer Philo's, in: Zeitschrift für wissenschaftliche Theologie, XXXI (1888), pp. 49—71 (in polemica con R. OHLE); L. MASSEBIEAU, Encore un mot sur la vie contemplative, in: Revue de l'histoire des religions, XVII (1888), pp. 230—232; P. WENDLAND, Die Essäer bei Philo, in: Jahrbücher für protestantische Theologie, XIV (1888), pp. 100—105 (contro R. OHLE); G. FAYOT, Étude sur les Thérapeutes et le traité de la vie contemplative, Thèse Montauban, Genève, 1889, pp. 117; J. NIRSCHL, Die Therapeuten, in: Der Katholic, LXX (1890), pp. 97—120; 214—238 (pp. 98—111: I. Die Schrift Philo's über das contemplative Leben); N. I. WEINSTEIN, Beiträge zur Geschichte der Essäer, Wien, 1892, pp. 92; KRÜGER, Beiträge zur Kenntnis der Pharisäer und Essener, in: Theologische Quartalschrift, LXXVI (1894), pp. 431—496; C. SIEGFRIED, Über die dem Philo von Alexandrien zugeschriebene Schrift 'vom beschaulichen Leben', in: Protestantische Kirchenzeitung für das evangelische Deutschland, XLIII (1896), pp. 972—982; J. M. STAHL, Zu Philons Schrift vom beschaulichen Leben, in: Rheinisches Museum, LI (1896), pp. 157—160; P. WENDLAND, Die Therapeuten und die philonische Schrift vom beschaulichen Leben. Ein Beitrag zur Geschichte des hellenistischen Judentums, in: Jahrbücher für classische Philologie, XXII. Supplbd., Leipzig, 1896, pp. 693—772; A. REGEFFE, La secte des esséniens. Essai critique sur son organisation, sa doctrine, son origine, Thèse, Lyon, 1898, pp. 104; E. ZELLER, Zur Vorgeschichte des Christenthums. Essener und Orphiker, in: Zeitschrift für wissenschaftliche Theologie, XLII (1899), pp. 195—269; V. ERMONI, L'Essénisme, in: Revue des questions historiques, LXXIX (1906), pp. 5—27; J. H. A. HART, Philo and the Catholic Judaism of the First Century, in: The Journal of Theological Studies, XI (1909—1910), pp. 25—42; CHR. BUGGE, Zum Essäerproblem, in: Zeitschrift für die neutestamentliche Wissenschaft, XIV (1913), pp. 145—174; I. ABRAHAMS, Philo on the 'Contemplative Life', in: Bypaths in Hebraic Bookland, Philadelphia, 1920, pp. 24—31; BAUER, Essener, in: RE., Supplbd. IV (1924), coll. 386—430; I. HEINEMANN, Die Sektenfrömmigkeit der Therapeuten, in: Monatsschrift für Geschichte und Wissenschaft des Judentums, LXXVIII (1934), pp. 104—117; ID., Therapeutai, in: RE., V A 2 (1934), coll. 2321—2346; L. MARCHEL, Esséniens, in: Supplém. au Dictionnaire de la Bible, II, Paris, 1934, coll. 1109—1132; R. GOOSSENS, La secte de la Nouvelle Alliance et les Esséniens, in: Le Flambeau, XXXV (1952), pp. 145—154; R. MARCUS, Philo, Josephus and the Dead Sea Yaḥad, in: Journal of Biblical Literature, LXXI (1952), pp. 207—209 (per l'identificazione della setta del Mar Morto con gli Esseni); B. J. ROBERTS, The Qumrân Scrolls and the Essenes, in: New Testament Studies, III (1956—1957), pp. 58—65 (scarsa esattezza delle testimonianze di Filone e di Giuseppe sugli Esseni); D. H. WALLACE, The Essenes and Temple Sacrifice, in: Theologische Zeitschrift, XIII (1957), pp. 335—338 (affermazioni di Filone al riguardo); J. CARMIGNAC, Témoignage de Philon, in: Revue de Qumran, II (1960), pp. 530—532 (sui Terapeuti); G. VERMES, Essenes—Therapeutai—Qumran, in: Durham University Journal, XXI (1960), pp. 97—115; E. F. SUTCLIFFE, The Monks of Qumran, as Depicted in the Dead Sea Scrolls, with Translation in English, London, 1960, pp. XVI-272 (i testi più importanti di Qumran, di Filone, di Giuseppe, di Plinio il Vecchio); G. VERMES, The Etymology of Essenes, in: Revue de Qumran, II (1960), pp. 427—443 (contributo anche di Filone); H. G. SCHÖNFELD, Zum Begriff 'Therapeutai' bei Philo von Alexandrien, in: Revue de Qumran, III (1961), pp. 219—240 (critica a G. VERMES); V. NIKIPROWETZKY, Les suppliants chez Philon d'Alexandrie, in: Revue des Études Juives, IVe Sér. II (1963), pp. 241—278 (sui Terapeuti); J. B. BURKE, Philo and Alexandrian Judaism, Diss. Syracuse, Ann Arbor, 1964, pp. VII-302 (microfilm); J. GOLDIN, Of Change and Adaptation in Judaism, in: History of Religions, IV (1965), pp. 269—294 (usa come fonte Filone); F. DAUMAS, L'activité de l'Institut français d'archéologie orientale durant l'année 1965—1966, in: Comptes Rendus de l'Académie des Inscriptions et Belles-Lettres, Paris, 1966, pp. 298—309 (scavi a Dikkela per identificare la sede dei Terapeuti filoniani); C. DANIEL, Zélotes et Sicaires et leur mention par paronymie dans le Nouveau Testament, in:

quelli negli stadi, gli indugi sulla legge mosaica in vista di insegnamenti
universali con quelli sulla legge giudaica della diaspora alessandrina per
celebrare con giustizia i processi del momento. Del resto avrebbero agito
assai stoltamente i suoi correligionari se per guidare l'ambasceria a Caligola,
dalla quale sarebbe dipesa la loro sorte, avessero scelto un vecchio asceta,
ignaro delle usanze sociali, digiuno delle norme diplomatiche, inesperto
della psicologia romana[317].

Numen, XIII (1966), pp. 88—115 (Cristo avrebbe alluso a queste tre sette denunciandone i
difetti); A. GUILLAUMONT, Philon et les origines du monachisme, in: Philon d'Alexandrie.
Colloque Lyon 11—15 Septembre 1966, Paris, 1967, pp. 361—374; M. DELCOR, Repas
cultuels esséniens et thérapeutes, thiases et ḥaburoth, in: Revue de Qumran, VI (1967—
1968), pp. 401—425; J. A. FITZMYER, Jewish Christianity in Acts in light of the Qumran
Scrolls, in: Studies in Luke-Acts . . . in honor of P. Schubert, London, 1968, pp. 233—257
(elementi comuni tra la comunità giudeo-cristiana presentata negli Atti e la setta Essenica
di Qumran); C. DANIEL, Les Esséniens et l'arrière-fond historique de la parabole du bon
Samaritain, in: Novum Testamentum, XI (1969), pp. 71—104; ID., Faux prophètes,
surnom des Esséniens dans le Sermon sur la montagne, in: Revue de Qumran, VII N. 25
(1969), pp. 45—79; ID., Nouveau arguments en faveur de l'identification des Hérodiens
et des Esséniens, in: Revue de Qumran, VII N. 27 (1970), pp. 397—402; A. MARX, Les
racines du célibat essénien, in: Revue de Qumran, VII N. 27 (1970), pp. 323—342; R. T.
BECKWITH, The Qumran Calendar and the Sacrifices of the Essenes, in: Revue de Qumran,
VII N. 28 (1971), pp. 587—591; C. DANIEL, Un Essénien mentionné dans les Actes des
Apôtres, Barjésu, in: Muséon, LXXXIV (1971), pp. 455—476 (su Atti, 13,6—12); A.
GUILLAUMONT, A propos du célibat des Esséniens, in: Mélanges A. Dupont-Sommer,
Paris, 1971, pp. 395—404; A. STEINER, Warum lebten die Essener asketisch?, in:
Biblische Zeitschrift, XV (1971), pp. 1—28 (non si radicavano in un'antropologia filosofica,
come vogliono Filone e Giuseppe, ma nel pensiero biblico); 'Antike Berichte über die
Essener', ausgewählt von A. ADAM, 2. neub. und erw. Auflage von C. BURCHARD (Kleine
Texte für Vorlesungen und Übungen, n. 182), Berlin—New York, 1972, pp. VIII-88;
A. RAGOT, L'essénisme dans les apocryphes, in: Cahiers du Cercle Ernest Renan, n. XX,
74, Paris, 1972, pp. 3—8; Y. YADIN, L'attitude essénienne envers la polygamie et le divorce, in: Revue Biblique, LXXIX (1972), pp. 98—99, e 'Remarques' relative di J.
MURPHY—O'CONNOR, ibid. pp. 99—100; J. MURPHY—O'CONNOR, The Essenes and their
History, in: Revue Biblique, XCI (1974), pp. 215—244; M. HENGEL, Judentum und
Hellenismus ... (cfr. nota 291), pp. 394—453 (sul primo essenismo); C. DANIEL, Filon
din Alexandria membru de seamă al mișcării Eseniene din Egipt (Filone Alessandrino
membro insigne del movimento esseno in Egitto), in: Studii Teologice (București), XXVII
(1975), pp. 602—625; G. ORY, À la recherche des Esséniens. Essai critique, Paris, 1975,
pp. 80 (la prima fonte che esamina è Filone); G. VERMES, Essenes and Therapeutae
(Studies in Judaism in Late Antiquity, n. 8), Leiden, 1975, pp. 30—36.

[317] Per quanto concerne le testimonianze che Filone ci ha lasciate sulla situazione storica
contemporanea cfr. F. DELAUNAY, Philon d'Alexandrie. Écrits historiques, influence,
luttes et persécutions des Juifs dans le monde romain, Paris, 1ᵉ éd. 1863, 2ᵉ 1870 entrambe
di pp. XVI-389; H. GRAETZ, Die judäischen Ethnarchen oder Alabarchen in Alexandria,
in: Monatsschrift für Geschichte und Wissenschaft des Judenthums, XXV (1876), pp.
209—224; 241—254; 308—320; ID., Präcisierung der Zeit für die die Judäer betreffenden
Vorgänge unter dem Kaiser Caligula, ibid., XXVI (1877), pp. 97—107; 145—156; L. K.
AMITAÏ, Vae, vae victis. Romains et Juifs. Étude critique sur les rapports publics et privés
qui ont existé entre les Romains et les Juifs jusqu'à la prise de Jérusalem par Titus, Paris,
1894, pp. VI-136; J. NICOLE, Avillius Flaccus préfet d'Égypte et Philon d'Alexandrie
d'après un papyrus inédit, in: Revue de Philologie, N.S. XXII (1898), pp. 18—27; E. VON
DOBSCHÜTZ, Jews and Antisemites in Ancient Alexandria, in: The American Journal of
Theology, VIII (1904), pp. 728—755; U. WILCKEN, Zum Alexandrinischen Antisemitismus,

(Proseguimento della nota 317)

in: Abhandlungen der philologisch-historischen Klasse der K. Sächsischen Gesellschaft der Wissenschaften, XXVII (1909), pp. 783—839; J. JUSTER, Examen critique des sources relatives à la condition juridique des Juifs dans l'empire romain, Thèse, Paris, 1911, pp. VIII-140; ID., Les droits politiques des Juifs dans l'empire romain, Thèse, Paris, 1912, pp. XIII-104; B. MOTZO, La condizione giuridica dei Giudei di Alessandria sotto i Lagidi e i Romani, in: Atti della R. Accademia delle Scienze di Torino, XLVIII (1912—1913), pp. 577—598; J. HOROVITZ, Entwicklung des alexandrinischen Judentums unter dem Einflusse Philos, in: Judaica. Festschrift H. Cohen, Berlin, 1912, pp. 535—567; J. JUSTER, Les Juifs dans l'Empire romain. Leur condition juridique, économique et sociale, Paris, 1914, 2 voll., pp. XVIII-510 e VIII-338; M. RADIN, The Jews among the Greeks and Romans, Philadelphia, 1915, pp. 421; M. ENGERS, Die staatsrechtliche Stellung der alexandrinischen Juden, in: Klio, XVIII (1922—1923), pp. 79—90; L. FUCHS, Die Juden Ägyptens in ptolemäischer und römischer Zeit, Wien, 1924, pp. XX-156; H. I. BELL, Juden und Griechen im römischen Alexandreia. Eine historische Skizze des Alexandrinischen Antisemitismus (Beihefte zum Alten Orient, n. 9), Leipzig, 1927, pp. 52; A. MOMIGLIANO, Aspetti dell'antisemitismo alessandrino in due opere di Filone, in: La rassegna mensile di Israele, V (1930), pp. 275—286; A. SEGRÈ, Note sullo 'Status Civitatis' degli ebrei nell'Egitto tolemaico e imperiale, in: Bulletin de la Société Royale d'Archéologie d'Alexandrie, XXVIII (1933), pp. 143—182; A. LEPAPE, Tiberius Iulius Alexander, Préfet d'Alexandrie et d'Égypte, ibid., XXIX (1934), pp. 331—341; H. LEWY, Philon von Alexandrien. Von den Machterweisen Gottes. Eine zeitgenössische Darstellung der Judenverfolgungen unter dem Kaiser Caligula, Berlin, 1935, pp. 85; H. BOGNER, Philon von Alexandrien als Historiker, in: Forschungen zur Judenfrage, II (1937), pp. 63—74; G. BERTRAM, Philo und die jüdische Propaganda in der antiken Welt, in: W. GRUNDMANN, Christentum und Judentum, I, Leipzig, 1940, pp. 79—105; A. D. DOYLE, Pilate's Career and the Date of the Crucifixion, in: Journal of Theological Studies, XLII (1941), pp. 190—193; H. A. WOLFSON, Philo on Jewish Citizenship in Alexandria, in: Journal of Biblical Literature, LXIII (1944), pp. 165—168; E. M. SMALLWOOD, Some Notes on the Jews under Tiberius, in: Latomus, XV (1956), pp. 314—329 (Filone sull'espulsione dei Giudei da Roma nel 19 d. C.); ID., The Chronology of Gaius' Attempt to Desecrate the Temple, in: Latomus, XVI (1957), pp. 3—17 (validità della cronologia filoniana); C. ROTH, The Debate on the Loyal Sacrifices, A.D. 66, in: Harvard Theological Review, LIII (1960), pp. 93—97 (testimonianze di Giuseppe e di Filone sul rifiuto dei sacrifici in onore degli imperatori); S. REYERO, Los textos de Flavio Josefo y de Filón sobre las residencias de los procuradores romanos en Jerusalén, in: Studium (Avila), I (1962), pp. 527—556; P. J. SIJPESTEIJN, The Legationes ad Gaium, in: Journal of Jewish Studies, XV (1964), pp. 87—96; F. DE VISSCHER, La politique dynastique sous le règne de Tibère, in: Synteleia V. Arangio-Ruiz, Napoli, 1964, pp. 54—65 (notizie di Filone su Macrone, successore di Seiano e sulla sua politica a favore di Caligola); B. TAMM, Ist der Castortempel das Vestibulum zu dem Palast Caligulas gewesen?, in: Eranos, LXII (1964), pp. 146—169; J. HAMBROER, Theogonische und kosmogonische Mythen aus Rumänien, in: Zeitschrift für Religions- und Geistesgeschichte, XVII (1965), pp. 289—306 (testimonianze di Filone); S. ZEITLIN, Did Agrippa Write a Letter to Gaius Caligula?, in: Jewish Quarterly Review, LVI (1965), pp. 22—31 (fu composta da Filone); A. BAJSIĆ, Pilatus, Jesus und Barabbas, in: Biblica, XLVIII (1967), pp. 7—28 (il carattere di Pilato risulta inflessibile, privo di riguardi, caparbio più o meno come quello ritratto nella lettera di Agrippa I a Caligola: Legatio ad Gaium, 38); J. COLIN, Philon d'Alexandrie et la «lâcheté» du préfet d'Égypte (Philon, In Flaccum § 38, 41 et 43), in: Rheinisches Museum, CX (1967), pp. 284—285; J. SCHWARTZ, L'Égypte de Philon, in: Philon d'Alexandrie. Colloque Lyon 11—15 Septembre 1966, Paris, 1967, pp. 35—44; C. KRAUS, Filone Alessandrino e un'ora tragica della storia ebraica (Nobiltà dello spirito, n. 14), Napoli, 1967, pp. 262; H. HEGERMANN, Das hellenistische Judentum, in: Umwelt des Urchristentums, Berlin Ost, 1967, vol. I, pp. 292—345; G. ROSEN, Some Notes on Greek and Roman Attitudes toward the Mentally Ill, in: Historical Essays in Honor of O. Temkin, Baltimore, 1968, pp. 17—23 (umana concezione filoniana sulla follia); E. L. ABEL, Were the Jews banished from Rome

Pur sentendo il contrasto tra la vita contemplativa e quella attiva[318], pur sperimentando l'inquieto turbamento interiore prodotto dallo scontro di queste due vocazioni opposte ed irrinunciabili, evitò di farne un dramma lacerante e riuscì a comporre l'antagonismo in una superiore armonia. Suo massimo merito fu appunto di aver saputo conciliare nell'unità del suo spirito esigenze contrastanti, sia sul piano pratico che su quello teoretico. Infatti anche la cultura ebraica e quella greca del suo tempo erano ben lungi dal presentare un aspetto monolitico e nettamente caratterizzato: erano entrambe un confuso ribollire di esigenze molteplici, un indefinibile intrecciarsi di impulsi non ancora sedimentati, un incontrollabile sovrapporsi e divergere di correnti che non avrebbero saputo criticamente rendere un

in 19 A.D.?, in: Revue des Études Juives, CXXVII (1968), pp. 383—386 (nonostante l'attestazione di Filone non pare probabile); P. L. MAIER, The Episode of the Golden Roman Shields at Jerusalem, in: Harvard Theological Review, LXII (1969), pp. 109—121; A. N. SHERWIN-WHITE, Philo and Avillius Flaccus. A Conundrum, in: Latomus, XXXI (1972), pp. 820—828; G. DELLING, Philons Enkomion auf Augustus, in: Klio, LIV (1972), pp. 171—192; P. G. MAXWELL—STUART, Pollux and the Reputation of Tax Gatherers, in: Rivista di Studi Classici, XXII (1974), pp. 157—163 (le testimonianze di Filone sono studiate alle pp. 159—162); M. STERN, The Greek and Latin Literary Sources: The Jew People in the First Century (Compendia Rerum Judaicarum ad Novum Testamentum, n. I, 1), Assen, 1974, pp. 18—37; S. S. FOSTER, The Alexandrian Situation and Philo's Use of Dike, Diss. Northwestern Univ. Evanston, Ill., 1975, pp. 223 (microfilm); H. A. HARRIS, Greek Athletics and the Jews (Trivium Special Publications, n. 3), Cardiff, 1976, pp. VI-124 (indaga sull'atteggiamento dei Giudei verso l'atletica nei libri dei Maccabei, in Giuseppe ed in Filone); M. MALINA, Sailing to Alexandria: Philo's imagery, in: Studia Philonica, IV (1976—77), pp. 33—39; G. ROCCA-SERRA, Le stoïcisme pré-impérial et l'esclavage, in: Centro ricerche e documentazione sull'antichità classica, VIII (1976—77), pp. 205—222 (informazioni di notevole precisione sulla schiavitù si trovano in Filone, specie nel 'Quod omnis probus liber sit'); B. M. BOKSER, Philo's Description of Jewish Practices, in: Center for Hermeneutical Studies, Protocol Series, XXX (1977), pp. 1—11. Per testimonianze varie di Filone cfr.: R. HARRIS, An Archaeological Error in the Text of Philo Judaeus, Classical Review, XXXVIII (1923), pp. 61—63; F. PFISTER, Das Nachleben der Überlieferung von Alexander und den Brahmanen, in: Hermes, LXXVI (1941), pp. 143—169; F. PETTIRSCH, Das Verbot der opera servilia in der heiligen Schrift und in der altkirchlichen Exegese, in: Zeitschrift für Katholische Theologie, LXIX (1947), pp. 257—327; 417—444 (per Filone vedi pp. 306—312); R. PFEIFFER, The Image of the Delian Apollo and Apolline Ethics, in: Journal of the Warburg and Cartauld Institute, XV (1952), pp. 20—32; S. SAUNERON, Un thème littéraire de l'antiquité classique. Le Nil et la pluie, in: Bulletin de l'Institut Français d'Archéologie Orientale, LI (1952), pp. 41—48; L. ROBERT, Les colombes d'Anastase et autres volatiles, II: Les colombes d'Aphrodisias et d'Ascalon, in: Journal des Savants, 1971, pp. 91—97 (la libertà dei piccioni in queste due città è testimoniata da Filone in un testo conservato da Eusebio, Praeparatio Evangelica, VIII, 14); J. W. McKAY, The Date of Passover and its Significance, in: Zeitschrift für die Alttestamentliche Wissenschaft, LXXXIV (1972), pp. 435—447 (la datazione filoniana — De spec. leg. II, 155 — della Pasqua ebraica al plenilunio non ha alcun appoggio nell'Antico Testamento). È pure utile ricordare che, sull'epoca filoniana, si trovano dei contributi, talora abbastanza notevoli, nei due primi volumi del 'Corpus Papyrorum Judaicarum' editi da V. A. TCHERIKOVER e da A. FUCHS, Cambridge, Mass., I (1957), pp. XX-294; II (1960), pp. XV-283. — In questo volume (ANRW II 21,1) vedi C. KRAUS REGGIANI, I rapporti tra l'impero romano e il mondo ebraico al tempo di Caligola secondo la 'Legatio ad Gaium' di Filone Alessandrino, pp. 545—586.

[318] Leg. II, 85 p. I, 107, 14—15.

esatto conto di sè. Dominava l'effervescenza spirituale ed il grigiore speculativo che sono proprii di molte epoche di transizione. Di questo magma Filone fu il rilevatore ed in piccola parte il depuratore. Per esserlo in grande parte gli faceva difetto un'autentica genialità: egli era infatti l'uomo che si faceva rimorchiare dal singolo versetto entro i cui orizzonti restava sovente imprigionato; gli scarseggiava la potenza di chi raccoglie il materiale frammentario per disporlo in una costruzione architettonicamente nuova e sostanzialmente sua. Possedeva la finezza dell'analisi ma non la potenza della sintesi. Ha in complesso ragione il VÖLKER[319] quando scrive che egli si dedicava ad un verso dopo l'altro tenendo d'occhio solo il presente e quindi legandosi al testo biblico[320]; che non tutto quello che diceva era il suo vero pensiero ma che molto gli capitava sotto mano alla mercè del passo trattato; che il carattere omiletico della sua opera lo induceva a deviare dal tema e le associazioni di idee lo attiravano su sentieri marginali; che alle sue riflessioni si intrecciavano esortazioni ed ammonimenti.

Il pensiero di Filone è lontano dallo sviluppo rettilineo proprio del filosofo che si traccia una via individuale pur avvalendosi di disparati contributi, che egli ha comunque precedentemente assimilati ed unificati; lascia trasparire un'incertezza che non è imputabile al genere letterario impiegato[321]: alla gratuità insita nell'allegorismo si aggiunge la provvisorietà

---

[319] Fortschritt und Vollendung bei Philo von Alexandrien. Eine Studie zur Geschichte der Frömmigkeit, Leipzig, 1938, pp. 9—10.

[320] Per il testo dei Settanta usato da Filone ed i problemi connessi cfr. C. SIEGFRIED, Philonische Studien, in: Archiv für wissenschaftliche Erforschung des Alten Testaments, II (1872), pp. 143—163; ID., Philo und der überlieferte Text der LXX, in: Zeitschrift für wissenschaftliche Theologie, XVI (1873), pp. 217—238; 411—428; 522—540; B. PICK, Philo's Canon of the Old Testament and his Mode of Quoting the Alexandrian Version, in: Journal of the Society of Biblical Literature and Exegesis, (IV) (1884), pp. 126—143; F. C. CONYBEARE, Upon Philo's Text of the Septuagint, in: The Expòsitor, IV. Ser. IV (1891), pp. 456—466; ID., On the Philonean Text of the Septuagint, in: The Jewish Quarterly Review, V (1892—1893), pp. 246—280; VIII (1895—1896), pp. 88—122; H. E. RYLE, Philo and Holy Scripture or the Quotations of Philo from the Books of the Old Testament, with Introduction and Notes, London and New York, 1895, pp. XLVII-312; H. B. SWETE, Introduction to the Old Testament in Greek, Cambridge, 1900, pp. 372—380 (stessa paginazione nell'edizione del 1914 rivista da R. R. OTTLEY); A. W. L. SCHRÖDER, De Philonis Alexandrini Vetere Testamento, Diss., Gryphiae, 1907, pp. 50; W. L. KNOX, A Note on Philo's Use of the Old Testament, in: Journal of Theological Studies, XLI (1940), pp. 30—34; F. H. COLSON, Philo's Quotations from the Old Testament, ibid., XLI (1940), pp. 237—251; P. KATZ, Notes on the Septuagint, in: Journal of Theological Studies, XLVI (1946), pp. 30—33; ID., Philo's Bible. The Aberrant Text of Bible Quotations in Some Philonic Writings and its Place in the Textual History of the Greek Bible (The Kaye Prize Essay for 1947), Cambridge, 1950, pp. XII-161; R. MARCUS, A Textual-Exegetical Note on Philo's Bible, in: Journal of Biblical Literature, LXIX (1950), pp. 363—365; P. KATZ, Οὐ μή σε ἀνῶ, οὐδ' οὐ μή σε ἐγκαταλίπω, Hebr. XIII, 5. The Biblical Source of the Quotation, in: Biblica, XXXIII (1952), pp. 523—525; S. JELLICOE, Aristeas, Philo and the Septuagint Vorlage, in: Journal of Theological Studies, XII (1961), pp. 261—271; G. E. HOWARD, The «Aberrant» Text of Philo's Quotations Preconsidered, in: Hebrew Union College Annual, XLIV (1973), pp. 197—209.

[321] Sulla lingua, lo stile e l'attrezzatura retorica di Filone vedi L. COHN, Observationes de sermone Philonis, in: Philonis Alexandrini libellus de opificio mundi, edidit L. C. (Breslauer philologische Abhandlungen, n. IV, 4), Vratislaviae, 1889, pp. XLI—LVIII;

dei risultati ai quali, nella fattispecie, esso è fatto servire. Si direbbe che Filone non abbia la forza di elevarsi al disopra del suo trattato ma che il

E. Hatch, Essays in Biblical Greek, Oxford, 1889: pp. 109—130, Psychological Terms in Philo; per singoli vocaboli vedi anche le pp. 48 e 82—88; J. Jessen, De elocutione Philonis Alexandrini, nel volume celebrativo di H. Sauppe, Hamburg 1889, pp. 1—12; I. Unna, Über den Gebrauch der Absichtssätze bei Philo von Alexandrien, Diss. Würzburg, Frankfurt a. M., 1895, pp. 51; K. Reik, Der Optativ bei Polybius und Philo von Alexandria, Leipzig, 1907, pp. XII-197; A. Tschuschke, De πρίν particulae apud scriptores aetatis Augusteae prosaicos usu, Diss. Breslau, Trebnitz, 1913, pp. 25—31; A. W. de Groot, A Handbook of Antique Prose-rhythm. I. History of Greek prose-metre: Demosthenes, Plato, Philo, Plutarch and others; bibliography, curves, index, Groningen, 1918, pp. XI-228, particolarmente pp. 54—58 e 111—117; A. Allgeier, Semasiologische Beiträge zu ἐπισκιάζειν (Lk. 1,35) aus Theophylakt und Philo, in: Biblische Zeitschrift, 1920, pp. 131—141; A. Priessnig, Die literarische Form der Patriarchenbiographien des Philon von Alexandrien, in: Monatsschrift für Geschichte und Wissenschaft des Judentums, LXXIII (1929), pp. 143—155; M. E. Andrews, Paul, Philo and the Intellectuals, in: Journal of Biblical Literature, LIII (1934), pp. 150—166; F. R. M. Hitchcock, Philo and the Pastorals, in: Hermathena, LVI (1940), pp. 113—135 (parallelo tra la lingua di Filone e quella di S. Paolo); H. Tyen, Der Stil der Jüdisch-Hellenistischen Homilie, Göttingen, 1955, pp. 130 (largamente basato su Filone); G. Bertram, Ἱκανός in den griechischen Übersetzungen des ATs als Wiedergabe von schaddaj, in: Zeitschrift für die Alttestamentliche Wissenschaft, LXX (1958), pp. 20—30; J. P. Smith, Γένος in Philo on the Essenes (Hypoth. = Eus. Pr. Ev. 8. 11) = νόμος ?, in: Biblica, XL (1959), pp. 1021—1024; G. J. M. Bartelink, Zur Spiritualisierung eines Opferterminus, in: Glotta, XXXIX (1960), pp. 43—48 (trapassi di significato della parola μῶμος soprattutto in Filone e nei Padri della Chiesa); R. Arnaldez, Les images du sceau et de la lumière dans la pensée de Philon d'Alexandrie, in: L'Information Littéraire, XV (1963), pp. 62—72; A. Pelletier, Les passions à l'assaut de l'âme d'après Philon, in: Revue des Études Grecques, LXXVIII (1965), pp. 52—60; J. R. Baskin, Words for Joy and Rejoicing in the Writings of the Apostle Paul and Philo Judaeus, Diss., Princeton, 1966, pp. 495 (microfilm); A. Michel, Quelques aspects de la rhétorique chez Philon, in: Philon d'Alexandrie. Colloque Lyon 11—15 Septembre 1966, Paris, 1967, pp. 81—103; Á. P. Orbán, Les dénominations du monde chez les premiers chrétiens (Graecitas Christianorum Primaeva, n. 4), Nijmegen, 1970, pp. XIX-243 (per Filone: κόσμος, pp. 13—15; κοσμικός, pp. 89—90; αἰών, pp. 110—111; αἰώνιος, pp. 150—151); D. Solomon, Philo's Use of γεναρχής in In Flaccum, in: Jewish Quarterly Review, LXI (1970—71), pp. 119—131; J. Reiling, The Use of ψευδοπροφήτης in the Septuagint, Philo and Josephus, in: Novum Testamentum, XIII (1971), pp. 147—156; P. Courcelle, Verus homo, in: Studi Q. Cataudella, Catania, 1972, vol. II, pp. 517—527 (espressione usata ripetutamente da Filone in accezioni diverse che però tutte tendono a porre in evidenza i valori intellettuali e religiosi); M. Giusta, Ἀνευπροφάσιστος, un probabile ἅπαξ εἰρημένον in Filone, De aeternitate mundi 75, in: Rivista di Filologia e di Istruzione Classica, C (1972), pp. 131—136 (in luogo di ἂν εὐπροφάσιστα bisogna ammettere l'ἅπαξ: ἀνευπροφάσιστα); E. J. Barnes, Petronius, Philo and Stoic Rhetoric, in: Latomus, XXXII (1973), pp. 787—798; F. E. Morard, Monachos, Moine. Histoire du terme grec jusqu'au 4e siècle, in: Freiburger Zeitschrift für Philosophie und Theologie, XX (1973), pp. 332—411 (per Filone pp. 357—362); H. Cazelles, Eucharistie, bénédiction et sacrifice dans l'Ancien Testament, in: Maison-Dieu, n. 123 (1975), pp. 7—28 (l'inchiesta comprende anche la terminologia di Filone); E. Des Places, Un terme biblique et platonicien: ΑΚΟΙΝΩΝΗΤΟΣ, in: Studi in onore di M. Pellegrino, Torino, 1975, pp. 154—158 (soprattutto in Numenio d'Apamea ed in Filone). Assai utile per la precisazione dei termini filoniani è G. Kittel, Theologisches Wörterbuch zum Neuen Testament, Stuttgart, dal 1933 in avanti, che fa frequentissimi riferimenti allo scrittore alessandrino. — Nel presente volume (ANRW II 21,1) vedi T. M. Conley, Philo's Rhetoric: Argumentation and Style, pp. 343—371.

più delle volte vi rimanga immerso e quasi oppresso; di qui quella sua abitudine di cogliere, un po' indiscriminatamente, qualunque idea gli venga a tiro senza operare una selezione o un collocamento in prospettiva. È persuasiva la dichiarazione enunciata da R. ARNALDEZ all'inizio dell' 'Introduzione generale' che fa da premessa all'edizione delle opere pubblicata dalle 'Éditions du Cerf': „Gli scritti filoniani sono prolissi; la loro natura è difficile da precisare; non sempre si ricuperano esattamente lo stile ed il pensiero; si sente che non tutto ha la stessa importanza, ma non si può distinguere con certezza che cosa fosse per Filone l'essenziale."

Ai limiti dell'ingegno non corrisposero, per fortuna, quelli dell'anima. Se l'eclettismo della sua mente lo portò a servirsi di tutti i sistemi filosofici, l'equilibrio del suo temperamento lo preservò dagli estremismi ai quali essi potevano avviarlo sotto l'azione di rigorismi razionali disancorati dalla realtà: così dissente dall'intransigenza stoica, che con Crisippo poneva come obiettivo etico la totale estirpazione delle passioni, per condividere la dottrina dei Peripatetici, i quali consideravano le affezioni come necessariamente connaturate all'uomo di cui erano preziose collaboratrici per condurre una vita retta; così tende coscientemente a spostare il centro della moralità dall'ambito della pura intelligenza verso quello della volontà[322]. Al chiuso

---

[322] Sulle convinzioni etiche di Filone puoi confrontare L. Löw, Die Lehre Philo's vom Eide (1863), ripubblicato in: ID., Gesammelte Schriften, I, Szegedin, 1889, pp. 213—221; Z. FRANKEL, Zur Ethik des jüdisch-alexandrinischen Philosophen Philo, in: Monatsschrift für Geschichte und Wissenschaft des Judenthums, XVI (1867), pp. 241—252; 281—297; M. WOLFF, Die philonische Ethik in ihren wesentlichsten Punkten zusammengestellt, in: Philosophische Monatshefte, XV (1879), pp. 333—350; J. HAMBURGER, Die Ethik Philo's in ihrem Verhältniss zu den ethischen Lehren der Volks- und Gesetzeslehrer der Juden in Palästina und Babylonien, in: Populär-wissenschaftliche Monatsblätter zur Belehrung über das Judentum, V (1885), pp. 153—156; 177—180; 207—209; 231—232; S. TIKTIN, Die Lehre von den Tugenden und Pflichten bei Philo von Alexandrien, Diss. Bern, Breslau, 1895, pp. 59; J. C. C. CLARKE, The Exposition of the Bible by Philo, the Alexandrian Jew, in: Man and his Divine Father, Chicago, 1900, pp. 143—183; J. HEINEMANN, Philo's Lehre vom Eid. Eine quellenkritische Untersuchung, in: Judaica. Festschrift H. Cohen, Berlin, 1912, pp. 109—118; J. MANN, Oaths and Vows in the Synoptic Gospels, in: The American Journal of Theology, XXI (1917), pp. 260—274; H. BOLKESTEIN, Een geval van social-ethisch syncretisme, in: Mededeelingen van de Akademie van Wetenschappen te Amsterdam, LXXII, 1, Amsterdam, 1931, pp. 52; S. BELKIN, The Dissolution of Vows and the Problem of Antisocial Oaths in the Gospels and Contemporary Jewish Literature, in: Journal of Biblical Literature, LV (1936), pp. 227—234; ID., Philo and the Oral Law. The Philonic Interpretation of Biblical Law in Relation to the Palestinian Halakah (Harvard Semitic Series, n. 11), Cambridge, Mass., 1940, pp. 292, ristampato nel 1970, New York; F. W. KOHNKE, Das Bild der echten Münze bei Philon von Alexandria, in: Hermes, XCVI (1968), pp. 583—590 (virtù e valori morali attraverso all'allegoria della moneta); A. BENGIO, La dialectique de Dieu et de l'homme chez Platon et chez Philon d'Alexandrie: une approche du concept d'ἀρετή chez Philon, Mémoire de maîtrise, Paris, 1971, pp. 116; D. S. WINSTON, Freedom and Determinism in Greek Philosophy and Jewish Hellenistic Wisdom, in: Studia Philonica, II (1973), pp. 40—50 (trapasso da un accentuato determinismo nelle due culture ad una chiara affermazione della libertà, sostenuta soprattutto da Epicuro e nell'Antico Testamento, da Ben Sira e dalla Sapienza); A. NISSEN, Gott und der Nächste im antiken Judentum. Untersuchungen zum Doppelgebot der Liebe (Wissenschaftliche Untersuchungen zum Neuen Testament, n. 15), Tübin-

nazionalismo ebraico egli contrappose un universalismo che superava però il cosmopolitismo stoico fondato sul diritto di natura, in quanto era prodotto dalla comunione nella verità: per lui infatti la filosofia, contenendo semi di quella verità che risplendeva intera nella rivelazione mosaica, era chiamata ad integrarsi alla Bibbia. Ne conseguiva che Filone si sentiva cittadino del mondo in unione con i sapienti di tutti i tempi e di tutte le stirpi. Il suo ebraismo non era tanto razziale e cultuale quanto spirituale.

Di qui il suo atteggiamento di fronte all'Impero Romano che è quello di un suddito leale ma non di un cittadino animoso: accetta la realtà politica, perchè sarebbe assurdo respingerla e perchè offre effettivamente dei vantaggi, però in lui c'è assai più sopportazione che entusiasmo. Non deroga da nessuno dei doveri civici ma non vibra per lo stato: l'idea che Roma possa cadere non gli suscita nè emozione nè terrore. In fondo all'anima gli stagna l'indifferenza la quale non è solo dovuta al suo internazionalismo filosofico: anche il suo sentimento non si agita nè si riscalda[323]. La sua patria più autentica risiede in un ascetismo che, attraverso all'austerità, alla meditazione ed alla purificazione, innalza l'uomo nelle sfere terse della contemplazione divina. Il suo convinto ebraismo si allea benissimo con questa aspirazione: sono infatti i terapeuti giudei che incarnano nel modo più perfetto l'ideale di un misticismo equilibrato e vitale, come fu ancora la legislazione giudaica di Mosè che applicò ai costumi umani quella suprema razionalità alla quale era informata la legge universale regolatrice del

gen, 1974 (su Filone pp. 417—502); S. SANDMEL, Virtue and Reward in Philo, in: Essays J. Ph. Hyatt, New York, 1974, pp. 215—223; D. S. WINSTON, Freedom and Determinism in Philo of Alexandria, in: Studia Philonica, III (1974—75), pp. 47—70; D. LÜHRMANN, Henoch und die Metanoia, in: Zeitschrift für die Neutestamentliche Wissenschaft, LXVI (1975), pp. 103—116 (per la metanoia in Filone vedi il par. 4 pp. 111—114); D. L. MEALAND, Philo of Alexandria's Attitude to Riches, in: Zeitschrift für die Neutestamentlichen Wissenschaft, LXIX (1978), pp. 258—264 (sua posizione sostanzialmente ambigua). Vedi anche, in questo volume (ANRW II 21,1) D. WINSTON, Philo's Ethical Theory, pp. 372—416.

[323] Sulle opinioni politiche di Filone cfr. F. DELAUNAY, Note sur le système politique de Philon, in: Académie des Sciences Morales et Politiques, Compte Rendu, XCIX (1873), pp. 305—313; E. R. GOODENOUGH, Philo and Public Life, in: The Journal of Egyptian Archaeology, XII (1926), pp. 77—79; H. LEISEGANG, Der Ursprung der Lehre Augustins von der Civitas Dei, in: Archiv für Kulturgeschichte, XVI (1926), pp. 127—158; J. HEINEMANN, Die Lehre vom ungeschriebenen Gesetz im jüdischen Schrifttum, in: Hebrew Union College Annual (Cincinnati), IV (1927), pp. 149—171 (particolarmente pp. 152—159); S. TRACY, Philo Judaeus and the Roman Principate, Williamsport (Pennsylvania), 1933, pp. 55; E. LANGSTADT, Zu Philos Begriff der Demokratie, in: BR. SCHINDLER—A. MARMORSTEIN, Occident and Orient..., Gaster anniversary volume, London, 1936, pp. 349—364; E. R. GOODENOUGH, The Politics of Philo Judaeus. Practice and Theory, New Haven, 1938, pp. 123 (dove sostiene l'improbabile tesi di un Filone propagandista antiromano): a quest'opera H. L. GOODHART e E. R. GOODENOUGH hanno poi aggiunto come appendice 'A General Bibliography of Philo', pp. 125—321 (che per ampiezza e precisione merita ogni elogio) seguita dai rispettivi indici, pp. 323—348. Vedi inoltre G. DELLING, Philons Enkomion auf Augustus, in: Klio, LIV (1972), pp. 171—192 (l'encomio ad Augusto di Gai. 143—147 ha un'impronta personale, è in contrasto con il giudizio su Caligola ed evita naturalmente qualsiasi accenno all'apoteosi imperiale).

cosmo. I patriarchi di questa legge erano stati delle ipostasi viventi e quindi con la loro esemplarità potevano diventare efficaci paradigmi per l'uomo il quale, situato al centro della piramide ontologica che ha Dio come vertice e la materia come base, è esposto alle contrastanti sollecitazioni verso l'alto e verso il basso. Il dualismo platonico tra spirito e materia forma l'ossatura della dialettica psicologica filoniana, però l'Alessandrino vi immette un soffio mistico, intermittente nelle sue manifestazioni ma perenne nella sua presenza, che l'Ateniese non conosceva e non poteva conoscere.

La fisionomia spirituale di Filone sembrava fatta apposta per renderlo un isolato tra gli Ebrei: messo al bando dai sadducei per il loro intransigente conservatorismo, osteggiato dai farisei per la loro fanatica avversione all'ellenismo, ufficialmente ignorato dal rabbinismo, di matrice farisaica, per il suo attaccamento alle tradizioni, trovò invece una notevole fortuna tra i cristiani. La sua qualità di esponente di quella scuola alessandrina che aveva applicato alla Bibbia principi ermeneutici di alto interesse, il suo eclettismo filosofico che insegnava ad attingere con disinvoltura a tutte le fonti che promettessero di soddisfare man mano le esigenze del momento, la sua rielaborazione razionale del messaggio divino e la conseguente fondazione della teologia, la sua saggia contemperanza di vita attiva e di vita contemplativa, la sua partecipazione in ispirito di carità alle vicende politiche per salvare i suoi fratelli di stirpe e di fede, il suo atteggiamento politico prudente e distaccato, lo zelo apostolico con cui aveva cercato di interpretare l'inquieta agitazione culturale dei suoi tempi per adeguarvi l'insegnamento rivelato ed ovviare al pericolo dell'apostasia, il suo universalismo spirituale, il suo sincero ascetismo e forse soprattutto la sua profonda pietà e tensione religiosa che lo avevano portato, certo tra i primi in Israele, a vedere non il rapporto giuridico di alleanza tra Dio ed il suo popolo ma quello personale di amicizia con ogni singola anima, erano tutti validi titoli di raccomandazione presso i maestri della nuova fede. La coincidenza che proprio ad Alessandria sorgesse il Didaskaleion, che rinsaldò subito il connubio tra la scuola giudaica e quella cristiana della medesima città, servì da lancio all'opera letteraria filoniana che, in certo qual modo agganciata a quella dei Padri, non doveva andare perduta. Per una volta tanto poi anche i difetti erano destinati a collaborare con i pregi; infatti quello stesso carattere di ambiguità e di frammentarismo che ora disperde gli studiosi nelle più svariate ricostruzioni del pensiero filoniano doveva aiutare i teologi ecclesiastici porgendo loro un materiale facilmente suscettibile di essere riplasmato nelle loro speculazioni spesso fortemente personali. Il quarto secolo — epoca aurea della letteratura cristiana greca — vede Filone ispiratore, selettivamente filtrato ma non ignorato.

Se la critica più recente ha ridimensionato con risolutezza le concomitanze filoniane con il Nuovo Testamento, che in passato si era piuttosto corrivi nell'asserire, limitandole quasi solo all'Epistola agli Ebrei[324], ha

---

[324] Per accostamenti tra Filone ed il Nuovo Testamento puoi vedere, oltre a moltissimi commenti, edizioni e ricerche sui singoli scritti neotestamentari, J. B. CARPZOVIUS, Sacrae

(Proseguimento della nota 324)

exercitationes in S. Paulli epistolam ad Hebraeos ex Philone Alexandrino. Praefixa sunt
Philoniana prolegomena, in quibus de non adeo contemnenda Philonis eruditione hebraica,
de convenientia stili Philonis cum illo D. Paulli in Epistola ad Hebraeos, et de aliis non-
nullis varii argumenti exponitur, Helmstadii, 1750, pp. CLXIV-664; H. C. BALLEN-
STEDT, Philo und Johannes oder fortgesetzte Anwendung des Philo zur Interpretation
der Johanneischen Schriften, mit besonderer Hinsicht auf die Frage: Ob Johannes der
Verfasser der ihm zugeschriebenen Schriften seyn könne?, Göttingen, 1812, pp. 148;
A. GFRÖRER, Philo und die alexandrinische Theosophie, oder vom Einflusse der jüdisch-
ägyptischen Schule auf die Lehre des Neuen Testaments (Kritische Geschichte des Urchri-
stenthums, n. I, 1, 2), Stuttgart, 1831, 2 voll., pp. XLIV-534; 406; F. LÜCKE, Commentar
über das Evangelium des Johannes, 3. Aufl., Bonn, 1840, vol. I, pp. 290—294; 630—650;
C. W. NIEDNER, De subsistentia τῷ θείῳ λόγῳ apud Philonem Judaeum et Johannem
Apostolum tributa, in: Zeitschrift für die historische Theologie, XIX (1849), pp. 337—381;
P. F. KEERL, Philo im Neuen Testament, in: ID., Die Apokryphenfrage ... aufs neue be-
leuchtet, Leipzig, 1855, pp. 287—348; J. A. REUBELT, The Logos of Philo Judaeus and that
of St. John, in: Methodist Quarterly Review, XL (1858), pp. 110—129; B. JOWETT, St.
Paul and Philo, in: ID., The Epistles of St. Paul to the Thessalonians, Galatians, Romans,
with critical notes and dissertations, London, 1859, vol. I, pp. 448—514 (3ª ediz. ibid.
1894, vol. I, pp. 382—434); F. DELITZCH, Johannes und Philo, in: Zeitschrift für die ge-
sammte lutherische Theologie und Kirche, XXIV (1863), pp. 219—229; J. J. GAILLARD,
Essai sur l'origine de la théorie du Logos et sur les rapports de la doctrine de Jean avec
celle de Philon, Thèse, Strasbourg, 1864, pp. 39; B. BAUER, Philo, Strauss und Renan
und das Urchristenthum, Berlin, 1874, pp. 155; C. PAHUD, Le Logos de Philon et les rapports
avec la doctrine chrétienne, Diss., Lausanne, 1874, pp. 84; K. ANET, La notion du Logos
dans la philosophie grecque, dans Saint Jean et dans les Pères apologètes grecs, Thèse,
Liège, 1874, pp. 84; J. W. LAKE, Plato, Philo and Paul; or The Pagan Conception of a
'Divine Logos' shown to have been the basis of the Christian dogma of the Deity of Christ,
London (1874), pp. 76; J. RÉVILLE, La doctrine du Logos dans le quatrième Évangile et
dans les œuvres de Philon, Paris, 1881, pp. 181; P. J. GLOAG, The Logos of Philo and St.
John, in: The Presbyterian and Reformed Review, II (1891), pp. 46—57; D. C. THIJM,
De Logosleer van Philo en haar betrekking tot het Evangelie van Johannes, inzonderheid
wat den Proloog betreft, in: Theologische Studiën, XI (1893), pp. 97—137; 209—245;
377—442; J. CABANTOUS, Philon et l'Épître aux Hébreux ou essai sur les rapports de la
christologie de l'Épître aux Hébreux avec la philosophie judéo-alexandrine, Thèse, Montauban, 1895, pp. 79; H. VOLLMER, Die alttestamentlichen Citate bei Paulus textkritisch und
biblisch-theologisch gewürdigt nebst einem Anhang über das Verhältnis des Apostels zu
Philo, Freiburg i. Br.—Leipzig, 1895, pp. VIII-103; W. E. BALL, St. John and Philo
Judaeus, in: The Contemporary Review, LXXIII (1898), pp. 219—234; E. SACHSSE, Die
Logoslehre bei Philo und bei Johannes, in: Neue kirchliche Zeitschrift, XV (1904), pp.
747—767; W. F. ADENEY, The Relation of New Testament Theology to Jewish Alexandrian
Thought, in: The Biblical World, XXVI (1905), pp. 41—54; J. WATSON, The Philosophical
Basis of Religion. A Series of Lectures, Glasgow, 1907, pp. 190—247; J. D'ALMA, Philon
d'Alexandrie et le Quatrième Évangile, Paris, 1910, pp. VIII-117; H. H. WENDT, Das
Verhältnis des Prologs zum Philonismus, in: ID., Die Schichten im vierten Evangelium,
Göttingen, 1911, pp. 98—103; C. JOHNSTON, Paul and Philo, in: The Constructive Quar-
terly, I (1913), pp. 810—825; ID., The Logos in the Fourth Gospel, ibid., VI (1918), pp.
347—362; J. R. HARRIS, The Influence of Philo upon the New Testament, in: The Ex-
pository Times, XXXVII (1925—1926), pp. 565—566; A. VITTI, Christus-Adam. De
Paulino hoc conceptu interpretando eiusque ab extraneis fontibus indipendentia vindi-
canda, in: Biblica, VII (1926), pp. 121—145 (pp. 140—144: Theoria Philonis); F. BÜCHSEL,
Johannes und der hellenistische Synkretismus (Beiträge zur Förderung christlicher
Theologie, II. R., n. 16), Gütersloh, 1928, pp. 114; E. F. SCOTT, The Fourth Gospel. Its
Purpose and Theology, 2ⁿᵈ ed. Edinburgh, 1930, pp. 54—64; 146—160; G. KUHLMANN,
Theologia naturalis bei Philon und bei Paulus. Eine Studie zur Grundlegung der paulini-
schen Anthropologie (Neutestamentliche Forschungen, I. Paulusstudien, n. 7), Gütersloh,

(Proseguimento della nota 324)

1930, pp. 145; Y. H. HADIDIAN, Philonism in the Fourth Gospel, in: The MacDonald Presentation volume, Princeton, 1933, pp. 211—222; M. E. ANDREWS, Paul, Philo, and the Intellectuals, in: Journal of Biblical Literature, LIII (1934), pp. 150—166; M.-J. LAGRANGE, Les origines du dogme paulinien de la divinité du Christ, in: Revue Biblique, XLV (1936), pp. 5—33; J. N. SEVENSTER, Het verlossingsbegrip bij Philo vergeleken met de verlossingsgedachten van de synoptische evangeliën (Van Gorcum's Theologische Bibliotheek, n. 4), Assen, 1936, pp. 190; J. TERNUS, Paulinische, philonische, augustinische Anthropologie, in: Scholastik, XI (1936), pp. 82—98; N. J. HOMMES, Philo en Paulus, in: Philosophia reformata, II (1937), pp. 156—187; 193—223; H. G. MEECHAM, The Epistle of St. James, in: Expository Times, XLIX (1937—1938), pp. 181—183 (la redazione delle allocuzioni componenti l'epistola, pronunciate in Palestina, sarebbe avvenuta ad opera di un discepolo di Filone); W. L. KNOX, Parallels to the N. T. use of σῶμα, in: Journal of Theological Studies, XXXIX (1938), pp. 243—246; J. H. STELMA, Christus' Offer bij Paulus vergeleken met de offeropvattingen van Philo, Diss., Wageningen, 1938, pp. 140; R. B. MIDDLETON, Logos and Shekinah in the Fourth Gospel, in: Jewish Quarterly Review, XXIX (1938—1939), pp. 101—133; C. SPICQ, Le philonisme de l'Épître aux Hébreux, in: Revue Biblique, LVI (1949), pp. 542—572; LVII (1950), pp. 212—242; G. DELLING, Zur paulinischen Theologie, in: Theologische Literaturzeitung, LXXV (1950), pp. 705—710 (Filone e Paolo subordinano il τέλος della vita umana alla sovranità di Dio); D. J. THERON, Paul's Concept of ἀλήθεια (Truth). A Comparative Study with Special Reference to the Septuagint, Philo, the Hermetic Literature and Pistis Sophia, Diss., Princeton, 1950; S. V. McCASLAND, The Image of God according to Paul, in: Journal of Biblical Literature, LXIX (1950), pp. 85—100 (confronti soprattutto con Filone); C. SPICQ, Alexandrinismes dans l'Épître aux Hébreux, in: Revue Biblique, LVIII (1951), pp. 481—502; A. W. ARGYLE, Philo and the Fourth Gospel, in: Expository Times, LXIII (1951), pp. 385—386; R. M. WILSON, Philo and the Fourth Gospel, ibid., LXV (1953), pp. 47—49; H. P. OWEN, The Stages of Ascent in Hebrews V, 11—VI, 3, in: New Testament Studies, III (1956—1957), pp. 243—253; E. KÄSEMANN, Der Königsweg bei Philo, in: ID., Das wandernde Gottesvolk. Eine Untersuchung zum Hebräerbrief, 2. Aufl., Göttingen, 1957, pp. 45—52; E. SCHWEIZER, Die hellenistischen Komponente im neutestamentlichen σάρξ-Begriff, in: Zeitschrift für die Neutestamentliche Wissenschaft, XLVIII (1957), pp. 237—253; J. H. BURTNESS, Plato, Philo, and the Author of Hebrews, in: Luth. Quarterly, X (1958), pp. 54—64; D. M. CRESSAN, Imago Dei. A Study in Philo and St. Paul, Diss. Athenaei Sancti Patricii, Manutiae (St. Patrick's College, Maynooth, Ireland), 1959, pp. 62; P. BORGEN, Brod fra himmel og fra jord. Om Haggada i Palestinsk Midrasj, hos Philo og i Johannesevangeliet, in: Norsk Theologisk Tidsschrift, LXI (1960), pp. 218—240; C. COLPE, Zur Leib-Christi-Vorstellung im Epheserbrief, in: Festschrift für J. Jeremias (Zeitschrift für die Neutestamentliche Wissenschaft, Beih., n. 26), Berlin, 1960, pp. 172—187; S. LYONNET, L'hymne christologique de l'Épître aux Colossiens et la fête juive du Nouvel An (S. Paul, Col. 1,20 et Philon, De spec. leg. 2,192), in: Recherches de Science Religieuse, XLVIII (1960), pp. 93—100; J. COPPENS, Les affinités qumrâniennes de l'Épître aux Hébreux, in: Nouvelle Revue Théologique, LXXXIV (1962), pp. 128—141; 257—282; S. SANDMEL, Parallelomania, in: Journal of Biblical Literature, LXXXI (1962), pp. 1—13 (condanna dell'abuso di raffrontare il NT con i testi di Qumran, Filone, gli scritti rabbinici); L. H. SILBERMAN, Farewell to ὁ ἀμήν. A Note on Rev. 3,14, in: Journal of Biblical Literature, LXXXII (1963), pp. 213—215 (richiamo di un passo filoniano); S. G. SOWERS, The Hermeneutics of Philo and the Hebrews. A Comparison of the Interpretation of the Old Testament in Philo Judaeus and the Epistle to the Hebrews (Studies of Theology, n. 1), Diss. Basel, Zürich, 1964, pp. 136; P. BORGEN, Bread from heaven . . ., cfr. nota 4; R. CANTALAMESSA, Il papiro Chester Beatty III (P⁴⁶) e la tradizione indiretta di Hebr. 10,1, in: Aegyptus, XLV (1965), pp. 194—215; H. CHADWICK, St. Paul and Philo of Alexandria, in: Bulletin of the John Rylands Library, XLVIII (1966), pp. 286—307; R. SCROGGS, The Last Adam. A Study in Pauline Anthropology, Oxford—Philadelphia, 1966, pp. XXIV-139 (tra il resto studia il commento di Filone su Gen. 1—3); E. SCHWEIZER, Zum religionsgeschichtlichen Hintergrund der Sendungsformel, Gal IV, 4f., Rm

invece confermato gl'influssi da lui esercitati su taluni Padri della Chiesa. Oltre a Clemente e ad Origene, il cui rapporto è ormai diventato un luogo comune, circa come lo è l'influenza da loro operata sui Cappadoci, possiamo citare, come esiguo florilegio, il ricorso di S. Basilio e di altri come a mezzo di elevazione a quella μνήμη θεοῦ di cui pare che l'Alessandrino sia stato il primo a parlare in maniera esplicita[325]; l'identità dei fondamenti sui quali i Padri criticarono la filosofia greca[326]; qualche consonanza di

VIII, 3f., Joh III, 16f., I Joh IV, 9, in: Zeitschrift für die Neutestamentliche Wissenschaft, LVII (1966), pp. 199—210; R. A. Stewart, The Sinless High-priest, in: New Testament Studies, XIV (1967), pp. 126—135 (accostamenti tra l'Epistola agli Ebrei e Filone); B. Gärtner, The Pauline and Johannine Idea of 'To know God' against the Hellenistic Background. The Greek Philosophical Principle 'Like by like' in Paul and John, in: New Testament Studies, XIV (1968), pp. 209—231; A. Škrinjar, Theologia epistolae I Jo comparatur cum philonismo et hermetismo, in: Verbum Domini, XLVI (1968), pp. 224—234; F. Schröger, Der Verfasser des Hebräerbriefes als Schriftausleger (Biblische Untersuchungen, n. 4), Regensburg, 1968, pp. 360; E. Brandenburger, Fleisch und Geist, cfr. nota 36; L. M. Congdon, The False Teachers at Colossae. Affinities with Essene and Philonic Thought, Diss. Drew Univ., 1968, pp. 285 (microfilm); H. Braun, Das himmlische Vaterland bei Philo und im Hebräerbrief, in: Verbum veritas. Festschrift G. Stählin, Wuppertal, 1970, pp. 319—327; K. Hanhart, The Structure of John I, 35—IV, 54, in: Studies J. N. Sevenster, NT Suppl. XXIV, Leiden, 1970, pp. 22—46 (influenza di Filone su S. Giovanni in questo passo); R. Williamson, Philo and the Epistle to the Hebrews (Arbeiten zur Liturgie und Geschichte des hellenistischen Judentums, n. 4), Leiden, 1970, pp. XIV-602; D. A. Hagner, The Vision of God in Philo and John. A Comparative Study, in: Journal of the Evangelical Theological Society, XIV (1971), pp. 81—93; E. W. Smith, The Form and Religious Background of Romans VII, 24—25a, in: Novum Testamentum, XIII (1971), pp. 127—135; D. L. Balch, Backgrounds of I Cor. VII. Sayings of the Lord in Q; Moses as an Ascetic θεῖος ἀνήρ in II Cor. III, in: New Testament Studies, XVIII (1972), pp. 351—364 (sulla rinuncia ascetica al matrimonio in S. Paolo ed in Filone, Moses II, 66—70); P. Grelot, La naissance d'Isaac et celle de Jésus. Sur une interprétation «mythologique» de la conception virginale, in: Nouvelle Revue Théologique, XCIV (1972), pp. 462—487; 561—585 (pp. 561—574: l'esame di Filone, specie nel 'De Cherubim', esclude l'esistenza nel giudaismo ellenistico di un mito di maternità verginale); D. Lührmann, Pistis im Judentum, in: Zeitschrift für die Neutestamentliche Wissenschaft, LXIV (1973), pp. 19—38 (connessioni e diversificazioni tra cristianesimo e giudaismo: per Filone pp. 29—32); O. Giordano, Gesù e Barabbas, in: Helikon, XIII—XIV (1973—74), pp. 140—173 (accostamenti tra il mimo burlesco inscenato dagli Alessandrini contro la visita di Erode Agrippa — raccontato da Filone, In Flaccum 36—39 — e gli oltraggi a Gesù durante la passione); H. C. C. Cavallin, Life after Death. Paul's argument for the resurrection of the dead in I Cor. 15. I: An enquiry into the Jewish background, Diss. Uppsala (Coniectanea Biblica, N.T., Ser. VII, n. 1), Lund, 1974, pp. 301 (considerato anche Filone); L. K. K. Dey, The Intermediary World and Patterns of Perfection in Philo and Hebrews (Society of Biblical Literature, Dissertation Series, n. 25), Missoula, 1975, pp. XI-239; J. Bernard, La guérison de Bethesda. Harmonies judéo-hellénistiques d'un récit de miracle un jour de sabbat, in: Mélanges de Science Religieuse, XXXIII (1976), pp. 3—34 (su Filone pp. 15—27); XXXIV (1977), pp. 13—44; R. A. Horsley, Wisdom of Word and Words of Wisdom in Corinth, in: Catholic Biblical Quarterly, XXXIX (1977), pp. 224—239 (Filone e I Cor. 1—4).

[325] Cfr. I. Hausherr, Noms du Christ et voies d'oraison (Orientalia Christiana Analecta, n. 157), Roma, 1960, pp. 157—158.

[326] Falsità di molte sue dottrine e disaccordi tra i filosofi con conseguente sua inutilità come guida alla verità. Cfr. H. A. Wolfson, The Philosophy of the Church Fathers, Vol. I, second edit. revised, Cambridge, Mass., 1964, pp. 15—16.

Didimo[327]; importanti capisaldi del sistema di Gregorio di Nissa. Infatti il Cappadoce nel suo trattato sulla creazione dell'uomo si ispira espressamente a Filone[328]; dipende da lui nella dottrina sulla doppia creazione e sull'assenza di sessualità nell'uomo ad immagine di Dio, nell'assimilazione delle passioni a bestie feroci in connessione con immagini bibliche, nei temi della sobria ebbrezza, della tenebra luminosa e della veglia spirituale, proviene da lui o da Plotino per il motivo della fuga del solo verso il solo[329]; deriva da lui quando vede nella parentela dell'uomo con Dio mediante l'immagine un principio di conoscenza di Dio, quando considera l'anima umana come μεθόριος tra la natura immortale, a cui aderisce per mezzo della contemplazione, e quella mortale e quando rifiuta la qualità di immagine alle forme corporee per quanto felici[330]; si affianca a lui nella trattazione sulla virtù[331]. Le citazioni potrebbero diventare volume se si volesse fare uno spoglio sistematico della bibliografia riferita, ma sarebbero superflue, tanto più che agli influssi diretti, su quanti lessero le opere di Filone, andrebbero aggiunti quelli indiretti, su quanti le sue opere non lessero ma si nutrirono ugualmente del suo pensiero, attingendolo anonimo dal patrimonio comune di cultura nel quale era ormai entrato come componente precipua. Non va inoltre dimenticata l'osservazione di E. VACHEROT[332]: ,,Clemente e Origene citeranno frequentemente Filone: proprio alla sua scuola impareranno ad apprezzare e ad impiegare la scienza greca; il vero Platone, il Platone greco li avrebbe poco attirati. Ed effettivamente, nonostante l'incontestabile affinità delle dottrine, la teologia cristiana si sarebbe difficilmente adattata al platonismo puro; ma essa abbraccerà con ardore il platonismo orientale di Filone." Molti dei grandi autori ecclesiastici poi da lui non detrassero solo lezioni di speculazione teologica ma anche di introspezione psicologica; percorrendo infatti la strada aperta dagli stoici, egli illustrò il complesso gioco interiore messo in moto dalle suggestioni

---

[327] Cfr. W. A. BIENERT, 'Allegoria' und 'Anagoge' bei Didymos dem Blinden von Alexandria (Patristische Texte und Studien, n. 13), Berlin–New York, 1972, pp. 81; 94; 155; 157; — Didymos der Blinde. Kommentar zu Hiob. Tura-Papyrus, herausgegeben, übersetzt, erläutert von A. HENRICHS (1—2) e U. HAGEDORN, D. HAGEDORN, L. KOENEN (3) (Papyrologische Texte und Abhandlungen, n. 1; 2; 3), Bonn, 1968: Teil I: n. 35 p. 69; n. 93 p. 174; n. 183 p. 289; Exkurs II: n. 4 p. 315; n. 8 p. 316; Teil II: n. 28 p. 45; n. 43 p. 69; n. 48 p. 73; n. 49 p. 73; n. 67 p. 96; n. 88 p. 115; n. 93 p. 124; n. 94 p. 125; Teil III: n. 14 p. 226; n. 15 p. 227; n. 42 p. 237; n. 72 p. 249; n. 99 p. 257; n. 103 p. 260.

[328] Cfr. J. DANIÉLOU, Philon d'Alexandrie . . ., p. 173.

[329] Cfr. J. DANIÉLOU, Platonisme et théologie mystique. Essai sur la doctrine spirituelle de saint Grégoire de Nysse (Théologie, n. 2), Paris, 1944, pp. 56; 79—80; 290—291; 298—299; 41.

[330] Cfr. R. LEYS, L'image de Dieu chez Saint Grégoire de Nysse. Esquisse d'une doctrine (Museum Lessianum. Section théologique, n. 49), Bruxelles—Paris, 1951, pp. 49; 50; 64 e vedi 33.

[331] Cfr. E. G. KONSTANTINOU, Die Tugendlehre Gregors von Nyssa im Verhältnis zu der Antik-Philosophischen und Jüdisch-Christlichen Tradition (Das östliche Christentum, NF. Heft 17), Würzburg, 1966, pp. 63—69.

[332] Histoire de l'École d'Alexandrie, Tome premier, Paris, 1846, rist. Amsterdam, 1965, pp. 166—167.

terrestri e dagli appelli celesti, per cui fu particolarmente felice il Bousset quando lo definì come,,il primo grande psicologo della fede"[333].

Il paradosso che la storia della filosofia cristiana incominciasse con un ebreo fu sentito dai cristiani e fu da loro risolto sul piano mitico[334] ma non fu contestato. Era una venerazione che — riservandosi ovviamente ampio beneficio di scelta in accordo con le esigenze dell'ortodossia dogmatica — riconosceva nell'Alessandrino un maestro: il suo non era un insegnamento da accogliere in blocco ma era una ricchissima fioritura di suggerimenti illuminanti.

I Padri della Chiesa[335] insomma spigolarono e ringraziarono; invece qualche moderno entrò nel campo filoniano addirittura a mietere. E l'entu-

---

[333] Cfr. Die Religion des Judentums im neutestamentlichen Zeitalter, 2. Aufl., Berlin, 1906, p. 447.

[334] Cfr. note 272 e 276.

[335] Per gl'influssi filoniani sui Padri cfr. la nota 2, per quelli su altri scrittori e movimenti letterari successivi vedi S. WEISSE, Philo von Alexandrien und Moses Maimonides. Ein vergleichender Versuch, Diss. Halle a. S., 1884, pp. 31; C. BIGG, The Christian Platonists of Alexandria. Eight lectures preached before the University of Oxford in the year 1886, Oxford, 1886: la lezione introduttiva ha come tema: Philo and the gnostics (su Filone pp. 7—27); S. POZNANSKI, Philon dans l'ancienne littérature judéo-arabe, in: Revue des Études Juives, L (1905), pp. 10—31; H. GUYOT, Les réminiscences de Philon le Juif chez Plotin. Étude critique, Thèse, Paris, 1906, pp. 92; D. NEUMARK, Geschichte der jüdischen Philosophie des Mittelalters, Berlin, Bd. II, 1910, pp. 391—473; E. BUONAIUTI, Una reminiscenza filoniana nello gnostico Valentino, in: Bollettino di Filologia Classica, XXV (1918—1919), pp. 27—29; G. NEBEL, Plotins Kategorien der intelligiblen Welt (Heidelberger Abhandlungen zur Philosophie und ihrer Geschichte, n. 18), Tübingen, 1929, pp. 26—33; E. STEIN, De Celso Platonico Philonis Alexandrini imitatore, in: Eos, XXXIV (1932—1933), pp. 205—216; L. FINKELSTEIN, Is Philo Mentioned in Rabbinic Literature ?, in: Journal of Biblical Literature, LIII (1934), pp. 142—149; K. STEUR, Poimandres en Philo. Een vergelijking van Poimandres § 12—§ 32 met Philo's uitleg van Genesis I, 26—27 en II, 7, Purmerend, 1935, pp. XI-213; A. KAMINKA, Die mystischen Ideen des R. Simon ben Johai, in: Hebrew Union College Annual (Cincinnati), X (1935), pp. 149—168; I. LEVINE, Philo and Maimonides, in: ID., Faithful Rebels. A Study in Jewish Speculative Thought, London, 1936, pp. 43—56; L. FRUECHTEL, Neue Quellennachweise zu Isidorus von Pelusion, in: Philologische Wochenschrift, LVIII (1838), coll. 764—768; J. H. WASZINK, Die sogenannte Fünfteilung der Träume bei Chalcidius und ihre Quellen, in: Mnemosyne, Ser. III, IX (1940—1941), pp. 65—85 (per Filone pp. 74—85); G. QUISPEL, Philo und die altchristliche Häresie, in: Theologische Zeitschrift, V (1949), pp. 429—436 (lo gnostico Valentino sfruttò Filone); H. A. WOLFSON, Albinus and Plotinus on Divine Attributes, in: Harvard Theological Review, XLV (1952), pp. 115—130; R. CADIOU, Sur un florilège philonien, in: Revue des Études Grecques, LXX (1957), pp. 93—101; ID., Sur un florilège philonien. Notes complémentaires, ibid., LXXI (1958), pp. 55—60; R. J. Z. WERBLOWSKY, Philo and the Zohar, in: Journal of Jewish Studies, X (1959), pp. 25—44; 112—135; P. WILPERT, Philon bei Nikolaus von Kues, in: Antike und Orient im Mittelalter. Vorträge der Kölner Mediaevistentagungen 1956—1959 (Miscellanea mediaevalia, n. 1), Berlin, 1962, pp. 69—79; R. MONDOLFO, Un precorrimento di Vico in Filone Alessandrino, in: Miscellanea A. Rostagni, Torino, 1963, pp. 56—60; B. HEMMERDINGER, Karabas ou l'origine alexandrine du Chat Botté, in: Chronique d'Égypte, XXXVIII (1963), pp. 147—148; G. SCARPAT, Cultura ebreo-ellenistica e Seneca, in: Rivista Biblica ... Italiana (Brescia), XIII (1965), pp. 3—30; U. TREU, Ein merkwürdiges Stück byzantinischer Gelehrsamkeit, in: Byzantinische Zeitschrift, LVIII (1965), pp. 306—312 (per qualche interpretazione filoniana); M. SIMON, Éléments gnostiques chez Philon, in: Le

siasmo è stato tale da raggiungere i toni ditirambici. Il WOLFSON[336] infatti, seppure non senza pesantezza di stile, affermò: ,,Filone emerge dal nostro studio come un filosofo dal potente respiro e non come un semplice pasticcione in filosofia. Egli ebbe un'intelligenza così forte da riuscire a respingere le teorie di altri filosofi e da tracciarsi una via nuova e fino ad allora sconosciuta. Merita credito di originalità in tutti i problemi da lui trattati, poichè in questa particolare serie di problemi egli fu l'iniziatore di tutti i concetti fondamentali che continuarono ad essere discussi d'allora in poi attraverso la storia della filosofia. Come qualsiasi filosofo grande e originale nella storia della filosofia, Filone nella propria filosofia compì una reazione contro quella dei suoi predecessori e contemporanei ed in questo senso, come qualsiasi filosofo nella storia se non è esattamente studiato, può essere chiamato eclettico. In realtà la sua erudizione, come quella di un gran numero di filosofi in passato, fu grande e varia, e l'artificiosità della forma letteraria dei suoi scritti, ancora come quella di un gran numero di filosofi in passato, oscura sovente il suo pensiero; ma, nonostante tutto ciò, egli edificò un sistema filosofico solido, coerente e libero da contraddizioni, dato che tutto in esso è basato su certi principi fondamentali." E nella chiusa della sua poderosa opera lo studioso di Harvard, esaminando il periodo tra Filone e Spinoza, ribadiva: ,,Se noi scegliamo di descrivere questo periodo come medioevale, poichè dopo tutto esso viene tra una filosofia che ignorava la Scrittura ed una che si sforza di liberarsi dalla Scrittura, allora la filosofia medioevale è la storia della filosofia di Filone. Per circa diciassette secoli questa filosofia filoniana dominò il pensiero dell'Europa. Nulla di realmente nuovo apparve nella storia della filosofia europea durante quel periodo. I filosofi che vennero in lunga successione durante quel periodo ... scelsero soltanto di spiegare, ciascuno

origini dello gnosticismo. Colloquio di Messina 13—18 Aprile 1966 (Studies in the history of Religions, Numen, Supplem., n. 12), Leiden, 1967, pp. 359—376; A. J. CLAYTON, Remarques sur deux personnages camusiens, Hélicon et Scipion, in: Revue des Sciences Humaines, CXXIX (1968), pp. 79—90 (nel 'Caligola' di A. CAMUS Scipione pare totalmente inventato dal drammaturgo, mentre per Hélicon trovò il nome ed i caratteri essenziali nella 'Legatio' di Filone); M. PAGLIALUNGA DE TUMA, Séneca y Filón de Alejandría en la temática calderoniana, in: Cuadernos del Sur, 1969, pp. 90—105; H. BAUMGARTEN, Vitam brevem esse, longam artem. Das Proömium der Schrift Senecas De brevitate vitae, in: Gymnasium, LXXVII (1970), pp. 299—323 (paralleli anche con Filone); A. M. DI NOLA, Qabbalāh, in: Enciclopedia delle Religioni, V, 1973, col. 95 (tra i precedenti osserva Filone); B. A. PEARSON, Friedländer Revisited. Alexandrian Judaism and Gnostic Origins, in: Studia Philonica, II (1973), pp. 23—39 (Filone e lo gnosticismo); R. McL. WILSON, Jewish Gnosis and Gnostics Origins. A survey, in: Hebrew Union College Annual, XLV (1974), pp. 177—190 (tendenze gnostiche che risalgono al massimo al tempo di Filone); F. T. FALLON, The Law in Philo and Ptolemy: a note on the Letter to Flora, in: Vigiliae Christianae, XXX (1976), pp. 45—51 (riferisce testi di Filone sulla legge suscettibili di essere accostati a Tolomeo e conferma l'impostazione generale del QUISPEL che l'atteggiamento degli gnostici verso l'Antico Testamento risaliva ad ambienti giudaici e giudaico-cristiani); G. SCARPAT, Il pensiero religioso di Seneca e l'ambiente ebraico e cristiano, Brescia, 1977 (nal cap. 2° studia le analogie tra il 'trattato del Sublime' e le opere di Filone e soprattutto tra il 'De providentia' di Seneca e quello di Filone).
[336] Philo. Foundations of Religious Philosophy . . ., Vol. I, 1962, pp. 114—115.

nella sua via, i principi che aveva formulati Filone. Alla domanda, allora, 'Che cosa c'è di nuovo in Filone?' la risposta è che egli fu il costruttore di quella filosofia, proprio come la risposta alla domanda 'Che cosa c'è di nuovo in Spinoza?' è che egli la demolì[337]. Sulla stessa linea R. ARNALDEZ[338] dopo averne posto in risalto il valore come testimone della storia e della religiosità giudaica, dell'esegesi biblica, della cultura greca, proclama che Filone ,,esercitò una tale parte nella formazione della patristica cristiana e, attraverso ad essa, di tutta la teologia medioevale che risulta impossibile ignorarlo se si vuole vedere ciò che fu lo sviluppo della cultura cristiana, tanto nella storia dei dogmi che nella predicazione morale o nell'utilizzazione dei simboli biblici per l'insegnamento dottrinale. A questo proposito, Filone fu l'artefice principale di quest'opera gigantesca da cui provenne tutta la civiltà occidentale: l'unione intima del giudaismo e dell'ellenismo."

Sono iperboli, evidentemente; sono forzature prospettiche dovute all'errore di scambiare la fertilità di un metodo — di cui non fu d'altronde nemmeno lo scopritore — con l'eccellenza dei risultati prodotti; però sotto le dimensioni gonfiate si possono facilmente scorgere quelle reali. Nel momento in cui il pensiero cristiano si accingeva ad iniziare il suo lungo cammino Filone gli fornì utili indicazioni e modelli: la potenza e lo splendore della civiltà, cristiana non furono certo merito suo, ma fu suo merito di avere contribuito al suo successo, anche se questo sarebbe comunque sopraggiunto anche senza di lui. Il suo influsso sul cristianesimo fu più vistoso nell'epoca che va dalla metà del secondo secolo a quella del terzo e più fecondo nella seconda metà del secolo quarto. In questo periodo sorsero dei geni a lui superiori per organicità di pensiero e per fulgore d'arte, però questi grandi dottori si mossero anche sotto il suo stimolo e sotto il suo esempio.

---

[337] Op. cit. pp. 459—460.
[338] 'Introduction' a 'Philon d'Alexandrie', contributi del colloquio di Lione del 1966, Paris, 1967, p. 14.

Saint Ambroise et saint Jérôme, lecteurs de Philon

par Hervé Savon, Paris

Table des matières

La fin du IVe siècle en Occident n'est pas sans importance pour la destinée posthume de Philon. C'est à cette époque que l'œuvre de l'Alexandrin fait vraiment son entrée dans le monde latin et y éveille un écho durable. Deux œuvres surtout témoignent − fort diversement − de cette influence et de cet accueil: celle d'Ambroise et celle de Jérôme. On a voulu ajouter à ces deux noms celui d'Augustin: un passage du 'Contra Faustum' témoignerait d'une lecture directe de Philon par l'évêque d'Hippone[1]. Mais cette vue a été contestée par P. Courcelle qui a montré que c'était très probablement à travers le 'De Noe' d'Ambroise que l'évêque d'Hippone avait eu connaissance du texte philonien[2]. On se bornera donc ici à examiner l'influence de Philon sur ceux qui furent incontestablement ses lecteurs: saint Ambroise et saint Jérôme.

---

[1] B. Altaner, Augustinus und Philo von Alexandrien, eine quellenkritische Untersuchung, Zeitschrift für katholische Theologie, 65, 1941, pp. 81−99; repris dans Id., Kleine patristische Schriften, TU, 83, Berlin, 1967, pp. 181−193. B. Altaner fonde sa démonstration sur Augustin, Contra Faustum, XII, 39, CSEL, 25, pp. 365−366.

[2] P. Courcelle, Saint Augustin a-t-il lu Philon d'Alexandrie?, Revue des Etudes Anciennes, 63, 1961, pp. 78−85.

I. Ambroise

Philon est l'un des auteurs auxquels l'évêque de Milan doit le plus, et nous possédons la grande majorité des textes de l'Alexandrin qu'Ambroise a utilisés[3]. La plupart de ces emprunts ou de ces remplois ont été signalés et répertoriés par les derniers éditeurs de Philon et d'Ambroise. Ceux-ci ont d'ailleurs eu tendance à exagérer les similitudes et à ignorer les différences. Selon une formule de SCHENKL, Ambroise n'aurait apporté que les mots, les idées seraient encore celles de Philon[4]. Un jugement aussi extrême mérite sans doute un nouvel examen.

De fait, on risque fort de se méprendre en ne regardant que les passages où l'évêque de Milan reprend directement un énoncé philonien. C'est souvent dans un autre endroit du même développement que l'on peut découvrir la véritable signification de ce remploi. On s'aperçoit alors qu'Ambroise amende presque toujours — et parfois très profondément — les énoncés qu'il semblait au premier abord se borner à paraphraser, voire à traduire.

Pour observer le jeu subtil qui s'établit entre le modèle et l'adaptateur, le mieux est alors de s'adresser à des œuvres où cette espèce d'interaction est suffisamment continue. C'est le cas dans cinq traités de l'évêque de Milan que l'on peut considérer par excellence comme 'philoniens': le 'De paradiso', le 'De Cain et Abel', le 'De Noe', le 'De Abraham II', le 'De fuga saeculi'.

A vrai dire, une étude récemment parue rompt sur ce point l'unanimité des spécialistes. Ceux-ci pensaient jusqu'ici qu'Ambroise avait directement imité Philon dans ces cinq traités. Or, pour deux d'entre eux — le 'De paradiso' et le 'De fuga saeculi' —, E. LUCCHESI veut que l'évêque de Milan n'ait utilisé l'œuvre de l'exégète juif qu'à travers une source intermédiaire[5].

E. LUCCHESI part d'une certaine idée des méthodes d'Ambroise imitateur: «S'il arrive, écrit-il, que celui-ci (Ambroise) abandonne, quel qu'en soit le motif, un modèle longuement utilisé en échange d'un autre au cours du même écrit, on peut être sûr d'a v a n c e que, aussi longtemps qu'il en aura un sous les yeux, il s'en tiendra s e r v i l e m e n t à son dessein sans jamais s'en départir ou simplement y déroger, en faisant intervenir d'autres compléments de provenances diverses[6]». Et cela ne vaudrait pas seulement pour l'utilisation de Philon, mais, plus généralement, pour la façon dont l'évêque de Milan en use avec ses modèles.

---

[3] On me permettra de renvoyer à mon étude: Saint Ambroise devant l'exégèse de Philon le Juif, I—II, Paris, 1977. On y trouvera le détail des analyses dont les pages qui suivent résument les principaux résultats.

[4] Sancti Ambrosii opera, CSEL, 32, 1, p. XXIII. Cf. ibid., p. XXIV; 32, 2, p. XVII. En sens contraire: TH. FÖRSTER, Ambrosius Bischof von Mailand, Halle, 1884, p. 104. Mais le jugement de SCHENKL a généralement prévalu: v.g. J.-R. PALANQUE, Saint Ambroise et l'Empire romain, diss. Paris, 1933, p. 46.

[5] E. LUCCHESI, L'usage de Philon dans l'œuvre exégétique de saint Ambroise, Arbeiten zur Literatur und Geschichte des hellenistischen Judentums, 9, Leiden, 1977, pp. 53—88.

[6] Ibid., p. 53 (cf. la n. 1). Les caractères espacés sont de moi.

Partout où l'imitation cesse d'être mécanique et conforme à ce schéma, E. LUCCHESI suppose donc l'existence d'une source intermédiaire où était déjà accompli le travail de contamination et d'adaptation dont Ambroise est supposé incapable. C'est le cas des développements philoniens du 'De paradiso', où les 'Quaestiones in Genesin' ne suffisent pas à expliquer le texte ambrosien[7]. C'est aussi le cas du 'De fuga saeculi', où les matériaux provenant du 'De fuga et inventione' de Philon se trouvent disposés dans un ordre tout nouveau[8]. Quelle serait alors cette source intermédiaire? Des textes perdus d'Origène, répond E. LUCCHESI: les Τόμοι sur la Genèse, pour le 'De paradiso', les 'Homélies mystiques' pour le 'De fuga'[9].

C'est pour le 'De paradiso' que la démonstration de la *Mittelquelle* origénienne est surtout développée. E. LUCCHESI commence par rappeler que, dans son 'Exameron', Ambroise a utilisé Origène, à côté d'Hippolyte et de Basile. «Il est à supposer», par conséquent, que l'évêque de Milan «continue d'exploiter l'une et l'autre de ces mêmes sources dans le 'De paradiso' qui apparaît comme la suite logique sinon chronologique de l'Hexameron»[10]. Or la candidature de Basile se trouve écartée, «son Ἐξαήμερον s'arrêtant à la création de l'homme». Quant à l'utilisation d'Hippolyte par l'auteur du 'De paradiso', elle reste une pure possibilité qu'aucun indice ne vient par ailleurs rendre probable.

En revanche, E. LUCCHESI pense avoir deux raisons de voir dans Origène la source intermédiaire qu'il recherche. Il fait d'abord état des «références savantes d'Ambroise aux versions d'Aquila et de Symmaque». On en trouve dans le 'De paradiso', mais beaucoup plus fréquemment dans des passages de l''Explanatio psalmorum XII' et de l''Expositio psalmi CXVIII' qui sont précisément imités d'Origène. Le second argument est fourni par la longue section du 'De paradiso' où Ambroise s'attache à réfuter les objections d'Apelle. HARNACK a montré que ce développement devait venir d'Origène. LUCCHESI y voit la preuve que ce dernier est la source première et principale du 'De paradiso'[11].

Quant au 'De fuga saeculi', notre auteur l'associe à une «série . . . homogène» formée des traités suivants: 'De Abraham I', 'De Isaac', 'De Iacob', 'De bono mortis'. Tous ces 'sermons' auraient, comme le 'De Isaac', les 'Homélies mystiques' d'Origène comme source principale[12].

---

[7] Ibid., pp. 55 sqq.

[8] E. LUCCHESI s'étonne de constater que, dans ce traité, Ambroise «contrairement à sa technique coutumière d'imitateur consommé et quasiment servile, pour ne pas dire plagiaire, . . . devient tout à coup plus indépendant à l'égard de sa source . . . et se soumet moins au plan et à la distribution reçus d'autrui» (op. cit. p. 51).

[9] E. LUCCHESI, op. cit., p. 76; p. 84; cf. p. 80. En dépit de cette appellation longtemps en usage, il s'agit d'homélies mêlées — *homiliae mixtae* — et non *mysticae* (cf. G. BARDY, Commentaires patristiques de la Bible, dans: Supplément au Dictionnaire de la Bible, t. II, Paris, 1934, col. 88). Mais, contrairement à ce que semble penser E. LUCCHESI, nous n'avons aucune donnée précise sur le contenu de ces homélies. La place que leur attribue saint Jérôme fait seulement supposer qu'elles concernaient la Genèse (Jérôme, Epist. 33, 4, CSEL, 54, p. 255, 16; Rufin, Apologia contra Hieronymum, II, 23, 24, CCL, 20, p. 99).

[10] E. LUCCHESI, op. cit., pp. 75—76.

[11] Ibid., pp. 76—77.

[12] Ibid., pp. 78—85.

Cependant, cette démonstration apparaît vite assez fragile. Dans le 'De fuga saeculi', des développements entiers suivent de très près le 'De fuga et inventione' de Philon. Il en va tout autrement dans des traités comme le 'De Abraham I', le 'De Jacob' ou le 'De bono mortis': les rencontres avec l'œuvre de l'exégète juif y sont beaucoup moins précises et toujours occasionnelles. Il est donc arbitraire de leur attribuer une *Mittelquelle* commune, ces *Homiliae mixtae* d'Origène, dont nous ne savons presque rien.

Les arguments invoqués pour voir dans Origène la source principale de l'ensemble du 'De paradiso', s'ils sont plus précis, ne sont pas plus convaincants. Il ne fait aucun doute que le 'De paradiso', une des premières œuvres de l'évêque de Milan, est bien antérieur à l''Hexameron'[13]. On ne peut donc suivre E. LUCCHESI lorsqu'il suppose que l'auteur du 'De paradiso' «continue» à utiliser les sources dont il s'est servi dans l''Hexameron'. En revanche, Ambroise lui-même a pris soin d'indiquer une étroite continuité entre le 'De paradiso' et le 'De Cain'[14]. Or, l'inspiration directement philonienne de ce dernier traité n'est niée par personne, même pas par E. LUCCHESI; l'argument de la continuité probable des sources dans deux traités connexes est donc finalement plutôt défavorable à la thèse de la *Mittelquelle*. Quant aux versions d'Aquila et de Symmaque, on ne les trouve mentionnées que dans un seul passage du 'De paradiso'[15], ce qui paraît bien mince pour permettre d'identifier «la source première et principale» du traité. Enfin, le développement sur les syllogismes d'Apelle, marqué par une polémique fondée sur le sens littéral est, on le verra, d'un tout autre esprit et d'une autre provenance que les sections 'philoniennes' où domine l'allégorie[16]. Il doit donc y avoir au moins deux 'sources principales' du 'De paradiso'. Rien n'oblige à y voir deux ouvrages du même auteur.

Mais ce n'est pas seulement l'identification de la *Mittelquelle* qui apparaît problématique. La nécessité même d'en appeler à cette 'source intermédiaire' est déjà par elle-même des plus discutables. E. LUCCHESI part de l'idée qu'on se fait notamment depuis SCHENKL de l'attitude d'Ambroise vis-à-vis de ses modèles. Si, en effet, l'évêque de Milan ne fait que paraphraser quasi mécaniquement le texte qu'il a sous les yeux, toute combinaison de sources, toute addition notable, toute transposition, en un mot toute modification significative prouvera l'existence d'une source intermédiaire qui sera soit Origène ou Hippolyte, soit, en désespoir

---

[13] Ambroise, Epist. 45, FALLER 34, 1, CSEL, 82, p. 232: *Lecto Examero, utrum paradisum subtexuerim requirendum putasti, et quam de eo haberem sententiam significandum, idque velle te studiose cognoscere. Ego autem iam dudum de eo scripsi, nondum veteranus sacerdos.*

[14] De Cain, I, 1, 1, CSEL, 32, 1, p. 339, 2–6: *De paradiso in superioribus . . . quod dominus infudit, sensus invenit digessimus, in quibus Adam atque Evae lapsus est conprehensus. Nunc quoniam illa penes auctores non stetit culpa, sed quod peius est deteriorem invenit heredem, sequentem adoriamur historiam et ea quae secundum scripturas sunt adnexa divinas nostro opere prosequamur.*

[15] De paradiso, 5, 27, CSEL, 32, 1, p. 284, 2.6.8.

[16] HARNACK souligne que les chapitres 5–8 du 'De paradiso' – la discussion des objections d'Apelle – forment „*eine scharf abgegrenzte Einheit*" (Sieben neue Bruchstücke der Syllogismen des Apelles, Leipzig, 1890, p. 117).

de cause, un 'proto-Ambroise' anonyme[16a]. Or, c'est bien cette imitation 'servile' que l'on croit découvrir dans les traités où l'utilisation directe de Philon ne peut être discutée: le 'De Cain', le 'De Noe', même le 'De Abraham II'. En fait, si l'on ne se contente pas de parallèles ponctuels et littéraux — méthode normale chez des éditeurs comme MANGEY et SCHENKL —, si l'on envisage le texte d'Ambroise dans sa continuité, on s'aperçoit que l'évêque de Milan n'est jamais passif à l'égard de son modèle; même dans le 'De Cain' et dans le 'De Noe', additions chrétiennes, suppressions, interversions, altérations, critiques plus ou moins explicites témoignent d'une vigilance toujours en éveil: il s'agit moins d'une simple imitation que d'une r é a c t i o n au texte de Philon. A ce point de vue, l'opposition dont part LUCCHESI entre l'imitation 'servile' qui serait le fait du 'De Cain', du 'De Noe' et du 'De Abraham II', et l'adaptation originale dont témoigneraient le 'De paradiso' et le 'De fuga' perd sa force. Certes, il n'y a pas lieu de refuser *a priori* l'éventualité d'une source intermédiaire. Mais la question de son existence ne peut être utilement posée que si, ayant examiné avec soin les techniques d'adaptation dans les différents textes d'Ambroise, sans s'en tenir au postulat d'une imitation mécanique et servile[17], on observe entre deux groupes de traités d'importantes variations de méthode.

1. La rencontre avec Philon et le programme exégétique d'Ambroise

Il convient de s'interroger tout d'abord sur les conditions qui ont permis l'adoption et l'adaptation de l'allégorisme philonien par Ambroise. Le 'De paradiso' est ici un témoin privilégié. On y voit en effet le nouvel évêque s'essayer successivement à deux types d'exégèse. Tantôt c'est une interprétation dialectique visant à défendre la lettre de la Genèse contre les objections rationalisantes d'Apelle[18], objections dont l'actualité n'était pas affaiblie deux siècles après l'héré-

---

[16a] Ce postulat se retrouve dans un bref article du même auteur (Utrum Ambrosius Mediolanensis in quibusdam epistulis Philonis Alexandrini opusculum quod inscribitur „Quis rerum divinarum heres sit" usurpaverit an non quaeritur, Le Muséon, 90, 1977, pp. 347—354). Par ailleurs, E. LUCCHESI ne propose dans ces pages aucun parallèle origénien, ce qui serait cependant bien nécessaire pour prouver qu'Origène joue le rôle de *Mittelquelle* entre Philon et Ambroise.

[17] Cf. E. LUCCHESI, op. cit., p. 73: «Bien évidemment, pareilles multiplicité et variété d'inspiration seraient contraires au p o s t u l a t énoncé plus haut de l'unicité (de principe) des sources dans les traités exégétiques ambrosiens».

[18] De paradiso, 5, 28—9, 42, CSEL, 32, 1, pp. 284—300. Sur Apelle et son œuvre, voir HARNACK, De Apellis gnosi monarchica, Leipzig, 1874; ID., Sieben neue Bruchstücke der Syllogismen des Apelles, TU, 6, 3, Leipzig, 1890, pp. 111—120; ID., Der kirchengeschichtliche Ertrag der exegetischen Arbeiten des Origenes, I, TU, 42, 3, Leipzig, 1918, pp. 24 sq., 31, 33, 35, 37; ibid., II, TU, 42, 4, Leipzig, 1919, passim; ID., Marcion, Das Evangelium vom fremden Gott, TU, 45, Leipzig, 1921, pp. 213—230, 323*—339*; E. DE FAYE, Gnostiques et gnosticisme, Paris, 1913, pp. 155—166. Selon HARNACK (Marcion, p. 335*), l'origine apellienne de l'objection discutée en De paradiso 9, 42, serait douteuse.

siarque[19]. Tantôt c'est le passage résolu au sens allégorique[20], dont les formules vont être empruntées à l'exégèse philonienne. Après avoir tenté la première voie, Ambroise opte décidément pour la seconde. S'il peut ainsi reprendre la méthode allégorique de Philon comme un instrument commode, c'est qu'il admet les présupposés dont est parti l'Alexandrin. Pour s'en assurer, il suffit d'examiner les arguments opposés aux 'Syllogismes' d'Apelle. L'interdit jeté sur le fruit de l'arbre de connaissance est au centre de ce débat. Pour Ambroise, comme pour Philon[21], ce qui est demandé à Adam, c'est de ne point juger[22], de renoncer à distinguer lui-même entre bien et mal et de s'en remettre totalement, avec une confiance d'enfant, à la parole de son créateur et bienfaiteur[23]. Encore faut-il que cette confiance soit nourrie et protégée. C'est en ses moindres parties que l'Ecriture doit être reconnue comme le canal d'un enseignement divin[24]. Dans tous les passages, si brefs soient-ils, où la lettre semble scandaleuse[25] ou décevante, il faut donc qu'elle dissimule un arrière-plan auquel on ne saurait accéder sans ce détour[26]. Le texte en ce cas dit autre chose que ce qu'il exprime ouvertement: il est allégorie[27].

Le 'De paradiso' a une autre particularité: on y trouve le seul texte où Ambroise mentionne nommément Philon. Or c'est pour reprocher à l'Alexandrin de s'en être tenu, dans son exégèse, aux *moralia*, par incapacité judaïque de saisir

---

[19] Sur les aspects 'rationalistes' de la propagande des manichéens, v. Augustin, De Genesi contra Manichaeos, I, 1, 2, PL, 34, 173. Les arguments qu'ils opposaient à l'Ancien Testament, ceux qu'utilisait par exemple Faustus de Milève à l'époque d'Ambroise, sont parfois proches de ceux d'Apelle, v. g. Augustin, Contra Faustum, XXII, 4, CSEL, 25, p. 593, 20 sqq. Des écrits provenant d'autres sectes, également hostiles à l'Ancien Testament, jouaient d'ailleurs leur rôle dans cette propagande. C'est ce que montre un manuscrit qui circulait à Carthage vers 420, en y soulevant le plus vif intérêt: un texte du manichéen Adimante y voisinait avec un opuscule probablement marcionite (Augustin, Contra adversarium legis et prophetarum, I, 1, 1, PL, 42, 603).

[20] De paradiso, 1, 3, p. 266; 2, 11, p. 271; 11, 51, p. 308.

[21] Pour Philon, voir M. HARL, Adam et les deux arbres du Paradis (Gen. II–III) ou l'homme milieu entre deux termes (μέσος – μεθόριος) chez Philon d'Alexandrie, Recherches de science religieuse, 50, 1962, pp. 321–388.

[22] Ambroise, De paradiso, 11, 52, p. 309, 9–16.

[23] Ibid., 6, 32, p. 289, 13–20; cf. 6, 31, p. 288, 12–19; 12, 59, p. 320, 11–21.

[24] Ibid., 9, 43, CSEL, 32, 1, p. 300, 3–6: *Iterum videamus qua ratione dominus deus Adae dixerit ,,morte moriemini'', quid intersit utrum aliquis dicat ,,moriemini'' an addat ,,morte moriemini''; ostendere enim debemus nihil superfluum in dei esse mandato.* Cf. ibid., 12, 56, p. 315, 1–23.

[25] Le passage à l'allégorie se justifie même si le texte n'est scandaleux que pour une partie des fidèles: De paradiso, 2, 11, p. 271, 4 sqq.

[26] J. PÉPIN, A propos de l'histoire de l'exégèse allégorique: l'absurdité signe de l'allégorie, dans: Studia patristica, TU, 63, Berlin, 1957, pp. 395–413.

[27] Quintilien, Inst., VIII, 6, 44, éd. RADERMACHER, Leipzig, 1935, p. 124, 19–21: Ἀλληγορία *quam inversionem interpretantur, aut aliud verbis, aliud sensu ostendit, aut etiam interim contrarium*; ibid., IX, 2, 92, p. 167, 3–4: *Totum autem allegoriae simile est, aliud dicere, aliud intellegi velle* (cf. R. HAHN, Die Allegorie in der antiken Rhetorik, diss. Tübingen, 1967, pp. 59–68); Tertullien, Scorpiace, 11, 4, 25–26, CCL, 2, p. 1091: *Aliud in vocibus erit, aliud in sensibus, ut allegoriae, ut parabolae, ut aenigmata.*

les *spiritalia*[28]. Ce passage indique bien que l'évêque de Milan va situer les données de l'exégèse philonienne par rapport à une table de catégories herméneutiques déjà établie. Une analyse précise du vocabulaire d'Ambroise invite à discerner ici deux schémas. L'un, binaire et fortement antithétique, oppose l'interprétation littérale et l'interprétation spirituelle comme deux niveaux d'approfondissement[29]. L'autre, ternaire — *physica, moralia, logica* ou *mystica* —, apparaît plutôt comme un classement des enseignements de l'Ecriture, calqué sur celui des parties de la philosophie[30]. En adoptant ces divisions qu'il doit directement à une exégèse ecclésiastique marquée par Origène[31], Ambroise se place en fin de compte dans une tradition qui remonte, en partie, à Philon lui-même[32]. Il est vrai que l'évêque de Milan pousse plus loin que l'Alexandrin la réinterprétation de ces trois 'sagesses', surtout celle de la physique, qui ne consiste plus, pour lui, à se tourner vers la nature pour l'interpréter, mais à en comprendre le néant pour s'en détourner[33].

2. Ambroise censure Philon

En dépit des présupposés qui leur sont communs, il existe entre le juif d'Alexandrie et l'évêque de Milan de telles différences doctrinales que l'exégèse du premier ne pouvait être utilisée par le second sans de profonds remaniements. L'intervention d'Ambroise consiste d'abord à éliminer de l'allégorèse philonienne un certain nombre d'éléments incompatibles avec le christianisme, plus précisément avec la forme que lui avait donnée l'orthodoxie nicéenne.

Même dans les deux traités considérés souvent comme les plus servilement philoniens — le 'De Cain' et le 'De Noe' —, une analyse plus attentive révèle à

---

[28] De paradiso, 4, 25, CSEL, 32, 1, p. 281, 21—22: *Philon autem, quoniam spiritalia Iudaico non capiebat affectu, intra moralia se tenuit.*

[29] V. g. Ambroise, De fuga saeculi, 2, 13, CSEL, 32, 2, pp. 172, 22 — 173, 1; Expositio psalmi CXVIII, 12, 21, CSEL, 62, p. 263, 7—8. Sur le travail exégétique — la 'manducation' — qui permet de dégager la *gratia spiritalis* contenue dans le texte sacré: De Cain, I, 10, 42, CSEL, 32, 1, p. 374, 12—15; Expositio ps. CXVIII, 16, 28, pp. 366—367. Cette antithèse entre 'l'esprit' et la 'lettre' apparaît souvent chez Ambroise dans un contexte de polémique anti-juive: Expositio ps. CXVIII, 3, 26, p. 56, 9—10; 6, 24, p. 120, 21—26; Epist. 38, FALLER 10, 9, 89—93, CSEL, 82, p. 77. Cf. H. SAVON, S. Ambroise, t. I, pp. 57—61.

[30] Les textes essentiels sont: De Isaac, 4, 22—30, pp. 656—661; Explanatio psalmi XXXVI, 1—2, CSEL, 64, pp. 70—71; Expositio ps. CXVIII, 1, 2—3, pp. 5, 24 — 6, 23; Expositio evangelii secundum Lucam, prol., 2—5, CCL, 14, pp. 1—4. Cf. H. SAVON, op. cit., t. 1, pp. 65—78.

[31] Voir notamment Origène, Commentarium in Canticum Canticorum, prol., GCS 33, pp. 75, 6 — 79, 21.

[32] Philon reprend le *topos* des trois parties de la philosophie (De agricultura, 14—16; De mutatione nominum, 74—76; De specialibus legibus, I, 336), mais il en modifie profondément l'esprit: Quod omnis probus liber sit, 80.

[33] La physique selon Ambroise a pour maxime: *Vanitas vanitatum et omnia vanitas quae in mundo sunt constituta* (Expositio evangelii secundum Lucam, prol., 2, 28—29, p. 2; cf. Eccl., 1, 2).

chaque pas les corrections que l'évêque de Milan apporte à son modèle. Cet examen permet également de discerner quels sont les adversaires toujours actuels qu'Ambroise vise à travers ce prédécesseur déjà lointain. Si les thèmes purement philosophiques ne font encore l'objet que de critiques occasionnelles[34] et de réserves latentes[35], bien que déjà significatives, la polémique contre les juifs et les ariens marque profondément ces deux opuscules. Par un paradoxe qui tient à l'entreprise même d'Ambroise, bien des exégèses proposées par Philon le Juif sont finalement retournées contre la Synagogue[36]. Ici et là, on sent la présence de l'importante communauté juive de Milan[37]. Un développement comme celui qui est consacré à la mort de Moïse semble bien renvoyer à un thème classique de controverse[38]. Mais la lutte contre l'arianisme tient plus de place encore. L'analyse montre qu'elle inspire souvent les corrections qu'Ambroise apporte à son canevas philonien[39]. Ces retouches se comprennent d'autant mieux que les tenants d'un certain subordinatianisme pouvaient, comme Eusèbe de Césarée[40], invoquer les thèses de Philon sur le Logos et sur les puissances divines. Ambroise, qui dénonce volontiers le 'judéo-arianisme', se montre alors particulièrement vigilant.

[34] De Noe, 5, 11, p. 420, 21—23: *Tempus quidem omnium hominum in conspectu dei et in eius voluntate est, non enim, ut vulgo aiunt, fatale decretum allegatur*; cf. Philo, Quaestiones in Genesin, I, 100, éd. J. B. AUCHER, Venetiis, 1826, p. 71 (sur ce texte, v. H. A. WOLFSON, Philo. Foundations of religious philosophy in Judaism, Christianity, and Islam, t. I, Structure and growth of philosophic systems from Plato to Spinoza, 2, Cambridge, Mass., 1948, pp. 329—330). Ailleurs, l'attaque contre la philosophie prend la forme d'une simple addition au développement de Philon (et non plus d'une critique implicite de celuici): Ambroise, De Cain, II, 9, 27, p. 401, 22—25 (cf., Philon, Quaestiones in Genesin, I, 68); De Noe, 25, 92, p. 478, 3—5 (cf. Philon, Quaestiones in Genesin, II, 59).

[35] Ambroise, par exemple, écarte tacitement la thèse stoïcienne des προηγμένα qu'il trouve dans le texte de Philon qui lui sert de canevas: De Cain, II, 2, 9, p. 385, 14—15 (cf. Philon, De sacrificiis, 34, 112—114). On trouvera un dossier plus complet dans: H. SAVON , op. cit., t. I, pp. 89—96.

[36] De Noe, 19, 70, p. 464, 14—21 (cf. Philon, Quaestiones in Genesin, II, 44, A 122—123); 13, 45, p. 443, 13—27 (cf. Philon, Quaestiones in Genesin, II, 15); De Cain, I, 2, 5, p. 341, 10—20 (cf. Philon, De sacrificiis, 1—3). Sur ces différents textes, voir H. SAVON, op. cit., pp. 96—110.

[37] Voir notamment: De Noe, 19, 70, p. 464, 21 sqq.

[38] Philon voit une preuve de la supériorité de Moïse dans le fait que le lieu de sa sépulture est resté ignoré (De sacrificiis, 10; cf. Dt., 34, 6). Ambroise répond implicitement en montrant que si le tombeau de Jésus a été connu de nombreux témoins, c'était en vue de prouver sa résurrection (De Cain, I, 2, 9, p. 344).

[39] De Cain, I, 1, 2, p. 339, 13 sqq. (cf. Philon, Quaestiones in Genesin, I, 58, AUCHER, p. 41); I, 8, 32, p. 367, 2—3: *verbum enim dei non, sicut quidam ait, opus est, sed operans* (cf. Philon, De sacrificiis, 65: Ὁ λόγος ἔργον ἦν αὐτοῦ); I, 8, 32, p. 367, 9—22 (cf. Philon, De sacrificiis, 66—68); De Noe, 26, 99 (cf. Philon, Quaestiones in Genesin, II, 62). Cf. H. SAVON, op. cit., t. I, pp. 118—129.

[40] Un fragment grec de Quaestiones in Genesin, I, 62, que l'on vient de citer, nous a été précisément conservé par Eusèbe de Césarée (Praeparatio evangelica, VII, 12, 14 — 13, 3), qui y trouve la preuve que la 'théologie des Hébreux' appuie sa théologie du Logos. En sens contraire, les tenants de Nicée dénonceront le 'judéo-arianisme': Athanase, Orationes contra Arianos, II, 17, PG, 26, 181 C; Basile, Adversus Eunomium, I, 23, PG, 29, 254 C; ibid., IV, 3, PG, 29, 564 C; Synode romain de 382, Canons 23 et 24.

Cela semble même l'avoir conduit à réviser radicalement une exégèse pourtant traditionnelle dans l'Eglise, celle des trois visiteurs reçus par Abraham à Mambré[41].

Le commentaire allégorique de la vie d'Abraham — le 'De Abraham liber secundus' — est pour Ambroise l'occasion d'affronter cette religion cosmique qui était devenue la doctrine officielle de la 'réaction païenne'. Ici encore, l'évêque de Milan rompt délibérément avec la politique relativement conciliante suivie par Philon à l'égard des grands thèmes de la spiritualité hellénistique. Mais un examen détaillé des pages où Philon[42] et Ambroise[43] commentent le sacrifice de quadrupèdes et d'oiseaux offert par Abraham[44], montre bien qu'il ne s'agit point ici d'une simple différence de tactique. L'Alexandrin reprend à son compte, apparemment sans arrière-pensée, deux grands thèmes de cette religion cosmique où confluaient les héritages de Platon et de Pythagore: l'harmonie des sphères[45] et l'éther, ce cinquième élément pur et indestructible[46]; Ambroise, au contraire, estime fallacieux d'attribuer à l'univers créé ne serait-ce qu'une apparence d'autonomie et de lui reconnaître un principe interne de stabilité et de permanence[47]. Quant à l'harmonie, il faut la chercher dans l'âme vertueuse[48], ce quadrige qui est apparu à Ezéchiel[49] et qui figure, selon l'évêque de Milan, les quatre parties de l'âme[50].

3. Ambroise christianise Philon

Comme dans tout baptême, la christianisation suit l'exorcisme. Cette christianisation est parfois réalisée par des moyens extrêmement simples. Le changement d'un seul détail peut permettre à Ambroise de donner à l'exégèse qu'il reprend une signification toute nouvelle. C'est ainsi que, dans un passage du 'De Cain', la modification d'une prescription rituelle[51] annonce un renversement

---

[41] Ambroise, De Cain, I, 8, 30, p. 365, 1–11 (cf. Philon, De sacrificiis, 59), commentant Gn., 18, 2sqq. A l'idée de trois visiteurs de dignité inégale — Dieu et ses deux puissances (Philon) ou le Christ et deux anges (v. g. Justin, Tertullien, Origène, Novatien, parfois Ambroise lui-même) — l'évêque de Milan substitue celle des trois personnes de la Trinité. Cf. H. SAVON, op. cit., t. I, pp. 129–137.

[42] Quaestiones in Genesin, III, 3–8.

[43] De Abraham, II, 8, 50–60, CSEL, 32, 1, pp. 603–613.

[44] Gn., 15, 7–11.

[45] Quaestiones in Genesin, III, 3, AUCHER, pp. 171–173.

[46] Ibid., III, 6.

[47] De Abraham, II, 58, pp. 611, 19 – 612, 2, Ambroise avait pu lire dans Cicéron que la *quinta natura* conférait à l'âme un statut proprement divin (Tusc., I, 26, 65 – 27, 67).

[48] De Abraham, II, 54, p. 608, 4–21.

[49] Ez., 1, 5–24.

[50] De Abraham, II, 8, 54, p. 607, 9–15. Sur cette division de l'âme et ses origines, et notamment sur la nature de la quatrième partie — le διορατικόν — voir H. SAVON, op. cit., t. I, pp. 150–161.

[51] De Cain, I, 8, 31, p. 366, 13–17: *Et ideo patres nostri festinantes manducabant pascha, succincti lumbos et pedes suos calciamentorum exuentes vinculis et tamquam onus*

de perspective: la liturgie de la Pâque n'est plus, comme chez l'Alexandrin, le reflet historique d'une réalité supra-terrestre[52], mais devient l'annonce figurative de ce qui sera vérité en Jésus[53].

Le plus souvent, cet effort de christianisation entraîne la transposition subtile de développements entiers. On peut alors parler d'une véritable *retractatio* chrétienne, procédant souvent par étapes successives. Le 'De paradiso' déjà offre un bon exemple de ce procédé, avec l'explication des quatre fleuves du paradis[54]. On y voit en particulier comment les références néo-testamentaires viennent introduire une certaine temporalité dans le schéma philonien[55]. Mais le modèle le plus achevé de cette *retractatio* chrétienne — au moins avant le 'De fuga' — c'est dans le 'De Cain' qu'il faut le chercher, dans la dizaine de pages où l'évêque de Milan raconte à son tour le débat de Volupté et de Vertu[56]. Il est frappant de constater que cette *syncrisis*, qui s'était conservée sans altération substantielle de Prodicos à Philon[57], fait l'objet chez Ambroise d'une révision radicale où intervient sans doute un certain goût baroque pour la variété, le mouvement[58], la méta-

---

corporeum deponentes, ut essent parati ad transitum. Philon, en revanche (De sacrificiis, 63) reste fidèle au texte de l'Exode (12, 11) enjoignant de participer au repas pascal les sandales aux pieds: Καὶ γὰρ τὸ Πάσχα ... προστέτακται ποιεῖσθαι ... τὸν σάρκινον ὄγκον, τὰ ὑποδήματα λέγω, περιειληφότας. Depuis 1580, les éditeurs d'Ambroise cherchent à harmoniser son texte avec la prescription de l'Exode, ce qui explique le 'non' abusif que SCHENKL a placé devant *deponentes*. Sur le sens exact de περιειληφότες dans le passage de Philon, voir H. SAVON, op. cit., t. I, p. 212.

[52] Philon, De sacrificiis, 63: Διάβασις γάρ ἐστιν οὐ θνητή, ἐπεὶ τοῦ ἀγενήτου καὶ ἀφθάρτου τὸ Πάσχα εἴρηται ... οὐδὲν γάρ ἐστι τῶν καλῶν, ὃ μὴ θεοῦ τε καὶ θεῖον.

[53] Ambroise, De Cain, I, 8, 31, p. 366, 18–20: *Ideo pascha domini dicitur, quoniam et tunc in typo illo agni veritas dominicae passionis adnuntiabatur et nunc eius celebratur gratia.* Faisant appel notamment à Exode, 3, 3, et 3, 5, Ambroise voit habituellement dans l'abandon des sandales le fait de se libérer des *carnalia integimenta* (H. SAVON, op. cit., t. I, pp. 207–210), dépouillement dont la passion et la mort du Christ représentent l'accomplissement suprême.

[54] De paradiso, 3, 12–18, pp. 272–277 (cf. Philon, Legum allegoriae, I, 63–84; Quaestiones in Genesin, I, 12–13). Il n'est pas certain que la suite du développement d'Ambroise (3, 19–23, pp. 277–280), où les vertus symbolisées par les fleuves sont mises en rapport avec les *tempora* de l'histoire humaine, provienne directement des textes parallèles de Philon (De Abrahamo, 7–55; De praemiis et poenis, 7–56). Une dépendance au moins indirecte semble en tout cas certaine.

[55] Cf. H. SAVON, op. cit., t. I, pp. 218–239.

[56] De Cain, I, 4, 13–24, pp. 348, 3–360, 13. Cf. Philon, De sacrificiis, 19–45.

[57] Cf. I. ALPERS, Hercules in bivio, (diss.) Göttingen, 1912; M. C. WAITES, Some features of the allegorical debate in Greek literature, Harvard studies in classical philology, 23, 1912, pp. 9–19. Les écrivains chrétiens ont utilisé à leur tour l'apologue de Prodicos, ainsi Justin (Apologia II, 11, 5), Basile de Césarée (De legendis gentilium libris, 5, 71–72), Grégoire de Nazianze (Carmen de se ipso, 45, 231–234, PG, 37, 1369–1370). Mais les changements qu'ils y ont introduits n'approchent pas des bouleversements apportés par Ambroise.

[58] C'est ainsi que le 'discours de Volupté' fait place, chez Ambroise, à deux scènes animées: une scène de séduction (De Cain, I, 4, 14, pp. 348, 23 – 350, 14) et une scène de banquet (ibid., pp. 350, 14 – 351, 21).

morphose[59], mais qui semble due surtout à l'originalité du message chrétien. Le jeu des abstractions personnifiées, où le spiritualisme philonien se trouvait à l'aise, est bien vite troublé par le réalisme évangélique, ce qui aboutit à une «mise en abîme»[60] où le contenu finit par absorber le contenant[61]. En même temps, l'eschatologie chrétienne se substitue à cet eudémonisme de la vie présente que l'apologue illustre encore chez Philon[62]. Enfin, Ambroise nous livre dans ce texte essentiel un des principes de sa méthode d'adaptation: remplacer les développements profanes de l'Alexandrin par le recours au «langage nu de l'Ecriture»[63]. Ce qui ne l'empêche d'ailleurs pas d'utiliser un passage célèbre du 'Pro Gallio' de Cicéron pour donner vie et couleur à son développement[64].

4. Métamorphoses des thèmes philoniens: de Platon au Nouveau Testament

Dans le 'De fuga saeculi' — vraisemblablement le plus tardif de nos cinq traités[65] —, les textes du Pentateuque jouent encore un rôle capital, mais ce ne

[59] L'image du lacet, encore conventionnelle et galante chez Philon (De sacrificiis, 29, éd. COHN-WENDLAND, t. I, p. 213, 12) devient chez Ambroise le point de départ de correspondances scripturaires (I Tim., 3, 7; 6, 9 [version longue]; II Tim., 2, 26; et — Expositio psalmi CXVIII, 14, 36, p. 322 — Mt., 27, 5) qui lui permettent de passer sans rupture de Volupté à Satan: De Cain, I, 5, 15, pp. 352, 25 — 353, 4; cf. 14, p. 349, 1; 15, p. 352, 20; 16, p. 353, 8.11.24. Quant aux premiers mots de Vertu — *Palam adparui tibi non quaerenti me* (De Cain, I, 5, 15, p. 351, 25) — ils sont empruntés à Isaïe (65, 1; cf. Rm., 10, 20), et, depuis Justin, la tradition chrétienne considérait qu'ils étaient prophétiquement prononcés par Jésus (cf. H. SAVON, op. cit., t. I, pp. 268−271).

[60] Le mode de composition nommé ainsi par A. GIDE a été redécouvert par la critique contemporaine, mais il est lié à l'allégorisme patristique et médiéval; voir J. RICARDOU, Problèmes du nouveau roman, Collection «Tel quel», Paris, 1967, pp. 171−180; L. DIEKMANN, Repeated mirror reflections: the technique of Goethe's novels, Studies in Romanticism, 1, 1965, pp. 171−180; B. MORRISSETTE, Un héritage d'André Gide: la duplication intérieure, Comparative Literature Studies, 8, 1971, pp. 124−142.

[61] Cf. H. SAVON, op. cit., t. I, p. 315. Cela est d'ailleurs conforme à l'idéal ambrosien de la relation corps-esprit: *Dicit dominus: „Calicem quem mihi pater dedit non vis ut bibam illum?"* (Io., 18, 11)). *Bibit enim corpus suum qui corporalem fragilitatem spiritali absorbet adfectu et quasi in mentem animumque transfundit, ut interioribus exteriorum inbecillitas hauriatur* (Ambroise, Expositio evangelii secundum Lucam, VII, 100, p. 248). Cf. Philon, Quaestiones in Exodum, I, 19, A 462.

[62] Cf. H. SAVON, op. cit., t. I, pp. 319−321.

[63] Ambroise, De Cain, I, 6, 22, p. 358, 14−17 (tout le passage est une transposition audacieuse de Philon, De Sacrificiis, 34).

[64] De Cain, I, 4, 14, p. 350, 15−24; cf. Cicéron, Pro Gallio, fragm. 1, éd. MÜLLER, IV, 3, Leipzig, 1879, p. 236, 26−33. Immédiatement avant ce remploi du 'Pro Gallio', on remarque une réminiscence virgilienne (Aen., I, 637−641).

[65] On pense généralement que le 'De fuga saeculi' a été composé après 388, voire après 391: F. H. DUDDEN, The life and times of St. Ambrose, Oxford, 1935, t. II, pp. 684−685. Récemment, faisant appel aux résultats de la *Quellenforschung*, F. SZABÓ (Le Christ créateur chez s. Ambroise, Studia ephemeridis Augustinianum 2, Roma, 1968, 21 sqq.) a proposé la date de 386: on remarque dans ce traité des réminiscences plotiniennes qui invitent à le rapprocher du 'De Isaac', mais on n'y trouve pas la 'mystique du Cantique des Canti-

sont plus eux qui donnent à l'oeuvre son unité et sa structure. Celle-ci est thématique, au lieu d'être exégétique. N'étant plus lié par l'ordre du texte sacré, Ambroise peut du même coup prendre plus de libertés à l'égard de Philon. Le 'De fuga saeculi' permet donc de voir jusqu'à quel point l'évêque de Milan s'est réellement assimilé la méthode et les allégorèses qu'il doit à l'Alexandrin.

De cet ensemble de variations subtiles sur le thème de la fuite, un bloc philonien nettement reconnaissable émerge dès la première lecture: le développement consacré à la législation mosaïque sur les cités de refuge. Mais, ici, il faut compléter sensiblement les indications des éditeurs. La présence du texte de Philon se prolonge en effet bien au-delà de ce que signalent les apparats. C'est qu'Ambroise procède en deux étapes. Tout d'abord, il reprend l'exégèse de l'Alexandrin en éliminant tout ce qui lui paraît incompatible avec le christianisme orthodoxe[66]. Ensuite, cette allégorèse est exposée à nouveau, mais interprétée cette fois à l'aide de catégories empruntées à l'Epître aux Romains[67]. Cela aboutit à un singulier renversement. Cinq des six directions indiquées par Philon à l'âme désireuse de fuir le sensible et le péché apparaissent comme autant d'impasses[68]. Le seul refuge qui ne soit point illusoire, c'est la mort du Verbe fait chair, symbolisée par cette mort du grand-prêtre dont Philon était incapable de découvrir l'interprétation véritable[69].

On ne trouve point dans le reste du 'De fuga saeculi' de développement où le canevas philonien soit aussi longtemps, aussi constamment suivi. Les pages consacrées par Ambroise à divers épisodes de l'histoire de Jacob[70] utilisent deux sections assez distantes du 'De fuga et inventione'[71]. Ailleurs, ce sont quelques phrases du traité philonien – deux citations d'un passage célèbre du 'Théétète'[72] – que l'évêque de Milan reprend[73], transforme et dont il va jusqu'à tirer les *leitmotive* de son opuscule[74]. L'analyse de ces remplois et de leur

ques' qui, sous l'influence d'Origène, va marquer l'œuvre d'Ambroise à partir du 'De Isaac' précisément; le 'De fuga saeculi' serait donc peu antérieur à ce traité. Ces arguments ne sont pas convaincants: le Cantique joue déjà un rôle important dans le 'De Cain', et Ambroise semble choisir ses sources avant tout en fonction du sujet qu'il doit traiter.

[66] Ambroise, De fuga saeculi, 2, 5–13, CSEL, 32, 1, pp. 165–173; cf. Philon, De fuga et inventione, 87–118. Ambroise écarte ce qui, chez Philon, évoque les puissances comme substances distinctes ou implique la subordination du Logos.

[67] De fuga saeculi, 3, 14–16, pp. 173–178 (cf. Rm. 1, 15–17; 1, 19–20; 2, 2; 2, 4; 2, 12).

[68] Cf. H. SAVON, op. cit., t. I, pp. 343–347.

[69] De fuga saeculi, 3, 15, pp. 175, 23 – 176, 4. Au § 16, pp. 176–178, Ambroise prend le contre-pied de l'interprétation négative de la mort du grand-prêtre, que l'on trouve chez Philon, et rattache ce thème à celui de la première cité, caractérisée par la justice: comparer De fuga saeculi, 3, 16, p. 176, 8 – *ad ostensionem iustitiae suae* (Rm., 3, 25) – et 3, 14, p. 174, 1 – *iustitia enim dei in eo revelatur* (Rm., 1, 17).

[70] De fuga saeculi, 4, 19–23, pp. 179–183; 5, 26, p. 185.

[71] Philon, De fuga et inventione, 44–52; 143–144.

[72] Théétète, 176a–b (Philon, De fuga et inventione, 63); 176b–c (De fuga et inventione, 82).

[73] De fuga saeculi, 4, 17, p. 178, 3–13. La reprise de Théétète, 176a–c, est en partie littérale, même si Platon n'est point nommé. On trouve un remploi plus discret – mais certain cependant – du même passage en De fuga saeculi, 7, 39, p. 194, 4–16.

[74] Cf. H. SAVON, op. cit., t. I, pp. 367–375. Dès le début de son traité, l'évêque de Milan a donné un équivalent évangélique à l'exhortation du philosophe: *Non enim potest percipere*

orchestration mène à une conclusion à première vue paradoxale. D'une part, il est clair que, de Philon à Ambroise, le contenu philosophique s'est encore appauvri. Sous une certaine permanence des formules, les thèmes du 'Théétète', transmis par Philon, changent de sens chez Ambroise; la métaphysique fait place à l'histoire sainte. C'est ainsi que la permanence du mal ici-bas n'apparaît plus comme une nécessité de nature, mais comme l'effet d'un libre choix − toujours révocable − de la pédagogie divine[75]. D'autre part, le 'De fuga saeculi' d'Ambroise semble plus proche du 'Théétète' que ne l'est le traité de Philon. L'évêque de Milan fonde en effet sa rhétorique du détachement sur la reprise incessante de l'exhortation de Socrate (Théétète, 176a−b) qui n'était guère, chez l'Alexandrin, qu'un ornement occasionnel. Cependant, ces emprunts philosophiques n'ont qu'une portée très limitée. L'usage qu'en fait Ambroise et qui peut être rattaché aux techniques de l'*amplificatio*, reste presque exclusivement littéraire.

De ces analyses, quelques conclusions générales peuvent, semble-t-il, être tirées. Ce sont notamment les suivantes:

1. − L'utilisation de Philon par Ambroise déborde largement les zones de correspondance plus ou moins littérale que signalent les éditeurs. Souvent, la référence au texte de l'Alexandrin explique encore la structure et le contenu de bien des pages où le langage de l'Ecriture et de la tradition ecclésiastique a entièrement recouvert les images et les formules proprement philoniennes.

2. − En même temps, la liberté d'Ambroise vis-à-vis de son modèle est bien plus grande qu'on ne le reconnaît généralement. Il faut retourner la formule de SCHENKL et constater que l'évêque de Milan a l'art de conserver les formules tout en changeant leur contenu. L'idée qu'Ambroise imite servilement ses modèles, sur laquelle E. LUCCHESI a fondé sa démonstration, doit donc être abandonnée.

3. − Les multiples corrections apportées au modèle − suppressions, additions, transpositions − trahissent une vigilance constante, un dessein sûr, une doctrine cohérente. Ambroise, tel qu'il nous apparaît dans ses traités, n'a rien d'un prédicateur pressé qui assemblerait un peu au hasard des matériaux hétéroclites, quitte à leur apporter quelques amendements improvisés.

4. − Ce qu'Ambroise veut exorciser chez Philon, c'est l'idée d'un monde trouvant en soi sa consistance, créé sans doute et administré par son Auteur, mais selon des lois immuables, expressions définitives et abstraites de la volonté générale de Dieu. C'est aussi l'idée d'un bonheur qui ne suppose pas une transmutation de l'homme et qui consiste simplement à reconnaître cet ordre cosmique auquel président des pensées divines qui ont l'universalité et la permanence des idées platoniciennes. C'est, enfin, cette subordination du Logos et cette hiérarchie des puissances qui semblent laisser le vrai Dieu dans un infranchissable éloignement.

---

illud quod est et est semper, nisi prius hinc fugerit. Unde et dominus volens patri deo adpropinquare ⟨*ad*⟩ *apostolos ait:* „*surgite, eamus hinc*" (Io., 14, 31). (De fuga saeculi, 1, 4, p. 165, 14−16.)

[75] De fuga saeculi, 7, 39, p. 194, 4−16; cf. Philon, De fuga et inventione, 63−64 (Platon, Théétète, 176 a).

5. — Les mêmes exégèses philoniennes qui exprimaient ces vues qu'il condamne, Ambroise les met au service d'une vision religieuse toute contraire. C'est la chair de Jésus, visible et palpable, qui est pleinement réelle[76], tandis que les idées platoniciennes sont des ombres vaines[77]. Notre condition et notre devenir ne s'expliquent ni par des nécessités de nature, ni par des lois générales, mais par des volontés particulières et imprévisibles de Dieu. L'univers est promis à la destruction et le bonheur est seulement au-delà de la mort. Le salut ne s'obtient point par une simple contemplation, mais par une participation à la fois symbolique et concrète à la mort du Verbe Incarné, vrai homme et vrai Dieu.

6. — Cette antipathie foncière pour la métaphysique du platonisme n'empêche point Ambroise d'en reprendre la rhétorique et d'en utiliser les images. A l'occasion, il peut emprunter celles-ci à Plotin, voire à Platon lui-même, mais c'est par l'intermédiaire de Philon qu'elles lui parviennent le plus souvent dans nos cinq traités.

7. — L'originalité d'Ambroise par rapport à son modèle s'affirme aussi dans la démarche de son exégèse. Il la veut plus purement biblique: souvent des recours à l'Ecriture viennent se substituer aux 'ornements étrangers'mis en oeuvre par l'Alexandrin. Ambroise dispose à cet effet d'un réseau de correspondances beaucoup plus riche que celui dont jouait Philon. Au Pentateuque s'ajoutent les autres livres de l'Ancien Testament et surtout ceux du Nouveau. La diversité des versions multiplie encore le nombre des associations qui s'offrent à l'évêque de Milan. Cette exégèse est enfin plus mobile. Ambroise possède à un haut degré l'art de la surimpression et de l'ambiguïté, qui permet les transitions insensibles ou surprenantes et favorise les glissements les plus audacieux, les métamorphoses les plus convaincantes.

8. — Cet art n'est jamais gratuit. La séduction des images, l'habileté des enchaînements, l'agencement des préludes et des reprises, comme la disparition des repères dont Philon avait muni ses traités sont autant de moyens de soumettre l'esprit du disciple et de l'inciter à se laisser conduire.

9. — De plus, ces détours, ces correspondances soudain apparues, tout ce cheminement imprévisible convenait parfaitement à la communication progressive d'une réalité mystérieuse, en un mot à une initiation.

10. — L'allégorisme ambrosien témoigne, en même temps, du goût d'une époque: il est un bon exemple de ce 'maniérisme' où l'Antiquité tardive s'est complu[78].

---

[76] Ambroise, De fuga saeculi, 4, 23, p. 183, 6—12.

[77] Ibid., 5, 27, p. 185, 19—22; cf. 8, 51, p. 203, 23 — 204, 2. Ce dédain contraste avec les propos favorables tenus par Philon dans une des pages adaptées par Ambroise, qui omet cette mention flatteuse: De fuga et inventione, 63 (τις καὶ τῶν ἐπὶ σοφίᾳ θαυμασθέντων ἀνὴρ δόκιμος).

[78] Sur la notion de maniérisme et son application à l'Antiquité tardive: E. R. CURTIUS, Europäische Literatur und lateinisches Mittelalter, 2e éd., Bern, 1954, pp. 277—305, et, parmi les travaux plus récents, H. FRIEDRICH, Über die Silvae des Statius . . . und die Frage des literarischen Manierismus, dans: Festschr. für Fritz Schalk, Frankfurt am Main, 1963, pp. 34—57. E. BURCK, Vom römischen Manierismus, Darmstadt, 1971 (c.r.: W. SCHETTER, Gnomon, 47, 1975, pp. 556—562); J. FONTAINE, Le mélange des genres dans la poésie

II. Jérôme

1. Références à Philon éparses dans l'œuvre de Jérôme

Ambroise ne cite Philon qu'une seule fois; encore est-ce pour lui reprocher son *affectus iudaicus*. Jérôme, au contraire, mentionne à plusieurs reprises l'Alexandrin, et les formules qu'il emploie, jointes au contexte où elles apparaissent, semblent plutôt élogieuses[79]. Josèphe et Philon sont qualifiés par lui de *viri doctissimi Iudaeorum*[80]. Philon est appelé ailleurs *vir disertissimus Iudaeorum*[81]. Jérôme souligne qu'on voit en lui un 'second Platon' ou le 'Platon juif'[82] et semble souscrire à ce jugement. Bien plus, le moine de Bethléem reconnaît lui-même que son livre sur l'interprétation des noms hébreux dépend d'un original philonien[83], et il consacre à l'Alexandrin une notice de son catalogue des 'écrivains ecclésiastiques'[84]. On croirait donc aisément que l'œuvre de Jérôme représente une étape importante de la destinée posthume de Philon.

Mais ce sont là des apparences trompeuses. S. von Sychowski[85] et C. A. Bernoulli[86] ont montré que la notice du 'De viris illustribus' n'était guère qu'un plagiat d'Eusèbe de Césarée. Quant à l'ouvrage de Philon sur les noms hébreux, Jérôme n'en a eu connaissance qu'à travers une adaptation d'Origène: c'est lui-même qui en prévient son lecteur. Restent les mentions occasionnelles, mais, là encore, il faut être prudent. Au moment même où il emprunte purement et simplement à Eusèbe la liste des ouvrages de Philon, Jérôme donne à entendre qu'il les a tous eus entre les mains[87].

Ces mentions éparses ne suffisent donc pas à prouver une lecture directe. Jérôme sait, par exemple, que Philon a consacré un livre aux Esséniens[88], qu'il a

---

de Prudence, dans: Forma futuri. Studi in onore del Cardinale M. Pellegrino, Torino, 1975, pp. 755–777.

[79] Cf. P. Courcelle, Les lettres grecques en Occident de Macrobe à Cassiodore, Paris, 1948, pp. 70–71.

[80] Epist. 29, 7, 1, CSEL, 54, p. 241, 17.

[81] Liber interpretationis Hebraicorum nominum, praef., 1, CCL, 72, p. 59.

[82] Epist. 70, 3, 3, CSEL, 54, p. 704, 13. Cf. Epist. 22, 35, 8, p. 200, 7–8: *Philo, Platonici sermonis imitator.*

[83] Liber interpretationis Hebraicorum nominum, praefatio, pp. 59–60.

[84] De viris illustribus, 11.

[85] S. von Sychowski, Hieronymus als Litterarhistoriker, Kirchengeschichtliche Studien, II, 2, Münster i. W., 1894, pp. 96–97.

[86] C. A. Bernoulli, Der Schriftstellerkatalog des Hieronymus, Freiburg i. Br., 1895, pp. 15–16 et 115–117.

[87] De viris illustribus, 11, éd. E. C. Richardson, TU, 14, 1, Leipzig, 1896, p. 15, 11–12: *Sunt et alia eius monumenta ingenii, quae in nostras manus non pervenerunt.* Cf. P. Courcelle, op. cit., p. 70.

[88] Jérôme, Adversus Iovinianum, II, 14, PL, 23, Paris, 1845, 303 (Vallarsi, 343); cf. Epist. 22, 35, 8, CSEL, 54, p. 200, 7–9. Dans les deux passages, Philon est cité en compagnie de Josèphe.

longuement expliqué le sens des vêtements du grand-prêtre[89], qu'il a repris la division platonicienne des âges de la vie[90]. Il invoque son autorité pour prouver que la poésie hébraïque n'était pas dépourvue de mètres[91]. Ce sont là finalement des points de détail, et on remarquera que jamais Philon n'est cité seul. Est-il nécessaire de penser que Jérôme a eu chaque fois entre les mains le traité qui fait l'objet d'une référence aussi épisodique[92]? En tout cas, même si ces apports provenaient tous directement de Philon, leur ensemble apparaîtrait bien mince à côté de ce que Jérôme doit, par exemple, à Josèphe[93].

Il n'y a aucune raison, il est vrai, de ne tenir compte que des passages où Philon est expressément nommé. Comme Ambroise, Jérôme a pu utiliser l'Alexandrin sans le citer. Il est clair que, dans ce cas, plus l'emprunt soupçonné est minime, moins il est facile d'en identifier exactement la source. Faut-il croire par exemple que c'est directement au 'De somniis' de Philon que Jérôme doit l'étymologie de Ramesse: *commotio turbulenta*[94]? C'est beaucoup plus vraisemblablement à Origène, dont les 'Homélies sur les Nombres' proposent conjointement les deux étymologies attribuées par Jérôme à des *quidam*: *commotio turbida* ou *turbulenta* et *commotio tineae*[95].

2. Dans quelle mesure la lettre 64 de Jérôme (à Fabiola) est-elle 'philonienne'?

On le voit, nous n'avons guère rencontré jusqu'ici que quelques références ponctuelles, parfois douteuses, en tout cas sans grande signification. Il est temps d'en venir à des emprunts beaucoup plus étendus, ceux qu'on a cru déceler dans la

---

[89] Jérôme, Epist. 29, 7, 1, p. 241, 14–18: *Iosephus ac Philo . . . multique de nostris id latissime persecuti sunt.*

[90] Jérôme, Dialogus adversus Pelagianos, III, 6, PL, 23, 576 AB (VALLARSI, 789).

[91] Jérôme, Praefatio in librum Iob, PL, 28, 1082 A (2e éd., 1141 A): *Quod si cui videtur incredulum, metra scilicet esse apud Hebraeos, legat Philonem, Iosephum, Origenem, Caesariensem Eusebium, et eorum testimonio me verum dicere comprobabit.*

[92] C'est ainsi que la référence à Philon à propos des mètres de la poésie hébraïque a toute chance de provenir d'Eusèbe, Historia ecclesiastica, II, 17, 13, GCS, 9, 1, p. 148, 3–5 (citation textuelle de Philon, De vita contemplativa, 29, éd. COHN-WENDLAND, t. VI, pp. 53, 16 – 54, 2).

[93] Cf. P. COURCELLE, op. cit., pp. 71 sqq.

[94] C'est l'hypothèse de P. COURCELLE, op. cit., p. 71 et n. 3, qui rapproche Jérôme, Epist., 78, 3, 2, CSEL, 55, p. 53, 5, et Philon, De Somniis, 1, 14: (Ῥαμεσσὴ) ἑρμηνεύεται . . . σεισμὸς σητός (cf. Nm., 33, 3).

[95] Origène, Homiliae in Numeros, XXVII, 9, GCS, 30, p. 268, 18–19. Sans doute la seconde étymologie – *commotio tineae* dans le latin de Jérôme et de Rufin – se trouve aussi chez Philon, mais, cette fois-ci, dans le De posteritate Caini, 55. Cependant, il n'est pas vraisemblable que Jérôme soit allé chercher ces étymologies dans deux traités différents de Philon, alors qu'il les trouvait réunies dans une homélie d'Origène sur le thème même qui faisait l'objet de sa seconde lettre à Fabiola: les *mansiones* des fils d'Israël au désert. Sur l'onomastique de cette 'Homilia XXVII in Numeros' d'Origène: R. P. C. HANSON, Interpretations of Hebrew names in Origen, Vigiliae Christianae, 10, 1956, pp. 115–119 et 122–123.

lettre 64 à Fabiola. Cette *epistula* est en fait un petit traité exégétique: Jérôme y commente différentes dispositions de la loi mosaïque ayant trait aux prêtres. Le plus ancien manuscrit connu, le Spinaliensis 68, du VIIIe siècle, en résume ainsi le contenu: *de cibis sacerdotalibus et veste pontifica* (sic)[96]. L'utilisation de Philon dans ce texte a été souvent relevée par plusieurs auteurs, mais, jusqu'ici, on n'a pas, semble-t-il, tenté d'analyser cette dépendance dans le détail. Cette analyse, au moins partielle, semble s'imposer pour notre propos. Elle doit permettre de mieux délimiter l'importance et de mieux déterminer la nature des réminiscences philoniennes chez Jérôme. Elle rendra en même temps possible une comparaison avec les analyses du philonisme d'Ambroise dont on a esquissé plus haut les résultats. Ce parallèle sera d'autant plus significatif qu'il s'agit d'un texte où domine l'interprétation allégorique ou tropologique de l'Ecriture[97], qui avait, semble-t-il, les préférences de Fabiola[98].

Des deux parties qui composent, on l'a vu, cette *epistula*, c'est la première qui est pour nous la plus intéressante. Dans la seconde, en effet, la plus développée de beaucoup, celle qui explique les vêtements du grand-prêtre, Jérôme utilise surtout Josèphe et Epiphane. Les emprunts éventuels à Philon ne peuvent alors représenter qu'un appoint[99]. En revanche, c'est Philon et lui seul que l'on cite comme source de la première partie, de cette *praefatiuncula* qui est, en réalité, un petit traité 'de praemiis et cibis sacerdotum'[100].

Sans doute, le correspondant de Fabiola ne nomme pas ici l'Alexandrin. Il semble même présenter d'entrée de jeu les interprétations qu'il va proposer comme spécifiquement chrétiennes[101]. A elle seule, une telle déclaration ne prouve évidemment rien, et, à défaut d'indications explicites de Jérôme lui-même, il va falloir examiner avec une particulière attention les pages du 'De specialibus legibus' où Philon traite précisément des mêmes thèmes que le début de cette

---

[96] Titre analogue dans le Bambergensis B. IV. 21 du VIe siècle (le plus ancien manuscrit du 'De viris illustribus'): *De cibis sacerdotum et de veste pontificis* (cf. F. CAVALLERA, Saint Jérôme, Paris, 1922, t. II, p. 136).

[97] Sur la notion de *tropologia* chez Jérôme: A. PENNA, Principi e carattere dell'esegesi di S. Gerolamo, Roma, 1950, pp. 110–117. Cf. P. JAY, Le vocabulaire exégétique de saint Jérôme dans le Commentaire sur Zacharie, Revue des Etudes Augustiniennes, 14, 1968, pp. 3–16.

[98] Cf. A. PENNA, op. cit., p. 30.

[99] Pour l'utilisation de Josèphe et d'Epiphane, v. l'apparat de HILBERG dans Jérôme, Epistulae, CSEL, 54, pp. 597–613. Cf. P. COURCELLE, op. cit., pp. 72–77.

[100] Epist. 64, 8, 1, CSEL, 54, p. 595, 12–15. Cette dissertation préliminaire que Fabiola n'avait pas demandée apparaît comme une pièce rapportée: Jérôme a voulu honorer sa correspondante d'une longue lettre (printemps 397): P. NAUTIN, Etudes de chronologie hiéronymienne, Revue des Etudes Augustiniennes, 20, 1974, pp. 268–269.
Le 'De specialibus legibus' de Philon est considéré comme la source probable de ce développement (Epist. 64, 1–2): VALLARSI, S. Hieronymi Opera, 2e éd., Venetiis, 1772–1776, t. I, p. 35 (PL, 22, 608); P. COURCELLE, op. cit., p. 70 et n. 6.

[101] C'est ce qu'implique, semble-t-il, l'allusion à II Cor., 3, 13–15 faite dès les premières lignes de la lettre: Ep. 64, 1, p. 586, 13–587, 2.

lettre à Fabiola. Conformément à la démarche de l'exégèse hiéronymienne, une telle analyse doit être menée à deux niveaux: l'*historia* et la *tropologia*[102].

3. Le développement sur les *praemia sacerdotum* (Jérôme, Epist. 64,1–2): sens littéral et interprétations rabbiniques

L'*historia*, ici, ce n'est point la narration d'événements passés, c'est un ensemble de prescriptions juridiques déterminant quels sont les morceaux des animaux sacrifiés qui reviennent de droit aux prêtres. Philon et Jérôme trouvaient ces dispositions dans deux passages du Pentateuque.

Ce sont d'abord quatre versets du Lévitique concernant les sacrifices ʿpacifiquesʾ[103]. Deux parties de l'animal immolé sont attribuées aux prêtres: la poitrine et la cuisse droite, dans la Septante: τὸ στηθύνιον . . . καὶ τὸν βραχίονα.

Un second texte – Deutéronome, 18,3 – témoigne d'une législation sensiblement différente. Ce qui, cette fois, doit revenir au prêtre, c'est l'épaule, les mâchoires et l'estomac de l'animal offert en sacrifice. Remarquons que les versions grecque et latine ne font point de distinction entre le membre postérieur et le membre antérieur de l'animal immolé, et qu'elles emploient dans les deux cas le même mot βραχίων ou *armus*.

Voilà donc l'*historia* qui va servir de base aux développements allégoriques de Philon et de Jérôme. Chaque fois que l'un et l'autre seront simplement fidèles au texte biblique, sans gauchissement ni interpolation, nous n'en pourrons naturellement rien conclure. En revanche, les divergences entre les interprètes et la lettre qu'ils prétendent expliquer doivent retenir toute notre attention: selon que ces écarts sont communs à Philon et à Jérôme ou au contraire ne se retrouvent que chez l'un d'entre eux, l'utilisation du premier par le second a chance d'avoir été plus importante ou plus réduite.

On peut d'abord observer que le plan d'ensemble des deux développements est identique: Philon et Jérôme commencent par expliquer le texte du Lévitique pour passer ensuite à celui du Deutéronome; mais c'est là une démarche trop naturelle pour que l'on puisse rien en conclure.

En revanche, une petite phrase initiale où Jérôme annonce en quelque sorte sa *divisio* pose plusieurs problèmes. Le correspondant de Fabiola, pour montrer l'insuffisance du sens littéral, vient de rappeler l'exclamation de Paul – «Dieu se soucie-t-il des bœufs?[104]» – et il poursuit: «Sûrement pas! Encore moins du foie du bœuf, du bélier, du bouc, et de l'épaule de la patte droite, et du ventre, où sont

---

[102] Cf. A. PENNA, Principi e carattere dell'esegesi di S. Gerolamo, Roma, 1950, p. 58–167; A. VACCARI, I fattori dell'esegesi Geronimiana, dans ID., Scritti di erudizione e di filologia, Roma, 1958, t. II, pp. 147–170.

[103] Lv., 7, 31–34 (cf. Ex., 29, 27; Nm., 18, 18). On reprend ici la traduction française consacrée par l'usage et qui évoque les *hostiae pacificae* de la Vulgate. Il serait plus exact de parler de ʿsacrifice de communionʾ. Sur ce rite: R. DE VAUX, Les sacrifices de l'Ancien Testament, Les cahiers de la Revue biblique, 1, Paris, 1964, pp. 31–48.

[104] I Cor., 9, 9.

digérés les excréments. Deux de ces parties sont reçues par les prêtres pour leur nourriture, la troisième, Phinéès la mérite dans le combat[105]». Quand on a présent à l'esprit les textes du Lévitique et du Deutéronome que Jérôme entreprend d'expliquer, on ne peut être que grandement surpris de ce préambule. Sans doute l'*armus dextri pedis* − expression singulière −, c'est le βραχίων ou l'*armus* dont parlent l'un et l'autre texte. Quant au ventre, c'est la troisième partie de l'animal sacrifié que le Deutéronome attribue aux prêtres. En revanche, ni la poitrine ni les mâchoires ne figurent dans cette énumération où elles auraient dû normalement prendre place. Et surtout, le Lévitique, pas plus que le Deutéronome, ne prévoit que les prêtres auront le foie en partage. Or, aucune de ces anomalies ne se retrouve dans le texte de Philon que nous supposions avoir servi de modèle à Jérôme.

La difficulté est d'autant plus sensible que, dans la suite du texte, ces singularités disparaissent. Il y est bien question du foie, plus précisément du lobe du foie. Mais Jérôme dit que les prêtres l'offrent à Dieu, non que cette partie leur revient, ce qui est conforme aux dispositions du Lévitique.

En même temps, la poitrine et les mâchoires, dont l'omission nous avait surpris, sont normalement citées par Jérôme comme revenant en droit aux prêtres. Elles font, à ce titre, l'objet d'une explication tropologique sur laquelle nous aurons à revenir.

On est donc tenté de penser qu'à la suite de quelque accident le mot *pectus* a disparu de la phrase d'introduction. Et, de fait, la tradition manuscrite fait preuve sur ce point de beaucoup d'incertitudes. On s'en aperçoit surtout si l'on ne se contente pas des manuscrits en nombre trop restreint que HILBERG fait figurer dans son apparat[106]. La leçon *et armo dextri pedis*, qu'il retient, est bien celle des trois manuscrits les plus anciens[107]. Mais, à la place de *pedis*, on trouve ailleurs *pectus*[108], et *pectore*[109]. Des grattages, des ratures et des surcharges montrent qu'il s'agit là d'un passage peu sûr[110]. Tout s'expliquerait si l'on supposait à l'origine la leçon *pectusculo* donnée par l'édition d'ERASME[111] et reprise par celle de MARIA-

---

[105] Jérôme, Epist. 64, 1, 2, p. 587, 6−10: *Numquid de bubus cura est deo? Utique non. Multo magis de iecore bovis, arietis, hircorum et armo dextri pedis et ventre, quo stercora digeruntur, quorum duo in esum accipiunt sacerdotes, tertium Finees meretur in praemio.*

[106] HILBERG utilise sept manuscrits, s'échelonnant du VIIIe au XIIe siècle. Or, on connaît aujourd'hui près de cent cinquante manuscrits de la lettre 64 (B. LAMBERT, Bibliotheca Hieronymiana manuscripta, t. I B, Steenbrugis, 1969, pp. 702−707). Il est vrai que ce sont souvent des *recentiores*. On pourrait du moins ajouter aux sept codices utilisés par l'éditeur du GCS huit manuscrits antérieurs au Xe siècle. Sur l'éd. HILBERG, cf. A. VACCARI, Bolletino Geronimiano, 2, Biblica, 1, 1920, pp. 386−390: „*Il numero e la qualità dei manoscritti consultati dovrebbe sovente essere ben maggiore*".

[107] Epinal, 68, s. VIII; Munich, lat. 6299, s. VIII ex.; Vienne, lat. 865, s. IX.

[108] *Armo dextro pectus*: Zurich, Reichenau 4, s. IX; Vatican lat. 355, s. IX−X; Paris, B.N., lat. 1871, s. X; Berlin, lat. 18, s. XII; Paris, B.N., lat. 11631, s. IX; etc.

[109] *Armo dextro pectore*. Cette leçon semble l'emporter au XIIe siècle − Paris, B.N., lat. 1756; 1876 (St. Martin de Tournai); 1884 (St. Amand); 1885; 12164 (St. Germain) etc. . . . − ainsi que dans les manuscrits plus récents.

[110] V.g. Paris, B.N., lat. 1866, s. IX; 1869, s. IX; 16841, s. XI.

[111] Opera Hieronymi, Basileae, apud J. Frobenium, 1524−1526, t. III, p. 57.

NO VITTORIO[112]. La chute de la finale aurait donné la leçon *pectus* qui ne se serait plus accordée avec le contexte, et aurait provoqué les corrections divergentes *dextri pedis* et *dextro pectore*. L'incohérence qui nous arrête disparaîtrait du même coup: les mots *de iecore bovis, arietis et hircorum* seraient une formule de transition et l'énumération qui suit *et armo dextro, pectusculo et ventre* annoncerait la *divisio* du texte de Jérôme. Mais on ne sait si la leçon *pectusculo* n'est qu'une conjecture du grand humaniste ou s'il l'a réellement lue dans un manuscrit aujourd'hui disparu. On ne peut donc guère attendre d'un texte aussi incertain qu'il jette quelque lumière sur le problème des sources de la lettre de Jérôme.

A la fin de la même phrase, en revanche, un détail pourrait bien être plus instructif. On y lit, en effet, que Phinéès a mérité d'avoir en partage le ventre de l'animal à titre de récompense. Or cela ne se voit nulle part dans le texte biblique. Il est dit seulement au livre des Nombres (25,7−12) que, pour avoir transpercé le couple pécheur qui avait provoqué la colère de Yahvé, le prêtre Phinéès obtint de Dieu une alliance de paix, une alliance de prêtrise éternelle. Il n'est pas question d'une autre récompense, et celle que mentionne Jérôme à deux reprises[113] est également ignorée de Philon. Etant donné l'importance prise par la figure de Phinéès − ou plutôt Pinḥas − dans le judaïsme post-biblique, on peut supposer que Jérôme utilise ici une tradition rabbinique. C'est ce que vient confirmer une rapide enquête. Pinḥas avait transpercé le couple impudique par le ventre (Nm., 25,8). La Haggadah a rapproché ce détail du récit et le verset du Deutéronome (18,3) qui prescrit de donner au prêtre, outre l'épaule et les mâchoires, l'estomac de l'animal sacrifié: les mâchoires parce que Pinḥas avait d'abord prié, l'épaule parce qu'il avait brandi la lance, le ventre parce qu'il avait transpercé le ventre des deux pécheurs. Cette interprétation est évoquée dans plusieurs textes, dont le plus ancien est le Sifré du Deutéronome qui rassemble des traditions antérieures au IIIe siècle[114]. On peut donc supposer que Jérôme doit à ses contacts avec l'enseignement des rabbins de Palestine la tradition dont il fait état − moins complète, il est vrai, puisqu'elle n'explique ni le don de l'épaule ni celui des mâchoires. En effet, non seulement l'interprétation que rapporte ici Jérôme est absente de Philon, mais elle relève d'un courant de pensée tout contraire au sien. Chez l'exégète alexandrin, le symbolisme conduit, comme on va le voir, à une vérité morale universelle[115], tandis que l'explication midrashique rattache le rite ou la prescription à un événement bien particulier de l'histoire du peuple hébreu[116].

---

[112] Opera Hieronymi, Romae, 1571−1576, t. III, p. 43.

[113] Epist. 64, 1, 2, p. 587, 9−10; 2, 1, p. 589, 5−6.

[114] Siphre zu Deuteronomium, éd. L. FINKELSTEIN, Breslau, 1935, p. 215 (Shofᵉṭim, 18, 165); B. Ḥûl. 134 b; Midrash Aggadah, Agadischer Commentar zum Pentateuch, Wien, 1884, 2e part., p. 148 (Pinḥas, 13); autres références dans L. GINZBERG, The legends of the Jews, t. III, 4e éd., Philadelphia, 1954, p. 389.

[115] C'est ainsi que, selon les Legum allegoriae, III,242, la lance brandie par Phinéès représente le Logos, la Madianite symbolisant la nature séparée du chœur divin, frappée au ventre afin qu'elle ne puisse plus enfanter le vice. Dans le De mutatione nominum, 108, la lance de Phinéès est le *logos* aiguisé et acéré qui transperce la passion par la matrice. Cf. De posteritate Caini, 182; De confusione linguarum, 57. Lorsque Philon rappelle, en suivant la lettre, ce que fut la récompense de Phinéès, il s'en tient à ce qu'il trouve en Nm., 25,

Le texte de Jérôme – envisagé du point de vue de l'*historia* – présente une dernière anomalie. En dépit des expressions employées[117], il entend la prescription du Deutéronome, 18,3, non pas d'un animal offert en sacrifice, mais d'une bête de boucherie abattue pour la consommation courante: *Ceterum et alia tria . . . de privato et de macello publico, ubi non religio, sed victus necessitas est, sacerdotibus membra tribuuntur: brachium, maxilla et venter*[118].

Or cette interprétation qui gauchit le sens obvie du texte biblique est également celle de Philon[119]. Faut-il voir là un argument déterminant en faveur de l'utilisation du 'De specialibus legibus' par l'auteur de la lettre à Fabiola? Certainement pas. En effet, ce n'est pas seulement Philon, c'est aussi la tradition rabbinique palestinienne, soucieuse d'éviter tout désaccord entre le texte du Lévitique et le verset du Deutéronome qui interprète ce dernier comme une prescription relative aux animaux abattus pour des fins purement alimentaires[120]. Et c'est l'attribution aux prêtres d'une partie de leur chair que l'on considérait comme la récompense de Phinées[121].

Ainsi, dans son interprétation 'historique' des dispositions relatives aux *praemia sacerdotum*, il est au moins un détail important que Jérôme n'a pu emprunter à Philon: celui qui fait intervenir le personnage de Phinées. Il n'est rien, en revanche, que n'expliquent suffisamment les textes du Lévitique et du Deutéronome complétés par les gloses des rabbins de Palestine.

4. Le développement sur les *praemia sacerdotum*: sens spirituel et allégorisme origénien

On peut imaginer que l'influence de l'auteur du 'De specialibus legibus' sera plus sensible dans l'exégèse tropologique de ces dispositions. De fait, à l'arrière-plan des interprétations de Philon et de Jérôme, on entrevoit nettement la même page de Platon: Timée, 69 d–71 a. Le philosophe y expose comment les différentes parties de l'âme ont leur siège dans différentes parties du corps: le principe divin et immortel dans la tête, la partie de l'âme qui participe au courage et à l'ar-

---

12–13: De vita Mosis, I, 304. L'exégèse philonienne est adaptée par Origène, qui fait du Christ le véritable Phinées (Homiliae in Numeros, 20, 5, GCS, 30, p. 198, 21–25: *Et ideo surgentes oremus ut inveniamus paratum semper istum 'gladium spiritus' per quem exterminentur et semina ipsa et conceptacula peccatorum ac propitius nobis fiat deus per verum Fineem ipsum dominum nostrum Iesum Christum, cui gloria et imperium in saecula saeculorum. Amen.*)

[116] Cf. I. HEINEMANN, Philons griechische und jüdische Bildung, Breslau, 1932, p. 77; S. DANIEL, Philon d'Alexandrie, De specialibus legibus, I et II, Paris, 1975, p. 97 n. 6.

[117] Cf. S. R. DRIVER, A critical and exegetical commentary on Deuteronomy, Edinburgh, 1895, p. 215.

[118] Jérôme, Epist. 64, 2, 1, pp. 588, 19 – 589, 3.

[119] De specialibus legibus, I, 147: Ἀπὸ δὲ τῶν ἔξω τοῦ βωμοῦ θυομένων ἕνεκα κρεωφαγίας . . .

[120] B. Ḥul., 130a.

[121] Ibid., 134b.

deur guerrière dans le thorax, la partie désirante dans le ventre. C'est cette espèce de topographie psychique que Philon applique à trois des portions réservées aux prêtres par le Lévitique et le Deutéronome: la poitrine, les mâchoires et le ventre. Sur ces trois points, la comparaison avec Jérôme peut être instructive.

La signification que Philon attribue à la poitrine de l'animal sacrifié découle de la doctrine platonicienne qui en fait le siège du θυμός, de l'âme irascible[122]. Supposant que ce qui est réservé aux fils de Lévi, c'est la partie grasse et donc tendre de la poitrine, l'Alexandrin y voit le symbole de la modération du θυμός, de l'apaisement des sentiments agressifs. Et, comme l'épaule droite signifie, selon lui, la force, le courage, il considère que les deux morceaux attribués aux prêtres par le Lévitique représentent l'alliance de l'énergie et de la douceur[123].

L'exégèse de Jérôme est, à vrai dire, fort différente. C'est qu'il commence par critiquer expressément la localisation des parties de l'âme proposée par Platon. S'il nomme le philosophe, ce que Philon n'avait pas fait dans le passage parallèle du 'De specialibus legibus', c'est pour le contredire. Pour Jérôme, en effet, la poitrine est le siège non point du θυμός, mais de l'ἡγεμονικόν que l'auteur du 'Timée' plaçait dans la tête[124]. On reconnaît là une thèse déjà soutenue par les Stoïciens[125], mais c'est de l'Evangile que le moine de Bethléem se réclame ici. Trois textes de Matthieu lui servent à appuyer l'idée que le *principale* réside dans le cœur et par conséquent dans la poitrine: «Bienheureux ceux qui ont le cœur pur, car ils verront Dieu[126]»; «C'est du cœur que proviennent les pensées mauvaises[127]»; «Que méditez-vous de mal dans vos cœurs[128]?» L'association de la poitrine et de l'épaule prend donc un tout autre sens que chez Philon. Elle ne symbolise plus une énergie tempérée par la douceur, mais la pensée droite aboutissant à l'action bonne[129].

Cette modification profonde de l'exégèse proposée par Philon n'est pas due à l'initiative personnelle de Jérôme. En fait, ce dernier ne fait que reprendre ici un thème familier à Origène[130]. L'exégèse que ce dernier a proposée des dispositions du Lévitique, c'est bien celle dont la lettre de Fabiola reprend les grandes lignes: la poitrine réservée aux prêtres symbolise le cœur dont il faut extirper les mauvaises pensées; c'est du c œ u r, en effet, qu'elles p r o v i e n n e n t. Il faut les

---

[122] Platon, Tim., 70a–d.

[123] Philon, De specialibus legibus, 145–146. Sur l'alliance nécessaire de l'énergie et de la modération, cf. Platon, Resp., 375, 410; Pol. 306a–311c.

[124] Jérôme, Epist. 64, 1, 3, p. 587, 13–15; cf. Platon, Tim., 69d–e; 73c–d.

[125] Stoicorum veterum fragmenta, I, 148; II, 879–911. Cf. M. POHLENZ, Die Stoa, Göttingen, 1948, t. I, p. 87, t. II, pp. 51–52.

[126] Mt., 5, 8.

[127] Mt., 15, 19.

[128] Mt., 9, 4.

[129] Jérôme, Epist. 64, 1, 4, CSEL, 54, p. 588, 3–6: *Mereantur accipere praemium pectus et brachium: in pectore mundas cogitationes, legis notitiam, dogmatum veritatem, in brachio opera bona et pugnam contra diabolum et armatam manum, ut, quod mente conceperint, exemplo probent.*

[130] G. Q. A. MEERSHOEK, Le latin biblique d'après saint Jérôme, Latinitas christianorum primaeva. fasc. 20, Nijmegen, 1966, pp. 169–173.

brûler au feu de l'autel afin d'avoir un cœur pur et de voir Dieu[131]. Un peu plus loin, Origène ajoute que le *sacerdotis pectus* est rempli de «sagesse, de connaissance, d'intelligence divine»[132]. De même, Jérôme voit dans cette poitrine donnée aux prêtres le symbole non seulement des *mundae cogitationes*, mais de la *legis notitia* et de la *dogmatum veritas*[133]. On a reconnu au passage, dans le développement d'Origène, deux des versets évangéliques avancés dans la lettre à Fabiola pour soutenir la localisation du *principale* dans le cœur: Matthieu, 15, 19, et Matthieu, 5, 8.

Deux indices viennent confirmer que c'est bien à Origène et non à Philon que Jérôme emprunte son explication de la poitrine et de l'épaule. Le premier, c'est la mention du lobe du foie dont Philon très logiquement ne parle pas, puisque cette partie de l'animal est brûlée sur l'autel et non point remise au prêtre. Or, ce rapide excursus que l'on remarque chez Jérôme, on le trouve déjà chez Origène: il faut brûler non seulement les pensées mauvaises, mais encore le lobe du foie qui représente la colère ou le désir[134]. C'est le second de ces symbolismes que retient la lettre à Fabiola[135].

Le second indice n'est pas moins significatif. Dans le Lévitique, les noms des deux morceaux attribués aux prêtres sont accompagnés de déterminatifs: la poitrine du balancement ou de la contribution (*t^enûpah*), l'épaule du prélèvement (*t^erûmah*). La traduction du premier de ces mots n'a pas fait, il est vrai, l'unanimité chez les spécialistes[136]. Mais ce qui importe ici, ce n'est pas l'original hébreu, c'est la façon dont il a été compris par les versions grecques et latines. La Septante a traduit par τὸ στηθύνιον τοῦ ἐπιθέματος et ὁ βραχίων τοῦ ἀφαιρέματος. La Vulgate rend les mêmes expressions par *pectusculum elationis* et *armus separationis*.

Le sens qu'Origène donne ici au mot ἐπίθεμα est celui d'«ajout», de «supplément». Rufin a traduit par *appositio*[137]. Quel est donc cet ajout? C'est pour Origène la grâce du Saint Esprit[138]. L'interprétation est presque littéralement reprise par Jérôme[139], enrichie il est vrai par une seconde traduction proposée pour le mot hébreu: *praecipuum et egregium*[140]. Qui a donc fourni ou suggéré à Jérôme cette addition? Comme il cite en hébreu le terme dont la signification fait

---

[131] Origène, Homiliae in Leviticum, V, 12, GCS, 29, p. 355,28—356,3.

[132] Ibid., p. 356, 16—18.

[133] Cf. ci-dessus, n. 129.

[134] Origène, Homiliae in Leviticum, V, 12, p. 356, 3—6.

[135] Jérôme, Epist. 64, 1, 3—4, pp. 587,18—588,3.

[136] On a généralement traduit *t^enûpah* par «balancement»: v.g. A. VINCENT, Les rites du balancement (*tenoûphâh*) et du prélèvement (*teroûmâh*) dans le sacrifice de communion de l'Ancien Testament, Mélanges syriens offerts à René Dussaud, Paris, 1939, t. I, pp. 267—272. Mais le mot signifierait ici «contribution» selon R. DE VAUX, Les sacrifices de l'Ancien Testament, Paris, 1964.

[137] Origène (–Rufin), Homiliae in Leviticum, V, 12, GCS, 29, p. 357, 10.

[138] Ibid., p. 357, 14—16: *Restat ut apponatur ei gratia Spiritus sancti, et tunc fiet „pectusculum appositionis".*

[139] Jérôme, Epist. 64, 1, 5, p. 588, 11—13: *Ex quo intelligimus . . . additamento gratiae spiritalis talem virum institui.*

[140] Ibid., p. 588, 8—9.

problème — «*thenufa*» — il est permis de penser qu'il utilise ici une source palestinienne. On peut même évoquer le juif converti qui lui a enseigné l'hébreu et lui aurait du même coup transmis nombre d'exégèses rabbiniques[141]. Il est vrai que les évocations de cet *Hebraeus* ne sont pas nécessairement à prendre au pied de la lettre: il arrive que Jérôme ait tout simplement trouvé cet 'Hébreu' chez Origène qu'il se borne alors à copier[142]. Peut-être est-ce le cas ici. Peut-être le correspondant de Fabiola utilise-t-il un de ces 'Excerpta in Leviticum' qu'il fait figurer dans la liste des œuvres d'Origène[143], mais que nous n'avons pas conservés. Ce qui est certain, en tout cas, c'est que le 'De specialibus legibus' de Philon ne peut être la source de ces quelques lignes.

Dans l'expression «épaule de prélèvement», c'est l'idée de mise à part, de séparation qu'Origène et Jérôme mettent en valeur. Pour Jérôme, cette séparation est le fait des prêtres qui doivent se séparer par leur conduite de tous les autres hommes[144]. Aussi est-ce l'épaule droite qui leur est attribuée, symbole des œuvres conformes à la volonté de Dieu, et non la gauche, symbole des œuvres qui mènent au Tartare[145]. L'application que fait Origène de cette allégorèse est plus large: elle concerne tous les chrétiens[146]. Mais ce ne sont là que les variantes d'une même interprétation, alors que Philon a négligé les mots ἐπίθεμα et ἀφαίρεμα dans son explication de ce passage du Lévitique.

Pour la seconde partie de l'exposé de Jérôme, celle qui concerne la prescription du Deutéronome (18,3), nous n'avons pas de parallèle dans l'œuvre d'Origène, puisque nous ne possédons plus les homélies que celui-ci avait consacrées au cinquième livre de Moïse[147]. Ce qui reste possible, c'est d'examiner jusqu'à quel point Jérôme s'éloigne ou se rapproche des interprétations que l'on trouve dans le 'De specialibus legibus'.

On se rappelle que la prescription du Deutéronome, plus ancienne en fait que celle du Lévitique[148], attribue aux prêtres trois morceaux: l'épaule, les mâchoires, l'estomac — plus précisément, selon la Septante, la caillette: τὸ ἔνυστρον. L'épaule a déjà été interprétée à propos de la législation du Lévitique. Philon et Jérôme renvoient donc à leurs explications antérieures par des formules assez voisines[149]. Mais c'est là une rencontre peu significative que suffit à expliquer un plan lui-même banal.

---

[141] Les *interprétations* de cet *Hebraeus* sont mentionnées à plusieurs reprises par Jérôme. Voir les textes rassemblés par A. VACCARI, Studi di erudizione e di filologia, t. II, Roma, 1958, pp. 160—161.

[142] G. BARDY, Saint Jérôme et ses maîtres hébreux, Revue Bénédictine, 46, 1934, pp. 145—164.

[143] Jérôme, Epist. 33, 4, 2, CSEL, 54, p. 255, 16—17.

[144] Jérôme, Epist. 64, 1, 5, p. 588, 16—17.

[145] Ibid., p. 588, 14—15.

[146] Origène, Homiliae in Leviticum, V, 12, p. 357, 16—26.

[147] G. BARDY, Commentaires patristiques de la Bible, dans: Supplément au Dictionnaire de la Bible, t. II, Paris, 1934, col. 89.

[148] A. VINCENT, op. cit., pp. 271—272; R. DE VAUX, op. cit., pp. 32—35. Dt., 18, 3, appartiendrait à la plus ancienne couche du texte primitif: R. P. MERENDINO, Das deuteronomische Gesetz, Bonner bibl. Beitr., 31, Bonn, 1969, pp. 187—190.

[149] Philon, De specialibus legibus, I, 147: . . . τὸν μὲν βραχίονα διὰ τὴν ὀλίγῳ πρότερον εἰρημένην αἰτίαν. Jérôme, Epist. 64, 2, 2, p. 589, 3: *De brachio iam diximus.*

Pour les mâchoires, Philon propose deux exégèses[150]. La première nous ramène à la doctrine du 'Timée' sur la localisation de l'ἡγεμονικόν: les mâchoires sont prélevées sur «la plus importante des parties, la tête». En revanche, la seconde interprétation — les mâchoires sont les prémices de la parole — évoque plutôt la division stoïcienne de l'âme[151], que Philon reprend ailleurs à son compte[152]: l'ἡγεμονικόν, les cinq sens, la p a r o l e, la puissance génésique.

Dans le texte de Jérôme, ces références philosophiques disparaissent. Sans doute, les mâchoires sont-elles mises en rapport avec l'éloquence, donc avec la parole[153], mais c'est là une association si facile, si commune qu'on ne peut rien en conclure. On a vu, à propos de Phinées, que les rabbins palestiniens s'étaient servis d'un symbolisme analogue. Jérôme en fait d'ailleurs un usage tout différent de celui de Philon. Il n'est plus question, chez lui, de la structure de l'âme. L'allégorie devient avant tout morale: il faut que la bouche profère ce que le cœur a conçu. Si l'on tient à voir encore dans cette remarque banale quelque allusion au thème des parties de l'âme, on doit constater que le moine de Bethléem reste fidèle au schéma qu'il oppose un peu plus haut à Platon: pour lui, les pensées viennent bien de la poitrine et non de la tête. On est décidément fort loin du 'De specialibus legibus'.

On parvient à des conclusions analogues, en ce qui concerne le dernier morceau réservé aux prêtres: chez Philon, la caillette; chez Jérôme — de manière plus générale — le ventre. La dépendance de Philon à l'égard du 'Timée' est ici particulièrement nette. Il y a non seulement une communauté de thème — l'âme désirante parquée dans l'abdomen —, mais aussi des rencontres de vocabulaire et d'images qui ne peuvent être l'effet du hasard. La partie désirante de l'âme — ἐπιθυμητικόν chez Platon, ἐπιθυμία chez Philon — est appelée un θρέμμα ἄγριον dans le 'Timée', un θρέμμα ἄλογον dans le 'De specialibus legibus', et, dans les deux textes, le ventre, séjour de cet être irrationnel, est assimilé à une φάτνη, une crèche, une mangeoire[154]. Mais, chez Philon, une autre image vient se combiner avec celle de la crèche: l'ἐπιθυμία est comparée au porc qui se plaît à vivre dans un bourbier[155]. On reconnaît un thème souvent exploité par les Grecs et les Latins et qui remonte peut-être à Héraclite[156].

---

[150] Philon, loc. cit.: . . . τὰς δὲ σιαγόνας τοῦ τε κυριωτάτου τῶν μελῶν, κεφαλῆς, καὶ λόγου τοῦ κατὰ προφορὰν ἀπαρχήν.

[151] Aetius, Placita, IV, 4, 4 (DIELS, DG, p. 389). Cf. M. POHLENZ, Die Stoa, t. I, pp. 87—88; t. II, p. 52.

[152] De opificio mundi, 117; Legum allegoriae, I, 11; Quod deterius potiori insidiari soleat, 168; De agricultura, 30; Quis rerum divinarum heres sit, 232—233; De mutatione nominum, 110; De aeternitate mundi, 97.

[153] Jérôme, Epist. 64, 2, 1, p. 589, 3: *Maxilla eloquentem eruditumque significat, ut, quod pectore concepimus, ore promamus.*

[154] Platon, Timée, 70 e: . . . οἷον φάτνην ἐν ἅπαντι τούτῳ τῷ τόπῳ τῇ τοῦ σώματος τροφῇ τεκτηνάμενοι· καὶ κατέδησαν δὴ τὸ τοιοῦτον ἐνταῦθα ὡς θρέμμα ἄγριον.
Philon, De specialibus legibus, I, 148: Κοιλίαν δὲ φάτνην ἀλόγου θρέμματος, ἐπιθυμίας εἶναι συμβέβηκεν.

[155] Philon, loc. cit.: Καὶ συὸς τρόπον ἐν βορβόρῳ διαιτωμένη χαίρει.

[156] M. AUBINEAU, Le thème du 'bourbier' dans la littérature grecque profane et chrétienne, Recherches de Science religieuse, 47, 1959, pp. 185—214 (notamment 201—212). Pour la

La manière dont ces deux images sont associées et interprétées par Philon montre assez à quel point il est éloigné du platonisme classique. Dans le 'Timée', l'infériorité de l'âme désirante par rapport au νοῦς et au θυμός est sans doute nettement marquée. Mais c'est là moindre estime plutôt que mépris insultant: l'inférieur participe à l'harmonie de l'ensemble. Il en va tout autrement chez Philon. Le lieu où habite l'ἐπιθυμία n'est plus seulement une mangeoire, c'est un cloaque, le réceptacle des excréments[157]: tel est le bourbier où ce porc aime à patauger. Du même coup, le désir n'est plus simplement subordonné et assujetti, il est avili. A la constatation d'une infériorité de nature tend à se substituer une condamnation morale[158].

Si l'on passe maintenant à l'interprétation de Jérôme dans sa lettre à Fabiola, on constate que les dernières références platoniciennes ont disparu. La leçon morale s'est définitivement substituée aux spéculations sur la structure de l'âme humaine: le ventre «condamne tous les efforts des hommes et les plaisirs fugitifs de la bouche en leur donnant pour terme l'excrément»[159]. Deux citations pauliniennes complémentaires viennent appuyer cette leçon: «Les aliments sont pour le ventre et le ventre pour les aliments, et Dieu détruira celui-ci comme ceux-là»[160], cependant les débauchés «ont leur ventre pour dieu et mettent leur gloire dans leur honte»[161]. Deux références vétérotestamentaires se greffent en outre sur ce développement. La mention de la Madianite frappée au ventre est une seconde allusion à l'épisode de Phinéès[162]. Une citation du livre de l'Exode introduit en revanche un élement nouveau. On sait que Moïse, après avoir broyé le veau d'or, en mêla la poudre à de l'eau qu'il fit boire aux enfants d'Israël[163]. C'est pour Jérôme une leçon morale analogue à celle dont le ventre vient d'être l'occasion: rejetant aux latrines les restes de l'idole ainsi absorbés, les Israélites apprennent à mépriser ce qu'ils avaient auparavant adoré[164].

Une fois de plus, on voit combien le texte de Jérôme est loin de la page du 'De specialibus legibus' qui est censée lui avoir servi de modèle. Philon situe encore ses explications dans le cadre de l'anthropologie platonicienne, même s'il tend déjà à transformer la 'physique' en morale. Chez Jérôme, la réflexion philosophique s'est définitivement effacée devant le discours édifiant. En un sens, ces

---

littérature latine: P. COURCELLE, 'Connais-toi toi-même' de Socrate à saint Bernard, t. II, Paris, 1975, pp. 502–519.

[157] Philon, loc. cit.: Παρὸ καὶ τόπος ἀπενεμήθη σφόδρα οἰκειότατος ὁ τῶν περιττωμάτων ἀκολάστῳ καὶ ἀπρεπεστάτῳ θρέμματι.

[158] Philon, op. cit., I, 150: Ἐπιθυμία μὲν οὖν βέβηλος καὶ ἀκάθαρτος καὶ ἀνίερος οὖσα πέρα τῶν ἀρετῆς ὅρων ἐλήλαται καὶ πεφυγάδευται δεόντως.

[159] Jérôme, Epist. 64, 2, 1, p. 589, 5–7: Venter . . . universos hominum labores et momentanea blandimenta gulae stercoris fine condemnat.

[160] I Cor., 6, 13.

[161] Phil., 3, 19.

[162] Jérôme, loc. cit., p. 589, 5–6: venter . . . in scorto Madianitide sacerdotali pugione perfossus.

[163] Ex., 32, 20.

[164] Jérôme, Epist. 64, 2, 2, p. 589. 12–15: Vituli pulverem, quem adoraverat Israhel, in contemptu superstitionis in potu accipit populus, ut discat contemnere quod in secessu proici viderat.

quelques pages de la lettre à Fabiola représentent l'aboutissement de l'évolution amorcée dans le 'De specialibus legibus'. Mais l'écart entre le point de départ et le point d'arrivée est tel qu'il n'est guère vraisemblable que Jérôme ait utilisé directement le traité de Philon. Faut-il invoquer encore, pour ce dernier passage, quelque source rabbinique, en raison de l'allusion à Phinéès? Il est vrai que l'interprétation de l'épisode du veau d'or proposée par Jérôme ne semble guère conforme à l'esprit de la Haggadah qui a plutôt considéré cette absorption de la poussière de l'idole comme une espèce d'ordalie[165]. Les emprunts précédemment constatés inviteraient plutôt à penser encore une fois à Origène.

Il est temps de dresser le bilan de ces analyses. On a vu que les trois pages sur lesquelles elles ont porté pourraient représenter, selon les spécialistes, le plus étendu des emprunts de Jérôme à Philon. L'examen que nous avons tenté permet-il de confirmer ou d'infirmer cette hypothèse? Une réponse simple serait assurément imprudente, étant donné les méthodes de travail du moine de Bethléem. Voici, par exemple, ce qu'il écrit dans le prologue de son 'Commentaire sur l'Epître aux Galates' après avoir évoqué les travaux de ses prédécesseurs: *Legi haec omnia et in mente mea plurima coacervans, accito notario, vel mea, vel aliena dictavi, nec ordinis, nec verborum, interdum nec sensuum commemorans*[166]. Sans doute, les confidences d'un auteur ne doivent jamais être accueillies sans quelque précaution. Néanmoins, la lecture du début de la lettre 64 semble confirmer les indications de Jérôme: on a bien le sentiment d'une accumulation d'éléments de provenances diverses, plus ou moins altérés par les infidélités de la mémoire et enfin rassemblés dans un texte assez hâtivement composé[167]. Pour ce dernier point, il suffit d'évoquer la manière dont la *quaestio* de la localisation de l'ἡγεμονικόν est soudain introduite dans le cours de l'exposé. Il semble que Jérôme ne veuille rien perdre, par crainte d'être pris en flagrant délit d'omission[168]. C'est ainsi qu'à la fin de cette même lettre 64, il s'inquiète à l'idée que sa correspondante pourrait se procurer un ouvrage que lui-même n'a pu trouver: le traité de Septimius Tertullien sur les vêtements d'Aaron. Si c'était le cas, que Fabiola veuille bien ne pas comparer la goutte d'eau de Jérôme au fleuve de cet auteur[169].

[165] L. GINZBERG, The legends of the Jews, t. III, Philadelphia, 1911, p. 13; t. VI, Philadelphia, 1928 [1946], pp. 54—55 n. 281 (cf. Nm., 6, 11—28). Parmi les textes invoqués, v. notamment Ps.-Philon, Liber antiquitatum Biblicarum, II, 7, éd. G. KISCH, Notre Dame, Indiana, 1949, p. 148. L'interprétation allégorique de Philon (De posteritate Caini, 158—159) est également différente de celle de la Mishna et de celle de Jérôme: le veau d'or représente les plaisirs corporels broyés par la vertu.

[166] Jérôme, Commentarii in Epistolam ad Galatas, prol., PL, 26, 309 (VALLARSI, 369—370); cf. Epist., 112, 4. Sur la place tenue par la dictée dans l'activité littéraire de saint Jérôme: E. ARNS, La technique du livre d'après saint Jérôme, Paris, 1953, pp. 37—51.

[167] Cf. Epist. 64, 22, 2, p. 615, 5—11. Il est vrai que le début de la lettre pourrait avoir été composé antérieurement. Cf. ci-dessus, n. 100.

[168] Cf. A. VACCARI, Scritti di erudizione e di filologia, t. II, Roma, 1958, p. 167.

[169] Jérôme, Epist. 64, 22, 3, p. 615, 11—14.

Ces réserves étant faites, il reste néanmoins possible de discerner, malgré les altérations et les mélanges, certains des éléments qui entrent dans la composition des pages que nous avons étudiées.

Il y a d'abord le cadre général, celui d'une *Quaestio* qui naît du rapprochement d'un passage du Lévitique et d'un verset du Deutéronome. Ce cadre est identique chez Philon et chez Jérôme. Cela indique-t-il une dépendance ou bien s'agit-il d'un rapprochement banal, d'une sorte de lieu commun de la casuistique juive? Il semble difficile d'en décider.

Si l'on passe maintenant au contenu de l'exégèse, il paraît vraisemblable qu'il existe entre le 'De specialibus legibus' et la lettre à Fabiola un lien de filiation au moins indirect. C'est ce que suggèrent en particulier ces références à une page célèbre du 'Timée', que l'on trouve dans l'un et l'autre texte.

Il semble pourtant difficile d'envisager une dépendance directe: les exégèses de Jérôme diffèrent constamment et profondément de celles de Philon. En revanche, chaque fois qu'un texte parallèle d'Origène nous a été conservé, nous observons que Jérôme en est beaucoup plus proche qu'il ne l'est de Philon. On peut raisonnablement en conclure que, pour l'ensemble de ce développement, c'est à travers Origène que l'exégèse philonienne a été connue de Jérôme.

Sur certains points, on pourrait supposer que le correspondant de Fabiola a complété ce qu'il devait à Origène par des renseignements puisés aux sources rabbiniques. Mais, dans ces quelques cas, si la parenté de thème est évidente, le canal par lequel telle exégèse est parvenue au moine de Bethléem peut être discuté. On peut hésiter entre un *Hebraeus* connu de Jérôme et une exégèse rabbinique trouvée chez Origène lui-même.

Ainsi, une fois écarté le seul emprunt de quelque importance, l'utilisation directe de Philon par Jérôme semble se réduire finalement à fort peu de choses, en dépit de quelques mentions élogieuses et de la notice du 'De viris illustribus'.

Ce relatif manque d'intérêt ne saurait d'ailleurs surprendre. En se comparant au «père de famille qui tire de son trésor des choses nouvelles et anciennes», Jérôme a défini ainsi son programme: joindre à l'histoire des Hébreux la tropologie des chrétiens[170]. Pour la tropologie, les maîtres dont il se réclame sont Hippolyte, Origène, Didyme. En vérité, c'est du second qu'il est surtout tributaire. Pour l'«histoire des Hébreux», la principale source de Jérôme est l'œuvre de Josèphe. Il faut y ajouter un certain nombre d'interprétations et de gloses recueillies auprès des milieux juifs de Palestine. Entre Josèphe et Origène, il ne reste guère de place pour Philon dans les lectures et les intérêts du moine de Bethléem. La conclusion plutôt négative à laquelle nous sommes parvenus était, somme toute, assez prévisible.

---

[170] Jérôme, Commentarii in Zachariam, praef., 34–38, CCL, 76 A, p. 78: *Itaque imitari cupiens illum patrem familias « qui profert de thesauro suo nova et vetera »* (Mt., 13, 52) . . . *historiae Hebraeorum tropologiam nostrorum miscui, ut aedificarem super petram et non super arenam.* Le sens exact qu'il faut donner à *nostri* est indiqué par les noms que Jérôme vient de citer: Origène, Hippolyte, Didyme.

Si l'on en juge par les cas exemplaires d'Ambroise et de Jérôme, l'influence de Philon sur l'Occident latin à la fin du IVe siècle s'exerce en grande partie de manière indirecte. C'est à travers l'allégorisme chrétien, et notamment par l'intermédiaire d'Origène, que l'œuvre du plus philosophe des exégètes juifs continue à être agissante. Les œuvres bibliques de Jérôme le montrent fort bien. Cela est vrai aussi pour bien des traités d'Ambroise, très largement tributaires d'Origène. Ce que Philon continue à offrir à travers ces intermédiaires, ce n'est pas seulement un grand nombre d'interprétations 'spirituelles', plus ou moins profondément christianisées, c'est bien davantage: les principes, les catégories et les techniques d'une exégèse qui veut, au-delà de la lettre, retrouver toute science et toute sagesse, non seulement dans l'ensemble de la Bible, mais, à la limite, dans la moindre de ses parties.

Cependant, aux alentours de 380, à cette influence médiate et diffuse, vient s'ajouter l'utilisation directe et continue de plusieurs traités de Philon par Ambroise. On peut parler, à ce point de vue, d'un véritable retour à la source. Grâce à l'évêque de Milan, un nouvel ensemble d'exégèses philoniennes va être intégré au patrimoine des chrétientés d'Occident. Le cours de l'exégèse chrétienne n'en sera pourtant point infléchi: ces nouveaux apports philoniens vont être en effet interprétés, corrigés et modifiés sous l'influence de l'exégèse origénienne; ils vont être absorbés en quelque sorte par ce philonisme indirect qui est devenu l'apanage de l'Eglise. On observe donc, chez Ambroise comme chez Jérôme, une commune évolution des thèmes de Philon, en particulier un glissement constant de la métaphysique ou de la physique vers la morale. Un certain antiplatonisme chrétien, accentué peut-être par l'aventure du règne de Julien, a pu se conjuguer ici avec l'esprit pratique et concret des Latins. Il en résulte comme une dégénérescence des exégèses de Philon. Mais cet appauvrissement est compensé, au moins chez Ambroise, par le développement complexe d'un réseau de correspondances et de symboles dont la richesse poétique et la densité spirituelle sont souvent indéniables.

RELIGIONSGESCHICHTLICHE VERSUCHE UND VORARBEITEN

Ladislav Vidman

Isis und Sarapis bei den Griechen und Römern

Epigraphische Studien zur Verbreitung und zu den Trägern
des ägyptischen Kultes

Groß-Oktav. VI, 189 Seiten. 1970. Ganzleinen DM 62,–
ISBN 3 11 006392 1 (Band 29)

Hans Gerhard Kippenberg

Garizim und Synagoge

Traditionsgeschichtliche Untersuchungen zur samaritanischen Religion
der aramäischen Periode

Oktav. XIV, 374 Seiten. 1971. Ganzleinen DM 103,–
ISBN 3 11 001864 0 (Band 30)

Klaus Schippmann

Die iranischen Feuerheiligtümer

Oktav. XII, 555 Seiten, 1 Faltkarte und Falttafeln in Rückentasche und 85 Abbildungen. 1971.
Ganzleinen DM 148,–   ISBN 3 11 001879 9 (Band 31)

Walter Burkert

Homo Necans

Interpretation altgriechischer Opferriten und Mythen

Oktav. XII, 356 Seiten. 1972. Ganzleinen DM 103,–
ISBN 3 11 003875 7 (Band 32)

Fritz Gräf

Eleusis und die orphische Dichtung Athens in vorhellenistischer Zeit

Groß-Oktav. XII, 224 Seiten. 1974. Ganzleinen DM 80,–
ISBN 3 11 004498 6 (Band 33)

Preisänderungen vorbehalten

Walter de Gruyter Berlin · New York

RELIGIONSGESCHICHTLICHE VERSUCHE
UND VORARBEITEN

Christoph Elsas

Neuplatonische und gnostische Weltablehnung
in der Schule Plotins

Oktav. XVI, 356 Seiten. 1975. Ganzleinen DM 109,–
ISBN 3 11 003941 9 (Band 34)

Gerd A. Wewers

Geheimnis und Geheimhaltung
im rabbinischen Judentum

Oktav. XIV, 394 Seiten. 1975. Ganzleinen DM 80,–
ISBN 3 11 005858 8 (Band 35)

Richard Merz

Die numinose Mischgestalt

Methodenkritische Untersuchungen zu tiermenschlichen Erscheinungen
Altägyptens, der Eiszeit und der Aranda in Australien

Groß-Oktav. XX, 306 Seiten. 1978. Ganzleinen DM 110,–
ISBN 3 11 007443 5 (Band 36)

August Strobel

Das heilige Land der Montanisten

Eine religionsgeographische Untersuchung

Groß-Oktav. X, 310 Seiten, 13 Abbildungen und 24 Tafeln. 1980. Ganzleinen DM 112,–
ISBN 3 11 008369 8 (Band 37)

Michael Blech

Studien zum Kranz bei den Griechen

Groß-Oktav. XXXIII, 490 Seiten, 40 Abbildungen. 1982. Ganzleinen DM 116,–
ISBN 3 11 004157 X (Band 38)

Preisänderungen vorbehalten

Walter de Gruyter Berlin · New York